CHEEVER

CHEEVER

A LIFE

Blake Bailey

ALFRED A. KNOPF · NEW YORK 2009

This Is a Borzoi Book
Published by Alfred A. Knopf

Copyright © 2009 by Blake Bailey

www.aaknopf.com

Portions of this work originally appeared in the following: *The Believer,*
The Gettysburg Review, Harvard Review, Virginia Quarterly Review,
and *Vice.*

Grateful acknowledgment is made to The Estate of John Cheever for the
use of photographs, documents, letters, and other archival material and
unpublished text by John Cheever.

Material from the following Alfred A. Knopf titles appears courtesy of
Random House, Inc.: *Bullet Park, Falconer, The Stories of John Cheever,*
Oh What a Paradise It Seems, and *The Journals of John Cheever.*

Knopf, Borzoi Books, and the colophon are registered trademarks of
Random House, Inc.

Library of Congress Cataloging-in-Publication Data
Bailey, Blake.
Cheever : a life / by Blake Bailey.—1st ed.
    p.   cm.
"This is a Borzoi book"—T.p. verso.
Includes bibliographical references.
ISBN 978-1-4000-4394-1
1. Cheever, John.   2. Authors, American—
20th century—Biography.   I. Title.
PS3505.H6428Z53 2009
813'.52—dc22
    [B]   2008042277
Manufactured in the United States of America
Published March 12, 2009
Reprinted One Time
Third Printing, October 2009

For Mary, Marlies, and Amelia

I've never intended to be patronizing. As a child I was told to remember, at all times, that I was a CHEEVAH. I thought this bullshit had cured me.

—*John Cheever to Frederick Exley*

Fred, remember you are a *Cheever.*

—*John Cheever's advice to his younger son*

I am nothing and everything is a nothing and I want to play out the role to the end; and if I am less than nothing I am a wayward boy, angry at Mummy and Daddy and a little queer to boot; and how does this square with the image of a cheerful man of forty-five who has been given everything in the world he desires but a degree of unself-consciousness.

—*John Cheever, Journals*

. . . it is too much to ask that people who spend very much time in a world of their own, as all writers do, should immediately and invariably grasp what is going on in this one.

—*William Maxwell*

Contents

PROLOGUE 3

CHAPTER ONE {1637–1912} 7

CHAPTER TWO {1912–1926} 18

CHAPTER THREE {1926–1930} 33

CHAPTER FOUR {1930–1934} 50

CHAPTER FIVE {1934–1935} 63

CHAPTER SIX {1935–1938} 79

CHAPTER SEVEN {1938–1939} 94

CHAPTER EIGHT {1939–1941} 101

CHAPTER NINE {1941–1943} 115

CHAPTER TEN {1943–1945} 129

CHAPTER ELEVEN {1945–1946} 137

CHAPTER TWELVE {1946–1949} 146

CHAPTER THIRTEEN {1949–1951} 162

CHAPTER FOURTEEN {1951–1952} 177

CHAPTER FIFTEEN {1952–1954} 193

CHAPTER SIXTEEN {1954–1956} 212

CHAPTER SEVENTEEN {1956–1957} 230

CHAPTER EIGHTEEN {1957} 239

CHAPTER NINETEEN {1957–1959} 251

CHAPTER TWENTY {1959–1960} 266

CHAPTER TWENTY-ONE {1960–1961} 280

CHAPTER TWENTY-TWO {1961} 293

CHAPTER TWENTY-THREE {1962–1963} 302

CHAPTER TWENTY-FOUR {1964} 322

Contents

CHAPTER TWENTY-FIVE {1964} 340

CHAPTER TWENTY-SIX {1964–1965} 355

CHAPTER TWENTY-SEVEN {1966} 370

CHAPTER TWENTY-EIGHT {1966–1967} 384

CHAPTER TWENTY-NINE {1967–1968} 399

CHAPTER THIRTY {1968–1969} 408

CHAPTER THIRTY-ONE {1969–1970} 422

CHAPTER THIRTY-TWO {1969–1970} 433

CHAPTER THIRTY-THREE {1971–1972} 444

CHAPTER THIRTY-FOUR {1972–1973} 462

CHAPTER THIRTY-FIVE {1973} 473

CHAPTER THIRTY-SIX {1974} 486

CHAPTER THIRTY-SEVEN {1974} 495

CHAPTER THIRTY-EIGHT {1975} 507

CHAPTER THIRTY-NINE {1975} 516

CHAPTER FORTY {1975–1976} 524

CHAPTER FORTY-ONE {1976–1977} 536

CHAPTER FORTY-TWO {1977} 547

CHAPTER FORTY-THREE {1977} 560

CHAPTER FORTY-FOUR {1977–1978} 571

CHAPTER FORTY-FIVE {1978–1979} 583

CHAPTER FORTY-SIX {1979} 596

CHAPTER FORTY-SEVEN {1979–1980} 612

CHAPTER FORTY-EIGHT {1980–1981} 625

CHAPTER FORTY-NINE {1981–1982} 634

CHAPTER FIFTY {1982} 648

EPILOGUE 661

Acknowledgments 681

Notes 685

Index 739

CHEEVER

PROLOGUE

ON APRIL 27, 1982, less than two months before his death from cancer, John Cheever appeared at Carnegie Hall to accept the National Medal for Literature. While his colleagues stood and cheered ("John had nothing but friends," said Malcolm Cowley), Cheever hobbled across the stage with the help of his wife, Mary. Months of cancer treatment had left him bald and pitifully frail, shrunken, but his voice was firm as he spoke. In his journal he'd referred to this occasion as his "Exodus" and reminded himself that literature was "the salvation of the damned"—the lesson of his own life, surely, and the gist of what he said that day at Carnegie Hall. "A page of good prose," he declared, "remains invincible." As John Updike remembered, "All the literary acolytes assembled there fell quite silent, astonished by such faith."

Seven years before—his marriage on the rocks, most of his books out of print—Cheever had tried drinking himself to death. He was teaching at Boston University, beset by ghosts from his awful childhood in nearby Quincy: "There were whole areas of the city I couldn't go into," he said later. "I couldn't, for example, go to Symphony Hall because my mother was there." Updike was living on the opposite end of Back Bay at the time, and when he'd visit the small furnished apartment Cheever had taken near the university ("no more lived-in than a bird perch") he'd notice the first dusty page of *Falconer* stuck in the typewriter. One night he came to take Cheever to Symphony Hall, and was disconcerted when the older man emerged naked on his fourth-floor landing while the door swung shut behind him. Fortunately, there was no automatic locking mechanism, and Updike assumed the role of a dutiful if slightly exasperated son: "[Cheever's] costume indicated some resistance to attending symphony but I couldn't imagine what else, and I primly concentrated on wedging him into his clothes." That winter Cheever went for long, staggering walks along Commonwealth Avenue, rarely wearing an overcoat despite freezing weather (his father had warned him that overcoats make one look Irish). Finally he sat next to a bum and the two huddled together, sharing a bottle of fortified wine. When a policeman threatened to arrest him, Cheever gave the man a look of bleary, aristocratic reproach: "My name is John Cheever," he drawled *(Cheevah)*. "You're out of your mind."

He came to himself in the Smithers Alcoholism Treatment and Training Center on East Ninety-third Street in Manhattan, where for twenty-eight days he shared a bedroom and bath with four other men. He couldn't remember leaving Boston. As for Smithers, it was grim: he was told that a man had recently jumped out the window in the ward where he slept; he was taunted in group therapy for pulling a fancy accent. "Displaying much grandiosity and pride," one of his counselors noted. "Denying and minimizing grossly." The staff was particularly struck by Cheever's tendency to laugh at "inappropriate" moments: little giggles would erupt while he recalled, say, a time he'd hurt his family. On the telephone with his daughter, however, Cheever would become tearful and say he couldn't bear it another day. And yet he sensed that an early departure would amount to suicide—and he wanted to live, oddly enough; he wanted to finish *Falconer.* "Cheever's is the triumph of a man in his sixties," Bernard Malamud said of his colleague's miraculous resurrection. "Here he'd been having a dreadful time . . . but he stayed with it. And through will and the grace literature affords, he saved himself." After his wife drove him home from Smithers on May 7, 1975, Cheever never took another drink.

Less than two years later, he appeared on the cover of *Newsweek* over the caption "A Great American Novel: John Cheever's 'Falconer.'" (He'd also been the subject of a 1964 *Time* cover story, "Ovid in Ossining.") After reading *Falconer,* the article proclaimed, "one has the ecstatic confidence of finishing a masterpiece." Large claims were made for Cheever's place in world literature: "Long before Donald Barthelme, John Barth and Thomas Pynchon began tinkering with narrative conventions, Cheever had unobtrusively disrupted the expected shapes of fiction. As was the case with Faulkner in France, Cheever has been unexpectedly recognized and honored in Russia for the corrosive criticism of American civilization his understated fiction implies." The fact that all but one of Cheever's story collections were out of print was described as "a scandal of American publishing."

This was remedied the following year, 1978, when *The Stories of John Cheever* became one of the most successful collections ever published by an American writer. The book remained on the *New York Times* best-seller list for six months and won the Pulitzer, the National Book Critics Circle Award, and the American Book Award. Cheever (appalled) was introduced as "the Grand Old Man of American Letters" on a Boston talk show. The bookish middle class, it seemed, identified en masse with Cheever's vision of suburban alienation; his "corrosive criticism" of their culture was mitigated, perhaps, by what the author himself wryly called his "childlike sense of wonder."

Cheever was determined to put his resurgent celebrity to its best use. As Cowley observed, "Yankees are distinguished, and tormented as well, by having scruples." Cheever—a consummately scrupulous, tormented Yankee—paid off old debts to the people and institutions that had been kind to him in harder times. He served on the board at Yaddo and, as chairman of the American Academy's grants committee, read at least a hundred new novels a year. He rarely declined offers to give readings, no matter how humble or remote the venue, though he'd despised such obligations in the past. "He was like a man who puts his affairs in order before setting out on a journey," said Cowley.

He even seemed to come to terms, at long last, with what he called "the most subterranean eminence in [his] person"—a fear that he was a sexual (as well as social) impostor. "Here is some sort of conflict," he wrote in 1963, though it might have been any year; "a man who has homosexual instincts and genuinely detests homosexuals. They seem to him unserious, humorless and revolting." Thus, even at the best of times, a shadow was cast over his happiness, though he often tried counting his blessings with a sort of wan bemusement: a loving family, a beautiful house, friendly dogs, talent, fame, on and on. Still the shadow remained, whatever the surface facts of his life ("I wake from a dream"—he wrote in his journal—"in which I am committing a gross and compulsive indecency").

Falconer had been a catharsis of sorts—the story of a man who makes peace with himself, partly in the form of a homosexual love affair—and shortly after he finished the novel, Cheever also seemed to find peace. While visiting the University of Utah Writing Program in 1977, he met a young man who had none of the attributes of a "sexual irregular," as Cheever would have it: "His air of seriousness and responsibility, the bridged glasses he wore for his nearsightedness, and his composed manner excited my deepest love . . ." The young man's name was Max, and, in some form or another, he remained in Cheever's life until the end. Cheever often wondered if he were being succored by the ghost of his beloved older brother, Fred, or some other long-lost friend; at any rate he seemed more inclined to accept his own nature, such as it was. "Life is an improvisation!" he liked to say, especially in later years.

Certainly life had turned out better than he ever could have hoped as a lonely, starving artist in the Depression, in flight from a family life that was "bankrupt in every way": "I remember waking in some squalid furnished room," he wrote, two years before his death, "probably with a terrible hangover and very likely with a stiff and unrequited prick." At such times he used to comfort himself with dreams of future love and success—and now, fifty years later, it had all come true. "And so I woke . . . with a wife and the voices of birds, dogs and children but what I had not anticipated was the sound of a brook. And so it seems to be more bounteous than once I could have imagined." But then a curious afterthought: "It could, of course, be more horrifying."

CHAPTER ONE

{ 1637–1912 }

"MANY SKELETONS IN FAMILY CLOSET," Leander Wapshot wrote in his diary. "Dark secrets, mostly carnal." Even at the height of his success, Cheever never quite lost the fear that he'd "end up cold, alone, dishonored, forgotten by [his] children, an old man approaching death without a companion." This, he sensed, was the fate of his "accursed" family—or at least of its men, who for three generations (at least) had seemed "bound to a drunken and tragic destiny." There was his paternal grandfather, Aaron, rumored to have committed suicide in a bleak furnished room on Charles Street in Boston, a disgrace too awful to mention. One night, as a young man, Cheever had sat by a fire drinking whiskey with his father, Frederick, while a nor'easter raged outside. "We were swapping dirty stories," he recalled; "the feeling was intimate, and I felt that this was the time when I could bring up the subject. 'Father, would you tell me something about your father?' 'No!' And that was that." By then Cheever's father was also poor and forsaken, living alone in an old family farmhouse on the South Shore, his only friend "a half-wit who lived up the road." As for Cheever's brother, he too would become drunken and poor, spending his last days in a subsidized retirement village in Scituate. No wonder Cheever sometimes felt an affinity to characters in Ibsen's *Ghosts*.

Despite such ignominy, Cheever took pride in his fine old family name, and when he wasn't making light of the matter, he took pains to impress this on his children. "Remember you are a *Cheever*," he'd tell his younger son, whenever the boy showed signs of an unseemly fragility. Some allusion was implicit, perhaps, to the first Cheever in America, Ezekiel, headmaster of the Boston Latin School from 1671 to 1708 and author of *Accidence: A Short Introduction to the Latin Tongue,* the standard text in American schools for a century or more. New England's greatest schoolmaster, Ezekiel Cheever was even more renowned for his piety—"his untiring abjuration of the Devil," as Cotton Mather put it in his eulogy. One aspect of Ezekiel's piety was a stern distaste for periwigs, which he was known to yank from foppish heads and fling out windows. "The welfare of the commonwealth was always upon the conscience of Ezekiel Cheever," said Judge Sewall, "and he abominated periwigs." John Cheever was fond of pointing out that the abomination of periwigs "is in the nature of literature," and it seems he was taught to emulate such virtue on his father's knee. "Old Zeke C.," Frederick wrote his son in 1943, "didn't fuss about painted walls—open plumbing, or electric lights, had no ping pong etc. Turned out sturdy men and women, who knew their three R's, and the fear of God." John paid tribute to his eminent forebear by giving the name Ezekiel to one of his black Labradors (to this day a bronze of the dog's head sits beside the Cheever fireplace), as well as to the protagonist of *Falconer.* However, when an old friend mentioned seeing a plaque that commemorated Ezekiel's house in Charlestown, Cheever replied, "Why tell me? I'm in no way even collaterally related to Ezekiel Cheever."

Cheever named his first son after his great-grandfather Benjamin Hale Cheever, a "celebrated ship's master" who sailed out of Newburyport to Canton and Calcutta for the lucrative China trade. Visitors to Cheever's home in Ossining (particularly journalists) were often shown such maritime souvenirs as a set of Canton china and a framed Chinese fan—this while Cheever remarked in passing that his great-grandfather's boots were on display in the Peabody Essex Museum, filled with authentic tea from the Boston Tea Party. In fact, it is Lot Cheever of Danvers (no known relation) whose tea-filled boots ended up at the museum; as for Benjamin, he was all of three years old when that particular bit of tea was plundered aboard the *Dartmouth* on December 16, 1773. Also, there's some question whether Benjamin Hale (Sr.) was actually a ship's captain: though he appears in the Newbury Vital Records as "Master" Cheever, there's no mention of him in any of the maritime records; a "Mr. Benjamin Cheever" *is* mentioned, however, as the teacher of one Henry Pettingell (born 1793) at the

Newbury North School, and "Master" might as well have meant *school*master. Unless there were two Benjamin Cheevers in the greater Newbury area at the time (both roughly the same age), this would appear to be John's great-grandfather.

The ill-fated Aaron was the youngest of Benjamin's twelve children, and it was actually he who had ("presumably") brought back that ivory-laced fan from the Orient: "It has lain, broken, in the sewing box for as long as I can remember," Cheever wrote in 1966, when he finally had the thing repaired and mounted under glass.

> My reaction to the framed fan is violently contradictory. Ah yes, I say, my grandfather got it in China, this authenticating my glamorous New England background. My impulse, at the same time, is to smash and destroy the memento. The power a scrap of paper and a little ivory have over my heart. It is the familiar clash between my passionate wish to be honest and my passionate wish to possess a traditional past. I can, it seems, have both but not without a galling sense of conflict.

To be sure, it's possible that Aaron had sailed to China and retrieved that fan—as his son Frederick pointed out, most young men of the era went out on at least one voyage "to make them grow"—but his future did not lie with the China trade, which was effectively killed by Jefferson's Embargo Act and the War of 1812. By the time Aaron reached manhood, in the mid-nineteenth century, the New England economy was dominated by textile industries, and Aaron had moved his family to Lynn, Massachusetts, where he worked as a shoemaker. But he was not meant to prosper even in so humble a station, and may well have been among the twenty thousand shoe workers who lost their jobs in the Great Strike of 1860. In any event, the family returned to Newburyport a few years later and eventually sailed to Boston aboard the *Harold Currier*: "This, according to my father," said Cheever, "was the last sailing ship to be made in the Newburyport yards and was towed to Boston to be outfitted. I don't suppose that they had the money to get to Boston by any other means."

Frederick Lincoln Cheever was born on January 16, 1865, the younger (by eleven years) of Aaron and Sarah's two sons. One of Frederick's last memories of his father was "playing dominoes with old gent" during the Great Boston Fire of 1872; the two watched a mob of looters, the merchants fleeing their stores. The financial panic of 1873 followed, in the midst of which Aaron—driven by poverty and whatever other devils—apparently decided his family was better off without him. ("Mother, saintly old woman," writes Leander Wapshot. "God bless her! Never one to admit unhappiness or pain . . . Asked me to sit down. 'Your father has abandoned us,' she said. 'He left me a note. I burned it in the fire.' ") After Aaron's departure, his wife seems to have run a boardinghouse to support her children, or so his grandson suspected ("If this were so I think I wouldn't have been told"), though Aaron's fate was unknown except by innuendo. As it happens, the death certificate indicates that Aaron Waters Cheever died in 1882 of "alcohol & opium—del[irium] tremens"; his last address was 111 Chambers (rather than Charles) Street, part of a shabby immigrant quarter that was razed long ago by urban renewal.

According to family legend, Sarah Cheever was notified by police of her husband's death and arranged for his burial in stoic solitude, without a word to her son Frederick until after she'd served him supper that night. Among the few possessions she found in his squalid lodgings was a copy of Shakespeare's plays, which came to the attention of a young John Cheever some fifty years later, at a time when he himself was all but starving to death in a Greenwich Village rooming house. Noting that "most of the speeches on human ingratitude were underscored," Cheever wrote an early story titled "Homage to Shakespeare" that speculates on the cause of his grandfather's downfall: "[Shakespeare's] plays seemed to light and distinguish his character and his past. What might have been defined as failure and profligacy towered like something kingly and tragic." As a tribute to kindred nobility, the narrator's grandfather (so described in the story) chooses "Coriolanus" for his older son William's middle name, rather as Aaron had named *his* older son—John Cheever's uncle—William Hamlet Cheever.

WHEN ASKED how he came to keep a journal, Cheever explained it as a typical occupation of a "seafaring family": "They always begin, as most journals do, with the weather, prevailing winds, ruffles of the sails. They also include affairs, temptations, condemnations, libel, and occasionally, obscenities." These last attributes were certainly characteristic of Cheever's own journal, though one can only imagine what other men in his family were apt to write; the few pages his father left behind were more in the nature of memoir notes, benign enough, some of them quoted almost verbatim in *The Wapshot Chronicle* as the laconic prose of Leander Wapshot: "Sturgeon in river then. About three feet long. All covered with knobs. Leap straight up in air and fall back in water."* When Cheever first encountered these notes, he found them "antic, ungrammatical and . . . vulgar," though later he came to admire the style as typical of a certain nautical New England mentality that "makes as little as possible of any event."

During his hardscrabble youth, Frederick was often boarded out at a bake house owned by his uncle Thomas Butler in Newburyport, where he slept in the attic with a tame raven and relished the view from his window: "Grand sunsets after the daily thunder showers that came down the river from the White Mountains," he recalled, with a lyric economy his son was right to admire. Life at the bake house was rarely dull, as Uncle Thomas was a good friend of abolitionist William Lloyd Garrison, and the house served as a station for the Underground Railroad. John Cheever often told of how pro-slavery copperheads had once dragged his great-uncle "at the tail of a cart" through the streets of Newburyport—though Cheever always saw fit to call this relative "Ebenezer" (a name he liked for its Yankee savor), and sometimes it was Ebenezer's friend *Villard* who was dragged, or stoned as the case may be. At any rate, the story usually ended with an undaunted "Ebenezer" refusing a government contract to make pilot biscuits for Union sailors—and indeed, as Frederick wrote in his notes, "[Uncle Thomas] said [biscuits] not good enough for sailors of US to eat. Others did it made big coin." John vastly improved that part of the story, too: "A competitor named Pierce," he related in a letter, "then accepted the [biscuit] contract and founded a dynasty" that became *Nabisco*, no less—which, for the record, was founded by Adolphus Green (not Pierce) in 1898.

"Bill always good to me," Frederick wrote of his much older

---

*The parallel passage in Frederick's notes reads as follows: "On the way [from Newburyport to Amesbury via horsecar] you saw sturgeons leap out of river—they were 3–4 feet long—all covered with knobs." One might add that, as Cheever suggests, his father was quite diligent about noting the weather—always, for instance, in the top right corner of the letters he wrote his son. Thus, from October 10, 1943: "Cold this AM 45 [degrees] Big wind from East No. East. Heavy overcoat—woodfire and oil kitchen."

brother, who apparently filled the paternal vacuum, if only for a while. Bill "called [him] down" when Frederick stepped out of line, and paid a friend—Johnny O'Toole at the Massachusetts Hotel ("Very tough joint")—to give Frederick haircuts as needed. John Cheever always used his uncle's more evocative middle name, Hamlet, when referring to this rather romantic figure: "An amateur boxer, darling of the sporting houses, captain of the volunteer fire department ball-team"— a man's man, in short, who, like his namesake in *The Wapshot Chronicle*, went west for the Gold Rush. "[There] isn't a king or a merchant prince in the whole world that I envy," Hamlet writes his brother Leander in the novel, "for I always knew I was born to be a child of destiny and that I was never meant . . . to wring my living from detestable, low, degrading, mean and ordinary kinds of business." By the time the real-life Hamlet arrived in California, however, the excitement of 1849 had faded considerably, and he later settled in Omaha, where he died "forgotten and disgraced"—or rather he died "at sea" and "was given to the ocean off Panama," depending on which of his nephew's stories one chooses to believe. Cheever invariably described his uncle as a "black-mouthed old wreck" or "monkey," since their occasional meetings were not happy. "Uncle Bill, Halifax 1919," John's older brother noted beside a photograph of a prosaic-looking old man rowing his nephews around in a boat. "Bill Cheever came from Omaha for a visit—the only time I ever saw him. He wasn't much fun." A later meeting with John would prove even less fun.

With Hamlet seeking his fortune a continent away, it was necessary for young Frederick to help support the household. From the age of ten or so, he "never missed a day" selling newspapers before and after classes at the Phillips School, where he graduated at the head of his class on June 27, 1879, and was presented with a bouquet of flowers by the mayor of Boston. In later years he'd wistfully recall how the flowers wilted before he could take them home to his mother, and on that note his formal education ended: "Wanted to go to Boston Latin," he wrote. "Had to work." For so bookish a man (he spent much of his lonely dotage reading Shakespeare to his cat), the matter rankled, and he'd insist on sending his sons to good private schools while boasting—à la Leander ("Report card attached")—of his own high marks as a boy.

For the next fifty years, Frederick Cheever worked in the shoe business, always bearing in mind the fate of his poor father, whose life was "made unbearable by lack of coin": "The desire for money most lasting and universal passion," he wrote for his own edification and perhaps that of his sons. "Desire ends only with life itself. Fame, love, all long forgotten." While still in his teens, he worked at a factory in Lynn for six dollars a week (five of which went to room and board) in order to learn the business; a photograph from around this time shows a dapper youth with a trim little mustache, his features composed with a look of high purpose, though its subject had glossed, "Look like a poet. Attic hungry—Etc." John Cheever would one day find among his father's effects a copy of *The Magician's Own Handbook*—a poignant artifact that brought to mind "a lonely young man reading Plutarch in a cold room and perfecting his magic tricks to make himself socially desirable and perhaps lovable." In the meantime, once he turned twenty-one, Frederick began to spend almost half the year on the road selling shoes ("gosh writer has sat in 1001 RR stations . . . 'get the business' or 'get out'"), often bunking with strangers and hiding his valuables in his stockings, which he then wore to bed.

Apart from the pursuit of "big coin," Frederick's early manhood was something of a lark. A great lover of the theater ("Powerful never forget it," he wrote of Henry Montague's performance in *Romeo and Juliet*), he took extra or "supe" roles at Boston's Hollis Street Theatre for fifty cents a performance, wearing tights and carrying spears into battle for big Shakespearean productions, and playing zany pranks on his fellow supes to pass time offstage: "Swiped the other chap's pants— left a bum pair—h——l to pay—did not show up again second fellow, out a pair of trousers—but 'actor's' life, you know." He not only saw James O'Neill's famous performance in *The Count of Monte Cristo*, but swore that O'Neill had been a boon companion whom he, Frederick Cheever, had drunk under the table at the old Adams House ("a memory I'm inclined to believe," his son remarked, "since I can drink Yevtushenko to the floor"). But his favorite recreation by far was the beach, for he always fancied himself a man of the sea: "On beaches the joy and gall of perpetual youth," Leander rhapsodizes. "Hear Neptune's horn. Always raring to go." For most of his life, Frederick kept a wide-waisted catboat and liked nothing better than sailing around Boston Harbor—preferably with a female companion—as a way of unwinding after grueling but increasingly lucrative sales trips. So things stood for Frederick Cheever until the end of a happy, protracted bachelorhood in 1901.

· · ·

OF HIS MOTHER'S FAMILY CONNECTIONS Cheever also made a romance—much of which he evidently believed, since he wrote it down in his journal as fact: "The only photograph I have of my grandmother shows her in a long apron. Her father was knighted by Victoria and Grandmother was (I think) friends of some ladies in waiting; but I think they had settled for a degree of plainness." Cheever claimed his great-grandfather was Sir Percy Devereaux, lord mayor of Windsor, who agreed to pay a remittance to his "bounder" son-in-law, William Liley, as long as the man left England and never returned.* Liley, perhaps broken in spirit, died on a horsecar shortly after arriving in America, and so left his three young daughters fatherless and poor. But Cheever's mother, Mary Devereaux Liley, never forgot her family's genteel beginnings in Old Windsor (though she herself was born in the industrial city of Sheffield, well to the north), and kept a picture of Windsor Castle in her home. As for John Cheever, his wife and children sometimes mockingly referred to him as the Lost Earl of Devereaux: "He'd ask me if I wanted some cauliflower," his daughter, Susan, recalled, "and I'd say, 'Wow! What a lucky girl I am, to be served cauliflower by the *Lost Earl of Devereaux*!' "

Cheever's maternal grandmother, Sarah, bristled at her poverty in the New World, proclaiming she was "a very well-educated English woman" who could hem a handkerchief and speak French, which she insisted her family practice each night at the dinner table. For the most part, though, she was glad to have left England, where there was little in the way of women's rights and she was unable to pursue her dream of becoming a fireman. Whether she achieved that dream, to whatever degree, is unknown; with her friend and fellow feminist Margaret Deland—author of *John Ward, Preacher*, and other novels—she ultimately devoted herself to the rehabilitation of unwed mothers who had (or might have otherwise) turned to prostitution. Ultimately, the two women took as many as sixty outcast mothers into their homes and taught them basic housekeeping skills, helping them find work via

---

*"Sir Percy Devereaux" did not exist, at least as lord mayor of Windsor; however, a Sir Joseph Devereux (born 1816) was indeed mayor of Windsor, and what's more was knighted by the Queen in 1883—but this man could not have sired Cheever's grandmother, whose full maiden name was actually Sarah Ann Devereaux *Bill*.

advertisements in the *Boston Herald*. In the meantime, too, as Cheever liked to point out, his grandmother and Mrs. Deland "provided themselves with good maids," and privately he was more rueful: "My mother's and my grandmother's houses," he wrote, "were always full of strays—orphans, bastards, prostitutes."

Two of Sarah Liley's daughters did not inherit her zest for good works, though both seem to have contributed something to their nephew John's personality. From his aunt Anne he might have derived some of the chilly hauteur he affected when threatened in certain ways, to say nothing of his wish for a "traditional past." Anne comported herself like the displaced gentry she believed herself to be, dubbing her oldest son "Devereaux" and cultivating a clipped British accent. When, later in life, she returned to Windsor in hope of glimpsing the family demesne, her husband Jim Armstrong—an affable Scot who took pains to deflate his wife's pomposity—furtively bribed a cabbie to drive them to the grandest estate he could find. "Just as I remember it!" Anne sighed. "There was nothing slummy about Aunt Anne," Cheever noted in 1968, by which time he hadn't spoken to the woman in over a decade—ever since she'd recognized herself in the quirky, imperious Honora Wapshot—though Cheever claimed she'd forgiven him once she remembered he was "a split personality."

If so, she might have been thinking of the side of her nephew's psyche that reflected the influence of her sister Florence, whom she sometimes cut dead in public because of the latter's incorrigible eccentricity. Florence was a painter who asked to be addressed as "Liley," wore Spanish shawls, and smoked cigars. She became a rather notable illustrator of children's books as "Florence Liley Young," though she regarded herself as a serious artist and was generous in sharing her enthusiasm. Cheever never forgot sitting on a riverbank watching his aunt Liley teach landscape painting to the cook—"*Cherchez le motif!*"—and among his favorite mementos was her portrait of himself as a slouching, apple-cheeked young artist, which, years later, as a man of means, he framed in gilt and hung in his library at Ossining.* "[Liley] interests me most," he wrote, "because of the importance art played in her life as it does in mine. Shortly before her death she said— 'One thing I really must do is go to the museum and see the Sargent

---

*Florence also painted a companion portrait of Cheever's brother, Fred, as the sturdy young burgher he was then in the process of becoming.

water-colors of the Milton quarrys. They are so beautiful.' This was exactly what she felt."

Cheever liked to think he had somewhat less in common with his mother, who was altruistic like Sarah Liley and also had "settled for a degree of plainness." In 1901, she graduated from the Massachusetts General Hospital School of Nursing, and she had already become a head nurse when she married Frederick Cheever. Where or how they met is not a matter of record, though it seems an unlikely alliance. For many years, Frederick had devoted himself to his mother while pursuing what his sons agreed was a robust love life. In his journal, Cheever wrote that his father had proposed out of pity ("a profound weakness") because his mother was "expected to die of tuberculosis"—though Cheever's wife always insisted it was her mother-in-law who had married against her will: "He persuaded her to give up her career, which she loved, and marry him," she said. "That's what a woman was supposed to do (I did something like that myself)." The truth, perhaps, was somewhere in the middle. Her older son, Fred, described Mary Liley Cheever as "quite beautiful" in her youth, and John remembered his father as being powerfully attracted, at least for a while: "He was constantly kissing my mother and blowing down the back of her neck. I remember his exclaiming, at some rented summer house: Oh what a burden of light that cobweb holds! It was his style and also mine."

Deprived of a nursing career, Mary Liley Cheever flung her astounding energy into all sorts of social-service endeavors. She was a "Madame President" type (as Cheever put it), who organized cultural events and raised money for libraries, progressive schools, and beautification projects; she cofounded the Woman's Club and the Current Events Club, and as her star rose she was called upon to give public lectures on such topics as feminism and the Armenian famine—so often, in fact, "that the word *mother* evoked for [Cheever] a lectern and a large hat." She rose to every challenge with an almost brazen level of commitment. When war was declared against Germany, she scooped up her husband's beer steins and smashed them with a hammer; she plowed up her lawn to plant potatoes; she organized parties for rolling bandages and potting vegetables. In sum, she was the sort of "do-gooder" who "distributed skinny chickens to the poor"—a woman who, like Sarah Wapshot, "had exhausted herself in good works . . . As a result of all these activities the house on River Street was always filled with dust, its cut flowers long dead, the clocks stopped." Nor was this the only drawback, domestically speaking. As her husband would shortly learn, "a woman who has just attended a stirring lecture on hospital conditions . . . [comes home] in a frame of mind that makes it difficult for her to be embraced."

Looking back, Cheever wondered if there was maybe something a little mad about his mother's zeal. As a boy he'd been mortified again and again by her "unseemly departures": "She had marched out of church in the middle of a sermon on the vanity of good works," Cheever wrote in his journal. "She marched up the aisle and out of the concert hall at the first notes of *Sacre du printemps*. She marched out of committee meetings, theaters, restaurants and movie houses at the first hint of anything unsavory, daring or improper. The single memory [I] preserved of [my] mother was of a woman dressed in black, hastening up an aisle." And though it was true that her sense of propriety was easily affronted, Cheever came to suspect her indignation was more a pretext for one of her various phobias. His mother would gasp for air if caught in a crowd or confined in any way, hence her pathological need to escape. Also, she had a "primitive horror of being photographed," such that her own son had little idea what she'd looked like as a younger woman until, one day, he discovered her portrait in an old Woman's Club program; when asked about it, she explained that her look of composure had been managed by holding her infant son—John himself—on her lap ("I was cropped").* At the time it might have seemed like so much winsome eccentricity, but it was less amusing later, when Cheever himself became a virtual prisoner of anxiety. "I blame her, I do," he wrote a week after her death in 1956, "for having conveyed some of her morbid fears to me." But then, as he wrote of his fictional alter ego, "Poor Coverly blamed everything on Mrs. Wapshot. Had he seen a falling star he would have blamed his Mother."

---

*A home movie survives from the thirties or forties in which Cheever's mother is seen walking briskly past the camera with a tight smile. When the photographer persists, she thrusts a hand toward the lens. One thinks of Honora Wapshot: "In all the family albums she appeared either with her back to the camera as she ran away or with her face concealed by her hands, her handbag, her hat or a newspaper."

CHAPTER TWO

{ *1912–1926* }

CHEEVER ONCE WROTE, "I have no biography. I came from nowhere and I don't know where I'm going." He put a slightly finer point on this when he remarked to an interviewer that he had "no memory for pain," which effectively eliminated a large part of whatever biography he had. Which is not to say he wouldn't talk about the past—on the contrary, he was forever telling stories about himself. "From somewhere—" said Updike, "perhaps a strain of sea-yarning in his Yankee blood—he had gotten the authentic archaic storytelling temper, and one could not be with John Cheever for more than five minutes without seeing stories take shape: past embarrassments worked up with wonderful rapidity into hilarious fables"—the main point of which was that life (his life) was a parlous but giddy affair. However, if one asked him to elaborate, a curious thing was apt to happen: suddenly Cheever would talk about something else—indeed, before one had even realized that the subject had been changed. "I always felt there was a blank behind John," said the writer Hortense Calisher. "For an anecdotal man, he'd skip over his background."

Cheever was at once the most reticent and candid of men. "Life is melancholy," he said, "which isn't allowed in New England." Mortality and bodily functions and so forth were not big topics of conversation in Cheever's childhood home, nor was anything else that adverted to human frailty or might lead to a quarrel: "Feel that refreshing breeze," his mother would say when the mood turned tense, or perhaps she'd call attention to the evening star. "If you are raised in this atmosphere," remarks the narrator of "Goodbye, My Brother," "I think it is a trial of the spirit to reject its habits of guilt, self-denial, taciturnity, and penitence, and it seemed a trial of the spirit in which Lawrence [the narrator's brother] had succumbed." A part of Cheever had succumbed as well, while another part roared its defiance to the world. On sexual matters especially, Cheever was almost insistently forward. He would answer fan mail with ribald anecdotes of the most intimate nature, and rarely hesitated to discuss a mistress or some other indiscretion with his children. At the Iowa Workshop, the sixty-one-year-old Cheever positively accosted colleagues to let them know that, the night before, he'd had a nosebleed and an orgasm at the same time! With a twenty-two-year-old girl! "[W]ith what delight, and agony, I read about [Boswell's] pursuit of Louisa," he wrote in his journal. "And how troubled I am by the intensity of my feelings. It may be no more than the reactions of a man who was raised, let us say, where the subject of food was overlooked. . . . So it is with joy, with glee, perhaps with boorishness that we can at least admit our appetites and the deep pleasure of requiting them."

But it was one thing to admit his appetites, another to discuss the "intensity of [his] feelings." As his daughter observed, "He focused on the surface and texture of life, not on the emotions and motives underneath." With family and friends in particular, Cheever was obliged to show a brave, jovial face—though strangers and chance acquaintances were, again, something else. "I am quite naked to loneliness," he announced to a startled journalist, and that sort of thing was typical. "[W]ith dad our sense of his past pain comes mostly from inference," said his son Federico, "and from observation of oddities in his behavior—fear and disgust turned up in the oddest places. . . . If the problems he died with were, in fact, the same ones he left Quincy with at 17, then they followed him through more twists and flips than anyone could have expected."

FREDERICK LINCOLN CHEEVER, JR., was born on August 23, 1905—almost seven years before his only brother, John—and he often spoke of his happy childhood. Both parents adored him: his mother grew plump and stayed that way because Fred had weighed only three pounds at birth, and she'd had to eat and eat to feed him; his father called him Binks because he resembled a cherubic little boy in an advertisement with that name.* Father and son went sailing together in Quincy Bay for many years while John was either unborn or too small to join them. He would always be too small. Meanwhile Fred grew into a manly, likable fellow whose athletic prowess was his father's greatest pride. "Everybody loved [him]," Cheever wrote of Coverly's older brother, Moses, "including the village dogs, and he comported himself with the purest, the most impulsive humility. Everybody did not love Coverly."

By the time John was born, his parents' marriage had become strained at best, and his conception was the result of some rare, tipsy lovemaking after a Boston sales banquet. "As my mother often pointed out," Cheever said, "she drank two Manhattan cocktails that evening. Otherwise I would have remained unborn on a star." His father— whose heart was already filled by Fred and the everyday joys of commerce—did what he could to dissuade his wife from having another child, even inviting an abortionist to dinner. It was a story that haunted Cheever the rest of his life, such that he couldn't help mentioning it time and again (often with a slight chuckle), and finally wrote it into *Falconer.* Not surprisingly, he saw fit to blame his mother for having the bad taste to tell him of the episode—this, as he wrote in his journal, by way of "seiz[ing] the affections of her son": " '[Your father] comes from very bad stock [she said]. It isn't his fault that he doesn't love you. He doesn't know anything about love. He didn't want you to be born.' . . . And what sense can the boy make of these lies." Most of the time, though, Cheever found it all too plausible: "I remember my father's detestation of me as I feel the roots of some destructive vine—the vine, of course, being my bewildering love." His lifelong need to requite this love would lead him to "invent a father" in *The Wapshot Chronicle,* but still his eyes smarted with tears ("oh foolishness") when he'd observe some chance tenderness between a father and son.

With whatever reluctance on his parents' part, John William Cheever† was born on May 27, 1912, in a two-story clapboard house at 43 Elm Avenue, near the trolley tracks. Within a few years, the family entered the period of its greatest affluence, ascending Wollaston Hill

---

*John would have no such charming nickname. He was either called Joey, a name he loathed, or the more generic Brother—because he was, after all (in his parents' eyes foremost), Fred's brother.

†He was named William after his (despised) uncle Hamlet, and kept the name under wraps as much as possible.

to an eleven-room Victorian house on Winthrop Avenue. Leather prices spiked during the war, and by his own recollection Frederick Cheever sold five hundred thousand dollars' worth of elegant, hand-made shoes in a single six-month period of travel—"night after night in the stifling coffin of a Pullman berth," as his son later imagined it, "because he had traveled all over a broad country selling shoes so they could join the golf club and buy gasoline for their cars."* John remembered a milestone day when his father ("pleased and embarrassed") picked him up at school in a brand-new Buick sedan of robin's-egg blue, complete with a flower vase and silk curtains. Such a powerful machine went well with the man's bespoke clothing, his Masonic finery, not to mention the other posh cars parked outside the Unitarian church where Frederick attended services as a matter of demonstrating prosperity rather than piety.

On the surface, at least, it was an idyllic time—and so Cheever was likely to describe it. "They were kindly and original people," he said of his parents some fifty years later, and to the writer John Hersey he spoke of his childhood as "extremely sunny." But privately he found a lot of "disorder and blindness" in his own memories: "If I were writing about someone else I could say honestly I think that he was well-fed, fair, blue-eyed, tanned from a summer at Dennisport or in some third-string white mountain hotel . . . believing that he loved and was loved by everyone in the world. To recall those years as an orderly development from youth to manhood does not come naturally to me at all."

---

*In the midst of his post-*Falconer* celebrity, Cheever would claim his father had actually been a partner in the manufacturing firm of "Whittredge and Cheever," which had a factory in Lynn where Frederick took his son John once a year to blow the whistle. However, Ben Cheever pointed out that his father, in the 1964 *Time* cover story, had described Frederick as a mere salesman ("a commercial traveler with a flower in his buttonhole"): "I assume the factory had not yet been invented," said Ben, with due skepticism. As with many matters relating to Cheever's past, the truth remains nebulous. Among Frederick's notes is a vague reference to one "MH Whittredge" ("Saratoga every season—clothes"), presumably the same "Myron H. Whittredge" who appears in an old family album. Perhaps this was the man who brought Frederick into the business as a salesman, but whether the two were actually partners remains unknown—there's no record of "Whittredge and Cheever" in the various city directories, and Frederick gives his occupation in every federal census as "Salesman." But wait: he appears in the 1932 Quincy directory as a "shoe mfr," and writes in his notes: "I have produced in essential material for 50 years. Given employment to many. Invested in equipment, material." Here one throws up the hands—except to add that Fred Jr.'s children never heard about any "shoe factory."

The idealized New England of St. Botolphs in the Wapshot novels ("an old place, an old river town") might suggest a desire to return to this happier time, or else to create a happiness that never existed. Whatever the case, Cheever was a little bemused by his own aversion to revisiting his "sunny" childhood in terms of reality rather than myth, and only seldom would he pick through the actual details—as nearly as he could recollect them—and wonder at the seeming innocence of it all. Each day had been pretty much like the next: his father always rose at six and took a cold bath ("howling like a walrus"), then played a few holes of golf before a hearty breakfast of fish hash or chops. And so it went:

> I and the dog walk with him to the station, where he hands me his walking stick and the dog's leash, and boards the train among his friends and neighbors. The business he transacts in his office is simple and profitable, and at noon he has a bowl of crackers and milk for lunch at his club. He returns on the train at five, and we all get into the Buick and drive to the beach. We have a bathhouse, a simple building on stilts, weathered by the sea winds. . . . We change and go for a long swim in that green, dark, and briny sea. Then we dress and, smelling of salt, go up the hill to have supper in the cavernous dining room. When supper is over, my mother goes to the telephone. "Good evening, Althea," she says to the operator. "Would you please ring Mr. Wagner's ice-cream store?" Mr. Wagner recommends his lemon sherbet, and delivers a quart a few minutes later on a bicycle that rattles and rings in the summer dusk as if it were strung with bells. We have our ice cream on the back lawn, read, play whist, . . . kiss one another good night, and go to bed.

Cheever described the Quincy of his childhood as a "pleasant, relaxed" middle-class suburb where all the women had gardens and everybody went to the more or less democratic "Neighborhood Club" for black-tie dances. There was a social hierarchy, of course, but it was relatively flexible: "[W]e were always allowed to play touch football with the Winslows and the Bradfords," Cheever remembered in the *New York Times*, adding that his family's maid had been no less than the daughter of "an Adams coachman and she once ate all the brandied sugar lumps around the plum pudding and was found on the wooden floor of the kitchen (this was before linoleum) dead drunk, giggling

helplessly and contributing a bearing or milestone for our recollections." An examination of this chestnut vis-à-vis the journal gives a little insight into Cheever's methods as a raconteur. It was true his family
occasionally hired the coachman's daughter for "large family dinners,"
though usually their maids were "girls sent out on probation from
some reform school," and it was almost certainly such a girl who pil-
fered those sugar lumps, as Cheever recalled a "violent scene" when a
girl was sent back to the reformatory for that very offense: "She gathered me in her arms, crying despondently. My mother pried me out of
her embrace. I expect I was about five." Whenever such a "breakdown
in service or finance" occurred, it fell mostly to Cheever's grandmother
Sarah to take up the household chores until another waif could be supplied. And while the old woman was nothing but bitter toward the men
of the family for using her as a menial ("we had failed her, not only as
providers but as men"), she was most displeased by the conduct of her
youngest daughter, whom she called a "cretin," thereby winning her
grandson's lasting regard. When she lay dying of a stroke, the seven-
year-old John sat at her bedside reading aloud from *David Copperfield*.

Thanksgiving was a great event in the Cheever home—the sort of
thing for which the coachman's daughter was presumably pressed into
service. What Cheever particularly remembered was his mother's
habit of collecting "strays" for the table. For weeks ahead of time—on
beaches and buses, in train stations or "the lobby at Symphony Hall
during the intermission"—his mother would approach whosoever
seemed lonely, poor, infirm, preferably all three, and invite them to the
stately house on Winthrop Avenue for the annual feast. The mellow
Cheever who waxed reminiscent for the *Times* viewed his mother's
motives as a poignant blend of noblesse oblige ("pride and arrogance")
and "her respect and knowledge of the cruelty of loneliness." When
the holiday arrived, the children of Wollaston played touch football or
hockey on the millpond, then repaired to their homes at noon. This
was a day when gluttony was forgiven even by the Cheevers, since an
overloaded table was one way of expressing "sentiments that were . . .
too profound and tender ever to be mentioned." Finally, once the
guests had departed, Frederick Cheever stood by the door and
declared, "The roar of the lion has ceased! The last loiterer has left the
banquet hall!"

By far the most memorable Thanksgiving was not a happy one,
though it offers a useful glimpse at the ethos in which Cheever was

raised. One of the strays invited for that year's feast was Miss Anna Boynton Thompson, a cousin of Cheever's father and one of the most celebrated spinsters in nearby Braintree. A classical scholar who received her doctorate from Tufts, Thompson taught at Thayer Academy for almost fifty years and had startled her neighbors during the Great War by standing on her balcony each night and appealing loudly to the heavens for peace. "She thought of all sensuality as a mode of ignorance," Cheever observed. In 1922, Miss Thompson was fretful over the Armenian famine, and so became incensed at the sight of the Cheevers' laden table: *How can you do this when half the populations of this world are starving?*" she exclaimed. "Anna departed," wrote Cheever (on whom she made such an impression that he'd pause guiltily over his meat during the lean years of World War II). "Six weeks later she was found in her cold, classical library in Braintree, Massachusetts, dead of starvation."*

One might bear in mind a curious affinity between the dour Miss Thompson and her cousin John—who combined, as Updike put it, "the bubbling joie de vivre of the healthy sensitive man and the deep melancholy peculiar to American Protestant males." Born under the sign of Gemini, the heavenly twins Castor and Pollux, Cheever considered his own nature to be "truly halved," and his aunt Anne Armstrong was hardly alone in supporting this view: "What you have to remember," his wife, Mary, insistently repeated, "is that John was a split personality." Though the words "boyish" and "pixie" are constantly used to evoke the giddy, hilarious Cheever, he could also be curt, cruelly sarcastic, relentlessly harsh in judging friends and family and especially himself. Henry Adams thought a divided nature was the inevitable result of growing up in New England and Quincy in particular ("the stoniest glacial and tidal drift known in any Puritan land"): "The chief charm of New England," he wrote in his *Education*, "was harshness of contrasts and extremes of sensibility—a cold that froze the blood, and a heat that boiled it—so that the pleasure of hating—one's self if no better victim offered—was not its rarest amusement. . . . Winter and summer, then, were two hostile lives, and bred two separate natures."

---

*Lillian Wentworth, the Thayer historian, wrote me helpfully as follows: "Anna Boynton Thompson died January 28, 1923, at age 76. . . . The police found Anna dead, sitting at breakfast in the kitchen. Medical examiners determined death was caused by cerebral hemorrhage and hardening of the arteries."

The profound ambivalence with which Cheever beheld the world was even more pronounced in regard to his birthplace. On the one hand, it was "a red-blooded and a splendid inheritance" to grow up in such a "powerfully sensual" environment, where one was barraged by the smells of wood smoke and flowers and the sea. "I've often wondered what makes us old Quincyites so randy," Cheever wrote a stranger who was trying to sell him insurance. "Must be the sandy clams we dug at Wollaston Beach in those wonderful days of our youth." Cheever made much of the fact that he'd lived less than a mile from Merrymount, where Morton had erected his Maypole and "jollity and gloom [had contended] for an empire," as Hawthorne would have it. "[T]he difference between the legend and the present has always been amusing," Cheever wrote in 1934, shortly after leaving Quincy for good. "It is now the most despicable, contrite tract of Dutch Colonial Houses I have ever seen. I've always wanted to go down there with a jug of firewater and a couple of sluts and raise a maypole."

To CHEEVER'S MIND, Anna Boynton Thompson "in her cold, classical library" served as an emblem for the "Athenian twilight years" of fin-de-siècle Boston, when even provincial families of the South Shore placed a high premium on culture. This was particularly true in Cheever's house, where reading aloud ("All of Dickens, from beginning to end, read and reread") was the chief entertainment and a successful novelist (Mrs. Deland) often paid visits. Indeed, the entire extended family cultivated a certain artistic and intellectual flair. There was the painter Aunt Liley, of course, whose pianist son Randall studied at the Eastman Conservatory, while even the snobbish Aunt Anne founded a Shakespeare Society, and Frederick Cheever "could be called on to recite 'Casey at Bat.'" (Frederick, again, was a great fan of Shakespeare in his own right, though perhaps defensive about his lack of formal education. In any event, he disliked arty pretentiousness, and tended to play the rube when things got thick. "If you want to hear the *pianer*-player you'd better come in," he said when the great Rudolph Ganz came for tea. "Mr. Ganz is about to tickle the ivories.") As for Cheever's mother, she took a particular hand in her sensitive younger son's education. Even when pregnant—"casting around for some way of improving the destiny of an unwanted child"—she made a point of attending every concert of the Boston Symphony,* and later took John to the theater, though an especially good play would make him almost ill with excitement. After a performance of *The Merchant of Venice*, the eleven-year-old dismayed his parents by rushing downstairs the next morning to get started on the rest of Shakespeare; and one time, too, his mother brought him to see *Hedda Gabler*, thinking it a musical, and was unable to budge her son once she'd been hideously disabused.

Cheever's precocity as a storyteller became something of a local legend. His fourth-grade teacher at Wollaston Grammar, Miss Florence Varley, never forgot the first time John "rose glibly to the occasion": "To my utter surprise," she recalled half a century later, "he told a fairy tale that lasted about ten minutes. His classmates listened as avidly as they did whenever I found time to read to them from Rudyard Kipling's *Jungle Book*." She refrained from praising the boy, because she assumed he was simply repeating something "he had read, or heard sometime"; but soon John convinced her he could make up such stories on the spot. For his part, Cheever never had any clear idea what he was going to say when asked (more and more often) to tell his classmates a story—but once he opened his mouth, a beguiling fabric of "exaggeration" and "preposterous falsehoods" never failed to synthesize. Miss Varley thought it a gift from "departed spirits," whereas the writer Wilfrid Sheed observed that, in Cheever's case, memory and imagination were "not two faculties but one mega-faculty," such that his everyday experiences were "improved" as soon as they happened and "halfway to being publishable" within a week—or, as Cheever himself liked to say (claiming to quote Cocteau), "Literature is a force of memory that we have not yet understood."† It was around this time, at any rate, that Cheever decided to make a career of his uncanny

---

*Which may have had the desired effect, as Cheever's musical tastes were narrow but passionate. As his wife remarked, "He was a nut about certain music. He played nothing but the Beethoven quartets for years. Also he loved *Tosca*—listened to it over and over." Cheever also enjoyed playing some of the easier Chopin preludes on the piano, and could sing the entire score to *Guys and Dolls*. When asked about his favorite music on New York's classical station, WQXR, he remembered hearing Tchaikovsky's Fifth Symphony when he was fourteen and thinking, "That's the way I feel about life"—a piquant remark, since the symphony reflects Tchaikovsky's struggle with what he called Fate, often interpreted as his secret homosexuality. The Fifth begins ominously but ends in a mood of triumphant joy.

†"Come, John, you know I made that up," Cheever remarked to John Hersey, when the latter asked to be reminded of the source of that fascinating quote.

knack and told his parents as much: "It's all right with us if you want to be a writer," they replied, after some deliberation, "so long as you are not seeking fame or wealth."

Writing was a suitable occupation for a pudgy, unathletic boy who preferred to stay home playing with his puppet theater. If other children visited, they often found themselves on the opposite side of the proscenium while John manipulated the puppets from above and provided their voices, or, if he had a more elaborate show in mind (for which he'd invite the whole neighborhood and charge a penny per), he'd put his visitors to work making sets or dyeing materials for the costumes. His friend Rollin "Tifty" Bailey got the impression that John was wholly absorbed in his own world, that he hardly noticed others, and was therefore startled when he read "Goodbye, My Brother" some twenty-five years later in *The New Yorker*. Cheever, it seemed, had paid better attention than Bailey thought—appropriating not only his nickname "Tifty" for the "rather undesirable" Lawrence Pommeroy, but also the relevant backstory. As Bailey explained, "When I was small, the sound of my little shoes on the runner carpet in the upper hall sounded to my father like *Tifty-Tifty-Tifty* . . ." And finally, for what it's worth, Bailey had to admit he rather identified with his fictional namesake: "I *did* tend to see the bad side," he said. "If you know what's bad, you can face it."

Cheever's public manners were pleasant enough, for his mother's strict sense of propriety was "rigidly observed" by the family. At the end of any social event, he always made a point of bowing to the hostess and thanking her for a good time—though occasionally (if he had an audience) he might add a puckish "My mother told me to tell you so." Such little rebellions were subtle, and no wonder. It was ill-advised to trifle with his "impetuous" mother, who abruptly defenestrated the puppet theater when it caught fire one day ("It was the intelligent thing to do," Cheever mused in retrospect, "but I was shocked"). "You sweep like an old woman!" she berated him, yanking a broom out of his hands, whereupon he carved his name on the cover of her sewing machine—a rare and probably unrepeated act of (overt) retaliation, since afterward "she trashed [him] with a belt until [he] bled." The woman's vigor was nowhere in evidence, however, when it came to showing affection. "My mother was not demonstrative in any way," said Cheever, who came to emulate such restraint toward his own children, though he was, arguably, free enough with his feelings otherwise.

He often signed letters with "Love" even to casual friends—usually "Best" or "Yours, John" to his children—and Updike's first wife, Mary Weatherall, remembered how Cheever went around gleefully hugging people in Russia.

His mother's lack of tenderness was partly a matter of New England decorum, of course, but was also influenced by Mary Baker Eddy's teaching that "God is both father and mother" and hence the proper source of such loving-kindness. Cheever had been christened in the Episcopal Church, though a few years later his mother "veered wildly into Christian Science" and thereafter adhered to its principles with the sort of fanatical devotion she brought to all larger pursuits. Every Wednesday she attended testimonial meetings, where (as family legend has it) she arrested a tumor by confessing to her fellows that she was "enchained by the flesh" and needed their prayers. Later, too, at the age of seventy, she broke her leg in the bathtub and set the bone herself—then, after five weeks in bed ("a severe trial for her," wrote Frederick, "with her natural speed and energy"), she refused any sort of elastic bandage and would only grudgingly use a cane. Moreover, she expected the same stalwart self-reliance from her children, as John discovered when he developed pulmonary tuberculosis at the age of twelve: "I think of myself when I was spitting blood," he remembered, "left alone in a dirty house. The sheets soaked with fever sweat, the rags I was given to spit in, stained with blood. . . . In the village [my mother] at the lectern, introducing an Armenian refugee."

Unassisted by modern medicine, Cheever's lungs took a long time to heal, and he became even more of a loner and (reputed) mama's boy. Once his convalescence was over, he continued to plead ill health in order to excuse himself from gym class and other games, though such lies filled him with "self-loathing and remorse"—all the more so in light of his brother's vaunted athleticism and regular-guy charm: "[T]hat boy of summer," Cheever recalled. "Quarterback . . . Captain of the undefeated hockey team. Happy with his friends, nimble with his girls, he loved his muzzy and dazzy." Fred's heroics even extended to sticking up for his delicate little brother, like the time he punched an Irishman at Braintree Dam for saying that John looked like a girl when he skated. But mostly Fred was too old and popular then to take much of an interest in John, who desperately wanted help with his "effeminate wing" so he could play baseball like the other boys: "I used to get out of bed in the middle of the night and practice pitching," he wrote in his journal. "Neither my brother nor my father would help me; there seemed to be a conspiracy on their part to keep me out of their male demesne." The trauma would become fodder for a bleakly amusing story in 1953, "The National Pastime," which begins, "To be an American and unable to play baseball is comparable to being a Polynesian and unable to swim." The narrator remembers having to beg a game of catch with his cold, unloving father (a malign ur-version of Leander Wapshot), who "stretched [him] out unconscious" with a throw to the back of the neck: "When I came to, my nose was bleeding and my mouth was full of blood. . . . My father was standing over me. 'Don't tell your mother about this,' he said."

Later in life, Cheever's public remarks about his father were characterized by a sort of sensible regret that they weren't able to "requite" one another because of the "age difference," and—after all—"in that particular period, intimacy between fathers and sons was fairly uncommon." In his heart, though, he never forgave the man for rejecting him as a child. "I can't recall taking a walk at his side although I walked with the fathers of my friends," he wrote, allowing, however, that his "memory may be blocked" in that respect (as indeed it may have been, since he'd once remembered those morning walks to the train station with the dog). "Baseball, football, fishing—we shared none of this." The only father-son outings Cheever did recall were virile entertainments such as horse races and boxing matches, during which Frederick would shout, *"Are you men sisters?"* or *"Hit him with a stool!"*—this for John's benefit, perhaps, as Frederick was worried by then that he'd "sired a fruit." His older brother, Hamlet, had practically told him so during one of his rare trips east ("as one of the founders of the Elks") when Cheever was twelve. The old man looked over his runty nephew and said, "Well, I guess you could play tennis." "That was all he said to me," Cheever remembered. "My poor father, defending his own virility, said that his oldest son played hockey and football; but the lecherous, selfish old goat spoke with the authority of a tribal chieftain who, at a glance, had rejected me as a warrior or any other kind of man." Hoping to prove otherwise, the boy went to a burlesque theater that afternoon, where the "jades with their flabby breasts" failed to arouse him. "My scrotum ached with dismay and I went home on a local in pain."

With Hamlet's "tennis" crack somewhere in the back of his mind, the adult Cheever would often assert his manhood with a conspicuous

interest in sports (except for tennis) and other kinds of strenuous physical activity. He flung himself into icy pools and skated with a masculine swagger; he professed to love the Red Sox (in fact he preferred the
Yankees) and baseball in general, interrupting a 1969 *Paris Review*
interview to watch the Mets win the last game of the World Series.
And yet his "wing" remained weak and still he heard "the voices of
[his] long-dead detractors, Uncle Hamlet and Mother and Dad. 'He
will never amount to anything. Dismal obscenities in furnished rooms,
drunkenness, loneliness and despair is all he will ever know.' . . . Isn't
this something of what I suffered."

"THE CLIMATE WAS ANXIOUS," Cheever wrote of his early adolescence; Fred was away at Dartmouth winning glory on the varsity
hockey team while, at home, his parents kept a weather eye on their
weakling second-born. They suspected the worst ("You sweep like an
old woman!") and let him know, obliquely and otherwise, that sexual
inversion was a terrible fate. Naturally, Cheever despised himself for
having such impulses, splitting wood to cleanse his thoughts of an
"obsessive" erotic need—not only a need for Janet Weil and Sally
Bradford, but also "Arnold and Gordon and Faxon and Tubby." And
the more he was browbeaten, the more he was apt to pursue his
"merry games of grabarse" as a means of "parting from Mother"—
the sexual equivalent of carving his name on the lid of her sewing
machine. Both had painful consequences. With or without a lash, the
woman possessed "the authority of an executioner" as the embodiment of social custom—"a world of white gloves and dancing pumps"
that Cheever associated with a fraught childhood memory:

> It was autumn. We went over to the R.'s barn and had a penis-
> measuring contest, followed by an orgy, but when it was over I felt
> so guilty and ashamed of myself, so sorrowful and uneasy. . . . I went
> home and ate a sandwich and was put by my mother into a bath so
> hot that it made my skin pucker and made the touch of everything
> unpleasant. . . . I couldn't find my dancing pumps. I connected this
> with my lewd behavior in the morning. . . . I went into the closet,
> got to my knees, and said the Lord's Prayer three times, noticing . . .
> that my dancing pumps, in a serge bag, hung from a hook above
> me. At least this much of my prayer was answered, but I was filled
> with terrible longings. . . . I would have run away, except that my

mother was a matron that afternoon [at dancing school], and anyhow where would I, in my blue serge, find a haven?

For a while, he found a haven of sorts in his friendship with Fax
Ogden, which he later described as "the most gratifying and unself-
conscious relationship I had known." Even their sex play struck the
adult Cheever as larky and harmless (though in general he was "frightened and ashamed" of such memories), and he didn't hesitate to suggest as much to his wife and children. According to his journal, it was
Fax who first learned the joys of masturbation from a man sitting
beside him at a vaudeville show: "F[ax] went home and gave it a try and
told me about it at school. Lying in bed that night I jacked off while listening to a philosophical radio commentator. The orgasm was racking;
my remorse was crushing. I felt I had betrayed the fatherly voice on the
radio." Happily, the remorse passed, and soon the two were masturbating each other as often as possible—in movie theaters, in the golf-club
shower, and especially at Boy Scout camp on Gallows Pond, in South
Plymouth. The camp was "one of John's happiest memories," according to his wife: He and Fax earned their junior lifesaving certificates,
and one year John won the treasure hunt and was awarded a watermelon. Rainy days were best of all, as the two boys could stay in bed
and practice, indefatigably, their favorite pastime ("When one bed got
gummed up we used to move to another").

They also attended the same progressive elementary school, Thayerlands, for which Anna Boynton Thompson had bequeathed her
home near the Thayer Academy (high school) campus. Cheever
entered as a seventh-grader in 1924, the school's inaugural year, and
was well suited to its determinedly creative atmosphere. He served as
poetry editor of the yearbook, *The Evergreen,* to which he contributed
some of his own verse, including at least one rather impressive stanza
from "The Brook":

> Arched with birches in Gothic style,
>   Traced in crystalline rain,
> Like a tall and slender window
>   In Notre Dame on the Seine.

"John never has a grudge against anyone," reads his character summary, "and is always a good sport"—a consensus view, it would seem.
His teacher Grace Osgood remembered him as pleasant and "eager

to learn" ("a very different young person," she noted, from the one who later made a notorious exit from Thayer), and other classmates described him as "a tease" and "full of fun." "Make it Posture Week, not Weak Posture!" Cheever quipped in *The Evergreen* (though he does not appear on the "Posture Honor Roll"), where he was repeatedly mocked for being a poor speller ("WHAT WOULD HAPPEN IF . . . JOHN CHEEVER learned how to spell?"). Clearly he and Fax were both regarded as class wags, and everyone found it "great fun" to watch them perform in an eighth-grade production of *A Christmas Carol*, with Fax appearing as Scrooge and John as his jolly nephew Fred in a swallow-tailed coat.

"I think of substratas of aloneness," Cheever wrote in 1972, remembering a sad day when "Fax walked off the playing field with his arm around someone else." After his sophomore year at Thayer, Fax transferred to Culver Military Academy in Indiana; he and Cheever would meet only once again, almost forty years later, after which the dejected Fax would occasionally call while in his cups: "Weren't we happy, Johnny? Weren't we really happy?"* Back at Thayerlands in 1926, the boys were given prints of snow-laden evergreens in lieu of diplomas ("thought to be inhibiting"); Cheever's bore the inscription "John, be true to yourself."

---

*In 1979, Cheever told an interviewer that his "closest [childhood] friend, a man named Faxon Ogden," was probably dead: "Someone called from Thayer last winter and I asked them to check back on Fax, and it was 'address unknown.' " On October 28, 1980, David Oliver of Thayer wrote a letter to the Culver alumni office asking for Ogden's address on behalf of "a classmate who remembers him warmly"—almost certainly Cheever, who perhaps saw fit to check on his friend one last time. The letter was returned with a Wilmington (Delaware) address typed at the bottom—though, as it happened, Fax had died almost ten years before.

CHAPTER THREE

{ *1926–1930* }

T HE DEPRESSION CAME EARLY to New England, and by the mid-twenties the shoe industry was all but dead. This, of course, was not openly discussed in the Cheever household, though John could tell his father was becoming dispirited. He overheard the man say to a neighbor, while raking the driveway, that he was prepared to die. As Cheever would later tell it, Frederick had sold out of the shoe business (whether that meant the manufacturing firm of "Whittredge and Cheever" or some lesser concern is, again, a mystery) and gone into an investment partnership with another fellow, alternately named "Mr. Forsyth" and "Harry Dobson" in Cheever's journal. One day, while playing his four holes of morning golf, Frederick espied what appeared to be a coat hanging from a tree near the fairway; naturally, this proved to be none other than Forsyth or Dobson, hanged. After that, Frederick gave up golf and began crying at the breakfast table: "He'd say good morning to me and then look out the window and say something about the weather and then his face would break . . . and he'd start making noises like a winded runner."

Fortunately, he was married to a resourceful woman, who saved the family from certain ruin by opening a gift shop in downtown Quincy.* In fact, it was becoming more and more common at the time for middle-class women to go into business for themselves—what with canned foods and labor-saving devices that lessened the drudgery of

---

*Her first shop was opened at 9 Granite Street in 1926 and later moved a block or so away, to 1247 Hancock Street, where it remained for many years.

housekeeping—and certainly this came all the more easily to an old feminist like Mary Liley Cheever. Indeed, one might even venture to say that as a gift-shop proprietress she'd found her niche: genial and motherly, she was able to strike an instant rapport with most customers, who came to regard the Mary Cheever Gift Shoppe as the place to go for something a little better than the usual dime-store bric-a-brac. It was true that Mrs. Cheever could be a bit pushy at times. As she herself confided, a little ruefully, the harder she tried to "match the purchase to the person," the more determined the person became to buy what she or he had picked out in the first place.

John was aghast that his mother had gone into trade: "[A]fter this I was to think of her, not in any domestic or maternal role, but as a woman approaching a customer in a store and asking, bellicosely, 'Is there something I can do for you?' " Nor was it simply the doorstops and china dogs and doilies that she foisted on a public consisting mostly of her former peers, but the very furniture out from under her family's backs. "You can't sell this," John would remonstrate, "it doesn't belong to you." To which the woman would sensibly reply, "Well, do you have $100?" She even sold his own bed (and decades later, at a Sutton Place party, Cheever bumped into an old Quincy acquaintance who informed him that she herself had bought one of the family beds). It wasn't long before his mother's almost demonic élan began to bear fruit. In 1929, she opened a second store, the Little Shop Around the Corner, purveying dresses and accessories reflecting "the same exclusiveness and beauty which is already evident in her gift shoppe," as the Quincy *Patriot Ledger* reported. Mrs. Cheever relished her success, such as it was, and became every inch the plucky, hard-boiled businesswoman: "She routed thieving gypsies," her son recalled, "brained an armed robber with a candlestick and cracked jokes with the salesmen."

The vulgarity of it all was an "abysmal humiliation" to Cheever, whose innate sense of alienation was burden enough. Nor did he ever quite recover from "the trauma, the earthquake," of his family's awful decline. Anything smacking of gift-shop knickknackery would always repulse him to the point of illness—and there were other triggers, too, some of them rather odd. Rollin Bailey's father was the director of a local bank, and John was never invited to play on their tennis court, two blocks above the Cheevers' house on Wollaston Hill. "Suddenly I remember with painful clarity a fight I had with Rollin Bailey, forty years ago, on the gravel walk of his mother's garden," Cheever wrote in 1965. "In a way I had been victorious, but I had only a painful sense of having disgraced myself and my family." Cheever would forever associate that disgrace (and also, perhaps, his irksome memories of Uncle Hamlet) with the posh *thwock* of tennis balls, and couldn't bear to be anywhere near the game; whenever his friends the Boyers would start a friendly tournament on Whiskey Island, Cheever would remove himself to the opposite shore. As for Rollin Bailey, he last saw his old friend on a troop train returning north during World War II; by then Cheever was on his way to becoming a well-known *New Yorker* writer, and he treated Bailey with a kind of cordial disdain that made the man feel "like less of a person."

At the best of times, Cheever would joke about his family's downfall, announcing that he was one of the "poor" or "wrong" Cheevers. As with other compartments of his personal legend, he had a ready-made story about how the schism had come to pass. The "right" Cheevers had been distinguished doctors in the Revolutionary War, and John's father had impudently written to one of their worthier descendants—Dr. David Cheever of Cambridge—and offered his body for dissection at the medical school.* The proper Cheevers were appalled at the prospect of a relation (however distant) flouting the Christian burial service, and thereafter banished Frederick and his whole raffish branch to the South Shore. John Cheever, for his part, affected to accept his exile in a spirit of roguish insouciance: "They could have their humorless Boston respectability with its piss-pot social rules and regulations and its dumpy Richardsonian architecture," as Susan Cheever put it. At the same time, he was quite pleased to be a *Cheever* (and a Devereaux to boot), because he believed somewhat in the idea of "breeding"—rather as his brother Fred expressed it in a late-life letter to his daughter Sarah: "My underlying conviction is that any Cheever has a great destiny, great ability, great force, grace and love of the world. This is inbred and not many people have it. It is a matter of breeding, and I have the great conceit to know that this will be a heritage to your child." John Cheever rarely went that far, though

---

*John Cheever's wife thinks Frederick may well have written such a letter—*not* as an impudent gesture but rather because (like both his children) he became a great writer of eccentric letters in later life. Also, he was drunk a lot: "Perhaps he was depressed that day," she opined, "and thought, this is *one* thing I can do—give my body to science."

he did think his "sound digestion" and "able dick" were the result of a lucky inheritance "that no amount of venereal or alcoholic abuse could impair."

The part that shamed Cheever—the part he sometimes took pains to conceal—was a dreadful suspicion that his family had become poor and outcast *not* as a result of some stylish revolt against "piss-pot" respectability, but because they were, at bottom, strange and vulgar people. In his journal he worried that he would "have to pay" when his origins caught up with him: "I have been a storyteller since the beginning of my life, rearranging facts in order to make them more interesting and sometimes more significant. I have turned my eccentric old mother into a woman of wealth and position, and made my father a captain at sea. I have improvised a background for myself—genteel, traditional—and it is generally accepted. But what are the bare facts, if I were to write them?" For his own edification he often wrote the facts. There were, for example, the soiled underpants hanging from a nail on the bathroom door ("When I complained about this I was slapped down"). There was the player piano his father had won in a raffle, which was later supplanted (anecdotally) "with a glistening parlor grand, some Schumann on the rack"; in fact, the instrument was upright, mice-infested, and the tunes it played when one pumped the pedals were not Schumann sonatas but dance-hall hits like "Lena from Palesteena." There was the cat to whom his father read Shakespeare. And finally there was the coral-embroidered, homemade dress his mother wore to Symphony Hall, to which she never bothered to bring tickets: "Young man," she'd say, "I am Mrs. F. Lincoln Cheever and my seats are number 14 and 15." Actually, Cheever was somewhat inclined to mention that spectacular dress and certain other details—her tricorn hat, say ("what shit," he glossed privately)—because they "[made] the cast seem charming and eccentric when it was neither."

"Eccentric," in this context, is meant to suggest a desirable originality—that is, as opposed to *un*desirable, as opposed to *aberrant:* "Sexual losers, sartorial losers, bums at the bank," Cheever wrote of his family. "Unclean outcasts whose destiny, written in the stars, was to empty garbage pails and pump the shit out of septic tanks but who, through some cultural miscalculation, imagined themselves being carried off the Lacrosse field on the shoulders of their teammates and then dancing with the prettiest girl in the world." Such an outcast was something Cheever never intended to be, and so he spent much of his adult life "impersonat[ing] squares" and living among them, despite his own "passionate detestation of the establishment." And much the same may be said of his brother Fred, who rebelled against his own Babbittry by becoming an "exhaustively" offensive drunk, and later a sixty-something hippie riding a Harley around the South Shore.

Cheever was a great believer in Satchel Paige's advice not to look back lest you see something gaining on you. "I'm tickled to know that the letters still serve," he wrote Josephine Herbst when she mentioned rereading their old correspondence, "although I always throw the damned things away myself. Yesterday's roses, yesterday's kisses, yesterday's snows." Nor did he keep carbons of his stories, or (so he claimed) copies of his own books. Cheever worried that, if he got in the habit of dwelling on the past, he might also be inclined to dwell on the fact that his father was a failed salesman and his mother ran a "cluttered gift shop" and that hence, with an origin like that, he should have ended up "a slightly drunken gas-pumper" rather than a distinguished author with "the airs of a disenfranchised but charming duke of the holy Roman empire." As for souvenirs, there were "the antiques and heirlooms out of Cheever's Yankee past," as one journalist observed—meaning the ivory fan, the Canton china, the lowboy from Newburyport, and of course Aunt Liley's portrait of the artist as a young man. "Gene [Thaw, an art-dealer friend] frames the portrait," Cheever noted in 1977, "[and] my whole past takes on authority and substance." It wasn't his *whole* past, of course, and sometimes—when he was speaking of his dear old days at Thayerlands, or the time his cousin Randall spent at Eastman Conservatory—his wife would laugh at him: "'When I was at Thayerlands,'" she'd mimic, "and what is this *Eastman Conservatory . . . ?*"

THAYER ACADEMY WAS an old-fashioned New England day school that had no truck with the progressive, "child-centered" principles of its junior school. Founded by Sylvanus Thayer—the so-called Father of West Point, a man who opposed "dissipation of every kind"—the school sought to instill a sense of "duty, industry, and honor" in its students while stuffing their heads with the kind of knowledge required for college entrance exams. The atmosphere was, in almost every sense, austere: the school couldn't afford to heat its buildings in the winter, so students wore earmuffs and mittens while poring over

Latin verbs; as for Cheever, he was constantly reminded of the "intellectual Atlantis" of his stern cousin, Anna Boynton Thompson, whose collection of plaster friezes from Periclean Athens ("a large cast of absolutely naked men") covered the walls of the main building.

Cheever did not shine in such a climate, though at the time he was not shining generally. Sloppy and depressed, he refused to improve his abysmal math skills ("What future is there for a man who can't deal with figures?" his anxious mother had remarked while John was still in grade school), nor did he make more than a token effort in classes that might otherwise have interested him. His freshman English teacher, Louise Saul, remembered him as a young man who did perfunctory work and "didn't take well to discipline"; in her class and in history, he managed a low C, while receiving D's or E's (failing) in pretty much everything else. Meanwhile he was an almost total outcast, and never forgot his "nearly animal resentment": "Second-hand clothes that didn't fit, lost friends, athletic incompetence, poor marks, no pocket money, bad food in a dark lunch-room where nobody much wanted to sit with me. . . . the member of a deposed family."

During his second year he transferred to Quincy High, where he could fail at no expense to his family,* whom he'd begun to help support with a job delivering the *Quincy News* in a Model T. Cheever enjoyed the independence of driving alone to little towns along the South Shore—Houghs Neck, Braintree, Milton—especially during the World Series, when he'd make an extra trip at dusk to deliver a late edition including box scores and full accounts ("It made me feel good to be the one delivering the good news"). When he got home, though, his mother would sometimes make him wash up and put on his brother's "safety-pinned tuxedo" so he could keep up appearances at some "backstreet cotillion." His grades continued to sink: for the fall 1928 semester he received a 77 in English and French, a 66 in Latin; the next semester his grades in those classes were, respectively, 55, 45, and zero.

One reason (of many) for Cheever's apathy was that he was too consumed with his own reading to bother with mundane schoolwork. Even as a child he'd spent summer vacations hiding in a canoe to read Machiavelli, and now that he was a lonely, inquisitive teenager he read

---

*Thayer tuition was $180 a year. Frederick made the first payment of sixty dollars on November 6, 1926, after which all payments were made by his wife.

"everything." Then and later, his favorite novel was *Madame Bovary*, not only because of its "absolutely precise" writing, but also a *c'est moi* identification with its heroine: the novel, said Cheever, was "the first account we have of controlled schizophrenia," a phenomenon he was somewhat familiar with. He reread the book over and over as an adult and could recite long passages word for word—in English, though he generally advised friends to read it first, if possible, in Flaubert's glorious French.* When reading Proust's *In Search of Lost Time* he always stuck to his native tongue, but to read the entire masterpiece in whatever language, at age fourteen, is astonishing enough. "It must sound awfully precocious," Cheever conceded in a 1969 interview, but it appears to have been no idle boast. He also reminisced in his journal about "how disturbed" he'd been, as a boy, to learn of Baron de Charlus's secret homosexuality: "This was in the house in Quincy where the clash between what I read and my surroundings made an intolerable discord," he wrote, while reflecting that he himself had "none of the ebullience it must take to lead a double life" (though at the time he was leading such a life, to some extent, ebulliently or not).†

In an altogether different category was Hemingway, whose importance to Cheever is hard to measure. Much of Cheever's apprentice fiction reads almost like deliberate homage (or parody), but there was more to it than that: "I remember walking down a street in Boston after reading a book of his," Cheever wrote after Hemingway's suicide in 1961, "and finding the color of the sky, the faces of strangers, and the smells of the city heightened and dramatized. The most important thing he did for me was to legitimatize manly courage, a quality that I had heard . . . extolled by Scoutmasters and others who made it seem a fraud. He put down an immense vision of love and friendship, swal-

---

*One of Cheever's friends was Francis Steegmuller, arguably Flaubert's greatest translator into English. Asked in 1956 why he was working on a new *Bovary* translation, Steegmuller explained that the current Modern Library edition (translated by Karl Marx's daughter, Eleanor Marx Aveling) was a "really poor job with awful mistakes": "My friend, John Cheever, loves it, though," said Steegmuller. "He's read it so many times in that way that he doesn't want it changed or improved on. It's his idea of 'Bovary' though he knows it's absurd. Well, that's my goal, to convert John Cheever."

†Tanya Litvinov, Cheever's Russian translator and intimate correspondent, remembers a curious impression on meeting Cheever for the first time in 1964: "I thought at the moment he was a *Charlus* for some reason." The oddity of the thought came back to her many years later, when Cheever's bisexuality was revealed after his death.

lows and the sound of rain." A little later, Cheever met the great man's widow and was thrilled to learn that Hemingway had once rousted her out of bed to read "Goodbye, My Brother." As time went on, though, Cheever became more ambivalent about his lifelong hero: reading the posthumous *A Moveable Feast* (with its unseemly reference to "Scott [Fitzgerald]'s cock" and so on) made Cheever feel as if he'd met "some marble-shooting chum of adolescence who has not changed." Finally, at the height of his own fame, Cheever seemed to worry that readers would overestimate Hemingway's (passing) influence on his work, the earliest samples of which he'd labored to keep out of the public eye. "What have you learned from Ernest Hemingway?" asked a well-meaning admirer at the Ossining Library. "Not to blow my head off with a shotgun," Cheever replied.

He also read Faulkner,* with whom he had a more subtle affinity but an affinity nonetheless. As Malcolm Cowley pointed out, both men were autodidactic high-school dropouts with "enormous confidence in their own genius," and Cheever also cultivated his "little postage stamp of native soil" à la Faulkner's Yoknapatawpha (postage stamps *plural* in Cheever's case, as he mythologized—inimitably if less ambitiously—such diverse locales as provincial New England, the Westchester suburbs, and the lost midcentury Manhattan that "was still filled with a river light"). Both writers, too, were attracted to the sprawling, picaresque novels of the eighteenth century—though, as with Hemingway, Cheever would sometimes hesitate to admit the breadth of his debt to Fielding (whose work he'd consumed "intravenously"). "Oh no, no," he hemmed when a visiting graduate student asked about Fielding's influence on the *Wapshot* novels. Cheever's wife had overheard the exchange, however, and sniped "That's not true! You've been reading *Tom Jones* again!"—then vanished back into the house.

The fact was, Cheever had read so much as a young man, and

---

*When Faulkner won the Nobel in 1949, Cheever showed he could still channel Hemingway with the best of them, imagining what Papa might say if he were to write a letter for the occasion to the *New York Times*: "I think it's fine that Bill Faulkner got the Nobel Prize. . . . The Nobel Prize is like that purse they give in Verona for the shot who bags the most sitting ducks on a clear day. There are other kinds of shooting, but they don't give prizes for it. There is the kind of shooting that you get in the Abruzzi in the May snows and underwater shooting and the kind of lonely shooting that you have when you take your sights in a pocket-mirror and bring down a grizzley [sic] over your left shoulder but they don't give prizes for that kind of shooting. Mr. Thomas Hardy and Mr. Herman Melville did that kind of shooting but they never got any prizes."

come so far as a writer, that he could honorably deny *any* particular influence—there were simply too many. "I seem to be running down," he wrote a few months before his death, "but as a very young man, choosing a career, to be a serious writer seemed to be to emulate heroes. Thackeray, Dickens, George Eliot, Ernest Hemingway all seemed to me heroes."

H E   W A S   B A D L Y   I N   N E E D of heroes. In the space of a few years, his father had gone from a jaunty golf-playing burgher to a sodden failure with a hacking cough who always seemed to be sitting on the porch with nothing to do. Everybody in the neighborhood knew about "poor Mr. Cheever": he'd taken to drink and odd behavior; he wore the shabby cast-off clothing of his dead friends. His son John "deeply resented his defeatism," but resented his mother's strength even more. Her latest venture was a restaurant she'd opened in a family farmhouse in nearby Hanover, where Frederick was relegated to an outbuilding and fed only after the last customer had left. John came to understand such contempt as unique to wives in New England and peculiarly evident in his mother's case. "Why don't you want to eat with me?" his father would say, following his wife around the house. The woman could hardly bear the sight of her idle, drunken husband, and would either eat standing at a sideboard with her back to the room ("For Christ's sake," Frederick would protest, "what have I done to deserve this?"), or remain at table to indulge in a bit of chilly repartee. "Don't these chops taste good?" she once asked, and when her husband replied that he hadn't "been able to taste anything for ten days," the woman sweetly observed, "Well, it doesn't seem to have spoiled your appetite."

At last they stopped talking entirely, communicating (if at all) in the form of written indictments. One day Frederick presented his wife with an exhaustive list of malfeasances; she tossed it, unread, in the fire, whereupon he announced he was going to the beach to drown himself. She told her son as much—with an exasperated sigh—when he came home for dinner that evening, and John took the car and raced after his father:

The beach was deserted, the sea was calm and I had no way of knowing if it contained, full fathom five, his remains. The amuse-

ment park was open and I heard some laughter from there. A group
of people were watching the roller coaster where my father, waving a pint bottle, was pretending to threaten to leap. When he
was finally grounded I got him by the arm and said Daddy you
shouldn't do this to me, not in my formative years. I don't know
where I got that chestnut. Probably from some syndicated column
on adolescence. He was much too drunk for any genuine remorse.
Nothing was said on the way home and he went to bed without his
supper. So did I.*

The episode was part of a repertoire of comic anecdotes Cheever
told about his father, in life as in fiction. There was also the time he
found the man "drunken, debauched and naked but for a string of
champagne corks," as well as the time his father drank all the sherry
and then tried to cover his tracks by pissing in the decanter. "I have
finessed these scenes," Cheever wrote a friend, "but when he failed me,
and he did a thousand, thousand times, I found my cock and balls in a
wringer. I was determined not to lose that sense of locus that I would
have lost if I dismissed him as a tragic clown." By way of mitigating his
resentment (not to say his own dreadful fear of failure), Cheever struggled all his life to comprehend his father's predicament. "He did not
even give me bus fare," he mused; "but he didn't have it, and I think his
spirit was pure." Cheever was especially haunted by papers he'd found
after his father's death—a heartbreaking testament of the man's losing
struggle to preserve self-esteem. There were "at least fifty" rejected
applications for menial jobs at shipyards and factories; promotional
schemes for selling cheese and soap chips and automobiles; dotty letters to heads of state and other luminaries. One long correspondence
was particularly telling: Frederick had been very proud of his four-
digit license plate ("3088"), because a low figure marked him as one of
the first automobile owners in Massachusetts and hence a man of substance; alas, his son Fred had forgotten to renew his license one year,

---

*Cheever wrote of this episode repeatedly in letters, journals, and finally in *Fal-
coner*, where he called the fateful beach "Nagasakit." In *The Wapshot Chronicle*, Leander
ferries his customers aboard the *Topaze* to the amusement park at "Nangasakit" Beach,
which appears to be the same fictional locale with an "n" added. Both are almost certainly based on Paragon Park at *Nantasket* Beach in Hull, about ten miles from Wollaston, which featured a large roller coaster such as the one Frederick rode so boozily.
Cheever was known to frequent the beach in his childhood.

and the coveted number was snapped up by an Italian politician. Frederick (who despised foreigners) wrote many indignant letters, and finally stopped driving altogether.

Naturally Mrs. Cheever was to blame. As John maintained, she never let the men of her family forget who the breadwinner was—and, to make the emasculation complete, she even insisted they do housework.* "I'm a businesswoman!" she'd gloatingly proclaim. Cheever remembered coming home from his newspaper route and finding the flowers dead, the furniture covered in dust, his father drunk. Desperate to cheer things up a bit (and since it was expected of him), John would rush about tidying the place before his mother returned from work. Then, after a dinner prepared in part by himself, he and his drooping father would wash and dry the dishes. ("I have got so [I can] polish the dishes better than [I] used to do," Frederick wrote his son years later, "when you and I teamed up on that job—quote—'Polish them Dad!' ") Cheever never got over the bitterness of their mutual humiliation— "a bronchitic and routed old man picking a thread off the rug and a youth, famous for his salad dressing." Later, as head of his own family, he created "an ideal Polynesian culture" (as his son Federico put it), for which the primary motto was "That's women's work!"—sternly repeated whenever Cheever caught a son of his hefting a broom or helping with dishes. Men scythed and split wood; housework was "bad for the hormones."

Meanwhile his mother gleefully bought a car and painted it herself ("imply[ing] that . . . neither my father nor I had the gumption"), then pressed her son into service as a chauffeur. Every morning he drove her to work, and returned in the evening at five; often Mrs. Cheever would be chatting with a friend or completing a sale, in which case John would cool his heels in a tiny office, amid stacks of broken china and the pervasive odor of "candle fat, sweat, . . . and hot radiator paint." It was, perhaps, the least he could do, seeing as how the gift shop kept the family afloat (for a time), but mostly he associated its sweaty bouquet with "the gall and chagrin of failure." That is, despite the best efforts of "a vigorous but disturbed woman"—as Cheever would have it—most of her business ventures came to a bad end. She

---

*"Well, she *did* damage my father," said Cheever with an edge of annoyance during an otherwise benign TV appearance in 1981, "and my father's well-being was very much my concern."

soon sold the dress shop; the restaurant in Hanover "struggled on" for a few summers, though days passed without a single customer: "The waitresses—country girls dressed in quaint costumes designed by my Mother—hung around the three dinningrooms [sic] and the lobster and chicken that was all she served would spoil." This was followed by something called the Oribe Tea Barn in Jaffrey, New Hampshire, which lasted a few weeks before Mrs. Cheever telephoned her son one night to come get her. "When I asked what had happened she raised her face as though for a blessing and sighed: 'I was much too popular.' "

Cheever also associated the gift shop with a sense of personal impotence. ("Did *you* used to work in the gift shoppe?" Cheever's wife would tease him, stirring memories that caused "an actual sensation of discomfort in [his] scrotum.") Later—when he sought the cause of his malaise in Freud—he discovered that his family was a virtual paradigm for "that chain of relationships" (weak father, dominant mother) "that usually produces a male homosexual." But things were even worse in Cheever's case. His mother (he came to suspect) had a "terrifying ambivalence" about homosexuality, deploring it on the one hand but wanting to castrate him on the other, the better to guarantee "a gentle companion for the lonely years of old age." Thus, when his wife would catch him, say, reading the theater page of the *Times* ("an incriminating piece of effeminacy"), Cheever would recall the Freudian shrink who'd told him, in so many words, that he'd married his mother—a *ghastly* thought. Could it be that the elder Mary Cheever had kept him tied to her "faraway apron strings" after all? "Come back, come back," he imagined her crying, "my wretched, feeble and unwanted child."

Whatever her designs, the fact remained that all three members of the household were crushingly miserable. The mother distracted herself with work, the father with drink and solitary quirks, while the son was left to shift for himself. His parents loathed each other and pretty much ignored him, except as a pawn or buffer; one year they both completely forgot his birthday. It was a lot to bear for anybody, especially a hypersensitive boy who found himself fleeing trolley cars because of a morbid awareness of other people. The main reason he became a storyteller, he said, was "to give some fitness and shape to the unhappiness that overtook [his] family and to contain [his] own acuteness of feeling." Later, with his own children, he often made a game of his favorite coping mechanism—picking out strangers in public and imagining their wallpaper, what they ate for breakfast, and so on. It worked and it didn't. Once, drunk, he confided to his son that he could hardly bear to take the train to New York anymore: "[E]very stranger's face," he said, "is like the last hand in a game of poker in which my life is at stake."

WHILE AT QUINCY HIGH, Cheever won a short-story contest sponsored by the *Boston Herald*, after which he was invited back to Thayer on a probationary basis. The idea was for him to receive special instruction from a revered English teacher, Harriet Gemmel, without the distractions of math or Latin. The academy was taken aback, however, by the more eccentric Cheever who returned in the fall of 1929—a "total kook" (so the consensus went) who flaunted his disdain for the place, interrupting teachers with pointless questions and taking pains to look as bored as possible. Also, whereas he'd neglected his personal appearance in the past, he now seemed to cultivate dishevelment as a kind of writerly ideal: "On more than one occasion," said a friend, "we classmates would collect a few pennies and escort him to the barber shop."

Miss Gemmel understood, and even looked kindly on her shaggy protégé when he'd stay behind in her classroom long after the bell rang, vividly absorbed in his writing. Eulogized in the yearbook as "our more-than-teacher, seeing guide, / Who understands our faults, but trusts our strength," Miss Gemmel gave Cheever tea and cookies at her home on Sunset Lake and shared the fruits of her more-than-teacherly wisdom. In the story Cheever was soon to write, she appears as the "very nice" Margaret Courtwright, a "slightly bald" woman who adores Galsworthy and warns the young narrator away from the "sex reality" of writers such as Joyce. "When I told her people laughed at Galsworthy she said that people used to laugh at Wordsworth," Cheever wrote. "That was what made her so nice."

The sardonic prodigy—reading his way through Proust and Joyce and Hemingway, et al.—soon decided that the likes of Harriet Gemmel didn't have much to offer him. As for Thayer at large, Cheever later observed that it "existed not to educate us in any way but to make us admissible to Harvard University"—where he claimed a scholarship had awaited him, though he sensed an Ivy League career would prove "disastrous."* Thus he became even more recalcitrant, ignoring his lessons ("I refused to commit to memory the names of Greek playwrights whose work I had not read") and smoking behind the tennis court—the last an offense for which he was repeatedly warned and finally expelled. Or so he usually claimed.

Thayer's headmaster at the time was Stacy Baxter Southworth, a beloved figure known throughout greater Braintree as "Uncle Stacy." "From someone who remembers Stacey [sic] Southworth vividly," Cheever inscribed a copy of *Falconer* for the Thayer library, and once, on television, he praised the man as "extremely understanding and vastly intelligent." Southworth was, in fact, keenly aware of John's troubled home life and more than willing to be patient (he'd excused him from math and Latin, after all), if only the boy would meet him halfway and buckle down to his studies a bit more. But John refused, and that was that. "The young man was not expelled from the Academy," wrote a furious Southworth three weeks after Cheever's "Expelled" appeared in *The New Republic*. "He left entirely on his own volition in the late spring season, presumably because of the added attraction of the May orchard blossoms, which he characterized in his unique way." Another unique characterization in Cheever's story (among many) was that of the headmaster's "gravy-colored curtains," which occasioned a lot of knowing snickers behind Uncle Stacy's back.

Shortly after leaving Thayer in March, Cheever took a job in the stockroom of the Shepherd Company in Boston, a large department store, where he presumably pored over *The New Republic* during lunch breaks. Judging from "Expelled," he'd become quite familiar with a few of the left-wing magazine's pet issues. For example, the governor of Massachusetts—a Republican Cadillac-dealer named Alvan T. Fuller—was a particular target for having refused to commute the sentences of Sacco and Vanzetti, and so in his story Cheever mentioned "the Governor" who comes to the narrator's prep school and delivers a Memorial Day harangue against the "Red menace." Meanwhile a gal-

---

*Peter Benelli, a later headmaster at Thayer, agreed with Cheever's assessment of the school circa 1930: "I was approached by angry graduates who were never taught to write," he said. "Mostly they were just prepped for achievement tests." Cheever's claim that he was bound for Harvard is more dubious. At the time, fewer than 10 percent of Thayer graduates went to Harvard. With Cheever's miserable academic record at a school of rather modest reputation, it's hard to believe anyone (much less Cheever) seriously considered him Harvard material.

lant history teacher named Laura Driscoll is fired for daring to suggest that Sacco and Vanzetti were innocent. Miss Driscoll also serves to embody the higher possibilities of modern pedagogy, as opposed to the "ruthlessly regimented" system that still prevailed, whereby "children were being crammed with meaningless miscellaneous information"— or so *The New Republic* reported in a "symposium" on progressive education that ran throughout its June 1930 issues. "When Laura Driscoll dragged history into the classroom," Cheever wrote, "squirming and smelling of something bitter, they fired Laura and strangled the history"; such a maverick as Driscoll had no place in a school where "people didn't care about Chartres as long as you knew the date."

Cheever commended his story to the attention of a young associate editor, Malcolm Cowley, whose first book of poetry, *Blue Juniata*, had struck the young Cheever (so he remarked in his cover letter) as the work of a sympathetic soul. Cowley read the precocious slush-pile manuscript and agreed: "I felt that I was hearing for the first time the voice of a new generation," he recalled sixty years later. So emphatic was his advocacy of Cheever that his fellow editors decided to suspend a long-standing rule against publishing fiction.

"Expelled from Prep School" by "Jon" Cheever (as he'd spell his name for the next five years) was the lead story in the October 1 issue, prefaced by a little note from the editors explaining that its author had recently been expelled "from an academy in Massachusetts . . . where education is served out dry in cakes, like pemmican." It's an astonishing debut. At age eighteen, Cheever had evolved a voice that alternated seamlessly between droll, oddly precise details ("a soft nose that rested quietly on his face") and flights of somber lyricism: "The year before I had not known all about the trees and the heavy peach blossoms and the tea-colored brooks that shook down over the brown rocks. . . . I wanted to feel and taste the air and be among the shadows. That is perhaps why I left school." Here and there, Cheever's adulation of Hemingway lets him down a little, as when he resorts to a kind of lumbering irony: "Our country is the best country in the world. . . . Dissatisfaction is a fable. . . . It is bad because people believe it all. . . . Because they marry and reproduce and vote and they know nothing." For the most part, though, the story is a curiously self-sufficient performance— "alarmingly mature," as Updike put it, "with a touch of the uncanny, as the rare examples of literary precocity—Rimbaud, Chatterton, William Cullen Bryant, Henry Green—tend to be."

Years later, when asked what it felt like to sell a story to *The New Republic* at such a tender age, Cheever cocked his head and replied, "It felt precisely . . . eighty-seven dollars, that's what it felt like." That may have been what it felt like to his parents, too, who suddenly developed an avid interest in their son's literary career: "Have you been writing today?" they kept asking him, bruiting it about Wollaston that their celebrated boy was working on a novel. In the meantime another notorious local dropout, Curtis Glover, sought out Cheever for his views on educational reform. Two years before, Glover had made the front page of the *Boston Herald* by abruptly leaving Dartmouth to live in the woods like Thoreau. Cheever enjoyed Glover's visit in the same spirit of jaunty mockery that informed his narrative voice: "[Glover] was tall, blonde, with a pink and white complexion, wide hips and a loose mouth," he reported to Cowley. "[H]e laughed through his nose, ate his toast with a knife and fork and read the 'new republic' faithfully." For the time being, at least, Cheever finally seemed to be having some fun.

But it came at a certain price. Among respectable people, Cheever was more a pariah than ever: simply to write for such a "radical" magazine as *The New Republic* was bad enough, but to play "fast and loose with the truth"—as Stacy Southworth noted in a letter to a sympathetic Thayerite—was unforgivable, even in a purported work of fiction. "Laura Driscoll," for instance (the firebrand Sacco-and-Vanzetti supporter), was an obvious surrogate for Mary Lavinia Briscoe, late of the history department. In Cheever's version of her departure, the headmaster had reported to students in chapel that she had "found it necessary to return to the West": "Then Laura got up, called him a damned liar, swore down the length of the platform and walked out of the building." This, Southworth fumed, was "a tissue of falsehoods": "I was glad to cooperate with her in securing a fine position in St. Louis," where she had moved "to enlarge the scope of her experience." Nor was the woman known to have any particular convictions about Sacco and Vanzetti one way or another, though in any case "she surely appreciated the freedom of expression which she enjoyed [at Thayer]."

By far the worst of it was Cheever's heartless treatment of his mentor, Harriet Gemmel, the woman he'd slurred as a balding Galsworthy connoisseur. "[T]ragic indeed," said Southworth, who knew only too well how wounded the woman had been. Thayer staff and students, the citizens of Braintree and beyond—almost everyone was aware of the pains Miss Gemmel had taken with the obnoxious youth, and was equally up in arms.* So they remained. "Personally, had I the choice, I should not invite John to visit or to speak at the Academy," protested his old teacher Grace Osgood when Thayer invited its most famous alumnus to give the commencement address in 1980 (the year his grandniece Sally Carr graduated). Cheever, said Osgood, had made too many "inaccurate" and "cruelly unkind" statements "about gentle, gracious, bright people who were truly trying to help him."

As it happened, Cheever had no interest in accepting the invitation. In fact he'd been asked before, in 1968, when Headmaster Peter Benelli had paid a personal visit to Ossining in hope of persuading him. As ever, Cheever presented his guest with a whacking martini and then grew solemn. His memories of Quincy, he said, were "very painful," and he would never return to the area for any reason.† As for Benelli's eminent predecessor—well, the very name put Cheever in a pious mood. "Without Stacy Baxter Southworth," he liked to say, "I would have ended up pumping gas in some place like Walpole." Such piety depended somewhat on his audience, however. To a fellow disgruntled alumnus, Cheever mentioned an old photograph he'd seen of Uncle Stacy: "[He was] wandering under some Elm trees in a light rain performing some traditional and foolish ceremony," Cheever wrote. "God have mercy on his soul."

---

*Miss Gemmel survived the attack and continued teaching at Thayer for many years. Hugh Hennedy (class of '47) was also given tea and cookies at Sunset Lake, and will attest that the woman was still teaching *The Forsyte Saga* in its entirety almost twenty years after Cheever's departure. "His portrait of her dazzles me every time I look at it," said Hennedy.

†As we shall see, he returned to the South Shore only twice after his mother's death in 1956: for his brother Fred's funeral and for his own.

CHAPTER FOUR

{ 1930–1934 }

JOHN AND HIS BROTHER had not been close when Fred left for Dartmouth in 1924, but when he returned two years later (because of the family's financial straits) the age difference no longer mattered as much. Also, Fred felt an obligation toward his gifted sibling, who was all but entirely alone in the world except for their embattled parents. Fred had settled briefly in Framingham, a few miles west of Boston, but as often as possible he'd drive to Quincy in his Model A roadster and, in effect, rescue his little brother. "[W]hen the situation was most painful and critical," Cheever remembered, "my brother entered my life and played out for me the role of mother, father, brother and friend."

The two brothers—Fritz and Joey—were almost inseparable for the next five years or so. They took a sculpting class together and read the same books; they spent long days at the beach or simply driving and talking about things. At one point Fred was between jobs and moved back to the house on Winthrop Avenue, where he witnessed firsthand what a shambles his family had become. There was, of course, the constant bickering (or fraught silences) between his parents, but most appalling was the deterioration of his father, whose behavior was markedly odd with or without alcohol. One or both of the boys often stayed out late at night, and one of Frederick's rituals involved locking them out of the house; one night young Fred had to force a window to get back in, and his father fired a pistol at his head. "The explosion woke me," John recalled, "and I ran downstairs and saw the two men in the dining-room and the hole in the wall. My

brother was very pale. 'You shouldn't have done that, Dad,' he said."
For a while the brothers tried sliding into the house through a coal
chute, until Fred found a job and took an apartment on Beacon Hill, a
cosmopolitan world where John began to spend more and more time.
"[M]y sense of freedom may have been erotic, my balls and my cock
hung in my pants in a serene condition, no longer my Mother's errand
boy . . ."

His genius validated by *The New Republic*, "Jon" endeavored to
become the sort of idle, brooding bohemian his mother was apt to
abhor. Growing his hair to his shoulders and affecting a large amethyst
ring, he whiled away the hours in his room playing the accordion amid
a pall of incense. (One assumes his mother was duly shocked; certainly
Cheever was shocked, many years later, whenever the soigné *New Yorker*
author considered his younger self: "I was·*some* kid in those days,"
he told the *Times* with "horrified amazement," while privately he
wondered how a boy with an amethyst ring had grown into "a decent,
likable and healthy man as I think myself." At other times, suffice to
say, he saw the connection more clearly.) Nor was the performance
entirely for his mother's benefit, as he'd begun to receive invitations
to dine among older, rather distinguished company. Cheever—though
he "knew the forks"—was still a small-town boy behind the Wildean
façade, so nervous in any sort of sophisticated gathering that he could
scarcely lift a spoon to his mouth. It was around this time that he
discovered the usefulness of alcohol: "The next engagement that
threatened to arouse my shyness I bought a bottle of gin and drank
four fingers neat. The company was brilliant, chatty and urbane and so
was I."

He and Fred soon became regulars at raffish saloons like Cohen's
and Sharkey's on Howard Street—"the arse-end of the city," as
Cheever put it. Strippers from the Old Howard burlesque theater
hung out in such places, and soon Joey was adopted as a mascot of
sorts. A venerable stripper named Boots Rush took a particular shine
to the lad, letting him lift her off a stool whenever she got tipsy enough
to regale the crowd with "Leave It to the Irish." Mischievously, perhaps, Cheever invited his old neighbor Rollin Bailey to accompany
him to a party in the arse-end part of town—an occasion Bailey
recalled as being "like a dream," so alien was it to his genteel Wollaston upbringing. Volatile men and women ("all foreign") rattled around
a dingy walkup apartment, drinking and laughing, and John seemed

very much one of them. "Yesterday, sitting in the sun," Cheever wrote in 1971, "I recalled my life among the burlesk stars. A frightful bore, highly colored with alcohol."

He preferred being alone with his brother—it was "the most significant relationship in [his] life," he later told a psychiatrist. "It was like a love affair." Whether it was an *actual* love affair is hard to say, though it appears not to have been entirely platonic. All his life Cheever spoke of an "ungainly closeness" to his brother, describing their attachment in his journal as "a sterile and perverse love," while certain details he let drop in conversation would seem almost to clinch the matter. Many years later he told Allan Gurganus (on whom he had an open crush) that he and his brother had shared a bed when he was an adolescent and Fred a young man: "He implied it had been the erotic romance of his life," said Gurganus. Above all, Fred seems to have served as a kind of ideal parent figure—a man he could easily confide in, as he'd never been able to confide in his father, and moreover a source of tenderness that had been all but entirely absent in his relations with either parent. When the brothers showered together, for example, John freely admitted he was worried about his sexual development, and Fred was able to reassure him. That the solace Fred offered was sometimes (in whatever form) physical is not in doubt: "I still long for the warmth and support I was given by his arms," Cheever wrote.

Any separation from Fred was an almost intolerable wrench, and so, in the summer of 1930, John was crushed when his brother departed for Germany. Interested in the idea of "breeding" even then, Fred was fascinated by the budding experiment to establish a state along racial lines, and finally he could no longer restrain himself from crossing the Atlantic to learn more about National Socialism. John (who would always lack his brother's zest for big ideas) lay weeping on the sofa in Fred's empty apartment in Boston: "I wept for a love that could only bring me misery and narrowness and denial; and how passionately I wept."

John was perhaps well cared for in his brother's absence, as they'd become part of a rather louche circle of intellectuals who tended to espouse socialism of one kind or another and gravitated around the frank bohemia of Beacon Hill. As Cheever reported to Cowley (in e. e. cummings–esque lower-case), "prescot [sic] townsend will very nearly give me his house in provincetown for a month." Prescott Townsend was then a thirty-six-year-old dandy who frequented "tearooms" such as the Green Shutters on Cedar Lane Way (a narrow street where Fritz and Joey would presently take an apartment), which featured enormous martinis quaffed discreetly from porcelain cups amid a din of radical palaver. Townsend's greatest fame would come later, as founder of the Boston Mattachine Society, a pioneering gay-rights advocacy group. Known as "Foxy Grandpa," he had exotic digs in Provincetown that were a kind of caravansary for like-minded youths who were either attractive or interesting (and Cheever, at the time, was both).*

Another Boston mentor was the poet John Wheelwright, a Brahmin socialist who lived on Beacon Street with his sister in (as Lincoln Kirstein put it) "a suite of red-and-black Pompeiian chambers." Cowley and Wheelwright had been fellow Harvard aesthetes, and Cowley might have been startled by the extent to which his new discovery "Jon" was getting around—as the latter informed him, he and "Jack" were friends: "[H]e is very nice, very guarded," Cheever wrote of the poet. "[D]espite his attempts to be a period piece or a distinguished snob he is probably one of the most sincere, affectionate, charming people in Boston." Wheelwright's sexual inclinations were as mutedly unorthodox as the rest of the man. He wrote bitterly of "those who split the monism of love into the dismal triad of heterosexuality, bisexuality and homosexuality," and once made a shy attempt to kiss the poet Howard Nemerov. What passed between him and Cheever will remain a mystery, though Wheelwright's endearing quaintness was (according to Cheever's journal) part of the confection that became Honora Wapshot.

With a certain wistful hilarity, Cheever often spoke of a memorable encounter with Henry Wadsworth Longfellow Dana, the poet's notorious grandson and proprietor of the family mansion on Brattle Street in Cambridge. Known for cultivating protégés, the fifty-year-old Dana gave Cheever a modest allowance and once invited him to Craigie Castle (as the mansion was known) for a lavish dinner. Later they went to the theater, after which Dana suggested they return to Brattle Street for a taste of his grandfather's brandy. "While I was waiting for him to produce the brandy," Cheever recalled,

---

*One of Townsend's later boarders was the young John Waters, years before he made his name as director of *Pink Flamingos* and *Lust in the Dust:* "It was like living with a lunatic Swiss Family Robinson," Waters recalled. "Part of the apartment was made out of a submarine, and trees grew right up through the living room."

he got out of his clothes. I remember turning around and being surprised by the sight of a plump, white, naked man. I think I was more amused than anything else although I can see now the bitterness of having one's erotic drives seem clownish. I thanked him for the evening and politely said goodnight to the naked spectre. He railed at me. "You claim to be an independent spirit," he said, "and yet you don't dare have a little harmless fun. You're just tied to your mother's apron strings." I left the room with him in pursuit. The front door was locked but I found the key in a marble daisy on the left.

Naked or not, Dana was a rather comic figure (he reminded Cummings of the comedian Jack Benny), though Cheever's memory of the man assumed a poignant dimension as time passed. "I could not imagine a man so old, racked with sexual ardor," he wrote Gurganus in 1974. "You may very well feel the same about me."

FRED WAS EXCITED by what he'd seen in Germany, and the following summer he proposed a return trip with his brother. John didn't see why not; his novel was stalled and he hadn't been able to follow up his *New Republic* coup with another sale. Meanwhile Fred had gotten a promising job in the advertising department of Pepperell, a textile manufacturer, and was happy (as ever) to pay for the whole thing. On a rainy day in July, then, they sailed for Bremen, where they caught a slow train to Munich and watched the swastika-laden scenery.

Apart from the beer, John wasn't particularly impressed by Germany, and he was appalled by Nazi militarism. "Everything I saw meant war," he later wrote Cowley, "although no one, especially Bruce Bliven [chief editor of *The New Republic*], seemed interested in my accounts of the National Socialist Party." Fred was exalted, however, and would always speak of the trip as one of the great adventures of his life. He adored the Führer's insistence on discipline and was touched by the renascent pride of the German people, whose mettle was evident in the superior merchandise they produced.* He breezily made

---

*For the rest of his life, Fred made a point of buying German cameras, binoculars, etc., and claimed to be the first person in Massachusetts (circa 1950) to own a Volkswagen. And while he and Hitler fell out over World War II and the Holocaust, Fred con-

friends with total strangers, eager to canvass their views on the com-
bustive Zeitgeist of 1931, and thereby gained a number of lifelong
pen pals. John apparently kept his own counsel (Fred remained under
the impression that his brother had relished the trip almost as much
as he), but a fissure had begun to form in the relationship. Indeed,
John's memory of that summer was so troubling he managed to repress most of it ("I have no memory for pain")*—claiming many years
later, for example, that he'd never once gone to France because his
infantry comrades had been slaughtered on the beaches of Normandy;
in 1931, however, he and Fred *did* stop in Paris, whence Cheever
reported the following "Talk of the Town" item for *The New Yorker:*
"On the Quai de Louvre, we are told, is now a sign on a lamp post:
'Pietons avant de traverser, allumez le signal.' One pushes the button, a
bell rings, a red light gleams; then, while the traffic halts, one crosses
statelily."

When he returned to the States, Cheever sought the literary advice
of a new acquaintance, the gay communist biographer Newton Arvin,
who pronounced the young man's work "contemptible" because it
failed to address the problems of the working class. Cheever promptly
hitchhiked to Fall River and took a room in a slum occupied mostly by
unemployed mill workers. The product of this experiment was "Fall
River," an impressionistic sketch of local bleakness that reads like
something a young Hemingway might have written if he'd fallen under
the influence of Newton Arvin. Cheever thus evokes an abandoned
mill: "On the floors and on the beams and on the brilliant flanks of
steel the mist of the web was covered with dust like old snow." The
images of dust and dead leaves and stark hilly distances recur often in
Cheever's early stories, suggesting a somewhat too avid study of the
famous first paragraph in *A Farewell to Arms.* Fortunately, elegant
Hemingway pastiches on proletarian themes were at the height of
their vogue, as most of the arty little magazines had been replaced by

---

tinued to find a certain validity in the man's racial theories. "We had a funny conversation once in the early sixties while driving between Connecticut and Boston," said his
daughter Sarah, who distinctly remembered her father's observation that "blacks
[were] inferior because of malnutrition"; he then dilated on the relatively superior
nutrition and educational opportunities of white Germans.

*"Untouched by the magic of fable, whole areas of experience have disappeared,"
Alwyn Lee wrote in his 1964 *Time* cover story on Cheever. "This includes an early
walking tour of Europe with his brother Fred."

organs of radical propaganda. An example of the latter was *The Left: A Quarterly Review of Radical and Experimental Art*, whose manifesto announced "the disintegration and bankruptcy of the capitalist system"—as did "Fall River," more or less, which appeared in that journal's Autumn 1931 issue.

Cheever found he didn't like writing about hunger and cold, much less living in a Fall River slum, so he returned to Quincy and reverted to a more apolitical mode. "It had rained hard early in August so the leaves were off the trees," the story "Late Gathering" begins. "In the sunlight the hills were like scorched pastry and when there was no sun the meadows were gray and the trees were black and the clean sky parted in firm lines down onto the smooth horizon." Let it serve as a testament to Cheever's precocity that, at this point, it was almost impossible to distinguish his prose from the master's. But while Cheever had mastered the style all right, his content needed work. Both "Late Gathering" and his next story, "Bock Beer and Bermuda Onions," are mostly concerned with a middle-aged war widow named Amy who runs a boardinghouse in the country and presides over events that resist analysis. What's notable about the second story is the enigmatic motif of its title, which is sounded throughout but never explained: "[Amy] thinks about her forty-fifth April and the great symbol and seal of spring as Bock beer and Bermuda onions." Such ambiguity had a nice modernist savor, whatever else it lacked, and both stories were placed in reputable journals. "Late Gathering" appeared in the second issue of *Pagany*, founded by a high-school dropout from Lynn named Richard Johns, with whom Fritz and Joey shared a bottle of bathtub gin ("One could tell it was bath-tub gin," Cheever later recalled, "because the bottle contained a large, perfectly preserved spider"). The other story was published in Lincoln Kirstein's *Hound & Horn*, alongside the work of T. S. Eliot, Marianne Moore, E. E. Cummings, and—perhaps most auspiciously for Cheever's purpose—Hazel Hawthorne.

As Fred Cheever would later describe her, Hawthorne was "one of the original beats"—a woman who'd married young, had many children, then left her minister husband to explore the world and work on her writing. Around the time she met John, she'd married Morris Werner—the biographer of P. T. Barnum and Brigham Young—and henceforth divided her time between Greenwich Village and Provincetown, while dividing herself among a great many men (including both

Cheever brothers). A descendant of Nathaniel Hawthorne, she was "the Compleat Wasp"—as writer Roger Skillings put it—"who had entirely slipped the noose of respectability . . . a grand figure, much admired, said to have competed for lovers with her beautiful daughters." She was introduced to Cheever over lunch with Kirstein and another editor, both so tall that John and Hazel (as she recalled) had to "hop along" to keep up with them. The diminutive Cheever was otherwise undaunted, however, feistily arguing some point about Henry James with the aristocratic Kirstein. Later he confided to Hawthorne, a little sheepishly, that he'd been drinking all morning to get his courage up for the lunch.

The thirty-year-old Hawthorne was charmed by the witty teenager ("What I always liked best about John," she said, "was his *persiflage*") and invited him to New York, where he slept on a sofa in Hazel and Morrie's fifth-floor apartment on Waverly Place. Beginning with that visit—the first of many—the couple spared no effort to launch Cheever in literary Manhattan. Through the Werners he would eventually meet Cummings, Sherwood Anderson, Edmund Wilson, John Dos Passos, James Agee, Walker Evans, and many others. "Their kindness," he said, "was exhaustive and indescribable." Hawthorne also lured him back to Provincetown, where she introduced him around the famous playhouse; the emancipated atmosphere appealed to Cheever, and he decided to rent a studio there in the early spring of 1932. His roommate was another *Hound & Horn* contributor, Charles Flato, a young man with a hunchback (from a childhood bout with polio) who was working on a biography of Mathew Brady. The two lived in a creaky, unheated shack on a wharf, where the water splashed through the floorboards at high tide. Spring came late that year and they shivered over their typewriters, punching away with their gloves on, subsisting on whatever fish was left over from their neighbors' daily catch.

By far the most important connection Cheever made through the Werners was Cummings—"Estlin"—whom John admired as much for his literary genius as for his stylish poverty despite an impeccably *haut* Cambridge background. When the two first met, Cummings was at a particularly low ebb in his affairs: "His hair was nearly gone," Cheever recalled, "his last book of poetry had been rejected by every estimable publisher, his wife was six months pregnant by her dentist and his Aunt Jane had purloined his income and had sent him, by way of compensation, a carton of Melba toast. He bit into the toast and exclaimed—oh so wonderfully—'Now I know why they call it Melba.'" Cummings was, for Cheever, an elusive ideal of sorts: "The only Yankee on the American literary scene," he remained happily married to his third wife, Marion Morehouse, while residing for decades in the same little apartment on Patchin Place (around the corner from the Women's House of Detention, where the poet would blithely hail the whores by name as he passed below their barred windows); effortlessly hilarious, Cummings could imitate everything from a ticket-punching machine to "a wood-burning locomotive going from Tifflis to Minsk," and his everyday "windupthechimney" voice became a key ingredient of Cheever's own. "A writer is a *Prince!*" Cummings declared, and he touched his sword to Cheever's shoulder: "Get out of Boston, Joey! It's a city without springboards for people who can't dive."

While testing the water in New York, Cheever also paid a visit to his patron at *The New Republic*, Malcolm Cowley, who was impressed by the young man's winning smile and "stubborn jaw." Cowley was not the heroic figure that Cummings was, but he would prove more useful over the long haul. As Cheever wrote him in 1977, "You taught me to be polite to [*New Yorker* editor] Katharine White, by-pass the French symbolists, train a retriever with a fresh egg, buy my shoes at Fortnum & Mason, catch a trout and keep my literary sights high and earnest. My gratefulness is vast." Cowley also invited the nineteen-year-old prodigy to what was perhaps his first New York literary party, where he was greeted by Cowley's first wife, Peggy, and shown to the bar. As Cheever remembered:

> I was offered two kinds of drinks. One was greenish. The other was brown. They were both, I believe, made in a bathtub. I was told that one was a Manhattan and the other Pernod. My only intent was to appear terribly sophisticated and I ordered a Manhattan. Malcolm very kindly introduced me to his guests. I went on drinking Manhattans lest anyone think I came from a small town like Quincy, Massachusetts. Presently, after four or five Manhattans, I realized that I was going to vomit. I rushed to Mrs. Cowley, thanked her for the party, and reached the apartment-house hallway, where I vomited all over the wallpaper.

Cowley took pains to remind the young man that he had Voice of a Generation potential and was therefore obliged to produce a novel, whereupon Cheever presented him with a few sample chapters. Alas, they wouldn't do as a novel, Cowley was sorry to report: along with their blatant debt to Hemingway (most notably "Cross-Country Snow"), "each chapter was separate and came to a dead end." The latter was a problem Cheever would struggle with for the next twenty-five years or so, and arguably never quite resolve.

WHEN FREDERICK CHEEVER sold out of the shoe business, he invested the proceeds in Kreuger and Toll International Match. On March 12, 1932, Ivar Kreuger shot himself in a Paris hotel room rather than face creditors, and Cheever's father lost his "anchor to windward," as he called it. For a long time, the Cheevers had borrowed against the big house on Winthrop Avenue, and when they couldn't pay their mortgage or fuel bills, the bank foreclosed. As John would later tell it, he'd overheard an argument one night between his father and "Mr. Pinkham" (owner of the local Granite Trust), whom his father indignantly informed that he, Frederick Cheever, was a "human employer of forty-two people whose birthdays and names he remembered, and coldhearted Mr. Pinkham simply dealt with money." The next *day*, said Cheever, his family was routed out of their house, which was summarily razed to the ground. The house was indeed razed, but it took a few months at least, and of course Frederick had not been a human employer for many years (if ever) when this finally came to pass.

John's parents went their separate ways: Mrs. Cheever took an apartment on Spear Street, near the gift shop, and the wretched Frederick washed up at the desolate old farmhouse in Hanover, where he slept in front of a fireplace to keep from freezing to death. Hardly able to care for himself, Frederick might have perished if not for a shell-shocked veteran named McDonough who used part of his pension to buy groceries and cigars for the poignant old man, and also helped shovel snow and chop wood. A *lot* of wood: in winter the temperature dropped to thirty below, and (since there was no running water) Frederick had to "bathe" by stripping naked and rolling around in snowdrifts; so galvanized, he spent the rest of his waking hours stoking the five fireplaces to such an uproarious glow that drivers slowed along the highway a quarter-mile away, wondering if the place was on fire. "Never a one of them stopped to see the prisoner," Frederick lamented.

Before cruel Pinkham had sent the bulldozers to Winthrop Avenue, Mrs. Cheever arranged for some leftover furniture to be hauled to her sons' new apartment at 6 Pinckney Street, on Beacon Hill near the Common. She pretended to be nothing but pleased that John was striking out on his own (under Fred's protective eye), but as the brothers backed out of the driveway for the last time, their headlights struck the old woman's face—"gleaming with tears," as John recalled, though neither brother remarked on it at the time. The better part of their sympathy remained with their father. Every weekend they drove to the farm in Hanover, despite its forbidding lack of creature comforts. "I still remember," wrote Cheever, "I will remember forever, shivering and reading by the fire long after everyone else had gone to bed, getting up and walking down the cold hallways, the odd flights of steps, out to the woodshed and peeing off the stoop." By day, the brothers picked up where the helpful McDonough had left off—chopping wood and planting gardens in warm weather—and for a while it pleased John to be such a good son to his forsaken father. But the man wasn't especially grateful. When he wasn't gloating over plans to raise goats and make a fortune on cheese, he'd maunder in a tipsy, self-pitying way: "I can't smell a rose!" he announced one day. "I have grown old. If I can't smell a rose I can't smell the east wind, I can't smell rain, I can't smell smoke and if the house catches fire I will burn to death . . ." On it went. Other times he'd retire to his room and read to the cat (which he'd found on the road with a broken hip and nursed back to health).

Nor were things much better in Boston. The brothers' apartment wasn't as cold as the farmhouse, perhaps, but it didn't have five fireplaces either; at one point they took a hacksaw to the main heating pipe and diverted steam with a rolled-up magazine. Such hardships might have been romantic if the rest of life were going well; by then, however, John had taken a dreary newspaper job and dropped his persona as a South Shore Rimbaud.* The company he kept as a cub reporter was decidedly less glamorous than the Werners' circle in New York or the languid bohemians of Beacon Hill. "I can remember night after night," he wrote a couple of years later, in very different circumstances, "drinking parties on Milton Street, leaving my place half-

---

*Cheever is listed in the 1933 *Boston City Directory* as a "reporter," and he vaguely spoke of the workaday routine he had to maintain at the time ("get[ting] out of work at five o'clock" etc.). No details of his employment are otherwise known, and perhaps it's safe to say that this was the sort of pain for which Cheever had "no memory."

cocked, going out for supper with a bunch of people I didn't want to see then and never wanted to see again, coming out of night-clubs in Copley Square, impatient with the girl I was with, glad to get away from the dance music and not wanting to go back to the place where I lived." The main reason he didn't want to go back ("lurching into lamposts [sic]") was "mortal boredom": "To finish the day's work and pass a football in the failing light was not enough for me."

But even boredom might have been bearable if not for a mortifying love triangle involving the brothers and a pretty Canadian named Iris Gladwin, whom John had met a few years back at Quincy High. John and Iris were the same age, and when by chance they were reunited in that sculpting class at the Museum of Fine Arts, the two began courting—which meant, of course, that Iris saw a good deal of Fred as well, since one brother was rarely without the other and they shared almost everything. Sizing things up, Iris came to the sensible conclusion that a man with a steady job was a better prospect than a would-be writer who hitchhiked to Fall River at the drop of a hat.

"Other than Malcolm's word and a few published stories, I have little to recommend me," Cheever wrote in April 1933 to Elizabeth Ames, director of the Yaddo artists' colony. "I am planning to be a writer and have been working for the last year on apprenticeship prose. At present I am trying to write a handful of good short stories." Such a modest, even perfunctory, request for admission suggests that Cheever was still a bit reluctant to leave his brother; in any event, Mrs. Ames replied with like brevity that perhaps he should try again next year. Cheever didn't seem put out. He thanked Cowley for recommending him, and added, "I don't expect to do anything worth publishing for five years or so. There is a lot of time."

Then another year passed—a bad year, one suspects. The brothers moved to 46 Cedar Lane Way, even closer to the arty heart of things, where it might have become clearer than ever that that particular garden was closed, at least where John was concerned. Meanwhile two years had passed since his last published story, and almost four since that marvelous debut in *The New Republic.* "The idea of leaving the city for a short while . . . has never been so distant or so desirable," Cheever wrote again to Mrs. Ames in March 1934, promising to work hard on a novel (about the incongruities of Boston life) if she saw fit to extend an invitation. Vague desperation was a better tack than modest ambivalence, and this time the hostess of Yaddo consented.

John seems not to have mentioned his decision to Fred one way or the other, and perhaps he wondered to the end whether he'd actually be able to leave. One day in June, though, he simply packed his bags and shook his brother's hand: "Fred, I'm leaving." "Oh, are you?" Despite the decorous reticence, it was a parting ("impetuous, visionary, and dangerous") that would haunt Cheever the rest of his life. "Oh brother, brother, why has thou forsaken me," he repined thirty-four years later. A putatively happy man at the time—prosperous and acclaimed—he'd never stopped longing for the one person who loved him as he wished to be loved. "[C]rowding fifty-six I want my big brother to come back and be my love," he wrote, "and when he comes, pious, artistic and floundering in sentimental self-deceptions, I can barely stay in the room with him."

CHAPTER FIVE

{ 1934–1935 }

YADDO, FOR CHEEVER, was a majestic summons back to his true calling. There was his artistic calling, of course, but more: a Gatsbyesque aspiration to the good life—in this case embodied by a fifty-five-room Tudor mansion situated among 440 acres of pleasant woodland and gardens and statuary and lakes, all within walking distance of the famous Saratoga Race Course and other mansions along Union Avenue (the most beautiful street in America, or so Henry James considered it). It was true that the mansion bequeathed by Spencer Trask for artistic purposes was a bit of an eyesore, but from Cheever's perspective it was a big improvement over a freezing ramshackle farmhouse in the sticks or a seedy bachelor flat on Beacon Hill.

The origin of Yaddo is a well-known and remarkably bleak story. Trask (the Wall Street financier who backed Thomas Edison) bought the property in 1881 as a place of summer respite for his poetic wife, Katrina, after the death of their first son. According to lore, it was the Trasks' second child, Christina, who came up with that beguiling name, *Yaddo*—the four-year-old's version of "shadow," as in the flickering shadows of wind-tossed trees, which the girl took to be the spirit of her dead brother: "Call it Yaddo, Mama, for it makes poetry!" Little Christina was soon among the shadows, too, as was her little brother, Spencer Jr., since both were ill-advisedly allowed to kiss their mother when she was thought to be dying of diphtheria. Katrina survived; the children died within two days of each other. A year later a fourth child died, whereupon Katrina devoted herself to more ethereal pursuits. One day, walking with her husband, the woman had a vision: "Here will be a perpetual series of house parties—of literary men, literary women and other artists. . . . Look, Spencer, they are walking in the woods, wandering in the garden, sitting under the pine trees—men and women—creating, creating, creating!" The man saw her point and set up a nonprofit corporation to maintain the estate as a retreat for people "usefully engaged in artistic and creative work"—but before the dream was realized, a freight train ran a red signal near Croton and smashed into Spencer Trask's private car. He was the only person killed. For a few more years, Katrina mourned her decimated family, comforted by the couple's mutual friend, George Foster Peabody, whom she finally married ("the romantic culmination of a rare triangular friendship") less than a year before her death on January 7, 1922. Her ghostly presence still abides in the mansion, or such is the impression created by a portrait of the woman in a billowy white shift ("poor Katrina's shower curtain," as Cheever called it).

A year after Katrina's death, Peabody was still in the process of carrying out her wishes with the help of an eighteen-year-old assistant,* Marjorie Waite, when the two were visited by Waite's widowed sister from Minnesota, Elizabeth Ames. Peabody was struck by Mrs. Ames's enthusiasm for his project and asked her to draw up a plan, which she accomplished with such insight and energy that Peabody named her executive director on the spot (or, in Cheever's more picturesque version: "When a beam of light caught Mrs. Ames's lovely face, Mr. Peabody decided that it was she who had been chosen"). In most respects he chose wisely. By 1926, Mrs. Ames had refurbished the mansion, erected outbuildings, hired a large and efficient staff, and was ready to welcome her first group of artists as the hostess of Yaddo.

"Hostess" was one way to put it. "For the first twenty-five years," said Malcolm Cowley, "Elizabeth Ames *was* Yaddo." No detail, however niggling, was likely to escape Mrs. Ames's notice. With her guests as a whole she communicated via bits of advice tacked on the mail table; more intimate messages were written on blue paper and left, like ill-boding tarot cards, in guests' lunch baskets. ("When you have a suggestion to make please do not ask to see any of the servants," she admonished composer Marc Blitzstein. "They have strict orders not to receive requests from guests. They may go only through me.") Guests

---

*So to speak. Three years later, Peabody formally adopted Miss Waite, as was customary for May-December romances in those days.

ignored such prompts at their peril, to say nothing of the more general commandments for which these notes served as gentle reminders. A temperate (though not entirely teetotaling) Quaker, Mrs. Ames forbade the consumption of alcohol in common rooms, though guests could furtively tipple behind closed doors. As for even more private matters—these, too, were closely monitored. When one woman chose to disregard a blue note deploring (tactfully) her entertainment of several different men after hours, she returned to her room to find that her double bed had been replaced with a single.

And yet Mrs. Ames's Victorianism was a bit on the quasi side. She herself was something of a feminist and radical, and hardly averse to a little fun: in August she made time for the horse races like everyone else and sipped her share of champagne. Nor was she a prude in her own affairs, nor was she likely to object if (as Cheever noted) "a distinguished man or woman took a lover"—key word "distinguished," as talent was everything, or anyway a great part in gaining Mrs. Ames's favor. Charm was important too, so that the woman's paradoxes were nicely reconciled by the following (oft-repeated) observation: "If Elizabeth Ames was fond of you, she'd do anything for you. If she wasn't, forget it." And if you protested, well, she was pretty much deaf as a post for most of her adult life, and would simply elect not to listen. To the very end, though, the likes of Cheever were encouraged to shout amiably into her ear.

Mrs. Ames hewed to the Trask vision of a "house party" in those early years, and a stay at Yaddo was (as Cowley recalled) like a summer visit "to a Newport 'cottage' owned by robber barons." If guests chose to sleep in, then breakfast trays laden with Trask silver were placed outside their doors with a gentle knock; as for the elaborate dinners, one reported in proper attire or not at all. After the stock market crashed, standards were necessarily lowered. Most artists could scarcely afford a new pair of shoes, and were grateful to have a roof over their heads, much less a platter of *confiseries* when they gathered downstairs at four o'clock. Yaddo's budget was strapped too, and some of the more enduring guests were asked to work for their room and board. John Cheever, in fact, became the first in a permanent tradition of "SAPs"—"Special Assistants to the President," as they were later called, a position that in Cheever's case involved chopping wood, shoveling snow, and doing whatever other donkey work needed to be done. Fortunately, the rigors of Hanover had prepared Cheever well for such labor, which he never minded in any case, since it was manly and distracted him from dark thoughts.

The privations of the outside world, as well as a not-so-subtle "climate of repression" (as Cheever put it) under the Ames regime, led to what has been called "the Yaddo effect": an obsession with food and sex and high jinks in general. Cheever was something of a pioneer in this respect, too. Each morning he slid down the banister and whacked the bronze Aphrodite on her rump; he left hats on statuary and splashed naked in the atrium pool; and once he installed the left-wing author Mary Heaton Vorse in a souvenir sleigh (given to Katrina by the Queen of the Netherlands) and shoved her down the grand staircase: "Hooves of fire!" the woman cried. As for sex, he often reflected on the "practical and colorless fucking" that he and a certain writer's wife used to practice, when young, on every flat surface in the mansion (not to mention "every garden, field and streambed"). From such exertions a naked Cheever tiptoed back to his room one night, bumping into a startled group of guests in the hallway: "[M]oving with great Hermian grace," Gurganus recounted, "he bounded directly past them, smiling and—just as he drifted past, offered the explanation of his casualness: 'I'm a ghost.'" To the very end, indeed, with both sexes, Cheever retained a certain Hermian vigor: "I have been sucked by Ned [Rorem] and others in almost every room," he reminisced during a visit in 1977, "and tried unsuccessfully to mount a young man on the bridge between the lakes."

As for the rest of "the Yaddo effect," food was never as high a priority for Cheever as drink, no matter how repressive the climate. At first he abided by house rules and drank in his room, leaving an impressive pile of empties outside his door for the maid, or else he'd repair with other thirsty colonists to the New Worden Hotel in town. All too often, though, he had to suffer the company of bores at dinner—sanctimonious radicals, effeminate poets, and the like—a trial he was loath to endure soberly. The problem was solved when he broke into the Trask wine cellar and found a vast supply of brandies that had turned clear over time, which he then drank out of his water glass even when seated right beside Mrs. Ames.

Not surprisingly, the two were a little slow in warming to each other. Elizabeth Ames was forty-nine in 1934—when Cheever (twenty-two) first came to Yaddo—and took a dim view of puerile high spirits, at least in people she didn't like. "I am told that he is twenty-two years old," she wrote in 1930 of the novelist Leonard Ehrlich (who would become the love of her life), "and somehow a twenty-two year old novelist does not greatly stir my enthusiasm"; most young novelists of her acquaintance, she primly continued, had proved "more infantile than anything else." Far from being an exception, Cheever was a rule unto himself, and Mrs. Ames was obliged to lecture the youth about "unwise attachments" and so on. When his second of two visits in 1934 ended on a slightly sour note, Cheever wrote a friend about a dream he'd had in which he'd thrown a platter of jellied salmon at Mrs. Ames's face: " 'I'm glad you did, John,' she said firmly and calmly, 'I'm very glad you did it. I'm glad to know how you feel towards me.' 'I'm also very glad I did it,' I said, going up and shaking her hand. 'I'm sincerely sorry but I'm glad I did it. Now we both know how things stand. There won't be anymore subterfuge or deceit between us.' " Nevertheless, she kept inviting him back, and one day she began to cry as he said goodbye to her. "I realized for the first time," said Cheever, "that our relationship was not simple."

Not only would he become a favorite of Mrs. Ames—even a surrogate son—but the servants loved him too, and took to calling him Lord Fauntleroy. This was important to Cheever for a number of reasons. "Only dogs, servants, and children know who the *real* aristocrats are," he liked to say. Though artists were forbidden to mix with staff (as Marc Blitzstein had been sternly reminded), Cheever would appear in the kitchen almost every morning to gossip with the cook, Nellie Shannon, while she fixed his breakfast. He was also fond of the superintendent, George Vincent, whom he'd insist on helping with chores around the estate (whether it was expected of him or not) as well as any problems the man might have with a guest or underling. "Do you want me to talk to him?" Cheever would offer. "I'll talk to him." Both Shannon and Vincent and certain other employees remained at Yaddo for fifty years or more, and became Cheever's lifelong friends. "[W]ho can come back to the scene of his early manhood," he wrote in 1961, "and find not a chair, not a thread, not even the faded asters in the silver bowl have changed. . . . Someone has remembered all my favorite dishes; spare ribs, ham and turkey, peach soufflé." One of his happiest memories was returning after a long absence and overhearing a parlor maid say, "Master John is back! Master John is back!" As Gurganus remarked, "He was living out some sort of magisterial fantasy of being master of the house, which he deserved to be in terms of his gift and his decency and his sweetness."

"It's the only place I've ever felt at home," Cheever said of Yaddo, and all his life he endeavored to pay the debt. For decades he served on the board of directors, and donated money when he could spare it. Without Yaddo he would not have survived the Depression, at least as a writer, and throughout his life it remained an oasis where he could work in peace until four in the afternoon, then have drinks and a swim and a good dinner with (usually) congenial company. No wonder he wept as he kissed an elderly Nellie Shannon goodbye after one of his last visits in the late seventies, when he thought he might never return.

THOUGH HIS FIRST VISIT to Yaddo wasn't especially productive— he wrote nothing publishable—Cheever did meet a soulmate of sorts, or so he thought at the time. Fresh out of Dartmouth, Reuel Denney was a poet whose first collection, *The Connecticut River*, would win the Yale Younger Poets Award five years later. But what eventually earned Denney at least "a footnote to scholarship history"—as his *Times* obituary noted—was his contribution to the sociological classic *The Lonely Crowd* (1950), which he co-wrote with David Riesman and Nathan Glazer. Denney was perhaps Cheever's first real friend since Fax Ogden, and it was more than a little significant that he bore "a startling resemblance" to Fred. Having left the one and found the other, Cheever came to associate both with a sense of youthful communion. "A fleeting longing for some kind of once-enjoyed tenderness," he wrote twenty years later—"Fred or Reuel."

Based on his later writings, it seems fair to say that Denney was largely unaware of the impact he'd had on Cheever, though Denney's memories of that summer were also "dominated" by their friendship: "I was one of the first to recognize [Cheever's] great talent," he wrote shortly before his death in 1995, "and I remember well the shock of admiration and envy with which I first heard his unpremeditated outpouring of conversational wit, criticism, and well-turned narrative." Cheever felt an almost pathetic gratitude for having found an intelligent, talented, and withal regular-guyish contemporary who responded to his personality and work: "Sympathy and patience, let alone understanding for my or our interests is rare," he wrote Denney. "[A]nd once found it can be stimulating and helpful as hell. Which it has been." For the previous five years—and most of the years before—Cheever had been close to only one human being; such profound alienation in his "formative years" (the telling phrase that had sprung to his lips as he helped his drunken father off the roller coaster) would arguably leave him with a blurred sense of identity the rest of his life. He tried to articulate the trauma to Denney in various ways. When, for instance, the latter mentioned his time at Fred's alma mater, Cheever replied that he'd gone to a Dartmouth football game the year before and ended up "feeling lousy":

> [S]eeing the importance you give those four years and their associations I naturally feel that I have missed something. . . . I cannot, as you can, at a point of loss or discovery, identify myself with a generation, a college, a class or industry. At the most it amounts to a handful of men and women of various ages and nationalities that I know because I like. . . . The thing I miss most is an ability to identify myself with a group. When you are lost you are completely lost. This resulted during the first winter in a confused, defensive idea of myself.* But that's all over now. I know who I am.

Cheever had formed his latest sense of who he was in direct opposition to who he'd been—that is, rather than a radical bohemian who cultivated burlesque stars and Beacon Street aesthetes, he was now a cynical traditionalist who regarded his leftist contemporaries with a majestic (if peevish) detachment. "Being likened to a decadent intellectual makes me sore," he wrote Denney. "I accept no interpretation of history, read no direction in the past, have no brief for progress. I fail to see why the thirteenth century should be any blacker than the nineteenth." He was, in short, somewhat in the throes of a "sane conservative" phase influenced, in part, by Henry Adams.† Fred was also a lifelong Adams fan, and had recently loaned his brother a volume of the great historian's letters. Adams was congenial in a number of ways, not least because Cheever was "born in the shadow of the house where [Adams] wrote some of the *Education*" (and of course his family had hired their coachman's daughter); also, the desperate reversals of Cheever's adolescence had left him susceptible to Adams's bleakly deterministic view of history: "There is something immense and significant," Cheever wrote of the dying Adams circa 1918, "in that dod-

---

*Cheever refers here to that "first winter" after his *New Republic* story in October 1930, when he definitely rejected the regimentation of mainstream society—including college—and began wearing an amethyst ring, etc.

†Cheever's outlook was also compounded, perhaps, of the droll Republicanism of his new hero, Cummings, who'd visited Soviet Russia in the late twenties and found it a dreary place, and now insisted that President Hoover be recalled to office.

dering figure standing on the beach at Newport as if he could see them bombing Rheims and dismantling Chartres." If anything, Cheever found himself more pessimistic than all that. What with the Depression and the rise of oppressive regimes throughout Europe and Asia, history seemed in a downward spiral that might even have startled Adams. For his part, Cheever deplored such contemporary works as Malraux's *La Condition humaine* because it "read form into a scene of such violence," whereas he himself was inclined to "admit the futility of art in the present or near future." This included fiction, and perhaps reflected a passing frustration with his own work as much as a larger *Weltschmerz*. Whatever the case, Cheever was considering some rather bizarre literary projects, such as writing short biographies of Adams, Poe, and Hart Crane—"a simple disarming analysis of the three men and their ends drawn from a viewpoint as personal as if they were my ancestors."

Such was the young man who found himself at Yaddo in the summer of 1934. And let it serve as evidence of Cheever's amiability, then and later, that he was able to mix with what should have been (except for Denney) a pretty inimical cast of characters. James Farrell was there, writing the last volume of his *Studs Lonigan* trilogy; a hard-boiled Irishman from Chicago, Farrell was a little bemused by Cheever's elaborate Yankee manners, but liked him well enough to toss a baseball back and forth. Muriel Rukeyser, the radical lesbian poet, became a good friend for the next decade or so. Even Leonard Ehrlich would warm to Cheever over time, and vice versa, though Ehrlich embodied the sort of naïve idealism that drove Cheever up the wall: "He's a liberal, a gentleman and a romantic," he wrote of Ehrlich, "and he makes me feel like a bloody son of a bitch with his concern over the defense of political prisoners and his desire to preserve a free and inquiring spirit in a highly questionable world."

Cheever's only serious work that survives from that summer is "Letter from the Mountains," a response to the misguided utopianism of his peers at Yaddo and beyond: "I think of Europe as a rat-toothed bitch," he declared with Poundian scorn. "Even up here I often have a sense of something cracked." This odd document (a continuation of his dialogue with Denney, who'd left Saratoga at the end of June and gone back to Buffalo) suggests that Cheever had taken to heart Cowley's advice about writing on behalf of his generation, which might have suited Cheever's wistful desire to "identify with a group," the more explicitly the better: "Born in the vicinity of nineteen-twelve"— his own birth year—"we come as strangers to this wreck." Cheever suggested that his generation, victimized by its elders, was drifting helplessly from one great war to the next. At last he fixed the time and place of this fatalistic manifesto ("July, 1934/the Adirondacks") and mailed it off to Cowley, who doubtfully tried to interest his colleagues at *The New Republic:* the manuscript was "diffuse," he admitted, but perhaps they should publish it "as a picture of the state of mind of the youngsters." The piece was rejected as "defeatist."

ONE OF MRS. AMES'S blue-papered notes appeared in Cheever's lunch basket toward the end of July, and he returned to Boston for a week or so before moving to New York. To avoid unnecessary strangeness, he took a six-by-eight apartment in the same rooming house, at 633 Hudson, where he'd stayed during a previous visit in 1931: "[A]cross the street from me," he reported to Denney, "sits the same old man in the same yellowed underwear." The place was mostly occupied by unemployed longshoremen, and Cheever's own room was so exquisitely squalid that Walker Evans would later photograph it— a quintessential Depression tableau—for the Museum of Modern Art.

Cheever didn't have a lot of choice in the matter. For the time being, he was living on a weekly allowance of ten dollars from Fred; this covered his three-dollar room as well as a certain amount of stale bread, raisins ("I almost destroyed my teeth, but I needed the iron"), and a daily bottle of milk divided into five portions. As Cowley remembered, "His only capital was a typewriter for which he couldn't often buy a new ribbon"—nor could he summon much energy to write. Some days he'd simply sit in Washington Square with a friend and discuss the phases of starvation ("It was the torpor we objected to"), and once he actually collapsed on Hudson Street. On the brighter side, he liked to recall the kindly longshoremen who were always trying to help the boyish, dapper little Yankee in their midst: they urged him to get work with the government, perhaps attend an extension class or take the post-office exam. In the meantime Cheever lay on his bed dreaming—determinedly—of a wife and family, wealth and fame, while "motors and klaxons and breaks and river-whistles" clamored outside his window. Sometimes, too, a bit of gravel would clatter against the glass, and there in the street would be Fred.

"Hudson Street is a far cry from anything in Boston," he wrote Mrs. Ames, "and so far the difference stands in favor of Hudson Street." Except for his constant hunger, Cheever was glad to be back among people who mattered. He was seeing a lot of Hazel and Morris Werner again, which meant he was seeing Agee and Sherwood Anderson and Dos Passos, as well as a good deal of his beloved Cummings. The latter shared his dislike of Edmund Wilson—another regular at the Werners'—whom Cummings ridiculed as a secret homosexual who needed to ride a motorcycle so he could have something vibrating between his legs. The poet, said Cheever, had "one of the finest tongues of the century," but was also "immensely considerate and just" and never mocked people who were hurting or helpless. In general, the atmosphere *chez* Werner was a nice mixture of New England manners and Greenwich Village irreverence. As Cheever described a typical party, "[I]t was a fine night with Morrie yelling that their food was talking while their conversation was getting cold and Hazel insisting that she hadn't raped x and that x hadn't raped her but that the bed had come up and hit them both. They are nice people, all of them with the characteristics of Cummings. Sharp tongues and patient sympathies."

Nor did Cheever neglect his friends from Yaddo, despite the "strenuous" contrast between their humorless radicalism and Cummings's tipsy shtick (his "facetious telephone calls to the municipal offal department"). Cheever listened with an earnest deadpan while Rukeyser and her fellow poet Sol Funaroff lectured him about the necessity of using literature to elevate the proletariat, and sometimes he'd tag along to some sordid venue so he could watch them put their ideas to work. "On Saturday night Muriel gave a reading of her poetry to a group of boogies in Harlem," he wrote Denney, observing that most of the audience was both "drunk and high": "[M]y impression was that this was not the crowd to approach or the way or place to approach them." Again, the miracle is that Cheever remained friends with such people—though not without a certain amount of chafing on both sides. Later he'd claim that, while still in his early twenties, he was labeled "the last voice of the decadent bourgeoisie" in *The New Masses*; if so, it was perhaps a bit of reprisal on the part of an exasperated Funaroff, the magazine's poetry editor.

Occupying a stolid middle ground were the likes of Cowley and his friends at *The New Republic:* "Nice people to drink beer and shuck corn with," as Cheever put it. At once grateful and slightly resentful of

Cowley's patronage, Cheever would always regard the man with a kind of risible filial impiety. At the time he characterized him as "dull, slow, with an eye . . . for the second rate," though he allowed that Cowley was likable enough and "useful" up to a point. There was, however, in his attitude toward Cowley (and most of the world) a considerable dissonance between heart and head. Frances Lindley remembered a dinner with the two men shortly after Cowley's mother died in 1935: "Malcolm produced a couple of childhood silver spoons, and John was tender toward him," she said, invoking the episode as an instance of Cheever's conspicuous "sweetness" when young. But always, too, a certain distance. As Cheever noted that previous autumn in New York, his floating among such diverse worlds was, above all, a good education: "I know more about the history of literature and the conduct of men and women than I could have learned at Harvard."

An actual Harvard diploma, though (or even one from Thayer), would have come in handy while trying to get a decent job at a magazine or newspaper. Under the circumstances, the best Cheever could do was occasional work writing plot synopses for M-G-M at the rate of five dollars a book. It was a hard-earned paycheck. The novels were divvied out by a Mrs. Lewton, a somewhat elusive figure who did not allow her employees to choose their own reading. "I've done one lousey detective story and am at work on a romance by a woman named or called Brada Field," Cheever reported that first week; a week later he'd gotten started on a thriller by Sarah Gertrude Millin, about whom his only comment was "Phrrft." On Wednesdays, when he wasn't waiting around for Mrs. Lewton, he waited around the offices of *The New Republic* with a crowd of other down-and-out literati, including the legendary bohemian Joe Gould (dressed in newspapers), since Cowley assigned book reviews on that day. Despite his good intentions, though, Cowley had far more reviewers than he could possibly use, and only gave books to Cheever (a reluctant critic, no matter how hungry) when there was a good thematic fit.*

---

*As in the case of Philip Stevenson's *The Gospel According to St. Luke's*—a "quite uninteresting" prep-school novel that Cheever reviewed a few months after "Expelled" appeared—or *Silas Crockett*, by Mary Ellen Chase, a novel about New England's decline that struck a particular chord with Cheever, who boiled it down as follows: "Silas Crockett, the first in line, is a sea captain of the prosperous China trade. . . . Reuben of the third generation is forced to pilot a ferry boat and sell the splendid furniture and portraits of his fathers in order to make a living; and Silas of the fourth goes to work

The hot weather and Sarah Gertrude Millin were too much for Cheever, and after less than three weeks on Hudson Street he begged Mrs. Ames to take him back. She relented, letting him know that the mansion would close in mid-October and that he might be asked to make a "small contribution" if he elected to stay. Cheever was ecstatic, and after collecting his latest paycheck from Mrs. Lewton, he boarded a bus for Saratoga—arriving, rather fatefully, during the last weekend of the racing season. That Saturday, at a time when Mrs. Ames expected him to be sequestered with his work, Cheever and a painter named Martin Craig jumped a fence at the back of the estate and blew their money on the horses. Mrs. Ames let the incident pass. When, however, a few weeks later, Cheever and Craig failed to appear at dinner because of an unauthorized engagement in town, a blue note appeared in Cheever's lunch basket: "It now seems best to set your departure for Monday, October 8th," Mrs. Ames sweetly informed him. "Perhaps after a month or so it will be possible to make some arrangements for you to come back either by contributing something for your board or perhaps doing some outdoor labor of which there is always plenty to do here at Yaddo."

Cheever was dismayed—"the lowest of the low"—though he might have been a bit relieved, at least, that his exile wasn't permanent. Also, Mrs. Ames had been decent enough to give him sufficient notice (two weeks) to make other arrangements; since he was dead broke, of course, he had to ask Fred and Iris (now married) to come pick him up in the roadster and let him regroup at their apartment in Weymouth for a few weeks before returning to New York. As for Mrs. Ames's invitation to return for the winter as a part-time laborer, he declined: "There is no possibility [at Yaddo] for exploration, danger, discovery," he wrote Denney. "In buses, trains, boats, hotels, rooming houses you meet people open handed. But here there is supposed to be a cessation of all life, all human relations. Which is the cheapest way of all, I think, of spending time." He knew it wouldn't be long, though, before the "open handed" life began to pall, and in the meantime he wisely took pains to mollify Mrs. Ames: "I have a lot of things to thank you for and

---

in a herring factory. . . . [T]he glorious seaboard of the China trade means to most of us . . . empty harbors and fugitive mill towns and the smell of the tourist camps and a cretin at the gas station. And all this, to Yankees of the new generation, is a story less for reverence and delicacy [that is, as Mrs. Chase chooses to tell it] . . . than for immense indignation and wonder."

I am sincerely grateful," he wrote. "It was one of the best summers, in every way, I have ever known."

NEW YORK MEANT MRS. LEWTON, though Cheever continued to spend much of his free time, fruitlessly, looking for steadier work. He wasn't getting a lot of writing done. What remained of his time and energy had to be conserved for summarizing potboilers; then, too, there was the simple unpleasantness of writing on Hudson Street, where he shared a sagging mattress ("stinking of lice-preventive") with a heavy typewriter. Most of the time he just didn't feel up to it. "I am certain of my own voice and I have a mindful of stories," he wrote, "and coming back here I smoke butt after butt and read the newspaper and lie on my back looking at the ceiling."

An ever more frequent companion was Walker Evans, though Cheever disapproved of the photographer in many respects. Almost ten years older, Evans had allowed his personality to congeal into a weary façade of pseudo-gentility—as Cheever put it, "a hopeless impersonation of the upper-middle class," including a mumbly accent of sorts. In other words, the friends had a little too much in common, though Cheever coveted at least one notable dissimilarity: Evans was wholly devoted to his art, such that the rest of him was almost an excrescence. And Cheever had to concede that, in Evans's case, the sacrifice of charisma had been worth making: "[Evans's photographs] are, for all of their contempt, snobbery, preciocity [sic], an impressive record," he wrote. "There are beautiful shots of razed houses, vacant lots, a tin ceiling smashed and twisted, peeling bill-boards. His pictures of Saratoga are much better than the ones [Lincoln] Kirstein printed."

Meanwhile the two discovered other things in common. "I feel confident that we are going to be involved in a *war*," Evans would say, "and that I will be *killed*." Thus resigned to his fate—as Cheever also professed to be—Evans didn't see that it made any difference whom one slept with, and no doubt detected some such attitude in his young friend. "When I was twenty-one," Cheever recalled, "Walker Evans invited me to spend the night at his apartment. I said yes. I dropped my clothes (Brooks). He hung his (also Brooks) neatly in a closet. When I asked him how to do it he seemed rather put off. He had an enormous cock that showed only the most fleeting signs of life. I was ravening. I came all over the sheets, the Le Corbusier chair, the Matisse Lithograph and hit him under the chin. I gave up at around three, dressed and spent the rest of the night on a park bench near the river."

For Cheever it would always be one thing to have sex with a man, another to spend the night with him. The latter was a taboo he would rarely if ever violate until a ripe old age—although, under whatever circumstances, he'd once caught a glimpse of Walker Evans sitting naked at the breakfast table and seemed haunted by the memory: "[W]hy should [Evans]"—he mused forty-three years later—"drinking his coffee seem to have between his legs not a source of burgeoning but the circumspect and humble equipment for knitting a pair of socks?" Henceforth Cheever suspected that certain kinds of sex had the unsavory effect of "tax[ing] one's posture."

But even in those days there were people who thought Cheever's posture (so to speak) was also a bit off. "We all knew John was sort of gay," said Betty Hewling, a copy editor at *The New Republic* in the thirties. And though Malcolm Cowley would later deny having seen "any sign" of his protégé's bisexuality, Cheever's journal decidedly suggests otherwise: "[Cowley] was father, brother, friend and might have jingled my participles," he wrote in 1962. "There was this in the air, I think, but neither of us wanted it enough to forgo the rest of the world. He's always been jumpy on the subject but never opaque." Cheever remembered being "reproached" by Cowley for even considering a homosexual lifestyle: "Such a course [said Cowley] could only end with drunkenness and ghastly suicide"—as it had, indeed, for Cowley's friend Hart Crane. A very young Cheever had met Crane, and (thanks to Cowley) had a lively idea of what had led to Crane's suicide, since Cowley's first wife, Peggy, had been romantically involved with the poet, and on the same ship, when he threw himself overboard.* Crane thus became a totemic figure to Cheever: an artist who'd succumbed to

---

*Cheever's version of Crane's death was singularly unflattering to Peggy Baird Cowley. As Cheever told it, Crane was hysterically despondent after being beaten by a sailor to whom he'd made advances. "I have to talk!" he cried to the former Mrs. Cowley, on finding her at last in the ship's beauty parlor. "I'm having my hair done," she replied, and so Crane hurled himself into the sea. Presumably this was some simulacrum of the version to which Malcolm Cowley was privy, though Cheever might have added the beauty parlor and much of Peggy's callousness. Certainly Malcolm himself didn't lack compassion toward his first wife: "Poor Peggy," he wrote Cheever. "She died about 1970 in Dorothy Day's Catholic Worker farm in Rivoli. . . . The services, at which I was the only old friend present, were conducted by a hippy priest with long dirty hair."

the "Orphic cycle" of self-destruction, which in Crane's case was a direct result of his role as a "tragic homosexual." That Cheever would endure (it seems) his first twenty years of married life without succumbing to temptation was at least somewhat due to Crane's example. "If I followed my instincts," Cheever wrote, "I would be strangled by some hairy sailor in a public urinal. Every comely man, every bank clerk and delivery boy, was aimed at my life like a loaded pistol."

Reuel Denney had never "known or suspected" his friend's "dual sexuality" except in retrospect, once it became widely known after Cheever's death. Denney was then struck by something odd, after all, in Cheever's "attitude toward women," which had seemed "to combine a strong sense of need for women's attention on his part with a hostile resentment against the fact that the need existed." Cheever confirmed this resentment in so many words, referring to his "*duty* [my italics] to respond to females," as though it was something of a burden. On the one hand, he wanted a socially acceptable "sanctuary for [his] cock," but above all he wanted a family: "I wanted to marry almost every girl I slept with, I wanted to marry and have sons and a home and I flatly deny that this was a guise of sexual cowardice, that I didn't have the courage to pit my homosexual instincts against the censure of the world. I didn't find the world that contemptible."

An early vehicle for social acceptability was Dodie Merwin, a pretty and spirited nineteen-year-old whom Hazel Werner had met in Provincetown and recommended to Cheever. By the time he called her, she'd moved to a little apartment on Barrow that shared a courtyard with the famous Chumley's Bar, not far from the squalor of Hudson Street (or, later, the squalor of Bethune). She and Cheever got on easily together. They took long walks around the Village, stopping at Sutter's Bakery, near Merwin's apartment, or any number of bars along the way. Both were adventurous, especially after a few drinks. On snowy nights, when the streets were empty, they'd ski beneath the old elevated train on Sixth Avenue, sometimes as far as Bryant Park.

Like most, Merwin was charmed by Cheever—and yet, for all his breezy wit, she detected something a little studied, detached, in his manner. "He always had this kind of chuckle," she remembered. "He'd say something with a sort of self-deprecating look and burst into a chuckle. The remarks were always acute—they amused *himself*. And if successful, he'd repeat them with that grin. He'd toss his head a little and look wise." Always, too, there was a tacit insistence on surface matters. If one was sad, and wished to confide, Cheever would make a sympathetic face and say the right things, more or less. He was kindly. But, as Merwin noticed, "He didn't communicate by eye. He looked at you straightforwardly enough, but his eyes were opaque. You got the impression he was thinking about his writing." Or (often the same thing) he was thinking of something he didn't want to discuss—his brother, Fred, say, or Walker Evans: "He didn't seem comfortable" with either subject, Merwin recalled. Nor would he ever be. "He would never talk to me about his brother," said his son Federico. "He would never talk to me about his years in New York, with the exception of a few carefully crafted and well-worn stories, and all that stuff was with him and would show up in the journals. I don't think I realized how much the past, and alternative presents (and that goes into bisexuality), were always with him."

Cheever's amiable self-absorption was especially evident in his sexual approach—which, as Merwin put it (with a sort of wondering understatement), was "perfunctory and quick": "It didn't seem to be initiated by the other person," she said. "It was self-initiating and -sustaining." A few years later, when Cheever lived near Dupont Circle in Washington, Merwin would pass through a creaking gate when she visited his brownstone; the creak would alert Cheever to her arrival. "No sooner did you get into his apartment than he's got you on the couch," she said. "And that's it. Now you can go out for the evening. And he was happy. I can remember looking at him kind of quizzically and thinking, 'Is that all there is?'" Many others, men and women alike, would wonder the same thing.

What also remained consistent over the years was Cheever's drinking. Even as a young man he had an enormous thirst, always on display in social situations, when sobriety seemed out of the question. Watching him polish off a dozen Manhattans at a single sitting—all the while chuckling and telling stories at an almost frenzied clip—Merwin got the impression that reality was a little too much for Cheever to bear. "He simply never faced himself, or when he did he didn't like what he saw," she said. "And nothing relieved him." William Maxwell made a similar observation after his friend's death: "He wanted to understand the world but he didn't want to understand himself."

CHAPTER SIX

{ 1935–1938 }

WALKER EVANS LEFT NEW YORK in January 1935 to take a long photographic tour of the South, and Cheever moved into his basement studio at 23 Bethune, two blocks east of the Hudson. If anything the studio was even more ghastly than Cheever's previous dwelling, and odd reminders of the place would forever send him into tailspins. While reading the *Times* in 1980, Cheever saw a photograph of a tubular chair very like the Le Corbusier in Evans's studio, where his younger self had "sat when [he] was truly lonely, hungry, impoverished and cold"; almost half a century later (and even more depressed), he wondered if that era had "introduced a strata [sic] into [his] makeup that is only now becoming apparent."

He was still trying to make ends meet with occasional scraps from M-G-M, but the work was erratic and weeks passed without a paycheck. "I don't know how I'll get along unless I sell a story," he wrote Denney, a few days after moving to Evans's studio. It was, perhaps, the worst time in history to be starting out as a writer. In 1934, only fifteen authors in the United States sold fifty thousand or more books, and the magazine market was even more straitened; advertising was at an all-time low, and many of the mass-market, high-paying "slick" magazines had either shrunk or folded. One night Cheever was bemoaning his fate at Cowley's house in Connecticut—where on weekends he'd often cadge a meal*—when Cowley suggested he try a different approach.

---

*In exchange for which he sometimes babysat for his future son-in-law, Robert Cowley, then a toddler.

"Your stories are too long for other magazines to accept from new writers," he said. "Tomorrow, try writing a story of not more than a thousand words, say three and a half of your pages. Write another of the same length on Sunday, another on Monday, and still another on Tuesday. Bring them all to the office on Wednesday afternoon, and I'll see if I can't get you some money for them."

For some time Cheever had suspected his work was too self-consciously arty, not to say derivative, and he was determined to curb its "refinement, discretion, excessive detail, lack of action." The constraints imposed by Cowley proved to be the ticket, as though Cheever were a discursive poet whose talent suddenly blossomed in the sonnet form. Three of the four shorts he'd written in as many days would find their way into print. Cowley was able to buy one—"The Teaser" (about an aging stripper)—as a "color piece," since *The New Republic* still didn't publish much fiction. Another story, "Bayonne," eventually appeared in *Parade* (not the Sunday supplement, but a would-be periodical that died after a single issue in 1936). The others were sent to Katharine White at *The New Yorker*, who met their twenty-two-year-old author a few days later at a *New Republic* party. As she wrote him afterward, "I thought we were taking one [story] and it turns out that I was right. I enclose our check for 'Buffalo.' The other one we didn't like so well."

"Buffalo"—the first of 121* stories that Cheever would eventually publish in the magazine—didn't amount to much, though it's interesting as a starting point. Titled after the city where Reuel Denney was then teaching high school, the little sketch was much in keeping with what was then becoming known as the "*New Yorker* short story": a character-driven mood piece with a slight twist at the end. Told in flat, declarative prose reminiscent of the magazine's most prolific fiction writer, John O'Hara (and therefore reminiscent, still, of Hemingway), "Buffalo" concerns a young man who develops a crush on a pretty waitress, only to learn in mortifying fashion that the middle-aged, nondescript baker behind the counter is her husband. Again, the story isn't much; comparing it to Cheever's later work is like comparing Michelangelo's *David* to an Olmec head.

Cheever's breakthrough had come just in time. "Things got lower

---

*The first one *sold*, that is: it wouldn't appear in the magazine until the June 22, 1935, issue, about a month later than "Brooklyn Rooming House" (May 25).

and lower," he wrote Denney, "and then I sold a mediocre story for forty-five dollars. Ever since then I've been going around like a kid with a broken bank buying scotch and sodas and dating up everyone I could lay my hands on." But he didn't rest long on this modest laurel. Within two weeks, he'd hired the prominent left-wing literary agent, Maxim Lieber, who also represented (at one time or another) Saul Bellow, Carson McCullers, Thomas Wolfe, Nathanael West, and many others. His first act on Cheever's behalf was to rush another story, "The Cameos," to *The New Yorker.* Katharine White's reply was just as swift, and suggests that Cheever had already forgotten Cowley's advice: "This story," wrote Mrs. White, "we can't believe is for us. It is too much the routine short story, the sort of thing the monthly short story magazines use rather than the sort of thing we use. . . . We are anxious for more from Mr. Cheever and hope he won't go the way of most fiction writers when they try for ambitious long stories, i.e., we hope he won't just turn out conventional 'Short Stories.' " In little more than a week, Cheever submitted "Brooklyn Rooming House," a more suitable slice-of-life about a landlady's futile struggle to keep her house "respectable" despite the ravages of the Depression. The story was accepted on condition that Cheever respond to a few minor points, including a typical quibble from the editor in chief, Harold Ross: "She can't ask about her roomers' habits *every* time she meets them in the hallways, can she?"

A year would pass before Cheever sold another story to the magazine, though hardly for lack of trying on the author's part. "I should be interested to know *how* Mr. Cheever works," wrote Mrs. White, as the manuscripts piled up on her desk; "his stories often sound as if they were pretty hastily put together. . . . I wish he'd try a little editing of his own work before he submits stuff." That was a taller order than she might have expected. Cheever's payment for "Brooklyn Rooming House" was double what he'd gotten for "Buffalo," and fully eighteen times as much as M-G-M was willing to pay for a synopsis that often ran as long as twelve typed pages. For the first time ever, really, it occurred to Cheever that he might actually make a living as a writer, and for him the matter was especially urgent. As a high-school dropout he'd learned the hard way that he was virtually unemployable, and it was too late to remedy the matter—too late, indeed, for the world at large, as Cheever (and Walker Evans) would have it: "I've never imagined making a living out of this machine but . . . there isn't time for much else and there doesn't seem to be much time anyhow." And then, why *not* write fast, if one could? As Gurganus put it, "John was a sprinter, not a dental technician." As a young man he could easily write almost twenty pages a day without changing a word; "editing," for the most part, meant tearing up a piece he deemed a failure. "Haste is a great limitation that can be traced back to my magazine experience," he wrote in 1976. "The story was written, paid for, printed and applauded in the space of a week. Why should I have tried to make them more substantial?" It was an aesthetic choice, too, as Cheever liked the kind of *movement* that came from writing fast: "[G]ood prose," he wrote Denney, "reminds me of a walking figure, preferably young."*

At Cowley's urging he started another novel, though he suspected the form was a little passé. Such was the chaos of his own life, and modern life in general, that he wondered if he could express it in terms of a long, conventional, cause-and-effect narrative. As a kind of warm-up, he wrote "Of Love: A Testimony," a longish but hardly conventional narrative that he sold to the less commercial *Story* magazine. As much as anything Cheever wrote, it reflects the fatalism he felt as a member of a doomed generation. "Before I left Hanover for the last time [1934]," he wrote Cowley thirty years later, "I spaded the vegetable garden and planted a potato patch. . . . I thought that I would never return to eat the potatoes I had planted (I don't like potatoes) and that in the years ahead the approach of war would trim and color most of my impulses; and in fact, pretty much from the time we sailed from Antwerp in August '31 until the day when I joined the army this turned out to be true."

Something of the sort applies to "Of Love: A Testimony," the most notable achievement of which is its peculiar originality—the way Cheever uses formal quirks to convey the disorder of his times. "It would be something as casual as the bartender's greeting," the story abruptly begins, "as clear as a legal confession of murder. 'I was born in

---

*It's not enough simply to say that Cheever wrote fast. Some stories seemed to come to him all of a piece, almost word for word, especially in the early years; but as one may discern by examining Cheever's typescripts at Brandeis, some stories—both his better *and* lesser efforts—were torturously worked over, often at the exacting behest of *New Yorker* editors. It's worth mentioning, too, that as a *novelist* he always progressed with the most painful difficulty—constantly making notes as he groped his way forward.

a two-apartment house. . . .' " Without any explanation of what this odd little salvo signifies (though one is reminded that what follows will be a *testimony* of sorts), the characters are then evoked in a leisurely manner—young people leading unremarkable lives—with a rather heavy emphasis on the larger historical context (all but entirely absent, except by implication, in Cheever's mature work): "[Julie] was conceived four years before they shot the arch-duke in Sarajevo and while they were building battlements in the Prussian woods. It seems, for that generation of her class, as if every tradition were broken by the smoldering books, by the murdered millions, by the shattered statuary and the election of fools." Such a hopeless course of events leads Julie, born 1911, to destroy a promising love affair with compulsive acts of infidelity. "Maybe I'm promiscuous," she says to her stricken lover, Morgan. "But I was afraid. . . . It seemed as if we had too much, too much." Expressing the vast collective nihilism in so many words, with a bit of random fornication, is bound to seem melodramatic; but then the story reverts to the quirky impressionism of its opening, until the narrator breaks frame to consider Morgan's future: "Make him employed or unemployed, put him in a strange city without money or on board a train leaving the city for some place like Niantic or South Norwalk for a week-end . . ." The reader, in short, is left to choose the character's destiny, but in any case the inner result (as well as the pitiless course of history) will remain the same.

CHEEVER HAD COUNTED ON a small advance for his novel from Harrison Smith at Cape and Smith, which had published Cowley's *Blue Juniata*. But his chat with Smith went poorly. The man told him that "a story writer and a novelist are two different birds": "He asked me how long I'd been writing," Cheever reported to Cowley. "Ten years—I said; true enough. He looked at me dubiously, nearly sadly—And this is all you've done? . . . Ten years."

After a while, the prospect of being a laborer at Yaddo didn't look so bad, though what Cheever really wanted was a job at Lake George, about thirty-five miles north of Saratoga, where Yaddo had recently taken over three small islands called Triuna. He pictured a long, larky summer of swimming and climbing mountains and chasing college girls. He let Mrs. Ames know that he was ready to make himself "generally useful," particularly in an aquatic capacity: "While we were talk-

ing about Triuna, one evening last summer, you mentioned the fact
that you would need someone to run the launch. . . . I can drive, swim
well enough to be intrusted [sic] with a boat . . ." But Mrs. Ames was
still, perhaps, a bit broody with respect to Cheever's shenanigans the
summer before; she responded with gentle bemusement that Cheever
(an able-bodied young man, after all) still hadn't found proper employment. "I have almost always worked," Cheever replied, more desperate
than indignant. "But about two years ago the possibility of holding
these jobs stopped. I have no trade, no degree, no special training.
Straightforward application for any kind of work from a bus-boy to an
advertising copy-writer has been completely ineffectual." The
woman's heart was a little wrung, and Cheever was allowed to return to
Yaddo for what amounted to an indefinite stay. The highlights were a
very brief trip to Lake George and a few pleasant days at the racetrack;
the rest of it was monastic to a fault—a great fault, as Cheever saw it.
"Yaddo still goes on if anybody should have forgotten," he noted, after
several months at the Trask mansion. "At six thirty every night Emma
rings the chimes and we all file into the hall and the dinning [sic] room
and speak as if we were afraid of waking someone. . . . The month of
August has seemed like a year."

   At last he escaped to Manhattan, returning to his little room on
Hudson Street and an old dilemma. "I can't get a WPA job because I
can't get on relief because I can't establish residence," he wrote Cowley. "And there don't seem to be any other jobs." As the holiday season
drew near, he tried to get work at a department store; however, after a
long day of waiting in line with other applicants, he shook so badly
from hunger and fatigue that he flunked the interview. At this decidedly low point, Walker Evans hired him as a darkroom assistant at
twenty dollars a week. The photographer had just been given the enormous job of filling some sixty portfolios with images from the African
Negro Art exhibition at the Museum of Modern Art. He'd hired a
Dutch artist named Peter Sekaer as his second-in-command, and
(once the actual photo-taking was done) reinstalled Cheever in his
Bethune Street studio with many, many prints to wash and hang in the
bathroom. Then Evans left town ("to chase some woman in Tennessee," as Dodie Merwin recalled), and Cheever was alone again in a
dingy basement. "I'm not doing the work I should do and I feel like
hell," he wrote in mid-November. A few weeks later the electricity was
cut off, since Evans had neglected to pay the bill. Cheever typed by the

light of a plumber's candle. "[P]oor John can't sit over there in the dark," Sekaer appealed to Evans; "and anyway there are something like 50 more prints to be done."

Such privations did not affect Cheever's politics much. Over the course of the next year, as civil war raged in Spain, many of his leftist friends became even more *engagé*—forming Marxist reading clubs and joining the Lincoln Brigade to assist the Loyalists against Franco. Cheever was sympathetic but aloof, and in the radical atmosphere of the Village and Yaddo he was often berated for his attitude. "C'mon, Cheever, join up!" said the artist Anton Refregier, but Cheever responded to all such appeals with the same pleasant demurral, and managed as ever to keep most of his friends.

"Last night at three o'clock," he recorded in the early pages of his journal, "I heard a drunken woman on 11th street screaming: 'I'm the United States of America!'" Cheever would always care more about the lone drunken woman than he would about ideological systems one way or the other, which (he believed) failed to take account of the vagaries of human nature—particularly an all-consuming selfishness that remains constant regardless of systems or the historical moment. Shivering in Evans's dark basement studio, he wrote an almost novella-length apologia titled "In Passing" that, to his utter amazement, was bought a few weeks later by *The Atlantic Monthly*. ("I can't seem to figure it out," he wrote Denney. "I guess I'll go out and buy some shoes.") The story's narrator is a young man like Cheever who leads a hard-scrabble, itinerant life—this after his middle-class Boston family loses their money and faces eviction from the fine old house where the narrator grew up. In Saratoga for the racing season, the narrator meets a communist named Girsdansky who has come to organize the city's Negro workers. Whether speaking face to face with the narrator or addressing a bored, harassed crowd, Girsdansky gives the same canned rant about the "dictatorship of the proletariat," while the narrator observes that "his talk [has] the clarity and dryness of a book." Meanwhile the scene at the racetrack serves as a gross but invigorating counterpoint to Girsdansky's vision—the gamblers clamoring around the bars and betting windows with "nothing in their faces but a love of money and the incorrigible dream of big money." Cheever leaves little doubt as to which dream will prevail. Returning to Boston at the end of the season, the narrator notices a lone speaker on the Common—Girsdansky, attended by a few odd stragglers, though he addresses his speech to "the trees and the wind and the sky as if he were addressing thousands."

"In Passing" was a nice catharsis for the author, and also helped put an end to a long run of failure that had followed those heady *New Yorker* sales almost six months before. Indeed, Katharine White had begun to wonder whether they'd been too hard on the young man, whose flurry of submissions had abruptly ceased toward the end of 1935. "I hope he hasn't deserted us entirely," she wrote Lieber, who reported that his client was now preoccupied with a novel, under contract with Simon and Schuster since December. *Sitting on the Whorehouse Steps and Empty Bed Blues*—the book's provocative and perhaps provisional title—was a "long narrative," said Cheever, as opposed to an actual novel ("a bad word anyhow"): "I'm doing exactly the same thing I would do with a story," he wrote. "But it will be ten times as long as a story and I will have just that much more room to move around. It will, quite incidentally, be topical. And probably forgotten as quickly as yesterday's newspaper." Clearly the problems of his generation continued to exert a pull, though Cheever's better instincts had already begun to militate against fiction that was merely timely.

Hoping to stretch his four-hundred-dollar advance, Cheever returned to Yaddo in February as a kind of general caretaker in the off-season. For a while, the only other guest was Josephine Herbst, who was twenty years older than Cheever and as famous as she'd ever be. Her trilogy of novels—*Pity Is Not Enough* (1933), *The Executioner Waits* (1934), and *Rope of Gold* (1939)—reflect her socialist sympathies, though she disliked being "ghettoized" as a "proletarian writer." Shortly before coming to Yaddo that winter, she'd spent months in Germany writing about Hitler's regime for the *New York Post*, and she compared notes on the subject with Cheever while huddling in the kitchen drinking rum. It was the beginning of an odd but lifelong friendship. Quietly dubious of Herbst's politics and literary merit, Cheever nonetheless found her a jolly companion with an almost inexhaustible fund of anecdotes, as the woman had known practically everyone—including Hemingway, whom she'd once forced (at the point of a shark rifle) to turn his boat around in a hurricane and head for land. As a proper socialist, she gave friends the run of her rickety old farmhouse in Erwinna, Pennsylvania, which the young Cheever would come to regard as a kind of personal pied-à-terre. In turn, Herbst would spend a number of holidays with Cheever's family, becoming a beloved figure to his children. "I thought of her not as a distinguished writer," Ben Cheever remembered, "but as a small woman in an orange serape who smoked heavily and kept saying, 'For Heaven's sakes.' " By then the world, too, had stopped thinking of Herbst as a distinguished writer, whereas Cheever's star would continue to rise—a state of affairs that would lead to some interesting friction between the two.

Another writer bound for obscurity, Nathan Asch, also came to Yaddo for a few weeks that spring. Son of the Yiddish writer Sholem Asch, Nathan had published an experimental first novel in 1925, *The Office*, while living in Paris and befriending Herbst, Hemingway, and other expatriates. After a handful of well-regarded stories in *The New Yorker*, Asch continued to write novels that nobody would publish and quietly faded away. To Cheever he became a cautionary figure of sorts—a writer whose grandiose ambition was out of proportion to his talent. "Poor Nathan," he wrote Herbst in 1952. "I can remember him saying in Washington: It's all running through my mind like quicksilver! What a book I will be able to write!" For the next few years, at any rate, he was a good occasional companion to Cheever, each man playing the antic role of surrogate son to Herbst, whom they sent cards and wires on Father's Day.

CHEEVER FINISHED A DRAFT of his novel in April ("I'm not as satisfied with it as I would like to be"), and a few weeks later managed to sell another story to *The New Yorker*. "Play a March" is a slight but artful vignette about an out-of-work accordion player and his wife, who is so busy consoling herself with pipe dreams that she won't let her husband practice his instrument. ("By the way, is 'John Cheever' right?" asked a puzzled Wolcott Gibbs on accepting the story. "Seems to me your first pieces were signed 'Jon.' ") Braced by the sale, Cheever did a quick revision of his novel and dropped it in the mail, then celebrated with a road trip to Cape Cod. By then he'd inherited his brother's Model A, which, after years of gadding about the South Shore, was quite a bit the worse for wear. Morris Werner considered it another subject for Walker Evans, but Cheever loved the stalwart jalopy: "It takes almost no gasoline, no oil, and I've had no tire trouble," he proudly reported. However, since the car had no windows or heater, Cheever's winter travels were necessarily curtailed.

In May, he paid his family a lingering visit. His father—broken by the hardships of Hanover—had reconciled with his formidable wife and resigned himself to an obedient dotage in downtown Quincy, where he whiled away his days at the Thomas Crane Library. For the next twenty years, John would also affect a sort of obedience toward his mother, nursing a vast resentment in secrecy. And when he found himself losing patience with both parents, there was always Fred, who lived more and more prosperously in the nearby town of Norwell. In the old days he and Joey had often discussed the nature of their respective "Belle Isles," but by 1936 Fred seemed content to the point of smugness. He and his family* lived in a well-appointed rental on Stetson Road, and presently Fred would build a Swiss-chalet-style house near the river. He treated his brother with a kind of jovial condescension, joshing him about his feckless hand-to-mouth lifestyle and dirty-neck friends. Fred was rooting for the fascists in Spain, while in his spare time he wrote a book titled *A Song for These States*, extolling the glories of his Yankee heritage and American democracy in general. "We disagree on everything," John noted after that May visit. "Any desire, higher than that for warmth and security, seems to have died out in his frame and with that he has cultivated an immense contempt for those poor, sad fools, living on the fringes of society, who have been unable to rent a house in the country, stuff it with antiques, dress their wives attractively, produce beautiful children and come up the gravel drive-way at dusk to love, sherry, supper, wood-fires and the editorials of the Boston Evening Transcript."

Cheever was coming to terms with his own sense of exile. "I'm a stranger here and I guess it's just as well," he wrote Denney. There were times, though, when he felt overwhelmed by a nostalgia that would never quite go away, whatever he saw fit to say about it. "But my days here are numbered," he wrote in 1936, and so they were.

WHILE ANXIOUSLY AWAITING WORD from Simon and Schuster (he was hoping they'd finance a second book so he could move to Maine "and have a boat and a girl and a lot of good liquor"), Cheever was relieved to learn that Mrs. Ames was willing, at last, to let him run the

---

*Fred's daughter Jane had been born in 1935, and three more children would follow: David, Sarah, and Ann.

launch at Lake George. "My father keeps telling me," he wrote her, "and asking me not to forget, that one whistle means a starboard passing, two, a port passing, three a salute and four means astern. I've also been studying Marine engine instruction books." Mrs. Ames wasn't entirely reassured. Stiffly she replied that insurance on the old Fay & Bowen absolutely stipulated that he keep the speed under twenty miles an hour "at all times."

The pleasant islands of Triuna are spanned by a fanciful ninety-two-foot bridge built by the Trasks, and for the first month of the summer Cheever had the place mostly to himself. He did chores and shooed away trespassers and ate big meals prepared by "a distinguished woman named Daisey MacAfee Bonner." In July he was joined by a young writer named Eugene Joffe, and the little town of Bolton Landing filled up with "a lot of nice girls" on vacation from colleges such as Skidmore and Beaver (a name that delighted Cheever). He was happy to give them rides in his boat, letting them aquaplane at speeds that probably exceeded twenty miles an hour, but his heart belonged to Lila Refregier, the ponytailed wife of his friend Anton. "[I] always hoped that something, the love of a beautiful woman, would cure my ailments," he wrote in 1967. "I thought that Lila would lead me away from my jumpy past."

By then his romance with Dodie Merwin, though still occasionally carnal, had cooled somewhat; she was an outdoorsy sort who liked going off to the woods and getting dirty, cutting her own firewood and so forth, which perhaps reminded Cheever a little too much of his mother ("flinging up weeds [in her garden] as a dog flings up dirt"). Lila, however, was chic: she and Anton barely made ends meet—he painted murals for nightclubs, and she taught the odd class in costume design—but when she did get a few dollars ahead, she liked to buy stylish high-heeled shoes and silk hats. She admired the same thing in Cheever: "He was a very dapper young man," she said, remembering his gray flannel trousers, tweed jacket, button-down shirt, and "always polished" shoes. (In regard to the last, Cheever once breached a curious point of etiquette: "I remember Lila . . . burst into tears after a cyclonic orgasm," he wrote in his journal, "when she discovered that I had not taken off my shoes.") The Refregiers had rented a house in Bolton Landing for the summer, and at first Cheever was equally charming to both; but after a while he could hardly be bothered to greet the husband when he asked for Lila on the telephone. Finally the man pressed a mutual friend, Frances Lindley: was Lila in love with John? "I could honestly answer 'I don't know,' " said Lindley, "though of course I knew well they had been sleeping together." Eventually the romance became more of a comfortable friendship, and, like Merwin, the woman would continue to think fondly of Cheever, with only the faintest unnameable qualm: "Joey was such a nice person," she said many years later, "a basically decent person, with something in him that kept him from being completely decent."

Be that as it may, the first phase of the fling ended with the summer of 1936. Suddenly everyone was gone—the Refregiers, the college girls, even Eugene Joffe. Cheever wanted badly to leave, but he was broke again and still hadn't heard from Simon and Schuster; and even if he could afford gas, his car's steering gear was shot. "I woke one morning with a hangover and not a red cent," he wrote Herbst, "and God only knows how I'll get out of this place."

As ever, he tried writing his way out, but Katharine White at *The New Yorker* wasn't making it easy for him. "I am sorry that we don't like this story of John Cheever's at all," she wrote of "Frère Jacques," about an *engagé* man ("interested in the Spanish trouble") and his fey mistress, who treats bundles of cornmeal, flour, or laundry as if they were the baby she longs for. "It is meant to be very serious and sad," Mrs. White went on, "and somehow the child mistress . . . seems more ridiculous and half-witted than touching." This is perhaps too harsh, but anyway the story's interest is stylistic. Like "Play a March" and other stories Cheever wrote around this time, it owes much to Hemingway's "Hills Like White Elephants"—a short two-character sketch written almost entirely in elliptical dialogue. In "Frère Jacques," the man and woman banter awhile to no apparent purpose—this while the man tries to read a newspaper ("anxious to find who was holding Madrid")—before the reader learns they aren't married, which somewhat explains the woman's loony determination, at the end, to sing "Frère Jacques" to a laundry bundle: "He was frightened, then, for . . . if she had been screaming and crying and drumming her heels on the floor, her words couldn't have held more finality and estrangement than the simple persistent words of that song." Cheever was eventually able to sell the story to *The Atlantic Monthly*, and Mrs. White may have been surprised when it was selected for *The Best Short Stories of 1939* and singled out for praise in the *New York Times* ("really illuminates the contemporary scene"). It would hardly be the first time one of Cheever's *New Yorker* rejections met with a (relatively) happy ending.

A week later, Cheever mailed the magazine another story of no particular distinction ("A Picture for the Home"), which proved to be his ticket off the islands of Triuna. "I haven't appreciated anything as much as I did that, in a long time," he wrote Wolcott Gibbs, who'd expedited the check. Cheever was glad to leave, but within a month or so he was back at Yaddo: Simon and Schuster had asked—evidently without enthusiasm—for extensive revisions. "I've got to go over the whole novel again, word for word," he sighed to Herbst. The manuscript, however, is lost to posterity; Cheever rarely mentioned it again, except to say that he'd used his revision notes to write "short things" out of financial necessity.

LILA REFREGIER (AND OTHERS) would sometimes badger Cheever about his dependence on Yaddo: high-school dropout or not, surely he could get *some* kind of job—and indeed he could. "I have a chance of a WPA job," he wrote after leaving Lake George in October, "but I sincerely don't want it. And I have another chance of traveling all over the country with Walker Evans. . . . I'm not crazy about that either." The fact was, he'd grown used to a freewheeling life, and starvation was no longer an immediate danger. He'd ingratiated himself with Mrs. Ames so successfully that he could come as he pleased to Yaddo or Triuna, and whenever he sold a story he'd simply hop back into his roadster and go spinning along the Hudson for a holiday in Manhattan, where he was entertained by a widening circle of friends.

At the marble tables of the Lafayette Hotel on University Place, he'd spend hours playing backgammon with the artists Niles Spencer and Stuart Davis. Or, in Chelsea, he'd call on the Refregiers—if both were home—and contrive to take Lila away on a cheap date enlivened by the excitement of illicit love: they rode the Staten Island Ferry for a nickel, or walked to the Central Park Zoo, or took the Fifth Avenue bus from Washington Square to Harlem and back. Sometimes, too, they'd go to a boozy salon at the Werners' apartment or that of his friend Eleanor Clark, who (though a year younger than Cheever) was already a leading light of the intellectual left—a frequent contributor to *Partisan Review* and *The Nation*, not to mention Trotsky's translator in Mexico.* Or if Cheever simply wanted to relax and eat a good meal, he'd visit his friend Dorothy Dudley, an easygoing fat lady from Biddeford, Maine, who for many years worked as the registrar at the Museum of Modern Art. Cheever was struck by Dudley's habit of falling for self-destructive heels: maudlin drunks and consumptives who treated her badly despite an unwavering solicitude on her part. "Some day," Cheever wrote in his journal, "I must write a story about women like Dorothy and call it The Widow."†

But soon enough the money always ran out, and Cheever would return to Yaddo and live awhile with other perennial guests who enjoyed Mrs. Ames's favor for one reason or another. At the time there was Leonard Ehrlich, her lover, a valetudinarian in his late twenties whose only novel—*God's Angry Man*, about abolitionist John Brown— was already years in the past. There was also Loyd (Pete) Collins, another one-novel writer, who was then married to Cheever's friend (and future editor at Harper) Frances Lindley; Cheever found Collins "a good drinking companion" and continued the friendship for three decades on that basis. And finally there was the more accomplished Daniel Fuchs, whose novels about his youth in Brooklyn had sold poorly despite wide acclaim.‡ "It was a pretty idyllic time," said Fuchs, remembering the "wonderful, choice people" at the Trask mansion, the long nights tippling at the Worden, where he once chided his friend John to get more serious about his career. "What are you waiting for?" Fuchs demanded. "For the world and life to get integrated," Cheever replied.

It wasn't that Cheever lacked ambition. He worked hard, but still loved the world a little too much. "When I was younger," he recalled

---

*Perhaps needless to say, Clark was another friend who gave Cheever a hard time (his entire life) over his lack of political conviction. She particularly nagged him for writing "frivolous" (apolitical?) realism, which she dismissed as a "blind alley." Noting Clark's work in *Partisan Review* and two other like-minded publications, Cheever wrote Herbst: "It's the vision of those three sheets lined up on a book-shelf with their air of profound compromise, unjustifiable snobbishness, and phoney calm, that makes me so happy in my rank, blind alley."

†The first mention of what would become, several years later, "Torch Song"—one of Cheever's best stories.

‡Fuchs went on to have a very successful career as a Hollywood screenwriter. In *Bech: A Book*, Updike alludes to him as the Jewish writer who "turned his back on his three beautiful Brooklyn novels and went into the desert to write scripts for Doris Day."

in the midst of later fame, "I used to wake up at eight, work until noon, and then break, hollering with pleasure; then I'd go back to work through to five, get pissed, get laid, go to bed, and do the same thing again the next day." Dodie Merwin, for one, knew the drill: when she paid a visit to Yaddo, it was understood that she took a backseat to Cheever's writing; if he managed to finish before sunset, they'd go skiing awhile before joining the others at the Worden and so to bed. Underlying Cheever's high spirits was a seething determination. "He wanted terribly to be respected," said James Farrell's wife, Dorothy, who got to know Cheever well at Yaddo. "I have this image of him: John Cheever squaring his shoulders, confronting the world."

Respect meant money as well as artistic achievement, and after being stuck at Yaddo for most of 1937, Cheever wrote an unabashedly trashy story for the slicks. "His Young Wife" is about a stand-up guy named John Hollis who marries a charming but "impulsive" girl much younger than he; both are "very happy" until she meets, at the track, a dissolute rogue her own age—but in the end, she sees the wisdom of staying with honest John ("crying like a young kid over the rediscovery of her own immense happiness"). *Collier's* bought the story for five hundred dollars, a fabulous sum, but then dispatched a troubling wire to Saratoga: they'd lost the typescript and would appreciate the author's sending a carbon. The problem, of course, was that Cheever never bothered to keep carbons, and thus had to spend another three or four hours rewriting the thing from scratch. "[W]hat's happened between now and then," he wrote Denney, "has been pretty much the spending of that money. It enabled me to leave here whenever I felt like it, which was often and I shunted around a lot between here, Boston and New York." Before leaving Yaddo that first time, he took Daniel and Sue Fuchs to Albany for a victory feast and then purchased a bottle of fine champagne for Mrs. Ames. Finally he came to Quincy as a conquering hero, lauded as such by a brief item in the *Patriot Ledger*: "A literary career which is growing quietly but steadily is that of John Cheever, son of Mrs. Mary Cheever of Spear Street . . ." Frederick is nowhere mentioned—almost as if his wife were wistfully casting ahead to widowhood—but then he had no pull at the *Patriot Ledger*.

CHAPTER SEVEN

{ 1938–1939 }

THE *COLLIER'S* MONEY lasted until the spring of 1938, when the twenty-six-year-old Cheever finally surrendered to the inevitable. His friend Nathan Asch was an editor for the Federal Writers' Project's American Guide Series, and was happy to recommend him to the program's director, Henry Alsberg, who took Cheever's word for it that he could manage the English language with "clarity, ease and meaning." Hired as a junior editor at twenty-six hundred dollars a year, Cheever joined thousands of writers who would last out the Depression with a boost from the Works Progress Administration—an honorable roster that includes Bellow, Nelson Algren, Richard Wright, and others of like distinction.

At best Cheever was bemused by the situation. "Every time I saw a beggar in the streets [of Washington]," he wrote Mrs. Ames, "I used to wonder why anyone would choose that way of making a living; why didn't they go to work for the government?" A beggar's lot, as many saw it, was only slightly more demoralizing: those employed by the WPA (called "We Poke Along" by its detractors) bore "a stigma of the lowest order," as writer Jerre Mangione put it, "a dark and embarrassing symbol of a time of their lives when circumstances beyond their control compelled them to admit, on public record, personal defeat." It was especially bad for Cheever, whose family took a dim view of New Deal slackery, and whose own Yankee scruples were such that— four decades later, blessedly solvent—he'd try to return his first Social Security check. On the other hand, there was something to be said for collecting a regular salary: with his fifty dollars a week, Cheever was able to help his family, pay down his debt to Mrs. Ames, and put aside a little in the bank to finance a novel once he'd done his time. Perhaps most gratifying was slipping the odd tenner under the table to his wretched father, augmenting what must have been a very meager allowance: "Have the Bill Fold and the X [$10] enclosed—and thank you John boy," wrote the grateful old man, who usually blew it on a big lunch at Locke-Ober.

Cheever thought Washington a dreary place. He'd taken a room at Mrs. Grey's boardinghouse, where he dined with librarians, government clerks, and "an old lady who sits at the head of the table and says all WPA workers are lazy and good-for-nothing." Cheever found it hard to argue: his fellow employees were hopeless drones, and he kept his distance lest he be tainted by their dullness and mediocrity. Worst of all was the job itself, which wasn't quite the boondoggle he'd hoped for; as Dodie Merwin put it, "he let himself accept their pittance," though he was "insulted" that such work was substantial enough to keep him from his writing. As for the social life, it was about as good as it would ever get in Washington. The evidence of his co-workers notwithstanding, Cheever wasn't the only talented young person who'd come to feed at the public trough, and the atmosphere was akin to that of a large college campus. Before long, Cheever was sleeping with a girl who worked in the archives and going to a lot of embassy parties; often drunk and "under the influence of Fitzgerald," he liked asking cabdrivers to help him knot his black tie. Later he'd go so far as to claim a certain glamour for the era, though he knew it wasn't really so: he was just another "broody clerk," the parties were third-rate, and it depressed him to chat with people about their civil-service classifications; what's more, his girlfriend had buck teeth and gave him "a bad case of crabs." One of the only good times was a weekend spent in Maryland, alone, riding a rented horse around the countryside.

So the summer passed. *The New Yorker* had begun to wonder, again, what had become of one of its most promising young writers. "What about John Cheever?" wrote William Maxwell, a new fiction editor. "It is almost a year since we have had a look at anything of his, and we'd like very much to have him in the magazine again." Cheever wanted nothing better than to oblige. He tried writing at night and on weekends, but his output remained "pathetically small": his FWP duties left him frazzled and depressed, all the less willing to forfeit valuable drinking time to punch out stories, which—even when he did buckle down—just weren't flowing with the old facility. The one thing he'd finished in five months ("like pulling a tooth") was another racetrack yarn for *Collier's* titled "Saratoga," about a boy and girl who grow up with gambling in their blood (etc.) but finally quit the horses and get married. One senses Cheever's misery in almost every line. In fact, he considered taking the *Collier's* money and running back to New York, then and there, but instead he moved out of Mrs. Grey's to a more private arrangement near Dupont Circle, which proved to have a bedbug problem.

The strain was such that even his vaunted affability began to fail him, and he had a final falling-out with Dodie Merwin. She was also living part-time in Washington, and the two would sometimes escape to New York in his Model A. Returning—no doubt morosely—from a weekend trip, they'd just crossed the Pulaski Skyway into the Jersey Meadowlands when the roadster was sideswiped and sent shambling off the road. Cheever got out and was pensively inspecting the flat tire, the steaming engine, when Merwin tried to lighten things up with a little laughter. "He got *furious*," she remembered. "I think he wouldn't let me back in the car. I don't know how I got back to New York, but whatever happened, we didn't go on to Washington together." Cheever's rigid back—as he stomped off to find a garage—was the last she'd see of her old friend for many years. And once, later, while crossing the Pulaski Skyway, Cheever mentioned the quarrel to his wife, whose sympathy was entirely with Merwin.

By November, after six months on the job, Cheever had had enough. He told Alsberg that his assignments "seemed neither interesting nor useful," and certainly not worth sacrificing his own work. But Alsberg valued his talents well enough to coax him into staying on a bit longer, in exchange for which he let Cheever return to New York and help edit the second volume of *The New York City Guide*. Lou Gody, the editor in chief, would later claim that the *only* job given to one of America's greatest writers was editing copy ("twisting into order the sentences written by some incredibly lazy bastards," as Cheever put it), but in fact Alsberg had canvassed his input on key points of content and given him a free hand in revising weak copy as well as generating his own. "Cheever thinks that the [introduction] ought to be somewhat condensed and be made a little less conventional," he wrote the director of the New York office. "He thinks he can do this very quickly without spoiling the article. . . . Another point I took up with

Cheever was the idea of having a very factual little piece at the beginning of the whole book telling a few things about the greater city."

Though glad enough to be back in a town where he could buy liquor on Sundays, Cheever was less than enthralled by Alsberg's confidence. Skipping both Christmas and New Year's, he sequestered himself in the Chelsea Hotel and flailed through mounds of god-awful copy, the better to resign by the end of January and never look back. A year before his death, he was greeted at the American Academy and Institute of Arts and Letters by Jim McGraw, an old FWPer like himself. "Hey Johnny," said the jovial man, "it's a long time since I last saw you on the Writers' Project!" "I don't want to talk about it," said Cheever, and walked away.

THAT SUMMER (1939) HE WAS BACK running the launch at Lake George and "dreaming out a book." Earlier he'd been at Yaddo, but had fled as soon as the summer guests began to arrive. "Yaddo, in season anyhow, has become impossible," he wrote. "The must those yellow carpets exhale, the lame conversation, and the pathetic picture my colleagues in numbers of more than five can produce, is more than I can take." Besides, there was a "good deal more license" at Lake George in terms of "drinking, screwing, etc." The latter activities—plus water-skiing—took up most of his time. He was having a strenuous affair with an older woman, a gorgeous brunette named Peg Worthington who was on the rebound from a dull marriage. Worthington liked drinking almost as much as Cheever, and "sang [his] praises as a male" more than any woman he'd ever known. The two had befriended a playboy named Comstock who had his own boat, a powerful GarWood that ran rings around the old Fay & Bowen; Cheever never forgot the excitement of skiing into a rain squall at blazing speed—or for that matter the whole heady, hedonistic spree: "That was the summer when I used to screw P[eg] in the old matchboard bedroom and we used to steal [Comstock's] father's scotch," he reminisced in his journal. "Even today the smell of scotch reminds me of that summer. We used to drink and neck and tear up and down the lake between the narrows and the village."

The lark ended in apposite fashion for a man who'd been so preoccupied with the fate of his generation: Worthington left for Reno "to divorce a stuffed shirt named Harold," and a few days later Germany invaded Poland. The news, said Cheever, was "a howling wind that shakes the island"; suddenly Bolton Landing was deserted, the lake was calm, and oddly, elsewhere, the world was sliding toward disaster. For a while, Cheever was grateful for the relative tranquillity. His friend Pete Collins had also come to the lake, and was a good if taciturn companion. (The man's aloofness was later put in perspective when Collins admitted that his wife had left him just prior to his departure for Lake George.) "We got on one another's nerves some," Cheever wrote Denney, "but we worked all morning, water-skiied all afternoon and worked all evening for three weeks. It was a cold and a lonely stretch, but walking up to the post-office at six in what used to be the football season, playing darts with the mountaineers, watching them shutter the lake houses and draw up the boats, was a lot more memorable than Skidmore's hysterics or those goddamned martinis we used to put away." Cheever would later reflect on how comfortable he'd felt in Collins's company. They slept "beararse" in the same narrow bed "without any trouble"—indeed, such was the serene asexuality between them that Cheever didn't mind walking from bed to bathroom in a state of rampant (but impersonal) arousal, making Collins laugh by pissing straight up in the air. In the evenings Collins kept him company while he went for a solo swim ("beararse" again) in the cold water, whereupon he'd take a hot bath and report to dinner in coat and tie. Once, he asked Collins, who cooked, why the plates weren't warmed: "That's a very peculiar request," said Collins, "from a horny, penniless bastard stuck on an island on a mountain lake at the beginning of duck season."

Cheever might have remained on the island for quite a while longer (and thereby altered his destiny in any number of ways) were it not for the intervention of his new editor at *The New Yorker*, William Maxwell. One day in 1938—shortly after Maxwell had moved to fiction from the art department—Katharine White had "turned Cheever over to him." Not only was Maxwell persistent in soliciting Cheever's work, but he tended to suggest revisions rather than rejecting stories outright. The first "casual" he bought, "Washington Boarding House," was a result of this process. Rejected with encouragement toward the end of Cheever's tenure at the FWP, the piece was later revised and resubmitted to Maxwell, who bought it at a higher rate than Cheever had ever been paid by the magazine. Maxwell's attentiveness was all the more flattering—and his editorial advice valuable—because he himself was already, at age thirty, the author of two well-regarded novels, *Bright*

Center of Heaven and *They Came like Swallows*. For most of his career, though, his own reputation would be eclipsed by the greater fame of the writers he edited: Nabokov, Salinger, Welty, and (as Maxwell put it) "three wonderful writers all named John"—O'Hara, Updike, and Cheever.

Like many *New Yorker* fiction editors—but more so—Maxwell cultivated friendships with his writers: he wrote long personal letters applauding their successes and commiserating over their failures; also, he was good about rushing payment, especially to writers such as Cheever in almost constant distress. No matter how desperate the writer, though, Maxwell was never apt to let sentiment interfere with his critical judgment. Though exquisitely tactful, and eager to help if warranted, he was rigid about rejecting work that fell below his standards. While Cheever was still at Lake George, for instance, Maxwell rejected his story "The Simple Life" because it violated an old Ross taboo against stories "concerning writers and their difficulties," which (as Maxwell wrote Geraldine Mavor in Lieber's office) "have been the difficulties of writers since time began." That said, Maxwell was careful as ever to accentuate the positive: "We have great hopes for Cheever and feel that even in this story there is that special quality which he gives to his things and which is exactly right for the New Yorker."

By then Maxwell had already made it possible for Cheever to leave Lake George. A few weeks before, he'd written Cheever asking if he could come to the city and discuss "Nothing Has Happened," a story Maxwell rather liked but thought only "half done." Cheever replied: "This finds me stranded on an island, surrounded by deep water, without the means for a trip to New York. If you would return NOTHING HAS HAPPENED with your suggestions, I'm quite sure I could fix it up within the week." A few days later, Cheever received a detailed, single-spaced page of suggestions and duly revised the story (renamed "The Happiest Days"); by the end of October he was back in Manhattan with money in his pocket. It was the beginning of a friendship that would prove both rewarding and deeply tortured. "I appreciate your personal interest in John," Mavor wrote Maxwell at the time. "You have done a great deal toward helping us sell regularly to the New Yorker." Quite so: before 1939, Cheever had published a total of five stories in the magazine; by 1940, he was averaging almost a story a month.

Thus Cheever was already launched when Maxwell resigned that year to concentrate on his own writing, and more than a decade would pass before he resumed duties as Cheever's fiction editor. In the meantime, the two occasionally met in New York. In the early days, especially, Maxwell was struck by Cheever's "immense charm": "One of my college friends happened to be visiting us when John came to dinner," he recalled in 1993. "And John's conversation was so pyrotechnic that my friend spoke of it all the rest of his life as something wonderful that had happened to him, that he had had dinner with Cheever."

CHAPTER EIGHT

{ *1939–1941* }

MORE THAN FIVE YEARS had passed since Cheever had broken with his brother—more than five years without a fixed
address, drifting between Boston and New York and Saratoga, often poor and (whatever the company) more or less lonely.
Now, as 1939 drew to a close, he again faced "the grey light of New
York apartments": Peg Worthington had returned to the city from
Reno, and "after the usual ring-around-the-rosey" had decided "very
wisely" to marry an editor at Viking, Marshall Best. "There was a wedding breakfast at Beekman Place a couple weeks ago," Cheever
reported in January, "with champagne, tears, beluga, and a German
band playing the Wedding March, I saw them off to Guatemala, a light
snow falling, and ended up in traffic court on a drunken driving rap.
That was the end of the summer."

More than ever at loose ends, Cheever had returned that autumn to
the Chelsea Hotel and told friends to address letters care of his agent.
"I don't know where to go," he wrote Denney. "I'm not up to taking
a house alone in the country and I don't know of anyone I can live
with." It seemed as though all his old friends and lovers were getting
married—Denney included (the year before)—each secure in the love
of at least one person amid the looming threat of war. Cheever, meanwhile, lay on a bed at the Chelsea and fought away thoughts of suicide.
"I didn't want to sleep alone anymore," he'd often remark, when asked
why he'd gotten married.

. . .

WHATEVER ELSE CHEEVER WOULD SAY about his marriage over the years, he wouldn't call it dull. "I think of how thrilling our life has been," he wrote in 1979 (at a time when he and his wife were barely on speaking terms). "We have been welcomed all over the world, we have become rich, our children are splendid, and all of this began when we met in an elevator on a rainy autumn afternoon." The elevator was at 545 Fifth Avenue, where Cheever had gone to visit his agent's office and check galleys of "The Happiest Days." Going up, both he and the pretty young woman had noticed each other, albeit for different reasons. Hers was a heart easily moved to pity, and the young man standing beside her was vividly pitiful: "[H]e was kind of slumped over and he was little," she remembered. "He was very little." He was so little the sleeves of his tweed coat covered his hands, and he seemed the worse for hunger. Cheever, in turn, had noticed the young woman because—well, she was pretty, and about the right size, and when she got off on the same floor and entered Lieber's office, he thought, "That's more or less what I would like." So he sat beside her typewriter and read his galleys. "And I asked her for a date. And presently married her."

Mary Winternitz—the woman so randomly chosen—had a remarkable past. Her mother was Dr. Helen Watson, daughter of the co-inventor of the telephone, Thomas A. Watson ("Mr. Watson, come here—I need you!"), and her father was the legendary dean of the Yale School of Medicine, Dr. Milton Winternitz, known to friends as "Winter" or "Guts." Helen Watson was one of the first women to take a medical degree from Johns Hopkins, and had shocked her gentile New England family by marrying her pathology professor—a brilliant, dynamic Jew who had entered college at age fourteen and begun teaching medicine seven years later. During his fifteen years as the Yale dean, Winternitz turned a failing school into one of the world's great research facilities, thereby prevailing over the rampant anti-Semitism of that time and place. For the most part he succeeded by refusing to make an issue of Jewishness one way or the other—to a fault, some would say, since Jewish students enjoyed no favor in his eyes, and their numbers continued to be restricted under his leadership. On his daughter's Sarah Lawrence application he listed his religious preference as "Congregational" (though he noted that the applicant's paternal grandparents were Jewish), and Mary herself had not learned of her own Jewishness until eighth grade, when she was asked by others (who knew) to play Shylock in *The Merchant of Venice*.

Cheever summed up his wife's early life as follows: "a cruel and beautiful mother, a violent father, a miserable childhood." Fair enough. "I was the child she didn't want," Mary said of her mother, who let her know that she'd been hopefully conceived as a male play-mate for her brother Tom; the mother's next attempt ended in miscar-riage, but she finally gave birth to a son, Bill, the baby of the family and "everybody's favorite." When Mary was seven, her mother was hospi-talized with a mysterious illness, and the two hardly saw each other until the woman's death five years later.* At the time, Mary's older sib-lings (two sisters, a brother) were away at boarding school, while Dr. Winternitz sequestered himself in the laboratory ("My own work is extremely confining," he wrote on that college application, "and so I fear I see little of the children"). "I really grew up alone," said Mary. "My mother wasn't there, my father was busy, and I was an odd charac-ter in school. I was very much alone and got in the habit of being alone and I like being alone." Such prolonged introspection in her formative years—"I grew up leading other people's lives" (i.e., by reading books)—had, it seems, some curious results. In 1970 a psychiatrist puzzled over the fifty-two-year-old woman's "very little-girlish speech and behavior," which Susan Cheever regards as "a need" on her mother's part to remain a child—the way, for example, she kept her youthful looks into her sixties, or the way her high-pitched voice used to induce strangers, on the phone, into asking if her mother was home. As for Cheever's view of the matter, he generally focused on the "vio-lent father" aspect. As he alleged in his journal, his father-in-law had beaten Mary with a belt when she was a child, and even at the best of times the man's standards of perfection were daunting. "Mary is an average girl from most standpoints except for a rather keen intellect," Dr. Winternitz noted for Sarah Lawrence. "She is fairly attractive, but this could be increased if her posture was better and if she took a little more pains with her appearance." He was loath, however, to give such advice: "because" (he added) "I am fearful of imposing my will on the children."

Things did not improve when Dr. Winternitz married, in 1932, the New Haven socialite Pauline ("Polly") Webster Whitney, widow of

---

*"Even now, in a family of doctors, no one seems quite sure what was wrong with Helen," Susan Cheever wrote in her memoir *Treetops*. "Her son Bill, a doctor, says it was nephritis, or kidney disease. Her daughter Jane tells me it was a blood disease—streptococcus septicemia—and that they found the cure with the discovery of sulfa drugs a year later."

Stephen Whitney. "MEDICAL HEAD CRASHES SOCIETY BY WEDDING SMART SET LEADER," the *Waterbury Herald* announced. In keeping with her set, Polly esteemed people who were *attractive*—a catchall term for witty, good-looking, well-mannered, etc.—and while she thought Mary and her brother Bill were all right, the other Winternitz children were hopeless. Worst of all was the oldest, Elizabeth, called Buff because of the way she'd lisped her name as a child. When the girl dropped out of Vassar in 1934 and was subsequently diagnosed as manic-depressive, it was Polly's emphatic opinion that she should be sterilized. Polly's children from her first marriage—Stephen, Freddy, Louisa, and Janie— were tall, blue-eyed, and charming, hardly the type to consort with a bona-fide lunatic, or even the latter's relatively normal (but also short and awkward) siblings. "Perhaps Winter imagined the merging of the two families as a surgical transplant," Susan Cheever wrote in *Treetops*, "a transplant that would bring together the worldliness of the Whitneys with the seriousness and intelligence of his own children." It didn't work out that way. With the not-so-tacit support of their mother, the Whitney children patronized and persecuted their stepsiblings; and though Mary may have become all the more withdrawn and insecure, she also adapted in ways that would arguably serve her well in married life.

Rather than join her combative family at their estate in New Hampshire, Mary spent the last two summers of college broadening her horizons. In 1937, she toured New England with the Emergency Peace Campaign, a collection of young lefties determined to save the country from another ruinous foreign war. "Each breath you draw," Miss Winternitz declaimed, "brings you nearer to organized slaughter. *You* face conscription. . . ." The following summer she and a friend went on a bicycle tour of France, and Mary was abashed to learn that the French were appalled at her for opposing American involvement in the war. Otherwise it was perhaps the happiest time of her life. Before college she'd attended the International School of Geneva and become fluent in French, which made her travels around the Provençal countryside all the more pleasant. Indeed, during the long domestic decades that lay ahead, she would often yearn to return to France, but her husband always refused. He claimed it was because of his comrades at Normandy and so forth, but, as his daughter wrote, "I think he avoided France because of my mother's infatuation with the country, and because she spoke the language and he didn't."

MARY DIDN'T LOSE TIME flexing her linguistic muscles with Cheever. "The folly of a fool," she once murmured—in French—when her impoverished boyfriend waxed ecstatic over a *New Yorker* sale. Both seemed a little ambivalent in the beginning. What Cheever remembered about their first date was that his future wife had arrived three hours late; what she remembered was the taste of Scotch (she'd never tried it before) and boredom. Cheever was holding forth about life at Yaddo, which might have struck the idealistic young woman as a bit frivolous, at least as Cheever told it. "I didn't want to hear about the love affairs of Leonard Ehrlich and so on," she later remarked.

But Cheever had made up his mind: 1940 would be a pivotal year. "[T]he girl I'm going to marry is on 67th street," he informed Denney, "my roots are in the forgotten valley of the North River, my agent is on Fifth Avenue, and money burns a hole in my pocket." The place on Sixty-seventh was a mansion with stained-glass windows ("and a cellar full of rats," as Cheever recalled), where Mary rented the master bedroom—or rather *had* rented the master bedroom, until she lost her latest job as secretary and reader for Thomas H. Uzzell, proprietor of a correspondence school for aspiring writers and author of *Narrative Technique*. ("Thank you for letting us see your work," Mary had typed to potential students, before an efficiency expert had advised Uzzell to let her go. "You will find my book *Narrative Technique* useful . . .") After parting with Uzzell, she was reduced to living on a monthly allowance from her grandmother, and the landlady ("a bit of a bandit") moved her to a tiny room in the back of the mansion.

By then Cheever had become something of a fixture around the place. "I was alone in the city," said Mary, "and he kind of moved in. That's the only way I can describe it." For Cheever it was a place that offered a warm body as well as an improvised meal of sorts (Mary, lacking a kitchen, cooked chops on a hot plate and fresh peas in a percolator). And when she was moved to the servants' quarters, he saw a chance to be helpful—finding affordable rooms for both of them at Rhinelander Gardens on West Eleventh, a picturesque if not very elegant locale. The artist Robert Motherwell had an apartment beneath Mary's (a calling card with his Paris address was tacked to the door); Cheever's own studio was a few steps down the hall, near the noisy front of the building. ("Tomorrow will complete two weeks in which I have done no work," he noted after moving in. "The comings and goings in an apartment house on Saturday and Sunday are distracting and I am broke.") The main benefit was being near friends in the Village: the Werners also lived on Eleventh and promptly gave a party for the couple, and Cummings was around the corner on Patchin Place.

Cheever worried whether he'd be able to support Mary in the style to which she'd become accustomed—which, of course, was a style he longed to possess. Mary's family occupied an Italianate villa on Prospect Street, near Yale, but what might have been even more alluring in Cheever's eyes was their fifty-acre summer estate in New Hampshire, Treetops. Thomas Watson had bought the place and designed the little guest cottages that dotted the hillside, but it was Mary's father who hired a notable New York architect to draw up plans for the Stone House, where the staff was installed and Dr. Winternitz held court. Each night at six o'clock, the guests would convene at the house for drinks, and during his early visits, at least, Cheever was a somewhat wary and critical observer. His prospective father-in-law, he noticed, was often a vulgar tyrant, especially after a few drinks ("he would tell a pointless obscene story in mixed company," Cheever wrote, "spit into the fire, belch"); as for the mistress of the house—never mind her children—she was a silly, pampered snob out of touch with a world that was verging on disaster. But withal Cheever was covetous, and knew it. While at Treetops he wrote in his journal:

> The misanthrope thinks: You are all children of distinguished men and women. You went to the schools your fathers went to, you were introduced into their clubs, people will do much for you in memory of your father whereas I, I, I, was, in a commercial hotel after a sales banquet, conceived by accident and the quarreling over my existence began long before I had even seen the light of day. My father brought a murderer to the house. While you, the misanthrope thinks, were walking from the class to the playing field at Saint Pauls and Yale, I was living in the furnished rooms of the lower west side on stale bread and skimmed milk. . . . How fatuous and complacent you all are. Yes thank you, the misanthrope thinks when he is offered a second brandy, and he thinks when will you ever learn that this fine costs eight dollars a fifth. I used to live on less than that a week.

But Cheever liked the brandy, and found himself softening toward the people who offered it—extraordinary people, whatever their shortcomings, and obviously fond of him. Whenever he visited the villa in New Haven, Dr. Winternitz would take him away to the den or laboratory and speak brilliantly on some medical topic for exactly fifty-five minutes. After listening to one such lecture on "the chemistry of courage," Cheever observed in a letter to Herbst: "He would like to reduce personality to terms of salt and potassium, being a man who has always been overwhelmed by the mysterious forces of his own temperament." Cheever had his own temperamental forces to contend with, some of them not dissimilar to his future father-in-law's. Meanwhile he came to view the man's wife as a soulmate of sorts. In her company—drinking martinis and gossiping over games of backgammon—Cheever became all the more *attractive*, whatever his social insecurity; in fact, it might even be fair to say that his *boulevardier* persona was partly evolved as a result of Polly's influence. Nor did the couple object to the charming young man's relative poverty; he was writing stories for *The New Yorker*, and a distinguished person at a dinner party had assured them that was a big deal.

Perhaps to force the issue, Polly came to New York one day and confronted her stepdaughter over lunch: "Your sweater is on backwards," she said, "and I hear you are living in sin." With respect to her sweater, the young woman replied that she liked it that way, and at least technically she was innocent of the other charge. Dr. Winternitz didn't bother to consult his daughter at all. "What are your intentions?" he sternly inquired of Cheever, who was happy to put the man at ease. The only problem was that Mary herself wasn't at all sure she was ready for marriage, and once (in response to some cutting remark) she told Cheever she wanted to "end the business" then and there. But he ignored this—he already had the family's blessing, after all—the way he ignored most of her contrary opinions. "Oh, the Sarah Lawrence girl!" he'd say, or words to that effect.

WRITING FOR *The New Yorker* was one thing, but Cheever knew that his reputation as a serious (*and* commercial) writer would remain suspect until he'd published a novel, an even more urgent matter now that he was getting married. Casting about for a subject, he vacillated between something "topical" and something more personal—close enough to his own experience, that is, to hold his interest for a few hundred pages. Again and again, rather in spite of himself, he reverted to his humble origins in that forgotten valley of the North River. "My heart is in a stuffy living room in a middle class suburb after a heavy dinner," he wrote, "listening to the philharmonic, dealing a hand of bridge or making talk. My heart is there and Polly's drawing room and the blinding tennis courts in the July sun and the fox hunt in Rockleigh and the track at Saratoga and the slopes of Cannon Mountain and all the rest of it seem thin." And lest he forget his colorful, troubling family history, his old Yankee father was at pains to remind him of its narrative possibilities. The man offered his son all kinds of "material" in the form of yarns about maritime New England, the post–Civil War era, the glory days of the shoe business, on and on. Likewise, when Cheever considered registering as a New York resident on his Social Security application, his father was duly shocked: "John boy—Quincy your hometown—Massachusetts your state—*hope you make it here*— not so many Yids or Bulgarians . . ." Probably he hadn't learned yet that his son's fiancée was descended from Austrian Jews.

During a visit that summer to Quincy, while Cheever was listening to one of his father's spiels ("Dad's just been in telling me about New-buryport in the 70's"), a woman from the *Patriot Ledger* arrived to interview him for "a feature story about hometown boy doesn't make so good," as Cheever wrote Mary, adding that he "got [the reporter] off the subject" of himself as soon as possible. Such "exceptional modesty"— so noted in the article ("Quincy Youth Is Achieving New York Literary Career")—would remain a byword of Cheever's public image in perpetuum. "I really haven't written anything worth reading yet," he told Mabelle Fullerton of the *Patriot Ledger,* conceding that he was "at work on a contemporary novel with a New England background." Afterward he seemed chagrined that he'd revealed even that much. Despite his being declared "one of the white hopes of American literature," Cheever ended his visit to the South Shore in a state of "great moodiness and discontent": "I drove back to [Fred's house in] Norwell and drank a lot of Tom Collins in the kitchen, snapping crossly at everyone," he wrote. "The evening was spent in brooding and brooding over the novel."

The novel—about a family called Morgan—was not going well. He'd hoped to have at least a chapter and outline to submit in September, but so far he had little to show for a long summer's worth of fretting. Part of the problem was the constant distraction of money work:

"Writing for the New Yorker leaves me feeling tired," he wrote in May, after his fifth story of the year had appeared in the magazine, "tired and lazy. Tired of the language, that is." Also, the disappointment of his previous novel lingered. Years later Cheever would recall (for the benefit of a young man writing a dissertation) that his novel for Simon and Schuster had been a highly experimental affair—"a deliberately digressive, episodic, avant-garde work with a shifting point of view." He claimed that the publisher had been quite enthusiastic about it, suggesting, however, that a seasoned editor such as Cowley help "whip it into shape"; Cheever had been so affronted by the idea (he said) that he'd dropped the manuscript into a garbage can that very afternoon. Both the publisher's enthusiasm and Cheever's brash integrity are doubtless exaggerated (if not entirely apocryphal), though it does seem likely the work was experimental to some extent, in keeping with Cheever's view at the time that a novel ("a bad word") had to reflect the fragmented experience of his generation.

The problem was how to apply such innovation to what was, essentially, an exercise in nostalgia. "In trying to recapture what I want to recapture I keep returning to an afternoon at the farm in Hanover," Cheever wrote in his journal that summer. "I have been burning tent catipillars [sic] out of the apple trees. . . . I can hear mother working in the kitchen. Fred is painting his boat. After that I went down to the wood-shed and talked with Fred. The door stood open and I could smell the wet grass outside and hear the brook. Dad came down and told us about the boats he used to build." The novel that would follow from this Proustian evocation was a family chronicle titled *The Holly Tree*, after a tree in Hanover that Cheever believed was "the largest holly in the Northeast and very probably planted by some English settler." Cheever had once imagined his mother writing him a letter in wartime, insisting he come home and protect the holly tree—a symbol of tradition amid the modern darkness. That, anyway, was the idea. "The book is a pain in the neck," he wrote Mary in August. "I start it and stop it about six times a day, revile and abuse myself, leer at the novels in the book-case and write long descriptions of my problem. . . . [A]ny conventional story or narrative seems to eliminate the qualities of modern life that interest me. . . . The desk is covered with notes reading: 'a realistic piece populated with grotesques, a grotesque populated with familiar characters,' etc." Whatever approach he took, he'd only become more certain over time that his material would (*must*) consist of some account of his youth, whether idealized as a lost Eden or a mirror of man's divided nature or what you will. "One thing is clear," he wrote four years later, still brooding over *The Holly Tree*. "I've got to write the Morgans out of my system." At that point he only had twelve more years to go.

RATHER THAN LET HER LIVE in relative sin at Rhinelander Gardens, Mary's parents had spirited her away to Treetops for the summer; Cheever had moved to Muriel Rukeyser's vacant apartment at 76 Bank Street. Mostly he hacked out stories and brooded over his novel, but when the world was too much with him, he'd take off to Yaddo and stay drunk awhile. That summer he befriended a young writer named Flannery Lewis, who, beginning in 1937, had published three books in three years; unknown to himself, one imagines, he would never publish another, and would vanish almost entirely as a writer and a man. For the time being, he staggered around Yaddo cracking up furniture and insulting Katherine Anne Porter, of all people. "Porter is wonderful," Cheever had written at first, having observed the woman sweetly patronize some boob named Ekstrand. "What do you write? Ekstrand asks, leering. Oh, not very much, Porter says, very little really, almost nothing. I mean do you write books or what, Ekstrand asks leering." A few days later, however, Cheever decided Porter "[wasn't] so wonderful": "La Porter and Joffe and Flannery and I went down to the Worden last night and the great conversational style was an awful disappointment," he wrote Mary. "[She] began with Auden, George Davis, etc. She was side-tracked for a few minutes into talking about her experiences with aviators in the last world war, but then she went back again to Auden, Davis, MacAlmon, Escott . . ."

Cheever would pay a valedictory visit that summer, but it wasn't the same without Lewis (banned for pissing in the atrium pool). Mrs. Ames urged him to stay on through the fall, and even offered to hire Mary as her secretary—a "very kind" but "impossible" offer, Cheever decided. For the foreseeable future, the Yaddo phase of his life was over. "If there is anything in my memory that could be called pre-war it is Yaddo," he wrote Herbst in 1944. "Oh those fountains, oh those box lunches, oh that stained glass window at the head of the stairs."

Though he longed to join his fiancée at Treetops, Cheever stayed put on Bank Street despite having to sleep in the bathtub to avoid bedbugs. He was eager to prove himself as a provider, and (except for his stalled novel) was doing a rather good job of it: That summer (1940) he published three stories in *The New Yorker* and three in the slicks—two in *Harper's Bazaar* and "a stinker" in *Collier's*—and in the meantime pursued, fruitlessly as ever, some sort of regular employment. When he got word that a junior editor at *The New Republic* had been "taken off to the booby-hatch," he raced over to fill the breach—too late: "Some other ghoul" had already gotten the job. In the end he accepted an advance from *The New Yorker* that required him to churn out stories faster than ever, while in his journal he girded himself for the task:

> It is still, even in writing for the New Yorker, a question of feeling strongly, of being alive. It can be the first thing you see in the morning; a wet roof reflecting the bleak light, the suspicion that your wife's legs under the table may be touching the legs of someone else, the happiness of burning up the road between New Haven and Sturbridge on your way home. In signing a contract with the New Yorker there are certain apprehensions as if writing were a mystery, something as chancey as a long shot on a wet track with mud all over the silks and the bums crowded in under the grandstand out of the rain. I have twelve stories to write and they'll be good.

One is reminded a little of Chekhov snatching up an ashtray to explain his writing method—that is, forming a story around the kernel of an object, an image, an emotion, and letting one's intuitive gift take over from there. Indeed, Cheever may well have had Chekhov in mind as he faced the challenge of writing stories at such a demanding pace and yet imparting, each time, some fresh glimpse of the world. Certainly Chekhov was becoming a greater influence on his work. The laconic mannerisms of Hemingway were giving way to a more discursive, playful style, the banality of incident suggesting—but lightly—an underlying sadness. "Read [Chekhov's] the Black Monk for perhaps the 100th time," Cheever noted in 1954, "all different times of life. I found it as clear and forceful as if I had looked up into the blue sky and seen a hawk strike a pigeon. . . . How precisely he brings a group into focus." Such an affinity was fostered all the more by Cheever's association with *The New Yorker*, whose slice-of-life fiction was nothing if not Chekhovian. As the young Irwin Shaw pointed out, a typical *New Yorker* story occurred in a single time and place, and all the dialogue was "beside the point." A virtual model of the form is Cheever's "The

Happiest Days"*: Suggested by Katherine Mansfield's "Bliss" (and hence by Chekhov), the story consists of a long, frothy dialogue in which a man discovers—implicitly—that his wife is having an affair with a man named Borden: " 'I'm going to be a war profiteer,' Borden said. He was lying with his face on the grass and his voice was indistinct. Each word added to the weight of the hatred Tom felt for him."

Sometimes Cheever was too Chekhovian even for *The New Yorker*, which rejected "I'm Going to Asia" as lacking "direction or focus."† The story, in certain respects, is almost a rehash of "The Happiest Days": both feature a family group (give or take the odd neighbor/lover) sitting around having a random chat about the weather and whatnot, with here and there a bit of innuendo about the war or some private sorrow. In "The Happiest Days" the exposition is supplied by an omniscient narrator: " 'Oh, look at that cloud!' Mrs. Morgan exclaimed. Her husband had hanged himself from an apple tree on a suburban golf course in 1932, and since his suicide she had supported herself, first by teaching contract bridge and then by running a dress shop." In "I'm Going to Asia," however, the narrator is almost wholly effaced, and readers are left to negotiate the oblique dialogue on their own. The title refers to a game in which each member of the Towle family says, "I'm going to Asia and I'm going to take" some object (an anesthetic, a trunk, a dress), which—if it satisfies some mysterious requirement known only to one player (but not the reader)—will enable the person to "go to Asia." (An anesthetic enables one to go to Asia; a dress does not.) Meanwhile a cynical son, Freddy, grouses about the war: "You just sit around here as if nothing had happened. Well, something has happened. Our world has ended." So it goes, until finally the two threads are brought together at the end, when old Mrs. Towle complains about losing the "Asia" game because of the dress she wanted to take: " 'I'd *like* to go to Asia. . . . There isn't any war in Asia, is there? Or is there?' "

Racking his brain for story ideas—let alone a novel—didn't leave energy for much else, and Cheever found himself becoming "something of a recluse": "My daily activity has been limited to bathing, shaving, watering the hyacinth Mary bought me, and smoking two

---

*Aptly included in the first anthology of *New Yorker* fiction, published in 1940.

†Though too ambiguous for *The New Yorker*, the story, oddly enough, appeared in *Harper's Bazaar* (September 1940) and was included in the *O. Henry Memorial Award Prize Stories of 1941*.

packages of cigarets." At such times his main companion was his journal, where he stored the sights and sounds and smells which might prove useful as story fodder, as well as the private sorrows which he was all but incapable of sharing with the world, at least in raw form. Cheever would later claim that he'd begun keeping a journal as a much younger man, but the earliest surviving pages were evidently written toward the end of 1939*—that is, shortly after meeting Mary (and making up his mind to marry her). This makes sense as a starting point, since the journal was primarily conceived as an exercise in professionalism; no longer a gadabout youth living off the charity of Yaddo, he couldn't afford to let salable impressions go to waste. As Susan Cheever explained, "He never said to himself, 'This is good material.' He didn't think that way. What you see in his journals is what he had to do instead, which is to write down everything that happened and see what rang and what didn't ring."

But, again, the journal was both a laboratory for fiction and a means of exorcising demons and fine-tuning the work-in-progress known as John Cheever. That summer, so much alone, he brooded with particular anxiety about his earlier amethyst-ring-wearing self, and prayed that he would have the "courage and decency" to assume the "grave responsibilities" of married life: "I have been evasive, God knows, but I have also come of age." So he hoped. Also—lying in bed between stories, smoking and scratching his bedbug bites—he indulged in idle reveries about the kind of bon vivant he saw himself becoming:

> I find myself driving up the road to Treetops in a large car, creaming the Whitneys at tennis, a game I've never learned how to play, giving the head-waiter at Charles' five dollars and instructing him to get some flowers and ice a monopole of Bollinger, deciding whether to have the Pot au Feu or the trout merinere [sic], I can see myself waiting at the bar in a blue cheviot suit, tasting a martini, decanting a bottle of Vouvray into a thermos bottle to take out to Jones' Beach, coming back from the beach, burned and salty . . . moving among my charming guests, greeting the late-comers at the door.

---

*Harvard misdates the first journal as having been started as early as 1934; there is no evidence, internal or otherwise, to support this. A few early entries are explicitly dated from 1940; the first pages (undated) appear to have been written during the last weeks of 1939. After 1940 Cheever rarely dated his entries.

But still he remained on Bank Street, though it was almost September, as if he was afraid of testing romance against reality. Only when the bed-bugs had become "ravening" and carpenters descended on the place and began "pulling things apart" did Cheever hit the road at last for New Hampshire—not in a "large car," of course, but the same old Model A.

He needn't have worried. After being treated as family by a lot of "amiable people," he "shouted and sang" as he drove back to New York a week or so later. "We will have a good life darling," he wrote his bride-to-be, "a wonderful and beautiful life."

MARY WINTERNITZ wasn't so sure about that, but on the other hand it pleased her to marry "somebody considered a catch" by her family, who never thought she'd amount to much. For both her and Cheever, in fact, it might have seemed a happy outcome to ghastly protracted childhoods—and not a moment too soon, under the circumstances. "We just decided not to wait much longer with everything so uncertain," Mary wrote her father in early 1941. "Why not take what you can get while you can get it?"

And so they were married on March 22, in front of the fireplace at 210 Prospect Street in New Haven. The Episcopal chaplain of Yale, Sidney Lovett, officiated, though the modest ceremony was not religious or even especially conventional, given that Mary ("serious-minded radical as I was") wore a "severe" gray suit with a corsage on her shoulder. Fred was Cheever's best man, while Mary was attended by her troubled sister Buff. Most of the other guests were also immediate family. Frederick Cheever (Sr.), looking tinier than usual, glanced around the villa in a nervous, furtive way, and—bumping into Bill Winternitz—piped, "I'm the old one!"

"I do condescend to take thee as my wedded husband was the gist of her marriage vow," Cheever wrote years later, in a characteristically bitter mood. At other times, he realized just how lucky he'd been: His wife, after all, was pretty and bright and talented all in her own right, and was moreover blessed with a very fortunate "grasp of ambiguities," as Cheever observed. Mostly she was stoical. As she remarked to the *New York Times* (almost thirteen years after her husband's death), "My maternal great-grandmother came out of nineteenth-century New England, where you do what you have to do."

CHAPTER NINE

{ 1941–1943 }

FOR THEIR HONEYMOON they spent a few pleasant days at Herbst's old house in Erwinna—"Venery Valley," as Cheever named it, after the preferred way of passing time. During their first year of marriage, especially, the place was a beloved refuge for the couple; later, as an exhausted army private, Cheever would lie on his bunk and reflect on those lost, lazy days in prelapsarian Pennsylvania: "shopping in Frenchtown, building a fire to burn the damp out of the house, the first drink at four o'clock on the nose, the second drink at four-fifteen, the venery, the eating, the noise of the brook and the ice-box motor at night, morning sunlight, breakfast, a walk into French-town maybe or raking hay or cutting wood." As for their hostess, Josie, she was already on her way to becoming "a rambunctious ruin" (as Mary put it), whose constant and often peevish chatter struck Cheever, even then, as a bit much—but no matter: "I feel that the house is my own," he wrote in his journal. "I see Mary and I living there after we have been married eight or nine years."

In the city they rented a two-room apartment at Sailors' Snug Harbor on Eighth Street near Fifth Avenue—the heart of the Village and only a few brisk footsteps from the Brevoort Hotel, where Cheever did much of his drinking. Even by Village standards, it was a remarkably alcoholic time: "I feel the presence of despair," Cheever wrote, having listened awhile to the radio news, which was getting so bad he could hardly see the point of writing anymore, much less staying sober. Night after night he found himself "spilling martinis all over the Brevoort" with regulars such as Niles Spencer and the amiable

lush Coburn ("Coby") Gilman. When their friend Dorothy Dudley decided to wait out the war at home in Biddeford, the three
men "drank her out of her apartment" and so inherited bits of wardrobe left over from her various ill-starred romances ("Coburn got a
linen suit, Niles got a blue serge, and I got a check"). Meanwhile his
disreputable Yaddo sidekick Flannery Lewis had also married and
moved to the Village; whether at Sailors' Snug Harbor or the Lew-
ises' place over the Black Cat Club, the wives would sit and sigh while
their husbands quaffed as much as four quarts of whiskey a night—
or so Cheever reckoned, penitently, in the midst of yet another stupendous hangover.*

A more wholesome companion was the man who'd succeeded Maxwell as Cheever's editor at *The New Yorker*, Gustave ("Gus") Lobrano.
A tall, courtly Southerner, Lobrano preferred outdoor diversions such
as badminton at his suburban home in Westchester, or fishing at an old
family lodge on Cranberry Lake in the Adirondacks. Lobrano was
only ten years older than Cheever, who nevertheless felt a filial urge to
please the man as he tried to please Dr. Winternitz and had failed (as
he saw it) to please his own father. Lobrano had taught Cheever to fish,
and thus introduced him to the whole rugged ethos of the sporting life:
the moose head over the fireplace, the chilly outhouse, the oddball furniture, the crack-of-dawn slogs through dense woods. "The big point
is this is a man's world," Cheever wrote after a visit to Cranberry Lake.
"Raised in a matriarchal environment by an iron woman I am profoundly used to feminine interference, feminine tastes. Here there is
no trace of it. . . . I returned with the world in focus for the first time in
weeks, the possessor of much self-respect."

Cheever also befriended one of Lobrano's foremost discoveries,
Edward Newhouse, who would eventually publish more than fifty sto-

---

*An intriguing aspect of one's research is learning something of the fates of forgot-
ten writers—a sobering lesson in the evanescence of literary fame. Take the strange
case of Flannery Lewis. For a few more years, he and Cheever were boon (if occasional) companions, though Lewis's behavior became more and more erratic as his
drinking worsened, until one day he left his wife and daughters and simply disappeared. Hoping to locate Lewis for an interview (while realizing that the odds of finding him alive were slim), I came across a listing in New Orleans and spoke with a
woman who claimed to be a relation. Lewis had recently died, she told me, but yes, the
listing had been for Flannery Lewis the writer. When I mentioned Cheever, she said
that Lewis had often spoken of their friendship, though the two had never met again
after the late 1940s.

ries in the magazine. What the two writers had most in common, as Cheever put it, was "an inability to draw the parts of [their] lives together." In that respect, Newhouse had come an even longer way than Cheever—all the way from Hungary, in fact, whence Newhouse had emigrated at age twelve, shed his accent, and reinvented himself as a cosmopolitan Anglo-Saxon litterateur. Cheever characterized his friend's "inscrutable" persona as an "unholy mixture of Budapest and the Ivy League," while conceding that "inscrutability has its charm"— as he knew better than most. In one form or another, the friendship would last a very long time ("To Eddie, My oldest friend in the world," Cheever inscribed a copy of *Falconer*), though always a certain distance obtained, perhaps because of a mutual awareness of each other's pretenses. Neither had finished high school and yet both found themselves in the company of sophisticated, accomplished people*—this by the force of their own talent and charm, of course, such that each might have wondered who in the end would go further. But all this was mostly latent in the old days: the *young* Cheever, Newhouse recalled, was funny and generous and "not at all concerned with image."

AFTER MORE THAN TEN YEARS of fatalistic anticipation, Cheever was almost relieved when war was finally declared in December. It was "very exciting" to mill with the masses in Times Square while the news of Pearl Harbor whipped around the Times Building, and afterward he and Mary "slipped out of the heavy-drinking set" and waited, with a kind of suspenseful tranquillity, for their lives to change. It wasn't that Cheever was eager to fight in a war: he promptly asked Cowley, who'd gotten a desk job in Washington, to "keep [him] in mind" if anything should open up, since he didn't rate his chances very high as a soldier. "All I know about war," he wrote Herbst, "is what I saw in the movies ten years ago, and I still believe all of it; the screams, the amputated hand on the barbed-wire fence, and the trench rats." But civilian life seemed absurd under the circumstances, and besides he was tired of living on advances from *The New Yorker*. When he had waited five months, then, he finally decided to enlist after a last idyllic week at

---

*Company that included their spouses and in-laws. Newhouse married (the same year as Cheever) one of the world's most distinguished violin teachers, Dorothy DeLay, whose pupils included Itzhak Perlman.

Treetops—a last savoring of the good life that, rather miraculously, he'd managed to achieve after thirty difficult years. "Goodbye, goodbye, goodbye, for in the Army there is no past," he wrote in "Goodbye, Broadway—Hello, Hello," published a month after his May 7 enlistment. "You are not married or single, rich or poor, a brilliant young man or a fool."

John Cheever, about to be absorbed into the army, reported to Fort Dix as a slightly taller and better-educated man than before: according to his service record, he was five foot six on that day in May (rather than five five and a whisper), and had finished high school as well as a year of college (Harvard, no doubt: his wedding announcement had noted that he'd studied there). So much for personal mythology. Fort Dix was "like a Boy's Camp" where one was either working hard or "sitting on fenceposts" staring at flat vistas. After a week or so, Cheever got a typhoid shot and boarded a train bound for Camp Croft in Spartanburg, South Carolina—a land of "razor-back hogs, grits, thin-bloodedness, spindly peach orchards, poorly attended American Legion parades on hot afternoons and a cultural bleakness that gleams through all [its] adornments," as Cheever would remember the city and the South as a whole.* On arrival, the men were given new clothes and a big meal ("The food is very good and the table-manners of my buddies are bound to improve in such an atmosphere"), whereupon basic training commenced: rifle and bayonet drill, grenade throwing, and the like, as well as abrupt confinement to barracks for a long night of washing floors and windows while their sergeant got drunk at the Post Exchange.

"Our sergeant is a strange and interesting man," Cheever wrote Mary. "He comes I think from the back-woods of Tennessee or Mississippi, from an unsocial, hard-working people. He has no friends and his one idea is to make his platoon the best in the company. He has an hysterical temper." This sergeant, a young man named Durham, had let his men know from the start that he wasn't afraid of them and didn't give a damn what they'd done in civilian life. In the blazing heat he drove them through "five poisonous gases without [their] masks" and

---

*As personified by Randall Jarrell, the poet, whose beard and accent struck Cheever as having an aversively regional savor: "He reminds me of the dirt roads leading in to the garrison town of Spartanburg [sic]," Cheever wrote, and proceeded with the description given above.

over an obstacle course, again and again, then *again* after dinner if he wasn't satisfied. "I don't care if you faint," he shouted, after a man fainted, "but if you're going to faint, tell me about it! You might die of sunstroke and I'd get the blame." It didn't help that Durham was drunk much of the time, nights especially, when he'd roust the men out of bed and make them bump into one another as they tried frantically to make sense of his incoherent commands.

Cheever's fellow soldiers were a diverse group. As he wrote Cummings, there was "an ex–smoke eater named Smoko, a clerk from the Chase National Bank, a waiter from the Hotel Westbury, two night club MCs, the wine steward from the Pierre, and a dozen or so longshoremen, steam-fitters, elevator operators." On payday (fifty dollars a month), most of them went to Greenville, where the more cretinous were given Mickeys, robbed, and put in jail for the weekend. Cheever and a few weary older men decided, after that first paycheck, to share a taxi to the more distant town of Hendersonville, where they sat around the veranda of a shabby-genteel hotel drinking bourbon and chatting with friendly civilians. As they began to leave, "an old ex-prostitute or ex-actress" accosted them: "Goodbye, boys, and God bless you," she said, weeping. "Remember, *this* is what you are fighting for."

"[M]ail call is the high point in my busy life," he wrote Lobrano. It was odd reading letters amid the dusty bleakness of Spartanburg and learning that, somewhere, life went on much as before. Morrie Werner was still drinking at Bleeck's as his wife Hazel lay on a beach in Provincetown; *The New Yorker* was making do with a higher number of female and homosexual employees; Cummings was spreading himself as sunnily as ever around the Village, while sympathizing with his younger friend's predicament. "I too have slept with someone else's boot in the corner of my smile," he wrote Cheever, enclosing an autumn leaf and a five-dollar bill. There was also a flurry of antic correspondence from old Frederick, who let his son know he was writing letters to his daughter-in-law, too ("Don't bother to answer them," John advised her, "and don't bother to open them unless they interest you"). Frederick's letters began with the usual lyric evocations of the weather ("Another grand morning . . . the breeze 'up and down the mast'—'wouldn't blow a butterfly off the mainsail' ") and proceeded with a lot of folksy advice about soldiering, such as using castor oil to polish one's boots and always peeking into same "to make sure that no practical joker [has] put an egg in the toe." A great fan of Soviet pluck,

Frederick had also favored Stalin with a letter ("an old time Yank's appreciation of himself, his people and his country") and bet his son a Coca-Cola that the Soviet leader would respond with a personal note. ("No word in reply from Premier Stalin," he reported two weeks later. "Give me 30 days.") As for Fred Jr., he was color-blind and hence disqualified from active service; instead he worked as an "employee relations" consultant to the War Department in Washington, to which he traveled each month with an air of great secrecy. To John he confided that they were "having a lot of trouble with negros."

After six weeks of boot camp, Cheever spent a weekend with Mary at a Greenville hotel. He was in bad shape: whippet-thin and so nervous he couldn't sleep ("When I saw you in Greenville it was kind of a strain"). Sergeant Durham was in the midst of some sort of meltdown, and this made life unpredictable for his men. For hours at a time he'd stay in his room and drink steadily while an ominous silence prevailed in the barracks. One night the men were undressing, or already in bed, when Durham suddenly emerged "with his fatigue hat pulled down over his ears, fully dressed in blue denims and leggings. He had evidently fallen into a drunken stupor and he thought it was morning." It got so bad Cheever began to feel sorry for the man. A burly private had given Durham an awful beating one weekend in town, from which he returned a day or so later with "his face sewed up and a pair of dark glasses to cover his eyes." He seemed, at last, a broken man, announcing ("very drunk") that his girl in Texas had just lost two fingers in a sawmill. But this proved only a lull before the biggest storm of all: On the final day of boot camp, he insisted the men fall out of barracks in fifteen seconds. "[T]his turned out to be a physical impossibility and after several men had hurt themselves falling downstairs he settled for eighteen seconds."

Cheever was more eager than ever for a desk job, and to this end Harold Ross wrote Colonel Egbert White of *Yank*, an army magazine with offices in New York: "I have a nomination of a writer if you want one. He is John Cheever, who has written some of the best short stories we've run in recent years, and is one of the leading and most promising short story writers there is, in our estimation here." Stout praise, which Cheever was "sure" would do the trick, though he was a little disappointed to learn he'd have to finish basic training first ("but Dear Jesus I hope and pray that they will be able to do something then"). Alas, it turned out he wasn't the only writer who'd had such hopes:

"[*Yank*] simply got over-manned," Ross explained to Irwin Shaw, "and also they faced a new order . . . that hereafter such outfits could not request men by name. If Yank wants a writer now all they can do is request a writer."

IN AUGUST, Cheever and his platoon were sent further south to Camp Gordon in Augusta, Georgia, which he thought resembled Harvard of all places ("The barracks are white clapboard with small-paned windows and brick chimneys")—an ironic resemblance for any number of reasons, including a certain incongruity of milieu. "I have never seen such poverty; in land, in people's faces, and in education," Cheever wrote Mrs. Ames. "Sometimes I think of the dilapidated countryside the nineteenth-century Russians wrote about. Here are the idiot children, the tin-roofed farmhouses, the scrub-trees, eroded soil, religious cults, etc." For a few days he was even "homesick for Camp Croft and Sergeant Durham," but then some Special Service officers found out he was a writer and took him off the bayonet course for a while to work on a radio skit; Cheever hoped it might lead to something permanent in lieu of *Yank*. In the meantime his regular army duties included standing guard over a lot of "southern boys who run around the [prison] yard like a pack of dogs." The delinquent rednecks ("Their offense is usually desertion") endeared themselves to Cheever, who couldn't help admiring their shamelessness and soon became one of the more lenient guards. While presiding over "hard labor" with a loaded rifle, he'd accept and subsequently mail "the voluminous correspondence" hidden in the prisoners' shoes, though he knew they weren't supposed to mail more than a single letter a week.

Cheever's attitude toward the South—or Southerners anyway— went from wary hostility to a sort of bemused fondness. Certainly it was a different world: "When the conductor shouted 'Columbia' this morning"—he wrote Mary after returning from leave—"he might have shouted Berlin or Zagreb and the 'I reckons' and 'yawls,' etc. sounded as strange as German or whatever they speak in Zagreb." For the most part, though, he found the locals a fun-loving bunch, especially the working-class soldiers, who were often blessed with a refreshing lack of inhibition. "Ain't that pretty?" a man named Calib asked Cheever in the shower, referring to his freshly painted passion-pink toenails and fingernails. Cheever—on the lookout for material, at

least as a raconteur—offered his services as reader and scribe to some
of the illiterate Southerners, whose letters (both written and received)
were a lifelong source of delight. One man solemnly dictated a request
for special leave so he could witness his brother's execution ("the first
electrocution in the family"); a spurned young woman wrote—and
Cheever read aloud—" 'Don't you remember what you done to me on
the floor? Didn't you mean it?' . . ." In general Cheever preferred the
company of regular guys—illiterate, Southern, or otherwise—whose
weekend high jinks in Augusta tended to attract the notice of military
police. Every weekend the city swarmed with soldiers, and Cheever
was loath to miss the whole Hogarthian spectacle—the teeming juke
joints and even the relatively staid places where locals tried to show
their GI guests some Southern hospitality: "[We] went to a dance at
the Eagle Club, Eyrie number seven, believe it or not," Cheever
reported. "I danced for about one minute with a southern beauty of
about eleven who was uneasy about dancing with a Yankee."

But a month at Camp Gordon was perhaps too much of a good
thing, and Cheever was ecstatic when he was granted a ten-day furlough in mid-September. The memories would stand him in good
stead for the rest of his time in Georgia, and indeed for much of his
married life thereafter. "[O]h Christ what fun," he wrote Herbst.

> The Cheevers had plenty of lettuce and I took a taxi from here to
> the city of Columbia, South Carolina, a distance of some seventy-
> six miles, pulling on a bottle of sour-mash bourbon. The train for
> New York pulled out of Columbia at three AM and I still had some
> whisky left when we pulled out of Washington the next after-
> noon. . . . I hit New York about nine o'clock, sober and very, very
> happy. Mary was waiting, all shined up and dressed up, the apart-
> ment was clean and shining, there were bottles of scotch, brandy,
> French wine, gin, and vermouth in the pantry, and clean sheets on
> the bed. Also joints, shell-fish, salad greens, etc., filled the ice-box.
> We did exactly as we pleased for eight days which is more than a lot
> of people can say lying on their death beds.

And there was more: On the last day, he went to the Plaza Hotel for a
meeting with Bennett Cerf of Random House, who promptly agreed
to publish a volume of his stories and sealed the deal with a check for
$250. Finally—after a calming five o'clock cocktail at Longchamps on

Twelfth Street—Cheever went home to tell Mary and walked into a surprise party in his honor, "involving nine Winternitzes, and a lobster dinner at Charles'." Returning giddily to Camp Gordon, he may have wondered if it were all a dream—a notion dispelled by a note from Cerf: "Just a line to tell you how pleased I was to meet you the other day and to know that you are now a full-fledged Random House author." Cheever replied that he'd been going around camp telling everyone that he was about to have a *book* published—"a fact that impresses no one," he added, "because their idea of a book is Superman or Flash Gordon."

For Cheever, success was always a goad to work harder, and now that Durham was no longer ranting at him, he returned to writing stories for *The New Yorker.* "I have my schedule down now," he wrote Mary, "so that I go into town on Friday nights and do my eating and drinking, have my hangover during inspection, and spend Saturday night at the typewriter." One night a week (plus the odd stolen moment in vacant offices) didn't give Cheever much time to chisel his prose, but the magazine's editors were willing to be liberal: many of their finest writers were unavailable for the duration of the war, and besides they wanted as much fiction about army life as possible. Within two weeks of his furlough, Cheever obliged them with "The Man Who Was Very Homesick for New York," much of which is summed up by its title: a soldier longs to leave his army camp in Georgia and return to his beloved city, and a sudden neural paralysis gives him the chance to do so; however, with a resurgence of de rigueur patriotism, the man decides to stay put and disguise his injury ("Gordon brought the gun up to the salute and held it there, with the sweat and the tears pouring down his face, until the anthem was ended and they were given the command for the order"). Lobrano thought the story "really first-rate" and swiftly posted a check ($365) to Maxim Lieber; he also showed the manuscript to Maxwell. "There was a nervous, little letter from Bill Maxwell," Cheever noted. "He thought it was so beautiful he couldn't stand it."

Cheever's army stories lack the stylistic flair of his prewar *New Yorker* fiction, but neither are they frankly trashy, like some of the stories he'd written for the slicks. Rather they stand as good conventional fiction—impressive for what they reveal of Cheever's growing versatility, an ability to modulate his prose, as it were, to suit the market. The army furnished plenty of material, which Cheever sifted for the most vivid scenes and details, as well as an eye for what was likely to fly with the Public Relations Office. He worried (for example) about his Durham story, "Sergeant Limeburner," since he'd written it "for [his] own pleasure" and thus lovingly rendered the sergeant in all his lurid brutality. But because he needed money, too, Cheever was relieved when the censors returned his manuscript without a word changed, perhaps because Durham/Limeburner's bullying is made to seem a good thing, at least by army standards: "You'll appreciate his training when you get into combat," a soldier remarks to Limeburner's men. "You wouldn't want him as a friend, but when it comes to the Army, he's got a good head." Another story, "The Invisible Ship," was based on an episode in which Cheever's company was restricted to barracks after money was stolen from one of the older men; the thief was never caught—though he is, violently, in the story—and his victim was sent home to tend the family farm in North Dakota. The actual captain who imposed the restriction had a small wart on his nose that Cheever transposed to his chin for fictional purposes; otherwise the portrait squares with the reported facts: "[The captain] was an odd-looking man with a forced composure in his oval face and a wart on the right side of his chin. Two years as an officer in the field had given him an exaggerated cant to his head and an exaggerated and springy walk, as though he were always passing in review."*

The extra *New Yorker* money was needed to bolster the meager income of an army private—which Cheever remained, even as certain of his friends were promoted to corporal or sergeant, at least, while Newhouse was already a major with an office at the Pentagon. It was perhaps the first time Cheever had really regretted his mathematical ineptitude, not to mention his overall lack of formal education, since his score on the Army General Classification Test wasn't high enough (110 or above) to qualify him for Officer Candidate School. "I feel like a dope," he wrote Mary, asking her to send a book "on easy ways to get a high IQ": "[M]aybe I can raise myself out of the moron class. If I can't you'll have to swing along with a moron." A year or so later, when he tried again for OCS, his friend Major Newhouse (soon to become Lieutenant Colonel Newhouse) had to pull strings to arrange for him

---

*In a letter to Mary, Cheever described the man as follows: "[H]e has an up-turned nose with a small wart on it. He walks with his head way up, moving a little as though the arches of his feet had been broken."

to retake the test in Washington, and even helped him prepare—but Cheever scored "108 or something," as Newhouse remembered, and never rose above the rank of technical sergeant. "Three stripes," wrote his father, "good boy John. You got it the hard way—no transparent cellophane commissions, in the noncoms."

ALL THAT AUTUMN it was rumored that Cheever's regiment would soon be sent overseas, and before that happened he and Mary wanted to start a family. During a weekend pass in late October, they met at a fine hotel in Richmond that featured baby alligators in the lobby fountain, and within a month or so Mary knew she was pregnant—none too soon, or so it seemed: after Christmas the camp became a staging area for embarkation to Africa. The men were ordered to prepare their wills and assign personal power of attorney; they were inoculated with potent antitoxins and told "that the women in Africa have the old, familiar venereal diseases." Then, suddenly, in late January 1943, emergency status was lifted and life returned to normal. It was oddly a bit of a blow. Cheever got another seven-day furlough to New York, after which Georgia seemed bleaker than ever. "On Lincoln's Birthday I went into Augusta for the first time since returning from New York," he wrote Lobrano. "Obviously Lincoln's Birthday isn't much of a holiday in Georgia and the damned Georgia whores and the damned bad whisky are beginning to make the barracks attractive."

Things began to look up, a little, when Cheever was transferred to Special Services a couple days later and declared editor of a weekly regimental newspaper, *The Double Deucer*. Paired with a cartoonist, Lin Streeter (best known for "Pat Patriot, America's Joan of Arc"), Cheever tried to make the newspaper as entertaining as possible, spoofing such hackneyed features as the Inquiring Reporter ("I don't know how the Major will take it, but I'm sure the men will like it"). Meanwhile he almost fell in the line of duty. On a cold day in February, an officious lieutenant insisted on helping him build a fire in the Recreation Hall, near the newspaper office, and ended up burning the place to the ground. With flames licking at his feet, Cheever ran out the back door with a typewriter and the stencil for the latest *Double Deucer*, which became "a special fire issue": when copies arrived from the printer, he and Streeter singed the bundle with a blowtorch as if it had been yanked from the fire in the nick of time.

Cheever's first collection, *The Way Some People Live*, was scheduled for publication in early March, and though he was careful to pretend otherwise, Cheever had rather high hopes for the book—that it would improve his literary career, of course, but also do him some good with the army. He reminded Cerf to make sure copies were distributed among editors and officers alike, as well as to see about lining up sympathetic reviewers such as Herbst. And though he was glad to accept input from Random House on what stories to include, it was Cheever's own idea to arrange them in a kind of loose chronological order, ending with his induction story, "Goodbye, Broadway—Hello, Hello,"* thus imposing a kind of thematic scheme that wasn't lost on the book's most admiring reviewer, Struthers Burt: "The earlier stories have to do with the troubled, frustrated, apparently futile years of 1939 to 1941," Burt would presently write in *The Saturday Review of Literature*. "This gives the book the interest and importance of a progress toward Fate; and so there's a classic feeling to it." In the meantime Cheever was dismayed by his publisher's trade announcement: it was one thing to languish amid the darkness of Georgia, another to be described to the world as a "young Southerner." As he instructed Cerf, "My family settled in Salem in 1632 and haven't strayed further east than Dedham for a long time."† Cerf mollified the author as to his lineage, and assured him that the work at hand was "a mighty fine collection": "I know you have no more illusions about the sale of a book of short stories than have I, [but] I think the critical acclaim will delight us both."

He was right about the sales. Published in a first printing of 2,750, *The Way Some People Live* sold just under two thousand at full price; the rest were either remaindered or pulped. The reviews were mixed. Most conceded Cheever's talent and hoped for better things, while damning him as a quintessential (and therefore trivial) writer of *New Yorker* fiction. Rose Feld's critique in the *New York Herald Tribune Book*

---

*The published collection ends with four additional stories—"Problem No. 4," "The Peril in the Streets," "The Sorcerer's Balm," and "The Man Who Was Very Homesick for New York"—but the basic idea remains the same: that is, two of the last four stories are concerned with aspects of army life *following* induction (and were published in *The New Yorker* after Cheever had initially suggested the book end with "Goodbye, Broadway—Hello, Hello"), whereas the other two are concerned with the effects of war on the civilian world.

†For what it's worth: Ezekiel—the first Cheever in America—arrived aboard the *Hector* in 1637, and settled in New Haven for many years thereafter.

Review was representative: "To the extent that in the writing world any material—sketch, article, newspaper report, fiction—is called a story, John Cheever's book . . . may be called a collection of stories"; such stories, however, were little more than "moments or moods caught in the lives of his characters, pointed in quality, but inconclusive in effect." Cheever's tone of remote pessimism was also condemned, as if he were regarding his characters with the same haughty nonchalance that Eustace Tilley fixes on that butterfly. In the *New York Times Book Review*, William DuBois stressed the author's connection with the magazine by way of explaining the "peculiar epicene detachment, and facile despair" of the stories. Such charges were not unwarranted: for the past eight years, ever since Cowley's advice that he shorten his work, Cheever had been training himself to write the sort of muted, elliptical "casual" that went over at *The New Yorker*, rarely allowing himself the luxury of longer, more ambitious stories. Reviewer Weldon Kees emphasized the difference: though Cheever's *New Yorker* stories ("among the best that have appeared there recently") were similar to the point of tedium—at least when "read one after another"—the long, anomalous "Of Love: A Testimony" gave a glimpse of what Cheever was "capable of doing when he has room enough in which to work for something more than episodic notation and minor perceptive effects."

As for Struthers Burt, in hindsight he seems prophetic, though it's hard to figure how he could have made such extravagant claims on the basis of *The Way Some People Live.* "Unless I am very much mistaken," he declared, "when this war is over, John Cheever . . . will become one of the most distinguished writers, not only as a short story writer but as a novelist." Far from finding the stories trivial, Burt applauded their revelation of the "universal importance of the outwardly unimportant," and thought the author's apparent pessimism was in fact a laudable grasp of human ambiguity ("a deep feeling for the perversities and contradictions, the worth and unexpected dignity of life"). Like other reviewers, Burt noted a certain monotony in Cheever's *New Yorker* fiction and cautioned the author lest his "especial style" harden into an affectation: "Otherwise the world is his."

Cheever took both praise and blame with a grain of salt—remarkably so for a first-time author. He was amused by DuBois's crack about his "facile despair," seeing the justice of that and other complaints. As he wrote Mary, "[A]ll in all—even though they don't like me—the reviewers seem to be very diligent and earnest people, anxious to help a gloomy young writer onto the right path, and to safeguard the investments of their readers." Ultimately the book's most bitter critic would be Cheever himself—the mature Cheever, who, improbably enough, had proved Struthers Burt to be absolutely right. "I find all this early work intensely embarrassing and wish it would vanish," he wrote in 1968, having devoted himself to destroying every copy of *The Way Some People Live* that he could lay his hands on. The author of the *Wapshot* novels and five or six of the finest American short stories was appalled that he'd ever been capable of such lazy, formulaic work. Writing of F. Scott Fitzgerald in the late sixties, Cheever pointed out that even the man's trashier stories "were not rueful vignettes or overheard conversations"—an apt description of Cheever's juvenilia—"but real stories with characters, invention, scenery and moral conviction." Cheever's best work would have all that and something ineffably more.

CHAPTER TEN

{ 1943–1945 }

I N APRIL, Cheever returned to Fort Dix, where it was only a matter of time before his regiment was shipped overseas. Occasionally he'd affect a bravura eagerness to kill Germans—as opposed to dawdling away his days at an army camp, at least—but in more lucid moments he hoped that some well-placed officer would hurry up and do something about the promising writer who'd remained an infantry private because of a low IQ. And so it came to pass. A month after his book was published, Cheever got word from Cerf that a former M-G-M executive named Leonard Spigelgass—now a major in the Army Signal Corps—wanted to see him as soon as possible. At the urging of mutual friends, Spigelgass had read *The Way Some People Live* and been vastly impressed by the author's "childlike sense of wonder."* As Mary Cheever wrote her father, "Between long-distance calls to Frank Capra and Louis B. Mayer, Spigelgass told John that he considered it unpatriotic for him to be in the infantry and that he would 'make with the General' immediately to get him into movie work." Both John and Mary were skeptical of what seemed a lot of Hollywood hyperbole, but a few days later the transfer went through and Cheever was whisked away from Fort Dix in a jeep while his comrades watched in awe.

The 22nd Infantry Regiment—minus John Cheever—was finally sent to England in January 1944, and a few months later suffered heavy

---

*The origin of that marvelous phrase vis-à-vis Cheever. It was later adopted by friends and family to mock (often rather pointedly) Cheever's reputation among certain of his more admiring critics.

casualties at Utah Beach. Survivors were decimated in the long European campaign that followed, and sometimes Cheever would reflect, wistfully, on their fate: "I try to remember the names of my dead friends," he wrote on Memorial Day, 1962. "Kennedy? Kenelly? Kovacs? I can't remember." Finally, in 1978, an old Camp Gordon acquaintance, David Rothbart, sent Cheever a journal he'd kept to commemorate the heroism of their old regiment. Cheever stayed up all night reading and remembering his comrades—name by name—as he realized that "every last one of them" had been killed. "You and I are survivors, of course," he wrote Rothbart the next morning, "and to be survivors seems to involve some responsibilities that I find onerous."*

WITH A BABY on the way the Cheevers needed a bigger apartment, preferably with a courtyard or patio of some sort, but of course money was a problem. Finally they settled for a cramped ground-floor flat on West Twenty-second Street in Chelsea—something of a slum at the time, with a large population of Irish prostitutes. The couple tried to make the best of it, putting a fence around their tiny yard and planting a garden: "We spend all of our Sundays rooting around in the soot and cat-shit that pass for soil in our yard," Cheever wrote Herbst, "trying to grow lilies out of crushed bluestone, coal ash and garbage." Once the garden was finished, they took to eating brunch alfresco and pretending to be middle-class while the life of the neighborhood bustled around them *("Don't you call ME a whore!")*.

In the early hours of July 31, 1943, Mary gave birth to an eight-pound daughter, Susan Liley Cheever. One of the father's "most intense" memories was holding Mary in his arms during the long labor, all the more grateful for being there when he learned that another woman, sharing the room, had to suffer the ordeal alone because her husband was in Africa. Mostly the couple were thrilled to be parents. A few days after returning to Chelsea, they were visited by Dodie Merwin—now married and living on Cape Cod—who was struck by how radiant with fatherhood Cheever seemed; though warm

---

*As a classification specialist, Rothbart was kept off the line, and so lived to send Cheever that poignant journal. When Cheever himself died a few years later, an obituary appeared in the regimental newsletter that would have made him very happy: "John contributed to the IVY LEAF and DOUBLE DEUCER, and although he was even then something of a celebrity, he was a very regular guy who used to drink beer in the PX with the rest of the guys."

and gracious, he firmly prevented Merwin from entering the room where his wife was nursing.

Each morning Cheever took the Eighth Avenue subway to the old Paramount Studio in Astoria, Queens, where he wrote scripts for *Army-Navy Screen Magazine* in keeping with the Signal Corps motto: "Make it clear, make it logical, make it human, and drive home the necessity of learning now, not when you get into battle." The subjects ranged from crucial aspects of combat to something as mundane as brushing one's teeth or using a hammer correctly (one of Cheever's colleagues remembered a seven-reel disquisition on *How to Carve a Side of Beef*). Intrigued by the difference between written and spoken language, Cheever would fret for hours, at first, over the crucial mot juste—almost always a verb, divested at length of the various modifiers he'd weighed. Soon he was one of the fastest and most effective writers, known for the "lean purity" of his language. "There wasn't enough work for him," Major Spigelgass recalled. "He was a writing machine."

Perhaps the best part of Signal Corps life was the company of illustrious peers such as Irwin Shaw, William Saroyan, cartoonist Charles Addams, and others—a fraternity of talent where rank hardly mattered. To underline the egalitarian ethos, writers and artists addressed one another by surname only, and when some B-movie-producer officer would insist they "flatten their backs against the wall when [he] pass[ed], god*dam*mit," Privates Shaw and Cheever would ignore the man and blithely retire to their offices. Finally, in an effort to impose some modicum of military discipline, drills were ordered in the streets of Astoria at the crack of dawn. Saroyan was said to have alighted on the parade ground, hungover, from a chauffeur-driven Rolls.

Cheever nursed his own hangovers at Borden's ice-cream parlor, where he'd have coffee and bagels with his friends John Weaver, Don Ettlinger, and Leonard Field. The kindly Weaver was known as "Good John" to Cheever's "Bad John"—a distinction earned by the latter's drinking and malicious wit. Ettlinger was a handsome, buoyant man who'd been signed as a screenwriter by Twentieth Century–Fox while still in college; in 1943 he was twenty-nine and well established in a career that would span the next four decades, as would his friendship with Cheever. Leonard Field shared adjoining kneehole desks with Cheever, and would also remain in touch for many years, picking up tabs for their semiannual lunches at Sardi's and reciting his woes as a not-very-successful theater producer.

By noon the headaches had dissipated somewhat and it was time to start drinking again. If the writers were flush, they'd race into Manhattan for an elegant lunch at "21" or another midtown restaurant, Au Canari d'Or, calling ahead to order martinis and pots de crème, so they could (in theory) return to their desks by one o'clock. The lunches, said Ettlinger, were "wild and hilarious": The overdressed matrons would stare aghast at the "so-called GI's" rocking with laughter and toasting their unbelievable good luck—at peace, for the moment, with their "occasional guilt that they were having too good a time and not getting shot at."

Another Signal Corps veteran, playwright Arthur Laurents, characterized Cheever's frequent inebriation as "protective"—a way of dampening the discomfort he felt as a bisexual among "relentlessly macho" types such as Irwin Shaw, to say nothing of all the other gay and bisexual men in the Signal Corps.* "Lennie, your mascara's running," Ettlinger was obliged to inform Major Spigelgass while the two filmed the invasion of an Aleutian island. Most knew about Spigelgass, who observed that it was "very clear to the ex-Hollywood and ex–New York people" who was and wasn't gay. Knowing it was one thing, admitting it another. Even the outré Spigelgass maintained a rather tongue-in-cheek public façade; Laurents saw a psychoanalyst for what was then viewed as a moral and mental sickness. Laurents could recall only one openly gay man in the Signal Corps—a "terrible drunk" in the animation department who concealed (or perhaps flaunted) his taste for rough trade by wearing a decorative patch over whichever eye happened to be black at the moment. As for Cheever: "He wanted to be accepted as a New England gentleman," said Laurents, "and New England gentlemen aren't gay. Back then you had no idea of the opprobrium. Even in the Signal Corps, even in the film and theatre world, you were a second-class citizen if you were gay, and Cheever did not want to be that."

What Cheever wanted, above all, was to be a successful writer and family man—not necessarily in that order—and things were going well on both accounts, or so it seemed. His life in New York had "never been so well regulated, moderate, and quiet," he wrote in the autumn of 1943. "Mary meets me at the door with a floury apron in the

---

*When asked how he knew Cheever was bisexual, Laurents invoked the play *Bell, Book and Candle*, by John Van Druten: "They [the witches in the play] know each other simply by looking in the eye. You just know."

evenings. We eat dinner, play with Susan, read the paper, and go to bed." But even then there were a few things wrong with that picture. A fellow writer and drinking buddy, Ted Mills, remembered how "terribly intolerant" Mary was when her husband came in late, and the couple gave Laurents the impression that, at bottom, "they disliked each other": "Both were always making these snippy remarks—always with a giggle. John always giggled when he said something mean."

The Cheevers' seedy apartment in a sinister part of Chelsea was far from ideal, but finances were as tight as ever, and there was a dire shortage of housing during the war—hence their decision, presently regretted, to move into a five-floor town house at 8 East Ninety-second Street with two other couples. The man who found the place was a Signal Corps acquaintance, John McManus, whose wife Peggy was the niece of Alfred Stieglitz and a schoolmate of Mary's at Sarah Lawrence. So that part made sense, but they still needed a third couple to split the two-hundred-dollar monthly rent and exorbitant fuel bills. When John Weaver and his wife, Harriett, declined, Cheever thought to approach Reuel Denney, then working as an editor at *Time*. The two had scarcely kept in touch since Denney's marriage five years ago, but Cheever was glad to vouch for his friend as a nice, bookish fellow who'd likely make a fine housemate. The unknown quantity was his wife, Ruth.

Mary took pity on the woman—who struck her as awkward and oddly dressed—and so invited her (with her small son, Randall) to Treetops in the hope of making friends. The visit was not a success: Ruth spent an inordinate amount of time scrubbing the bathroom floor in her cabin, and couldn't be persuaded to follow the family custom of appearing for drinks and dinner at the Stone House *without* toddlers; also—though the two women were hardly en rapport by then—she liked to confide certain details about her marriage that made Mary uncomfortable. As for the town-house arrangement, it soon headed for the shoals. The women had agreed to divide cooking duties, and Ruth was hurt when the others seemed to dislike her codfish. More serious, or anyway curious, was the woman's tendency to wash her hair in the kitchen sink even though there were eight bathrooms in the place. As for the boy, Randall, he would sit on the steps and spit at Peggy McManus for some reason, until one day she slapped him and was promptly rebuked by his mother, who refused to let anyone "touch or chastise" her child.* Reuel Denney, for his part, naturally sympathized with his wife and took her side, and even began to feel a bit persecuted himself, what with the way John McManus persisted in addressing him as "Whit" (after his *Time* boss, Whittaker Chambers). And the breach grew wider one night when neighbors called the police because little Susan Cheever was banging her head against the wall; the police assumed (according to Ruth Denney) that this was the sound of an illicit, radical printing press located in the Denneys' bedroom, and they attacked the couple in bed. When Reuel resisted, he was pistol-whipped and dragged away in handcuffs to the Harlem station.

The only member of this strange ménage who benefited was Cheever, keeping his Signal Corps buddies in tears of helpless laughter each morning as he related the latest mishap. Indeed, it was too good not to share with the world, and so he began spending nights writing "funny, funny pieces for *The New Yorker*"—six in all—titled "Town House." Apart from whatever satisfaction he took in making hay of his disastrous living arrangement, Cheever denigrated the serial as the sort of middlebrow fluff then in vogue (e.g., *Life with Father*): the literary equivalent of a sitcom. In fact, Cheever's own stories amounted to a stylish, nuanced comedy of manners—another increment in his chameleonic progress as a writer. "Look, I hope you don't mind," he said to Ruth Denney before the first installment appeared. "I put you in a story and it's not terribly flattering." This was a breathtaking understatement. "She ate as though she were participating in a contest, trying through practice to pare seconds and minutes from her eating time," he wrote of "Esther Murray," the character modeled on Ruth Denney (as she herself concedes). "She smacked her lips, overloaded her fork so that it sometimes spilled its load before reaching her mouth, and scratched her arm on the edge of the table." Nor was Cheever's own wife spared. Though her "Town House" counterpart is mostly sympathetic, even in those days her husband was apt to score points through his fiction—in this case indicting what he regarded as

---

*Mary Cheever and Peggy (McManus) Murray and others have attested to the vagaries of Ruth Denney, who—alive and well and living in Hawaii as of 2004—denies almost everything: "Codfish was not a thing I cooked," she said, nor did she remember washing her hair in the kitchen sink. And though she was "very sorry" that her child did, in fact, spit at people, "I certainly didn't defend him for spitting."

her maudlin capacity for pity: "It was the naive, erratic, and indefatigable pity of an amateur social worker, and it had crossed their marriage with many stray animals and strange people."

Though his domestic travails were sublimated somewhat into art, Cheever longed to escape and see the war before it was too late. Once again he was jockeying for a transfer to *Yank*, for which he hoped to cover the aftermath of the D-Day landings, ideally in the company of his old regiment. At the last moment, though, his superior in the Signal Corps, Manny Cohen, refused to let him go: "He used to be president of paramount," Cheever wrote, "and he decided that Yank was RKO or 20th Century Fox and that he was not going to let them have one of his writers." Cohen promised to make amends "any minute" by sending him abroad with the Signal Corps, and so Cheever was "given injections for everything but bubonic plague" and told, over and over, to wait a bit longer. Nearly a year passed, until finally, in April 1945, he was put on a train to Los Angeles, where he got a belated plague shot and woozily awaited transport in the Biltmore Hotel, next door to a roomful of younger servicemen ("hanging out of their windows, yelling, throwing bottles, glasses . . . singing obscene songs, and challenging one another to fights"). Such was the secrecy of his assignment—somewhere in the Pacific—that Cheever could only write about "dreams and reading" in his letters home, and mostly he stuck to the latter: "I had bought a copy of 'The Best Known Novels of George Eliot,' and I read Adam Bede into the Los Angeles station," he reported to Mary. "Adam Bede and his unlucky friends didn't strike me as being any more unhappy than the Cheever family." A few days later he was still in Los Angeles and halfway through *The Mill on the Floss*.

Finally he arrived in Manila—a smoking ruin where "absolutely nothing over waist-high" remained. An old man sat amid the rubble trying to interest Americans in purchasing a ten-year-old magazine; also for sale were monkeys and birds and "a dried fish strong enough to smell up a city block." Japanese money blew around the streets. The beaches and jungles of Guam—Cheever's next stop—were something of an improvement: the public-address system played Strauss waltzes, and one could get a good milkshake, though liquor was unavailable west of Honolulu. Sober, then, and keenly susceptible, Cheever took his typewriter to the beach and wrote another "Town House" story; he also swam and "crack[ed] coconuts" with a sailor who'd taken a fancy to him. Many years later, Cheever would claim that he'd "changed to another beach" as soon as this friendship had "seemed about to become sentimental"; but his journal implied that he'd stayed put, since that sailor in Guam would become one of the lifelong elect who (however briefly encountered) would "wander at will into [his] dreams, undress and wait to be gentled," as Cheever noted in 1961.

By mid-June he was back in New York, where he was welcomed with a party at Ettlinger's apartment that didn't break up until three. He and Ettlinger were together again on VJ Day (riding around in a cab shouting *"La guerre est finie!"*), and a few months later Cheever was mustered out of the army after three and a half years. Except for occasional teaching jobs, it was the last regular employment he'd ever know.

CHAPTER ELEVEN

{ 1945–1946 }

A FTER A RESTFUL VISIT to Erwinna, the Cheevers returned that summer to the town house and a "saga" of "disorder, hysteria, and vermin"—as Mary wrote Herbst—that "should be sung to the lyre." One day Mary heard the unmistakable sound of a Flit gun being used in the Denneys' room, and discovered that Ruth had been spraying a secondhand mattress she'd recently acquired, which explained the sudden infestation of bedbugs. Ruth Denney denied (and still denies) that bedbugs had traveled farther than her own room, but the other couples had already been bitten, and a terrible row ensued. Thus ended the unhappy experiment once and for all (though Cheever, at least, had a theme for his sixth and final "Town House" story).

As luck would have it, the Cheevers managed almost immediately to find a nice, somewhat affordable apartment on East Fifty-ninth near Sutton Place. "Here we are," wrote Mary in late July, "living like the wicked rich surrounded by swells and movie magnates and the reproachful stares of doormen and other dignitaries whom we can't afford to tip." The place wasn't as posh as all that, but it was a definite improvement over their previous apartments: there was a sunken living room large enough for cocktail parties, a bedroom and bath for little Susie, and a ninth-floor view of the Queensboro Bridge ("the interminable funeral procession . . . to the enormous graveyards in Long Island"). Cheever even had an office of sorts. Almost every morning for the next five years, he'd put on his only suit and ride the elevator with other men leaving for work; Cheever, however, would proceed all the way down to a storage room in the basement, where he'd doff his suit and write in his boxers until noon, then dress again and ascend for lunch.

Sometimes he despised New York, and resented having to keep up with his dapper fellow tenants in the elevator—but they reminded him, too, that a writer was just as entitled to middle-class comforts as a lawyer or stockbroker. Though he could barely pay the rent, he'd presently insist on sending his three-year-old daughter to a private nursery school, loading her into a taxi each morning and instructing the man to drive, whatever her protests, twenty blocks uptown to the Walt Whitman School ("She enjoys herself tremendously when she gets there but she has decided that she does not like to leave the nest in the mornings"). By the time she came home in the afternoon, Cheever was free to take her on long walks around the city—indeed, his "favorite New York" was the one he'd discovered with his children in these postwar years. Sometimes they'd walk to the Central Park lion house, or the apex of the Queensboro Bridge, or the docks along the East River ("where I once saw a couple of tarts playing hopscotch with a hotel room key"). And when he felt like stopping for a drink, he'd take Susan along to the Menemsha Bar on Fifty-seventh, where she was enchanted by a little electric waterfall. Finally, at night, he tucked her into bed and told stories about Faustina, the perfect little girl who loved serving her parents breakfast in bed and keeping her room clean. So poignant were his memories of early fatherhood that Cheever would always associate a sense of homecoming with these few blocks near Sutton Place—the "happiness that clings to the shoeshine parlor, the laundry, the drugstore, the vacant store and the butcher's," he later wrote. "[But also] an incurable longing, the basic loneliness implanted in [me] by the miserableness of early life."

Cheever remarked to friends—with a mixture of wit and real self-pity, perhaps—that he thought his parents were "terribly disappointed" he'd survived the war. In fact, he and his parents were mutually well meaning, more or less, if a little bewildered by one another. At her shop in Quincy Square, Mary Cheever was a beloved figure: her granddaughter Jane remembers how people were always coming in from the street just to say hello and chat. But with her son, whom she rarely saw, she seemed divided between a pose of prideful self-reliance and a real need to confide her sorrows. Cheever didn't make it easy for her. Though always polite, he'd find himself boasting about his illustrious in-laws, the grandeur of Treetops, by way of reminding her of the better life he'd rather defiantly made for himself; she in turn would counterpunch with trumped-up claims of business success or her old friendship with Margaret Deland, the crusading novelist. Such visits left Cheever vaguely unhappy, wishing he'd been kinder—but he couldn't help it. The old woman embarrassed him. "The bars are down at Milton Academy!" she'd sigh, forgetting that her daughter-in-law was half Jewish. Cheever's remarks in his journal—after one of his mother's occasional buying trips to the city (during which she'd always insist on staying at the Martha Washington Hotel near Madison Square)—reflect an aching perplexity:

> I haven't seen mother for eight months. When I first came into the room she was sitting on the Hitchcock chair by the door looking ill at ease and so exhausted that her face seemed mottled. She was dressed in black, she wore a pair of corrective shoes curled a little with long use, the long underwear she was wearing reached to below her knees and showed as she sat there and the black enamel of her cheap stick had begun to wear off at the handle. . . .
>
> I forget these people's plainness. Mother made her own bed at the hotel. She took us for dinner to a place called Paddy's Chop House. It was crowded and noisey and she enjoyed herself. When I'm with mother the bridge between the house in Wollaston, the farm, the apartment in Quincy, and the life I have or would like to have in New York seems broad and sometimes untenable.

With his father the bridge was nigh insurmountable, though perhaps there was a certain comfort in conceding as much. At least the man no longer threatened to drown himself or dive off a cresting roller coaster—on the contrary, after eighty years "on this oblate spheroid" (as he liked to say), Frederick seemed at peace with the world, wishing only to make amends. "John that's all that makes life worth living—someone else, other than just yourself," he wrote, part of a larger paean to the wife he'd once despised. As a father, too, he was more dutiful than ever, avidly interested in his son's career, or at least careful to seem that way: he read *The New Yorker* at the library each week and would praise not only John's latest story, but everything else about the magazine ("its layout sure sparkles in all departments . . . and ads, are highest grade mdse. See Altman—Tiffany—etc etc"). For all his apparent mellowing, though, he never quite reconciled himself to idleness, forever plotting to make a comeback of sorts. Not long before his death, he tried to get a payroll job at the Bethlehem Hingham Shipyard, but as usual it didn't work out: "'Too old' as it looks," he laconically noted in a letter to John; "1865 scares them when they read it in my formal application." A week later, the episode had marinated a bit, and this time he related it to "John Mary and the Baby" as an extravagant escapade (*much* abridged below):

> Got a phone call Th'sgiving at 10AM . . . visions of folding money for Xmas . . . interview with Dept Head—who was to detail my tasks—arrange hours pay etc. Signed some 35+ papers—some call for 3 sigs to a sheet—talked or was talked to by 30+ window ladies . . . Then fingerprint both hand . . . then picture taken (with smile) . . . then physical exam—pulse, heart, sight, hearing, scars . . . *Passed all above* was to go to work 29 Monday . . . *7 Days a week* . . . but in MD exam room "strip"—got down to BVDs—MD asks, "How old are you?"—told him honest . . . (he had OKd all tests— "very good very good indeed" earlier)—He barked . . . "You need not go further. Too old."*

In subsequent letters he kept repeating the story every so often—in a comic, tragic, or tragicomic mode, according to mood—because, like his son, he was a born raconteur who couldn't help fine-tuning a tale until he'd nailed it, but also because he was old and getting a bit dotty. To the extent that he was aware of this (as when he misplaced a flashlight in the icebox), it made him sad: he was becoming a Burden. "My letters from now on will not be at as great length," he mawkishly promised his son. "Am alone—very much alone—and start a brief letter but runs into words—words words and more words, but will not inflict it on you any more—(till next time)."

Death came on July 26, 1945; Frederick's heart stopped beating while he sat in a wing chair sipping tea. The son felt a sense of shock— such a profusion of letters, abruptly curtailed—as well as remorse for

---

*Cheever incorporated the episode in a draft of *The Holly Tree*, though arguably his version lacks the comic brio of his father's. Aaron (the name of the Frederick/Leander character at that point) ends up feeling grossly humiliated by the whole ordeal: "They told me to take off my clothes. . . . Then they said I was too old."

having failed his father in various ways over the years. (A little later he felt a pang of kinship, too, when his mother bitterly admitted that the old man had left a final indictment on his desk—clearly meant to be read after his death—"excoriating her" as a wife, mother, and house-keeper. "She had worked so hard to support a helpless old man, and her only reward was castigation. Sigh—how deep were her sighs.") "It was a very long association," his mother remarked as the coffin was lowered into the ground, and Cheever stepped forward to recite Pros-pero's soliloquy (as requested)*: "Our revels now are ended . . ." Cheever got through the ordeal with the help of alcohol, which he needed for any number of reasons: "[T]his plainness for which whisky seems to be my bridge," he wrote in his journal that day. "My mother was a nurse. My desire to escape seems constant. That's why I talk about the W[internitz]'s. These are plain, plain people and I am one of them."

CHEEVER'S PREWAR REFUGE had been Yaddo, and after the war it was Treetops, where he was again treated as Lord Fauntleroy. While the Winternitz and Whitney children wrangled and vied for their par-ents' approval, Cheever remained (for the most part) serenely above the fray. For years to come, his relations with Polly and Winter would be something of a mutual admiration society. These, after all, were the parents he deserved: a brilliant, eccentric scientist and a woman of wit and social distinction, the one holding forth on poisonous gases and such, the other remembering the night she danced the Castle Walk with Representative Hamilton Fish. And though Dr. Winternitz was given to "storms of petulance" and perverse cruelty, even this was strangely comforting to Cheever: He, too, had a rotten temper, truth be known, and was certainly a very odd person in his own right, and it was heartening to see a fellow eccentric make such a success of life. Besides, Winter went out of his way to mitigate his worst qualities where Cheever was concerned—in "penitence" (thought Cheever)

---

*Or did he? In 1977 he told John Hersey that he did, though at other times (as Susan Cheever noted in *Home Before Dark*) he claimed to have "refused"—all this a reflection, no doubt, of his profoundly mixed feelings toward the man. Whatever the case, he made amends in *The Wapshot Chronicle*, at the end of which a weeping Coverly recites the speech at Leander's graveside. "We are such stuff as dreams are made on" is inscribed on Frederick's headstone.

"for all the unkindnesses he has done to his sons," but also, perhaps, because his son-in-law was such a good companion to Polly. When dinner was over and the others drifted away, Cheever would mix a batch of martinis and pass the time swapping gossip with the woman. His own stories were benign enough ("My demeanor is generally tame"), but Polly became biting when drunk and would ruminate bitterly over some fresh tiresomeness on the part of her step-relations. She also liked to be naughty: "Polly was one of those decorous and witty beauties whose familiarity with dope-addiction and cock-sucking was consummate," Cheever wrote. It was fun when she'd coax him into the library, say, to show him some dirty pictures—less so when she'd project her son Freddy's inclinations onto Cheever. "Was your friend nice?" she'd leer, when Cheever returned from a day's hiking, as if that were his usual ruse for a homosexual rendezvous. "Why yes," Cheever would reply, jaunty as ever, and they'd laugh and break out the backgammon board.

In fact, the wistful pleasure Cheever always took in robust, manly activities was fully satisfied at Treetops, where he was positively eager to finish the day's writing so he could spend an afternoon chopping wood and scything with the family gardener, a Latvian communist named Peter Wesul. ("His name is pronounced weasel," Cheever wrote Maxwell. "He was bitten by a weasel and he has to tell people that he was bitten by a mink.") The man fascinated Cheever. A dead ringer for van Gogh, he had the proverbial mystic bond with the earth and single-handedly cultivated a garden that could feed twenty-five people every summer. Most beguiling to Cheever, however, was the man's wizardry with a scythe. "This was part of my father's self-invention as a man of the soil," Federico explained. "The magic of a scythe is almost undeniable. It requires a kind of balance and grace to use, and with that very long blade there are elements of the whole masculine deal. Also, of course, he was well aware of that scene in *Anna Karenina:* Levin and the peasants was never far from my father's mind when scything." This is true: "When I scythe I think of Tolstoy," he admitted to Tanya Litvinov in 1977. "How universal is the experience, I think, when what I really think is that I am one of the last aristocrats in the county who can wield a scythe." For the rest of his life, when Cheever was feeling blue about work or finances or sexual temptations, scything was almost as great a balm as alcohol, and he owed his mastery of this neolithic wand to Wesul, who presented him with a sharpening stone ("kind of like a diploma") when their lessons were done. Also, in a veiled way, Cheever sympathized with Wesul's contempt for bourgeois frivolity. "I got too much to do," the gardener Nils rails against his employer in Cheever's "The Common Day," one of several stories exploring the tension between a Wesul-like hired man and his alleged superiors. "Move the lilies. Move the roses. Cut the grass. Every day you want something different. Why is it? Why are you better than me? . . . You sit there. You drink. God damn you people." Such a rant would have delighted Cheever in real life, though he'd be careful to condole with its victims afterward.

When he wasn't scything with the resident man of the soil, Cheever was discreetly commiserating with the Whitneys in their war against the misfit Winternitz clan. Like Polly, he made (qualified) exceptions where his wife and her brother Bill were concerned, but the other three siblings were fair game. "There are a lot of Mary's family here now and a good deal of venom is generated at the dinner table," he wrote John Weaver. "When I left the table last night Polly pulled me under a syringia and hissed: 'They say he used to eat flies at Hamden Hall and now I believe it.' " Still in a category of her own was Mary's maid of honor, Buff, whom the Whitney children mercilessly abused because of her dumpy figure and odd behavior. Cheever, too, invariably described her as "Mary's unstable sister" and made amusing references to her overeating. That first summer after the war, it got so bad that Buff went berserk and threatened to kill the cook ("Mary's sister is as crazy as a bed-bug," Cheever reported), whereupon she was driven away to a mental hospital in Rhode Island. At one such place Buff would meet her future husband, Walter, a chemist with a Ph.D. and social manner that made his wife seem glib by comparison. Once, the man misinterpreted (or understood all too well) one of Cheever's witticisms and challenged him to step outside and fight, but Cheever only laughed and resumed his conversation. There were times, though, when the whole internecine comedy became a bore, and then Cheever would escape to New York, alone, so he could work in peace and see a few friends. While Buff was still regaining her composure at Butler Hospital, Cheever was celebrating Ettlinger's marriage to Katrina Wallingford, heiress of a grain-elevator fortune: "[They] came into town on their way to Berne (Suisse) where they are going to live," he wrote Herbst. "It was hot and we drank gin and champagne at the Plaza."

· · ·

THE ETTLINGERS SOON RETURNED to the city and took an apartment on Sutton Place. "I used to put a gin bottle in the window and an
Edith Piaf record on the phonograph"—Cheever later remarked to the
couple, only half in jest—"and hope that the Ettlingers might just possibly drop in to keep me company but you almost never did." Cheever's
working day usually ended at lunch, and the long afternoons made him
restless. The fact was, he did see a fair amount of his friends Don and
Katrina—the families often spent Christmas Day or New Year's
together—but Ettlinger had resumed his busy career writing for *Kraft
Television Theater*, and would soon find a permanent niche as head
writer for the soap opera *Love of Life*. Cheever, a loyal friend, would
sometimes watch the show in various bars, and when Ettlinger sued
CBS for ripping off his idea for a series titled *Our Miss Booth* (which
CBS had rejected before making *Our Miss Brooks* with Eve Arden),
Cheever would walk to Foley Square on fine afternoons and listen to
his friend testify ("Now and then he flashes the jury a youthful smile
with just a hint of modesty in it and you ought to see them lay back in
their swivel chairs," he wrote Weaver). On the surface, the two could
hardly have been less alike: Ettlinger was tall and princely, Cheever
short and rather plain; Ettlinger was wealthy, and Cheever struggled to
get by. But of course they had talent and charm in common, not to say
a tendency to conceal their deeper natures with artifice of one sort or
another: "His split person," Cheever observed of Ettlinger after a
drunken evening. "That his social graces, his wit, spring entirely from
evasion. The sense that he might commit a murder and that all my
friends have been potential criminals." Cheever might have been writing about himself, though there's only a slight implication of that in
the context of these cryptic remarks.

In those days—as Pete Collins's second wife Elizabeth pointed
out—"Everybody drank like a fish, but Pete thought Cheever was an
alcoholic as early as the late forties." What with the long afternoons to
kill, Cheever often began his evenings with a considerable head start,
and the social results would sometimes (as he put it) have "all the characteristics of an automobile accident." There was Cheever the antic,
happy drunk, who one night in 1946 danced the "atomic waltz" with
Howard Fast's wife, Betty, on his shoulders, until she put out a cigarette in his ear and he flung her to the floor. There was Cheever the
mean drunk, whose dry wit would suddenly turn vicious at some vague
point ("What right have I to calumniate these gentle people?" he
reproached himself). And finally—more and more often—there was

Cheever the bored and even boring drunk, pickled by the long day's drinking and wishing only for bed: "The conversation [last night] hit a very low level," Cheever reflected in his journal (the only type of writing he could manage in the grip of his nastier hangovers). "I discussed with Dave some shirts I had bought at a sale and he told me about his disappointments with a tropical worsted suit."

One of his more stimulating companions was the writer Irwin Shaw, whose larger-than-life personality excited both love and envy in Cheever. The two had in common the Signal Corps and *The New Yorker*, though already Shaw was becoming the kind of "money player" who wouldn't have to suffer Harold Ross's legendary stinginess much longer. Even then Cheever secretly considered himself the better artist, and it galled him that Shaw got most of the glamour. Their rivalry was manifest in touch-football games they played in Central Park on Sundays. Though heckled as a runt, Cheever was all business when Shaw was on the opposing team, and once managed to slip past him for a touchdown—a slender triumph, since otherwise Cheever was constantly reminded that he could scarcely afford the sweetness of Shaw's company: "[T]he cost of this comfortable life is fantastic," he wrote Herbst, after a skiing weekend with the Shaws in Vermont ("drinking martinis and playing parchesi"). The same applied to his friendship with the Ettlingers, who were then in the process of buying the artist Waldo Pierce's house in Rockland County, where they would consort more and more with show-business neighbors such as Burgess Meredith and Paulette Goddard, Helen Hayes and Charles Mac-Arthur. On returning (by bus) from a New Year's visit, Cheever noted his envy and wondered if he and his family would ever have a house of their own—while at the same time surprising himself with such petty materialism:

> Last night, folding the bath towel so the monogram would be in the right place (and after reading a piece on Rimbaud by Zabel), I wondered what I was doing here. This concern for outward order—the flowers, the shining cigarette box . . . I was born into no true class, and it was my decision, early in life, to insinuate myself into the middle class, like a spy, so that I would have an advantageous position of attack, but I seem now and then to have forgotten my mission and to have taken my disguises too seriously.

CHAPTER TWELVE

{ *1946–1949* }

THE YEAR 1946 had begun on a promising note: Cheever signed a contract with Random House for a novel (still some version of *The Holly Tree*) and received a rather generous advance of forty-eight hundred dollars. Both Broadway and Hollywood were showing interest in the "Town House" stories. And meanwhile, advance or no, Cheever was broke again: "I got out of the army in November and the work I've done since then you could put in a peashell," he wrote Herbst in January. "I want to start on a book but I still have to write three stories and God knows when I'll get those done." According to his journal, he wrote himself out of debt by late spring, when at last he returned to the novel he'd abandoned shortly before his enlistment in 1942. "And now we face the Holly Tree again," he noted with bleak apprehension. Reading over the thing with the vast objectivity of four years, Cheever tried hard to like what he saw ("It seems good; it seems good"), but mostly he noticed that it was, as ever, the work of a short-story writer: each chapter ended with a dying fall, a bit of provocative irony that went nowhere. "You must use suspense," Cheever hectored himself.

His editor at Random House was the well-respected Robert Linscott, whose letters to Cheever over the next seven or eight years were rarely other than tactful and encouraging, while Cheever, for his part, always did his best to seem hopeful. "This letter is to thank you for the great pleasure I had in reading your admirable story in last week's New Yorker, and to tell you how eagerly I'm awaiting the manuscript of your novel," Linscott wrote in July 1946, almost seven months after

Cheever had signed a contract for a novel he'd started writing (as both men knew) several years before. "How goes it, and do you still expect to complete it this year?" The novel was coming along "nicely," Cheever replied, and yes, he thought he might have a draft by late November; he repeated the deadline in a letter to the Ettlingers, almost as if to persuade himself of its plausibility, though he also confided a certain dread: "I like the story but I keep asking myself: Is there a character in this book you would enjoy meeting? . . . It troubles me. I love a great many people and the color of the sky, but this doesn't describe my work." A year later, at Treetops, he was still wondering whether to inflict these characters on the world, in whatever form, while letting Linscott know there was "a fairly good chance" he'd return to the city with a draft in September. In August, however, he learned that "eggs in the city [were] a dollar a dozen," and so he put the novel aside, again, to grind out stories.

Based on his journal notes, plus a number of surviving typescript pages and his correspondence with Linscott, *The Holly Tree* seems to have been composed almost entirely of scenes and people that would later find their way into *The Wapshot Chronicle*. This was the material Cheever was determined to "write out of [his] system," and his perseverance in the face of repeated failure—fifteen years (or more) of tinkering and starting over—is simply astounding. The version that evolved in the forties, after the war, concerned an Ur-Wapshot family alternately named Morgan, Flint, or Field: an elderly couple, Aaron and Sarah, and their sons, Tom and Eben. The gift shop was always part of the story, as was the blithely promiscuous Rosalie and Aaron/Leander's abandoned child who haunts him as a haggard spinster—and so forth. "All moderately dull material," Cheever admitted in his journal. What was missing, perhaps, was the transformative magic wrought by a special point of view: the tender and forgiving humor of *The Wapshot Chronicle*, a love of humanity and the "color of the sky," as it were. It's telling that nothing equivalent to Cousin Honora existed in the novel's early stages—no composite, that is, of Cheever's quirky aunts and cousins and (foremost) mother—perhaps because such a character was inconceivable until enough time had passed for Cheever to view these people with a certain degree of detached loving-kindness. In the absence of such nostalgia, Cheever resorted to melodrama as a means of lifting the miserable facts of his early life above the mundane. Of the character most like himself, for example, Cheever wrote in his journal: "Tom would have tried to kill himself when he was sixteen. Perhaps out of jealousy for his brother. This and any other irregularity in his conduct he would be very anxious to conceal. The effort to present the front of a college man." All this was certainly true of Cheever himself—minus (in all likelihood) the suicide attempt—but almost beside the point in regard to Coverly Wapshot, the benign neurotic that this character would eventually become.

By the end of 1947, Cheever still hadn't produced a manuscript, though he claimed a longish one existed, and finally Linscott suggested he write an outline, at least, to give the salesmen something to work with. Cheever reluctantly obliged, though he doubted he could convey what was best about the novel—the actual writing—and so took pains to play this up in the outline, which itself is quite cleverly written:

> The writing, or the surface of the book, which has concerned me a good deal, seems to me clear and reliable. I speak of the writing since it seems very important to me . . . that it should appear decorous and beautiful and I sometimes think of the story as having the polish, the sentimental charms of a greeting card with an obscene message. . . .
>
> The story centers on a family; the Fields. Aaron, Sarah and their two sons, Tom and Eben. There is much of a country that I love in this book—much scenery, much rain, many semi-colons—for these are bewildered children in a beautiful garden.
>
> The story begins in 1936 and has in it's opening the appearance of something to be read in bed on a rainy night in an old house.* . . .
>
> Sarah Field . . . is stout, she has yielded her beauty without a struggle, she has attended a White House reception, dreamt of carnal relations with Padarewski and two bibles have come apart in her hands. . . .

Having sold the atmospherics of the book (and emphasized his own cleverness wherever possible), Cheever tried to relate the plot with

---

*Cheever adored this phrase, this image, and thought of using it in almost every novel he wrote. He liked to say that "fiction is our most intimate means of communication," and the idea of telling his readers a story while they are safe and cozy in bed seemed to please him. Finally he was able to use the sentence in slightly different form at the beginning (and end) of his last novel, *Oh What a Paradise It Seems:* "This is a story to be read in bed in an old house on a rainy night."

similar élan. The first part of the book consisted of various threads that would later be woven into *The Wapshot Chronicle*. The second part was absurdly melodramatic and perhaps never written at all, except in tentative bits and pieces. Aaron was to escape the blackmail of his spinster daughter by hiding in Detroit, while Sarah "commits a dreadful murder"—the particulars of which Cheever wisely omitted in his outline, as well as whatever pyrotechnics he would perforce bring to bear in resolving such complications. The novel was to end (à la *Wapshot*) with Aaron's funeral.

"That's a wonderful presentation of your book," Linscott generously replied. "You have certainly whetted my appetite for the book, and I shan't be happy until I read it." He would not be happy, then, for a long time. Three months later, with no end in sight, Cheever felt like "the only man in the East Fifties who hasn't finished his novel"; meanwhile the usual financial setbacks made it imperative that he get back to story writing and stay there for a while. "I want to write short stories like I want to fuck a chicken."

It was unfortunate he felt that way. Apart from the foundering progress of his novel, the late forties (and 1947 in particular) were miraculous years for Cheever. He was well on his way to becoming one of the best fiction writers at *The New Yorker*, and hence (when considered in the company of contributors such as Nabokov, O'Hara, Salinger, and Shaw) one of the best writers in America. Cheever later remarked that the magazine had accepted almost everything he wrote in those days "as long as there wasn't any explicit sexual intercourse," and in fact rejections did become relatively rare as Cheever's work continued to change and improve in startling ways. Though he belittled his stories, and longed to be a novelist, Cheever was almost morbidly aware of his *New Yorker* readership and eager to please. "It was one of the most felicitous relationships between readers and writers I think that ever existed," he said of this golden age. Cheever loved the immediate gratification of writing for the magazine—not only the quick (if meager) paycheck, but the marvelous idea that he could communicate in print "with estimable men and women" as soon as (sometimes) a week or two after he'd written a story! And how delightful (for such a lonely man) when these same readers would write personal letters validating, in effect, his most vital feelings about life. Indeed, when he met these readers in the flesh, he was elated by their praise and stricken by any sign of indifference. When, for example, a woman at a cocktail party applauded the *New Yorker* work of one Robert McLaughlin—but had never heard of Cheever—the latter brooded despondently in his journal: "The stories she liked by McLaughlin were obvious and done without any talent, and I was disappointed to find that she did not remember, and had never noticed the cutting edge I work so hard to give my prose. . . . Who knows the difference."

Cheever was determined to make them see the difference. Having finished the last of his "Town House" stories in March 1946—and perhaps sensing he was in danger of becoming the sort of slick writer whose proper peers were the likes of Robert McLaughlin rather than O'Hara, Shaw, et al.—Cheever challenged himself to write something with "more size and passion": no more "rueful vignettes," in other words, "but real stories with characters, invention, scenery and moral conviction." What followed was "The Sutton Place Story," which appeared in *The New Yorker* that June*—a somber look at the tawdry private lives of the Manhattan middle class, as witnessed by a little girl named Deborah Tennyson, who "knew about cocktails and hangovers." Through a series of delinquencies committed by the negligent adults in her life, Deborah ends up (disastrously) in the care of a genteel semi-prostitute named Renée. The narrator casually evokes the woman's sordid nature, as if it were the sort of thing any quasi-respectable New Yorker could relate to: "She had begun to notice that she always felt tired unless she was drinking. . . . When she was not drinking she was depressed, and when she was depressed she quarreled with headwaiters and hairdressers, accused people in restaurants of staring at her. . . . She knew this instability in her temperament well, and was clever at concealing it—among other things—from casual friends like the Tennysons."

The story of a child who runs away from adult corruption—and is almost lost forever—certainly possessed the moral conviction to which Cheever aspired, and the contradictory impulses of his characters had rarely been so well portrayed. In the meantime, as a self-styled "spy" among the middle class, Cheever liked to imagine the secrets of his innocuous fellow tenants in that building near Sutton Place, and he continued to brood on this theme—namely, "that genuinely decorous men and women admitted into their affairs erotic bitterness and even greed," as he put it (a little self-mockingly) in his preface to the *Stories*. As an early treatment, "The Sutton Place Story" would serve as

*The earliest story that Cheever—or rather editor Robert Gottlieb—saw fit to include in the definitive collection, *The Stories of John Cheever* (1978).

a springboard to greater things, possibly leading the author to ponder a more interesting way of becoming, so to speak, a narrative fly on as many walls as possible. The solution would involve a dose of magic. "[I'm] facing the need for change in my work," he wrote in 1947. "The physical world is very important to me but dry descriptions of the details of its beauty are not enough."

Cheever would later invoke Kafka as his main influence for "The Enormous Radio," but when Dodie Merwin first read the story, she immediately recognized Cheever's own peculiar anecdotal style: "He had the most hilarious sense of going on tangents. He would build this absolutely perfect portrait of the times and the places and the people— and all of a sudden it would *shoot off* somewhere." Consider the opening lines of "The Enormous Radio": "Jim and Irene Westcott were the kind of people who seem to strike that satisfactory average of income, endeavor, and respectability that is reached by the statistical reports in college alumni bulletins. They were the parents of two young children, they had been married nine years, they lived on the twelfth floor of an apartment house near Sutton Place, they went to the theatre on an average of 10.3 times a year, and they hoped someday to live in West-chester." Rather than dramatize the Westcotts' ideal ordinariness with a lot of tedious narrative detail, Cheever simply states the matter with a droll statistical flourish ("10.3 times a year"). The only way the couple deviates from the norm, he informs us, is in their extravagant love of music, hence the need of a brand-new radio. Thus, as Irene West-cott settles down to listen to this ungainly machine, Cheever goes off on one of his tangents: "A crackling sound like the noise of a burning powder fuse began to accompany the singing of the strings. . . . [S]he began to discern through the Mozart the ringing of telephone bells, the dialing of phones, and the lamentation of a vacuum cleaner." This is Kafka's approach, too: Before the reader can object to the idea of a man transformed into a dung beetle, the thing has been done with absolute naturalism, from Gregor Samsa's "armor-hard back" to the "rigid bow-like sections" of his abdomen. And so with Cheever's radio: a hot "crackling" is precisely the sound a radio makes (circa 1947) when changing signals, but the description also resonates with infernal overtones, as Irene discovers that this particular radio allows her to eavesdrop on neighbors. "Irene shifted the control and invaded the privacy of several breakfast tables. She overheard demonstrations of indigestion, carnal love, abysmal vanity, faith, and despair."

The story is typically interpreted in terms of Edenic myth—the satanic radio bestows on the Westcotts the knowledge of evil—and one supposes this was fine with Cheever, whose main objective was to "put things down as they appear and to leave the spore of myth and allusion to the reader." He knew his fanciful exaggerations had mythic dimensions, and so be it; however—quite like Kafka—he deplored his work's being reduced to "banal allegory." In the case of "The Enormous Radio," the obvious Edenic gloss doesn't quite fit—unlike Adam and Eve, the ultra-normal Westcotts have *always* been corrupt, and the radio simply reminds them of this: "You made Grace Howland's life miserable"—Jim Westcott berates his wife toward the end of the story—"and where was all your piety and your virtue when you went to that abortionist? . . . You packed your bag and went off to have that child murdered as if you were going to Nassau." And finally, once the radio is "fixed," it still insists on confronting the traumatized pair with the hopeless suffering of a fallen world: "The voice on the radio was suave and noncommittal. 'An early-morning railroad disaster in Tokyo,' the loudspeaker said, 'killed twenty-nine people. A fire in a Catholic hospital near Buffalo for the care of blind children was extinguished early this morning by nuns. The temperature is forty-seven. The humidity is eighty-nine.' "

"The Enormous Radio" was included in that year's *Best American Short Stories*, and was also selected for a *Best of the Best* volume published a few years later. More gratifying, perhaps, was Mary Cheever's reaction: "It made a big difference in how I felt about the man I was married to and how he was spending his time." From then on—while the evidence mounted—she would have to consider their marital and financial woes in the context of caring for a potentially great writer. Even Harold Ross was moved to praise the story (a rare enough occurrence, lest a writer think about asking for more money): "I've just read 'The Enormous Radio' . . . and I send my respects and admiration," he wrote Cheever a few weeks before the story was published. "It will turn out to be a memorable one, or I am a fish. Very wonderful indeed." And a few months later the man sent *another* personal message ("unquestionably excellent") when the magazine published "Torch Song," Cheever's equally surreal tale about a woman who battens on sickly, violent men, cheerfully enduring their abuse because of a "lewd" infatuation with death.

Ross tended to dislike any writing that smacked of the experimental or highfalutin, and one might have expected him to balk at Cheever's straying from strict realism. As an editor, though, Ross specifically insisted on an almost pathological clarity of *detail*, such that the reader never had to look twice at a sentence to gather its meaning, or wonder what exactly was happening in a given scene. If anything, such a quibbling passion for verisimilitude ("This story has gone on for 24 hours and no one has eaten anything") may have contributed something to the precision of Cheever's own style, and sometimes Ross's edits were inspired: "In 'The Enormous Radio' he made two changes," Cheever recalled; "a diamond is found on the bathroom floor after a party. The man says 'Sell it, we can use a few dollars.' Ross had changed 'dollars' to 'bucks,' which was absolutely perfect. . . . Then I had 'the radio came softly' and Ross pencilled in another 'softly.' 'The radio came softly, softly.' "

In later years, when Cheever would wax nostalgic about his early association with *The New Yorker*, he'd claim a close acquaintance with Ross and elaborate on the man's legend as a lovable grotesque— a "scratcher and nosepicker" who used to make Cheever jump in his chair by saying "fuck" a lot at the lunch table. "I doubt very much if those lunches ever took place," said Maxwell after Cheever's death, pointing out that Ross kept his distance from fiction writers as much as possible. Indeed, it seems the two only spoke in person once, when Lobrano introduced them at the Algonquin. "A few days later," Cheever remarked to Newhouse, "I saw [Ross] in the elevator and he didn't recognize me." Still, he was fond of the *idea* of Ross, and liked to tell of how desolate he'd been when he got news of the editor's death— such that he could hardly bear reading about it eight years later in *The Years with Ross*: "I leafed through the Thurber book on Ross last night," he wrote Maxwell, "and when I read the part where Hawley says: 'It's all over' I burst into tears. I couldn't stop."*

IN THE MARGIN of one Cheever story—where a character comes home from work and changes clothes before dinner—Ross scribbled, "Eh? What's this? Cheever looks to me like a one-suiter." He had guessed right, but then he ought to have known. Toward the end of the

---

*"Ross is dead," Cheever noted in his journal on December 6, 1951, then proceeded to other matters: "Dinner party despatched [sic] on Sat. Hotchkisses, Boyers, Maxwells. An annoying waste of time."

Ross era, Cheever was paid between five hundred and one thousand dollars a story, which meant that in a good year—with bonuses and occasional sales to other magazines—he made a little more than five thousand dollars. As he later reflected, "I think Ross's feeling was that if I was paid any more . . . I would get prideful, arrogant and idle." Things were bad enough in 1947 for him to break down and let his wife take a job teaching composition at Sarah Lawrence, about which he was alternately grudging and derisive. "[S]he comes home with a briefcase full of themes written by young ladies named Nooky and Pussy," he wrote Herbst; "but these nicknames would give you no indication of what these themes are about." As for the pittance she was paid, Cheever reminded her that Newhouse's wife earned at least a hundred a week teaching the "fiddle" at Juilliard, but (he supposed) it was "too late for Mary to take up a musical instrument." Nor would he allow her to console him when he was feeling hopeless about things, having learned from childhood that it was shameful to be caught without a stiff upper lip. At best he'd evade her sympathy with the usual quip and giggle, but when his mood was especially foul he'd "whip out at [her]," so that Mary learned to hold her tongue ("I did lots of tongue holding in those days"). But really he couldn't help it. Toward the end of that year—in some respects his most artistically successful yet—he was almost at the end of his rope. Of a bad day in October, he wrote in his journal:

> I tried to work with no success and early in the evening Gus called me and said they were not going to buy the Mink Decade [story]. This means I'm out a thousand dollars and six weeks work. Bob Linscott came for dinner and told me that Irwin [Shaw] had completed his novel and that it was magnificent. I didn't talk particularly well and drank quite a lot. I woke at four in the morning. The struggle for recognition then, for money, even for success in my own terms seemed hopeless, and I felt . . . that I had betrayed my pure and gentle family, and because of this the desire to kill myself was strong.

While pondering suicide Cheever was his old jovial self among friends, though one day Ettlinger spotted him walking along First Avenue. About to say hello, he suddenly noticed the haunted look on Cheever's face—"such a powerful expression of sadness" that he quickly ducked behind a building until his friend had passed.

No matter how dejected Cheever got, he was quite determined to finance a private education for his daughter, and hence his main anxiety the following spring (1948) was whether she'd be accepted at the elite Brearley School. Not only did they accept the four-year-old, but their "charming letter" applauded the "independence and extraordinary maturity" she'd shown in her interview; Cheever—passing along the good news to Polly and Winter—wondered whether such glowing terms could possibly be used to describe his "fat and wayward daughter." Almost from the moment of her birth, he'd begun to suspect she wasn't going to be the slender, perky debutante he longed for, and before she'd reached the age of reason he found ways of letting her know she was disappointing him. "Sue is about the same," he wrote the Ettlingers, when the girl wasn't quite three. "For a minute or two I thought she was going to get thin; but it didn't happen. Then I thought she might learn to swim; but no." Perhaps forgetting that he himself had been chubby and unpromising as a child, Cheever was forever browbeating his daughter about her weight, banning candy and cookies and other snacks, with predictable results: "[W]hen I picked her up at the party there was frosting in her ears, several pieces of candy in her mouth . . . so that I'm afraid all of our hard work has been undone."

Mary Cheever's thirtieth-birthday gift, as she'd always say, was the birth of her second child, Benjamin Hale Cheever, on May 4, 1948. "We think he's handsome, intelligent, wirey, and strong," Cheever reported to friends, "and actually he's very unlike Sue." So at least the boy was born on good terms, though perhaps it helped that his father's financial prospects were looking up at the time. Two years before, dramatic rights to the "Town House" stories had been sold (netting Cheever $173) to Bernard Hart and Clinton Wilder, who'd hired Herman Mankiewicz to write an adaptation. The latter had won an Oscar for his *Citizen Kane* screenplay, but by 1946 he was often drunk, and the first (and only) act of his "Town House" play was, by Cheever's account, a cliché-ridden disaster: "All the people came out of a bad picture . . . a football bore, an old gentlemen [sic] with a tough, wisecracking cutie." Mankiewicz was fired, and the property changed hands a few times, floating in limbo until the beginning of 1948, when it was picked up by one of Broadway's top producers, Max Gordon, who signed George S. Kaufman, no less, to direct and co-write (with Gertrude Tonkonogy). Cheever, though he received only fifty-two dollars a month until the play was in the black, was so bucked that he hired a maid to help his burdened wife with the housework: "This maid has a gray uniform with an apron . . . and is no great shakes as a cook," Cheever wrote, "but at noon we all cram ourselves into the vestibule, ring a little bell and she brings in a plate of deviled ham sandwiches and trails after her a rich blend of patchouli and Nuit d'Armour [sic]."

As opening night approached, Cheever was frankly "stage struck." He'd taken to passing his afternoons at the Lyceum Theatre with Kaufman and Gordon, watching rehearsals and "saying No thank you very much to hundreds of women with strawberry hair." On September 1, he and Mary went to Boston for a two-week tryout at the Colonial Theatre, and once again Cheever was interviewed by the enduring Mabelle Fullerton of the *Patriot Ledger* ("Former Quincy Boy Courting Miracle"), who described the author as a combination of Peter Pan, Voltaire, and Bambi. Cheever remarked that all the actors in *Town House* were "wonderful" ("just as I realized them in the stories"), and even wrote his own puff piece for the *Boston Post:* "From the shelter halves of Guam [i.e., where he'd written one of the "Town House" stories] to the new, comfortable seats in the Colonial Theatre is a fairly long way for an idea to have come," he concluded, "and I for one am very glad that it made the trip." On opening night he and Mary checked in at the Ritz, had dinner with family and friends, then repaired en masse to the theater. The show, Cheever decided, was "a sentimental and moderately funny piece of bunk": "Max Gordon waltzed Kay Brown around the lobby and said they were going to sell it to the pictures for a million dollars."

Two days later, a few qualms had crept into his head, and he returned to watch another performance in sober solitude:

> It seemed vulgar, mechanical, and unfunny. Going out to Quincy on the midnight bus I felt a depression that seemed to transcend that particular evening and those circumstances and to return me to a moment in my youth when perhaps I stepped into a cold and empty house. . . . We have lived insecurely for so many years that the thought that this trash might bring us a steady income has seduced and corrupted my judgement.

His better judgment was confirmed when the play opened on September 23 at Broadway's National Theatre. In the meantime Cheever had done his best to salvage the thing with a flurry of revisions, while Kaufman had "shine[d] it up" with "so many gags . . . that it sounded like a recitation from a joke book." As for the producer, Max Gordon, he'd spent twenty-six thousand dollars on the set alone: a full-sized cutaway of an Upper East Side town house. To no avail. Don Ettlinger, who'd cringed through opening night, remembered the final product as being crammed with a lot of "terrible" gags, and the *New York Times* agreed ("a thin, loose, mechanical whizzbang that never explodes across the footlights"). The play closed nine days later, after only twelve performances. "I don't quite know who to blame, with the exception of myself," Cheever wrote his in-laws. "[N]ow and then I feel sorry for myself because I had such wonderful ideas for spreading the money around, but it's a speculative business and I'm glad we confined our speculation to day-dreaming."

In his journal Cheever wrote, "We are as poor as we ever have been. The rent is not paid, we have very little to eat. . . . We have many bills." Determined to write "a story a week," he was rejected four times in a row by *The New Yorker*, which meant he wouldn't be receiving a yearly bonus, either.* Faced with dire poverty, and forced into writing "lifeless and detestable" fiction, Cheever chided himself for entertaining an "unreasonable" degree of petulance ("This is a patriarchal relationship, and I certainly respond to the slings of regret, real or imaginary"). At length he dug himself out of his latest hole with an easy lampoon for the slicks titled "The Opportunity," about a seemingly dull-witted girl who passes up a choice part in a Broadway play because (as she is not too dull-witted to notice) "it stinks"; viciously denounced for her integrity, she yet evades the "[s]corn, ridicule, abuse, and disgust" that are heaped on everyone associated with the play, which closes after five performances in Philadelphia. The story sold to *Cosmopolitan* for $1,750, Cheever's highest price yet, and perhaps served as a somewhat satisfying coda to the whole *Town House* debacle.

Meanwhile Irwin Shaw's first novel, *The Young Lions*, was a big hit; moreover Shaw's wife had remarked to Cheever that, in the novel's home stretch, her husband had written at the inspired pace of seventeen pages a day! "This seems to me seriously lacking," Cheever noted,

---

*He managed to sell two of these rejected stories to *Harper's*, "The Reasonable Music" and "Vega." The second—an odd tangent for Cheever in certain ways, though by no means inferior—was a long story inspired by Peter Wesul's farouche daughter, who rarely showed herself or spoke. It appeared in the December 1949 *Harper's* with illustrations by a young Andy Warhol.

after a long and mostly sober night of reading. "Knowing the fierce-ness of competition among writers I sometimes feel that my knowl-edge of Irwin, my love of Irwin may have buried some malevolence deep in my judgement but it is my judgement that this is not much of a book." Be that as it may, his friend was now a bona-fide celebrity, and while lunching at the Algonquin, Cheever found himself smiling and nodding at the news that Irwin had just returned from Cap d'Antibes and was getting a big welcome-home party from Frank Capra, etc. "I keep telling myself that this cannot go on," Cheever wrote, "no, no, no, that this is all wrong."

CHEEVER HAD NOT REVISITED Yaddo since his raucous stays in the summer of 1940. Around that time he wrote a friend, "Elizabeth [Ames] has closed the door of Yaddo in my face remarking that my interests in Saratoga seem to center on the skiing, the riding club, and the Worden Bar & Grill." The two remained fond of each other, though, and continued to write and promise to get together at some point.

A reunion of sorts was hastened by a peculiar series of events in the spring of 1949. On February 11, a front-page story in the *New York Times* reported that General Douglas MacArthur's intelligence staff had identified Agnes Smedley, author of several books on Red China, as a Russian agent. Smedley was ill and destitute by then, and had lived for almost six years (1943 to 1948) at Yaddo as, essentially, one of Mrs. Ames's charity cases. The War Department presently withdrew its charges, citing lack of evidence, though not before a couple of FBI agents came to Yaddo to interview Mrs. Ames, her guests, and her sec-retary—the last of whom, it so happened, had been acting as an informer for the past five years: "[W]henever I heard people talking very brilliantly red," she said, "I have written down their name and address and dropped it off . . . for forwarding to the FBI." This, of course, was not altogether surprising, since Mrs. Ames had in fact demonstrated a partiality toward radical authors: there was her long-time lover, Leonard Ehrlich, as well as a list including Josie Herbst, Eleanor Clark, Muriel Rukeyser, and many others. Amid the furor of the Alger Hiss case, and the McCarthy era soon to come, this was con-sidered a very dubious state of affairs.

At the time there were only four guests in residence: Robert Lowell, Flannery O'Connor, Edward Maisel, and Elizabeth Hardwick. When FBI agents told Lowell that Yaddo was "permeated with Communists" and suggested that Mrs. Ames had been protecting a Russian spy, the poet—drinking heavily, in the grip of religious mania, and on the brink of perhaps the worst breakdown in his colorful career— rallied the other guests against Mrs. Ames and demanded a meeting with local members of the Yaddo board. Mrs. Ames, said Lowell, was "a diseased organ, chronically poisoning the whole system"; he insisted that she be fired immediately or else he'd continue his crusade on a larger scale; indeed, he felt as if he were fighting "against the Devil himself." The board members, not a little shaken, assured the poet that they'd pursue the matter at their regular meeting in New York a few weeks later. Meanwhile the main topic of cocktail gossip in literary Manhattan was whether Yaddo was or was not a hotbed of communist traitors.

"John Cheever was wonderful in his loyalties," said Eleanor Clark, "and Elizabeth [Ames] was one of them." Clark recruited Cheever and three others—Alfred Kazin, Harvey Breit, and Kappo Phelan—to draft a letter of protest against the witch hunt. "We feel that the charge currently being brought arises from a frame of mind that represents a grave danger both to civil liberties and to the freedom necessary for the arts," they wrote. "We feel this charge involves a cynical assault not only on Elizabeth Ames's personal integrity, but also on the whole future of Yaddo. . . . We regard their [Lowell et al.'s] action as a thoroughly foolish and nasty performance, dangerous to the extent that it weakens any sober fight against Communism." The group collected fifty-one endorsements and appeared personally before the directors on March 26. After five hours of discussion, the board decided to censure Lowell and absolve Mrs. Ames (who nevertheless was divested of her power to extend visits to whomsoever she pleased). Recovering in a nursing home afterward, the embattled woman wrote Herbst*: "I do not know how I should have come through these dreadful two months if that little staunch Committee of which John is a member had not sprung into action over night, working swiftly and wisely. It is all a

---

*Herbst would benefit in a similar way from Cheever's friendship. Because of her lifelong interest in left-wing causes—and because her former husband, John Hermann, was an actual party member—the State Department accused her of communism and refused to issue her a passport. On November 9, 1954, Cheever submitted the following affidavit in Herbst's defense: "Nothing that she ever did or said would have led me, or now leads me, to believe that she was a member of the Communist Party."

miracle." Almost thirty years later, Cheever wrote in his journal: "Lowell is dead and God have mercy on his soul."

THE PREVIOUS SUMMER Cheever had finally shown a fragment of his novel to Linscott, who (as Cheever later noted) "found so little worthwhile that I was never able to look at the manuscript again." After a long bout of story writing and other distractions, Cheever "slowly regrouped [his] forces for another trial," but after months of effort he felt even more discouraged. The novel wasn't working. Even the prose was weak—full of "affectations" and "bad poetry," perhaps by way of overcompensating for an absurd plot and dreary characters. "What is wrong with Aaron, a question I have asked a hundred times and may have to ask a hundred times more," Cheever wrote. "He is not taken from life, but I did not mean him to be." Aaron—the character that would someday become Leander Wapshot, an even more pictur-esque version of Frederick Cheever—was a man who suffered the same basic ills as Frederick (old age, poverty), but with neither the man's zaniness nor his benignity. As for the author's determination to demon-ize Aaron's wife, Sarah, simply because she opens a gift shop—well, obviously, it made no sense: "The descriptions of her enterprise make opening the shop a natural development," Cheever reflected (with a fair-mindedness he could rarely muster in his own mother's behalf). "She also does this because they want money."

At the end of almost ten years of sporadic work on *The Holly Tree*, Cheever was utterly stymied and broke as ever. Forced again to write short stories, he conceded temporary defeat in a sheepish (but stub-bornly hopeful) letter to Linscott:

> I am writing principally to say that I will not have a draft for you by the end of this month [January 1950]. No one regrets this more bit-terly than I; but I cannot die whenever I announce another delay. . . . If you should feel, as Mary does, that I closet myself all day merely to take cat-naps I would be delighted to talk with you, to tell you how the book has changed over the years and to con-vince you that this is not a still-born project, an illusion, that my way is not hopelessly obstructed by some deep spiritual impedi-ment and that I am not willfully tinkering with some old pages. I never read what I think of as the right, the durable chapters without some satisfaction and their number has increased steadily since fall.

Linscott replied with his usual equanimity ("I have told you many times we would rather wait for a really good novel than take an almost good novel prematurely"), but Cheever wasn't much consoled. As one decade dwindled into the next, he felt more than ever like a failure: "Sitting on the sofa, surrounded with friendly people, I kept saying: I am not doing well, I am not doing well enough. I must take a line on the novel, strong enough to get me out of bed in the morning."

CHAPTER THIRTEEN

{ 1949–1951 }

MARY CHEEVER SUSPECTED there was something fundamentally wrong with her marriage almost from the start,
though she'd had no serious boyfriends before Cheever and
certainly knew almost nothing about homosexuality. Nevertheless, as
she put it many years later, "I sensed that he wasn't entirely masculine." She got a slightly more definite inkling in 1948, when she and
her husband saw the original Broadway production of *A Streetcar
Named Desire* ("As decadent, I think, as anything I've ever seen on the
stage," Cheever wrote). The leitmotif associated with Blanche's dead,
homosexual husband* stuck in Mary's head, and led to a subtle, perhaps only semiconscious epiphany: "I saw a connection there." Did she
discuss it with Cheever? "Oh Lord, no. Oh Lord, no. He was terrified
of it himself."

"I can remember walking around the streets of New York on a summer night some years ago," Cheever wrote in 1952. "I cannot say that
it was like the pain of living death; it never had that clear a meaning. . . .
The feeling always was that if I could express myself erotically I could
come alive." After several years of marriage, and burdened with almost
every sort of anxiety, Cheever found it more and more of a strain not to
yield to temptation. In his journal he called himself "the walking
bruise," a sensation he would attribute to Coverly Wapshot—"one of
those men who labor under a preternaturally large sense of guilt that,
like some enormous bruise . . . could be carried painlessly until it was

---

*A polka tune Mary Cheever still remembered fifty-five years later.

touched; but once it was touched it would threaten to unnerve him with its pain." Cheever was almost daily unnerved, almost daily reminded of his damnable secret (as he saw it), and such was the loneliness of his suffering that he considered returning to the church in hope of comfort.

His greatest fear was that his wife would discover his illicit desires. Because of this—and because his career at the time seemed to have "all the characteristics of a failure"—he was especially sensitive to any sign of discontent on her part. One night, when she asked to be alone for a while, Cheever's pride was so wounded that he considered asking for a separation or divorce, though he knew such an impulse was "perverse": "There is some part of her that is not gregarious or affectionate, that has never been yielded to me or to anyone else without pain. She was alone much when she was a young girl and the habits of solitude sometimes return to her. Now and then, by a complete absence of privacy, she feels suffocated. She is entitled to this—I recognized it when I met her and married her." This was Cheever's reasoned, objective view, and it could hardly have been more empathetic; his actual behavior was another matter, and so Mary tried to hold her tongue. Still, there were many distant looks and "tremulous sighs," duly noted by Cheever, who imagined his wife in the midst of some "tragic adultery" or anyway wishing to seem that way.

Perhaps to show how well he understood, he wrote "The Season of Divorce," about a woman named Ethel—gifted in her own right— whose life is "confined" to housewifery by her husband's modest salary. For a while she hangs her college diploma over the kitchen sink as a pathetic joke ("I don't know where the diploma is now," the husband-narrator remarks), and is tempted by the passionate appreciation of a man named Trencher, who sends roses on her birthday while her husband forgets the occasion entirely. One of the woman's outbursts stands as a rather remarkable apologia given the times—all the more so in comparison with Cheever's later, decidedly less compassionate portraits of talented, unfulfilled women: "In Grenoble," Ethel says, "I wrote a long paper on Charles Stuart in French. A professor at the University of Chicago wrote me a letter. I couldn't read a French newspaper without a dictionary today, I don't have the time to follow any newspaper, and I am ashamed of my incompetence, ashamed of the way I look. Oh, I guess I love you, I do love the children, but I love myself, I love my life, it has some value and some promise for me and

Trencher's roses make me feel that I'm losing this, that I'm losing my self-respect. . . ."

Such a dark view of the distaff middle class was galling to Harold Ross, who preferred to give his readers (chiefly female) a little uplift in their fiction. Later Cheever would claim that Ross—while picking his nose and scratching himself and jumping about in his chair—had once admonished him, "Goddammit, Cheever, why do you write these fucking gloomy goddamn stories? . . . But I have to buy them. I don't know why." He might have bought them, but he sometimes hesitated to print them, letting almost two years pass before he published a grindingly lugubrious story titled "The Pot of Gold," about a nice young couple named Whittemore who endure a life of constant disappointment while clinging to the lower rungs of white-collar Manhattan. A dream of success sustains them, coloring their dreary lives with a wan golden light that Cheever paints into the story with deft, incidental strokes, as when Laura Whittemore chats with another deprived wife amid "the sorry and touching countryside of Central Park": "Vaguely, boastfully, the two women discussed the irons their men had in the fire. They sat together with their children through the sooty twilights, when the city to the south burns like a Bessemer furnace, and the air smells of coal, and the wet boulders shine like slag, and the Park itself seems like a strip of woods at the edge of a coal town." All the Whittemores' schemes come to nothing in the end, and the light seems to fade as they find themselves poor as ever and middle-aged to boot. Left at that, the story would rank with Chekhov at his most laughably desolate; but perhaps as a sop to Ross (as well as an oblique tribute to his wife's forbearance), Cheever tacked on a sappy ending in which Ralph Whittemore realizes that the gold he sought was always there for the taking: "Desire for [his wife] delighted and confused him. Here it was, here it all was, and the shine of the gold seemed to him then to be all around her arms."

"The Pot of Gold" and "The Season of Divorce" were included, respectively, in the 1951 O. Henry Award *Prize Stories* and *Best American Short Stories*, though Cheever gloomily concluded that "Pot of Gold," at least, was "not a first-rate story": "It is deeply felt but it is morbid," he wrote in his journal. "It is a morbid story with a sentimental resolution. It was a step in the right direction, perhaps, but don't do this again."

.   .   .

As THE NEW YORKER prepared to celebrate its twenty-fifth anniversary with a famous gala at the Ritz, Cheever took stock of his affairs. Both his lack of money and certain limitations in his work were linked, undoubtedly, to his dependence on the magazine, and he wondered how he might improve as a writer and yet continue to support his family. His friend Irwin Shaw was now cheerfully scribbling left-handed screenplays for Sam Goldwyn—while retaining (for the time being) his reputation as a serious writer—and for Cheever it was exquisite agony to hear Shaw complain, blithely over lunch, about how much money he'd have to make *this* year in order to pay taxes on his earnings from *last* year, and so on.* Cheever, meanwhile, was momentarily pleased that he'd sold a recent story and could almost afford to take his family to Martha's Vineyard for the summer; also, his friend Lennie Field had agreed to loan him a car. But of course such contentment was fleeting: "I am tired of borrowing and hedging and living like a bum," he complained in his journal, adding that he again felt like killing himself ("I have so little to pass on to my children"). One would scarcely have guessed that he had only to accept money from his wife, who—on the death of her Watson grandmother in the late forties—had begun to receive a modest inheritance every quarter. Only in moments of the most hopeless penury, though, would Cheever stoop to borrowing from her ("It wasn't *genteel*," she explained), and for many years, at least, he'd insist on covering household expenses out of his own pocket. Indeed, as a decent if tenuous member of the middle class, he was even loath to accept the hospitality of a grateful Mrs. Ames, who urged him to return to Yaddo after a long absence. "I cannot, in good conscience, accept an invitation," he wrote her, "knowing that a younger and a needier man would benefit . . . more than I." Instead he advised her to invite his old friends Pete and Elizabeth Collins (the latter an abstract artist), whom he knew to be poor but industrious.

"Tonight Ross is giving a party for seven hundred people to celebrate the twenty-fifth anniversary of the magazine and I am going to wear a tuxedo which I bought in a second-hand clothing store on East

---

*At the time Cheever was fascinated and appalled by Shaw's flair for being a "money player." As Newhouse pointed out, Shaw lived in the "real world" of "cause and effect" that dictated the three-act plots of movies and radio serials and best sellers; Cheever, however, "operated in a fantasy world" that was conducive to a more subtle artistic (and social) approach. "Put it this way," said Michael Bessie, Cheever's future publisher. "What Irwin couldn't have known about John was quite a lot, whereas I don't think there was much about Irwin that John couldn't easily know."

End Avenue," Cheever wrote Herbst on March 18, 1950. "I got some studs at Woolworths and a ready-tied black tie in a store in Times Square. We are going with Hazel Werner who is going to wear a night-gown and with Morrie who is also wearing a second-hand dinner jacket and I guess the city will probably never see such a concentration of hair-dye, hand-me-downs, and five and ten cent store jewelry." The lavish bash was a landmark event for New York's literati, who packed the Ritz grand ballroom and spilled into the Oval Room amid a constant din of music and laughter and tinkling glasses. Cheever got very drunk and "skipped around the dance floor" until half past three, when he piled into a taxi with Shaw and others to pay a visit to Shaw's bedridden wife—or so Cheever dimly remembered the next day, amid a "profound physical and spiritual depression": "A lot of people complimented me on my stories," he noted a little doubtfully, "and I hope that I can at least take from this some confident feeling that people are interested in seriousness and that I have been able to preserve in spite of the pages of The New Yorker, many of my own characteristics."

The magazine imposed constraints on fiction writers—of length, subject matter, and language—that, Cheever thought, had reduced his work to a "contemptible smallness"; the best solution was to finish his novel, but of course that wasn't panning out and the failure was affecting his everyday mood as well as that of his "gloomy goddamn stories," as Ross would have it. And yet Cheever knew his work was improving and would continue to improve if only he could "achieve some equilibrium between writing and living"—less drinking, more discipline, and the rest would follow: "I must bring to my work, and it must give to me, the legitimate sense of well-being that I enjoy when the weather is good and I have had plenty of sleep." The place where he felt best was Treetops—what with "the smell of wood smoke and the noise of the wind," which almost erased his "dread of falling, of loneliness and disgrace"—though he'd rarely been able to work there, or quite do justice to its peculiar atmosphere in his fiction. Finally, though, after four evocative postwar summers, he was able to write a long, ambitious story, "The Day the Pig Fell into the Well," about a Winternitz-like family called the Nudds who gather each year at their house in the mountains and tell stories, or rather parts of the same story.

Cheever completed a draft in late 1949 and continued to revise for a few months; because of the length, however (as well as complexity and mature themes, perhaps), the story would not appear in *The New Yorker* until 1954. Returning galleys at last, Cheever felt obliged to explain a few points to Maxwell, who was apt to enforce a certain Rossian literality: "It is supposed to operate something like a rondo and I don't think the chronology can be too exact. . . . The story is intentionally sketchy—Hartley is supposed to be a good man without my saying so. . . . [T]he story asks a lot from the reader and repays him with the noise of the wind up the chimney." As in Cheever's early, elliptical finger exercises—his rather simplistic Chekhov pastiches—much of the story's meaning is suggested by understatement; but in terms of sheer technical mastery, and depth of feeling, the story's relation to those apprentice efforts is that of, say, *The Cherry Orchard* to the jocular newspaper sketches of Chekhov's youth. "Remember the day the pig fell into the well?" the Nudds are forever asking each other, and so the family members take up their familiar parts of "this chronicle of small disasters"—about a summer day long ago when the pig drowned and Mr. Nudd had to swim ashore with Aunt Martha because their boat sank and young Esther got thin and had her first affair with a poor neighbor and so forth. As the past is examined, piece by piece, the sadness of the present transpires "softly, softly," rather like the insidious voice of Cheever's enormous radio. There is an accumulation of parenthetical asides—bits of exposition that become darker and darker: "Mr. Nudd's part in the narration was restrained (Aunt Martha was dead)"; "But their memories of the war were less lasting than most memories, and, except for Hartley's death (Hartley had drowned in the Pacific), it was easily forgotten." So the story proceeds, quite like a rondo, circling back to the past, the pig, while the present unfurls "like magicians' colored scarves"—novelist Anne Tyler's apt phrase for the marvelous legerdemain of Cheever's best work. Finally, the entire span of the Nudds' lives is evoked and somehow sadly transcended all at once: "There had been the boom, the crash, the depression, the recession, the malaise of imminent war, the war itself, the boom, the inflation, the recession, the slump, and now there was the malaise again, but none of this had changed a stone or a leaf in the view [Mrs. Nudd] saw from her porch." Thinking it over, she realizes in a single sinking moment that "none of them had done well"—and rouses herself by asking the others if they remember the day the pig fell into the well. "It had begun to blow outside," the story ends, "and the house creaked gently, like a hull when the wind takes up the sail. The room with the people in it looked enduring and secure, although in the morning they would all be gone."

Rightly pleased with this magnificent story,* Cheever showed it in typescript to his long-suffering Random House editor, Linscott, who pronounced it "the best you have ever written" (while wondering, perhaps, how Cheever could compress the material for four or five novels into twenty-odd pages and yet not be able to complete a novel per se). With that time-consuming triumph behind him, Cheever hoped to find a little peace and quiet that summer (1950) so he could more briskly "pry a saleable story out of [his] head." He drove to Treetops in Lennie Field's expensive-looking Packard, which belied his overdrawn bank account and helped him cash (and bounce) a twenty-five-dollar check at the local grocery store. As for Treetops, he had even less luck working there than usual—the families were as combative as ever— though he thought he might make some fictional use of the cook that summer, "a crazy Pole": "At night when the dishes are done she butters a loaf of bread and goes out to feed the chipmunks, porcupines, birds, and fishes. 'Eat, eat, eat,' she shouts at them." Cheever stayed a month, wrote nothing of merit, and proceeded en famille to a nice rented house at Seven Gates Farm on Martha's Vineyard—more than he could afford, of course, but working conditions now struck him as "perfect": "This house is remote and quiet and fish is plentiful and cheap," he wrote Lobrano. "Some kind neighbors take Mary and the children to the beach in the mornings and don't return them until one or two. Then at six I take them to the beach again where we usually cook supper."

With all the time and quiet and scenery he could possibly desire, Cheever remained morose and unproductive. "It's been sort of a fuckedup summer," he wrote Herbst. The cliffs of Gay Head were stunning, the beaches ditto, but he couldn't help thinking the whole thing was about to "sink into the ocean." Moreover, he looked askance at "the hosts of people with white shoes" who gathered on the island every year for softball and cocktail parties and dances; Cheever found them nice enough but scorned their frivolity and felt envious, as always, toward their rather too vivid gentility. "At the West Tisbury fair I felt lost," he wrote in his journal.

---

*Despite (as he wrote in his journal) his wife's finding it "pessimistic and morbid"— piqued, no doubt, by this portrait of wistful losers who bear at least a passing resemblance to her own family.

It was last summer's feeling of being a stranger in a closely integrated community. . . . The dance at West Chop was a charming
archaism; the old people sitting around the wall, musical chairs, the
pretty girls. I walked on South Beach and tore my hair. Why? The
sea was blue. . . . West Chop does not really interest me. It proves
how insular and foolish a social group can become when they are
able to isolate themselves, how this transparent illusion of superi-
ority sustains them. It was close to high-comedy, the husbands and
wives falling in love with one another; men and women of forty
stealing kisses in the backs of cars.

On his desk was the beginning of a gloomy story titled "The
Backgammon Game." Cheever could hardly bear to look at it. He
wanted to write something "funny, beautiful, light," but a constant
"undertow of depression" dragged him away from any such effort—
hollow at any rate—and back to the beach, alone, pacing, worrying
about his debts, marriage, everything. "After lunch I walked along the
beach; low tide, gold beards on the rock. . . . I kept thinking: but it is
only a summer day, these are only debts . . . it is only a summer day." At
length, he returned ("sadly") to where family and friends had finished a
picnic, and saw his wife swimming with a neighbor named Florrie:
"Mary's head was light. Florrie's head was black. . . . After a little while
they walked out of the waves. They were both naked. The sight filled
me with great joy."

This was a start, but only a start. Back in Manhattan by mid-
October, the first order of business was imparting the usual bad news
to Linscott: "This is a report on the long-delayed novel and it isn't
good. Of the work I did since Christmas I sold only one story and I had
to work on articles and stories all summer. It was an anxious summer
and one result of this was that I wrote in a peculiar mixture of sentimentality and laconism that has meant throwing away three of the five
stories I completed." Pausing perhaps to consider this, Cheever concluded with an almost audible sigh: "It is still my principle aim in life to
write novels . . ." That settled, he returned to "The Backgammon
Game" and realized, reading it over, that, "like some kinds of wine, it
had not traveled. It was bad." The story was about a family named
Pommeroy who play backgammon for "life and death" stakes: one
brother wins the other brother's wife; Mrs. Pommeroy loses rights to
her children, and so on.

Cheever put the manuscript aside and looked over his journal notes from that summer—perhaps he'd find something cheering there—but no: all was sadness and bitter mockery. The way his neighbors in West Chop had carried on at the yacht-club dance—recounting old football triumphs and larky bonfires and such—was simply pathetic, or so he'd seen fit to perceive it ("The lights and passions of youth have gone down and having been replaced with no other lights and passions they are like people who have suffered a loss of faith"); indeed, such childishness was a universal failing in this country and class ("how the nation like a miserable adult, turns back to the supposed innocence of its early life"). The only whisper of happiness in the whole petulant account was the line about his wife and Florrie walking out of the sea. "I had spent the summer in excellent company and in a landscape that I love," he later wrote, describing the genesis of one of his greatest stories, "but there was no hint of this in the journal I had kept." Cheever reflected that the worst side of his nature—the dour, conscience-haunted Yankee who considered all forms of earthly pleasure "merely the crudest deceptions"—was getting the better of him and his work, and he felt a sudden impulse to exorcise this dreary spirit. Thus he contrived the image of "a despicable brother"—himself, in effect—and wrote the words "Goodbye, My Brother."

The story that followed was even longer than his intricate narrative about the Nudd family, but this time he finished in a joyous, week-long burst of inspiration ("I think it is myself, writing with the fewest obstructions"). Though Cheever almost never wrote in the first person—wary of lapsing into garrulous imprecision—he sensed a measure of "ambiguity in [his] indignation" and so required a slightly unreliable narrator, a soi-disant "good brother," to describe the "despicable brother," Lawrence. At the outset this narrator announces, a little defensively, that he is a teacher: "I am past the age where I expect to be made headmaster . . . but I respect the work." As for Lawrence, he is a bleak prig who has been something of a misfit in his own family ever since childhood, when he was dubbed "Tifty the Croaker" and "Little Jesus." Still, the Pommeroys "are a family that has always been very close in spirit," and when Lawrence pays a rare visit to their summer home at Laud's Head, everyone is eager to make amends. Lawrence, however, is unchanged, and loses no time alienating himself. "Is that the one she's sleeping with now?" he says of his sister Diana's latest affair, and also points out that the family house "will be in the sea in five years": "The sea wall is badly cracked. . . . You had it repaired four years ago, and it cost eight thousand dollars. You can't do that every four years." Such remarks are obnoxious, but not inaccurate: arguably the sister *is* "a foolish and a promiscuous woman," and probably it *is* folly to keep wasting good money for a sea wall that will only continue to crack, and certainly (apropos of another mean remark) the mother *does* drink too much.

That said, most of Lawrence's opinions are only *attributed* to him by the narrator, who distorts his brother's pessimism in order to make it seem more fatuous and nasty than it is. When, for example, Lawrence watches the family play backgammon for money, the narrator *imagines* the man's absurd indictment of them all, as follows: "*I may be wrong, of course* [my italics], but I think that Lawrence felt that in watching our backgammon he was observing the progress of a mordant tragedy in which the money we won and lost served as a symbol for more vital forfeits." This, of course, is an idea lifted from Cheever's own abortively portentous story, "The Backgammon Game"; the fact is, Lawrence's only explicit comment gives little hint of such dark musings: "I should think you'd go crazy . . . cooped up with one another like this, night after night." Likewise when the narrator imagines Lawrence's cynical view of a yacht-club party with a "come as you wish you were" theme (which results in the men dressing mostly as football players and the women as brides), Cheever paraphrases his own caustic remarks in the journal: "And I knew that Lawrence was looking bleakly at the party . . . as if in wanting to be brides and football players we exposed the fact that, the light of youth having been put out in us, we had been unable to find other lights to go by and, destitute of faith and principle, had become foolish and sad." Again, whatever the relative truth of this observation, the narrator is actually projecting on Lawrence his *own* suspicion that he and the others have "become foolish and sad." To be sure, Lawrence is a "gloomy son of a bitch" (as the narrator calls him), but ultimately he's little more than an abstraction— an embodied point of view that is "elegiac and bigoted and narrow" and that the narrator, confronting the disappointment of his own life, wants desperately to reject. The famous last paragraph, then, is a moving affirmation that yet seems to protest a little too much:

Oh, what can you do with a man like that? What can you do? How can you dissuade his eye in a crowd from seeking out the cheek with acne, the infirm hand; how can you teach him to respond to the inestimable greatness of the race, the harsh surface beauty of life; how can you put his finger for him on the obdurate truths before which fear and horror are powerless? The sea that morning was iridescent and dark. My wife and my sister were swimming—Diana and Helen—and I saw their uncovered heads, black and gold in the dark water. I saw them come out and I saw that they were naked, unshy, beautiful, and full of grace, and I watched the naked women walk out of the sea.

Malcolm Cowley pointed out to Cheever that the story's irony is so extensive that it is "troublingly uncertain" what the author means to say. Cheever replied: "The brother story, in its bare outline, was the story of one man. There was no brother; there was no Lawrence." In other words, it was to be the story of one man struggling with his demons— a struggle that would never quite be resolved in Cheever's life or work, such that his use of irony would, if anything, become even *more* elaborate, the better to have it both ways, light and dark (or neither). As for the ultimate "meaning" of "Goodbye, My Brother," Cheever was determinedly subtle: "I had hoped that the women—dark head and gold— coming out of the sea, would clear away any ambiguity," he explained to Cowley with characteristic diffidence. "I seem to have failed."

"GOODBYE, MY BROTHER" was promptly accepted by *The New Yorker*, though almost a year would pass before it appeared in the magazine, and Cheever was rather surprised it was accepted at all. He wanted to go on writing stories of greater length and complexity, to take a break from the soul-killing grind of writing "saleable" stories or, for that matter, his recalcitrant novel ("a form with which I seem unable to cope"). Explaining his decision to apply for a Guggenheim, he remarked, "I would like to write some stories that would not be inhibited in their length by the pages of a magazine nor in their content by the fact that the magazine might, after all, fall into the hands of a child." Though "Goodbye, My Brother" and "The Day the Pig Fell into the Well" existed only in typescript at the time, he chose to submit them (with "Torch Song") as samples of his best work, while writing "None"—again and again—in reply to such prompts as "College," "Degrees," "Accomplishments," and "Positions Held." "I'm not sanguine about getting a fellowship," he told Cowley, who'd written an urgent recommendation in his behalf ("He really should have a chance to develop his talent, which is now at a turning point"), along with Wolcott Gibbs ("one of the four or five ablest and most original [*New Yorker*] contributors"), S. J. Perelman ("I cannot think of anyone who has as exact and meticulous a knowledge of middle-class behavior and psychology"), and others. When Cheever was informed a few months later of his three-thousand-dollar fellowship, nobody was more surprised than he.

It came at a good time, since relations with Lobrano had soured over the past couple of years—beginning with that string of rejections after the failure of *Town House*, whereupon Cheever noted that his "long love affair with The New Yorker seems like an unhappy marriage, repaired now and then with a carnal exchange, a check." Matters took a turn for the worse when Lobrano responded unenthusiastically to "The Bus to St. James's," the only decent piece of writing Cheever had managed that summer on Martha's Vineyard. Lobrano had advised him to cut the story, and when that didn't work he asked to see the deleted scenes again so that he, Lobrano, could perhaps cobble together something salable. Cheever realized the suggestion was made in "pure kindness and helpfulness," but couldn't help feeling insulted: "I do resent the fact that my stories, imperfect as they are, must undergo so much manipulation," he wrote in his journal, "from people who are paid much more than I for tampering with my fiction." Lobrano had stumbled, then, while walking the tremulous wire between being a friend and being editor and banker, and may himself have been feeling a little put out two months later, when he took Cheever to lunch after accepting "Goodbye, My Brother" and proceeded to speak at length about the sale (for thirty-five thousand dollars) of a recent Newhouse story to the movies.* "I listened patiently to these triumphs," Cheever glumly reflected, "thinking that it is difficult to be petulant when you don't have a buck to get your hair cut . . ." But perhaps Cheever did allow himself a hint of petulance, because Lobrano promptly turned him back over to William Maxwell. What would prove a happier association—at least for the next ten years or so—began with Maxwell's editing "Goodbye, My Brother," which forever remained his favorite Cheever story ("John seemed to have a joyful knowledge that no one else had").

Cheever, with some misgivings, also admired Maxwell's highly autobiographical fiction—especially his 1945 novel, *The Folded Leaf,*

**I Want You, with a screenplay by Irwin Shaw, no less.

which Cheever vividly remembered reading for the first time in a Hollywood hotel room (presumably while taking a break from George Eliot's oeuvre). His admiration for that particular novel is worth considering. "The whole of my youth is in it," Maxwell once observed. Like at least two of his other novels, it touches on the sudden death of his mother when he was ten years old, as well as the suicide attempt that eventually followed. It's also regarded as one of the first serious novels in American literature about an overtly (more or less) homoerotic male friendship. "Bill never made a secret of the fact that he'd had a brief homosexual life before [his marriage]," said Shirley Hazzard. "He felt he was so sensitive he could never have friends or a normal life." A few years after his suicide attempt, Maxwell began an intensive seven-year course of therapy with the controversial Theodor Reik, a disciple of Freud who did much to popularize psychoanalysis in the United States with such books as *Listening with the Third Ear* and *Masochism in Modern Man*. Reik also treated Cheever's old Signal Corps colleague Arthur Laurents, who was struck by Reik's tendency to mention, somewhat luridly, the progress of another patient—Maxwell—perhaps because Laurents and Maxwell were seeking help for much the same problem. Laurents would presently decide Reik was a "charlatan," though Maxwell was nothing but grateful to the man ("He gave me a life"), and seems to have discussed the matter up to a point with Cheever, who remarked on his friend's "courage and perseverance": "I think of Bill who did penance for seven years with a screwy hungarian [Austrian] in order to conquer his partiality to death. And conquer it, he did." Shortly after finishing *The Folded Leaf*, Maxwell interviewed a beautiful young woman, Emily Noyes, for the job of poetry editor at *The New Yorker*; she wasn't hired, but the two were soon married and by all accounts were ecstatically happy with each other the rest of their lives.

Apart from his work as a writer and editor, Maxwell was legendary for his kindness, his vast empathy, a warmth he conveyed despite an ironclad sense of decorum. To some he gave the appearance of a man who was very carefully holding himself together. Laurents met him for lunch, at Reik's insistence, and naturally expected a discussion of their common problem (since, after all, Reik had mentioned a number of intimate details about Maxwell's sex life)—but the subject never came up: "We talked about writing," Laurents recalled. "He was very reticent." Not that he was apt to deny anything—he was too honorable for that. Once, in a gathering, he was approached by a man who rudely referred to a certain disreputable character from their mutual past. Gently but firmly, Maxwell replied—ending the exchange—that such matters were "very remote from [his] life now." For his part, Cheever thought his friend "terribly fastidious," and liked to tell of the time Maxwell had suddenly phoned to say he was coming to tea: "Mary went wild and cleaned, waxed, arranged flowers, etc. When he arrived everything seemed in order. Mary poured the tea. The scene was a triumph of decorum until Harmon, an enormous cat, entered the room, carrying a dead goldfish. It seemed to be our relationship in a nutshell."

Whether Maxwell was aware of Cheever's predilections is hard to say, though Cheever certainly knew about Maxwell and sometimes longed to air the matter between them, while worrying, too, over the "devastating turn" their friendship might take as a result. Reunited as writer and editor after Lobrano's defection, the two met for lunch at the Century Club; afterward Cheever wrote: "Here is an old friend, a boy to play with, an answer to the lonelyness that I still seem to carry from childhood and upon which I do not choose to act. And here is a man who is lonelier than I will ever be. He talked about childhood dancing school, his step-mother, this and that—rather in the end like a woman—and I talked about my parents, my brother, and held through it all the affectations of gentility. I avoided the looming truths."

Cheever would always esteem Maxwell's literary advice, and was properly grateful for the man's support in almost every department of life; this created a vague intimacy between them that, for various reasons, didn't quite translate into intimate words or acts—though with Maxwell, again, Cheever longed to find "some way of expressing our indignation at the fix we have got ourselves into, some reassuring nostalgia for what appears to be a lost and natural way of life." In the end, though, he was invariably disappointed with the actual fact of Maxwell and his "terribly fastidious" manner: as he often noted, he loved the man and always looked forward to seeing him, but he tended to feel "bored stiff" in his company.

TOWARD THE END of 1950, Cheever's apartment building changed ownership and would soon be turned into a cooperative. Present tenants were given eight months to move, which was imminent in the Cheevers' case anyway: their growing children were sharing a tiny bedroom and needed more space. Like so many of the postwar middle class, Cheever considered moving to the suburbs—better schools, cheaper housing, fresh air—though he had some typical misgivings: "My God, the suburbs!" he later wrote. "They encircled the city's boundaries like enemy territory and we thought of them as a loss of privacy, a cesspool of conformity and a life of indescribable dreariness in some split-level village where the place name appeared in the *New York Times* only when some bored housewife blew off her head with a shotgun." Be that as it may, his friend and fellow *New Yorker* writer E. J. ("Jack") Kahn, Jr., would soon be vacating his rented house in Westchester County, and invited Cheever to take his place. For a while the search continued for a larger but affordable apartment in the city, until Cheever neglected to pay his electric bill and the lights went out; he spent the night sitting in the dark, solemnly pondering his poverty. The next day he paid the bill and took a train to Westchester, where he arranged to rent the house ("with a sickly shade tree") in Scarborough-on-Hudson.

By far the most memorable farewell party was held at the Riverview Terrace apartment of their friend Margot Morrow. Cheever, tipsily complacent, was sitting on a first-story window ledge with his legs dangling outside when, suddenly, he went hurling through space and just missed being impaled on an iron-spiked fence. Ten years later, in an essay for *Esquire,* Cheever claimed to have jumped "in an exuberance of regret," but actually he went to his grave believing he'd been pushed by his great friend and *New Yorker* editor. Maxwell denied it: "I was standing on the sidewalk [at the time], talking to some of the guests," he said, then cited the testimony of a fellow guest, Jack Huber, who claimed a man from Minneapolis had done the pushing. Jack and this man "were standing at the window, and Mary Cheever joined them, and, indicating John, and in a joking manner, said 'What a poseur! Why doesn't somebody give him a push.' . . . None of them could see the spiked fence."

To Cheever, however, Maxwell's urge to push him was part of a deep-seated (and potentially deadly) ambivalence. "There's this chap named Marples who keeps saying that he loves me and then he tries to kill me," Cheever wrote in his journal, refining the episode for fictional use.* "He's a very quiet man, terribly sensitive, but he's a murderer." Maxwell later told the story for laughs, though he sensed Cheever was rather serious in his suspicions. "There was a paranoid side to him," he observed. "He was paranoid."

---

*Finally incorporated in *Falconer* as one of several attempts at fratricide on the part of Farragut's egregious brother.

CHAPTER FOURTEEN

{ 1951–1952 }

THE CHEEVERS MOVED to "the chicken house in Scarborough" on May 28, 1951, and Cheever predicted—with gloomy accuracy—that they'd live there for at least ten years. The house was located in a small corner of a vast estate, Beechwood, purchased in 1906 by the National City Bank tycoon Frank A. Vanderlip, who'd essentially invented the surrounding town of Scarborough. The gatehouse, Beechtwig, had been built as a machine shop and later converted to a cottage, occupied in 1939 by Vanderlip's daughter Virginia ("Zinny"), shortly after her marriage to Dudley Schoales*; the Cheevers, however, paid their monthly rent of $150 (sans utilities) to another daughter, Charlotte, who'd inherited the place "as a sort of booby prize" when her "marriage went blooey," as Cheever put it. Charlotte had added two upstairs bedrooms and a bath; downstairs were another two bedrooms, one of which was taken by the seven-year-old Susan and the other used as Cheever's workroom. Perhaps the best feature was a spacious living room (spacious because it had once housed two large drop-forges), whose walls would occasionally tremble and crack from the perpetual rumble of traffic on Route 9, the Albany Post Road, separated from the house by a low brick wall.

Cheever felt a little disoriented at first—broke and lonely ("wanting someone, anyone to come and drink my martinis")—but was heartened as always by the idea of living amid luxury, however para-

---

*This after the place had been hastily vacated by the novelist Richard Yates (age thirteen) and family, since Yates's impecunious sculptor-mother, Dookie, had neglected to pay rent for several months. The Beechwood estate is located near a street named Revolutionary Road—also the title of Yates's first and most famous novel.

doxically. From his front door he could look out on the lush "manorial lawns" leading to a large swimming pool that was "curbed with Italian marble, luscent [sic] and shining like loaves of fine sugar." He also liked the fact that he no longer had to bury himself in a basement storage room during working hours. Mary, too, was pleased by all the extra space, and promptly bought a used concert grand ("full of cigaret butts and moths") to grace the living room; lest it be strictly ornamental, Cheever took piano lessons from one Lavena MacClure, who in time would teach him to grope his way through some of the easier Chopin preludes.

There was a certain amount of piano playing and other cultural diversions in the amorphous Vanderlip mansion up the hill, where respectable neighbors and their children were invited for dinner and dances in the William Welles Bosworth ballroom. Frank Vanderlip's widow, Narcissa, was a formidable Swedenborgian who'd assumed a matriarchal role in the community, seeing to it that Susan and her friends (who called the woman "Monie") learned the forks, as well as how to rumba and fox-trot and waltz. Toward adults Mrs. Vanderlip tended to be somewhat more austere: a former suffragette who used to ride around in a chauffeur-driven Pierce Arrow, children in tow, berating the citizenry (*"If I can raise six kids and still stand up for women's rights, why can't you?"*), she was not one to suffer fools. Cheever wrote that "she played the meanest game of chopanose [he] ever saw," affecting to be deaf when convenient and treating unwanted guests like servants. Cheever, of course, was largely exempt from such bullying, adept as ever at ingratiating himself with grandes dames. With both fondness and writerly curiosity, he made a point of attending the woman's genteel gatherings and observing the local personages. As he wrote Eleanor Clark:

> Mrs. Vanderlip passed tea and sherry to celebrate the retirement of the local station master; a nice old man with the neck and head of a turtle. It was rainy outside and dark in the library where the rector, the banker, the church organist, the postmaster and his wife, the broker, the lawyer and the doctor raised their sherry glasses in the gloom and shouted: "Happy days, Kedney!" When the station master spoke his voice was very clear. "I didn't like it when I first come here," he said. "I said to my wife, I can't stand that bunch. I stuck it out for forty years so I guess I must have liked it." Applause, etc.

Before long Cheever had all the social life he could handle, as his friend Jack Kahn was the hub of a raucous (and not especially literary) group of neighbors. Cheever remarked to Herbst that these were "kind and gentle people," if a little *too* kind and gentle ("What I'd like is a good quarrel"); Kahn, however, remembered Cheever as "the most gentlemanly" of them all, at least in the early days. He was nice about chatting up bores and at least outwardly a good-natured loser at backgammon—paying up on the spot (as Kahn insisted) and totting the result on a score sheet the two maintained in an old copy of *A Bell for Adano*.

Through Kahn he met his first great friends in the area, Philip and Mimi Boyer, who lived in a large, ramshackle house in nearby Croton. The Boyers' *echt* Waspiness was enough to fill even Cheever's striving heart: Philip was a tall, hard-drinking Bostonian who'd attended both Groton and Harvard; he raised retrievers, played tennis, and drove Cheever to the Harvard-Yale game in a vintage Plymouth named Apple Pan Dowdy. Putatively a public-relations man, he was a great reader and friend of various *New Yorker* writers—St. Clair McKelway, Maeve Brennan, Geoffrey Hellman—but thought Cheever the most talented by far. Certainly the Boyers helped dispel any lingering notion on Cheever's part that his suburban neighbors would all be dull. Mimi Boyer was from old money—her father had been head of the Morgan Bank in Paris, where she'd grown up between the wars—and comported herself like something "out of Edward Gorey," as Federico put it. "I dress like this," she'd say, indicating the rags she wore in layers (old bath towels, pajamas, etc.), "because my mother is one of the best-dressed women in the world." In constant rebellion against her upbringing, and with the doting cooperation of her husband, she gave dogs, birds, and other beasts the run of her house until everything was covered in hair and feathers—not that one was apt to notice while in the presence of the woman herself, whose layered style of dress was due in part to the chills she suffered as a lifelong anorexic. "She has a discerning and a sensitive intelligence but she is a woman so wasted, so frail that she seems pitiable," Cheever mused. "She has gotten very eccentric in her middle age, wears several dresses, one on top of the other, serves her guests dog food by candlelight and wears carpet slippers to the theatre."

Mimi Boyer's family had a compound on Whiskey Island in the St. Lawrence, where Cheever would sometimes visit a few days in the summer. Here on this private island, with a view of Canada on one side and New York on the other, was a style of living to which Cheever could easily become accustomed. "I don't think the Kaiser will declare war, do you?" he'd suavely remark, reclining in the stern of an old mahogany launch, *The Wild Goose*, which ferried guests between Whiskey and Clayton, New York. Mostly Cheever chose to relax by himself on the island, away from the hateful sound of tennis balls, in an old Swiss chalet that was said to be haunted—said by Cheever, that is, who was reputedly able to describe certain of Mimi's bygone family with uncanny accuracy. His main company on the island, though, were not ghosts but dogs—an affable pack of Labradors who complained fearfully each night when rounded up to return to their pen, called Gomorrah. "You ought to call it *Eden*," Cheever suggested, and when they did, the dogs practically clambered over one another (said Cheever) trying to get back in.

Dogs, in fact, were the main thing he had in common with the Boyers. When the latter's black Labrador bitch, Queen Sable of Teatown, gave birth to a litter in 1952, Cheever bought a puppy and named her Cassiopeia, after the mother of Andromeda. For the next sixteen years, Cassie would be his most faithful and beloved companion—a dog whose "fleeting, warm and imperious smile" led Cheever to speculate on her various former lives. "She is rumored to have been a wealthy Jewess who left Leningrad in 1918 for Finland, her underwear stuffed with worthless Provisional Government Bonds," he wrote Tanya Litvinov. "She also claims to have been Chekhov's mistress, the Grand Duchess Anastasia and a Los Angeles prostitute called 'The Black Dahlia.' " At one point, the dog even seemed possessed by the spirit of Cheever's mother—whose heavy necklace looked remarkably like Cassie's tag-laden collar ("John, can't you try to be a little neater?" he thought he heard the dog say, shortly after his mother's death)—and in this incarnation, perhaps, she went on to found the Northern Westchester chapter of Dogs for Goldwater. Meanwhile she faithfully wrote lower-case letters to her "aunt mimi and uncle philip": "it wasn't too safe," she remarked of a family drive to Treetops, "because the old man [Cheever] had been booze-fighting since practically before dawn."

Another dog descended from one of the Boyers' bitches, Minerva, belonged to a man who would arguably become Cheever's closest friend, Arthur Prince Spear. At least weekly the two got together to walk their dogs to the Croton Dam, or skate on the Boyers' pond, or go for a swim, usually followed by martinis and backgammon at ten cents a game. In certain respects the lanky, crew-cut Spear was the kind of upstanding Yankee that elicited a wistful (though not unequivocal) admiration on Cheever's part: "Arthur is a fishing and drinking companion," he wrote Litvinov, "he votes the conservative ticket, goes to church twice on Sundays and is an impacted member of our traditional middle class but I find him excellent company. His wife Stella is the daughter of a Bishop and I won't attempt to describe her beyond saying that she plays the viola."* Whatever his credentials among the Westchester middle class, Spear was no Babbitt. His father and namesake had been a well-known painter of the Boston School, and Spear himself was born in Paris while his father was studying at Académie Julian. Later an art editor for the *World Book*, Spear was forced into comfortable retirement in the mid-fifties (when his company merged with Harcourt, Brace) and spent the rest of his life dabbling in rather arty avocations. In addition to his dutiful organ playing, he wrote books (anonymously) for local historical societies, studied architecture, and spent many assiduous years transcribing old family journals.† And though he was a model of rectitude in his everyday conduct, Spear was hardly averse to a bit of ribald humor and had a "quick eye" (Cheever noticed) "for the rearends of lady bicycle riders." Cheever couldn't help wondering if their easy affinity was too good to be true: "We seem to delight one another and I think—ah—there must be something wrong with this . . . there must be some deep unrequition that we share, we recognize, not one another's excellence, but one another's wounds. But this is baloney. We enjoy one another's company and there is nothing more to be said."

For their hikes to the dam, Spear and Cheever would often bring small bottles of bourbon or Gilbey's gin ("mother's milk") to enjoy while pondering the water, and indeed what all these people had in common, other than dogs, was a terrific fondness for alcohol. Every Saturday at noon, Philip Boyer would arrive at Cheever's house (or

---

*Spear attended services at the Presbyterian church across the street from Beechtwig, though he played organ for the Episcopal church (All Saints) attended by Cheever and Mrs. Spear. And Spear was, in fact, a decided political conservative. While in Moscow in 1964, Cheever took the trouble to send his friend a postcard— "Please don't vote for Goldwater"—to no avail.

†In the fullness of time, Cheever would become *very* bored with Spear's incessant talk about his Yankee progenitors, but at first he was delighted and even used the journals of Spear's grandfather Hezekiah Prince to flesh out bits of maritime lore in *The Wapshot Chronicle*.

vice versa), and the two would spend an hour drinking martinis and talking about dogs, while Mary occupied herself in the kitchen ("No matter what else needed to be done or had been planned for the family, the gin had to be drunk first," she recalled with abiding annoyance). "I cringe to think how much we drank," said Virginia Kahn, whose husband was in the casual habit of throwing up each morning before he fixed his coffee. The nice part was that none of them neglected their children. Boyer liked to bring a daughter or two along for his Saturday "errands," and Cheever taught his son Ben how to measure a drink by placing his little fingers along the side of a glass. One of Ben's early memories, in fact, was the sight of their bibulous neighbor Dudley Schoales crashing down the stairs into the dining room: "It wasn't the fall that made the evening remarkable," said Ben, "but rather the fact that the banker's highly polished shoes left scuff marks up above the handrail—scuff marks which could be seen and admired the next morning."

Usually Dudley was more graceful. A star athlete at Cornell in the twenties, he used to entertain the children by hurdling a sofa without spilling a drop of his cocktail. He and his wife, Zinny, both heroic drinkers, lived in a large renovated barn on the other side of the estate, and the two families saw a lot of each other. Cheever and Dudley were backgammon chums, but otherwise had little to talk about; the son of a Cleveland farmer, Dudley had married into the Vanderlips and become a partner at Morgan Stanley, for which he spent much of his time traveling abroad and philandering. "D[udley] still has the grace of an old athlete but the fine profile and the golden curls are long gone," Cheever wrote in his journal. "He rubs his hairy stomach and boasts of his sexual prowess. He is indebted to Z[inny] for her financial support." Cheever much preferred the wife ("a heavy kindly and intelligent woman"), and felt rather protective toward her; only a decade before, she'd worked with Ralph Ingersoll at the leftist newspaper *PM*, and now she passed her days caring for children, reading, chain-smoking, and drinking. Cheever joined her for the latter activities, taking a pleasant afternoon stroll across the estate to her house— the Cow Barn—where he and Zinny would sit for hours watching the light fade over the Hudson.

The pastoral aspect of Scarborough lent an almost wholesome dimension to the bacchanalia. Whatever the season or relative lack of sobriety, everybody loved playing in the gorgeous outdoors. Even the smallest child could romp around the walled Beechwood estate "without a leash" (as Dr. Winternitz put it), its wilderness an orderly world of slate paths and gardens and sheep, while young and old alike came from around the neighborhood to gather at the pool on sunny days. In autumn the sport was touch football, which Cheever continued to play with an almost antic zeal despite his size and pitiful wing. (In later years—feeling even more ill-used by *The New Yorker*—he'd cast back to a game of touch *chez* Kahn, when he'd found himself on the same team as Ross's successor, the diminutive William Shawn: "[O]n the third play I threw a wobbly pass in his direction. He tried to catch it, slipped and went down, crashing and tinkling like a tray of dishes.") And finally, best of all, winter came and Cheever went skating at the Boyers' or Kahns' or Schoaleses'. Young Joey Kahn was a playmate of Ben's, and often saw Cheever looking tired and unhappy in those years, but while skating at the Kahns' he was "charming, dashing," swishing around the ice with a radiant smile. One snowy day when there wasn't enough ice for a skating party, a happily plastered Cheever raced another guest down the pond's embankment, using aluminum row-boats as toboggans.

Amid all the revelry, though, Cheever never forgot that he was a writer, an observer as well as a participant. The suburbs of the Northeast were still an experiment of sorts—"an improvised way of life," as Cheever liked to say—and he was quite earnestly curious about things: given the cultural vacuum, what sort of traditions would be established by such a diverse group of educated, affluent people? Drinking was a common thread, of course, but there was also a certain amount of semi-sober grappling with civic issues and so forth. In Cheever's community it was almost de rigueur to concern oneself with the fortunes of the Scarborough Country Day School—a tiny progressive school in a perpetual state of fiscal embarrassment—and Cheever was no exception: Not only did he send all three of his children to the school, at one time or another, but he also served as trustee and faithfully attended PTA meetings and the like. For the benefit of old left-wing intellectual friends such as Cowley, Herbst, and Eleanor Clark, he affected to view the proceedings with a lofty, tongue-in-cheek detachment. "There has never been a more conscientious or a more difficult trustee [of the school]," he wrote Cowley.

> While we were arguing at a board meeting last week about the arrangements for a fund-raising dance at the country club (The Apple Blossom Fete) one of the reasons why I like this community

occurred to me. It's a great deal like the Village of Z in the Province of X in a second-rate Russian novel. We have all the stock types; the Governor-general, the Governor's socially ambitious wife, the drunken station-master, the old lady who once entertained the King of Siam, the over-worked doctor, the fortune teller and the idiot.

To Herbst he reported, deploringly, that the country club in question was "a depressing place to which Jews are not admitted," and that a vulgar five-and-ten-cent-store heiress named Mrs. Newberry had proposed that tickets to the Fete be sold at the incredible rate of forty bucks a head, and that people be seated by age, no less: "[I]t made the benefit in The Possessed seem like a picnic," he concluded. "Now the neighborhood is in an uproar. It's wonderful." Even Cheever's evening strolls around the leafy streets were in the nature of fieldwork, as he peered through lighted windows and witnessed, say, "a man in his shirt sleeves rehearsing a business speech to his wife who was knitting." Chatting with such men in person, Cheever discovered that many seemed to consider themselves "the peers of Milton": when Cheever identified himself as a writer, his interlocutors would almost invariably reply that, if only they had the time, they'd have written any number of novels by now.

Whatever their latent literary aspirations, Cheever's neighbors attached very little cachet to being an actual writer, and Cheever had to admit in his journal that he felt "out of water" and was "occasionally cut." What these people knew for certain about writing—based on Cheever's example—was that it didn't pay worth a damn. The neighbors ("in the advertising business to a man") lived in big houses and drove Cadillacs; Cheever drove a secondhand Dodge and lived in a "rented toolshed." And he was lucky to have even that much, as his would-be benefactors were careful to remind him. Every so often a Vanderlip daughter would drop by the toolshed with a well-heeled friend on the lookout for a country pied-à-terre. "Perfect!" the friend would say, oblivious to the fretful little man in the corner, making drinks for his guests. As Susan Cheever wrote, "When the rich people had left . . . my parents would huddle in their wake like refugees. As my father always reminded us, we had nowhere else to go. This sort of observation was often accompanied by a laugh."

Rest assured he was not laughing on the inside. In his early days at

Beechwood, while dressing for a social evening with prosperous neighbors, Cheever often found himself nervously rehearsing the "vital facts" of his father-in-law's career at Yale—realizing as he did so ("like a third person") that he was "still compelled by his father's failure to regale himself with the facts of his father-in-law's success." To some extent Cheever would always be the strange, friendless boy from a disgraced family, whose occasional scorn of the wealthy was in mitigation of an almost unbearable feeling of envy—but also, of course, he was an exceptional man and knew it, and wanted terribly for the world to know it too, and give him the admiration he deserved. "Every indifferent glance," he wrote, after one year in Scarborough, "every back turned to me by chance, every hint of indifference, real or imagined, sinks into my breast like an arrow dipped in poison. I am consumed." Gradually, though, he began to adapt somewhat. Rather than tell stories about his in-laws, Cheever acted all the more as if he himself were to the manner born, whatever his reduced circumstances as a (distinguished) writer. With, for example, a local friend such as Sally Swope—a Bostonian of unimpeachable pedigree—Cheever was almost "stuffy," as she recalled, in observing the dictates of their common (so to speak) background: "My father taught me that a gentleman only wears dark clothes after six o'clock," he'd drawl, then perhaps chuckle at the absurdity of it all. Generally he kept them guessing—was he really such a snob, or only pretending to be?—but in his heart he wanted very badly indeed to be considered "first-class," and fortunately there was more to it than wealth or breeding per se: "You and I will get along without the awkward and the ugly," he wrote in his journal. "They will ring your doorbell; they will bring you roses and pears; they will invite you into steerage. They disguise stupidity with seriousness; they sneer at the wit and grace they miss. . . . So the bores travel through infinity, a little below the waterline. Don't deceive yourself with illusions of equality. There is brilliance and there is stupidity."

DESPITE HIS ASSURANCES to Linscott about the accretion of "durable" novel chapters, Cheever had pretty much scrapped his previous drafts of *The Holly Tree* and started over from scratch in the summer of 1951—which is not to say he was telling a different story. Retitled *The Impostor,* the novel was still "the sad annal of a family that never amounted to anything," and focused mostly on the travails of a

Frederick-like character now called Leander. Though he gave out optimistic reports on his progress, the work went as fitfully as ever and he wondered, again, whether there was something "intrinsically wrong" with his material, which he suspected was not only depressing but dull. He was still convinced, though, that he had to write about his own past and get it over with, out of his system, since he felt a novel required some vital personal issue lest he find himself "writing off the surface."

The Impostor slogged along until, at the beginning of 1952, Cheever's debts outweighed the balance of his Guggenheim money; rather than go back to writing stories, he decided to "complete a rough draft as rapidly as possible and send it off to Bob." What he actually managed, by March, were a few relatively polished chapters—about a hundred pages in all—which he hoped were good enough to persuade Linscott to give him some money to finish or, failing that, at least a vote of confidence. When, however, he wrote Cowley that he thought this latest effort had "gone very well," his old mentor replied with decorous skepticism: "I'd begun to think that the only way you'd work up to a novel was simply by expanding a long story, or by fitting two or three long stories together, but now you sound as if you were writing a novel just—like—that." This would prove a prescient assessment of Cheever's novelistic approach, and meanwhile some such misgiving had occurred to him in regard to *The Impostor*, even as he tried to cheer himself up in his journal: "I think they will like it . . . [a]lthough it may seem to them jerrybuilt, unhealthy and comical. We will see."

At Random House the manuscript was received with "an all around air of profound embarrassment," such that Cheever suspected his editor had given the pages to an assistant "to read among her cats." As the days passed, one after another, Cheever waited for the telephone to ring while writing little more than the odd despondent note in his journal: "[I]f the work I've sent him is bad I have made some grave mistakes. My eyes are wrong, my heart is wrong, and I have been mistaken in listening for all these years to the rain." Writing to Herbst—two weeks had passed by then—he indulged in the usual jaunty stoicism, predicting that when the telephone did ring ("but it will probably never ring") he'd be told something along the lines of "We like some of it" or "We like the way you've handled the material, but we don't like the material."

This, as it turned out, was overly optimistic. Perhaps to force a verdict of whatever sort, Cheever arranged to have lunch with Linscott on a day (March 27) when he was in town anyway to see his dentist. The editor greeted him more sheepishly than ever, spoke of other matters as long as he could manage it, then finally announced that he didn't like Cheever's manuscript. At all. ("He had nothing generous to say about anything," Cheever noted afterward. "He looks at me as if I were a cistern or manhole into which 4,800 dollars had been dropped.") He thought the characters were unbelievable, that the overall negativism was not "timely"—and so on. When Cheever wondered aloud how he'd ever manage to pay back his advance, Linscott replied that Random House had insured his life via the contract, which Cheever took as a sober suggestion that he commit suicide. Thirteen years later (Linscott had been safely dead a year), Cheever related the following sad, comic, and largely apocryphal account of their meeting:

> When I reached the office [for lunch] they said [Linscott] was out. I waited nearly an hour. He presently drifted down the stairs, gave me his left hand and took me to a basement restaurant. He did not mention the book. He said he thought it worthless, that I should give up writing and try to make a living in some other way. As we parted he asked softly: "You wouldn't do anything foolish like kill yourself, would you?" "No," I said. These were the last words we exchanged.

Cheever was not quite suicidal, though he was getting there (again). During a follow-up visit with his dentist, he lay in the chair brooding: "I am like a prisoner who is trying to escape from jail by the wrong route. For all one knows, that door may stand open, although I continue to dig a tunnel with a teaspoon. Oh, I think, if I could only taste a little success." Meanwhile he needed to write more stories, and fast, but his confidence was shot. With much effort, he finally finished a long story that summer ("The Children"), but couldn't think what to write next. For a while he "loafed around the house" and complained that he needed more privacy, so he drove to Erwinna and visited Herbst for a weekend; then he loafed some more, absorbed the scenery on Long Island, and finally spent the rest of the summer at Treetops, where he "subsist[ed] on his mother-in-law's creamed chicken and [made] some delicate notes on the weather." "The Children" was published in the September 6 issue of *The New Yorker*; a year would pass before another of Cheever's stories appeared.

THOUGH CHEEVER CLAIMED he encountered no "deep spiritual impediment" to finishing his novel, the fact remained that he was trying to write an unflattering account of a family very like his own—featuring a domineering, gift-shop-owning mother—while his actual mother was still alive, if not altogether well. At age eighty she was very fat and ill with diabetes, and her face had a mournful way of collapsing when she removed her upper plate at night. She managed to keep busy, though. In recent years she'd closed the gift shop and begun selling hand-painted lampshades out of her house; sometimes when Cheever arrived for a visit he'd find the living room crowded with ladies and have to retreat to the kitchen or backyard, remembering the old days when he used to cool his heels in the back of her shop while she chatted with customers after hours ("I still feel the struggle—faintly—in my balls"). Though he tried hard to be nice to the old woman, her "depraved tastes" mortified him as much as ever—more—now that he had a family and lived in the posh *banlieue* of Scarborough (where, he noted, her "tastes and manners would not succeed"). When she insisted on talking business, Cheever would listen with a faint, flinching grin and imagine that she was deliberately tormenting him, and in front of his family no less. Her reactionary provincialism (as he saw it) pervaded all of New England. When he took Susan on a tour of Concord and other historical sites, a lady custodian at Emerson's house pointed to a portrait of the great transcendentalist and said, "*He* was a man of principle. Today [Senator] McCarthy is our only man of principle." Writing to Eleanor Clark, Cheever claimed to have given this woman a piece of his mind while "Susie blushed and sweated." A few days later, however, writing to Maxwell, he transferred the woman's McCarthyism to his mother: " 'Isn't MaCarthy [sic] wonderful?' old Mrs. Wapshot asked me before her welcoming kiss had dried. . . . It galls her that I am now her sole support and she announced—reflectively—that if I were only dead she would be handsomely provided for by the state. It would be like poor Coverly to notice that every stick of furniture in her house has claw feet."*

---

*The trip to Concord took place in April 1954, around the time Cheever had begun writing the final version of *The Wapshot Chronicle*, early fragments of which he'd

For what it's worth, Susan Cheever did not find her grandmother ("Bammy") the least domineering, nor did she consider the gift shop the "depraved" brainchild of a castrating vulgarian; rather she thought it the natural enterprise of a "craft-y" woman with a taste for pretty things. Indeed, she remembers Bammy as nothing but thoughtful and kind: the woman was always sending lovely little presents she herself had made—an embroidered dress, bits of jewelry—and liked to teach her granddaughter how to do practical feminine things like bake cookies and make a martini ("Just pass the [vermouth] bottle over the gin"). Fred Cheever's oldest daughter, Jane, also has nothing but fond memories of Bammy: "She would take me out to lunch and have my hair done, and then she'd buy me outlandish clothes that my mother would never want me to wear. She hadn't had daughters so I was the first girl she had a chance to play with." Lest the picture seem too idyllic, though, it's worth noting that Jane's younger sister Sarah thought her grandmother "a bit of a bitch," and never forgot the time Bammy asked her to help wrap a package by placing her finger on the bow: "She tied it so tight my finger almost came off." By then relations had soured between Bammy and Iris—Fred's wife—who chafed at her mother-in-law's bossiness and resented her husband's having to "prop up" the old woman (*pace* John's claim that he was her "sole support"). Because of the friction, Bammy's visits to the chalet in Norwell had dwindled to the odd Sunday dinner, though apparently Fred tried to compensate by going alone to visit his mother—or so she'd find ways of suggesting to John. "Would you like a drink?" she'd greet him when he came to Quincy, and if he answered "Yes, please," she'd go to the pantry and return with a sad little smile: "Your brother has drunk all the whiskey."

This was perhaps her decorous New England way ("Feel that refreshing breeze") of letting John know his older brother had a drinking problem, as he did. The brothers had rarely seen each other for the past ten years or so, but after one recent visit John had noted that Fred seemed "like a man in a labyrinth, who thinks that he is unobserved. Fumbling, lost, self-deluded." By then Fred had begun to alarm his family and alienate his neighbors, but at the same time he was still advertising manager at Pepperell and about to be promoted to the head of the Sheet and Blanket Division—a promotion that would

---

shown to Maxwell. Thus he refers to his mother as "Mrs. Wapshot" and himself as "Coverly," as he did habitually in his journal.

bring him to New York and closer to his brilliant little brother. Fred later wrote his daughter Sarah that the move to "an exciting place like New York" was "part of trying to deny [his] middle-class status," and in fact Fred shared and even surpassed his brother's ambivalent snobbery. On the one hand, Fred was tired of small-town bourgeoisie and wanted to be introduced to bright, sophisticated people—writers and artists—and perhaps he expected Joey's help with that. On the other hand, he wasn't a writer or an artist, or even particularly sophisticated; he was a businessman who considered himself an intellectual, too, and wanted credit for both—his success and his intellect—to say nothing of his winning personality ("Where there's a Cheever, there's *color*," he liked to say). In 1952, Fred bought an ivy-bearded Tudor in Briarcliff Manor, about a half-mile from Beechtwig.

John was horrified. He'd spent almost twenty years reinventing himself, adopting his mother-in-law, Polly, "as a phantom parent," ingratiating himself with the nobs of Scarborough—and here, lumbering out of the past, was his drunken Rotarian brother. "Hey, Joey!" Fred would hail him across a room of his peers, the local smart set, and what could John do but wave back and try not to wince? Nor did he overestimate his friends' dismay: this was certainly *not* what they'd expected from a brother of John Cheever. Mimi Boyer found Fred "gross, roughhewn," and actively avoided him, while for his part John urged the whole crowd to keep their distance, for Fred's sake as well as their own. Nor did it help that Iris and Mary Cheever despised each other. Iris sensed that Mary and her Scarborough friends didn't cotton to her and Fred, and she bitterly resented it—why didn't John and Mary *help* them more, and where did they get off anyway? Did *they* live in an elegant Tudor house? Did *they* have a daughter at Milton Academy, about to be presented to Boston Society at the Debutante Cotillion?* Besides, Iris was born in Canada to British parents, and knew plenty about the right way to serve tea and so forth; if anything Mary should defer to *her*.

Iris complained to her husband, but what could he do? He'd also picked up on the condescension and perhaps understood it all too

---

*Cheever had a mildly retarded cousin, Robert Devereaux Young (one of Aunt Liley's children), who was then running a freight elevator at the Sheraton Plaza Hotel—where Jane Cheever made her debut. "Life's little ironies," John's mother remarked.

well—at any rate he became more and more glum and drunken. Even John was startled by how badly things were turning out. "I think of F[red] who seems to me deeply unhappy," he wrote in his journal.

> I can't imagine how they think of me or how they anticipated thinking of me. It may have been little Joey; it may be unacceptable to them that I am not little Joey and this may again be vanity on my part. But why should I go to see him; with one exception, when we were alone, our meetings have been disastrous. He retires from a creative, a progressive human relationship into a drunken corner every time.

Fred may have been understandably chagrined that, far from being accepted on his merits as a successful, intelligent (and colorful) businessman, he was practically treated as a pariah. Thus he was less inclined to be gracious in praising his brother's different kind of success, and never mind that Fred fancied himself a writer, too. "We seem unable to grant one another excellence without losing ground," John wrote, though in fact Fred was delighted as ever by his brother's talent, always exhorting his children to read Uncle John's stories and later his books. And sometimes, when drunk, he'd drop his guard and let his old extravagant affection (and desperation) show: "Don't go, Joey, don't go," he pleaded one night as John was leaving along the bordered flowerbeds that traversed Fred's lawn. John thought his brother seemed almost frightened and wondered "what there was to frighten a man, surrounded by his family."

In time John would know the loneliness of being a bad drunk, estranged from friends and family alike; for now (given Iris's tendency to "complain passionately" about her husband) he might have surmised that what Fred wanted was a drinking companion, a little commiseration, since clearly his own family didn't fill the bill. For the past five years or so, his older children had been watering his gin, hoping to forestall the moment when Fred's joviality turned into something else—something ghastly that Fred himself was less and less apt to remember, such that he seemed almost puzzled when his children tried to remonstrate with him. As his daughter Jane recalled, "His attitude was 'Well, I don't think there's anything wrong. I'm providing for all of you.' " While in Briarcliff, she and her brother, David, finally went to a dry-out facility and spoke with a doctor, who assured them that little could be done until their father wanted to help himself. Fred gave no indication, however, of being anywhere near that point, and meanwhile his obnoxious behavior got worse. According to his brother's journal, he called Mrs. Vanderlip an "old bag" and almost made it a point, at parties, to "single out some woman of a conservative appearance" and ask her if she wanted to fuck him. "You're a lovely old bitch," he remarked to his daughter's future mother-in-law (to whom it was explained that there was nothing necessarily pejorative about the word "bitch" when spoken by Fred; it was interchangeable with "woman").

Sober, Fred was a kind, lovable, funny man (if a bit prickly and arrogant when put on the defensive), and the sober Fred decided that things weren't working out in Westchester. He was not sober, however, when he visited his brother to announce that he and his family were moving to Connecticut after less than two years in Briarcliff. "Going out F[red] gooses M[ary]," John recorded. " 'I hope we'll see more of you,' I whimper, 'now that you're going away.' " Though he felt nothing but relief as he watched Fred shamble off, he couldn't help feeling sorry for the man, and wistful too, as if he'd encountered a former lover "grown old and shabby": "But the fact is that we were once like lovers, that this has left an opening, a weakness in my mind, a lack, a longing, the chagrin of unrequition, a sexual tristesse."

CHAPTER FIFTEEN

{ *1952–1954* }

D URING THAT UNPRODUCTIVE SUMMER of 1952, Cheever tried to get a job writing for television ("because poor little Benjy is dressed in rags"), though he loathed the prospect. "The only thing to come my way so far is a husband & wife show," he wrote Herbst, "in which the humor begins with the fact that their name is Arbuckle. Fuck 'em." A few months later, something a little better came along: an adaptation for CBS of Clarence Day's *Life with Father* and *Life with Mother*, which had been successfully adapted as both a play and movie by Howard Lindsay and Russel Crouse. The producer of the proposed series, Ezra Stone, had been explicitly seeking a *New Yorker* writer who could evoke the memoir's genteel urban milieu, and finally picked Cheever when St. Clair McKelway and Patricia Collinge turned him down.

Cheever was paired with an experienced writer of radio sitcoms, John Whedon ("a quiet man with a twinkle, very like Cheever," Stone remembered), and soon the two finished a pilot script and were summoned to a story conference with the playwrights Lindsay and Crouse, as well as Clarence Day's widow—all of whom (especially Mrs. Day) had a number of "long-winded suggestions" to make on how to improve the script. "I don't recall whether or not [Whedon and I] exchanged notes but we certainly exchanged glances," Cheever wrote thirty years later for *TV Guide*, "and at the end of an hour we stood and said—in unison—that to adapt Clarence Day's memoirs to accommodate eight [sic] vastly dissimilar interpretations of the book was a project we did not wish to undertake. We left, slamming the door. So ended my experience with commercial television." In fact, Cheever and Whedon obligingly revised their script at least six times, but as it happened Stone had other writers working on the pilot, and a different script was eventually used. Cheever was paid a nominal sum for his trouble, and ultimately the project was taken out of Stone's hands and moved to the West Coast, where the show was produced for a couple of mediocre years. As Cheever told Dick Cavett in 1978, the last he heard from CBS was when someone called to insist he return his copies of *Life with Father* and *Life with Mother*.

One consolation (as well as a source of further dread) was that a second collection of stories, *The Enormous Radio*, was about to be published in the spring of 1953. Two years before, Cheever had broached the idea of a new collection with Linscott, who looked over some tear sheets and thought the stories "stand reading and rereading wonderfully well," but wanted to wait until they could be published "in connection with the novel." Cheever (who knew, of course, just how long such a wait might turn out to be) found an English publisher, Victor Gollancz, who was willing to split production costs with Random House. Linscott still resisted, however, and finally Cheever requested permission to cast about "for an improvident publisher." This proved to be Funk & Wagnalls, the encyclopedia people, who were "looking around desperately for the beginnings of a trade list," as Cheever noted.

For *The Enormous Radio*, Cheever selected fourteen strong stories which had been published since the war, at least two of them arguably classics (the title story and "Goodbye, My Brother").* Cheever was adamant about publishing the collection for two main reasons: he wanted to build a reputation outside *The New Yorker* that only a book could bring, and (perhaps more important, given his recent creative setbacks) he wanted to know where he stood as a writer—that is, to find out what serious critics thought of his work, "to get a clearer idea of where [the stories] fail and where they [don't] and to get some measure of the increase in breadth I should aim at." Naturally he expected the worst. Having sent galleys "to old, tender-hearted, soft-brained friends" in hope of getting a few blurbs, he inferred from a brief silence that he was being snubbed, and remarked that he might "have to fall

---

*"The Day the Pig Fell into the Well" was not included, since it hadn't appeared in print yet.

back on old Spigelgass" (what with the man's delight in his "childlike sense of wonder"). It might have seemed a good sign that he was interviewed for Harvey Breit's column in the *New York Times Book Review*, but after their lunch together Cheever fretted in his journal that he'd behaved in an "unstable" and "indiscreet" manner. On the contrary, he'd come across as a "tough-minded short-story advocate" (so Breit wrote), who considered the novel an "artificial" and "anachronistic" form—not an entirely disinterested apologia, under the circumstances, though actually Cheever's aesthetic ideas had changed very little over the years, reflecting his view of modern life as fragmented and nomadic: "The short story is determined by moving around from place to place, by the interrupted event. The vigorous nineteenth-century novel is based on parish life and lack of communications. . . . I've always noticed that just as people are about to tell you the secret they're transferred to another city. The way people drop out of sight. Really drop!"

In that same issue of the *Book Review* (May 10, 1953) was James Kelly's critique of *The Enormous Radio*, which was everything Cheever might have hoped for (if he hadn't been so morbidly insecure at the time). Kelly described the stories as "miraculous expressions of life among the middle-class have-not-enoughs," though he added (as did other critics) that the stories were less impressive when read one after another, as the reader discovered a certain sameness of theme and setting. "But not one can be called insignificant or shoddy or inadequately observed," Kelly concluded. "No American writer in business today is more on top of his genre than Mr. Cheever." William Peden, writing in the *Saturday Review*, was also enthusiastic: "John Cheever shows an absolute genius for taking the usual and transforming it into the significant. . . . [He] is one of the most undervalued American short story writers."

What Cheever was apt to notice most in Peden's review, however, was an incidental remark that his stories were "less spectacular" (albeit more likely to "improve with rereading") than those of J. D. Salinger, whose *Nine Stories* was published around the same time to ecstatic acclaim. Indeed, a comparison of the two books was the basis of one of the most wounding reviews of Cheever's career—all the worse given that the reviewer, Arthur Mizener, had become one of the nation's most prominent critics after the recent success of his pioneering Fitzgerald biography, *The Far Side of Paradise*. Appearing in *The New*

Republic, Mizener's review was framed as an assessment of the "*New Yorker* story," which Mizener thought a good thing for the most part: "If their limitations on subject matter are in the long run dangerous to real talent, they nonetheless provide a stiff course in the craft." As Mizener would have it, Salinger exemplified the Good sort of *New Yorker* writer—a brilliant craftsman who transcended the "limitations" of the form—and thus his place on the best-seller lists was "as it ought to be." Cheever, however ("not a writer of any great talent"), was the Bad sort—an empty craftsman, a craftsman *tout court*: "Congreve" (wrote Mizener) "once remarked that he selected a moral and then designed a fable to fit it. . . . It is the glaring fault of Mr. Cheever's stories that they all appear to have been produced in that way."

Salinger was a sore point. Five years before, he'd come to Cheever's and everybody else's attention with "A Perfect Day for Bananafish," which provoked a flurry of letters to the magazine *(Why did that man commit suicide?)*, including one to Lobrano from Cheever ("one hell of a story"). At measured intervals Salinger continued to publish such stories, and then became wildly popular with his novel, *The Catcher in the Rye*. On the one hand, Cheever deeply admired Salinger's particular gifts, his "excellent and supple" prose, and eventually pressed a copy of *Nine Stories* on his daughter; on the other hand, he thought there was something precious and contrived about Holden and the whole Glass family, and liked to remark, maliciously, that "Jerry" (Salinger) wouldn't let anybody make a movie of *Catcher* because he was too old to play Holden. And later, as Salinger's work became more meandering and eccentric, Cheever began to suspect the man was "very close to crazy."

Crazy or not, he'd written a novel (a novel!) that was already considered a modern classic, and his story collection was a best seller and would remain in print forever, whereas *The Enormous Radio* sold a few thousand and vanished—though not before its author was abused in the daily *Times* for being a misanthrope*: "Listening to this cacophony of hatred and despair," William DuBois wrote, "one harassed reader could only wonder if the human race, as Mr. Cheever views it, is worth

---

*And what about *Salinger's* misanthropy?—so Cheever may have protested. After reading "Seymour: An Introduction," he wrote a monitory note in his journal: "I am reminded of the bitterness in my own work, that bitterness that is not art but that is its opposite. So I would like to write a story that is all yellow, yellow, yellow, the brightest yellow."

saving." This rankled; as Cheever complained to Herbst, it was an "appalling" state of affairs "to find the self-designated intellectuals urging one to cheerup, cheerup and take the world for what it appears to be." At the same time he suspected that on some level they were probably right, and, despite a mostly favorable reception for *The Enormous Radio*, he saw "harsh and bitter years" ahead: "You may never get into the rose garden."

"I AM SO PROUD OF MY FAMILY," Cheever wrote in 1952. "I love to walk with them on a Sunday." Nothing made him feel closer to his ideal self than the role of paterfamilias, and he often remarked that the most important thing was to have children—"to procreate." "I suppose the happiest days of my life," he later wrote a friend, "were the days when Susie, Ben and Fred stepped into it." "He had a strong maudlin streak," said his younger son, who pointed out that Cheever was particularly drawn to scenes evoking "a basic Norman Rockwell image." Susan and her friend Sarah Schoales, for instance, would write playlets and perform them in front of the fireplace, while Cheever attended with a rapt look ("very riveted") and applauded vigorously. Perhaps inspired by such wholesome entertainments, he initiated a "very pleasant ritual" every Sunday evening whereby members of the family would recite poems they'd memorized during the week. In fact, it was the ritualistic side of family life that he seemed to like best, and nowhere was this more evident than at dinnertime: Mary cooked while Susan set the table, and once the food was arranged in serving dishes, Cheever said a formalized grace. Expanded for special occasions, it began with a bit of Cranmer ("Almighty God, maker of all things, judge of all men!"), followed perhaps by a more specific petition ("bless this table with peace"), and invariably including what became a mantra of sorts for Cheever—a quote from Benjamin Jowett's translation of Plato that he'd altered slightly to suit his own needs: "Let us consider that the soul of man is immortal, able to endure every sort of good and every sort of evil. Thus may we live happily with one another and with God."*

---

*Jowett's actual words: "Wherefore my counsel is that we hold fast ever to the heavenly way and follow after justice and virtue always, considering that the soul is immortal and able to endure every sort of good and every sort of evil. Thus shall we

Ben Cheever has a vague memory of being kissed or nuzzled by his father and feeling the bristles of his beard, but once he got a little older there wasn't much in the way of nuzzling. "Physical contact was not encouraged in our family," Susan recalled. "On parting, we aimed kisses at one another's cheeks, and there were brief hugs for special occasions. We shook hands a lot." Meanwhile, at her best friend Sarah's house, people were forever hugging and sitting on laps, which might explain why Susan tried to stay over as often as possible. Perhaps it also had something to do with Cheever's "thunderous rage" one night when she stayed for dinner without asking permission; the Schoaleses were so alarmed—Cheever had called their house, demanding his daughter come home at once—that they followed by car while Susan (nine or ten at the time) frantically pedaled home on her bicycle. As for the ritual poetry readings—as for rituals, period—partly they served to stave off the malaise that descended in their absence: "I wondered last night why the hours between five and eight, when we have supper, are so intensely uncomfortable," Cheever wrote. "Why do I have to stupify [sic] myself with gin to see them pass."

Cheever loved being a father in the abstract, but the everyday facts of the matter were often a letdown. He was dismayed by his oldest child, for one thing, as she continued to "overthrow his preconceptions" by remaining, as he put it, "a fat importunate girl." Cheever was pitiless in judging female beauty—"You were either a dish or a drudge," his wife repeatedly insisted—and when the young Susan failed to measure up, he was bewildered and sorry for all concerned. He'd wanted a "frail daughter," after all, a "wraith" with long blond hair who drove a sports car and went by the kicky name of Susie. In any event they did call her Susie, but to Cheever's mind the name didn't jibe with the hoyden who chewed with her mouth open and said all the wrong things ("How long does it take to hang a man?"): "The tragic instant"— Cheever wrote, during a bad patch when his daughter was all of eight— "when a parent loses faith with his child."

"They were *completely* unable to cope with me," said Susan Cheever, after some fifty years of blessed retrospect. The main issue, as her parents always saw it, was her weight—if only she looked right, everything else would follow—and in a way that was true, since they harassed her so relentlessly on the subject that her behavior was mostly a matter of

---

live dear to one another and to the gods . . ." Cheever's version says nothing about justice and virtue.

reprisal. They put her on diets, made her eat Ayds candies to cut her appetite, and kept up a constant running commentary on what she ate at dinner. Every so often, too, they'd invite her grossly obese pediatrician to the house so he could deliver a stern lecture to the little girl on the evils of overeating. Deprived of snacks and the like, Susan took to stealing food (and therefore eating many times what she would have eaten normally): she hollowed out cakes they were saving for company (leaving a "veneer of icing on top"); she rooted around in drawers, closets, and desks, searching for hidden chocolate and whatever else she could find. "They had no privacy," she said. "I read everything in the house, I was in every secret compartment of every desk, I became like a little criminal. I was lying, I was cheating, I was stealing. Their cruelty about my weight was not one-way. We were in a dance of death on that subject." Many years later, after Cheever had stopped drinking, he often assuaged his melancholy by gorging on cheese and crackers: "And I remember, as a father, how ruefully I separated my daughter from her crackers and cheese when all she sought, by stuffing herself, was to understand her place in the world."

At the time he didn't see it that way; rather he regarded himself as a loving, well-meaning, long-suffering father who was simply trying to talk his only daughter out of being fat, whereas she in turn responded with unsavory remarks and tics such as banging her head against the wall and constantly sucking her thumb. She wasn't doing well in school either, and finally (at age eleven) they sent her to a psychiatrist in White Plains named Dr. Sobel. Apparently the man didn't see what all the fuss was about—certainly the girl was intelligent enough ("She has a Cadillac motor in there," he observed). The parents were another matter: Dr. Sobel remarked that Mary was a "passive" personality, which (he opined) was why Cheever had married her, whereupon the affronted husband rose from his chair and stood protectively beside his wife. In his own version of the meeting, however, Cheever tended to omit that detail, informing Susan that what Sobel had *really* said (furtively taking him aside) was: "Be careful. If anyone looked at me the way your wife looked at your daughter, I'd suck my thumb too!"

Then as later, Cheever had his own way of seeing things, or at least of telling them. Around that time, he sent his daughter to summer camp (Kaiora) in Piermont, New Hampshire, about thirty-five miles north of Treetops. After visiting for a parents' weekend, he painted a desolate picture for Maxwell's benefit:

[Susan's] smile was broad and forced. She kept seizing my hand and saying: "I'm participating in everything, Daddy." She was shrill. . . . We watched her swim, stuff a balsam pillow, row a boat, play box-hockey and plunge into a game of kick ball in which she was the only enthusiastic participant (several of the players hid under the lodge) and the last member of the team—when it began to rain—to give up. . . . Then [after saying goodbye] Susie called after me and I went back. She was not crying but her eyes were full of tears. "You understand Daddy, don't you," she said "that I am homesick every minute of the day." I said that I did. . . . On Saturday Susie was to be in a play so we returned to see this. She smiled at us from the stage, sang Green Grow the Rushes Oh with a choir, kissed us lightly and ran off with a little girl named Justine Eliot. I've never seen her so happy.

Susan doesn't remember any second visit, and definitely no play or Justine Eliot. According to the journal, however, it does appear they returned at least once for her birthday—a visit that wasn't as bleak as the first, though hardly a red-letter day either ("It was not easy to talk with S[usan], but there was nothing sad"). As for that touching set piece he wrote for Maxwell, it was also characteristic of Cheever that he should castigate himself for having written it: "I yearned to discharge with competence and strength the responsibilities of a family man . . . [and] I glimpsed the lacks I show in turning my daughter's loneliness into a poor anecdote."

He would go on telling such anecdotes, though, which generally portrayed himself in a more or less sympathetic light. Twenty years later, while drinking with Raymond Carver and others at the Iowa Writers' Workshop (where he was effectively in exile from his family), Cheever mentioned that once, after yet another marital spat, he'd woken the next morning to find a message his daughter had written in lipstick on the bathroom mirror: "D-e-r-e daddy, don't leave us." Someone remarked that he'd seen that in one of the stories,* and Cheever replied, "Probably so. Everything I write is autobiographical."

Asked whether she'd ever written "D-e-r-e daddy" in lipstick, Susan was bemused: "I know how to spell, and I think what we wanted

---

*"The Chimera" (1961).

was for him to leave us. One thing about my father was he was always *there*, you could not get rid of him. He worked at home, he ate at home, he drank at home. So 'don't *leave* us'?" She laughed. "That was never the fear."

"I would like to move along," Cheever wrote, after a couple of years in Scarborough. "This may be some fundamental irresponsibility; some unwillingness to shoulder the legitimate burdens of a father and a householder. . . . It is partly the provincialism in the air that makes me want to kick over the applecart." Having spent much of his youth among writers and artists at Yaddo or in the Village—or wherever it struck his fancy to go—Cheever was disheartened by the effort of finding sustenance among the burghers of Westchester, even the best of them. After a typical dinner with the Schoaleses, for example, he wanly observed of Dudley: "And the rich banker, the man who negotiates loans of millions that will bring iron ore out of the mountains and carry natural gas across a continent is utterly delighted to have found in his garden a squash that is shaped like a sexual organ. I am not hurt or perplexed; I am only bored." For some time Cowley had been hectoring him to go abroad, suggesting his future as an artist was at stake, but Cheever simply couldn't afford it. As he wrote Eleanor Clark (who divided her time between Connecticut and Rome), "I keep writing a story that begins: 'We lived in Westchester for six months.' I think we'll be here for years."

As long as he was stuck here (he thought), he might as well make the most of it, but how? Sitting at a PTA meeting and listening to friends and neighbors ask silly questions, he couldn't help reflecting—again—how "stupid, depressed, and uncreative" they seemed. Also, in the harsh fluorescent glare, he noticed that one woman's face (a woman he'd always considered pretty) was actually "a wrinkled mask, her gold jewelry rattling and flashing like plumbers gear"—and so it went for them all, himself not excepted: "[H]ow pitifully exposed are all our struggles towards youth and beauty," he mused. "And if we look like a hobgoblin company . . . it is because we struggle so to hang onto a youth that is longone [sic]." He'd written about the struggle per se—indeed, he thought "the theme of aging children" was one of the most pervasive in *The Enormous Radio*—but he wondered whether he really understood, on a level of deep empathy, what was at the bottom of it:

"What I want is to live among this in love and charity; and for these feelings to have a clear value; not the vague sentiments of a Christmas card."

A breakthrough of sorts occurred at a civil-defense meeting. Gathered in a high school gymnasium with "the rayon blanket tycoon, the vice president of the Life insurance company, etc.," Cheever and the others discussed what they would do, as a community, when the Bomb fell. Cheever sensed, however, that the dire business at hand was little more than a formality, and what was really on their minds was the touch-football game that would follow the meeting—and this, he concluded, was as it should be: a childish, larky escapism had its uses, at least when the alternative was contemplating Doomsday. And of course he fully shared his neighbors' zest for the games of their youth (or rather, in Cheever's case, what he would have liked his youth to be), and it reminded him, too, of how Dudley was compelled to hurdle sofas when drunk. And finally all this tied nicely with an idea he'd been kicking around (after a creative doldrums that had now stretched on for many months): namely, the middle-aged suburban male as something out of Bulfinch—a Greek god, perhaps, or Narcissus crossing into hell and "lean[ing] from the boat for a last glimpse at his face."

"O Youth and Beauty!"—the first of Cheever's stories set in the Scarborough-like suburb of Shady Hill—was written a few days after that civil-defense meeting, and, despite a nominal pessimism, it reflects the joyful resurgence of Cheever's powers. This was due in part to a discovery that he didn't have to write an "excoriation of the suburbs" after all, adopting instead a tone of detached gaiety—a tone most characteristic of Cheever's mature greatness, a playfulness that would lead him at last to *The Wapshot Chronicle*. Having noticed his own boredom in reading the leaden openings of most *New Yorker* stories, Cheever determined to take an approach that would "refresh the attention of the reader": "At the tag end of nearly every long, large Saturday-night party in the suburb of Shady Hill," the story begins, then dives into a whimsical catalogue of tediums, "when almost everybody who was going to play golf or tennis in the morning had gone home hours ago . . . when the bellicose drunk, the crapshooter, the pianist, and the woman faced with the expiration of her hopes had all expressed themselves . . ." On it goes, almost half a page, when abruptly the sentence ends and we're brought to the nub of the matter: "Trace Bearden would begin to chide Cash Bentley about his age and thinning hair. The chiding was preliminary to moving the living room furniture." Once the furniture was arranged, Trace would fire a pistol out the window and Cash would begin hurdling furniture. "It was not exactly a race, since Cash ran it alone, but it was extraordinary to see this man of forty surmount so many obstacles so gracefully."

Cash, as Narcissus, is at length brought to hell when he breaks his leg and can no longer run the hurdle race; without that pistol shot to look forward to, that poetic demonstration of his abiding youth, the scales fall from his eyes and the parties of Shady Hill seem "interminable and stale." And lest we fail to grasp the man's dejection, a suave and witty narrator (who henceforth will intrude himself more and more into Cheever's fiction) is apt to apostrophize on the matter: "Oh, those suburban Sunday nights, those Sunday night blues! Those departing weekend guests, those stale cocktails, those half-dead flowers, those trips to Harmon to catch the Century, those postmortems and pickup suppers!" Cheever knew those blues all right, but he also knew the peculiar magic of those leafy streets, and he imparts this too with sensual immediacy—the "sense of being alive" that he found in Fitzgerald's work, and which he invokes here with a sudden switch to the present tense (the same way one is cued to the building excitement of Gatsby's parties): "Then it is a summer night, a wonderful summer night. The passengers on the eight-fifteen see Shady Hill—if they notice it at all—in a bath of placid golden light. . . . On Alewives Lane sprinklers continue to play after dark. You can smell the water. The air seems as fragrant as it is dark—it is a delicious element to walk through—and most of the windows on Alewives Lane are open to it." The night's fragrant nostalgia moves Cash to resume, foolishly, his hurdle races—to take a last look at himself in the water, as it were—until his wife (accidentally or not) shoots him dead in midair. No dénouement is necessary. "It seems allright to me," Cheever noted on finishing the story. "God knows I need the money. What to do next."

Cheever's next story (also set in Shady Hill) was one of his best, "The Five-Forty-Eight," though its raw materials were homely enough. His brother, Fred, had mentioned that he'd fired a secretary who seemed unstable, and afterward the woman had sent him a few threatening notes. (When Iris read the story, she was furious that John had plundered their lives for a donnée—it would be far from the last time—or rather *two* données: as John wrote in his journal, Fred would sometimes punish his wife "by refusing to speak to her for a week or two.") But the story is no more about Fred than "O Youth and Beauty!" is about Dudley. Mostly it was determined by Cheever's own alienation—his occasional sense that there were "two worlds," his own and everyone else's, that he was unloved and unloving, doomed to be "the lonely, lonely boy with no role in life but to peer in at the lighted windows of other people's contentment and vitality."

"When Blake stepped out of the elevator, he saw her," the story begins, *in medias res*, proceeding in somber, muted prose that seems the work of an almost entirely different man from the author of "O Youth and Beauty!" Not a flicker of humor is found in "The Five-Forty-Eight," since the reader is confined to the perspective of a humorless man incapable of love. "She had no legitimate business with him," he briskly decides of the woman waiting outside the elevator, and that fixes Blake's character once and for all. And yet one feels a vague sympathy for him—as he pauses, say, on a rainy street (the woman lurking somewhere behind him) to peer into a store window: "The window was arranged like a room in which people live and entertain their friends. There were cups on the coffee table, magazines to read, and flowers in the vases, but the flowers were dead and the cups were empty and the guests had not come. In the plate glass, Blake saw a clear reflection of himself and the crowds that were passing, like shadows, at his back." Here is perfect loneliness—a man divided from the domestic tableau in front of him (made desolate by his gaze) and the crowds passing behind him like so many ghosts. It is precisely the hell of a man "with no role in life but to peer in at the lighted windows of other people's contentment and vitality," a point sustained in almost everything Blake thinks and sees. Trapped on a train—the woman holding him at gunpoint—he wistfully notices the same advertisements at every station: "There was a picture of a couple drinking a toast . . . and a picture of a Hawaiian dancer. Their cheerful intent seemed to go no farther than the puddles of water on the platform and to expire there." Meanwhile the woman reads to him from a letter written in the "crazy, wandering hand" that had first signaled her instability, before he seduced and fired her: " 'Dear Husband . . . they say that human love leads us to divine love, but is this true? . . . I dreamed on Tuesday of a volcano erupting with blood.' " *Dear Husband* is a marvelous touch, and indeed the character ("Miss Dent") is a triumph of negative capability. Her bizarre behavior is somehow all of a piece, credible from beginning to end, and it even becomes possible to believe that—between her and

Blake—she will be the one made whole again. "[A]n extraordinary story," Maxwell wrote Cheever. "I was lost in admiration for the way you had done the girl, and for the way you brought it off, with the only possible, but completely unforeseeable, ending."

WRITING WELL made all the difference to Cheever's mood, and by the summer of 1953 he was far away from the dismal limbo of a year before. After a brief stay at Treetops, he took a room at the Hotel Earle on Washington Square and wrote three stories. Alone in the city—that precarious state—Cheever found it a splendid and even healthy place: "Walking on the streets I have never felt so well," he wrote in his journal. "The loneliness that seems to have pursued me is over. . . . [T]he quality of hurt and fear, the feeling of deprivation, all these limitations seem conquered." Such was his well-being that when he encountered his old, unloved acquaintance, Katherine Anne Porter, looking haggard and forlorn, he invited her to dinner at the Plaza. ("[She] kept chatting about American poetry and looking across the room to where a woman in a pale blue dress was eating watermelon," he wrote Eleanor Clark.) A few days later, still magnanimous, he left the city and took his family to Cape Cod, and once he got back to Scarborough he began working "so happily" that he hardly gave a thought to moving to Europe.

This lasted until New Year's Eve, when an annual *bal masqué* was held at the Swopes' barn on Teatown Lake. It was the community's biggest social event, involving months of preparation. During the Cheevers' first year in Scarborough, the theme had been "Come as a Clue to '52": Mary had dressed as Pax (white gown and shawl, laurel branch with olives entwined), and Cheever had borrowed a Saracen helmet from Mrs. Vanderlip. This time the theme was "How You See Yourself in Heaven,"* and Mary was chairwoman of the decoration committee. Weeks before Thanksgiving, even, dinner parties were held on the pretext of discussing décor (Heaven and Hell) and arranging such effects as a "wire-recording of the 'strange tongues, horrible outcries, words of pain, tones of anger, etc.'" As for the actual party, it

---

*"If I have to go," Cheever wrote a friend in October, "I'm going to go as the late Warren G. Harding." In fact, he went as a Chinese acrobat, or so he claimed twenty years later; Mary was "the seven-eyed Sybil."

began well and ended in disaster—"a trauma," as Cheever would always remember it.

That night, as always, there were early cocktails and a sit-down dinner, a stop at the Beechwood gala to pay homage to Mrs. Vanderlip, until finally they arrived at the Swopes' barn, where Cheever swung the women around in widening circles, the way he'd learned at the Masonic Temple in Wollaston. Shortly after midnight ("moved by profound love and some alcohol"), he asked his wife to dance but was "rudely" repulsed—and the next thing he knew (or thought he knew), she'd disappeared into the parking lot with another man, Rod Swope, Sally's handsome brother-in-law. ("I never did," said Mary, "but I'd like to.") Cheever sadly recounted coming home around three, alone, and washing away his makeup and all traces of false beard. In the wan light of dawn Mary herself came home, and, despite Cheever's determination to be "just" and "cheerful," she regarded him with "looks of aversion and grief " for weeks and even months to come. "If I ever see R.S. again"—Cheever scrawled in his journal—"I will bash him in the nose." Such sentiments were promptly transmuted into a story, "Just Tell Me Who It Was," about a man who suspects his wife of cuckolding him at a fancy-dress party; it was the fourth story in Cheever's bonus cycle at *The New Yorker*, and hence resulted in an extra 15 percent payment on that story as well as the previous three. This, however, was small comfort.

It wasn't just other men who worried Cheever, but anything Mary did that seemed to indicate a waning interest in wifely duties. Her participation in the League of Women Voters, for example, excited an almost hysterical chagrin, which as usual Cheever cloaked with a lot of good-natured ridicule in his letters: she was a "comical character," he wrote, who got up early every morning and nailed signs to trees alerting "the ladies" to their latest meeting, while he, Cheever, hid "in a neighbor's attic." In fact, he feared nothing less than total abandonment, suspecting that her interest in the League of Women Voters and Rod Swope was all too justified. Impotence had become an issue in their marriage, and this was a very vicious cycle for Cheever. Any failure to perform resulted in proliferating anxieties, which drove him deeper into drink and further impotence; rather than blame drink and certain other factors, though, Cheever would find ways of blaming his wife—she was cold, self-involved, and so on—which in turn heightened her own exasperation and caused her to reject him in actual fact.

Beneath it all, of course, was an escalating terror of homosexuality, and living among the dauntingly normal citizens of Scarborough didn't help. Alleged "sex perversion" was a bigger stigma than ever— the fifties were a time of rampant homophobia, of government witch hunts and random police raids—and there was a lot of heavy, nervous joking at suburban cocktail parties. "Jumping at every mention of homos," Cheever wrote in his journal, which in the early months of 1954 was filled with self-loathing on the subject. "He speaks scornfully of effeminate men lest he be misunderstood and as he scorns his own effeminacy," Cheever wrote of an acquaintance. "And in making this harsh judgment I might say that I sometimes seem to live behind a veil of ignorance myself." That was perhaps an understatement, though in Cheever's case it wasn't so much ignorance as visceral revulsion. Every encounter with suspected homosexuals ("with their funny clothes and their peculiar smells and airs and scraps of French") struck him as "an obscenity and a threat," such that his own impulses were unbearable and had to be numbed with alcohol or blamed on his wife. But then homosexuality was only part of the problem, as even Cheever could see. Reading the psychoanalyst Karen Horney one night, he realized that he was "implicated in the neurotic picture," given his insatiable need for love and approval (often caused by "parental indifference," said Horney), and never mind his pathological jealousy: he strained himself to write kindly, witty, intimate letters to almost total strangers; his public persona was unassailably charming (belied withal by the depressive paranoia of his journal); he followed comely people around on the street; he felt an "erotic, childish" hankering almost all the time, and regarded himself (rightly) as "a punching bag for the beauty and virility of the world." But why speak only of the neurotic's "frustrations," he wondered, when "a good deal of poetry and charm can be involved"?

Perhaps, but the fact remained that he was impotent, and often drunk before lunch. Finally, in April, he decided to see the Sing Sing psychiatrist, Bernard Glueck, a young man who'd struck him as having a "vigorous mind" when the two met at a party in 1952. Cheever told his wife that he was going because of impotence per se, but with Glueck he openly broached the matter of "homosexual concerns" along with his worsening (and not unrelated) problems with impotence and alcohol. At their first session Glueck was reassuring enough, but Cheever was wary at the prospect of any sort of long-term psychoanalysis. As he wrote in his journal, he found the "atmosphere of the confessional" distasteful, and was hesitant as ever to probe deeply into the past ("to regale myself with my interesting history"). Besides, he was feeling better already, what with the quickening spring weather, and decided after two or three meetings to manage on his own—to accept anxiety as simply the "dread disease of poets."

And then he suspected that plenty of nonpoets suffered too. Even among his most prosaic neighbors, he noticed a certain "breakdown of perspective" in middle age: "Bald-headed men" who suddenly took up painting, or played the *Moonlight* Sonata with their windows open ("this ardent invitation to some lonely chamber-maid"). Any one of them might slip along the tightrope of propriety: commit adultery, seduce the babysitter, "bugger the tree surgeon," but (in most cases) they didn't—*Cheever* didn't—because "to do any of these things would so damage the health of my self-esteem that I would be dealing with the obscenities of death." Or, as he put it in the story he began to write, "The village hangs, morally and economically, from a thread; but it hangs by its thread in the evening light." When at last Cheever finished "The Country Husband"—almost three months after his first tentative notes—he was so exalted that he drove at once to Maxwell's house in Yorktown Heights, to wait while his editor (ill with bronchitis) read the manuscript in bed. Maxwell would always remember his own sense of "rapture."

"To begin at the beginning" (the story opens), Francis Weed is rocked out of his daily torpor with a picturesque airplane crash on the first page of the story. The airplane goes down through "a white cloud of such density that it reflected the exhaust fires," while the only sound is that of the pilot "singing faintly, 'I've got sixpence, jolly, jolly sixpence. . . .' " Not only does Francis survive, but the whole incident is made to seem immediately unreal. Returning to New York (the crash was outside Philadelphia), he encounters his old friend Trace Bearden on the train to Shady Hill, but the man can scarcely credit that Francis has been in a weather-related crash, since, after all, that late-September day in New York is as "fragrant and shapely as an apple." As for Mrs. Weed and their children, they are too "absorbed in their own antagonisms" to give Francis a proper greeting, much less listen to his story about miraculously escaping death. Indeed, when Francis asks his wife if they might try eating dinner apart from their squabbling children, the woman brings him crashing back to earth in a different sense: "Julia's guns are loaded for this. She can't cook two dinners and lay two tables. She paints with lightning strokes that panorama of drudgery in which her youth, her beauty, and her wit have been lost." Meanwhile the spirit of anarchy—embodied by a black retriever named Jupiter—frolics amid the staid gardens of Shady Hill: "Jupiter crashed through the tomato vines with the remains of a felt hat in his mouth."

Such is the banality of Francis's life—his Weedness—that the airplane crash might have been forgotten and everything restored to normal, were it not for a subsequent encounter that piques his memory and leaves his senses "dilated" (momentously for one so absorbed in the quotidian present: "He had not developed his memory as a sentimental faculty. Wood smoke, lilac, and other such perfumes did not stir him, and his memory was something like his appendix—a vestigial repository"). At an otherwise unremarkable dinner party, Francis recognizes the housemaid as a woman he saw in France during the war. Punished for fraternizing with Germans, she had had her head shaved and was forced to strip naked in the public square. Aglow with the strangeness of that memory—of that whole incongruously vivid time—Francis goes home to find their usual babysitter, a crone, replaced by a lovely seventeen-year-old named Anne Murchison. The girl begins sobbing in his car because of a nasty exchange with her drunken father, and Francis tries to comfort her: "The layers of their clothing felt thin, and when her shuddering began to diminish, it was so much like a paroxysm of love that Francis lost his head and pulled her roughly against him." At first the girl seems shocked and pulls away, but at her door she kisses him "swiftly," and Francis falls in love.

Such a love will not end well, of course, but for a while Francis is a man risen from the dead (or for that matter "a punching bag for the beauty and virility of the world"). The next morning he stands tingling on the platform, waiting for his train, when he sees "an extraordinary thing": in a passing window, a beautiful nude sits in her roomette "combing and combing" her golden hair. Ecstatically Francis watches the vision pass, when suddenly he's visited by an emissary from Shady Hill—old Mrs. Wrightson, who wants to talk about her quest for the right sort of curtains. "I know what to do with them," Francis finally interrupts her. "What?" "Paint them black on the inside, and shut up." This exhilarating exchange proves the high point of Francis's rebellion. As his furious wife reminds him, Mrs. Wrightson wields a terrible

power in the village—she decides which girls will go to the assemblies—
and by insulting her Francis has consigned them all to pariah-dom.
Worse, it turns out that Anne Murchison is engaged to a pimply youth
named Clayton, who for good measure lectures Francis on the shortcomings of the life to which he's doomed to return: "[Shady Hill]
doesn't have any future. So much energy is spent in perpetuating the
place—in keeping out undesirables and so forth—that the only idea of
the future anyone has is just more and more commuting trains and
more parties. I don't think that's healthy." At last the abject Francis is
driven to confess his love to a psychiatrist, Dr. Herzog, who advises
him to console himself with woodwork; ten days later he's in the cellar
building a coffee table. "Francis is happy," the narrator announces,
with vertiginous irony.

And so the story winds down with a last, virtuosic montage of
Shady Hill at twilight: a wistful neighbor, Donald Goslin, goes on
playing the *Moonlight* Sonata with excessive *rubato;* little Toby Weed
pretends to be a spaceman; the naked, aging Babcocks race around
their hedge-screened terrace ("as passionate and handsome a nymph
and satyr as you will find on any wall in Venice"); an evocative cat hob-
bles onto the scene "securely buttoned into a doll's dress, from the
skirts of which protrudes its long hairy tail." Finally Jupiter reappears:
"He prances through the tomato vines, holding in his generous mouth
the remains of an evening slipper. Then it is dark; it is a night where
kings in golden suits ride elephants over the mountains."

Cheever wrote this "arty ending" (as he called it) out of sequence,
in a flash of inspiration, and felt that he'd perfectly synthesized the disparate elements of an exquisitely intricate story.* Some have criticized
the ending as anticlimactic and evasive, but of course Cheever was
rarely interested in resolving the loose ends of a neat linear plot; rather
he sought to compose a harmonic set of impressions, in this case a
picture of the suburbs rendered in a spirit of "love and charity" that yet
reflected "the real limitations in such a community." Francis is

---

*With such a passage in mind, Cheever once wrote that he knew "no greater plea-
sure" than drawing together disparate incidents in fiction "so that they relate to one
another and confirm that feeling that life itself is a creative process, that one thing is
put purposefully upon another, that what is lost in one encounter is replenished in the
next and that we possess some power to make sense of what takes place." When he
later taught writing, one of his favorite assignments was to have students take seven or
eight dissimilar things and put them into a coherent scheme.

thwarted and properly so, though he finds a drop of (ambiguous) comfort in woodwork; meanwhile Jupiter prances free, as do the Babcocks, and after all it's a kingly night of (almost) infinite possibilities. In later years, Cheever wasn't averse to pointing out that Nabokov, no less, had mentioned "The Country Husband" as one of his "half-a-dozen particular favorites," explaining its mechanism in very agreeable terms: "The story is really a miniature novel beautifully traced, so that the impression of there being a little too many things happening in it is completely redeemed by the satisfying coherence of its thematic interlacings."

At the end of that difficult year, then, Cheever could take comfort in having made better and better art out of a supposedly neurotic outlook, and there were more tangible rewards as well. "The Country Husband" won first prize in the O. Henry Awards, and was also included in *Best American Short Stories* (and finally adapted as a feature-length film for *Playhouse 90* on CBS—this while Cheever was mercifully in Italy: "I saw a script before we sailed," he wrote the Boyers. "They changed everything but the title"). Around that time, too, he went to Washington to receive the Benjamin Franklin Magazine Award for best story of 1954: "The Five-Forty-Eight." For the moment, at least, he stood at the top of his genre, and in the midst of such eminence he visited his mother in Quincy. "I read in the newspaper that you won a prize," she remarked. "Yes, mother," he replied, "I didn't tell you about it because it wasn't terribly important to me." "No," said the old woman, "it wasn't to me either."

CHAPTER SIXTEEN

{ 1954–1956 }

Toward the end of the summer in 1954, Cheever got a telephone call from the poet Paul Engle at the University of Iowa Writers' Workshop: would he like to come out and teach for a year? Cheever—longing once again to leave Westchester ("even if I were traveling in the wrong direction")—enthusiastically accepted the offer. Then he waited. Finally, a brief note arrived, explaining the position had been filled. "Mary thinks that the University called the New Yorker and asked for Jean Stafford's telephone number and got mine by mistake," he wrote Herbst. Still, the idea had been planted, and so ("to vary this landscape somewhat") he accepted a job at Barnard, beginning in January 1955, to teach a single two-hour writing class every Monday afternoon.

At first Cheever was intimidated by his small group of honor students. He'd never taught his own class and had no degree, and for a while he found himself wasting time at his writing desk "giving imaginary lectures"—some of them rather abstruse: "[F]or the Barnard girls" (he reminded himself in his journal) "there is the statement that writing fills in that discrepancy between what we mean to be and what we are; between our very real vision of life and its possibilities and those experiences that gall us." True enough, though what stuck in his students' minds were his more down-to-earth insights. He mentioned, for example, that it would be much harder for them to pursue writing as a career than it had been for him in the Depression, when it "wasn't a crime" to be a writer without a job—that said, they needn't act like bohemians to succeed, and he warned them explicitly against sleeping

with editors (particularly at *The New Yorker*). Privately Cheever wondered at his own sententiousness, and one night, brooding as usual, he
suddenly realized it was a "mistake" to take the job so seriously.

Cheever's students remember him as helpful, modest, and soft-
spoken. Sometimes he'd give them assignments ("Write a description
of Richard Nixon"), but mostly he was content to read his own work
and listen to theirs. "Most of the girls are so subtle you can't tell
whether the characters are alive or dead and there is a good deal of
loneliness and moonshine, etc.," he wrote Eleanor Clark, though in
the classroom he kept his sarcasm in check. Which is not to say he
wasn't critical when warranted. One woman liked to write erotica, and
Cheever would listen to her stories with a polite poker-face—evidently
finding them distasteful, but willing to be patient. He raised one mild
objection, however, when she described a man abruptly withdrawing
his penis and thus forgoing climax: "There is no recorded instance in
history when a man was able to do this," he said. It was a fairly typical
observation. Regardless of what they chose to write—and generally
Cheever thought it a good idea for them to write what they knew—he
insisted that characters behave in a plausible manner, and (reminiscent
of Harold Ross) that the reality of a story be made accessible to readers
with vivid, specific detail. One of his students, Judith Sherwin (who'd
already published a poem in the *Atlantic**), wanted to write something
akin to magical realism, and thought Cheever's strictures precluded
this. But of course Cheever was no stranger to magical realism; he simply insisted that, while revising, Sherwin "put in a few signposts"—that
is, the kind of details that make up a believable world.

Mostly his students adored him. They balked when he asked them
to memorize "Fern Hill" for its lovely cadence; a week later, though,
three of his best students came to his office and recited the poem in
unison. Such moments made it almost worthwhile, but not quite:
teaching was too much effort ("[it] takes the skin off your back"), no
matter how relaxed his approach. Besides, his novel was finally taking
off and he resented distractions of any kind, especially the muddling
static of apprentice prose. Toward the end of his second and last term,
he was doing little more as a teacher than reading aloud from *The Wapshot Chronicle*—not that his students seemed to mind. As one remarked,

---

*A number of Cheever's Barnard students went on to become professional writers—
among them Sherwin, Emilie Buchwald, Irma Kurtz, and Piri Halasz.

"It was an honor to be sitting there, at age nineteen, with this writer on the cusp of greatness."

Such greatness was the result of a truly mulish persistence. After his last, disastrous meeting with Linscott in March 1952, Cheever had very nearly given up the idea of ever writing a novel at all. "I think maybe I might stick with short stories," he wrote, then immediately proceeded to argue with himself: he'd never make any real money as a short-story writer, or establish a durable reputation; a novel was "massive, longlived," whereas the short story "has the life expectancy of a mayfly." Still, a long year would pass before he could dust himself off and try again. "It's been my intention for the last twenty-five years to complete a sustained piece of fiction and I feel sure that I will," he wrote Linscott in early 1953, adding, however, that he'd abandoned his previous draft *in toto* after the editor's scathing appraisal, and hadn't made any progress since.

To Cowley he reiterated the necessity of writing a novel—as a career imperative, if nothing else—but complained that he found the genre "bankrupt." Cowley replied that perhaps he shouldn't try to write a "conventional" novel at all, but rather pursue one of the alternatives Cowley had mentioned before: namely, either write what amounted to a long short-story—"take some situation like the one you treated in Goodbye, My Brother and work back (not forward) till the characters assumed their full roundness"—or else take two or three stories "and weave them together." The latter method evidently struck a chord with Cheever, but structure wasn't his only problem. There was also the question of *tone:* "[t]he irresistable attraction [that] satire, irony, the memory of Fielding have for me," he wrote, having made a breakthrough of sorts with the darkly exuberant "O Youth and Beauty!" With a somewhat Fieldingesque treatment in mind, then, he wrote "The National Pastime" in the summer of 1953—an attempt to recast Leander in a more comic, malevolent mode. This was the father he was never able to "requite": the gruff, distant old man who refused to play baseball with him; the self-absorbed zany who wore a fez and read to his cat. In the story, Leander writes in his will, " 'To my changeling son, Eben . . . the author of all my misfortunes, I leave my copy of Shakespeare, a hacking cough . . .' The list was long and wicked [the narrator-son observes] . . . the piece of paper was evidence of my own defeat." For the purpose of his novel, though, Cheever preferred to make peace with his father's ghost rather than the opposite, and anyway the wacky, fez-wearing Leander was perhaps too thin to sustain over the course of a long narrative. "[The story] seems like a model of wrongness," he wrote Maxwell, "although I might be able to use some of it later in a different light."

Next he wrote "Mrs. Wapshot," still another attempt to get his mother down on paper. In her final incarnation in the novel, Sarah Wapshot is a single-minded but essentially pious and gentle woman; the heroine of "Mrs. Wapshot," however, is much closer to the real-life model (still abiding in Quincy at the time, it bears repeating). "She is a very enterprising woman," Mr. Wapshot explains to his sons. "She used to go alone to those dark streets in Boston where the rag-pickers were and buy rags by the car-load. When she and her friends had made enough quilts to cover every coolie in China they had a bazaar and sold the quilts for the benefit of the Armenians." This unpublished story is over thirty pages in manuscript, and the Wapshot cast is still evolving: the father is a gentle apologist for his wife's vagaries, and dies in the early pages; there are three sons—Moses, Coverly, and William—the last a divinity student, while in this version Coverly is based somewhat on the author's piano-playing cousin, Randall Young. At any rate Cheever was not surprised when *The New Yorker* rejected the story as diffuse ("a series of eddies and whirlpools"). "My plan to write a novel piecemeal seems frustrated," Cheever wrote.

But a piecemeal approach was the only way to proceed, given his finances. Indeed, the journal suggests that the first usable part of *The Wapshot Chronicle* was the "Clear Haven" episode—begun in early 1954—which appears in the last third of the published novel. "Clear Haven" originated as a lampoon of the Vanderlips' ghastly mansion—to say nothing of Mrs. Vanderlip herself (who, like Cousin Justina Wapshot Molesworth Scaddon, was a great believer in celibacy)—but a long time would pass before Cheever could figure out how to relate it to the rest of his material. In the meantime he put it aside to write what he hoped would prove a salable, self-contained story about the Wapshots, "Independence Day at St. Botolph's [sic]," which appeared that summer in *The New Yorker* and was partly cannibalized into the first and fifth chapters of his novel. In the magazine story, Leander is named Alpheus,* a ferryboat captain who loves "boarding-house

---

*There is no evidence in Cheever's notes (after 1950 or so) that he ever intended to call this character anything but Leander. Probably the name was changed in the magazine to avoid confusion with the Leander of "The National Pastime," published in *The New Yorker* about nine months before.

widows, seaside girls, and other doxies," and freely consoles himself with same after learning that his high-minded wife doesn't like to be "embraced." On Independence Day, Mrs. Wapshot discovers her jewelry box has been rifled and assumes, tearfully, that Alpheus has robbed her in order to run away with a randy widow. In fact, Alpheus has hocked the baubles to buy fifty dollars' worth of fireworks: "He was in high spirits, for he knew there would never again be such a display at the farm."

For the actual Leander of the novel, though, Cheever wanted something more than simply a colorful scoundrel, and hence considered "breath[ing] some fire" into the character by including his "autobiography"—that is, a document based on Frederick Cheever's notes about his youth during the gaslight era of old New England. The problem was how to turn his father's "antic" and "vulgar" writing into a properly elegant prose style. "Having revised these lines as Gide might have written them," Cheever later wrote, "I realized that my father was a better writer than I, and using his style I went on then to invent a character and a life that would have gratified him." At the time, Cheever wrote two chapters of Leander's journal (sometimes quoting his father verbatim) and rather doubtfully gave them to Maxwell, hoping for a little feedback at best. Maxwell was not only wildly enthusiastic ("I was mad about that journal"), but willing to publish the whole thing almost word for word in *The New Yorker* as "Journal of an Old Gent." For Cheever it was the crucial turning point: "So many of my plans for books have backfired, withered and vanished," he wrote Maxwell after getting the news. Now, however, he had both confidence and money enough to continue—though little existed of the novel except a few bright scraps: the first part of Leander's journal; the Independence Day parade in St. Botolphs; and bits of "Clear Haven" (which might or might not fit into the ultimate design). As Cheever noted in early February 1955, "[W]hen I drink a martini after dark the book seems to unfold before my eyes like a roll of pianola music . . . but in the clear light of morning I have my troubles."

A MONTH AFTER THIS WATERSHED, Linscott decided to pull the plug. "It is nine years now since we advanced you $4800 to write a novel and two years since the last report of 'No progress,' " he wrote on March 2, 1955, with unwonted severity. "Meanwhile our finance department has been pressing me to make some sort of arrangement for repayment." The man added, pro forma, that of course he'd prefer a complete, publishable manuscript, but in lieu of this he suggested that Cheever "undertake to pay us back in installments." After further negotiation (epistolary), Linscott agreed to release Cheever if he could repay half the advance, and Cheever began casting about for a savior ("I wonder if any publisher will pay as much for a forty-three year old writer"). In the meantime, expecting a modest windfall from the television sale of "The Country Husband," he took his family to Nantucket for the summer.

He'd rented a big, rickety old Boston cottage* atop a bluff on the narrow northeastern tip of the island, in Wauwinet, with spectacular views of the ocean on one side and the bay on the other. "I am able to spend a good deal of money on liquor," he wrote the Spears, "because we have found a sea pond that is teeming with steamers, cherry stones, oysters, and blue crabs and we can count on a good deal in the way of free groceries." One day the family was frolicking naked in the little pond, digging for clams, while the dog Cassie furtively removed their discarded clothing: "When we climbed back to the sand dune that afternoon there was nothing but one shoe," Ben remembered. "My father had to slink back to the house naked, and then return with clothes for the rest of us." The place was isolated but hardly deserted; nearby was a family-owned hotel with little cottages, and the Cheevers had plenty of social life. They hired a well-born young woman named Cordelia ("Dilly") to help look after the children and teach them how to sail, as well as to team up with Cheever in the local yacht-club races—a "disaster," as Mary recalled: "They found themselves going backward. John came from an old maritime family, so he liked to believe he knew something about sailing."

He was fretful about finances: the television deal was still in suspense, and always nagging at the back of his mind was that unpaid Random House advance. "These old bones are for sale," he wrote Simon Michael Bessie, a senior editor at Harper & Brothers whom he'd met at a Westchester lunch. He mentioned the price—twenty-

---

*The house had belonged to Sally Swope's aunt, who'd recently died of cancer. "Sally was reluctant to use it so soon after her aunt's death," her son David explained, "so she let the Cheevers have it."

four hundred dollars—and warned Bessie that the novel "may or may not ever be written," but in any event he was tired of running into Bennett Cerf at parties and invariably being greeted (after a few fumbling moments of nonrecognition) with "Oh yes, of course—uhhh—*Cheever!* . . . How's that novel coming?" If Bessie saw fit to repay the advance, said Cheever, he must never ask how the novel is coming. As it happened the man was also on Nantucket that summer, and a few days later Cheever was gazing pensively out his window at the harbor, when suddenly he descried a dazzling yacht on the horizon. Presently the boat was anchored and a dinghy rowed ashore containing a dapper fellow dressed in flannels and a navy blazer: Bessie. "I'm looking for John Cheever!" he announced, and thus a bit of literary history was made. So Cheever told it. Actually, Bessie had simply phoned the author and asked where he should send the check. In due course, though, he did sail a modest catboat into the harbor and pay Cheever a visit. "He has a slender face, glasses, a nimble mind, I think, liberal and perhaps prosaic," Cheever noted after their meeting. "I'm not sure that he will like what I do, and it doesn't much matter. I've got to get to work."

The months that followed were among the happiest of Cheever's adult life. Four days a week he worked on *The Wapshot Chronicle*, and his leisure was savored all the more as a result of his steady progress. The grail was almost within his grasp—a novel!—and he felt a thrilling sense of "having overwhelmed [his] detractors . . . of having a headlong and exciting role to play." Suddenly the suburbs seemed a golden place—a paradise of creativity and fellowship. On weekends he drank martinis and raked leaves and played piano or recorder in a Baroque ensemble—this amid the usual games of scrub hockey and touch ("A lovely afternoon; the women cheering; Tommy Brooks running with the football under his sweater"). He and Mary got invitations for parties almost every Saturday night, and the next morning at eight o'clock (no matter how bad his hangover) Cheever duly appeared at the communion rail.

Such was his renewed sense of belonging that he joined the Scarborough Fire Company and persuaded a few neighbors to follow his lead—a tight group, said Cheever, who "ate roast beef and drank India Pale Ale," whereas Briarcliff firemen settled for baloney and Rheingold. What particularly appealed to Cheever, or at least piqued his interest, was the chance to mix with the indigenous population, the Italian and Irish who'd lived in Westchester long before the commuting crowd had moved in after the war. It always pleased Cheever to be accepted by working people: Peter Wesul at Treetops, Nellie Shannon at Yaddo, and Angelo Palumbo, the Beechwood superintendent and fire-company veteran, who organized cookouts and taught Cheever and his friends how to use the equipment. Cheever found it "small-town stag and pleasant": he got a kick out of whooping around in the Diamond T fire engine, playing the spotlight on his comrades when they ducked behind the truck to take long beery pisses. As a writer he was made secretary, and soon began typing his letters on Scarborough Fire Company stationery: "As you can see from the letterhead," he wrote Herbst, "I have gone way up in the world. . . . I have my own exclusive club—a brotherhood of 29 manly, hard-drinking, courageous fellows. . . . As my father used to say: What a bully life!" Or so he liked to think. Worried that his new friends would doubt his commitment, he made a point of attending the many social functions—"and attending" (he wrote in his journal) "I must eat clams and drink beer and clams and beer make me sick. Life. Life." After a few months he bestowed the office of secretary on his fellow writer Jack Kahn and promptly resigned.

By then, however, Cheever's thoughts were on higher things—not just his novel but his immortal soul, and indeed the one seemed to remind him of the other. "While I was writing the book I would walk around the streets," he later recalled, "staring into the faces of embarrassed strangers and asking myself what glad tidings could one bring them? . . . I settled for a book that closed with praise of a gentle woman and The Lord God of Hosts." Cheever had been a churchgoer for many years, often explaining that he'd regained his faith as a result of falling in love for the first time, or, as he sometimes put it, "because of an experience of sexual ecstasy so great that I felt impelled to respond through liturgical gesture." But his most recent happiness—after the awful lows of the past decade—had reinvigorated his sense of a benevolent Creator ("[T]here is some love in our conception. . . . [W]e were not made by a ruttish pair in a commercial hotel"), and his need to express thanks was so powerful that he decided to be confirmed. As he explained to a friend, "[H]aving lived much of my life like an odd mixture of man and cockroach* I found, not so long ago, that the cockroach had left me and I am still now and then bewildered by the

---

*Cheever often referred to his depression as *le cafard*, "the cockroach" or (colloquially) "the blues."

strenuousness of my pleasure. . . . I keep telling the rector that I did not reenter the church because I travail and am heavy-laden, but because I was happy . . ."

The All Saints rector was Reverend William Arnold, who presided at Cheever's confirmation on October 16, 1955. With this man at least somewhat in mind, Cheever once told his son Ben that it didn't matter if the minister was a jackass—though there were times, plainly, when it did. "I will not go to church," Cheever recorded one Good Friday, "because B[ill] will insist upon giving a sermon and I will not have the latitude or the intelligence to overlook its repetitiousness, grammatical errors and stupidity." Arnold was an affable, tippling bachelor who liked to insinuate himself as much as possible into the life of the community, participating in local theater productions and cadging meals among his flock. What he knew about Cheever was that the latter wrote "articles" for *The New Yorker* and served enormous martinis, such that the garrulous ex–army chaplain was sometimes slow to leave in the evenings. "I'd ask you to stay for dinner, Bill, but I don't even know what we're going to have," Cheever once remarked, urging the man out of his chair just as Cassie wandered into the room with a leg of lamb clamped in her jaws (the meat was extracted and popped in the oven). Nevertheless Cheever stuck with All Saints, because it met his basic requirements: it used the Cranmer prayer book and was less than ten minutes away, and (as Susan Cheever pointed out) its altar was "sufficiently simple so that it [didn't] remind him of a gift shop." Also, the eight o'clock service was sermon-free, so he could have at least twenty-three minutes of relative peace each week ("a level of introspection that's granted to me at no other time"). Not one to proselytize, he rarely mentioned his faith except at odd moments when visited by the same happiness that had moved him to become a communicant in the first place: "There has to be *someone* you thank for the party."

HIS MOTHER clearly wasn't long for the world, and to the end Cheever chided himself to be kinder to the old woman: "He would have liked, somehow, to do it again," he wrote a few months before her death,* "to have them both behave differently, to spare her, in her old age, the sharp teeth of loneliness, helplessness and neglect." She was

---

*In his journal, Cheever often referred to himself in the third person, using alter egos such as "Coverly," "Bierstubbe," or "Estabrook."

nothing if not proud, however: having been (relatively) deserted by her children and scorned by an ungrateful, dissolute husband, she clung to her independence with something akin to bitterness. "I am eating a capon in front of my fireplace and I am *not* lonely," she proclaimed when Cheever phoned during her penultimate Thanksgiving on earth. He felt guilty about neglecting her, but not so guilty that he could bring himself to visit more than once or twice a year. At such times he'd keep a polite simper afloat while his mother chatted (perversely, he thought) about a lovely new mural at the corset shop, or a pleasant young man who was, after all, "a *regular* boy."

Probably the woman had no idea of the bruises she was stomping on—certainly her son wasn't one to enlighten her—and simply figured the best she could do was not be a bother. Toward the end, she sold her little house (giving her sons five thousand dollars apiece) and moved back to the dingy apartment up the street where she'd lived before her husband's death. "Empty rooms, torn windowshades, a glimpse of old age," Cheever mused while measuring her kitchen floor for linoleum. "[S]he is admirable; she did not ask for sympathy on her moving; and she is a very old woman." A month later she had a stroke. Cheever returned to find her "bedridden and helpless," her speech slurred; at first she made the usual show of heroic resilience ("systematically learning to write with her left hand"), but at some point dissolved into tears and said she wanted to die. Though Cheever was stricken by her misery, it simply wasn't in him (or vice versa) to respond with tenderness. "Left in the middle of the afternoon," he wrote afterward. "Deeply sorry to have arrived at no sense of requition. Here is an excellent woman, but her excellence cannot be applied. There is for both of us a sense of failure that I cannot assess."

At the beginning of 1956, her diabetes took a turn for the worse, and her sons arranged for a nurse to look after her. Before long, however, Cheever got a telephone call—the nurse had been fired—and he hurried back to Quincy on the train. "Who told you?" his mother demanded when he appeared at her bedside. With typical self-reliance, she was working her way through a case of Scotch, having been warned by the doctor that alcohol would kill her.* "You must not be upset

---

*This smacks of mythology, and one can only point out that it was a story Cheever stuck to, with little variation, the rest of his life. From his medical record at Smithers (dated April 10, 1975): "Father was a heavy drinker, mother was not, but at 82 developed diabetes [and] bought a case of scotch and drank herself to death."

when I die," she said. "I am quite happy to go. I've done everything I was meant to do and quite a lot that I wasn't meant to do." She died a few days later, having finally won her son's unequivocal esteem. "[A]lthough she was afraid of many things in her life—" he wrote, "crowds, confinement, deep water—she seemed to face death completely unafraid." So it was, on a snowy day in February, that Cheever paid his last visit to the scenes of his childhood, noting his "strong emotion" as he stood at his parents' graves in Norwell—one of the little towns in that "forgotten valley of the North River" where part of his heart remained. Mostly, though, the environs of Quincy reminded him of a time when he'd felt like "an ugly and useless obscenity," and he was glad to be shut of it forever.

His mother's death freed him in another crucial respect. "The Chronicle was not published (and this was a consideration) until after my mother's death," he told at least one interviewer, though of course he'd been trying to write (and publish) such a book for almost twenty years before her death. Perhaps it's fair to say, though, that his worst inhibitions were lifted, that he felt a bit easier about conferring his mother's quirks on Mrs. Wapshot and Cousin Honora—the latter's tendency to toss her unopened mail into the fire, say, or read *Middlemarch* over and over—not to mention his mother's death, which he would re-create with some exactitude when writing of Honora's death in *The Wapshot Scandal*. But, mother or no, he was determined to finish his first novel as soon as humanly possible—"to prove [Linscott] wrong" and liberate himself, at least somewhat, from the constraining label of "*New Yorker* writer."

Certainly the time was ripe: Cheever was finally receiving a degree of acclaim from his peers, something he'd fully expected after "The Country Husband." "I have written to myself imaginary letters of praise from Auden, Bellow, Trilling, Mizener," he reported in his journal the day after the story appeared—and the next day: "Still this low comedy of waiting to be complimented . . . Half asleep I saw letters so numerous that they had to be tied into bundles; but nothing this morning at the PO (which I visited twice) but a belltin [bulletin] from the League of Women Voters." Presently, however, some mail began to arrive. A. J. Liebling wrote that he considered Cheever the "American Chekhov" (an almost proverbial title in later years); Katharine White called him "one of our most original writers and one of the most gifted." And finally, when Malcolm Cowley became president of the

National Institute of Arts and Letters in 1956, Cheever began rubbing his hands together in earnest. "I guess you and I can look forward to a cozy old age—" he wrote Herbst, "snoozing in club chairs and eating the free food at testimonial dinners. I don't think he'll forget his old friends."

What Cheever was specifically hoping for—even counting on—was the Prix de Rome: a fellowship subsidizing a year's residence at the American Academy in Rome.* Cowley of all people knew how badly Cheever had wanted to go abroad these last five years or so; indeed, it was Cowley who kept insisting such a move was essential, lest Cheever lapse into hopeless provincialism. But apparently Cowley's endorsement wasn't enough, for that year's fellowship went to the poet John Ciardi.† Cheever, however, was not entirely overlooked: along with James Baldwin and five others, he was awarded a one-thousand-dollar grant in recognition of his "wry sympathy of heart, [which] has commemorated the poetry of that most unpoetical life, the middle class life of the American metropolis and its suburbs." Cowley may have sensed chagrin on Cheever's part over what amounted to a relative booby prize; in any case, he accused his old protégé of ingratitude when Cheever declined (in all modesty) to donate an original manuscript to an exhibition at the award ceremony. "I am crushed and miserable," Cheever promptly wrote the Institute librarian, Hannah Josephson, assuring her that a manuscript was in transit. "I know myself to be drunken and lazy, foolish and lewd, nervous and long-winded, runty and improvident, but God preserve me from ever being balky with such an old friend as you." ("Spent most of the morning writing letters to repair my fences at the institute," he wrote in his journal. "Malcolm pompous, I think.")

It galled Cheever that such occasional sops hadn't translated into anything resembling big money, whereas a mediocre rival like New-

---

*The American Academy of Arts and Letters, that is, whose fifty distinguished members were elected from the 250-member National Institute of Arts and Letters. In 1976, the two merged into the American Academy and Institute of Arts and Letters and is now a single, 250-member organization known as the American Academy of Arts and Letters.

†Getting beaten out of the Prix de Rome—by John Ciardi—would rankle forever. In 1979, Cheever was head of the jury awarding the prize, and thus phoned that year's winner, Joseph Caldwell, with the good news. "You yourself won, didn't you?" said Caldwell, filling an awkward pause. Cheever allowed that he hadn't. "Well," said Caldwell, "keep plugging!" Cheever didn't laugh.

house had scarcely written a word in five years because (as he was happy to explain) he'd taken his movie money and tripled it in the stock market; meanwhile his last (ever) novel, *The Temptation of Roger Heriott*, had been "aimed straight at the cockles of Sam Goldwyn's leathery old heart," as Cheever saw it. Irwin Shaw had also continued to prosper. Having sold *The Young Lions* to the movies and gone to Switzerland, he occasionally blew through New York and entertained Cheever, distractedly, in his hotel ("I read the Sunday paper while Irwin talked large sums of money with Hollywood"). But then Cheever was not a worldly man. For years his old Signal Corps buddy John Weaver had exhorted him to hire a proper Hollywood agent—Weaver's own agent and friend, Henry Lewis—but Cheever "kept putting it off": he didn't like haggling with show-business types, and he didn't want to be seduced, ever, into writing anything remotely like *The Temptation of Roger Heriott*. At long last, though, he did rather grudgingly assent to Hollywood representation, and roughly two weeks after "The Housebreaker of Shady Hill" appeared in the April 14, 1956, issue of *The New Yorker*, he got a call: Dore Schary of M-G-M had bought the rights for twenty-five thousand dollars. Cheever drank off a glass of whiskey, told his dog Cassie the news, and piously read *Winnie-the-Pooh* to Ben. "The reason I told the dog about it," he wrote Weaver afterward, "was because when Henry Lewis called there was no one here but Ben and me and the dog. Mary and Susie had gone to a movie called The Little Kidnappers. I don't believe that children Ben's age should be told about money and so that left me with the dog. . . . Then Mary came home, received the news sniffily, and went upstairs to sleep. This made me cross so I drank more whisky and sat broodily on the sofa thinking how with this money I could have prostitutes of all kinds, dancing to my whip." His journal corroborates this account, more or less, including the part about prostitutes.*

· · ·

---

*In fact, Cheever spent at least part of the money on an old friend. If he'd been awarded the Prix de Rome as expected, then Josie Herbst—now virtually destitute—would have gotten one of the thousand-dollar grants, since she'd been chosen as an alternate. Whether Cheever knew as much is unknown, but once he received the Hollywood money he promptly sent her a check "which should be spent on gin, shoes, and rose-bushes or anything else." Herbst would have to wait ten more bitter years before she finally got a grant from the Institute (largely at Cheever's behest).

ON A THURSDAY IN JUNE, Cheever finished a draft of *The Wapshot Chronicle* and dropped it off at a typing agency. The next day he drove his family to Friendship, Maine, where he'd rented the Spears' house (The Spruces) on a point overlooking the Atlantic. "Bostonians, rocks, sunsets, fir trees, a lovely coast line and at dusk the whole point awash with tea," Cheever wrote. "Lovely, lovely." The "Bostonians" were three or four sprawling Yankee clans who populated the point in summer, wandering around The Spruces calling "Yoo hoo, yoo hoo," while drinking martinis out of jelly glasses. Cheever was apt to receive them with perfect magnanimity. Perhaps for the first time in his adult life, he didn't have to worry about money, and, even better, his novel was finished, his wife was pregnant, and in the fall they were all going to Italy (and the Prix de Rome be damned). "Took Mary and the others out to Ram island in the outboard," Cheever wrote of a serenely typical day. "Boiled lobsters over a driftwood fire on the rocks . . . Back here, feeling no pain, ate some excellent chowder, dozed on the sofa listening to Vivaldi. Rain on the roof at four in the morning."

As long as his novel was out of sight, he was somewhat able to relish the accomplishment. He wrote himself congratulatory letters ("The Greatest thing since War and Peace"), while anticipating book-club deals, movie sales, every conceivable award. Indeed, he could hardly believe his good fortune—and so he began to doubt it. He suspected the book was, at best, unfinished and full of holes, imagining a letter from Harper & Brothers reminiscent of the rebukes he'd gotten from Linscott over the years ("you may have the beginnings of something here but we feel it would be best if you put this behind you and made a fresh start"). Several times a day he went to the post office, waiting for his freshly typed manuscript, but when it finally arrived he could barely look at it. Fearing the worst, he sent copies to Maxwell and Bessie. "And I'm still up in the air over the book," he brooded in his journal. "I think that Bill and Mike are reading [it] today. . . . A telegram cannot reach me here, but this does not keep me from writing them to myself."

"WELL ROARED LION," Maxwell wrote in his first telegram—which arrived safely—and then he sent another: "I don't expect to enjoy anything as much for a long long time. The places and people are all real, the 'hearty fleeting vision of life' is consistent and recognizably yours, and the writing is brilliant everywhere. I think it is going to be enormously successful." This, Cheever reflected, was the very thing he might have written himself, and made all the difference "between feeling alive and feeling like an old suit hanging in a closet." Maxwell said nothing about "holes" in the structure or making a "fresh start," and a week or so later he reported further that Shawn and Katharine White had also loved the novel, and wanted to publish two or three long sections in *The New Yorker*. Mrs. White even wrote separately: "One of the most cheerful things that has happened to me—and to the New Yorker—all this summer is the fact of our going to be able to publish the chapters from your book. . . . I know it will be a tremendous thing."

Heady stuff, and Cheever's elation lasted all of a day or two before he resumed brooding. He'd yet to hear from Bessie, after all, whose "prosaic" turn of mind had worried him ever since that meeting on Nantucket. It was one thing for Maxwell to like the book—he was a fellow artist: he understood Cheever's love of atmospherics, his need to listen (as it were) to the rain. Bessie, like Linscott, was liable to miss the point of all that. "I'm not prepared to remove any smells from this book," Cheever had declared in his cover letter. "I'm a very olfactory person and I will not be disposed to remove any smells." But Bessie hadn't minded the smells at all; he'd found the book delightful from start to finish, as had everyone else at Harper. Finally, almost a month after receiving the typescript, he even called Maine to say so: "Tell me!" he greeted Cheever. "How are Mary and the children? And how is Maine?" Cheever—overwrought, all but certain the long silence meant an imminent Linscottian raspberry—replied that Mary and the children were fine, Maine was fine, and how did Bessie like the book? Bessie said (in effect) that the book was *wonderful*, just wonderful, and he'd be happy to go into more "detailed criticism" in a letter; meanwhile they should have lunch and so on. "I seem to get nothing from Harpers but consternation," Cheever wrote Maxwell. "They have promised to send me a 'detailed criticism' and as Mary points out I can't wait to lay my hands on this and lose my temper."

A few days later, Bessie and Cheever met for lunch at the Ritz. As they sat down, Cheever abruptly announced (eyes slightly averted) that he was happy to return the twenty-four hundred dollars if Bessie didn't like the book; also he repeated that business about the smells. "John"—Bessie interrupted—"I tried to tell you for half an hour on the phone the other day what a wonderful book it is, and I'll be glad to start all over again, and somebody [Evan Thomas] said 'that it's the best thing that has happened to Harper's fiction in a long time' . . ." At length Cheever appeared to be mollified, but afterward wrote in his journal that he was still "not satisfied": "[Bessie] reminds me of other people who put one into the position of a patsy. They stuff you into taxi cabs, buy you plane tickets and buy you the drink you don't need and in the end they leave you standing alone at the bar, surrounded by your luggage and screwed." He did, however, decide to accept the situation ("I've settled"), but continued to suspect some nastiness in the offing. A week or so later, Mrs. White wrote that she'd recently chatted with Bessie (a friend), who went on and on about *The Wapshot Chronicle*: "He is very happy about it." "Harpers *seemed* to like it but it was very hard to tell," Cheever replied. "Your good opinion has fortified me over the summer and made me a loving husband and a patient father. Without it I would have got drunk and broken all the dishes."

For whatever reason, Bessie had expected Cheever to be something of a lightweight when they first met in Westchester a few years back (quite possibly Cheever had picked up on this), but was pleasantly surprised when the subject of Saul Bellow came up. "Bellow"—said Cheever on that occasion—"is the first American novelist of parts who writes neither in sympathy with nor in opposition to the Puritan tradition. He writes as if it didn't exist." This was high and insightful praise, coming from a writer whose own work was marred (so he thought) by an inordinate preoccupation with the Puritan tradition. Little wonder Bellow would always be Cheever's favorite contemporary, both as a writer and as a man—this even though they'd met on one of the worst days of Cheever's life. "These are the hardest days, hours anyhow," he wrote on March 27, 1952, after his bad, bad lunch with Linscott. "Then to an unhappy drink at the Commodore and a party at Eleanor's where Saul Bellow was."*

Bellow had yet to become an obsession, though Cheever had been impressed by *Dangling Man* ("Here is the blend of French and Russian that I like") and doubtless said so in lavish terms. Then, in 1953, Cheever read *The Adventures of Augie March* and (as he later put it

---

*Mary Cheever confirmed that this encounter at Clark's party was indeed the first time the two met.

while presenting an award to Bellow) "had the experience, that I think of as great art, of having a profound chamber of memory revealed to me that I had always possessed but had never comprehended." If anything, the book was even more overwhelming than these orotund words suggest. At the time, Cheever was writing his first Shady Hill stories, and had a sense of coming into his own powers at last; *Augie March*—as both a vision of life and a piece of writing—was an incitement to do better. "There is to learn that in writing of carnal love he shakes the gloom, the morbidity, the mud, and proseyness (an unclothed woman, etc.) that gets under my feet," Cheever wrote. "His optimism I share, having reached it by my own, crooked, lengthy, leaf-buried path. We cannot spend our lives in apprehension." But of course the book was not altogether pleasurable. Faced with "the challenge of a brilliant contemporary," Cheever tried hard to compare himself favorably. For one thing, he tended to find vernacular prose "distasteful" as a rule, but then his own relative precision was in the service of expressing "the genteel symbols of the middle class"—constricted, in short; small. Meanwhile he kept reading *Augie March* ("I read it backwards. I read it upside down in a bucket of water"), and finally wrote a letter to its author: if Bellow was as good as all that, then it was Cheever's "manifest destiny" to return to the South Shore "and pump gasoline at one of those service stations on the way to the Cape." In loftier moments, though, he considered Bellow's work an exalting reminder that literature was "a key part of the human enterprise"—and besides, "writing is not a competitive sport," as Cheever's public persona liked to say.

He might have been less generous if he hadn't been so smitten with the man. In the summer of 1956, Cheever was elected to the Yaddo board of directors, and when he returned to Saratoga for the meeting in September, his main concern was seeing Bellow: "At dinner I am conscious of being in the same room with Saul." The two went for a walk afterward, and Cheever remembered other "passionate friendships" which had begun at Yaddo—with Reuel Denney and Flannery Lewis—wondering why he should feel an almost "mystical" bond with a Chicago Jew. "I cast around for some precedent of two writers with similar aims who are strongly drawn to one another," Cheever mused. "I do not have it in me to wish him bad luck: I do not have it in me to be his acolyte." Nor did it seem to matter whether he had anything weighty to say with Bellow. The two had rapport—"we joke, fool, as I like to"—and Cheever couldn't help reflecting a little sadly on "poor BM" [Maxwell], "who never extends this pleasant feeling of friendship, who never quite seems to get out of doors except to bend over his roses."

The admiration was wholly mutual. "I loved him," said Bellow. "A wonderful man." Both were charming, difficult personalities, and both were at their best with each other on the rare occasions when they met. If anything Bellow was the more prickly of the two, alert to slights of any sort—especially from goyim—but with Cheever he felt "no sense of rivalry," and certainly never a hint of Yankee condescension. As he remarked in his eulogy, "It fell to John to resolve these differences [of background]. He did it without the slightest difficulty, simply by putting human essences in first place." Reduced to their essences, the two were fundamentally alike. "We share not only our love of women but a fondness for the rain," said Cheever. Or, as his wife would have it, "They were both women haters."

CHAPTER SEVENTEEN

{ 1956–1957 }

A FTER HE FINISHED a light revision of *The Wapshot Chronicle*, Cheever wasn't able to get any work done for a long time. He was tired of writing about (and living in) Shady Hill. For years now he'd been casting ahead to Rome—listening to *La Traviata* and *Tosca* again and again, as well as the odd conversational-Italian record—and now at last he was ready to sail. Such was his excitement that he'd hardly considered some obvious difficulties: none of them spoke Italian (records withal); they hadn't arranged a permanent place to stay or schools for the children; Mary was pregnant, and didn't see the point of having a baby in Rome, to put it mildly. Also, Cheever had elected to receive his M-G-M money in three annual installments for tax reasons, and now discovered he had surprisingly little in the bank once he'd paid for boat passage (first-class), trunks, clothing, and the like. And finally there was a more esoteric concern: "So [I am] afraid that I may fall in love in with a dirty duchess or a lonely grocery boy," he wrote a few days before sailing, "but this is after all not so remarkable; and with a gentle heart and a capricious cod what can you do but trust in the Lord and take your chances."

They departed on October 17, 1956, aboard the *Conte Biancamano* ("a cross between the Fall River Line and the old Ritz"). Cheever rose early and had a last drink with Angelo Palumbo, then a few more with the Boyers, who eventually drove them into New York. After a *bon voyage* party in their cabin, the ship pulled out of the harbor amid a shower of confetti and circus music. The gaiety lingered perhaps an hour or two: "Then fog, a heavy roll and everyone sick but me." The wind would blow for six long days. Cheever awoke "to the noise of smashing flower vases and medicine bottles," and when he emerged in the morning, most of the passengers were absent. Dressed in black-tie, he passed the time in an elegant bar or playing musical chairs with a few stragglers in the ballroom, all the while worrying whether the boat would sink. Finally the weather cleared somewhere around the northern Azores (Cheever went for a swim), and after stops in Lisbon, Casablanca, Gibraltar, Barcelona, Cannes, Palermo, and Genoa, they disembarked at Naples and boarded a train for Rome. "I am tired of the ship," Cheever wrote in his journal, noting a "peculiarly bad smell" that had pervaded the crossing: "The essence of it seems to have been one rough mid-afternoon when I was hanging onto an ornate piece of furniture with one hand and a glass of whisky with the other, the orchestra playing concert music to a room-full of empty chairs . . . and the unfresh smell."

Tired and disoriented, they hired a carriage in Rome and spent the first day sightseeing. At the Tomb of Augustus, Cheever thought his heart would break ("Is this all, is this all there is?"), and matters soon took a turn for the worse. Eleanor Clark had found them a temporary two-room apartment at La Residenza, an expensive *pensione* near the Villa Borghese Gardens; they'd been there all of four days when Ben's beloved mouse, Barbara Frietchie, died. Aboard the boat, the eight-year-old and his pet had been inseparable, winning second place in a hat contest (the hat featured Barbara clinging to the brim with a piece of cheese). Now, however, in the close quarters of La Residenza, the mouse's odor was especially pungent, and one night, after the children had gone down to dinner, Cheever stole into their room and sprayed the cage with perfume. The next day, Barbara Frietchie was dead. "Mary bought violets in the Piazza di Spagna," Cheever wrote Herbst. "Barbara was laid out in a candy box and I was commissioned to bury her in the Borghese gardens but the ground was hard and she got a sordid resting place." Worried that he'd be caught digging in the public garden with a spoon, Cheever finally chucked the mouse into a trash can, and when he returned to the apartment, his children were weeping hysterically and begging to go home.

The bigger picture was also grim. They'd learned in Palermo—where a pack of newsboys had run screaming through the streets—that Israel had invaded the Gaza Strip in response to Egypt's nationalization of the Suez Canal, and another world war appeared imminent.

This was the substance of Cheever's daily reading while he sat on a ratty sofa sipping bad gin and tap water; it also dominated the conversation at cocktail parties, where Cheever encountered a colony of Americans every bit as tedious and provincial as the ones he'd left behind in Scarborough: "They talk gaily about the certainty of war," he wrote Maxwell, "and with their Roman clothes and jewelry and their knowledge of good small restaurants they seem to be fulfilling ambitions that must have been formed in the kitchens and backyards of small and lonely American Towns." Given, too, that he was running through his money at a harrowing rate, that he could scarcely buy a newspaper without getting shortchanged, that he lacked the linguistic skills to remonstrate, and that "the dash of Roman men . . . reminded him of his own contested sexual identity," Cheever already felt so homesick that he couldn't imagine why he'd ever left Westchester in the first place. After an especially dreadful cocktail party, he almost decided to cut his losses and go—this after a week or so in Rome—but resolved to stick it out like "Scout camp" and see if the "storms of strangeness" would pass.

By then he'd looked at some twenty-five "indescribably dismal apartments" and was about to sign a lease on a "cubby-hole in the outskirts," but Eleanor Clark persuaded him to stay in the middle of town (bus service was terrible). With her help they found a rather stunning place: the *piano nobile* on the fourth floor of the Palazzo Doria, directly across from the Palazzo Venezia, where Mussolini had hailed the multitudes. The place mostly consisted of a cavernous, gold-ceilinged salon, divided by screens into reading, living, and dining rooms, in the last of which Cheever sat typing his letters (and little else) at an ormolu table: "There is only one chair in the salon where I can sit and have my feet touch the floor and there are two chairs where my feet don't even hang over the edge." Such grandeur didn't come cheap, but then Cheever had the added pleasure of regaling guests with tales of his romantic landlady, the Principessa Doria, an anti-Fascist who'd escaped the Nazis by hiding in a Trastevere cellar during the occupation. On the other hand, gas leaked in the grubby little kitchen, the drains were clogged, and there was only one water closet, with a toilet seat that pinched ("impulsive or hasty guests could be heard howling in pain behind the closed door").

Within a few weeks, Cheever was "on thin ice financially" and had to borrow from *The New Yorker*. As for his children, they were still crying themselves to sleep every night, but at least they were back in school: Susan at Marymount International ("a convent where they work the nose off her") and Ben at the Overseas School ("where he gets along mostly with Burmese"). The family's lack of Italian and basic cluelessness continued to make everyday life a strain. On Thanksgiving, Mary went shopping for the feast, but at five different shops (there were no supermarkets) the best she could manage was some bread, salami, and cheese. While Ben ate raw fish and rice at the home of his new Burmese friend, Ronald Aung Din, the rest of the Cheevers sat at a warped kitchen table and ate salami. Susan wept: "I don't like Rome," she said. "It's just like any other big city. It's noisy and dirty and expensive and the crowds are always running and what does it matter if you see a ruin now and then?" Cheever recorded the remark in his journal and wrote, "I think she is so right."

A week or so later—after a day "like a witches [sic] tooth"— Cheever came home from his Italian lesson and found a letter from a stranger in Philadelphia informing him that *Time* magazine had "panned the collection." The collection was titled *Stories* and included work by Cheever and three other notable *New Yorker* writers: Jean Stafford, Maxwell, and Daniel Fuchs. (The early *Time* review—"News from the Defeated"—wasn't really that bad: it called Stafford "the biggest name and most accomplished craftsman of the group" and didn't mention Cheever at all, though the four were collectively praised for their "competence.") The idea for the book had originated a few years back, when Cheever had met Stafford at a party given by their mutual friend Margot Morrow. Someone had asked the two why they hadn't published more story collections. As Cheever wrote in his "Authors' Note":

> The writers explained that—aside from the indifference of publishers—to collect short stories is something like marrying many times and collecting all your wives under one roof on a rainy day. Furthermore, collections of short stories are usually reviewed in tandem or four-in-hand and in an atmosphere of combativeness (X is more sensitive than Y) that overlooks the fact, known to most writers, that to make sense out of life is an exertion of uncommon cooperativeness.

Thinking no doubt of the invidious comparisons he'd suffered because of *Nine Stories*, Cheever had proposed that Stafford and he collaborate with Salinger on a collection of their most recent fiction; such a show of solidarity would perhaps appeal to the reviewers' better natures. Salinger, however, politely declined ("What a *very* nice idea!"), and Cheever recruited Maxwell along with their old friend Fuchs, wryly suggesting they title the book (in homage to Hawthorne) *Mosses from Four Old Manses.* The more generic *Stories* included five by Stafford, four by Cheever ("The Day the Pig Fell into the Well," "The National Pastime," "The Bus to St. James's," and "The Country Husband"), and three apiece by Maxwell and Fuchs. Reviews were sparse but admiring. In the *Times Book Review*, Richard Sullivan described the stories as "expert, worthy and honorable pieces of prose," while at least two other major reviewers singled out "The Day the Pig Fell into the Well," both as the best (William Peden) and the gloomiest (Orville Prescott) story in the collection.

Back in Italy, meanwhile, things were looking up at last. One day Cheever got in touch with a fellow expatriate, the novelist Elizabeth Spencer. His wife was pregnant and becoming rather frantic, Cheever explained, what with one thing and another; he wondered if they might borrow Spencer's maid for an afternoon. Presently a short, energetic woman wearing a cat-fur stole appeared, and promptly began "raising great Biblical clouds of dust in the middle of the sala," as Cheever wrote. *"I Cheevers hanno bisogno di me,"* the woman told Spencer ("The Cheevers have need of me"), to whom she sent her sister as a replacement. The new maid was named Iole Felici, and she would remain in Cheever's life until the end. For thirty-five cents an hour, she did the cooking, cleaning, minor repairs, and most of the child-rearing; she also dealt with various merchants who'd been robbing the monoglot Americans, and took it upon herself to hire a second maid, Vittoria, to help with heavy work. When Cheever tried to take out the garbage or carry his own groceries, Iole would scold him for making a *brutta figura* ("lousy impression")—a phrase that enchanted him.

Cheever's love of the language would prove an elusive, lifelong affair. In Rome he diligently attended La Società Nazionale Dante Alighieri, where a heavy woman "with a large amethyst brooch and a bum leg" scrawled verbs on the chalkboard and hissed *("psssst!")* for silence. To little avail. Aside from a few stilted phrases, Cheever was never able to master *la bella lingua*, whereas his wife got good enough to chat with the maids and keep secrets from him. Cheever's own attempts to communicate with his staff had a way of going awry. The teenage Vittoria would bring him breakfast in bed, but didn't understand that he preferred to eat his boiled egg from the shell, un-peeled. As his daughter remembered, "He studied the dictionary care-fully, finding the word for egg, the word for kitchen, and the word for peel. In the morning, when Vittoria appeared, he cleared his throat and carefully asked her not to peel the eggs in the kitchen. Vittoria shrieked, blushed, and rushed from the room in tears. What my father had said was, 'Do not undress in the kitchen, you egg.' The fact that Vittoria had been changing her clothes in the kitchen didn't help." But Cheever kept trying to learn, and eventually came to believe that Ital-ian was his "linguistic hole card," as he put it. People like Shirley Haz-zard, who really did speak the language, would sigh whenever a tipsy Cheever gave a telltale leer and began speaking "his ghastly Italian."

CHEEVER DIVIDED the American colony into "Academy and unAcademy," and found a fair number of "duds" in both groups. While unAcademy people were often provincial and generally foolish, Acad-emy people were dull in their own right and doubtless intimidated Cheever with their intellectual airs. In early December he attended a reception for Robert Penn Warren—Eleanor Clark's husband of four years—and reported afterward that he hadn't "been so uncomfortable since they discontinued the old 59th Street cross-town trolley cars." For the rest of his life, Cheever would see the Warrens once or twice a year, at Institute functions or the couple's Christmas parties in Con-necticut, but he and "Red" never became close—except perhaps for a single afternoon when he visited the Warrens' apartment in the Acad-emy complex atop the Janiculum, one of the highest hills in Rome. The two went for a walk along the Via Aurelia and discussed their var-ious projects and ideas. "We saw some pretty country, bought bread and cheese and ate it in the sunlight, throwing our scraps to a pair of tame magpies," Cheever wrote in his journal. "Then, walking back a terraced hill covered with sheep, he recited and Dante'd [i.e., recited Dante]. We must have walked sixteen miles. All very pleasant." Warren noticed, however, that Cheever tended to grow "impatient" when-ever the erudite Kentuckian resorted to "generalizations"—that is, the sort of formalist lingo he was apt to exchange with Cleanth Brooks. Cheever himself "always talked specifics"—nice little details from the books he loved—and privately mocked Warren as an "academic char-latan" who confused philosophy with literature.

Ralph Ellison was also at the Academy (he'd gotten his 1955 Prix de

Rome renewed for another year), and he and Cheever were friendly in a somewhat constrained way. "His face can shine with light," said the latter, "but it doesn't seem to shine for me." Though he would never admit it publicly, Cheever had found *Invisible Man* "longwinded"—an allegorical novel of ideas, after all—and when Ellison would start "talking about negros" and using terms like "mass motivation," Cheever would make a sympathetic face and cast about for ways of changing the subject. At the Academy, at least, he preferred the surrealist painter Peter Blume, whom he'd known in New York twenty years before; neither Blume nor his wife, Ebie, was inclined to discuss New Criticism or sociopolitical topics, at least with Cheever, who found them "about as clear, sweet and blue-sky as any people I have ever known."

And finally among the literary set (briefly) was Irwin Shaw, living like a movie star at the Hotel Excelsior and riding around Rome in a chauffeur-driven cream-colored sedan (or "canary-yellow convertible," as Cheever preferred to describe it). Now that Cheever had finished his novel and gotten a taste from the Hollywood trough, he could afford to laugh at Shaw's zanier excesses, to say nothing of his linguistic facility or lack thereof. "Irwin stopped at the [Excelsior] desk and asked for his mail in Italian," Cheever wrote a friend.

> He spoke such gibberish that [his companion] offered to interpret for him but he said that wouldn't be necessary. The governess of his son, he explained, was Italian and that was why he spoke so fluently. Irwin got his mail—a large bundle of it—and they went out to the chauffeur driven car that Irwin always has in Rome. "I'll ask the chauffeur to hold my mail," he explained and then made another assault on the bella lingua. "Si, si," the chauffeur said when Irwin had finished, "si signore." Then, as Irwin climbed contentedly into the back seat of the car the chauffeur trotted down the street and stuffed Irwin's letters into a mail-box.

Cheever's socializing was a more or less vapid way to kill time (which weighed heavily in the absence of any work), though he longed all the while "for a kind of unicorn"—something more romantic, that is, than a stale friendship or even a pregnant wife. Quite simply he wanted to be in love again, and in that respect he liked the strangeness of Rome. Walking the streets in New York, he was never quite free of "sexual and financial anxiety": he couldn't help sizing people up and deciding that one or another was richer or more virile or temperate than he. But in Rome he never saw "a recognizable homosexual or alcoholic": old men bussed one another on the cheeks, and the "cox-combery" of youth seemed to have little to do with class or sexual disposition. The mystery appealed to Cheever—the whole hopeful ethos of "arsehole jokes and golden piety that . . . adds up to an honest measure of our nature."

Of course, the pious side of Cheever's nature was devoted to his family, and he was duly grieved by the ordeals of a pregnant woman in a foreign land. Mary noticed that Roman men rarely gave up their seats to her on buses, and her obstetrician was downright "brusque and patronizing." At one point he diagnosed her with toxemia and told her to eat nothing but spinach (without oil or salt): "She did this for two weeks," Cheever wrote, "and then protested and the Doctor said: 'But I have gout and that's all I eat.' Mary said that he wasn't going to have a baby and he drew himself up and said, 'It's not my role in life.' " The onset of labor (on March 9) came as a blessed relief. The Blumes drove Mary to Salvador Mundi Hospital on the Janiculum, where she lay in a birthing room, along with nine or ten screeching Italians, and read her husband's copy of *The Woman in White* by Wilkie Collins. Cheever, meanwhile, was fretfully pacing the streets of a city whose aspect "seemed pitiless and cruel": "I went to the zoo for a Campari and found myself surrounded by hyenas, buzzards, wolves and grisley [sic] bears. Then I climbed up the roof of St. Peters but all the prophets had their backs to me." Arriving at the hospital, he found his wife "in great pain"—and alone, because her bookish decorum had resulted in neglect. A nun was summoned in the nick of time, and twenty minutes later Cheever was told he had *"un figlio robusto."* "I don't ever remember loving a child so much," he wrote in his journal the next day, after visiting the hospital with Susan and Ben. "I have a drink and feel very odd—the cold, I guess—and looking down from my balcony into the street I covet the freedom of young bucks in open cars going down to Ostia to raise hell, and observe how a man can be given nearly everything the world has to offer and go on yearning."

Cheever would not stop yearning, to be sure, but neither would he ever love another human being as much as his younger son, Federico.*

---

*He wanted to name the boy Frederick, of course—after his father and once-beloved brother—but ran into trouble with the birth certificate: there is no "k" in the Italian alphabet ("I gave up after an hour or two"). As a grown man Federico is generally called Fred, though I use the Italian by way of distinguishing him from other Freds in Cheever's life.

Though easily disappointed in people (particularly his family), Cheever noted toward the end of his life that Federico had always been "a source of boundless pleasure" and even his own "salvation"—quite true, if not unfailingly mutual. And Cheever wasn't the only one whose love of the boy was lifelong and unconditional. *"Il Duce! Il Duce!"* Iole cried ecstatically when they brought him home. Unmarried and childless, she spirited the baby away and would only yield him at nursing time. Dubbing him *picci*—"little one"—she did not abide contradiction on matters pertaining to his care: she ignored Princess Doria's complaints about the diapers hanging from one end of the balcony to the other, and when Cheever returned from the doctor with a bottle of brown medicine (a purgative of some sort), she snatched it out of his hand and poured it down the sink amid a long incomprehensible harangue of rapid-fire Italian.

CHAPTER EIGHTEEN

{ 1957 }

W HEN OBLIGED TO DISCUSS his almost total inability to work during those first months in Italy, Cheever would sometimes explain that he couldn't find the right sort of paper, or that he didn't have enough privacy in the Doria salon, or even that the ceiling was too high. Mainly, though, he was obsessively "woolgathering" about *The Wapshot Chronicle*. He couldn't help wondering what sort of reception the book would get, and this led to rereading it over and over ("I hope to become so bored and tired with it that I will forget it") in order to reassure himself. Usually he rather liked the book, and this in turn led to further woolgathering about fame and fortune—or at least a sale to the Book-of-the-Month Club, so he could really afford life as a leisured expatriate. As it happened, the club was all for it, except for one problem: the word "fuck." As Ralph Thompson (the editorial director) explained to his old friend Mike Bessie, the club had *never* distributed to its members a book with that word in it; therefore he wondered if the author might be persuaded to come up with some reasonable equivalent. Bessie got hold of Cheever in Rome and mentioned the money at stake, then told him about the hitch. There was a pause. Finally Cheever replied: "Mike, the answer is no. That's the right word. That's the *only* word." Bessie pointed out that the word had been changed when the passage had run in *The New Yorker*,* but Cheever remained obdurate—there were

---

*The line in question—"You've talked yourself out of a fuck"—was changed in *The New Yorker* to "Shut up, Melissa. Shut up."

things he'd do for the magazine that he wouldn't do for anyone else, and that was that. Thus history was made: *The Wapshot Chronicle* became the first-ever selection of the Book-of-the-Month Club that contained the word "fuck."

Cheever had continued to take a dim view of Bessie and Harper, whose attitude he likened to a large "Boston trust company with a very small investor." Then, in late February 1957, he received an advance copy of *The Wapshot Chronicle* and had to admit it was very handsome indeed; that same day he also received a complimentary letter from Bellow, all of which left him in grave danger of "commit[ting] the sin of pride": "But dizzy with excitement I went out to buy cigarettes," he wrote in his journal, "and the pretty girl at the cafe, quite a flirt, gave me a look of pure uninterestedness and so I am crushed and feel like myself again." And still he had a month to go until publication, and still he couldn't get back to work. Instead, he mentally wrote reviews ("I've written them all, even the Albany Times-Union") and allowed himself to wonder, late at night, what it would be like to open a copy of *Il Messaggero* and learn that he'd won the Pulitzer.

One of the first important notices, in the March 24 *New York Times Book Review*, seemed to portend no such result. "The 'New Yorker' school of fiction has come in for so many critical strictures lately that one almost wishes John Cheever, a talented member of this group, would confound the critics and break loose," wrote Maxwell Geismar, who went on to conclude that Cheever had not, in fact, broken loose, nor was his novel "quite a novel," or at any rate a very "serious" one. Rather it was mere "entertainment"—a "picaresque" that "didn't quite hang together." Other reviewers would also point out the novel's "episodic" or "fragmented" structure, and the main question was whether or not they thought this defect was transcended by its virtues. Most of them did. Two days after Geismar's mixed review, Charles Poore wrote in the daily *Times* that the novel was "a magnificently exuberant story of a Massachusetts sea-sprayed clan, rising, falling, rising again, entangled in plots of awesome adventurousness," and the *Washington Post* was similarly effusive: "Cheever's venture is exuberantly, cantankerously, absurdly, audaciously alive," wrote Glendy Culligan, who also found the book "brilliant, ebullient, alternately sad, funny and tender . . ." And then there were critics who thought Cheever had decidedly broken loose—not only advancing on previous work, but (as Fanny Butcher claimed in the *Chicago Sunday Tribune*) "add[ing] something new to the stream of American fiction." But perhaps the poet Winfield Townley Scott said it best: "It is difficult to think of another contemporary who can write without sentimentality and yet with so much love."

Love was very much to the point: "A dear book it is," Cheever would say of his first novel, never forgetting the terrible obstacles he'd overcome in writing it—a twenty-year effort to reconcile himself (in art, at least) with family demons, and thus find the strength to forge a style, a world, that was magnificently his own. As Rick Moody wrote in his foreword to a later edition, "Where did [Cheever] get the confidence to begin disassembling and reassembling American naturalist fiction, thereby helping to pave the way for the experimentation of the late sixties and the seventies? He got the confidence by writing *The Wapshot Chronicle*." Abandoning naturalism—in this case a literal and all-too-painful evocation of the past—was akin to walking out the "door" that had stood open for Cheever all those years he spent trying to dig his way out of jail "with a teaspoon," as he'd once put it. What this entailed was yet another reinvention of the young writer who'd once, long ago, been preoccupied with *history*—namely, the fatalism of a generation coming of age between the wars, during a Depression that had left one feeling rootless and doomed. In *The Wapshot Chronicle*, however, there is no history as such: no wars, no Depression, and very few "signposts" whatsoever. "I am a little troubled by the way Mr. Cheever plays fast and loose with time," wrote the critic Granville Hicks, noting (for example) that Hamlet's search for gold in California "must have happened in the 1890s" and yet is depicted "as if he were one of the original Forty-niners."* Just so, and this was one of Cheever's favorite effects: wiping the slate clean, as it were, the better to give his characters "a freedom to pursue their emotional lives without the interruptions of history." Likewise he cobbled together a mythical place, St. Botolphs, that "can't be found on any map" but rather represents "a longing for simplicity and coherence."

Ejected from this paradise, the brothers Moses and Coverly embark on a series of adventures in the disorderly modern world, with little regard on their creator's part for narrative continuity. As Cowley pre-

---

*Granville Hicks was a Yaddo director, whom Cheever tended to call (privately) "Granny." Little did Hicks know that the actual Hamlet Cheever had gone west in the same feckless, anachronistic style.

dicted, Cheever would always be an episodic writer, more or less, having persuaded himself that conventional cause-and-effect narration was silly and contrived, worthy only of parody—and on a deeper level, he was almost temperamentally incapable of constructing such a plot. "Perhaps you could have given the book a little more of a novelistic air by adding a few sentences here and there to answer some questions left hanging," Cowley remarked, noting that strands of the novel are abandoned and never retrieved. (What becomes of Rosalie from the first section? Leander's illegitimate daughter?) Cheever, with his usual breezy candor, replied that such questions were left unanswered because the author was "such a pig-headed fool": his editors had made all the same points, Cheever said, but he simply chose to ignore them, because "for once [he] was on [his] own and would not change or explain a word." And doubtless he liked it better *his* way, without a lot of deadly, quibbling logic. Cheever was, after all, an improvisational writer who trusted his instincts: he wrote scenes out of sequence, in bursts of inspiration, and when tangents or characters were exhausted in his mind, he dropped them and moved on to something else. "One never, of course, asks is it a novel?" he once wrote. "One asks is it interesting and interest connotes suspense, emotional involvement and a sustained claim on one's attention." In those terms, at least, Cheever was a consummate novelist, as were his eighteenth-century forebears, Fielding and Sterne.

And whatever its structural lapses, the novel has a high degree of thematic integrity. "St. Botolphs was an old place, an old river town," it begins, with repetitive insistence on *oldness:* permanence, tradition. In this pastoral setting, everybody knows everybody else ("It's only the Wapshot boys"), and such familiarity breeds a kind of grim sufferance for human quirks. During the wonderful tour of St. Botolphs in the third chapter, one encounters such curious specimens as Reba Heaslip ("SALUTE YOUR FLAG! ROBBERS AND VANDALS PASS BY!") and Uncle Peepee Marshmallow, who is adopted almost as a kind of village mascot, despite his tendency to wander around naked: "What could the rest of the world do for him that could not be done in St. Botolphs?" But the most elaborate and loving study of eccentricity—so incubated in the hothouse of a tiny New England town—is Honora Wapshot, who deliberately leaves lobsters behind on buses (fighting for their lives in a bag), and tosses her mail in the fire. The kindly and humorous narrator, however, is at pains to remind us that such a person is not to be regarded as a simple figure of fun: "[H]ow much more poetry there is to Honora," he remarks of her impulse to throw away mail, "casting off the claims of life the instant they are made." And such uniqueness has its poignant side, too, as people like Honora are scarcely aware of their own freakishness. Walking past a window, she overhears her servant laughing over her odd behavior: "[Honora] stops and leans heavily, with both hands, on her cane, engrossed in an emotion so violent and so nameless that she wonders if this feeling of loneliness and bewilderment is not the mysteriousness of life." Fortunately such paroxysms are passing in a noble soul, and Honora proceeds to eat supper with a "good appetite."

The most abiding human quality found in this old, stalwart place is the kind of Emersonian self-reliance embodied by Leander, who first appears at the helm of the *Topaze*—a larger-than-life character given to shouting "Tie me to the mast, Perimedes!" whenever he hears the merry-go-round at Nangasakit. Leander wishes to instill in his sons "the unobserved ceremoniousness of his life"—the kind of values that enable a man to *be* a man and enjoy life as it ought to be lived: "He had taught them to fell a tree, pluck and dress a chicken, sow, cultivate and harvest, catch a fish, save money, countersink a nail, make cider with a hand press, clean a gun, sail a boat, etc." In the better world of St. Botolphs, all this is enough, and one has the courage to be oneself, whatever that may be; amid the institutionalized conformity of the modern city, though, an assertion of anything smacking of the peculiar is swiftly punished. Screened by a personnel psychiatrist for his first job in New York, Coverly decides "Honesty [is] the best policy" and blithely admits, among other things, that he dreams of having sex with men and (once) a horse. To his surprise and dismay he is not hired, and presently comes to dread what he suspects is "a furtive strain of morbidity" (chiefly sexual) in his nature—whereupon it falls to Leander, of course, to reassure him: "Played the man to many a schoolboy bride," the father writes with manly frankness. "All in love is not larky and fractious. Remember."

St. Botolphs may be an Eden of sorts, but it is a fallen Eden, and the provoking odors of the place (the "smells" that had worried the author so much) are a constant reminder that flesh lusteth contrary to the spirit—surely the major theme of Cheever's work as well as his life. In the village, one is assailed by scents of wood smoke and salt marshes, or (indoors) floor oil and coal gas and perhaps a boiling fish: "A carp is cooking in the kitchen, and, as everyone knows, a carp has to be boiled in claret and pickled oysters, anchovies, thyme and white onions. All of this can be smelled." Such bouquet is a goad to sensual sport, and indeed the very name "Wapshot" suggests an aspiration to subdue one's animal passions: derived from the Norman "Vaincre-Chaud"— literally, "to defeat heat"—the name graces a family of "copious journalists" who have long been in the habit of using their diaries (as Cheever did) to reproach themselves "for idleness, sloth, lewdness, stupidity and drunkenness, for St. Botolphs had been a lively port where they danced until dawn and where there was always plenty of rum to drink." No wonder Coverly flees when he sees a stripper do "something very dirty" with a farm hand's hat at a "cootch show" on the fairgrounds, only to find himself "admiring squashes" while he tries to regain his composure ("The irony . . . was not wasted on him").

But if anything the novel is a celebration of "larky," robust sensuality of the sort suggested by Moses, who remarks to the tractable Rosalie, "What harm can there be in something that would make us both feel so good?" Far from being harmful, the point is made again and again that sexual commerce is one of the great consolations in this vale of tears, as when a young man aboard the sinking *Topaze* sees fit to reflect (potentially his final thought) on the "fair and gentle" way his girlfriend has just "spread her legs" for him. Certain extremes of celibacy are perceived as a form of meanness, most notably in the case of Cousin Justina, who "hatefully" forces Moses to traverse a quarter-mile of treacherous rooftop to get to his lover's bed each night. Such prudery is an excess almost as damnable as outright "lewdness," and both are degrading to the spirit. The danger of the latter is illuminated for Leander in his dream of "walking alone through hell," where he encounters a hideous old man who exposes his "inflamed parts"— intoning "This is the beginning of wisdom"—before walking away "with the index finger up his bum." Thus Leander spends his last waking hours on earth in a sort of purification ritual: attending church and then swimming away into the cold, beloved sea.

That human beings are sinful is never in doubt, but Cheever is ultimately more concerned with the possibilities of goodness—the goodness of God, no less, manifest in our own better instincts and the beauty of all creation. Despair is almost never final. Hobbled by a sense of aloneness, Honora soon recovers her appetite; Melissa's first husband, the egregious Beaver, rallies himself "at the nadir of his

depression" with visions of "cities or archways at least of marble" and
so absconds with Justina's jewels. And finally, most movingly, Leander
is succored by rain at the funeral of his first wife, Clarissa, a suicide:
"Wind slacked off in middle of prayer. Distant, electrical smell of rain.
Sound among leaves; stubble. Hath but a short span, says Father Fris-
bee. Full of misery is he. Rain more eloquent, heartening and merciful.
Oldest sound to reach porches of man's ear." Such a humanistic vision
was realized by Cheever in the course of making peace with a father
whom he could never properly love or understand. Coverly then, in
tears, recites Prospero's speech at his father's grave, and perhaps manages to "build some kind of bridge between Leander's world and that
world where he sought his fortune." But the idealized father is given
"the last word"—a page of advice for his sons on how to live happily in
the world, with a proper regard for both flesh and spirit: "Fear tastes
like a rusty knife and do not let her into your house," the novel concludes. "Courage tastes of blood. Stand up straight. Admire the world.
Relish the love of a gentle woman. Trust in the Lord."

Cheever's long ordeal in writing *The Wapshot Chronicle* would be
amply rewarded. The book sold more than twenty thousand in hardcover, and a subsequent Bantam paperback sold almost 170,000 in the
United States alone.* That spring in Italy, meanwhile, Cheever continued to woolgather over his imminent good fortune, dreaming one
night of the Eisenhowers alone in their White House bedroom:
"Mamie is reading the Washington Star. Ike is reading The Wapshot
Chronicle."

ZINNY SCHOALES CAME OVER in April, joining the Cheevers on a
trip to Venice for the St. Mark's Festival. Arriving in the rain at the
Hotel Europa, the group was refused rooms because of Federico's
squalling (Iole allegedly punched the desk clerk) and proceeded to the
Londra. The rest of the trip was "wonderful." They were woken the
next morning by all the bells of Venice pealing in honor of the festival,
and spent the day riding gondolas and attending concerts and watching the various religious processions. The drinks were nastier than

---

*The latter had "a vaguely suggestive cover," as Susan Cheever recalled, which her
father removed from every copy that came into his house. He asked his teenage daughter not to read *The Wapshot Chronicle*.

ever, though, and Cheever allowed himself the luxury of a celebrated tourist trap, Harry's Bar, "just to see how disgusting it was": "The second day I went in to make sure. . . . I took Mary back the next day to show her how disgusting it was and we stayed until closing."

A decent martini reminded Cheever that he was more homesick than ever. Federico was colicky and crying all the time, which left Mary exhausted and inclined to cry, too. As for Cheever, he was tired of playing host to a lot of dull Americans in his vast salon, and longed to get back into a proper working routine. The combination of idleness and drink tended to make him mean. One day Ben came home from an outing with friends—a warm, jolly (if a trifle déclassé) family whom Cheever described to his guests "with much unkind detail" while the boy stood there holding a pail of tadpoles. "Then the guests go," Cheever wrote in his journal,

> and when we come to the [dinner] table Ben is sobbing as if his heart would break for, having left people who I think of as needing my condescension he has come home to find his own house, as is so often the case, full of men and women drinking whisky and jawing. I speak to him, stupidly perhaps—I was too drunk to remember what I said—and this morning when I wake him he takes one look at me and buries his face in the pillows. He does not want to see me, touch me, he does not like my house or my friends. And standing in the Piazza Venezia beside a dirty beggar I get a crushing visitation of the shabbiness of my life.

Things improved somewhat with the arrival of Jean Douglass—Salinger's mother-in-law—a charming woman who enjoyed the company of children and soon began babysitting for the Cheevers, whose parenting style bemused her. "She likes to take care of [Federico]," Cheever wrote, "and like all baby-lovers she feels that his parents are giddy and unworthy and whispers things to him like: 'Did Mummy have a little too much wine at Tre Scalini, Federico?' " That sort of thing was benign enough, but one night the woman witnessed an episode that shocked and enraged her. Cheever had promised to take the thirteen-year-old Susan to see Renata Tebaldi sing the role of Desdemona in *Otello*; with Douglass's help, the girl had picked out her only suitable outfit, a pink dress she'd worn to dancing school. When she was ready to go, Cheever (drunk) walked in with Zinny, looked his daughter over, and stiffly declared: "You won't do." Douglass exploded, demanding he apologize at once or she'd never speak to him again; Cheever, cowed and ashamed, not only apologized but spent forty thousand lire on a new wardrobe for the girl. As Susan recalled, "Jean Douglass had just taken the skin off him, and for about six months he was completely different toward me." It helped that (as Cheever would have it) the girl was dressed *properly* for once. "Susie has a new dress and shoes with heels," he noted a few days later; "[she] feels very adolescent and pleases me. What a pleasure it is to raise a family."

The Wapshot Chronicle (and its reviews) behind him, Cheever was trying to get back to work with an almost alarming lack of success. For the time being, at least, he had nothing in particular to say—or rather nothing fit to print. Such was his desperation that he even considered writing ("oh so boldly") about the homosexual romps of his youth, perhaps having the stuff published privately in Europe. The notion, however, was short-lived: "I seem to have one, and only one axe to grind and this is the enormous and monotonous question of sexual depravity and I trust that I may see the face of the devil in some other guise." He thought it might help to get away from the commotion of Rome, so he bought a Fiat ("a rotten little car," as Mary remembered) and drove back and forth on weekends to a friend's country villa—an idyllic place with a fountain and willow trees, located at the bottom of a steep wall of stairs leading to the pleasant town of Anticoli.

Probably it was here that Cheever completed the one and only story he would write in Italy, "The Bella Lingua," rather inevitably about alienated Americans in Rome. Kate Dresser, a language teacher, tries to believe that the seedy life she's made for herself and her teenage son is better than going home to Krasbie, Iowa, where her father had been a trolley conductor. Meanwhile one of her students, a middle-aged businessman named Streeter, finds the city and its people unknowable and even a little sinister, as when he observes a man struck by a car: "The victim lay in a heap on the paving, a shabbily dressed man but with a lot of oil in his black, wavy hair, which must have been his pride. A crowd gathered—not solemn at all, although a few women crossed themselves—and everyone began to talk excitedly. . . . Streeter wondered why it was that they regarded a human life as something of such dubious value." A string of other, similarly aversive vignettes follow—where arguably one or two would do—most of them culled almost word for word from Cheever's journal, and indeed the whole story suffers from a diffusion of effect. Cheever himself realized he was showing rust, and advised Maxwell to "just put [the story] in a drawer somewhere" if he didn't like it. When Maxwell promptly bought it, Cheever assumed he did so out of friendship ("I wish it had been better"), and remained skeptical when Maxwell suggested he return to Rome in September 1958—financed by *The New Yorker*—and "write some more pieces with an Italian background."

By then it was summer and Cheever had almost had his fill of Italy, at least for a while. As a last adventure, he'd arranged to take the Warrens' place at La Rocca, an enormous sixteenth-century fortress in Porto Ercole—a move that began ominously, with rumors of a polio epidemic in nearby San Stefano. "Yes, the city is dangerous!" Cheever's doctor shouted over the telephone, having been called away from dinner. "Life is dangerous! Do you expect to live forever?" Under a pall of doom, then (Cheever smelled spoiled meat in the air), they departed after a slight delay, and were taken aback by the awesome beauty of the place as well as its daunting lack of amenities. The bedrooms—beetle- and scorpion-infested—were gloomy barracks with straw mattresses; the one toilet could only be flushed with a bucket of icy water drawn from a well (and there was no paper except a pile of old magazines); the courtyard was inhabited by a balding goat, a few elderly chickens, and a multitude of starving cats. And that wasn't all: "When we arrived here we found that the signorina had rented the place out as a movie set," Cheever wrote the Blumes. "There were two light generators in our yard and a small company of about forty-five people wandering around, acting, eating sandwiches and relieving themselves." Mary caught a bad case of impetigo and they almost gave up, but soon enough both the itchy pustules and the movie people vanished, and the Cheevers began to have fun. The village was populated by friendly peasant folk, mostly sardine fishermen and their families, who took a shine to the Americans: "When Ben walks down the street everyone shouts: Bengy, Bengy, c'iou Bengy and there was a dance on Saturday night. Susie went with an Italian family and danced with the beach-boys. The music was an accordion and a set of trapdrums."

The majestic cliffs and the purple Mediterranean stirred immortal longings in Cheever, and he spent many wistful hours sitting on a wall, sipping cocktails, and gazing at all the strapping fishermen gamboling about in the nude. One day a couple of youths carved a woman in the sand, then mounted her "with considerable agility and ardor" while Cheever's heart turned over. It was all so hopeless—and yet sometimes, with a sense of "gaiety and terror," he considered "follow[ing] his mischievous nose" and the world be damned—but he only sat there drinking and feeling old. "And it seems that we cannot reform our sexual natures," he wrote in his journal. "And there is a point where denial is sheer hypocrisy, with its train of gruelling and foolish anxieties. . . . I think how narrow and anxious my life is. Where are the mountains and green fields, the broad landscapes?"

As a condition for renting La Rocca, Cheever had agreed to hire the caretaker—an energetic middle-aged woman named Ernesta—as a cook. Eleanor Clark had warned him that Ernesta ("an absolute jewel") and Iole would despise each other, and she was right: Ernesta banned Iole from the kitchen, and Iole began blackguarding the woman at every opportunity. She told Cheever that Ernesta was taking kickbacks from merchants, and that her shiftless husband, Fosco, was siphoning gas from the Fiat. One day, too, Cheever returned from an afternoon swim to find a group of tourists milling around the courtyard taking pictures—they even took a picture of the startled, naked Cheever as he stumbled into his trunks. Outraged, he ran them off with a bucket of water and threats to call the police, whereupon Ernesta indignantly explained that at least one of the visitors was "the local Marquesa, paying a courtesy call." According to Iole, however, they were all Germans: Fosco had accosted a tour bus and sold them tickets at fifty lire a head.

The final blowup occurred in early August. Susan and Ben had begun filling their hats with figs from a tree near the lighthouse when Ernesta snatched the hats away and dumped the (unripe) figs on the ground. Iole scampered down from the terrace and the fight was on: she called Ernesta a big, filthy witch (*strega*), while Ernesta replied in effect that Iole was a whore (*mignotta*) and a piece of shit (*cacca*). An hour later Cheever put his family on a train to Rome, then returned to La Rocca and coldly paid Ernesta her wages. "What troubles me most are unkind feelings about Eleanor," he wrote afterward, "some timidity towards her that is best overcome with anger, some fear of losing her friendship or perhaps her advocacy."

They left Italy three weeks later, after a stop in Pompeii to examine the crater of Vesuvius, where Cheever was smitten by a Danish actress. He sat with her on the bus going back and was about to get her name when she suddenly disembarked, and Cheever was left feeling "sick with love." (He would moon over the encounter for years.) Two days later, in Naples, they boarded the *Constitution* with Iole in tow as well as four Japanese dancing mice (recompense for Barbara Frietchie). "After having wondered for so many months about the depth and reality of my love of Italy," Cheever reflected, "after having imagined this scene so many times, I stand at the stern deck, staring at the cliffs along the coast; it all slips and falls away as insignificantly and swiftly as a card house."

CHAPTER NINETEEN

{ 1957–1959 }

IT WAS A MORE BUOYANT Cheever who returned to Westchester in the fall of 1957. His time in Italy had enhanced his cosmopolitan airs, or so it seemed whenever he slung a lot of Italian-sounding phrases at Iole, his own *donna di servizio*, who cooked wonderful homemade pasta and changed the baby's diapers. While in Italy, he'd gotten letters from home that were all about "surly soft-ball games" and "great advances in amateur theatricals"—at this rate, said Mary, he'd never return to the States. But in fact Cheever was "very excited": *The Wapshot Chronicle* was a hit and its author a world traveler whose daughter would soon attend the posh Masters School in Dobbs Ferry. He was eager to tell old friends (and detractors) all about it at the Schoales's welcome-home party on September 14.

He was in for a nasty shock. "We think a skunk is in the woodpile," Zinny told him, calling him on the carpet at the Cow Barn. The word was out that certain characters in *The Wapshot Chronicle* resembled members of the Vanderlip family—for instance, the repulsive Cousin Justina seemed a caricature of Mrs. Vanderlip, and Justina's browbeaten "ward," Melissa, was likely modeled after Mrs. Vanderlip's daughter and namesake, Narcissa (Mrs. Julian) Street, who'd once been scolded for presuming to speak to her mother without first making an appointment. (And never mind the fact—so noted by Cheever—that Mrs. Vanderlip was "a dedicated feminist in favor of separate bedrooms and a minimum of sexual intercourse.") Nor was this the first time such rumors had circulated. A few years before, an "Iagoesque nuisance" had told the family that Cheever's reason for moving to Beechwood was to gather material for a book "implicating the late F. A. Vanderlip in the Teapot Dome oil scandal": "The family was galvanized," Cheever wrote a friend at the time. "People were telephoned to ask about my character, letters and copies of letters were sent here and there, and I was finally told the secret. I demanded apologies, and got none; but things have quieted down." Even then, truth be known, Cheever was not quite so innocent as he claimed: writing about stale political scandals was hardly his line, but right from the start he'd been intrigued by, say, a story about the time Mrs. Vanderlip had learned her paintings were forgeries, which was one of several chestnuts he was finally able to use in *The Wapshot Chronicle*.

Zinny warned him that he was in danger of being banished from Beechwood—a threat that had hung in the air for years. Narcissa Street, for one, had never liked him: Jack Kahn had been *her* pet, and now the resident writer belonged to Zinny. As for the mother, her favor toward Cheever had always been qualified by a kind of seigneurial hauteur, lest he forget whose estate he was (for the time being) squatting on. Perhaps Cheever explained to Zinny how an artist transmutes his material (much of which, in the present case, had been provided by Zinny herself), but at any rate she interceded so effectively that he soon received a magnanimous note from old Mrs. Vanderlip:

> I was awfully pleased to have The Wapshot Chronicle from you with your very pleasant little message. I am sure it must be very entertaining to be the author of such a controversial book, or perhaps to the younger generation it does not seem so controversial.
>
> You do not need to worry about anything you may say about Beechwood. Personally, I thought several points were very well taken. I have always been horrified by the roofs of this house. . . . There were other references that I recognized too, but I am very flattered to figure in even a remote way in a book by "one of the modern authors."

She couldn't resist the implication, however, that she'd found the work as a whole rather distasteful, with or without the "flattering" personal references: "Except for Leander I do not think you presented a really loveable character in the whole book, and I think, just for contrast, this is always pleasant in any novel or play."

The immediate danger was averted, but Cheever never again felt quite so welcome in Scarborough. For the most part he drifted away from the old crowd, including Kahn, who one day let him know that he (Kahn) had advised the Vanderlips to rent Beechtwig to the new headmaster of the Scarborough Country Day School. Cheever interpreted this as "the callousness of an intensely competitive nature"—and certainly, by then, Cheever was far more esteemed by the world than was Kahn. His social confidence was another matter, though that too seemed to be gaining somewhat. "In an upper-class gathering I suddenly think of myself as a pariah—a small and dirty fraud, a deserved outcast, a spiritual and sexual impostor, a loathsome thing," he wrote shortly after his return from Italy. "Then I take a deep breath, stand up straight, and the loathsome image falls away. I am no better and no worse than the other members of the gathering. Indeed, I am myself. It is like a pleasant taste on the tongue."

AMID THE PHILISTINE DOMAINS of Westchester or Wauwinet, Cheever sometimes repined over his "lack of literary companionship." When a young Elizabeth Spencer remarked, in Rome, that she wasn't keen to meet other writers, Cheever seemed slightly affronted: "Some of the nicest people I've ever known are writers," he replied. Even apart from the prestige, then, it must have been a pleasure for Cheever to be elected in May 1957 to the National Institute of Arts and Letters, where he took his place as one of 250 of the most celebrated personages in literature, art, and music. He even composed a ditty for the occasion: "*Root tee toot, ahhh root tee toot, oh we're the boys from the Institute. Oh we're not rough and we're not tough, we're cultivated and that's enough.*" In years to come, this august body would prove a comfort to Cheever, providing him with a kind of nominal respectability as well as all the literary companionship he desired. "I love my colleagues," he wrote a friend in 1975, "embrace them, kiss them, and sometimes weep with them over our cruel separation, but why is it that we only do this once a year?"

Whatever his irreverence, Cheever took his responsibilities within the Institute very seriously indeed. Soon after his election, he nominated Bellow ("the most original writer in America") and proposed a grant for Maxwell, whose own successful nomination he seconded a few years later. ("When I open my handkerchief drawer," Maxwell wrote Cheever, "there among the cufflinks is the rosette that you took out of your buttonhole and placed in mine, and the symbolism of this overcomes me, morning after morning.") But his greatest and certainly most grueling contribution was as a member (and thrice chairman) of the Committee on Grants for Literature, which obliged him to read stacks of novels by "young associate professors with scandalous affectations": "[W]hat is that old man doing at twelve o'clock noon?" he wrote Maxwell while in Wauwinet one summer. "He is pouring himself a glass of gin. What does he hold in his hand? He is holding a sensitive novel by a young man who wants to go to Rome. How can a drunken old man judge the merits of a sensitive novel? He cannot. What a cruel world is it where the destinies of the young lie in such shaken hands!" It must be noted, though, that in the actual presence of a sensitive young novelist, Cheever went out of his way to seem gracious and attentive—as the writer Stephen Becker put it, "[H]e would make [one] feel like the only other person in that room. . . . [T]o me he was affection itself, approval itself, whatever youthful brashness I displayed."

Meanwhile his own reputation was decidedly ascendant. *The Wapshot Chronicle* won the 1958 National Book Award—scoring a major upset over James Gould Cozzens's acclaimed best seller, *By Love Possessed*, whose stock had plummeted after Dwight Macdonald's career-destroying abuse ("By Cozzens Possessed") in *Commentary*.* Cheever's own feelings toward Cozzens were typically mixed. In his journal he opined that *By Love Possessed* was "excellent"—the product of a "loveless" but "broad intelligence"—and years later, when told that Cozzens admired his work, Cheever claimed to have been so appalled at winning the National Book Award that he'd considered sending Cozzens the blue Canton dishes his grandfather "is supposed to have brought home from China." At the time, however, he acknowledged at least one congratulatory note—Katharine White's—by writing how "pleasant" it was to win, "partly because I've always felt that Mr. Ross would not have liked By Love Possessed." And whatever else Cozzens had going for him, he didn't have "at least three good friends among the [NBA] judges"—as did Cheever, who cheerfully admitted as much. Actually he had two friends, William Maxwell and Francis Steeg-

---

*One could argue that Macdonald played kingmaker that year. He lavishly praised James Agee's posthumous novel, *A Death in the Family*, which went on to win the Pulitzer.

muller, as well as a staunch supporter in Elizabeth Ann McMurray Johnson; what he didn't know, and would never find out, was that Steegmuller had actually been the lone dissenter, preferring Malamud's *The Assistant*. Maxwell not only adamantly supported *The Wapshot Chronicle*, but afterward took Steegmuller aside and insisted they make it unanimous. "Bill was very protective of John," said Shirley Hazzard, later Steegmuller's wife. "He knew better than almost anybody how much John needed the reassurance, whereas someone else may not have cared all that much."

On the day of the award ceremony ("a gathering of nearly 1,000 writers, publishers and booksellers in the grand ballroom of the Commodore Hotel," reported the *Times*), Cheever was very nervous. After Clifton Fadiman presented him with a plaque and a check for one thousand dollars, Cheever recited a very brief speech "in a swift mutter that verged on unconscious discourtesy," as one observer recalled. He spoke about the loneliness of the writer and how much the writer depends on the "good opinion of strangers"; fortunately, said Cheever, there were still so many readers in America who, "beset with an unprecedented variety of diversions, continue to read with great taste and intelligence."* The audience sat in rigid silence, straining to hear, but suddenly it was over and Cheever was replaced on the dais by Randall Jarrell—then the poetry consultant to the Library of Congress—who proceeded to deliver a jeremiad that vividly contradicted Cheever's sunny view of the American reading public. As long as people preferred *Peyton Place* to the works of Proust, said Jarrell, they would be "enemies of [their] own culture"; he also said some hard things about *South Pacific* and the like. (As Cheever wrote a friend afterward, "Randall Jarrell, who had just washed his beard, made a long speech, the gist of which was that Bennett Cerf is a shit, that South Pacific is shitty and that people who look at the sixty-four thousand dollar question are virtual cocksuckers.") An even graver ordeal had to be faced the next morning, when Cheever appeared with Robert Penn

---

*Among Cheever's papers is a draft of a speech he wrote for some unknown occasion subsequent to the March 11, 1958, National Book Award ceremony: "It is very gallant of you to come here tonight and it is also quite gallant of me, since I find this kind of thing quite difficult. The last time I spoke to any sort of gathering was in receiving an award and in this connection I said how much a writer desires the good opinion of strangers. Three newspaper men in the audience reported . . . that from my manner, my demeanor on the platform I needed the good opinion of strangers in the worst possible way."

Warren (the poetry winner) on the *Today* show. Outside the studio window on Fifty-second Street "were about four hundred women milling around and holding up signs saying: HELLO MAMA. DORIS. SEND MONEY. GLADYS. HELP. IDA," Cheever noted.

> I was asked to wait in a green room where there was a chimpanzee drinking coffee, a man with a long beard and a lady in Arab costume practising a song. . . . [I]t took two strong men pushing and pulling to get me into the studio and everybody on the street shouted: It's Gary Moore. I sat down at a baize-covered table and quivered like a bowlfull of chicken fat for fifteen minutes and then I drove Mary home. Mary took the check away from me and Ben hung the plaque up in his clubhouse . . . so I may not be any richer but I sure am a hell of a lot more nervous.

· · ·

IN SEPTEMBER, Cheever published his third collection, *The House-breaker of Shady Hill*, a slender volume of eight stories that yet included some of his best work: "The Country Husband," "The Five-Forty-Eight," "O Youth and Beauty!," and "The Sorrows of Gin." Cheever had reservations about the book ("it is a nothing, turkey warmed over in some instances, four times"), though it stands as an important artifact of the postwar era—as Jonathan Yardley would observe some forty-six years later, *The Housebreaker of Shady Hill* is the work of a great writer at the height of his powers, who at the time had "rivals but no superiors in the national literature." Contemporary reviewers also had a sense of Cheever's growing significance. Herbert Mitgang praised his "beautiful control" in the daily *Times*, while William Peden observed in the *Book Review* that Cheever "is one of the most urbane moralists of our times; he is also one of the most entertaining story tellers." A few reviewers, however, suspected there was something a little vapid about the work—most insistently Richard Gilman, calling Cheever (in *Commonweal*) a "culture-hero to the barbecue and Volkswagen set" who was, whatever his satirical gifts and fine prose, "essentially a sentimentalist": "It is all adolescent at bottom and not simply because Cheever is portraying a world of adolescent values," Gilman concluded. "In the end he shares them." This is harsh and simplistic, though not entirely without justice. In his lesser stories, at least, Cheever was more and more apt to finesse his own ambivalence—toward almost everything, but especially traditional suburban values—with a lot of mystifying irony. In "The Worm in the Apple,"* for example, Cheever appears to mock his own occasional pessimism. Examining the case of the (seemingly) contented Crutchmans—who engage in all the trite, neighborly diversions—the narrator looks for unsavory truths but finally suggests that the "worm" may be "in the eye of the observer who, through timidity or moral cowardice, could not embrace the broad range of [the Crutchmans'] natural enthusiasms." The story concludes with a line that might be interpreted one way or the other, echoing the final line of that bottomlessly ambiguous novel, *Bullet Park*, published ten years later: "they got richer and richer and richer and lived happily, happily, happily, happily."

The tone is a bit shrill, perhaps reflecting the exasperation of a man who (at least for a while) wanted to write about something other than the suburban middle class—or not at all: "I seem unable to get my hands on anything," he noted almost six months after returning from Rome. "It may be a question of discipline but why write about things that bore and disinterest me." More than anything, he wanted to get on with another novel, but at the moment he was completely out of ideas and couldn't afford it besides: *The Wapshot Chronicle* had sold better than expected, but it wasn't enough "to keep a family of five in shoe-leather," as he remarked to Herbst. Writing for money as opposed to pleasure, then, he regurgitated more Italian material into a long story titled "Boy in Rome," about a young American who remains in Rome because his father is buried in the Protestant cemetery there. At one point the narrator breaks frame and makes his own boredom explicit with a rambling parenthetical digression: "(But I am not a boy in Rome but a grown man in the old prison and river town of Ossining,† swatting hornets on this autumn afternoon with a rolled-up newspaper. . . . But my father taught me, while we hoed the beans, that I should complete for better or worse whatever I had begun and so we get back to the scene where [the boy] leaves the train for Naples.)" This curious bit of metafiction seems less a formal innovation than a frank admis-

---

*The story is worthy of particular consideration because it was hitherto unpublished—that is, written specifically for *The Housebreaker of Shady Hill* and thus intended to tilt the thematic balance somewhat.

†Ossining is only a few miles away from Scarborough, though of course Cheever had yet to move there when he wrote the story. That Ossining is a famous prison town was perhaps deemed pertinent to the homesick protagonist's predicament.

sion of failure, and though Cheever regarded the story as "close to parody," the fact remained that he'd worked on it for six weeks and wanted money for his trouble—hence, a little reluctantly, he sent the thing to Maxwell, who seemed almost startled by its badness: "[It] doesn't work, everybody feels. . . . I guess what it is is that you really don't care what [the boy] does with his passport or himself. One doesn't, the reader doesn't, meaning, surely, you didn't. And all the other ingredients—the palace, the expatriate mother and so on, are from other stories of yours." Cheever apologized ("I have not written so feebly in eight years"), though in fact he was offended by Maxwell's tone—and, feeble parody or not, he allowed "Boy in Rome" to circulate among seven magazines (at least) before finally dumping it on *Esquire* for a thousand dollars.

One problem was that Cheever's life had simply become more distracting. The little house was crowded now with a crying baby and a flamboyant maid, while the telephone rang more frequently, too, what with Cheever's growing celebrity. As a young man starting out in the Depression, he'd gotten used to writing wherever he could find a flat surface, and was never pompous about the trappings of his profession: he worked in odd spare rooms and seemed almost to welcome distractions such as runaway mice or the arrival of a drinking companion. Amid one of the worst slumps in his career, though, Cheever decided he could use a little more privacy after all, and rented a room over a real-estate office near the train station. This entailed a short walk each day in his working uniform of "wash pants" and seedy crewneck sweaters (one or the other usually torn), and presently he was stopped by police on suspicion of vagrancy. Cheever was furious, and refused to give his name or address. "I do not like to have this slight irregularity in my habits misinterpreted," he fumed in his journal.

Under the circumstances, Cheever was drinking more heavily than ever, and this made him peevish about things. To the Blumes he confided that the gist of his recent journal entries was as follows: "Drank too much; talked too much or just: Drank too much or sometimes Drank too much; very choleric. I don't do anything about this because as I tell Mary it's the way I *feel* about life." More often than not, he awoke in a condition of physical and emotional distress: his hands shook, his kidneys ached, and he felt a depressive anxiety about everything and nothing—his family was in danger, financial ruin was imminent, and what was that smell of smoke (was the house on fire)? Such a "liverish grasp of disaster" could only be relieved by one thing—

another drink—and Cheever found himself longing for the "noontime snort" in the middle of the morning. The prospect of mixing with friends was another source of thirst, which in turn had a corrosive effect on his genial public persona. "Phil [Boyer] leaves without saying either thank you or good night," he wrote in his journal. "He has often done this before, but tonight I have no patience and when he calls to apologize I tell him he is an ill-mannered bore." Cheever also ticked the man off for drinking up his liquor, tracking "dog-shit all over [his] rugs," and making "dirty passes at [his] wife." The next morning, however, he awoke feeling "confused and sad" and eager to make amends.

Such "choleric" outbursts were a minor loss of control, as Cheever saw it, next to the ghastly possibility of succumbing to "certain forms of concupiscence." Thus, in the early phases of drunkenness at least (and depending on the company), Cheever had come to seem even more fretful, shy, and constrained than the mannerly person he was when sober. "He became physically self-conscious, as though he were feeling a sensuality he was at pains to conceal," said Michael Bessie, who'd suspected from the beginning that Cheever was bisexual. Given his restless, questing libido, combined with worsening alcoholism, Cheever had begun to worry it was only a matter of time before he disgraced himself in some public way. One morning, after a literary party in Connecticut, he vaguely remembered meeting William Styron and feeling "unselfconsciously happy"—but now, hungover, he felt only a strange misgiving he couldn't explain to himself. Styron, however, remembered the encounter vividly: With a "kind of urgency in his voice," Cheever had proposed the two go for a walk, and Styron (tactfully declining) had the definite impression the older man was "putting the make" on him. In any event, drunk or sober, Cheever's ultimate prophylactic was to remind himself that he was, above all, a *father*—loath to give his sons any reason to think such conduct was "acceptable": "Walking around New York in a condition of intense harassment my principal anxiety is that my sons may walk on the same streets and experience the same pain."

He was also a husband, and his constant intoxication was taking a further toll on his marriage. "I am a solitary drunkard," he wrote in the summer of 1958.

> I take a little painkiller before lunch but I don't really get to work until late afternoon. At four or half past four or sometimes five I stir

up a Martini, thinking that a great many men who can't write as well as I can will already have set themselves down at bar stools. After half a glass of gin I decide that I must get a divorce—and, to tell the truth, Mary is depressed, although my addiction to gin may have something to do with her low spirits. The gin flows freely until supper and so do my memories of the most difficult passages in our marriage; and I think of all the letters I have received from literary ladies implying that my experience with the sex must have been unnaturally difficult and that I deserve better. How right they are, I think. . . . So the gin flows, and after supper the whiskey. I am even a little sly, keeping my glass on the floor where it might not be seen. Mary does not want to speak to me, to be sure. Her looks are dark and impatient. I rustle up a glossary of little jokes to prove the sweetness of my disposition, but she does not laugh. She does not even listen. She does not want to be in the same room with me.

In moments of middling sobriety, at least, Cheever was still able to grasp that his alcoholism "may have something to do" with his wife's depression, but as time passed he was more apt to regard her as "capricious," and often reminded himself of the insanity in her family. Such instability, he reasoned, would also explain her lack of tenderness in bed: that summer he calculated that she'd rebuffed him ("I ask for what I do not really want and being refused lie contentedly between the sheets") no fewer than thirty-seven times in a row. "What about the times you couldn't get it up?" she rejoined, lucidly enough, but that was her fault too. She spiked her hair with a lot of uninviting steel curlers; she sighed; she looked "victimized"—and so on. It was just too much trouble: "I think tonight this fortress is not worth the assault, siege, ladder work and sometimes broadsword fighting that might be involved," he noted.

As if all that weren't enough, Cheever was also worrying about the Bomb. During a visit to Yaddo, he lay awake thinking "that if the world should end [he] would not be with [his] children." He thought he detected an "unearthly green light" in the west, and was almost convinced that atomic testing had ruptured the atmosphere, both physical and moral: "The most useful image I have today is of a man in a quagmire," he wrote that year, "looking into a tear in the sky. . . . Something has gone very wrong, and I do not have the language, the imagery, or the concepts to describe my apprehensions. I come back again to the quagmire and the torn sky." The "quagmire" was the nihilism that followed from a sense of imminent doom. Reading manuscripts for a fiction contest at Barnard, Cheever was astonished by the decadence— impotent rapists, sadistic homosexuals, and the like—contrived by a lot of well-groomed college women, and he wondered how an affluent nation should be "imitating the moral collapse of Germany in the twenties." Meanwhile he wrote a story that year, "The Wrysons," about a dull suburban couple who experience the malaise of the nuclear age in terms of their own well-concealed "oddness." The wife keeps dreaming of the hydrogen bomb, while the husband relieves his own elusive dread by baking (furtively, late at night) Lady Baltimore cakes, since he has no other interests or inner life to speak of. One night the couple's oddnesses converge: the husband falls asleep and burns his cake, while the wife smells smoke and thinks the world is ending. " 'The Wrysons' very bad," Cheever reflected, finding his prose "complacent" and the story itself "nasty, nothing more." Nevertheless the little satire was a telling indication of things to come.

A year that began in triumph ended in a Westchester hospital room, where Cheever spent New Year's Eve "in the company of a dozen faded roses" (sent by Maxwell) "and a copy of *La Garabaldina* [sic]." For years now he'd referred to himself as "an old man, nearing the end of his journey," and when a "rotten headcold" persisted for a few weeks, the forty-six-year-old Cheever began to feel sorry for himself in earnest: "Mary's love of me does not seem to include my infirmities," he wrote Weaver. "She seems lost in some race memory where primitive men, once they began to sniffle, stripped themselves naked, lay down in the snow and let themselves be eaten by crows." It was almost a relief, then, when the doctor assured him he had "something as manly and straightforward as virus pneumonia," though it was perhaps too much of a good thing when X-rays showed a large spot on his lung that seemed to indicate a resurgent case of tuberculosis. Cheever noted in his journal that he'd made "all the arrangements for his death," but soon the spot cleared and he was left convalescing with Maxwell's roses.

Alone with his thoughts, Cheever brooded over his recent refusal to write a blurb in behalf of Updike's first novel, *The Poorhouse Fair.* "He seems to me an unusually gifted young man," he wrote the Knopf publicist, "but perhaps not as a novelist. His eloquence seems to me to retard the movement of the book and to damage his control." Cheever had kept an eye on Updike ever since the latter's stories had begun appearing in *The New Yorker* in 1954; he told his Barnard students that Updike was one of the most promising writers of his generation, though almost in the same breath he remarked that Updike seemed a bit *too* talented—"too pretty"—for his own good. But in the hospital his better nature kept reproaching him, and he couldn't resist writing a second note to the publicist: although, alas, his opinion of the novel hadn't changed, for the sake of his own "peace of mind" he wanted to reiterate that he considered Updike "unusually brilliant." And to Maxwell (their common editor at the *The New Yorker*) he also wrote of his troubled conscience, repeating that he'd been "disappointed" by *The Poorhouse Fair* but had liked Updike's most recent story in the magazine—except, that is, for "the shaven armpits of the poor girls playing pingpong. One should never remark idly on the armpits of ladies." Such a punctilio went to the heart of a certain dialectic between the writers. For Updike's part, his first published story in the magazine, "Friends from Philadelphia," had been conceived as a riposte to "O Youth and Beauty!": "I thought to myself, 'There must be more to American life than this,' " Updike remembered, "and wrote an upbeat little story, with an epiphanic benefaction at the end, to prove it." When the story was "accepted into that exalted fold," Updike felt a sense of debt to Cheever for having provided "the crystallizing spark"; Cheever, meanwhile, continued to brood over the uses to which Updike put his gifts, to say nothing of how those gifts compared with his own.

"It was nice while you were away to have a dry toilet seat," his wife greeted him when he returned from the hospital, or so he reminded himself whenever he was feeling especially ill-used. Mostly he wondered how he might deploy such a perfect insult in his fiction. Again and again he weighed it for this or that story or novel, until finally, almost twenty years later, he gave it to Farragut's despicable wife in *Falconer*.

AT LOW POINTS in his drinking career—whenever he made one of his children cry, for instance—Cheever would reflect on his brother's decline and wonder at how little he, John, seemed to be learning from Fred's example. The latter was seven years older, and his alcoholism was accordingly more advanced. Fred's phobias were such (John claimed) that he could scarcely board an airplane or go higher than the seventh floor of a building unless he was "pissed." Also, because of the shakes, he'd come to dread business dinners where he was served soft drinks rather than cocktails: "I [used to] sit at a table with a bunch of big shots and be afraid to pick up the tomato juice," he wrote John in 1967, ten years after he'd been fired by Pepperell. His dismissal was if anything belated. Apart from his obvious drinking problem, Fred had become openly contemptuous of the whole "corporate freeze," as he called it. Like many drunks, he had a grandiose view of himself, and indeed was not without a certain intellectual flair. One day in the late fifties, John and Susan bumped into Fred at Grand Central Station; the brothers had been somewhat out of touch since Fred's move to Connecticut, and so repaired to a dark bar, briefly, to catch up. Susan, a perceptive teenager by then, was struck by her uncle's "brilliance": "It was August, and Fred said, 'Oh my God. I've just been up to the Frick, because when you look at those Constables, it really cools you off.' " John, however, seemed uneasy at the thought of his tipsy, idle brother whiling away an afternoon at the Frick, and soon made excuses to part.

Now a "freelance advertiser," Fred had become all the more determined to prove the world wrong. He'd revised and expanded *A Song for These States*—his paean to Yankee individualism, begun some twenty years before—and kept a copy of the enormous manuscript on his desk even as it was rejected again and again. At the same time, he seemed more thrilled than ever at his brother's success: they were both *Cheevers*, after all. His son David, in college at the time, remembered the "glowing" letter Fred had written when John won the National Book Award: "He had this outward pride," said David, "but there was a lot of unexpressed conflict, too: why the hell didn't he have talent like that?" Which is not to say Fred despaired of his own talent, or lost faith in his fundamental excellence. His well-to-do neighbors had come to regard him as a drunken misfit, a perception Fred encouraged by drinking more conspicuously than ever and mocking any overture of disapproval or pity with the same "stupid and impenetrable smile on his face," as John would have it. "I only want to educate my neighbors," Fred liked to say, though he managed to educate (as in *épater*) more than his neighbors. Invited to Beechtwig for Thanksgiving in 1958, Fred arrived "like a blast, a thunderclap of obscene misery": drunk before dinner, he indulged in a lot of fractious jocularity before passing out in a wing chair, whereupon (John observed) "His daughter pitilessly took a photograph of him, asleep with his mouth open."

When John alluded to his brother's life in "The Five-Forty-Eight,"

Fred let it pass without comment (despite his wife's indignation); but when "Journal of an Old Gent" appeared in 1956, and Fred recognized certain of their father's notes reproduced as "fiction," he gave John a call: "What are you *doing?*" he asked, clearly unnerved by the ramifications. John related this anecdote to his Barnard class and then appended a moral: "Ignore your family," he said, "and just keep writing." And so (shortly after that Thanksgiving debacle) Cheever wrote "The Scarlet Moving Van," about a pedantic drunk named Gee-Gee (for "Greek God," after the promising youth he used to be) and his long-suffering wife, who wear out their welcome in one "felicitous" suburb after another. "They've got to learn," says Gee-Gee, regaling his "stuffy" neighbors with a jig and a dirty song. "I've got to teach them." The nature of his lesson, the narrator determines, is that decorum and felicity per se are the worst self-deceptions: "the happy and the wellborn and the rich . . . would not be spared the pangs of anger and lust and the agonies of death." Fred Cheever may or may not have agreed, but he would have been hard-pressed not to recognize himself in the portrait. For one thing, he'd recently broken his ankle and taken to rolling around his house in an office chair ("My office is the house"); the fictional Gee-Gee, similarly impaired, gets around "half riding in a child's wagon, which he propelled by pushing a crutch."

The story appeared in the March 21, 1959, issue of *The New Yorker,* at a time when Fred had pretty much retired to his bedroom to drink full-time.* Shortly before, Iris had summoned John to Connecticut to discuss her husband's condition, and at one point Fred lumbered into the room and joined them. "His face is swollen almost beyond recognition," John wrote afterward. "I think his brain is damaged. . . . His conversation makes no intellectual or human sense." After a few min-

---

*Within a week or two, Fred suffered the collapse that led to his hospitalization, described below. Was there any connection? It's impossible to say. At the time Fred was probably in no condition to read anything, though certainly he would have read the story later with (one imagines) something less than delight. But, as we shall see, Fred remained inscrutable on the subject of his various incarnations in John's fiction. The rest of Fred's family were less inscrutable. His daughter Sarah bitterly remarked that Uncle John used Fred as a "classic drunk" in his work, and Iris was enduringly furious. In his journal John describes her "exhaustive" attack on one of his stories (unnamed), as well as his own sheepish response: "She seems like one of the orphic harpies and I am driven into a regressive fastidiousness that I detest. She is predatory, lumbering, and faced with this massiveness I don't actually simper but I become retiring, wounded and feeble."

utes, Fred gave up trying to make sense and called his dog—a toy poo-
dle, dressed in a tutu, that Fred had taught to dance on its hind legs
while he waved a cracker in the air. ("For a moment F[red] seems
happy and I do not mean anything uncharitable by observing this.")
Finally Fred went back to bed, while John and Iris agreed that a thorough physical examination was in order, "to see how far gone he is."
But matters came to a head before anything definite was arranged. As
Susan Cheever remembered, either Iris called to say her husband was
killing himself, or Fred called and slurred something like *"She's trying
to kill me, Joey!"* In any case John drove back to Weston with his daughter and found a fraught domestic scene. "Something terrible had happened," said Susan, "like [Fred had] thrown something at [Iris] or she'd
thrown something at him. And she was kind of skulking around." With
his daughter's help, John got the bloated, red-faced Fred into the car
and drove him to New Haven Hospital, where Dr. Bill Winternitz had
his office. "Well, Joey, nice of you to drop by the club," Fred muttered
(more or less) as he was poured into bed. Throughout the ordeal,
according to Susan, her father's demeanor was mostly stoical: "He
wasn't cranky to Fred, just *Ugh:* exasperated. Looking up to the heavens to make sure God saw that he was taking care of his brother, who
he wanted God to know was a real pain in the ass."

Fred was found to be suffering from alcoholic malnutrition and an
enlarged liver; on the brighter side—according to Bill Winternitz—he
"laughed a lot and seemed apologetic." Why was such an affable man
bent on destroying himself? As Bill reported to his brother-in-law, a
psychiatrist thought it was due to some obscure childhood trauma—
which, John reflected, must have been his own birth: "He was happy,
high-spirited, and adored, and when, at the age of seven, he was told
that he would have to share his universe with a brother, his forebodings
would, naturally, have been bitter and deep. . . . I have felt for a long
time that, with perfect unconsciousness, his urge was to destroy me. I
have felt that there was in his drunkenness some terrible cunning."
Alarmed that his brother's fate could prove to be his own, John pored
over his journal and was appalled by the obviously "progressive"
nature of his disease. "I look up the telephone number of Alcoholics
Anonymous," he noted, after taking Fred to New Haven. "Then, my
hands shaking, I open the bar and drink the leftover whiskey, gin, and
vermouth, whatever I can lay my shaking hands on."

CHAPTER TWENTY

{ 1959–1960 }

CHEEVER ONCE REMARKED to his son Ben that he'd had many
fathers and that Ben should try to have many fathers, too. In
Cheever's own life, one of the "critical turning points" (his
words) had been finding a father—Dr. Milton Winternitz—who commanded his utmost respect and affection and even reciprocated as
much, after his own volatile fashion. Over the years Cheever had
repaid the man's kindness by being, in effect, a good son: deferential,
hardworking (scything with Peter Wesul and so on), witty and charming. From the beginning, though, he'd had serious reservations about
both parents-in-law—Winter was a tyrant, Polly a shrew—and as
Cheever's place in the world became more secure, he was less and less
comfortable with the rather obsequious role he'd come to play at Treetops. Returning from his sumptuous year in Italy as a proper paterfamilias, he felt less obliged to laugh at Polly's "gossipy and uncharitable"
remarks about Mary's mad sister (though of course he couldn't stand
Buff either), and as for his father-in-law, Cheever now found the man
almost insufferable. As Winter's storied tenure as dean of the Yale
School of Medicine receded further into the past, he'd become all the
more inclined to indulge his perversities at Treetops. He toiled like a
bitter martyr in the kitchen, say, making breakfast and mopping the
floor, as if he'd been forced to do so by the sheer worthless laziness of
his family; but if anyone tried to help, he'd throw an "insane tantrum":
"Here are the unreasonable and insatiable hungers of our egotism," his
son-in-law mused.

Cheever's last visit to Treetops while Winter was still alive was in the summer of 1958. Winter greeted him at the Stone House with a petulant attack on *The New Yorker*, while Polly immediately began to impart "some gossip about Philadelphia": "They talk loudly and at cross-purposes and when her back is turned he makes a face at her and says she is a stupid bitch." Later Cheever and Polly went away for martinis and she resumed her usual waspish spiel about her ghastly stepchildren: Buff was crazier than ever, Tom a troublemaker, and Mary "obtuse and neurotic." In the past Cheever would have obliged her with at least a chuckle—and probably did so on this occasion—but he was not laughing on the inside. "Where is my sense of humor?" he chided himself. "I can enjoy these antics but I think they threaten my happiness." By far the greater part of his grievances, though, were directed against Winter, whom he'd come to blame for the precarious state of his marriage. He reminded himself, again and again, that the bitter old man had beaten Mary with a belt when she was a child, and now the memory of that violence had returned to haunt her—indeed, this was the true cause of her "capricious" depressions ("she cannot, quite understandably, face this"), which she saw fit to blame on Cheever. "I have come to think of [Winter] as the king of a hades where M[ary] must spend perhaps half her time," he concluded. "There is no doubt about the fact that he is a source of darkness in our affairs." Thus, after that last visit, he announced to his wife that he would not be returning to the "beauty and embarrassments" of Treetops: he loved Polly and Winter, he said, but he loved her and the children more, "and the two seem incompatible."

True to his word—though Winter was very sick by then, and wanted to see him—Cheever arranged to spend most of the following summer (1959) in Europe, alone, first at a PEN conference in Germany and then (by way of the Brenner Pass) in Austria and Italy. "This is the *best*; this is it," he wrote Maxwell from the Carlton Hotel in Frankfurt. "I go to cafes, dance with Dutch girls, climb mountains, attend passion plays. Oh boy." Actually, he found the conference "very dull" and his fellow delegates "not much" ("wouldbe writers, former writers, the authors of cook books, etc"). And while he was, at first, almost as excited as he would have had Maxwell believe—Frankfurt seemed "literally risen from known ashes," and the "comely, kind" citizens were nothing but hospitable—he soon began picking out unsavory details, such as the odd legless beggar, the one-eyed man renting boats, and so forth ("the tragedy is brought home to you sooner or later"). And of course the exhilaration of traveling alone soon began to pall, though he still had almost six weeks of vacation ahead of him. On his last night in Frankfurt, he ran into some fellow English-speaking PEN delegates in a bar and was mortified when he wasn't invited to join them: "I walked around the streets, looking for some place where I could get supper without being seen and so exposing my aloneness."

The rest of the vacation followed the same pattern: excitement on arrival at some new place, followed by loneliness and boredom. He was delighted to return to Venice ("although I wonder if I am worthy of the spectacle"), and his high spirits were promptly rewarded with a happy coincidence: cruising down the Grand Canal in a vaporetto, he spotted his old Signal Corps buddy (whom he still met for lunch every so often at Sardi's), Leonard Field, drinking coffee on the terrace of the Hotel Gritti. As he wrote their mutual friend John Weaver, "I began to wave my arms and yell: 'Lennieee, Lennieee,' and he finally recognized me. I couldn't get off the boat until San Marco's but then I ran back to the Gritti and Virginia [Field's wife] came down and we went to the Lido and in the very next cabana was Nancy Mitford and Victor Cunard. Swam in the same water with them and everything." That was precisely the sort of thing Cheever liked writing to his friends, but no further anecdotes happened in Venice, and soon he moved on to Rome, where he took a room at the Academy. "[Rome] is like coming back to a school where one had a tough time and finding it all small and pleasant," he wrote in his journal. For the first week or two, he sat sipping gin in the golden dusk, savoring his own independence. His wife's letters had been full of complaints (finances, her sick father, etc.), and Cheever found himself remembering her "not as the loving woman [he had] known but as a threatening, derisive and unhappy figure." He couldn't help wondering what it would be like to spend the rest of his life in Italy. But then he began to worry: What if Mary wanted to divorce him? What if he never saw his children again? "I am lonely and bewildered," he wrote. "I feel very melancholy and wonder how I can make sense, order, give value to my life." The first step, he figured, was to return home immediately.

He almost didn't make it. In the middle of the Atlantic, one of the airplane's port engines caught fire, and the captain turned around and tried to land in Shannon, then London, but both airports were fogged out. Finally they made it to Orly in Paris, where passengers were given coffee and reboarded on "another seedy-looking plane" that "labored across the heavens for another seventeen hours." Cheever—"unafraid" the while—placidly read *Lolita* during the second flight and wasn't surprised when he phoned home from Idlewild and found nobody there but Iole and the baby: the others, naturally, were in New Hampshire with Mary's dying father. "I [had] not expected her to be [home]," he noted matter-of-factly in his journal—but soon he felt a touch of chagrin, calling his wife at the hospital in Hanover and (rather like Francis Weed in "The Country Husband") trying to regale her with the story of his brush with death. She seemed too upset to pay much attention. He would have liked a little sympathy, at least.

Winter clung to life for almost a month, repeatedly asking to see his son-in-law, but Cheever stayed put. "I have seen him make a spectacle of a head-cold," he remarked knowingly (hypochondria was another thing the two had in common). Mostly he was annoyed by the claim on Mary's attention: every time the doctors thought Winter was finally about to die, she'd have to drop everything and race back to New Hampshire; then he'd rally again, "to everyone's astonishment, some people's embarrassment and a few cases of indignation," as Cheever wrote Herbst. He himself was among the indignant ones: "It gets me down, it gets me down," he wrote in his journal. "The death watch of a great man but bathing the baby and washing the breakfast dishes forces me into a sullen frame of mind." And still he didn't visit the man, though he could hardly claim anymore that Winter was faking: the latter had stopped eating a month ago, and must (as Cheever conceded) "be skin and bones." In fact, as time passed, Cheever's irritation over the extra housework gave way to grudging admiration ("how great his energies and his powers of endurance"), though he was no more inclined to go to New Hampshire. Meanwhile he sensed some increased friction in his marriage. Mary refused to speak to him except in "biting and derisive" terms, and he suspected her of ruining meals on purpose—putting grenadine in an artichoke sauce, for example ("I do not mind a light supper," wrote Cheever, "but I mind what I think is the sullenness that lies at the bottom of these spoiled dishes"). He might have been right; certainly she didn't see the point of discussing her complaints, such as they were. "Reproach Cheever?" she said, recalling the episode. "He was in a different world."

Dr. Winternitz died the night of October 3, while the Cheevers were attending Phil Boyer's fiftieth-birthday party at Snedens Landing.* "Winter is dead," said the pithy message awaiting their return (Cheever reflected that the man "always had some violence of poetry"). At the funeral in New Haven, Polly seemed cold toward Cheever, and he got the impression she was "in the process of casting [him] off": "I am unhurt by this but I can't help wondering why." As for Winter, whatever his thoughts toward the end, he went ahead and bequeathed his vast, dandyish wardrobe to his son-in-law—they were about the same size, after all—including some nice Peal shoes and silk bow ties and a vicuña coat Cheever would cherish forever.

CHEEVER'S RELATIONS with his children had become more strained since their return from Italy two years before—partly because of his drinking, and partly because they were older and more complicated. "Susie is in the throes of adolescence and not very good company," Cheever reported that year to the Warrens. More than ever, he wanted her to be pretty and demure like his friends' daughters—particularly Linda Boyer and Pammy Spear, much admired by Cheever—but instead she continued to eat too much (as he saw it) and slump around with an unhappy scowl on her face. "S[usan], twenty pounds overweight," he ruefully observed, "shaped, to my fine eye, like a barrell [sic], wearing azure stockings and a purple scarf, her hair dirty and unkempt." At such times his eye would drift to other, perkier girls ("that one at the corner, that one waiting for a bus, that one coming out of Plummers") and he'd long to be young and in love again.

Sarah Schoales had been "puzzled" by Cheever's decision to send her friend Susan to the Masters School in Dobbs Ferry ("Dobbs for snobs!" she'd teased her), perhaps unaware that Pammy Spear also attended the school and Cheever very much wanted his daughter to emulate Pammy. "He was constantly engineering situations in which my imperfections would be highlighted vis-à-vis Linda and Pammy," Susan remembered. One such occasion was when he took her and

---

*As Susan Cheever related in *Treetops*, "When Winter died in 1959 at the age of seventy-four, the autopsy found that his body was riddled with ulcers. . . . [I]n the end, they perforated his stomach lining and killed him." As for that birthday party for Phil Boyer, Cheever described it as a "big blowout" hosted by his fellow *New Yorker* writer St. Clair McKelway. When he first received the invitation, though, Cheever had noted his reservations: "I am tired of [Boyer's] lechery, tired of the rudeness and the frustrations of his friends, tired of alcoholics, tired of promiscuous women in their middle forties, tired of finding myself back in this train of thought."

Pammy to hear the great classical guitarist Andrés Segovia at the Century Club—"hoping" (as he wrote a friend) "to prove to [Susan] that the pleasures of respectability are not necessarily boring. I think she was impressed although there was a certain amount of pushing at the sandwich tables." This was cruel, but then Cheever only wanted the best for her: over and over he insisted that if she'd only improve her looks (lose weight, curl her hair, etc.) *and* her attitude—why then she'd have lots of dates, like Linda and Pammy, instead of sitting in her room all night reading books and stuffing herself. As it was, she seemed to be turning into the very sort of eccentric, precocious "sorehead" he'd been at Thayer, and (whether or not the similarity occurred to him as such) he wanted better things for her. When she'd complain about her insipid schoolmates and rotten teachers, the author of "Expelled" would advise her to be "still and patient and watchful"—but evidently she insisted on making trouble. "Susie comes home with the news that she is on some sort of probation," he wrote when she was sixteen.

> Her negativism, her digressive negativism are thought to be bad attitudes in class. Our conversation begins in soft voices but then I begin to shout, she cries and throws herself onto her bed, I order her to get up and eat dinner and tell her if this were in Italy I would hit her over the head with a piece of wood, and Federico, catching the harsh or ugly notes in my voice, begins to cry. We sit down to a gloomy table. I read. At eight o'clock sharp the wind springs out of the north with gale force, an inundation of snow and rain. Susie goes for a walk in the storm. Later I speak with her. "I'm indifferent," she says. "I'm a mass of intelligence adrift. I don't care if I sleep in the street."
>
> "Oh, you don't," say I, as the wind flings the rain against the windows. "Would you like to go out and sleep in the street this evening?" Here is sarcasm, fruitless and obscene.

Such unkindness (when he was aware of it) filled Cheever with remorse, and one of the ways he tried to make amends was with a sincere effort to be friends with the girl. His advice about her looks was, in a sense, meant to be friendly, and also they stayed up late at night discussing books and whatnot (often she was so exhausted in the morning that she could hardly stay awake at school). They talked about Yeats and Stendhal and the friendship of Dickens and Wilkie Collins, and sometimes Cheever would digress about certain personal woes (wondering later if he'd been "merciless" in doing so). But even in the midst of such intimacy there were certain points of decorum which tripped the girl up like so many landmines ("S[usan] asks me who was the Marquis de Sade and I blow skyhigh again")—though later, sober, Cheever was usually sheepish or downright miserable about losing his temper, if not quite able to apologize. Another touchy subject was the few but intense friendships the girl had made at Masters, a place where the headmistress had been fired because she was suspected to be a lesbian; Susan was also enamored of a charismatic teacher (female) who lived with another teacher (female), all matters that made her father nervous "for reasons [she] didn't understand." Under the circumstances, he might have been relieved when she finally decided to transfer to a boarding school (Woodstock) in Vermont, where at least she was happy, but he was *very* disappointed and told her so. One advantage to her absence, however, was that he could sustain himself with reveries of her returning as the daughter he'd always wanted ("Her figure is perfect, her face is slender and lovely"), though it only made matters worse when his hopes were dashed all over again. As he wrote that spring, he didn't understand Susan at all: "I've fed her, bathed her, taken her up in the night, plucked thorns and splinters out of her feet, loved her . . . but now when I speak to her she weeps and slams the door, hides in the woods on a fine Sunday morning, seems on the one hand merry and on the other to carry some unanswered question."

Ben was now old enough to be a considerable disappointment in his own right: as his father was at pains to remind him, he too needed to lose weight and do better in school and (especially) take an interest in sports like other boys. As Federico remarked many years later, "Ben, poor Ben, bore the brunt of all this masculine hoopla and accepted it with the fatalism [with which] he has accepted almost everything in his life." Cheever, a great reader of Freud, was not consoled by the news that homosexual tendencies are somewhat innate in all people; rather he became even *more* vigilant in cultivating a proper ethos for his older son. "Speak like a man!" he'd say, driven up the wall by the boy's high-pitched voice, not to mention his giggling ("You laugh like a woman!"). And while perhaps a little boy can't help what his voice sounds like, he didn't have to *choose* to speak that way—as Ben sometimes did, forming little two-legged creatures out of his hands and making them talk to each other in tiny piping voices ("*Stop* that nonsense!"). Also, he liked to dance in front of the bathroom mirror—pretending he was a gun-slinger who could dance so well that he dodged bullets—until one day his father walked in: "That," said Ben, "was the end of my dancing in front of the mirror."

In addition to such ominous behavior, the boy had a bed-wetting problem and couldn't read very well. His parents decided to invite his "hated teacher" to dinner, the better to discuss their concerns in depth and perhaps ingratiate themselves in some helpful way. It soon tran-spired, however, that Cheever's romantic interest in the teacher "pretty much blotted out" (as Ben put it) any immediate academic mat-ters. ("Ben's teacher for supper—how pretty girls refresh and compli-ment our feelings—and later to a concert and, during a Bach chorale, guess what I was thinking about.") Years later Ben was diagnosed with exophoria, which causes one eye to wander and diminishes depth per-ception (affecting athletic endeavors too); at the time, though, his par-ents didn't know what to make of his terrible marks in school, and deemed it best for him to repeat second grade while in Italy. Since his old, pre-Italy friends had all been promoted, the boy grew even more lonely, depressed, and apt to wet his bed, and finally (like his sister before him) went to a psychiatrist.

Cheever's worries deepened when the ten-year-old Ben befriended an effeminate boy named Richie Henry, whose family had moved to the carriage house next door.* For two years or so, the boys were almost inseparable: they'd disappear for hours, playing Monopoly or reading in the basement, or else go for long bicycle hikes and stop by the woods to explore. As for Cheever, he couldn't help seething whenever he laid eyes on Richie: "[He] often stands with both hands on his hips in an attitude that I was told, when I was a boy, was the sign of a congen-ital queer. . . . He is attached securely to my son and I do not like him." But of course the source of his misgivings was a taboo subject, such that Cheever's erratic behavior was an all-but-total mystery to the boys. Once, they returned from a long bicycle hike and were sitting under a tree when Cheever "came rip-snorting out of the house" and

---

*"Effeminate" was Cheever's invariable epithet for the boy, and it appears to have been the *mot juste:* "At the time I had no idea of my sexuality," said Richie, a very good-humored (and gay) man in his fifties when we spoke. "My family never made an issue of it. But later I asked an old junior-high friend if she thought I was effeminate, and she said, 'Yes, I certainly did.' "

began shouting at Ben about some nominal grievance—this while looking at the other boy, whose bicycle he kept shaking for emphasis: "He seemed to be directing his anger at *me*," Richie remembered, "and at the end of his tirade he threw my bike on the ground. I was flabbergasted." Nor could he fathom Cheever's coldness one Halloween, when the boys went trick-or-treating together; Richie was already in costume when he came for Ben, and Mr. Cheever gave him a very hard stare before finally calling his son to the door. As it happened, he was "rigid with indignation": "A friend of Ben's," he wrote Weaver, "who has always seemed to me on the delicate side, showed up at the door in high-heeled shoes and an old evening dress, rouged to the ears and blooming." Ben, especially, was nonplussed by it all. His father seemed forever berating him over trifles: *You've been gone* how *long picking blueberries? And that's all the blueberries you've picked? And why didn't you go to the football game with everyone else? Where have you* been *all this time—?* "What I claim to feel is that he has turned his back on the beauty of the autumn day, the green playing field, and the decent people," Cheever wrote in his journal, "but what I really fear is that he has been indulging in the vices of my own youth, smoking cigarettes and masturbating in the moldy-smelling woods. . . . So I seem to pour onto his broad and tender shoulders all my anxiety, my guilt."

He wanted to be the right kind of father—not like his own father, in short, the dreaded "passive father" of Freudian lore. This meant enticing his son onto fields of glory: reminding him to practice his soccer passes ("although he would sooner take his tame mouse for a walk"), kick a football, and by all means learn a seemly love for baseball, that *sine qua non* of American manhood. "When I was seven years old," Ben remembered, "he told me that if I picked a team, he would take me to a game, and after that he'd help me follow the standings in the newspaper. He gave me a list of teams." Ben picked the Baltimore Orioles, and Cheever asked why. "Because Oriole is such a pretty name," the boy explained. And yet Cheever persevered. One of the great morbidities of his own youth had been an effeminate wing (the fault of a passive father), and his own son would be spared that, if possible. As Ben wrote in "The Boy They Cut," Cheever would often coax his indifferent, exophoric son to play catch with him.

We'd go outside. He'd throw the ball at me. I'd drop it.

"I'm sorry," I'd say and pick the ball up and throw it back.

He'd throw the ball again. Again I'd fail to make the catch. "Sorry," I'd say. . . .

"For Christ's sake, stop apologizing," he'd say.

"Okay," I'd say. "I'm sorry."

But at last they discovered a mutual love of the outdoors: Cheever delightedly taught his son how to fish, and Ben became an avid reader of *Field & Stream* (which, he said, "you could read without having any questions about your sexual identity"). When he expressed interest in a twenty-two-dollar kayak kit ("Hours of Paddling Fun!"), Cheever bought it for him at once, and wasn't the least dismayed when Ben wrecked the thing a week later in the Croton River; he promptly bought him another, better kayak. Ben—nothing if not eager to please, and sensing he was on a roll of sorts—zestfully took up a lot of manly chores, like felling trees and splitting wood, for which his grateful father paid him fifty cents an hour. Sometimes after these exertions the boy would reward himself with a bubble bath—until one day his father found him reclining among the suds. *"Who do you think you are?"* he roared. *"Some kind of* STARLET?!"

Nobody could say he didn't care—and really, at bottom, he had almost nothing but sympathy for the sensitive little boy. When Ben would leave the dinner table in tears and go hide under his bed, his father would sometimes lie on the floor beside him and (as Ben recalled) "talk to [him] through the dust bunnies." And there were many times when the boy would get scared at night and crawl between his parents— then wet the bed. "We did the best we could," Ben decided, many years later.

FRED CHEEVER WAS TRYING to stay sober, but he was having a hard time finding work, and he still had children to support. One day in early October 1959—Dr. Winternitz had just died—John got a call from his brother asking if they could "discuss some business," and the two met for lunch. "Fred talks on about his trip across the country in August and finally I ask him, as gently as possible, what is on his mind," John wrote. "'Nothing,' he says, 'nothing,' but as I press him a little I find that he plans to open a men's-clothing store in either San Juan, Puerto Rico, or Palo Alto, California. . . . I ask him if he would like some money. No, this will not be necessary; but we drive back to the house and I write him a check for five hundred dollars. He puts this in his pocket and leaves." Within a few weeks, Fred got a salesman job for the Hearst Sunday supplement, *American Weekly*, but he seemed in poor health ("fat and very lame") and of course he could always start drinking again. John had borrowed from *The New Yorker* to make up the "loan" to Fred, which he realized was likely the first of many: "[A]t the moment I have nine dependents," he wrote Weaver. "This is one hell of a burden for my childlike sense of wonder."

It was a bad time to be strapped for cash. In the past few months, Cheever had flogged himself into writing as many stories as possible ("wanting to prove to myself that I can"), but the work wasn't very gratifying anymore, except materially. He often felt as if he'd done about as much as he could in the short form, at a time when most writers of the first rank were focusing almost exclusively on novels. Also, he was more embarrassed than ever to be associated so closely with *The New Yorker*—appearing constantly amid the "bland poetry" and "bad cartoons," he wrote, had begun to seem a kind of "confinement": "I must realize that the people who read my fiction have stopped reading The New Yorker; I must realize that the breach here is real and happy." And yet, three and a half years after finishing *The Wapshot Chronicle*, he had only the vaguest idea what his next novel would be about. A story he'd published earlier in the year—"The Events of That Easter," about an egg-hunt contest gone awry—seemed part of something bigger, but he was far from certain what; all he knew, more or less, was that he wanted to write a Wapshot sequel treating "Coverly as Apollo and Moses as Dionysus," since the theme of fraternal competitiveness was on his mind at the moment.

He refused, however, to say even that much when he asked Harper for an advance at the end of the year, or, for that matter, when he applied for another Guggenheim: he simply stated, as was true, that he wanted to work on a novel without ("for once") having to support himself with story writing at the same time. Harper gave him $6,850— a paltry sum for a writer of his stature (though Cheever might have wanted it that way)—and meanwhile he worried that he'd queered his chances for a second Guggenheim by "smash[ing] into" the foundation's president, Henry Allen Moe, at the Century Club ("what with the gin and one thing or another"). When he was, in fact, awarded a fellowship, Cheever asked for the same amount he'd gotten ten years before—three thousand dollars—since he only needed roughly ten thousand (he said) to "feed, shelter and educate" his family, and he hoped the Harper advance would account for the rest.*

"My one New Year resolution," he wrote Herbst at the beginning of 1960, "is that I Will Not Write Anymore Short Stories, so help me God." It was a resolution he'd soon break, but first he tried his hand at writing a play, which, if he could bring it off, might sell for big money. A few surviving notes indicate *The Rules of the Game* was to be a three-act teleplay satirizing the nuclear age in some mysterious way; there was a scientist named Simon who "could be employed by [Edward] Teller," and evidently this character was to appear on a quiz show involving soundproof booths (the *Game* of the title, though Cheever had yet to invent the *Rules*). Between acts, Cheever planned to include a couple of mock commercials for a tonic called Elixircol that restored youth and protected one from "excess radioactivity." After a few weeks, though, Cheever gave up ("The play just seems to lack density and everything else") and cannibalized the commercials into a story, "The Death of Justina," which he quickly finished with great satisfaction: "I think B[ill] will say tearfully that it is brilliant," he noted (then added a little doubtfully, "It will be interesting to see").

The core story of this complicated tour-de-force is suggested by the title: Justina, an elderly cousin of the narrator Moses's wife,† dies during a visit and sits gaping on the sofa while Moses learns, to his chagrin, that he is prevented by a zoning ordinance from disposing of the body. As his doctor explains, "A couple of years ago some stranger bought the old Plewett mansion and it turned out that he was planning to operate it as a funeral home. We didn't have any zoning provision at the time that would protect us and one was rushed through the Village Council at midnight and they overdid it. It seems that you not only can't have a funeral home in Zone B—you can't bury anything there and you can't die there." The doctor suggests that Moses drive his guest to Zone C ("beyond the traffic light by the high school") and "just say that she died in the car." When Moses indignantly appeals to the Mayor, the man objects that such "morbidity" could easily get out of hand ("People don't like to live in a neighborhood where this sort of

---

*He was given thirty-six hundred dollars this time.

†One presumes that Moses is Moses Wapshot and the title character is Cousin Justina from *The Wapshot Chronicle*, but Cheever doesn't constrain himself with a lot of intertextual exactitude: the story's Moses reflects on the "neglected graves of [his] three brothers," whereas the novel's Moses has only one brother, Coverly.

thing goes on all the time"), but finally agrees to make an exception when Moses threatens to bury the woman in his backyard. The funeral, however, is a very gloomy affair on the outskirts of town, where the dead "are transported furtively as knaves and scoundrels and where they lie in an atmosphere of perfect neglect."

Such anyway is the pretext for an elaborate rumination on the denial of death in a pre-apocalyptic world. At the outset Moses informs us that he's just given up drinking and smoking on doctor's orders, as a result of which his senses are so dreadfully heightened that he sees a face in his breakfast muffin ("As you can see, I was nervous") and for the first time perceives the awful breadth of despair beneath the paralyzing gentility of Proxmire Manor: "Above me on the hill were my home and the homes of my friends, all lighted and smelling of fragrant wood smoke like the temples in a sacred grove, dedicated to monogamy, feckless childhood, and domestic bliss but so like a dream that I felt the lack of viscera with much more than poignance—the absence of that inner dynamism we respond to in some European landscapes. In short, I was disappointed." Even the "anthracite eyes" of a melting snowman seem to regard the scene with "terrifying bitterness." The same malaise prevails at Moses's office, where he is prevented from attending to poor Justina by his gum-chewing tyrant of a boss, who insists he stay behind to write a commercial for Elixircol, "the true juice of youth." Rebelling against a world in which "the solemn fact of death" cannot be respected or even admitted, Moses writes a scathing parody: *"Are you growing old? . . . Are you falling out of love with your face in the looking glass? Does your face in the morning seem rucked and seamed with alcoholic and sexual excesses and does the rest of you appear to be a grayish-pink lump, covered all over with brindle hair?"* And so on, hilariously. (There are three commercials in all, the last consisting verbatim of the Twenty-third Psalm.) A further element in this zany (yet somber) fantasia is a dream Moses has on the night of Justina's death: in a vast supermarket he sees thousands of shoppers— obviously citizens of his own "beloved country," there being a farrago of races, colors, and creeds, all dressed with "sumptuary abandon"— pushing their wagons amid harshly lighted aisles and deliberating over ambiguous victuals: "Nothing was labeled. Nothing was identified or known." At the checkout counters they are met by "brutes" who rip open their parcels and cause the shoppers to show "all the symptoms of the deepest guilt" at the sight of what they have chosen, whereupon they are pushed out the door and taken away, moaning and crying, into the darkness. "What could be the meaning of this?" Moses asks, and the answer seems to lie somewhere in Hawthorne's injunction at the end of *The Scarlet Letter:* "Be true! Be true! Be true! Show freely to the world, if not your worst, yet some trait whereby the worst may be inferred!" Or, as Moses reflects after Justina's oddly shameful funeral, "How can a people who do not mean to understand death hope to understand love, and who will sound the alarm?"

Large questions, to be sure, and one could go on and on—such that the story (surprisingly short) strains a little at its all-too-visible seams. But then, too, it's funny and profound and unlike any story written at the time, which might explain why *The New Yorker* "summarily rejected" it: "B[ill] says the satire lacks support and I suppose he means that it is over-intense." Cheever responded with his usual show of equability. As he wrote Maxwell, he thought he'd just go ahead and break the story into its constituent parts—that is, save the dream sequence and commercials for some other project (probably the novel), and sell the Justina plot to a lesser magazine like *The Reporter.* On further reflection, however, he decided against this. Instead he sold the story (intact) to *Esquire*, and later—with the rejection of "Justina" (and other stories) decidedly in mind—remarked of Maxwell: "If you don't grow and change he baits you; if you do grow and change he baits you cruelly." At the time he expressed a similar sentiment in his journal, albeit in the words of an old adage from his father: "If you run they'll bite you. If you stand still they'll fuck you in the arse." At any rate Cheever loved the story, and for the rest of his life he generally chose to read it at any public gathering. If the audience responded well, he knew they were the right sort and would favor them with a second story. And almost always, delightedly, he'd announce that *The New Yorker* had rejected "Justina": "They thought of it as an art story," he'd say with breezy contempt.

CHAPTER TWENTY-ONE

{ 1960–1961 }

A FEW DAYS BEFORE the fifties ended, Cheever wrote in his
journal that he'd been watching his beloved Benny Goodman
on TV one night when he began to weep ("I am like a boozy
sponge") at the thought of having "lived in great times and known
great men": Cummings, Bellow, Warren, Ellison, and so on. Then, a
few pages later, he wrote: "I think bitterly of the solitude of my life,
that I know no writers, that weeks and months pass in which I see
almost no one, living in a haunted house by the railroad tracks."

Minus his time in Italy, Cheever had lived almost eight years in
Westchester and had wanted to leave for most of them. He was tired of
being snubbed by businessmen at cocktail parties, and tireder still of
what passed for cultured companionship. A rather good friend, Kenneth Wilson, was editor of Reader's Digest Condensed Books, and
though Cheever liked Wilson all right, it was jarring for him to consider that he squandered his time "in the company of people who con-
dense books." As for the rest of his circle—the Kahns and Boyers,
et al.—he regarded them as "a society of the bored and disappointed,"
and was now gaining a bona-fide reputation for saying "atrocious
insulting things" (as Ginny Kahn put it) when drunk. By mutual agreement, then, Cheever's life among the local gentry had become a somewhat more solitary affair, and when he did attend the odd cocktail
party, he couldn't help noticing the "cursory service" he received from
part-time bartenders, who realized Cheever had not been asked "to the
X's, the Y's and the Z's." The main exception to all this was Art Spear
("the best company I have these days"), who shared a boyish delight in

such escapades as swimming "beararse" in the Hudson and waving at passing trains. Cheever liked to woolgather over the prospect of taking Spear to Rome and showing him the sights ("Why that is a corker, he says")—but really, when all was said and done, he had to admit that theirs was not a very profound attachment: "[I]f he moved to San Francisco tomorrow it wouldn't make much difference," Cheever noted, a few pages after imagining Spear in Rome.

In April 1960 he went to Yaddo, and while walking along Union Avenue he noticed that a mid-Victorian mansion, the Drexel House, was for sale at the remarkably low price of fifteen thousand dollars. The house was something of a wreck, as Saratoga had declined since its fin-de-siècle glory days: a number of other rickety mansions along the street were also for sale, if not altogether forsaken. But Cheever liked the idea of savoring the vistas of his youth amid relative splendor, as well as having easy access to artistic peers at Yaddo. "There will be the boredom and the bigotry of a raffish small-town," he conceded, writing a friend, "but I think it's about time that we tried another way of life." A week later, he brought his family up and showed them around the Drexel House—the airy bedrooms and porte-cochère and large, creaking veranda. "Mary seemed to like the house," or so he thought, oblivious perhaps to the dim glare she'd given that whole gloomy block, to say nothing of her impression of the Worden, where they stayed in a suite that (as Cheever observed) "smelled of old poker-decks and cigar ends." Nevertheless, he met with a banker and was all set to sign the papers when, a few nights later, he noticed his wife weeping over the dishes: she did *not* want to live in Saratoga, she said, and that was that. "I'm quite pissy about my disappointment," Cheever wrote.

Just because Mary was opposed to living in a moribund spa town did not mean she was opposed to moving per se. "I was tired of living in someone else's playpen," she said, and in fact had been looking at houses for years, perusing the real-estate news almost every night. Nothing had quite clicked, though, until one day late that summer, when she found a lovely stone-ended Dutch Colonial farmhouse on five acres of the Van Cortlandt estate in Ossining.* "M[ary] claims to

---

*Later, when holding court for journalists (the apple wood crackling in his fireplace, the heirlooms on display), Cheever often pointed out that his house in Ossining had been built in the eighteenth century "and so handsomely restored by Eric Gugler

have dreamed of [the house] long before she saw it," Cheever wrote in his journal. "It's the most wonderful thing ever to happen to me, she says. I will faint, I will swoon." For Mary the best part was the natural beauty of the place—what with its view of the Hudson, its little brook and apple orchard, all of it sequestered in a private valley. Cheever also made note of the brook, as well as the "stately living-room" and (perhaps the clincher) "enough bedrooms for us but not enough for Mary's sister to come and stay. I shall buy it."

So he thought. The house cost $37,500, and officers at the Knickerbocker Mortgage Company and Bank couldn't help wondering how a self-employed man in his late forties, with little in the way of personal assets, proposed to pay for such a spread. With some slight trepidation, Cheever suggested they get in touch with Milton Greenstein, a lawyer at *The New Yorker* who handled payroll matters and might be expected to cosign a mortgage on the magazine's behalf. Greenstein—"a pathological cheapskate," according to one editor—had always thought Cheever a bit on the profligate side, but this took the proverbial cake. "Freelance writers," he told Maxwell, "should *not* own property." At the time Cheever had been having second thoughts, but when Maxwell ("tactlessly") repeated this remark, he made up his mind. Mary contributed a ten-thousand-dollar down payment out of her own savings, and Cheever persuaded Dudley Schoales to cosign a mortgage for the rest ("and all I have to do now," he wrote Cowley, "is to write a short story a week for the next twenty years and turn out plays and novels in the evenings"). For a day or two he may have gloated over trumping *The New Yorker,* before reminding himself that (in addition to other misgivings) he was now positively doomed to remain amid the "crushing boredom" of Northern Westchester:

> I feel imprisoned, angry and bitter and when I think of taking a walk with A or drinking with B I only feel more bored and disappointed. Everything I look at, the gateposts, the rooftops across the street, the majestic elm—they all seem like old ticket stubs to plays that bored me. Nothing is interesting. And I think angrily of the house, that I am trapped within the circle of the commuting area

---

in the 1920's" (as he wrote for an architectural journal in 1976) "that it has lost its historical status . . ." Such status was never actually conferred, since the house was built in 1928, though the land was acquired in 1799 or thereabouts.

that spreads out around the city, as clearly defined as a stain, that M[ary] wants the pleasures and none of the risks of my life.

. . .

THEY WEREN'T MOVING until January, and in the meantime Cheever did a fair amount of traveling. Rust Hills had invited him to San Francisco to appear with Philip Roth and James Baldwin for an *Esquire*-sponsored symposium titled "Writing in America Today." The program began October 20 at the Berkeley campus, where Cheever was scheduled to speak followed by a panel discussion; Roth would speak the next night at Stanford, and Baldwin the third night at San Francisco State. It was not a miscalculation to invite a Wasp, a Jew, and a Negro, two of whom were young and reputedly angry about things, while the third was supposed to be the suave embodiment of the Eastern literary establishment. As the *New York Times* reported, "It was the general hope that Cheever, Roth and Baldwin would disagree violently about practically everything and that San Franciscans would not have seen anything so lively since Kerouac and Ginsberg left town." In fact, Cheever got along fine with Baldwin—they'd met at the Institute— and he admired *Goodbye, Columbus* so extravagantly that he'd been moved to write a little note to Roth's publishers: "This is not for publication because I don't believe in setting a good book afloat on a spate of quotations but I would like to thank you for the immense pleasure I took in the Roth stories. It was my wife who said that she is very grateful to Mr. Roth for having proved to her that somebody lives in Newark."

And so the three were pretty much en rapport among themselves, if not always with their audiences. That first night, Cheever was (as ever in public) very nervous, excusing himself to take a calming swim in the Berkeley pool before mounting the dais, where he read "Some People, Places, and Things That Will Not Appear in My Next Novel"— a numerical list of items (with witty, illustrative vignettes) which Cheever wished to eliminate from his own work and, as far as possible, the work of others. "Out with . . . explicit description of sexual commerce," he proclaimed, "for how can we describe the most exalted experience of our physical lives, as if—jack, wrench, hubcap, and nuts—we were describing the changing of a flat tire?" He also wanted to dispose of "all lushes," and perhaps gave Baldwin pause by declaring a moratorium on "all those homosexuals" too—a statement mitigated somewhat by the (personally fraught) rhetorical question that followed: "Isn't it time that we embraced the indiscretion and inconstancy of the flesh and moved on?" Finally he asked the audience to consider the career of one Royden Blake, who'd begun by writing "bitter moral anecdotes . . . that proved that most of our deeds are sinful," before entering a "decade of snobbism, in which he never wrote of characters who had less than sixty-five thousand dollars a year." Toward the end, Blake found himself in a rut, writing about all the tedious things Cheever had just proscribed: "You might say that he had lost the gift of evoking the perfumes of life: sea water, the smoke of burning hemlock, and the breasts of women. He had damaged . . . the ear's innermost chamber, where we hear the heavy noise of the dragon's tail moving over the dead leaves." Such an ecstatic vision was the very thing Cheever longed to recover, for (he asked in closing) how otherwise could one "hope to celebrate a world that lies spread out around us like a bewildering and stupendous dream?"*

Having described what he viewed as his own predicament, Cheever spoke of the "abrasive and faulty surface of the United States in the last twenty-five years," which had led to the coarsening of American fiction: "[H]aving determined the nightmare symbols of our existence, the characters have become debased and life in the United States in 1960 is Hell." Under the circumstances, Cheever concluded, "the only possible position for a writer now is negation"—which jibed nicely with Roth's own manifesto ("the alienation of the writer in America from a grotesque contemporary society") and drew an ovation from Berkeley students. According to the *Times*, however, older members of the audience were indignant, "climb[ing] and totter[ing] to their feet" to accuse Cheever of "deliberate obscurity" and "anti-Americanism."

Some People, Places, and Things That Will Not Appear in My Next Novel was the title of Cheever's next collection, and this particular piece was reprinted as "A Miscellany of Characters That Will Not Appear," in which a number of items from the magazine version were deleted. One such item had borrowed verbatim from the eccentric preamble to "The Death of Justina"—which ran the same month in *Esquire* (November 1960) as "Some People" in *The New Yorker*!—and another was a transparent attack on Salinger, though Cheever would later claim, "The only writer I meant to attack was myself [i.e., in the person of Royden Blake]." The Salinger-slurring item called for the elimination of "all autobiographical characters who describe themselves as being under the age of reason, coherence, and consent" and included a little parody of *Catcher in the Rye:* "I mean I'm this crazy, shook-up, sexy kid of thirteen with these phony parents, I mean my parents are so phony it makes me puke . . ."

Cheever responded with an air of patient, wistful politesse. Asked why he bothered to write at all if he thought everything was so terrible, Cheever replied, "I write to make sense of my life."

But when his next collection was published a few months later, Cheever himself was repulsed by his bitterness: "Love never enters these pages and the prose seems precious. Here is a display of my worst characteristics and a devastating self-portrait of a man in a decline . . ." Having just returned from a book-signing in New York, Cheever was doubtless in low fettle when he wrote this; in any case it's too harsh. *Some People, Places, and Things That Will Not Appear in My Next Novel* is hardly "devastating" evidence of decline, though perhaps it's a slight comedown from the two superlative previous collections. At least half the stories (including "Boy in Rome" and "The Wrysons") are mediocre by Cheever's standards, but "The Death of Justina" and "The Scarlet Moving Van" are proof of how cogently he was responding to the times—"a sort of apocalyptic poetry," as Cowley put it, "as if you were carrying well observed suburban life into some new dimension where everything is a little cockeyed and on the point of being exploded into a mushroom cloud." Such a viewpoint was also noted by the reviewers— likewise as a good thing, for the most part. Charles Poore praised Cheever's "remarkable inventiveness" in the daily *Times*, and David Boroff in the *Book Review* singled out "Justina" as "masterly" and thought the collection as a whole reaffirmed Cheever's "prowess and defines anew the terrain features of the curious suburban Gehenna his characters inhabit."

But story collections were not going to pay for a life of landed ease on the Hudson, and hence Cheever appealed to his Hollywood agent, Henry Lewis, to find him a screenwriting job. Less than a week after he returned from San Francisco, the telephone rang at midnight: Jerry Wald of Twentieth Century–Fox wanted Cheever to write a treatment for an adaptation of D. H. Lawrence's *The Lost Girl*, the hitch being that he'd have to work in Hollywood for a few weeks—a big hitch, as Cheever saw it, and despite the money he almost refused. The prospect was ominous for a number of reasons. As he considered other writers who'd accepted such work, and been tainted by that milieu, he couldn't think of "anyone who [had] come out of it intact." The most baleful example was Irwin Shaw, whose most recent fiction had struck Cheever as almost awesome in its vulgarity, as if written expressly for the movies. Enumerating the characters of one Shaw novel, Cheever noted, "X is a terrible man, Y is afraid, Z is a beast. Ten years ago [Irwin] would have trimmed and modified all these judgements."*

A far more troubling concern was whether Cheever could, as he put it, "keep [his] nose clean." After almost twenty years of tortured monogamy, Cheever had begun to hope that he'd put "the sins of [his] childhood" behind him forever; besides, the world seemed to be getting a little more tolerant on that score. Watching Gore Vidal on TV that year, Cheever was impressed by how "personable and intelligent" the man seemed: "I think that he is either not a fairy," Cheever reflected, "or that perhaps we have reached a point where men of this persuasion are not forced into attitudes of bitterness, rancor and despair." But then, two months before Cheever's departure for Hollywood, Newton Arvin was arrested at Smith College for possession of homosexual pornography—a controversy that was "huge" in Cheever's household, as Susan remembered: "Maybe I heard Malcolm [Cowley] talking about it—this innocent man hauled off to jail by brutes because he was homosexual. I may have asked Daddy, in all innocence, how that could happen. Now I know he was scared out of his mind." At the time of his arrest, Arvin was director of Yaddo's executive committee, and Cheever may have expressed a quiet sort of solidarity by refusing an offer to replace him. But any open discussion of the matter made him "very unhappy and ill-tempered," as he wrote when Susan asked why homosexuality wasn't legalized. As it happened, in Cheever's home state of Massachusetts, where Arvin had been arrested, sodomy was classified as an "abominable and detestable crime against nature," often resulting in lengthy prison terms.†

Cheever feared that such a long isolation in the alien, decadent

---

*Eventually—with the spectacular success of *Rich Man, Poor Man* in 1969—the transformation would be complete. As Cheever succinctly described this massive potboiler: "It is the history of an emigrant family, much fucking."

†After his arrest, Arvin was ordered to have a psychiatric examination that resulted in a "classic homosexual profile," as Barry Werth wrote in his excellent account of the Arvin affair, *The Scarlet Professor.* Whatever one may think about the state of psychoanalytical theory circa 1960, it's interesting to consider Arvin's profile in light of Cheever's own history: "[Arvin] was fixed at a prepubertal stage of development and consequently sought solace in an inner world. . . . He was insecure as a result of early parental conflicts. He had a strong affinity for his mother but resented her dominance. At the same time, he had an indifferent and inexpressive father to whom he yearned to be close. . . . This compensatory longing for affection from other men, he was told, was the chief source of his depression."

world of Hollywood would fatally impair his better instincts, and in his journal he agonized over "the Hollywood problem": "It is true that I do protect my perhaps unstable and dangerous nature . . . with properties and affections that have the force of clemency and continence, and that Hollywood represents for me, at least, financial and sexual corruption." One "immense consolation" was the proximity of his old friends John and Harriett Weaver, who lived in the Hollywood Hills. "She is a sweet, pretty woman without a line on her face and he is a most gentle, affectionate, and excellent man," Cheever reassured himself, and to the Weavers he expressed a seemingly comic wish that their "kind presence will guide [him] away from violent drunkenness and disgusting venereal embroilments."

THE WEAVERS ARRANGED for Cheever to stay at the Chateau Marmont—a few blocks from their house—where the management grandly informed him that he'd been given the "Mitzi Gaynor Suite." It was small comfort. What struck Cheever most about his lodgings was the constant racket from the Sunset Strip outside his window, where he could observe an enormous papier-mâché chorus girl advertising the Sahara Hotel in Las Vegas. Los Angeles was "the magnification of all our vices," he wrote, with special reference to the large metaphorical chorus girl. Finding it hard to get out of bed in the morning, Cheever would pick up the telephone and order an elaborate breakfast by way of goading himself into the shower before he committed suicide. As for the Weavers, their hillside sanctuary only served to remind him of the domestic security he'd left behind in Westchester. For the rest of his life he was haunted by a curious memory (among others) from that visit to Hollywood: standing alone on the Weavers' terrace, he'd heard Harriett flush a toilet and address a casual remark to her husband. "The sensation of my aloneness was stupendous," Cheever remembered.

On the surface he affected to be cheerfully bemused by the oddities of Hollywood life. He told friends about his "fancy hotel apartment" at the Marmont, and proudly noted that his carnation-filled parlor had a water cooler in the corner. "I ran up a bill of a hundred dollars a day," he wrote Maxwell, "but it was all so deluxe that I was terribly ashamed of the cigarette burns in my dressing gown and the fact that much of my underwear is torn. I had a white Lincoln Continental convertible"—actually a Ford Falcon—"which I never took out of the garage and when someone at the pool said: 'There he is; that's Cheever' I dove in and lost my trunks." That he raffishly clashed with his environment was a matter of pride—part of his studied disdain for the "sumptuary laws," the point being, of course, that such a vividly civilized man could dress howsoever he liked. "My God, John," said Harriett Weaver when he appeared in her kitchen wearing a navy Brooks suit, "your crotch!" Cheever was about to leave for Twentieth Century–Fox to meet Jerry Wald, but Harriett demanded he hand over his pants. A few minutes later, when Henry Lewis arrived to pick up his client, he found Cheever sitting in his boxers sipping a martini while Harriett ironed the wrinkles out of his crotch.

As he loitered around the studio waiting to see Wald, Cheever ran into his old friend and *Stories* collaborator, Daniel Fuchs, now a gray-haired man whiling away his days in an office that reminded Cheever of "a side-parlor in the Hotel Gladstone." Fuchs advised him to treat Wald "like a demented child," and subsequently Weaver reported to Mary that her husband was following a serial about Marilyn Monroe in the *Mirror* so he and Wald could "talk more intelligently": "They talk about Saroyan's tax problems, Yves Montand ('an alley cat') and the works of D. H. Lawrence, especially *Ulysses,* which seems to be Mr. Wald's favorite." As a matter of fact, Wald was a kind, affable man who respected good writers and warmed to Cheever in particular. He claimed to have no problem with Cheever's request to spend a month in the Midlands soaking up Laurentian scenery, but as for his more earnest desire to work at home in Scarborough, Wald refused. He assured Cheever that he'd do his best to make him comfortable: the writer would have his own secretary, office, and nameplate, and be left entirely alone.

Though he liked Wald "immensely," Cheever seemed miserable to a degree that puzzled his colleagues, among them Ivan Goff and Ben Roberts, two writers from his Signal Corps days. Occasionally Cheever would stop by their offices to borrow gin—there was no alcohol in the Fox commissary—and vaguely complain about the place, which he described in a letter to Cowley as a "literary graveyard." Mostly, though, Cheever holed up in his own office ("an old bath-house at the edge of the lot") and worked steadily, the better to return to his family as soon as possible. He submitted a finished draft of his treatment in early December, only to learn that he had to wait ten more days for the studio's verdict. Meanwhile he stuck as closely as possible to the Weavers, but even their wholesome company wasn't much of a diversion from the usual dark thoughts. Walking along Malibu Beach of an afternoon, Cheever picked out squalid details—swastikas painted on a wall, or "curious domestic scenes such as a blonde in an adhesive-tape bikini helping a drunken man up a flight of stairs." He also obsessed over the brazen, ubiquitous homosexuals who seemed to be tempting him at all times. "I think there is a fag beside me at the lunch counter," he somberly recorded in his journal. "He drums his nails impatiently and who but a fag would do this?" He prayed for the surf to wash them away.

After a few days of unwanted leisure, Cheever sensed he was beginning to slip. A casual meeting with the actor Dean Stockwell was a terrible ordeal: though Cheever didn't doubt the actor's heterosexuality ("His tender looks are aimed at girls"), he felt afterward as if his penis "had been put through a mangle." His dinner with the singer Peggy Lee, however, caused no such consternation. Cheever was intrigued by Lee's Chinese garden, the dwarf trees sagging with Christmas ornaments, as well as the loutishness of Lee's boyfriend, who called her "baby" and kept saying, "It's going to be cool."

One night, toward the end of his visit, Cheever brought a friend to the Weavers' house for dinner—a writer in his mid-thirties named Calvin Kentfield. The two had met a decade before at Yaddo, and kept somewhat in touch through Maxwell, who'd edited some of Kentfield's fiction for *The New Yorker*. At Yaddo, Cheever had been impressed by the young man's looks and charm, but the years had been unkind to Kentfield. His first two books had gained little recognition, and he'd been forced to support his wife and daughter with long stints in the merchant marine—which provided a lot of nautical literary fodder, but was otherwise a strain. A heavy drinker, Kentfield brawled with other sailors, and in 1958 he fell off a gangplank and broke his kneecap on the deck below. By the time he was reunited with Cheever in Hollywood, Kentfield was missing two front teeth and walking with a limp. Also, he was recently divorced from his beloved, long-suffering wife, Veronica ("the true image," he called her in one book dedication), who only a year before had borne him a son.

Cheever duly noted his friend's defects—the limp, the missing teeth, "the face weathered by whisky and time. . . . He is late for everything and sometimes doesn't come at all." One afternoon the two went to a Finnish bath together and sat around chatting "beararse," and a couple nights later, after dinner, Cheever asked Harriett Weaver if she'd like to read his journal. She accepted the small three-ring binder and read politely for a minute or two, then smiled and returned it to Cheever without comment. Her eyes had fallen on the latest entry:

> I spend the night with C., and what do I make of this? . . . Perhaps sin has to do with the incident, and I have had this sort of inter-course only three times in my adult life.* I know my troubled nature and have tried to contain it along creative lines. It is not my choice that I am alone here and exposed to temptation, but I sin-cerely hope that this will not happen again. . . . I trust that I have harmed no one I love. The worst may be that I have put myself into a position where I may be forced to lie.

Let it serve as a measure of Cheever's distress that he felt compelled to seek immediate absolution—even implicitly—from a kindhearted per-son; nor would it be the first time he went about it in this manner. (Cheever had prepared the Weavers with an amusing spiel about how his "seafaring progenitors" had all kept journals, "secure in the knowl-edge" that their oldest sons would burn the things once they were dead.)

After his encounter with Kentfield, Cheever was more desperate than ever to escape Hollywood—"he seemed to think he was impris-oned here," Fuchs recalled—and was almost ecstatically grateful when Wald told him he was free to go. Home in time to spend Christmas with his family, Cheever boasted incessantly of having "bussed" Peggy Lee, and made a point of listening to her records with a lovelorn expression. By then his children were used to odd confidences of one sort or another, and joked about the "stacks of satisfied starlets" he'd left behind in California.

. . .

---

*This seems as good a place as any to make the indelicate point that Cheever almost certainly meant *oral* intercourse. One has it on good (and diverse) authority that he was just as entitled to the claim Farragut makes in *Falconer*: "When I die you can put on my headstone: 'Here lies Ezekiel Farragut, who never took it up the ass.' " Or, as he wrote in his journal in 1967 (and elsewhere in so many words), "I have no conscious desire to have anyone put their cock up my backside."

"AFTER LEAVING C.," Cheever wrote four years later (while engaged in a flirtation with another, better-known writer), "I suffered the worst agonies of my life for a month. Why should I ever let myself in for such pain again?" That winter, after he returned from Hollywood, Cheever was outwardly occupied with the move to Ossining and the labors required to pay for it—a hectic time that he seemed to take in stride, albeit boozily as usual. In fact he was consumed with an almost suicidal self-loathing. His imagination was crowded with sordid daydreams of the "unwashed sailor" (Kentfield), which could only be subdued with huge doses of alcohol. Not surprisingly, he was more impotent than ever with his wife ("there is not a spark of life in the old root") and worried that, for his sins, he'd now become decisively homosexual. When, a month later, Wald offered him two thousand a week to come back and write a screenplay, Cheever was tempted to accept—certainly he needed the money, but the thought of seeing Kentfield "[took] the lead out of [his] pencil" all over again. Wald persisted, proposing that Cheever was the only man to write "a big, important film that will explore, investigate and interrogate all the people residing in the sub-urbs," but Cheever continued to beg off. He never wrote for the big screen again.

Nor, it seems, did he ever see Kentfield, who continued his long decline. After finishing his third book, *All Men Are Mariners*—which took five years to write and vanished with hardly a trace—Kentfield devoted himself all the more to emulating the feckless lives of his heroes, Malcolm Lowry and Hart Crane. Returning to Sausalito after a chaotic sojourn in Mexico, he promptly fell down some stairs ("or in fact *up* them," he wrote a friend), breaking several ribs. "He is lost and I know something about this," Cheever wrote in 1964, after reading Kentfield's final story in *The New Yorker*, about "alcoholism and whores in Mexico." A few years later, as chairman of the grants committee, Cheever discreetly inquired of Maxwell whether he knew anything of Kentfield's whereabouts; he doubted he could get Kentfield a grant, but he thought the committee might make some charitable gesture if things were as bad as he suspected.

Things were bad, all right, though Kentfield persevered for nearly fifteen years after that meeting in Hollywood, and even managed to produce an autobiography of sorts, *The Great Green*. This did not lead to a surge of interest in his work, however. Nor could he stop drinking, though he'd made a last-ditch effort to get help from Synanon, a spin-off of Alcoholics Anonymous that had evolved into a cult of sorts. When they demanded he prove his commitment to sobriety by shaving his head, Kentfield threw in the towel. "Local Writer Falls from Cliff" read the headline in the *Point Reyes Light* on September 11, 1975. "Kentfield's nude and battered body was found Thursday morning at the bottom of a 500-foot cliff at Palomarin," the newspaper reported, along with some other curious details. Kentfield had left a hastily scribbled will of sorts, advising his beneficiaries that his most valuable possession, a ramshackle van, needed a new clutch and fuel pump. By way of explaining his suicide, he mentioned his disillusion with Synanon and suggested the reader consult chapter ninety-three of *Moby-Dick*, "The Castaway," in which the sailor Pip has a near-death experience that leaves him indifferent to the world: "[T]herefore his shipmates called him mad. So man's insanity is heaven's sense . . ." Kentfield's son may have taken this to heart in some obscure way, for he fell to his death from almost the identical spot twenty-five years later.

A 1978 journal entry reveals that Cheever knew something of Kentfield's fate. At a time when Cheever was sober, celebrated, and "terribly lonely," he seemed to think it was Kentfield's estranged wife who had driven him past the cliff en route to a rehab clinic. "I want to stop and have my last drink," he imagined Kentfield telling the poor woman, before he got out of the car. As far as anyone knows, though, Kentfield died alone.

CHAPTER TWENTY-TWO

{ *1961* }

IN JANUARY, Cheever moved to Ossining—about five miles from Beechwood and thirty miles from Manhattan, on the eastern shore of the Hudson. "We know that it commands the greatest views except for the Bay of Naples," Cheever was fond of saying (tacitly paraphrasing Tocqueville) once he'd become the town's most celebrated resident. At first, though, he was nothing if not conflicted. For one thing, he was still suffering "overwhelming anxiety" about the Kentfield affair and his sexuality in general ("I wonder . . . if by repressing these instincts I don't crush myself"), and this led to the question of whether such "a shabby and ridiculous figure" was worthy of so grand a demesne. He found himself standing frozen in one room or another—bemusedly examining the pilasters in the library, the cheerful yellow walls of the dining room, his grandfather's Canton handsomely on display—and wondering what on earth he was doing there. It was a long way to come for the seedy but self-sufficient youth knocking about in an old roadster during the Depression, living in rooming houses and fourth-rate hotels. "I feel very much like a bum," he wrote Peter Blume a few days after moving in, "and think that what I would like most to do is grow a long beard and recite dirty poetry in my underwear at the YMHA. This revery alternates with an imaginary evening party in which I say things like: President de Gaulle may I present my old friend Peter Blume?"

He expressed both the pleasure and pain of being a homeowner—at last—with quasi-deprecating humor. A previous occupant had named the house Afterwhiles (inscribed on the gateposts), and Cheever took to calling it Meanwhiles, mocking the pomposity of naming one's house while calling attention to the fact that one lived, no less, in a house with a name. Perhaps he also meant to suggest the transitory nature of the arrangement. Things began falling apart as soon as they moved in. One day it was the water pump, then the oil burner, plus the roof leaked, and finally, when his publisher, Cass Canfield, came for dinner, a sewer line burst under the stairs and squirted the man. And while Cheever rallied to keep the house in repair, the grounds began to deteriorate too: the elm trees blighted and died, the pond (dubbed the Turgenev Memorial Tarn) clabbered into a swamp, the little bridge collapsed, and the overall effect "rivaled the jungles of Borneo," as Federico put it. Within a few months Cheever was half seriously composing an advertisement to sell the place ("Stone ended 18th Century manor house, etc."), though he was pleased to show it off to an old rival like Shaw. "Irwin came for lunch and said that we both got what we wanted," Cheever wrote: "i.e. I got a picturesque old dump and he got a Swiss chalet and a taxfree two million in Geneva."

Perhaps his first real houseguest was Josie Herbst, who would admire the place, he expected, "with gusto and sincerity." In the past, Herbst had always been a vivacious presence, especially toward the children, but in recent years a strain of acerbity had begun to get the best of her. During their last encounter at Yaddo, in 1959, Cheever had noted how she "force[d] the conversation into a false and evasive vein" ("Yes, you say, we are all frustrated and miserable, we are all poor"); but mostly he was sympathetic, and afterward resumed his long campaign to get her a grant from the Institute—"not for her work," he wrote then-secretary Louise Bogan, "but for a nonstop literary conversation that must have begun in Sioux City around 1912 and is still going strong. . . . She is also old, sick, poor and quite embittered." No grant was forthcoming, however, and when Herbst arrived in Ossining two years later (hefting a cat carrier), she looked older and quite a bit more embittered. As Cheever drove her home from the train station, she immediately began blasting the Institute: "They're a bunch of stuffed shirts," she said. "Nobody any good is a member." At last Cheever told her that if she didn't desist he was going to stop the car and leave her on the side of the road. The next morning she stayed in bed so long that her hosts feared she'd died in the night.

Fortunately she survived the weekend, and in her wake left a large, balding "kitten" named Blackie who (she explained) had belonged to the poet Delmore Schwartz's estranged wife, Elizabeth Pollet. This was quid pro quo: many years ago, the Cheevers had unloaded on Herbst a cat named Harriet who'd proved ill-suited to their small New York apartment; the cat had thrived in the wide-open spaces of Erwinna, and it was Herbst's hope that Ossining would have the same tonic effect on Blackie. The latter—whom Cheever promptly renamed Delmore—spent a few days hiding under furniture and then began spraying the walls, until a veterinarian suggested he be neutered. "If the knife should slip," said Cheever, "there would be no recriminations." The castrated Delmore was not a whit more amiable: he pissed in Cheever's shoes and ate flowers off potted plants, and once made a point of "dump[ing] a load in a Kleenex box while [Cheever] was suffering from a cold." Herbst, it seemed, had placed a curse on Cheever's house, and consequently the two friends fell out of touch for a while. In the end it was Cheever who made amends, writing to assure Herbst that he'd allowed Delmore not only to live but to prosper: "He is very fat these days and his step, Carl Sandburg notwithstanding, sounds more like that of a barefoot middle-aged man on his way to the toilet than the settling in of a winter fog but he has his role and we all respect it . . ." By then the writers' respective careers had diverged even further, and when Cheever complained that his long-awaited wealth and fame made him "intensely uncomfortable," Herbst replied that he could ease the pain a little by loaning her a hundred bucks to pay the electric bill. Cheever gave her at least that much ("I'm glad you asked"), and two years later—enlisting the support of Bellow and Warren—he finally got her that grant from the Institute. This restored her to the public eye somewhat, and the following year she was tapped to serve on the fiction jury for the National Book Award.

CHEEVER'S NEIGHBORS on Cedar Lane were Ted and Sally Ziegler. Ted, an energetic polio survivor, was himself an author (*Men Who Make Us Rich*), which perhaps had something to do with what appeared to be a defensive attitude toward his more famous neighbor. After their first dinner together, Cheever noted the "sharp edges to Ted's personality" and suspected he'd made a bad impression for some reason— confirmed a few days later, when Cheever went to get his mail and noticed that Ziegler, working outside, abruptly seized his papers and stormed into his house, slamming the door. From there matters went downhill, though long placid intervals passed when the two didn't speak at all. Every few years, however, the feud would get hot again. Ziegler took up the French horn in middle age and began practicing outdoors at night, until Cheever "marched up the hill" and threatened to "fire off [his] shotgun at intervals of five minutes." That was in 1967; nine years later, Ziegler suddenly began railing at Cheever about his dogs ("For fifteen years his wife hasn't been able to take a walk, his daughter has been terrified, his old cat is miserable . . ."). Meanwhile one of Ziegler's sons, Andrew, sometimes found himself in the midst of these imbroglios and would notice an odd tangy odor he couldn't quite identify until the Proustian moment, many years later, when he took his first sip of gin and "immediately thought of John Cheever."

Partly as a means of staving off (or sweating out) those first drinks of the day, Cheever had become a great taker of walks, for which the pastoral environs of Cedar Lane were well suited. His favorite route was along the Croton Aqueduct—a forty-five-minute (or so) hike through the woods and along the Croton River leading at last to the fabulous spectacle of the Croton Dam, which Cheever especially liked to show companions in spring, when the 180-foot marvel overflowed ("in spate") and the crashing water could be heard a mile away. "This is the second largest cut-stone mortised structure in the world," Cheever would always explain to first-time visitors, adding in later years, "—and one of the last things on the planet to be seen by Neil Armstrong before he was hurled into space."

On his way home from the aqueduct pathway, Cheever would often stop for a drink at Shady Lane Farm, which Aaron Copland had sold in 1960 to the Italian poet and novelist Antonio Barolini ("a member of the Vicenza aristocracy," Cheever was apt to point out). Barolini was a gentle eccentric who tended to greet Cheever with a great hug and buss on both cheeks, calling him "my dear" and affably declaring his love. The two would then retire to Barcaloungers and attempt to communicate in a curious pidgin accompanied by florid gesticulation— until one day Cheever noticed Barolini had begun speaking entirely in English, translating even the simplest bits of Italian. ("Is too bad you cannot read my article, he says. But I can read Italian I say shyly. No reply.") "I am loving the Beatles," Barolini suddenly announced in 1964. Cheever asked if he'd seen them on TV or bought their records, and the man presently explained that he was referring to "George and Helene Beatle" who lived in Croton. These were the Biddles; indeed,

Cheever had kept up a witty correspondence with George for many years. The old man was a well-known artist from an eminent Philadelphia family; his brother Francis had been attorney general in the Roosevelt administration, and George had used his influence with FDR (an old Groton and Harvard classmate) to help establish the WPA's Federal Art Project. Soon after the Cheevers moved to Cedar Lane, Biddle presented them with an enormous Muscovy duck—"Duck Biddle"—who presided over the Memorial Tarn until he was devoured by neighborhood dogs.

Such congenial locals were a comfort, as Cheever was suffering from "inhibitive megrims" which made it "as difficult for [him] to leave [his] quaint old house in the country as it is difficult for an impacted wisdom tooth to leave its seat in the jaw-bone." His anxiety over the Kentfield affair would not go away, inflaming an old dread that he was an "impostor" whose iniquity would surely be discovered and his "chosen way of life" destroyed. He became more and more wary of any sort of taxing social encounter. One of his very few outings in 1961 was the Institute lunch in May, a "painful bore" where he found himself acting as minder for John Knowles ("I never dreamed I'd take a leak with Robert Graves and [Fredric] March," the man quipped) and wincing as Glenway Wescott read award citations ("You have made a GAME of the sport and a sport of the GAME!"); afterward the Cowleys and Blumes came to Cedar Lane for dinner and began chatting about a married football star who, they happened to know, was a pederast. "They continue to talk about married homosexuals," Cheever fretted in his journal. "I don't seem to know any. . . . Glenway with his lisp and fancy-work prose gives me a pain in the neck."

It got so bad that Cheever could scarcely drive across a bridge without suffering a full-blown panic attack, as if he were being physically chastised for leaving the safety of his home. "Poor X," he wrote.

As he approached the bridge there would be an excruciating tightening of his scrotum, especially his left testicle, and a painful shrinking of his male member. As he began to ascend the curve of the bridge it would become difficult for him to breathe. He could fill his lungs only by gasping. This struggle to breathe was followed by a sensation of weakness in his legs, which would presently become so uncoordinated that he could legitimately worry about being able to apply the brakes. The full force of the attack came at the summit of the bridge when these various disturbances would seem to affect his blood pressure and his vision would begin to darken.

This terrifying experience was evoked in a story he wrote that year, "The Angel of the Bridge," in which the narrator comes to perceive his phobia as the manifestation of some vague disenchantment with "modern life"—abruptly cured by a young hitchhiker who carries a small harp and serenades the narrator with an old folk song: "She sang me across a bridge that seemed to be an astonishingly sensible, durable, and even beautiful construction designed by intelligent men to simplify my travels, and the water of the Hudson below us was charming and tranquil." Such a bizarre *deus ex machina* was the very sort of "marvelous brightness" to which Alfred Kazin would perceptively refer (a few years later) as a dubious effort on Cheever's part "to cheer himself up." It was an effort that would only become more strenuous, and nothing akin to an angelic hitchhiker was likely to make it otherwise.

Marooned to some extent in Westchester, Cheever continued to see a certain amount of the white-collar crowd, who remained a rich source of material. That was the summer of the Berlin Crisis, a few months after the Bay of Pigs, and one night Cheever spent an evening at the Boyers' with some banker guests and an architect named Art Malsin whom he'd always despised. "Micks in the White House!" they complained. "Bomb Cuba!" ("On and on it goes," Cheever wrote Biddle, "and I spend most of my time counting to ten so that I won't be intemperate and expose myself as an enemy agent.") Around that time, too, Mrs. Vanderlip had decided to "hydrogen-proof" her vintage bomb shelter, built during the Great War, and the whole paranoid ethos inspired Cheever to write one of his most entertaining satires, "The Brigadier and the Golf Widow." The story begins, "I would not want to be one of those writers who begin each morning by exclaiming, 'O Gogol, O Chekhov, O Thackeray and Dickens, what would you have made of a bomb shelter ornamented with four plaster-of-Paris ducks, a birdbath, and three composition gnomes with long beards and red mobcaps?'" This fanciful shelter belongs to Charlie Pastern, the "brigadier" of the Grassy Brae Golf Club, who spends his days "marching up and down the locker room" shouting, "Bomb Cuba! Bomb Berlin! Let's throw a little nuclear hardware at them and show them who's boss." For all his bravado, though, Charlie proves to be a pathetically unhappy man stuck in a loveless marriage while expiring under an avalanche of debt. To distract himself, he begins an affair with a promiscuous matron named Mrs. Flanagan, who ultimately demands a key to his bomb shelter in exchange for her favors. When this gets back to Charlie's wife, she is duly vexed: "He had dragged her good name through a hundred escapades, debauched her excellence, and thrown away her love, but she had never imagined that he would betray her in their plans for the end of the world." Finally, as she prepares to leave the wretched Charlie (who has lost Mrs. Flanagan too), she relates her epiphany: "You *want* the world to end, don't you? Don't you, Charlie, don't you?" A funny, poignant dénouement follows in the form of a letter from the narrator's mother, who reports that Charlie subsequently went to jail for grand larceny, leaving his family destitute, while the now divorced and similarly bereft Mrs. Flanagan was last seen standing beside the bomb shelter "like a mourner," until the new owner sent a maid down to shoo her away.

That dénouement led to the first explicit clash between Cheever and Maxwell, whose friendship had been on the mend since the latter's brisk rejection of "Justina." A few months before, Maxwell had even gone so far as to accompany Cheever to the dentist—a gesture of almost maternal solicitude that had moved Cheever, who reflected in his journal: "He has for more than twenty years, encouraged and supported me, it was he who got me an award and took me into his club* and now he sits beside me at the dentists to cure my anxieties. It is a friendship I think [of] today with no jealousy, no dependence, none of the imbalance of the lover and the beloved." At other times, suffice to say, Cheever was very much inclined to dwell on the "imbalance" ("[Bill] was a man who mistook power for love," he'd later remark), though it's not enough to say he merely concealed his misgivings— rather he seemed determined to abolish them with good behavior, almost as if he were reproaching himself for having such ignoble thoughts in the first place. As Maxwell put it shortly after Cheever's death, "He tried to separate things so that he could be my friend and I

---

*In 1958, Maxwell had nominated Cheever for membership in the prestigious Century Club on Forty-third Street—a privilege that meant a lot to Cheever, though as ever he was at pains to downplay it: the main point of membership, he liked to say, was "to have a place to pump ship in midtown."

wouldn't be responsible for anything *The New Yorker* did that made him angry." To a large degree, though, Maxwell *was* responsible, and Cheever was never quite so foolish as to think otherwise.

In the present case it was Maxwell, and Maxwell alone, who decided that the little dénouement to "Brigadier" was superfluous—he didn't share Cheever's taste for abrupt tonal changes, whimsical digressions, or really anything that diverged (much) from straightforward realism. Cheever, however, thought the final image of Mrs. Flanagan, standing forlornly beside the bomb shelter, was imperative to the story's integrity. ("Did you know that *The New Yorker* tried to take that out?" he remarked in *The Paris Review*, still indignant eight years later.) What's more, the cut was presented to Cheever practically as a fait accompli.* Dropping by *The New Yorker* to correct galleys, Cheever had noticed a page missing at the end—just like that—whereupon he asked Maxwell to meet him for lunch at the Century. As he wrote Weaver, "I kept the conversation . . . on the subject of his wife and children but when we said goodbye he asked about the cut. 'Do anything you want,' I said and walked over to the station where I bought a copy of Life [magazine] in which J. D. Salinger was compared to William Blake, Ludwig von Beethoven and William Shakespeare."

Salinger, it bears repeating, was a sore point: *Franny and Zooey* had been published that September and had dominated the best-seller lists ever since, at a time when Cheever was struggling to get on with another novel while supporting himself, as ever, with inventive—but relatively less acclaimed (and now maimed)—short fiction for *The New Yorker*. Reading the *Life* tribute, Cheever went into a "slow burn" and began drinking heavily, until finally he phoned Maxwell in a rage; writing to Weaver, he recounted his rant thus: "You cut that short story . . . and I'll never write another story for you or anybody else. You can get that Godamned sixth-rate Salinger to write your Godamned short sto-

---

*It should be noted that drastic, peremptory editing was *not* Maxwell's style, as Cheever himself pointed out: "[I]t has been my experience that Bill intends stories to be printed exactly as they are written," he remarked in 1957, and surviving manuscripts bear this out. Vis-à-vis Cheever, at least, Maxwell usually restricted himself to the odd marginal comment. "Don't believe it," he wrote beside a line in "The Bella Lingua," where Cheever had written, "To be a trolley-car conductor in Krasbie was a position of some importance . . ." Cheever deleted the line. "What *is* a shapely day?" the literal-minded Maxwell queried a bit of description in "The Country Husband" about a day "as fragrant and shapely as an apple." Cheever (happily) retained the line.

ries but don't expect anything more from me. If you want to slam a door on somebody's genitals find yourself another victim. Etc." According to Maxwell, it was the "only time" Cheever really showed anger toward him, and as he admitted, "I blundered. I thought there were two endings and one was better." That said, he also claimed (albeit at a distance of some twenty-five years) that he'd only removed the "second ending" in a preliminary "working proof," so that Cheever could "see how it would read in print": "[The story] wasn't about to go to press," said Maxwell. "It wasn't scheduled." Not so. That fulsome Salinger article ran in the November 3, 1961, issue of *Life*; "The Brigadier and the Golf Widow" appeared the following week (November 11) in *The New Yorker*. As Cheever asserted at the time, "[T]he magazine had gone to press and they had to remake the whole book and stay up all night but they ran [the story] without the cut."

When it was over, Cheever wrote in his journal that he felt "troubled": "The whole incident seems senseless and indigestible, perhaps because I cannot accept the degree of my dependence upon the tastes of others and in general my lack of success." Success or no, he seemed genuinely remorseful for having insulted Salinger so rashly: "I admire Salinger, of course, and I think I know where his giftedness lies and how rare it is," he wrote in a mollifying letter to Maxwell. "Another reason for my irritability is the fact that I am never content with my own work; that it never quite comes up to the world as I see it. This is not to say that I despair of succeeding; I think I may—but I am touchy."

CHAPTER TWENTY-THREE

{ 1962–1963 }

O N THE FIRST DAY of the new year, 1962, Cheever noted that
he hoped to finish his novel—now titled *The Wapshot Scandal*
(though he wasn't yet sure what constituted the "scandal" in
question)—by the spring. "I think of the enormous responsibilities and
burdens that have, very recently, overtaken fiction," he wrote four
months later; "to hold the attention of an audience whose attention is
seriously challenged; to describe with coherence a society that has no
coherence; to discover or invent links of precedence and tradition
where there are none; to look into the moral questions of the hydrogen
bomb; to renew a sense of good and evil." A tall order, all that, and no
wonder his progress was slow. Spring came and went, and that summer
he wrote that he hoped only "to report here soon that the middle section of the Wapshots has fallen into shape"—but then added, "I expect
that I will continue to report here that I drink too much."

Often he drank because he was worried, and not all his worries
were ill-founded. He was fifty years old and had published almost 150
stories—many among the best of the postwar era—as well as a novel
that had consumed half his life: could he go on like that forever?
Meanwhile his financial obligations were crushing. He awoke (earlier
and earlier) in the grip of the *cafard*, and lay in bed thinking about
things ("eviscerated, insubstantial") until it was time to have breakfast
and get to work—but all too often the work went badly, which made
him even more anxious and presently despairing, until a state of total
pitiless sobriety was simply out of the question. Then he would sneak a
drink or two and wait for lunch, when he could legitimately drink

more, after which he'd try sweating it out with a long walk or a scything session. Young Federico was always "terrified" to see his drunken father tottering off with the big unwieldy scythe over his shoulder: "I was never sure if he was going to come back with all his limbs."

It helped a little that Cheever managed to find humor in his own low spirits. He became more and more fond of the refrain that he was an "old man nearing the end of his journey," and he noticed that, like his mother, he was apt to indulge in "copious sighs" as well as the bleak little proverbs that accompanied them ("There's not enough rain to water the garden," he'd quote her, "but enough to keep you indoors"). And—like his father-in-law—he often assumed the role of martyr in order to put others subtly in the wrong: "Oh, don't worry about me, dear," he'd sigh, having served his wife and family with generous portions so that nothing was left for him but a potato and a puddle of grease. "This is *plenty* for me." His children took to calling him Eeyore, and once Susan presented him with an empty honey jar and a dead balloon.

Another way of shaking off the torpor of the *cafard* was to remind himself, emphatically, of certain abiding virtues that made life beautiful. As he wrote in his journal at the end of that disappointing spring, "I wake at three or four—soft moonshine from the west—and half-rising in bed exclaim: Valor, Love, Virtue, Compassion, Splendor, Kindness, Wisdom, Beauty, Vigor! The words seem to have the colors of the earth and as I recite them I feel my hopefulness mount until I am contented and at peace with the night." For years he'd resort to that little incantation when all else failed to rouse him (his recital was wan at times), and meanwhile it provided the spark for "A Vision of the World," about a man who rebels against "incoherent" reality by imposing the logic of his dream life. In sleep the narrator keeps encountering an oddly heartening, quasi-Slavic phrase—"*Porpozec ciebie nie prosze dorzanin albo zyolpocz ciwego*"—but when he urgently repeats this to his vapid wife, she dissolves in tears. At last, waking once more "in despair," he suddenly, ecstatically grasps the (implicit) meaning of the dream motto—"Valor! Love! Virtue!" etc.—and so achieves a peace that passeth understanding.

One imagines that Cheever resorted to his incantation more than a few times when thinking of his brother, Fred, who had fallen off the wagon in spectacular fashion. For a while, according to his daughter Jane, Fred had been not only sober but almost content—or rather he was "wonderful in the morning," though afternoons weighed heavily and his mood darkened as the once-beloved cocktail hour came around. On weekends he'd drive into town with his youngest daughter, Ann, whom he'd ask to wait in the car while he went around the corner to buy meat or hardware; the waits became longer, until one day the fourteen-year-old girl noticed a telltale odor when her father returned (wreathed in smiles). Then, one Sunday afternoon in 1961, Fred paid his first visit to Cedar Lane; he was obviously tipsy and had a funny story to tell. "What is involved seems almost beyond my comprehension," John wrote. "He is drunk. He has lost his job and will not be given another. And in his drunkenness he has tried to find a college roommate, an old friend of forty years ago, a homosexual friend for all I know* . . . and has ended up in the jail of the town where our prominent and respectable parents shaped a life for themselves and for us, and he refers to this whole series of events as an uproarious joke. I think this is insanity." In fact, Fred may well have sought his old Quincy friend in the hope of getting some lead on a job, a matter that made him understandably desperate. He was pushing sixty, and his problems had become well known among former associates; he'd called every conceivable friend and connection, but no one could help. Almost every day he went into the city and sat around employment agencies, returning so drunk in the evenings he could hardly stagger off the train. Finally Iris called John in despair: Fred was back in his room and keeping himself drunk; she couldn't take him anywhere, since he'd only slip away and hide until the only thing she could do was go home and wait for the police to call. "But oh my god, my god how he must suffer," John wrote. "Can I see it, can I feel it? He has completely lost his sense of reality."

Iris eventually enlisted the aid of a psychiatrist, who advised her to leave home immediately and let her husband "sink or swim"; in the meantime the man would check on Fred every so often and try to keep him alive. Iris took the keys and cut off the telephone, then went to visit her mother in Florida. Ann went to live with sympathetic neighbors. Fred (except for the psychiatrist) was totally isolated. His daughter Jane lived in the South Shore town of Hingham, where she had a

---

*Perhaps the only instance in Cheever's enormous journal where he uses the word *homosexual* (or some explicit equivalent) in the context of his brother, though it obviously colors our interpretation of certain other passages.

family of her own; David had "escaped to the west" (Boulder) and worked in a bank; Sarah had left home after her father's breakdown in 1959, when she was eighteen, fed up with playing buffer and go-between to her feuding parents ("Finally I thought, 'This is not my problem'"). While her mother lingered in Florida, young Ann went by the house each day to feed the dog, but at least two weeks passed before she saw her father again. ("His favorite word for me was *diffident*. I didn't know what it meant at the time, but finally I looked it up. He was right: I *was* timid and intimidated. It was a put-down. He was a very bright man.") When Fred emerged at last—to be hospitalized—he was scarcely recognizable: "His skin was sagging all over him," said Ann. "White, pale. Just a bag of flesh."

But Fred remained first and foremost a *Cheever*, and Cheevers were men of destiny and force: it was a matter of breeding. When he returned to Cedar Lane a few months later, he was fat and beaming and full of advice. John attributed his heartiness to alcohol, and observed him with exasperated detachment. "He has endured many disappointments, indignities, and injustices and in his determination to rally he has developed a crude mockery of cheerfulness. Everything is wonderful, simply wonderful." At such times John tended to retire into his "fastidious" manner, though on this occasion he probably couldn't resist the odd sarcastic aside, which might have provoked Fred into an even more pointed heartiness; in any case, John would always refer to this conversation as an argument of sorts, and by way of having the "last word," Fred remarked, "Whatever else I have, I have four beautiful children. Loving, wonderful children." John guardedly allowed that his son David was "very loyal," which angered Fred: "He lifts his face," John wrote, "swollen now with years of drink, and says, 'They're all loyal to me.' I have seen them scorn and disobey him, and they have all run away from home. There is not a grain of truth in this pitiful claim to love."*

Fred's remarks about his children's love—innocuous enough on the

---

*There was, in fact, more than a grain. Though Fred's children were naturally anxious to distance themselves from an unbearable situation, they continued to care deeply for their father. "I separated the alcoholism from the man," said his son David, and even the more estranged Sarah wrote to her father at the time, "I love you. . . . I have a great deal of respect for you. . . . It hurts both you and me to have me tell you to stop drinking. Or to have me tell you to go to AA. Or for me to see you in such bad shape."

surface—seemed to infuriate his brother: he brooded over them for years. In a nutshell, they seemed to express all of Fred's maddening perversity, and perhaps in a general way suggested just how lost in self-deception a man—his "only, only brother," no less—could become. Where would it end? "F[red] calls and he will call again," John noted later in 1962. "I suppose he needs money. If he's at the club says F[red] to M[ary] then I'll go there; and here is the nightmare I have already worked out in detail. I am sitting in the reading room, looking at La Nouvelle Revue Francaise when I hear his loud voice in the downstairs hallway. It is the voice of a totally broken spirit shored up by a pint of lemon-flavored gin." And there was another, even more disturbing nightmare that seemed parlously close to realization: "I was planning to take him trout fishing up at Cranberry Lake," John said, a year after his brother's death, "which is just miles away from everything in the wilderness, and I realized if I got him up there he would fall overboard. I would beat him with an oar until he stayed." It was the kind of obsession that drove one to drink.

AT A COCKTAIL PARTY he gave in the sixties, the publisher Sol Stein remembered how Cheever had glared at another celebrated guest, Leslie Fiedler, whose sweeping critical studies of American writers had omitted any mention of Cheever. Indeed, the only notice he'd received from anything resembling academia was in Ihab Hassan's *Radical Innocence* (1961), which had described *The Wapshot Chronicle* as a "collection of quaint episodes" that were "far from unified." But that summer a promising overture came from Frederick Bracher, a respected scholar at Pomona College: "My credentials for this overdue bit of criticism are a relative freedom . . . from academic bias, a dislike of the current critical jargon . . . and a real, and I hope true, feeling for your work." He proposed to write the first serious study of Cheever, focusing mostly on *The Wapshot Chronicle*, and wondered if he could put a few questions to the author. Cheever responded with great wooing enthusiasm, discussing at length his rationale for omitting certain historical and topographical details from the novel in order to create a more universal world and so forth. Bracher duly incorporated these points in his paper ("*The Wapshot Chronicle* is loosely situated in time and space . . ."), which so delighted its subject that he literally couldn't put it down ("He's reading Professor Bracher's paper *again*," said Susan): "That you should have undertaken to diagnose so unarchitectural a work as mine seems to me one of those admirable pieces of generosity that keeps the world from flying apart," Cheever wrote with abject gratitude.

Academic critics, however, didn't share Bracher's esteem for the well-known *New Yorker* writer. *The Hudson Review* returned the paper with a printed rejection slip ("the first I've ever received," Bracher noted), as did a lesser journal out of Purdue, until finally a reworked and shortened version—"John Cheever and Comedy"—was published in *Critique: Studies in Modern Fiction*. A few months later Bracher came to New York, and Cheever took him to lunch at the Century: "He is generous, intelligent and colorless and I feel somehow that I fail him," Cheever wrote afterward, sensing he'd drunk too much and been in bad form generally. To Bracher, of course, he wrote with ornate graciousness: "[C]onsidering the complexity of all human relationships, the powers of gin, the stuffiness of the clubrooms and the bitter weather outside, I hope that somewhere along the line I made my pleasure in meeting you apparent."

Cheever would go on corresponding with Bracher for years, and when he was at Yaddo that September (1962), it was Bracher to whom he confided that he couldn't "ever recall having been so discouraged and melancholy." He'd gone there hoping to finish *The Wapshot Scandal*, only to realize the prospect remained as distant as ever. And then, a day or two after he arrived, his old hero Cummings died at home of a cerebral hemorrhage. That night Cheever talked of Cummings with two Yaddo friends, Curtis Harnack and his wife, Hortense Calisher. Harnack had also known the poet, and amid long ruminative pauses, the two swapped remembrances. "The body of Cummings might have been there in its coffin," said Calisher, "and in a way it was. I was at a wake." Cheever had seen Cummings a few years before at Susan's school in Dobbs Ferry, where the poet had agreed to give a reading. As Susan remembered, the two men had warmly embraced in the headmaster's office: "The force and openness of their affection for one another seemed to shake that airless, heavily draped room." Afterward they drove the poet back to Patchin Place, stopping for hamburgers at White Castle, where Cummings railed wittily against his arthritis as well as the silly teachers at Susan's school. As Cheever liked to point out, the poet had "perfect style": "I think of Cummings, who played out his role as a love poet into his late sixties. There was a man."

A further source of unhappiness at Yaddo was, as Cheever saw it, the ever more visible presence of homosexuals, though of course they were hardly a novelty there. As a much younger man, Cheever had warily taken tea with composers David Diamond and Marc Blitzstein ("thinking, without censure, that their world was very unlike mine"), and now, twenty-five years later, here was Blitzstein still—and still vaguely "ungainly," it seemed to Cheever: "I think that this is not the force of an invincible society but the invincible force of nature that demands that we take procreative attitudes and loathes the gymnastics of perversion." Be that as it may, the force of society (as opposed to nature) was much on Cheever's mind too—it was society, after all, which had left Newton Arvin "stripped of everything." Before and after that unfortunate man's fall, Cheever had militated at board meetings in favor of building a swimming pool at Yaddo, and now the thing was done at last. Every afternoon, then, Cheever sat beside the water watching the sun-bathing youths and reminding himself of his devotion to attitudes of procreation. "But my itchy member is unconcerned with all of this," he glumly noted, "and yet if I made it in the shower I could not meet the smiles of the world." Arranging his towel, Cheever felt again like "a practiced and consummate impostor" and concluded that he was "heading for ruin."*

As a self-proclaimed (and often drunk) impostor, Cheever was increasingly poor company around his family. His daughter and he were especially apt to clash, as she got older and more assertive and perhaps eager to get a bit of her own back. These days, when he began to lecture her about her weight, instead of bursting into tears she was just as likely to call him a "troll" and slam the door in his face. Of course, Cheever had always encouraged (and certainly modeled) a sort of mocking banter among family members, such that the dinner table was characterized as a "shark tank" and a "bear pit." At the best of times, no one appreciated a well-aimed barb as much as Cheever, even

---

*While at Yaddo, Cheever had witnessed Marc Blitzstein's will "by chance," and so was summoned to the probate in 1964 when Blitzstein died—beaten to death by Portuguese sailors in Martinique. Sharing a cab to the courthouse with Aaron Copland ("I cannot find a trace of the fact that he is queer but my examination is unremittent"), Cheever found the whole business "shocking" and "unimaginable" and longed more than ever "to love what is seemly and what the world counsels one to love . . . a lighter destiny than to court a sailor in Port-au-Prince [actually Fort-de-France in Blitzstein's case] who will pick your pockets, wring your neck, and leave you dead in a gutter."

when he was the target, but these were not the best of times. "You have two strings to play," said Susan, at pains to deflate her father's occasional pomposity. "One is the history of the family, the other is your childlike sense of wonder. Both of them are broken." Cheever exploded, and even managed to force her into tears again. "I think, abysmally bitter, that Orpheus knew he would be torn limb from limb," he wrote; "but he had not guessed that the Harpy would be his daughter."

The previous year, she'd begun attending Pembroke (the women's college at Brown), and hated it; she wanted to transfer to Bennington, but Cheever refused—he'd also talked Pammy Spear into choosing Pembroke, and *she* liked it just fine. Soon, however, Susan gave him reason to regret his obduracy. That spring she brought home a boyfriend named Webster, a Brown dropout whom Cheever described as having tight pants and a "Bottom-the-Weaver haircut": He and Susan "read Reich aloud to one another and play junky music. I keep routing them out of one another's bedrooms." For years Susan had heard her father's speeches about what she ought to do (lose weight and curl her hair) in order to get lots of dates, like Pammy and Linda, so now it pleased her to canoodle with Webster in plain sight. "No necking in the parlor!" Cheever erupted, finding her tracing a finger along the hair beneath Webster's navel. They slept until noon, ate enormous meals, and forced Cheever into such a "bilious humor" that he'd have to leave the house and scythe away his grievances ("jockeyed into the position of a heavy fatherinlaw"). When Webster departed after one of his visits (walking with "his yachtsman's stoop"), Cheever noticed that his daughter seemed forlorn, and sought to commiserate after his fashion. "It is not possible to talk to you," she said. "You say what you don't mean and you mean what you don't say."

Ben, at least, was falling in line. "I cannot say truthfully that I have never felt anything but love for him," Cheever reflected. "We have quarreled, he has wet his bed, he has waked strangling from nightmares in which I appeared as a hairy werewolf, dripping with gore. But all of this is gone. Now there is nothing between us but love and goodnatured admiration." Ben's love of the outdoors (his kayaking and whatnot) had gotten the ball rolling in the right direction, but his redemption was complete that fall, when he announced that he'd made the varsity football team. As a freshman! He forbore to mention that no *junior* varsity team existed for the six-man squad at Scarborough

Country Day, or that he was probably the least popular man on the team, or, finally, that his status as a second-string center was "the athletic equivalent of wheelchair competition," as Ben put it in sober retrospect. No matter. Cheever was thrilled that his son was staying after school for *football practice*, and more than happy to pick him up afterward, at whatever hour, and buy him a loaf of fresh bread at the Italian bakery. It helped that, as Ben recalled, his father never actually attended games (except once: "I go to see my son play football although he does not get off the bench"). And things just kept looking up from there. Later that year Ben was accepted to a boarding school in Connecticut, Loomis, whereupon his father ("beaming like a foolish swain") escorted him to Brooks for a proper wardrobe: two suits, a tweed jacket, a dozen shirts, a raincoat, trousers, the works ("Never having been to boarding-school, and wearing at his age, tailless shirts, my underwear fastened with a safety pin, I am made very happy by this performance"). At Loomis, however, Ben was cut from the football team after two days. His father was crushed.

ANOTHER NEW YEAR DAWNED, 1963, and still Cheever struggled on with his novel. It wasn't falling into place, and was far too gloomy for a writer whose work had been celebrated for its "wonder" and "brightness," a writer who was trying, once again, to hear the dragon's tail swishing among the leaves: "[L]ast night I dreamed I was a Good Humor man, ringing a small bell and urging people to try the seven flavors of discouragement," he wrote Weaver. "There are, between you and me, more than seven." By the end of March, he was able to report that the end and the beginning seemed all right: "But the middle, aiie, aiie. The middle is wreckage." He'd taken to sleeping (he said) with the manuscript between his legs; he'd made bargains with the devil. Finally, as another spring came to an end, he didn't finish so much as arrive at a point where he couldn't think of anything else to write or revise. It was time to send the thing to Maxwell, who if nothing else would be sympathetic. In his journal, Cheever drafted a sheepish cover letter: "A great many people felt that the Chronicle was not a novel, and the same thing is bound to be said about this, perhaps more strongly. I do hope you'll like it, but if you shouldn't I will understand."

Maxwell did not respond with his old alacrity, and Cheever wondered if the novel had "embarrassed him into speechlessness." Mean-

Above, left: John's father, Frederick Lincoln Cheever, age twenty, when he was learning the shoe business. "Look like a poet. Attic hungry—Etc.," he wrote next to the photo. *Above, right:* John's uncle, William Hamlet Cheever. Like his namesake in *The Wapshot Chronicle*, Hamlet went west for the Gold Rush—thirty years too late. *(Courtesy of Jane Cheever Carr)*

Left: One of the few surviving photographs of John's mother, Mary Liley Cheever—whose phobias included a "primitive horror" of having her picture taken—as she appeared in the *Wollaston Woman's Club Magazine.* Her look of composure, she later explained, had been managed by holding the infant John on her lap. *(Courtesy of Thomas Crane Public Library)*

Right: Frederick Cheever and his beloved firstborn, Fred, whom he liked to call Binks.
(Courtesy of Jane Cheever Carr)

Left: Fred and his younger brother, John.
(Courtesy of Jane Cheever Carr)

Below: John as a baby. His father later wrote him, "You were as bald as a billiard ball, for 6 mo[nth]s as a kid—but you caught up later on hair-game—as all the Cheevers—'wear a lot of hair'—till the final curtain." *(Courtesy of Jane Cheever Carr)*

Right: Front row, seated left to right, John's cousins Devereaux and Donald Armstrong, Fred Cheever, and their cousin Randall Young. John is seated with his maternal grandmother, Sarah, who endeared herself by calling his mother a cretin.

(Courtesy of Jane Cheever Carr)

Left: John (far right) with some playmates in the genteel suburb of Wollaston.
(Courtesy of Jane Cheever Carr)

Below: John Cheever, outside the house at 43 Elm Avenue, Quincy. "Floating around in melancholy," he later wrote, "I recall my claim that my life was brightly lighted by the sun until my adolescence. But there is a photograph of me, taken, I think, when I was seven, that would refute this. The face is of a boy whose father regretted his conception and wished that he was not alive."
(Courtesy of Jane Cheever Carr)

Right: Frederick Cheever and sons. *(Courtesy of Jane Cheever Carr)*

Above: Clockwise from left: Fred Cheever, Janet MacDonald ("my first real girlfriend," Fred had glossed in the photo album), and John, sullenly wearing what appears to be a wig. "[T]hat boy of summer," John wrote of his brother's youth. "Happy with his friends, nimble with his girls, he loved his muzzy and daddy."
(Courtesy of Jane Cheever Carr)

Right: Fred and John Cheever.
(Courtesy of Cheever family collection)

Left: The Cheevers' eleven-room Victorian house at 123 Winthrop Avenue, which was repossessed and razed by the Wollaston Cooperative Bank in 1932.

Right: Anna Boynton Thompson, a classical scholar who considered "all sensuality as a mode of ignorance," according to her cousin John. She left the Cheevers' Thanksgiving feast in a rage. *(Courtesy of Thayer Academy)*

Left: In an eighth-grade production of *A Christmas Carol*, John (at left) played nephew Fred to his best friend Fax Ogden's Scrooge (at right). Many years later a tipsy, dejected Fax would occasionally phone Cheever late at night: "Weren't we happy, Johnny? Weren't we really happy?" *(Courtesy of Thayer Academy)*

Right: A jovial-seeming Cheever in the midst of a miserable adolescence. *(Courtesy of Cheever family collection)*

Above: Malcolm Cowley in his office at *The New Republic.* "I felt that I was hearing for the first time the voice of a new generation," he remarked of the eighteen-year-old Cheever's first published story, "Expelled." *(Courtesy of Robert Cowley)*

Right: John and Fred's passport photos for their trip to Germany in the summer of 1931. John was appalled by Nazi militarism, but Fred would always be something of a Germanophile, later claiming to be the first person in Massachusetts to own a Volkswagen. *(Courtesy of Jane Cheever Carr)*

Below: Dodie Merwin, one of John's first serious girlfriends. *(Courtesy of Dodie Merwin Captiva)*

Above: A group photo from Cheever's first visit to Yaddo in 1934. Yaddo would become a second home to Cheever (seated at right on the bench), while its director, Elizabeth Ames (seated center, wearing a white dress), was something of a surrogate mother. Other guests included the poet Muriel Rukeyser (standing at left) and *Studs Lonigan* author James T. Farrell (over Cheever's left shoulder). *(Copyright © Gustave Lorey and the Yaddo Corporation)*

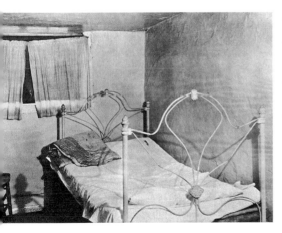

Left: Cheever's first room in the city at 633 Hudson Street was photographed by Walker Evans as a typical Depression tableau. *(The Metropolitan Museum of Art, The Horace W. Goldsmith Foundation Gift through Joyce and Robert Menschel, 1993 (1193.361) © Walker Evans Archive, The Metropolitan Museum of Art)*

Right: The young author. "Quincy Youth Is Achieving New York Literary Career," his hometown paper, *The Patriot Ledger,* proudly reported. *(Courtesy of Cheever family collection)*

Right: Cheever with an unidentified companion at Triuna Island, Lake George, where Cheever piloted a Fay & Bowen launch on behalf of Yaddo.
(Courtesy of Cheever family collection)

Left: Cheever and his fiancée, Mary Winternitz, at her father's estate in New Hampshire, Treetops.
(Courtesy of Cheever family collection)

Right: Mary Cheever, around the time of her marriage in 1941. "My maternal great-grandmother came out of nineteenth-century New England," she remarked after her husband's death, "where you do what you have to do."
(Courtesy of Cheever family collection)

Above: The Signal Corps. Seated, from left to right, are Don and Katrina Ettlinger, (unknown), and John Cheever. Their gatherings, said Ettlinger, were often "wild and hilarious," despite their "occasional guilt that they were having too good a time and not getting shot at." *(Courtesy of Cheever family collection)*

Right: Scything in New Hampshire. "When I scythe I think of Tolstoy," said Cheever. "How universal is the experience, I think, when what I really think is that I am one of the last aristocrats in the country who can wield a scythe." *(Courtesy of Cheever family collection)*

Above: A relatively placid family gathering at Treetops in 1948. Standing from left: John and Mary Cheever (holding Ben), Mrs. Pauline "Polly" Winternitz, and Ethel Whitney. In front: Dr. Milton Winternitz, Janie Whitney Hotchkiss, Susan Cheever, Steven Whitney, and two cousins.

Left: Katrina and Don Ettlinger, shortly after the war. (*Courtesy of Cheever family collection*)

Left: Mary toasts the holiday with her children, Ben and Susan, while her stepmother, Polly, looks on. (*Courtesy of Cheever family collection*)

Below: Cheever at a costume party in the early fifties. (*Courtesy of Cheever family collection*)

Above: Susan Cheever in the midst of her less-than-idyllic childhood. "They were *completely* unable to cope with me," she remembered. (*Courtesy of Cheever family collection*)

Left: Mary and John at a picnic lunch in Westchester. (*Courtesy of Cheever family collection*)

Below: Mary (at right) sang in a church choir with various Westchester friends—in this case, Philip Boyer and his daughter Linda. (*Courtesy of Cheever family collection*)

Bottom: Mimi Boyer and Cheever enjoy the cocktail hour on Whiskey Island. (*Courtesy of Cheever family collection*)

Left: Cheever's beloved black Labrador, Cassiopeia. (*Courtesy of Cheever family collection*)

Below: The Cheevers traveled to Italy first-class aboard the *Conte Biancamano* ("a cross between the Fall River Line and the old Ritz"). (*Courtesy of Cheever family collection*)

Right: Ben, with his pet mouse Barbara Frietchie, aboard the *Conte Biancamano*. A few days after the family arrived in Rome, the mouse died and "got a sordid resting place," as Cheever reported.

Above: The piano nobile of the Palazzo Doria, Rome, where the Cheevers lived from 1956 to 1957. (*Courtesy of Cheever family collection*)

Right: "I don't ever remember loving a child so much," Cheever noted in his journal, the day after Federico's birth in Rome. (*Courtesy of Cheever family collection*)

Left: The Cheever's *donna di servizio*, Iole Felici, with her beloved *picci* ("little one"). (*Courtesy of Cheever family collection*)

Right: Cheever's brother Fred in 1957, around the time he lost his job at Pepperell. (*Courtesy of Jane Cheever Carr*)

Left: Cheever's editor at *The New Yorker*, William Maxwell. "He said that he loves me," Cheever wrote, once the friendship had begun to go sour, "and I have often said that he mistook power for love." (*Courtesy of Alfred A. Knopf*)

Top: The Cheevers' house in Ossining, where they moved in 1961. (*Courtesy of Cheever family collection*)

Above: Cheever's favorite neighbor, Sara Spencer, whom he privately referred to as Mrs. Zagreb. He often used her swimming pool (fed by an artesian well), and she never seemed to mind if Cheever was drunk or naked or both.

Right: Fred Cheever at home in Weston, Connecticut, 1963. "I only want to educate my neighbors," he liked to say, as his drinking became more conspicuous. (*Courtesy of Jane Cheever Carr*)

while, the *cafard* seemed to become an almost corporeal presence; it spoke, late at night, in Hemingway's voice: "This is the small agony. The great agony comes later." Cheever would get out of bed and chain-smoke in the bathroom—thinking the book was unpublishable, a disgrace—and finally go back to sleep, only to wake later and find the *cafard* worse than ever, smelling of "cheap handsoap" for some reason. "I wake, sucking air and scyth [sic] the orchard thinking that if I do any less I will know the torments of hell."

Finally, on his fifty-first birthday, Cheever took a matinal slug of whiskey and gave Maxwell a call: "He seems plainly unenthusiastic about the book if not gravely troubled by its failure. This is the devastation of my most intimate aspirations and dreams." Doubtless Maxwell sensed as much, and so the kindly man called back a couple days later to say he'd reread the book at once and found it quite wonderful after all (words to that effect). Cheever thanked him effusively, though on reflection he decided to keep the novel's dedication ("For W.M.") in the vitiated form to which he'd emended it: "The initials are intended to represent the lack between what I mean to write for you and what I produced. If it seems better in galleys I'll add the illiam and the axwell." But apparently it seemed no better, and so the dedication remained; nor was Cheever ever really persuaded that Maxwell liked the book, and he was right to be skeptical. Ten years after Cheever's death, Maxwell admitted that he'd much preferred the *Chronicle* "because it is the most realistic": "[I]n *The Wapshot Scandal* he began to play ducks and drakes with plausibility and the psychological consistency of his characters . . . in order to be freer, more fanciful, more didactic, more violent." Cheever would continue to be less plausible and so forth—as Maxwell would have it—and the rift would continue to widen.

Facing imminent ruin, or so he thought, Cheever became all the more caustic on the subject of his wife's duties at Briarcliff Junior College, where she'd begun teaching part-time the year before. Once again Cheever invoked Newhouse's wife, Dorothy (the renowned violin teacher), as an example of a working wife who was paid *decently*, at least, at *Juilliard*, whereas Mary taught a bunch of debutantes how to spell *cat* "at an eighth-rate college." ("Now, John," she'd reply, "it's a fifth-rate college and you know it.") The pittance she made, said Cheever, was just enough to force them into a higher tax bracket. (In fact, the pittance—about three thousand dollars a year "at most"—

went to Iole for looking after Federico on the two or three mornings a week that Mary taught, while her Watson inheritance continued to pay about ten thousand dollars of their annual expenses.) But of course these were nominal quibbles, beyond which lay an old trauma. "I think again and again and again of the mixed rewards of sexual equality," Cheever seethed in his journal. "I have been looking at them, it seems, for three generations. Grandmother's love of her children was sparse and capricious she was so busy redeeming whores. Mother's love was chancy, she was so deep in women's club politics. And now M[ary] going off to teach freshman English burns the breakfast." For this she'd relegated her celebrated husband to housewifery while she corrected themes "for her pleasure." After a bitter stint of babysitting, Cheever felt tainted and even depraved: "I read Hannah Arendt on the repulsive moral chaos in Fascist Germany and turn these facts back on myself. I am the immoralist, and my failure has been the toleration of an intolerable marriage. My fondness for pleasant interiors and the voices of children has destroyed me." The banality of evil indeed.

It was true Mary could be strident about "women's liberation" (a rather novel topic in 1963, even among the liberal middle class), until her exasperated husband would flee to Shady Lane Farm and commiserate with Barolini, who had similar problems with his American wife. She wanted to write, he said, she coveted his success, and being Italian he was far more mystified than Cheever: why would a woman not want to care for her husband and children? Cheever explained that American women of their generation were the most miserable in history, terribly bitter about giving away the best years of their lives to marriage, and eager to share their sufferings with men: "[E]ducating an unintellectual woman," Cheever remarked, "is like letting a rattlesnake into the house. She cannot add a column of figures or make a bed but she will lecture you on the inner symbolism of Camus while the dinner burns." He cited the case of his poor old friend Kenny, reduced to polishing silver while his wife poked away at her opus on the late novels of Henry James. And perhaps he mentioned, too, a time not long ago when Mary (hastening to teach debutantes) had left Federico home alone with a bad cold—or rather she'd left him alone with Cheever, who had his own work to do; her solution was to give the sickly boy a pot lid and wooden spoon with which to signal his father if things took a turn for the worse.

Such were the materials for a vindictive tour-de-force titled "An

Educated American Woman," which appeared that November in *The New Yorker.* The story opens with a sprightly, ingenious gambit—Jill Chidchester Madison's verbose and pretentious "item" for her college alumnae magazine, wherein she breezily reports that she remains married to her "unintellectual 190-pound halfback" while writing a critical biography of Flaubert and serving as president of "every civic organization in the community": "I still find time to band birds and knit Argyle socks," she concludes. What she does *not* find time for, needless to say, is being a decent wife and mother. Her kindly ex-halfback husband, Georgie, not only is forced to polish the silver (while wearing an apron), but also does most of the caring, in every sense, for their adorable four-year-old son, Bibber. After a long night of housework—and never mind his day job—Georgie finally goes to bed, hoping for some well-earned lovemaking, but Jill interrupts their embrace with a spontaneous recital of Flaubert *en bon français.* Bewildered and hurt by Georgie's angry response ("God damn it to hell!"), she thereafter devotes herself wholeheartedly to stopping the construction of a four-lane highway. One night Georgie comes home to find Bibber abandoned and burning with fever: Jill is in Albany, appearing before the highway commission, while the babysitter (leaving a note on the bloodstained pillow) has been called away. Bibber dies, and Georgie never forgives his wife. "I thought then how inferior he was to Jill, how immature," remarks the laughably unreliable (and hitherto invisible) narrator, who wants never again to see the "cruel and unreasonable" Georgie. Here again is Cheever's guileful irony: such a narrator is disingenuous if you like, or sincerely deploring if you don't.

Cheever might have suspected he'd gone too far this time—though perhaps not. Four years before, noting the constant presence of "predatory women" in his fiction, he'd conceded that this particular motif amounted to a "serious weakness in [his] vision; a crack." But when readers asked Cheever, in person, why he seemed to dislike women so much, he'd look puzzled and protest that he *loved* women ("but"—as he wrote in his journal—"when I am kicked and spat on I must say so"). As for Bibber's death at the hands of a self-absorbed, civic-minded mother, Cheever once wrote the following in regard to Forster's *Where Angels Fear to Tread:* "The death of a child seems to be idle and repulsive and I think that in fiction, much as in life, we may not, without good reason, slaughter the innocent, persecute the defenseless and infirm, or speak with idle malice." That was in 1959.

By 1963 he'd evidently changed his mind, or else felt there was "good reason" for disposing of Bibber. In any case, he was shocked when his wife confronted him in the pantry: "It was wicked of you to kill the child," she said. "I do not reply," he wrote afterward, "to say that I feel as if the last of my literary plumage had been plucked off my back; I do not suggest that we set up a censorship desk where my subject matter will be judged . . ." Later that night, Cheever was still "rigid" with indignation—and, by his own confession, *very* drunk—weeping over this latest affront to his autonomy while piously teaching the alphabet to his "little, little son."*

By then he'd already written "The Ocean" (though it wouldn't appear in print until the following summer), one of his most brilliant and bizarre stories, and perhaps his most cruelly deliberate caricature of Mary Cheever. The wife in the story, named Cora, is an eccentric and possibly mad woman who expresses malice with a "musical voice" pitched "in the octave above middle C." The narrator—a gentle, well-meaning husband—has reason to think she is trying to murder him: she douses the salad with lighter fluid ("You left the lighter fluid in the pantry," she explains, "and I mistook it for vinegar"), and seems to have sprayed pesticide on the veal cutlets. In spite of this, her husband feels nothing but tender concern when she stands madly watering the lawn in a rainstorm, and wonders how to coax her back inside before the neighbors see ("Should I say that a friend was on the telephone? She has no friends"). The narrator also has a daughter named Flora, who has dropped out of college "to live in a Lower East Side tenement with a sexual freak"; the couple occupy themselves by artily gluing butter-flies to a skeleton purchased from a medical supply house. Finally the narrator rebels against "sadness, madness, melancholy, and despair," and antically writes the word "luve" all over the house for Cora to see, then magically escapes to a serene English countryside where his wife and daughter are nowhere to be found: "I lay on the grass and fell into a sweet sleep."

---

*Cheever's Russian translator, Tanya Litvinov (who loved Cheever and vice versa), was also revolted by the story. While translating *The Brigadier and the Golf Widow* in 1965, she wrote that she was "side-stepping the Educated woman for the while . . . I'm woman enough to resent its unfairness." As for Mary, she was quoted in *Time* a few months after the story appeared: "I did go to one or two meetings of the League of Women Voters," she coolly remarked, "but I do think he should not have killed the lit-tle boy."

"Maybe he *was* wicked," Mary Cheever speculated after her husband's death, though in time she would achieve a remarkably lucid detachment. "No," she said, when asked whether he'd based certain characters on her. "He used details about me and other women, but his characters came whole out of his own strong feelings. I'm not saying obsession." She paused. " 'His own obsessions' is correct, actually." Fair enough. Thirty years before making this observation, however, she decided never to fight with the man again (if possible), since her words would only end up in his fiction.

AFTER READING "THE OCEAN" in typescript, Maxwell called Cheever and told him he was at the top of his form and needed to work very hard. This he did. Before the summer was over, he wrote another story ("Montraldo") and finished revising *The Wapshot Scandal*, after which he left for Yaddo and wondered what to do next. "You can kick around Narcissus," he wrote in his journal, after a hungover day at the pool. Mythography was very much in vogue at the time, particularly applauded by academic critics such as Fiedler and Hassan; Updike's *The Centaur* had just been published to great acclaim, and Cheever himself had expressed an intention to "rewrite Bulfinch"—which he did to some extent in a series of recent vignettes titled "Metamorphoses," baldly modernizing the myths of Orpheus and Actaeon and others. But Cheever's imagination was such that he hardly needed recourse to Bulfinch. He was forever going off on "tangents" (as Dodie Merwin had put it), compulsively transforming the world into something more resonant, funny, and meaningful. As for "kick[ing] around Narcissus," he had in mind a fellow Yaddo guest whom he was meeting for the first time that September, composer Ned Rorem, who'd just broken his ankle and was hobbling about with a little plaster cast. As a reader of Freud, Cheever tended to equate homosexuality with narcissism, and in this respect the (almost) forty-year-old Rorem struck him as a kind of wistful, aging boy: "[H]e seems, in halflights, to represent the pure impetuousness of youth, the first flush of manhood," Cheever wrote. "He intends to be compared to a summer's day, particularly its last hours and yet I think he is none of this."

Here was a tangent leading to Cheever's greatest story, and while he'd dispense with explicit parallels to Narcissus, he retained the idea of fading youth as well as the name Ned. But Rorem was not the only boyish middle-aged male on his mind—indeed, it was one of Cheever's own defining traits, as he often admitted (with amusement and rue) in his journal. Though he played the dignified squire in his elegant farmhouse, part of him had never changed from the freewheeling youth who refused to get a job or pin himself down in any way; at age fifty-one he still flung himself into icy pools with vigorous abandon, got drunk whenever he felt like it, and was always poised to fall in love or escape. As Maxwell put it with (perhaps) faintly exasperated affection after his friend's death, "He lived as a child would live if a child were able." Remaining young is a "mode of hope," as Cheever would say—everything lies ahead—and in this respect he was also thinking of his brother, Fred. "You can draw a line easily enough from the summery boy to the club drunk, but where did . . . the phony hopefulness come from?" Fred's hopefulness in the face of total disaster—for both himself and his family—struck his brother as an object lesson in the ruinous consequences of self-deceit, a fate he rightly feared for himself. "I clear my throat, reset my shoulders, put out my cigaret in the same abrupt or jerky way of my brother. I move in the same vigorous and decisive way . . . that arises from, in his case, incomprehensible despair." Such were the ideas that began to transpire as he wrote "The Swimmer," which he later explained as being "about the irreversibility of human conduct."

Once he knew that he was no longer evoking Narcissus, staring into a single pool, he gave Neddy the freedom to swim from one pool to the next (as he himself liked to do), encountering elements of his past along the way. Soon Cheever suspected he had "a perfectly good" novel on his hands—there were some thirty pools in all—but then something began to happen: "It was growing cold and quiet," Cheever later recalled. "It was turning into winter. Involuntarily. It was a terrible experience, writing that story. I was very unhappy. Not only I the narrator, but I John Cheever, was crushed." As he began to find the core of the story, he threw away pages and took yet a different approach. The main technical challenge, he realized, could not be sustained over the course of a novel: that is, Neddy could not plausibly repress the truth for some two hundred pages, and the magic involved in making the seasons change in a single afternoon was better accomplished with a few deft strokes, such that the reader scarcely notices until it is dark and cold and Ned, suddenly, is the embodiment of "an old man nearing the end of his journey."

"It was one of those midsummer Sundays when everyone sits around saying, 'I *drank* too much last night,'" the story famously begins. Neddy Merrill—who has "a vague and modest idea of himself as a legendary figure"—is drinking gin at the Westerhazys' (no less) when he's struck by the delightfully original idea of going home along the "quasi-subterranean stream" of pools from his friends' house to his own. He names this the Lucinda River, after his long-suffering wife, who also "*drank* too much" and now disappears from the story with a flick of the author's wand (lest she say a word more and spoil the effect): "When Lucinda asked where he was going he said he was going to swim home." For a while Ned's journey proceeds auspiciously: he walks beneath "flowering apple trees" to his first pool, the Grahams', and then encounters a pleasant cocktail party at the Bunkers', where he's ecstatically kissed by the hostess and "eight or ten other women" before being served by a "smiling bartender." A faint minor-key trill is sounded around the halfway point, when Ned ducks into the Levys' gazebo to wait out a cloudburst: "Then there was an explosion, a smell of cordite, and rain lashed the Japanese lanterns that Mrs. Levy had bought in Kyoto the year before last, or was it the year before that?" Thus the first hint that Ned's mind is blurred—and since the story is, after all, from Ned's point of view, one might begin to wonder (if only half consciously) whether it's really a "midsummer" day at all*: "The rain had cooled the air and he shivered. The force of the wind had stripped a maple of its red and yellow leaves and scattered them over the grass and the water. Since it was midsummer the tree must be blighted, and yet he felt a peculiar sadness at this sign of autumn." Ned, too, begins to shed leaves as he journeys from past to present, illusion to truth, his strength waning with every step. "We've been *terribly* sorry to hear about all your misfortunes, Neddy," says an old friend, vaguely remarking on rumors that he'd sold his house and that something has happened to his "poor children." Ned hastens away, but the Lucinda River becomes more treacherous, until the natives themselves—first welcoming, then at least sympathetic—rebel and turn nasty. At a parvenu's party he's scorned as a "gate crasher" and snubbed by the bartender ("to be rebuffed by a part-time barkeep meant that [Ned] had suffered some loss of social esteem"), but the harshest

---

*One of the story's pleasant ambiguities is whether the seasons change as a matter of magical realism or as an aspect of Ned's delusions.

wound is inflicted by an old mistress, who ridicules this latest "legendary" exploit with a casual insult compressing a novel's worth of exposition: "Good Christ. Will you ever grow up?" And so the constellations of autumn—"Andromeda, Cepheus, and Cassiopeia"—wheel into the sky, and what the weeping Ned will find at home is now a foregone conclusion: "He shouted, pounded on the door, tried to force it with his shoulder, and then, looking in at the windows, saw that the place was empty."

The end. The particulars of Ned's calamity—the fate of his "poor daughters," his financial losses, his housing arrangements (do he and Lucinda live full-time at the Westerhazys'?)—are left to the reader's imagination, such that Ned's darkened house seems all the more haunted. One wants to go back to the beginning and search for clues, see how the trick works, or simply reimmerse oneself in the pleasures of such a perfect story. "'The Swimmer' is a masterpiece of mystery, language and sorrow," said Michael Chabon, who made the nice point that the story has "mythic echoes . . . and yet is always only the story of one bewildered man, approaching the end of his life, journeying homeward, in a pair of bathing trunks, across the countryside where he lost everything that ever meant something to him." Years later, when asked about the story's "mythic" content, Cheever laughed and replied that such matters were better left to those who "teach fiction . . . at the level of veterinary medicine": "It's much easier for the teacher and easier for the student who has no particular interest in literature to dissect a story than to be moved by it." By then he'd cheerfully abandoned any thought of "rewrit[ing] Bulfinch"; as "The Swimmer" proved once and for all, his own myths were good enough.

HAVING RECENTLY FINISHED a novel as well as one of the century's finest short stories, Cheever decided to ask *The New Yorker* for a raise. As a New England gentleman he hated to talk about money, but really the time had come: the upkeep on his picturesque farmhouse was onerous, two of his children were in private schools, and his drunken brother was constantly asking for handouts. Besides, it wasn't as if *The New Yorker* couldn't afford it. According to a *Wall Street Journal* article, the magazine was wildly prosperous, having the highest per capita ad rate of any national magazine (twice that of *Life*), and "probably" the highest profit margin at 10 percent.

What was at issue were the terms of Cheever's "first look" agreement, which paid him a yearly bonus in exchange for a first reading of anything he wrote. It also stipulated a word rate, which varied from author to author and was a matter of considerable secrecy. This was based on one of Ross's byzantine systems. Having decided that the magazine's fiction was getting too long (moving away from the frothy "casuals" he preferred), Ross provided what he hoped would prove an incentive for shorter work: he doubled the word rate on the first two thousand words, after which the rate was half or less in certain cases. Shaw's minimum rate in 1945, for example, had been "34–15," or thirty-four cents a word for the first two thousand and fifteen cents thereafter (later the system was revised to the "first 2,000 words or first half of wordage, whichever greater"). Ross also established a system that assigned grades to stories, ranging from C− to A, which dictated the price of a story. Maxwell always gave any story he accepted an A ("on the ground that it was not a cent too much"), and in Cheever's case would hasten over to bookkeeping, figure out the exact price of a given story, and order an immediate check up to 75–80 percent of the total, the balance to be paid on publication ("Sometimes," he recalled, "this process would be forgotten, and John would be distressed when the check was small on publication").

Perhaps because he took such pains, Maxwell was touchy on the subject of money; also, as Brendan Gill once noted, though Maxwell "seemed the gentlest of men," he was "on some level of his being . . . tough as nails." Cheever knew this as well as anybody, and privately mocked his friend's "gentle and tender" manner when imparting bad news of some sort, particularly bad news for which Maxwell was largely responsible—a rejection, say, or the fact that one of Cheever's stories had been stuck "behind the cartoons" ("One is always being pushed into second class"). Once, at a dinner party in Scarborough, Mary Cheever had adamantly told Maxwell that he ought to pay her husband better, whereupon Maxwell had stormed out of the house (only to find he'd left his headlights on and couldn't start his car; Cheever came out and pushed him down a hill and on his way).

In any event, Cheever's request for a raise went over badly— "embarrassing and painful," as he wrote in his journal. Eventually he'd make a funny story out of it: as Susan Cheever remembered, "[H]e often set it on Christmas Eve and threw in a snowstorm and the suggestion that he couldn't afford to buy presents for his children." In fact,

Cheever did complain that he was "harassed by indebtedness," and—though he loved working with Maxwell, of course—he simply had to make more money. Maxwell threw up his hands: he was only a part-time editor, he said, and couldn't change the payment system; with the best will in the world, he suggested that Cheever might be able to do better elsewhere.

Through the falling snow—as he liked to tell it—Cheever walked to a pay phone on Forty-fourth Street. ("I remind myself of my brother," he noted at the time; "sitting in a pay-phone, trying to make some business arrangements. . . . Since he has failed and since I look like him I seem bound to fail.") Cheever hadn't had an agent to handle his stories since he and Lieber parted company in the forties,* but now he called Candida Donadio, whose clients had been listed that year at the "red-hot center" of *Esquire*'s "literary universe." She told him to give her a few minutes, then called back: *The Saturday Evening Post*, she said, would pay him twenty-four thousand for a first-look contract and a minimum of four stories a year, which would roughly triple his *New Yorker* income.

He returned to Maxwell's office and reported the offer. "Great consternation" ensued: Mr. Shawn was summoned, along with the magazine's treasurer, Hawley Truax, and together the men tried to reason with Cheever. He was, of course, one of their most illustrious fiction writers, but they simply couldn't afford to pay him the sort of money that would support his lavish lifestyle ("I am accused of improvidence"); as Maxwell claimed, "To do so we would have had to make an exception of him, and that would make others furious." In the end, as Cheever put it, he was offered "a key to the men's room and all the bread and cheese [he] could eat": "The Saturday Evening Post has offered me twenty-four thousand, The New Yorker has offered me twenty-five hundred, and I will take the latter, I'm not sure why." Actually (in addition to the alleged bread and cheese), the magazine had raised his first-look bonus to twenty-*six* hundred, and added a clause that allowed him to submit his work elsewhere from time to time; also,

---

*Edith Haggard at the Curtis Brown agency had negotiated Cheever's book deals and foreign sales until her retirement in March 1963, after which he severed relations with the agency. As for short stories—his main source of income at the time—Cheever's later agent, Lynn Nesbit, pointed out, "*The New Yorker* made it clear they didn't like agents fussing around. It was a gentlemen's club, and they dealt with each other in a gentlemanly way."

his minimum word rate was fixed at "18–9." But as Ben Yagoda would reveal in his comprehensive book on the magazine, *About Town*, "Cheever didn't realize how low this was." Not only had Shaw gotten almost twice as much in 1945, the young Updike's bonus in 1964 was thirty-five hundred, and the younger-still Shirley Hazzard got two thousand and a word rate of 20–10.

Forty years later, Ben Cheever read Yagoda's book and was taken aback: How could this be? After his father's death, he and Maxwell had become close friends—indeed, Maxwell was a surrogate father of sorts—and so he approached the man: *Did he know?* Maxwell replied that he'd had no idea; it was shocking to him too. Yagoda, however (who pored over the whole massive archive of *New Yorker* editorial correspondence at the New York Public Library), doesn't think this likely: "Whoever was editor of a particular writer knew what that particular writer was paid," said Yagoda. "That particular editor would know the rates of all the writers he worked with." Maxwell's writers included Updike and Shirley Hazzard, among others with presumably higher rates than Cheever's. But then, Cheever was (as his daughter would say) a "patsy" when it came to money: Yankee reticence or no, it was a subject that made him extremely uncomfortable ("Perelman screams and I guess it keeps his prices up, but I can't"). Which is not to say, necessarily, that he didn't know when he was getting screwed. Toward the end of 1975, as Maxwell was about to retire from the magazine, Harold Brodkey (one of Maxwell's discoveries) told Cheever that Maxwell had been "financially, intellectually and emotionally dishonest" with Cheever, who reflected, "Some of this I know to be true."

CHAPTER TWENTY-FOUR

{ *1964* }

A FEW WEEKS AFTER SUBMITTING the final draft of *The Wapshot Scandal*,* Cheever had lunch at the country estate of his publisher, Cass Canfield, who lovingly recited one of his favorite passages from memory. Everyone seemed excited about the book except its author. Cowley had found it a "pure delight" and praised Cheever's "power of invention" with an almost paternal pride: "That riot of the housewives over the plastic easter eggs: it's a Breughel vision of hell. I've been disturbed by the slowness of readers in realizing that your work is completely outside the New Yorker pattern or any other; that it's something unique in contemporary fiction." But Cheever was unpersuaded. Right up to publication, he continued to suffer "seizures" of melancholy: "I have a feeling that [the novel] is not only a failure—it is an odious crime—and the world is whispering about it at my back."

Such fears were somewhat dispelled by Elizabeth Janeway's front-page rave in the January 5, 1964, *New York Times Book Review:* The novel, she wrote, was "a riotous, slapstick, tragi-farcical show of the world today." And perhaps Cheever was particularly gratified by her remarks on "mythic elements" such as the maenadlike housewives, Melissa Wapshot's "suffering for her Adonis," and so on: "More than anyone except perhaps Nabokov (and he does not suffer from Nabo-

---

*In 1959, Mike Bessie had left Harper to co-found a new publishing house, Atheneum, and was startled by Cheever's refusal to follow him. *The Wapshot Scandal* was edited at Harper by one of Cheever's oldest friends, Frances Lindley.

kov's plunges into pure grotesquerie), [Cheever] is able to use the objects, the scenes and the attributes of contemporary life for the purposes of art." Two days later, Charles Poore concurred in the daily *Times*, noting that the book "should be on everybody's list for the best novel of the year." In his journal Cheever reflected that he found it "disconcerting" to be "embraced by an institution," though he couldn't resist showing the Poore review to Maxwell over lunch that day. The latter's response, he wrote, "seemed close to unfriendly": "I do not understand the nature of this friendship; I think I never have."

Most of the other notices seemed to indicate that the world was indeed realizing (as Cowley would have it) that Cheever was a good deal more than just a proficient writer of *New Yorker* fiction. "I can think of no other writer today who tells us so much about the way we live now," Joan Didion observed in the *National Review*, while Cheever's (secretly despised) colleague at the Institute, Glenway Wescott, applauded the novel on the front page of the *New York Herald Tribune Book Week* as an improvement over its vaunted predecessor—"a true novel, not just a *nouvelle* expanded, not a set of stories strung along like matching or contrasting beads on arbitrary string, not a disguised memoir or autobiography." Wescott also wrote Cheever a personal note, expressing his almost feverish gratitude: "[N]ow and then, as it were by chance, a particular book comes along, and it's a love affair."* A few prominent reviewers, however, delivered the sort of pans that Cheever had anticipated with such terror. In *The New Republic* ("Sugary Days in St. Botolphs"), Hilary Corke wrote that Cheever's Wapshot novels were marred by "unredeemable carelessnesses and loosenesses of construction" as well as "arrant sentimentality." And perhaps the most distinguished reviewer of all, Stanley Edgar Hyman, began his review in the *New Leader* with this rather prescient salvo: "When a highly-esteemed story writer tries a novel and fails at it, in this amazing country, he is rewarded just as though he had succeeded. . . . John Cheever's *The Wapshot Chronicle* won a National Book Award. In *The Wapshot Scandal*, Cheever has again tried, and

---

*The following year, when *The Wapshot Scandal* was awarded the William Dean Howells Medal from the Academy of Arts and Letters, Wescott was one of Cheever's main detractors: "[H]e forced some perfect stories into a somewhat loose, somewhat arbitrary novel," Wescott demurred—in direct contradiction to his *Book Week* review—noting his own preference for Katherine Anne Porter's *Ship of Fools*.

again failed, to make short story material jell as a novel. As a two-time loser, he can probably expect the Pulitzer Prize."

One could also make the case that Cheever was deemed a "failed" novelist by certain critics for the very reason that he was regarded as a story writer first and foremost; as with its predecessor, the structure of *The Wapshot Scandal* may be reduced to the formula of three or four long stories rather loosely (in terms of linear plot) plaited together. Moreover, as Maxwell asserted (and Hyman made a similar point), "the psychological consistency of characters" is sacrificed somewhat by the author in order to be "freer" and more "fanciful." When we last see Melissa Wapshot, for example, she's wandering around an Italian supermarket like "Ophelia," madly chanting commercial jingles ("Mr. Clean, Mr. *Clean*"); reading Cheever's notes, we learn that he considered using Coverly's wife Betsey for this scene, before randomly deciding to "throw it to Melissa"—in other words, it was the set piece that mattered rather than the characters, most of whom are mutable ciphers responding to their respective predicaments. But then, if one insists on well-rounded characters, there's always Honora, who remains perfectly herself from start to finish, and that's arguably as it should be: Honora embodies the more coherent traditions of an old, dying world, whereas Melissa and Betsey reflect the alienating chaos of modern times.

The Wapshot Scandal begins and ends during Christmas in St. Botolphs, where a "shine of decorum" still prevails "at the time of which I'm writing"—the latter phrase perhaps the most recurrent in Cheever's work, fixing time beyond history, again, though we are told that it's "late in the day." Thus the "shine of decorum" in St. Botolphs is little more than "a mode of hope," and everywhere a disparity is noted between appearance and reality. Even the apparently "benign" rector, Mr. Applegate, is in fact a cynical drunkard who seems to hear his parishioners' silent prayers in all their maddening banality: "It was the feeling that all exalted human experience was an imposture, and that the chain of being was a chain of humble worries." And yet there is still a redemptive sense of connection in St. Botolphs: carolers serenade their fellow townsfolk, the telephone operator knows everyone by name, and people do not judge their neighbors' social prestige ("as they presently would") based on the relative lushness of their Christmas trees. But meanwhile, at the Missile Research and Development site at Talifer, where Coverly now works and lives, the impending

Apocalypse has imposed a mood of paranoiac isolation. Across the street from her tract house, Betsey Wapshot observes a man falling to his death while installing storm windows, and returns to her television rather than violate "security" concerns by getting involved. This, then, is what passes for a "shine of decorum" at Talifer, which is decidedly more hypocritical than hopeful. Near an abandoned farm with its deceptive "bucolic imagery" is the "dark, oil-colored glass" of the administration center—"buried six stories beneath the cow pasture"—and viciousness, in one form or another, is forever bursting to the surface. Coverly brawls with a loutish neighbor over a stolen garbage can, while in the background a missile rises brightly against the horizon. As for the Teller-like director of Talifer, Dr. Cameron, he boasts of skiing expertly down a steep slope at dusk (whereas in fact he furtively rode the lift both ways), and one page later reveals to Coverly that a bird is calling him by name ("Cameron, Cameron, Cameron"). In such hands rests the fate of the earth.

The degree to which readers are polarized over the question of structure in *The Wapshot Scandal* (or any of Cheever's novels) seems ultimately a matter of taste. George Garrett singled out the book's *craft* as one of its most "outstanding" features, while Corke (et al.) thought it an architectural fiasco and certain reviewers seemed almost to take personal offense—Robert Kirsch of the *Los Angeles Times* deplored the author as "weary, bored and confused," and of course there were times when Cheever was inclined to agree. In due course, though, he'd arrive at a more charitable view, describing his second novel as "an extraordinarily complex book built around non sequiturs really." And so it is: *The Wapshot Scandal* bulges with sideshows and discordant (to the humorless) bits of slapstick, but it is actually *built around* such moments. To take perhaps the most notable instance, the entire novel (more or less) is conveyed in microcosm through the self-contained parable of Gertrude ("Dirty Gertie") Lockhart, who over the course of a four-page anecdote slides into alcoholism and promiscuity and finally suicide.* "Her downfall began not with immortal longings but with an

---

*Such digressions serve the same purpose as, say, the dumb show in *Hamlet*—indeed, a Hamlet motif is yet another ingredient in this generous, sprawling novel, an incidental spice Cheever uses whenever he happens to think of it. Like Hamlet's father, Leander's ghost haunts the early pages as an emblem of protest against the decadent modern age ("Oh, Father, Father, why have you come back?"), and then vanishes altogether—*qua* ghost anyway—after only forty pages or so. Talifer is a kind of

C H E E V E R

uncommonly severe winter when the main soil line from their house to the septic tank froze. The toilets backed up into the bathtubs and sinks. Nothing drained." Unable to find an available plumber in all of Parthenia, Gertrude hires a derelict to dig a ditch for two dollars an hour plus all the whiskey he can drink, and the two end up in bed together. The woman's decline continues as her appliances break down one by one, leaving her isolated and helpless and faced with the awful fact of her own "obsolescence." One day she throws herself at the milkman in drunken despair, after which the oil burner stops working and no repairman can be found on short notice: "It was very cold outside and she watched the winter night approach the house with the horror of an aboriginal. She could feel the cold overtake the rooms. When it got dark she went into the garage and took her own life." The lonely nomadism of modern life is such that Gertrude's husband can find no friends among their neighbors to attend the funeral; instead he musters a few "near strangers" whom they'd met "on various cruise ships." Finally, as a kind of parenthetical rim-shot, we are told that the "oil-burner repairmen, electricians, mechanics and plumbers who were guilty of her death did not attend."

Melissa, as it happens, is a passenger on the train bearing Gertrude's remains back to Indiana, and it is Melissa's story that is mostly foretold here. In his notes to the novel, Cheever reminded himself to emphasize "the lonely and erotic nature of man, that all the splendid ceremonies, the music and the bells, meant to honor and contain his drives, the atmosphere of loneliness and bewilderment is never expunged." In a world where nuclear oblivion seems imminent, and life in any case is "bitterly disappointing"—bereft of "splendid ceremonies" or much in the way of spiritual fulfillment—one is apt to overindulge one's carnal appetites. Lonely Gertrude, without even the creature comforts afforded by working appliances, consoles herself with drink and sex until she's driven to suicide; Melissa takes up with the nineteen-year-old grocery boy, Emile, because she thinks she's dying of cancer: "The image, hackneyed and poignant, that came to her was of life as a diversion, a festival from which she was summoned by the secret police of extinction, when the dancing and the music were at their best." But human beings are meant for better things than

---

Elsinore, with Cameron its murderous king; *Gertrude* Lockhart evokes Hamlet's tragic, debauched mother; and Melissa is explicitly likened to the mad Ophelia.

dancing and rutting; the erotic, for Cheever, is ideally a symbol of divine love, and animal despair can only be transcended by the soul's aspiration toward the "illustrious." The Dionysian Melissa does not end up dead like her farcical counterpart Gertrude Lockhart, though her eventual life in Rome does seem a living death of sorts, as she divides her days between dubbing Italian movies and thereby impersonating fallen women through the ages ("She was the voice of Mary Magdalen, she was Delilah, she was the favorite of Hercules") and wandering around a supermarket ("Mr. Clean, Mr. *Clean*") in search of food for her oafish paramour. In a separate but "parallel" story line (so noted by Cheever), Coverly also has a brush with death—a mysterious hunter fires an arrow at his head just as he stoops to tighten his shoelaces—but consequently takes a more Apollonian route: "Coverly's resolve to do something illustrious settled on a plan to diagnose the vocabulary of John Keats." Feeding the poet's oeuvre into a computer at Talifer, Coverly discovers that a list of Keats's most frequently used words results in an odd, lyric pensée about the flawed nature of humankind (and hence restates the novel's main theme): "Silence blendeth grief's awakened fall / The golden realms of death take all / Love's bitterness exceeds its grace / That bestial scar on the angelic face / Marks heaven with gall."

Fittingly, the novel ends with a Last Supper of sorts at Honora's house in St. Botolphs, attended by eight guests from the Hutchins Institute for the Blind. These wretches have been invited at Honora's behest—her last request as she proudly drinks herself to death, departing a heartless world embodied by the Internal Revenue Service, which has hounded her all the way to Europe and back. Indeed, an entire way of life seems to be passing with Honora, beginning with her beloved old house, which like a "carapace" seems to dwindle into "cobwebs and ashes" along with its tenant. Her posthumous hospitality toward the blind Christmas guests—"the losers, the goners, the flops"—seems a final act of ceremonial kindness, as well as a timely reminder of human misery and death. One thinks of Cheever's injunction in "The Death of Justina": "How can a people who do not mean to understand death hope to understand love, and who will sound the alarm?" At this late hour in history, we are thus urged to consider our fragility, and mutual dependence, as well as our ultimate purpose as immortal beings. Not to do so is to end up like poor Moses, a hopelessly drunken reprobate who can no longer bear to consider his life in the sober glare of

(Christmas) morning: "The brilliance of light, the birth of Christ, all seemed to him like some fatuous shell game invented to dupe a fool like his brother while he saw straight through into the nothingness of things."* At the end of the novel, the temporal world is fading away, and Cheever's favorite bit of Plato in the final paragraph ("Let us consider that the soul of man is immortal . . .") seems a relinquishment of all that. "I will never come back," the narrator concludes, "and if I do there will be nothing left, there will be nothing left but the headstones to record what has happened; there will really be nothing at all."

AFTER MONTHS of grueling anxiety—redeemed at last by "booming" sales† and mostly excellent reviews—Cheever decided he needed a vacation and asked Mary if she'd like to visit Italy again. She countered with the suggestion that they go to Paris instead—she'd yearned to return for some thirty years now—but Cheever petulantly refused ("I am fatuous and disgusting") and even decided to stay home rather than travel alone. When he announced as much to his family, however, "They seemed so terribly disappointed"—he wrote Weaver—"that I announced again that I would leave for Rome on Sunday and so I shall." The first thing he did was savor the grandeur of Porto Ercole again, staying with the Australian writer Alan Moorehead (*Gallipoli*) and his wife, Lucy, whom he'd befriended in Italy seven years before. After a few days of sitting on the beach with Mrs. Moorehead—who discussed her husband's "ruthless infidelity" with a kind of doting detachment—Cheever proceeded to Rome and took an apartment at the Academy. Lonely as ever and searching for love ("someone who will take care of my needs"), Cheever ended up dining with fellow guests almost every night and feeling the "institutional blues, those old Yaddo blues." He returned to Ossining at the end of January.

Through the Mooreheads he'd recently met another Australian, Alwyn Lee, who, after a picaresque career as a Melbourne journalist, had come to the States during the war and joined the staff of *Time*. As a former colleague reminisced, Lee "had a unique reputation even

---

*When first conceiving the novel, Cheever had meant for Moses to play a larger role—the "Dionysian" part largely taken over by Melissa. It's possible that Fred Cheever's grinding decline in these years left his brother disinclined to dwell on his fictional surrogate. In Cheever's working notes, anyway, references to Moses dwindle away until we come to this: "MOSES: nothing much. He's a goner."

†*The Wapshot Scandal* eventually sold almost fifty thousand copies in hardback.

among the extraordinarily alcoholic group of writers" at the magazine. One day in 1958, a researcher had passed Lee's office and observed the following: "Lee lay on the floor, under his desk, with only his feet visible. Half kneeling, half peering into the dark hollow, stood Henry Grunwald, present Editor in Chief of Time, Inc., asking plaintively, 'Are you all right, Alwyn?' " Lee's first appearance on Cedar Lane was also memorable. As Ben Cheever wrote, "I came home from school to find a tall, slender Australian in a suit and vest attempting cartwheels on the lower lawn. My father was standing off to one side watching." Despite his own vagaries, Cheever tended to find overt eccentricity distasteful, and Ben felt certain his father would take an immediate dislike to the tipsy Australian. But not at all: he found Lee a "first-rate" raconteur and was in awe of his larger-than-life persona. "[Alwyn] had a series of ardent and eccentric attachments to barkeeps, whores, unemployed actors and an international spy called Hong Kong Harry," Cheever recalled after Lee's death. "He had been, as a youth, the sexual and political terror of Melbourne and when his face was in the shadow you could see how comely he had been. In the light, of course, his face was heavily scored. He drank two quarts a day."

Such was the man who proposed to write a cover story about Cheever for *Time*. At first the latter demurred as a matter of course—all such publicity was "abominable"—but Lee insisted: they were kindred spirits, he said, pointing out that they'd been born the same year (1912) in spring (or rather Cheever had been born in May and Lee in October—"the Australian spring"). Cheever claimed that he and Ben promptly absconded to Vermont to escape the predations of *Time*, but actually the trip was an expenses-paid "research" boondoggle for which he was accompanied by Lee and an assistant. ("In the bar after dinner," Cheever mused in his journal, "Lee picks up a girl who dumps him out of her Volkswagen three miles from town. He walks home but still shows up for breakfast, bathed, shaved, dressed for skiing.") It wasn't long, however, before the lark began to pall. When Cheever returned to Ossining, he found the artist Henry Koerner installed in Susan's bedroom, painting one of Cheever's shirts. Afterward, Koerner remarked that he'd included Cheever's pet doves in his cover portrait "because they seemed . . . to symbolize the peaceful world with which Cheever surrounds himself "—unaware, perhaps, that his placid host had suspected him all the while of seducing Mary and was "prepared to murder" Koerner if this should prove to be the case.

Cheever's general paranoia about the project was not unjustified. A second reporter, Andrew Kopkind, soon arrived from California and began interviewing family and friends.* One night Cheever got an idea of just how deeply the man intended to dig: "What have you done wrong?" Fax Ogden inquired, phoning from Delaware. "To have this friend of my adolescence, who I have not seen for forty years, brought into the picture is strange and unnatural," Cheever wrote. It got stranger still. When Cheever had first agreed to cooperate ("it's better this way than hiding in the bathroom like Salinger who never seemed to find his way out"), he made only one request: *Leave my brother in peace.* Kopkind, however, lost no time running Fred to ground in Connecticut, and soon it transpired that he was indeed searching for "smut." The Warrens almost kicked the man out of their house for asking unseemly questions about Cheever's marriage ("I remember that son of a bitch!" said Red Warren twenty years later), and certain other friends, Cheever noticed, seemed "uneasy" around him these days, as if worried they'd said a little too much to Kopkind.

In public Cheever affected a breezy, nothing-to-hide scorn: he claimed to have advised one group of friends to say he was impotent, the other that he had "two cocks." He wrote the following set piece, word for word, to various correspondents:

> Sally Ziegler, a small-town Georgian who lives in the cottage on the hill, has been preparing herself for the TIME interview for a month. On Friday the doorbell rang and she let the man in. "I don't approve of this kind of sneaky journalism," she said, "but the truth is that I know a lot about him because I can see him from my windows. I mean to say that I know he's a very heavy drinker and I often see him out there at twelve o' clock noon with a martini cocktail in his hand. And he sometimes chases his wife through the orchard in full view of my children. And he almost never wears his bathing-suit when he goes swimming and I've always thought there was something peculiar about men who go swimming without their bathing suits. But as I say I don't approve of this kind of gossip and if you'll ask me some suitable questions about his habits I'll try to answer them to the best of my ability." Then the man said, "Lady, I'm your Fuller Brush representative."

---

*Kopkind went on to gain a certain degree of fame as one of the sixties' leading radical journalists, a frequent contributor to such magazines as *Ramparts* (one of whose founding editors was Susan Cheever's third husband, Warren Hinckle).

Cheever's private attitude was far less debonair. Once his face appeared on "four million newsstands" in late March (he fretted), he'd be exposed for all time as "impotent, homosexual," to say nothing of all the other sins he'd committed in his almost fifty-two years. "So the boundless continents of anxiety appear," he wrote after one sleepless night. "I will be described as an impostor, a bum sponging off the government and the corporation of Yaddo, a cheap social climber, an imitation gentleman."

No doubt Kopkind turned up something of that sort, but it was not to be found in Lee's elegant puff piece, "Ovid in Ossining." Far from being described as (essentially) a snobbish crypto-homosexual, Cheever was praised for the "moral vision"—the *pietas*—that was everywhere evident in his work: "John Cheever, almost alone in the field of modern fiction, is one who celebrates the glories and delights of monogamy." The better aspects of *The Wapshot Scandal* were incisively discussed (Lee was a first-rate critic), and its supposed flaws were explained away as ingenious formal effects: "Cheever is not a great expositor of character. Fiction as character study belongs to the Victorian novel, and this, he believes, is as obsolete as the world it moved in—the tight, homogenous community, before mass communications smoothed out the world and blurred individuality. This tends to make his novels seem disjointed, but he defends it on the ground that disjunction is the nature of modern society."

Astonished by Lee's "transcendent generosity," Cheever invited the man over for a celebratory walk to the dam. When Lee complained of the cold, they returned to the house and sat around a fire. "I'm frightfully sorry," said Lee, lowering his whiskey, "but I'm about to go into the torture of little ease." Cheever looked puzzled, and Lee clarified that he was about to die and needed to find a bathroom. "He goes to the bathroom, vomits, returns, goes to the bathroom again," Cheever wrote in his journal. "I hear him spitting out his guts and crying pitifully. When I open the door I find him lying in the bathtub." Cheever helped the dying man out of the tub and put him to bed with a hot-water bottle, then phoned for an ambulance. "You're not going to die, Alwyn," he said, taking Lee into his arms. "The tenderness in this scene was marred by the fact that I had a sharp pain in my arse," Cheever related to a friend. "Standing, I saw that I had sat on his false teeth. 'Godamn it Alwyn,' I said, 'you just can't leave your false teeth anywhere.' At this The Angel of Death—a conservative and humorless spirit—vanished. The ambulance arrived and he made a miraculous recovery." Lee's near-fatal attack of pancreatitis had yielded, for Cheever, that choice business about the false teeth, which eventually became a linchpin moment in *Falconer*.

Another curious outcome of the *Time* story was a meeting at the Century with his old "boy chum" Fax. "This is no reunion to be turned into a story," Cheever wrote of the rather melancholy occasion. The middle-aged Fax was a homely man "with a sad song to sing": his public-relations business was failing, and he seemed to dislike his wife and children. He thought perhaps he'd write a textbook or a television show ("something that will bring in large and sudden sums of money"). After lunch the two walked along Forty-third Street with their arms around each other's shoulders for old times' sake, and in parting Fax asked Cheever where he could get a whore ("I suggested the elevator man at the Iroquois but you know with a face like that he might have some trouble"). Every so often, in years to come, Cheever would get late-night phone calls from Fax, always a bit drunker and sadder, and generally wondering if Cheever was interested in some vague "business venture." Then, around 1970, the calls stopped.

CHEEVER USED TO SAY that he had "two conspicuous lacks": a singing voice and a self-image. By the latter he meant (on one level) a *public* image, the lack of which was due, he said, to "a genuine horror of notoriety" engendered by his Yankee upbringing; also, sober, he was a desperately shy man who felt oppressed by strangers. He tended to drink before any public appearance and then would "smile, smile, smile" until his face ached—what else to do?—and afterward he felt so ashamed of himself that he drank more. "I feel like a remorseful masturbator," he wrote after a recent reading, "holding his aching, softening cock in one hand while sperm runs down the wall paper like the white of an egg." But then he always professed not to care about fame: literature, he was fond of saying, was like a vast impersonal "stream." He himself had been influenced by everything since the Egyptian Book of the Dead, and though his own work might be forgotten ("it wouldn't disconcert me in the least"), it would forever be part of that "stream" running into the future. Asked about his father's "stream" concept, Federico laughed: "To say he stood on the shoulders of giants is to say he's Isaac Newton. It's a wonderful kind of double play. You say 'Ah, I'm nothing in the great stream of things,' but in saying that you put yourself in the great stream of things."

His appearance on the cover of *Time* increased his visibility in the stream, and also gave him the beginnings of an image—that of a "serious and likable person," no less, not to mention one of the great writers of his generation. He began to be noticed on the street, and didn't really mind it at all ("Me tickled"): now perhaps he'd be fussed over in restaurants and whatnot; his barber might tack his picture to the wall. Meanwhile his mailbox was stuffed almost daily with *Time* covers to autograph, and Cheever was only too happy to oblige. This serious and likable, witty and gifted author began to worry about things like publicity photos, and was dismayed when others failed to share these concerns. Shown an advertisement featuring her husband's likeness, Mary remarked: "What are they going to do with it, pin it up in the post office?" "Should there be some way of seeing this humorously," Cheever fumed in his journal, "I would be most grateful. Gin seems to be the only way out."

What Cheever anxiously sought in these photos, perhaps, was some further confirmation of the image so perfectly captured by *Time*, which had initiated (as Federico put it) "the media shakedown cruise for the new landowning Cheever." "[Cheever] wears Brooks Brothers shirts with their conspicuously missing pockets and would never consider having a mongrel dog," Alwyn Lee noted, alongside pictures of the tweedy author and his faithful retrievers, strolling around his Westchester estate. And lest he seem an arriviste—a cartoon gentleman like John O'Hara, with his spats and hard-finish suits—Cheever wore clothes as though he'd been born in them: one collar-point of a button-down shirt was carefully unbuttoned, his crewneck sweater was gone in the elbows, and his "wash pants" were rumpled and stained. Real aristocrats (to say nothing of real *men*) didn't worry about whether their creases were ironed, as long as the label said Brooks and certain other touches were right. "I *am* a Wasp, my God, look," he remarked (with his usual protective irony) to a journalist: "Palms over a Seth Thomas clock on Maundy Thursday!" His next remark, perhaps, would be some drawling reference to the century in which his farmhouse was built ("Pushkin and Sterne were still alive"), followed by a footnote about how it was completely "restored" (the audible quotes were a further level of irony) by Gugler in the twenties. "Cheever was not, I think, content merely to be an artist," said

Maxwell. "He wanted a place in society, to lead the life of upper-middle-class people as he saw it (with some idealization, I think). He would have liked to have had lots of money, entertained beautifully, been socially the best there was."

The main aspect of this personage was his curious accent. Was he a Cambridge Brahmin? British? What? It was hard to pin down. Philip Roth pointed out that it wasn't really a New England accent at all—"more like an upper-class New Yorker, someone like Plimpton, perhaps." This was close, though Cheever's accent was somewhat more mutable than Plimpton's. When appearing on *The Dick Cavett Show*, or putting an impudent barkeep in his place, Cheever became almost a parody of the pompous toff ("like Thurston Howell III on *Gilligan's Island*," the writer James Kaplan observed, "or Chatsworth Osborne in *Dobie Gillis*"), but at other times—relaxed, cracking jokes—he sounded not unlike a boy from the South Shore with an English mother. "I knew John before he had an accent," said Jerre Mangione, his old FWP colleague from the thirties, and Mary Cheever also seems to remember when her husband had a more conventional way of saying "idear" for "idea" and "Cheevah" for "Cheever." No matter. Most agree that Cheever's accent became a well-assimilated part of his persona—"a suave, fictional dialect," as the poet Dana Gioia put it, "[that] seemed to have the force of ancient authority, as if he were some New England Homer standing at the apex of a long oral tradition."

Nor would it be accurate to say that the persona itself—in its finished form—was false. "He saw what he wanted and he became it," said Allan Gurganus. "That's what Cary Grant said, who started with Archie Leach: 'I made up the name Cary Grant and then I became him.' " One thinks of F. Scott Fitzgerald—or rather Cheever did, noting the disparity between Fitzgerald the vulgar, drunken prankster and Fitzgerald the artist, Fitzgerald the well-meaning father who "preserved an angelic austerity of spirit," as Cheever wrote in *Atlantic Brief Lives:* "Noble might be a better word, since as a boy in what had been the frontier town of St. Paul he had considered himself to be a lost prince. How sensible of him. His mother was the ruthless and eccentric daughter of a prosperous Irish grocer. His gentle father belonged to the fringe aristocracy of the commercial traveler, moving from Syracuse to Buffalo and back again. How else could he explain his giftedness?" Needless to say, Cheever might just as well have been writing about himself. Also like Fitzgerald (and any number of American writers), he was a wistful snob—simultaneously enchanted and repelled by a materialistic culture where artists, no matter how great, remain outcasts to some extent. Fitzgerald, finding his grandfather listed in the St. Paul Social Register as a "grocer," penciled in the word "wholesale"; Cheever, feeling belittled in some way, would pull an accent and become the lost prince of Wollaston. And yet the part of him that remained Archie Leach, so to speak, was a humble man who felt tender toward the other Archie Leaches of the world.

"I can't connect my life," Cheever remarked once in the late seventies. "That person in the Army wasn't me. And there was a whole life before that that I can't connect either." There were other lives, too, until finally he became the world-famous writer and Westchester squire. "It is strange to relate that I never had such a clear impression of knowing someone so well as on the first evening I met John Cheever [in the fifties]," said Elizabeth Spencer. The two remained friends over the next twenty-five years, though Spencer never again felt remotely as close to Cheever. "But I continued to believe that that funny and charming person was the real one."

IN HIS JOURNAL, Cheever described himself as "a fat slob enjoying an extraordinary run of luck," and no wonder. Earlier that year, the producer-director team of Alan Pakula and Robert Mulligan (*To Kill a Mockingbird*) had bought the rights to both *Wapshot* novels for seventy-five thousand dollars. On April 3—while Cheever's radiant face still lingered on a few newsstands—he went to Los Angeles to finalize the deal and discuss the possibility of adapting the novels himself.

He was met at the airport by Pakula's wife, the actress Hope Lange—"a pretty young woman whose company I enjoy," Cheever noted, quietly enough, of the person who would become a lifelong (if sporadic and mostly platonic) mistress, for lack of a better word. Lange had debuted in the movie *Bus Stop* (1956) and earned an Oscar nomination the following year for her best-known role, in *Peyton Place*. By 1964 she was thirty and temporarily retired, the better to devote herself to family. Charged with entertaining Cheever that first night, Lange would later remember that "he had his New England mumble and suit on": for an hour or so, he sat stiffly sipping drinks and glancing uneasily around the Pakulas' orange basement playroom, until Lange put *Guys and Dolls* on the phonograph (Cheever loved the sound track even more than *Tosca*) and a wonderful time was had by all.

After that, Cheever made little attempt to disguise the fact that he was smitten with Pakula's wife. He shined his shoes, shaved twice a day, and gazed at her with dewy fascination, whatever the company. Most of the others found it oddly endearing, and Lange's younger brother, David, even viewed Cheever as an ideal father figure of sorts ("a writer of consequence, witty")—while Cheever in turn was impressed that David was dating Natalie Wood. One night the young man picked up Cheever at the Beverly Hills Hotel and the two went cruising around the neighborhood; as they passed Glenn Ford's house David mentioned he knew the man, and Cheever ("acting like a naughty boy") said, "Let's go see him! I've got to have something to tell the kids." So they went, though the midnight visit was "pretty dull," according to David, since Cheever was shy and Ford was sleepy.

The one person who seemed to hold out against Cheever's boyish charm was Alan Pakula. While they were dining together one night, Cheever noticed that the man "seem[ed] cross" with him for some reason, and finally Pakula's brother took him aside and explained things. Mortified, Cheever delivered a little speech the next day to the effect that he loved Hope as he loved "the light of day," which may or may not have done the trick; afterward Cheever cursed himself for indulging in such a "vain and indecent flirtation" ("Improve, my soul, improve"). Nevertheless, he arranged to say goodbye to Mrs. Pakula on his way to the airport, and was alarmed to find she wasn't home. Thinking her husband had "forbidden" her to see him again, Cheever spent much of the transcontinental flight drinking gin in the toilet, and when he got home that night (presumably worse for wear) he lost no time telling his wife and seven-year-old son "about [his] emotional embroilments." The next week or so passed in an agony of worry: "Why should H[ope] have stood me up, oh why oh why?" he wrote, thinking his "drunken and immature behavior" had ruined the movie deal: "There will be a desperate call from Henry [his agent], a prolonged lawsuit, etc." But at last he got a call from Hope, who explained that she'd had to run an errand the day of his departure, that she was *very* sorry, and meanwhile everybody loved and missed him. "I've never wanted anything more from the world," Cheever sighed to his wife, "than to be rich, famous and loved."*

---

*Though Cheever would see more of the Pakulas (especially Mrs. Pakula), the *Wapshot* movie was never made. According to David Lange, Tad Mosel wrote a screenplay that was deemed "professional but not quite filmable." A pity, as the cast would

"Will success spoil John Cheever?" his family joked, and for a few weeks, at least, it seemed the opposite was true. He gleefully deposited a fat Hollywood check at the local bank (whose employees were gratifyingly incredulous) and began spreading the wealth—lavishing gifts on his wife and children, paying off part of the mortgage, and treating himself to a sporty new Karmann Ghia convertible. In June he and Mary went back to Italy with Alwyn and Essie Lee, more or less retracing the steps of Cheever's previous visit: Mary "flash[ed] her rubies and diamonds on the deck of the Mooreheads' yacht" in Porto Ercole, where they spent the balmy days sipping gin and eating lobster and playing backgammon. Cheever was glad not to be a solitary traveler again, if a bit piqued by Lee's flashy Italian (and agitated by the comely youths "pos[ing] on the rocks and the headlands" of Sperlonga).

By July, however, the "dog days" had returned to the Hudson Valley: "I have the disposition of an adder," Cheever reported. This had become a yearly cycle, ever since Cheever had decided that Treetops was "an inbred group of neurotics"—no longer mitigated, even, by the presence of a few charming Whitneys, since they'd been banished after Winter's death. Still, Mary insisted on making the trip (and taking Federico and the dogs), though she tried to mollify Cheever by filling the freezer with precooked meals and reminding friends that he'd be in need of their hospitality. To no avail: "Alone, alone," he brooded in his journal, "eating boiled eggs while you [Mary] stuff yourself and play mahjong with your mad sister." Such was his restless desolation that he entertained friends whom he could scarcely bear anymore, or never much liked in the first place. Art Malsin ("Bomb Cuba!") made an appearance one night, and wanted to discuss Negro writers vis-à-vis the Civil Rights Act: "[James] Baldwin is a homosexual," Cheever recorded the gist of it. "Baldwin is a negro. Ergo most negros are homosexual. One of the results of the civil rights bill will be to legitimize homosexuality." Which, of course, was another sore subject: lonely, bored, and drunk, Cheever felt as vulnerable as ever to unsavory temptations, and the more he tried to distract himself, the more the world conspired to remind him. When Alwyn Lee went back into the hospital, Cheever volunteered to give his wife rides from the train station: "My motives are 1 to occupy myself and 2 to help her. She gets

---

have been illustrious if Pakula and Mulligan had gotten their way: Spencer Tracy (Leander), Katharine Hepburn (Honora), and Robert Redford (Moses).

into the car with a newspaper clipping that says gin-drinkers are determinedly married to conceal their homosexuality."

Fortunately, a rather wholesome alternative was right across Cedar Lane, at the lovely hilltop "chateau" (as Cheever described it) of a merry divorcée named Sara Spencer. For years the woman had combed *The New Yorker* each week to see if Cheever's name appeared at the end of any stories, and was therefore delighted to learn in 1961 that her favorite writer had become a neighbor. Soon they had struck up a friendship of sorts, but only recently had things become really interesting. One day Spencer had taken the liberty of carrying a large bundle of Cheever's mail down to his house, and while he sorted through it, he remarked, "I get letters from all over the world, and yet I'm desperately lonely." Appalled that this wonderful, witty man—this world-famous writer who'd recently graced the cover of *Time*!—had been abandoned by a callous wife, Spencer gave Cheever the run of her house and somewhat acceded to his overwhelming "appetite for sexual tenderness," as he put it. That summer he'd published a story titled "Marito in Città," about a married man who has a larky affair with an aging seamstress named Mrs. Zagreb, which was how he invariably referred to Spencer in his journal.* "I take Mrs. Zagreb to a restaurant in Peekskill and have a jolly wrestling match on her sofa," he wrote of a night in August. "You could use a young man, say I. I could use three or four young men, says she." The two could talk about almost anything, it seemed: Spencer was a shrewd businesswoman who owned several apartment buildings in the Bronx, and sometimes, amid the afterglow of whatever went on between them, she gave Cheever financial advice. Indeed, he felt so comfortable with this kindly, worldly matron that he even mentioned his "homosexual instincts": "Oh baby, she said, you're not queer; you love women more than any man I ever knew, you're all man, all male."

No wonder he forgave her for being middle-aged (at least), though it wasn't a matter he could forget entirely. Again and again he tabulated her defects—her face had evidently been lifted at least once ("the firmness of her chin contrasted with the slackness of her neck"); she dyed her hair in the "silvergilt" pattern of aging blondes; her legs and breasts "show the mileage they've traveled"—and yet: "[S]he is so eas-

*Fifteen years later, when Hope Lange began to show her age, she too became "Mrs. Zagreb" in the journal.

ily approachable that I am delighted to be with a woman who does not flinch at my touch." She also had a fine swimming pool* and skating pond, and never seemed to mind if Cheever was drunk or naked or (usually) both. All she asked was that he sign a legal waiver absolving her of any liability in the event of accidents.

---

*A pool "fed by an artesian well," which Cheever gave to the Westerhazys in "The Swimmer."

CHAPTER TWENTY-FIVE

{ *1964* }

A MID THE (SOMETIMES) LONELY doldrums of that summer, Cheever consoled himself with thoughts of his "somber and mysterious trip to Russia in October," as part of the State Department's new cultural-exchange program. Previous emissaries had been obvious candidates such as Steinbeck and Erskine Caldwell, what with their proletarian themes, while Edward Albee had gone in 1963 on the strength (mostly) of his *Death of Bessie Smith*, since American racism was another favorite topic among Soviet readers.

The first Cheever story to be translated into Russian was "The Superintendent" (1952), about a humane, competent building super named Chester, who mediates squabbling among his crass, bourgeois tenants (" 'You get her stuff out of there, Chet,' Mrs. Negus said, 'and I'll give you ten dollars. That's been my apartment since midnight' ").* The translator was Tatiana Litvinov, whose father, Maxim, had been Stalin's foreign minister before the war.† In 1961, she'd written Cheever a letter explaining that a friend of hers—an *éminence grise* of

---

*A 1980 edition of Cheever's *Selected Stories* (Moscow: Progress Publishers) includes ten canonical stories along with three specimens of juvenilia chosen for their congenial themes: "I'm Going to Asia," about a frivolous bourgeois family who willfully ignore the tides of history which threaten to engulf them; "The Pleasures of Solitude," about a selfish old woman who savagely beats an urchin with her umbrella; and "Frère Jacques," about an *engagé* man who reads about the Spanish Loyalists while his vapid mistress sings to her laundry bundle.

†He was replaced in 1939 by Molotov, who went on to negotiate the "nonaggression" pact with the Nazis. Maxim Litvinov, known for his friendly overtures to the West, served as ambassador to the United States from 1941 to 1943.

Soviet literature, Kornei Chukovsky—had recently loaned her a copy of *The Enormous Radio*: "I loved the stories so much that I began translating them there and then." The first three translations were immediately published in *Novy Mir (The New World)* and *Znamya (The Banner)*—"our two most popular literary magazines"—and now Litvinov wanted to translate the rest of the book as well. Nor was her love of such stories as "The Season of Divorce," "The Pot of Gold," and "Torch Song" (her favorite) based on elements of anti-capitalist satire or socialist realism: "Your stories have a special appeal for us Russians," she wrote, "brought up as we are in the Chekhov tradition of sympathetic irony"—a point she clarified with a note in the margin: "What I like about the stories among other things is that they made you grieve for the people without feeling sentimental about them." Litvinov's translation of *The Enormous Radio*, published in 1962, was a particular success among other writers, who seemed to agree with Litvinov that Cheever's work "belonged to Russia and had to be got back." According to the *New York Times*, he'd also been discovered by a "lost generation" of Russian youths who were "alienated from Soviet goals and strongly oriented toward almost anything Western," including the Twist, blue jeans, and long hair. Whatever pleasure Cheever took in this information, however, would have been dampened somewhat by the fact that *Catcher in the Rye* was far more popular ("almost a status symbol") than any work of his. On the other hand, there was little question of Salinger's traveling on behalf of the government.

A week before his October 1 departure, Cheever went to Washington for his State Department briefing. "I was told that my liberty would be in danger, that my possessions would be rifled, my conversations bugged, and my walks shadowed," Cheever would later recall (adding—inaccurately—"Nothing of the sort happened"). He was also asked whether he had any vices they should know about. "I've always been a very heavy drinker," Cheever replied with a grin. His interlocutor then wondered if there was anything the KGB could use against him as blackmail leverage, and Cheever replied (perhaps after a tense pause) that he thought not.*

---

*When the ordeal was over, Cheever visited the suburban home of F. Scott Fitzgerald's daughter, Scottie Lanahan, where he was received by her then husband, Jack: "There seems to be cheese spread on his mouth and he has been drinking. He treats me, first, as if I were trying to sell encyclopedias but presently we settle down to drink." Eventually Mrs. Lanahan arrived and began to complain about the recent pub-

In a state of tipsy exhilaration, Cheever arrived in Moscow at midnight and heard, amid the shushing rain, what sounded like *cheep cheep cheep*. This was a delegation of some fifteen Soviet writers, headed by Vasily Aksyonov, all of them calling *Cheever Cheever Cheever*. Any lingering unease he might have felt was dispelled by his hosts' almost overwhelming enthusiasm: they fell upon him, embracing and back-slapping and "pour[ing] vodka into [his] ears." Indeed, this was the kind of wide-open affection for which, on some level, Cheever had hankered ever since his glacial childhood on Wollaston Hill. ("But why," he'd written the year before, "having known so little contentment, do I think continuously of a world, a scene, in which comely men and women greet one another eagerly and with love.") After a number of toasts, the writers dropped Cheever at his hotel—the cavernous Ukraine—where he washed his socks in the bathtub and got a few hours of sleep. At his publisher's office the next morning, Cheever was seated at a "felt-covered" table and given brandy, coffee, and cakes. "Then a man comes in with the boodle [royalties] and counts it onto the felt," he wrote Weaver. "Then you say Bolshoi Spaseba and the publisher gives you a big smelly kiss, right on the bouche."

In some ways, it was very near paradise. After years among the philistines of Westchester, Cheever found himself revered by a people to whom books mattered "tremendously": to be a writer in Russia, he said, was "like being a priest of some functioning religion"—and to be an American writer (*pisatel' amerikanskii*) was to be a sort of demigod. But then, the presence of any American was "like the arrival of a mail order catalogue in an especially provincial neck of the woods": "We represented Marlborough [sic] cigarets, freedom of speech, opinion and movement, an uncensored literature, soap, toilet paper, serviceable and inexpensive automobiles and decent clothing." Cheever rose to the occasion with vigorous conviviality. Where English failed, he marshaled a few Russian phrases he'd learned before the trip, along with an eccentric brew of Italian, French, and vodka-fueled expostulation. "It seemed as if he were in sort of a cloud," said Bill Luers, a young officer at the U.S. Embassy who saw a lot of Cheever. It was not, however, a lonely cloud. "Soubletsky put an arm around my shoulders and I put my arm around his," Cheever wrote of a typically spontaneous, ineffable friendship. "He ordered a bottle of vodka and we clanked our

---

lication of Hemingway's posthumous memoir, *A Moveable Feast*, wherein the size of her father's penis (among other things) had been impugned.

glasses and began to drink. Our conversation consisted mostly of repeating the word Printemps. I suppose he meant by this that he would see me in the spring . . . or perhaps he simply meant that in spite of the gloom of the early winter in Moscow we should remember that spring would come again."

Cheever had a tendency to slip away without telling anyone, and this was clearly disconcerting to the authorities. The exchange program was still something of a novelty, and neither side wanted any "bad incidents." In theory, Cheever was supposed to be accompanied by his "interpreter" from the Writers' Union, Giorgio Breitburd, a nice-enough fellow who (according to Litvinov) was a KGB agent. At gatherings Cheever would pump his new friends with eager questions about every aspect of their lives, while Breitburd hovered and sighed and looked at his watch and reminded him of other engagements. And when Cheever managed to escape his minder, it was seldom for very long: "Wherever we went," said Litvinov, "we'd suddenly come across [Breitburd]." When at last she explained the man's function to Cheever, he shrugged and said he wasn't afraid. "Well," she said, "you'd better be afraid."

When sober—that is, not often—Cheever did know the odd moment of fear. Waking at 3:00 a.m. in Azerbaijan, he was racked with homesickness and worried that he'd be kidnapped ("Will I have anything better than a single bed in a country where I do not speak the language"). But the next day his anxiety was eased by a bracing swim in the Caspian Sea, after which he flew to Tbilisi in Georgia ("the country of argonauts, Prometheus and Medea") and was driven "through oceans of sheep" to a monastery in the mountains. Next was Kiev and another picturesque drive to Yalta, where he visited Chekhov's final villa. "Welcome to the house of Anton Pavlovich Chekhov," the guide exclaimed in every room. "In house of Chekhov were being entertained Stanislavsky, Rachmaninoff . . . and the great Maxim Gorki." Afterward he lunched with the poet Margaret Aligher, and the two went swimming in the Black Sea. Near the beach was a dilapidated statue, its wire rigging exposed: "Chekhov?" asked Cheever. "Da, da," his companion sadly admitted. After further investigation, however, she rushed back to Cheever with some good news: "Was not Chekhov. Was Pavlov." Finally, on October 14, Cheever returned to Moscow and noticed that the ubiquitous portraits of Khrushchev had all vanished; people were marching around waving flags and Brezhnev posters. Breitburd said he was "sorry for the old chap"—Khrushchev, that is, who'd been deposed that day—a "brave" remark, said Litvinov.

Cheever also struck up friendships with Andrei Voznesensky and Yevgeny ("Zhenya") Yevtushenko, both famous in a way that was almost unimaginable in the West, not only as poets but as daring spokesmen for greater artistic freedom. Khrushchev had denounced Voznesensky as a "bourgeois formalist," and Yevtushenko's most famous poem, "Babi Yar"—an indictment of Nazi and Russian anti-Semitism—would not be published in his own country until 1984. "How many letters do you get?" Yevtushenko asked Cheever, who said he got maybe ten or twelve a week. Yevtushenko beamed: "I get two thousand a *day*." That was the sort of thing that excited Cheever's love. "Everybody says that [Voznesensky is] a better poet than Zhenya and he definitely thinks this himself," said Cheever; "but my affection for that incontinent and self-destructive ego-centric makes Andrei's gleaming face seem a little complacent." Cheever's crush on Yev-tushenko (platonic) was confirmed when he saw the man perform at a public reading, which was more like a rock concert than a literary event: for two hours, the flamboyant poet dashed around the stage reciting from memory, while the ecstatic crowd threw flowers. "I seem to love him as I love most natural phenomena," Cheever wrote, though he was more restrained about the poetry itself: "[Zhenya] writes always of a new world, its failures and promise. I know that the paradise he speaks of is populated by stupid and drunken peasants. The cows are scrawny, the children are hungry, the wheat crop is blighted and the trains are late but I would much sooner hear him speak than listen to the mumbling of my colleagues."

Cheever admired and perhaps even preferred Voznesensky's work, but quietly deplored the way the serious young man sipped water when others were toasting with vodka. No such qualms applied to Yev-tushenko, who fully reciprocated Cheever's admiration in this respect. "You drink like Siberian worker!" he declared, adding that Cheever's face was perfectly "working class." Then he gave the puzzled American a big kiss. ("Was best compliment," Yevtushenko explained forty years later. "Because he didn't look like an intellectual. What was great in John Cheever, when he came to Russia, he was very childishly curious about things. He created atmosphere of sincerity around him. The real artists, they are never peacocking. That is the great quality of the John Cheever character.") When the two wanted to speak freely, they'd take a bottle to Pasternak's grave and sit there on the bench; it was a common spot for such chats, as it seemed impervious to eavesdropping, and Yevtushenko's home, of course, had long been bugged. Years later, however, when Pasternak's daughter-in-law wanted the bench repainted, a bugging device was found in one of the hollowed-out concrete legs.

Whatever his awe of Yevtushenko, Cheever's most abiding attachment was with Tanya Litvinov, whom he'd first met at a reception given by the editorial board of *Inostrannaya Literatura (Foreign Literature)*. While publisher Boris Ryurikov "was booming along" about "common aims" and so forth, Cheever and Litvinov ducked behind a bowl of fruit and whispered about one thing and another. ("You could talk about anything with him," she remembered. "As if you were going on with some conversation that had begun long, long ago. It was absolutely wonderful.") Litvinov had begun translating "The Swimmer" and wanted to know *why*, exactly, Neddy was obliged to swim from one pool to the next, but Cheever mostly wanted to talk about her. ("Tanya," he noted afterward. "A very quick woman. A suit, a man's haircut, bad teeth, quick laughter, quick smile . . . She speaks of her mother; never her father. An intractible woman, I think. A light, feminine fierceness, having lived a life that would best be understood by a lunatic.") At one point Cheever produced a few well-thumbed family photographs from his wallet, and Litvinov remarked that Susan looked like a Russian girl ("he took it—as I intended it to be—as a compliment"), and when he gave her a somber publicity photo of himself, she said, "Mr. Cheever on his guard." "Always am," he replied.

With Breitburd in tow, as ever, Cheever and Litvinov were driven to Kornei Chukovsky's dacha in Peredelkino, a writers' settlement a few miles outside Moscow. The eighty-two-year-old Chukovsky had not only discovered Cheever for the Russians, but also written an admiring preface to Litvinov's translation of *The Enormous Radio*. The two men loved each other at once. Chukovsky said that Cheever looked just like his old friend H. G. Wells, with particular reference to a pen drawing he'd kept from the twenties. He also produced a number of other souvenirs—Oxford robes, an Indian headdress—and asked Cheever to add his name to the distinguished list of visitors in Chukovsky's guest book. "May I kiss you?" Cheever asked, saying goodbye, and Chukovsky said he supposed it was all right, since they'd never meet again.* Ten years later, Cheever told Raymond Carver that

---

*After his visit to Russia, Cheever often sent copies of *The New Yorker* to Litvinov, who shared them with her friend Chukovsky. Said the latter, "I'm getting conditioned

one of his fondest memories was falling asleep that evening with his head in Tanya's lap during the drive back to Moscow, and then waking just as the lights were coming on in the city ("note how this is the dream of a little boy sheltered by his mother," said Carver). Cheever was supposed to go to the Bolshoi that night with Breitburd, but the man wanted to write his report on the Peredelkino meeting, so he gave his ticket to Litvinov. Left alone for once, the two decided to skip the Bolshoi and spend the night walking around Moscow. As they passed the zoo—closed at that hour—Litvinov indicated a place in the fence where the stakes had been loosened, and Cheever excitedly insisted they squeeze inside. Litvinov was tempted, but then imagined the headline in *Pravda:* "American 'So-Called Writer' Caught Spying on Soviet Animals!" She told him that he would be "non-grataed" and sent home, while she would end up in the Gulag.

Cheever's friendship with Litvinov would continue—with occasional interruptions both personal and political—the rest of his life. "We all enjoy your letters tremendously and they are the only letters I have ever saved," he wrote her a few months after his return to the States.* Whenever his friends went to Russia, it pleased Cheever to put them in touch with her, so he could hear about their meeting afterward and vicariously partake of her company. The summer after Cheever's visit, for example, Art Spear and his wife went to Moscow "on some sort of International Amity Excursion," after which Spear and Litvinov exchanged affectionate letters for years. Spear returned with some stories written by Litvinov's English mother, Ivy, which Cheever passed along to Maxwell with the result that (1) a number were published in *The New Yorker*, and (2) Maxwell and Tanya also became lifelong friends. "We had a heartwarming reunion with the Maxwell's," she wrote Cheever in 1978, after she and her family had defected to England. "They took Vera [her daughter] and me to an Italian restaurant in South Kensington and we poured our monologues into the

---

to the ads, and quite enjoy looking at the girls I'll never kiss, the cars I'll never drive, the sweaters I'll never wear, the shoes which will never pinch my toes, the places I'll never visit . . ." The list went on, and ended with "the cemetery I'll never recline in." He died in 1969.

*This is true. Though Cheever corresponded with hundreds of people over the course of his life, the only surviving letters I found among his papers—kept in an old sewing box in his library—were a few letters from his children, various odds and ends, and perhaps fifty letters from Litvinov.

din." By then she and Cheever had grown apart in more than a geo-
graphical sense, though they both felt there was some inviolable aspect
of their friendship that transcended worldly differences: "I am sure
that when I die and you (many years later) die we will meet at once and
have a very stimulating eternity," Cheever wrote.

CHEEVER HAD TO DISPOSE of his publisher's rubles while in Russia,
and one day he told Litvinov he wanted to stop and buy a football.
"What do you want a football for?" she asked. "Well," he said, "I'll toss
the ball with the other John." The "other John" was Updike, who
arrived with his wife Mary in the middle of Cheever's month-long
visit. Cheever was nothing but eager for his American colleague's company, though his opinion of the man's work remained problematic; in
the privacy of his journal, at least, he found it hard to pay him an
unadulterated compliment. "Read Updike's new book with pleasure,"
he wrote of the collection *Pigeon Feathers* (1962), adding: "with mixed
feelings but always with pleasure; what we call pleasure." He continued
to disapprove of the way Updike "retard[ed] the movement" of his narrative with excessive detail, though at the same time he found the
details oddly compelling: "[H]is prose has that pace, that intensity that,
when we put down the book and step out of the house on to the road,
we have a heightened acuteness of feeling." Meanwhile the public
Cheever was a veritable fount of praise and good works in the younger
man's behalf: "I sincerely admire the brilliance of your equipment," he
wrote Updike earlier that spring, calling his own prose "so much
shredded wheat" in comparison. The year before, he'd nominated
Updike to the National Institute of Arts and Letters, and as a National
Book Award judge he'd been "instrumental" (his word) in pushing *The
Centaur* ahead of Pynchon's *V.*—though afterward, as ever, he was
bemused by his own generosity: "Sometime I like the thought of
[Updike] and just as often he seems to me an oversensitive changling
[sic] who allows himself to be photographed in arty poses."
    In any event, Cheever was at his ebullient best when Updike arrived
in Russia with his attractive wife. "He greeted us with glee," she
remembered, "as if all three of us were about to embark on an enormous adventure in a place as outlandish as the moon." Cheever, well
adapted by then, acted as a kind of ideal host and tour guide, telling
stories and jokes as the three of them were herded around schools and

catacombs and the like; what might have been a "glum" ordeal, said Updike, became "as gay as an April in Paris." Certainly "Big John" (Cheever) and "Little John" (Updike)—a distinction based on age rather than size—gave the impression of being "really chummy," as Litvinov put it: "John was proud of [Updike] like an uncle." And sometimes, when Cheever and the Updikes were alone together in their hotel rooms, they'd gossip and gripe about their Soviet minders (despite the bugs, into which they often made a point of speaking), or chat about their children and even their literary careers. Cheever cheerfully admitted that he was fed up with *The New Yorker*, and found it "a considerable relief " to be less dependent on its vagaries. "Cheever's confession made me sad and, yes, exultant," Updike later wrote: "one less competitor for that delicious glossy space . . ."

Even then Updike couldn't resist keeping his hand in, finding time "in one neo-czarist hotel room or another" to order his impressions into a few poems that Cheever described as "assinine" [sic] when they appeared in *The New Yorker* the following June. By then Cheever had decided that Updike was rivalrous, and had rearranged his Russian memories accordingly. "At the University of Leningrad"—he wrote a fellow writer—"[Updike] tried to upstage me by reciting some of his nonsense verse but I set fire to the contents of an ashtray and upset the water carafe." Lest one think this is so much lighthearted hyperbole, much the same thing appears in Cheever's journal, where he brooded over the way Updike "hogged the lecture platform" and even stepped in front of him when pictures were taken. Cheever also liked to describe, in letters, how he and Updike competed to see how many of their books they could dump on the Russians: "[Updike] then began distributing paper-back copies of the Centaur while I distributed hardcover copies of The Brigadier. The score was eight to six, my favor. . . . On the train up to Leningrad he tried to throw my books out of the window but his lovely wife Mary intervened. She not only saved the books; she read one. She had to hide it under her bedpillow and claim to be sick. She said he would kill her if he knew."

Cheever's ambivalence toward the gifted young man isn't all that puzzling. For one thing, he was intimidated by Updike's intellectual versatility, which he scorned or praised according to mood. "John reviews a French novel in his most graceful and erudite manner," Cheever noted in 1971 (when Updike was in good odor for the moment). "This would be beyond me and I do not understand all the words and have forgotten, if I ever knew, what is the Descartian man.

He writes with that authority and comprehension that makes it seem as if writing—literature—was the legitimate concern of a distinguished man." Which was well and good, of course, but when Updike was holding forth in such a "graceful and erudite manner" for the benefit of Russian audiences, it was perhaps an uncomfortable reminder that Cheever himself (as he'd blithely admit in less invidious circumstances) had "no formal education, no critical inclinations, no critical vocabulary and no long-range perspective of literature." Thus, if Updike "hogged the lecture platform," it was largely a matter of having more to say; also, the recent translation of *The Centaur* had made him a darling of Russian youth, though the courteous Updike was at pains to redress the imbalance as best he could: "At one of our joint appearances, I blush to remember, observing our audience's total ignorance of Cheever's remarkable work, I took it upon myself to stand up and describe it, fulsomely if not accurately, while my topic sat at my side in a dignified silence that retrospectively feels dour."

By the time Updike wrote these words, he'd read Cheever's shockingly uncharitable account of their trip in the latter's posthumous *Letters*, which includes that antic fantasy about the lovely Mary Updike hiding Cheever's book under her pillow to read on the train. It was true that Cheever was charmed by Updike's wife and vice versa, though it's unlikely this caused any friction between the Updikes; if anyone was envious it was Cheever, who already felt considerable chagrin over his own Mary's absence.* Nevertheless, Cheever's journal suggests some particle of truth to the train story: "While Mary [Updike] and I danced in Leningrad," he recalled in 1976, "she told me that [her husband] could not endure having a book of mine in his room . . ." Whatever Mary had actually said ("why should [Updike] forbid his wife to read my stories or even mention them," Cheever fretted at the time), no doubt her dancing partner laughed it off amid the relative amity that prevailed in Russia.† Mary Updike remembered how "bereft" she and her husband felt while saying goodbye to Cheever, who was so

---

*Cheever told Litvinov that his wife had declined to accompany him because of anti-Semitism in Russia—though of course it may have been for any number of reasons. Whatever the case, he felt very bitter about it: "Wasn't it *sleazy* of her not to come?" he said. Litvinov had never encountered the word "sleazy" before.

†When I asked the former Mary Updike (now Weatherall) about her alleged remarks, she was mystified and absolutely denied saying anything of the sort, even in jest: "John [Updike] *loved* Cheever's writing," she said. "We both read everything he wrote."

eager to resume their friendship that he called the couple ("unsober") as soon as they returned to the States. "He is unyielding, really inscrutable," Cheever wrote of Updike's phone manner. "Can it be that he dislikes me. How could such a thing come to pass! Chekoslovakia [sic] is worth a good two or three weeks, he says, talking like a travel agent." Cheever was devastated by the snub (as he saw it), and wondered over its import for months: "I cannot bring [Updike] into focus because I cannot believe that he would take such an instantaneous dislike to me. . . . He may be so intensely competitive that he finds my existence an exacerbation but I find this difficult, I find it impossible to imagine." The following summer Cheever and his family vacationed in Wellfleet, Massachusetts, and when he got the impression that Updike was reluctant to visit him there—though Updike did, in fact, visit him there—Cheever made up his mind for the time being: "I would go to considerable expense and inconvenience to avoid [Updike's] company," he wrote a friend that June. "I think his magnanimity specious and his work seems motivated by covetousness, exhibitionism and a stony heart."

TOWARD THE END of his Russian visit, Cheever still had a lot of rubles to spend, so one night on a train he bought Romanian champagne for all his fellow passengers. Afterward two men approached him and asked if he'd like to buy something really interesting—a genuine seventeenth-century icon (which hangs in Cheever's house to this day). Later, as he was secreting the sacred artifact in his suitcase along with his fur hats and football, Yevtushenko called at his hotel and said he had a present for Cheever. "No, no," said the poet, when Cheever indicated his already bulging suitcase, "this is nothing you take with you. This is something special." The two drove a while to a "sort of slum" outside Moscow, where Cheever was introduced to the artist Oleg Tselkov—in disgrace at the time—who produced a number of paintings for his inspection ("brilliant, progressive, and heretical," Cheever observed). "So!" said Yevtushenko at last. "He cannot show his painting. He cannot sell his painting. He cannot discuss his painting. My present to you is the invincibility of his painting."

Cheever left Russia the next day. "When the train from Leningrad crossed the Finnish border we all cheered, sang, and got drunk," he wrote. "It was like getting out of prison. I sat in the Amsterdam air-port with a gin and tonic and thought with longing of vast, slothful Mother Russia but had I been asked to return I would have fought with my life." Lonely and exhausted from the whole fraught adventure, Cheever still had one more stop to make in West Berlin, where he was supposed to give a reading at the Amerika Haus. Perhaps his greatest fan in the city was a forty-year-old writer named Paul Moor, who as a young man in Texas had been a devotee of *The New Yorker* and particu-larly John Cheever. Reading of the latter's arrival in the newspaper, Moor learned from the Amerika Haus that Cheever was staying at the Hilton, and promptly gave him a call. He (Moor) was a friend of the Styrons, he said, offering to put himself at Cheever's disposal for the duration of his stay. Cheever was delighted—all the more so when he discovered that Moor could quote long passages from his work, and seemed insatiably curious as to how that glorious work had come into being. "May I kiss you?" Cheever asked, with lingering Slavic brio, after a particularly enjoyable evening. Moor accepted the buss as inno-cent, since Cheever had lengthily discussed his passionate attachment to Hope Lange.

That last night in Berlin, Cheever invited Moor up to his room for a nightcap. "I've had some very pleasant homosexual experiences," he suavely declared, filling Moor's glass. Moor was "thunderstruck": it was true that he himself was gay, and he'd assumed that Cheever had figured as much, but . . . what about Hope Lange? ("As for Paul [Moor]," Cheever wrote Litvinov, "I think he was or may be a homo-sexual. . . . This would account for the funny shoes and the tight pants and I thought his voice a note or two too deep.") At any rate, Moor responded to this unexpected sally with a guarded nod—"I adored him as a writer, but not physically"—and the evening passed without fur-ther incident.

Moor kept in touch with a stream of letters, to which Cheever courteously replied, until Moor came to New York in June 1965 and the two met for lunch at the Algonquin. Saying goodbye on Forty-fourth Street ("He was on his way to *The New Yorker* office to do some-thing catty about John Updike," Moor recalled), Cheever suddenly gave the man a tight and definitively final embrace, after which the let-ters from Ossining dwindled to nothing. "I would like to live in a world in which there are no homosexuals," he wrote of Moor, "but I suppose Paradise is thronged with them."

· · ·

FOR MONTHS after his return from Russia, Cheever spoke of little else. He'd refined the whole experience into a nice comic routine, commencing with his arrival on that rainy night in Moscow (*cheep cheep cheep*) and proceeding amid the Georgian sheep, the songs, the drinking, the mistaken statue of Pavlov, and culminating in a "fifteen minute impersonation of Yevtushenko." He distributed fur hats among his friends, whose company he found more intolerable than ever. "There is no self-consciousness at all about the banality of the conversations," he wrote of a Westchester dinner party. "One goes on calmly for hours about the difficulty of getting a plumber; the difficulties of getting a boy into college; the expense of fertilizing the lawn." Cheever determined not to go to any more such parties if he could help it, because they did "severe damage to [his] spirits and [his] health." Staying home, then, and drinking in his yellow wing chair, he ruminated over all the emotional things he'd say about the Russians at the State Department debriefing: "They gave me no trouble. They gave me friendship and at least the illusion of love." What's more, he thought his rapport with all these affectionate people had changed quite a few minds about the United States, and surely all that was to the good. Indeed, this appears to be what he did say, more or less, and perhaps that's why the FBI made Cheever the subject of "internal security interest." In 1967, the agency intercepted a note from Cheever to Ryurikov of *Foreign Literature:* "I am not a political person and I have no informed opinions on Socialist Culture," he brashly asserted; "but I cannot let the occasion of your 50th anniversary pass without saying how vivid my memories of the greatness of your country and your people remain." Cheever sensed that he'd excited some sort of unsavory official notice ("My name is mud"), but he didn't much care. For a long time he continued to receive gushing letters from his Russian friends, and his own letters were cherished and often read aloud in public by Litvinov or Frieda Lurie (Updike's minder), who wrote him a few weeks after his return: "We all miss and love you inspite of the broad ocean between us."

Cheever needed all the love he could get—though it seemed, at first, that absence had made his wife's heart grow fonder. She and Federico had met him at the airport, and the three had stayed up late while Cheever told stories and handed out presents; better yet, Mary had "bounded into bed" with him and "declared her undying love." "All my anger is idle and a waste of power," he decided, but not for long. "[I]n a blaze of gin and self importance I announce at the [dinner] table that I will not be harried by . . . an English instructor," he wrote in December. All the old problems had briskly returned to the fore: Mary neglected him in favor of grading themes and whatnot, which in turn made him drink too much, and drink made him impotent, and impotence led to an all-purpose paranoia that his wife was less and less apt to pacify. If he wasn't satisfying his wife in bed, Cheever reasoned, then she must be satisfying herself elsewhere, and he applied this syllogism even to the most unlikely scenarios—the way (for instance) his old friend Spear behaved whenever he picked up Mary for choir practice: "A[rt] usually goes through the routine of being a young man taking a young woman away from an old coot. M[ary] usually swings her tail and giggles." Cheever put up with this unseemly charade for as long as he could decently stand it, then put his foot down in no uncertain terms: "I rail, I swear. . . . I say that when A[rt] comes I will beat him up, I will disfigure him. She goes to the telephone to warn him. I break the connection. . . . I roar, oh Christ, decide not to drink anymore, think bitterly that they will make a great couple; the educational junkheap and the Audubon Society of [which] he is president." Sober, of course, he felt the usual crushing remorse—toward Spear—and apologized. But as for his marriage, he figured it was a goner and considered getting a divorce:

> What other dignified course is left to me. I am treated like a wretch, fit to be cooked for a cuckolded, malodorous, supported by a suces fous [sic], comical, impotent, opinionated, uneducated, short-cocked and illbred. But waking at two and three I remember a love so pure and fresh, sighs and cries of pleasure . . . engorgements and revelations that I think it is this I should remember. To be practical I will always have M[ary]'s lengthy and mysterious depressions to cope with but I can hope that these will diminish.

Meanwhile his brother was becoming a hardship again. In the summer of 1963, that unsinkable man had pulled himself together and gotten a job as advertising manager of *Stores*, the publication of the National Retail Merchants Association. By then, however, he had borrowed so much money from the bank that his wages were confiscated to pay the debt, and soon he was drinking again and trying to sell subscriptions to *Life* over the telephone. This was so irrefutably hopeless that his wife, Iris—who'd been working as a clerk in a gift shop—decided to call it quits for good, and Fred began to go under for what appeared to be the last time. "I call Fred who makes no sense," his brother wrote. "Uds the seet smell of sugsess, he says. . . . I can only try to imagine the excruciating pain he suffers. I expect he can kill himself or come close to it and I will call this morning to see if he should be taken to a hospital."

That was August 1964. In mid-November—two weeks after John returned from Russia—Fred appeared at Cedar Lane looking sober, relatively fit, and rather chastened. He was going to AA three times a week, he said, and attending the Unitarian church on Sunday. More than ever he was unabashedly worshipful of his celebrated little brother, as if their family connection was the last source of self-esteem he had left. (After their meeting, he related to his daughter Sarah, among other things, that Updike and her uncle John "can do the twist beautifully, and they drew admiring crowds. The Russians just aren't built to do it.") When Fred remarked that he made ends meet with freelance work for the Famous Writers School, John replied that he'd been offered a chair at Harvard ("I'm not sure this is true," he wrote in his journal, "and if it were it would have been a terrible mistake on the part of the University"). At length Fred came to the point: "He describes his bookshop, his dream; old fashioned lamps, hooked rugs a rolltop desk, really a gem, he says. Why do I find this so embarrassing. Do I come from a family of born shopkeepers, people who dream of shelves, inventories, firesales." As if to reproach himself for unkind thoughts, John agreed to loan Fred five thousand dollars for the bookshop, and shortly thereafter they drew up papers at a lawyer's office, where Fred told jokes in a Jewish accent.

Within less than a year, his dream—the "eagle i" (lower case) bookstore in Westport—had come to an end, and he was "trying to establish a sales pattern" for a small FM radio station. As he explained to his children, he'd "put his whole heart and soul" into making a go of the "eagle i," but had to close the place when Uncle John refused to loan him any money. "F[red] telephones," John noted, roughly a month after the "eagle i" had expired. "Are you all right, he asks, are you sure you're all right? What he wants is six hundred dollars, bringing my loans for less than a year to eight thousand. When he was drunk he always used to ask: Are you all right, are you sure you're all right."

CHAPTER TWENTY-SIX

{ 1964–1965 }

CHEEVER AFFECTED TO BE INDIFFERENT to reviews, and liked to say that he made a point of leaving the country so he wouldn't have to bother with them: he'd been in Italy when *The Wapshot Chronicle* was published, and went again when the sequel came out seven years later. The truth was, of course, that Cheever scrutinized almost every word of every review from the *Times* to the *Salt Lake Tribune*, though he did keep up appearances by kiting off to Russia when his fifth collection, *The Brigadier and the Golf Widow*, was published that October. *"Where the hell are the reviews?"* he complained in Leningrad, as he had rather high hopes for the book, which included some of his best work ("The Swimmer," "The Ocean," and the title story).

The reviews were mostly positive, as usual, though some of them sounded a vaguely troubled note about the direction of Cheever's work. An anonymous reviewer for *Newsweek* remarked that his sensibility was becoming "so weird that it veers perilously close to Charles Addams," and the *Washington Post* worried about Cheever's increasing "pessimism," while conceding "the gloomy brilliance of his prophecy." Orville Prescott, in the daily *Times*, called Cheever "one of the most gifted, original and interesting of contemporary American writers of fiction," and considered all sixteen stories worthwhile—however: "Four seem to me less successful than the rest and these are all rather sinister fantasies." Prescott—a champion of virile realists à la Cozzens and Marquand ("our American Galsworthy")—was referring, of course, to such stories as "The Swimmer" and "The Ocean." One of the most presumptuous and damning assessments of Cheever's work as a whole was John Aldridge's long review in the *New York Herald Tribune Book Week*. Cheever, he declared, "is one of the most grievously underdiscussed important writers we have at the present time"—a claim that might have made Cheever smile, though the smile was liable to die horribly as he read on. Aldridge thought that Cheever's *Time* cover and National Book Award had actually precluded serious critical attention, for these honors were regarded (in serious circles) as "a kind of good housekeeping seal of middlebrow literary approval": "It was no accident that *Time* should have offered Cheever to the world as a kind of crew-cut Ivy-League Faulkner of the New York exurbs." Cheever's vacuous characters took refuge in "small, arbitrary" rebellions, or in pathetic, misguided nostalgia, or in daydreams "not of Walter Mitty-ish grandiosity, but of almost girlish modesty and poignance." The Walter Mitty reference was wont to remind Cheever of the time Irving Howe described him as a "toothless Thurber" in *Partisan Review*,* and never mind the "girlish" crack. As for the weirdness of Cheever's sensibility, Aldridge—like that *Newsweek* reviewer—also invoked Charles Addams: "Somehow the nightmare tonalities of his work come to seem after a while a little too coy and cloying, the postures of psychic torment a little too much like the smartly macabre decor of some Fifth Avenue shop window in which creepy mannequins stand around draped in the latest creation by Charles Addams." Evidently, though, Aldridge had not despaired of Cheever, as he closed by echoing Gertrude Stein's hectoring but hopeful advice to the young Hemingway: "Begin over again and concentrate. For he [Cheever] does not yet disturb us enough."

Cheever dismissed Aldridge as little better than a vandal, while privately agreeing with him somewhat. "I seem neither sane enough nor mad enough," he wrote in his journal shortly after the review appeared. He'd been looking over some old work and had found even the best of his stories "circumspect" and "small." The resolution of one, for example, "The Cure"—about a man who begins to go mad when his wife leaves him, until she returns and he feels fine again—was "superficial," a characteristic problem, though Cheever felt reluctant

---

*"At the [Academy] ceremony on Wednesday," Cheever wrote Maxwell in 1960, "Irving Howe, who once described me as a Toothless Thurber with a graying prose style, appeared to have very little hair, all of it grey and seemed . . . to have no teeth at all."

to go "any deeper into that storm."* For his new novel, however, he wanted to be disturbing in earnest—a task, he wrote Litvinov, that he approached "warily": "[I]t is like letting oneself into a labyrinth." A year before, he'd written what was perhaps the first incubatory note for a story that would become *Bullet Park:* "a man who looks in the windows of buildings all over the world trying to find an interior a yellow room where he will be happy." As Cheever continued to ponder this man (apparently mad to some degree), it occurred to him that such a character might serve to "introduce violence, in order to dramatize a moral dilemma, into a landscape, a way of life that might be characterized by its monotonous lack of violence." Even then, vaguely, Cheever liked the idea of an attempted "crucifixion" in the suburbs (let Aldridge call *that* "coy and cloying"): "I would like to write a gothic novel," he wrote, "without being caught in the act."

The better to gather these disparate thoughts, Cheever went to Yaddo in February 1965 and found himself sharing a bathroom with Maxwell's old protégé Harold Brodkey. Thirty-four at the time, Brodkey seemed already in decline. With Maxwell's help, he'd published his first *New Yorker* story, "State of Grace," in 1953—a year out of Harvard—and five years later his collection *First Love and Other Sorrows* had made him a minor literary celebrity; in the years since, however, he'd published only two more stories in the magazine, and (so he told Cheever) he'd resorted to "hacking trash" for a living. He'd also entered what he later called his "binary" sexual phase, a matter he elaborately impressed on Cheever: "B[rodkey] talks about sexual orgies (two) he has participated in, a position I have never heard of, and the homosexual community which he seems to know well. . . . He is young, one might say wayward and immature. So we dance, play psychic games, then ping pong and I go to bed feeling lonely, lonely, oh lonely." For a number of reasons, all disturbing, Brodkey reminded Cheever of Calvin Kentfield ("he is, as C[alvin] was, in the process of selfdestruction"), but when the beguiling young(ish) man "embraced" him in the "winter twilight," Cheever couldn't help putting reason aside for a while: "I think that I am in the throes once more of a hopeless love."

Fortunately the visit lasted only a few days, and Cheever soon came

---

*This entry is misdated as "1963" on page 191 of the published *Journals*, no doubt because the pages are jumbled in the original journal manuscript. Internal evidence suggests it was written around January 1965.

to his senses. A wistful letter from Brodkey left him feeling vaguely disgusted: "I want hearty and robust friendships; not men who write emotional letters to one another." Reflecting on the flirtation—and probably it was no more than that—Cheever decided the "book of the month club had something to do" with Brodkey's ardor. A bit later, he invited Brodkey to Cedar Lane, and amid that heartening domestic tableau he wondered how he could have ever taken such a man seriously: Brodkey, he noticed, had exchanged his "dismal beard" for a mustache, and adopted or refined an accent that was distinctly on the "faggoty side." This, he concluded, was the quintessential "mirror person"—the Freudian homosexual doomed to abide in the "barren country" of prenatal narcissism: "I think of Brodkey in St. Louis," Cheever mused, "falling in love with himself because there was no one else so intelligent handsome and rich in the neighborhood; and how bitter this marriage was." Every so often Cheever would cast back to those three or four days at Yaddo, and shudder over the way Brodkey had forever been fishing for compliments: Did his beard look all right? Had his tan begun to fade? And meanwhile, at *The New Yorker*'s offices, a young (and later celebrated) writer was startled one day when Brodkey accosted her to announce that Cheever was *gay*. "Oh, but he is!" Brodkey insisted, when the woman seemed skeptical. "I had an affair with him!"

AT THE BEGINNING of May, Cheever and his wife boarded the *Twentieth Century Limited* for a weeklong vacation in Chicago, where Cheever had agreed to serve as a visiting writer in Richard Stern's fiction class. He'd engaged a roomette on the swanky *Century* in the hope of "[tying] on a can," but when he climbed down to his wife's berth she determinedly feigned sleep, and her recalcitrance continued for most of the trip: "Mary complains about the smell of the hotel, the smell of the train, the smell of the world." Stern, too, was startled by Mary's sharpness toward Cheever—"I felt defensive for him," he said, and the feeling was mutual: "[Stern's] wife greets the guests but says nothing for the rest of the evening," Cheever observed in his journal. "[Y]ou realize that it was he who bathed the children and put them to bed; it was he who cooked the goulash. She has not spoken to him for a week." The two unhappy husbands enjoyed each other's company, at least, and Cheever also had a pleasant lunch with Bellow. The year before, he'd read *Herzog* and been rather comforted to find it a sub-par performance, or so he thought: "The fear that he was without parallel, that I should always be second or third best seems to have faded . . ." Thus he was able to relax even better in Bellow's company, enjoying the man's "erudite, bellicose and agile" mind without feeling the usual inferiority.

Perhaps his happiest encounter, though, was with a total stranger. "Mary flew back on Thursday and I took the Twentieth Century Friday night," he wrote Weaver, "carrying a lot of nice, serious books. . . . Well the engine took fire somewhere east of Gary and in the confusion I got horribly mixed up with a broad from Evanston who was drinking rusty nails. This went on until three when the conductor told us we couldn't play strippoker in the observation car." The "broad" in question was one Sherry (Mrs. Donald H.) Farquharson, who was taking the trip with a girlfriend to see a few shows in New York. They were sitting in the club car when (as Mrs. Farquharson recalled) Cheever came over and asked, "May I join you?" ("[I]t pleases me to make friends when I travel," Cheever once noted.) Before Cheever could even mention it himself, the women realized they'd seen this very face on the cover of *Time*, and a "delightful" evening ensued: the three had drinks and dinner, and later Cheever did in fact coax Sherry to the observation car and ply her with Rusty Nails; the vivacious matron was not, however, so far gone as to play strip poker with a new acquaintance, who in any case was a perfect gentleman throughout. Indeed, he called her in New York the next day and asked her to have lunch with him, but she had to decline—with regret that persisted for decades—because of a previous engagement.

Just over a week after his return, Cheever was awarded the William Dean Howells Medal from the Academy of Arts and Letters for the most distinguished novel of the last five years. He claimed to feel appalled at the honor ("Mother would have been indignant"), not only because of his Yankee humility, but also because he didn't have a high opinion of the novel in question and found the very concept of such an award ridiculous. Repeating his usual chestnut about literature not being "a competitive sport," Cheever added, "I don't think that you can divide American fiction into five-year periods." Perhaps an even more compelling reason for his distaste was an uncomfortable awareness of just how dubious the politicking had been this time—that is to say, even more dubious than usual. "I had lunch with Ralph Ellison and

asked him if he knew what sonofabitch had put me up for it," Cheever
wrote Helen Puner, a neighbor.

> He said angrily, that it was he and that it had been uphill work.
> Louis Kronenberger abstained. Everybody else wanted to give it to
> Saul except Glenway Wescott who had promised it to Katherine
> Anne. She wanted it. She's crazy about jewelry. The reason Ralph
> insisted that I get it was because when Ralph and Saul lived
> together in Tivoli Saul, stepping out onto his terrace one morning,
> slipped and fell into a pile of dogshit. He asked Ralph if he couldn't
> train his dog. . . . A bitter quarrel ensued. Saul's tongue is longer
> and sharper than Ralph's and Ralph evened things up by getting me
> the medal.

In all likelihood, Ellison's zealous support of *The Wapshot Scandal* over
Herzog had little to do with a quarrel about dogshit, but may well have
had plenty to do with the fact that Cheever had helped Ellison get into
the Century Club a few months before. Because of the racial issue, it
was apparently no easy task. In the summer of 1962, Cheever's old
friend Lib Collins had visited Cedar Lane with the Ellisons and Albert
Murray; she later distinctly remembered Cheever telling Ellison (in
effect), "I'm sorry, but they won't let you in, and that's all there is to it."
Eventually, however, Cheever managed to pull it off with the help of
Red Warren, to whom he wrote: "I am very fond of Ralph and would
not want him to suffer that unreasonable bitterness that seems to
overtake grown men when they are turned down by even so artero-
sclerotic an organization as ours."

On the day of the award ceremony, May 19, Cheever awoke feeling
"crushed" with malaise, and when Mary told him that she intended to
teach a class even though (as he saw it) it would make them late, there
was a nasty exchange: "Her voice goes up an octave and cracks," he
wrote in his journal while waiting for her to return. "It seems the voice
of a child; then the voice of some female mouse in an animated cartoon." He told Weaver that he "took some gin" to calm down ("cheap
bourbon" in his journal), and when he arrived at the auditorium, "The
secretary took one look at me and said: 'Every single year, someone has
to be carried out feet first.' " It was, in fact, a lively ceremony. Academy
President Lewis Mumford ("who seems to be losing his marbles,"
Cheever wrote) kicked things off by denouncing the Vietnam War as a

"moral outrage," whereupon artist Thomas Hart Benton stormed off the stage and later threatened to resign. Finally it was time to present the Howells Medal, and Ellison made an orotund speech about laughter in the face of the "chaos that we've made of our promise": "It is John Cheever's achievement to have made us aware not only of what our laughter is about, but of that tragic sense of reality, that graciousness before life's complexity which is its antidote." By comparison, Cheever's own remarks were almost aggressively modest, perhaps reflecting his considerable cynicism toward the proceedings. "Thank you very much, Ralph," he began.

> When *The Wapshot Scandal* was completed my first instinct was to commit suicide. I thought I might cure my melancholy if I destroyed the novel and I said as much to my wife. She said that it was, after all, my novel and I could do as I pleased but how could she explain to the children what it was that I had been doing for the last four years. Thus my concern for appearances accounted for the publication of the novel.

Mumford was far from alone in his outrage over Vietnam; already in 1965 a number of artists and intellectuals had pledged to boycott White House functions in protest. Cheever, however, was not among them, and so looked forward to meeting LBJ at a reception for Presidential Scholars in June. Susan was graduating from college a few days before, and that morning, as he prepared to leave for Providence, Cheever spotted a three-and-a-half-foot snapping turtle making its stately way across his lawn. Firing ten shotgun shells into its head, Cheever mused that the ancient reptile "seemed to possess the world much better than I—I with a shotgun, my hands shaking from a cocktail party." ("The gun blasts really shattered the usual serenity of that suburban milieu," Andrew Ziegler recalled.) As it happened, Cheever's fellow *New Yorker* writer S. J. Perelman was getting an honorary degree at the Brown commencement, and later the two met for drinks and learned they were both attending the president's reception. They decided to "get stoned" at the Hilton and then walk over to the White House together and heckle John Updike, who was scheduled to give a reading. Cheever's resentment toward his younger colleague had only deepened. In Chicago he'd given Stern the impression that Updike was a kind of "pet hate," and a week or so before the White House affair he'd written in his journal, "The arrogance of Updike goes back to the fact that he does not consider me a peer." He did, however, consider *Salinger* a peer, or so Cheever had bitterly concluded.

"The Updikes were [at the White House] and I did everything short of kicking him in the trousers," he wrote Litvinov afterward. The evening had begun with a buffet supper on the lawn, where Cheever had mingled with fellow luminaries such as John Glenn, Stan Musial, Marianne Moore, and John O'Hara, who joined Cheever (said he) in "banging folding chairs together" when Updike got up to speak. Years later Updike was again mortified, retrospectively, when he discovered Perelman's account (in a letter to Ogden Nash) of what followed: "[Updike] read extracts from three works of his to the assembled scholars, which I couldn't personally hear as I was overtaken by the characteristic nausea that attacks me when this youth performs on the printed page. But Cheever brought me tidings that all three extracts dealt with masturbation, a favorite theme of Updike's. When I asked Cheever whether Lady Bird was present, he informed me that she was seated smack in the middle of the first row. What are we coming to?" In his own correspondence, Cheever claimed to have remarked to President and Mrs. Johnson that Updike kept autographed copies of *The Centaur* in his underwear, and in his journal he wrote: "I am high and a little drunk and am rude, I think, to John. The result of this is that I like him better than I did. He reads three descriptive passages and I find them very bad." Reflecting on these matters, Updike later wrote that only *one* of the three extracts he'd read that evening was (obliquely) about masturbation, and as for the shock of "finding [him]self discussed with such gleeful malice" by two of his greatest idols—it was "chastening, perhaps edifyingly so": "In fact, I know now, the literary scene is a kind of Medusa's raft, small and sinking, and one's instinct when a newcomer tries to clamber aboard is to stamp on his fingers."

Later that summer, the Updikes came to Wellfleet and lunched with Cheever, who'd calmed down considerably after his cathartic rudeness at the White House: "I think that we will never be friends because I think we both dread the sort of self-consciousness involved but we are for this day at least amiable companions." And then, as in Russia, the presence of Updike's wife helped sweeten Cheever's mood: "Having missed the size of her breasts in Moscow . . . I am curious and pleased to see, in a bathing suit, that they are splendid."

. . . .

By August, Cheever's *cafard* had become so overwhelming that he feared losing his mind. For years he'd routinely taken the tranquilizer Miltown and now worried that he might become hooked; besides, the present emergency seemed to call for something stronger—something that might even discourage him from drinking, much less popping Miltown. His regular doctor, Ray Mutter, prescribed a "massive tranquilizer" that left Cheever "as collected and stagnant as the water under an old millwheel." Indeed, he was so collected that he felt "rather glum," yearning for his usual tendency to woolgather and take the world lightly, at least when drunk. Thus, after a week or so, he reported that he'd "kicked the pill" and resumed drinking ("jibbering slightly").

The coming of autumn got him down: Susan and Ben would be leaving, Federico would be in school most of the day, and Mary would resume teaching. The last was an exacerbation that his marriage could ill afford at the moment, especially in the absence of buffering children. For a long time Mary had tended to retire (with a "shuddering sigh") to the farthest side of their bed, and now Cheever spent most nights in a separate room at the top of the house. Mary claimed this was simply a matter of practical necessity ("he used to scratch me with his toenails; also he was a restless sleeper, and he snored"), but Cheever took it hard: "I think pissily in bed that since we sleep separately, as we do, this fact should be published and not concealed under a bedspread. I think I will tell people that I am forced to sleep alone."* Not for the first time, he considered divorce—but again he couldn't quite bring it off. Why should *he* go, after all, when he'd just spent ten thousand dollars repairing the front porch? "And to tell the truth I am, alone, utterly incompetent. I step into a bar where there are some whores and my cock seems to strike an affirmative attitude of limpness. Nothing doing, it says. . . . It seems to be a homeloving cock, attached to simple food, open fires and licit ejaculations." Two out of three, however, did not a full marriage make, and Cheever was determined to regain his conjugal rights. "The battle rages on," he recorded that September. "Is it that you detest me, I ask, or that you detest men? I don't

***

*This he did. "He slept upstairs in a tiny room, like a boarder," Sara Spencer (a.k.a. Mrs. Zagreb) deploringly recalled.

detest men, she laughs. I conclude that she is ghastly, then wicked, then evil." Still mulling over the breadth of her turpitude, he saw, or thought he saw, Mary and Essie Lee (who'd just given Mary "a present of some trousers," no less) hugging in a manner that struck him as decidedly peculiar: "Suddenly I conclude that she is a lesbian. This would explain the rebuffs I'm given, the moodiness and melancholy, it would explain everything." Perhaps, but looking back he couldn't find much in the way of hard evidence—and then, whatever her proclivities, and however much he swore and swore to divorce her, the fact was that he felt "terrified" (when sober) that she'd end up leaving *him*. "People named John and Mary never divorce," he wrote, resignedly, as autumn got under way. "For better or for worser, in madness and in sameness, they seem bound together for eternity by their rudimentary nomenclature. They may loathe and despise one another, quarrel, weep, and commit mayhem, but they are not free to divorce."

Happily there was always the refuge of art, and so Cheever turned to writing a rabidly misogynistic satire titled "The Geometry of Love," about a mild-mannered "freelance engineer" named Mallory who endeavors to understand his wife's cruelty through Euclidean theorems, but finally sickens and dies. It was the first story Cheever had finished in over a year, and at first he rather liked it. Certainly the opening is among his most memorable: "It was one of those rainy late afternoons when the toy department of Woolworth's on Fifth Avenue is full of women who appear to have been taken in adultery and who are now shopping for a present to carry home to their youngest child." The "imposture" of adultery among the housewives of Remsen Park, in the story, was somewhat inspired by Cheever's recent suspicions over his wife's constant, wistful sighing, as well as the trouble she took with her appearance whenever she went shopping in town: "She has all the airs and graces of someone involved in a tragic love." As for the comic viciousness of Mallory's wife as he lies dying in the hospital ("Nobody seems to miss you"), this reflected an earnest concern on the author's part that he might get sick, and then what? "I do not expect M[ary] to have the graces of a nurse," he wrote, "I only expect her to sit for a little while at the foot of my bed, in a kindly way but this I think I won't have." These elements of the story, however mean-spirited, are often funny and effective, but the surrealism—Mallory's magical use of geometry (Gary, Indiana, vanishes as a result of his efforts)—is vague and unconvincing, and no wonder: Cheever's knowledge of Euclid was pretty much limited to one year of plane geometry at Quincy High, for which he'd earned a D.

He began to have misgivings as soon as he submitted the story, and for the right reasons: namely, he realized that it had been "motivated by unreasonable hatefulness" and its garish surrealism was such that he might be "declared mad." He wasn't far wrong. In recent years, Cheever's fondness for the "implausible" had caused increasing dismay at *The New Yorker*, and this time they "threw in the sponge," as Maxwell put it: "[Cheever] was the first person I ever saw try to do this and I just stood there with my mouth open. He tried things that people felt weren't possible in fiction. It turned out that anything was possible in fiction." By the time Barthelme and Barth and Coover and other post-realists had become (briefly) dominant figures on the scene, Maxwell realized that he'd underestimated stories such as "Justina" and "The Swimmer"—the latter of which was not only stuck "behind the cartoons," as Cheever would have it, but behind an Updike story too. ("This seems to me unintelligent and perhaps mean, but then one encounters much of both.") Then *and* later, however, Maxwell viewed "The Geometry of Love" as positive proof that Cheever was "losing his powers" because of alcohol. Indeed, the man was so troubled that he took it upon himself to stop in Ossining and reject the story in person. "I was drinking gin and romping with the dogs," Cheever wrote a friend. "[Bill] looked at me sadly, patted me gently, said that the story was a ghastly failure and implied that I had lost my marbles." Legend has it that Cheever became furious, but that would appear to be an exaggeration*: "I could not, with a skinful and surrounded by so many loving animals, take him seriously and I reminded him, cruelly, of all the other stories they had rejected and of all the editorial crap I've put up with over the years." Afterward, though, Cheever wondered whether he'd been "needlessly harsh"—if not actually "furious"—while

---

*Maxwell's friend Shirley Hazzard said of the incident, "At its time [it was] quite a famous story of Cheever being uncontrollably angry," and Maxwell's *Times* obituary also gives a version of the story (attributed to Brendan Gill), characterizing Cheever as "furious" and Maxwell as "courtly." But one may recall that Maxwell himself said "the only time" Cheever ever really showed anger toward him was during the "Brigadier" episode in 1961, and Cheever's journal bears this out: "Spears come and suddenly Bill whom I have not seen for months. He does not like my Euclid story and *I am not disturbed* [my italics] as I think I am meant to be. I am a little drunk. I remind him of the stories he has turned down, the editorial foolishness that I have tolerated, etc."

suspecting, too, that Maxwell was right. Nevertheless, he decided to give the story to Candida Donadio, who promptly sold it to *The Saturday Evening Post* for three thousand dollars. "This cheered me."

For nearly two decades, Maxwell's rejections had often been emotional and financial calamities for Cheever, but never again—and so he felt "cheered," and cheerfully he indulged in a kind of impudence that had been hitherto absent in their friendship: "I look forward to having the book," he wrote of Maxwell's 1966 collection, *The Old Man at the Railroad Crossing and Other Tales*, "and I am determined to write you a letter to explain that while I liked some of the pieces and was unenthusiastic about some this plainly has nothing to do with their merit." This mocked, lightly, one of Maxwell's typical gambits, in which the editor professed, with delicate modesty, that a given work of Cheever's was (but only in his opinion) a failure. As for their less and less frequent personal meetings, Cheever tried to be sociable—he liked to make things go—but usually found it heavy sledding: Maxwell seemed more solemn than ever, and sometimes even pointedly unfriendly; if Cheever didn't labor to carry the conversation, a "massive silence" had a way of descending. "He said that he loves me," Cheever wrote, shortly after the "Geometry" rejection, "and I have often said that he mistook power for love and the fact that he is now powerless may explain the chill." In years to come, however, there would be many times when he missed Maxwell's insight, discretion, and generosity—and yes, even his old "power," since it gave a diffident man the license to speak frankly, and after all (Cheever conceded) there wasn't "anyone better" as a critic.

"What disturbs me," Maxwell said after Cheever's death, "is not that we stopped talking but that we kept on talking and never said what we thought. I never spoke out." Apart from aesthetic differences, Cheever's fame after the *Time* cover had made him a different and rather distasteful man—at least to Maxwell, to whom he couldn't resist holding forth about his flirtation with Hope Lange and so forth. "B[ill] calls to say that Eddie [Newhouse] had a heart attack in a taxi cab," Cheever noted in August 1967.

> He has just returned from visiting him in the hospital. . . . I think I will not go to see him because I do not like to admit that such a thing could happen to a friend and perhaps to me. I tell B[ill] that I have just returned from a week in Naples with Sophia Loren. I am

not quite sure of his reaction. It could be anger. I remember his saying that my life was charmed and I remember his writing with anger and bitterness about people who consider their lives to be charmed. What fools they are!

It could be anger. Perhaps, but to some extent Maxwell blamed himself: "I didn't say, 'For Christ's sake, John, will you stop talking about actors?'—or anything that would have been decent to have said."

IN LATE DECEMBER 1965, Cheever was invited back to Chicago, with Ellison and Norman Mailer, to address the annual meeting of the Modern Language Association; the putative topic was "the relationship of the novelist to the country's power structures." Cheever, however, saw it as an opportunity to air (entertainingly, he hoped) certain qualms he had about Mailer and others. He'd been "pleased and excited" by *The Naked and the Dead*, whose ambition had left him feeling dejected over "[his] own confined talents"; but Mailer's most recent novel, *An American Dream*—about Stephen Rojack's lurid quest for sensation in the face of a deadening society—struck Cheever as "repetitious and fetid": "In describing intercourse in detail [Mailer] is limited by the fact that only three orifices are involved and so is forced into repeating himself." If American writers (as Mailer, Roth, and others suggested) were obliged to keep pace with the outrageous unreality of current events—Vietnam, race riots, rampant pornography—then it wouldn't be long, thought Cheever, before the more delicate, abiding pleasures of literature became obsolete.

Cheever had chatted with Mailer at an Academy gathering in 1960, and though the exchange was friendly enough, Cheever thought he detected a fellow "sexual impostor" in Mailer's "great affectation of bellicosity": "I think I see a man, a touching one, in the throes of confused sexual longings, and forced into a painful pose, a painful imposture." Affected or not, such a bellicose man would not be ridiculed with impunity, and before the MLA meeting Cheever wrote friends that he'd "trimmed [his] weight to 138 lbs." in order to "tangle with Mailer." When the day arrived, however, he began to have second thoughts ("Will I be able to deliver my speech? Will gin help?"), and was so late for a pre-speech luncheon that his host, Robert Lucid, phoned Mary Cheever in Ossining: "Well, you've got to find him!" she said, alarmed at the possibilities. Fortunately Cheever arrived a few minutes later, dressed for battle in a tailored suit and immaculate pearl-gray Brooks Brothers hat, which (said Lucid) "he kept glancing at during lunch to be sure it hadn't disappeared."

The session was the most crowded in recent memory: some two thousand scholars packed a room at the Palmer House, while others listened outside on the PA system. Ellison got things started with a pompous, leaden address that "seemed to puzzle the audience," as Richard Stern wrote in *The New York Review of Books*, but Cheever's speech—"The Parable of the Diligent Novelist"—left everybody (but Mailer) "ablaze with pleasure." Cheever told of a man who quits the seminary to become a writer, until one day ("when he was busily trying to describe the sound of a winter rain") he glances at the *Times* and realizes that, given the violence of his age, such an occupation is "contemptible"; thus he becomes a war correspondent in Saigon. When this begins to pall, he returns to New York and writes a pornographic novel titled *Manhattan Beach Boy*, but it doesn't seem convincing enough: "He saw that the sexual candor of men like Miller, Updike, Mailer and Roth was not a question of their raw material but of their mastery of the subject." Therefore he embarks on a spree of buggery and exhibitionism, and in the course of "confronting those barriers of consciousness that should challenge a writer" he also turns to alcohol and drugs: "His writing, while he is drugged, seems to him stupendous but when he reads it over during his few sober moments he realizes it is worthless." Ultimately, he becomes a spy and is run over by a taxi in Moscow: "Writing a novel," he gasps, dying, "becomes more difficult each day."

Mailer was "pissed": "In those days I took myself very seriously," he recalled, "and was indeed embattled." He regarded Cheever as a lightweight—"darling of *The New Yorker, Time* cover boy, that sort of thing"—a lapdog of the establishment, in short, which was constantly sniping at Mailer back then. Clutching the microphone and glaring at Cheever (who gazed benignantly back), Mailer delivered "a corrosive, brilliant, hit-and-run analysis of the failure of American novelists to keep up with a whirling country," as Stern described it. "There has been a war at the center of American letters for a long time," Mailer declared. This began as a "class war" between realists like Dreiser who attempted to produce novels "which would ignite a nation's consciousness of itself," and genteel entertainers who appealed to "an uppermiddleclass [looking] for a development of its taste. . . . That demand is still being made by a magazine called *The New Yorker*." In the end, said Mailer, both impulses had "failed," and literature was now being superseded by movies and television.

That, anyway, was the gist of it, and when it was over the academics "thundered applause" (Stern). "I am impressed by Mailer's delivery," Cheever wrote, "but in retrospect most of what he has to say doesn't parse." Mailer glared at him a bit more, but finally they made amends and retired en masse to the Playboy Mansion, where they sat chatting in the Grotto Bar while swimmers fluttered past a glass wall; occasionally, said Cheever, "young women wearing nothing but artificial eyelashes" would wander into the bar "doing cross-word puzzles," then glance at the middle-aged literati sitting there, and withdraw.

After Cheever's death, Mailer finally got around to reading his work and felt "a great sense of woe": "Why didn't I know that man?" At the time Cheever sensed Mailer didn't like him much, but decided to like Mailer all the same—especially when Mary attacked Mailer "as the sort of common brute whose only use for women is to get them on their backs": "It is the old plaint of the feminist and I think with terror that my love is turning into one of those tweedy women with strained faces who teach freshman English at fourth-rate colleges," Cheever reflected, but was soon cheered by a visit from his fun-loving neighbor Sara. "Mrs. Zagreb shows up on her way to a party, decked with sparklers and a ruby as big as a fig. She is, I announce, the sort of a woman who doesn't consider lying down for a man to be a chore. I give her a drink and flirt."

CHAPTER TWENTY-SEVEN

{ *1966* }

THE EXCITEMENT OF CHICAGO faded, winter deepened, and Cheever went back to being depressed. He felt like a "prisoner" in his own unhappy home, and longed to escape more often, but his *cafard* was such that the local train had become "a kind of gethsemane." Somewhat confined, then, to the pleasures of Ossining, he lunched with Art Spear and the like, until Spear dubbed their weekly gatherings the Friday Club. The other members were also gentlemen who didn't keep regular hours. Spear was "Founder," Cheever was "Membership," the folksinger Tom Glazer was "Treasurer" (good at figuring tips), and the witty alcoholic Alwyn Lee was "Entertainment"; later, when Lee moved to Italy (and presently died), he was replaced by John Dirks, a cartoonist and sculptor. Various others came and went over the years. "What all the Friday Club gang had in common," said Federico, "was the belief that they were artists exiled to Ossining. Spear was the only exception: he was solid in ways the rest of them were not." Cheever wasn't even the most famous of the group, arguably, as Glazer had become something of a national phenomenon with his 1963 novelty hit, "On Top of Spaghetti," sung (with a chorus of endearing children) to the tune of "On Top of Old Smoky." As for John Dirks, he was the son of Rudolph, creator of *The Katzenjammer Kids*, which later became *The Captain and the Kids* and was taken over—grudgingly—by John, who was foremost a sculptor of metal fountains.

Around noon, the group met for drinks at one of their houses, where wives were allowed to serve hors d'oeuvres as long as they vanished afterward. The men ate at various restaurants in the area, though perhaps their favorite was a raffish Italian place called Gino's ("The Oldest Seafood House in Croton"), where a bantering waitress named Pam became the "Ladies Auxiliary." In a *Times* piece about the Friday Club published a few days after Cheever's death, Mary Dirks was quoted as saying that the men were "electrifying conversationalists, full of jokes and wild laughter." Cheever would not have agreed. He liked to hear Alwyn Lee hold forth, but if others assayed witticisms or would-be aperçus, Cheever was liable to snort or mumble some rejoinder which, if audible, tended to sting. As he wrote about Glazer in his journal (which served as a veritable ledger of *esprit de l'escalier* insults vis-à-vis the Friday Club), "I am the one who tells the jokes. He is meant to listen." Indeed, it was Glazer who rankled the most. In his freewheeling, folksinging youth, he'd drifted (like Cheever) from one flophouse to the next, and Cheever thought he remained redolent of such dwellings. That Glazer seemed to fancy himself an intellectual was perhaps the most galling part, especially after his "On Top of Spaghetti" success; Glazer himself was inclined to belittle the tune, and liked to focus instead on his more serious efforts in the tradition of Leadbelly and Burl Ives, as well as his work as an archivist ("but we all know," Cheever noted, "that his principle [sic] source of income is singing commercials").

John Dirks also came in for a certain amount of subtle abuse. With Lee's departure, Cheever insisted on referring to his replacement as the new "Entertainment," even though Dirks rarely said a word, funny or otherwise. "[H]is comic strip and his fountains bore me," wrote Cheever, who thought Dirks's "provincialism" was matched only by that of his spouse. Mary Dirks was a Radcliffe alumna who taught English and theater at Briarcliff, which she satirized in a novel titled (in homage, perhaps, to her friend Cheever) *The Bagleigh Chronicle*. As a playwright and an actress, she also participated in a number of productions given by the Beechwood Players, a community-theater group based in Scarborough.* Cheever regarded her as the sort of shrill, pitiful dilettante who assuages her frustration, in part, by "french kiss[ing] in pantries," though at other times he found her "pleasant and intelligent" and properly rebuked himself for making such "unkind and unnecessary" remarks, if only in his journal.

---

*Model for the "Laurel Players" in Yates's *Revolutionary Road*—the company whose catastrophically awful production of *The Petrified Forest* leads to April Wheeler's decline and eventual suicide.

In those days he mostly kept his malice *in camera*, or limited to the odd elliptical mumble, largely in deference to his old friend Spear: Cheever would have liked to emulate the man's decency, his enviable solidity, or in any case to be somewhat worthy of it. After lunch the two would take their dogs for a walk to the dam, then pass the afternoon playing backgammon, while Spear canvassed his friend's opinion about whatever old family document he was studying at the moment. Cheever always obliged in whatever way he could: "John called early this AM to say come over at 11 and talk about the 19th century letters which I had asked him to look at," Spear wrote Litvinov. "He, as you would know he would, read through the whole dull manuscript and indicated one third to discard." ("Art talks about editing his great-grandfather's journal; has talked about this for ten years. I say yes and no, concealing my impatience with politeness and wondering does he do the same for me.") Anyway it was something to talk about, other than dogs and neighbors and church. And certainly Cheever appreciated such a "fine friendship . . . without a trace of jeopardy," though it would never occur to him to mention anything truly personal, much less tormenting, which at best would have only puzzled the wholesome Spear. "[John] is in good shape," the man cheerfully reported as late as 1974, when Cheever was entering the last stages of suicidal alcoholism.

No matter what his condition, though, Cheever generally managed the drive to Yaddo every September for the board meeting, and during his visit in 1962 he'd met a twenty-nine-year-old poet named Raphael Rudnik to whom he took a shine ("I think that he will introduce me to a younger generation"). Rudnik, for his part, never forgot his first encounter with Cheever: "I was dozing in a chair by the pool, and saw this little man walk up. I heard him reading a book—an extraordinary book. But when I opened my eyes there was no book, he was just talking!" That night or the next, Rudnik gave a reading of his poetry and received a cherished compliment from Cheever, who said he felt that "everything was all right with the language" after hearing Rudnik's work—and what's more, he meant it. Cheever was then having a bad time with *The Wapshot Scandal*, and wrote in his journal that Rudnik's poetry had reminded him of "how [he] would like to write." The friendship was sealed when Cheever discovered the young man had a "good wing" to boot, and so invited him to Cedar Lane for Thanksgiving and Christmas dinner that year—and almost every year thereafter. "That house was the great good place for me," said Rudnik. "John was a delightful person. I would see darker things, but [they] didn't denigrate the fact that this was a joyous occasion for everyone."

The next year at Yaddo, Cheever met another young poet, Natalie Robins. "I don't know why he liked me," said Robins, who was a little startled when Cheever got in touch after Yaddo, inviting her to come for Thanksgiving and bring her boyfriend, Christopher Lehmann-Haupt. Along with Rudnik, the couple became a fixture at holiday meals for many years—though the tradition got off to a shaky start, since that inaugural Thanksgiving was less than a week after JFK's assassination. Cheever, rather gloomy at first, said he'd been "glued to the television," but his mood lightened as he watched the young people play touch football in the post-prandial twilight ("it was something he liked people to do," said Lehmann-Haupt, "a memory of what people *ought* to do on an occasion like that"). "I have an anxious seizure on Thanksgiving morning," Cheever wrote afterward, "and during the next twelve hours I drink nearly a fifth of whiskey. This is dangerous, odious and obscene. I barely see Raphael who leaves empty beer cans all over the place. Natalie wears a purple dress and her boyfriend is an attractive young man with a vaguely familiar look, that sense of kinship. . . . I am proud of my wife, my sons, my daughter, my house and this holiday, sometimes so difficult, passes with pleasure."

Two years later, the Cheevers went to Christopher and Natalie's wedding at the Algonquin, and that December (1965) Lehmann-Haupt published one of his first pieces in the *New York Times*, reviewing a new edition of *The Man Who Loved Children*, by Christina Stead. At the subsequent Christmas dinner on Cedar Lane, the young man asked Cheever what he'd thought of the review. The latter was "polite but definite": "You failed to catch the spirit of the book," he said. Lehmann-Haupt felt "soundly rebuked," but decided not to take it amiss—especially in view of Cheever's touching devotion to Natalie. Every year the two would sit in front of the fireplace, hugging and holding hands, at perfect ease with each other. "I felt his need to hold on to me," she remembered, "as if it grounded or anchored him."

Mary Cheever was also warm and motherly, and it occurred to the couple that they'd been adopted as "surrogate children." As such, it struck them as odd that they "never saw" Cheever show any affection toward his own children, for all his blatant doting on Natalie; the contrast was so uncomfortable that Ben once said something bitter to Lehmann-Haupt, later explaining that his father acted as if he loved

Christopher and Natalie more than him. And indeed the couple had to wonder: Was Cheever's restraint some sort of Wasp thing? Was he warmer to Natalie because she was Jewish? If so, it soon became clear that Jewishness per se was no guarantee of his favor. One Thanksgiving he asked Natalie to bring her mother, a middle-class widow from New Jersey "whose idea of good fiction was Danielle Steel": "She was totally bewildered by the Cheevers, who didn't accommodate her at all," Lehmann-Haupt recalled. "In the car going home she burst into tears. She couldn't understand their attitude. They were mean to her, both Mary and John—making sarcastic remarks. It was the only time we can remember them being mean." ("Natalie's mother comes," Cheever wrote. "She is the sort of woman who speaks in clichés, asks the price of everything. What a charming setting she says of our diningroom. That highboy was a nice purchase.")

Despite the (mostly) good times, the couple now wonder whether their friendship was ever anything more than "superficial." It was true Cheever played the role of "literary father" to Natalie—but then Lillian Hellman had been a literary mother of sorts: "She'd always ask me for pictures of my children," said Robins, "but none turned up among her effects after her death." Rudnik, too, had reason to wonder about the man he regarded as a revered mentor. "Rafael [sic] calls from a bar," Cheever noted in 1966. "I guess he is drunk or drinking. I am troubled to think that what appeared to be a simple friendship is becoming unsimple." Apart from whatever transpired at their holiday meetings on Cedar Lane (that "great good place" for Rudnik), Cheever realized he knew "very little" about the poet and was more or less content to keep it that way.

When he wasn't cultivating the young and gifted at Yaddo, or enduring another lunch with the Friday Club, or meeting (more and more rarely) some literary acquaintance at the Century, Cheever was alone, except for a small son and a wife who often wasn't speaking to him. During "seizures" of loneliness in the past, Cheever would occasionally ride the train and chat "anxiously with strangers," but he didn't like the train anymore; there was also Mrs. Zagreb, but that only worked in moderate doses. Desperate for almost any company at all, he'd sometimes respond to letters and calls from random admirers with invitations to visit.* As he

---

*He was easily reached by telephone, as his number was always listed—and is, for that matter, listed as of this writing, twenty-five years after his death.

was reminded again and again, however, people who presume to make friends with their favorite authors tend to be a little on the eccentric side. "An admirer arrives on Saturday," Cheever wrote in his journal. "He has a bad facial tic and has been confined to Bellevue and Hillsdale. He rants, shouts, attacks President Kennedy and has some nice things to say about Hitler. I tell him to calm down and he does. Why, I wonder, should my admirers always be mad."

In 1965, Cheever received a letter from Frederick Exley of Watertown, New York, who'd been moved to get in touch with him after hearing Bellow say on Montreal TV that Cheever was his favorite writer. Exley was a fan of both men. "A man named Exley wrote to say that he liked the stories," Cheever subsequently related to Weaver. "I thanked him briefly. He then called collect from Miami and asked me to post five hundred dollars bail. He had just smashed up a saloon and knew I would understand." Exley did, in fact, have a long history of alcoholism and mental illness, though his assumption that Cheever would meet his bail wasn't nearly as bizarre as Cheever implied. First of all, the bail was only *two* hundred (duly noted in Cheever's journal), and moreover Cheever had *not* replied "briefly" to Exley's letter(s), but rather at lavish and witty length, since Exley was one of his few interesting correspondents at the time. It was Exley to whom he wrote those scurrilous Updike indictments, as well as some of his most inspired set pieces: "Coming in late last night I opened the ice-box and grabbed a piece of cold meat, swallowing a false tooth which included a plastic backside and two sharp hooks." The tale went on, serial fashion, in Cheever's next letter, wherein he described a visit to the dentist, who informed him with great dismay that the tooth couldn't be passed "without medical assistance." And so the punch line: "It is true that when I fart these days it sounds like a police whistle but I suffer little pain and it's very easy for me to get cabs."* After several letters, Cheever figured that Exley was ready for a visit to Cedar Lane, and was disappointed when the disturbed young man stood him up; concluding that Exley had been offended by the "cursory" nature of his most recent letter, Cheever hastened to explain: "If my note to you seemed cursory it was meant to be since your last letter contained so many

---

*In the published *Letters*, Ben Cheever explained that the false tooth was actually lost in a swimming pool: "There was in any case no significant alteration in the tone or volume of my father's farts."

provocations and snappers that if I'd risen to them all it would have taken me a day to reply. I meant to be cursory but not unfriendly." Three years later Exley would stun almost every soul in Watertown by producing his quasi-fictional masterpiece, *A Fan's Notes*, but meanwhile he was just another drunken lunatic with delusions of grandeur, and Cheever happily kept writing him all the same.

Cheever particularly enjoyed hearing from students: it meant his standing in the academy might go up a tick or two in the near future, and also such people were a little less likely to be certifiable. In 1966, an undergraduate at Georgetown, George McLoone (hoping "to obtain a direct quote" for a paper he was writing), queried Cheever about the importance of *environment* in his work—and lo, the famous author replied: "Environment plays, I hope, a very superficial part in my stories. . . . When I exploit an environment—Rome or St. Botolphs—it is for the purpose of illuminating people." Thus began a correspondence that spanned almost eight years and several personal meetings. When McLoone followed up with a phone call, Cheever urged him to catch a train to Ossining and bring a friend if he liked. McLoone did so, and when Cheever noticed that the friend—one Tommy Sullivan from the Bronx, who was at Georgetown on a baseball scholarship—wasn't keen on discussing literature, he invited the boys to go for a swim at Sara Spencer's house (she waved at them from inside). "The water was icy cold," McLoone remembered, "but it didn't seem to faze [Cheever]. Tommy was an athlete, and even he had trouble with the temperature." McLoone's four or five subsequent visits were made alone: Cheever always picked him up at the train station and drove him back roughly two hours later, and was never less than convivial—"a witty, impish guy with a twinkle in his eye"—and once he seemed downright ecstatic: "Mary!" he called down from the library. "George is doing his master's thesis on me!"

By far his most reliable attachment (and in many ways his most profound) was with his black Labrador, Cassie. "The old dog; my love," he wrote in his journal.

> That she always got to her feet when I entered the room. That she enjoyed men very much and was conspicuously indifferent to women. That her dislikes were marked and she definitely preferred people from traditional and if possible wealthy origins. That she had begun to resemble those imperious and somehow mannish

women who devilled my youth: the dancing teacher, the banker's wife, the headmistress of the progressive school I attended.

In her dotage the dog had become all the more loving toward her master. She lay at his side and made comforting wheezing noises while he brooded in his wing chair, and when it came time for bed, he'd push and coax the whimpering, arthritic beast up the stairs so that neither of them would have to sleep alone. One day she fell in the snow and couldn't get up again, and Cheever carried her home and presently called the vet to put her down. "She was a wonderful companion and I loved her dearly but I shed very few tears," he wrote Litvinov. "Fred cried for about an hour. We had her for fifteen years and she led a very active and useful life . . ."

THE SUMMER OF 1965, after her graduation from Pembroke, Susan went to Tuskegee, Alabama, in order to "teach the Antigone to negroes," as her father put it. When she returned—joining the family in Wellfleet—she spoke excitedly of her often dangerous encounters with white segregationists, while Cheever nodded and sighed and wished she were married. For years he'd been arranging the details in his mind: he, wearing a morning coat, would guide her down the aisle while an eighteenth-century pavane played ("I give her away first at All Saints, then at St. Pauls in Rome") and a crowd of "substantial" guests from the Social Register watched in admiration. As it was, she would have to go on teaching in the fall at the Colorado Rocky Mountain School in Carbondale. ("My guidance counselor at Pembroke told me, 'All our best girls are engaged. Sorry, but you have to look for a job.' It wasn't just my father.") All was not lost, however: one of her fellow teachers, as luck would have it, was none other than the young Ned Cabot, of the *Boston* Cabots. Tippling in the wee hours, Cheever gloated over the possibilities: first, of course, he'd have to discuss the union with Ned's father . . .

[W]e meet at my club. He has the bony face of his caste, his family but is pleasant. He explains to me the difficulties of becoming Mrs. C[abot] and hopes S[usan] understands them. In the nature of things in Boston Mrs. C[abot] is bound to be an institution. She must be a director of the hospital, leader of the Sewing Circle, a member of the admissions committee for the Chilt Club and she must distribute one hundred thousand dollars a year among the worthy. Is S[usan] capable of this. I say that I know her to be capable but that she must herself express her willingness to be an institution. . . . How pretentious, vulgar and absurd is this revery but it seems to improve my spirits.

Absurd, perhaps—but what sweet revenge against all the Wollaston nobs who'd murmured about his drunken father and shopkeeping mother! What a swipe at Rollin Bailey and his tennis court! "He always wanted his children to *belong*," said Federico. "He wanted them to join country clubs, sail skiffs in Nantucket Harbor. That was important to him. But," he added, "at the same time it was very threatening, and he did what he could to prevent it from happening."

When Susan told her father that Ned would be flying back with her at Christmas and spending a night in Ossining on his way to Boston, Cheever was delighted and insisted on picking them up at the airport. For the occasion, of course, he'd fortified himself with gin, though this wasn't baldly obvious until Ned was crammed into the boot of Cheever's two-seat Karmann Ghia and inhaling Cheever's breath point-blank whenever Cheever turned around to make eye contact (his little car lurching this way and that). They were crossing the George Washington Bridge when Ned suddenly remembered that he'd promised to stay with a cousin on Riverside Drive; Cheever remonstrated to no avail. As Susan later wrote, "My father finally concurred, behaving, I'm sure he thought, in a way that Ned would recognize as the mark of a gentleman. We dropped him off at the corner of Eighty-sixth Street; a light snow began to fall."

But again it's worth bearing in mind, perhaps, that Cheever only wanted the best for his daughter, and was naturally worried about her becoming an old maid. "I think she is a courageous, intelligent and unhappy young woman," he reflected. "I wish I could do more for her." Meanwhile the little he could do, as ever, was remind her that fat girls don't get husbands. "I find S[usan] picking at scraps in the icebox. Oh kick it, I say. Go to hell. She hurls the line at me, laughing . . ." And with that, the pavane began to fade—the striped tent, the champagne—it was all going up in smoke. "I look for someone supple and lovely like the young women who pose for girdles and find myself up against a strong, independent and contentious spirit who does not seem to dream of children gathered at her knees, arranging roses, waiting at dusk for her beloved spouse."

By contrast, Ben returned from his first year at Loomis a conquering hero. "Ben, who is my favorite, returned on Friday," his happy father reported. "I damn near swoon every time I see him." The seventeen-year-old had lost his baby fat and become stocky, handsome, and even rather athletic, holding his own on the wrestling and lacrosse teams. "I love you not for the person you are," Cheever had told him as a boy, "but for your possibilities." What he wanted was a young man who wasn't an Orioles fan because of the pretty name; what he wanted, above all, was a son who wasn't "hungry, artistic, worried and broke," as the young John had been. And so his wish had come true—or, as Ben put it, "to some extent I was able to imitate that"—though there was little in the way of profound communication between the two. "The attachment seems to resist any analysis," Cheever noted at the height of his somewhat abstract esteem. "I simply love him. His skin is clear, his face is muscular; we mostly joke." Of course, there were still times when Ben would step out of character and startle his father with some unself-conscious remark, like the time he observed that boys at a school dance had seemed more attracted to one another than to girls. "Let us be manly and raise manly sons," Cheever sternly intoned. ("I think he is fine and pray that he won't have a troubled life," he fretted afterward.) And Ben, it seemed, was ever more determined to take such proverbs to heart; during a subsequent visit, he got off the train with a strange woman who appeared to be in her thirties. As he explained to his parents, he and the woman had struck up a conversation (Cheever had always advised him to make friends on the train), and finally he'd invited her to have dinner with him, perhaps see Ossining in the morning. And so dinner came and went—a bit of a strain, to be sure—and when Ben awoke the next morning, his new friend was gone.

For the most part, Ben had a pleasant relationship with his father during these years. Cheever was proud to have such an amiable, good-looking son, and proud of himself for "shield[ing]" the boy from the privations he'd suffered at that age. Above all, he was lonely, and thought it "very natural" to take "vicarious pleasure" in reliving his youth through Ben. The best times were summers, when Mary and the others were at Treetops and the two men had the house to themselves. For dinner they'd heat up some Stouffer's roast-beef hash and put the tray between them on the porch: "We'd each have a fork," Ben remembered, "we'd eat toward the middle, and whoever ate fastest got the most. . . . We were always laughing, and he was in his fifties then." Cheever's vicarious impulses were especially piqued by the presence of Ben's perky girlfriend, Lynda—the sort of girl who "waves to everyone," Cheever noted with approval: "There's Charlie, there's Louise, there's Helen. Yoo Hoo . . . I find the company of the young very heady and am in some danger of mistaking myself for one of them." Cheever was pleased to drive the couple around in his Karmann Ghia, musing over how impressed the girl must be with his sporty roadster, to say nothing of his "faithful and pedigreed dogs, [his] charming stone house [and his own] personal gifts."

On New Year's Eve that year (a week or so after Cheever had given Ned Cabot a lift from the airport), Ben and Lynda had some friends over and were listening to loud music, while Cheever hovered nearby and his daughter cloistered herself upstairs, "eating Triscuits [as she remembered] and reading Hawthorne." At some point she came down and asked if they could lower the volume a little, as she couldn't find a room in the house where she could read in peace. "S[usan] complains about not having a room in which she can read," Cheever wrote. "I say that if she had a date I'd see that she had a room." This went over badly. *"Fuck you!"* his daughter replied, bolting upstairs and out the terrace door and into the snowy night, her father in shambling pursuit. *"Do I have to hide in the woods to get away from you?"* she cried, while he called and called her name. The rest of the holiday she spent reading in the attic with a chair propped against the door. "Christmas was for some reason not as pleasant as I had hoped," Cheever reported to Litvinov. "I love the children passionately and the house was full of them and their guests but something went wrong." He didn't elaborate.

Federico, not quite nine at the time, was largely exempt from his father's occasional cruelty—though on the surface, at least, he was an ideal candidate. Chubby, clumsy, glum, and unpopular, he was a veritable catalogue of flaws crying out for his father's correction. "I am teaching Fred how to pass and catch a football," Cheever solemnly announced when the time came, though it wasn't long before he had to admit it was hopeless. Federico made his older brother look like a prodigy: Ben could catch the odd ball if one really persevered, but Federico *never* did—he defied the law of averages. Next Cheever tried bowling: "F[ederico] has no grace, no aptitude and I display the impatience of a father. There's no point in my paying good money to watch you roll the ball down the gutter. . . . Later he cries. 'All I have is a good memory,' he says. 'I'm fat, people make fun of me.' The force of this remark." Federico, in short, was poignantly inept, and perhaps he reminded Cheever of himself at that age: much the youngest, that is, and generally regarded as a lost cause. Whatever the reason, his love for the boy was "massive." After Cheever's death, Ben was approached at a party by Harold Brodkey, who consolingly told him how much his father had loved his children. "Oh no," said Mary Cheever, overhearing the exchange. "The only one of the children he ever *really* cared about was Fred!"

The screenwriter Eleanor Perry had read "The Swimmer" when it first appeared in *The New Yorker*, and immediately decided it would make a wonderful movie. She and her husband, Frank, a director, had made a critical splash with their first effort, *David and Lisa* (1962), but Eleanor's script for "The Swimmer" floated around the studios for almost a year before it was finally picked up by Sam Spiegel at Columbia. In the spring of 1966, Cheever was notified that shooting would begin that summer in Westport, Connecticut (less traffic noise than Westchester), and his first response was to make plans for leaving the country. On the other hand, Burt Lancaster had agreed to play Neddy, and the prospect of meeting the famous actor and any number of other glamorous Hollywood types (and perhaps telling Maxwell about it afterward) proved an aching temptation, and in the end Cheever became a frequent visitor to the set. At first, though, he was daunted, and asked Spear to come along for moral support; he also stopped in Greenwich and bought a pint of whiskey. "This helps to settle my nerves but my drinking seems erratic," he wrote in his journal. "After several martinis, some wine and 1 Milltown [sic] I somewhat settle down." Thus sedated, he did in fact enjoy meeting the fifty-two-year-old Lancaster, who struck him as "both young and old, masterful and tearful," as well as remarkably committed to the role. Though an acrobat, a boxer, and a horseman, Lancaster could scarcely swim a stroke, and had been working since April with the UCLA swimming coach, Bob Horne. After shooting was finished that morning, the actor put on a bathrobe and had a poolside lunch with Cheever and the Perrys, after which Cheever (evidently over the worst of his shyness) "jump[ed] beararse" into the water.

Perhaps the main reason he commuted so faithfully to Westport was a teenage actress named Janet Landgard, who played a sexy ex-babysitter. (One of the main padding devices in the movie is a long, lyrical interlude in which Lancaster cavorts around the countryside with Landgard and therefore feels, at least for a while, young and vigorous again.) "She was a nothing actress and not very pretty," Mary Cheever observed of the young woman—whose career had begun with *The Donna Reed Show* and pretty much ended with *The Swimmer*—but Cheever thought she was marvelous, and was thrilled when the Perrys asked him to do a "talismanic" cameo opposite her and Lancaster. The scene was a poolside cocktail party, and the prop man had been filling Cheever's glass with Scotch for almost four hours before he finally got his call. As he wrote Weaver, "What I was supposed to do was to shake hands with Lancaster and say 'You've got a great tan there Neddy.' Things like that. I was supposed to improvise. . . .

> So we rehearsed about a dozen times and then we got ready for the first take but when this dish [Landgard] came on instead of shaking hands with her I gave her a big buss. So then when the take was over Lancaster began to shout: "That son of a bitch is padding his part" and I said I was supposed to improvise and Frank [Perry] said it was all right. I asked the girl if she minded being kissed and she said no, she said I had more spark than anybody else on the set. . . . Lancaster heard her. Anyhow on the second take I bussed her but when I reached out to shake Lancaster's hand the bastard was standing with his hands behind his back. So after the take I said that he was supposed to shake hands with me and he said he was just improvising. So on the third take I kissed her but when I made a grab for Lancaster all I got was a good look at his surgical incision in the neighborhood of his kidneys. We made about six takes in all but our friendship is definitely on the rocks.*

Shortly after shooting ended in August, the whole project got "into very deep and stormy water," as Cheever put it. Spiegel saw the rough cut and was flummoxed: What the hell was the man's motivation for swimming across the county? It made no sense! When the Perrys

---

*Though Cheever's blink-and-you-miss-it cameo is hard to follow, he appears to say to Landgard, "I'm John Estabrook," then busses her, whereupon Lancaster takes her briskly away from him (without shaking hands), asking "How ya doin' Kevin?" "Great, great," Cheever drawls as the camera moves on.

defended the arty ambiguity at the heart of Cheever's vision, Spiegel gave them the sack and hired a young Sydney Pollack to shoot a few "mop-up" scenes on the Coast. These included a long, tempestuous confrontation between Neddy and his mistress (played by Janice Rule), and a "Teamster's Union hose-type rainstorm" at the end; Spiegel also hired Marvin Hamlisch to compose the score, which one reviewer said "would sound overly passionate in a Verdi opera." Among these complications, Cheever was principally worried about his paycheck: he'd gotten a measly ten thousand dollars up front, and would not receive the fifty-thousand-dollar balance "until 120 days after they made a final print."

Almost two years after the initial shooting in Westport, *The Swimmer* was somewhat grudgingly released in May 1968. Cheever was furious when Mary refused to attend the New York premiere, and considered taking Mrs. Zagreb instead ("in her limegreen Thunderbird"), but finally went with Spear and sat between the Perrys, who got screen credit after all. "It is not a great picture but it is faithful to the story and at the end when he returns to the empty house grown men weep," Cheever wrote Litvinov the next day; as for Lancaster, Cheever thought he was "great in the part—lithe and haggard—and the sense of an odyssey, a life a man moving through space, time and water is there." The critics, however, were almost categorically vicious. Perhaps the kindest was Vincent Canby in the *Times*, who professed to like the movie despite its being "uneven, patchy," and "occasionally gross and mawkish." More representative was Joseph Morgenstern's pan in *Newsweek*, which derided the movie as a ludicrous melodrama with a visual style akin to that of "a shampoo commercial."* "I don't think the picture would ever have been great but Sam Spiegel really fucked it up," Cheever remarked, a few months after his first, rather glowing critique. "He fired Frank and got a man named Pollock [sic] to put in the fancy dissolves . . . and reshoot the last ten minutes in Beverly Hills. Frank and I wanted Miles Davis for the music but instead we got a sixty-five all-girl string orchestra. Etc."

---

*On November 25, 2001, Steve Garbarino published a piece in the *New York Times Magazine* ("Leave It to Cheever") in which he made a case for rediscovering the movie as a perfect fable for the post–9/11 zeitgeist: "[I]n many ways, [Neddy] is a symbol of America now, a once presumably safe haven that has been forced to tighten its belt, put up its guard, find new footing and stay afloat while lamenting its lost innocence in a time of terrorism. Like Neddy, America can no longer rely on its charm. . . . And like our country, we find ourselves rooting for 'The Swimmer' down to the last drop."

CHAPTER TWENTY-EIGHT

{ 1966–1967 }

CHEEVER THOUGHT *Bullet Park* would be an improvement over *The Wapshot Scandal*, though it wasn't any easier to write and was badly stalled by the summer of 1966 ("Just the sight of a typewriter gives me an acute pain in the gut"). He decided to put the novel aside and work on a couple of stories he'd been considering for the past year or so: one concerned an old expatriate poet who becomes consumed with obscenity, the other was a malicious portrait of Antonio Barolini, who'd been getting on Cheever's nerves lately ("Perhaps I can write a story about him"). The bumptious aristocrat had solicited a blurb from Cheever for his first novel, *A Long Madness*, translated from the Italian and published by Pantheon in 1964. "*Una lunga pazzia*," Cheever would say, giving the Italian title, then add, "*Un lungo romanzo* [A long novel]!" Cheever hated writing blurbs in any case ("The mortal boredom of reading the fourth-rate novels of my drinking companions"), but was all the more piqued when Barolini's effort sold fewer than four hundred copies, despite his endorsement. Also, the man's constant whinging about his wife struck even Cheever as unseemly, though of course he found the woman insufferable, too. One day she phoned him to say she'd gotten "stuck" writing her novel, and wondered if he had any advice: "Oh for heaven's sake, Helen, take a walk around the block!" he snapped, banging the receiver down. So, yes, he had to concede that Barolini's wife was "truly difficult," and he also sympathized with the way the poor man had to suffer the oafish condescension of their neighbors: "Like most Italians in this country he is taken immediately for a semi-comic member of the lower class; a gardener, fruit peddler a clown. They call him Tony, this nephew of a countess." Such were the basic ingredients for an untitled story Cheever presently wrote, in which the main character is a feckless aristocrat named Marcantonio ("Boobee") Parlapiano: "[Boobee] did not understand that men in America do not complain about their wives," the narrator observes. By way of faint disguise, Cheever gave the fictional wife an operatic rather than literary ambition, but Helen Barolini recognized her husband at once and found the story "very objectionable."

"[I] have written two stories just to keep my hand in," Cheever wrote Litvinov. "One of them is quite dirty and the other is quite boring and I think I won't publish either of them." As it happened, though, Cheever needed the money—he hadn't accepted an advance yet for *Bullet Park*—so he mailed both stories to *The New Yorker* (one still untitled), "because I like to put things in the mail," as he said in the cover letter. The magazine accepted the "boring" story, and thus Cheever gave it the most perfunctory possible title, "Another Story"*; as for the "quite dirty"—and far superior—story, "The World of Apples," it was predictably rejected and sold instead to *Esquire*. "Apples" had been somewhat inspired by the "unsavory dreams and reveries" which had beset Cheever for much of his life, but especially now that he was sleeping alone. Asa Bascomb, the poet in the story, is a disaffected New Englander who lives in the Anticoli-like town of Mount Carbone; one day he happens on a couple copulating in the woods, and afterward finds himself incapable of writing anything but pornography: filthy ballads ("The Fart That Saved Athens"), limericks, or simply the word "fuck" over and over. This, for Bascomb, is a profound sickness of the soul. Like his creator, he tends to associate obscenity with self-destruction—a matter of peculiar urgency, since four other poets "with whom Bascomb was customarily grouped" have all committed suicide ("but Bascomb in his stubborn, countrified way was determined to break or ignore this link—to overthrow Marsyas and Orpheus"). At one point the old man is vaguely tempted by the charms of a repulsive male prostitute, who seems "angelic, armed with

---

*Such was Cheever's disdain for the piece that he didn't include it in his next collection, *The World of Apples*, a slender volume that could have easily accommodated it. That he didn't object to its later inclusion in *The Stories of John Cheever* was perhaps due to his faith in editor Robert Gottlieb's judgment.

a flaming sword that might conquer banality and smash the glass of custom"—but rather than succumb to such ultimate corruption, he makes a pilgrimage to the sacred angel of Monte Giordano, to whom he prays: "God bless Walt Whitman. God bless Hart Crane. God bless Dylan Thomas. God bless William Faulkner, Scott Fitzgerald, and especially Ernest Hemingway." Having invoked his literary idols— men whose imaginative labors had left them painfully alienated and in some cases suicidal—Bascomb completes his purification by standing beneath an icy waterfall, as his father had done before him, and then returns home to write "a long poem on the inalienable dignity of light and air that . . . would grace the last months of his life."

"Another Story" would appear in the February 25, 1967, issue of *The New Yorker*—more than two and a half years after Cheever's previous appearance in the magazine. One reason for the long absence was that he was simply writing fewer stories, though one could also argue that he feared rejection now that Maxwell had "written [him] off as an improvident, evil-minded, alcoholic breakdown." While proceeds from the movie *The Swimmer* were still in suspense, however, Cheever grudgingly—and apprehensively—sent Maxwell the masterly first chapter of *Bullet Park* ("Paint me a small railroad station then . . ."): "I think Bill will praise it," he wrote in his journal. "I think then that he will be very sad and will, by innuendo, suggest that I have lost my marbles and my gifts." When Maxwell did, in fact, praise and publish the piece, Cheever had mixed feelings at best ("I was happier as an outcast"). By then he was irate over the rise of Donald Barthelme and similar writers, whose stories began to dominate the magazine's pages in the late sixties, when surrealism and black humor were in favor—the sort of fiction, in other words, that had excited the editors' dismay when Cheever had written a less blatant version of it a few years before. "[T]he stuntiness of Barthelme disconcerts me," he wrote Maxwell in 1969. "One can always begin: 'Mr. Frobisher, returning from a year in Europe, opened his trunk for the customs officer and found there, instead of his clothing and souvenirs, the mutilated and naked body of an Italian sailor.' Blooey. It's like the last act in vaudeville and anyhow it seems to me that I did it fifteen years ago." Privately he referred to Barthelme as "Shawn's chosen surrealist," and in moments of particular (and more and more frequent) bitterness, he'd rail against the magazine for publishing so many of his "imitators" while neglecting him, as if it were a matter of deliberate malice: *"I've done so much for them and they treat me like this!"*

This wasn't simply petulance on Cheever's part—it was a legitimate aesthetic grievance. Quite apart from the evolving taste of *The New Yorker*, he was deeply troubled by the "cataclysmic" vogue for post-modern experimentation, which waxed in outrageousness as time went on. In later years, he would deplore the incoherence of such widely praised novels as Gaddis's *JR* ("less than rubbish"), lamenting the "lost sense of literature as a voice that appeals to a communal sensibility." As for all the talk about the "death of the novel," Cheever considered it the sort of thing "one leaves to boors": "That the complexities of con-temporary life have overwhelmed the novel would be claimed only by someone who knew nothing of the history of the novel and of the novel's dependence upon change," he wrote indignantly to *The New York Review of Books*. "I think not that the novel has been overwhelmed by the complexities of contemporary life, I think the novel is the only art form we possess that has approached any mastery of this storm." Perhaps the greatest offender, in Cheever's view, was John Barth, whose sprawling works were built around idle metafictional tricks ("The sort of Pirandellismo that is used everywhere by everyone"), to which Cheever himself had resorted, but sparingly, almost from the beginning of his career (q.v., "Of Love: A Testimony" in 1935). He liked to tell of a time when he and Jean Stafford had been at a dinner party with Barth: "Jean said, drawing me aside, but not so far that Barth couldn't hear what she was saying: 'John, your reputation in American literature is very, very shaky. God knows what will happen to it, but if you put a knife in his back, you will be immortal.' "

Though he opposed experimentation for its own sake, Cheever was also an innovator who applauded any approach that made some useful contribution to what he understood to be literature—that is, an attempt to make sense of our lives. He adored *The Armies of the Night*, Mailer's take on the so-called nonfiction novel in which he (Mailer) appears, ingloriously, as a third-person character participating in the 1967 March on the Pentagon. Such a work made nonsense of the novel's supposed obsolescence, and was damnably readable besides. "[Mailer] is so wonderfully tough, sassy and brilliant that I find him the most cheerful figure on the literary scene," Cheever wrote Litvinov. "He can also be a brute, a bore, a pig and a bluff but not in this book." Even Mailer's "fetid" insistence on lurid sexual detail was becoming more palatable to Cheever: "The World of Apples," after all, had been his most explicit work yet, though even in that story he wrote "F--k" with hyphens and spoke of "flaming sword[s]" rather than penises and whatnot, which were so abundant in the work of certain contemporaries. Updike, for one, had proved that writing frankly about sex could be good art as well as good business: "John's new novel (Couples) has made him a millionaire," Cheever reported a bit sadly in 1968. "It is obsessively venereal but the descriptions of undressed women are splendid."

Cheever would soon get on the bandwagon where sex was concerned, but writing about politics was pretty much out of his ken. The only fictional use he would ever make of his Russian material, for instance, was in the (rather dirty) 1972 story, "Artemis, the Honest Well Digger," where a few scenes set in Moscow serve the purpose of deploring the intrusion of politics into matters of the heart. But really it was the heart alone that interested Cheever. "Novels are about men and women and children and dogs," he'd say, "not politics." He could admire but not emulate Mailer's "mastery" of that particular storm, and his indifference was the same in life as in art. He was a conventional liberal who generally agreed with the *Times* editorial page; he was against Vietnam and racism and so forth. But when it came to making his views public—much less marching in support of them—he'd rather not: "I will not march because I am lazy, suffer from agoraphobia, will probably have a hangover, am afraid of the reactionary bullies who will hiss and boo me . . . am shy, timid, a born bystander, etc."

When Susan announced—a year after Tuskegee—that she would spend the summer working for civil rights in Jackson, Mississippi, Cheever did not conceal his exasperation. "The children are home but Susie goes off to Mississippi next week to teach and be stoned," he wrote Maxwell. "It will be miserable and dangerous." He attributed her zeal to a "rampant" blood strain originating with such abolitionist forebears as his "great uncle Ebenezer" (Thomas Butler rather, who may or may not have been persecuted by copperheads in Newburyport). In fact, his feelings on this point were even more tortured than usual. At night he lay awake sensing Susan was in danger, and wondering whether he should brave a trip south ("with my numerous phobias") and charm the local peckerwoods while absconding with his daughter—who soon phoned, in any case, asking for $350 in emergency funds, which Cheever promptly wired from White Plains. Likewise, when Ben went off to Antioch College in 1967, and did a few de rigueur days in the Cincinnati jail because of his part in an antiwar protest, Cheever was "proud of him" and managed to persuade the Western Union office to stay open late while he raised nine hundred dollars in cash for bail. Later, he claimed to have refused an invitation to give a speech in Cincinnati ("I told them I would not make a potholder in the city that had arrested my eldest son"), but more often than not he found his children's posturing a bit much: "As for Ben he was reclassified 1-A on Friday," he wrote, shortly after the Cincinnati incident. "Susie was particularly incensed and wanted to send him to Stockholm on the next plane. . . . I went to the draft board on Monday where the reclassification was declared a clerical error. Ben goes his feckless way."

The times were changing at such a rapid rate, though, that even Cheever's sixty-one-year-old brother was becoming part of the Scene. After two years of sobriety, Fred moved to Boulder, Colorado, in the fall of 1966 to be with his estranged wife and three of their children, who'd originally gone west to get away from him, but now found him delightful. Ann had scarcely known her father as a sober man, and was struck by how "knowledgeable and compassionate" he was: he liked to "rap" (his word) about the thriving counterculture in Boulder, and meanwhile he bought a motorcycle and dumped his wizened, chain-smoking wife for a thirty-five-year-old physicist named Sabine, for whose benefit he got monkey-gland injections.

But the more things changed the more they stayed the same, at least in one respect: "Dear Joey," Fred wrote, not long after his arrival in Boulder. "For no explainable reason except perhaps over-exertion in moving, my bad ankle has become a problem and for the past three weeks I haven't been able to walk on it." He'd managed to keep his PR job at a local radio station, he said, but his salary had been halved until he could return to work, and therefore he wondered if John could "underwrite [his] next two months to the tune of $1,500 or $2,000," which would allow him to feed himself and go on paying Ann's tuition. John patiently replied: "I'm enclosing a small check because it's all I have. I can't produce two thousand dollars out of thin air and I don't know who can. . . . If Annie would write and tell me what she needs in the way of tuition I will see what I can do about this. I realize that this will be embarrassing for Annie but it seems to be the only way of doing it." One year later, Fred was sufficiently back on his feet to take a trip to England, stopping for a night in Ossining before catching his plane. While John simpered and drank and wished his brother would go away (even the man's rejuvenation was vaguely unsettling), Fred went on about the splendors of Boulder and reminisced about the family. "After twenty-five years of acute alcoholism, paranoia and marital mayhem," John wrote Exley, "[Fred] appears at sixty-two, handsome, intelligent, sober and well-dressed. We sat up late, the Good Brother and the Bad Brother. The Good Brother (me) drank nearly a quart of bourbon while the Bad Brother sipped a gingerale. At breakfast the Bad Brother was all charm and composure. The Good Brother was one fucking mess."

BY THE MID-SIXTIES, Cheever's furtive trips to the pantry were an almost daily ritual. The morning's work was usually done by ten-thirty, whereupon he'd retire either to the terrace if the weather was fine (he could hear the telephone ring and see people come and go) or down-stairs to his wing chair, where he'd sit chain-smoking and pretending to read while casing the situation: Iole, perhaps, was puttering around the kitchen and would have to be distracted, or else his wife and/or children were lingering over their coffee and newspaper. Meanwhile the gin bottles sang and sang. When the coast was clear, Cheever would hit the pantry like a shot and pour a few "scoops," but if the others were still hanging around as late as half past eleven or so, he'd often excuse himself (irritably) and drive to the liquor store, then park in some leafy area on the way home and "take a big pull at the bottle, spilling a lot of gin over [his] chin."

He knew he was destroying himself, but the prospect of stopping or even tapering off seemed preposterous. Sometimes he felt all right when he woke up (albeit hungover to some greater or lesser degree), but within an hour or two the *cafard* would "[move] in like tear-gas," and if he didn't get a drink he'd suffer an almost maddening malaise. Better to drink and calm down and wonder, sometimes tearfully, what was to become of him. "I keep reading biographies of Fitzgerald and I always get to bawling at the end," he wrote a friend. "I read on a ter-race where no can see me and when he goes out to Los Angeles for the last time I start crying and I weep right through to the end." Perhaps this was meant to be taken somewhat tongue in cheek, but in fact Cheever could hardly have identified more with Fitzgerald, whose "torments" (and fate?) seemed very like his own. "Shall I dwell on the crucifixion of the diligent novelist?" he wrote, thinking of Fitzgerald.

"The writer cultivates, extends, raises, and inflates his imagination, sure that this is his destiny, his usefulness, his contribution to the understanding of good and evil. As he inflates his imagination, he inflates his capacity for evil. As he inflates his imagination, he inflates his capacity for anxiety, and inevitably becomes the victim of crushing phobias that can only be allayed by lethal doses of heroin or alcohol."

As it was, his condition was literally paralyzing. The "gethsemane" of train travel—and he did, after all, have to go to the city now and then—would begin on the platform, where he was attacked by a vertigo so severe that he'd clutch a column, anything, lest the pavement "fly up and hit [him] between the eyes." Then, if he actually managed to get on board, his panic would mount until sometimes he had to get off in the vicinity of Tarrytown or Yonkers; otherwise he'd "get bombed" (more so) in the toilet or perhaps take one of his "massive" tranquilizers, which left him floating in a limbo wherein his "hands seem[ed] to drop off." And it wasn't just trains, but almost any form of travel whatsoever: "I bitterly resent these infringements on my life," he wrote. "I can barely walk, I plainly cannot drive, I can't cross bridges and since we have been taught that we received what we deserve I wonder what I have been guilty of to suffer so." But he never wondered long. On the rare occasion when he was able to goad himself all the way to Manhattan, he'd come face to face with the horror his body had been warning him against (always beginning with a painful, telltale tug in his scrotum): "Walking on Madison Avenue I had been tormented with the thought that my sins would be discovered although I claim to have committed no sins. My children will vilify and disown me, my loving dogs will bark at me, even the cleaning woman will spit in my direction."

Under the circumstances, the shelter of his marriage was more important than ever, though it was also a humiliating reminder that he was all but incapable now of performing the procreative act. As he wrote in his journal of an aptly named persona, "If he [Fallow] could make love to a woman it proved that he was not the sexual criminal he sometimes thought himself to be. His manhood seemed to reside between Priscilla's legs." He and Mary still tried from time to time, but it was no use: at best he could get started a bit, but rarely (if ever) finish. To pre-empt failure—and rebel against his wife's terrible power—Cheever adopted the stratagem of insulting her when sex seemed imminent, with the predictable result that she would then refuse to proceed, or at least protest at some length, in which case Cheever was known to quote Moses Wapshot: "You've talked yourself out of a fuck." ("He liked to say that," Mary recalled. "Of course, the fallacy of that is, who would *want* to fuck anybody who talked to them that way?") By way of reprisal, Mary could be somewhat pre-emptive herself: "I can't bear to be gentled by an impotent man," she remarked, departing to cook potatoes rather than endure his tentative caresses. "I'm not impotent with other women!" he called after her (admitting in his journal, "This is a damned lie, since all I've done is neck with other women").

Finally Cheever had had enough of his wife's "needless darkness"—obviously, she was a "castrator" like his mother, and moreover a "serious manic-depressive" like her sister. "She naturally resists this admission and looking around for some other explanation for her profound unhappiness she has settled on me," he reflected. "This accounts for the depth of her aversion to me, the intensity of her hatred." Lest he "destroy [him]self " by "accommodat[ing] her madness," he decided to present his case to a reputable psychiatrist, David C. Hays. During their first appointment in July 1966, Cheever explained to Hays that he was there for his wife's sake, adverting to the history of insanity in her family and noting her particular resemblance to Buff. He could no longer abide her moodiness and "tongue lashings," he said, and advised Dr. Hays to have a talk with her and help her understand her problem in clinical terms. "So I go to the shrink," he wrote. "I feel much better talking to him. He does seem a little angular, a little inclined to contradict and interrupt. . . . Mary will go see him, and how wonderful it would be if we could clear this up." Mary was happy to comply. When the doctor inquired about her "moodiness" and so on, she sweetly replied that Cheever was far moodier than she, and though it was true she was cold at times, this was simply a defense ("she has built up an armament," Hays noted, "so that he can't hurt her anymore"). When Cheever observed how cheerful Mary seemed after chatting with the man, he was delighted: "[T]he trouble seems over, the ice is broken. . . . I adore her, worship her, love her, live within her and wake in the morning for the first time in weeks without a cafard. I would like to wake her, embrace her, kiss her, screw her, screw her and screw her again but instead I go downstairs and make the coffee." Meanwhile Dr. Hays had jotted down the following in regard to Cheever: "egocentric, narcissistic, evasive . . . very active fantasy life."

The couple went together for the next session, the resolution of which Cheever had pictured in terms of "a musical comedy": "We would embrace, kiss on the threshold of his office and tie on a can after the children had gone to the movies." But he was brutally disappointed. "The picture, as I saw it, was that I, an innocent and fortunate creature, had married a woman with deep psychic disturbances," he grimly recorded afterward. "The picture, as it was presented to me, was of a neurotic man, narcissistic, egocentric, friendless, and so deeply involved in my own defensive illusions that I had invented a manic-depressive wife." While Dr. Hays outlined a program of treatment—individual *and* group therapy for the husband, whereas the wife needn't return except for an occasional joint session—Cheever mentally impugned the man's credibility. He wore garters, for one, holding up socks that had silly clocks printed on them; he used a lot of "specious jargon" like "meaningful" (fourteen times), "interpersonal" (twelve), "longitudinal" (nine), and "structure" (two); and, worst of all—by far—he'd never read any of Cheever's books!

Mary and Federico departed for Treetops, and Cheever was left to brood alone. It was the "friendless" part that really rankled. By God, just the other day he'd gone to Westport with his great friend Art Spear, and lunched with Burt Lancaster, no less! And even as he sat there brooding (so he reported to Weaver), the telephone rang: "[I]t was Esquire saying that they were doing a spread of Janet Landgard and that Janet had asked if dear Mister Shiffers would please write her captions because she didn't want her captions written by anyone but Shiffers and I said that I would write the captions and that's the way things stand." Also, as luck would have it, Hope Lange and Alan Pakula were in town with their friend Sharman Douglas—daughter of the former ambassador to the Court of St. James—and the three took Cheever to East Hampton for the weekend. Thus he returned to Dr. Hays with his guns loaded, taking a seat and silently noting the tacky *objets* all over the office ("Does he know anything about music, literature, painting, baseball? I think not"); then, hearing the word "friendless" again, he returned fire: "I said that I had just had a very friendly weekend with Hope, Alan, and Sharman . . ." But Hays only shook his head: "He explained that I had developed a social veneer—an illusion of friendship—that was meant to conceal my basic hostility and alienation." (The next day Cheever wrote his wife, "[Hays's] mouth seems a little blubbery and he is not always successful in keeping his hands away from it.")

Despite his dislike of Hays's characterizations, Cheever seemed willing to cooperate up to a point. When Hays, a Freudian, asked him about his childhood, Cheever obligingly touched on what seemed the most salient issues: his father had wanted him aborted, and growing up he'd found himself caught in the middle of a "power struggle" between his parents, which his mother had won, thereby planting a fear of women as the "predatory sex." That said, Cheever wanted to hurry along to what he viewed as the root of his anxieties: "I would like to discuss, to ventilate, my homosexual problems," he wrote before the subsequent (fourth) session, to which he arrived bearing an auto-graphed copy of *The Wapshot Chronicle*. As Cheever began (with "some circumspection") to broach the matter of homosexuality, Hays made it clear that he wanted to talk about the mother more—a lot more. When Cheever mentioned his dalliance with Sara Spencer, for exam-ple, Hays speculated that the woman was perhaps his "good mother" and Mary his "bad mother," or so Cheever might have (unconsciously) conceived it. Be that as it may ("Who profits by concluding that Mrs. Zagreb is my mother?"), the patient tried to retrieve his previous thread, asking if he could speak about his brother, Fred; Hays gave him "a frightfully condescending smile" and suggested they'd get around to that later. As Cheever mused, "[I]t would be a thousand dollars or more before I could say what was on my mind."

"Some years ago I went to a psychiatrist who told me I was obsessed with my Mother," he later wrote Litvinov. "When I told him that I liked to swim he said: Mother. When I told him that I liked the rain he said: Mother. When I told him that I drank too much he said: Mother." Toward the end Cheever began arriving late, tipsy, and tended to be sort of suavely impertinent. "I lost a fifty-dollar bet with Mary about your religion," he announced at the outset of their penultimate (eighth) session: he thought Hays was an Irish Catholic, but in fact he was Jewish, as Mary had claimed. For his part, Hays would urge the patient, repeatedly, to participate in group therapy too, but the latter refused or simply evaded the subject. Finally—when Hays reiterated that Cheever seemed to project onto his marital relationship certain unresolved conflicts with his mother—Cheever flatly declared, "I don't like to talk about any of these things." Then (in a "very friendly" way, Hays recalled) he said he wouldn't be coming back anymore, but thanked Hays all the same and said he'd helped a little, which may have been somewhat sincere: "I realize that my own infirmities contribute to [Mary's] unhappiness," he wrote, after deciding to quit therapy.

"The microscopic scrutiny I bring to every note of her voice, every footstep, is a morbid exacerbation of our incompatibility but it cannot account for those weeks and months when I am the object of every disappointment and dislike in her world." This was a fair synthesis, more or less, and then there were times when Cheever was inclined to accept even the most damning of Hays's insights: "And drunk I think perhaps the shrink is right, perhaps I am capable only of parasitism, dependence and imposture disguised as love . . ."

ONE WEEK after his final session with Hays, Cheever managed the long drive to Yaddo for the annual board meeting, Tappan Zee Bridge and all. He was aghast, however, by what he found there: the eighty-one-year-old Elizabeth Ames was virtually surrounded by homosexuals, despite her stern assertions about excluding them whenever possible. This was the same "terrifying ambivalence," thought Cheever, that he'd detected in his own mother—that is, an impulse to condemn perversion on the one hand, and to castrate her son on the other, the better to ensure "a gentle companion" in her lonely old age. Actually, Cheever wasn't quite sure about some of Ames's entourage, but at least one—Ned Rorem—he knew to be "a famous cocksucker": "N[ed] who I've been told claims, in his public confession, to have been blown and buggered by half the French Academy . . ." The "confession" was Rorem's recently published *Paris Diary*, a remarkably candid account of gay culture that had elevated Rorem to the status of "America's official queer, goyim division," as the author put it.

That night Rorem had an unexpected visitor: Cheever, festively waving a fifth of Scotch. For three hours or so, he went on and on about his recent psychotherapy, his drinking problem, the link between writing and screwing, and finally, when the bottle was empty, he put a hand on Rorem's leg. "I was reluctant," the composer recalled, "since I wasn't particularly attracted to him physically. But Cheever sort of broke my heart, he was so wistful. 'I simply have to,' he said." Cheever seemed "very naïve sexually"—he only wanted oral sex, as if other possibilities hadn't occurred to him—and afterward he was "like a high-school boy, romantic in the extreme": "I've never felt this way before," he said, claiming that he hadn't been with a man in some thirty years, and meanwhile caressing Rorem in a way that seemed "sort of cursory."

"Oh what good children we are!" Cheever wrote the next day. "How I rush to present myself at the breakfast table at eight AM, bright, shaven, proof of the fact that I did not get drunk last night and do something I should not have done." For the next week or so, at any rate, the two were a couple: buzzing around the countryside in Cheever's roadster, having picnics together and chatting about one thing and another while Cheever gulped gin from a thermos. "[He] was obsessed with homosexuality," Rorem later wrote, "as though hoarding lost time. Learning about my orgasm fantasies (squalid, narrow and sadomasochistic), he was anxious to show that *his* were elating, like being on a crimson staircase toward a silver tower that bursts open to a sky of golden stars." With Rorem's assistance, Cheever ascended those stairs three or four times a day, and his long struggle with impotence was nowhere in evidence. Nor was he very discreet about things—once they did it under a Ping-Pong table—seeming almost to invite discovery: "My God, there's Hortense [Calisher]! . . . They know! . . . But I'm glad. . . . No I'm not." Several years hence, while writing *The Later Diaries*, Rorem described the liaison and likened Cheever to Proust's Baron de Charlus, though he deleted these bits on the advice of his publisher's lawyer. "I wouldn't have minded," Cheever remarked, once the book had been safely expurgated.

His infatuation with Rorem ended almost the moment he left the "precious and unreal environment" of Yaddo; amid his dogs and souvenirs, Cheever rationalized his behavior as little more than an attempt "to offend [his] elders." "I want to get back into the rousing, rainswept country of love," he wrote—meaning heterosexual love— but where to begin? Ruefully he reflected that "perhaps fifty women" had offered their favors in recent years; for various reasons, though ("firstly because I might be incompetent"), he'd turned them all down. And whoever the fifty were, they'd certainly vanished by then, as Cheever found himself at an almost total loss. For a moment he thought he might marry Sharman Douglas, but then he had to admit he'd only met her once in his life and had already forgotten what she looked like. As for Mrs. Zagreb ("a matron in her fifties, whose feet are killing her"), she hardly seemed a suitable mistress for a world-famous author, and truth be known it wasn't a very torrid affair: "He beseeches her to love him and she sometimes kisses him, roughs his hair and fondles his whatsis but if he tries to go further she says: be good, be good, now please be good." And finally, if he were perfectly honest with himself, he didn't want a mistress at all—quite simply, he wanted to be a proper husband with a loving wife. "I am sad," he wrote that fall; "I am weary; I am weary of being a boy of fifty; I am weary of my capricious dick, but it seems unmanly of me to say so. I say so, and Mary most kindly and gently takes me into her arms. I don't make out, but lie there like a child. Patience, courage, cheerfulness."

Things got better, for a while, when Susan called from Colorado to say she was quitting her job and coming home to marry Malcolm Cowley's son, Robert, a thirty-two-year-old divorcé with two children. Cheever was bemused—it almost seemed "a little incestuous"—and not quite inclined to celebrate until he'd received confirmation from the prospective groom, whom he promptly invited to lunch at the Century. When he asked Cowley what his intentions were, the man began to stammer: "A you, you sound comes into his speech," Cheever noted. "He asks me to tell him about my daughter. It seems to me a strange question for a man in love and my answers are inconclusive." Even stranger, perhaps, was what appeared to be Cheever's genuine puzzlement on that point: "I seem to know so much about her that I know nothing," he wrote the senior Cowley. "She doesn't break promises, tell lies or read the newspaper over one's shoulder at breakfast. She's intelligent, unpunctual, fearless and plays the record player very loud. It's about all I know." But really it hardly mattered—she was getting married, and what a relief. That would be the end (Cheever hoped) of her quixotic interest in civil rights and such, nor would there be any more scenes like the one that had spoiled the holidays the year before. Indeed, when he saw the couple together at Christmas, they "seem[ed] so happy that it infect[ed] [them] all": Cheever beamed and beamed ("I should get to my knees and thank heaven"), while Mary said she wanted to kiss everyone, even her husband, and did so.

At the beginning of a hopeful new year, Cheever wrote: "My bowels are open, my balls are ticklish, my work moves, my children are well and unprecedentedly happy, I love my wife, my house is warm, so why should I wake in the throes of melancholy." Why, indeed. For one thing he worried that word might spread of his tryst with Rorem, who, after all, was hardly celebrated for his discretion (and God only knew what the others at Yaddo had seen or heard). The following summer, anyway, when Rorem asked him to write a blurb for his new book, Cheever saw a chance to distance himself in a decorous way: after the whole Barolini fiasco, he replied, "I resolved never to do this again or to use friendly endorsements on my books." So that was that. Still, he remained rather fond of Rorem and made a point of lunching with him almost every year at Yaddo, though he found the man's narcissism trying: "[Ned's] ego seems in spate," he wrote, "crystaline [sic] and uninteresting."

CHAPTER TWENTY-NINE

{ *1967–1968* }

CHEEVER'S TRUCE WITH MARY lasted perhaps a month, before their marriage began to make "its annual journey towards the rocks," as he wrote Litvinov. Ever more drunken, Cheever was less and less apt to dissemble his bitterness, while Mary continued to refine a subtle method of guerrilla warfare. Arriving separately at a dinner party, Cheever made a point of throwing his wife "a look of implacable hatred," and when he later sobered up and apologized, she benignly replied that she was "so used to [his] contempt she didn't notice it." Also, she made a point of conspicuously breathing through her mouth in his presence, and when he solicitously inquired whether she had a cold, she explained that he reeked of gin.

In February 1967 he escaped to Yaddo, and was relieved to find that all the homosexuals had cleared out; in their place was a captivating youngish woman who'd written an acclaimed biography of a great Romantic poet. "I would be a fool to claim that I am falling in love but I am immensely grateful for her company," Cheever wrote. "Of all the people I have become attached to here this is the only seemly attachment, the only one with promise." Their attachment appears to have been based on a single meeting (maybe two) at a restaurant near the racetrack, where Cheever exerted his charm and established the sort of instant (if ephemeral) rapport noted by many. For her part, the woman observed that Cheever seemed perhaps a little defensive about his lack of education, and he in turn thought he detected a touch of scholarly "sternness" in her manner, but decided this was relatively slight: "[H]ow natural it is that I, having been surrounded for so long by women who wield their intellectual gifts like battle axes should fall in love with someone whose intellect is of such excellence that she carries it like some simple gift."

And he *was* in love. She'd given him a friendly—perhaps even tender—kiss goodbye, and when he came home to his glum wife, Cheever felt "invincible" in his determination to marry the other woman and start a family. They'd made a date to lunch in the city—a meeting so fraught with possibilities that Cheever could scarcely face it without sneaking a lot of gin before and during his morning train, endeavoring to sweat it all out at the Biltmore steam room, where he caught an unhappy glimpse of himself in the mirror: "I see a puffy old man with pink feet, sparse pubic hair and a short cock." Not surprisingly, the date proved a little anticlimactic for both parties: Cheever was so drunk he could barely follow the thread of his own well-worn stories, and lurching to embrace the woman, he almost burned a hole in her chesterfield with his cigarette. Meanwhile he observed that she wasn't as young as he recalled, nor as pretty: "Her backside is broad from all those years in libraries, there is a definite heaviness to her voice and her taste in clothing is dreary." Alone again with his reveries, though, he decided that these "were trifling and opaque matters that love will cure," and so wrote her a letter that seemed to lay his cards on the table: "[T]his is a proposal of marriage. . . . I will dedicate my new novel to you. I expect you to dedicate your book to me. We will appear together on the book jacket, photographed in the garden of our 18th century farmhouse on the grassy banks of the Limpopo River." Perhaps he figured this was droll enough to be taken as a joke in case it didn't go over, but on second (and doubtless more sober) thought, he decided it was less than realistic, at least for the moment, and put the letter aside for later consideration.*

Susan and Rob Cowley were to be married on May 6, 1967, and as the date drew near Cheever's own marriage was pretty much at its nadir; he couldn't help wondering about the propriety of playing a principal role in a ceremony that, for him, meant "slander, contumely, mutilation, etc." Nevertheless, he threw himself into the preparations with admirable zeal. At first he planned to hold the reception at the Century Club, but was reminded of a by-law forbidding such affairs;

---

*The unmailed letter may be found in the pocket of one of Cheever's journal notebooks at Harvard.

then he decided the ceremony would take place at St. Mark's in-the-Bowery, where a quaint little graveyard could be used for the reception—though the minister had warned him (said Cheever) "that if he didn't have a squad of policemen every bum in lower New York would crawl into the tent, piss in the punch bowl and throw empty Petri wine bottles at [his] Mother-in-law." What was important to both Cheever and his daughter was that it be a proper Episcopalian service using the original Cranmer. Rob Cowley was therefore enjoined to write a letter to the bishop of New York "to the effect that [he] wasn't really married [previously] despite [his] two children," as Cowley recalled.

The night before the wedding, Cheever and his wife took a hotel room in the city, and the next morning he attempted to engage her in a bit of amorous play: he crawled into her bed and she crawled out the other side and got into his bed; when he invited her to sit on his naked lap, she "[made] an exclamation of distaste" and grimly watched television. Thus rebuffed, Cheever spiked his orange juice with gin and went about his day (solitary martinis in a "dark, pleasant bar"; the pre-wedding lunch at Lüchow's), until the time came to pick up his wife and daughter in a limousine. Driven to the tenement on Waverly Place where Susan was living, Cheever couldn't find her name on the mail-boxes and began ringing random doorbells and yelling *Susie! Susie!* from the street. Presently his daughter appeared in her wedding dress—she and her mother had been drinking champagne and getting ready—and at length they arrived at the church and hastily took their places while Purcell's Trumpet Voluntary began to play. Cheever noticed that his daughter seemed frightened ("I don't remember much," she said, "because I was really lit"), and was glad to offer his arm: "In how many hotel and other lonely beds have I imagined myself greeting her at the church door (Why he might be her brother he looks so young) and leading her, with a superb mixture of ceremoni-ousness and humor, down the worn red carpet." So he'd mused years before, and now the thing was happening at last.

Cheever had hired a fancy caterer who spread a green felt carpet around the graves and erected a tent, into which passing derelicts peeped at the festivities. There were some two hundred guests in all. An elderly Josie Herbst sat chain-smoking in her serape (she had less than two years to live), and Mrs. Zagreb "raked the male guests" and finally pointed to Peter Blume: "That's what I want next." "Everyone acted in character," Cheever reported. "Mary's unstable sister seized two vases of flowers and carried them out to her car. Her husband— a shy man—retired to a nearby saloon and got drunk at his own expense. Mary—very chic—upstaged Susie and nearly ran off with the groom. Fred, attended by his Italian [Iole], ate six pieces of cake and I kissed eighty-three women and drank a pint of bourbon." In fact Cheever had rarely been happier—in marked contrast to the groom's parents, who sat dourly in a far corner of the tent: Muriel Cowley had been ill, and the cold, blustery day wasn't helping, and Malcolm was furious that Rob hadn't visited his mother *once* in the days prior to the wedding. "What a beautiful party it is!" Cheever kept exclaiming, hoping perhaps that his high spirits would prove infectious. "You," said his wife, "are the spectre at the feast."

THAT SUMMER Cheever was enticed by *The Saturday Evening Post* to interview Sophia Loren on location in Italy; in exchange for taking his first "hack job," the magazine offered to pay expenses for him and his family as well as provide them with a car and driver. When Cheever told Mary as much, she agreed to accompany him but "[did] not seem cheered."

Cheever was worried that his *cafard* would ruin the vacation, but it seemed to "miss the plane" and only caught up with him intermittently. Eager to use his Italian, he began "gabbling like a turkey" as soon as he, Mary, and Federico arrived in Rome, where a chauffeur met them at the airport and drove them to the fishing village of Sperlonga: "This is all white-washed staircases leading to the sea," he wrote Litvinov, "and at six in the morning, American time, we were eating tomatos and mozzarella and sporting in the waves." Afterward Cheever went his own glamorous way for the most part, leaving Mary to show Federico around the ruins of Pompeii while he chatted up the movie crowd. He found Loren "intelligent and capable," albeit unwilling to bare her soul for the sake of a little publicity, even at the behest of so famous and charming an author. "She has the tact and discretion of a public figure," Cheever wrote for the *Post*. "She will not break the dishes, get stoned, do a belly dance or calumniate Lollobrigida or Mia Farrow." Hoping to end the visit on a more personal note, he asked Loren for a kiss goodbye and she cheerfully obliged him. "She wrote, she wrote, she loves me," he gushed to Maxwell that October, when his article appeared and the actress cordially thanked him for same. "Yesterday in the mail-box among the spiders, autumn leaves, bills and magazines was a vast envelope from the Palazzo Colona. . . . What a lovely child."

By then he could ill afford to let himself get too excited about things, as he'd been afflicted by a severe case of prostatitis. For a week or two he weathered the worst of it (burning urination, painful swelling, worrisome discharge), before downing "three scoops of gin" and visiting a venerable urologist in White Plains, who sensibly advised him not to drink so much. Cheever conceded the problem, but wondered whether there was more to it than that—indeed, whether perhaps he'd "suffered from an unstable prostate since adolescence," as he wrote his regular physician, Ray Mutter.

> The infection seems closely allied to my basic sexual nature and it seems that the blowup could have been caused by alcoholic and other excesses brought on by my anxious and greedy urge to take more than my share of brute pleasure. . . . It has also occurred, to my uninformed mind that some of the phobias, from which I've suffered in the last years might have some connection with this capricious gland since the pain always begins in the scrotum. . . . I have felt, since my early twenties that that whole part of me was apt to be foolish.

One wonders what the amiable Mutter made of all that; in any event, Cheever remained disconcerted by some of the more sinister etiological implications: Was he being punished for his sins? Would he be racked with pain every time he became aroused (licitly or otherwise)? When the illness persisted, he asked Litvinov to say a prayer for him at St. Basil's, which seemed to have some slight mitigating effect. His drinking, however, remained as bad as ever, and he considered the case of Rossini, the composer, whose happiness had been similarly threatened by depression and urinary problems: "What excites me is that after nearly ten years of pain he recovers completely and goes into a robust middle age," Cheever noted, "as I intend to."

But for now he was still in the doldrums, both physically and creatively. Encountering "The Country Husband" in an anthology, Cheever had to admit that his recent efforts in the genre were vastly inferior. The story he was writing at the time, for instance—"Percy"—

was little more than straight memoir about his aunt Florence Liley, the painter, whose story he'd considered writing as long as twenty-five years ago: "Thinking idly of Liley on the trainride," he'd written in his journal at the time, "it seemed that to convert a biography into an anecdote is a kind of terrible perfidy or betrayal for which you should be made to descend into hell." Amid his present illness, however, he found the reminiscence easy and oddly comforting to write ("It served me as a kind of bedtime story"), and besides he suspected—correctly— that it was the sort of thing *The New Yorker* would buy. Also, he needed to pause again and regroup in his work on *Bullet Park*, which he worried was turning into a facile "indictment" of the suburbs: "The admissions committee at the club does not scandalize me. Neither does the fact that D. has sold a bond issue for Franco." On the other hand, if he wasn't writing an "indictment"—and surely *some* of the satire (however muddled by irony) was directed against modern suburbia—then what exactly *was* he writing? Faced with a number of hard-to-solve ambiguities, Cheever steadied himself with the idea that his novel was, at bottom, "an uncomplicated story about a man who loved his son"—a kind of updated *William Tell*, in other words.

With this in mind, Cheever spent the rest of the year working on a long sequence in which the protagonist's son, Tony Nailles, is stricken with sadness and takes to his bed. "Tony's melancholy is not a symbol of the spiritual bankruptcy of Bullet Park," Cheever reminded himself. "Melancholy is some part of the human condition and he is its chance victim." When he'd finished the section, Cheever could finally envision the novel all the way through to the end; in fact, he thought these pages were the best he'd ever written, and his confidence was boosted further when Maxwell bought the entire excerpt and proposed to publish it as "Tony in Bed." Presently, though, he infuriated Cheever by asking him to cut at least two galley pages: "A short story is as precise as a poem and it cannot be slashed," Cheever brooded in his journal, while betraying (as usual) only a hint of peevishness to Maxwell and agreeing to make the cuts. When his *Swimmer* money came through in April, however, Cheever abruptly canceled the story and gleefully returned the $4,147.50 payment to the magazine. In the meantime another excerpt, "The Yellow Room"—previously rejected by Maxwell ("the narrator isn't a man of very much particularity")—had appeared in the January 1968 *Playboy*, the first of several appearances Cheever would make in the magazine: "They pay well and they are hospitable,"

he wrote a friend, "and the tits aren't any more distracting than the gir-
dle advertisements in the New Yorker." As for the latter, it would not
publish another Cheever story for seven years.

CHEEVER FINISHED A DRAFT of *Bullet Park* in mid-July, though he
kept the news to himself until his agent called and pronounced the
work "magnificent," whereupon he and Mary went out to celebrate
and ended up ("for reasons that I can't recall") quarreling bitterly. Matters escalated, and it began to look as if this time, surely, divorce was
imminent, until the two were found in the library giddily poring over
travel brochures. Less than a week later, they departed for Ireland with
Federico. In the parking lot of Shannon Airport, Cheever got in on the
wrong side of the rental car and promptly had a minor collision; after a
few calming Irish coffees, he drove a replacement vehicle south across
the mountains. For the next few days, he fished for salmon in the
shadow of a beautiful ruined castle, humming with bees, and (while
spending a night in the village of Adare) chatted with a priest about
local history, particularly the noble Dunraven family. Driving on to
Galway, Cheever sang a ditty he'd composed off the top of his head
about the Duke of Dunraven's fateful journey to America.* Very like
the duke in his song, Cheever drank an enormous quantity of Irish
whiskey, and even startled himself at one point when he realized he'd
polished off an entire fifth of Jameson Crested Ten in half an hour.

Cheever's impromptu ballad would be his last composition for a
long time. Toward the end of August, he completed some very minor
repairs to *Bullet Park*, then became so blocked that he even stopped
writing in his journal: weeks passed without a single word, perhaps the
first time he'd neglected this daily chore since his years in the army.
"Ropesville," he tersely wrote in one of his infrequent entries. "Marti-

---

*To this day Federico remembers his father's song almost word for word ("As they
say about ABBA, it's full of hooks") and is happy to sing it, as follows: "The Duke of
Dunraven, he snored in his sleep / He frightened the turkeys, the cows, and the sheep /
He drank Irish whiskey from morning to night / And [something something] was a
horrible fright. [REFRAIN:] Dunraven, Dunraven, come back to your hearth / Come
back to Adare, the place of your birth / The rooks are all grieving / The brooks are in
spate / Come back and inherit your broken estate." Federico stopped there, but
explained that a number of further verses tell of the duke's adventures in the New
World, where he discovers such delicacies as "dehydrated taties" (potatoes) and "fresh
frozen peas."

nis for breakfast or thereabouts. It takes three to get me fixed." His days passed in a browned-out fog. When Donadio called to impart the happy news that he'd gotten a large advance from his *English* publisher, no less, Cheever was able to express a seemly incredulity, but afterward had no idea of the figure in question. A few weeks later, he somehow managed to catch a train to New York, go over his "Percy" galleys with Maxwell, regale a stranger at the Biltmore bar about his career as a jockey, then return to Ossining with only a fleeting recollection of the whole adventure.

His wife was unsympathetic, and it didn't help that she seemed to dislike *Bullet Park*. "Of course I cannot judge the book," she said, "because I know in every case the facts on which it is based. Hammer is revolting . . ." Cheever thought this rather hard, since after all there was "some correspondence" between Hammer and himself. He was still mulling it over when Mary announced that one of her Briarcliff students had run away from home, and needed a place to stay for a while. "So off one goes again to find some spare room, tool shed, office, loft, or garage," Cheever complained to Exley, though in fact he was allowed to keep his little room off the terrace, while his wife's student, Martha, was installed in a "mouse-infested room behind the kitchen," as Federico described it. Martha (whom Cheever privately called "the waif" or "stray") was a thin, prettyish, depressively self-absorbed young woman who seemed mindful nonetheless of the inconvenience she was causing in the midst of an already tense situation—which is to say, she tried to be polite to Cheever, who at the time required a special brand of tact. "What a ghastly color," she remarked of some medicine Cheever had fetched when she was ill. "I fly into a rage," he noted, "and say that the least she could do would be to refrain from complaining about the color of her medicine. She cries. I apologize."

That was during the first, relatively placid stage of Martha's visit. Soon Cheever decided that the girl had a "fleeting bloom of attractiveness" and that he might as well enjoy the arrangement while it lasted: "Dazzy had, after all, been looking for a young mistress and found one sleeping in the spare room. If you behave like a damned fool, he said to Muzzy, you can expect some consequences." But Martha was impervious to his charm—more so, indeed, than just about anybody he'd ever met. His wit left her stone-cold, she flinched at his caresses, and was amused (in a bad way) when he "prance[d] around in [his] underwear."

At length it occurred to Cheever that she perceived him as a "drunken comical and flabby old man," and hence he began despising her in earnest. He especially resented the way she distracted Mary from her wifely duties. One evening, when served a dish he'd always affected to like, Cheever roared *"Meatballs!"*—shambling out the door and off to a proper restaurant meal, while Mary and Martha bemusedly watched him go. He became convinced the women's relationship was "unsavory," and said so, emphatically, on an almost nightly basis. Matters came to a head when Cheever interrupted a "tender conversation" (as he put it) by wandering downstairs stark naked; as Mary recalled, she and her guest "tried to be polite," but couldn't quite stifle their giggles. This, it seemed, was not the response Cheever had expected.

The girl was gone by December, and Cheever resolved to treat himself for the holidays. A lot of publicity was scheduled for *Bullet Park*, and he was worried about his smile: his teeth had always been a disaster—snaggled, capped, and brown—and his dentist advised him to get rid of them once and for all. After the procedure at Phelps Memorial, Cheever remained incoherent long after the anesthesia wore off, hardly recognizing his own family; it was Rob Cowley's impression that "he'd had no alcohol that day and couldn't function." Once Cheever got used to the dentures, at any rate, he took to flashing them with cheerful regularity. "Wipe that artificial smile off your face," said his exasperated wife. "The only thing artificial about this smile is the teeth," he replied.

The day after Christmas, he took his family to Curaçao, where they stayed at a little resort on a remote part of the island. Cheever begged off while the others snorkeled; he claimed that he couldn't put a tube in his mouth "lest [his] smile fall to the bottom of the sea," but in fact he was terrified of swimming over the abysmal depth of the continental shelf. Mostly he drank gin and tonic, read Graham Greene, and flirted with his wife—the two had entered yet another of their weirdly renascent phases. "We had adjoining terraces," Susan remembered, "and I looked over and she was sitting on his lap, and I was like *whoa*." The usual status quo became evident, however, when Federico began to sob on the airplane. Ben, sitting beside him, asked what was wrong, but the boy only shook his head. "I thought it was because he'd been stuck with this problem, that we'd deserted him," said Ben. "I thought, 'This is bad. This is really bad.' "

CHAPTER THIRTY

{ 1968–1969 }

D AYS AFTER FINISHING *Bullet Park*, Cheever signed a lucrative two-book contract with Knopf, ending his happy thirteen-
year association with Harper & Row. Meeting his new editor,
Robert Gottlieb ("A pleasant young man"), Cheever was uncharacter-
istically insistent that Knopf make it worth his while, since otherwise
he had no good reason to leave Harper. "I'm afraid I was a nuisance
about money," he wrote Gottlieb afterward, "but I have this nightmare
where I push a super-market wagon across River Street—macaroni
and cold cuts—and am either run down by Roth in his Daimler or
buzzed by Updike in a new flying machine." The whole business left
him in an awkward position with Harper: Frances Lindley had labored
extensively over *The Wapshot Scandal* ("page after page of ruled paper
with comments and queries," as she recalled); without her efforts, said
Cheever, the novel "would have withered and died unknown." Squea-
mish as ever to admit that money exerted a pull, Cheever explained to
her that he'd been discouraged by "gossip" about "so many changes at
Harpers" ("I felt as if the firm as I knew it had vanished"), and then
retreated into a quip: "I've changed everything—my doctor, my
lawyer, my dentist and my liquor dealer. I've even asked Elizabeth
Ames to resign from Yaddo. As you can see, I'm running wild."

Actually, his role in removing Ames was the result of long, sober
deliberation. Several years earlier she'd finally acceded to one of
Cheever's pet proposals—the building of a swimming pool—only to
change her mind at the last instant, again, fearing her guests would
behave dreadfully in and around water. Cheever was furious: "I believe

we have voted for the swimming pool seven times now," he wrote Cowley, "and to have the vote of any representative body disregarded this many times seems to me to reflect seriously on its usefulness. . . . [I]f the pool is overlooked again I would like to resign."* And this, of course, was part of a larger grievance. Ames's conduct as director had always been a bit on the peremptory side, and now that she was all but totally deaf and a little demented, too, she'd become a tyrant. "*No!*" she shouted into the telephone when an eminent critic called (during working hours) and asked to speak with a resident artist. At the time, the critic in question was visiting the ladylike Anne Palamountain, wife of the Skidmore president, who vividly remembers her own first visit to Yaddo. It was late at night, and her new friend Cheever had proposed that she and her husband follow him (amid a lot of antic shushing, lest the despot be roused) to a back door of the Trask mansion; making their furtive way into the main hall, they encountered an equally apprehensive Philip Roth creeping down the stairs. "Ames had everyone terrified," said Palamountain. It got so bad that Cheever himself had begun to dread the place—"the demesne of a powerful and weary old lady," whom he blamed, moreover, for cultivating "the company of emasculated men" and hence leaving him at the mercy of Rorem and the like: "There are never any attractive or available women and in my desperation for company I find myself drinking with homosexuals." Still, a part of him would always be fond of Mrs. Ames, and he took care to relate his decision to her in the most gracious possible terms: "This, of course, has nothing to do with our long and affectionate friendship, or with the fact that you have been my most intimate confident [sic]. Without Yaddo, as you've managed it, it would have been impossible for me to be a writer. . . . [But] I am convinced that a change is in order and I know you have the strength and intelligence to assess such an opinion." At the subsequent board meeting, when Ames conceded her resignation, Cheever spoke movingly of her "imperturbable, humorous and fair" treatment of the (very) odd assortment of artists she'd hosted over the years: "This is a life and a triumph."

---

*The pool was built, of course, and Cheever made the most of it. During his visits he held court there almost every afternoon—often in the nude, despite the relative modesty of certain peers. Hortense Calisher, for one, never forgot her shock when a naked Cheever popped out of the water and sat beside her, chatting amiably about one thing and another.

·   ·   ·

As 1968 CAME TO AN END, Cheever summed up his recent life as follows: "I've written nothing since the novel was completed and have spent a lot of time posing for photographers and mouthing crap about the essential prophetic nature of literature." Knopf had paid dearly for *Bullet Park* and insisted the author do his part in promoting the book, always a dreary prospect for Cheever and even more so in this case. He thought he liked the novel all right, but he didn't want to *talk* about it—certainly not in terms of its deeper meaning, or (God forbid) its autobiographical elements, though he knew these were precisely the sort of questions he'd be asked. As he worried in his journal, "I don't know whether to admit to Sheed that I suffer from melancholy and that the incantations were invented to get me, not Tony [Nailles] out of bed." Sheed was Wilfrid Sheed, an estimable novelist in his own right, who would soon be interviewing Cheever for a big feature in *Life*. Cheever knew what to expect when the magazine called before-hand and asked him to give a cocktail party and play a game of touch football for the photographer. "Clichés of suburban life!" he sighed in a separate interview. "This is not the way I live. I told [*Life*] they have to take me as a boozy recluse." To illustrate this, Cheever downed mar-tinis for the duration of the *Life* shoot, though he agreeably tossed a football and stood in the Vanderlips' empty swimming pool and so on. As for Sheed, Cheever would later boast that he'd gotten the man so plastered that he (Sheed) had had to come back and finish the inter-view later—and even then Cheever was as evasive as ever, letting Sheed know that he could interpret *Bullet Park* however he liked, as long as he didn't mistake it for "crypto-autobiography." "After a few more questions have been detonated like this," Sheed wrote, "you have the impression you are supposed to have: that the work is everything, the writer is nothing."

What the writer was, in fact, was lonely and depressed and desper-ately alcoholic, and no amount of wealth or fame seemed to help much. The good news kept pouring in: the Book-of-the-Month Club had paid fifty thousand dollars to feature *Bullet Park* as an alternate selection; Bantam had offered seventy-five thousand for paperback rights (though Knopf was holding out for twice that much); the first printing had been bumped to fifty-five thousand. "Celebrate!" said Gottlieb, but Cheever didn't quite know where to begin. His dogs were gone at the moment (Mary had taken them for a long walk), and it occurred to him that he "[didn't] seem to have any chums"—or chums he cared to see, at any rate. Toward Christmas, his publisher put him up for two days at the St. Regis Hotel so he could give more interviews, and so he did—gleefully ordering bottles of gin up to his room ("Guess what the bill is? Twenty-nine dollars! Wait until Alfred Knopf sees that!") as well as bottles of whatever the interviewers were having, and meanwhile nobody seemed to find anything amiss about this witty, boyish man who appeared to be drinking himself to death. "In fighting the hootch I seem to be fighting something much stronger than my own character," Cheever reflected as the new year began; "I am overwhelmed by the spirits in the gin bottle. What, under the circumstances, does one do. Pray. Join AA."

Then, too, he began to wonder whether his book was really worth all the fuss: "Sometimes I recall a chapter that seems competent. Sometimes the book returns to me as sloppy, trifling and worthless." As his paranoia began to swell, he projected these doubts onto his editor, Gottlieb, whom he suspected of deliberately "cut[ting]" him at the Century Club, as well as "exploit[ing] every possibility for anxiety and self-doubt"—this despite all the money and attention Knopf had lavished on the book, and never mind Gottlieb's constant reassurance and enthusiasm. Indeed, the editor had expressed only a single significant qualm: "Perhaps you remember that when we first talked," he wrote Cheever, "I said that the only thing that I didn't love about the book was that it stopped—I wish it had gone on longer. . . . [T]here is an abruptness there." Cheever said he would try to "enlarge the last chapter," but didn't—either because he was too blocked by then to write any further, or perhaps because he simply decided that he preferred the ambiguity of his original ending. Whatever the case, Gottlieb continued to make encouraging noises and even mentioned that Cheever's old nemesis, Bennett Cerf, was "very impressed and moved" by the novel.

In more temperate moments, Cheever reminded himself that *Bullet Park* was, if nothing else, "better than the Scandal," and that he'd basically fulfilled his own aims, to wit: "a cast of three characters, a simple and resonant prose style and a scene where a man saves his beloved son from death by fire." Let the reviewers do their worst, then, though Cheever hardly expected as much; on the contrary, his friend Lehmann-Haupt had brought good tidings on that score, or so it seemed. Lehmann-Haupt, then an editor at the *Times Book Review*, had asked Cheever whom he would choose to review *Bullet Park* if the choice were his. "Ben DeMott," said Cheever. "Good!" said Lehmann-Haupt. "Because that's who you're getting." To both men, DeMott had seemed the perfect fit: a Waspy Amherst professor, he'd written a judicious review of the *Scandal* for *Harper's*—applauding the novel as a witty (if episodic) evocation of the modern world's "living hell"—the sort of thing, in short, that Cheever had in mind when he remarked to an interviewer at the St. Regis, "I would rather have an informative [review] than a silly rave." In this case, though, a "silly rave" would have done nicely, given that DeMott's review was slated for the entire front page, and would be accompanied on page 2 by Lehmann-Haupt's interview with the author. Not long before the review appeared on April 27, however, Cheever got a call from his agent: Lehmann-Haupt's sidebar piece, which was nothing but admiring, had been bumped to the back pages—a bad sign. As Susan Cheever remembered, "My father seemed suddenly very frail."

DeMott's review (enticingly titled "A Grand Gatherum of Some Late 20th-Century American Weirdos") faulted Cheever for everything from his "sad, licked lyricism" to his "carelessness, lax compositions, perfunctoriness" to the "broken-backed" structure of his novel:

> And finally—most important maybe—there's the problem of story style vs. novel style. Except when tricked up in gothicism, fantasy or allegory, the novel is a world of explanations, and the story is a world of phenomena. . . . [Cheever's stories] say that nowadays a man falls in love with his baby sitter and heals himself by buying a lathe . . . and by the time the reader of any of them thinks to ask, What? What was that? Why? he's into the next tale in the book. No explanations offered or required.

With novels, DeMott suggested, authors are obliged to provide some explicit rationale for their characters' behavior, and this was conspicuously absent in *Bullet Park*. But then, one might just as well make a similar observation about DeMott's review—that is, before the good reader can ask, What? But isn't the present novel exempt from such "explanations" *precisely* because it's intended as "gothicism, fantasy or allegory"?—DeMott has already clinched his argument, as far as it goes: "John Cheever's short stories are and will remain lovely birds—

dense in inexplicables and beautifully trim. But in the gluey atmosphere of 'Bullet Park' no birds sing." And so it went for other reviewers who judged the novel in naturalistic terms: The plot "is not at all convincing," said Charles Nicol in *The Atlantic Monthly;* Hammer "is no more interesting than any other lunatic," said Guy Davenport in the *National Review* (Davenport also echoed a number of his colleagues in describing the novel's ending as "false and shockingly inept").

Granted, *Bullet Park* is a strange performance, and it was a bad sign that even reviewers who were nothing but well disposed to Cheever seemed a little puzzled. A few months before her review appeared in the *Washington Post Book World,* Joyce Carol Oates had been quoted as saying that she was Updike's and Cheever's "ideal reader" ("whatever they write I read immediately, and I read it again two or three times"), so it made sense perhaps that she and Updike were en rapport in regard to *Bullet Park:* neither thought the book amounted to a novel, properly speaking, but rather that it worked (as Updike wrote in the London *Times*) "as a slowly revolving mobile of marvellously poeticized moments," or, as Oates put it, "a series of eerie, sometimes beautiful, sometimes overwrought vignettes." Oates knew better than to worry whether the plot was "convincing" or not, pointing out that Cheever was if anything bent on making his plot as outlandish as possible; and yet, for all the novel's seeming absurdity, said Oates, it conveyed a sense of "terror . . . as deadly, more deadly, than any promised in the glib new genre of 'black comedy.' Cheever has been writing such comedy for decades." John Leonard, whose review appeared in the daily *New York Times,* also realized that conventional narrative was beside the point, and praised the novel as Cheever's "deepest, most challenging book." And finally a synthesis of sorts was found in Anatole Broyard's *New Republic* review, which suggested that the book was a little too fraught with oddities, that Cheever had apparently gotten carried away by his own virtuosity: "He is determined to be surprising or original, even at the cost of incredulity."

Such a range of opinion (and general puzzlement) indicated obtuseness on the part of certain reviewers, but also the possibility that Cheever's own intentions were so intuitive, and subtle, that in some respects they were obscure even to himself. In the novel's formative stages, he'd noted: "I count on my experience with Fred [his brother] and the division in my own spirit but I haven't made much progress." He seems to have begun, then, with his old obsession over the duality of human nature and his own nature in particular: dark and light, flesh and spirit, grossness and aspiration. However, when readers later interpreted *Bullet Park* along these lines—suggesting, for instance, that Hammer and Nailles were opposite sides of the same person—Cheever balked: "Neither Hammer nor Nailles were meant to be either psychiatric or social metaphors; they were meant to be two men with their own risks. I think the book was misunderstood on those terms." It bears repeating that Cheever had a horror of simplistic allegory, and would naturally prefer to regard his own creations as somewhat rounded, distinct personages—but obviously Hammer and Nailles also serve a metaphorical purpose, underlined by their almost flippantly suggestive nomenclature: "Lying in bed that night Nailles thought: Hammer and Nailles, spaghetti and meatballs, salt and pepper . . ." And lest we miss the point, the narrator also observes that their doubleness extends to a rather exact physical resemblance: "They were about the same weight, height and age, and they both wore a size-eight shoe."

Whether or not the two characters were *originally* conceived as complementary opposites—that is, as an easy metaphor for a divided personality—Cheever ultimately developed the idea into something more complex (and even, at times, opaque). Some critics have made the point that Hammer and Nailles are actually quite similar, and the novelist John Gardner suggested that the main difference is merely a matter of luck: "Nailles's blessing is that he is married to a good woman and has a son, whereas Hammer is married to a bitch and is childless." But while it's true that Nailles's marriage is happier than Hammer's, one should bear in mind that Mrs. Nailles's devotion to her husband is something of an imposture: on at least three occasions, she has nearly succumbed to extramarital temptation, only to be saved each time by some happy accident ("a fire, a runny nose and some spoiled sturgeon eggs"); accidental or not, though, she regards "her virtue as a jewel—an emblem—of character, discipline and intelligence." So it goes, then, to some extent, with Hammer and Nailles: it's not that one is good and the other evil, but that Nailles's failings are bridled by a rather naïve reverence for social convention, and also perhaps (as Gardner would have it) by his relative happiness and luck; in actual fact, though, his failings differ from Hammer's mostly in terms of *degree*. For example, both Hammer and Nailles are homophobic, for the common reason that they fear homosexuality in themselves. "I wish it didn't exist," Nailles admits to his son, explaining that the only reason he joined the Chemists Club was so he could have a place to "pump ship" in midtown other than the Grand Central toilets, where he feared "getting into a moral crisis" every time he was accosted by a homosexual. For his part, Hammer escapes the attention of a "faggot" on the beach by helping a family fly their kite—an act of conspicuous wholesomeness—though afterward he's enraged by the unnerving potentialities of his own nature: "The faggot had vanished but I longed then for a moral creation whose mandates were heftier than the delight of children, the trusting smiles of strangers and a length of kite string." Likewise, too, Hammer and Nailles are both in their fashion prone to depression, alcoholism, and murderous tendencies. Nailles's weaknesses, however, are mostly under control, whereas Hammer's incipient criminality is revealed by his long first-person rant in Part Two; afterward, when the narrative reverts to the third person, the reader sees—from outside—how strenuously Hammer works to impersonate a relatively "normal" person such as Nailles: "[Hammer] had a nervous way of shifting his head, setting his teeth and bracing his shoulders as if his thinking consisted of a series of resolves and decisions. I must cut down on my smoking. (Teeth-setting.) Life can be beautiful. (Shoulder-bracing.) I am often misunderstood. (A sudden lifting of the head.) Nailles' manner was much more serene." Nailles may be more "serene," but when Hammer reveals his inner self with a casual suggestion that Nailles shoot his beloved old dog, the latter is so infuriated that "for a moment he might have killed Hammer."

Like his wife, Nailles prefers to believe in his own happiness and virtue, just as he takes for granted the happiness and virtue of his neighbors in Bullet Park—a typical Cheeverian suburb where decorum prevails at all costs, while misery and corruption and even human mortality are denied whenever possible. "I think [Bullet Park] stinks," says Hammer's wife, Marietta, at an otherwise genteel gathering. "It's just like a masquerade party. All you have to do is to get your clothes at Brooks, catch the train and show up in church once a week and no one will ever ask a question about your identity." When she then proceeds to castigate her cipherlike (but actually homicidal) husband as a "doormat," the other guests politely make their excuses to leave rather than endure this unsavory spectacle of marital unhappiness. Thus Mrs. Hammer serves much the same purpose as Gee-Gee in "The Scarlet Moving Van," whose drunken tirades are meant to instruct his neighbors ("They've got to learn. . . . I've got to teach them") in the inevitability of "anger and lust and the agonies of death." As for Nailles, he is a kind of ideal candidate for such edification. "Well I suppose there's plenty to be sad about if you look around," he remarks to his son, "but it makes me sore to have people always chopping at the suburbs. . . . The living is cheaper out here and I'd be lost if I couldn't get some exercise. People seem to make some connection between respectability and moral purity that I don't get." What Nailles doesn't "get," of course, is that the vaunted "respectability" of a utopia such as Bullet Park is a sham: his charming neighbors the Wickwires are drinking themselves into early decrepitude, while Mr. Heathcup tries assuaging his misery by painting his house until he finally gives up and kills himself. For Nailles, however—a soi-disant "chemist" whose real job is merchandising Spang, a mouthwash, thereby devoting himself to the denial of such everyday unpleasantness as bad breath—all infirmity belongs to some abstract "principality" far away from Bullet Park, and it bemuses him to receive occasional reminders of such a place in the form of a postcard, say: "Edna is under sedation most of the time and has about three weeks to live but she would like a letter from you." No wonder that when he first observes Hammer (at church), he decides that his would-be destroyer is a man of "invincible" excellence—because, after all, he *appears* to be. "I go on about the vulnerability of Nailles," Cheever reflected in his notes, "of a man who was so absolutely of his time and the conveniences of his society that he was utterly defenseless at the appearance of an alien set of values."

Nailles's best quality is also the source of his vulnerability—namely, his extravagant love of family, "[which was] like some limitless discharge of a clear amber fluid that would surround them, cover them, preserve them and leave them insulated but visible like the contents of an aspic." His ability to demonstrate this love, however, is constrained by the narrow propriety of life as a Bullet Park paterfamilias. When, for instance, he finds some dirty pictures concealed in his son's dictionary, he quietly disposes of them and just as quietly informs the boy, without censure, that he has done so. Trusting as ever in appearances, he simply assumes that Tony accepts his decision as being for his own good; if, however, Nailles were to turn on Tony's tape recorder—one of the many generous gifts he delights in giving his son—he'd discover that all was not so well in their relationship: "You dirty old baboon," the young man intones on the tape, "you dirty old baboon . . ." Indeed, Nailles is so shocked when his son finally reveals his true feelings— his disdain for a father who wastes his life "pushing mouthwash"— that he responds by trying to "split [Tony's] skull" with a golf putter, and so precipitates the melancholy that leaves his son languishing in bed.

Part One of the novel—concerning Nailles and the world of Bullet Park—though a bit on the desultory side, nonetheless has a kind of poetic coherence. In the first chapter we are shown around the suburb with the mysterious Hammer and his real-estate agent, while a suave omniscient narrator remarks on the lives of various characters encountered along the way. As Updike and Oates pointed out, the plot unfolds in a series of vignettes—"moments"—related by a sort of nuanced repetition. The charming Wickwires, for example, are presented as representative citizens who constantly hurt themselves with a lot of drunken accidents—then, after an exquisite four-page set piece, they vanish without a trace for more than two hundred pages; finally, as the novel is ending (and only the careful reader will remember the Wickwires at all, much less their drunken tendency to hurt themselves), they reappear, charming as ever: he with court plaster over one eye and she in a wheelchair. "I don't work with plots," Cheever remarked in his *Paris Review* interview (and throughout his career in so many words). "I work with intuition, apprehension, dreams, concepts. . . . Plot implies narrative and a lot of crap." Fair enough. On the other hand, one can see DeMott's point about the "broken-backed" structure of the novel: Part Two—Hammer's monologue—seems a mystifying digression from all that has gone before. Nailles, the erstwhile protagonist, disappears Wickwire-like for some seventy pages, and the tone of the book is entirely different—indeed, we seem to have stumbled into an altogether different novel, or rather a string of diffuse non sequiturs. A letter from Hammer's mother rambles on for several pages, serving no discernible purpose except to establish that she is barking mad, which might have been established with a sentence or two—with, say, her assertion that she can divine the sort of person who has preceded her in certain hotel beds: "It is a simple fact that we impress something of ourselves—our spirits and desires—on the mattresses where we lie and I have more than ample evidence to prove my point." Much attention is also lavished on Hammer's oddball father, a muscle-bound drunk who models his physique for caryatids holding up parts of various

Munich hotels; when at last Hammer finds the man—passed out, naked, and wearing a necklace of champagne corks (as Cheever claims to have found his own father)—nothing comes of it. Hammer leaves. "What I wanted was verisimilitude and improbability," Cheever explained to Litvinov, who confessed bewilderment over these episodes. "[Hammer's mother's] letters—and Taylor holding up all those buildings—are meant to seem true and false. It seems to me that conventional narrative is untruthful these days and that one has to divine an inner narrative. Oh ho." "Oh ho" is a phrase to which Cheever often reverted; usually it implied a kind of risible doubt over the merit of his own pronouncements.

One might argue that Hammer's story is bizarre and incoherent because Hammer himself is mad, and so he proceeds according to the dreamlike logic of madness. His primary quest, after all, is to find "a room with yellow walls" and thereby cure his *cafard*, because he finds such an ambience uniquely cheerful. He is so determined that when he finally discovers the yellow-roomed house of one Dora Emmison, he proceeds to ply her with drink and thus cause her to die in an automobile accident—whereupon he buys the house and is happy for a while. Then his wife, Marietta, repaints the house pink and his *cafard* returns. At this point, the reader is perhaps too dumbfounded to wonder why the man doesn't simply buy a can of yellow paint. John Leonard, in his generous critique of the novel, suggested that Hammer "isn't intended to be believable" because he is "an aspect or fantasy of Nailles's mind . . . an *Other* fashioned from anarchic depths, a creature of repressed libidinal ferocity." It may be so; one pictures Cheever nodding his head and wondering if that's what he meant after all. Indeed, it would explain just about everything, if not for the consummate banality of Nailles's mind: how could such a man begin to imagine a quest for yellow walls, a father who models for caryatids, the whole fantastic rigmarole?

As for Hammer's motive in attempting to murder Tony Nailles—it seems wholly random, contradictory, and yes, perfunctory. At first Hammer appears to be motivated by his mother's manifesto condemning the "spiritual poverty" of American life; exiled in Kitzbühel, the woman explains why she refrains from returning to her homeland: " 'I would settle in some place like Bullet Park. I would buy a house. I would be very inconspicuous. . . . I would single out as an example some young man, preferably an advertising executive . . . a good example of a life lived without any genuine emotion or value. . . . I would crucify him on the door of Christ's Church,' she said passionately. 'Nothing less than a crucifixion will wake the world.' " When Hammer hears this, he sensibly concludes that his mother is "a crazy old woman"; but later, for whatever reason (because of his rage over the "faggot" on the beach?), he decides his mother's plan is "sound" and proceeds to carry it out to a nicety, hoping eventually to murder Nailles, whose photograph he accidentally finds in a dental journal. Why Nailles? Because he's the very sort of vapid ad-man his mother had specified? Because of his idiotic commercials for Spang? Not at all: "It was infantile to rail at this sort of thing, Hammer thought. It had been the national fare for twenty-five years and it was not likely to improve. . . . Hammer had chosen the victim for his excellence." *What* excellence? Nailles's happy home life? The author doesn't say, nor does he say why Hammer decides (in a one-sentence afterthought) to murder Tony instead.

Perhaps the most controversial part of the novel is the last few pages, where Nailles saves his son's life. Years later Cheever wrote in his journal that the scene "was almost never understood" and he wondered if he "could have done better." If he was still wondering at that point, then he must have felt as though he'd accomplished at least something of what he'd intended: namely, a scene in which Nailles is able to "implement" his love for Tony in some redemptive, heroic fashion, and thereby recognize the reality of evil as embodied by Hammer and reflected somewhat in himself and the rest of humanity. And yet this climactic episode—so essential to the novel's gravitas—is written almost as slapstick. In oddly flat, declarative prose, Cheever describes his determined murderer, Hammer, dragging the unconscious Tony to the altar and dousing him with gasoline—then deciding to pause and smoke a cigarette and go on smoking as long as it takes for Nailles to drive home, fetch a chainsaw, and return to the locked church:

"Hammer?" [Nailles calls from outside]
"Yes."
"Is Tony all right?"
"He's all right now but I'm going to kill him. First I want to finish this cigarette."
. . . [Nailles] made a diagonal slash across the door and broke it

easily with his shoulders. Hammer was sitting in a front pew, crying. The red gasoline tank was beside him. Nailles lifted his son off
the altar and carried him out into the rain.

And then—quite abruptly, just as Gottlieb said—the novel is over. We
are told with slapdash brevity that Hammer confessed to attempted
homicide and was quoted in the newspaper as explaining that he meant
"to awaken the world" (but *why*, given that he'd asserted earlier that he
accepted the world for what it is and rather was motivated by his victim's "excellence"?), and so we are brought to the final sentence: "Tony
went back to school on Monday and Nailles—drugged—went off to
work and everything was as wonderful, wonderful, wonderful, wonderful as it had been." Now, if this be irony—and four "wonderful's"
would seem to suggest as much—then we must surmise that life is *not*
wonderful in Bullet Park and never was, and besides Nailles still needs
to take tranquilizers just to get through the day. So nothing has
changed; but if that's true, then what's the point of the whole triumphant rescue? What, for that matter, is the point of the novel? As
Joyce Carol Oates concluded her review, "Irony so pervades Cheever's
writing that one cannot tell where whimsy [ends] and a real nastiness, a
profound nastiness, begins. Is everything wonderful in Bullet Park? It
may well be." If one of our most prominent novelist-critics (and an
"ideal reader" of Cheever to boot) was perplexed, it's safe to assume a
lot of general readers were, too.

But at the time, the reader whose opinion mattered most was Benjamin DeMott. After he "dumped on [the book] in the *Times*," said
Cheever, "everybody picked up their marbles and ran home." Knopf
stopped advertising, and sales petered out at just over thirty-three
thousand copies—a little better than dismal, given all the advance hype
and Cheever's reputation. Still, he affected to take it in stride. After all,
he'd made enough money to last him at least two years, he said, "and
one couldn't ask for more." But how long was two years, under the circumstances? Cheever had taken four years to write *Bullet Park*, and
perhaps five times as long to work his way to some acceptable version
of *The Wapshot Chronicle*, and never mind that he was now an almost
hopeless alcoholic who felt only the faintest impulse to write anything.
Federico never forgot his own sense of dread that Thanksgiving, when
he overheard Lehmann-Haupt say to his father—who nodded
benignly ("Oh, really?")—that the novel didn't really hang together

and DeMott had been right.* Behind the insouciant façade, though, Cheever fully shared his younger son's dread. Before long, he decided he didn't like *Bullet Park* either ("I think something misfired"), and was only a little cheered, two and a half years later, when John Gardner wrote a long vindication of the novel for the *Times Book Review*, declaring that its detractors had been "dead wrong": "*Bullet Park* is a novel to pore over, move around in, live with. The image repetitions, the stark and subtle correspondences that create the book's ambiguous meaning, its uneasy courage and compassion, sink in and in, like a curative spell."

Perhaps, but at the time it seemed too little, too late—at any rate there was no particular resurgence of interest, and Cheever continued (for the rest of his life, really) to brood over the DeMott review. Sometimes he agreed with the man, agreed with Lehmann-Haupt, and went on thinking the book was a botch; at other, more spirited moments, he accused DeMott of "plugging for tenure at Amherst," and meanwhile his loathing for academics—considerable at the best of times—became even more pronounced. A year or so after *Bullet Park* had quietly disappeared, Cheever responded to some pompous remarks from one of his wife's Briarcliff colleagues by hurling a glass of bourbon at the man. "I aimed for the head but I got him in the stomach," he wrote Litvinov. "He is a frustrated professor of English and I have come to consider frustration a most dangerous human condition."

---

*Cheever got his own back by damning Lehmann-Haupt's journalism with fainter and fainter praise: "Well, Christopher," he observed a few years later, "you've settled in and become a highly—ah—*reliable* reviewer."

CHAPTER THIRTY-ONE

{ 1969–1970 }

I N 1968, HOPE LANGE had resumed her career with a starring role in the sitcom *The Ghost & Mrs. Muir*, about a spirited widow who moves her family into an old New England cottage and befriends its resident ghost. Each week Cheever watched the show and made casual asides to Federico (his perennial TV companion) suggesting that he knew a lot of inside dope about the pretty actress who played Mrs. Muir. By then Lange had separated from Alan Pakula, and in early 1969, during a trip to New York, she gave Cheever a call and the two went skating at Rockefeller Center; either that time or the next, the relationship became carnal—or rather as carnal as Cheever could manage: "We rip off our clothes [at the Biltmore] and spend three or four lovely hours together," he wrote in his journal, "moving from the sofa to the floor and back to the sofa again. I don't throw a proper hump, which disconcerts no one . . . so it's all finger-fucking, sucking, tongue-eating, arse-kissing, bone-cracking embraces and earnest declarations of love . . ." A woman of extravagant candor, Lange would later characterize Cheever as "the horniest man [she] ever met" (impotence withal), if a bit "overly concerned with his own needs": "[He was] like a high-school quarterback who wants to get his rocks off," she said, echoing the consensus opinion.

Though meetings with the actress were sporadic at best, Cheever rarely missed a chance to boast about his "mistress" whatever the company, particularly if his wife was in earshot. "I suppose it's possible to love two women," he sighed, clasping Mary's hand across the dinner table, having returned from a tryst in time to sit down to a nice home-cooked meal. ("He may be unfaithful," said Mary, "he may be a drunk, but he always came home for dinner.") Often his references to Lange were merely in passing, though he could be spiteful if he thought the occasion warranted it. "I'll be taking the train back with you," he announced to some overnight guests (and indirectly his wife) at breakfast; "I have a date with Hope." One night he even phoned his daughter—as if casting about for a loved one to share his happiness— and said he was leaving her mother at last and marrying "the most beautiful woman in the world." But of course this was never really in the cards. For one thing, Lange could hardly understand half of what Cheever was saying, because of his muttering accent; besides, he always had to catch an early train back to Ossining. And finally, for all his gloating infatuation, Cheever had to admit (at least to himself) that his feelings didn't run all that deep—Lange was simply "the sunny side of the street," as he put it: "[Hope's] brightness precludes shadowy and immortal longings. . . . It is only that [I am] happy and light-hearted in her company."

Still, he was disgruntled enough at first to consider following his lover to the Coast and starting anew, until one day in March he suffered what seemed a rather minor skiing injury. As he wrote Lange, "Swooping (or so I thought) among the trees in the orchard I went down like a tray of dishes and tore all the ligaments in my left knee." Fitted with a plaster cast from hip to foot, Cheever was gratified when his wife responded with sweet solicitude (as ever in the case of any stricken creature, be it husband, dog, or deer*), and he supposed it might even prove a good thing, for a while, to "substitute physical pain and infirmity for melancholy." It didn't, however, work out that way: not only did Cheever's *cafard* increase ("it fills the house like smoke"), but the injury took a long time to heal, and meanwhile Cheever began to bloat with alcoholic edema. More than ever, writing was out of the question—indeed, he found it hard to type a single declarative sentence. The best he could muster, on a good day, was a few lines in his journal and/or a distressful letter or two. "I can't write you a story," he wrote Maxwell. "I can't write anyone a story. I know that Bullet Park is not that massive but six months later I still feel poleaxed. Twice I seem to have had a donnee but I don't seem to have any motive for following through." Rather than blame his funk entirely on a failing liver and

---

*Notwithstanding Cheever's occasional expressions of self-pity to the contrary.

attendant malaise, Cheever figured he'd exhausted some aspect of his career (such as writing about "the minutiae of upper-middle-class life"), and would simply have to wait and be patient until some fresh aesthetic approach presented itself.

And so the willpower that had driven Cheever to become one of the greatest writers of his time—despite everything—was now reduced to restraining him, a little, from racing to the pantry for his first drink of the day. "First scoop at half past nine," he'd tabulate, or "Held off this morning until eleven-twenty-two." Whereas in the past he'd taken care not to let his family see him drinking before lunch, these days it was a little too much to ask. One morning Cheever was pretending as usual to read the *Times*, his antennae tingling while his wife moved around in the kitchen—arranging flowers, cracking eggs, and finally (just as he thought she was about to go outside and hang laundry) unfolding the ironing board "to [his] absolute horror": "She seldom, if ever, irons, and this maneuver seemed to me unfair. I supposed she was going to iron the wrinkles out of the dress she would wear to lunch. This oughtn't to take more than five minutes, but five minutes was more than I could wait, and in full view of my wife, and the world, I went in the pantry and mixed a drink. It was eighteen minutes to eleven." Amid such petty embarrassments and racking hangovers, Cheever wondered and wondered why he drank so murderously much—after all, his wife was being nice to him for a little while, ditto his dogs and children, and there was plenty of money in the bank. At the Yaddo meeting that year, Cheever listened with a lugubrious face while Philip Roth went on about the shortcomings of fame: Since *Portnoy's Complaint*, he'd been mobbed for autographs wherever he went and could hardly go to the theater anymore, etc. By way of reply, Cheever said he was quitting everything—Yaddo, Institute, Century, everything—and letting younger folk like Roth take his place. "I've had my career," he sighed, "and now it's over."*

As Cheever's gloom that autumn suggests, his recent therapy with a new psychiatrist hadn't borne much fruit. "Today I go to see Dr. Silverberg," he'd written in his journal on May 20, 1969 (his first entry in

---

*Roth had written Cheever a tactful letter enumerating the *pages* he'd liked in *Bullet Park*, to which Cheever replied: "[M]any thanks for putting down the page numbers. I checked them all. I thought Portenoy [sic] great from page one straight through to the end."

at least two months). "Hip Hip Hooray." Next entry: "Hip hip hooray. I see Dr. Silverberg but I am too sauced to remember anything about his appearance beyond the fact that he wears a ring." Dr. J. William Silverberg's notes serve to corroborate this: "[Patient] seems quite drunk . . . and forgets what he had said a few minutes before." One thing the patient definitely (if superfluously) said was that he was "drinking too much," and the following week he elaborated that he'd been depressed for quite a while. There were a lot of problems in his life—trains, bridges, phobias of one sort and another—but his "most important conflict" was homosexuality: "I've never confessed this to anyone before," he said, admitting to a total of three encounters in his lifetime, most recently in December.* All this was due, he speculated, to the pressure he felt having to "prove his sexual prowess over and over again"—a statement that led happily to the subject of Hope Lange, who nowadays figured in his ritual for getting out of bed in the morning, thus: "Hope is coming and she's beautiful and loves me and I *must* get up . . ." And what about his wife? "At present she's quite rejecting," Cheever said, adding (with a slight chuckle) that the reason was "unclear" to him.

After the first few sessions, Cheever decided he'd "exhausted [his] secrets" and returned to the delicate mischief he'd practiced on Dr. Hays. "But I'm concerned about *you*," he'd say when Silverberg tried directing him back to the matter at hand. At one point the doctor mentioned he was planning a trip to Rome, whereupon Cheever seized on the subject again and again—hotels, restaurants, monuments the man simply *must* see in order to have a satisfactory experience. As with Hays, Cheever presented Silverberg with an autographed copy of *The Wapshot Chronicle*, and even invited the man to have dinner with his family. And sometimes, still, he'd drop all the tourist talk and resume his role as a proper analysand: for all his success—he announced one day—he felt like "a wreck of [him]self," though he *did* try to be "good

---

*Though of course Cheever had a compulsion to discuss homosexuality—especially with psychiatrists—he tended to fudge the facts. He may have had an encounter in December 1968, but there's no evidence of this in his journal or elsewhere. But even if he were lying about such an episode, his total number of at least semi-verifiable homosexual encounters to that date would number more than "three": one counts Fax, Walker Evans, Kentfield, Rorem, to name only the most obviously carnal, and bearing in mind his nebulous intimations about Brodkey, Fred, and various chums of his youth.

tempered" about things (citing his recent leg injury). When the doctor pursued such remarks with questions about (say) Cheever's "need for a passive-dependent role," the latter would dodge away and insist they keep chatting as if they were guests at a cocktail party. And so it went until "a rather diffuse rambling final session" in mid-July, when Cheever wondered aloud what he was gaining from all this. Silverberg wondered, too: despite the odd soulful revelation, Cheever had never asked him for a bit of advice, seeming instead to be "much concerned with how people [were] reacting to him and giving him enough applause for his charm, wit, and success." In any event, Cheever phoned later that summer and officially terminated therapy (politely, of course), and meanwhile Silverberg arrived at much the same conclusion as his predecessor: "[Cheever's] major personality trait is his narcissism, and underneath it all is tremendous self-doubt."

IN THE MIDST of all this, Mary decided ("a little like Zelda," said her suffering husband) to give a lavish black-tie dinner gala in honor of Susan and Rob Cowley, who were leaving that July for a long sojourn in Majorca. Outside the house on Cedar Lane were a tent and dance floor and four-piece band, while the illustrious local literati—the Ellisons, Maxwells, Warrens, et al.—came to pay tribute to the promising young couple. The whole glamorous bash might have been an almost perfect success were it not for a memorably long line to the only available bathroom, not to mention a host who seemed far too drunk even by the standards of the present gathering (though, as ever, he tried to be ingratiating: "You'll notice there isn't anybody from *Knopf* here!" he whispered to his old friend and Harper editor, Frances Lindley).

A month later, the Cheevers followed their daughter and son-in-law to the coastal town of Deya, demesne of the poet Robert Graves. Along for the trip was Cheever's niece Ann, the idea being that she'd look after the twelve-year-old Federico while the adults enjoyed themselves. "Uncle John was a terrible traveler," she recalled. "He didn't like to fly, and before every takeoff he'd lean across the aisle and cross himself on the chest." Also, he was disastrously unorganized, and had to be shooed from one place to the next lest they miss a plane or lose luggage. (Ann's luggage, for one, was lost; she borrowed clothes for most of the trip.) Susan had arranged for them to stay in a quaint little pensione owned by one of Graves's sons, but Mary found the place dreary and raffish. When she complained about the towels, Cheever advised her to get along then to the Madrid Ritz, where the towels were better—a magisterial dismissal that delighted him, in part because he could actually afford the Ritz (for now). Meanwhile, in Deya—where Cheever remained with niece and son—the pensione was less than three dollars a day, wine was nine cents a bottle, and Cheever seemed moderately content to limp among the olive and lemon trees each morning down to the sea, where he'd swim and read and then limp back to a little café for gin and tonic. One night he had dinner with Graves and entourage, which consisted mostly of the genial Cheever feeding the great man questions about the White Goddess and so forth ("he is a kind of prince, scourge, God and war-memorial," Cheever wrote a friend, while describing Graves in his journal as "slippery and sinister"). At some point, too, Cheever developed a crush on the pretty Dutch wife of another literary expatriate (a biographer), and once Federico caught a glimpse of his father sitting with the woman at dusk—"her looking a bit awkward, him looking hungry."

That hungry look was well known to Ben's girlfriend, Lynda, who was about to become part of the family. While in high school, the girl had been a fetching cheerleader who was somewhat disaffected from her straitlaced parents, and hence amenable to her doting future father-in-law. "I spend a lot of time kissing her, and she doesn't mind," Cheever gleefully mused in the summer of 1967. "What about a man making out with his son's date? What about that?" The idyll ended with a nasty shock, however, when Cheever found an unmailed letter from Ben to Lynda describing him and his wife as "the two most self-centered animals in the creation"—this after he'd given the boy a brand-new sports car (a white Austin-Healey Sprite)! Once Ben had departed for his freshman year at Antioch (in the sports car), Cheever sublimated his grief by drafting a high-minded rebuttal to "Tony Nailles" in his journal: "You say that we are the most self-centered people in the world when, in fact, our love for you verges on fatuity," etc. At other times Cheever considered subtle forms of reprisal, such as "disinherit[ing]" his son as a correspondent: "I will deprive him of the delight and humor of my letters," he reflected, but decided this was "contemptible petulance" and so continued to sign himself "Best, Father" and "Yrs, John." ("There is some capriciousness in the love I feel for my children," he'd observed some years earlier. "I seize their

CHEEVER

love greedily when I need it; and am indifferent, callous when my needs lie elsewhere.")

That Christmas (1967) Ben had returned from Ohio with a beard and shaven head, having proved his mettle as a peacenik with his three-day stint in the Cincinnati jail. "You don't know anything until you've been roughed up by the Man!" he reportedly told his father, who called him Myshkin. Ben made it clear that he'd grown away from his elders, but, having said that, continued to keep his father company and talk about whatever was on his mind. Antioch students had to spend part of each year on a work assignment, so after Christmas Ben went back to the small Dayton suburb of Vandalia, where he was supposed to work as a newspaper reporter. As it happened, Vandalia didn't have much use for another reporter, and he was soon laid off. Far from taking the news amiss, his father promptly offered to send money. "If he was sober and you were in trouble," said Ben, "he was great. It was always possible, though, in three months or four weeks from then, he'd get drunk and say, 'Can't even hold a job!' "

By the summer of 1968, Cheever was often drunk, and his son had arguably become an even more representative member of his generation. The two didn't mix so well, though not exactly for lack of trying. Soon after he came home for a summer visit, Ben and one of his Antioch friends brought a guest to Cedar Lane—a somber thirteen-year-old named Ellen (the friend's sister), who'd run away from a strict father to the drug-ridden streets of the East Village. The Cheevers professed to keep an open-door policy (the Martha debacle was still a few months in the future), and Cheever did his best to be an engaging host. Clowning for the girl one night, he placed a cork table-mat on his head. "Queen for a day," the girl quipped. "The remark, perhaps innocent, seems to fell me," Cheever wrote in his journal, fretfully recounting a dream in which the girl told him, *Your whole life is a lie. I can see right through you. . . .*" Still disconcerted, perhaps, Cheever threw a heavy crystal glass at another of Ben's friends, Doug Brayfield, a "beautiful young man" (Ben remembered) who fancied himself a poet; no one can remember the exact provocation—apart from the poetic airs—though later Cheever admitted to Dr. Silverberg that he'd been agitated by homosexual desire for one of Ben's friends.* In what might

---

*Brayfield later read Cheever's published *Journals*, where he found himself described as "barefoot [with] a fan-shaped beard and fuzzy hair." He found this "wide

have been a further attempt to rally himself, Cheever dropped his trousers at a subsequent party and began chasing one of Mary's comelier Briarcliff students. The girl was a good sport about things, but Ben was appalled and tried to intercede. His father paused, pants around his ankles, and regarded his son with considerable asperity. "When did you start wearing a red necktie?" he demanded at last. Rather than remind Cheever of his own sartorial lapse, Ben found himself abashed: "Oh my God," he thought. "What *am* I doing wearing a red necktie?" ("Never wear red necktie," Leander Wapshot had bluntly advised his sons.) Observing that Ben often seemed cowed by his famous father, certain of his friends tried to be protective—especially a "fearless and bohemian" girl named Nina, who made hay of the fact that Ben had broken up with Lynda that summer. "I'm coming to rescue you from your father," she'd say, before conspicuously dragging him upstairs to bed for hours on end, reappearing only for dinner. Cheever—doubtless more offended by the girl's dislike of him than by her brazenness—laid down his fork one night and called her a whore. He was very drunk, of course, but it still caused a ripple.

A year later Ben had reconciled with Lynda, who in turn was getting on better with her parents, while all concerned had cooled toward Cheever. When he returned from Deya on September 2, 1969, his son informed him that he and Lynda were to be married two days later. For the occasion Ben had hastily purchased a suit at an Ossining haberdasher that fit him "the way suits fit bears and chimpanzees in the circus," as his father put it; because of the suit, Ben's mother wept bitterly during the ceremony. When it was over, Cheever merrily rang the church bell while the newlyweds roared away on a motorcycle; the guests repaired to a reception at the home of the bride's parents, where Cheever's old friend Sally Swope swore that she'd seen actual plastic flamingos on the front lawn. "Her Father is in charge of security at IBM," Cheever wrote Litvinov. "He is a pleasant, slender man with a thin and absolutely permenant [sic] smile. . . . She must have been quite a pretty woman. They neither drink nor smoke nor do they read."*

---

of the mark": "I often wore sandals in those days, but never walked around barefoot; I had a full beard, but it was well-groomed and close . . . and my hair couldn't possibly be described as 'fuzzy.' "

*As Ben noted in the *Letters*, "I am no longer on speaking terms with my former in-laws, but I must point out in their defense that they each used to smoke a package of Salems every day."

Sizing up the flamingos and so forth, Cheever weaved over to Lynda's mother and contrived to put her at ease over what he perceived to be their relatively modest means: "*He's* never going to make any money," said Cheever, meaning his Myshkin-like son, "but it doesn't matter, because I have plenty of it!"

In the months and years that followed, Cheever observed with bemusement while his son defected more and more to his in-laws, alleged flamingos and all. Lynda's parents liked to visit the couple in Ohio and even attend classes with them, and during holidays Ben seemed to ration his appearances on Cedar Lane as frugally as possible. His mother-in-law fussed over him as if he were her own darling boy; his father-in-law taught him how to tune cars and such. Since the man really didn't bother with much in the way of intellectual diversion, he spent most of his leisure hours happily engaged in home improvement. Cheever once gave the couple a lift to Lynda's house, where he was intrigued to find her father meticulously patching holes in his driveway with a little caulking gun; indeed, the driveway was so immaculate "you could eat breakfast off it," as Ben recalled. "If that's what you really like to do," said Cheever affably, "you should come over to our house, because we have a much larger driveway and much more satisfactory holes!" Lynda's father might have kept his permanent smile afloat, but the rest of his face turned crimson with rage. "A few of those incidents went a long way," said Ben. "My older son seems seriously to have switched his allegiance from me to his father-in-law," Cheever wrote shortly after the wedding. "This is no cause for feeling, merely something to be observed."

As for the whole hippie thing, Cheever tried to make light of it with remarks about "Myshkin" and the like, but he found it a little dispiriting. The blond cheerleader type was a solemn ideal of his, and now that such a girl had married his son, Cheever expected them to have a brilliant, elegant life together. Instead, Ben's beard grew longer and more Christlike, while his fetching wife sat around sewing psychedelic patches on his bell-bottoms. But then, that was the ethos of Antioch in those days, and when the Cheevers came to Yellow Springs for a visit in early 1970, Ben took pains to soften the blow. He and Lynda bought a big roast beef (though they weren't sure how to cook it), as well as a new table, curtains, and an ounce of premium marijuana. The last was for themselves, to steady the nerves a bit; stoned out of his gourd, Ben drove his customized van to the airport that afternoon to collect his parents and younger brother—"a nightmarish ride": "It was like I was talking Greek and he was talking Serbian," Ben remembered, though perhaps he underestimated his father's own mellow intoxication. ("We take the plane to Ohio," blandly noted the latter. "My beloved son meets us and we dine with his much beloved wife.") Another treat Ben had planned was lunch with Louis Filler, an eminent cultural conservative whose dim view of the younger generation seemed to square with Cheever's. (When Ben had boasted about a paper he'd written on the subject of Chagall, his father erupted: "Five minutes from here at the Union Church there are *nine* of Chagall's windows! And yet you'd never bestir yourself to look at them, and *that's* the trouble with your generation!") But of course this was an awful mistake: no academic alive was likely to ingratiate himself with Cheever, who moreover wasn't even able to weather the ordeal with a few cocktails because of the local blue laws. "So," said Ben, "Daddy's thinking gin, and Louis Filler's thinking Meeting of Two Great Minds." When Filler remarked that some modicum of sociological knowledge was imperative to the making of great literature, Cheever "laid him out": *Sociology hasn't a thing to do with literature!* etc. Filler fell silent and pretty much stayed that way.*

After the visit, relations with the couple deteriorated rapidly. Ben's wife not only stopped flirting with Cheever, she hardly spoke to him, and even refused his well-meaning invitations to dinner and whatnot. "I will *not* go over there for dinner!" he overheard her yelling in the background when he called Ben on the telephone. "I can't *stand* that old man!" Even worse was the cringing way his son tried to remonstrate with her, using a lot of unctuous endearments like "Monkey" and "Honeybear." Cheever wondered in his journal, "Is it possible that because of the ups and downs of our marriage he has come to feel that married happiness even if it means the loss of intelligence and character is desirable?" In practice, the whole Cheever family did their best to help Ben see how silly and victimized he seemed. *"That's the way Lynda likes it!"* was the constant, singsong, mocking refrain, especially when there were other guests to be entertained. Of course, they knew it was the essence of Ben's nature to placate—after all, he'd spent his

---

*On his return from Yellow Springs, Cheever promptly got to work on an early version of "Artemis, the Honest Well Digger," in which the title character has an affair with the wife of J. P. Filler, scholarly author of the best-selling monograph, *Shit.*

entire life trying to please a demanding father, who responded by dubbing him (a little backhandedly, perhaps) "the peacemaker." Living up
to his reputation as such, Ben solicitously followed his father out to the
rock garden one night, since the man was very drunk and likely to fall
and hurt himself. "You're pathetic," said Cheever, when his son sat
beside him.

For the next seven years or so, the two spoke only "in curt, tele-
graphic sentences" (as Ben put it), and for only one reason. After college Ben had found it necessary to cut his beard and get a job—a very
ill-paying one, as it turned out, at the *Rockland Journal News.* Lynda's
parents did their best to help the struggling youngsters—they paid
some of the rent and finally bought them a house—so Lynda thought
it only fair that the elder Cheevers do their part as well. Once a month,
then, under considerable duress, Ben would visit Cedar Lane and
spend a few minutes asking his father about his lumbago and so forth,
while the latter dourly awaited the dun. "My dearly beloved son comes
in the middle of dinner to ask for money," Cheever wrote in the mid-
seventies. "He has not come to the house in two years for any other
reason. I can hear his wife say, 'Go over and ask your father for some
money.' . . . I wish he wouldn't always ask me for money. I wish I didn't
know that he was ordered, commanded, to ask for money."

CHAPTER THIRTY-TWO

{ 1969–1970 }

WHILE BEN WAS GROWING UP, one of his father's most
vehement strictures was against masturbation: *Never do it*,
he'd say; *it's vanity, self-love, and it ruins you for women.* Ben
had heard this so many times that he was surprised to find, after his
father's death, that the man had not only masturbated quite a lot himself, but recorded the matter almost as copiously. "Jerking off I wonder
if I would sooner be between H[ope]'s legs or down N[ed]'s throat," he
wrote around the time of Ben's wedding, when his own marriage was
especially stagnant. Cheever was known to make the point that his constitution required at least "two or three orgasms a week"—but where
to find them? That indeed was the rub. Even Mrs. Zagreb wasn't putting out these days. She was happy to give him a drink and commiserate about his wife's frigidity—but still (as she reminded him), he *was*
married, and that was that. "It's all your fault," Cheever told his wife in
so many words, mentioning their neighbor's newfound compunction.

Every so often he announced to the Friday Club that he'd met a fascinating, attractive woman, and would canvass his cronies as to the
advisability of leaving his wife. (Within a week or two, usually, he'd
deny having ever considered such a thing: "Oh, nonsense! I couldn't
think of leaving Mary . . .") That autumn of 1969, his latest dream girl
was Shana Alexander, the forty-four-year-old editor of *McCall's*, whom
he'd met through his old friend Zinny.* "I seem, after three encoun-

---

*Alexander went on to greater fame as an author and, especially, debater—taking
the liberal side (opposite James J. Kilpatrick) for the "Point-Counterpoint" segment
on *60 Minutes*.

ters, to have fallen in love with S[hana]," he wrote, though he cautioned himself not to get carried away: "I seem to consider the women I love to be my inventions and when they forget or change the parts I've written for them I am disconcerted and at times disinterested." Alexander may or may not have conformed to Cheever's invention, but in any case she remembered him—vaguely—as "cute," albeit in a decidedly nonsexual way ("a little nut-brown guy with twinkly eyes"). Probably those "three encounters" were the extent of it, more or less, but that was all Cheever needed to contrive an affair of sorts. Besides, the practical side of things tended to be overwhelming, to put it mildly. "I am a man, a free man," he resolved in the spring of 1970, when Hope finally returned to town: "I will drive into New York, I will take a hotel room, I will screw H[ope], and take S[hana] to the big dancing party. Pow." Cheever proceeded to make elaborate preparations: he packed "a brown suit for the seduction and a dark suit for the party," made sure he had enough Seconal and Miltown, bolted a quick TV dinner, wrote a note to Mary, reserved a hotel room—all the while drinking, of course—until at last he lugged his bag out to the car and took off. "[I] observe that my vision is bad, my driving dangerous. . . . I turn back at the gas station and drive home. I destroy the note, cancel the hotel reservation, unpack my toothbrush and my pills, undress, and climb into bed. I sleep soundly."

Little wonder he preferred fantasy. Almost everything about his subsequent meeting with Hope, for example, was lovely—except certain aspects of the meeting itself. He got up that morning free of *cafard* and was able to ignore, serenely, his wife's "contemptuous and weary voice" while he downed "three heavy scoops" to brace himself for the train, where a woman sitting beside him "seem[ed] appalled and terrified by [his] presence and perhaps by the fumes of gin that must roll off [him]." As for Hope, she appears to have done her best as always, but Cheever couldn't entirely deceive himself about his own performance: "It is not as good as it was a year ago. I somehow—hooch and a head cold—can't get quite on the beam. . . . She laughs at my jokes and says that I look much better than I did. Stoned and with a runny nose, I don't see how this could be possible. We lunch and return to the room, but the kissing is halfhearted, and when I suggest a fuck she says gently that she somehow doesn't feel like it." But it was worthwhile, perhaps, just to confide in his wife afterward ("I talk freely about H.") and regale the Friday Club with yarns about Alan Pakula's being "after [him] with a pistol" and so forth. During Hope's divorce proceedings, however, it transpired that she was actually seeing a lot of Frank Sinatra. As Cheever wrote a friend, "Hope and Alan are getting a divorce but I seem, through some sleight of hand, to have ended up with Alan."

CHEEVER FITFULLY RESUMED WRITING FICTION, though he sensed he'd lost a degree of "keenness" and that his work-in-progress, "The Fourth Alarm," was little more than an "anecdote." Perhaps hoping for reassurance to the contrary, he wrote Maxwell that he was "doubtful" about the story and didn't want to publish it under his name ("I don't want to return on these terms"); Maxwell took him at his word, and rejected it. With this in mind, one suspects, Cheever not only went on to publish the story under his name (in the April 1970 *Esquire*), but even gave it pride of place in his next collection, *The World of Apples*.* Cheever's first story in two years had been somewhat inspired by the nude revue *Oh! Calcutta!*, which had recently opened Off Broadway; wondering what he'd do with his valuables (wallet, keys, watch) if asked to strip naked and appear onstage, Cheever proceeded to imagine a protagonist whose prosaic wife takes a role in a naked play, *Ozymanides II*. The man's favorite childhood movie had been a quaint tale about a horse-drawn fire engine that saves the city when other, more modernized engines fail, and he reflects on this while watching his wife simulate copulation in public: "Had nakedness—its thrill—annihilated her sense of nostalgia? . . . Should I stand up in the theatre and shout for her to return, return, return in the name of love, humor, and serenity?"

The quirky little story is entertaining enough, but hardly the sort of thing to make Cheever's competition stop and take notice. And who were his competition? He wanted nothing less, ever, than to be considered in the same breath with Bellow, Updike, Roth, et al., and yet *The New Yorker* was rejecting his work, while running almost monthly stories by his hated epigone, Barthelme. Cheever claimed to be writing an elaborate parody—sometimes a story, sometimes a whole book *(The*

---

*He took a similar approach to his two previous collections: *Some People, Places, and Things* opens with *two* stories rejected by Maxwell—"Justina" and "Brimmer"—while *The Brigadier and the Golf Widow* opens with the title story, which (one will recall) Maxwell had tried to truncate in galleys.

Man Who Rented Garter Snakes)—that was "meant to demolish Barthelme," though in fact he wasn't writing much at all. While wooing (as it were) Shana Alexander, he'd promised to contribute something to *McCall's* titled "A Pure and Beautiful Story"—the genesis of what would become, *very* gradually, "Artemis, the Honest Well Digger." "I am disappointed in Artemis," he noted, after several months of work. "It lacks density and enthusiasm and my search for another method has not been successfully completed. Keep trying."

One problem was that his working day was getting shorter and shorter, and of course he worked in the midst of ghastly hangovers. Still, coming down to breakfast at the start of each day, he tried to capitalize on the brief interval of sobriety by wishing his wife a pleasant "Good morning," and it was disconcerting when even this was answered with contempt. For his son's benefit, he tried to mitigate such darkness by engaging the boy in a kindly patter of jokes, and persevering with a patient smile when his wife maintained her stony, unamused silence—but for *what*, he wondered, was he being punished? He hardly ever raised his voice, he didn't rant or rave, though perhaps he'd remark in passing, oh, on the quality of the roast, or some fatuous intellectualism on her part. "I was the grown-up in the house," said Federico, "and I wasn't a very successful grown-up. I remember saying, 'Okay, I've got a piece of paper and I'm going to put a black checkmark next to each of you whenever you say something mean to the other one.' After half an hour he had about twenty-five checkmarks and she had about three."

Both parents asserted that they stayed together for the boy's sake, and in fact the boy seemed unhappy in almost every department of life. As he recalled, "I was fat and unpopular and dyslexic and smart—an incredibly deadly combination." Like his brother before him, Federico had to repeat a grade at Scarborough Country Day, where he was a laughingstock on the soccer field and often got in locker-room fistfights, which he always lost. Miserable beyond words, he couldn't help bursting into tears from time to time, whereupon his father would invoke their ancient lineage: "Fred," he'd say, with perhaps a heartening jostle, "remember: *You are a Cheever.*" When this didn't seem to work and—like his brother before him—Federico went on wetting his bed to boot, his parents sent him to Dr. Silverberg. (Despite the ineffectuality of his own recent treatment, Cheever liked the man: he was a good listener and laughed at the right moments.) Silverberg noted that

Federico was a "fat rather depressed" child, and was struck by his behavior in the waiting room: for almost an hour he sat there staring into space; he hardly moved; there were magazines to look at, but he didn't seem to notice. As for the boy's observations, they were made with a kind of numb detachment, as if it hardly mattered one way or the other. He had few friends his own age, he said, but had managed to get by on his own, or in the company of adults, mostly his father. And what about his father? "He's fairly nice. He's a good father, but he lives in a world of his own."

The adult Federico maintains this view: his father was nice enough, and usually they got along fine. "But you have to realize," he added, "for most of my childhood I was like a bit part in a Eugene O'Neill play. I was furniture. Certainly I was fat and unpromising, and that was pointed out to me, but he had a wife whose themes were extremely well developed over thirty years; he had my brother, who would come over exclusively to borrow money, and Susan was married to his former editor's son. He could have much more fun with them than he could with me." Often, to be sure, Cheever would call the boy a gluttonous slob or some such, and the boy would (tacitly or otherwise) concede as much: he *was* a gluttonous slob. When he wasn't at school, he sat in his room eating and reading, or eating and watching TV— at any rate, eating. "Fred is on a diet which seems to involve eating everything in sight excepting spinach," Cheever wrote his older son. It was like that—all in good fun, mostly, and well meaning in the sense that it called attention to a real problem. The Lehmann-Haupts have an abiding impression of Federico playing on the library floor while his parents stand over him making ironical comments about his self-sufficiency and their relative ineptitude as parents. The boy seems not to notice. "There was something prodigious about Fred," said Lehmann-Haupt. "He seemed to build a cocoon. I felt that *he* was the one who would get out alive."

Behind the impassive façade was (among other things) enormous grief and rage, which had to come out on occasion. The first time Federico hit his father was after a soccer match. Exhausted and demoralized as ever, he returned home to find his father being drunkenly cruel to his mother, and when he began to protest, his father walked away. "I think I actually wanted some part of our life to be about me," Federico remembered. "He was walking away and I said *No, no* and I hit him on the back." Another time, Cheever was sitting at the head of the table in a special antique chair, which he smashed by falling over (drunk) when struck in the chest by his son, who was bigger than he as of age thirteen. ("If your father's going to be a drunk, it's good if he's five foot six.") There were other such incidents, and they always seemed to have a calming effect on Cheever, who would then realize how low he had fallen. Also, he knew the boy loved him; each was pretty much all the other had. Federico had never been particularly close to his mother ("I remember trying to play games with her as a kid, but I couldn't"), whereas his father, if anything, was accessible to a fault: he sat through dreadful TV shows just so he could chat with the boy during commercial breaks; he even helped with homework. "He wanted to be a good father," said Federico. "He wanted passionately to be a good father."

Meanwhile Cheever's wife was becoming more independent than ever. Through her teaching she'd come to realize that others perceived her as charming and intelligent, quite apart from her being Mrs. John Cheever. More and more she was taking pains with her appearance, buying stylish clothes, and openly flirting with other men. "He's looking worse and worse," said Susan, "and needing more and more nursing, just as she's ready to rock. Sort of a disaster." At the time, perhaps the greatest tonic for Mary was her poetry writing, which not only served to reassure her that she was creative in her own right, but also brought her in touch with other talented women, most notably the poet-novelist Sandra Hochman. During a session with Dr. Silverberg, Federico pointed out that his father was especially moody of late because his mother was seeing a lot of Hochman, whom his father detested. To this day, however, Hochman is convinced that Cheever was one of her biggest fans. They'd met in the early sixties at a party. Hochman had recently won the Yale Younger Poets Award, and Cheever mentioned he was friendly with Dudley Fitts, one of the judges, who'd encouraged him to read Hochman's work. Then, in 1970, she completed a novel, *Walking Papers*, which Cheever also professed to admire—in fact, he liked it so much that he was willing to forgo his usual rule against blurb writing and provide her with *two*, no less, as follows: "I haven't been as thrilled by anything as much as *Walking Papers* since *Jesus Christ Superstar*"; "I love this writing. I think Sandra Hochman is terribly funny." Hochman used the second one. ("Read Sandra," Cheever noted while scanning her novel. "So what.")

As if the woman's literary pretensions weren't bad enough, she was also a devoted feminist and hence a perfect scapegoat for Cheever's marital woes.* Divorced from a successful businessman, the well-heeled Hochman invited Mary to spend a week in St. Croix sans men—a vacation that made Ossining seem, for Mary, bleaker than ever. Greeted by Cheever on her return, Mary sighed: "I'll make myself a rum drink in memory of my happiness." For weeks she spoke of little else, or so it seemed to her husband, who couldn't help picturing "two undressed women giggling in a bathroom" when Mary mentioned tie-dyeing her friend's underwear. Indeed, this detail struck Cheever as almost definitive, though he couldn't quite bring himself to accuse his wife openly of lesbianism ("I know her reply would be: Are you a fairy?"), nor could he entirely overlook the chance that "this is the fantasy of a tortured neurotic who is drunk most of the time." Also, he had to admit that Hochman—despite her feminism—hardly behaved like a lesbian. At the time she was seeing an Armenian named Harout, who introduced himself as an architect and played a lot of backgammon with Cheever while the women talked poetry and the like. Hochman always thought the two men were great pals. "I open the door and find Harut [sic]—the unemployed waiter, stud, bore and companion of the flighty poetess," Cheever wrote. "They often drop in on Sunday night just as the meat is coming out of the oven." He also described the boyfriend as a "gymnast."

Whether because of lesbianism, feminism, other men, or some fiendish combination of the three, the fact remained that Mary was being *very* unloving, and Cheever was fed up. Since they seemed unable to discuss anything without nastiness, he insisted she see a psychiatrist again—a sympathetic one, that is, who was likely to comprehend *his* side of things. "He talks about David Hays seeing his wife and telling him she was normal and that he had ruined her life," Dr. Silverberg noted during one of his sessions with Cheever. "He resented this, finds me supportive." Silverberg it was, then—who if anything was even more well disposed to Mary than Hays had been, though frankly he found the whole family a little bizarre:

Problem [he wrote on Mary's file card]: Patient comes at the urging of her husband, who wants her to be less hostile to him. It is clear that in actuality it is he who is hostile and demeaning to her and has

---

*Hochman is perhaps best known for her 1973 documentary, *Year of the Woman*, a seminal contribution to the then rather nascent Womens' Rights Movement.

been through the whole marriage. Patient is a sensitive intelligent woman, much spunk, but also strong feelings of inadequacy and . . . little girlish speech and behavior. . . . She hasn't been in love with her husband for a long time but has a great sense of loyalty and devotion. Sort of that she's taking care of an important creative person. This is her first line of rationalization for putting up with his anger, narcissism, drinking, etc. The second line is the children, who are very devoted to him and also have her protective attitude towards him. Patient has a fair understanding of her complex husband, [but] is unaware of degree of his homosexual side.

Mary would go on seeing Silverberg for almost a year—it was nice to talk about herself for a change, without fear of derision or rebuke—though, as she later remarked, "it didn't solve anybody's problems." As for Cheever, he met with the psychiatrist only once more (roughly a month after his wife's first session), and was nettled to find the man groping, à la Hays, for some tactful way of saying that "*he* [Cheever] distorts rather than Mary." Cheever pressed one of his journals on Silverberg, evidently hoping it would prove exculpatory in some way. The doctor warily opened it: "It seems"—he noted—"to be largely an intimate sexual journal and [Cheever is] quite obviously uncomfortable about it." Perhaps Silverberg hadn't read the right page; in any event, Cheever snatched it back and never returned (though in parting he invited the man, again, to come "see [his] house and meet the maid," and later he sent Ben to meet with Silverberg, too).

THAT SUMMER (1970), Cheever was a delegate to the International PEN Congress in Seoul. He'd invited Mary to accompany him, but she worried that her acceptance "implie[d] rapprochement," and by then she was seriously considering divorce. But finally she relented: not only would she remain in the marriage for at least another year (until they could enroll their son in boarding school), but she would also go to the Far East, with Federico as buffer.

On June 22, the three Cheevers took a seventeen-hour flight to Tokyo, stopping to refuel in Fairbanks, Alaska, where a large contingent from the University of Akron boarded, each of the faculty wives carrying a bottle of hometown water. Cheever observed them from the back of the airplane ("What a waste of time to ridicule them"), where he situated himself near the liquor station. In Tokyo the smog was so bad that people were wearing surgical masks, and mostly the Cheevers stayed put in their room at the posh Okura. In Seoul, however, Cheever was relegated to the pedestrian Tae Yun Kak, whereas more favored delegates—such as Updike—stayed at the Chosun, where the conference was being held. Because of their different lodgings, Cheever and Updike saw little of each other except for a brief meeting at the Chosun bar, where Updike observed that his colleague's drinking "was beginning to drag on him visibly." Cheever in turn liked to tell how Updike had dutifully visited tourist sites like the Thirty-eighth Parallel, while Cheever had gone to a high-class geisha house where a beautiful girl named Saw stroked his privates and fed him fish, nuts, and mushrooms.

The American delegation included a black activist writer who, with his wife, had befriended the Cheevers. Federico found the man "extraordinary": he (the writer) told a fascinating account of his experience in a segregated army camp during World War II; also, though companionable enough, he was not at all "inclined to be deferential," like their other black friend, Ralph Ellison. Federico wasn't the only one in the family who'd been impressed. On her return to the States, a radiant Mary Cheever told Silverberg that she'd fallen in love with the man and was now meeting him every so often in New York ("heavenly"). Everything was better now: she and John were getting along because she no longer felt the need to "rise to his every prod or bait"; in fact, she was so mollified that she didn't mind obliging him a little in bed, patiently helping him keep it up long enough to reach climax.

"I mount my beloved, and off we go for the best ride in a long time," wrote the ecstatic Cheever, who couldn't believe his luck and wasn't inclined to look deeply into the matter. Susan and Rob Cowley had recently returned from London and were living on Cedar Lane for the time being—reason enough to make both Cheevers happy: John gained an audience, and Mary a confidante for her love affair. "Where's your mother?" Cheever asked Susan, who looked puzzled before remembering "something about a sale at Lord & Taylor's." Cheever—"blissfully" happy—smiled and went his way. "I walk the dogs in a heavy rain," he wrote that autumn. "Water lilies grow at the edge of the pond. I want to pick some and take them home to Mary. I decide that this is foolish. I am a substantial man of fifty-eight, and I will walk past the lilies in a dignified manner. Having made this decision, I strip off my clothes, dive into the pond, and pick a lily. I will be dignified tomorrow."

It ended with a bang rather than a whimper. "On Tuesday we were lovers and on Wednesday warriors," Cheever wrote shortly after the lily-picking entry. "I am told that I am an insane shit, that even when I am loving I am a shit." He simply couldn't fathom it. Was it because she was about to lose her job at Briarcliff? (The academic dean had been fired, and a number of faculty members had threatened to resign in protest.) But no, she seemed almost to welcome that. What, then? The nominal catalyst had been a well-meaning remark he'd made about a screenplay she was writing; as Mary conceded to Silverberg, her husband's advice had been "actually appropriate, but she blew up because she felt it was an unfair inference." What she meant by that is unclear, but of course the main reason for her distemper was that her lover seemed to be rejecting her, and the sight of Cheever may have been maddening under the circumstances. "What I will forget and never mention is what I heard at dinner," Cheever wrote. " 'What is worse for a woman: to marry a man with a bad prostate or to marry a homosexual?' But where does this venom originate?"

He'd never know, and by the end of autumn they were back in their separate bedrooms to stay. Eager to escape on almost any pretext, Cheever accepted an invitation to go to Egypt for a week or two and give a lecture at Cairo University—a lonely, drunken blur, only the broad outlines of which (the Temple of Luxor, a swim in the Nile) Cheever saw fit to retain. Actually, one encounter did prove distinctly memorable. Killing time between a solitary dinner at the Cairo Hilton and a reception of some sort, Cheever went for a walk in a nearby park:

> I was joined almost at once by a young man who asked if he could join me in my walk. I couldn't see him in the fading light but he seemed comely and amiable. . . . He led me almost at once to a park bench where he unzipped my fly and took out my cock which was all smiles, ready for fun and juicy. I politely did the same for him but his pants were rags, half the fly-buttons were gone and his cock was like a dead bait worm. . . . When I zipped up my trousers and stood to leave he struck me and made a grab for my wallet. I punched him and got back into the circle of bright light that surrounds the Hilton.

One might dismiss this as a finger exercise or a fever dream, but eight years later—when such liaisons (minus the violence) had become more common—Cheever revisited the memory in passing: "I see the folly of my loves and that good fortune has kept me from dying of stab wounds in a park in Cairo."

CHAPTER THIRTY-THREE

{ 1971–1972 }

WHAT CHEEVER REQUIRED in his own fiction, he often said, was a sense of *urgency:* "Is what I have to say urgent, and do I suppose it would be of any urgency to people who read my books?" Ever since *Bullet Park* he'd found it hard to write a single urgent sentence, and so he'd inched his way, nonurgently, through "Artemis, the Honest Well Digger," which he finally completed at the beginning of 1971. It was promptly rejected by *The New Yorker*, as Cheever must have expected, since he knew the editors were reluctant in those days to run stories with lyrical descriptions of seminal discharge ("like the fireballs from a Roman candle") or characters who write monographs titled *Shit.* That aside, the story is soberingly mediocre, especially given that Cheever took almost nine months to write it—that is, to contrive a somewhat random, sprawling plot for his Russian material. Artemis lands in Moscow, of all places, purely by way of escaping an entanglement with his client's wife; then, within forty-eight hours, while Khrushchev is rather incidentally deposed, Artemis gets deported because of an exalting (but perfunctory to the reader) affair with his guide, Natasha. The story works best as travelogue, and is either too long or too short, depending on how you look at it. It's a measure of Cheever's desperation that he considered expanding it into a novel—thus compounding an already long and joyless labor—though artistically he was right in suspecting that the narrative per se was slight, and could only be brought up to snuff by throwing good money after bad, so to speak. Wisely, he decided to cut his losses: "Esquire wants to buy it but they'll only pay fifteen hundred," he wrote

Ben. "Considering the length of time it took, this is less than Susie makes on the Tarrytown paper.* Harpers is out and the Atlantic still doesn't know about orgasims [sic] and that's that." Not quite: *Playboy* certainly knew about orgasms and was willing to publish just about anything Cheever wrote; "Artemis," then, would appear in the January 1972 issue.

Cheever gave two reasons for his creative funk: "1. I drink too much. 2. I've written too much. . . . When, walking in the woods these days, I am struck by an idea, a metaphor or a phrase it takes me several minutes to realize that I've already used it." Actually, this was only half true: Cheever's gift (and curse) was an imagination that went on working no matter how drowned in alcohol; it was the follow-through that bored him nowadays. Tipsily oracular one night, he lectured Mary on the subject of artistic *bouleversement* (upheaval), and became excited in spite of himself as he began to consider the *bouleversement* of time, morals, and perhaps his own work. His mind "swelling like a cabbage in the rain," Cheever remembered a convoluted story about some Wollaston neighbors—"a novel in fact"—which he'd tried writing when he was fifteen or so. One of his childhood girlfriends had been a descendant of the great Puritan William Bradford, though she was one of the "wrong" South Shore Bradfords (resembling Cheever in that respect). The girl's family had a sordid destiny: her mother was something of a shrew, and her father had taken up with a disreputable widow and sired a bastard son (years later, at summer camp, Fax warned Cheever not to be seen with the boy); meanwhile Mrs. Bradford had invested most of their modest fortune in four diamond rings, which her older daughter stole out of spite, hoping to hock them in Boston so she could abscond to Paris. At any rate, the fifty-eight-year-old Cheever was now eager to apply his thoughts about *bouleversement* to this childhood memory (changing the name Bradford to Cabot), though his enthusiasm waned as soon as he sat down to write: "Who cares about the wrong Cabots this morning. Not I . . . I cannot feel that the world will be any better for their story or any worse without it. I will make some notes."

That was in January 1971, shortly after finishing "Artemis"; months later, he was still poking away, though not entirely without result. For years now Cheever had wanted to make momentous

*Susan had begun working as a reporter for the *Tarrytown Daily News*.

changes in his work ("I want a new cadence, a new perspective, a new vocabulary"), and he found that his story about the Cabots lent itself to an experiment in "digression," as he put it. One of the favorite novels of his youth had been Gide's *The Counterfeiters* (which of course Cheever always referred to, socially, as *Les Faux-monnayeurs*), what with its intriguing metafictional narrator accosting the reader with constant reflections—digressions—on his story and characters. Returning to Gide's novel some two years *after* he'd finished "The Jewels of the Cabots," Cheever experienced an almost unsettling shock of recognition: "I was either influenced unconsciously by the Counterfeiters when I first read it or there is an extraordinary coincidence here. The ambiguity of Gide, if that is the word, seems to be what I've been driving at for years." And it wasn't simply a matter of Gide's narrative approach, but also a particularly congenial theme, which Cheever expressed as follows: "[T]he sense that what we part from forcibly and with deep regret is what we love and know best and our departure is impetuous, visionary and dangerous." Thus Olivier runs away from home in *The Counterfeiters*, and thus any number of Cheever's characters (Geneva Cabot, Moses and Coverly, Ezekiel Farragut, to name a few) say goodbye to their homes, their haunted pasts, in order to forge identities in the greater world, as Cheever himself had done.

His hope was to "change key" in writing "The Jewels of the Cabots"—to take nonlinear narrative to another level, jarring the reader out of the dream world of conventional fiction—though he couldn't help wondering if his experiment had gone awry. "Footnotes might help," he wrote, while revising the story in May; "help that is to express a loss of self-confidence." In a desperate effort to push past his doubts and ennui, Cheever finished the story "aided by gin"—a measure he'd hitherto managed to avoid in his serious work (or so the evidence suggests)—and when the thing was done, he scarcely knew what to make of it. "I will give the Cabots to Bill [Maxwell] and his enthusiasm will be boundless," he fancied. "He will drive over here from Yorktown and embrace me, etc." It wasn't to be. According to Cheever, Maxwell replied, "I'm happy to have been born in the same century as you, but as God is my witness this is not a story." In any case, he rejected it.

Not for the first time, one regrets Maxwell's conservatism (not to say his lack of sympathy toward an old friend in dire need of encouragement). At the very least, "The Jewels of the Cabots" is a fascinating failure, and perhaps an essential step toward the sort of reinvention that would enable Cheever (once sober) to proceed with *Falconer*. The story's persistent digressiveness may seem, at times, an almost boorish distraction from its titular subject, but in fact the Cabots are almost beside the point—little more than a means of piquing the narrator's memory in a contrapuntal manner. Early in the story, for example, the narrator recalls Mrs. Cabot's yearly diatribes at St. Botolphs Academy on the evils of drink and tobacco, which remind him (at great length) of his own mother's provincial intolerance. "Miss Peacock's has changed," she "sadly" remarks of her granddaughter's school. When her son fails to grasp her meaning, the woman explains, "They're letting in Jews":

> "Can we change the subject?" I asked.
> "I don't see why," she said. "You brought it up."
> "My wife is Jewish, Mother," I said. My wife was in the kitchen.
> "That is not possible," my mother said. "Her father is Italian."
> "Her father," I said, "is a Polish Jew."
> "Well," Mother said, "I come from old Massachusetts stock and I'm not ashamed of it although I don't like being called a Yankee."
> "There's a difference."
> "Your father said that the only good Jew was a dead Jew although I did think Justice Brandeis charming."
> "I think it's going to rain," I said. It was one of our staple conversational switch-offs, used to express anger, hunger, love, and the fear of death.

And hence the point of Cheever's digressiveness, which reflects the very nature of things in St. Botolphs—a place where the nastiness of life (whether embodied by genteel anti-Semitism, or more blatantly by Uncle Peepee Marshmallow and Doris the male prostitute) is swept under a rug of digressive propriety ("Feel that refreshing breeze"). Consequently the narrator himself, a product of that milieu, can't help shying away from unpleasant facts. "Why would I sooner describe church bells and flocks of swallows?" he remarks, remembering a time in Rome when he overheard an unseen woman railing at a man, "You're a God-damned fucked-up no-good insane piece of shit. . . ." Considering this—the sad case of the Cabots, St. Botolphs, the world at large—the narrator wishes he could express some heartening *truth*, as opposed to the merely sordid "facts": "My real work these days is to write an edition of *The New York Times* that will bring gladness to the hearts of men." At the same time he chides his own evasiveness as "puerile, a sort of greeting-card mentality"—and he does manage, finally, to confess the unpleasant "facts" about the Cabots: namely, that Geneva stole her mother's diamonds and fled to Egypt, whereupon Mrs. Cabot poisoned the girl's father. But we also learn that Geneva's escape—however tragic in other respects—has at least resulted in her own happiness. In a brief dénouement, the narrator visits her many years later in Luxor and finds her fat, happy, and married to a nobleman. And so the story ends: "On the last day I swam in the Nile—overhand—and they drove me to the airport, where I kissed Geneva—and the Cabots—goodbye."

The valedictory note is apt. In *Falconer*, Cheever would attain the kind of synthesis hinted at in "The Jewels of the Cabots": he would describe the squalor of prison, a living hell, without any trace of squeamishness, and yet ultimately manage to transcend the mere "facts" and bring "gladness to the hearts of men" ("Rejoice, he thought, rejoice"). Until then, however, he was pretty much done as a writer, and never again would he complete another ambitious, first-rate short story.* "The Jewels of the Cabots" appeared in *Playboy*, naturally, and was included in both the *O. Henry Prize Stories* and *Best American Short Stories* for 1973. Reviewing the latter for the *Times*, Anatole Broyard reckoned that Cheever had cast "a very wide net, but it may be too heavy for the craft"—a fair point. Despite its relative lack of focus, though, the story remains an impressive achievement, especially considering what a wreck the author was when he wrote it. And it's poignant to consider, too, that he persevered largely in the hope of winning back the approval of Maxwell and *The New Yorker*; that failure in particular seemed to break his spirit to some extent, at least as a short-story writer. "My friendship with The New Yorker seems over," he reported after the "Cabots" rejection. "Playboy seems to be all that is left, alas." Somewhere in the abstract, though, he knew he'd eventually prevail over his detractors. As he noted in his journal that following spring, "I

---

*"Cabots" is the last story in *The Stories of John Cheever*. Though Cheever published six more stories (not including novel excerpts) in his lifetime, Gottlieb saw fit to exclude three of the four preceding the 1978 *Stories*, and almost certainly would have excluded the last two—*very* weak—stories of Cheever's career in the event of a posthumous volume.

will write a story beginning: Noone reads the fiction in the New Yorker anymore."

"I DIDN'T GO TO SING SING to gather material any more than I got married and had children to gather material," Cheever would remark, post-*Falconer*, when asked about the two years he spent teaching inmates at Sing Sing. In a way, this is true. When he first volunteered in the summer of 1971, he was just finishing "The Jewels of the Cabots" and had little idea what to write next. With no meaningful work to do, no outlet for his imagination, he was liable to go mad. Indeed, the process seemed well on its way. Often alone and drinking all day, Cheever found that his legitimate anxieties about life—money woes, marriage, health, work—had a way of inflating into rampant paranoia, until by nightfall he'd drunkenly imagine that snakes or stray dogs or burglars (doing poor bobwhite imitations) were about to infiltrate his house. Sometimes he slept with a shotgun at his side. One night Ben dropped by, thinking his parents were away: "I was in the dining room when my father appeared at the top of the stairs. He was bare-assed and had the shotgun clutched in both hands. I don't believe it was loaded. He invited me to stay for a drink, but I declined."

Getting out of the house, then, was a good idea, but it also seems fair to say that Cheever went to Sing Sing in the hope of finding new material. He felt as though he'd "exhausted his old landscapes." The previous year, for instance, while walking along Union Avenue in Saratoga, he'd seen "exactly twenty-seven details that [he] had used in stories—a wooden tower, old parimutuel tickets, a three legged dog, an iron deer, a dying elm, etc." If anything it was worse with respect to New York, Rome, greater Boston, and the suburbs. Years later (a few months after finishing *Falconer*), Cheever would speak of the "stamina and courage" that Chekhov had shown in attempting to "vary his magic," late in his career, by traveling thousands of miles to the penal colony in Sakhalin. Cheever could achieve much the same thing without leaving town, and doubtless something of the sort came to mind when the Sing Sing chaplain, George Kandle, approached him that spring after a reading. There were some two thousand inmates, said Kandle, and only six instructors. "Tomorrow I go to Sing-Sing to talk with the warden about giving a course in the short story to convicted drug-pushers, etc.," Cheever wrote Ben. "If you don't hear from me you'll know what happened. Clang."

Thirty or so curious felons showed up for the first class, where Cheever explained that writing was an exercise "in making sense of one's life by putting down one's experiences on a piece of paper." A Black Panther with one tooth in his head responded by writing and reciting a long, caustic manifesto against white society. "I find the place depressing," Cheever reflected, "not for sinister reasons, but because of boredom." Most of his students agreed, and soon he was down to a total of six. Since even these diehards had almost never cracked a book, Cheever decided to donate the Boyers' set of Harvard Classics to the prison, which proved a more intricate business than he'd expected. When he and Federico carted the boxes into the processing room, a guard detained them for half an hour until the gift could be properly inspected. At first Cheever was haughty (*Now see here, my good man*), then furious when the guard refused to let him retrieve some cigarettes from his car: he demanded to see the warden, the education director, someone in *authority*, by God, while his son begged him not to make a scene. "I think there was a level of incredulity about whether in fact the inmates were going to gain a lot from Charles Eliot's bookshelf," said Federico, though it appears Cheever was able to coax a few of them into reading (or at least listening to) the odd passage. Gleefully he reported that one of his "murderers, bank robbers, [and] drug-pushers" had exclaimed, "Oh what a cool motherfucker was that Machiavelli."

Even if Sing Sing hadn't resulted in *Falconer*, it would have served to replenish Cheever's fund of anecdotes. "I had hoped to do something like Camus," he wrote Gottlieb after that first year, "but the raw material—misery and death—is disconcertingly farcical." Three students in particular seemed to endear themselves to Cheever, and each was colorful in his own way. A Puerto Rican named Stacy had blown a man's head off with a Luger, though like most inmates he claimed to be innocent ("It went off by accident"); the *real* reason they'd locked him up, he said, was the power he wielded as "the biggest pimp in New York." One of his notable compositions was about a family man who ends up raping a teenage boy, and sometimes he'd get a sudden donnée and drop it in the mail to Cheever ("Stacy writes a letter in which he describes threatening to break a whore's legs backwards, that sage and gentle man"). Stacy and his wife, a Jewish prostitute, had sired two sons who lived in a local orphanage, and one day Cheever took them out for lunch and bowling. Another student—easily his most talented—was a black man named David, whose most memorable work in Cheever's class was something called "The Pit-Wig Papers," about a man who develops Afro wigs for armpits; David also wrote about a woman who got a sexual charge out of being pelted with tangerines.*

By far Cheever's most abiding relationship was with Donald Lang—a pale, emaciated white man and "serious loser" (Federico) who'd spent half of his thirty-one years behind bars for armed robbery. At Sing Sing, Lang had been working as a clerk for Reverend Kandle, who thought Cheever's class would go nicely with a correspondence course Lang was taking in rhetoric and composition. As Lang saw it, a proper man of letters was someone like Hemingway; he didn't know what to make of this runty guy with the faggoty accent who said things like *One expects* ("I thought, 'One *what* . . . ?' "). Lang pegged his teacher as a showoff, a phony who came to Sing Sing because it gave him something to chat about at cocktail parties. Cheever, for his part, thought Lang was insane: "He repeats himself, repeats his name and is deeply suspicious," he wrote in his journal. "I give him two magazines and he asks darkly: what is your motive." Even during class Lang was sometimes rabidly hostile ("Donald mentions an undercover faggot and I jump in my seat"), until Cheever earned a measure of respect during the Attica uprising in September. As at Attica, the majority of inmates at Sing Sing were black, and prison officials felt certain they'd riot, too, if given half a chance to organize. "You'd make a great hostage," Cheever's students observed, while Lang put the matter more bluntly: "I wonder where a little shit like you gets the balls to come in here." But Cheever remained unperturbed—"I don't think anybody will hurt me, Lang"—and went on teaching, regardless of the danger. "You had to admire him for that," said Lang, who would learn over time just how much Cheever identified with prisoners. "[I]f the cons and I were lined up against a guard," Cheever told an interviewer, "I was all with the cons."

Once he had their trust, he was careful not to lose it. Caskie Stinnett, editor of *Travel & Leisure*, solicited a piece on what it's like for prisoners, who, after all, enjoy little in the way of travel if not leisure,

---

*David got out of prison in 1972, resuming his considerable career as a writer and character actor. He wrote a play about prison life that was performed at the Public Theatre in New York, and later became a staff writer for *The Cosby Show*. More impressive still was his ten-year stint as one of the lovable denizens of *Sesame Street*.

but Cheever (who found the idea "interesting" and certainly needed the money) declined: "He explained that his acceptance by the inmates was an extremely sensitive thing," Stinnett recalled, "and that it could be easily derailed." And meanwhile, of course, he was hoarding his material for a higher purpose. Almost every set piece in *Falconer*—almost every detail—appears somewhere in Cheever's journal entries about Sing Sing, based on information he'd extracted from inmates: a robbery gone awry, for instance, when the victim, chained to his refrigerator, had dragged the thing out of the kitchen and down the hall to the nearest telephone; or the way Stacy went to the infirmary each morning to get his methadone, and was almost beaten to death by "assholes" (guards) when he caused a ruckus in the midst of withdrawal; or the way convicts were photographed for loved ones standing next to a Christmas tree. Nobody, however, was grilled as relentlessly as Lang, who was grateful for Cheever's help in getting him paroled that December. Lang gave Cheever nice details about, say, the cats in the mess hall, one of which was clubbed by an asshole on the "goon squad" named Tiny, who organized beatings of difficult inmates ("dead by natural causes"). Lang also described an elaborate plan of escape he'd worked out as chaplain's clerk, whereby he'd disguise himself in a surplice and board the helicopter of a visiting ecclesiastic. Most fascinating to Cheever were Lang's stories about the casual homosexuality of prison life. Movie night, for example, was an excuse for mass blow jobs: "As soon as the lights went down [Cheever wrote] so too did Larry and Petey and Harry and Georgie and a real freak who called himself Margot. 20th Century Fox presents was wasted on us and even with that loud music they play for the credits you could hear slurping noises. Cocksucking is very noisy. . . . [One guy] stood right up and said, Hey men I just came seven times. Everybody clapped."

THAT CHEEVER MANAGED to pursue his Sing Sing duties for two years is more than a little remarkable. At home, the situation deteriorated almost daily. Each morning, as Cheever put it, he did "everything but shout 'fire' " to clear the pantry so he could get at the bottles, and his body continued to bloat in protest. Shortly after he began teaching that summer, he was stopped by police while driving home—very, very slowly—from a dinner party at the Cowleys' house in Connecticut. "Put me in jail!" he angrily expostulated. "If it's a crime to drive carefully, put me in jail!" The policemen, who couldn't fail to notice that the gentleman reeked of alcohol, diffidently insisted he take a Breathalyzer test. A few weeks later, Cheever recounted the sequel while thanking an admirer for sending him a copy of *Inquire at Deacon Giles's Distillery*, a temperance tract by an alleged nineteenth-century forebear, George Barrell Cheever: "I trust he hasn't heard—in heaven, his resting place—that his great-nephew was arrested last month for drunken driving. I didn't hit anything but the State Police stopped me at two in the morning and asked me to breathe into a bag. The bag exploded."

Cheever's license was suspended for sixty days, and so he had to ride shotgun when he went to Treetops later in July for his daughter's twenty-eighth birthday. One reason he was willing to make the trip—however "painful" in a logistic sense—was that he'd gone out of his way to get Susan a special present. As she remembered, "[He] knew I was a fan of *New Yorker* cartoonist Ed Koren, and he surprised me with a drawing Koren had done at his request featuring a crowd of furry creatures shouting 'Happy Birthday, Susie.' " It was a festive occasion for all but Cheever, who hadn't been to the Winternitz estate in almost ten years and felt haunted by the place. While Mary and her brother Bill swapped stories about their illustrious father, Cheever ruminated (as ever) about how the "great man" had beaten his children with belts and so on—the ur-trauma which explained so many of his difficulties with Mary. "Thirty years ago," he sadly reminisced, "when we were courting, I used to leave the guesthouse, where everyone seemed asleep, and walk, naked, through the woods to this cottage, where we made love." Thirty years later, the cottage was a less hospitable place, and Cheever caught an early ride home with Susan the next day, huddled with dogs and a bottle of Scotch in the cramped backseat of her car.

That year Mary was writing some of the best poetry of her life, she thought, and Cheever tried to be encouraging. Certainly his public utterances on the subject were meant to be politic. "Mm-hm," he answered when asked on TV whether he read her poems. "Where is she published?" the interviewer pursued. "Not often," Cheever said, after a flustered pause; "and I can't remember the names of the magazines." At the time she'd never been published at all, though several years later her poems would be collected in *The Need for Chocolate*, and Cheever always declared the book "first-rate" when asked. "Oh, she writes about men, women, children, dogs, landscapes," he ventured in a 1981 interview. "She writes not at all, as far as I can figure out, about her husband." This was very disingenuous; as it happened, Mary's favorite poem was about her marriage, and Cheever despised it. Though it was originally titled (circa 1971) "A Long Time Married," she changed the title to "Gorgon"—the better to suggest (as she explained) the "very powerful, slightly malevolent woman" who persisted in her husband's imagination, and appeared in his fiction, regardless of anything she said or did. The poem begins: "I have sometimes complained, husband, / that as you feinted, shadowboxed and blindly / jived to that misty monolithic woman in your mind / I have been battered, drowned under your blows." But that wasn't the part that bothered Cheever. Rather, the narrator mentions how her husband "fuss[es]/and nicker[s] at [her] breasts"—which reminded Cheever of the time Mary had asked him (rhetorically) if he could "imagine how revolting it is to have an old man kiss her breasts." Anyway, he thought "Gorgon" was in the worst possible taste, which might account for his tight grimacing smile (ten years later) while declaring her poetry "first-rate" on TV.

He was less tactful about her latest job. Since leaving Briarcliff that year, she'd begun teaching an adult creative-writing workshop at the local high school. Sometimes she'd announce at dinner that one of her students (sensitive businessmen and the like) was especially gifted, and, if others seemed receptive, she'd produce an actual sample of prose and read it aloud at table. Cheever would light a cigarette. "Oh yes," he'd murmur, "oh that's brilliance for you all right"—managing to suggest not only that the work was ghastly, but that the person whose teaching had resulted in such work was also a fair subject for ridicule. Which is to say, these impromptu readings had a way of ending badly: Mary would leave the table in tears, or else Cheever would rise with a sort of final, drunken exasperation and retire upstairs (followed by elephantine crashing noises as he negotiated the narrow halls). "Who do you think you are, she asks," Cheever wrote of one such battle. "The voice is tremulous, musical, highly emotional. What am I. An imposter, usurper, a broken down alcoholic. I am your husband, I say."

Given his writer's block and dicey domestic situation, Cheever spent almost the entire autumn of 1971 on the road. After a visit to Whiskey Island in September, he proceeded to Yaddo for the annual meeting and had a very satisfactory tryst with a painter exactly half his age. "There's something about a drinking bond," the woman said,

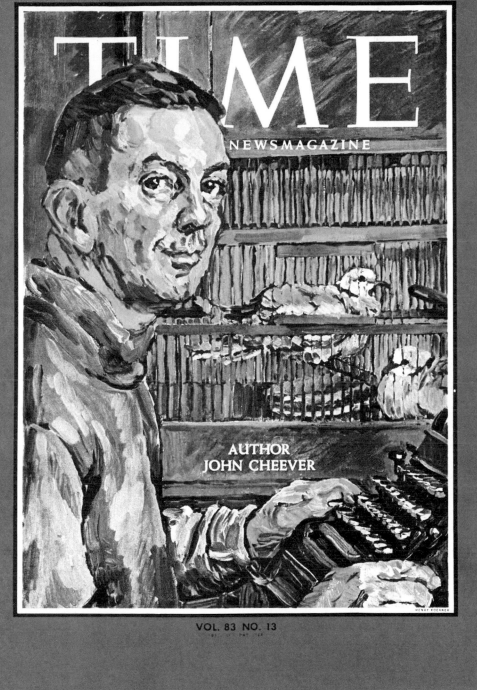

TIME

NEWSMAGAZINE

**AUTHOR
JOHN CHEEVER**

VOL. 83 NO. 13

Cheever appeared on the cover of *Time* magazine's March 27, 1964, issue.

Right: Cheever's Russian translator and intimate correspondent, Tanya Litvinov. (*Photograph by John Swope, courtesy of John Swope Trust*)

Above and right: During his trip to the Soviet Union in 1964, Cheever felt an instant rapport with his jovial hosts from the Writers Union. Being a writer in Russia, he said, was "like being a priest of some functioning religion." (*Courtesy of Cheever family collection*)

Top: A tipsy-looking Cheever endures an earnest gathering of Soviet writers, including the poet Yevgeny Yevtushenko (second from right), whom Cheever adored. The feeling was mutual: "You drink like Siberian worker!" the poet admiringly obscrvcd.
(Courtesy of Cheever family collection)

Left: Yevtushenko, Cheever, and John Updike.
(Copyright © Nancy Crampton)

Bottom left: Josephine Herbst at home in Erwinna, 1965.
(Courtesy of Cheever family collection)

Left: Burt Lancaster, Arthur Spear, and Cheever on the set of *The Swimmer* in Westport, Connecticut. Cheever had a brief cameo in the movie ("I'm John Estabrook").

Below: Cheever in front of Ossining's most famous landmark, Sing Sing prison. "Paradise on earth," he said of his adopted hometown. (*Copyright © Harry Benson*)

Right: Cheever and his eleven-year-old son, Federico, whom Cheever chided for being chubby ("Fred is on a diet which seems to involve eating everything in sight excepting spinach"). Federico, in turn, kept a weather eye on his father's drinking. (*Copyright © Harry Benson*)

Right and below: The actress Hope Lange, whose friendship with Cheever became (somewhat) carnal in 1969 and continued, after a fashion, until Cheever's death. During an early date, the two went skating at Rockefeller Center, and Lange snapped this photo of Cheever in his best suit.

Right: Skiing in his orchard, Cheever tore the ligaments in his left knee a month before publication of *Bullet Park* in 1969. "The substitution of physical pain and infirmity for melancholy seems not to have worked," he wrote in his journal. "I am simply saddled with both." (*Courtesy of Cheever family collection*)

Left: Federico and his father fishing on Whiskey Island. (*Courtesy of Cheever family collection*)

Below: John, Mary, and Federico traveled to Tokyo and Seoul for the International PEN Conference in 1970. (*Courtesy of Cheever family collection*)

Left: Cheever engaging in one of his favorite activities. Like Neddy in "The Swimmer," he would *hurl* himself into pools, no matter how icy. (*Courtesy of Cheever family collection*)

Left: Cheever doted on Natalie Robins as if she were a surrogate daughter, though she never saw him show affection toward his own children. (*Courtesy of Cheever family collection*)

Right: Cheever and Frederick Exley in Iowa City, 1972. Exley—whose name is virtually synonymous with alcoholism—was startled by how much Cheever drank. (*Courtesy of Cheever family collection*)

Left: Cheever and family with Donald Lang, a former inmate at Sing Sing, who for a while was Cheever's most frequent companion. Clockwise from top: Lynda and Ben Cheever, Mary and grandson Joshua, Federico, Lang, and Cheever. (*Copyright © Nancy Crampton*)

Left: Dennis Coates wrote a doctoral dissertation on Cheever's novels and was friendly with his subject until 1978, when Cheever read the dissertation. (*Courtesy of Dennis Coates*)

Right: Allan Gurganus at Yaddo, 1974. "A[llan] seems . . . to magnify the incongruities between my social and my erotic drives to the point of combustion," Cheever wrote. (*Courtesy of Allan Gurganus*)

Left: A despondent Cheever in his bleak two-room apartment on Bay State Road, where he lived from 1974 to 1975 while teaching at Boston University and drinking himself to death. "This place is straight asshole," he reported to friends. (*Copyright © David L. Ryan/ Boston Globe*)

As Cheever wearied of his old Westchester circle, he went out of his way to befriend younger men, such as poets Raphael Rudnik *(above)* and Philip Schultz *(left)*. (*Courtesy of Raphael Rudnik and Philip Schultz*)

Falconer reached number one on the *New York Times* best-seller list, around the time Cheever appeared on the cover of *Newsweek*. (Newsweek *[3/14/1977]* © *Newsweek, Inc. All rights reserved. Photo © Duane Michals, courtesy Pace MacGill Gallery New York*)

Above: Susan interviewed her father for the *Newsweek* cover story. "I have had many, Susie," he replied—when asked (apropos of *Falconer*) whether he'd had any homosexual experiences— "all tremendously gratifying, and all between the ages of nine and eleven." (*Copyright © Bernard Gotfryd*)

Right: Cheever's best friend in Westchester was Arthur Spear, a Goldwater Republican who knew little of Cheever's inner life. "[Art] would be capable of having me burned at the stake," Cheever mused in his journal. (*Copyright © Nancy Crampton*)

Left: Cheever and Gore Vidal, playing backgammon in Bulgaria. (*Courtesy of Cheever family collection*)

Above: Clare Thaw and Cheever admire a Cézanne. (*Courtesy of Eugene Thaw*)

Below: Cheever presents the Gold Medal of Honor to Saul Bellow at the National Arts Club. "Saul's genius is inestimable," he wrote in his journal. "With Saul on the team the game is real and the stakes are not self-aggrandizement . . . fame and wealth." (*Copyright © C. J. Zumwalt*)

Left: Cheever receiving an honorary degree from Harvard in June 1978. (*Courtesy of Cheever family collection*)

Right: Cheever won the 1979 National Book Critics Circle Award for *The Stories of John Cheever*. He appears here with fellow winners Maureen Howard and Garry Wills. (*Copyright © Nancy Crampton*)

Left: In 1979 the Bulgarian government provided Cheever with a fetching young interpreter, Alexandra. (*Courtesy of Cheever family collection*)

Left: Carving the holiday meat was a ritual Cheever took very seriously. (*Courtesy of Cheever family collection*)

Above and left: In later years, Cheever began to enjoy public readings and book-signings, though he'd despised such obligations in the past. "We laugh. We blush. I sign a book. Here is that experience of intimacy we try so hard to explain. We are, in short, not alone." (*Above: Courtesy of Cheever family collection; left: Courtesy of Jane and Barrett Clark*)

Above: The modest, self-mocking Cheever was less in evidence once he became famous, and he was more inclined to have his likeness preserved for posterity. (*Courtesy of Cheever family collection*)

Right: Cheever was delighted to be associated with top-drawer merchandise.

Rolex. For those who set the measure of the times.

John Cheever

Best-selling novelist and master of the short story. An award-winning author who savors the bittersweet taste of American life in timeless narration. Just as detail illuminates John Cheever's writing. Just as detail inspires every Rolex craftsman. Created like no other timepiece in the world. With an unrelenting, meticulous attention to excellence in a world fraught with compromise. The Rolex Oyster Perpetual Day-Date Superlative Chronometer. A great work designed to stand the test of time.

ROLEX

Left: Cheever and Susan, shortly after she finished her first novel, *Looking for Work.* Cheever was relieved to find that the heroine's father was a Columbia professor who parted his hair in the middle and not (as he put it) "an old man who is too drunk to dance the Charleston." (*Copyright © Nancy Crampton*)

Right: Cheever in the fall of 1981, shortly after his urologist had assured him that his cancerous kidney had been removed in time. Cheever suspected otherwise. *(Copyright © Stathis Orphanos)*

Left: To the end, dogs were a great consolation to Cheever. *(Courtesy of Cheever family collection)*

Right: Cheever with Janet Maslin and her mother, Lucille, at Ben and Janet's wedding on Christmas Eve, 1981. The couple had hastened to marry when Cheever was diagnosed with terminal cancer three weeks before. *(Courtesy of Cheever family collection)*

Left: John Updike delivers the eulogy at Cheever's funeral in Norwell, Massachusetts. (*Courtesy of Cheever family collection*)

Right: After the funeral. (*Courtesy of Cheever family collection*)

Left: Pallbearers (on left side of casket) included Federico, Ben, and Max Zimmer (wearing glasses). (*Courtesy of Cheever family collection*)

remembering the episode. "I've been sober for twenty years, but I was a bit of a drinker to say the least." Cheever was in good form and made the woman laugh, and perhaps in tipsy gratitude (since she needed a laugh at the time) she performed fellatio on him—thereby supplanting both Shana Alexander and Hope Lange as Cheever's top dream girl for the next two or three years. "My incantation is that I am lying in a four poster bed with S——," he wrote almost a year later.* "It is a large bed. This is in her Vermont farmhouse." And then, the year after that: "I think of S——. Why do I love a girl with such a husky voice, I ask. She kisses me. Why do I love the oldest man in the world." The woman (like certain others) was bemused to learn that she'd played such a prominent role in Cheever's fantasy life; as she pointed out, their meetings after Yaddo were "casual at best."

In October, he flew first-class to Chicago—compliments of Hugh Hefner—for the *Playboy* International Writers' Convocation, where he joined the likes of Sean O'Faolain, Alberto Moravia, John Kenneth Galbraith, and some sixty other *Playboy* contributors to discuss such topics as "Paranoia: The New Urban Life Style" and "The Future of Sex." The gathering was so high-minded that, during parties at the Mansion, Bunnies were chaperoned by a former housemother at Vassar. Cheever availed himself of the good liquor and kept smiling. Buttonholed by an earnest young writer who asked if he'd ever altered his work to suit an editor, Cheever gravely replied, "Not since I came into my inheritance." Richard Todd, reporting on the event for *The Atlantic Monthly*, noticed how Cheever "nodded elaborately in approval" when Arthur C. Clarke (of *Space Odyssey* fame) described a future in which offices would be obsolete: "Don't commute, communicate!" he exhorted the panel, while Cheever sent a paper airplane gliding down the table. Hef presented his guests with *Playboy* credit cards and VIP International Keys, but the highlight for Cheever was meeting his beloved Bellow at the Riviera Health Club. He arrived while Bellow was still on the racquetball court, and agreed to chat afterward in the steam room—an Olympian encounter that Cheever evoked six years later, while presenting Bellow with yet another award: "Saul appeared from the clouds, stark naked and wearing a copious wreath of steam. I stood in my own cloud. As we shook hands I said, as I am pleased to say tonight, that our friendship is obviously not of this world."

And finally, in November, Cheever was invited back to the Soviet

---

*The woman's name (given in the journal) is omitted here.

Union for Dostoevski's 150th-birthday celebration, for which he brought his younger son as companion and caretaker. The two had never been alone together for a long vacation—unchaperoned, as it were—and, looking back, Federico regarded this as perhaps the time he really "got to know [his] father." On the flight to Moscow, they sat together for as long as it took for the seatbelt light to go off, whereupon Cheever adjourned to the back of the plane for cocktails; when he didn't return, Federico stood peering into the gloom until he spotted his father (animatedly talking) seated beside a female passenger (listening). Landing in a blizzard, they were met by old friends and interpreters, Giorgio Breitburd and Frieda Lurie, who explained that the Dostoevski festival was in Riga and that Cheever would not like it in Riga; rather they would go to Tbilisi. "[A]nd so," Cheever later recalled, "while the speeches, concerts and parades in honor of Dostoevski raged in snowbound Riga, we swam in the rivers of southwestern Georgia and ate Homeric feasts." The sheer quantity of food bordered on life-threatening—almost twenty courses at a single meal—but the "primary indoor sport" was drinking, and Federico promptly got drunk for the first time in his life. Before he could really savor the experience, though, his even more sodden father lost control of his bowels. As the adult Federico reflected, "Washing out his pants in the bathtub of a hotel room in the Soviet Union sticks with me as one of the high points or low points of my role as keeper of my father."

But of course Federico had been taking care of his father for years now (finding his glasses and car keys; helping him stagger down the hill from Mrs. Zagreb's house), so that no chore was entirely a surprise, and for the most part they got along fine. In fact, Cheever liked to say that the only serious fight (verbal) they ever had was in Leningrad—on the banks of the Neva, amid swirling gusts of snow—because Federico wanted to see the battleship *Aurora* and he didn't. "If you think," Cheever shouted, "that I am unable to abandon a fourteen year old boy in a blizzard in a strange country you are greatly mistaken." On returning to their hotel, however, Cheever bought "an uncommon display of caviar" and the two embraced, apologized, and tucked in. Also, back in Moscow, Cheever brought his son along for a lavish dinner with Yevtushenko, who appeared in a floor-length otter coat with mink trim and presented the boy with a bottle of pepper vodka to help cure his cold. As ever, the poet served as a wistful reminder that writers were heroic figures in Russia. At the restaurant, he breezed past a line of freezing would-be patrons out on the sidewalk, and while driving in the snow he made a wild U-turn in the middle of a busy street, a maneuver that (in stark contrast to Cheever's recent treatment by the New York State Police) was regarded as little more than a winsome flourish: *"Write more poetry!"* said an affable traffic cop, once he caught a glimpse of the driver.

By the time Cheever got around to calling Tanya Litvinov, both he and Federico were exhausted. Cheever had been drinking even more than his son realized: "[I] kept ducking into closets, toilets, etc.," he wrote Exley. "Glug, Glug. Even in the Kremlin"—that is, even during a visit with President Nikolai Podgorny, who proudly showed off a shoeshine machine in his office. Unused to drinking himself, and never mind the eating, Federico had come down with raging diarrhea and was glumly consuming large brown tablets pressed on him by Yevtushenko. As for Litvinov, she'd recently lost a front tooth and looked shabby; her mother told her she was "mad" to go out looking like that, but she loved Cheever and thought she'd never see him again, so she stuck a piece of wax to her gums and met him at the Hotel Ukraine. The wax dissolved. "It was awful," she remembered. "My tooth was missing. John was drunk. The hotel restaurant was miserable. And Fred with his brown pills. Suddenly John opened his pocketbook to show me all his money, which he wanted to give me so I could buy a coat. I was furious. I said, 'Look, if you want to give me money for *samizdat* [underground publications], I'll be really glad.'" Cheever— obliged to be a good guest of the nation, and always a little worried that he'd be kidnapped and sent to Siberia—clapped his wallet shut.

"The flight back from Moscow is painful," he wrote. "A gray day."

A FEW DAYS BEFORE Cheever left for the *Playboy* conference, Zinny Schoales choked to death while eating a steak sandwich. "The face is haggard," Cheever noted of his old friend shortly before her death. "Alcohol and pain." To be sure, Zinny's last days were bleak. She used to say that she stayed interested in life by reading the obituaries first thing in the morning to see how many more of her old friends had died; then, revived somewhat by coffee and cigarettes, she'd spend the rest of the day tippling. Her children were grown up and gone away; her philandering husband traveled the world for months at a time. Zinny told Cheever she considered murdering the man, and once left photographs on the coffee table of a female praying mantis devouring its mate. "Z. is dead," Cheever wrote in his journal. "It was a relationship in which I think I took more than I gave." At the memorial service, Cheever delivered a eulogy that Zinny's older daughter remembered as "astounding"—in the middle of which a man arrived to fix the grandfather clock, dismayed to find that its owner had departed from the cares of this world.

By then Cheever could hardly afford to lose a stalwart confidante like Zinny, with whom he had more than a few things in common. "The company I used to keep when I was alone has scattered," he reflected, a few months after her death. The Boyers had moved to Guatemala shortly after his recent visit to Whiskey Island ("when you left you seem to have pulled the plug," Cheever wrote them), George Biddle was enfeebled and soon to die, and the rest of Cheever's friends could only take him in measured doses, if at all. It wasn't that he was a mean drunk—though he often was—so much as a boring, pathetic one. At parties his drawling accent would become incoherent as he told the same stories over and over, laughing at his own garbled punch lines, and almost invariably lapsing into pidgin Italian. One day his fellow Friday Clubber Tom Glazer came over to say that his friends were worried about him. Cheever had always regarded Glazer as an oaf, but now he was almost touched: "If he is worried about me he must like me. Cha cha." Subsequently he introduced the folksinger to Mary (who'd known him for many years) as follows: "I'd like you to meet my very great and good friend, Tom Glazer." Then he whispered, "I have no friends."

There was little reason to go to New York anymore, though Cheever was sometimes bored and lonely enough to suffer the miseries of train travel. "Wouldn't you rather talk than read?" he'd ask fellow passengers, desperate for any distraction. Usually they preferred to read, though some would pause a moment to point out that Cheever was drunk. And if he made it all the way into New York, the "painful alienation" that had roused him to go in the first place would only grow worse. Maxwell was cold these days, and other friends had gone or changed. "What has happened to this place where I used so happily to pound the sidewalks?" he mused. "Where has my city gone, where shall I look for it? . . . In the steam room at the Biltmore, in L[ennie Field]'s panelled apartment, in the skating rink, in the Park, in the Plaza . . . ?"

And so he stayed mostly in Ossining, though summers were almost unbearable, since Mary went to New Hampshire and he didn't have so much as a warm body to cook for him. "I am one of those lonely men you see eating London Broil in Chinese restaurants" was a constant refrain, especially when cadging meals from sympathetic neighbors. "I have entertained John Cheever most of the summer," Mary Dirks reported in a letter to friends. "[H]e drinks far far too much and one memorable evening I had to pick him up bodily from the terrace and stuff him with food, after which we managed to have a good long talk about American writers and the gossip that surrounds such creatures as Bellow and Updike and poor dead O'Hara." Cheever loathed Mary Dirks, and it is sobering to reflect just how wretched he must have been to sing for his supper thus. Indeed, he might well have succeeded in drinking himself to death, or having some nasty accident, were it not for the constant shadowing presence of his younger son. More and more, Federico had become the father and John the wayward boy: the latter had to be told not to swim naked in other people's pools, not to use the chainsaw when drunk—on and on—while the former patiently absorbed the insults Cheever inflicted on whosoever presumed to look after him. "Both Susie and I grant [Federico] absolute maturity," Cheever remarked as a sober man, mindful of the burdens he'd placed on his son. "We both feel that, in his earlier life, he had a successful but unbrilliant business career, married twice and raised seven children."

In the midst of that endless summer of 1972, Cheever wrote, "What I would like is some nice, clean heterosexual companion. Should I advertise?" What he got was Donald Lang, who fit the stated requirements imperfectly at best, but in other respects suited Cheever just fine. When Lang first got out of prison, Cheever had driven him to a halfway house in Poughkeepsie, but now he was back in Ossining, living in a tiny bedroom at the Dirkses' house; a talented carpenter and electrician, he worked for a local theater company and did odd jobs for Cheever and his friends. "Are we going to feed the thief [*il ladro*], too?" Iole would ask while serving lunch, though soon enough she and everyone else got used to him. For a long time he'd "blow in" almost every day—or disappear for weeks, according to whim—and he and Cheever would do the same things Cheever did with any friend: drink on the porch, walk in the woods, watch baseball, or take pool-hopping treks à la "The Swimmer" (though some of Cheever's wealthier neighbors balked at having the wiry ex-con romp in their pools). Cheever

did his best to help Lang acclimate to the outside world. He'd discreetly show him, by example, how to comport himself at cocktail parties and such, though Lang continued to prefer a more raffish element.
Usually he hung out at a black bar in Ossining called the Orchid
Lounge, and one night he got in a disagreement that resulted in his
beating a man with a crowbar. As Cheever wrote a friend, "Lang called
me from jail early Tuesday morning and I spent three hours (in my
very best suit) talking to the backs of black and white police officers. . . .
At around noon I got to a judge, who set bail. I got the cash and out
came Lang, unshaven, unwashed and carrying his shoe-laces. I wondered what your reaction would be, he said. Say thank you, said I.
Thank you, said he, and we, for the second time, stepped out of jail
into the sun. . . ."

Lang was far from imperceptive, and soon figured out that Cheever
needed him at least as badly as vice versa. Cheever often insisted on
greeting Lang with a bone-cracking hug ("It took time to get used to
that")—the sort of physical contact he'd always craved but was too
sheepish, now more than ever, to seek among his family. Lang got the
rest of the picture, too: though Cheever had a wide circle of acquaintances, he didn't seem to have a really "tight friend" in the world—certainly no one with whom he could relax, as with Lang, and display his
profound disdain for so-called decent society. "Once you got to know
him," said Lang, "he had no façade at all. If he felt like diving into a
pond, he just did it." He also accompanied Lang to such places as the
Orchid Lounge, where they'd sit for hours chatting with Lang's girlfriend, Peaches, whom Cheever described as "a very nubile, 17 year
old black . . . very ethnic and very funny and refreshing." Lang's multi-
faceted love life, in fact, was a source of endless fascination to Cheever.
Before he'd gone to Sing Sing, Lang had dated a prostitute named
Kathy who once "took on the Yankee ballteam": "There ain't a decent
fuck in that ball team," she'd allegedly remarked, "and Mickey Mantle
is the dirtiest, most disgusting man I ever knew." Lang's own sexual
appetites were strange and unappeasable: whenever he got sick, he
said, he'd go to bed and "beat [his] meat" until he couldn't ejaculate
anymore, though he went right on beating it ("feels great, but nothing
comes out the end").

In the course of one such conversation, Lang suddenly asked
Cheever if he had any "buddies." Loath to seem utterly bereft,
Cheever replied that Art Spear was his buddy. Lang was incredulous:

"You two old guys are *buddies?*" It transpired that Lang was thinking of a different kind of buddy—the kind of buddies Lang and Cheever became for a while, or so it seems. At one point Lang fell into a stone quarry, drunk or high, and knocked out most of his teeth; Cheever helped buy him a set of dentures, then felt oddly heartsick when Lang came "bound[ing] up the stairs" to show off his new smile: "I feel bypassed," Cheever wrote in his journal, "in fact I feel lonely. . . . I might write a story about an older man who fell in love with a [toothless] youth. . . . The young man returns with a beautiful smile . . . and the lover sees that a bridge of porcelain and plastic has ruined his happiness." Be that as it may, he couldn't resist showing off the "comely" Lang to his agent, Candida Donadio, who was convinced the two were "emotionally involved"; and then, years later, Cheever confessed to a male lover that he'd had a "brief affair" with Lang—who, he added, "is now on drugs."

Most agree the drugs probably killed Lang. At any rate, he and Cheever gradually fell out of touch: Cheever got sober and began writing again, while Lang returned to the black community he'd gotten used to in prison. "Lang's car has been parked by the bank for a week," Cheever observed in 1976, a few weeks after finishing *Falconer.* "He could be sick or dying or gone on drugs and I look for him. I find him getting soup for Peaches in a restaurant. . . . I seem to love him." A few months later, Lang wrote a note thanking Cheever for helping him complete his five-year parole (he'd celebrated, said Cheever, "by getting pissed and falling down a flight of stone steps at the Soul #4 Bar and Grill"), and they continued to cross paths until the very end—or rather Cheever's end. Lang's came a few years later: one person said he collapsed while shoveling snow in front of the Star of Bethlehem Baptist Church, but John Dirks thinks he was found dead in his squalid little room on Spring Street. "He just burned himself out," said Dirks, though he added that Lang had stayed out of prison, as far as anyone knew.

CHAPTER THIRTY-FOUR

{ 1972–1973 }

CHEEVER SEEMED PERMANENTLY IMPAIRED by alcohol. His face and extremities were swollen, his speech was slurred, and almost any kind of physical exertion made him dizzy to the point of fainting. Most ominous, perhaps, were the spells of "otherness" he began to experience in the spring of 1972: "With a hangover and a light fever I distinctly get the impression that I am in two places at once," he wrote. "I am aware of my surroundings here—rain and the beech trees and [also] I smell the coal gas and see the furniture in the old house in Quincy. Have I gone mad?" These frightening lapses continued, until Cheever was finally persuaded to attend an Alcoholics Anonymous meeting at a local church. He found it "dreary": "The long speech I have prepared seems out of order and I simply say that I am sometimes presented with situations for which I am so poorly prepared that I have to drink. . . . I am introduced to the chairman, who responds by saying that we do not use last names." For the next three years, whenever the subject of AA came up, he'd explain that he'd gone to a meeting where someone had blurted out, "Hey! There's John Cheever!"—though (as we see) he'd found it even more distasteful that he wasn't, in fact, allowed to utter that celebrated name. In any case, he decided AA wasn't for him, and besides: "I think detoxification would kill me dead."

He persevered with his writing after a fashion, but the best he could do were disparate little vignettes that he sometimes tried stringing together into stories. The first inkling of *Falconer* ("Sauced, I speculate on a homosexual romance in prison") appeared in his journal that

April, around the time he became troubled with "otherness," which may explain why he'd failed to write anything further on the subject (except notes) almost eight months later: "Since I know so much about addiction and incarceration why can't I write about it? All I seem able to do is to howl: Let me out, let me out. What did I ever do to deserve this? I am both a prisoner and an addict." Though he could no longer make his material cohere into good art, it continued to marinate somewhere in his brain, and occasionally he'd come out with some non sequitur that hinted at his obsession: "I think I'd be perfectly capable of killing my brother"; "I have no moral objection to homosexuality, it's just that I've never quite got the hang of the plumbing . . ." Meanwhile he told interviewers he was working on a "massive" novel ("You'll be able to lift it to the sound of outboard motors"), the progress of which was so painfully, painfully slow that he was determined to stop writing for good once it was done.

With nothing but time on his hands, Cheever was tempted to accept an invitation from his friend Exley to give a reading that autumn at the Iowa Writers' Workshop—though he was far more wary about traveling than he'd been even a year before. "I breakfast on scotch and Librium," he warned his host, "am having an unsavory love affair [Lang?], and suffer so from Agraphobia [sic] that it takes me a pint of liquor to get on the train." Perhaps the deciding factor was sheer curiosity. After seven years of lively, candid correspondence, he and Exley had met in the flesh only once, and then briefly, when the latter received the Rosenthal Award at the 1969 Academy of Arts and Letters ceremony—this a direct result of Cheever's efforts. As chairman of the Committee on Grants for Literature that year, Cheever had proposed *A Fan's Notes* for the Rosenthal (given to "that literary work . . . which though it may not be a commercial success, is a considerable literary achievement") by way of killing two birds with one stone: (1) promoting the cause of a worthy novel written by a friend (of sorts), while (2) scuttling Donald Barthelme, whose collection *Unspeakable Practices, Unnatural Acts* had hitherto been considered the favorite. "[A]fter his last story in The New Yorker I cannot take [Barthelme] seriously," Cheever wrote his fellow committee members. "This leaves me with Exley." The poet Phyllis McGinley fired back that to eliminate Barthelme "on the strength of one failed story" seemed "captious"; besides, she "didn't find Exley up to his reviews." Lest he appear to rule by fiat, Cheever diplomatically circulated a ballot including the names Exley, Malcolm Braly, and Richard Brautigan (but not Barthelme).

Even Exley—whose name is virtually synonymous with alcoholism—was impressed by Cheever's drinking. As he recalled, "No sooner were we on the highway [from the Cedar Rapids airport] that John reached into his raincoat pocket, pulled out a beige plastic pint flask containing gin, invited us to have a belt, we declined, John took a healthy swig and returned the flask to his pocket." Exley showed his guest to a room at the Iowa House, then inquired whether it would be all right if a nice young man came to interview him for the campus newspaper; Cheever was happy to oblige. "I like Exley," he said, when asked what writers he admired. Any others? "I like Exley." *Nobody* else? "I like Exley." So it went. Since Cheever had arrived a few days early, he and Exley filled the interval with a pleasant routine. Each morning they'd meet at the downstairs cafeteria for "shaky cups of coffee," then embark on an all-day round of campus saloons. "Hi Fred! . . . Hi Ex!" shop clerks yelled from their doors as the two writers shambled along. When Cheever expressed amazement at his friend's celebrity after only ten weeks in town, Exley "beamed modestly" rather than explain that the clerks were hoping to be introduced to Cheever, whose arrival had been widely trumpeted in the local press.

Perhaps Exley should have mentioned as much, since Cheever's self-esteem was at a very low ebb, which meant a certain amount of compensatory haughtiness was almost inevitable. The writer Vance Bourjaily's wife, Tina, had gone to the trouble of birthing a lamb, feeding it only the best grass, assisting in its slaughter, and roasting it to perfection in a pastry crust for their distinguished guest—in return for which she received a bit of muttering condescension. As she remembered with lingering pique, "[Cheever] sat on his pompous ass at the dinner table saying 'Imagine eating *d'agneau en croute* in Iowa!' He probably never tasted a finer one unless he had eaten at the four star restaurant out in the wilderness of Southern France where they gave me the recipe." Likewise, when Exley tried to talk him out of reading a story as lengthy as "Justina"—with worsening laryngitis yet—"John drew himself up to his full five-feet-five and in his insufferable tones proclaimed something like, 'Ah've read "The Death of Justina" in Moscow, Leningrad, Stockholm [etc.] . . . and if it's good enough for those places it's damn well good enough for Iowa City.' " Sure enough, his voice began to fail around the middle of his reading at the Clapp

Recital Hall ("Hoarseness is not, thank God, a symptom of Clapp," he remarked), and afterward he complained to Exley about the size of the audience: "I thought you said Styron packed the place!" In the company of students, however (especially Exley's twenty-one-year-old girl-friend), Cheever was at his funny, self-effacing best, and in hindsight he viewed the visit as an almost unqualified triumph. "That was great fun although I do worry about all the tabs you picked up," he wrote Exley. "We seem to have something basically in common, something more lambent, I hope, than hootch and cunt."

Indeed, Cheever had found Iowa City so "serene" that he considered teaching there the following year, when Bourjaily was planning to take a sabbatical. Jack Leggett, the workshop director, was all for it, and everything seemed in order except a few "imponderables," as Cheever put it: "I don't know what to do about this house, [and] my marriage is in the annual dumps . . ." Mary, to be sure, was not keen on the idea of going to Iowa with her drunken husband, who moreover was likely to kill himself if allowed to go alone. The discussion escalated into mutual threats of divorce, until finally it was decided that they would all go their separate ways in the fall of 1973: Mary would remain in Ossining, while Cheever went to Iowa and Federico to boarding school (Andover). "Who cares?" Cheever said when friends wondered how he'd manage alone in the sticks. "Feed me to the pigs."

APART FROM THE USUAL DOMESTIC CRISES, nothing much happened to Cheever between his Iowa trip in November 1972 and the publication, in May, of *The World of Apples*, which coincided almost exactly with a long-overdue brush with death. One episode in the interim seems exemplary. That spring he was invited to give a reading in Provincetown, where he'd spent many happy days in his youth. "It's easier to get to Egypt," he replied by postcard to Molly Cook, chairman of the Fine Arts Work Center, who replied that she and writer Roger Skillings would be happy to retrieve him in Ossining. What ensued, as Skillings wrote the poet Stanley Kunitz, was "a kind of nightmare." Following directions provided by Cheever, they arrived at the house of a "large florid whitehaired man" who appeared to be in the process of repairing TV sets. "Who do you think I am?" he finally asked, having served them jelly jars of vodka. They told him. "Oh no," he said, "I'm Johnny Curtains, Cheever lives up the road." They found

Cheever in high dudgeon and drunk, as he'd gulped a great deal of gin while waiting for them to arrive. He soon calmed down, however, and insisted on reading them a story from his advance copy of *The World of Apples;* with Mary and Federico in bemused attendance, Skillings lit a joint and settled back to listen. "I can tell it better than I can read it," Cheever said after an "interminable" attempt to negotiate the text, and so he did while his wife devised a map to the Watergate Inn in Croton, where Cook and Skillings were to spend that Friday night.

Cheever had been drunk yet dignified, lordly even, in his own home, but a very different Cheever began to emerge on the road to Provincetown. A "perfectly suited" Art Spear went along as a minder of sorts, though both pulled freely from flasks (gin in Cheever's, sherry in Spear's) and were plastered by the time they stopped for lunch at a diner in South Dartmouth, where Cheever indulged in a lot of Fitzgeraldian hazing of the waiter. That night, before the reading, Cook and Skillings had planned to take their guest to dinner at Ciro and Sal's Restaurant, but when the time came he was nowhere to be found. After a frantic search, Skillings spotted him wandering down Commercial Street: "[Cheever] gave me an immense long hug," Skillings noted, "which gave me the willies because I thought he'd gone to sleep." An elderly Hazel Hawthorne, one of the great benefactors of Cheever's youth, exuberantly greeted him at the restaurant— "*Joey!*"—and Cheever responded with a kind of bewildered bonhomie ("he barely knew her," said Cook). The poet Mary Oliver was supposed to introduce Cheever at the Work Center, which was mobbed for the occasion, but before she could work her way up to the podium, Cheever had already begun: "[H]e read The Death of Justina very well considering," Skillings related to Kunitz, "but his heart wasn't in it, and then everybody went over to the barn for a party where he kept sticking his tongue in my mouth and asking me how could I resist him." Cheever explained that he'd "discovered homosexuality at Sing Sing" and wanted to give it a try, but Skillings resisted being pinned to the bed and finally persuaded him to desist. Art Spear was presumably elsewhere.

It got worse. Spear caught a plane the next day, but Cheever gave no sign of leaving: nice people were providing drinks and food, he liked the scenery, and anyway why go home? "We were little drudges," Cook recalled, "and he expected it. He would thank us politely, but not enthusiastically." On Sunday, because of the blue laws, Skillings had gone round to friends' houses borrowing Scotch for Cheever, and very early on Monday Cheever said that he needed a morning drink "for the first time in [his] life." Guiding him to a liquor store, Skillings observed the visible effort on Cheever's part not to "bolt behind the store and take a belt." The bottle was empty by noon, and meanwhile Cheever never stopped talking: "He talks mechanically and repeats himself," said Skillings, "reminiscences without point or perspective . . ." Expecting dinner, Cheever reported once again that night to Molly Cook and Mary Oliver (both "grey with fatigue"), after which he resumed making passes at Skillings. "Why do you find me so repulsive?" he demanded. "I won't hurt you! I don't even know what the ritual is!" This went on until midnight, when Cook finally coaxed him back to his room and tucked him into bed. "I've lost all my friends," he said, gazing into her eyes. "I'm lonely."

They got him a ride back to Ossining the next day. "In Provincetown I see the beach, the dunes, the ocean," he wrote in his journal. "How beautiful it is. I see an old friend [Hawthorne], smoke four joints and have a number of unsuitable erotic spasms. Why should people not respond to my caresses. I'll never know."

SUSAN CHEEVER APTLY DESCRIBED *The World of Apples* as "a slim collection of the ten stories [her father] had eked out during the 1960s, in between novels, traveling, and alcoholic interludes." The title story might almost (but not quite) be ranked among Cheever's best, "The Fourth Alarm" and "The Jewels of the Cabots" are eminently readable and interesting, while the rest are divided between the relatively weak and the nearly embarrassing.* Two reviewers, Thomas R. Edwards in *The New York Review of Books* and Ronald De Feo in the *National Review*, summed up the volume with the same phrase—"rather tired"— nor were they alone in wondering at how little Cheever had to show for himself since his previous collection almost ten years before.

That said, *The World of Apples* received some of the best reviews of Cheever's career, his admirers seeming to realize that the time was ripe

---

*As an example of the latter, the collection's most recent story consisted of three trite, unrelated anecdotes that Cheever had dumped on *Playboy* under the title "Triad" (reprinted in *The World of Apples* and *The Stories of John Cheever* as "Three Stories"). The first sketch is narrated by a middle-aged man's stomach, and—except for the elegant prose—reads like a funny story swapped among Rotarians.

to rally support for such a superlative (and evidently discouraged) writer, especially after the beating he'd taken over *Bullet Park*. "Yes, this collection may give comfort to Mr. Cheever's detractors," wrote his old friend Christopher Lehmann-Haupt in the daily *Times*. "But it also gives aid to those of us who have always thought of him as our foremost writer of short fiction, as our most telling explorer of the geography of the heart." Both the *New York Times Book Review* and the *Washington Post Book World* featured extravagant front-page encomiums, by Larry Woiwode and D. Keith Mano respectively: "Cheever is as much a master of the short form as Chekhov, and should be recognized as such," said Woiwode; Mano likened the author to Proust. Cheever was naturally gratified: "Apples seems to have done much better than Bullet Park," he wrote a friend. "I got a spate of reviews yesterday in which I am praised, all across the country, for my sophistication, my insouciance, my elegance and charm."

The moral support came at a good time. For several months now, along with the usual dizziness and chest pains, Cheever had found it harder and harder to breathe; it was especially bad in the morning, though he'd conveniently discovered that whiskey alleviated the problem somewhat. On the morning of May 12, however, he seemed to be suffocating: coughing uncontrollably, he lay abed quaffing Scotch and smoking cigarettes in hope of some relief, until his family persuaded him to go to the Phelps emergency room. As his doctor, Ray Mutter, remembered, "All the cardiologists and internists and everybody were swarming all over him to try to get him out of [heart] failure." Cheever was found to be suffering from "dilated cardiomyopathy," an often alcohol-related condition in which the left ventricle fails to eject blood at a proper rate, drowning the lungs and causing the heart to enlarge. Had he waited a little longer to go to the hospital—another drink, another cigarette—he would almost certainly have died. ¯

For three days he lay calmly recovering in the Intensive Care Unit, and then ("like clockwork," said Mutter) he lapsed into delirium tremens, which had killed his unfortunate grandfather Aaron. Because Cheever's heart was too weak to withstand heavy doses of tranquilizers, he was in for a long bout—almost five days—during which his foremost hallucination was that he was in a Soviet prison somewhere in Moscow. He thought the intercom speaker above his bed was a Bible they wouldn't let him read, that the rumbling food carts were prisoners being trucked from one place to another. In a panic, he yanked tubes out of his arms and lashed out, physically and otherwise, at anyone who came near him. Susan brought him a copy of the *Times Book Review* with the Woiwode rave on the cover, which Cheever thought was a confession he was supposed to sign; he cursed her and threw it on the floor. Meanwhile Federico patiently explained, over and over, that they *weren't* in a Moscow prison ("if you've ever been to Phelps Memorial Hospital," he later remarked, "you'd know that's not the most implausible hallucination you could come up with"), and when his father demanded proof, he retrieved a sign written in English: "Oxygen: No Smoking."

However *in extremis*, Cheever did not forget his own importance* and was very high-handed toward the hospital staff (or Soviet jailers, as it were). Susan worried that he'd be treated roughly if left unattended, and insisted that at least one family member stay by his bed whenever possible. Even the estranged Ben was pressed into service (over his wife's objection): at one point he noticed his father groping about the sheets for a cigarette; then the latter espied what he thought were the lights of a tavern (actually a nurses' station), and asked his son to trot over and get him a pack of Marlboros and a martini. As Ben wrote in the *Letters*, his father's voice became "haughty and crisp" when Ben tried to explain where they were:

> "Are you completely without imagination and initiative?" he asked. "If that is not a bar, then why don't you go and find one? And when you've found one, if you're capable of finding a bar in a state that is crammed with them, then why don't you buy that pack of cigarettes for me and a double martini?"
>
> "I don't think I should, Daddy."
>
> "Well, then, I'll just get up and do it myself," he said. . . .
>
> Then he started to get up. This excited the heart monitor, and I was afraid of what the oxygen tubes would do to his nose, so I grabbed the rail of the bed and made a barrier of myself. First he struggled, then he lay back down. Then he hit me in the chest with his forearm. It didn't hurt, but it did surprise me. He was furious. "You've always been a disappointment as a son," he said.

---

*Along with the rave reviews for *The World of Apples*, that same week he was also nominated to become one of the elite fifty in the American Academy of Arts and Letters.

Finally, Cheever was moved to a barred bed and placed in a webbed straitjacket. With almost laudable bravado, he managed to fish a razor out of his bedside table and cut himself free, then he laboriously squirmed his way out through a hole at the foot of his bed and collapsed onto the floor. "This brought the cops," he wrote, "and I was put into a second straitjacket—leather with brass bindings and four padlocks." When the cardiologist visited that night, Cheever roared, "I've been *shackled*!"

After some three rocky weeks in the ICU, Cheever's heart began to improve. Applauded for his "spectacular" recovery, he celebrated by wheeling himself into the hall at three in the morning and having a cigarette with his son-in-law. Around this time Jack Leggett called him at the hospital and told him to focus on getting well and forget about coming to Iowa. "Don't be silly," said Cheever, "of *course* I'm coming!" In fact he was terrified he'd begin drinking again and end up killing himself, and on his sixty-first birthday he went to see a Phelps psychiatrist named Frank Jewett, whom Cheever dubbed "The Boots" because of the man's preferred form of footwear. His main incitement to drinking, Cheever admitted as usual, was homosexual anxiety, and he went into some detail about his recent encounters with young men. Jewett—intrigued by the whole *"Death in Venice* plot," as he put it, and perhaps a little doubtful as to whether the puckish Cheever was entirely serious—couldn't resist discussing the matter with his old med-school pal Ray Mutter, who was convinced that Cheever was toying with the man. Laughing heartily, he related the whole "homosexual" business to Susan, who was both amused and exasperated: how was her father ever going to get better if he didn't quit clowning and level with these people? "Come on, Daddy," she said. "Why did you go and tell 'The Boots' that you were homosexual?" After a pause, her father laughed: "I guess I just don't like psychiatrists."

Home again after almost a month in the hospital, Cheever felt a happiness at being alive that was "indescribable": "There is a sinister shrink in the wings who says that my euphoria is regressive," he wrote Weaver, "that I am high because I'm forbidden to do what I don't like to do (emptying the garbage) and that if I don't take his advice I'll end up in the stews. I've told him to kiss off." A month of sobriety had wrought a dramatic change: his bloated body seemed to deflate, his blue eyes stood out in his head again, and he treated his family with a sort of wan, remorseful courtesy. He was still a very sick man: his left ventricle remained "unruly," and his heart did a "clog dance" whenever he tried climbing stairs. Still, in the absence of drinking, he longed to be more productive. Sitting in his wing chair or out on the porch, he sipped iced tea and wrote "on air" bits of *Falconer* he'd been kicking around for over a year: the protagonist's murder of his brother, the man's love affair with the convict "Joey" (a name he'd understandably change to "Jody" in due course). In the meantime Gottlieb (et al.) knew about his precarious health and what had led up to it, and seemed hesitant to give Cheever another high advance. Nor could Cheever, in good conscience, complain much, since he'd yet to write a single finished word of the novel in question: "A nightmare is that I will die suddenly and some editor—Bob [Gottlieb] perhaps—will find no trace of the book," he wrote that June. "I ought to leave something that looks like a book. So my long vacation continues." A few weeks later, Gottlieb came around with a hundred thousand dollars, and sometime in August Cheever finally managed to write a few "inarticulate and clumsy" pages of *Falconer*.

One problem was rust; another was that he'd begun drinking again. Doing so, he'd followed to the letter the classic pattern of the alcoholic who gets sober in response to some crisis, then thinks he's capable of drinking moderately and almost immediately reverts to his previous condition or worse. In Cheever's case it would get much, much worse, though it began with a trifle: "I drink perhaps a tablespoon of whisky," he noted in mid-July. "The effects are splendid, beyond anxiety, but I suppose I should confess this." A page later, he wrote: "Alone, I drink a whisky after dinner. It tastes very good. It seems to do me no harm but I must be very careful about this." Cheever would have found a reason to drink in any case, but since it was summer the most satisfying reason was readily at hand: his wife was going away to Treetops, and if that weren't callous enough, she was taking the whole family with her—all but Cheever, who felt very sorry for himself even though the decision to stay behind was, as ever, his. "I might state the facts," he wrote, explaining to himself why he wanted to drink again, "that I am a very lonely man of sixty-one, malnourished, living alone with a cat, suffering from a heart condition and trying to write off a debt of one hundred thousand dollars before I die." Still, he made a miniature stand of sorts. Home alone that first day, he poured his gin down the sink and tried to get some work done; then he lunched with friends and went for a swim at Mrs. Zagreb's. A drab day. His work went badly or not at all, and he found himself "less spontaneous" with friends. That same night, then, he consoled himself with two whiskeys ("I revel in these, wallow, smear, engorge myself"), and the next day he drove to the liquor store and replenished his gin.

Federico returned from Treetops after a week or two, and soon discovered that his father was drinking again. Caught in the act, Cheever said that Mutter had allowed him to have two drinks a day*; Federico didn't buy it and demanded he stop. For a while Cheever drank furtively and somewhat moderately, and from time to time would even ask his son's permission; this being denied—emphatically—he'd sneak a drink anyway. Meanwhile he worked on the only real writing he accomplished that summer: a brief testimonial on the savory elegance of Suntory whisky, in return for which a Japanese PR man arrived one day with a case of the stuff. "I was nervous about it," Federico recalled, "and I think in one of his moments of pique he told me he'd drunk some of it to hurt me." Federico promptly poured the rest of it into the sink, then phoned his mother in a panic and begged her to come home right away. But of course it was too late—had always been too late, though Cheever promised once again to abstain. "The gin bottle, the gin bottle," he wrote.

> This is painful to record. I go to the post office and stay away from the gin shop. "If you drink you'll kill yourself," says my son. His eyes are filled with tears. "Listen," say I. "If I thought it would benefit you I'd jump off a ten-story building." He doesn't want that, and there isn't a ten-story building in the village. I drive up the hill to get the mail and make a detour to the gin store. I hide the bottle under the car seat. We swim, and I wonder how I will get the bottle from the car to the house. I read while brooding on this problem. When I think that my beloved son has gone upstairs, I hide the bottle by the side of the house and lace my iced tea.

By the end of August, Federico and Mary had exhausted their arguments and Cheever was drinking openly again. They avoided him in disgust, while he in turn felt sorry for himself and affected to look forward to Iowa. As he wrote a friend, "I'm not at all sure what I'm getting into or getting out of but there seems to be a time for departure and this seems to be it."

---

*"The doctor tells me that I cannot drink for the rest of my life," Cheever wrote that summer. "I have a cardiomyopathy and a drop of alcohol in my bloodstream would be dangerous. I can always go to another doctor."

CHAPTER THIRTY-FIVE

{ *1973* }

Cheever would later indulge in a certain amount of gloating over what a great time he'd had in Iowa, but the first weeks were grim. He was installed in Room 436 of the nondescript Iowa House, where the rooms were precisely those of a small-town Midwestern hotel—the stark gumwood furniture, the beige walls, the black and white TV bolted to the dresser. Cheever was so lonely he wrote letters to almost everybody he knew, including the Dirkses and Tom Glazer; he'd sit in taverns wistfully observing the tables full of lively undergraduates, none of whom seemed inclined to accept his company.

Knowing hardly a soul, he spent those first days traipsing around town—pausing every so often to catch his breath and worry about his heart—en route to the movies: *Last Tango in Paris* was a lot of pretentious "rubbish," he thought, so he crossed the street to watch a Western and presently *Godspell* ("a highly estimable piece of work"). Afterward he'd sometimes visit an Irish tailor over a Chinese restaurant to check the progress of a navy three-piece he'd ordered (his "best suit" for many years); then, as evening fell, he'd either take an Italian lesson or go to the odd social engagement—the latter a dreary ordeal for a shy man who was trying to curb his drinking. Ron Hansen, who'd signed up for Cheever's workshop, became acquainted with his teacher at the writer John Irving's house (where Hansen lived in the basement and babysat Irving's children). Cheever had come to dinner wearing his new bespoke suit with an Academy badge in the lapel, and Hansen politely asked what the badge signified. "He explained the American Academy of Arts and Letters to me," Hansen recalled, "as if he were prepared to be patient about anything now that he'd accepted a visiting professorship."

Life improved once he actually began teaching, and no wonder: all the best graduate students had assigned themselves to Cheever's workshop, and if a missile had hit the class, at least three of the leading lights of that generation would have been eliminated—Hansen, T. (Tom) Coraghessan Boyle, and Allan Gurganus. Once he settled in, Cheever would find such a concentration of talent invigorating ("when we bring off a seminar it takes three men to get me off the ceiling"), but at first it was a lot more daunting than teaching convicts. "We were a bunch of ragtag hippies," said Boyle, "and he had no experience with such people"—or so it seemed. Cheever, wearing his tidy new suit and badge, would look dismayed at the "critical brawls" that took place during a typical workshop session, and by way of imposing a level of civility, he'd bring his accent and elegant manners to the fore. Gurganus remembered that Cheever was initially "very nervous, and the more nervous he got the more hauteur he affected and the more gargly and Katharine Hepburn–y his talk became." Gurganus, a worldly young man in his mid-twenties, was able to put his teacher somewhat at ease: while in the navy, he'd discovered a copy of *The Brigadier and the Golf Widow* aboard the USS *Yorktown* ("because of the military title someone thought it had some vital application to national security"), so he knew that Cheever was more than simply a realistic "suburban writer," as the others rather dismissively perceived him. Also, Gurganus was good-looking and quite insouciantly gay—as Cheever noted, "a versatile and brilliant young man who . . . dispels any doubts I have about his sexual nature with a clear-eyed self-possessed presence."

Because Gurganus had an enlightened reverence for his teacher, he was willing to put forth his best effort in completing the menial "drills" Cheever saw fit to assign: "Write me a love letter in a burning building," he'd say, or "Give me seven or eight disparate objects or incidents that are superficially alien and yet profoundly allied." This was nothing less than the sort of thing Flaubert had taxed the young Maupassant with, but Iowa students found it annoying: they were working on their own novels and stories, and didn't like being treated as if they were rank amateurs. Gurganus, however, submitted homework that was good enough to publish: "Seven Details the Major Critic of the Show Felt to Be Overexplicit" would later appear in *The Atlantic Monthly*, as would another story about an incestuous brother and sister seeking Aztec funeral urns in a burning building. As for Cheever, his constrained manner soon dissolved under the force of his enthusiasm. "Marvelous! *Marvelous!*" he'd gush. "Oh *gosh* that's invigorating . . ." Nor was it simply a matter of soigné former sailors. "You're *wonderful*," he told the shaggy Tom Boyle. "We're equals!"

It was different when he didn't like a story. Gurganus later worked with Stanley Elkin—a "genius teacher" who provided a study in contrast: "[Elkin] was like an architect looking at a building and telling you exactly where the stresses were," said Gurganus. "John would either say *yes* or *no*. Either it would do or it wouldn't do. He said yes to me more often than he said no, but it was frustrating when he said no, because it was hard to get him to tell you what could be changed." The most disheartening part was that he tended to be right, though it often required a lot of painful labor in the dark to discover why this should be so. Gurganus admitted that his own *no* stories were, in fact, buried at last in files somewhere ("with all the Christian rites and honors"), and even Cheever's formidable contemporary Hortense Calisher conceded the "ruthless" accuracy of his literary judgments: "Come now, Hortense, that's a fudge," he'd say when she'd protest that she was still reading a book and hence uncertain as to its merit. "You can read a page and tell if it's alive or dead." In workshop, Cheever would express rejection with a vaguely grim poker-face, perhaps a slight shrug, which was tantamount to a loud and insulting harangue. And if a student made the mistake of pressing him as to *why* a story didn't work, or (worse) how it might be improved, Cheever would respond with a sort of pensive sarcasm: "If that character is supposed to be *gay*," he might say, feigning careful deliberation, "maybe you could *show* as much by having him lick his fingers and wipe his eyebrows . . ." As Hansen explained, "He meant to suggest that the story was such a mess that even a detail like that wouldn't help."

Whether or not Cheever liked a student's work also seemed to depend on whether he found the person *attractive* in the comprehensive sense intended by his mother-in-law, Polly, or the "metaphysical" sense, as Gurganus would have it: "Just as you either got a story the first time or you didn't, people were either attractive or unattractive." Cheever ran the workshop like a "very nice cocktail party," and he liked people to amuse him. One woman, however, was definitely unamusing to Cheever. She was fortyish, had two children, and was overweight and dowdy and wore funny glasses. Once, when Cheever was reading a story to the class, she apologetically remembered that she had to go pick up her children at school. Cheever lowered his book and gave her a hard stare. "I am *not* going to stop reading this story for you." There were many such episodes, one of which sparked a remark in Cheever's journal: "I lash out at a middle-aged woman with harlequin glasses who has left her family to pursue her literary career. She has little if any talent but my distemper is probably personal." That Cheever would find such a woman distasteful requires no elaboration. However, classmates remember her as really quite likable and talented; what's more (and this was well known), she'd been abandoned by her husband, *not* vice versa. "John couldn't find one thing to praise in her work," Gurganus recalled. "He smelled her bad luck and her poverty and her ordinariness, and maybe he felt it was wrong to encourage her if he didn't think she had a future."

Mostly, though, Cheever was the soul of kindness and tact, and was even prepared to forgive his students' dislike or (more often) total ignorance of his own work. "I'm terribly out of mode," he said again and again. "Nobody reads me anymore." The young Tom Boyle agreed: like so many of his peers, he worshipped at the feet of "experimental" writers such as Barthelme and Barth, and particularly liked to invoke the latter's *Sot-Weed Factor*. Finally—diffidently—Cheever allowed that he didn't much care for Barth, and even had the temerity to suggest that he himself was experimental. "All writing is 'experimental,' Tom," he said. "Don't get caught up in fads." Boyle inwardly scoffed and continued to regard Cheever as "an old stick in the mud"—until he finally got around to rereading Cheever's work with care. To this day he's still reading it, though it's been a long time since he's read any Barthelme or Barth. "Anyone can write a Barthelme story," said Boyle. "No one can write a Cheever story."

It was all the same to Cheever—most of the time. "Look in my closet," he'd say (wearing his bespoke suit). "Two shirts and two pairs of wash pants." Then he'd shake his head with a sad little chuckle. As for all the patronizing young geniuses at Iowa, well, let them have their fun. "Ah yes, I loved your book," he told the poet Michael Ryan, who'd recently won a prize. As Ryan wrote many years later in "Meeting Cheever":

> And you, inconsolable bell-bottomed cliché
> of wounded-by-the-world angry young poet
> who became me as strangely as years become today,
> replied, "The book's not published yet."

And so the poem ends:

> . . . Where was the future with its bloody claws?
> Brilliant John Cheever is a handful of ash.
> I would be finished with what I was.

. . .

CHEEVER SOON GAVE UP his occasional sobriety. Jack Leggett liked to tell of the time he'd been called to the phone at a party where Cheever had already drunk "twelve or thirteen martinis"; the caller proved to be none other than Cheever's doctor: "Whatever you do," the man said, "*don't let him drink.* He could drop dead at any moment!" After less than a month on campus, Cheever was visited by his old Signal Corps buddy John Weaver, who was stopping in Iowa on his way home from a research trip. Weaver was under the impression that his ailing friend had gotten sober at last, but the morning after his arrival Cheever insisted they go to a bar, and when Weaver left to catch his plane a few hours later, Cheever was "stoned": "I left Iowa never expecting to see him again," Weaver remembered.

Cheever knew he was killing himself, but he claimed to be too depressed *not* to drink. Over and over, to whosoever would listen, he spoke of how "inadequate" he felt as a husband and father, laying the blame on himself with mawkish insistence, as if it might ease the shame. (Rather like the tippler in *The Little Prince*, he drank because he was ashamed, and was ashamed because he drank.) On the other hand, he didn't really want to die either. Once, overcome by dizziness, he staggered to the grassy bank of the Iowa River and sat down. It was a crystalline autumn day, and he watched the students walk by as through an impenetrable pane of glass. The "tangible world" was receding, he couldn't even cry out, and this "vision of youth"—so coveted by the helpless observer—would be the last thing he'd ever see. "If I die," he told Gurganus, "I've given your name to the hotel, and I have instructed them to call you any hour of the day or night, and as soon as you get the call, I want you to come and get these journals out of here, because I'm afraid they'll fall into the wrong hands." He showed Gurganus the twenty or so loose-leaf notebooks under his desk, and the young man (amid token protest: "Oh, don't be ridiculous, John") promised to do exactly as told.

Cheever's despair was belied somewhat by all the fun he seemed to be having. "I shout myself hoarse at football games," he wrote Spear, "take young women to concerts, dance the Virginia Reel, play football, lecture on the problems of modern fiction and generally splatter myself over this part of the mid-western landscape." As one of the most famous writers ever to grace the faculty, Cheever was literally welcomed with open arms wherever he went. One day a stranger embraced him in the elevator, and when Cheever inquired as to whom he owed the pleasure of such a charming salutation, the man introduced himself as the president of the university, Willard "Sandy" Boyd. Cheever became a regular guest in the man's home, where he knew he was dealing with quality because, after all, there was Messiaen on the piano's music stand! When it came to splattering himself around the landscape, though, Cheever preferred the company of young people. Ron Hansen was dating one of the few women in the workshop, Sarah Irwin, whom Cheever found "friendly as a cocker spaniel" and took to a number of football games. Passing a thermos of Scotch and huddling under a lap rug, the two would cheer the hapless Hawkeyes before returning to Iowa House for long, drunken soul-chats. "I'm displaced and *lonely*," Cheever would say ("drawl[ing] out the word with a terribly hollow *oh* sound—lo*h*nely," Irwin recalled), telling as ever the saga of his marriage—how there's "always a lover and a beloved" and his wife was decidedly the latter. ("I talk with M[ary] on the phone and these conversations are always poor," he wrote around that time. "I make the sign of the cross and can barely keep from hanging up.") Worried that Irwin's boyfriend would get the wrong idea, Cheever proposed they pay him a visit one Saturday afternoon, and the three sat around the floor of his basement apartment drinking wine and popping cashews. The dapper, mannerly Cheever kept startling the couple with the odd bombshell: "I was at Yaddo last month," he remarked in passing, "and there was this sculptor who kept following me around, so finally I just let him blow me and that was the end of it." While Hansen and Irwin listened with widening eyes, Cheever added, "Fellatio is the nicest thing one human being can do for another."

Hansen and Irwin also accompanied their teacher to a bluegrass festival, where he managed to disconcert them for a different reason. Joining a touch-football game, Cheever frisked about, howling with laughter and gasping for air, while his minders wondered if they should do something before it was too late. Fortunately, Cheever noticed that (as Irwin put it) "the other players were moving around him like something fragile as an egg, and he did not wish to spoil the game." Next he jumped on a picnic table and began dancing a jig, then scampered up the hill to join a Virginia reel. As he noted in his journal, "I romped into this with such enthusiasm that I damned near had a heart attack, and ended up (happily) sitting on a pile of horse buns." Even in quieter circumstances, Cheever hardly behaved like an old man nearing the end of his journey. The night after the festival, Irwin stopped by his room for a drink—perhaps to make sure he was still breathing—and at one point Cheever tenderly kissed her foot and placed it against his chest. Things began to go further ("I had a great deal of admiration and affection for John," said Irwin—"that plus the Scotch"), but both had qualms about Hansen and decided to keep things on a platonic basis.

Cheever's most constant female companion, however, was not Irwin. One day he was reading beside the river when a young woman approached: "Good afternoon, Mr. Cheever," she said, launching into a spiel about how she'd read everything he'd ever written and wanted *so* badly to be in his class, but she was only a first-year and they wouldn't let her in. ("I sit on the river banks with [Elaine],* an intelligent young woman with a slight gauntness in the face.") Cheever said he'd take care of it, and got her into his literature class. Meanwhile he began asking her to have drinks and dinner with him. "People were falling all over themselves to have ten minutes with him," she remembered, "and he wanted to be with me." Elaine was able to appreciate, vividly, that she was in the presence of greatness, and Cheever did his best to oblige her. Eating a hamburger at their usual hangout, The Deadwood, he began reciting one of his stories from memory; the girl listened, spellbound, and afterward checked the actual text in her room and realized that he'd "told [her] the story literally word for word."†

Elaine repaid the compliment of Cheever's regard by making herself indispensable. Whatever else she was, she was foremost his keeper. "We set up certain signals," she said, "like, if we went to someone's house or whatever and I saw that he was getting sloppy, I'd give him the signal that we had to leave, and we'd leave. He'd say, 'Oh, we have

---

*Her name has been changed here.

†"One way I can find out if I like something I've done"—Cheever remarked during a 1969 interview—"is if I can tell it and it's all right. . . . So one day last summer I said, 'Look, Ben, I've written a novel. Do you want to hear it?' And Ben said, 'Yuh.' And so I went absolutely all the way through it from 'Paint me a small railway station' to 'wonderful, wonderful, wonderful as it had been.' "

to go. Miss Moody* has another engagement.' " Leggett, for one, attested to this peculiar dynamic: in public, at least, Elaine appeared to have the upper hand, almost as if she were "exercising marital rights." Naturally people began to talk, and perhaps to put the girl at ease, or simply because he wished to unburden himself, Cheever announced one day that he had something very important to tell her. "He was really a wreck," said Elaine. "I think he thought I was going to reject him or have a fit. He told me he was gay." As she remembered it, Cheever made a point of emphasizing *gay* as opposed to bisexual, though Cheever's journal suggests otherwise: "I go back with [Elaine] to her dormitory. My sexual iridescence [Cheever's term for a sort of ravenous versatility] is spread out with more breadth than ever before. . . . Look, look at grandfather. Leaving a girl's room in a dormitory at half past three in the morning." Not that Cheever minded being seen in that kind of compromising situation; on the contrary, he made a point of telling his drinking companions at Iowa—and later his family—all about his sexual exploits with the young woman. Then and later, she vehemently denied having sex with Cheever, though it wasn't something she wanted to confront him about. In private, he was very much the master and she the disciple.

It was Gurganus who brought out the boyish swain in Cheever. "You look fan*tas*tic!" Cheever would gush when the two met for Sunday strolls along the river. "What a handsome man you are!" In his journal Cheever deplored how this Eagle Scout and Vietnam veteran would "swing his hips" when he walked. As ever, the most admired male evoked the strongest homophobia. But otherwise he found the young man's openness "highly desirable" and relished his company. The two could talk as equals: Gurganus would give his "generational opinion" of Cheever's contemporaries (most urgently Bellow and Updike, the only rivals Cheever cared to acknowledge), and delighted the older man by admiring many of the same books as he.† On one end of their walk they'd feed grass to the buffaloes at the zoo, until finally they came full-circle to Iowa House, where Cheever would try coaxing

---

*Last name has been changed, though perhaps it's worth noting that Cheever almost invariably used this form of address: "Miss Moody."

†To give the most interesting example, J. R. Ackerley's *My Father and Myself,* in which the author writes with pioneering frankness of his own homosexuality, as well as the discovery of his manly father's louche past. The book would serve as a model, among others, for Susan Cheever's *Home Before Dark.*

his protégé upstairs for some Scotch and whatnot. However, if there wasn't any concrete business to accomplish—a manuscript to discuss; a dying man's last request—Gurganus would usually decline. ("We part the student and the teacher," Cheever noted a little ruefully.) Which is not to say Gurganus failed to reciprocate Cheever's delight in his company. "[John] was so entertaining, he was so wonderful, so alive to the moment," said Gurganus. One of his fondest memories was sitting with Cheever in the River Room restaurant at the Iowa House, the two telling each other stories about their fellow diners—a game at which Cheever seemed eager to be bested. Gurganus would indicate, say, a plump middle-aged couple eating with their Down-syndrome daughter, and speculate as follows: "His third marriage, her first, the daughter a 'love-child' of his youth (first cousin, out of wedlock) who had become an unconscious millstone for him, ruining with her hapless demands marriage after marriage, job after job, since he still refused to have her institutionalized. Today was the day wife number three had found a home for poor Margerie and this was to be her last veal cutlet as a free girl . . ." Cheever would bunch up in his chair, ecstatically tickled, an ideal audience. "Gosh, but we had fun," Gurganus recalled. "Sex alone would have spoiled it."

Even at the best of times, though, Cheever's ambivalence about homosexuality was never entirely forgotten. He often doted quite openly on Gurganus, but if the student responded with some sort of well-meaning tenderness, Cheever would fret over what he perceived to be the young man's sudden effeminacy, not to say his shameless teasing: "[Allan] flirts with me," he wrote. "The more he flirts, the more he seems like a woman. He shifts his shoulders . . . and gives me long, bone-making gazes, but we stay within four feet of each other." It galled Cheever, and would go on galling him to the end: Gurganus could play sandlot football; he was so perfect in many ways—witty, well read, gifted—if only he weren't so *homosexual*. And, given that he let himself be known as gay, the least he could do—or so Cheever manifestly believed—was go to bed with him! Their relationship was summed up nicely by an encounter (of sorts) that Halloween. Gurganus was at a Gay Liberation costume party in the basement of the Unitarian church; dressed as a German sailor, he was dancing with another costumed youth when he looked up and saw Cheever gazing down at him from the basement window. Years later, Gurganus couldn't help vacillating a little in evoking that look on Cheever's face:

on the one hand, he seemed a wistful von Aschenbach, or was it a bane-
ful Peter Quint, or for that matter "some Victorian urchin looking into
a bakery through a cloud made with his own breath"? Doubtless it was
something of all three.

ONE OF CHEEVER'S MORE INNOCENT overnight guests was the
thirty-five-year-old Raymond Carver, who lived on a different floor of
the Iowa House but couldn't be bothered to stagger back to the elevator. The two were a very odd pair indeed: Carver was a burly working-
class fellow with frazzled hair and sideburns—"a truck-driver or
master-sergeant type," as Leggett put it. They'd become acquainted
when Carver sought Cheever's help in tying his necktie prior to a faculty party. What they had in common was a love of literature and
drink. Carver had yet to publish his first book of fiction, and was
thrilled to meet Cheever and just sit there listening to him ("I'd never
heard anyone use the language like that"). He made himself useful by
giving Cheever lifts to the liquor store, preferably the moment it
opened at ten o'clock. As Carver remembered of one such run, "[T]he
clerk was just unlocking the front door. . . . John got out of the car
before I could get it properly parked. By the time I got inside he was
already at the checkout stand with a half gallon of Scotch."*
     Cheever had a more temperate friendship with the young John Irv-
ing, who, like Carver, was still laboring in relative obscurity at the time
(he'd published two novels to little acclaim). He and Cheever had a
weekly ritual of watching *Monday Night Football* and eating homemade
pasta, and once they escorted the writer J. P. Donleavy to his reading.
(Cheever wrote of *The Ginger Man* in 1959: "[It] amuses me and has,
real or false, the dingdong litany of the Welsh and the Irish.") Irving
had met Donleavy and his wife at the airport, and was startled by the
man's absolute lack of civility: Donleavy let him know that he never
read living writers, and wondered aloud if they were in Kansas; later he
told Irving's students that any writer who lowered himself to teaching

---

*"Dear Ray," Cheever wrote in 1977, "I'd be very happy to tell the Guggenheims
how good I think you are and having driven with you to the liquor store with a flat
tire . . . I'm happy to hear you're off the sauce." Carver later dedicated a story to
Cheever—a homage titled "The Train," which picks up where "The Five-Forty-Eight"
leaves off: "The woman was called Miss Dent, and earlier that evening she'd held a gun
on a man."

"wasn't capable of teaching them anything." When Irving introduced Cheever, the Irishman ignored them both and resumed chatting with his wife about her headache; Cheever tried a few conversational sallies, then said, "Do you know, Mr. Donleavy, that no *major* writer of fiction was ever a shit to another writer, except Hemingway—and he was crazy?" Donleavy looked blank *(Who is this bloke?)*, and nothing further was said. "Surely you're *not* going in to see that man read?" Cheever called to Ron Hansen, as the latter queued up on the sidewalk with an SRO crowd. For his part, Cheever repaired to a bar, but later showed up at a party in Donleavy's honor. Disgusted to a find the man surrounded by acolytes, Cheever beckoned Hansen and Irwin into another room: "Let's get people to come to *our* party," he said, and began booming *"Ho ho ho!"* as provocatively as possible.

Finally, in November, largely at Cheever's behest, the Romanian writer Petru Popescu arrived—a man who lived, or so Cheever delighted in saying, on "Julius Fuck Street" in Bucharest (actually *Fucik* Street). The two had met three years before, in Egypt, on a plane from Cairo to Luxor. Popescu was wearing a "drab commie suit," and Cheever—very drunk, of course, but farsighted too—paused in the aisle and gazed at him owlishly. "Yevgeny!" he said at last. "How are you?" Popescu replied, "I am not Yevgeny Yevtushenko, although you are John Cheever." The latter, underestimating his popularity in the Soviet bloc, became alarmed: here at last was the secret agent sent to kidnap him for some mysterious transgression against the State. In fact, Popescu was far more anti-Soviet than Cheever. During a long night of drinking in Luxor, he spoke of his longing to defect, though he worried about the difficulty of reinventing himself, Nabokov-like, as a writer of English. Cheever listened sympathetically ("I've rarely seen an individual who was more delicate and more respectful of other people," said Popescu), and later arranged for the young man to come to Iowa under the auspices of the university's International Writing Program. Popescu made the most of it—smoking pot with students, drinking with Cheever, generally relishing "all the experiences of the West"—and was so impressed that he defected four years later and became a prolific American novelist.

When Cheever went home for Thanksgiving, he was pardonably pleased with how well he, a dying man, had managed for months on his own. He took Federico and Rob Cowley to lunch with the Friday Club, and exuberantly held forth about the "earthly paradise" he'd found in the Midwest: The country was absolutely *gor*geous, and he a*dored* the students and faculty and vice versa. His wife agreed to visit him a week or two later, and Cheever did his best to be a good host. Leggett gave a dinner party for the Cheevers and other dignitaries, while Cheever himself arranged an elaborate, well-attended reception at the Triangle Club on campus: "Mary was a very handsome woman and he loved showing her off," said Gurganus. "Nobody really knew why he was there and not at home."

"Again I have no idea of where the fault lies," Cheever wrote after his wife's departure. "I have to ask for a goodbye kiss and that is fleeting." Perhaps it had something to do with his drinking, which had gotten so bad that he could scarcely conceal it to any seemly degree. His young consort Elaine remembered that she was "looking at [her] watch" by then—that is, counting the hours until she could drive him to Cedar Rapids and put him on a plane. The witty, modest gentleman who'd chuckled at his two pairs of "wash pants" and deferred to the promptings of "Miss Moody" had all but vanished, replaced by a drunken bully whose main topic of conversation was his own unappreciated greatness. For Elaine it was bad enough having to bear the brunt of these rants alone, much less to observe his mortifying rudeness to others. One night he agreed to meet a group of Christian Scientists for dinner, before which he'd spent several hours getting drunk with Elaine. "Well! I've just finished spending the afternoon with Miss Moody and we had *plenty* to drink," he greeted his mother's coreligionists in the lobby of the Iowa House. As Elaine recalled, "They were dumbfounded—*and* he was late! This was a big event for these people, and he just treated them like dirt."

Another subject Cheever pursued in his cups was his sexual prowess. "Mary says I'm impotent," he'd rail, "but I'm *not*!" Whether he succeeded in proving as much is a mystery; in public, at any rate, he did his best to appear insatiable. In addition to her role as keeper, Elaine served as a prop for these performances. One of her most vivid memories is the time Cheever was visited by a poor graduate student who lived in nearby Amana and made a pilgrimage in a blizzard, with his wife, to speak with the great man. The young couple sat on one of the narrow beds in Cheever's room, while Elaine and Cheever sat on the other. "So while this guy was trying to talk with him and have a visit," said Elaine, "John was trying to paw me and kiss me." At last it came time for their visitors to depart—to hitchhike in the snow, that is, back to Amana. As they waited for the elevator, Elaine took Cheever aside and proposed to give them a lift, but he had other plans and adamantly vetoed the idea. A few days later ("he thought I was out of earshot"), Elaine heard Cheever tell the young man that he *wished* he'd given them a ride, but "Elaine had things to do."

Reading Cheever's journal, one would think that December had been an idyllic time for the two. "The last days," he wrote. "I do not sleep alone at all. We [he and Elaine] embrace strenuously as if we could leave a fossilized impression on one another." To the end, though, he couldn't make up his mind whom he preferred—Elaine or Allan—until the latter resolved the dilemma, for the time being, by pursuing other interests ("Alan [sic] . . . has vanished"). Elaine it was, then, who spent a final "sublime" night with Cheever, then drove him to the airport without, it seems, conspicuously checking her watch.

They met for the last time a few years later, when Elaine attended one of Cheever's readings at Harvard. Afterward they walked across campus and then paused to say goodbye. The sober Cheever, at least, seemed quite capable of remembering how badly he'd behaved. "Elaine," he said, "you really were very kind to me."

CHAPTER THIRTY-SIX

{ *1974* }

OR A FEW DAYS Cheever mooned over Allan and sometimes Elaine, but what with Christmas and family and so forth, the whole Iowa episode seemed to fade into the mist like Brigadoon ("I remember no one from Iowa and so I think, alas, alas, no one remembers me"). As an irrepressible raconteur, however, Cheever couldn't help regaling his wife and children with tales of his legendary prowess, referring as often as possible to the young woman who wrote him such ardent love letters. Beyond a point, Mary seemed to take the whole performance amiss, and after a startling confrontation ("she hurled at me the fact that I am responsible for all her misery"), she pretty much stopped talking to him again. This had the usual lowering effect on Cheever's morale: "I am in a very bad or self-destructive routine," he wrote in January 1974. "M[ary] leaves at seven, long before daybreak these days. I stir somewhat later, drink coffee barearse, get sauced and never approach this machine with the clear eye and the clear head that I need. . . . Work, discipline, self-respect."

The reason Mary had to leave so early was that she'd taken a job at the Rockland Country Day School in Nyack, a rather long drive across the bridge. One evening she mentioned that she had to rush off to rehearsal, explaining that they were giving a pantomime to raise money for the school: she was playing Cinderella, while the rest of the cast would appear in drag. Of these rehearsals Cheever noted, "I don't really want her to remain here—she wouldn't speak to me anyhow— but the pantomime sounds bizarre." The more he thought about it, the more troubling it seemed, and finally he couldn't resist driving all the way to Nyack (unknown to his wife) to attend an actual performance, which proved worse than his most ghastly imaginings. The headmaster (a man Mary considered attractive) came onstage wearing a wig, joined by a female science teacher dressed as a man: "They sang a duet about how you separate the men from the boys on Fire Island," Cheever observed. "With a crowbar." By the time Mary appeared for her wedding to Prince Charming (a young woman), Cheever had seen enough; when the stage preacher asked if anyone objected to the union, Cinderella's affronted real-life husband bolted to his feet. "*Yes!*" he bellowed, stalking up the aisle. "*She's already married! To me!*" The audience laughed it off, more or less, but Mary was embarrassed all the same.

This was another episode that would someday give Cheever a pang of remorse ("I was a fool"), but at the time it only affirmed his indignant sense of alienation. "I will leave here with no regrets at all," he wrote a few days later, having accepted a professorship at Boston University for the fall. "I will take nothing, not even my own books, not even my ikon. . . . I will pack my bag and walk out the door." In conversation with the poet George Starbuck, head of the writing program at BU, Cheever had candidly mentioned that he'd almost drunk himself to death the previous spring—but all that, he said, was in the past. Meanwhile he told friends that his eventual departure was "a decent way of ending things" with Mary, and though he was privately worried about returning to the part of the earth where he felt most haunted, he liked the idea of being a full professor; besides, Federico would be in nearby Andover.

Still, there were many months to endure until he packed that one small bag, and suddenly it became important again that, almost half a continent away, there were comely young people who cared about him ("Iowa is my life line, my kapok vest and why don't I use it"). Confessing with a great show of sheepishness that he wanted to go to Iowa for a dubious purpose, Cheever asked Caskie Stinnett of *Travel & Leisure* whether he'd finance the trip in exchange for an article about town and campus. Stinnett was happy to oblige (if a little "uncomfortable" over how "guilt-ridden" the poor man seemed), and thus Cheever returned to Iowa in early February "to celebrate Miss Moody's birthday," which was actually a month later. Gurganus was then in New Orleans for Mardi Gras ("I rather wish this so"), but Elaine seemed flattered by the visit, albeit a bit on the wary side. As Cheever alleged in his journal—

and told various friends and acquaintances, including his physician—she'd asked him to keep his clothes on during sex "so that if [he] dropped dead there would be no embarrassment." As he wrote Weaver, "I have been fucking a twenty-two year old graduate student who wakes me in the middle of the night to ask: Are those your own teeth? . . . It's a long way to go for that sort of thing but I'll probably do it again."

When he returned to Ossining, however, it wasn't Elaine he had in mind while wrestling with the urge to write "I love you" a "hundred times, a thousand times"—though he realized that this was "aimed at the wrong customer": "I write an advertisement for the New York Review of Books: 'Revolting, elderly, alcoholic novelist desires meaningful relationship with 24-year old aristocratic North Carolinian with supple form and baroque biceps. Little gay experience but ready learner. Etc.' " The Carolinian in question was Gurganus, of course, who'd come to dominate Cheever's thoughts to a disturbing degree—disturbing because it was all so hopeless. Or was it? Around Valentine's Day, Gurganus sent Cheever some of the better stories he'd written in workshop, including one titled "Minor Heroism" that Cheever had found so promising he'd even been willing to offer concrete editing suggestions (*How about a little more of this? And perhaps a little less of that?*). Cheever sent the story to Maxwell, and became almost unbearably excited when his old friend paid him a visit that Saturday (the first, perhaps, since his doleful rejection of "The Geometry of Love" in 1965): Maxwell thought the story was wonderful, but now it was up to Shawn—who, Maxwell cautioned, had "never taken a story about a homosexual." That Monday, Cheever drank martinis and waited anxiously by the phone, dying to get the go-ahead to call Gurganus with good news; as it happened Maxwell had already called him. "Yeah, and I'm Mae West," Gurganus remembered saying when Maxwell introduced himself. The latter, soft-spoken as ever, insisted he was indeed from *The New Yorker* and would very much like Mr. Gurganus's permission to publish "Minor Heroism." "That was one of the nicest things I've ever participated in," Cheever wrote Maxwell afterward; Gurganus would always consider it "the kindest thing anybody's ever done for me."

It came with a few strings, though, or so it seemed. A day or two later, Cheever wrote a playful love letter describing "the modesty of [his] demands": "All I expect is that you learn to cook, service me sexually from three to seven times a day, never interrupt me, contradict me or reflect in any way on the beauty of my prose, my intellect or my person. You must also play soccer, hockey and football. I once asked myself (while skating) if Allan and I became lovers would I have to give up scrub hockey?" As a matter of fact, Cheever had given up scrub hockey (if he'd ever properly picked it up) almost before Gurganus was born, but this was by way of pointing out, subtly, that any ideal chum of Cheever's would have to swing his hips less and whack a ball or a puck more. Gurganus was subtle, too, in letting Cheever know that he had other plans. "The closings of your letters disconcert me," Cheever wrote. "We started off with love, and moved into respect, devotion and affection. . . . I suppose we'll go through sincerely, truly, and end up Dictated but unsigned." Gurganus had no particular objection to signing off with love (especially after the "Minor Heroism" sale), as long as he let Cheever know that this was more of an *agape* type of love, since his erotic drives were decidedly occupied elsewhere. In his journal, Cheever brooded over the "string of lovely boys" Gurganus never failed to mention ("How dare he refuse me in favor of some dimwitted major in decorative arts"); meanwhile he asked Gurganus to consider whether such callow youths "appreciate the excellence of your character and the fineness of your mind."

The best Gurganus could do was insist that he loved Cheever—after a fashion. When the semester ended in May, he paid homage in Ossining, where Cheever was waiting for him at the train station ("like being met by Melville on the docks," said Gurganus). Deeply moved, already tipsy, Cheever held his beloved's hand as he drove them to a restaurant, where he drank heavily over a long lunch and was glowing by the time they returned to his car. Their waitress was also leaving at the end of her shift, and Cheever rammed into the back of her car. "She got out and saw that there was no visible damage," Gurganus remembered, "and she wagged her finger at him, knowing full well that he had all the power and she had none. It was an extremely embarrassing, painful thing, though he didn't seem embarrassed."

Apart from Cheever's drunkenness, snobbery, and age (almost fifteen years older than Gurganus's *father*), the young man had other qualms. Cheever, he sensed, longed to play Pygmalion—to introduce him to people who mattered, take him places, nurse his talent—but, as Gurganus put it, "I was much too vain to be Mrs. anybody, even Mrs. Cheever." And finally, of course, he'd picked up on Cheever's hints about hockey and so on, the odd jaundiced look at his hips, and could well imagine what it would be like to wake up with such a man. "The only men I know who live together as lovers I cannot take seriously," Cheever wrote two years later (while determinedly looking for a male lover). "It is one thing to tear off a merry piece behind the barn with the goatherd but one wouldn't, once your lump is blown, want to take it any further."

CHEEVER'S NEED TO RATIONALIZE his homosexual impulses—and explain them to the world, if possible, in some acceptable form—led to one of his most incoherent stories, "The Leaves, the Lion-Fish and the Bear." Almost three years earlier, he'd made a note in his journal about "the vast and sternly concealed abyss of unrequition in my relationships to my brother, my father and my friends." The abyss that separated Cheever from the "legislated world" seemed a reasonable premise for a story about the transcendence of one's secret fears, beginning with the image of a literal abyss: the continental shelf around Curaçao, a "submarine cliff" that drops thousands of feet into blackness— "a metaphor for something mysterious in [the narrator's] own nature." What follows are five vignettes that are likely to strike even the most sympathetic reader as haphazard—and no wonder, since Cheever mostly patched them together out of various passages in his journal. The second vignette, a distasteful encounter between the narrator and his brother Eben, would later be used in *Falconer*. However, the vignette that mattered most in terms of Cheever's purpose—where he finally comes to the point, as it were—concerns a homosexual encounter between a traveling salesman and a hitchhiker, both eminently "normal" men under normal circumstances: "The ungainliness of two grown, drunken, naked men in one another's arms was manifest, but Estabrook felt that he looked onto some revelation of how lonely and unnatural man is and how bitter, deep, and well concealed are his disappointments." The abyss resides in us all, then, and such means of bridging it are only seemly. The story ends with a coda in which a feisty old lady recovers an antique chamber pot from two thieves after a high-speed chase—the point being that people are capable of great things once their fears have been conquered, or something to that effect.

There was no question of showing the story to *The New Yorker*, and it was possible that even *Playboy* might balk for once. Only two weeks before, however, as luck would have it, Gordon Lish at *Esquire* had offered "three thousand for anything, sight unseen"; for "The Leaves, the Lion-Fish and the Bear" he was willing to pay twenty-five hundred, which Cheever was presumably happy to get. When he reread the story two years later, he found it "disjointed and not very good"— though he reversed himself in 1980, offering it to a publisher of expensive vanity editions, Stathis Orphanos. Then at the height of his fame, Cheever had decided the story succeeded, as few before it, in making homosexuality "understandable and valid in the realm of everyday life," as he explained to a friend. The story was therefore "quite important" to him, and he was "delighted" to have it reprinted in so handsome an edition.*

In 1974, he was happy to be writing anything at all, given that he was suffering from fainting spells and washing down his digitalis and Seconal with larger and larger doses of liquor ("a half-pint a day," he informed Dr. Mutter). Marooned in Ossining, fed up with the vagaries of Donald Lang and the dullness of the Friday Club, Cheever looked forward to regular visits from a handsome young scholar named Dennis Coates, who was writing about Cheever's novels for his dissertation at Duke. The two had met the previous summer, while Cheever was still convalescing from heart failure. Captain Coates was on his way to West Point, where he'd taken a job as an English instructor while continuing to work on his dissertation; since Ossining was only a short drive down the river, he visited his subject every month or so to interview him, then kept visiting because he'd come to regard Cheever as a friend and vice versa.

One day in April, Cheever came downstairs and announced that he'd just finished a story; would Denny like to hear it? The young man was more than honored: it felt "like a gift" being the first person to hear a story by John Cheever. The two sat at the dining-room table, where Cheever covered Coates's hand with his own and began to read "The Leaves, the Lion-Fish and the Bear." Coates thought the story was wonderful (distracted, perhaps, by the beauty of its prose), and made no connection between his covered hand and the masculine

---

*For Orphanos, Cheever simply removed the section that had already appeared in *Falconer*: "[I]n my considered opinion," he wrote the publisher, "the story is improved by this deletion." Certainly it wasn't harmed by it.

brand of homosexuality evoked in one of the vignettes. Afterward, though it was rather chilly outside, Cheever proposed they take a walk in the woods, and at one point asked the young man to hold him. Coates was happy to give his frail companion a warming embrace, but became flustered when Cheever tried to kiss him: he was fond of John, and certainly wanted to be friends, but not like that! Cheever affected to be almost as innocent as Coates: "To me it's all love," he said, and the two lay together (chastely) to get out of the wind and go on chatting about things.

When Coates returned in early June, it was warm enough to go swimming, so Cheever suggested they make a round of his neighbors' pools. He swam naked and urged his friend to do likewise, but Coates went on wearing a pair of baggy, borrowed trunks. As they sat on the edge of a pool, Coates sadly remarked that Cheever seemed "the most unloved man [he'd] ever known": "I feel like I'm watching a tragedy, and this is the second act." The naked man indignantly denied it: "I am one of the most loved men on earth!" he protested, elaborating at length about how he'd vied with Sinatra for the heart of Hope Lange, and so forth. "Your crack about my being unloved still rankles," he wrote Coates. "I ask everybody—everybody—if they love me and they all say yes. The girl from Iowa writes daily to say I'm beautiful. . . . In any case if I am unloved I shouldn't be forsaken and please come over. The swimming's great."

In fact, Cheever felt very forsaken and didn't hesitate to say so, at least to his family: he was a dying man, for all they cared! When Cheever wasn't recuperating in bed, he staggered about the house with a drink in his hand, wondering what he'd done to deserve such indifference. One day he suffered a series of painful spasms in his chest, and rather than call his available daughter ("I am cranky with Susie"), he tried instead to reach Coates at West Point, and subsequently implied to his psychiatrist, Jewett, that he drank (and was therefore dying) because of his sad situation at home. Jewett replied that Cheever invented his problems to justify his drinking, and insisted the patient check himself into a dry-out clinic—whereupon Cheever ended their relationship: "The memory of strait jackets and cruelty is still vivid."

Federico resumed his role as caretaker when he returned that summer from Andover, finding his father both craftier and nastier. Cheever stashed bottles all over the property and sometimes slipped away to get drunk in peace. Calling around to their neighbors one day,

Federico located his father at Mrs. Zagreb's, and, waiting on the phone, he glanced down and spotted a half-pint of gin in one of Cheever's boots. Ever more vigilant, he began accompanying his father to parties, though Cheever was less amenable to "signals" than he'd been with Elaine in Iowa. "Oddly," said Federico, "one of my memories of that summer was to think that, because of everything that had happened, I would have lines on my face when I returned to school and that would bring me more respect." But then the very fact that he now had a refuge of sorts, another life to return to, made him less apt to panic over his father's heedless self-destruction; because of the boy's relative detachment, Cheever tended to accuse him, too, of being unfeeling. For Federico it was more like exhaustion: "I remember Susie and I taking a walk," he remarked, "and her saying, 'He's dying.' I felt no surprise."

Susan had also begun to distance herself, with arguably better reason. That spring her marriage broke up, and she was chagrined to find her father going out of his way to console her ex-husband, who also found it "kind of appalling." One day the two men sat commiserating in a gas line, passing a flask, and Cheever freely admitted that he'd always wanted a blond "Linda Boyer type" for a daughter. He even urged Rob not to pay alimony, since the man was already burdened with two children from a previous marriage. As for the married man Susan had "[run] off " with—*Ramparts* editor Warren Hinckle— Cheever referred to him as a "wretched buffoon," citing the time he'd squashed a banana into Federico's typewriter. For her part, Susan seemed to respond to her father's latest rejection by working harder than ever to step out of his shadow. While at the *Tarrytown Daily News*, she won an Associated Press writing award ("People stop me on the street and ask if I'm really her father," said Cheever), and in 1974 she was hired as religion editor at *Newsweek*. Toward her father she was alternately solicitous and bullying. Particularly at the dinner table— "the shark tank"—she let him know in quite pointed terms what she thought of his manipulative self-pity, and Cheever seemed at a loss to respond: "He would look hangdog, as if he deserved it," one guest remembered.

The more wretched he became, though, the more incessantly he talked about his young "mistress" Elaine. Here, after all, was a person who loved him as he *deserved* to be loved. More than once his son called him a "shit" and told him to shut up already ("It's one thing to have affairs," said Federico, "another to trot them out exclusively to cause pain"), which only seemed to validate Cheever in his roguishness. When Mary announced that she was going to Treetops, as always, for a few weeks in August, he reached for his usual cudgel: *Elaine* would come stay with him, he said, and he wouldn't even require Iole on the premises. Mary seemed all in favor of the idea, and even phoned Elaine in Maine: John *was* rather ill, she explained, and hated to be left alone; would Elaine be willing to come and take care of him for a few weeks? Not only did Elaine decline, she declined vehemently: "Why don't you divorce him?" she said. "How can you *stand* him?" Perhaps Mary chose not to relate the girl's exact response to her ailing husband, who at any rate claimed to have been swayed by the better angels of his nature: "[Elaine] is not here," he reported to Coates. "In a fleeting moment of common sense I realized that this is Mary's house and that [Elaine] is unwelcome. [Elaine] is sulking in Maine."

In August, then, Federico was again left alone to care for Cheever, who was finding it harder and harder to get out of bed and whose ankles had swollen ominously. Finally the boy burst into tears and demanded his father go to the hospital and dry out, or else he was leaving for good. When Cheever kept insisting he was fine, his son got in the car and drove away, while Iole berated her employer with a lot of histrionic Italian; by the time Federico had driven around the block, Cheever was willing to go. According to his admission report at Phelps, he informed the doctors that his drinking had been "minimal" in Iowa—but alas: "On return home to a tense emotional atmosphere, he again began consuming larger quantities of alcohol until the present time his intake is approximately that before he originally became ill." Treated with vitamins and Valium, Cheever was able to avoid another bout of the DTs and by the fifth day he appeared to be successfully withdrawn. Dr. Mutter gave him the usual stern lecture, and Cheever returned home and resumed drinking within a day or two.

"If I just *leave* you awful people," he said to his disgusted family, "everything will be *fine.*" At the same time, he seemed to be hoping they'd come to their senses and beg him to stay. "He was an invalid," said Federico. "The notion that he was going to leave his oppressive wife and be happy was obviously absurd. He was no more capable of doing his own laundry than . . ." He paused. "I won't make the dangerous and inflammatory similes. We let him go. Fatigue was a big item."

CHAPTER THIRTY-SEVEN

{ *1974* }

B Y WAY OF DECLARING his independence, one of the first things Cheever did in Boston was order stationery: "John Cheever / 71 Bay State Road / Boston, Massachusetts 02215." This enabled him to write despondent letters about how much he despised his new lodgings, and never mind the "sinister" part of town where he found himself, Kenmore Square ("part student, part slum"), whose most prominent feature was a school for embalming, or so he rarely failed to point out. At his (peremptory and belated) request, an apartment had been found for him in a handsome bow-front brownstone on a leafy street near campus, though it was hardly ideal for a lonely alcoholic with a bad heart: not only was it four flights up, but the interior was bleak and Cheever was disinclined to personalize it. "[There] is no point in listing the contents of these two rooms," he wrote shortly after his arrival. "It is much too decorous and efficient although there is dirty clothing on all the chairs." His main attitude was one of bewilderment: he'd worked hard all his life—attained the pinnacle of his profession!—only to be banished by his family to two furnished rooms in Boston, where he expected to "end up penniless and naked" like his poor grandfather Aaron, what with the predations of the Plymouth Rock Laundry.

He found some consolation in long walks beneath the shady elms of Commonwealth Avenue: "I start with the Lief Ericson [sic] monument and go on to the president of the Argentine who is massive. He is fol-lowed by [William Lloyd] Garrison (with whom my great uncle was tarred and feathered).* . . . Then we have George Washington and the Ritz Bar. I return here by the river and clock it at about six miles." But even these constitutionals were tainted by memories of happier days—those jolly walks along the Iowa River with Allan, swapping jokes and feeding the buffaloes. "He hasn't sent me a thing," Cheever remarked that first lugubrious week, gazing teary-eyed at the Charles. In the absence of some suitable companion, he was thrown back all the more on memories of his miserable youth, when he'd considered himself "a patsy, a Joey, basically a second rate clown." The whole abortive return to Boston, in fact, called to mind "the last pages in Proust": he kept running into people from the past—or their ghosts—who knew him as the wayward son of a gift-shop proprietress, rather than a world-renowned author with a supposedly patrician pedigree.

As for his relations with the university, they began with delinquencies on both sides and went downhill from there. As a last-minute replacement for Jean Stafford (who was allegedly drinking even more than Cheever), the relatively obscure Ivan Gold had been hired to teach the other workshop section; consequently most students had requested Cheever, whose classes were swamped. He repeatedly asked that the situation be remedied, but found the administration "quite mysterious" at best: the head of the English department wasn't returning his calls (he finally met the man by accident, standing at an adjoining urinal), and George Starbuck of the writing program seemed alarmed at the very sight of him. "I did *not* rise to the occasion of John's troubles," Starbuck later admitted, "did not effectively love or help him, floundered stupidly between catering to him . . . [and] pursuing some coherent plan of stern-but-supportive intervention." And yet his wariness was at least somewhat understandable, since Cheever—quite apart from his disastrous alcoholism—had given signs of being very high-maintenance indeed. First he'd demanded that Starbuck find him suitable lodgings, then he let it be known that Iowa had "provided" him with a graduate student who served as a kind of secretary-*cum*-mistress-*cum*-nurse, and he expected BU to do the same. As Starbuck recalled, "There was (carefully) plenty of twinkle in his voice . . . as he urged this. Pixie mischief. But he *did* urge it, and tell me he needed just that to keep him on an even keel." Starbuck, however, balked at "play-

---

*His great-uncle Thomas Butler, that is, the Newburyport abolitionist and would-be biscuit tycoon whom Cheever generally insisted on calling "Ebenezer."

ing procurer" even for so distinguished a colleague, whose invidious comparisons between Iowa and Boston usually ended with " . . . and every night [in Iowa] there was someone to suck my cock!"

For the first month or two, Cheever was able to function as a teacher. Precisely because he drank before classes (vodka mostly, since it was relatively odorless), he remained fairly alert and often held forth in an engaging way. His remarks tended to be incisive, and sometimes led to worthwhile tangents about his own writing and what seemed to work for him. He found his students "responsive and contentious"—if not especially talented—and made a point of learning their names quickly and finding out what sort of books they liked (*Gravity's Rainbow* was the rage, and Cheever also professed to like it—or rather he liked it better than Vonnegut's work, which was almost always the other favorite). He assigned "drills" as ever, though these were received with even less enthusiasm than at Iowa. As an exercise in "describing the indescribable," one of his students—a semi-famous novelist's son, who fancied himself experimental—read an endless list of synonyms for "Death" from Roget's *Thesaurus*. A long silence followed. "It's a found object," the young man explained. Cheever threw his head back and studied the ceiling. "From now on," he said at length ("sound[ing] like Alfred Hitchcock after a pint of gin," one student observed), "all found objects shall be designated 'FOs.' "

Not surprisingly, Cheever couldn't be bothered to read his students' work outside of class, seeming to think it was more than sufficient that he had to listen to it. Asked about a large manuscript on his coffee table—a novel, as it happened, by the semi-famous novelist's son—Cheever closed his eyes and shook his head; when, however, he returned the manuscript (exactly one week after the epigone had given it to him), he declared it "perfect": "Submit it to a New York publisher and they'll publish it right away!" ("I never got it published," the author reported thirty years later.) All graduate students, in fact, were required to get two professors to read and sign off on their thesis work, and whenever they managed to run Cheever to ground and ask for his signature, he was always happy to give it. "Oh yes *very* good," he'd mutter, when they asked if he liked the work in question.

Whatever remained of Cheever's willpower was entirely reserved for showing up; outside the classroom, he barely functioned at all. His most constant companion (at least that first semester) was a graduate student named Laurens Schwartz, who'd been one of Red Warren's

protégés at Yale; perhaps because of this connection (and/or the manuscript he purported to have read), Cheever had recommended the
young man for a full scholarship at BU. Schwartz endeavored to return
the favor. Since Cheever "had a tendency to walk out of his apartment
nude," Schwartz would meet him several mornings a week to make
sure he was properly dressed. Dirty clothes were strewn about the
rooms; the butcher-block table in the kitchen was covered with empty
bottles and rotting fruit (brought by Mary). Trembling from head to
toe, unable to speak, Cheever would walk with Schwartz to a seedy
hotel bar on the way to campus, where a rock-faced waitress in a
miniskirt would wordlessly bring her only customer a double vodka on
the rocks. As Schwartz recalled, "Cheever was like one of those toy
birds who peck at a water glass: he'd lower his head, sip, come up, and
repeat. Maybe halfway through, he'd finally be able to pick up the
glass." He'd also tentatively attempt speech, and after a few garbled
phrases would begin to make some kind of sense, whereupon he'd
become tearful, as if his own words were unbearable to hear. His life
was *such* a mess: he had no clean clothes, the proprietor of the Plymouth Rock Laundry was a bandit, and for the last seventeen days he'd
subsisted entirely on oranges and hamburgers. On it went. Meanwhile
he tried to light a cigarette, the matches falling one after another from
twitching fingers; Schwartz, snatching the embers out of Cheever's lap,
once counted thirty matches to light a single cigarette. Over and over
Schwartz implored the decrepit man to see a doctor, but Cheever
seemed more interested in maundering about his woes than in doing
much about them. "It was like taking care of a child," said Schwartz,
echoing his various predecessors.

Word traveled fast that Cheever was an all-but-hopeless drunk.
The eminent Harvard psychologist Henry A. Murray—creator of the
Thematic Apperception Test, as well as a notable Melville enthusiast—
had thrown a welcoming party for Cheever, a mistake neither he nor
any of his guests was likely to repeat. On arrival, Cheever shoved an
armchair into the middle of the living room, where he drooped slack-
jawed for the rest of the evening, cigarettes turning to ash in his fingers
and crumbling to the carpet. Michael Janeway had found Cheever's
condition "heartbreaking." As a boy he'd received a kindly, encouraging letter from Cheever, who was friends with his mother, Elizabeth.
Now a thirty-four-year-old editor at *The Atlantic Monthly*, Janeway had
arranged to meet Cheever at the Ritz Grill with the magazine's editor

in chief, Robert Manning, another of Cheever's old acquaintances. Any hope of soliciting a story dissipated over the course of lunch, as their guest emptied multiple mini-carafes of martinis amid a sodden monologue on his ruined marriage and the like. As Janeway recalled, "The message was (his and mine), 'You don't want to get too close.' " Cheever's only putative confidant among peers was the poet John Malcolm Brinnin, a colleague at BU whom he often met for Wednesday lunches at Locke-Ober. "We were intimate but not close," Brinnin remarked after Cheever's death, perhaps alluding to the evanescent nature of their rapport under the circumstances. "Should I not remember you when next we meet," Cheever apologetically wrote the poet in 1978, "it will only be an aspect of my clumsiness and will not at all mean that I have forgotten your kindness to me during that trying winter in Boston."

As for Updike, he too was estranged from a wife named Mary, and living in Back Bay about a mile from Cheever. The similarities ended there. They'd met by accident in September, outside Brooks Brothers, where Cheever had invited Updike to join him while he blithely purchased two pairs of tasseled loafers, though the tassels gave him very slight pause. (He subsequently told Schwartz that he'd "trained" Updike never to inquire about prices when shopping for clothes.) That done, the two adjourned to the Kon-Tiki bar at the Park Plaza, where Cheever instructed the waiter with great urgency to bring him *doubles* ("as if a drink that was merely single might in its weakness poison him"). Saying goodbye on Commonwealth, Updike paused to watch his "wobbly" colleague walking away under the elms: "I felt badly," he remembered, "because it was as though a natural resource was being wasted. Although the covetousness in me, and stony heart, kind of rejoiced to see one less writer to compete with."* Cheever likewise noted the "conspicuous ego clash" between the two, and yet remained galled as ever by Updike's failure to cultivate warmer relations. "Updike never calls me," he complained. "We bump into each other and it's like old times, but he never calls me!" Updike did, in fact, call him—but at measured intervals. There was that night at Symphony

---

*Speaking here in a 1994 BBC documentary, Updike was doubtless paraphrasing Cheever's remark about him in a 1965 letter to Exley (quoted on page 350), which Updike had posthumously discovered on page 245 of the *Letters:* "[Updike's] work seems motivated by covetousness, exhibitionism and a stony heart."

Hall when Updike had helped the naked Cheever get into his clothes, and another time when he took him to the Museum of Fine Arts to see an old Garbo film, which proved to be sold out; after dining instead at the Café Budapest, Updike was startled when Cheever bolted out of the car in Roxbury to buy cigarettes "at a dark and heavily grated corner emporium."

Later, reading *Falconer*, Updike seemed to recognize the novel's first sentences as the very ones he'd spotted on a sheet of paper stuck in Cheever's typewriter—always the same dusty sheet, unaltered. Whether Cheever made any further progress in Boston is unlikely.* A visitor from nearby Bradford College, James Valhouli, had read parts of Cheever's Boston journal (later destroyed) and found them "incoherent," while Laurens Schwartz observed that Cheever could hardly type: "He used his forefingers, punching out each letter at one-second intervals. . . . He wrote two lines and suddenly faded out." The reason he made that one attempt in Schwartz's presence—drunk, late at night—was that he intended to rewrite one of the young man's stories ("I'm going to get it published for you"), having mentioned that he'd rewritten "Minor Heroism" and even parts of Updike. This, of course, was the pathetic braggadocio of a man who hadn't done a first-rate piece of work (as he saw it) since *Bullet Park* six years before, and had begun to suspect his career and perhaps his life were over. When Candida Donadio sent him a copy of the acclaimed new novel by Joseph Heller (another of her clients), *Something Happened*, Cheever read a few pages and threw it out the window. Because he liked it.

EVEN CHEEVER HAD TO CONCEDE a "Vesuvian maternalism" on Mary's part while he languished in Boston. She brought him groceries almost every weekend, and would stay the night to tidy up and take care of his immediate needs. One day Schwartz was holding down the fort while Cheever was out buying vodka, when Mary suddenly swept into the apartment with a large bag of apples she'd brought from New

---

*Much of an early draft of *Falconer* was written on Cheever's "Bay State Road" stationery, which doesn't necessarily mean he wrote it in Boston; probably he used the stationery simply because he had a lot left over. Be that as it may, the draft affords a fascinating glimpse of how Cheever worked when inspired. Page after page is virtually unpunctuated, unparagraphed, unrevised in any way, yet the actual *words* are almost identical to the published version.

Hampshire. Identifying herself to Schwartz, she proceeded to collect the empty bottles from the kitchen table and replace them with apples (even though a number of old apples and oranges were still there, gathering mold). "That's good," said Schwartz, casting about for some pleasantry. "I try!" she said, and walked out the door.

Though it was only a short bus ride from Andover, Federico visited his father in Boston perhaps a total of two or three times. It was true Cheever made an effort to pull himself together ("He didn't answer the door naked," Federico noted; "I should consider myself relatively fortunate"), but the whole picture was "just too depressing": his apartment was always a shambles (Mary's efforts withal), and in the midst of what was obviously an excruciating bout of semi-sobriety for his son's benefit, Cheever was not only dour but a little senile, or so it seemed. They'd eat at a nearby Greek place (Aegean Fare) where Cheever took most of his meals, and would talk about anything but "the gorilla sitting on the table," as Federico put it; that the boy no longer bothered to scold his father for drinking was a measure of how hopeless things had become. As for Ben and Susan, they couldn't bring themselves to visit at all, and the disenchantment was mutual. Cheever often remarked that his older son didn't have any *push:* he was a henpecked husband who seemed content to waste his life in a worthless job, sponging off his parents. Which was mild compared with what he had to say about Susan, whose affair with Hinckle never ceased to rankle: "She's going to marry a chap who just wrote a book about lemons,"* he'd say, adding that he didn't think much of the book *or* the chap, and going on from there. One day his old friend Newhouse phoned Ben at the *Rockland Journal News:* he'd just visited his son at Harvard, he said, and at Mary's behest had delivered some groceries to Bay State Road, where he'd found Cheever "sodden drunk"—crawling around on all fours! Someone had to *do* something, he said, but Ben threw up his hands. As he pointed out in the *Letters,* "I'd had trouble dissuading him from having a smoke in the intensive-care unit."

The family member who deserved most of the credit for keeping Cheever alive was his brother, Fred, who called every day and met John for lunch at least once a week. At the age of sixty-nine, Fred had begun to mellow somewhat after many fitful years of trying to find himself— to carve out a niche worthy of the name Cheever. A few years before,

---

*If You Have a Lemon, Make Lemonade (New York: Putnam, 1974).

he'd left idyllic Boulder after his children had taken up their lives else-where, and now he was back on the South Shore, selling ad space for various radio stations and weekly newspapers—one job after another, each ending with the inevitable clash between Fred and his employers, than whom he always knew better. "Your [job] title and year in which you assumed it," the Dartmouth Alumni Department benignly in-quired in 1971, to which Fred snapped, "Communications Time-peddler, 1970—don't be silly." Nor was it only station managers and newspaper editors and alma maters who had to be straightened out, but also the president of the United States and his benighted minions. "Dear Mr. Nixon (sic)," read a typically opprobrious salutation to a 1970 letter in which Fred demanded to receive a refund for overpay-ment of his income tax, lest he withhold future taxes in protest against the war in Vietnam. Two years later, he also berated John Ehrlichman about an "inept" comparison the man's boss had made between mod-ern America and Disraeli's England: "This, to my mind, is the heart of Mr. Nixon's own problem. He has no sense of continuing world his-tory, no weltgeist, no historical perspective as it really is and not as he wishes it to be."

Fred's own *Weltgeist* (he remained something of a Germanophile) was much affected by the campus protests of the time—or rather vice versa, as he saw it, since he regarded himself as a kind of proto-hippie who was "a college drop-out way back in 1926"; in the years following, to be sure, he'd lost his way amid the "corporate chairs" at Pepperell (albeit as "one of the young centaurs . . . [who had] introduced many of the current advertising and marketing methods of the industry"), but eventually he'd "walked out" because he was "stultified" (as opposed to being fired for drunkenness), and now was living life on *his* terms: a free man. Thus Fred explained the background of a book he completed in 1970, *Who Are the Revolutionaries? The Coming Revolt Against the Middle Class*, which he envisaged as essential reading for "the 18–25 college guy and doll who wants . . . some justification for his or her protests." The agent Perry Knowlton at Curtis Brown decided to "encourage" Fred on the basis of a lukewarm report from one of their readers, who'd found *Revolutionaries* "potentially an excellent manu-script," though it didn't quite hold together ("I don't catch the connec-tion between the discourse on Henry Adams . . . [and] the diatribe against the middle-class").

Duly encouraged, Fred concluded it was only a matter of time before he was climbing the best-seller lists. A few weeks after he received that encouraging report, he wrote his son in Hawaii, "If the book delivers the money I expect, Honolulu is on my itinerary." Such was his confidence that he began planning other books and articles, rather than revising his previous book as suggested. Of a piece titled "Quo Vadis Advertising," Fred advised Knowlton to sell it to *The New Yorker* since, after all, his name *was* Cheever ("Perhaps I've delineated in non-fiction what my brother has been writing about all these years"); he informed his brother that he'd gotten started on a new book about the communications industry ("I would hope that it would make McLuhan appear very much out-dated and superficial") and wanted to know how to go about applying for a Guggenheim. (John tactfully replied that applicants usually had to publish at least one book first, whereupon Fred wrote back asking for a loan of six hundred dollars "or whatever part of that you might be able to dig up.") For almost a year Fred bombarded Knowlton with harangues about the marketability of *Who Are the Revolutionaries?*—as witnessed, say, by the *Weltgeist*-shaping success of Charles Reich's *The Greening of America*, which proclaimed the triumph of the hippie lifestyle and thereby "covered the same ground" as Fred's (even more marketable) book. Finally Knowlton wearily returned the manuscript: quoting one of Fred's many pitches, he wrote, "Perhaps, as [one reader] said, 'it should be published,' but I'm really not enthusiastic enough about the book to be the man to do the necessary selling job."

Fred remained undaunted, since he was optimistic by nature and had long ago incorporated failure into his personal philosophy ("there is a kind of destiny . . . that takes a toll of some sort which we get back in the form of new experience"). For a while he continued to think his book would ultimately be published and become "quite an influence for good," but in time he let go of his literary ambitions and devoted himself to playing the part of a local eccentric in Plymouth: a plump old man with longish hair who liked to rap with the kids and roar around town on his motorcycle. His brother, John, couldn't help being reminded of their mother (who'd played a not-dissimilar role in Quincy), and tended to report that he and Fred were "estranged." Dennis Coates was therefore surprised when he interviewed Fred for his dissertation in 1973, learning that the man loved and admired his brother and had always assumed the feeling was absolutely mutual. "I thought, 'This is *important*,' " Coates recalled. " 'John needs to appreciate this.' "

Up to a point, he did. "Poor Fred began to drink again and is in the hospital with heart trouble," John wrote Coates the following year. "However he is showing uncommon intellectual and physical stamina and will live. What a family." After decades of chagrin, John was moving toward a sort of amused (if still rather wary) acceptance of Fred—admiration, even. If nothing else, the man had persevered despite killing setbacks, proving his mettle as a *Cheever* and serving as a kind of bellwether for John's own decline and eventual resurrection. Notably, Fred's alcoholic relapse in 1974 would be his last. A social worker at the hospital had urged him to take a hard look at his past in order to understand *why* he drank, but Fred (very like his brother) would have none of it: "I don't want to go *back*," he said, "I want to go forward! And if you can't help me with that, you can go *now*." The man went, while Fred henceforth resolved to become a devoted (rather than occasional) member of Alcoholics Anonymous.

In his brother's company, however, Fred never seemed to proselytize. Whether John was drunk or (relatively) sober, Fred loved listening to his stories—"funny and very relevant"—and was simply thrilled to be reunited after so many years. One day John was entertaining a student, Rick Siggelkow, when Fred arrived for lunch in a very odd-looking car with a bulbed horn attached to the driver's side. ("What's *this*?" Siggelkow furtively murmured to his teacher, who sighed, "Oh, just something he put on his car.") Invited to come along, Siggelkow was fascinated by the dynamic between the two. John got things started with a bit of generic patter ("Can you believe it? Here we are, a couple of old men living alone in furnished rooms"), but Fred was determined to draw Siggelkow into their conversation, with the apparent object of building up John: "How's the class going? Isn't John a great teacher? Isn't he a *wonderful* writer?" Speaking of John's work led to a certain amount of reminiscence on Fred's part about family and friends who'd appeared in fictional form, and every so often he'd pause to explain these alter egos to Siggelkow. "He knew John's canon inside and out," said the latter. "I kept waiting for some nugget to drop about the role of the brother [in John's work], but it didn't. Fred seemed cheerfully oblivious of the fact that he himself was a recurring character." Meanwhile, no matter how many martinis he drank, John remained keenly alert in Fred's presence, ready to pounce the moment his garrulous brother went too far—as, for instance, when Fred inquired about Mary: "John just froze up," said Siggelkow, "and Fred knew enough not to pursue it."

THE OTHER FAMOUS PERSON in the BU writing program was the poet Anne Sexton, whom Cheever found "aggressive" and mostly avoided. The two had met at a faculty dinner hosted by the dean, where both engaged in a kind of caustic banter meant to shock their less illustrious colleagues and perhaps each other. Ivan Gold remembered sensing a "visceral distaste" between the two; Brinnin and Starbuck tried to distract the dean and his wife at the other end of the table: "Did they overhear *that*?" the two men worried with each new explosion of naughtiness from Cheever and Sexton. Whatever their incompatibility otherwise, both were alcoholics who'd distanced themselves from family in order to drink in peace, and Sexton somewhat endeared herself to Cheever by spiking his coffee with vodka at tedious faculty meetings.

Sexton killed herself on October 4, 1974, and Cheever "never quite got over this." Even though Sexton had been suicidal for most of her adult life, nobody really expected it: her friend Brinnin was under the impression that she'd "never been so happy," whereas Ivan Gold had found her "sardonic, nervous, full of a crazed energy." For his part, Cheever seemed to regard the tragedy as emblematic of the whole ghastly situation—aspects of which included the apathetic, feckless administration of a "fourth rate" university near an embalming school in an utterly, utterly dismal part of Boston. Cheever boycotted the memorial service, threatening to resign on the spot and go home.

But home to what? Over Thanksgiving his family tried to rouse him out of his funk with the usual "shark tank" persiflage, an occasion to which Cheever was decidedly unable to rise. "Susie said that I put on a rather bad show," he wrote Coates afterward, "and I shall try to do better at Christmas." This was not to be. Returning to Cedar Lane a month later, Cheever appeared to be on the verge of death—an impression he soon confirmed by coughing uncontrollably and turning blue. This, of course, was the same old heart trouble, and once again he went to the hospital and stayed a few days to dry out. Perhaps to underline the gravity of his predicament, a young priest visited his "extraordinarily bleak" room at Phelps. Cheever, wearing pajamas, bemusedly knelt on the linoleum floor and received Holy Communion, then said "Thank you, Father," and watched the man depart.

Back home he demanded a drink, and when his family protested, he asked if he might take a Valium instead; given the go-ahead, he swallowed three and poured himself a drink. During the Christmas feast, a hush fell over the table as he tried to eat peas: time after time, suspensefully, the trembling fork ascended, only to spill its savory burden at the crucial moment. At last a spoon was suggested. "I regret to tell you," said Cheever (putting the fork aside), "that you have a father who is dying." A look went around the table, and Federico said, "We have a father with a taste for melodrama." This eased the tension somewhat, though it was precisely the sort of thing Cheever was apt to find "unfeeling." On New Year's Day, he became enraged when his family advised him to eat lentils "in order to ensure an income": after crashing upstairs to his room, Cheever yanked the cover off his bed and fell over backward, unconscious.

"So I am heartily sorry," he noted exactly one year later. "We have all survived."

CHAPTER THIRTY-EIGHT

{ *1975* }

THOUGH HE'D ALMOST DIED over the holidays, Cheever returned to Boston for the spring semester and the situation duly deteriorated. Sadly he reported to the Friday Club that the place was "straight asshole" and his students had become "sluggish." He'd persuaded Updike to visit his combined classes for a two-hour Q&A session that Cheever abruptly terminated after less than an hour (evidently startling Updike), because his overawed students had proved unresponsive. "You had an opportunity to ask John *Updike* questions," he subsequently told them in a seething voice, "and nobody said a damn thing." After that, he seemed to give up. He went through the motions, more or less, but didn't bother to disguise his drunkenness or do much in the way of teaching. He also kept a rather flexible schedule. "Should we go looking for him?" his worried students murmured one day when he was fifteen minutes late for class. An expedition was forming when they spotted their teacher shuffling past the door. "Mr. Cheever?" they called. "Mr. *Cheever?*" An elegant voice floated down the hall: "*Ye-esss . . . ?*" "We sort of talked him back into the room," one student recalled. "He returned with this big grin and went around the table kissing all the women and shaking hands with the men." That was a relatively good day. More and more Cheever seemed utterly unprepared, and would either read one of his own stories or just sit there looking depressed until his students gradually drifted away. One youth expressed his contempt by removing his shirt, climbing on top of the circled desks, and stalking around the room while Cheever gazed at him in quiet puzzlement.

On bitter-cold days he could be seen walking bleary-eyed along Commonwealth, wearing only a tweed jacket with the collar turned up. When hailed by acquaintances or well-wishers, he'd start violently, as though awakened from a nightmare, which usually served to discourage further intercourse. Peter Benelli—the Thayer headmaster who'd invited Cheever to give the commencement address in 1968— was stopped at a red light when he noticed the school's most famous alumnus standing at the corner, unmoving, his haggard face vacant and staring. Benelli worried that he'd be picked up by the police, which almost certainly happened once or twice, though it appears Cheever went to Massachusetts General under his own steam. Dr. Robert Johnson, a heart specialist, remembered the way Cheever bridled at being treated like a common drunk: not only was he a reputable *novelist*, he informed Dr. Johnson (and later Elliot Brown, the hospital's chief of social services), but he also enjoyed considerable stature among the families of Boston. The latter illusion seemed to gain importance as a sense of his own literary distinction waned. While lunching in February with a colleague, Dean Doner, he mentioned that *The New Yorker* was giving its fiftieth-anniversary party that day. "You're not going?" asked Doner, with suitable amazement, whereupon Cheever bitterly admitted he hadn't been invited: "I've written more goddamn words for them than anyone else," he said in effect, "but I suppose I've become an embarrassment."* Before lunch, while feeding a meter outside the restaurant, Doner had dropped a quarter into the gutter, which was running with dirty water after a heavy rain. When they returned to the car, Cheever said he'd rather walk back to campus; Doner glanced in his rearview mirror and saw Cheever groping around the gutter in search of the dropped quarter.

His last month in Boston was a free fall. Raphael Rudnik—who'd heard of Cheever's distress and had an intuition that he was about to kill himself—tried to cheer up his old friend with a visit, but found him "unreachable." The only thing Cheever wanted to think or talk about was drinking. When Rudnik tried to get him to eat, Cheever said, "If I eat, can we go out to drink?" Rudnik pointed out that he was already on the verge of passing out. "Yes," said Cheever, "but *you're* not." Perhaps the last social engagement (formal) that Cheever kept was a din-

---

*According to Maxwell, the anniversary party was "staff only, not even spouses, much less contributors."

ner with Sally Swope at her father's house on Louisburg Square. He arrived an hour late in pouring rain, slipped on the steps and cracked his head on a newel post; a maid bandaged the gaping wound, and Cheever tardily joined the others at table. From that point on, he tended to decline invitations and discourage visitors. "I'd love to see you here but I can't think of anything more selfish," he wrote Coates. "There's nothing much to see or do and I am very gloomy. Your remarks about a tragedy may in the end be right." Meanwhile, if indeed he was dying, then he supposed he might as well indulge the rest of his appetites, too. Buying a "cock magazine" struck him as "a blow for common sense" (though he couldn't quite decide how to dispose of the thing), and he also brought at least one male prostitute back to his apartment, "hurry[ing] him out the door" once their business was concluded.

Around this time, he sat next to that bum in the park and asked for a "pull" from the man's bottle,* and soon he began hoping he'd be hit by a car while walking in traffic. When Rick Siggelkow stopped for a visit, Cheever insisted on giving the (much taller) student a pair of dark, lightweight Brooks Brothers suits: "Now you have two suits to use for a summer funeral," he remarked. (Siggelkow mused that this was a "very Cheever" thing to say: "Everything was always evocative of something else. In other words, he didn't just give me two suits, he gave me 'two suits to use for a summer funeral,' and the way he said it, you could see yourself standing at that funeral wearing those suits.") While the two were drinking, Cheever began to cough and gasp for breath, finally asking the young man to call for an ambulance—then, quite adamantly, changing his mind. "You really have to *go*," he said, closing his eyes and sitting rigidly back in his chair, "or something's going to happen we're both going to regret." Siggelkow ("terrified") protested, but Cheever demanded he leave immediately, and when the student glanced up from the bottom of the stairs, Cheever was looking down at him with a forced, cordial, miserable smile (this a matter of "New England breeding," Siggelkow figured).

At his brother's insistence, Cheever resigned his teaching position in late March, though not before calling the department head a "delinquent asshole." His bitterness was general, and when a man came by his apartment to collect the telephone, Cheever ripped it out of the

---

*See prologue.

wall and threw it at him. Toward his students, however, he was nothing but apologetic: speaking with averted eyes, he allowed that he'd been treated shabbily by the university, but his problems ran deeper and he simply couldn't go on; for the remaining six weeks of the semester, he told them, Updike would take his classes and the students would be far better off.

Free at last, Cheever spent his final days on Bay State Road in the usual manner. The Sunday before his departure, he gave Ivan Gold a call: "I'm faring rather poorly," he announced, asking whether he might borrow a bottle of gin. Gold happened to have an almost untouched fifth of Gordon's on hand, and was even willing to throw in a bottle of Noilly Prat: he and Cheever had not been close, and Gold saw this as a belated chance to "talk with a master." But when Cheever arrived (the two lived only a few brownstones apart, which was doubtless part of Cheever's rationale in choosing a donor), he gave no sign of wishing to stay. Gold's three-year-old son thought Cheever looked like a monkey and said so repeatedly (Gold explained he was actually saying "marquis"), and Cheever regarded both the boy and the two convivial cocktails in Gold's hands with equal dismay. "I scrubbed the plan and ushered him out," Gold remembered. "From the window I watched him scurry with the loot back to his dark sanctuary."

When Fred failed to reach John on the telephone (unaware of its sudden removal), he became concerned and rushed to Bay State Road, where he found his brother naked and incoherent. He got him dressed and drove him back to Ossining. The next day, Fred wrote his son a circumspect account of the episode, noting that he was "in deep concern" about John: "He is such an extraordinary person, not only very knowledgable and bright, but kind and loving, [and] it would hurt many, many people if anything were to happen to him." Such was Fred's haste in rescuing his brother that he didn't bother to retrieve any manuscripts, or, for that matter, John's false teeth and Academy badge, which were eventually found in the bedroom dresser.

"I MUST HAVE BEEN QUITE DRUNK and mad," Cheever wrote a few weeks later, realizing that he remembered nothing of the drive back to Ossining (during which he'd drunk a bottle of Scotch and then urinated into the empty bottle), or even his subsequent hospitalization at Phelps, where he was found to be suffering from a degree of brain damage in addition to a failing heart. Given one more chance to choose between life and death, Cheever seemed on the whole to prefer living—defiant of the expectation that he should go on fulfilling the "Orphic myth." Where he differed with his wife and doctors was in how, exactly, to proceed with his recovery. Jewett, the psychiatrist, had arranged for him to be admitted to the Smithers Alcoholism Treatment and Training Center on the Upper East Side of Manhattan, which involved an "intensive" twenty-eight-day inpatient treatment program. Balking at the prospect of incarceration, Cheever phoned his daughter and insisted she find out whether the program was affiliated with Alcoholics Anonymous, because he refused to get mixed up with a "bunch of Christers." Susan did so, and someone at Smithers denied the connection—falsely, but in accord with AA's principle of anonymity. Cheever would later concede that the lie had saved his life, but at the time he was decidedly ambivalent, and even tried to jump out of the car when Mary drove him to Smithers on April 9.

All things considered, he was in remarkably good fettle on arrival: he seemed fairly lucid, and his vital signs were normal. After his typewriter was turned upside down to check for contraband, he was given the abbreviated Shipley IQ test (scoring, as ever, in the high-average range) and the Minnesota Multiphasic Personality Inventory. It was the screening interview that gave counselors pause: Cheever's memory was "apparently poor," they noted, since he denied ever having blackouts, DTs, or any psychiatric treatment (aside from "some marriage counseling" five years before), though his medical records plainly contradicted him on all these points, and never mind the patient's claim that "all his trouble *began* [my italics] with the suicide of a close friend [Sexton!] last year." Despite such "minimization," he seemed otherwise cooperative, relating well (if reservedly) with staff and patients alike. "A bummer; not really bad, but not good," he wrote in his journal that second day. "At breakfast I am asked not to sit at a particular table. We do not play musical chairs around here, says an authoritative woman of perhaps forty, a little heavy." But he hadn't much time to dwell on his social progress. Between meals ("meat and rice and Jell-O"), he was shunted from lectures to group sessions to individual meetings with one humorless staffer or another, and such free time as he enjoyed was supposed to be spent poring over the wisdom of AA founders "Bill W." and "Dr. Bob." As he wrote Spear, "The indoctrination here is stern, evangelical, protestant and tireless."

The main objective of such a program is to break down the alcoholic's denial, and Cheever proved a difficult patient precisely because he seemed so tractable, at least for a while. Asked about his appetite (he loathed the food), he'd answer "Fine." Sleeping all right? "Fine." Are you an alcoholic? "Yes." But in fact he found it almost impossible to believe that he had much in common with the other "dismal" patients, the milieu being nothing if not democratic. "I share a bedroom and a bath with four other men," he wrote. "1. is an unsuccessful con man. 2. an unsuccessful German delicatessen owner. 3. an unemployable sailor with a troll's face and faded tatoos [sic], and 4. a leading dancer from American Ballet."

For the most part, Cheever's demeanor was detached and vaguely ironical. One doctor, becoming emotional during a lecture, noticed the quick look of amusement on Cheever's face. Which is not to say that his judgments were always dismissive, or that he was less than attentive; rather he was keeping his own counsel, and doing his best to stay out of harm's way, since he found Smithers a brutal place where vulnerability was apt to be punished. "During group analysis a young man talks about his bisexuality and is declared by everyone in the group but me as a phoney," he observed in his journal. "I perhaps should have said that if it is phoney to have anxieties about bisexuality I must declare myself a phoney." Years later Cheever was still complaining that the staff had been "pitiless" about the young man's bisexuality, even to the point of hounding him out of the program. That the director of Smithers, LeClaire Bissell, was herself an open lesbian would suggest he'd willfully missed the point—namely, that one shouldn't use sexual issues, one way or the other, as an excuse to drink. "The director," he noted, "toward whom I have some complicated vibrations, says that a healthy person can adjust to acceptable social norms. The banality of a TV show, certainly acceptable, is what makes me want to drink." That was the kind of attitude (*the* world *is to blame in all its deadening banality, especially given one's higher sensibility*—etc.) that provoked the staff into insisting, after a week or so, that Cheever stop writing so much in his journal and start concentrating on the Twelve Steps. Resignedly he wrote his brother, Fred, "They don't want me to work and it seems best to play along with this and everything else."

So Cheever played along, or so he might have thought, but it only got worse. He was heckled mercilessly for his affectations. For example, he'd long cultivated a tendency to pause with a kind of strained look, as if groping for words, gathering strength, before coming out with some mellifluous pronouncement; observing this, one counselor noted that he seemed "on the verge of belching" and was "very impressed with self." As for his literary reputation ("he insists [his novels] have been very successful"), only a handful of people at Smithers knew Cheever from any other drunk, and nobody really cared in any case. Sensing as much—though naturally wishing to be identified with his achievement—Cheever "almost surreptitiously" presented an autographed book to his personal counselor, Ruth Maxwell, who promptly returned to the subject of his drinking. At length Cheever responded as if he were forced to chat with some tiresome guest at a dinner party—as if he were bored to death with the same old subject but willing to go along as a matter of politeness. "I'm really allright but I can't say so here because only the hopeless lush claims to be allright," he wrote Weaver. "That's a point of view I'm discouraged from taking because I've ruined my life with false light-heartedness." This was irony, of course, and yet even Cheever's friends had often wondered at his constant, nervous "outward tremor of laughter" (as Shirley Hazzard put it), sometimes at *very* odd moments; as for the people at Smithers, they were openly startled by it. "Why are you *laughing?*" they demanded again and again, as Cheever tittered at some grindingly miserable memory from his youth, or some cruelty he'd inflicted on his children.

Bullied at every turn for his "false light-heartedness" and "grandiosity," Cheever retreated into a vast, fraudulent humility. "Oh, but of *course* you're right," he'd mutter (in so many words) when challenged. Nobody was fooled or amused. Carol Kitman, a staff psychologist, remarked that Cheever reminded her of Uriah Heep: "He is a classic denier who moves in and out of focus," she wrote in her progress notes. "He dislikes seeing self negatively and seems to have internalized many rather imperious upper class Boston attitudes which he ridicules and embraces at the same time. . . . Press him to deal with his own humanity." Told he was just like John Berryman, Cheever ("humbly") replied, "But he was a brilliant poet and an estimable scholar, and I'm neither." Yes, said the counselor, but he was also a phony and a drunk, and now he's *dead;* is that what you want? Cheever affected to take this sort of thing in stride, though in fact it was a ghastly humiliation. "Non posso, cara," he'd weepily tell his daughter during his daily call from a communal pay phone. "Non posso stare qui." He sounded so defeated that Susan worried he wouldn't last another day, and began parking her car outside the *Newsweek* building so she could leave work immediately and rush him to the gentler Silver Hill in Connecticut, where she'd made a reservation just in case. "Fifteen patients have fled since I joined the fun," Cheever reported to Spear on April 21. "It's quite sad in this part of Siberia."

But Cheever stayed put, and gradually began to make progress. A more tolerant attitude toward his fellow patients seemed to help. At first he'd been appalled by the "human garbage" he had to share quarters with: they stole from one another; they refused to clean their pubic hair out of the bathtub. Unable to dissemble his distaste, Cheever himself became roundly disliked; when it was his turn to wait on tables, he was so anxious over potential hazing that he spilled a dish of peas into a woman's lap. Confronted in group sessions for being aloof and snobbish, Cheever finally broke down and assured the others that he was taking things "very seriously" indeed. By the time Mary, Susan, and Ben came for a Sunday visit, Cheever appeared to be almost at peace with his environment. "Alcoholism seems to be an infirmity of the lower classes," Mary observed, peering around the dining room, but Cheever's own gaze was humorous and fond. "I always liked running with a crowd of whom my mother disapproved," he later remarked, "and Smithers did that." Around the middle of his stay, "a lame black who knits and crochets" moved into his room and proved every bit as disaffected as Cheever had been two weeks ago: "He says that if he were strong enough to carry his suitcase down the stairs he would leave. I've offered to take his suitcase down but he doesn't answer."

Toward the end, it was the prospect of leaving that sometimes worried Cheever. "I call Mary from time to time and she is full of complaints," he wrote Maxwell. "The bank can't add, the dogs (4) are muddy, the lawns are dry, Susie has followed a worthless man to Chicago, and by innuendo her husband is in a dryout mansion on east 93rd." In his journal he wrote a more somber account of the conversation (Mary had been "very bad-tempered," mainly because his lost bank statements—abandoned in Boston—had led to a two-thousand-dollar overdraft): "This sort of thing provokes my drinking," he concluded. "It makes me afraid to return." The staff at Smithers were also somewhat afraid on his behalf. When Mary failed to appear for a scheduled conference, one of the counselors gave her a call; with glacial politeness she explained that they couldn't tell her anything about her husband she didn't already know after thirty-four years of marriage—but not to worry, as she had no intention of leaving him ("he's an old man who needs to be taken care of"). "She seems to operate in a very passive aggressive way," the counselor noted, "and to have given up on her husband who is now just somebody she'll have to care for until he dies." Informed of her position, Cheever seemed unsurprised if a little self-pitying, remarking that he'd always been the more "giving" partner in the marriage.

When Cheever was released on May 7, his prognosis was "guarded" ("Consensus is that p[atien]t is so wrapped up in self that there is no room for anything else"). Ruth Maxwell had laughed out loud when Cheever suddenly announced that he'd never drink again, but Dr. Robert de Veer was convinced Cheever had actually accepted that he was an alcoholic and therefore had *no* excuse—be it a bad marriage or a banal TV show—for drinking, ever. One of Cheever's students in Boston had been particularly skeptical that such a drunken man could ever get sober, and one day he received a postcard from his old teacher with a terse message:

"See?"

CHAPTER THIRTY-NINE

{ *1975* }

"To go from continuous drunkenness to total sobriety is a violent wrench," Cheever wrote, the day after he'd been "sprung" from Smithers. "Laughter seems to be my principal salvation." In certain ways, he had plenty to laugh about. There was the sheer absurdity of being sober and nothing but, as well as the fact that he suddenly looked and felt twenty years younger. Lila Refregier, his old girlfriend from forty years ago, had seen the 1969 Sheed article in *Life* and been saddened by how bloated and boozy Cheever seemed; in 1977, however, she caught his first appearance on *The Dick Cavett Show* and found him "as young and handsome and well groomed as ever." Around that time, John Hersey described the sixty-four-year-old Cheever as looking "like a man of 34 who has been to a hilarious but awfully late party the night before." Until Smithers, he could hardly walk uphill to his mailbox without huffing for air; now he had energy to burn, and before long he breezed into a department store, grabbed a five-speed bicycle off the rack, and rolled it to the checkout counter. The clerk began to protest that he'd grabbed the pre-assembled demonstrator, but Cheever slapped his money down ("This is the one I want!") and walked out. For the next few years, he took long bicycle rides almost every afternoon: either the five-mile "large circle" or two-and-a-half-mile "small circle" around the extended neighborhood; when he needed a breather, he'd pull up to a random driveway and help himself to the *Times*, popping it back in the tube after a thorough perusal and pedaling away.

He felt a powerful urge to mend fences, though this would prove

something of a mixed blessing. Deeply ashamed of the Boston interlude, he promptly wrote Starbuck "a lovely kind note" (as the latter
recalled) regretting that he'd been such a disappointment as a colleague, and also, of course, he thanked Updike, whose "immense kindness" in taking over his classes had undone some of the chaos of his
"sinister and obscure departure." The process of making amends was
facilitated, in turn, by the eagerness of "people from the remote past"
to resume their friendships with Cheever now that he was sober. Meeting friends again without the benefit of alcohol, however, was practically tantamount to meeting them for the first time—a bit of an ordeal
for such a shy and hypersensitive person. Lunching with Newhouse a
month after Smithers, Cheever was reminded that his friend was a
"very decent man," yet he found himself becoming "bored to the point
of questioning [his] reason." Tom Glazer, too, if such things were possible, seemed even duller than Cheever remembered—ditto the entire
Friday Club, whose members would later speak with great jollity about
how Cheever, sober, had served them larger drinks than ever ("giant
martinis in jelly glasses"), the poignant subtext being that he was
simply trying to make them a little interesting. When even the company of his jaunty old friend Don Ettlinger seemed a letdown, Cheever
was tempted to blame himself: "I wonder if one of my alcoholic self-
deceptions was the illusion of boyish charm." One day a mutual
acquaintance, Marion Ascoli, joined him and Ettlinger for lunch in
Tarrytown—a "somewhat labored" occasion that became even more so
when Cheever drove her home: "I used to be an alcoholic," he ventured after a long silence. "Yes," said Ascoli, "I'd heard about that."
Silence. "My marriage is breaking up." "Oh, that's a shame." End of
conversation.

For the rest of his life, AA meetings would serve as his main source
of social diversion. Two or three times a week, he'd drive to various
parish houses around Westchester, usually after dinner when the urge
to drink was strongest. Fred helped him get started by going along for
a few meetings right after Smithers, pleased to find himself back in a
mentorly role vis-à-vis his little brother: "[If John] can do [AA] on an
amusing and semi-humorous basis," he wrote his son, "it will be a great
help to him and I'm quite sure, a lot of fun for all those who attend the
meetings." This would prove a prescient summary of his brother's AA
experience. Cheever continued to find absurd the whole metaphysical
aspect of AA ("lack[ing] the coherence of a redneck cult"), but, that

said, it was the only thing that worked—a constant reminder that alcoholism was "an obscene mode of death." And then, quite apart from
the therapeutic benefit, Cheever did manage to enjoy himself after a
fashion. He found solace in the simple mantra "My name is Jawn and I
am an alcohaulic," and if called on to speak further, he rarely failed to
entertain. Luxuriating in his persona as a rather seedily genteel old
lush, he'd wryly tell of past and present sorrows: his "wife of a hundred
years" who wasn't speaking to him, his children whom he'd never
really understood, and so on.

Mostly Cheever was keen on listening to others tell their stories,
the better to recycle them into funny anecdotes and perhaps even fiction. "He certainly didn't respect anybody's confidence," Federico
recalled. "Much as he made fun of the sentimental, badly told
tragedies, I think he ate them up and I think they kept him straight."
Some of the more dreadful scenes at AA meetings would excite a peculiar dialogue between the charitable, sober Cheever and the malicious
rogue he now sought to repress. Watching a pathetic old man in an
"ill-fitting suit" accept a cake with thirty-eight candles commemorat-
ing his long, long sobriety, Cheever was tempted to point out that "he
could have done as well dying of cirrhosis, but that would be sinful."
That would be sinful: What Cheever kept learning from AA was that
being sober was a matter of sacred dignity, and that people from every
conceivable class and background could be essential to one another.
Only with fellow alcoholics could he comfortably discuss his own loneliness and bewilderment. " 'Yesterday was a memory, tomorrow is a
dream,' says a man who is dressed like a gas pumper and has only three
front teeth," he wrote in his journal. "From what text, greeting card, or
book he took the message doesn't matter to me at this hour." At other
times, to be sure, he might laugh at such a chestnut—but such laughter
("acid, scornful and motivated by pitiable defensiveness") was an irksome betrayal of the better person he longed to become.

He was fortunate in his choice of sponsor, Bev Chaney, a bookseller
who had a deep and appreciative knowledge of Cheever's work. Almost
until the day of his death, Cheever relied heavily on the man to keep
him sober. Whether he was feeling a little blue or (often enough) suicidal, his sponsor was an unfailing anchor—ready at a moment's notice
to help him over a bad patch with a bicycle ride or meeting. The two
also spent a fair amount of time visiting other alcoholics in trouble, an
aspect of AA that meant a lot to Cheever. When Hope Lange told him

that her brother David was drinking too much and refusing to go to AA, Cheever insisted he had *no choice* and called him immediately: "I will not allow you to hurt yourself," he said. "Now stop it." Such was his reputation as a successfully reformed drunkard (an almost unheard-of phenomenon among American writers of the first rank) that even Truman Capote sought his help—again and again and again. "We really need you, Truman," said Cheever on the telephone, while lunch guests waited for him to return to the table. "We need your prose. . . ." As Cheever stood there precisely rediscussing the reasons Capote should check himself into Smithers (as Capote would, eventually, with less enduring results), he grimaced and rolled his eyes for his guests' benefit.

The fact was, a part of him chafed at being perceived as "a fucking do-gooder": it was galling to remember his mother's bandage-rolling for the Red Cross, her delight in giving "skinny chickens" to the poor and so forth; on the other hand, Cheever owed his life to the kindness of fellow alcoholics, and felt an inescapable sense of obligation. Perhaps his most extended effort was in behalf of Zinny's son, Dudley Jr., who'd opened a restaurant in the area and then (as Dudley Sr. put it) "took to sampling his own liquor." Having watched the young man's mother drink herself to death, Cheever took Dudley to AA meetings and tried to be something of a father to him. "We play backgammon," he wrote in his journal. "[Dudley] is so stupefied with drugs and drink that the game is meaningless. . . . I put my hand over his and say: 'This is not right, this is not right at all. You are drugged, you are lost.' He mumbles some agreement but I know from my own past how little he has heard, how little he cares." Cheever took almost every possible measure to save the man: he phoned various family members (one of whom was in Jamaica at the time), confronted doctors, and finally drove to Dudley's house and insisted he get in the car. "You're an alcoholic like me," he said. "I'm going to take you to Phelps, and that's going to be it." After drying out, Dudley went to a rehabilitation clinic in New London, Connecticut, and was sober for almost a year—then relapsed, and relapsed again, until finally Cheever despaired of him. ("I preferred him to my own father," said Dudley after Cheever's death. In 1987 Dudley himself died, age forty-five, of a brain embolism.)

As perhaps some Higher Power appreciated, it was burden enough looking after one's own salvation. A month after leaving Smithers, Cheever chided himself: "I make the sign of the cross a dozen times a day. Cleanse the thoughts of my heart, etc. Rejoice, rejoice. Can't you take this as a gift given? Must you, like a broody child, remark that the toy that fills your heart with pleasure will soon be broken and thrown away?"

IF CHEEVER HAD HOPED that sobriety would improve his marriage, he was soon disabused. "I've changed violently," he wrote, "but nothing else seems to have changed. Looking for a good-night kiss, I find the only exposed area to be an elbow." Mindful that his drinking had been "a grave problem," and given that he was, by nature, averse to confrontation, Cheever tried to show his contrition with deeds rather than words. As his daughter recalled, he seemed to realize for the first time "that the house wasn't cleaned by gremlins," and diffidently inquired how one went about working the dishwasher and such; he also learned to feed himself in some rudimentary way. His newfound self-reliance, however, would have to be its own reward. That first summer post-Smithers, he cheerfully welcomed his wife back from Treetops with a batch of groceries he'd bought all by himself: "I lean for a kiss. There is none. If my questions are answered at all they are answered with a sigh. The groceries I brought are worthless, the corn is questionable, and would I mind if it is thrown away? 'Not at all!' I exclaim, which means that it will be served. This is perversity and madness." He tried to remember that his "grave problem" had taken an awful toll over the years, abrading "the excellence [he knew] Mary to possess"; he also bore in mind ("with profound sympathy") her miserable childhood, the thought of which sometimes moved him to lavish acts of tenderness. Once, she returned from an antique store in Pleasantville, bemoaning the fact that she'd left behind a gorgeous, chrysanthemum-patterned Imari bowl because it was too expensive; while she was cooking dinner, Cheever slipped out and bought it for her. "He changed and she didn't," said their daughter, though Mary didn't see it quite that way: "He was perhaps a little more civil," she reflected, "and occasionally put on an act of being very loyal and loving. Sometimes it was credible, sometimes it wasn't."

Perhaps as a further goodwill gesture, Cheever returned with her to Treetops early that fall. Another incentive might have been the absence of Mary's "mad sister," Buff, who in 1972 had been hit by an express train in Pennsylvania—her body obliterated without a trace, or so legend has it. ("I will not speculate or comment," Cheever noted on hearing the news, "except to say that Mary loved her very much.")* The visit served as a final reminder of why he'd declined to go back (but once) these many years: the house was frankly shabby, its furniture and rugs having "missed their date at the municipal dump," and the main topic of conversation, still, was the Winternitz patriarch, to whom everyone pithily referred as "MCW" ("Remember when he tore down all the windowshades and jumped up and down on them"). Driving back from New Hampshire with his wife, Cheever felt "relaxed and happy"—perhaps because he knew he'd never return, or bother to complain about his wife's returning.

He began to get along with his children a little better, and to speak of them with pride rather than rueful malice: "Fred got honors at Andover and is (by my lights) marvelous," he wrote Weaver. "Susie is an editor at Newsweek and Ben, very handsome and expensively dressed, is on the staff at Readers Digest." It was a particular relief whenever Federico came home, since it meant that Mary was civil for the sake of appearances and Cheever had someone other than the dogs to keep him company. His relationship with Ben remained problematic. Even though the young man had gotten a better job at *Reader's Digest*, he still borrowed money on an almost monthly basis, as a matter of both necessity and principled hostility. Cheever was alternately bewildered ("I think he has felt that to succeed as a husband and father he must find me contemptible") and hostile in turn. While a visitor bemusedly watched, Ben drove up to the house one day and asked his father, on the porch, if he needed anything in town: "Get me the number one best-selling nonfiction book," Cheever muttered, whereupon Ben went inside, spoke with his mother, and departed without a further word (possibly to retrieve the book). Meanwhile Cheever enjoyed an enduring truce with his daughter. To a friend who'd recently sired a baby girl, he wrote advising the man to "put her little feet on the path" leading to a job like Susan's: "Thus she will have perfect teeth, lovers, husbands, a large salary and unlimited expense accounts." This was admiration, albeit a trifle backhanded. Susan's "lovers," after all, still included the "charming, corpulent alcoholic" Warren Hinckle, and

---

*One can't help pointing out the eerie similarity between Buff's fate and that of "Shinglehouse" in *Bullet Park*, who, after being sucked under an express train, leaves naught but a "highly polished brown loafer lying on the cinders."

Susan's own drinking made her father "uneasy." "I got two clues that he was aware of this," she remembered. "He took me to [AA] meetings, but he may have just liked having the company. Also, when we met for lunch, he'd already have ordered my drink. That's something alcoholics do for each other."

Despite a slightly improved domestic life, Cheever was often bored, lonely, and beset by terrible longings. Once his morning work was done, he'd invent reasons to get out of the house and go to the post office, the bank, the laundry—anything that brought him into contact with other people. Sometimes, still, he'd drop by Lang's hovel and invite the ex-convict to come have a beer later on, though Lang usually didn't show, and Cheever would have to find other ways to fill the time. "I write Lincoln Kirstein what I think is an entertaining letter and he returns a brochure with his initials and his address on the envelope," Cheever noted that November; "and writing to Laurens [Schwartz], because I have little else to do, I think that my epistolary profligacy is a little absurd." The highlight of Cheever's week was Sunday night, when the miniseries *Poldark* was aired on public TV: "Poldark! Poldark!" he'd excitedly announce, running around the house. The only drawback to *Poldark* was its lack of commercials, a genre Cheever had come to find oddly entertaining, even when they were "contrived, banal and obscene."

What he wanted most of all was a lover, since he could no longer rely on alcohol to drown his ravenous libido. Along with a renascent boyishness, however, sobriety had also brought with it a harshly objective awareness of what it meant to be pushing the age of universal retirement. "I love my son," he wrote; "my cock can shoot a pint; these facts are as relevant as my daughter saying that I look like one of those old men who celebrate their last birthdays by swimming the river and whose unappetizing photographs are sometimes—but not always—printed in the paper." Even at the best of times, the aging Cheever didn't think much of his looks: wincing at publicity photos, he'd remark that he had the "face of a ferret" and was, even worse, round-shouldered and *short*—reminiscent, he thought, of "the small museum guard in a worn uniform who says softly, 'It is beautiful, isn't it?' " This was too bad, as Cheever found that most of his erotic urges were now definitely homosexual, and he was haunted by memories of the middle-aged Henry Wadsworth Longfellow Dana, shedding his clothes at Craigie Castle almost half a century ago and standing there, plumply nude, while the eighteen-year-old Cheever fought back laughter and ran for the door. Found among Cheever's papers on Bay State Road was a letter from Gurganus, who'd written wistfully of their Sunday walks along the Iowa River and declared that his love was "without precaution or moderation." The sober Cheever was apt to cast a coldish eye on this sort of thing ("Allan seems to be skirmishing again"), but when Ganymede appeared in person—as he did that summer of 1975 in Ossining—Cheever once again found himself ardently trying to hold hands while working the steering wheel ("A[llan] seems . . . to magnify the incongruities between my social and my erotic drives to the point of combustion").

Underlying such autumnal turbulence was a sense that time was short. Perhaps the most disturbing reminder of this was his spells of "otherness," which, if anything, had gotten worse since he'd given up alcohol. A pre-Smithers CAT scan had indicated "severe atrophy of the brain," which in Cheever's case seemed to affect his prodigious memory in curious, almost ineffable ways: "A strain of music, heard from upstairs, does not remind me of a moment in my past; it reminds me of a thousand moments in any place I may have been; Asia or southern Massachusetts." In the midst of these "seizures," or whatever they were, Cheever would forget where or even who he was; also, a certain elusive hallucination tended to recur, having something to do with Ginny Kahn and Exley standing on a beach in Cape Cod perhaps, the latter singing a forlorn jingle that Cheever couldn't quite parse. If he ever managed to possess the memory, he felt certain he'd go mad. Meanwhile, even on relatively lucid days, he sometimes felt an almost unbearable estrangement from the world: "I am in a bell jar or worse since I seem to respond to nothing that I see," he wrote. "I remember being as depressed in Rome. A cigaret butt in a cup, a formation of dust under a table seemed to represent the utter futility of staying alive."

CHAPTER FORTY

{ *1975–1976* }

Along with his other sorrows, Cheever was pretty much broke. "I am so deeply in debt that even if the novel at hand is completed and successful I will remain poor," he reflected in his journal. "I am close to tears; I mean this." It got so bad that he even had to give up his coveted membership in the Century Club. A club official had written him an admonishing note in regard to (as Cheever put it) "[his] sordid deliquesence [sic] as a dues payer," and Cheever drafted a reply accepting his fate as persona non grata, at least for the time being: "However I shall pay my back dues when I've finished the book at hand and—if the book succeeds—apply for readmission." Such matters reminded him, all over again, that *Falconer* would have to be a best seller to justify its advance and cover his debts, and never mind sending Federico to college and keeping his own body and soul together while trying to get his work done. Fortunately, at the darkest hour, Candida Donadio managed to negotiate a forty-thousand-dollar movie option from Paramount on the strength of a single published chapter in *Playboy*.

It was now more imperative than ever that he finish *Falconer*, which remained at a rather formative stage after almost five years of occasional contemplation. "I still claim that my muse is around but there isn't much evidence," he wrote, two months after Smithers. While he was looking in old journals for "situations that might be connected," it occurred to Cheever to confect another hodgepodge (à la "The Leaves, the Lion-Fish and the Bear") that could be sold for ready cash. The result was "The Folding-Chair Set," which Cheever explained to one befuddled reader as "the story of [his] life told by innuendo"—a pompous way of saying that it was a collage of random anecdotes about his family, loosely sutured by the recurring phrase "we were the kind of people." Among the material incorporated into the story (much of it also used in *Falconer*) was an account of the time his drunken father had pretended to ponder suicide while riding a roller coaster, as well as several derisive glimpses of his brother—portrayed as a boorish oaf who insists on summoning waiters by clapping his hands, who springs to his feet and doffs his Tyrolean hat when a band in Kitzbühel plays "Home on the Range" (which he mistakes for the Austrian national anthem): "I mention this only to illustrate the fact that we were the sort of people who endeavor to be versatile at every level," the narrator dryly remarks.

William Maxwell was planning to retire from *The New Yorker* at the beginning of 1976, and Cheever would later claim that "The Folding-Chair Set" had been meant as a "finger-exercise" to commemorate the occasion. It seems rather doubtful, however, that he intended any such tribute when he first submitted the story, or that Maxwell would have accepted it even if he had. Happily, Maxwell was out of the office for a few weeks, and so the story fell in the hands of one of his successors, the twenty-eight-year-old Charles ("Chip") McGrath, who idolized Cheever and recognized his prose immediately despite the protective (or tongue-in-cheek) pseudonym he'd used for such a "trifling piece": Mrs. Louisa Spingarn.* Though McGrath realized the story would have been rejected if it were by almost any other writer, at the time he and others were simply thrilled to have an actual submission from *Cheever*, to whom the magazine had been paying an annual "first-look" fee for many years without any real expectation of receiving further work.

Cheever was almost giddily pleased that the young man had recognized his style *and* bought the story, though his pleasure turned to anxiety when he arrived on the nineteenth floor to meet McGrath for lunch. *"Do you know who I am?"* he demanded of the receptionist, who plainly didn't, causing Cheever to throw a "minor fit" until he spotted a mentally impaired messenger from the old regime: "There's a familiar face!" During lunch, McGrath was struck by how hard Cheever was

---

*Also the name of the benefactress in *Falconer* who ("IN MEMORY OF HER BELOVED SON PETER") pays for the inmates to be photographed next to a Christmas tree.

trying to impress him: he'd just come from the New York Public Library, Cheever grandly announced, where he'd been conferring with the "eminent woman" in charge of looking after his papers. Afterward he wrote a friend, "I am pleased that my work, these days, makes [the magazine's editors] intensely uncomfortable"—noting that they'd deleted "a nasty crack at Borges and Barthelme" from what was, after all, his first *New Yorker* story in seven years. Nor was this altogether an idle boast. One of Maxwell's last acts as an editor was to reject a section from *Falconer*: "We are very grateful to John for letting us see this," he wrote Donadio, "but the massacre of the cats was too much for us."

The improbable success of "The Folding-Chair Set," whatever its merits, was a great boost to Cheever's morale: he felt as though he'd shaken off a curse, and was eager to make the most of his changing luck. In the old days, when his creative powers and work ethic had been at their best, he'd almost always made a point of getting on with his writing rather than dwelling on some passing triumph. "I must get back to the Cardinal if I have to work in declarative sentences," he urged himself as soon as "The Folding-Chair Set" was behind him. The "Cardinal" was the late-middle section of *Falconer*, in which Jody miraculously escapes from prison via the Cardinal's helicopter—one of the first sequences Cheever wrote, and perhaps his favorite. When it was finished, he excitedly gathered his family around the fire and read it aloud ("They were all very pleased with it"). After that, rather to his amazement, the book began to fall into place, even the stray bits he cannibalized from old stories and journals—anything to keep his momentum going. Just to be working again made him so ecstatic that he deliberately rested on Fridays, lest he get so "high" with creative jubilance that he end up "brain[ing] Tom Glazer with a dinner-plate" at their lunches with the Friday Club.

"UP THE RIVER to Yaddo for the first time in many years without the company of alcohol," Cheever wrote at the outset of a long September stay. As luck would have it, Gurganus was working as special assistant to the president (or "the John Cheever job," as some called it), and when Cheever arrived in his room at the Trask mansion, he found flowers and presents from his protégé; he couldn't help thinking, however, that if Gurganus *really* loved him he would have been waiting impatiently at the bus station in Albany. Despite such high expectations, Cheever seemed undismayed when Gurganus again refused ("kindly and politely") to sleep with him: "I enjoy his company and would enjoy his skin," Cheever mused, "but I miss neither."

With Gurganus, he paid his first visit in a long while to the ninety-year-old Elizabeth Ames, who appeared to be waiting for a train—what with her fur stole and tightly clasped handbag—in the parlor of her cottage, Pine Garde. Cheever greeted her with the usual obliging roar ("HELLO THERE, ELIZABETH!"), and she peered up at him with evident pleasure. "John! What a *coincidence*! Fancy meeting you here!" Evidently thinking it was some time in the distant past, she treated Cheever like the charming young man whom she'd first adopted as a surrogate son, while Gurganus was "the boy in white pants" whose name she could never quite place. As Cheever put it, "she decided that the people she loved and admired—many of them long dead—were alive and working in the mansion, the fools and the bores . . . were dead." For a while she politely inquired about Carson McCullers and the like ("Oh, I don't think Carson's doing so well, Elizabeth . . ."), then, growing tired, she pointedly told her nurse to "put that call through" to her brother, who'd been dead since the Great War. "Well, John, this *has* been a coincidence," she said, dismissing him. "If you're ever in Minneapolis again, *do* stop by."

Leaving Pine Garde, Cheever seemed all the more eager to attach himself to a younger generation. An abstract artist in her late twenties, Melissa Meyer, found that the only free seat at dinner was next to Cheever, the most dauntingly famous person in the room. Since the table was discussing quaint towns in the area, Meyer couldn't resist putting in, "Last year I went to Cohoes to buy shoes with Hortense." Cheever was transported: "Oh, what a *wonderful* sentence! May I use it?" Thus endeared, Meyer was invited to join him for drinks at the Gideon Putnam Hotel, where a van-and-trucking convention was in progress. After an hour or two of giving her his sober, undivided attention, Cheever guided her back to the convention and slipped two metal signs ("for your studio") under his jacket: "KENTUCKY" and "POSITIVELY NO SMOKING IN VAN OR IN RESIDENCE." During the same visit, he befriended the poet Philip Schultz, in part because the young man had proved to have a "good wing" while tossing a football with Cheever. One night the two were having a manly chat about women while Gurganus, seated nearby, rolled his eyes and repeated the odd word with broad sarcasm. If Cheever noticed, he gave no sign.

He was reunited with Schultz later that year in Boston, where Cheever had arranged to give a reading at the offices of the Harvard *Advocate* in order to "strike some sort of peace" with the city. "I must repair my farewell scenes there," he wrote Laurens Schwartz; "and everything is going so splendidly here that I'm sure I'll be able to weather what I think to be a sinister, provincial and decadent part of the world." To prove his point, he promptly paid a visit to Kenmore Square, where a bitter wind continued to blow amid the funeral parlors and embalming academy. "That place is asshole," Cheever reiterated, but the rest of the trip was a lark. Schultz, then living in Cambridge, attended the *Advocate* reading and laughed in all the right places; then the two got in a taxi and struck up a conversation with the cabbie, who waived his fare once he learned that Cheever was in his car. As the latter reported: " 'Hot shit,' [the cabbie] said, 'Apples, Bullet Park, the Wapshots.' I gave him a copy of the Brigadier. Everybody was laughing." It got better the next day, when Schultz announced ("jumping up and down") that he'd just won a grant for three thousand dollars. "This is just the beginning of *many* good things for you," Cheever said with paternal pride, treating the poet to baked oysters and tournedos at Locke-Ober.

Perhaps the most definitive act of reconciliation came after his lunch with *Atlantic* editor Robert Manning, who again solicited a story. Cheever wrote it in his head while leaving the restaurant, then typed it up in his hotel room: "I was *hot*," he said later. "When you're hot you can write anything—timetables, grocery lists, stories, anything." "The President of the Argentine" is more than a timetable or grocery list, though somewhat less than a fully realized story; as a witty confession of the author's fall from grace, however, it serves as an interesting artifact. The piece opens with a quick parody of (and commentary on) old *New Yorker* fiction: "How like sandpipers were the children on the beach, she thought, as she stood by the rusty screen door of their rented house on Nantucket. Zap. Blam. Pow. Here endeth my stab at yesterday's fiction. No one's been reading it for forty years." Instead, the reader is told of a desolate day when the narrator was almost arrested in Boston, while trying to put a hat on the president of the Argentine. By way of familial context, he also describes the alcoholic exploits of his eccentric old Yankee father—who once, for instance, drank all the sherry and pissed the decanter full. "[T]he piece is shapeless and self-indulgent," one *Atlantic* editor wrote in a circulating memo, "as well as periodically tasteless"; "a lazy exercise," wrote another, who thought it "boil[ed] down to whether we want Cheever in the magazine that badly. I, for one, don't need him." Richard Todd, however, found the piece "funny and affecting," and Michael Janeway agreed: "Also," he pointed out, "it's in some ways meant for us as 'a Boston story,' from the bad Boston season of his life." For that reason, primarily, the story was purchased for twelve hundred dollars, appearing in the April 1976 issue. "I prefer your books," Schultz remarked. "The story is like your dinner conversation."

By then Cheever had pretty much forgotten the thing. *Falconer* was going so well that he'd treated himself to another vacation in late January, heading to Stanford for a reading while Federico (soon to graduate from Andover) toured the campus. Cheever's minder was Dana Gioia, a graduate student and lifelong fan*; in a curious coincidence, he'd been at Harvard the year before, when he'd arranged for Cheever to read at a "weekly literary table" for undergraduates. Unfortunately, the well-attended event coincided with Anne Sexton's suicide, and Cheever decided to stay home that night (as he might have done in any case). "Intoxicated by the news of Cheever's [Stanford] visit," Gioia remembered, "I mentioned it to some undergraduates, but soon learned that none of them knew who he was. Undismayed, I decided I would show them and went off to the university bookstore only to discover that all but one of his books were out of print."

Cheever behaved, in the best possible sense, like a man who realized his books were out of print. "Absolutely perfect," he declared, when Gioia showed him his "tiny concrete-block cubicle" at the Florence Moore dormitory (Federico was staying elsewhere with Andover friends). Cheever had nothing much to do until his reading, and each day Gioia would find him sitting alone in the common room, reading and smoking, happy to go for a walk or a drive or whatever else Gioia had in mind. Such were his radiant good spirits ("the joy of having been resurrected from the dead," as Gioia put it) that freshmen in the dorm actually enjoyed having their meals with Cheever: "His conversation never excluded them," said Gioia. "It was intelligent without being intellectual, informed but not pedantic. And he was very funny. After all, as he once said, 'You can't expect to communicate with anyone if you're a bore.' "

What little star-treatment Cheever might have expected was fur-

---

*Gioia went on to a distinguished literary career, becoming chairman of the NEA in 2002.

ther precluded by the unexpected arrival of Saul Bellow, whose wife, Alexandra, was considering a position in the math department; Bellow's presence implied that he might be interested in a package deal, though Cheever intimated to Gioia that what Saul *really* wanted was to get away from his previous wife in Chicago. The two writers had rarely been further apart in stature: Cheever was virtually forgotten, whereas Bellow had just published *Humboldt's Gift* and would presently win the Pulitzer and Nobel Prizes. Also, Cheever could hardly have been more gracious and charming, while Bellow seemed to *suffer* whosoever had the temerity to approach him. "Literature is not a competitive sport," he snapped (quoting a friend) when Gioia asked him what contemporary fiction writers he admired; having put the youth in his place, Bellow abruptly continued: "Wright Morris, J. F. Powers, and a man standing in this room . . . *John Cheever.*" The latter was doubtless flattered, but hardly awed. As Bellow prepared to give an impromptu reading, Cheever conspicuously relinquished his front-row seat to an old lady; then, sitting on the floor, he whispered to Gioia, "I can *hear* Saul, but all I see are a shiny pair of reading glasses peeking over the microphones."

When it came time for Cheever's own reading, he was introduced by the head of the writing program, Richard Scowcroft, whose "elegiac tone" confirmed the general impression that Cheever was washed up. And yet he seemed to enjoy himself all the same. His duties at Stanford discharged, he flew to Los Angeles and spent a few days sitting around the Weavers' heated pool, where the old friends took turns delivering mock eulogies of each other. He also had a pleasant lunch with Hope Lange: "That her voice may be shrill," he wrote in his journal, "that her looks may be passing, that there is very little correspondence in our tastes are things I know and don't care about at all." He could hardly wait to get home and tell family and friends all about it: the way they'd kicked off their shoes at the restaurant and played footsie under the table, their kiss beside the streetlight in Sherman Oaks, the possibility that she was coming east in the spring.

THAT SPRING (1976), Cheever was so busy with *Falconer* that he could hardly bother to write letters, and what few he wrote tended to be on the same subject. "All writers suffer terribly from delusions of omnipotence and I am in the throes of this," he wrote Litvinov, who'd since defected to Hove, England, near Brighton. "I feel, at the moment, that if I wanted to go to Hove I would simply have to stand on the sunny terrace, flap my arms and ascend. I would, of course, break my neck." Standing on that sunny terrace with his daughter one day, Cheever happily announced, "He gets out. Farragut gets out." The discovery that his fictional alter ego would soon be free—from prison, from addiction, from various kinds of fear—made Cheever himself feel, perhaps for the first time in his life, that everything was going to be absolutely all right:

> I think the work is successful and that I may be rich and famous. I claim not to care. I can always scythe my fields and walk in the streets. It is the strangeness of this excitement that I must examine. Why should it seem so strange to succeed? I do not mean pride or hubris. I mean only to have solved most of my problems and to have exploited, to the best of my intelligence, my raw materials.

After finishing the novel on Good Friday, he went to Trinity Church in Ossining "to say [his] prayers," and was "nearly run over by Donald Lang" as he departed. Somehow it seemed a good augury.

Once the manuscript was out of his hands, however, Cheever began to fret: "Around four I think that Falconer is a poor fantasy, that it will interest only a few cranks with corresponding fantasies." He was even sensitive to the response of his typist, who failed to express a proper regard for the work at hand ("I am accustomed to tears and declarations of love") when asking Cheever where to send the bill. His mood continued to darken as he awaited the publisher's verdict. He wrote Coates that he "[didn't] really give a shit for what anyone else thinks"—yet wrote in his journal of a recurrent daydream in which Gottlieb came to Ossining to kiss him on the mouth (or, conversely, called to say that he and Donadio "feel that there is a great deal of work to be done . . ."). After a long week of silence, Gottlieb's actual reaction was, if anything, an anticlimax. According to Cheever, the editor quipped that *Falconer* might be "too noble to sell," and though he was moved to say the usual tactful things, too, on the whole he seemed neither overwhelmed nor terribly disappointed. "I want a friend, an enthusiast, a lover," Cheever reflected, "and he is none of these."

By the end of the summer, Cheever's sense of omnipotence had decidedly waned. Charles McGrath had found nothing in *Falconer* that could be used as a *New Yorker* story, though he considered the novel "a miracle" and was nothing but generous in his note to Donadio: "It's not very often that we get a story from a novel, and I sometimes worry that when we do it must be because there's something wrong with the novel. In any case, there's not a thing wrong with The FALCONER [sic]; it's splendid, and I think it will be a great success." It was one of the kindest rejections Cheever ever received, and would help cushion the blows that followed. Gordon Lish at *Esquire* (still riding high after publishing excerpts from Capote's notorious work-in-progress, *Answered Prayers*) returned a heavily blue-penciled manuscript to Cheever, then rejected the novel altogether. But the big money, of course, was in movies, and Cheever was particularly anxious to hear from Paramount via his new Hollywood agent, an associate of Donadio ("[he] screams a lot, says blah blah blah and seems to take it up the ass," Cheever observed); he soon learned, however, that Paramount had not renewed its option on *Falconer*—this without any apparent negotiation on the part of Cheever's agents, who'd quarreled with each other and were no longer on speaking terms. "My discontents are quite simple," Cheever wrote Donadio, whose days were numbered. "I am sixty-four years old, I have a seriously damaged heart and a nineteen year old son to support and to discover—entirely by chance—that no one is representing Falconer for film came as blow." The final blow came in September, when Cheever was notified that the Book-of-the-Month Club had found the novel "shocking" and had decided to pass on it. At that point Cheever felt "robbed" all around, though he was disposed to be philosophical: "I am the sort of iconoclast," he wrote Litvinov, "who will ridicule the establishment endlessly and expect to be seated at the head of the table. They sometimes protest."

In the meantime he'd been distracted by graver matters. On May 28, his brother had died of a massive heart attack (his third). Just a few weeks before, Fred had moved into "one of the dandy little apartments" of Wheeler Park, a subsidized housing development for the elderly in Scituate; then he'd paid a last visit to his brother, who knew immediately that Fred was near death. "This is a commonplace evening, a great improvement," John noted afterward, while Fred was characteristically more effusive: "Just back from a fine visit with John who is in great shape," he wrote his son. "He asked about you, as always, for he has a most sincere and proud interest in all the kids. Remember?—he took Nan [Fred's daughter Ann] to a short trip to

Europe a few years ago and still talks about what a wonderful gal she was." Fred had constantly mentioned Ann's trip to Majorca over the years, extravagantly proud of this rare intersection with his brother's family; he also mentioned the novel John had just finished, though he didn't refer to their parting exchange (as John often would): "Fred, I killed you in my novel." "That's splendid, Joey. That's splendid."

John had been struck by a memory of his mother's decision to end her suffering by drinking herself to death ("[I] think of her as uncommonly clear and strong") at almost the exact moment, he later learned, that Fred had died. "I cry," he wrote in his journal.

> He seems, as most people I love have seemed, to be lost, to be suffering a loneliness more painful than anything experienced in life. I read the prayer book, but—other than that God will not be a stranger—the descriptions of life everlasting are not what I have in mind. The next day my sorrow seems visceral. . . . Susie and I talk about the family. I am inclined to make a legend of the Cheevers, and this can easily be done, but it seems idle to me. I will write a eulogy, including the fact that my brother wasted half his life. . . . We seem to have got the provincial eccentricities of New England, but we seem to have got them wrong.

Philip Schultz said that his friendship with Cheever really began when the latter remembered his brother tenderly—"instead of (as usual) belligerently"—a few days after Fred's death. John spoke of the "communion" between them in the old days: how "protective and fatherly" Fred had been; the way he'd thrown gravel against John's window on Hudson Street. Schultz had been moved to tears, and felt as though he were crying for Cheever, too, who as usual found it difficult to express sorrow except with a kind of constrained cheerfulness.

On June 3, however, when he attended Fred's funeral at the First Parish Church in Norwell, he became cheerful in earnest. Looking around the seventeenth-century church at the flowers ("Yes, yes, Louisa Hatch did the flowers"), the high, lighted windows, the mourners with their "sailboat tans, white hair and mannered wives," Cheever gleefully realized that this was "the world into whose umbrella stands [his] brother used to piss": "The text was Tillich, Cummings, and Eliot and not a tear was shed," he wrote Gurganus. "It was splendid." Nor was Cheever inclined to shed any more tears, confessing to himself that he didn't really miss Fred—for whom life had been "mysterious and thrilling," after all, whereas "death was of no consequence": "Some clinician would say that, while I part so easily with my brother, I will, for the rest of my life, seek in other men the love he gave to me."

A POSTSCRIPT OF SORTS: In the midst of mourning his brother—on June 1, to be exact—Cheever received a phone call around 4:00 a.m. "This is CBC," the man said. "John Updike has been in a fatal automobile accident. Do you care to comment?" Cheever burst into tears. "Oh, was it personal?" the man asked. "He was," Cheever sobbed, "a *colleague*."

One of the signs that Cheever was mellowing with age and sobriety was his ever more gracious, even tender, attitude toward Updike, especially after his rival's kindnesses in Boston. Cheever had recently nominated him to the Academy ("He is forty-three but one might put excellence above age"), and after Cheever received the tragic news that night, he couldn't get back to sleep. "He was a prince," he wrote in his journal, and began drafting what appear to be formal remarks for the press: "I think him peerless as a writer of his generation; and his gift of communicating—to millions of strangers—his most exalted and desperate emotions was, in his case, fortified by immense and uncommon intelligence and erudition." The eulogy proceeded ("John, quite alone in the field of aesthetics, remained shrewd," etc.) until it began to get light outside and Cheever left off to feed the dogs. Finally he called his daughter at *Newsweek* and asked her to check the story with the CBC and the Boston and Ipswich police. Updike, it turned out, was home in bed. The call was a fraud.*

For the rest of Cheever's life, he felt more and more easily reconciled to the fact that he and Updike were conjoined in the public imagination, for better or worse; he even rather enjoyed ("without presuming any familiarity") the idea that they'd been "chosen to play out the roles of a father and son." In 1977, Cheever attended the wedding of Updike's daughter Elizabeth and always made a point of dropping warm little notes to his colleague on the occasion of a new book,

---

*A quite reputable novelist (who'd been drunk that night, and who will remain nameless here) later confessed to making the call—or rather calls *plural:* he'd also phoned Updike's first wife and perhaps certain others.

or to make some deprecating comparison to his own work or reputation: "In yesterday's mail I was cordially invited to Notre Dame on the strength and mastery of the Maple stories," he wrote Updike in 1979. "I think you don't know me well enough to know how vile I can be but in this case I was retiring and pious." He also repeatedly told the press that Updike was the "most interesting writer of his generation"—the last three words being perhaps the crucial nuance, bringing us nicely back to Cheever's ambivalence, which never did quite fade. When Updike's novel *Marry Me* was published shortly before *Falconer,* Cheever all but prayed on his knees for its failure, and two years later he was furious to learn that "Updike's fourth-rate novel [*The Coup*]" had a larger first printing than his own *Stories.*

CHAPTER FORTY-ONE

{ 1976–1977 }

SHORTLY AFTER FINISHING *Falconer*, Cheever arranged a summer vacation in Romania, courtesy of *Travel & Leisure*. He gave various reasons for this: his Romanian friend Petru Popescu, he said, was "such a striking example of egocentricity that I have wanted to check on his origins"; also, he had a lot of time on his hands before the publication of his novel in February 1977, and little appetite for writing in the meantime, or wrangling with editors over how to make *Falconer* "more readily appreciated by a larger readership." But the main reason was simpler than all that, and applied just as well to the other travels Cheever would undertake in the months ahead: he was lonely. Days passed without his wife's saying a word to him, and when he tried to steal a kiss, she'd avert her cheek or fill her mouth with a cookie. "[W]atching Casablanca on TV I weep freely," he wrote that summer. "My need for love, for tenderness, is painful and dangerous. . . . Oh God, I need it." As for Romania, Popescu had assured him that he had a wide readership there, and thus he hoped to find "sexual engorgement" with an admirer of whatever gender.

In that respect he was disappointed, though he could hardly fault the hospitality of the Romanian government. Provided with a chauffeured Mercedes and "an amiable guide who liked to play backgammon and swim," Cheever was driven some two thousand miles, from Bucharest to Câmpulung to Suceava along the Russian border—a trek affording him plenty of material for a *Travel & Leisure* paean to the tree-shaded, two-lane highways of that folksy old country: "In Romania one drives mostly on such roads, and it is not only the past recaptured, it is the return to some serene human scale where one can admire the geraniums in farmhouse windows and wave to strangers." But Cheever didn't really care about the geraniums, and even the picnics in the mountains, where one ate wild boar and listened to Gypsy music, were spoiled somewhat by vulgar tourists ("drunken Jews from New York"), to say nothing of his own indelible loneliness. "I see loving couples and would love to be among them," he wrote. "I think, on waking, that I am deserving. And I worry for hours about the temptation of an erotic consummation with a man." Worry though he might, the object was nowhere in sight, and he returned to Kennedy Airport in a foul humor: "[T]he Customs man threatened to confiscate some Moldavian Easter Eggs I had bought in a nunnery and I told him to shove them up his ass," he wrote a friend. "Then I shouted at a perfect stranger: 'If you had a dumb wife who knew you were coming in from Bucharest where do you suppose she'd be?' Then I felt a hand on my shoulder. It was my beloved Federico."

But apart from Federico, who left for Stanford that September, there were very few people whose company he much enjoyed anymore—certainly not that of his oldest, "fourth-rate" friends ("What am I doing among them"). There was Newhouse, of course, who kept a well-appointed office with a lovely old desk at which (mercifully, as Cheever would have it) he hadn't written a word of fiction in more than ten years; after one of their tedious lunches, the man settled himself in Cheever's wing chair and, solemnly puffing a pipe, urged his friend to invest in common stocks. "You are," said Cheever, "a bore." And what would such bores think, he often wondered, when *Falconer* ("a romance between a drug addict and a hustler in prison") was actually published? Would it not confirm their worst suspicions? Watching Art Spear as he brooded over the backgammon board, Cheever realized that his boon companion "would be capable of having [him] burned at the stake." He also began to suspect that certain members of his old circle had already discovered his secret. Mary Dirks, in particular, was apt to boast (or so it seemed to Cheever) of her ability to detect homosexuality in even the most unlikely people: "She is the provincial sorceress and why, one might ask, with her supernatural powers of divination, has she failed as an actress, a teacher, a lover, a cook and a housekeeper." Mocking the poor woman as "the provincial sorceress" (or "muse of the provinces") seemed to comfort Cheever, and he developed the theme at length in his journal. Her dinner parties, he wrote, were like "Stations of the Cross," involving exhaustive innuendo about homosexuality and ending for the guests around three in the morning, when they retreated en masse to their toilets, "racked with diarrhea" from a rancid lobster mousse. "Some day I will get her down," Cheever vowed.*

"You are lonely, aren't you?" said Philip Schultz, who'd moved to New York the previous March and become one of Cheever's steadiest and most tolerable companions. (Cheever promptly related Schultz's remark to Dennis Coates—then stationed in Germany—by way of underlining the two men's common instincts on the subject.) Schultz was trying to live off his three-thousand-dollar grant, and Cheever identified with the struggling young poet: he, too, "hadn't a pot to piss in" when he'd moved to Hudson Street more than forty years ago, and yet he'd persevered and was determined to help Schultz do the same. The latter joined perennials such as Rudnik and the Lehmann-Haupts for holiday gatherings on Cedar Lane, and for a while he also came for regular Sunday brunches (Mary had a motherly impulse to feed him), after which he and Cheever would toss a football or take long bicycle rides. Zooming down a hill one day in November, Cheever hit a patch of gravel and "went cock-a-hoop over the handlebars," badly gashing his forehead. Almost twenty-five years later, Schultz resumed a then-dormant poetry career by writing "The Eight-Mile Bike Ride," an elegy for Cheever that recounted the "looping red trail eight miles long" that dribbled from Cheever's wound as he walked his bicycle home. Refusing to wash his face, much less see a doctor, Cheever was smeared with gore when his wife and daughter returned from a walk and rushed to comfort the stricken Schultz.

The high point of the friendship came the following year (1977), when Viking accepted Schultz's first book of poems, *Like Wings*, on Cheever's recommendation. When given the news, Cheever actually jumped up and clicked his heels, and when *Falconer* and *Like Wings* were both nominated for National Book Awards, he seemed happier for Schultz than himself. After that, however, the two began to lose touch—or, as Schultz explained, "John became famous again." In later years, on the rare occasions when they met, Schultz couldn't resist mocking Cheever's self-importance—asking, for example, the same

---

*A vow he kept in his last novel, *Oh What a Paradise It Seems* (see page 55 *re* Sears's second wife).

question twice ("Saul wrote to you? . . . Saul *wrote* to you?"), whenever Cheever said something pompous. "I flare up at him, call him a horses ass," Cheever noted in 1980—but then reminded himself, wistfully, that Schultz had been "a great friend when his friendship was needed."

A friendship perhaps better suited to Cheever's evolving persona was with the prominent art dealer Eugene Thaw and his wife, Clare, the latter of whom he'd met at an AA meeting a few months after Smithers. Clare had noticed Cheever previously ("a gaunt figure in a seersucker coat [with an] unhappy face"), and one night he sat beside her and sighed, "Oh this is so goddamned *boring*. Why don't we have a cup of coffee?" Thus began a post-meeting ritual of repairing to the Thaws' splendid Stanford White house in Scarborough, where Cheever would wittily complain about his awful marriage, or eavesdrop on Eugene's long-distance negotiations with, say, Norton Simon in Los Angeles. "Good *niiight*," he'd drawl at the end of the evening, then turn to Eugene: "What is it now? One-point-six or one-point-*two*?" He also delighted in ridiculing the parvenuish Sleepy Hollow Country Club, whose golf course abutted the Thaws' lawn. One night the three had dinner there, Cheever casting a radiant gaze on the panoply of madras and green; for weeks he mordantly reminisced about his "dinner at Sleepy."

Not that he was categorically averse to the flashy, nonaristocratic rich. For example, his old friendship with Mrs. Zagreb—whom he'd reverted to calling Sara in his journal—had become "quite humorous and innocent," now that he was no longer an importunate drunk appearing at random intervals to use her pool and drink her liquor. That summer he was asked by *Newsweek* to make a few remarks on the occasion of the Bicentennial, and, while pondering the American experiment, he was moved to dash off a note to Sara to the effect that the "love of one's neighbor" was a virtue that seemed to flourish in our democracy: "I think you ought to know this since you are my neighbor." Cheever's love, in these twilight years, became a cozier, quieter affair. Sunday mornings, after church, he'd buy fresh croissants or brioches at Say Cheese in Ossining Village, then have breakfast with Sara while watching the horse races on television. As he mused toward the end of his life, "I swim and chat with S[ara] and while this is not a complete engagement it seems to be one of those consolations that travelers settle for, indeed it is sometimes for these consolations that one travels."

· · ·

DISAPPOINTED IN ROMANIA, Cheever agreed to give readings that autumn at Bennington and Cornell with quite the same goal in mind: "I think in terms of the appearance of some lover who will undo me, engorge me and grant me a contentment I have nearly forgotten." It occurred to him that "close to three years" had passed since he'd actually gone to bed with a willing partner (the occasional piece of quick, hired sex didn't count), and now it seemed that his best hope lay in finding a tractable protégé in some university English department. This involved a great deal of soul-searching, however: "I could not possibly exploit or debauch a young secretary," he chided himself; "one cannot take this much of another man's life." But it was, quite definitely now, a *man* he wanted, though he worried that, once he'd committed himself to that path, it would lead to his destruction. In the past this intuition had always dissuaded him from cultivating long-term homosexual affairs. As he'd reflected some twenty years before:

> What is involved is a relaxed acceptance of the bisexual nature of man and the realization of the fact that excesses of perverse love, unlike other forms of love, compounds perversion and spreads it all through the personality, for once you are absorbed in unnatural matters your conduct becomes unnatural, the lures you use to attract your prey are disfiguring, your attitude toward the most rudimentary and vital forms of organized society . . . become implacably scornful. It is a fine line between the admission of natural bisexuality and the excesses of perversion.

And then, too, what would his family think? What, above all, of his beloved Federico, who Cheever often worried would be approached by the sort of predatory homosexual that Cheever (by his own lights) now considered becoming—what would Federico, having encountered such a person, think of his own father? Quite simply, Cheever could not succumb to his desires without abandoning certain of his fondest convictions; and so, in the end, he decided to abandon them. "I lie in the sun, nearly overwhelmed by the thought of the phantom lover who will destroy my life," he wrote that October. "For an hour it seems that I must part from all of this; the trees, the clearness of the autumn light, even the old dog." And yet he felt he had no choice ("this is a destiny") but to pursue the "darkness in [his] heart" and find his "destroyer."

Such a person was not to be found at Bennington, though Cheever watched with furtive interest as a tall, dark youth went around the train station approaching the sort of seedy old men who linger on benches once the arriving passengers have dispersed. Cheever had been told to expect a woman, Melissa Fish, but at the last moment Peter Pochna (to whom Cheever had been described as a man "no longer young") had gone instead; when Pochna approached the dreary codger nearest Cheever, the two finally met. Before his reading, Cheever had dinner with Bernard and Ann Malamud, the poet Stephen Sandy, and other students and literati, whom he regaled again and again with the train-station story (the would-be Cheevers becoming more numerous and decrepit with each telling). Later, he put in a brief appearance at a party in his honor, saw nothing he liked, and retired to his room at the Fruitrich guesthouse, where he drew himself a bath and turned on the TV: "I got into the tub and pretended that the room was full of people. It was full of voices. But I am tired of such loneliness."

That left Cornell, where Cheever had been the first in a distinguished roster of writers—Walker Percy, Eudora Welty, Brodkey, and others—invited to perform at the Chekhov Festival. "For the master I'll come for bus fare and a roof over my head," Cheever had replied, though his host, James McConkey, insisted he accept an airline ticket and the usual one-thousand-dollar honorarium. (Cheever typically donated his honorarium checks to the college literary magazine or some such institution.) At Cornell, however, his reception was even less auspicious than at Bennington: "I am met at the airport in Ithaca," he noted, "not by a beautiful youth but by Professor and Mrs. McConkey!"

Still, he looked forward to a packed auditorium at his reading, for which he'd gone to the trouble of writing a long meditation on Chekhov titled "The Melancholy of Distance." As he reminded his audience, "I am, after all, one of perhaps ten American writers who are known as the American Chekhov; but then I have been described as the Budd Schulberg of New England." Cheever made light of the vogue among New Journalists and the like to claim that modern reality "outstrips the inventiveness of the imagination": under Alexander III, he pointed out, there had been "bands of whooping Cossacks riding on the ghettos to murder men, women, children and infants"—and yet

Chekhov had not been discouraged, even amid "the darkness of a censored press," since, after all, his subject was the "deep giving and taking" between human beings of any historical moment. Cheever concluded with a splendid instance of Chekhovian obliquity from *Uncle Vanya*—the one time in this very personal, anecdotal lecture that he bothered to quote the master at all (evidently from memory)*: "The [final] scene is one of sadness and despair. Then Astrov goes to the map on the wall and exclaims: *How hot it must be in Africa.* . . . Here is a new and thrilling element brought to the universality of loneliness, here is Chekhov's mastery of the melancholy of distance. The line is written for an actor and it can be laughed or wept or dropped like a stone: its force remains unchanged. How hot, etc."

Cheever knew whereof he spoke, and once again he ended such an evening alone in his room: "I meet no destroyer," he forlornly recorded; "I may never. . . . What I remember most vividly, most usefully is leaving the reception in my honor. I would like to pluck someone from the gathering for my pleasure but I will not, I cannot. . . . No liquor, no sex, no love, no friendship, nothing but a cigaret and The New York Times." As it happened, the graduate student who was most admiring of Cheever's work (the only one, indeed, who knew much about him at all) was a married woman named Frederica Kaven, and hence the two were thrown together for much of the weekend. Cheever tried to be a lively companion, but when Kaven remarked how "funny" his stories were, she noticed a definite flicker of sadness in his eyes—as though he was thinking that people remembered him, if at all, as *funny*.

Kaven, at any rate, was elected to drive him to the airport, where he was informed that his flight had been delayed because of engine trouble. "I'm taking the bus!" he cried in alarm. That left some three hours to kill. For a while they chatted over coffee at Kaven's house, and finally Cheever was standing in a tavern across from the bus station, trying (unsuccessfully) to get a sandwich; Kaven never forgot how a dusty ray of sunlight seemed to be pointing at Cheever—a frail, tweedy figure among the afternoon drinkers ("a person who never had a chance," she thought for some reason). After he kissed her goodbye on

---

*"I can find nothing in Chekov to quote," Cheever wrote Gurganus, "I can find almost nothing of Chekov to read and what I've done is to invent a Chekov as I think he would have invented a Lermontov under the same circumstances."

the cheek, Kaven paused on her way to the parking lot: "I'll be looking for your next book!" she called back to him. "What's it called again . . . ?" "*Falconer!*" he shouted vigorously.

ON THE FIRST DAY of 1977, Cheever predicted (with greater accuracy than he might have imagined) that the new year would prove to have "some true newness to it." There was *Falconer*, of course, as well as a week at the University of Utah in late January—a prospect that struck Cheever as "deliciously promising": as he'd been reminded over the past few months, illustrious writers are hardly novelties at prestigious eastern colleges, but out in the desert of Utah he seemed more likely to find a student aching for his patronage. And yet, again, he was almost startled by his own hideous excitement: "Is self-destruction my destiny, am I perverse? Will I read into a cruel or a bestial face the promise of romantic love? Can this be my death?"

The head of the writing program at Utah, Dave Smith, had encouraged the more promising students to submit work in advance of Cheever's visit, since their famous guest had agreed to spend a few hours a day in individual conferences. Perhaps the best writer in the program, however—a Ph.D. candidate in his early thirties named Max Zimmer—wasn't interested: he'd satisfied his curiosity by reading a couple of Cheever's stories and hadn't found them congenial; besides, he'd begun work on a vast, Pynchonesque novel about the West that had recently caught the eye of E. L. Doctorow, no less, so he figured he didn't need Cheever's help. But Smith insisted he arrange a conference, and finally took it upon himself to submit one of Zimmer's stories, "Utah Died for Your Sins," which Cheever did, in fact, find "very exciting." Thus Zimmer was presented with a fait accompli: "Cheever's getting out of a seminar at two o'clock," said Smith, "and I want you to be there to meet him." Reluctantly he complied, appearing before Cheever at the appointed hour—a shaggy, bespectacled young man wearing cowboy boots and accompanied by a small Airedale on a leash. But what enchanted Cheever most, perhaps, was that Zimmer "had none of the attributes of a sexual irregular"; what he'd always wanted, after all—as Gurganus put it—was "somebody who was literary, intelligent, attractive and *manly*, but gay on a technicality in a way."

Arguably Zimmer was not gay in even a technical sense—but then, as Dave Smith pointed out, "there was some difficulty in knowing who the real Max was." Already he'd gone through a number of curious changes in his life. His parents were devout Mormons who'd emigrated from Switzerland when Zimmer was a boy. At age nineteen, he'd gone back to Europe as a missionary and discovered a love of writing while editing (irreverently) the mission's newsletter. He soon returned to Utah, however, having been excommunicated for a sexual indiscretion—a fact he was compelled to confess ("gruesome") to his congregation back home. Then, a year or so later, he endured the ordeal of reinstatement so he could marry a Mormon woman and, not incidentally, win back the affection of his father and namesake, to whom "nothing mattered more than [having] good Mormon kids." For a while Zimmer was able to play that role, until almost the day of his college graduation with a degree in engineering: "The sixties were breaking open," he remembered, "and engineers were getting jobs building toasters for Motorola in Arizona, stuff like that, and that's not my life." So once again he turned his life upside down: "I left the church, divorced a perfectly good woman, and went full-hog into English and writing."

The story that Cheever had claimed to find exciting, "Utah Died for Your Sins," would later be included in *The Pushcart Prize III: Best of the Small Presses,* but otherwise seems hardly in line with Cheever's tastes, given that it is frankly experimental and lacks what Cheever was apt to call *velocity.* It opens with a disquisition on a deer-killing method that involves embedding a razor in a block of salt, so that the animal obliviously bleeds to death without injury to its internal organs. Next is a long description of a man customizing a car, then using the car to romance a woman until the affair goes vaguely wrong. At last we encounter a character named Seymour Utah, who may or may not be the bereft mechanic: Utah has thief-proofed his motorcycle helmet by sticking razors in the padding, but apparently forgets and claps the helmet on his own head—whereupon, like a deer or a Christ figure, he slowly bleeds to death from this crown of thorns while riding into the desert. What does it mean? "It is a story about a man who allies the mysteriousness of women to the mysteries of machinery," Cheever conjectured.

With a momentous air, Cheever invited the author back to his room at the Lake City Motel, an uncommonly grungy place near campus. (Dave Smith had offered to reserve him a room at one of the better hotels in town, three or four miles away, but Cheever wanted to be within walking distance and seemed to enjoy complaining, wittily, about the lack of basic amenities such as a telephone or a bath plug.) Once they were situated—Cheever with a six-pack of sodas, Zimmer with Wild Turkey—they began talking about books and writing and, of course, Zimmer's future. The first thing he had to do, said Cheever, was get out of Utah; one did not make a literary career in Utah. Cheever would be glad to arrange a place for Zimmer at Yaddo that summer—he was a board member; he would take care of everything— and so on, for some four hours. "And I was, like, *Wow*," said Zimmer.

> Because at this point I was pretty eager to get out of Salt Lake myself. I'd been in school too long, and ever since I'd walked away from the church, my wife, and my engineering degree, my father wouldn't have anything to do with me. Essentially I hadn't had a father in three years at that point, so Cheever really struck a chord. I looked at him and thought, "Boy, here's a guy who's in control and who's an authority in the life I've chosen to lead, as well as a father figure who actually embraces what I'm doing."

For the rest of Cheever's visit, Zimmer was his companion of choice. "No, thank you, I'll just have Max take me," he'd say whenever Smith offered a ride to this or that function. On the last day, Zimmer arrived at the Lake City Motel to give Cheever a lift to the airport, but Cheever was tired and wanted to lie down for a while. He asked Zimmer to lie beside him. Zimmer was a little "alarmed," but did as he was asked; then, while they spoke, Cheever took the young man's hand and guided it to his crotch. Zimmer felt a "slight hardness under the corduroy pants" and tactfully withdrew his hand—forever remembering the moment (as he would write in his journal five years later) "with dizzying revulsion." ("I have a seizure of lewdness and arrogance that seems to me sinful," Cheever wrote at the time, "that is deserving of punishment. I am more frightened than remorseful.") Until then, the sum of Zimmer's gay experience had been an experimental romp in junior high school, as well as a few minutes of mutual masturbation with a fellow Mormon—but those partners had been his own age. He wasn't altogether sure what to make of the present episode, though he prayed it was an aberration, since he'd already set his heart on leaving Utah and going to Yaddo and so forth. In any event, when Cheever asked for a hug as they were leaving, Zimmer obliged him; the embrace lingered until a maid paused in the open doorway. "I experienced a profound stirring of love," Cheever remembered, while Zimmer felt a further surge of "confusion and revulsion."

Cheever proceeded to Stanford to visit Federico and give another reading. In a rather fraught coincidence, Gurganus was also at Stanford as a Stegner Fellow, and when Federico showed his father to his room at Dinah's Garden Hotel on El Camino Real in Palo Alto, there was a conspicuous bowl of fruit waiting with a note attached: "Nothing could be finer / than the thought of you at Dinah's / exiled to El Camino / at the mirth of your bambino." Cheever wasn't much amused, and when the three met for dinner, he seemed determined to put the waggish young man in his place. "Everybody knows that," he said haughtily, when Gurganus quoted an aperçu from Randall Jarrell's satirical novel, *Pictures from an Institution* (to wit, how the buildings of a fictional college based on Sarah Lawrence—Gurganus's alma mater— seemed half designed by Bottom the Weaver and half by Mies van der Rohe). Gurganus perhaps had no idea of Cheever's loathing for Jarrell, but the rest of the evening was like that, too: "I was the whipping boy," he recalled. "He was showing a member of his family that I didn't matter much." Only once, really, was their old rapport in evidence, when Gurganus eagerly raised his hand after Cheever's reading. "Tell me, Mr. Cheever," he said. "Do you write with a typewriter or in longhand?" Cheever composed himself and replied, "I inscribe on stone tablets."

As he left Dinah's to catch a plane to Los Angeles (and Hope Lange), Cheever spotted a wet playing-card facedown on El Camino Real. He turned it over—the two of clubs. "From that moment onward my erotic, familial and financial life would soar," Cheever wrote eighteen months later. "So much for portents."

CHAPTER FORTY-TWO

{ *1977* }

"TRUST IN THE LORD," Cheever noted, once he'd returned from that eventful trip to the West. "Use your intelligence, keep your skin clean." He tried to reassure himself that his motives were pure where Max was concerned—he simply wished, after all, to "give [Max] some freedom from the darkness of that place"—and he expressed (albeit equivocally) similar sentiments in the letters he began sending the young man at the rate of two or three a week: "Firstly this is a no-shit friendship and I have assumed you into no league. I thought your work first-rate before we met and it is you—whom I scarcely know—and your work that will move the train. That I love you has nothing to do with the case. The young and the old are meant to pool their advantages and with luck this is what we will do." Cheever promptly endeavored to prove his sincerity. He sent "Utah Died for Your Sins" to McGrath at *The New Yorker*, even though the story had already been accepted by a little magazine on the other coast, *Quarry West*—but in any case, and for a number of reasons (one of which was the word "fuck"), the story wasn't right for *The New Yorker*. Cheever also sent a copy to the president of Yaddo, Curtis Harnack, with a peremptory little note: "The various dead-lines and other formalities don't seem to prevail under the circumstances. Zimmer is thirty-two and I know him to be civil, clean and industrious."

Meanwhile, back in Utah, the object of all this generosity was at once flattered, puzzled, and not a little anxious. One of the most famous authors in the world was devotedly promoting his work, not to mention writing him constant letters in which he (Cheever) was perfectly willing to "talk about his dick," among other things: "And I was thinking, 'God, how'm I gonna answer these letters?'" Max wonderingly remembered.

> I'm just a hick from Utah. I could not answer every one he sent me. The hazard was that my letters would be so boring that he'd lose interest in me and that would be the end of the friendship. So it would take me a day to write a letter back to him. Of course I didn't have a model to go by except the letters he'd written me, so I tried to write him back in the same way—the same voice, the same kind of frankness, same kind of cynicism, sophistication and stuff. That was tough.

It was tough for Cheever, too. Determined not to get involved in anything "furtive or compromised," he repeatedly reminded himself, and Max, that he was as red-blooded as the next fellow . . . more! He'd been married for thirty-six years, raised three splendid children, and was dating a famous Hollywood actress, who, it so happened, had come to New York just the other day and had lunch with him: "She is terribly pretty and good company but I am not, this afternoon, deeply in love," he wanly admitted in his journal, while writing Max that the "taste of [Hope's] lipstick on [his] mouth" had helped him endure "a tedious interview with Knopf." Lange, whether or not she actually excited him, served the imperative purpose of proving that he was "in there swinging" where women were concerned: "I will not abdicate my position in the procreative, heterosexual world," he rallied himself—but alas, all too often this sort of thing just didn't help much. The facts remained: his marriage was moribund, he rarely saw Hope, and he couldn't stop thinking about Max. Between desperately asserting his manhood and tentatively declaring his love, Cheever's letters to Max began to assume a kind of contrapuntal quality. "That a man of sixty-four should fall in love with a graduate student seems to me highly unlikely and perhaps it will seem so when we meet again. . . . I could not describe the importance of your embrace. I truly wish you no trouble." And a week later: "I think of this as a great back-slapping friendship in which no one is lonely and I don't want to get into your pants."

Max was perhaps relieved to know as much, though it hardly mattered by then. The die was cast. Everybody knew he was bound for the fabled East: Sponsored by John Cheever to spend three months at

Yaddo! Hero of the Utah writing program! And even if he were to have second thoughts—and he had them—what possible reason could he give for staying? The only thing that remained to be done for his Ph.D. was a dissertation—his novel—and he could write that anywhere. He was thirty-two. It was time to leave home and hope for the best.

"How cruel, unnatural and black is my love for Z[immer]," Cheever wrote that spring. "I seem to mean to prey on Z's youth, to drive Z into a tragic isolation, to deny Z any life at all. Love is to instruct, to show our beloved what we know of the sources of light, and this may be the declaration of a crafty and lecherous old man. I can only hope not."

IT WOULD BE HARD to overstate how important the success of *Falconer* was to Cheever. It wasn't simply another *Bullet Park*–like critical debacle he feared, but also the awful prospect that his novel would be perceived as even remotely confessional. Meanwhile some of his most well-meaning colleagues had mixed feelings. Malamud had congratulated Cheever on the "extraordinarily good detail" of the whole prison experience, while alluding to the curious resemblance between Farragut and the author, and admitting, worse, that he didn't "deeply feel [Farragut's] suffering or growth of compassion." (Graciously—and rather tellingly—Cheever agreed: "There is some spiritual ungainliness about the man that makes him barely worth saving.") Cowley's response was similar: he thought individual aspects of the novel were "extraordinary," but Farragut didn't "seem to [him] all of a piece." Both writers apparently had a hard time believing that such an otherwise civilized—not to say familiar—personage as Farragut could also be a bisexual, incarcerated, fratricidal drug addict. What Cheever clung to, in moments of terrible doubt, was the wholehearted endorsement of the present Nobel laureate: "Well, I expected the best and that's exactly what I got in Falconer," Bellow wrote. "It's splendid. . . . You should sell hundreds of thousands of copies, unless the country is farther gone in depravity than I think."

Bellow wasn't wide of the mark, oddly enough, though this wasn't entirely due to the country's discerning readership. Rather, Susan Cheever's influence at *Newsweek*—coupled with the ecstatic enthusiasm of their reviewer, Walter Clemons—had moved the editors to consider putting a writer on their cover, something they permitted only once every two years or so.* Cheever had been summoned to lunch at the Newsweek Building, where he was careful to eat no more than a single lamb chop ("I didn't want them to think I was a rube or hungry") while the editors asked him a lot of questions and eyed him rather doubtfully. As Cheever wrote a friend, "Then one of them said that with my face on the cover there would be a drastic drop of news-stand sales but then another man said this was true of all serious writers. After this I went out on a local and called Knopf to tell them the news and the PR man said, 'I've been successful.' "

The *Newsweek* feature would include an interview between the subject and his daughter ("A Duet of Cheevers"), for which Susan came to Cedar Lane on a cold, rainy afternoon in February. For five hours the two sat in front of the fireplace, and Susan, in her introduction, evoked the Cheeverian ambience of the scene with the same good effect as Alwyn Lee's *Time* piece thirteen years ago ("Three golden retrievers lie before the fire on an Oriental carpet . . ."). After a couple of hours, the two began to relax and talk more like father and daughter, and during this phase of the interview the following (published) exchange took place:

> Q: Did you ever fall in love with another man? I mean, because of the homosexuality in *Falconer*, people are certainly going to ask you that.
>
> A: The possibility of falling in love with a man seems to me to exist. Such a thing could happen. That it has not happened is just chance. But I would think twice about giving up the robustness and merriment I have known in the heterosexual world.
>
> Q: Well, have you ever had a homosexual experience?
>
> A: My answer to that is, well, I have had many, Susie, all tremendously gratifying, and all between the ages of 9 and 11.

Thus Cheever seemed to brush the matter aside with an easy quip. In fact, as Susan recalled, the moment was quite a bit more fraught than the text suggests. "I have had many, Susie," said Cheever—then, mark-

---

*Bellow had been the last (September 1, 1975), because of *Humboldt's Gift;* before that, Joyce Carol Oates had been featured (December 11, 1972) around the time of *Marriages and Infidelities.*

ing the startled look on her face, he added with the usual tremor of laughter, "all tremendously gratifying, and all between the ages of 9 and 11."

The *Newsweek* cover was scheduled for the March 14 issue, and in the meantime the early reviews of *Falconer* seemed to indicate that critics were either staunchly in favor or staunchly opposed. A few days after Susan's interview, Cheever was contacted by the *Saturday Review:* John Gardner's piece was so enthusiastic that they were sending a photographer to Ossining. "John Cheever is one of the few living American novelists who might qualify as true artists," Gardner raved. "His work ranges from competent to awesome on all the grounds that I would count: formal and technical mastery; educated intelligence; what I call 'artistic sincerity,' which implies, among other things, an indifference to aesthetic fashion . . . and last, validity, or what Tolstoi called . . . the artist's correct moral relation to his material"; as for *Falconer,* it was "an extraordinary work of art." Cheever wrote in his journal that Maxwell had taken credit for this coup ("Bill calls then to say that this was his doing"), and it was also Maxwell who gently alerted him to the "noncommittal" *Time* review. Cheever rushed into town looking for the February 28 issue, until he found one in a drugstore. The photograph, he thought, was "ghastly," and the review wasn't much better. "*Falconer* is strong on feelings," wrote R. Z. Sheppard, "even though they often overflow the novel's loose structure." Not only was the structure loose, but the strong feelings tended to be expressed in terms of "sententious observations" about the suffering of prisoners and so on: "Another sententious observation would be equally true," Sheppard sternly pointed out (as if the book in question were a sociological tract): "crime's victims are no strangers to grief." Absorbing this, Cheever had a "bad few hours," but finally was able to persuade himself that *Time* had "shit on [the book]" by way of undermining the imminent *Newsweek* feature.

For the crucial daily *Times* review, Cheever had petitioned Lehmann-Haupt to ensure the services of John Leonard, lest the job fall to another *Times* reviewer, Anatole Broyard: "[Leonard] is sympathetic and I can't forget what I've been told about Anatole's review of Bullet Park." Cheever presumed to ask such a rare political favor in exchange for having agreed—at Lehmann-Haupt's urgent request—to write a Thanksgiving piece for the Living section, "Thanks, Too, for Memories." Unhappily for Cheever, *Harper's* had already commissioned a review from Leonard, and the review was bad: "Whatever happened to suburbia?" Leonard wrote, proceeding to take Cheever to task for deserting his proper subject in favor of distasteful, sensational material. "It is as if our Chekhov . . . had ducked into a telephone booth and reappeared wearing the cape and leotard of Dostoevsky's Underground Man."* Since Leonard wasn't available for the *Times* review, and Broyard had been blacklisted, Lehmann-Haupt went ahead and reviewed Cheever's "extraordinary new novel" himself: "After a first reading . . . I could report that I had devoured it hungrily, marveled at the grace of its prose, been given nightmares by its early passages, and come away from it with a sense of a world set right." That left Joan Didion's front-page notice in the *Times Book Review* of March 6, and although Didion had never been anything but lavish in her praise of Cheever, he worried all the same ("the rivalry between novelists is worse than the rivalry between sopranos"). But she, too, thought *Falconer* an "extraordinary new novel"—its author a consummate artist, whatever the ethos of his fiction. "'Falconer' is a better book than the 'Wapshot' novels, a better book even than 'Bullet Park,' for in 'Falconer' those summer lawns are gone altogether and the main narrative line is only a memory."

A few days later *Newsweek* hit the stands ("A Great American Novel: John Cheever's 'Falconer'"), and demand for the book exploded—unfortunately, there were no copies available. The first printing of twenty-five thousand had already sold out, and Knopf had yet to fill orders for forty or fifty thousand more. Cheever expected his agent to intervene, but Donadio was slow on the uptake. "My agent's brain seems gravely damaged," he angrily reflected. "I may call Knopf this morning and break my relationship but very little would be accomplished." Instead he decided to get rid of Donadio, albeit with such exquisite politeness that the woman hardly knew what hit her— only that Cheever was suddenly cool on the telephone, and eventually wrote her a gracious note: "I have neglected to thank you for your part in FALCONER. . . . It was you who got me the advance that let me imagine the book, it was your restraint that saw me through two heart

---

*"It doesn't seem fitting for me to write John Leonard but if you see him please tell him how accomplished I thought his review," Cheever wrote Lehmann-Haupt on May 1—bearing in mind perhaps that Leonard was a good man to keep in his corner, and after all the success of *Falconer* was assured by then.

attacks as well as drugs, alcohol and suicide without a nagging letter
and it was your confidence in the book that helped it through its rather
confused reception at Knopf." Having written as much, Cheever hired
a lawyer to sever the connection; Donadio ("a Jewish den-mother," he
once described her) was "devastated": "We did like each other a lot for
a long time," she later mused, proposing that she'd been fired because
she knew too much about her client's bisexuality, and not (as Cheever
explained to a friend) because she'd "gone completely insane."

All's well that ends well. Gottlieb saw to it that eighty thousand
copies of *Falconer* were rushed to the stores, and the novel spent three
weeks at the top of the *Times* best-seller list—ultimately selling almost
eighty-seven thousand in hardback and over three hundred thousand
in its first paperback edition. While it was still number one, Cheever
wrote his daughter a note: "The lesson let us help one another was not
lost on you."

"I LIKE TO THINK of *Falconer* as the sum of everything I've ever
known and smelled and tasted," Cheever told *Newsweek*, and this may
be as good a way of explaining the novel as any. Beyond the elaborate
prison metaphor—flawlessly detailed yet oddly dreamlike, as in much
of Cheever's best fiction—*Falconer* is perhaps his most deeply personal
work: a tabulation of his own singular afflictions, ordered as a parable
of sin and redemption. That said, the narrative bristles against the
logic of a pat allegory (or pat anything), and readers who attempt to fit
Falconer into any kind of formula are liable to be a little confused.
"Tentatively—very tentatively—one would have to say that it is about
coming to terms with humanity through the medium of homosexual
love," Lehmann-Haupt awkwardly ventured, while John Leonard
(who'd managed one of the most ingenious critiques of *Bullet Park*)
pretty much threw in the towel: "Sentence by sentence, scene by scene,
Falconer absorbs and often haunts. As a whole, it confounds."

As with *Bullet Park* ("Paint me a small railroad station then"),
Falconer opens with a resonant image:

> The main entrance to Falconer . . . was crowned by an escutcheon
> representing Liberty, Justice and, between the two, the sovereign
> power of government. Liberty wore a mobcap and carried a pike.
> Government was the federal Eagle holding an olive branch and

armed with hunting arrows. Justice was conventional; blinded, vaguely erotic in her clinging robes and armed with a headsman's sword. The bas-relief was bronze, but black these days—as black as unpolished anthracite or onyx. How many hundreds had passed under this, the last emblem most of them would see of man's endeavor to interpret the mystery of imprisonment in terms of symbols.

Having begun on a symbolic footing, the novel proceeds from there: Farragut is identified in terms of his sin and punishment ("fratricide, zip to ten"), and the place he inhabits, cellblock F, is "a forgotten place. Like Piranesi"—or, as the prison guard Tiny puts it, "F stands for fucks, freaks, fools, fruits, first-times, fat-asses like me, phantoms, funnies, fanatics, feebies, fences and farts. There's more, but I forget it. The guy who made it up is dead." It also stands for Farragut, Falconer, fratricide, forgotten, and so forth, and is a place of perfect forlornity— a purgatory where one may pause to consider one's predicament with little in the way of consoling distraction. Indeed, at the beginning of Farragut's captivity, the only relief from loneliness is the company of cats ("They were warm, they were hairy, they were living and they gave fleeting glimpses of demonstrativeness"), which are presently massacred. Lest one abandon all hope, however, we have it on the authority of Chicken Number Two—the mascot of cellblock F, prophet, Greek chorus, embodiment of human destitution—that Farragut's imprisonment is "a terrible mistake," that something good awaits him once he gets "clean" of addiction and its various impurities.

Until then, Farragut's alienation is complete. "Farragut was a drug addict and felt that the consciousness of the opium eater was much broader, more vast and representative of the human condition than the consciousness of someone who had never experienced addiction." His addiction helps ease a painfully keen awareness of his own homelessness in the world, an "otherness" that becomes so explicit at Falconer that his sense of time and space are "imperiled" (notably, on arrival, his watch is stolen by a fellow prisoner); ultimately, he feels so disoriented that he has to ask Tiny for occasional reminders of his whereabouts: "Tiny understood. 'Falconer Prison,' he would say. 'You killed your brother.' 'Thanks, Tiny.'" As for the pressures that have driven Farragut to such an outcast state ("Why is you an addict?"), certain familiar Cheeverian bêtes noires are suggested. There is, for one, the comically hateful wife who visits Farragut in prison only to mock and revile him—part of an old dynamic between the two, as we learn from flashbacks. Once, Farragut remembers, she'd taken off to Rome with an old friend (a woman of "very unsavory sexual reputation"), and when he tried to celebrate her return by cleaning house and lighting fires and buying flowers, she responded by curtly asking for a Campari: "Campari will remind me of my lost happiness." Farragut's own homecomings have been even less successful. Returning from a rehabilitation center in Colorado, he'd explained to her that his drug-damaged heart could not tolerate excitement, whereupon she pointedly slammed a door ("The effect to his heart was immediate"), and then slammed it again. Such murderous malice, on the part of putative loved ones, even preceded Farragut's birth. "One of his mother's favorite stories" concerned the time his father had invited an abortionist to dinner "in order to kill Farragut," and his brother Eben had also made attempts on his life—inviting him to go for a swim in Chilton Gut (a "well-known deathtrap" of sharks and riptides, as a stranger informs Farragut at the last instant while Eben runs off down the beach), and later pushing him out of a brownstone window and almost impaling him on a fence of iron spears. "[Father] wanted you to be killed," Eben taunts his brother at last. "I bet you didn't know that. He loved me, but he wanted you to be killed. . . . Your own father wanted you to be killed." Little wonder Farragut strikes back at his "hated origins" by trying to brain his brother with a fire iron.

Up to that climactic moment, the novel proceeds in a series of eddying digressions—memories, set pieces, particularly "Browning-esque monologues," as Gardner pointed out—the last a long-standing element in Cheever's work: to give two random examples, an incidental shoeshine man in "The Superintendent" confides at length that the smell of shoe polish gives him dirty thoughts, and a military chaplain in *The Wapshot Chronicle* harangues Coverly about his neglected church services and other sorrows. Such outbursts serve little purpose but to remind the reader, in passing, of Cheever's most abiding theme—loneliness, the terrible need to connect—and nowhere is the device more aptly pervasive than in *Falconer*. "Oh my darling," Farragut writes to "a girl he had lived with for two months when Marcia [his wife] had abdicated and moved to Carmel" (the girl is never mentioned again). "Last night, watching a comedy on TV, I saw a woman touch a man with familiarity—a light touch on the shoulder—and I lay in bed and cried. . . . I do not love, I am unloved, and I can only remember the raptness of love faintly, faintly." Even his loathsome brother Eben achieves a fleeting poignance in recounting an extravagant attempt to communicate with his wretched wife by wangling an appearance on her favorite game show, *Trial and Error.* Having fallen off a tightrope into a water tank before a studio audience, Eben rushes home and excitedly asks his wife if she caught him on TV. " 'She was lying on a sofa in the living room by the big set,' " he tells Farragut. " 'She was crying. So then I thought I'd done the wrong thing, that she was crying because I looked like such a fool, falling into the tank. She went on crying and sobbing and I said, "What's the matter, dear?" and she said, "They shot the mother polar bear, they shot the mother polar bear!" Wrong show. I got the wrong show, but you can't say that I didn't try.' " Eben's monologue is characteristic—a futile confession of loneliness, a voice crying out in a wilderness of other tormented, self-absorbed people. ("Stop fussing with my breasts," says the narcissistic Marcia to her husband. "I'm beautiful.") As for the prisoners of cellblock F, one by one they speak their pieces but remain forsaken, nightly retiring to a long cast-iron urinal called the Valley, where they stand without touching and "fuck [themselves]."

Farragut's redemption begins with his love for Jody, though he worries at first that this, too, may be so much lonely narcissism ("If love was a chain of resemblances, there was, since Jody was a man, the danger that Farragut might be in love with himself "). But while Jody is both vain and loquacious, he's also "a very good listener," and his monologues tend to be somewhat instructive—as when he lectures Farragut on the proper way to smile: " 'It has to be real. You can't fake this selling smile. . . . Now watch me smile. See? I look real happy— don't I, don't I, don't I, but if you'll notice, I keep my eyes wide open so I won't get disgusting wrinkles.' " Far from narcissistic, Farragut's love affair with Jody is all but selfless, leaving him both bereft and lighthearted when Jody flies away in the cardinal's helicopter. The rest of Jody's escape, though not ostensibly from Farragut's point of view (as is the rest of the novel), may be understood as a figment of his imagination—a hopeful fantasy foreshadowing his own liberation, which likewise will be assisted by an "agent from heaven": "It is exciting, isn't it?" the cardinal remarks to Jody, leading him to a Manhattan clothing store and then, twenty minutes later, setting him free on Madison Avenue. "[Jody's] walk was springy—the walk of a man going to first on balls, which can, under some circumstances, seem to be a miracle."

After Jody's departure from the novel, some forty pages of filler ensue—namely a long, mostly superfluous sequence about the riot at "Amana" (based on Attica), its effect on the guards and prisoners of Falconer. ("And what do I intend?" Cheever wrote, as he entered the final stretch of work on his novel. "A story about a man of forty-six who enters prison. He falls in love with Jody, who escapes; he is visited by his wife; he suffers the agony of drug withdrawal; and he escapes. You've got to have more narrative in your bag than that. So he must have some failed escapes. Other attempts and other relationships." The Amana scenes provide much of the latter.) These pages are diverting enough, though perhaps the only indispensable part is when the prisoners are kept from rioting by having their pictures taken beside a Christmas tree. Asked to complete a form giving the name and address of some loved one who will receive a print, Chicken Number Two writes, *"Mr. and Mrs. Santa Claus. Icicle Street. The North Pole"*: "The photographer smiled broadly and was looking around the room to share this joke with the rest of them when he suddenly grasped the solemnity of Chicken's loneliness. No one at all laughed at this hieroglyph of pain, and Chicken, sensing the stillness at this proof of his living death, swung his head around, shot up his skinny chin and said gaily, 'My left profile's my best.' " The compassion of the other prisoners, as well as Chicken's own blithe stoicism, prepare the reader for Chicken's role in the rebirth and liberation of Farragut.

Shortly after learning that he no longer needs his methadone fix ("You've been on placebos for nearly a month. You're clean, my friend, you're clean"), Farragut takes the dying Chicken into his cell and washes his elaborately tattooed body. Himself a somewhat priestly figure now, Chicken confesses Farragut ("Why did you kill your brother, Zeke?"), then grants him a kind of absolution, providing guidance into the mysteries of life and death:

> "How could you say you were fearless about leaving the party [i.e., dying] when it's like a party, even in stir—even franks and rice taste good when you're hungry, even an iron bar feels good to touch, it feels good to sleep. . . . I like you and I don't like the Cuckold and it's that way all down the line and so I figure I must come into this life with the memories of some other life and so it stands that I'll be

going into something else. . . . I'm very interested in what's going to
happen next."

Dying, Chicken gives life back to Farragut—goading him, after a fashion, to get out of prison and start over: "Oh, Chicken," Farragut cries,
realizing he's been sitting on the dead man's false teeth, "you bit me in
the ass."

Stowed in Chicken's burial sack, Farragut leaves prison feeling a
sense of boundlessness, a happy unburdening of his former self: "How
strange to be carried so late in life and toward nothing that he truly
knew, freed, it seemed, from his erotic crudeness, his facile scorn and
his chagrined laugh . . ." On the outside he is greeted almost immediately by a stranger—an "agent from heaven" who, as Chicken foretold,
takes a knowing shine to him ("I like your looks. I can tell you got a
nice sense of humor") and helps Farragut re-enter the world with the
gift of a new coat, a new identity. "Stepping from the bus onto the
street, [Farragut] saw that he had lost his fear of falling and all other
fears of that nature. He held his head high, his back straight, and
walked along nicely. Rejoice, he thought, rejoice." In art, at least, all
things are possible.

MAX ZIMMER HAD two younger sisters who lived in New York,
and a week or so after *Falconer* was published—the very week when
Cheever's face was on display at almost every newsstand in the
country—he flew east to take his youngest sister home to Utah in a
drive-away car. She was only nineteen, and recently her older sister
had led the family to believe that the girl was having suicidal thoughts.

Prior to his departure, Max had accepted an invitation ("And bring
your sisters!") to lunch at the Cheevers'; he thought it might cheer
things up a bit to show off his "great back-slapping friendship" with a
famous author, though during the meal he worried that his sisters
would say or do something gauche. Fortunately it seemed to go well
enough, and afterward Cheever offered to show him the Croton Dam.

They drove there in Cheever's brown VW Rabbit, and after a brief
walk alongside the roaring landmark ("in spate"), they returned to the
quiet of the car. "This is the second-largest cut-stone mortised structure in the world," Cheever was saying, "and one of the last things to
be seen by Neil Armstrong . . ." Max, who'd been admiring the struc-

ture in question, glanced at his companion and noticed his penis was out of his pants. With a slight tremor of laughter, Cheever left off chatting about the dam and suggested that Max "play with it." This, the young man realized, was the proverbial turning point:

> Here I was. With a man in his Rabbit, in a totally alien place to me. A man I'd pretty much staked everything on at this point. My sisters were down at his house with his wife, one of them was suicidal, and I thought, you know, "What if I say no? We're going to drive back to his place. He's going to raise hell, throw us out of the house, throw my sisters out of the house, and it's going to devastate my sisters, especially the one that I'd been told was suicidal."

Given what had happened at the Lake City Motel, perhaps this shouldn't have come as a complete surprise, and, truth be known, Cheever was hardly one to "raise hell" when his advances were rejected; still, Max worried he'd somehow be put in the wrong. Also, on whatever level, he sensed he was being punished. He'd left the church and deeply wounded his father—maybe he deserved this. "So anyway," he bleakly recalled, "I jerked him off. And it was just a gruesome thing to have to do."

"I say goodbye to Max precisely as I say goodbye to a very good friend," Cheever noted, benignly enough. "We may never meet again." Max, meanwhile, drove his sister across the George Washington Bridge in a heavy rain.

CHAPTER FORTY-THREE

{ *1977* }

THE DOWNSIDE of Cheever's *Falconer* fame was that many people did, in fact, assume he was gay. "Is your father a homosexual
drug-addict?" people asked Susan (in effect) for years to come.
Cheever was disinclined to evade the issue entirely. He didn't consider
himself gay, of course, though he freely admitted to Hope Lange that
he'd had a homosexual affair once (sic) because he was "terribly
lonely," but didn't care to discuss it. Also, when Dick Cavett sugges-
tively inquired whether he'd "turned a corner in *Falconer*," what with
its homosexuality and violence, Cheever manfully pointed out that
such themes were hardly new to his work.* But there were times, to be
sure, when all the speculation got him down. For one thing, he kept
getting calls from members of the Aesthetic Realism movement,
devoted in part to the conversion of homosexuals. A young man (one
of Cheever's lovers, as it happened) was visiting Cedar Lane when
Cheever received such a call: "Look," he heard Cheever say, "don't you
dare call me here again, or I'm going to take action against you!"

Mostly, though, he was deeply gratified by all the attention.
Granted, the sound of his "fruity accent" was a little dismaying when
he watched himself on *Cavett*, but then the mail started pouring in—
hundreds of letters from discerning, lonely people all over the country.

---

*A few of the more knowledgeable reviewers made the same point. In *The New
York Review of Books*, Robert Towers wrote that a look back at Cheever's earlier work
"reveals numerous occurrences of homosexual material—occurrences to which the
straight characters invariably respond with fear or distaste."

"I'm having a marvelous time," he wrote Gottlieb, noting that he'd just earned the "undying love of the President of the True Value Hardware Store in Eau Claire, Wisconsin." When he appeared on *Cavett* again the following year, he made a point of saying he answered all his letters, in the hope of receiving even more. "I think of myself as a fat boy," he wrote in his journal, "who answers all his fan mail with loving letters with the unseemly ambition, it seems, of gathering to himself more friends than his competitor enjoys." Nor were readings and book-signings the sort of morbid chore they'd been in the past; on the contrary, Cheever was avidly curious to see what kind of readership a book like *Falconer* attracted. "I'd be honored," he said, when the proprietor of a local bookstore—who'd hitherto found Cheever "unapproachable"—diffidently offered to host a signing the week of the *Newsweek* cover. ("They expect hundreds," Cheever gleefully wrote Weaver. "Mary plans to appear, towards the end of the afternoon, frightfully drunk, disheveled and with a torn dress that shows one breast. 'A Star is born,' she is going to scream, 'but only I know that the prick has toe-jam.' Confusion. TV cameras.") A year later, when he was more famous still, Cheever hired a limousine to take him to Caldor's, a vast department store where he signed books near a woman "demonstrating a food-chopper": "The customers and I are utter strangers," he mused. "We laugh. We blush. I sign a book. Here is that experience of intimacy we try so hard to explain. We are, in short, not alone."

He even consented to a modest book tour, which included a stop at the Greater Boston Book and Author Luncheon. Boston, he decided, was not such a bad place when viewed from a high window at the Ritz ("That the struggles of my late adolescence were battled out on the streets is impossible to recall"), and the various TV, radio, and print interviewers treated him like a favorite son. At the book luncheon he sat on the dais with the likes of Henry Cabot Lodge and Garson Kanin, each of whom stood to give a little speech plugging his book. "My name is John Cheever," said he when his turn came, "I was born in Wollaston." Then he sat down. During the autograph session that followed, *Falconer* was the only book that sold out, and among the mob around Cheever's table was a group of Thayer students brought by Headmaster Benelli, who'd last seen Cheever, two years before, standing on Commonwealth in a drunken stupor. This time Cheever was "cordial but shy," chatting briefly with students and signing a copy of *Falconer* for the Thayer library. When the school librarian wrote to thank him, she alluded to his local legend by urging him to return to Thayer and "snatch a smoke" on the grounds. "I am very happy to think of my novel in the library at Thayer and when I next come to Boston I shall certainly visit my old school," Cheever replied, with gracious insincerity.

By far the most controversial item on his agenda was an appearance at the International Conference of Writers at Sofia, Bulgaria, in early June 1977. A few months before (the day after his return from Utah and points west, in fact), Cheever had received "a delegation of Bulgarians who came down the icy driveway carrying wine, brandy and red roses," he wrote Litvinov. "They were like the jolliest of my friends in Moscow." Cheever would always be susceptible to such jollity: it heartened him to reflect on his high reputation in the Soviet bloc—where he was known as "the naive optimist"—and, especially in later years, he was so keen on returning that his family joked he would be "the first western writer to defect to the East." Not everyone was amused, however. That year the Bulgarian president, Todor Zhivkov, had brutally cracked down on social unrest in his country: some forty thousand party members had been purged, and a number of dissident writers hauled off to jail. Amnesty International called for a boycott of cultural activities in the country, while Soviet poet Vladimir Kornilov had appealed directly to Cheever, Updike, and Erskine Caldwell to renounce their participation in the writers' conference. "Bulgaria seems quite dark," Cheever wrote a friend. "The Russians called yesterday to ask exactly what my position will be. I keep saying that Mr. and Mrs. Cheever have accepted with pleasure the cordial invitation of the Bulgarian government and look forward very much to meeting the charming people of this friendly country and to admiring their celebrated landscapes." Tanya Litvinov was especially grieved by Cheever's attitude, and told him so in no uncertain terms. "You may have forgotten what I am like," he benignly replied. "Last summer the Romanians scornfully described the people of Bulgaria as possessing nothing but fresh vegetables and new, crusty bread. That's what I'm looking for, that and some escape from the fact that Falconer is an enormous success here and that it is not in my disposition to be famous." But Litvinov was far from the only friend who found such "innocence" appalling; at home, Eleanor Clark and Red Warren thought Cheever had "succumbed to [the] flattery" of a despicable regime, and regarded his conduct as "ignorance to the point of real evil, almost."

The truth was somewhat less dire. One is bound to repeat that Cheever was not a politically minded man, and he really did adore the warm, demonstrative people of Russia and Eastern Europe ("we embrace and shout in unison 'La grande poésie de la vie' ")—the whole "agrarian unspoiled literary culture" that had embraced the universal themes in his work. Cheever wished to show his solidarity with such people—and bask in their adulation—without alienating political leaders with principled gestures one way or the other, which in any case had proved worse than futile. In 1969, when Solzhenitsyn was expelled from the Soviet Writers' Union, Cheever had found the "stupidity and clumsiness and brutality, in fact, of the Russians" so egregious that he'd agreed to sign an international letter of protest with fifteen other cultural figures (chosen for their popularity in the Soviet Union), including Sartre, Updike, Arthur Miller, Stravinsky, Vonnegut, and Günter Grass. "And that was absolutely the end," he remembered. For years, all letters from Litvinov and others were stopped, and various Russian artists vanished from the public eye with scarcely a trace ("I guess the most conspicuous proof of their loss of freedom of speech is the fact that Yevtushenko, who has the biggest mouth I've ever seen in my long life on the planet, has been silenced," Cheever observed in 1976).

Besides, the Bulgarians really had been extravagantly flattering. Theirs was the only Soviet-bloc country publishing *Falconer* in translation—the Russians had banned the book because of its "perversions"—and moreover the Bulgarian ambassador, Lyubomir Popov, had paid a personal visit to Cedar Lane for Easter dinner. After a game of football (Susan and Philip Schultz versus Ben and the ambassador's chauffeur), Popov was conducted upstairs to the library, where he "unbuttoned his vest and cut a fart," according to Cheever. Tipsy with bourbon, the man bragged about how adroitly he'd dealt with LBJ, Nixon, Ford, and so on, until Schultz said something mildly deflating ("Oh, so American presidents come and go, but *you* outlast them all?") that infuriated His Excellency. Mary, Ben, and Susan tittered, but Cheever looked grim and later admonished Schultz for speaking out of turn.

On his return from Bulgaria, Cheever promptly reported to Litvinov that the trip had been "thrilling": "What political or social significance can one attach to swimming in the Black Sea? The English-speaking group consisted of Lord Snow, Gore Vidal and Anthony Powell [but not Updike or Caldwell]. I am, of course, a sentimental man, but it truly seemed to be a display of our capacity to enjoy one another. No more." No more for Cheever, anyway, who was particularly delighted to be reunited with Yevtushenko—not a whit worse for wear after his recent disgrace with Soviet officialdom. The flamboyant poet danced with Mary Cheever on a Black Sea beach, and dazzled his admirers wherever he went—rather to the disgruntlement of Gore Vidal, or so it seemed to Cheever, who liked to tell the following story:

> We kissed the mayor [of Sofia] and headed for the mountains in the limousine. This was Gore, Zhenya [Yevtushenko], Mary and me. In the snowy uplands we were met by throngs in peasant costume who danced and sang and set fire to a small lamb. Zhenya was in top form which is rather like watching a man pitch a no-hitter while playing the Rasamouvsky quartette at a moon-landing. Gore who does not eclipse gracefully, was burning. Anyhow we danced with the peasants and ate the lamb and when we left perhaps a hundred people gathered around Zhenya reciting his poetry and asking him to autograph their shirttails. Gore, who had stopped speaking, was writing postcards to Paul Newman. Our chauffeur, it seemed, was drunk and racing down the mountain we nearly went off a cliff. When some helpful peasants had put the car back on the road Gore said: "Had we gone off the cliff *I* would have gotten all the headlines." Zhenya brushed a feather off his knee and said, "only in the west, only in the west."*

Another memory that became a permanent part of Cheever's repertoire was his trip to the mountains of Macedonia to visit the famed Venga, a fat middle-aged woman who'd been blinded by lightning and given prophetic powers. Entering her cave, Cheever inquired why women didn't understand him and vice versa. "Women are jealous,"

---

*It is instructive to compare Vidal's version of this episode, which he evidently related without any knowledge of Cheever's more colorful tale. According to Vidal, the key occupants of the bus—not limo—were Cheever, himself, and William Saroyan. Since their driver seemed a bit reckless, Cheever remarked to Vidal, "If this bus overturns, Saroyan will be the only one the Bulgarian papers will feature." Whereupon the two paused to marvel at Saroyan's enduring fame in communist countries, even though the author of such Depression-era classics as *The Daring Young Man on the Flying Trapeze* was all but forgotten in the West, which may explain why Cheever never mentioned him in connection with the Bulgarian trip.

the oracle replied in so many words; "you understand them, all right!" Then she gave him a list of prominent Americans (including Jackie Onassis) who needed to stop drinking.

Changing planes in Frankfurt on his way home, Cheever had arranged a brief rendezvous at the airport with Dennis Coates, who waited fruitlessly around the gate before spotting Cheever by chance on a moving walkway. He was alone. "Where's Mary?" asked Coates, and after a moment Cheever pointed to another lone figure some distance ahead of them. "We don't sit together," he explained to his bemused friend.

SOMETIMES CHEEVER blamed his wife for driving him into "bizarre practices," and sometimes he thought Max was a surrogate for his dead brother ("I want a friend. I wanna friend"). Whatever the case, he tried very hard to keep things in perspective. As Cheever would have it, he and Max were just good pals who occasionally saw fit to indulge in a bit of "carnal tenderness." And now that the ice had been broken in that respect, Cheever was all the more willing to "talk about his dick," as Max discovered with no little foreboding. "If I sounded sinister yesterday morning [on the telephone], I was," Cheever wrote not long before Max was due to return to Ossining en route to Yaddo. "When I am hard-packed I get quite sinister but after I've ruined the wallpaper I think myself jolly and easy-going." In public, too, Cheever hinted rather broadly that he was not the conventional family man he seemed, while also stressing that he was worldly enough not to lose sleep about it. As he remarked to John Hersey before hundreds of undergraduates at Yale, "That one is in conflict with oneself—that one's erotic nature and one's social nature will everlastingly be at war with one another— is something I am happy to live with on terms as hearty and fleeting as laughter." In fact, his laughter was fleeting indeed, and quite often he was "bewildered and apprehensive," for he couldn't help identifying— now more than ever—with the objects of his lifelong loathing. "Brooding, as I must, about homosexuality," he wrote Max, "I stepped out of the post-office yesterday morning and saw Them. . . . The old one was very skinny with a few strands of hair, dyed a marvelous yellow. The youth had all his hair and everything else, I guess, and he might have seemed quite beautiful if he didn't have a mouth like an asshole. The old one would be seen to walk as if his asshole were a mouth. In the back seat was an obligatory Mastaff [sic], a massive, ornamental, brainless dog named after some international cocksucker. 'He'll keep me company when I am abandoned by Michael,' the old fairy will tell his guests."

Max agreed that such a scenario was distasteful, and ever since that episode at the Croton Dam he'd continued to rationalize the matter as best he could: maybe that sort of thing would be a *very* rare occurrence, or, better still, Cheever might come to his senses and call it off; he was married, after all, while Max was practically engaged to a fellow graduate student named Marilyn. In any event, the young man loaded his rusty BMW and drove—in triumph, as it seemed to family and friends—forty-five hours straight through to New York, stopping for a night in Ossining. On the way, he tried to think positive thoughts: Cheever had gotten him a place at Yaddo; his intentions were good, at least; he seemed genuinely interested in Max's career. ("I love you because so much green[n]ess lies ahead of you and that I should in any way shadow or darken this would be wicked," Cheever had written only a few weeks before.) Thus Max consoled himself, pulling into the driveway at Cedar Lane, but alas: "I knew before I left for Saratoga," he sighed, "that I'd have to give him another hand-job." ("[Max] seems a gentle fellow," Cheever wrote afterward, "perhaps no more.")

For a couple of weeks, Max enjoyed himself at Yaddo—"a bughouse": "I was just a stable boy from Utah, and everybody was fucking everybody." To a distinguished poet (female) Max confided his sorrows over his would-be fiancée, Marilyn, with whom he was in a bad patch; the poet listened, sympathized, and took him to bed. Then Cheever arrived for a visit, which was mostly spent with Max in a motel room, and that was something else entirely. In *Falconer,* Farragut finds that he can "kiss Jody passionately, but not tenderly," which was quite in accord with Max's memories of Cheever: "He would kiss me, and it was pretty brutal stuff. . . . Just this raw greed kind of thing.* I'm glad it wasn't gentle, to tell you the truth. I'm glad it was brutal, because that's the way I felt: this is a brutal thing I'm being asked to do, so it should be conducted brutally." And when it was over, there was little in the way of afterglow. Cheever was happy ("jolly and easy-going"): he'd crack open a soda or pour some tea and go back to whatever they'd been talking about—his work, Max's, baseball, some funny anecdote perhaps.

---

*"I know that my need for love can be gross, self-centered, a sort of greed," Cheever wrote in his journal.

"What I seem to want," Cheever noted, shortly after his return from Yaddo, "is a means of getting my rocks off with the least inconvenience, a degree of sentimentality and some decent jokes." So he hoped. What was supposed to be especially funny was what transpired in those motel rooms ("you know better than the next man that bearass I look like something found on the road-shoulders of route #134"), and indeed it was the larky, laughing, *casual* aspect of male sex that seemed to appeal most. With Max he needn't worry about his performance ("I was delighted to be free of the censure and responsibility I have known with some women"), or whether he looked bad or said the wrong thing. This was a back-slapping friendship, after all: "I took a shit with the door open, snored, and farted with ease and humor, as did he." But then if everything was so marvelous, Cheever wondered, why did he feel such "suicidal depression"?

Perhaps it had to do with his stubborn awareness that he was, to be sure, casting an awfully long shadow over Max's "green[n]ess": "Anyone who caressed and worshipped this old carcass would be someone upon whose loneliness, fear, and ignorance I preyed," he admitted that summer in his journal. "This would be the exploitation of innocence." Such a punishing degree of candor, however, could only be taken in moderate doses; usually he tried to persuade himself that Max was as happy (so to speak) as he was, or happy enough, and meanwhile he let it be known that there could be dire consequences if Max disappointed him. Gurganus, for one, was often invoked for Max's benefit, both as the embodiment of *true* homosexuality ("he suffers acutely from the loss of gravity that seems to follow having a cock up your ass or down your throat once too often") and as living proof that it was unwise to spurn Cheever's advances. As he told Max more than a few times, he'd helped get "Minor Heroism" published in *The New Yorker*, but now that he'd withdrawn his patronage, Gurganus would *never* appear in the magazine again.*

As for patronage, Cheever continued to hold up his end of the bargain, more or less, though he believed (as he wrote Max) that "to engage one's interest in the welfare and destiny of a younger writer is to eclipse and constrict one's own gifts." The easy part was using his

---

*As it happened, Gurganus did not publish another story in *The New Yorker* until 1995, though by then he'd become world-famous as the author of *Oldest Living Confederate Widow Tells All* (1989), which spent more than eight months on the *Times* bestseller list.

influence to get Max in the door: he gladly wrote recommendations for jobs and fellowships and so forth, and, more important, arranged for Max to have lunch that summer with Chip McGrath—who had, in fact, found "Utah Died for Your Sins" to be "quite promising" ("a mess, but a promising mess"). McGrath felt genuinely hopeful that it was only a matter of time before Max managed to "crack *The New Yorker*," especially with the guidance of John Cheever, no less.

But that guidance proved to be rather grudging and vague. "When I would bring him a piece of writing," Max remembered, "I was expecting him to actually sit down with me, the way I did with my students, and go through a story line by line, paragraph by paragraph. Details and stuff like that. But he only spoke in the broadest generalities." Reading one of Max's manuscripts that summer, Cheever commended his protégé's "voice" ("something I first got off a page in Salt Lake"), but was otherwise dismayed by what appeared to be "a catalogue of alienations"—which was pretty much the gist of his criticism, right up to the end. "The contempt you bring to this cast is very unlike you," he remarked of another effort. "Fiction is very like love in that there is something lost and something gained." Max didn't quite know how to apply such aphorisms to his work ("I'd turn them over and over in my head for days")—nor was vagueness per se the most daunting part of their arrangement. For much of his adult life, Cheever sincerely believed that sexual stimulation improved his eyesight and overall concentration; while driving late at night, for example, he used to ask Mary "to fondle [his penis] to a bone" lest he have an accident. As he put it, "With a stiff prick I can read the small print in prayer books but with a limp prick I can barely read newspaper headlines." And so with critiquing fiction. Whenever Max submitted a manuscript, Cheever would first insist that the young man help "clear [his] vision" with a hand-job; then (as Max noted in his journal) "you [Cheever] take my story upstairs and come back down with a remote look of consternation on your face and with criticisms so remote they only increase my confusion." Perhaps needless to say, this would eventually lead to a rather formidable case of writer's block.

But most of this was still in the future. That summer, after returning from Saratoga, Cheever began to get the impression that Max was avoiding him—a bit of a blow, because he'd hoped the two of them would spend that fall in Bennington, where Malamud had offered Cheever a three-month teaching appointment: "We would rent a quaint Vermont farmhouse and sleep in one another's arms," Cheever had proposed. "In the mornings we would work. In the afternoons I would teach and you would ski the down-hill trails." When Max didn't get back to him about that or much else, Cheever had to scrap the idea, and meanwhile he asked his old friend Rudnik (also at Yaddo) for news of Max. Rudnik replied that Max was getting "the wretch treatment" from his girlfriend Marilyn, and was thinking of paying her a visit in Baltimore, where—after dumping Max—she'd gone to work on her Ph.D. at Johns Hopkins. (Max had further intimated to Rudnik that his relationship with Cheever had taken a curious turn: "Max had the ability to talk about himself as if he were someone else," Rudnik observed. "A kind of detached acceptance.") Nor was Baltimore the only evasive action Max was considering. While at Yaddo he'd met Lewis Turco, director of the SUNY-Oswego writing program, who offered him a job. As Max recalled, "The first thing I thought was 'Where is Oswego?' And I looked it up on a map and saw that it was hundreds of miles from Ossining, and I thought, '*Good. Good.* I can get away from him without having my career destroyed.' "

He moved to Oswego in August, cutting short his stay at Yaddo, and soon reported to Cheever that he'd reconciled with his fiancée. "Your description of your love for Marilyn pleased me deeply," Cheever replied, "since it refreshed my sense of that genuineness of heart I so admire in you and made clear the fact that for both of us the love of a woman is without parallel. This seems in no way to diminish the need I feel for your company, in every way." Whereupon Max's notes became even more sporadic, until around Thanksgiving they stopped altogether: he and Marilyn had gotten married over the holiday. "I'm determined that this should end happily but I don't know where we are," Cheever had written him a few days before. "Often, when I lie down, I seem to hold you in the crook of my right arm and I wish to hell you wash your hair oftener."

The fact was, his heart was breaking. He was in love with Max, and if Max was gone, he didn't know where else to turn. "I may have lost the great gift of loving a woman," he wrote that autumn. "This is a parting of great vastness and why should it be forced upon me. There is my loneliness, the fact that I seem to want to return to the country of my brother's love, forswearing all the lights of the world." As for Hope Lange—his "golden-haired princess (dyed and well into her second face-lift)"—she now kept an apartment in the city, and sometimes

Cheever would bestir himself to have lunch with her; this was good for a few laughs and little else. The city made him nervous, and he was careful to catch an early train, anxious to get home before dark. But home, too, offered less and less comfort. His wife seemed to find him more abhorrent than ever. She told friends that she'd never bothered to read *Falconer*,* and gave its author the silent treatment on almost any pretext. Around the time of Max's defection, Cheever recorded a typical dispute: "Mary does not make coffee. I complain and so there is a quarrel. I cry. I cry because, at the risk of seeming petulant there seems to be nothing in my life but these corridors."

---

*The problem, more likely, was that she *had* read *Falconer*—noting the uses to which Cheever had put certain real-life episodes in crafting the villainous Marcia Farragut.

CHAPTER FORTY-FOUR

{ *1977–1978* }

CHEEVER CONSOLED HIMSELF with travel. A month after his return from Saratoga, he accepted an invitation to spend a few days at the Thaws' dairy farm near Cooperstown. It wasn't a bad trip: He painted a fence with Eugene, danced to the jukebox with Clare at a raffish restaurant, and attended a tea party at the elegant home of Mr. and Mrs. Henry Fenimore Cooper. But he was lonelier than ever—the sort of loneliness he used to feel at the Boyers' compound on Whiskey Island (listening to distant laughter and the soft, disturbing *thwock* of tennis balls): an odd man out, straining to ingratiate himself. "I seem to be one of those singular . . . old men who appear in summery reminiscences," he wrote afterward. "Kind to dogs and children, jolly mostly, sometimes witty, wearing old-fashioned clothes with a moth hole here and there, a fountain head of charming and eccentric memory. . . . That he hankers for the uncircumcised cock of the fourteen year old farmhand seems to be part of the picture." Next he spent a couple of weeks with Mary at the Wauwinet House on Nantucket—"as much of my past as I suppose Switzerland and the desert is of yours," he wrote the inscrutable Max; "although for the first time I feel somewhat estranged." While the other guests painted watercolors and flew box kites, Cheever rode a bicycle around the island and occasionally sought out backgammon partners ("one could die of boredom"). At one point he kissed an old one-night fling of his named Molly, who gently resisted being wrestled onto the bed, and perhaps it was just as well.

He'd been very excited about "returning to the banks of the Iowa

River" for a reading in the fall, but the reality proved rather desolate: his lodgings were "wretched," and most of the faces had changed. His old student Tom Boyle had stuck around to finish his Ph.D., and after the reading ("Justina" again) Cheever took the young man's hand and sighed, "Well, at least you're here." Then it was off to Washington, D.C., for a videotaped program with the thirty-two-year-old poet Daniel Halpern—a literary chat between the older and younger generations, sponsored by the United States Information Agency. Each man was convinced he'd disgraced the proceedings. Halpern had a bad case of strep throat and hardly said a word, or so he remembers, whereas Cheever found the young man "composed and articulate" and himself a disaster ("I clutch the arms of my chair, lick my lips nervously and am very slow to respond"). Away from the camera, the two found much to talk about. Cheever invited Halpern to his hotel room, where he poured him a glass of Scotch; when Halpern asked whether Cheever would be joining him, the latter explained that he didn't drink anymore but always kept a bottle on hand when he traveled ("I love to see it sitting there, and when it's empty I get another"). Both men had suffered terribly from phobias, and Halpern was struck by how "amazingly open" Cheever was on the subject, particularly as it touched on his problems with impotence. Afterward, Cheever wrote Halpern a few letters, which reflected the sort of bravura candor he seemed to reserve mostly for congenial strangers (he never saw Halpern again):

> Your psychiatrist and mine can't be the same but they entertain the same conclusions. When I told mine that I had happily fucked hundreds of women and quite a few men he said that this was a carapace that all neurotics build to dissemble their impotence.* I thought this over and fucked some more and reported to him that my carapace seemed so successful that I thought I would devote myself to it.

---

*Cheever is alluding here to the observations (circa 1966) of David C. Hays, which evidently continued to rankle. The "carapace" or "social veneer" that Hays attributed to Cheever (quite insightfully) was, said Hays, primarily meant to "dissemble" Cheever's "basic hostility and alienation," though perhaps Hays had also suggested that it dissembled his impotence, what with Cheever's constant talk about Hope Lange and the like.

But Cheever did not give Halpern the impression of a man so "happily" engaged: "I remember feeling sorry for Cheever. . . . There was a *wan*ness about him."

In January 1978 he took Mary to Russia, stopping in London to see Tanya Litvinov, who also noticed a wanness of sorts—odd, since Cheever seemed to have everything now: money, fame, sobriety. Frieda Lurie met the Cheevers in Moscow and took them to a plush suite at the Sovetskaya, thence to tea with Premier Kosygin's daughter and many cultural events, including a serenade of "Hold That Tiger" as played by the Novgorod High School Band. The whole experience, Cheever wrote Cowley, was "profoundly disturbing": "Some of the Russians by now are close friends . . . and to say goodbye there in the snow is an experience that it takes me weeks to comprehend." At other times he said the trip was simply exhausting—"not worth it"—and indeed the whole thing seemed a blur, as did all his other travels during the past eight months or so, going back to Bulgaria. "I seem these days to be intensely unhappy," he'd noted a few weeks before Russia, wondering if he'd still be alive in the spring: "This strikes me as obscene and contemptible. And yet I do suffer hours of loss that are quite painful and that I used to bridge with bourbon and gin." Not only had he begun thinking about suicide, but talking about it too: his AA sponsor, Bev Chaney, remembered the subject coming up "fifty, a hundred times" ("I wonder what it feels like to die").

When he returned from Russia, a seeming reprieve appeared in the form of a letter from Max—the first in months. Cheever plucked it out of the piles of backed-up mail and read it greedily: "He hinted at the indifference of his marriage and hinted—no more—at his love for me." This changed everything. All at once Cheever decided his life had been a sham ("a competent performance but a performance is always lacking"): He was *gay*, by God, and happy to say so for the moment, at least, in his journal. He promptly arranged a tryst in Saratoga for the following week, and called Max "twice a day" in the meantime to declare his love, unbothered by any trace of objectivity as to the young man's motives. As Max remembered:

> I would try to buy myself time and clarity periodically by procrastinating in answering his letters and phone calls and by putting off any visits for as long as I thought I could get away with. This was true particularly for the period after my marriage. But it always got

to where I believed I'd pushed him off dangerously long, long enough to where he would get fed up, end things, and do what he could to punish me.* . . . I knew that when I wrote the letter [in January] that he would want to see me, and that I was out of reasons for putting him off. . . . He arranged the rendezvous in Saratoga and I went.

The visit was something of a milestone for Cheever, to whom the greatest taboo about sleeping with a man had always been the actual *sleeping* with him: back-slapping friends might "get their rocks off" together, but only true homosexuals woke up in one another's arms. This time, however, he crossed the Rubicon. "After spending a night contentedly with you and your cock," he wrote Max afterward, "I expected to gain two hundred pounds, to make sucking sounds with my mouth when I asked for the pepper at breakfast and to invest in a yellow wig. . . . We must part, of course, but I think our parting will be as natural and easy as our meeting was." Cheever was, in fact, relieved to find that he and Max were "quite simply friends" in the morning, but (as he feared) there *had* been a certain awkwardness about finding himself in bed with a man—that is, once he'd gotten his rocks off. Waking in the middle of the night, Cheever had observed Max drinking whiskey and watching a bad movie, and had to admit that the young man was "far from a figure of any interest" at that moment. He tried to bear this in mind whenever he repeated the mantra—again and again in years to come—*We must part:* they were married men, after all, and at bottom Cheever had little desire to confess such an affair to the world.

On the other hand: he was still plagued with "capricious erections" and, without Max, what was an old man to do? "There are the matter-of-fact problems of my loneliness and my punctual accruals of semen that must be discharged," Cheever mused. "These seem as simple as the problems of a car, stuck in deep snow. One gets a shovel." On balance, then, he decided to postpone any sort of definitive valediction; when the time was right, surely Max himself would say something, and for now they were simply friends who helped each other. "Neither of us is homosexual and yet neither of us are foolish enough to worry about the matter," he wrote his friend reassuringly. "If I want your

---

*That is, by harming Max's writing career in some way, though it seems doubtful Cheever would have done anything worse than decline to help Max further.

cock or your mouth I know I have only to ask and yet I know there is so much better for you in life than my love that I can think of parting from you without pain. This, of course drives my cock up the wall." And how did Max feel? "Filthy and repulsed and bewildered and mortified and with no sense of reality for what I'd had to do and filled with his bullshit about how happy this all was," he recalled. "I always felt relieved, too, that it was over. The sense of having reset the clock . . . I could start from zero again in racking up time away from him until it came due again."

So Max went back to Oswego, while Cheever lingered in Saratoga for a few weeks, brooding about things ("And so what I seem to be afraid of is the voice of the world. . . . 'Have you heard? Old Cheever, crowding seventy, has gone Gay. Old Cheever has come out of the closet. Old Cheever has run off to Bessarabia with a hairy youth half his age' "). Every afternoon, he and Anne Palamountain—the Skidmore president's wife—would go skiing at the state park, and on Sunday they attended early services at Bethesda Episcopal and then had breakfast at the Gideon Putnam. "Every woman needs a man who's a friend she can tell *anything* to," said Palamountain, and Cheever was such a friend to her. This, however, did not work both ways. Once, when Cheever suggested that two of her other men friends—a dance critic and his athletic companion—were a couple, she answered as follows (so he reported to Max): " 'That,' Anne said sternly, 'is a purely platonic friendship. If it were anything else I would not entertain them.' " Therefore Cheever told the woman funny stories and kept his brooding to himself. Later she learned of his bisexuality and felt "terribly guilty" when she remembered how "troubled" he'd often seemed: "But we never discussed it, or else I was too obtuse to pick up on his hints."

CHEEVER WAS AT LOOSE ENDS in his work, too. The only matter that seemed "urgent" enough to write about was his own bewildering alienation, so he clipped newspaper articles about the possibility of life on other planets ("WATER DETECTED OUTSIDE EARTH'S GALAXY") and vaguely considered writing a novel about "cosmic loneliness." But his main project was a teleplay titled, tentatively, *The Hounds of Shady Hill.* In December he'd had lunch with Jac Venza, an executive producer at New York's public TV station WNET, who wanted Cheever to adapt three of his stories for television; Cheever had no objection to other writers' adapting his stories, but the only project that he personally wanted to pursue "as a lark" (larky as opposed to lucrative, since he'd only be paid Writers Guild minimum) was an original teleplay. As luck would have it, Venza thought this perfect for their projected series, *American Playhouse*, which would feature original works by American writers—a riposte to those who thought public television "[spoke] only with a British accent." Cheever had long toyed with the genre, from his Signal Corps days to his abortive work on *Life with Father* and even *The Rules of the Game*, and now there was a rather compelling personal reason as well: he wanted to collaborate with Hope Lange, which just might add a spark to their tired affair and reinvigorate his interest in the "procreative world." "I'm really working on the WNET show in which you play all the parts," he wrote Hope in April. "I really want to write a smashing show within the confines of traditional TV and I also want to work with you." So that, at least, was something to look forward to.

Meanwhile his literary life seemed disproportionately concerned with applauding the successes of Saul Bellow. On his return from Saratoga in late February, Cheever presented Bellow with the Gold Medal of Honor from the National Arts Club—only nine months after he'd presented Bellow with the Gold Medal for Fiction from the Academy of Arts and Letters. Bellow, of course, was the living author Cheever most admired (as he'd recently reiterated in the *Times*), all the more so since *Humboldt's Gift:* "Saul's genius is inestimable," Cheever had reflected while reading the novel. "With Saul on the team the game is real and the stakes are not self-aggrandizement . . . fame and wealth." So naturally it was a pleasure to see genius rewarded, especially given Cheever's personal fondness for the genius in question, though the Nobel Prize was perhaps too much of a good thing. On the bleak autumn day when Bellow was named the winner, Cheever took a dejected walk with Gurganus through Central Park, starting a little when they came to the statue of the nineteenth-century explorer Alexander von Humboldt: "Oh my God!" he said. "They're already putting up statues!" But once his initial dismay had passed, he gladly conceded the "exemplary and tireless grace" Bellow had shown as laureate*—this while presenting that first gold medal in 1977, an occasion

---

*Bellow's grace was such that he'd mentioned a number of other American writers who were also "acceptable" candidates: Mailer, Ellison, Wright Morris, and Cheever.

he remembered when presenting the second in 1978: "Saul was in Jerusalem and the medal was accepted by Tom Guinzburg, his publisher, and was, I like to think, the first time in the history of literature in which a writer has enthusiastically given a publisher a piece of negotiable gold."

That same year—that same month, in fact (February 1978)—Cheever had been passed over for the Academy's Gold Medal in the Short Story, a decision that Cowley protested as "outrageous": Cheever was the "best short-story writer" in the country, he wrote the committee, whereas, of the three writers nominated—Updike, Peter Taylor (the eventual winner), and Mary McCarthy—the last wasn't even "essentially a short-story writer." Cowley was subsequently informed that, as a matter of fact, Cheever had been suggested by every member of the committee; however, since he'd already received the Howells Medal, it "was mentioned" (passive voice) that perhaps they should "spread the honors around." Cowley was emphatically unpersuaded, pointing out that at least three previous Gold Medal winners—Faulkner, Cather, and Welty—had also received the Howells Medal. Finally it fell to Cheever himself to enlighten his old friend:

> The difficulty may be with Bill Maxwell who, having put me above Updike for years, now feels that I have had more than my share of everything and should be rebuked. It doesn't matter to me at all. . . . I gave a reading last night that included THE SWIMMER and I would much sooner have written that story—without a gold medal—than anything that has so far been accomplished by my dear friend Updike.

The difficulty had indeed been with Maxwell, and the motive was rather dubious, as he later admitted ("This has remained somewhat on my conscience"). He explained the matter as follows: While vacationing on Cape Cod during the summer of 1977—that is, a few months before he met with the nominating committee—Maxwell had been contacted by a *Times* reporter, Jesse Kornbluth, who was writing an article on Cheever. "I put [Kornbluth] off until I had called John to find out how he felt," Maxwell remembered. Cheever professed to take a dim view, and therefore Maxwell declined to be interviewed. When the article appeared, however, Maxwell was furious to learn that

Cheever himself had cooperated fully with Kornbluth—telling the infamous Telephone Story (about which more below) in the bargain, and making Maxwell (as he later put it) "look like a heel": "I thought, Why should I go on furthering John's career when he tells these whoppers about me?"

One can well imagine Maxwell's anger over the Telephone Story. After all, it was primarily Maxwell who had first seen to it, forty years earlier, that Cheever's work appeared regularly in *The New Yorker*; it was Maxwell who had insisted that *The Wapshot Chronicle* receive the National Book Award; it was Maxwell who had brought yellow roses to Cheever's bedside when he was ill, who had rarely failed to give heartening advice and encouragement when it was most crucially needed, and who *did* believe, incidentally, that Cheever was the best American short-story writer. All that said, however: the invidious Kornbluth article ("The Cheever Chronicle") did not appear in the *Times Magazine* until October 21, 1979—almost two years *after* Maxwell suggested that the Gold Medal nominating committee "spread the honors around." In other words, it is more accurate to say that Cheever's Telephone Story was in reprisal for the Gold Medal imbroglio (to say nothing of Cheever's suspicion that Maxwell had colluded in screwing him financially for many years) than vice versa.

At any rate, herewith the Telephone Story, which was based—*very* loosely—on the occasion when Cheever had asked Maxwell for a raise in December 1963.* As Cheever related to Kornbluth (my own comments appear in brackets):

> "I recall . . . that at the time of my first novel, *The Wapshot Chronicle* [actually a few months after he completed the *Scandal*], I had no money, I had holes in my shoes, it was raining [snowing?], and I was coming down with a cold. I had published nine stories in *The New Yorker* that year [circa the *Chronicle*, Cheever published five *New Yorker* stories in 1956, one in 1957; he published five in 1963, when the incident actually took place], and they had won every prize you can get [?]. . . . So I went to *The New Yorker* and said, "What will you give me for a piece of the book?" [By the "book" he presumably means the *Chronicle*—several installments of which Maxwell enthusiastically accepted for the magazine—but in any case that wasn't

---

*See pages 318–21.

the vital issue in 1963.] . . . Bill Maxwell said, "I can't tell you." I said, "I can't work that way." He said, "All right, I'll tell you," and he made me an offer of, I think, $2,000. And I said, "Bill, I can get more." "There's the phone," he said [well-meaningly, as Maxwell would have it]. "Try." I said, "How uncivil," and I went downstairs and called my agent.

"She phoned me in the morning [she phoned him a few minutes later, via a pay phone on the street] and said, "I've tried one magazine, *The Saturday Evening Post*, and they've offered $25,000 [$24,000 for a first-look agreement and a minimum of four stories a year, *not* for a "piece" of *The Wapshot Chronicle*]. Should I try somebody else?" And I said, "No, let's rest on that." It was terribly funny, because *The New Yorker* called and asked if, by chance, anyone had offered more money [actually Cheever had promptly returned to Maxwell's office and informed him of the *Post* offer, whereupon Shawn and Hawley Truax were summoned to remonstrate with him]. I said someone had, so they gave their counteroffer, which was a key to the men's room and all the bread and cheese I could eat [not exactly]. And I said, "Well, what the hell, I'll stay with *The New Yorker* [true]."

Apart from the vindictive element, it's possible Cheever had gotten on a raconteurish roll and simply told the story for laughs, the way he usually told stories—for the sake of entertainment rather than posterity—and, for what it's worth, Cheever himself was *furious* about the Kornbluth article. But anyway the damage was done: Maxwell and he stopped talking, and a number of mutual friends took Maxwell's side (Newhouse, for instance [rather happily for Cheever, perhaps], no longer made himself available for lunch). And yet it bears repeating that Maxwell had blocked his friend's Gold Medal some two years *before* the Telephone Story—and really, taken altogether, it was neither man's finest hour.

To a remarkable degree for a writer of his reputation, Cheever was still ignored by academia, and so he'd been rather excited to learn that Dennis Coates had returned to the States, at last, to defend his dissertation—the first book-length study focusing exclusively on Cheever's novels. Coates's approach had changed drastically, however, as a direct result of that episode in the woods four years earlier, which had led to an epiphany of sorts: "I thought, 'Oh my God, I've got to go back and reread all the books and really *get* it this time' . . . and there it was! It was all there. So that really allowed me to put the thing in perspective for the dissertation." The "thing" was Cheever's bisexuality, which for Coates had become a sort of skeleton key unlocking the real meaning of Cheever's work. "My life has always been an open book," the latter calmly replied, perhaps failing to consider the full implications when Coates mentioned his discovery. In any event, after receiving his Ph.D. from Duke that spring, Coates eagerly mailed his subject a copy of the dissertation—which began by boasting its author's "knowledge of John Cheever, the flesh and blood person," followed by a long biographical profile that proved as much. "I read Denny's dissertation," Cheever wanly noted, "in which he concludes that I was, as a child, a tubercular shut-in with a manly brother. In order to conceal my homosexuality I married, made my wife miserable and bitter and finally rose to greatness in my last novel by admitting my love for cock."

This précis is simplistic, but not inaccurate. Having made the point that the protagonist of each novel is "overtly modeled on the author," Coates invites the reader to consider the "oddity" of the "homosexuality theme," insofar as it "often surfaces without the benefit of a clear connection to what may otherwise be a fairly coherent creation. . . . Inevitably, explanations of these problems lead to revelations about the novelist himself." And that's not all: "This idiosyncrasy [i.e., the homosexuality theme] is closely related to what . . . appears to be the author's misogyny. . . . It is likely that this perspective is based on personal experience. Indeed, it accounts for the tenderness and humanity with which Cheever develops the homosexuality theme." So it goes for a couple hundred pages, more or less. Given what must have been his mounting, ineffable horror, Cheever's reply to Coates was impressively temperate: "My congratulations on having completed such a difficult task. I do find it particularly distressing when censure is involved in an assessment of my work and my life. You copiously quote from a man who obviously gets a stick prick at a blade of grass and you conclude that this has destroyed the women around him. I can't agree." Coates was mystified by what appeared to be a somewhat hostile reaction ("an open book"?), and promptly gave his favorite writer and good friend a call—but Cheever was "cold," and soon hung up.*

All this might have been very depressing indeed, had it not coincided with a far happier development in the academic world: namely, the announcement that Cheever would receive an honorary Doctor of Letters degree at Harvard's 327th commencement exercise in June. As Cheever wrote in his journal (possibly drafting remarks for the press), "To have been expelled from Thayer Academy for smoking and then to have been given an honorary degree from Harvard seems to me a crowning example of the inestimable opportunities of the world in which I live and in which I pray generations will continue to live." Of the many honors that would presently be lavished on Cheever, this was almost certainly the one he valued most: Harvard was the embodiment of Boston respectability, after all, a thing mocked and contemned and deeply coveted by Cheever, even more since that disastrous interlude at BU three years before.

On the great day, some fifteen thousand people gathered in the rain to hear Solzhenitsyn deliver a somber denunciation of the West (with its "revolting invasion of publicity . . . television stupor . . . intolerable music"). Since his name began with "C," however, Cheever was first in the procession of honorees—"Aleksandr brought up the rear"— including Bart Giamatti, Vernon Jordan, Jr., and Sir Seretse M. Khama, the president of Botswana ("a marvelous-looking man," said Mary Cheever). Hailed as "a master chronicler of his times," Cheever would have been almost perfectly happy, at least for the moment, if only there were someone who truly shared his happiness; but as he confessed to the Israeli president's wife ("a loving Russian"), he'd been "cold and hungry and lonely" in his life, and fully expected to be that way again. Mary had hardly spoken to him for weeks—practically the status quo by now—and she didn't say much in Cambridge, either, save the odd pleasantry for the sake of appearances.

Cheever's sense of utter destitution, despite his Harvard degree, was more than idle self-pity. Not only did he lack a sympathetic wife or lover, there really wasn't a soul on earth (except occasional strangers)

---

*Three years later, another scholar (R. G. Collins) happened to mention Coates's dissertation during a visit to Cedar Lane, whereupon his amiable host "flared up": "Oh he's totally discredited, he's not to be trusted at all! He went to see Fred, found him down and out, and got him to say a lot of lies . . ."

to whom he could confide his sorrows. Bill Maxwell and he were no longer friends, Denny had betrayed him, and Max had carefully distanced himself since that meeting in Saratoga. "Your letter was so circumspect and humorless that I haven't known how to reply," Cheever wrote Max in March, taken aback by what might have seemed a rather sudden lack of warmth. As for Hope Lange—never one for deep intimacies ("I don't really know you at all," Cheever had recently remarked)—she too was gone for the time being. One day that spring, she casually announced that she'd sublet her apartment and was leaving for the Coast in the morning. "What are you doing tonight?" Cheever had asked, concealing his slight chagrin. She was having dinner, she said, with the playwright Robert Anderson. "Robert Anderson wrote *Tea and Sympathy* years ago," said Cheever, "and has no other distinction."

CHAPTER FORTY-FIVE

{ 1978–1979 }

WITH THE SUCCESS of *Falconer,* many in the press wondered how it was possible that the short stories of (arguably) our finest living practitioner in the genre could be almost entirely out of print.* *Newsweek* called it "a scandal of American publishing," though Cheever himself was undismayed. He prided himself on not looking back, and when Gottlieb suggested they publish an omnibus collection, Cheever seemed puzzled. "Why do you want to do that?" he asked. "All those stories have already been published." But Gottlieb was certain the book would be a great success, and he was happy to take care of the whole thing: "I'll read every story you ever wrote," he said, "and I'll make a selection and show it to you, and any way you want to amend it will be fine with me." Cheever agreed, without much enthusiasm, though he expressly forbade the inclusion of anything from his despised first collection, *The Way Some People Live,* or, for that matter, anything previous to the stories collected in *The Enormous Radio.*†

Cheever's reluctance to live in the past—to save letters, to speak of painful memories except in the privacy of his journal, and so on—

---

*Technically *The World of Apples* was still in print, but almost impossible to find.

†Gottlieb's selection included every story published in the five previous collections, as well as two uncollected stories, "The Common Day" (1947) and "Another Story" (1967); he also included two stories from the 1956 *Stories* with Jean Stafford et al., omitting "The National Pastime." According to Gottlieb, Cheever's input was minimal: "My vague memory is that there may have been at the fewest one, and at the most three, stories that he wanted included and that I hadn't included."

included a profound reluctance to revisit his own work, an impulse he compared to "some intensely unhappy relationship with a mirror": "The work is done and to return to it seems idle in the strongest sense of the word—a demeaning sense of time squandered." Sometimes he claimed that he hadn't even bothered to read over Gottlieb's selection ("I would read three lines, and if they were all right . . ."), though in *Time* magazine he admitted that he had, in fact, overcome his usual aversion out of sheer curiosity: given the hundreds of stories he'd written in the past fifty years, he'd "totally forgotten some of them" and found reading them again a surprisingly pleasant experience. Indeed (as he wrote in his journal), he was occasionally "bewildered" by his own enthusiasm; while reading "The Day the Pig Fell into the Well," for example, he laughed out loud and finally began to cry ("I miss being interested in my work").

Gottlieb had suggested he write a preface, which proved a small masterpiece of shrewdness and charm. Rather apologetically, Cheever pointed out that the present volume had been arranged ("to the best of my memory") chronologically, and thus readers would have to endure the relative ineptitude of his early stories:

> The parturition of a writer, I think, unlike that of a painter, does not display any interesting alliances to his masters. In the growth of a writer one finds nothing like the early Jackson Pollock copies of the Sistine Chapel paintings with their interesting cross-references to Thomas Hart Benton. A writer can be seen clumsily learning to walk, to tie his necktie, to make love, and to eat his peas off a fork.

Nicely said, but of course the book opens with "Goodbye, My Brother"—one of Cheever's two or three greatest stories, written some twenty years after his first published effort and almost five years after the oldest piece in the collection ("The Sutton Place Story"); such "early" stories do not remotely entail the literary equivalent of learning to eat one's peas off a fork. Suffice to say, however, that if Cheever had seen fit to include work *prior* to 1946 (as opposed to destroying the evidence whenever possible), the reader might well have noted some "interesting alliances" to Hemingway, Chekhov, O'Hara, and Fitzgerald, to name a few. And though the mature Cheever had mostly assimilated his influences, there's a lingering trace of Fitzgerald, perhaps, in the most exquisite line of his preface: "These stories seem at times to be stories of a long-lost world when the city of New York was still filled with a river light, when you heard the Benny Goodman quartets from a radio in the corner stationery store, and when almost everybody wore a hat." In his little essay for *Atlantic Brief Lives*, Cheever had argued that Fitzgerald—far from being a dated relic of the twenties—was a "peerless historian" whose period details evoke the "excitement of being alive"; similarly, Cheever's reminder of a city bathed in "river light" conveys an entire epoch in a sort of magical amber.

The reception of *The Stories of John Cheever* was tantamount to a coronation, as reviewers seemed bent on topping each other's ecstatic, all but unstinting praise. Paul Gray of *Time* wrote that the book "chart[ed] one of the most important bodies of work in contemporary letters"; William McPherson opened his front-page review in the *Washington Post Book World* by declaring that "John Cheever's stories are, simply, the best." Such compliments seemed almost trifling, though, next to John Leonard's definitive proclamation in the daily *Times:* "It would be meaningless and impudent to commend one or another story in a volume that is not merely the publishing event of the 'season' but a grand occasion in English literature. For whatever the opinion is worth, John Cheever is my favorite writer." A number of Cheever's fellow fiction writers were likewise eager to give the master his due: "John Cheever is a magnificent storyteller," Anne Tyler wrote in *The New Republic*, "and this is a dazzling and powerful book"; "John Cheever is the best storyteller living," said John Irving in *Saturday Review*; and once again John Gardner (who'd extolled the merits of *Bullet Park* and *Falconer* as if to champion a great cause) chimed in, calling Cheever "the dean of the contemporary American short story."

Amid all the superlatives, Cheever proved elusive to reviewers trying to define his place "in the stream" (as he would say). Gardner, a brilliant analyst of literary craft, remarked on Cheever's "postmodernist experiments"—authorial intrusion, self-parody, etc.—by way of concluding that the "stories are realistic in the best sense of the word, anchoring the dream in the concrete example, nailing the reader to the page with ruthless attention to detail character by character, scene by scene." (One thinks of Cheever's advice to his Barnard student Judith Sherwin, the young woman who wanted to write magical realism: "put in a few signposts.") Cheever's virtuosity is such that one forgets how subtly the sense of a dream persists in his otherwise "realistic" fiction, or, as the case may be, how reality persists in the midst of a dream. "The Country Husband" and "O Youth and Beauty!" both adhere to the conventions of realism, more or less, though they involve a highly intrusive, lyrical narrator ("it is a night where kings in golden suits ride elephants over the mountains"; "Oh, those suburban Sunday nights, those Sunday-night blues!"), and slightly off-kilter details (a pilot singing "jolly sixpence" as his plane goes down; a man shot dead by his wife while he hurdles the furniture). No wonder the critic Robert Towers—who had remembered Cheever's work as "surrealistic and bizarrely plotted"—was startled to find that relatively few of his stories (the novels are another matter) could properly be classified as nonrealistic. "The Enormous Radio" and "Torch Song" are anomalous among the early stories, followed by a long period of essentially realistic work, until "The Death of Justina" and the increasingly bizarre stories of the mid-sixties—"The Swimmer," "The Ocean," "The Geometry of Love"—which began to disconcert *The New Yorker* until (as Cheever would have it) Barthelme found acceptance as "Shawn's chosen surrealist." But wait: "Although [Cheever] employs all manner of literary devices," said Richard Locke in the *Times Book Review*, "he writes for the most part as if Borges, Barth and Barthelme had never been born. He is a realist with the longings of a lyric poet and a wish for allegorical revelations." Perhaps, though one can't help wondering how Barth and Barthelme would have written if Cheever had never been born; at any rate, such a generalization suggests the bedeviling impulse on the part of critics (particularly academics) to find a writer's proper niche in the canon or "stream"—easily done in the case of Hemingway, Faulkner, Fitzgerald (never mind Barth and Barthelme), but not so much in Cheever's. Which may explain why posterity would eventually abandon his cause, at least for the present.

For the rest of his life, though, Cheever had the satisfaction of being duly canonized: he was "the dean of the contemporary American short story," after all, and had written a few beguiling (if problematic) novels as well. Moreover he was a best seller—a "money player," at last. "At the risk of sounding pious this is the first time a collection of short stories has been successful," he observed to a journalist. "I'm hoping the editors of periodicals will begin to regard the short story as a legitimate form of expression."

UP TO A POINT, Cheever seemed to enjoy the acclaim and keep it somewhat in perspective. "There are a few PR demands on my time," he wrote Weaver. "Yesterday afternoon Mrs. Vincent Astor sucked my cock in Caldors window for the benefit of the New York Women's Infirmary and afterwards I autographed copies of the collection." While *The Stories of John Cheever* was dominating best-seller lists (its striking red cover and giant signature "C" an almost ubiquitous sight among the reasonably literate), Gottlieb gave the author a gala dinner at Lutèce, where Cheever found himself sitting between Lauren Bacall and Maria Tucci (Gottlieb's wife)—"bask[ing]," as he wrote Max, "in that fragrance of beaver we both so enjoy" ("I sit between two lovely women," he wrote in his journal, "[and] think about my chum"). Bacall had kept an office at Knopf while working on her memoirs, and one day Cheever came in and flirted with her for half an hour or so. "He had an easy time talking to women and was good at it," Bacall remembered, though any sort of sexual charge was, for her, somewhat vitiated by his "debutante accent." Still, he was under the impression that the actress was "madly in love with him," according to Mary Cheever, whom he left at home when Bacall invited him to a party at her Manhattan apartment. "I think Betty [Bacall] has got me mixed up with the late Adlai Stevenson," he wrote his daughter afterward. "Why else would she keep sticking her tongue in my ear?" (Privately, he observed that Bacall had a "fourth-rate Bonnard over the sofa and—you guessed it—a large and ghastly Picasso over the mantlepiece.") Bacall was also on hand to celebrate when Cheever won the National Book Critics Circle Award in January 1979 (beating out Irving's *The World According to Garp* and, better yet, Updike's *The Coup*)—one of a multitude, said Cheever, who'd vied for his favors that day: "I was kissed by both Mary Gordon [another nominee for *Final Payments*] and John Irving and John Updike telephoned from Georgetown," he wrote Susan. "Your mother, of course, thought that GARP should have won. My humble remarks were greeted with an affectionate standing ovation and after having been kissed by about three hundred women and autographing things like deposit slips and shirt-tails your mother and I made our way, by spacious limousine, to 21 where there was a dinner for sixty in The Hunt Room, served by about eighty waiters. . . . Betty Bacall ate my right ear."

Cheever was more active than ever in public duties, becoming vice president of Yaddo and secretary of the American Academy and Institute of Arts and Letters (as it was now called), for which he also served a third term as chairman of the grants committee. It may have been the whole *noblesse* aspect of Academy work that appealed most, since for many years he'd been bored by his aging colleagues (a "death watch") and had skipped the various dinners and luncheons whenever possible. Formal meetings were an even more terrible crucible, during which Cheever would chain-smoke and suppress groans of impatience ("He might go into the men's room and jerk off. He just might"). Worst of all were the hundred or more novels he was supposed to read as chairman of the grants committee—autobiographical first works, mostly, in which the characters occupy themselves (as Cheever put it) with "wiping the steam off a windowpane and wondering what is the meaning of it all." Had he lived longer, anyway, it seems safe to say he would never again have served on the grants committee. "I suspect that my tastes, with old age, have become parochial and cranky," he wrote his colleagues that year. "I have, for example, just completed a book called BIRDY. This is about a demented man who would like to fly. My passion for gravity seems to have increased with age and I am constitutionally disinterested in a weightless life. . . . Considering the general mediocrity of the year I suppose we should honor John Irving for GARP." But despite his weariness with middling fiction (with, more and more, fiction in general), Cheever valued the good opinion of his peers and was mindful of their common predicament—so much so, indeed, that he could scarcely read an acquaintance's book without pausing every so often to "try and compose an observation that will be truthful and encouraging." After finishing *The Professor of Desire* (1977), for example, he wrote Philip Roth as follows: "[In 1959] I first read a paragraph or two of yours and came into the house shouting to Mary that Roth—whoever he was—had the most compelling voice I had encountered in years. I don't mean style; I mean voice—something that begins at around the back of the knees and reaches well above the head . . ." Roth was so impressed with the compliment that he attributed it, almost word for word, to E. I. Lonoff—the revered mentor of Nathan Zuckerman—in his subsequent novel *The Ghost Writer* (1979).

As one might have guessed, Cheever's celebrity did not have an ameliorative effect on his marriage. Some thought Mary got tired of (among other things) the frequent press attention—the photographers coming out to Ossining to take pictures of her husband splitting wood or sitting on top of a (rented) horse, the better to bolster his image as a Westchester squire. Then, too, Cheever was hardly averse to reminding her that the *world*, at least, seemed to love him. Even academics were beginning to churn out the odd monograph. As Cheever recorded, "A book comes, of which I'm the subject, and Mary says, 'People write those books for practically nothing.' " She also seemed rather deflating on the subject of Cheever's relative wealth. When he mentioned that he would bank half a million dollars before taxes that year, she suggested they sit down at the kitchen table and discuss giving the money away to a worthy cause ("We have never sat at the kitchen table," he mused, "she hasn't spoken to me for weeks"). He was nothing if not generous when he was flush: one of his first major purchases with the *Stories* windfall was a Blackglama mink for his wife— she picked it out at Bonwit's that October—though by Thanksgiving the goodwill had already evaporated. The Thaws came for the feast that year (along with Philip Schultz), and were struck by an almost paralyzing tension in the air. When Cheever said grace, Clare recalled, he muttered "on and on": "maybe [because] he could *talk* and didn't have to get down to the tension of sitting and eating. We got through it."

Christmas was better for the simple reason that Federico came home from Stanford. "The equilibrium that Fred brings to this establishment is inestimable," Cheever wrote. "[W]ith Fred here the enigmatic aspects of my life seem to be no more than shadows I have always hoped them to be." Nor could he fail to notice that Mary was transformed in their son's presence, chatting at table with perfect ease after so long a frost ("I glimpse how difficult I am for her as a husband"). Amid the largesse that Cheever freely bestowed at the time—cars, televisions, minks (one for Hope, too)—was a brand-new BMW 320i for Federico, this because the young man's girlfriend had dumped him with the words "Grow up and get a car!" "He is a most judicious, loving and comely young man," Cheever wrote that Christmas, while noting further that he (Cheever) had just given Bathsheba (the dog) "her check for $50,000."

In fact, relations had vastly improved with all his children, who had turned out miraculously well: Ben was rising in the ranks at *Reader's Digest* and running marathons; Susan had gone to France to work on her first novel. "My enthusiasm for you three is boundless," Cheever wrote her that autumn (signing himself "Yours, John"). He was especially pleased that Susan had finally broken up with Warren Hinckle. Two years before, when *Newsweek* was about to transfer Susan to San Francisco so she could marry Hinckle (who'd "sort of left his wife" but was still living with her), Cheever had invited his daughter to join him for a luncheon at the Ettlingers' house in Rockland County. "What do you think of Tad?" he asked afterward, referring to the elegant older man whose name she hadn't caught. When he told her that "Tad" was Calvin Tomkins, the notable *New Yorker* writer, Susan's "jaw dropped": not only was she a "huge fan" of Tomkins, but she'd once spoken to him at length on the telephone, when she interviewed him for a magazine piece on Buckminster Fuller. And so, while Susan renewed her acquaintance with Tomkins, Cheever "did some sleuthing" on her behalf—asking Ettlinger about the status of Tomkins's marriage (not so good). Things progressed nicely, and finally, in the summer of 1978, Susan took her father to lunch at Four Seasons and announced that she was quitting *Newsweek* and moving to France with Tomkins to write her novel; meanwhile she needed her parents to take care of Bathsheba, the dog. "And he said 'okay,' " she remembered, "and I felt it was him giving me his blessing, because running off to France was kind of a harebrained adventure. I had a really good job at *Newsweek*, and my father loved the fact that I had that job. But he was just thrilled." France and Tomkins, after all, were not San Francisco and Hinckle.

Cheever was, at first, less than thrilled by Susan's literary ambitions. There were the obvious reasons—it was a tough life, lonely and often impecunious—and reasons that were somewhat harder to express. One way to put it, perhaps, was that Cheever regarded himself as the rare sort of writer who communed with an actual muse, and anyone else presuming to do so was "throwing up a clay pigeon," said Ben, who'd once shown his father a story that his fifth-grade teacher had considered wonderful. "It's in the first person," Cheever remarked, "and you have to *earn* the right to write in the first person." Also, as Federico pointed out, their father's talent "emanated from the conflict in his soul, and it really isn't anything he would have wished on anyone else." So he'd discouraged his children from being writers, but, whatever he might have said, the actual example he set was rather compelling. "One gift I got from my father," said Susan, "was the lesson that writing was something you can *do*." Almost every morning of his adult life, Cheever had eaten breakfast and then gone to a room and typed for a while; in Scarborough he'd occupied a room next to Susan's, and sometimes her hamsters would escape and nibble his ankles. "Writing," his daughter concluded, "was something he did between rescuing hamsters and picking you up at school."

While she was in France, Cheever sent her a clipping from a local paper in which he was quoted (alongside a photo of himself in a dinner jacket) as plugging her forthcoming novel: "But she doesn't have to read mine," he'd added, "so I don't have to read hers." In fact, Cheever was eager to read his daughter's novel—for a number of reasons—though it was a pretty circumspect business on both sides. "I never showed my father anything I had written until it had been bought by a publishing house and was in final manuscript form," she remembered. "I didn't ask for help, and he didn't offer it. When he did read my novels, he was polite but perfunctory. 'I liked it very much,' he would say, or 'I thought it was fine.' " Whatever else he might have thought, Cheever was gratified to learn that her protagonist's father was a Columbia professor who'd written a study of Gide, and *not* (as he put it) "an old man who is too drunk to dance the Charleston." He'd remarked to a friend that he was aghast at the prospect of her writing a sort of *Daddy Dearest* roman-à-clef, and when this proved not to be the case, he underlined the point in a puff piece for *New York* magazine, "My Daughter, The Novelist": "We have both agreed that fiction is not crypto-autobiography. . . . The father of the heroine in her splendid novel, *Looking for Work*, parts his hair in the middle. I wouldn't be seen dead with a center part." Moreover—*pace* his caveats about being a writer—he noted that her career choice "seemed to prove that in some ways [he] enjoyed her esteem. One couldn't ask for more."

Particularly in the last couple of years, he'd also made an effort to win back the esteem of his older son, and to that end (once Susan and Tomkins had returned from France in the spring) Cheever invited the whole family to stay at the Ritz and watch Ben run in the Boston Marathon. Since it was Patriots' Day, April 16, they attended a re-enactment of Lexington and Concord, and later jostled among the crowd on Boylston Street trying to get close to the finish line—but it was hard to see much, and the day was chilly, so Cheever announced that he was heading back to the hotel. His daughter remembered watching him go: "As I look at his back in my mind's eye, I think, 'There was something *expectant* about the way he left the race.' " Ben, for his part, had already crossed the finish line and gone back to the Ritz, where a stack of messages was waiting from the *New York Times*, the *Boston Globe*, even the Quincy *Patriot Ledger*. He was soaking in a hot tub when Cheever stuck his head in the door: "You finished the marathon?" he asked. Ben nodded: "And you won the Pulitzer Prize."

The family assembled afterward in the Ritz dining room, where the chef produced an enormous blazing Baked Alaska. Cheever, chatting with reporters, was careful to mention his son's achievement as well as his own: "Ben finished the Marathon in under three hours and I won what is perhaps literature's most cherished prize. It was a day for athletic-esthetic celebration." To a *Patriot Ledger* reporter, however, he said what was perhaps foremost on his mind: "I never believed in my childhood days in Quincy that I would be sitting here as a fresh Pulitzer Prize winner." But there he was.

CHEEVER STILL AWOKE most mornings with an awful *cafard*, and—given so many happy things in his life—he couldn't help wondering whether his constant smoking had something to do with it. Since adolescence he'd smoked two or three packs of Marlboros a day, and before that he'd smoked cedar bark rolled in toilet paper ("smoking meant joining the company of robust men"). The first thing he did at his desk each day was light a cigarette, and indeed it was almost impossible to imagine working except in a cloud of smoke. Past efforts to quit had been unavailing. Twenty years before, he'd recorded holding off until noon or so, but, as he put it, his head kept "leaving [his] neck" and floating away ("I always catch it before it goes off towards the railroad tracks but it is disconcerting"). Such was his intense craving that Cheever wondered whether he was "requit[ing]" some erotic need, a notion that once led to his writing a story about a man who gives up smoking and goes mad, attacking a woman he mistakes for a Lucky Strike.*

In March, Cheever began attending SmokEnder meetings with a lot of frumpy matrons ("Helen Hokinson ladies") in White Plains: "[S]itting on a folding chair," he wrote, "a woman of little intelligence, charm or information says: Reward yourself. Make a trip to the five and dime. Reserve a best-seller at the public library. Buy yourself a rose." Cheever persevered withal: as instructed, he counted the butts in his ashtray each day, and tried distracting himself with long walks and train rides. It took about a month or so, but a few days after winning the Pulitzer (and two weeks after celebrating his fourth year of sobriety), Cheever was smoke-free. "[T]his has involved some serious

---

*Originally published in *The New Yorker* (March 7, 1964) as "The Habit," it appears in *The Stories of John Cheever* as the last of four sketches in "Metamorphoses."

redistribution of energies," he wrote Max. "It is very difficult to work, I have a hardon all the time and I keep losing my temper."

His *cafard* persisted as well, which he supposed had more to do with loneliness than nicotine after all. Back in November he'd finally wangled a trip to Oswego as a visiting writer ("Everybody at college was amazed that I was able to score a writer of Cheever's caliber," Max ruefully recalled), after which Max had written him a pointed letter about "the thrills of his wedding anniversary": "I am, quite plainly, the supplicant and I find the role self-destructive," Cheever brooded in his journal (where he'd begun referring to Max as "Rip Procrustes," by way of suggesting the latter's adaptability). In his own letters Cheever insinuated that he himself was hardly chopped liver: his was the world of "acclaim and substance," he was desired by famous actresses (plural), and yet for all that he remained enamored of some ex-Mormon nobody in Oswego. "On Friday I did an ABC tape on the American Male," he reported to Max in January. " 'In my long life,' I said, 'I have seen nothing more beautiful, splendid and mysterious than demureness in a woman.' The script girl blushed and asked if I was busy for lunch. I was. I bought Hope a $55 lunch and when she said goodbye to me, on her doorstep, I remembered how splendidly you grasp my loneliness." The key phrase was *on her doorstep*, as Hope failed to grasp his loneliness the way Max did. These days, when lunch was over, she always had to rush off somewhere—to exercise class, a rehearsal, the airport, anything to avoid grasping his loneliness. And while eating at those tony restaurants, Cheever wondered if other diners guessed at the sterility of their affair: "I am not ardent and I think I might appear to someone at another table as an aging homosexual, dedicated to some wayward asshole, but determined to appear straight," he noted after that fifty-five-dollar lunch. "I am lonely and lost."

A few days later, he phoned Ned Rorem and said he needed to see him as soon as possible, since Rorem was the "only homosexual" he knew in New York. Rorem invited him to lunch, but also cautiously asked his longtime partner—a thirty-nine-year-old musician named Jim Holmes—to be present. Cheever arrived early, stepped inside the door and dropped his pants, protesting his loneliness as he chased Rorem around the apartment. "Please come out!" he cried, when Rorem locked himself in the bathroom. "I'll be good!" At length Rorem sat warily on a sofa with Cheever (pants still down), until Holmes arrived— at which moment, said Rorem, "John forgot about me for the rest of his life." Over lunch they discussed their guest's loneliness, and afterward Cheever asked Holmes to sit and hold him a while. The next morning he phoned Rorem: would Ned mind terribly if he gave Jim a call? "[He] asks not one question about my relationship to JH," Rorem mused in his diary. "Suppose I went to his house and made passes at his spouse while at table with them both?"

As it happened, Holmes was also depressed at the time: for twelve years he'd been eclipsed by his lover's achievements, and it was gratifying to be needed by an even more famous artist, whom he found charming besides—albeit in a "childlike" way, said Rorem. "JH, with the air of Florence Nightingale tending the wounded, has seen John often, and found tranquility therein, the way maniacs are said to find tranquility as babysitters." The two met at various posh hotels ("I like to remember that we have made love in The Drake, the Plaza and the Hilton," Cheever wrote Holmes, "and I would like to feel your gentle hands on my cock in a hundred more hotels"), and as a result Cheever noted a vast improvement in his general outlook. But Rorem took a dim view. One day Cheever was visiting the Academy when he noticed the secretary chatting with Rorem on the phone, whereupon Cheever asked to say hello to his old friend: "We must have words together," Rorem said balefully. Cheever hoped to avoid even speculating on such a conversation, and really had to admit that parting with Holmes would be little more than a "physical inconvenience." But who needed the inconvenience? "That the pleasure I take in Jim's company should in any way seem destructive is to me unimaginable," he wrote Rorem. "I know how long your association has been and I can only imagine the depth of your love but I think that neither Jim nor I are inclined to challenge this."

The beginning of the end came, in any event, when Holmes manifested his "lack of maleness" by commenting on the upholstery of a given hotel's furniture ("Suddenly an abyss opens between them"). Since, however, the affair had provided Cheever with a crucial degree of equanimity where Max was concerned, he tried for a while to mold Holmes into a more pleasing form: "I think I am not particularly susceptible to the beauty of men," he wrote Holmes, "but I love your smile because I know it to be genuine and your eyes because I think them level and manly"; as for the paramount purpose of "large orgasims" [sic], they served to "put a man's feet back on the stern path we know life to be." Cheever also mentioned how much he enjoyed things like boxing matches in White Plains, which he attended once a month with members of the Friday Club. But it was no good. Whatever Max's shortcomings, at least he could "pass a football and catch a fish," whereas Cheever wondered whether Holmes could even ride a bicycle. And yet Max hardly answered his letters or phone calls anymore. "I am an old, old king in love with a silly creature who keeps the pigs clean," Cheever lamented.

CHAPTER FORTY-SIX

{ *1979* }

CHEEVER HAD COME A LONG WAY from the eleven-year-old boy who'd promised his proud Yankee parents never to seek fame or wealth in his literary career. His new agent, Lynn Nesbit, had negotiated a half-million-dollar advance on his next novel, and Cheever had invested much of the proceeds in short-term, tax-free municipal bonds—enchanted by the idea of making money without lifting a finger. "It would be a lie to say that I am disinterested in fame and wealth—I ardently desire both," he'd admitted in his journal after finishing *Falconer*. But then, really, the giddy pleasure he took in the accoutrements was more endearing than not. He adored riding in limousines, a mink-coated wife at his side, and would unabashedly exclaim over the splendors of a fine hotel ("this is the first time I've ever had a view of the park, you know, the first time," he told a *Washington Post* reporter while leaning "happily" out his window at the Plaza).

It was also characteristic of the sober, somewhat frail Cheever to be intimidated by certain high-powered public situations. When Susan had a book party at Elaine's for her first novel, she insisted that Elaine stand out on the street and make sure her father didn't just peek into the window and bolt; once he'd been drawn inside, he promptly glommed onto his old friend and Harper editor, Frances Lindley, with whom he could just sit and be Joey. "Some people seem to have a gift for public personality and I just don't have it," said the man who—in *some* respects—never quite got used to himself as a famous person. Almost anyone who wanted to visit Cheever was welcome (however grudgingly), and in his last years, at least, he would give readings or

signings for whosoever happened to ask. Also, the fact that he imper-
sonated the gentry even more blatantly than O'Hara or Marquand
was, on some level, rather playful: he was capable of laughing about the
horses he rented for PR purposes, the conspicuous brace of faithful
retrievers, the indefatigable scything and firewood-splitting and so
forth, while at the same time it was nothing less than the consummation of his fondest dream. Naturally he jumped at the chance to
be featured in a Rolex advertisement—*very* pleased that his name
was associated with top-drawer merchandise—after which he could
scarcely resist taking off his six-thousand-dollar Oyster Perpetual Superlative Chronometer and asking a friend ("Feel this!") to consider its
luxurious heft. Even better was being recognized on the street by deferential strangers—not simply as some run-of-the-mill *actor*, say, but
as the Pulitzer Prize–winning Dean of the American Short Story, who
moreover happened to be the same friendly-looking regular guy who
appeared in the jacket photos. "As his fame increased," his daughter
noticed, "he developed another smile for cameras and people he didn't
especially want to talk to. This smile left out his eyes and involved
exposing his lower teeth. He had a kind of tense *heh, heh, heh* laugh that
went with it."

For the most part he became a lot more pompous. In an earlier
phase of his fame—circa the 1964 *Time* cover, for instance—Cheever
had usually been willing to mock his own pretensions, whereas the
later Cheever often seemed to forget that the whole Elegant Paragon
of Literature thing was something of a pose. "There are people who
consider me, now that I'm sober, to be much more of a bore than I ever
was falling down," he observed in 1981, and among those who considered him thus were, first and foremost, his family. "He really was boring and insufferable," said Federico, who loved him dearly. "Because
he's thinking, like, gosh, he's arrived, he's made it. The first thing you
have to keep in mind is, he's a drunk who doesn't drink anymore. They
try to enjoy their lives. What does that mean? When you're a musician, people can ask you to play, and when you're a movie star, people
can ask for your autograph, but what does it mean to be a famous
writer? Well, you get to say pompous things. You get to talk about aesthetics and things like that. That's the goodies you get."

Cheever made the most of his goodies. In later years he deployed
his minimal French not only in referring to literary classics (*Le Rouge et
le noir*) but also, to the greatest extent possible, in everyday speech, as

when he'd mention an art opening ("I'm going to Peter's *vernissage*"). "I've never been any great shakes as a thinker," he'd frankly admitted to an admirer in 1967, and for most of his life he combined a distaste for intellectual cant with only a slight, wistful insistence that he be taken seriously as an intellectual in his own right. True, he'd never finished high school, but nonetheless he'd become one of the world's great writers, and naturally he wanted people to appreciate the fact that he'd attained a kind of eclectic erudition. But fame blurred discretion, and more and more Cheever's reach exceeded his grasp. "I've been reading Wordsworth's preludes," he remarked to Lehmann-Haupt (who could have sworn there was only one *Prelude*), and while riding home from Liz Updike's wedding with an acclaimed Whitman scholar, Cheever grandly held forth on the subject of poetry—or *poh-tra*, as he pronounced it. "John," his wife sighed at last, "knock it off about that poetry stuff."

Cheever's self-importance was rather in evidence during a visit from the young James Kaplan, who'd published a run of stories in *The New Yorker* and was eager to cultivate an acquaintance with one of the magazine's most fabled writers. Kaplan had heard that Cheever answered his mail, so he'd written a few diffident notes to which Cheever had replied with the usual lapidary epigrams.* Finally, Kaplan called to say he was coming north for Christmas and wondered if he could pay a visit to the great man. But of *course*, said Cheever, who obligingly gave directions to Cedar Lane.

"One learns to separate the writer from the writing," Kaplan reflected many years later, "and my meeting with Cheever was sort of my final lesson." The first thing Kaplan noticed was how "tiny" Cheever was—a long head shorter than Kaplan himself, who also noticed that the low-ceilinged house seemed built on its master's scale ("It reminded me of Diane Arbus's photo of the Jewish giant at home with his parents in the Bronx"). Cheever beckoned Kaplan to an easy chair in front of the fire, gave him a tumbler of his "best Bulgarian vodka," then sat opposite and waited. "I was nervous, and he was not helping me," said Kaplan, who wondered if Cheever even remembered

---

*"You ask if I have ever wavered in my vocation," Cheever wrote Kaplan on July 23, 1978. "I can think of nothing that I have undertaken—my marriage, my ascent of the Grande Sora, my romances, my parenthood, my citizenship—in which I have not wavered continuously. That's what makes it so thrilling."

who he was. Gulping vodka, he began to recite his entire publishing record, with particular regard to a long story he'd published in *The New Yorker*, "Love and Painting." "*Mary!*" Cheever shouted to his wife in the kitchen. "This is the young man who wrote the painting story!" Somewhat relieved, Kaplan proceeded to mention that he'd been helped along the way by his "revered mentor," William Maxwell—information that seemed to put Cheever on guard (just as Maxwell had seemed oddly reticent on the subject of Cheever). Then the phone rang: Herbert Mitgang of the *Times*, calling to interview Cheever about the *Stories* collection. While answering questions in a level voice, Cheever mocked his interlocutor with elaborate facial mugging for Kaplan's benefit; the young man smiled weakly and drank more vodka. After twenty minutes or so, Cheever hung up, and Kaplan—casting about for something to say—asked, "Do you drive?" As he later explained:

> I'd asked for a complimentary reason: I was thinking of Nabokov, who didn't drive. I was desperate. There was nothing to talk about. I was having an audience with John Cheever. On the one hand I wanted it to last, and on the other I wanted to get the hell out of there. So I ask: "Do you drive?" And *instantly*—he's not drinking—he flies into high dudgeon, to my horror: "I *drive*, I *ski*, I *mountain climb* . . . !"—a whole catalogue of accomplishments. My mouth was falling open.

Cheever abruptly concluded the interview and showed Kaplan to his car. Rising to his feet, Kaplan realized how drunk he was, and wondered whether he'd be able to drive all the way home in the snow. "It was a miracle I survived."

With old friends in the Friday Club, Cheever tried to be magnanimous. Art Spear jovially wrote Litvinov that they were all "basking in the reflected light" of Cheever's fame; for his part, Cheever reminded himself to feign interest in his friends' affairs (though they hadn't asked a single question about his Harvard degree) and be "as yielding and generous as possible in any controversy." There were limits, however. When Spear presumed to observe that he received "exactly the same mail" as Cheever, fame or no, the latter was forced to "snap at [his] dear friend," assuring Spear that he (Cheever) received "checks, love letters and invitations" in relative profusion. As for his long-standing animus toward Tom Glazer, it got worse in spite of himself, at least on paper. Cheever hadn't been very supportive when Glazer's wife left him in 1974, and ultimately Cheever decided the man was a "homosexual spinster" who chose to live in wretched, homophobic isolation rather than admit his true appetites. Nor did Cheever soften much when he heard a rumor that it was none other than Glazer's body that had been found recently, charred by the third rail at the Scarborough station; Glazer had been missing for a while, and certain neighbors had long considered him a likely candidate for suicide. "He was quite famous until he was discovered to be alive," Cheever noted in his journal, after the putative corpse had returned from an obscure folksinging gig in California.* "I can't judge the sincerity of my regrets. . . . He fills me with a dismay that I seem unable to conceal."

Always at his best with dogs, Cheever was comforted in these final years by a golden retriever named Edgar, whom his daughter described as a "boisterous, leggy, badly bred dog with a square head and a habit of dropping wet rocks on your feet." Edgar, a bitch, had been named Tara when she belonged to Ben, who'd "loaned" her to his parents when his son was born in 1972; Cheever changed the dog's name to "Shithead" before settling on "Edgar," and the two became almost inseparable. On summer nights Cheever would occasionally take Edgar to Burger King (fries for her, a sandwich for himself) and then to a Carvel stand for her favorite treat, a chocolate flying saucer. "Brisky-frisky!" he'd call, coaxing the dog upstairs to his bedroom, which would have been a very lonely place without her. "When [s]he wakes me, late at night, rooting noisily amongst [her] dingle-berries," Cheever wrote his daughter, "we exchange the most profound and tender smiles before we both return to sleep."

More than ever, Cheever took pleasure in being a familiar face in his adopted hometown, the virtues of which he extolled with impressive zeal. When Cheever was profiled by *People* in 1979, the magazine described Ossining as a "gritty enclave, dominated by Sing Sing penitentiary"; Cheever, indignant, rushed to disavow the slur in the local *Citizen Register:* "Paradise on earth," he said, "with its fine views of the Hudson, its unpretentious people, its good restaurants, its nearness to New York . . ." He meant every word of it, too, especially the part

---

*The whole strange saga was related in the *New York Times* (November 30, 1980, page WC3). The identity of the victim was unknown at the time.

about unpretentious people, many of whom regarded Cheever as simply a nice (if eccentric) old man who didn't have a job; indeed, until the years of his greatest fame, even the more literate townsfolk had a hard time placing their most illustrious citizen. Cheever noted how once he'd been approached in Kipp's Pharmacy by a man who thought he was Burgess Meredith, then David Wayne; finally the man became flustered and said, "But you're *somebody* . . ." "I *am* somebody," Cheever replied, "and I like living in a community where *everybody* is somebody." And this, in a way, was true—poignantly so. In 1935, at the outset of his lifelong exile from home, Cheever had written Reuel Denney: "I think, with a lot of satisfaction, about the town I came from with its ship-building plant and two-storey bank-building. And if you mention our name to the bar-tender or the clerk in the drug-store he'll say 'yeah, old man Cheever, had two boys etc.' " This, after all, was the world evoked in the *Wapshot* novels—what Seymour Wolk (owner of Kipp's Pharmacy, who considered Cheever a friend) called "the village kind of life where people *know* people." Whenever Cheever went downtown, he was looking for company. He practiced Italian with various merchants, he chattily worked the booths at the Highland Diner or the lines at the bank, and toward the end of his life he was indisputably a local celebrity—not just because he was Cheever the author, but because he was Cheever the citizen: the man who'd lived in the area for almost thirty years, who'd volunteered at the fire department and prison, who'd gone to AA meetings all over Westchester, and who always had a moment to stop and talk on Main Street. His family called him the Mayor of Ossining.

And so in his own hometown he insisted on doing all his shopping, even though local merchants knew that he'd always pay the sticker price, that he was constitutionally incapable of haggling—that he was, in short (as Federico liked to remind him), "the biggest mark in Ossining." Once, at a jewelry store in the Arcadian Shopping Center, he pointed to a bracelet he wanted to buy for his wife; the clerk picked up the wrong bracelet, which Cheever hastily purchased lest he embarrass the poor man. "There was a kind of little-boy quality about him," said Bev Chaney, and perhaps this was simply another aspect of being a *Cheever.* As he mused in his journal, "I am reminded of the claustrophobia that attacked my mother and my brother in department stores, clothing stores, all sorts of commercial interiors. I will buy anything if you will set me free." His bonhomie as "Mayor of Ossining" was one way of coping with such deep-seated, nervous uncertainty—part of a determined effort to feel at home in the world. He loved to linger in Barker's, a discount department store that was soothingly cavernous (like "the well-lived interior of an Unidentified Flying Object"), though it seemed to help that he'd struck up a friendship with the manager, Richard Van Tassell. Barker's was such a happy place that he and Natalie Robins would abscond there after the holiday feast, and when Natalie lost a child at birth, Cheever expressed condolences by writing her a long letter about Barker's ("The soapy, oriental perfumes in the air remind me of Woolworths in Quincy").

Spending time with unpretentious people, away from his usual public ethos, seemed to provide a blessed respite from being the tweedy, bow-tie-wearing John Cheever. Ray Mutter's nurse, Kay, sought to improve herself with courses at the local community college, but hesitated to bother Cheever with questions about a paper she wanted to write on "The Swimmer"; finally, though (at Mary Dirks's urging), she gave Cheever a call, and the two talked for more than an hour. After that, the nurse made a point of discussing Cheever's work with him whenever he came in for an appointment—which suited Cheever fine, since he liked to kill time in the afternoon by reading magazines in the waiting room (*after* he'd seen the doctor). Some-times, too, he'd drop by Dom's Friendly Service in Croton just to chat with the owner, Dominick Anfiteatro, who cherished Cheever's com-pany: "I couldn't wait when I'd see him, I'd run out there," said Anfiteatro. "When he left me, he left me on a high for a good part of the day." And just as Cheever used to enjoy laconic discussions about communism and whatnot with Peter Wesul at Treetops, he also liked to ride his bicycle to the Ascolis' farm to buy brown eggs and sit on a stone fence with the superintendent, John Bukovsky, who remem-bered speaking of "spiritual things." In church, on his knees, Cheever bitterly rebuked himself for—among other things—his irksome aver-sion to "unattractive" people (as Polly would have it) like that fat woman in the next pew, who was wearing the kind of mink stole "that used to be raffled off at Fireman's carnivals" ("But here then is my sin . . . to estrange myself from this stranger").

One never quite knew when some such sinful impulse would rear its head. Cheever was always happy to sign extra copies of his work for local booksellers—doing so in bed when he was dying from cancer—but woe unto the clerk who didn't *immediately* grasp that "the Collected" (as in, sharply, *"D'you have copies of the Collected?"*) meant the big red book. But then there was the time Cheever was signing books after a reading at the public library, and a woman handed him a ratty paperback that looked filched from a Dumpster; Cheever signed it with a radiant smile. Not long after, however, at a signing in Vermont, an elegantly dressed woman handed Cheever a copy of *The Wapshot Scandal* that had actual toothmarks on it, whereupon he loudly insisted she buy a fresh copy of "the Collected": *"That* I will endorse as you please," he railed, "though *preferably* to your dog, who is *obviously* the only Cheever lover in your household!"

"He was always at sea," said Federico. "He didn't understand how the world worked. He was forever cheated by tradesmen, he bought the most ridiculous cars at the most ridiculous prices his entire life. He had no profession. He'd spent his entire career as a writer. He was not a high-school graduate. So he could say [pompous voice], '*Listen*, my good man . . . !'—and this over time became a habit, second nature, when he was up against the wall." Being at sea also meant being the fat boy who wanted to be loved by everybody. "You don't even have to *answer* that kind of mail," Bev Chaney would say, over and over, when Cheever would anxiously confide that the Newburgh Kiwanis (whatever) wanted him to read but, well, he'd rather *not*. Once, a man he'd chatted with on the train a couple of times, Martin Amsel, found Cheever's name in the phone book and invited him to "be a speaker" at the local Lions Club. "I'm terribly sorry," said Cheever in a tired voice, "but I'm quite ill at the moment." A few weeks later, Amsel opened the newspaper and saw that he was dead.

AS PART OF AN EFFORT to mend fences with Ben and Lynda, Cheever had tried to help their troubled marriage by paying for his son to receive counseling from the family psychiatrist, J. William Silverberg. ("You're asleep!" Ben indignantly noticed at one point, and the man gave a violent start: "What makes you think that?") Cheever also invited the couple to join him for a trip to Bulgaria in the summer of 1979. Stopping in London, Cheever gave Lynda some money to go shopping, the better to spend a day getting to know his son again. "Sometimes," he confided, "I experience a loneliness as painful as intestinal flu." Ben could relate to that, since his wife rarely slept with him anymore; indeed, it was a little nettling for Ben to discover that their attractive Bulgarian translator, a very young woman named Alexandra, was sleeping with his father (a distinguished guest of the nation, after all). While the two skinny-dipped in the Black Sea, Ben worked out his frustrations with long morning jogs along the byways of Varna. ("The troupe we were traveling with was very bemused, because I had this flirtatious blond wife and yet I was getting up every morning at six to run. They felt I should have been screwing her instead of running so much. Which I also felt.") By the end of the year, Ben realized his marriage was going nowhere—this at a time, oddly enough, when his frigid wife wanted a second child—and so he decided to take a *Reader's Digest* junket to the Esalen Institute in Big Sur ("massages and blow jobs") by way of liberating himself. "On Saturday morning," his father noted, "our son Ben, after a week in a spiritual retreat where he got fucked, has left his wife and returned home [i.e., to Cedar Lane], for it seems only a few hours."

Actually he stayed a few months, though he and his father seemed to remain amiable strangers: "I think we do not know one another," the latter reflected; "I think it is our destiny that we never will." Ben might have agreed, at least in retrospect. "Well, it's going, and Daddy will be pleased," he announced to a guest one day, lighting a fire. "He had two great fears about me. The first was that I would not learn how to lay a proper fire, the second was that I would be a homosexual." Even now his father often remarked that he hoped Ben wouldn't have his own "difficult propensities," which Ben took to mean that his father hoped he wouldn't be burdened with talent—and that was a little wounding. Possibly to elucidate the matter, Cheever invited Ben to read his journals, and once sat beside him while he read; when Ben looked up, he noticed his father had been crying, though at the time he didn't connect this with all the obsessive references to homosexuality he kept encountering: "I didn't quite get it," he later wrote, "or maybe I didn't want to get it. I was also surprised at how little I appeared in the text. I was surprised at how little any of us appeared, except perhaps my mother, who was not getting the sort of treatment that leads one to crave the limelight."

Then one day Ben took a bicycle ride with his father and Max. The two young men had pulled ahead, chatting about their respective journals, when Max mentioned that he sometimes liked to use a kind of "shorthand" or "trigger phrase" rather than exhaust a memory by evoking it in detail. While living in Dobbs Ferry, for example, he'd gone to bed with a man who kept saying "you sweet thing," and so Max's entry for that day was simply: "You sweet thing." Ben was shocked: Had his father heard? What would happen if he found out? "He's gay!" Ben told his sister over the phone. "Max is *gay*! He made a pass at me!" Susan mentioned this to Calvin Tomkins, who just shook his head. "Ben is hysterical," he said.

Whether Max was any more gay than he'd ever been is a matter of conjecture; in any case he was no longer married and had, in fact, suffered a ghastly reversal of fortune. As a popular instructor in Oswego, he'd decided to stay put for another year before moving to Baltimore to be with his wife. Meanwhile he'd talked with some people in the English department at Johns Hopkins, who thought they might be able to find a place for him in the fall of 1979. ("I figured Hopkins is even farther from Ossining than Oswego," he recalled. "I'd really be free of him then.") But two weeks before the end of his last semester in Oswego—and not long after he'd tendered his resignation—his wife called and demanded a divorce; stunned, Max drove immediately to Baltimore, and during a long boozy dinner she confessed that she'd been having an affair with an older man.

"Max called on Thursday to say that he had broken with his wife and would be here on Friday," Cheever noted at the time. Max's lease was about to expire in Oswego, his old job had already been filled, Johns Hopkins had fallen through with a bang, he was estranged from family and church in Utah, and he needed a place to live (not to mention a means of support) as soon as possible. A girl he'd begun seeing in Oswego hailed from Westchester, and was home for the summer, so Max moved to an attic apartment in Dobbs Ferry—a few miles downriver from Ossining. "If the water was right and the tide ebbing I could swim it," Cheever gleefully wrote his protégé. "Now and then I ask my cock if it can't imagine that Zimmer might like to fuck someone his own age but it doesn't seem to hear me."*

And so—at Cheever's insistence—Max began coming round Cedar Lane three or four times a week, and for a while nobody seemed to suspect a thing. He and Cheever bantered like a couple of old cronies, as Max wasn't apt to be deferential, at least around others. When

---

*As I mention in the footnote on page 290, when Cheever refers to intercourse (in whatever terms) with a man, he does not mean *anal* intercourse but rather any activity resulting in orgasm.

Cheever made fun of Glazer, for instance—sneering at the way pizza cheese hung off his chin, or the man's maudlin tendency to recite his many woes—Max (who liked Glazer) called Cheever "a fucking brat." And everybody laughed, most of all Cheever. Why should anyone see anything amiss? Max wasn't the least effeminate, and he was far from the first young man to hang around the place—there had been Rudnik, Lang, Schultz, to name a few, as well as any number of school chums the children had brought home over the years at a moment's notice. Cheever, *qua* paterfamilias, had always kept an open-door policy: the more at table, the more he liked it. Even Federico—who was living near San Francisco in the days of Harvey Milk; who had several gay friends and thought it was sort of cool (for his friends) to be gay— never suspected a thing.

As for Max, he wasn't quite sure *what* to think, though he hoped his affable façade was working, more or less, and he was especially careful to be courteous to Cheever's wife. "Mary, Mary, Mary," he wrote in his journal; "how difficult it is to be alone with you, eating your pea soup at the table, when our knowledge of one another has such terrible foundations of deceit—and it is raw deceit in spite of any sophistica- tion." Did Mary know? If so, she never let on, though perhaps she found other ways to express her frustration—like the time she flew into a rage when Max, weeding the stairs leading to the driveway, unwit- tingly picked some sedum she'd planted. And yet Cheever himself seemed nonchalant about things, and Max "took [his] cues" from Cheever:

> If he thought it was okay to parade me in front of Mary and his children, then I guess it was okay. The fact that I didn't *feel* okay doing it was my problem. . . . Obviously it's what people in the East do, the way he takes it in stride. Sitting down at the dinner table with his family, an hour after I've given him a hand-job and he still has stains in his corduroys from it, I guess this is okay here. It's tear- ing *my* guts out, but Ben's being nice to me, and Susie—who should take a fucking plate and bust it over my head—and poor Mary, you know.

One way Cheever justified things was to remind himself that he'd spent much of his adult life in a state of relative self-denial, supporting his family (and often his brother's family) by grinding out stories for

The New Yorker, and what had he gotten in return? Bilked by the magazine and rejected by his wife and even his children at times (the fact that he'd often behaved abominably was all but lost on him in his worst moods of self-pity). "I have courted these responsibilities," he wrote, "but now it seems that they have eclipsed my truly carefree nature and lying in the arms of Procrustes . . . I feel a marvelous sweetness of freedom."

As for the "you sweet thing" episode: Max had been driving home from Ossining—drunk ("being with [Cheever] always included getting drunk"), desperately depressed—and had picked up a young hitchhiker, who put a hand on Max's inner thigh. "And I figured, okay," Max remembered, "let's see if this is something I really like. Let's see if it's just Cheever's age and the fact that I never had a say in it." Telling Ben was a tentative way to unburden himself and clear the air, though nothing much changed. Ben kept his own counsel and remained as nice as ever; Susan "sometimes had a flicker of wondering" but finally dismissed it ("I think the violent ups and downs of my father's life had exhausted all of us"). Meanwhile Max went on playing his role, whatever that was, always wondering what the Cheevers *really* thought of him. The slightest hint of rejection cast him into a panic of self-loathing, such as the time Susan seemed to shrink from a friendly kiss: "[W]hat child no matter how sophisticated wants to complicate his or her life with a kiss on the cheek from her father's homosexual lover," Max wrote in his journal. "Ben is lovely to me and by the end of dinner I find that I am being restored to some identity of my own, something other than that awkward manifestation of their father's sexual preferences." When, at the end of the evening, Susan crossed the room to kiss Max goodbye ("she knows, beyond doubt, what she is doing"), he felt almost pathetically grateful.

THAT SPRING Cheever had struck up a far less complicated friendship with Tom Smallwood (not his real name), a former undergraduate at BU. Tom had finished a novel and wanted to show it to Cheever, so he wrote his old teacher a letter mentioning that he'd moved to Manhattan and would love to get together at some point. Cheever replied immediately, and a few days later the two met for the first time in four years at the train station: "Are you Tom?" Cheever was asking another youth when the real Tom tapped him on the shoulder. Cheever apologized, explaining that he'd always been drunk when they'd met in the past.

Walking to Croton Dam ("the second largest cut-stone mortised structure . . ."), Cheever put his arm around Tom, who was taken aback and politely pulled away. Cheever let it go, but on the way back he began talking about homosexuality. He had a male lover, he said, and found it *very* troubling, since his "upbringing" hadn't made it easy for him; his grandfather Aaron had committed suicide (it wasn't clear whether he was linking this to homosexuality per se), and the disgrace was never mentioned in his family. Back at the house, Cheever kept returning to the subject whenever his wife drifted out of earshot. "Perplexed about what sons will think of him," Tom wrote in his journal afterward. "Masturbates frequently—messy, we agreed. . . . We gave each other a hug good-bye, which turned into a kiss." When Tom returned a month or so later, Cheever proposed another walk to the dam, pausing around the halfway point: "When I put my arm around you last time, you seemed repulsed." Tom explained that he'd only been a little surprised, and Cheever said he wanted to touch the young man's penis. They ducked behind an outcropping a few yards off the path. "I didn't cum," Tom noted, "but he certainly did. 'Felt great.' Seemed quite beholden to me."

The two continued to meet now and then for the rest of Cheever's life, and later Tom would look back on the friendship with unadulterated pleasure. Tom wasn't particularly conflicted about his bisexuality—he soon married and started a family—and Cheever seemed easy in his company, more apt to express affection as opposed to lust. The two cuddled and chatted in bed; they hugged and kissed goodbye. Because he knew Cheever to be very affectionate, Tom was bemused by the man's family dynamics. Cheever and his wife lived together like virtual strangers, and in her absence he was both derisive (mocking her high-pitched voice) and a little fearful of her. In spite of this, he affected a kind of disdainful bravado—"Screw them!"—whenever Tom worried about being caught *in flagrante* at Cedar Lane; however, with respect to his children (who were otherwise included in the dismissal), Cheever expressed remorse over how often they'd seen him at his worst—what a nasty drunk he'd been; all the times he'd promised to stop drinking, or drink less, and failed. Still, it was odd for Tom to observe how formal Cheever was in their presence, this man who loved to be held and kissed. Perhaps the fact that there were no strings attached to his friendship with Tom had something to do with the difference: "I did give him this novel I'd written," Tom recalled, "and he didn't like it that much, and it was, like, 'Okay, let's move on.' I never asked him for anything."

Meanwhile, now that Max was financially dependent on Cheever, the question of *his* writing career had assumed greater urgency, and occasionally Cheever betrayed some slight impatience on that point: "If you would write your fucking homework in as commanding and relaxed a tone as I find in your letter and bring into its closing the pace of a man walking easily—as you walk—to a railway station or a mailbox it would make me happy." And so Max would mull this over *(be commanding and relaxed; conclude with an easy walking pace)* while studying, again and again, Cheever's own work—since their common goal was getting Max published in *The New Yorker*, a trick Cheever had managed 119 times. Then, too, despite his initial enthusiasm for Max's work, Cheever had gradually discovered that his protégé was rather drastically on the wrong track. Besides being "a catalogue of alienations," Max's earlier stories had reminded Cheever "a little of Beckett"—static, impressionistic—and the fact was, he didn't find Beckett all that interesting. "Our differences seem quite simple," he wrote Max. "I write the fiction of cause and effect. You do not. But it would please me if you found a use for your extraordinary voice that seemed more universal."

Be universal. Don't write like Beckett. Max did his best to follow this advice—anything to get published in *The New Yorker*—one result of which was a novella titled "The China Doll," which Max would later describe as "[his] 'Reunion.' " The original "Reunion" is the shortest story in the big red book, a masterpiece of compression. The first and last phrases are "the last time I saw my father," and in between we are told not a syllable more than we need to know, to wit: Father and son haven't seen each other in three years; the man's *secretary* replies to the boy's letter; the boy realizes that, whatever happens, he is doomed to resemble his father somewhat. The rest is the reunion itself—a broad, virtuosic rendering of the father's swinishness and the son's quiet, presumably appalled, observation. "It reads like a streak," Maxwell wrote Cheever in 1962, "and is perfection at every point." But Max's "Reunion," alas, is a bloated, derivative mess. In fifty pages or so, the narrator describes a meeting with his disaffected Mormon father, and amid endless exposition about the man's religious scruples (and a lot of stuff about the mother, too) one hears constant, tinny echoes of the master.*

Whenever Max finished a story—less and less frequently—it would be forwarded to McGrath at *The New Yorker*, who was quite aware that Cheever was using him "as a reward for Max." And nobody, of course, was more painfully aware than Max himself: "Poor Chip. I would bring him these stories that I didn't even understand and he'd suggest revisions and I'd make the revisions still not understanding the story or knowing exactly where the revisions went. And then I'd bring them back to him, and the guy would try to get the stories accepted and then have to tell me no." By then McGrath would have liked few things better than to accept one of Max's stories—he was fond of Max, and never mind getting Cheever off his back—but that required the approval of more than one editor, and the others were less invested. Yet McGrath tried to stay upbeat, at least for Cheever's benefit: "I hope Max Zimmer hasn't been overly discouraged by this series of revisions. My belief in his work remains unaltered, and I think he's getting better and better." Sustained (if bewildered) by such encouragement, Max decided to get out of Dobbs Ferry and take a cheap winter rental in Southampton—to hole up and *write*, by God—coaxing a couple of his more devoted students from Oswego to take a year off and join him.

Two days after Max's departure in early September, his bereft mentor flew to New Hampshire to accept the Edward MacDowell Medal for "outstanding contribution to the arts," an award that was annually rotated among writers, visual artists, and composers. After a long and eloquent introduction from Elizabeth Hardwick, Cheever produced some "notes scribbled on the back of a shopping list" (so the *Times* observed), which mostly had to do with his present sorrow:

> The day before yesterday I was saying goodbye to a very dear friend and as I watched him go away it was only, I think, through

---

*Random examples: "the last time I saw my father" is the last line of Max's first paragraph; the father's aroma is evoked as his "sour and ambrosial odor as a male" ("the rankness of a mature male" in Cheever); the son calls his father a "son of a bitch"—twice, triumphantly—the same way Mrs. Henlein, the babysitter, ticks off Mr. Lawton in "The Sorrows of Gin." Max would concede this and more—indeed, this was his point in showing me the story in the first place: "It was written by a guy out fishing for his voice by trying on everyone else's," he wrote me. "The first line, in fact, is a direct steal from Updike." Updike, after all, was another successful *New Yorker* writer.

my grasp of fiction, through narrative and through invention that I could first reproach myself for loving him excessively and then attack psychiatry for having added the element of *prudence* to love—and then to have concluded that *imprudence* is a synonym for love, a conclusion I could not have reached were I not an author of fiction.

A rather imprudent confession, or so it looks on paper, though doubtless Cheever's mandarin persona had a beguiling effect on his listeners; in any event, nobody seemed to read much into it. But Cheever was not quite done confessing. The chairman of the award committee was his great admirer John Leonard, who spotted the guest of honor "slipp[ing] away" from a dance that night; he found the man sitting alone in his room, sipping some instant coffee he'd packed for the trip. At first Cheever tried to be charming, but he couldn't conceal his melancholy. "Sex is very important to me," he said, "and there is no sex in my marriage." Perhaps Leonard could find him an apartment in New York? Something in the East Sixties? His loneliness at home was simply unbearable . . . and so on, most of the night. For Leonard it was "terribly painful" to learn that his favorite writer, such a radiant artist, was one of the saddest people he'd ever met. Cheever would not have disagreed: "I wake this morning feeling how painful is my life," he wrote, "when I can, offhand, think of no one who leads a life with less pain."

CHAPTER FORTY-SEVEN

{ 1979–1980 }

CHEEVER'S FAME continued to grow in ways that might otherwise have been gratifying. In October, three adaptations of his stories were broadcast on consecutive Wednesdays as part of the PBS series *Great Performances*. Over the past year, Cheever had completed a problematic draft of his teleplay—now called *Kidnapping in Shady Hill*—but the project was in limbo while WNET sought financing; in the meantime Cheever had dreaded the adaptations ("God have mercy on us all"), a dread he conveyed in the press as a kind of lofty skepticism ("Any confrontation between the camera and the word is unhappy"). Such was Cheever's prestige, however, that the underfunded project had attracted a first-rate pool of talent: Wendy Wasserstein adapted "The Sorrows of Gin," starring Edward Herrmann and Sigourney Weaver; "O Youth and Beauty!" was adapted by A. R. Gurney, and starred Michael Murphy; and "The Five-Forty-Eight"—arguably the most successful of the three—was adapted by Terence McNally, directed by James Ivory, and starred Laurence Luckinbill and Mary Beth Hurt. Cheever was rather impressed in spite of himself (though he deplored the "scored music"), and even agreed to give publicity interviews in New York.

The programs might have served as a further reminder that Cheever owed much of his present distinction to stories he'd written many years ago, and whether he was still capable of working at that level was more than a little in doubt. He had almost nothing to show for the three and a half years since finishing *Falconer*, though he always told interviewers he was hard at work on "another bulky book." There was no book. "I seem unable to approach a frame of mind in which I can work," he'd mused around the time of his Pulitzer, and now work had gotten even harder, he claimed, without cigarettes. But finally he managed to write his first story in four years, "The Night Mummy Got the Wrong Mink Coat," quite possibly the worst thing he ever published. "That was the year everybody went to China if they hadn't already been there," the story opens with deliberate self-parody (rather like his preceding story, "The President of the Argentine," and perhaps in the same mood of pre-emptive apology). "All the women wore black, ankle-length mink coats and the men wore massive gold wristwatches with golden bands." The ensuing anecdote was based on an actual episode in which Mary had gotten the wrong mink coat while leaving a formal affair, then returned and exchanged it for the right one: The end. "It's a *very* silly story," said Mary, who reluctantly submitted it to *Westchester Magazine*, where she'd been hired as fiction editor. The hope was that—as Mrs. John Cheever—she'd attract "important" fiction and maybe even an original Cheever story, though Mary herself wanted to submit work from her adult-education class. "John was just cross that I was interested in other people's stories," she recalled, and for that reason (somewhat in jest) he'd submitted the "Mink" story under his old pseudonym, Mrs. Louisa Spingarn. *Westchester* rejected it ("They thought it was terrible"), and the editors may or may not have noticed when the same story appeared in *The New Yorker* a few months later. Such was Cheever's prestige.

"My wife's detestation of me seems at a high point," Cheever observed around the time of his penultimate *New Yorker* appearance. What passed for discourse between the two were curt rejoinders on Mary's part whenever Cheever attempted (disingenuously, she thought) to break the silence between them, though generally she tended to be as oblique as possible in expressing hostility ("This cookbook is a pack of lies!" she declared of a cookbook he'd given her), since she'd long ago despaired of any sort of fruitful remonstrance. According to Cheever's journal, "six months or even longer" had gone by until, one night, she ventured to speak to him directly at the dinner table, and then afterward—miraculously—sat "for a minute or two" on the same sofa where he himself was sitting: "This has not happened for years. . . . She does not actually sit beside me but she does sit near me in order to say that a book, given to me, is in her bedroom and that I am free to read this during the daylight hours. I thank her and we part. This is my union."

At the same time, he was finding less solace in his friendship with

Max, who returned from Southampton in May 1980 and took a basement apartment with his girlfriend in Westchester. His time on Long Island had not been a success: he was now so blocked that he could hardly finish a paragraph, much less a story, and the ramifications had left him "frightened witless." He felt utterly at Cheever's mercy. Fast approaching middle age, he'd burned his bridges in the hope of becoming a writer—a *New Yorker* writer—and without Cheever's sponsorship it was a far-fetched prospect, to say the least. Plus he had to eat. Working as an occasional factotum on Cedar Lane—feeding dogs, watering plants, other more sordid chores—Max had begun to grate a little on his master's nerves, since Cheever could no longer quite persuade himself that his protégé's affection was disinterested. He longed, however, not to succumb to "meanness of spirit" (the essence of which was, as he put it, "I don't want to play with you because you don't really love me"), but amid other frustrations it was a lot to ask. "Oh Max *fuck off*," he snapped one day, when Max was drinking too much Scotch (increasingly the case, for his host all but demanded it), and Cheever, meanwhile, had been waiting for a load of firewood to be delivered so he could leave for the airport. Around dusk, the wood finally arrived and the man began unloading it, but Cheever stopped him and said he wanted to inspect it first. As Max recorded the scene in his journal:

> "Green," [Cheever] said. "You can't sell me green wood." "It's not green. . . . It's been seasoned a year." . . . "It's green. Don't come here under cover of darkness and tell me it's not green. Get out of here." "Well, you motherfucker," yells the woodman. "You goddamn little cocksucker." . . . Then I realize that I am stunned from drinking Scotch and from being told to fuck off and from hearing the woodman cuss out Cheever.

Max jumped to work on the woodpile, praying that Cheever would "like [him] again" when it was all over. As he remembered twenty-five years later, "I thought, 'Now I've done it. Now he's going to finish me.' " As a matter of fact, some such thought had occurred to Cheever, albeit in less portentous terms: "I think that I must say goodbye to Max," he wrote shortly after the firewood episode. "We could not live together unless we had some simple occupation such as cycling fifty miles a day. This we have already done and he, as a young man, cannot make a life of bicycling."

CONDUCTING AT LEAST TWO gay relationships under the noses of his wife and children did not make Cheever more tolerant or comprehending toward those who presumed to do likewise. One day he felt so tormented that he confided something of the truth to an old Signal Corps buddy, whom he'd met for lunch in New York every so often for three decades. "What's the big deal?" the man said, meaning to console Cheever. "I like to get my cock sucked, too, now and then." Cheever looked back on the moment with lingering wonder: "When [he] told me that he liked having his cock sucked I decided, before he had completed the sentence, that I would never see him again as a friend and I never did." (His friend accepted Cheever's excuse that he could no longer bear to be in the city without wanting to drink.) But this was a mild shock compared with what was coming from another, even closer Signal Corps friend. "We dined with the Ettlingers about a month ago and it was like stepping into the crucial chapters of some extraordinary success story," Cheever had written in 1962. "They are all rich, happy, well-fed, well-staffed, well-dressed and enthusiastically at peace with the world. Don loves his program [*Love of Life*]. Katrina loves Don. The dogs and cats lie in one another's arms amongst the roses." So it seemed, and perhaps so it was. In any case, Cheever had fallen out of touch with Ettlinger during the worst of his alcoholism, but in recent years the two had resumed meeting almost weekly at a diner near the Tappan Zee Bridge, where each would bring the other updates about children, grandchildren, and wives. Then one spring day in 1980, as they were saying goodbye in the parking lot, Ettlinger announced that he was bisexual. "I've had hundreds of one night stands in the New York apartment," he said, or so the horrified Cheever recorded in his journal.

Ettlinger rarely denied the truth to his gay friends (or to himself, for that matter), and his marriage seems to have remained stable in a way Cheever's never was. Katrina once remarked to her husband, as they were pulling into the driveway of their home in Rockland County, "You know, you have this whole other life, and it has to do with men." Such a moment was surprising enough for Ettlinger to mention it to a friend, who claimed that homosexuality "wasn't an open issue" between the couple otherwise. Arthur Laurents—another gay Signal Corps friend—had been close to the Ettlingers before their marriage, and was "instrumental" in persuading Don to marry his wealthy, charming girlfriend: "Don and Katrina remind me of a scene I wrote in *The Way We Were*. Robert Redford broke up with Barbra Streisand and she calls him up: 'It's because I'm not attractive, isn't it?' I liked Katrina a lot. Don was too weak—he needed someone strong. Katrina wasn't conventionally attractive, but she was very bright and had a great body. He needed her more than she needed him." Cheever—with the perspicacity he brought to most areas of life—had sensed the truth about Ettlinger all along, but simply could not summon the dreaded word: "I do not mean to judge him," he wrote in 1954, "but perhaps I can say that here is a temperament . . . that cannot be judged by the standards our society has evolved. . . . There is a breadth here—libertinage or infantilism may be what I mean—that does not in any way diminish the love he bears his wife and his children."

But how could such things be? And why had Ettlinger decided, after so many years, to confide in a friend he *knew* to be homophobic, thereby losing at least "some particle" of his friend's esteem ("I think him to be a revealed narcissist," Cheever wrote; "something that I think I and my lover not to be")? It so happened that a mutual acquaintance, the novelist Joseph Caldwell, had suspected Cheever of being bisexual ever since reading "The World of Apples": "I thought, 'No *straight* man would get aroused by the sight of a hairy ass' " (as Bascomb does in the story); then, after reading *Falconer*, Caldwell was almost convinced. "Is Cheever gay?" he asked Ettlinger, who replied that his old friend was most definitely *not* ("*Anybody* else—James Cagney, whoever—but not Cheever"). And yet Ettlinger was intrigued enough to investigate further—hence his confession in the parking lot. "I got it out of him," he told Caldwell two weeks later. "He's bisexual all right." It wasn't information that Cheever had surrendered gladly ("I am not, with Don, disposed to bring in any of my deeper feelings on these matters"), and he continued to squirm at every mention of the subject, especially after Ned Rorem (via Laurents) had enlightened Ettlinger all the more.

But Ettlinger insisted on discussing it, perhaps because his heart went out to Cheever. "Lunching with my old friend Don leaves me quite confused," Cheever wrote, a few months before his death. "He claims to regret not having led the life of a homosexual. I find this unimaginable." By then, however, Ettlinger had managed to make inroads with Cheever, regaling him with stories about the life, or lives, he'd led these many years—one in New York, one in Pomona, and a certain amount of happiness with both. After one such conversation,

Cheever reflected, "I think that far from being ashamed of my androgynous nature I shall embrace and if possible enjoy this as a gift rather than an infirmity."

"I LOVE YOU VERY MUCH and my endeavors to dismiss this disconcerting love have been highly unsuccessful," Cheever wrote Max, after a short-lived attempt to distance himself. Indeed, now that the foundering young man was at his beck and call, Cheever began to introduce him to a widening circle of friends and writers—many of whom did arrive at the logical conclusion. Eugene and Clare Thaw noticed an "obvious intimacy" when the friends came over for one of their frequent swims, though it might have surprised Cheever to learn as much, since he was careful to avoid any public displays of affection. As for Max: "I remember meeting Updike once at some party, and I thought, 'Maybe they *don't* really know . . . but, yeah, they know. They know.' And again, it seemed okay with them. They acted like, 'Yeah, so you play with Cheever's cock. It's okay, I've met stranger people.' The shame was *incredible*, but I'd put on my good old Mormon-missionary smile and get through it." Max longed to have friends his own age, to have any "regular friends" period, but above all he wished he could go back to Utah—to a time, that is, before he'd been "swallowed"—so he could rediscover who he'd been and why he'd wanted to write in the first place. At the very least he wanted to get a job, but Cheever insisted he needed the time to write, or anyway to be free at a moment's notice for a trip, a swim, a bicycle ride, a party, or some chore on Cedar Lane.

In fact (though he now considered it "very unlikely"), Cheever had continued to hope that he could somehow railroad Max into print, if only to improve the man's spirits and confer a certain legitimacy on their relationship. But Max hardly knew where to begin anymore. He looked over the stuff he'd written for Cheever and concluded that he "might as well have spent the last two or so years fishing." Lunching one day in the *Reader's Digest* cafeteria, Max admitted his frustration to Ben, who kindly pointed out that his father "[wasn't] that great a teacher": "Some writers have a flotilla of students who follow them into print, but he's not like that."* Meanwhile Cheever continued to

---

*Actually, of course, quite a number of Cheever's students went on to impressive careers—Gurganus, Boyle, Hansen, some Barnard students—though arguably the more notable cases had little to do with Cheever's influence.

caution Max about his constant, Beckettesque gloom, insisting he write a story "in which suppuration, corruption and decay do not appear. . . . [R]emember that George Grosz could paint flowers." But Max had long since digested such advice and found it wanting, not to say "insidious": "[I]t might be a wholesale dissimulation for him," he wrote in his journal, "and one he perpetuates in order to surround the vileness, the evil, the horror of our relationship with a false aura of goodness and virtue and greenery." Once more it occurred to Max that his work, his very identity, was doomed if he didn't put some distance between himself and his teacher, who at length agreed to cover rent on a studio apartment in Manhattan for Max and his girlfriend. He also put Max in touch with his and Ettlinger's friend Joseph Caldwell, who happened to live right around the corner. One day Max dropped by and showed Caldwell a recent (and perhaps sunnier) story he'd written—remarking, however, that Cheever "wasn't impressed." Then, almost in tears, he added, "What does Cheever *want* . . . ?" "It was the saddest thing," said Caldwell. "You can't write to please somebody else, and I knew that was the end of Max as a writer. I thought, 'You poor guy.'"

What Cheever wanted, or sometimes thought he wanted, was his own New York apartment—an idea he'd been kicking around for a year or so, even before he'd broached the subject with John Leonard in New Hampshire. No longer would he have to worry (insofar as he worried) about sneaking around his wife and children and neighbors; he could start all over. On the other hand, starting over at age sixty-eight was a terrifying thought. He pictured himself (à la his days on Bay State Road) sitting alone in his apartment, "chain-smoking over [his] third martini," an elderly homosexual stood up by some young cock or another. And it was essentially a gay lifestyle he'd be leading, since he'd finally come to admit, once and for all, that he and Hope Lange were nothing but good friends. "You don't understand the first thing about women," she'd been telling him for years, and he'd done little to change her mind. The decisive episode had occurred after a recent lunch when, returning to her apartment, Cheever had dropped his pants and waited. "I can't help you," she said, and made a phone call. Cheever pulled his pants up, rushed downstairs, bought three dozen roses, and rushed back. Said Max (bleakly familiar with the incident and the basic MO): "It was like, 'What's wrong? Women like flowers. Now you're supposed to fuck me.'" Hope continued to chat on the phone, and presently Cheever got the message and left. The larger message, of course, was that home was where he belonged after all. His wife might not speak to him (much less sleep with him), but she was a warm body and rarely failed to have dinner waiting—"one of the great labors of history," as Cheever gratefully acknowledged: "She has often served me with bitterness . . . but night after night for a decade less than half a century she has brought food to the table."

Hope's retirement from the scene may have served as a catalyst for Cheever to start work on a novel he'd long been considering about "the erotic loneliness of an old man." Perhaps the most inhibiting factor had been the issue of bisexuality ("the astonishing iridescence of my nature," as Cheever liked to say), which if anything had become more momentous in recent years—and yet, another such book after *Falconer* would be tantamount to a public confession, and Cheever hadn't forgotten by a long shot the way Dennis Coates (for one) had glibly connected the life and work. But then, too, he had an obligation as an artist—a great artist—to be emotionally honest: "What I come on is that I am writing the annals of my time and my life and that any deceit or evasiveness is, by my lights, criminal." So that settled the point about bisexuality. Still, Cheever was loath to write about erotic matters only, and he cast about for some other, nobler aspect of life that had given comfort over the years, that had reminded him of the "intrinsic largeness of the human spirit" no matter what the sordid facts—which brought him back to nature, of course, and one of his favorite ways of communing with it, skating. Groping to begin, he explained the gist of his novel as follows: "I mean it's about what it's like to fuck a woman and then a man because the woman won't fuck you. But then there's this other thing about turning a lake into a dump so that it can be a softball field for crippled war veterans. I don't know what the two stories have in common. It could of course be the old man's skating pond that they are beginning to destroy."

Sometime that summer, at any rate, he got to work on what would become *Oh What a Paradise It Seems*, but the work went slowly or not at all; the ecstatic high he'd felt while writing *Falconer* was gone—quite gone—and he often wondered if he was losing not only his creative powers, but his sanity. He'd continued to experience the odd hallucination of Ginny Kahn and a drunken Exley, the latter singing a "forlorn jingle" that Cheever had taken to calling the "Ain't Got Nothing" song; when he tried to pursue the scene further, he'd suffer a memory lapse so profound that he felt utterly lost in time and space ("I [do] not, for a moment, know my wife's name or the name of my dogs"). Along with alcoholic brain damage, he suspected he was suffering from "[what] psychiatrists would call a traumatic rejection"—that is, a kind of hysterical amnesia, cued by the hallucination, at the bottom of which was some "cruelty in [his] youth" so ghastly he couldn't bear to face it. Whatever was happening to him, chemical or otherwise, left him so drained and alienated that he could hardly speak or even smile. "I seem in a contemptible frame of mind and am perhaps ill," he noted toward the end of September.

Despite his increasing malaise, he decided to go to Yaddo in October—a trip he viewed "with genuine dread," though the thought of staying home with a silent, scornful wife was even more intolerable. It would be his last visit. The handful of guests included a sculptor Cheever knew slightly from previous visits, Mary Ann Unger, as well as the novelist Joan Silber and the composer Lee Hyla—all of them relatively young and respectful toward the legend in their midst. Everyone noticed, however, that Cheever was a little off: he kept losing his train of thought, and took a vicious dislike to one of the guests, a fifty-two-year-old surgeon and writer named Richard Selzer, who (one learns from the journal) had struck Cheever as effeminate. When, at dinner that first night, Cheever learned that the surgeon was married, and moreover had children, he became implacably hostile ("I find him repulsive because he performs the same sexual acrobatics that I, as a terribly old man, am beginning to enjoy"). Affecting to break the ice, Cheever turned to Selzer and asked, "Richard, have you ever plagiarized?" Selzer struggled to keep his dignity: it was his first trip to Yaddo and he was excited about it, all the more so because Cheever, no less, was there. "I let it be known to him that I certainly wanted to be his friend, but no," the man recalled. "He began an attack in his little bitchy way. And he was good at being a bitch." When he wasn't putting Selzer in his place, Cheever entertained the table with old Yaddo stories that tended to stress his reputation as a cocksman, what with the many women he'd conquered on the couch in the Great Hall. The next day he was visited by Max ("we watch a ballgame, screw, have dinner, watch another game, and part, at my wish"), who everyone assumed was his lover, said Silber, despite his past exploits in the Great Hall.

"I'm working like a streak but I don't seem able to end the unreality blues when I leave the typewriter," Cheever wrote Max on October 12. Two days later, he tauntingly challenged Selzer (a heavy smoker) to join him for a twenty-two-mile bicycle ride around Saratoga Lake; Selzer declined, and Cheever (pleased) departed alone. Exhausted on his return, he nonetheless went to an AA meeting after dinner, then returned to his studio at Hillside Cottage to watch the World Series with Hyla, Silber, and Unger. During the seventh inning, he was chatting with Silber when suddenly he crushed the plastic cup of ginger ale in his hand. "At first I thought it was a joke about how crappy the plastic was," Silber remembered. "I started to laugh, then I realized something was wrong." After a long stare, Cheever's hands flew to his throat and he fell over backward, thrashing his legs and making strange gurgling noises.

It fell to Selzer to save his life. The surgeon, staying at Pine Garde, was wearing nothing but pajama bottoms when one of the women banged on his door: "Come quick!" she said. "John Cheever is dying!" Selzer ran barefoot through the woods and burst into Hillside Cottage, where he found Cheever "cyanotic-blue . . . and looking dead"; Selzer gave mouth-to-mouth resuscitation until Cheever started breathing again, and presently (in his pajama bottoms) rode in the ambulance to Saratoga Hospital, where he learned the doctors had gone home for the night. "Get me oxygen, an electrocardiogram, and I want to draw some blood, do some tests," he ordered a dawdling nurse. "And I want to examine this man. Get me a thalmoscope and a stethoscope and all of that stuff—and shut up!" Finally, when Cheever was "all plugged in and stable" in the ICU, Selzer went back to Yaddo.

Cheever was sitting up in bed when Selzer returned early the next morning. "I'm *not* going home," he said, when Selzer urged him to do so. "I'm here at Yaddo, I'm staying." When Selzer explained what had happened the night before, and mentioned the mouth-to-mouth part, Cheever became enraged. "What right have you?" he demanded. "That's rape! That's a violation of me!" At length Selzer replied that he was sending Cheever home in an ambulance whether he liked it or not ("I'm not going to have another thing to do with you"), and phoned Mary to let her know as much. "Well that's fine," she said. "Do that."

Back in Westchester, Cheever was thoroughly examined by Dr. Mutter, who found him in surprisingly decent health except for arteriosclerosis and a "Babinski sign"—the big toe going up instead of down when the bottom of the foot is scratched—indicating active swelling of the brain. The doctor told Cheever that he'd been abusing himself for sixty years ("I said that my scrotum hadn't retracted until I was eight and that I had been abusing myself for only fifty-nine years," Cheever quipped*) and consequently had a certain amount of scar tissue on the brain, an "irritable focus" which had been triggered by too much caffeine (up to a gallon a day of coffee and tea) as well as overexertion, hence a grand-mal seizure. He was advised to cut down on caffeine and take aspirin for his heart.

"Mr. John is back!" said one of the servants when Cheever arrived to complete his stay at Yaddo. He seemed little changed by his brush with death—tired, certainly, and somewhat embarrassed. "Oh God," he remarked to Silber, "can you believe Richard helped me?" As for Selzer, he decided to leave now that his tormentor had returned, and late that night, while packing, he heard a knock on the door. "May I come in?" Cheever asked. Selzer went back to packing, and his visitor stepped inside, sat down, and proceeded to speak about his childhood. "Well, John, I'm expected in the Operating Room at eight o'clock this morning," Selzer said at last. "I'm afraid I must ask you to leave." Cheever stood up and took a step toward Selzer, staring at him with curious intensity. "Shall I come see you in New Haven?" he asked. "I can't think why," said Selzer, struck by the notion that Cheever wanted to kiss him. For years he pondered the moment, until he learned of Cheever's bisexuality after his death. "I think, now, that he was attracted to me, and I think to defend himself against that, he abused me," said Selzer. "I felt guilty, because I thought: 'Well, I've failed to understand another human being.' "

"I'M AFRAID THE SEIZURE jarred my perspective and I've not yet dared look at the [pages] I wrote on the day of my collapse," Cheever noted. When he finally got around to it, his worst fears were confirmed: not only was his recent work poor—even bizarre—but the whole manuscript was a botch and would have to be done over. And he really didn't feel like it. He missed drinking, especially at night, when he seemed to come face to face with Hemingway's "Nada" ("the utter nothingness that is revealed to an old man"); and then, if he were dying

---

*Getting the math wrong: he was sixty-eight at the time.

and/or going mad, why bother? Why *not* drink? "I can laugh, and ask why can't I be a jolly old man who is finished with his work and is free to spend his twilight years on some sun-drenched island, having his asshole tickled with a peacock feather. I think I can't because I think I would resume my career as a drunkard which would be idiotic and obscene. Get to work."

There was also the fact that he'd accepted a sizable portion of his half-million-dollar advance, though he wasn't at all sure he could satisfy the contract, whether he felt like it or not. One day he read a novel in one sitting, and was horrified to find that the next day he couldn't remember a single detail. Indeed, the whole world seemed increasingly strange to Cheever, and vice versa. When Litvinov came to the States and visited Cedar Lane, she felt as though she were communicating with her friend "through a veil": "He hardly talked. Every now and then he'd go somewhere and come and bring some book and put it on the table, then bring another book, like an automaton, rather." Litvinov related the incident to Maxwell, who sadly observed that she was "describing a deeply disturbed man"; on the lighter side, he mentioned that Newhouse thought Cheever was secretly pleased by his seizures, since he could now liken himself to Dostoevski—not a bad aperçu, as it happened. "Did you know that I suffer from Grand Mal?" Cheever wrote a prospective biographer, James Valhouli. "I think this important since the seizures I've suffered, this late in life, seem allied to some of the insights in the stories." But privately he wondered, too, whether his condition was meant to reveal the "error in [his] ways":

> That fucking Max is punishable by death is the censoriousness of my childhood, Freud's revelation in Vienna, Dostoievsky's vision in Leningrad and the expounding of this by a school of sexual misfits. . . . I have prayed for sexual discretion and reasonableness a thousand times. I have prayed to be able to join the erotic glee that is so truly my sense of being alive with the spiritual guidance that has been my salvation.

By then he'd suffered a second seizure, on November 30, while playing backgammon with a friend and sometime Friday Clubber, Roger Willson. This time he was in the hospital for two days, and emerged feeling almost desperately weary—"quite old"—even more so now that he was taking the anticonvulsant Dilantin ("It's knocked the shit out of my childlike sense of wonder"). Happily, though, his marriage had shown a vast, practically overnight improvement. Always at her best as a caretaker, Mary found it easier to be loving now that her husband needed her so badly, while he in turn forced himself to be patient whenever she disagreed with him in some tacit or accidental way—by speaking kindly, say, of someone he despised. As he mused with laudable self-awareness, "I am inclined to consider any diversion from my thinking to be quarrelsome and perverse."

Thanks to their renewed amity, Cheever was able to face with composure and even pleasure the publication (in December) of *The Need for Chocolate and Other Poems,* a collection of Mary's work, which of course included what the author considered her finest poem, "Gorgon," with its lines about "life-denying husbandry" and (which Cheever never did quite forgive) "nicker[ing] at my breasts." A few months earlier, while the marriage was still on the rocks, Mary had suspected her husband of being mischievous when he presented her with a framed copy of the book jacket: "It was like, 'Look what *she* did!' It wasn't an entirely pure-hearted gesture." However, when the book was finally published, he was nothing but supportive. He went out of his way to praise her in the press, attended her signing at a local bookstore ("a triumph for her as a poet, a neighbor, a mother, a wife"), and on Valentine's Day presented her with a gold necklace and a little poem: "The need for chocolet is much finer / than the need for gold, / and I have hoped to find you / some of both, / While we have sought the ghost of love / together—and better yet, / Found something more enduring / than either gold or chocolet."

CHAPTER FORTY-EIGHT

{ *1980–1981* }

T HE WORLD SEEMED IN A RUSH to honor Cheever. On his return from Yaddo in late October, he'd gone to New York with Ben to receive the Abraham Lincoln Literary Award from the Union League Club. The occasion called for a speech, which Cheever saw as a nice opportunity to declare his place among aesthetic traditionalists ("[I'm] rather like the old Hudson River painters"), while deploring the incoherence and abstraction of so much contemporary art. "I will tell them that our two most conspicuous innovators—Pablo Picasso and James Joyce—never for a moment lost sight of the fact that our bewilderment in this world in which we find ourselves, is finite," he wrote Max (perhaps pointedly). The speech was a success, though afterward Cheever was confronted by a drunk who'd been offended by *Falconer* ("You used to be good, but then you started writing smut!"), until Ben stepped between them.

The laurels continued in spring. That April of 1981, Cheever received the American Book Award for the paperback *Stories*, and the following month he returned to Saratoga for an honorary degree from Skidmore. Standing on the dais, accepting the congratulations of his old friends the Palamountains, Cheever couldn't help but wonder at "the abyss between [his] public and [his] otherwise person." The abyss was more on his mind than ever, now that people were writing books about him. He'd kept warmly in touch with James Valhouli ever since 1971, when the young man had begun researching his dissertation on Cheever at the University of Wisconsin. But now that Valhouli had proposed a biography, he found Cheever's manner a little "offish":

there were days when Cheever seemed inclined to let Valhouli see a journal or two, other days when he thought not; sometimes he'd answer a question with candor and precision, other times he'd feign deafness and tell some irrelevant story. Finally Valhouli committed the fatal blunder: "He speaks of Coates' paper in which I am a tubercular, effeminate, solitary lover of men," Cheever wrote. "This story seems not worth telling." And yet the story *would* be told, in some form or another, and Cheever did his best to defuse the matter with evasion, bluster, or (especially) charm. When George Hunt—a sympathetic Jesuit from Le Moyne College in Syracuse—began writing a work of criticism that would touch, here and there, on the subject's life, Cheever lost no time addressing the issue of his "erotic adventures" with an affable note: "These seem never to have enjoyed any perspective in the dissertations I have read. I would not dream of challenging the authority of Venus but I have always felt that the tenderness and ardor that men and women often feel for their own kind is quite blameless."

His longing to escape meanwhile—from the responsibilities of work, the consequences of fame, and sometimes life itself—informed his last contribution to *The New Yorker*, a one-page set piece titled "The Island," which evoked a final, paradisal destination for bygone personages of every sort: "Here they all were—the greatest trombonist, the movie queen, the ballplayers, trapeze artists, and sexual virtuosos of yesterday—leading happy and simple lives . . . trapping shellfish, weaving baskets, and reading the classics." And with them, in spirit anyway, was one of the greatest writers: Prospero putting his wand away. Almost fifty years ago, Cheever had broken into the magazine with a modest sketch, and he was leaving that way, too, having descended, as it were, to the foot of a mountain. The editors realized they were getting "the last squeezings from the press," as McGrath put it, but were simply happy that Cheever had come back at the end. Or nearly the end: slowly—dutifully—he plugged away at his novel, which he now thought of calling *Work for the Night Is Coming*, or simply *Swan Song*.

A couple of weeks before "The Island" appeared in the April 27 issue, Cheever noticed that his beloved old dog, Edgar, was becoming very ill, and a few days later his own health took an abrupt turn for the worse. Finding it almost impossible to urinate, and passing blood when he did, Cheever was admitted to the hospital on April 17 "in acute distress." At first it didn't seem terribly serious: his prostate was enlarged again, and the bleeding was attributed to incipient kidney stones ("I had been hoping for some restraint on my erotic ardor and this seemed to serve," Cheever noted). However, when lab reports showed "irregularities" in his urine, Cheever was referred to a Phelps urologist named Marvin Schulman, who relieved the patient's immediate distress with a procedure that must have been intensely painful: a catheter with a spring-loaded blade was inserted into Cheever's ureter and then withdrawn, slicing through scar tissue and thus relieving the obstruction. "I felt like a Calla Liley [sic] with my stamen in the Waring Mixer," Cheever wrote Federico. Once he'd healed a little, though, he felt a certain gratitude toward the urologist; also, he might have figured that—given what had passed between them—it would be wise to endear himself: "[T]hank you for having cleared up my plumbing and for having left the relationship open-ended," he wrote Schulman that summer. "It is a pleasure to know that while my urinary tract has an understanding friend in Ossining, so also does the rest of me. In August I am one of those men who can be seen eating their fried potatoes alone in the Brasserie Suisse and I will call to see if you might join me."

Soon Cheever's pain and bleeding resumed, worse than ever, though he was determined to keep his good humor ("I take this all as a big joke since there really isn't anything else to be done"). At the beginning of July, Updike and his second wife came to Cedar Lane for lunch, and while Cheever had no appetite and looked "yellowish," he was a convivial host and even insisted on showing his guests the Croton Dam, where Updike's wife took a picture of the two writers. Looking at the photograph afterward, Updike was struck by how "visibly in pain" Cheever seemed: "Yet such was his vitality, and the dazzling veil of verbal fun he spun around himself,* that only the photograph made me realize how bravely ill he was that day." He was, in fact, only days away from a major crisis. On July 8, Cheever suffered another seizure and was rushed to the Phelps emergency room, where X-rays revealed a walnut-sized tumor on his right kidney. On July 14, the kidney was removed by Dr. Schulman, who declared the operation a success. As Cheever wrote in his journal, "I am told by the surgeon that the malig-

---

*Remarking, for example, that he'd been determined to finish his novel "even if [his] prick fell off," as sometimes seemed likely.

nity of my cancer was far from fatal and that the cancer was defenestrated very early in its career." Ben also spoke with the surgeon, and was also told that all would be well.

So Schulman might have thought at the time. Two days later, a pathology lab report indicated "transitional cell carcinoma," a generally low-grade malignancy that tends to be treated with electrodesiccation, in which recurring bits of cancerous tissue are burned away with electric current. In other words, the report was relatively good news. That same day, however—July 16—a *second* report was submitted to Dr. Schulman, indicating the presence of a deadly, "poorly differentiated" hypernephroma (common to heavy smokers) that spreads rapidly and requires immediate attention. Schulman sent both reports to Dr. Mutter, stapling a little note to the second one: "Attached is the revised report on John Cheever. Please destroy previous report and replace it with this one. Thank you."

Meanwhile Schulman stuck to the story offered by the *first* report (which incidentally remained in the file). "I returned from the hospital only yesterday morning and feel exactly like a man who has risen from the dead," Cheever wrote Art Spear on July 22. "Indeed, according to Dr. Schulman, that is what I am." And what of Cheever's longtime physician and friend, Ray Mutter? He, too, was in possession of the dire facts, and would eventually—four months later—be the one to break the news. However, back in July, Mutter simply assumed that Schulman was maintaining a postoperative follow-up, which naturally would have entailed discussing the prognosis and treatment options. "To begin with," Mutter explained, "this is a very complicated tumor and you needed a urologist to try to interpret it. Technically, it's a very difficult problem, and I'm sure that Schulman ducked it. He ducked telling John about it and he *should* have told John about it. It's shocking to me, too. I'm struggling with this because I'm sitting here thinking, 'Where did the ball drop between July and December?' " When it finally came to light that Schulman had been less than candid, various family members (including Bill Winternitz, a physician) had urged Mary to sue, but by then her husband was dead and she wanted to put the matter behind her. When asked many years later what she thought of Marvin Schulman, Mary said: "I hated him! He was one of those yucky people up to no good. He was making much of his association with Cheever, because he thought it reflected on his own importance." Then, ruefully, she added, "John liked people who played up to him."

Indeed, Schulman and Cheever cultivated a friendship of sorts (as we shall see), which might have been jeopardized if the urologist had told his patient frankly that he had less than a year to live. And if things were hopeless anyway, why not enjoy the friendship while it lasted?*

On some level, anyway, Cheever *knew* he was dying—whatever Schulman might say about little cauterizable bladder tumors—and he became severely depressed. "I conclude that these are the last weeks or months of my life," he wrote a few days after leaving the hospital, though he couldn't quite bring himself to confess the extent of his despair. He didn't want to burden his family, for any number of reasons—because he loved them, certainly, and because he'd spent a lifetime filtering a lot of unspeakable feelings through a façade of formality and laughter. ("I still feel very frail from the defenestration of my kidney and the loss has left me quite sentimental," he wrote Federico on July 24. "I sometimes cry when Edgar brings me a tennis ball.") Essentially alone with his misery, Cheever began hoarding pills in the drawer of his bedside table, until one day he blurted out that he was "frightened" while lunching with Don Ettlinger: "I wake up at night and I'm calling out 'Daddy, Daddy, *help* me,' and I've never called anybody Daddy in my whole life." He also told Ettlinger about the pills, which helped; afterward the thought of suicide began to seem "less important," and he decided to see a psychiatrist.

Schulman referred him to Donald Van Gordon in Croton, whose main impression of Cheever was one of total, exhausted surrender: the patient had skipped the denial and anger stages of grief (though he would revert to them later), and seemed melancholy but "kind of relieved," too, that the end was near; Van Gordon had never encountered a terminally ill patient who put up less resistance. Still, Cheever refused to succumb to an almost constant temptation to drink—"How *nice* it would be," he kept saying—nor had he stopped worrying what others thought of him. During his first visit to Van Gordon, Cheever presented the stranger with an inscribed copy of the paperback *Stories*: "To Donald Van Gordon, with profound gratitude."

Around this time, Cheever and Mary went to the Katonah Library for a reading by Eudora Welty, and while waiting in line they were approached by Dana Gioia, the young man Cheever had met at Stan-

---

*I'd very much like to hear Schulman's side of the story, but he died several years ago in a head-on collision.

ford several months after Smithers. As Gioia remembered of that final meeting: "[Cheever] looked thin, ashen, and painfully frail . . . seem[ing] half a century older than the quick, boyish man I had met only six years before."

SUBDUED BY ILLNESS, Cheever was capable of taking a more lucid view of his friendship with Max. "I sleep alone and wake to think how much happier things would be for Max if I were not around," he wrote that summer. With the psychiatrist he discussed the problem almost incessantly: Max wanted to take his girlfriend to Utah and perhaps reconcile with his family; Cheever realized he was "infring[ing]" on these plans, and really, under the circumstances, shouldn't he just let Max go? Finally? Van Gordon replied, sensibly enough, that Max would have to make that decision on his own, though Cheever perceived that "some power of decision" lay in his own hands for reasons that might have been hard to convey to a third party. In the meantime he imagined a jovial parting scene, both him and Max laughing: "Goodbye old man," Max would say. "It's too bad you never learned to change a tire."* This, Cheever knew, would be best for all concerned—but when it came to the point, he simply couldn't bear it. "If Max does not call by Thursday," he wrote, quite aware that Max was avoiding him, "I will call him and ask if he can do the driving next week."

"I am going to say goodbye," Max wrote in his own journal on July 30. "I am for the simple reason that I need to find the will to live again and the instinct for moving forward." Just over a week before, when Cheever was released from the hospital, he'd insisted that *Max* come to get him: Mary had an etching lesson, and Ben would be at work (though he'd offered to take the morning off), and Cheever didn't want to disrupt their routines. He also, of course, wanted to have his cake and eat it too, since he was therefore able to seem magnanimous to his family—a genuine impulse, after all—while at the same time enjoying Max's company. "She needed a vacation," he told Sara Spencer the fol-

---

*Perhaps an allusion to one of Max's more practical functions on Cedar Lane, since he was an excellent mechanic. But one thinks, too, of that line from "A Miscellany of Characters That Will Not Appear": "Out with this and all other explicit descriptions of sexual commerce, for how can we describe the most exalted experience of our physical lives, as if—jack, wrench, hubcap, and nuts—we were describing the changing of a flat tire?"

lowing week, when Mary left for Treetops. "It was pathetic," Spencer remembered, indignantly wondering (years later) what kind of wife would skip off to New Hampshire while her husband recovered—alone!—from cancer surgery. But of course Cheever wasn't alone, and (as Max's journal confirms) Mary had offered repeatedly to stay home and nurse him. For his part, Max had little choice except to go to Ossining. He'd set his heart on a trip to Utah at the end of August, but he was broke and money was hard to come by, since Cheever (as he freely admitted by then) was afraid of paying Max *too* much, lest he leave for good. "I have never, I think, had a more arduous thing to do in exchange for money, and I have been paid so poorly," Max wrote. "But what is it you do to rebel against an old man who says that being left by you will certainly not kill him but will make his life terribly hard." And still Cheever longed to do the right thing. He knew Max wanted nothing better than to go back to the city and be with his girl-friend, and to some extent Cheever wanted the same thing: he found the rituals of domesticity with a man—sitting on the porch reading together, chatting over steaks in a restaurant— "painfully awkward"; besides, he could make do as usual in August, going to AA meetings and watching baseball on TV. However: "I mustn't overlook the fact that I have a wayward cock to accommodate and so, I think, does he."

One of the drawbacks of lodging on Cedar Lane, for Max, was that he wasn't allowed to smoke; on the other hand, he was constantly encouraged to drink, and now he was also welcome to take as many Percodans as he liked, since Cheever didn't want to get hooked. One night Max took more Percodans than usual. Dr. Schulman was coming to dinner—that is, he and Cheever planned to have a drink at the house, then go to White Plains for dinner—and Cheever had made it clear that Max wasn't invited. As Max was about to clear out, though, Schulman arrived: a short, plump, rather awkward man who put Max in mind of a "very bad Truman Capote." As it might have seemed rude to leave at that moment, Max joined the two for a drink, but when he rose to refill Cheever's apple juice, Cheever put a hand over his glass and said, a little sharply, "No, Max. You go off and get your dinner." Flustered, hurt, and somewhat disoriented, Max picked up some take-out chicken and returned to Cedar Lane, but the two were still inside; Max circled around waiting for them to leave, and finally bolted his chicken on the shoulder of Route 134. At length he was able to return to the house and fall into bed, exhausted, but at some point he felt a tugging at his toes. "He's home, he's here," Cheever said to Edgar; then, to Max, "I hope I didn't seem uncivil to you this evening. It's just that he was such a handful I didn't feel comfortable with both of you here." Max couldn't get back to sleep after that, because his heart kept "racing, stopping, idling, jumping," and he worried that he was having a bad reaction to the alcohol and Percodan. First thing in the morning, then, he went to the hospital for an EKG, and was happy to learn that there was nothing wrong with his heart after all.

Once Cheever felt a little better, and Max had gone, he wrote a note to Tom Smallwood reporting that he was now "well enough to walk to the dam." The two hadn't met in many months and were delighted to see each other. As usual, they ate a good lunch and then walked along the aqueduct to a familiar outcropping, where Cheever was "rewarded with that vast serenity [he enjoyed] after a huge orgasm": "These young men, and there have been perhaps ten, who treat my sexual drives rather as if this were a condition of being wounded, have contributed greatly to my life in these last years. Traditionally these are felons, blackmailers and thieves but I have never known such innocence and generosity." And Tom, at least, regarded it as an even exchange: he didn't care much for the sex ("[I] kind of blocked [it] in my own mind"), but Cheever was marvelous company and loved having a congenial audience ("[Tom] has not heard any of the old, old stories such as that midnight on the Red Arrow express between Leningrad and Moscow when I ordered champagne for everyone on the train"). Crucially, too, Tom knew better than to overstay his welcome, and was generally the first to mention that it was time for him to catch a train back to the city.

Another nice aspect of the friendship was that Cheever could frankly discuss the gay side of his nature (with Max, the illusion of mutual heterosexuality was more imperative), and indeed, toward the end, he struck Tom as being "almost militant" about "mak[ing] up for lost time." Which appears to have been no idle pose. For a mortally ill man almost seventy years old, Cheever's libido remained intact to a degree that excites awe and even a trace of envy. A few weeks after his right kidney had been "defenestrated," Cheever complained of getting aroused "at the smell of bacon," and was quite willing to drag himself up several flights of stairs to a paid assignation in order to relieve this nagging affliction. And now that such encounters had become commonplace, Cheever seemed more and more bemused at all the fuss he'd made about his "androgynous struggle" over the years; reading old journals, he couldn't help finding the whole saga "hilarious" ("This is quite simply my life"):

> And so at breakfast [he wrote in September] I think of that chapter in my biography that describes how happily, at this time, he cultivated the friendships of several young men. He intended to encourage their literary aspirations, he enjoyed their company on bicycle trips and long walks and Louise Delshower claims to have encountered them several times in the woods, quite naked and howling loudly with sexual exertions. When cross-questioned he often said: Yes, yes, nothing could be more natural.

The widowed Helen Barolini, who lived near the aqueduct path, did in fact detect something amiss when—having read *Falconer*—she kept spotting Cheever walking along with some young man, though she never actually overheard their "exertions" ("I would also like to write about having an ejaculation with [Tom] and shouting loudly: 'This is journey's end' ").

Perhaps because he was more content in that department of his life, Cheever felt all the more beholden to his "venerable marriage," and wished to make some gesture to that effect. Early that autumn, he approached an architect friend from his Scarborough days, Don Reiman, and hired him to build an addition to the house that would serve as an etching studio for Mary, who'd been taking classes from a local artist and was quite passionate about it. The project cost upward of fifty thousand dollars in a difficult tax year, and while Cheever sometimes groused about wasting money, he always insisted it was something he wanted to do no matter what. Examining this impulse ("[my] gratefulness for Mary's willingness to live with so unstable a husband"), he wrote: "The word 'dear' is what I use: 'How dear you are.' It is the sense of moving the best of oneself toward another person. I think this was done most happily within my marriage, although I do remember being expelled to sofas in the living room, although not before the years had passed. I do recall the feeling of moving, rather like an avalanche, toward Mary."

CHAPTER FORTY-NINE

{ 1981–1982 }

CHEEVER HAD FINISHED a draft of *Oh What a Paradise It Seems* in June 1981, and, though uncertain of its merit, he was understandably pleased that he'd managed to write it at all. He expected Knopf to be a little disgruntled about the length (one hundred pages in published form), but he'd written the story he meant to write, more or less, and that would have to serve. As it happened, Gottlieb considered the book "beautiful," though he suspected the ending was too abrupt and suggested that Cheever write a "last movement" that would bring things to a more definite close. As with *Bullet Park*, Cheever was inclined to concede the point at first, resolving in his journal to make the "last chapter more dense"—but, once again, he seemed to conclude that the essential form of his novel had already been realized, or at any rate he had nothing to add.*

The other shoe dropped in September, when Cheever received a rather drastic contract amendment from Knopf. As Gottlieb later explained, "We had contracted for a full-length novel, and *Oh What a Paradise* was hardly that; there was no way it could possibly earn back so huge an advance (huge for the times). I did love it, though, and still

---

*I'd venture to suggest that Gottlieb's advice is reflected only in the book's last three sentences, where the narrator acknowledges some loose ends and decides to let them be: "But, you might ask, whatever became of the true criminals, the villains who had murdered a high-minded environmentalist and seduced, bribed and corrupted the custodians of municipal welfare? Not to prosecute these wretches might seem to incriminate oneself with the guilt of complicity by omission. But that is another tale, and as I said in the beginning, this is just a story meant to be read in bed in an old house on a rainy night."

do. John's reaction was, I'm afraid, a symptom of his deteriorating condition, something I only came to understand when I was working years later on the Journals." The amendment called for a second book "approximately 75–100,000 words" (more than twice as long as *Paradise*), for which Cheever would receive the remaining two hundred thousand dollars of his advance—which is to say, whereas he'd been expected to write *one* book for five hundred thousand dollars, now he was expected to write *two*. "Early in the evening I have read, for the first time, the new agreement with Knopf and when I wake at dawn I find myself in a rage," he wrote. "I remember being underpaid by the New Yorker, I remember being given a check for first-look that turned out to be an advance."

Cheever's rage would continue for a few days, then fizzle out. He was tired. Van Gordon, the psychiatrist, remarked on a "quality of wispiness" about him—the way he entered a room so quietly, so diffidently, one hardly knew he was there. Lynn Nesbit, his agent, was likewise struck by his "world-weariness" and wanted very much to cheer him up; to the best of her recollection, she'd offered to show the novel around and see if other publishers would match the original half-million or at least come close—but in the end, after venting his grievance, Cheever decided to stay with Knopf. "I find that I have misread my contract and that the rage and indignation with which I have been racked at dawn for several days was foolishness," he consoled himself. It's hard to say what Cheever had "misread"; his more businesslike daughter had read the amendment precisely as written and remained furious about it. "My father never would stand up for himself professionally," she said. "*Ever.* . . . And I thought, 'Enough!' And I yelled and screamed and carried on, and he *signed* it. Because he was a patsy."

Perhaps, but then Cheever felt obliged to his publisher: his wealth and fame would have been considerably less, after all, if Gottlieb hadn't pressed him to publish the *Stories.* During a radio interview in 1980, Cheever had been asked if he ever thought about switching publishers: "Why should I do that?" he replied. "Bob Gottlieb has been a *wonderful* editor. Knopf has done a *wonderful* job for me. . . ." Purely by chance, Gottlieb was listening that day.

AFTER THE CONTRACT DEBACLE, Cheever lost a certain amount of faith in his book—a process that had begun in earnest a month before, when he'd read Updike's *Rabbit Is Rich* in galleys: "I am delighted," he noted. "Indeed I am so covetous that I feel faint. But it is, this morning, I truly hope, a genuine sense of how serious an occupation this is." Eager to do his part for so "important" a novel, Cheever came to the city in October to appear with Updike on *The Dick Cavett Show*, where he seemed in decent fettle despite breaking his fly zipper just prior to taping (he kept his legs tightly crossed and looked flushed). After so many years of competitiveness (albeit mostly in Cheever's mind), the writers now seemed determined to out-praise each other. "I see [Cheever] do things effortlessly that I couldn't do with a great deal of effort," said Updike, and Cheever observed, "He is at the peak of his powers while I'm an old man nearing the end of my journey." At one point Cheever delivered himself of an extravagant paean to Updike's "inestimable" gifts, then chuckled, "Match *that* one." "I bet you wish you had Norman Mailer and Gore Vidal back on the show," said Updike. Indeed, the only hint of discord arose when Cheever allowed that he didn't—as Updike did—write much in the way of explicit sex scenes: "I do think the emphasis on our erotic life has always seemed questionable," he solemnly averred, adding a few days later (in a letter to Weaver) that Updike had "described erections so exhaustively that he's beginning to look like a big prick with a hair-piece."

No matter. The writers were resolving their sometimes murky association in a mood of almost perfect rapport. A month later, Updike wrote that he'd "read at a gulp" *Oh What a Paradise It Seems* and found it full of "brimming magic," whereupon Cheever replied that he'd meant to attach a cover letter to the galleys noting how "unenthusias-tic" he was about the book, in light of which Updike's praise was all the more "overwhelming." As for the Cavett show, Cheever had watched it alone in his kitchen the night before and deemed Updike "comely," whereas he himself "looked rather like a viper who was trying to break wind."

Meanwhile PBS had finally managed to get *American Playhouse* off the ground, and *The Shady Hill Kidnapping* was scheduled to air on Jan-uary 12, 1982, as the premiere offering of "the most ambitious and expensive single series in the history of public television," according to the *Times*. Three years ago, Cheever had gotten excited about the proj-ect when a reading of his teleplay was performed at the Public Theater by such notable actors as Kevin McCarthy, Maria Tucci, and Tammy Grimes (the last in the role Cheever was holding open for Hope Lange: "Hope is out on the coast," he wrote at the time, "playing the mother of a demented child in a two-part TV film"). Over time, though, he'd come to realize his script needed a lot of work—the PBS adaptations of his stories had been edifying in that respect—and when money suddenly became available in early 1981, Cheever was wide open to suggestions. His main collaborator was the director Paul Bogart (of *All in the Family* fame), who showed Cheever how to cut his teleplay by almost an hour and a half. Fortunately, this was easy to do. The "mysterious and oracular Bogart," as Cheever called him, pointed out that all the long descriptive bits would have to go, or else be converted to dialogue, ditto the "very peculiar" set pieces that seemed to bear little relation to the story proper.* But Cheever held firm on the five Elixircol commercials he'd written into the script, insisting rather absurdly that they played an "integral part" in the drama; in fact, he'd appropriated two of them almost word for word from "The Death of Justina," doubtless for the simple and sufficient reason that they delighted him.

He was not mistaken on that point: the commercials were by far the most entertaining part of the show. "The Surgeon General says that Elixircol has caused cancer in certain laboratory animals," intones a louchely preserved Celeste Holm.† "But who ever heard of the Surgeon General? Does he ever get asked anywhere? . . . Who wants to heed the warnings of a nonentity? Forget the Surgeon General." The tenor of these commercials harked back to a time when Cheever was at the height of his powers, driven to brilliance by (among other things) his indignation over a collective tendency to deny one's mortality in the midst of the nuclear age. But even at his most caustically satirical, there was always a softer, more wistful side to Cheever, a side that wanted to "cheer himself up," as Alfred Kazin had perceived. It is this side of Cheever—the glib transcendentalist—who wrote *The Shady Hill Kidnapping*. "What a paradise, what a kingdom it is!" exults his protagonist, Charlie Wooster (played by George Grizzard), as he sits in his backyard gazing out at a verdant suburbia. Nor is there any trace of irony here—caustic, wistful, or otherwise. Life *is* a paradise (particularly among the genteel middle class), or rather potentially, if only we

---

*In the opening scene, for instance, Cheever had indicated some dogs playing with what appears to be a ball but on closer inspection proves to be a human head. "What are you trying to tell me?" Bogart asked. Cheever thought about it, shrugged, and the scene was cut.

†A happy substitute for Hope Lange, who never did get on board.

can be a bit more mindful of just how precious we are to one another. The members of Wooster's winsome family are brought to this realization by the supposed kidnapping of Charlie's grandson, Toby, who wanders off for the day. This also serves as the premise for some broad-as-a-barn satire about the evils of bureaucracy: In order to pique the interest of an indifferent police department, Charlie's son Bob decides to drop a phony ransom note in the City Hall suggestion box; then a stuffy banker informs Charlie that he cannot receive a loan for the ransom unless he first agrees to build a swimming pool as "entre-preneurial collateral." And so on. As for the discontents of suburbia, they are touched on, lightly, by a kooky matron who entertains Toby while the community pursues its frenzied, oblivious search for the boy: "I have a nice husband, two beautiful children. We have so many con-sumer goods that we have a garage sale every autumn. But I terribly want *something* more. Guess that's why I like the thought of being in outer space. I'm so lonely I think there must be *someone* out there for me. I want to be kissed by a passing star."* This while Toby—too young to comprehend the spiritual bankruptcy of a materialistic soci-ety—cutely watches the skies.

Back when Cheever was writing some of the best fiction of the postwar era, a few captious critics chided him for having a sentimental streak: "He does not yet disturb us enough," said John Aldridge; "a toothless Thurber," said Irving Howe. It is interesting to imagine what the likes of Aldridge and Howe would have made of *The Shady Hill Kidnapping*. But Cheever had become a name, and most reviewers (not to mention Cheever himself) were willing to believe there was some-thing more here than meets the eye. Harry F. Waters of *Newsweek* was bound to admit that certain scenes were "as gooey as a box of Mallo-mars," though he discerned "flashes of brilliance" too; the *Boston Globe* applauded Cheever's teleplay as "bright, funny, accurate, and so damn well written that it makes the scripts for most fiction on television seem about as dramatic as a year-old issue of 'Plywood and Panel Mag-azine.'" According to the show's producer, Ann Blumenthal, *The Shady Hill Kidnapping* attracted one of the largest audiences ever for public television.

On October 30, ten weeks before the broadcast, Cheever had anx-iously attended an advance screening for friends and family at the

---

*A byproduct, perhaps, of Cheever's abandoned novel about "cosmic loneliness."

Henry Hudson Hotel on West Fifty-seventh. Mary and Ben mingled with the two hundred or so guests, but were elsewhere when Cheever took his seat in the front row and insisted that Tom Smallwood sit beside him. When the lights went down, he took Tom's hand and squeezed it slightly whenever he heard someone whispering, "It's really rather *good*, isn't it?" As he wrote in his journal, "I go to the city to see the TV show which is quite successful and which might contribute to my self esteem."

NOT LONG AFTER his kidney was removed, Cheever recovered enough strength to take short bicycle rides, but by the end of October he began to weaken again. His three days in New York for the screening party and other publicity (including a photograph session with Richard Avedon for the cover of WNET's magazine, *The Dial*) had left him not only exhausted but limping badly. Unable to get a cab, Cheever and Max walked many long blocks to Grand Central, and by the time Max helped him onto the train, Cheever could barely stay on his feet. A young woman named Martha Frey recognized Cheever from a reading he'd given at Vassar a few years back, and offered to carry his bag when they arrived at the Croton station. He was in no condition to protest, though he did speak up when she noticed his limp: "I am not at all infirm," he said. "Every day I bicycle around the block, up to twenty-five miles."

No more. As the pain in his leg increased, Cheever consulted with Mutter, who referred him to a chiropractor (oddly enough, given what he knew about Cheever's condition). The chiropractor suggested a traction device, which provided little relief. By Thanksgiving, Cheever was so ill he could hardly eat, and a few days later he reported to Mutter that he'd discovered "a whole new concept of what pain was." Little wonder: X-rays revealed that the cancer had now metastasized to his left ilium and femur, right ninth rib, and bladder. Schulman was able to burn away the bladder tumors, though he admitted in a postoperative report that they were likely to recur and that "the overall prognosis is, of course, poor." The day before the operation, Mutter had called Ben and informed him that his father was suffering from "unusually vigorous" bone cancer and would live maybe six months longer. Ben had planned to take his mother to *Nicholas Nickleby* that night—his father had paid for the tickets—and decided they might as well go; before the play, however, he broke the news to Mary, who afterward spent the "worst night of her life" alone in Susan's apartment. Two days later, she was in Mutter's office when he told Cheever the truth. As Mutter recalled, "It was the only time John wasn't happy, jovial, changing the subject from his own ills. The contrast made it terrible." Cheever embraced his wife and sat for a few moments "thunderstruck"; then he mentioned that Federico was getting married in California on Valentine's Day: "Will I at least be able to go to his wedding?" Mutter could promise nothing.

Max was waiting on Cedar Lane when the Cheevers came home, looking pale and lifeless. "The news is very bad," said Cheever with a little smile. On a number of levels, it was bad for Max too. He'd felt broken in spirit after his long stay in Ossining the previous August, and Cheever, perhaps sensing as much, had given him two thousand dollars for the trip to Utah with his girlfriend. "[Max] does seem to enjoy a dimension of freedom after his trip to the west and I intend to encourage this," Cheever subsequently observed. "We have had, I feel, a thoroughly enjoyable time together and now the time has come to part." Max would not have disagreed, but Cheever's increasing decrepitude made him hesitate; still, Max had all but definitely decided to make a clean break when Cheever came home, smiling bravely, and announced he had terminal cancer. "I thought, 'I can't do this now,' " Max remembered. " 'I've seen it through this far. However long it takes, I have to stick with it.' "

Susan was vacationing in California with Calvin Tomkins when Cheever called to give her the news; he told her that he'd also phoned Federico, who was coming home as soon as possible. "Some parents will do anything to get their kids to come home for Christmas," he quipped. Susan returned to New York and found her father lying resignedly in bed, waiting to die. She couldn't bear it: "I called Bill [Winternitz] and he told me to get him to Sloan-Kettering, and hurry. I went to Mutter, got the records, and was off to the races. Ray seemed surprised at the suggestion." Mutter's surprise was not unwarranted: the time for action had arguably passed months ago, even before Marvin Schulman had discovered the deadly malignancy in July 1981. At Sloan-Kettering, however, Cheever's case was picked up "enthusiastically" by a renowned expert on genito-urinary cancer, who seemed to think that an intensive program of chemotherapy and radiation stood a good chance of shrinking Cheever's tumors and possibly saving him. As Bill Winternitz recalled, "John was told by [the oncologist*] that his treatment would fix it: 'You'll be riding your bike in two weeks.' I thought that was obnoxious, and I've never felt good about Sloan-Kettering's treatment since then."

For much of that snowy winter, Max took a train to Ossining three times a week in order to drive Cheever to Sloan-Kettering at Sixty-eighth and York, where Cheever would doff his navy cashmere coat, tweed suit, gloves, and hat, then put on a gown ("those rags that are mandatory hospital dress") and go sit with other cancer patients in what he described as "a kind of laundromat," where he'd listen for hours to "vulgar and banal music" while waiting to have "a bolt of cobalt fired through [his] diseased bones." The waiting room wasn't altogether dreary, though. Looking around at his fellow sufferers, Cheever felt a powerful sense of solidarity with the "thousands and thousands" who were thus clinging to life, and meanwhile he couldn't help regaling Max with quick little stories about what these strangers were thinking, what their lives were like, on and on ("the guy's mind never rested"). Then at last Cheever's turn would come. "It was brutal," said Max. "They'd take him down this long corridor, with this strange aquarium lighting, and twenty minutes later he'd come back down the hallway in silhouette, dressed again in his tweed jacket, but just looking *fried*—lost, disoriented, his hair just [Max fluttered his fingers around his head and made a crackling noise] like he'd been electrocuted." Around ten o'clock, the two would drive back to Ossining, where Mary always had dinner ready, and Max would either spend the night or take a late train back to Manhattan.

"While my beloved wife and my good friend set the table for lunch I conclude that I will simply spend the rest of my life under the happy power of drugs," Cheever wrote after a few weeks of this. "That this is obscenely self-destructive seems a possibility. The pain in my chest is, at this hour, my main occupation." Cheever wanted desperately to believe what his doctors were telling him, but he suspected he was being a little deceived and that his suffering was pointless. As it was. And yet, for Cheever, it was no small triumph to recover his tenacity and go down fighting, though it made him cranky at times. *"Get out! And don't come back!"* he shouted at a doctor who'd proposed a

---

*Name omitted, though the man died in 1996. Unlike Marvin Schulman, he deserves, I think, the posthumous benefit of a doubt.

lot of bothersome tests (and worn tasteless clothing, or so an observer remembered). "Clare Thaw called and asked me the same thing," he said in a seething voice, when Max called to ask how he was doing after a session of chemotherapy. "I told her it was shitty and not to come and see me. I know very few people, Max—besides Clare Thaw—who would call and ask me that."

Mostly, though, Cheever was nothing but grateful toward family and friends, who indeed took every pain to comfort him in these final months. "My beloved daughter calls and she is a sort of paradise," Cheever wrote of a hospital stay in January 1982. "I bask in the many kinds of radiance she seems to bring into the room." To be sure, it was a little awkward when family visits coincided with visits from Tom or even Max. When the latter realized that he and Susan would be alone together while Cheever endured some lengthy procedure, he cast about for any excuse to flee; likewise, Tom felt a little superfluous when Susan arrived one day, six months pregnant, and found him sitting in the chair nearest her father. "Aren't you going to give your chair to a pregnant woman?" she asked. Cheever tended to be the calm eye at the center of these imbroglios. He insisted that Tom stay, and at other times would gently inform his daughter that he was expecting a lover (gender unspecified). Though he was too frail to "throw backgammon dice," as he wrote Clare Thaw, his erotic drives withstood even the worst ravages of cancer and its treatment. At home he would hobble into the woods to look at photographs of naked men, and a nurse once entered his hospital room while he and Tom were "stark naked and engorged on top of one another."

Cheever himself was "astonished at [his] lewdness": "That I can be lewd at all is paradoxical in the light of the love I receive these days from the family and one's friends and lovers. The great beauty of this seems in some way to transcend most physical drives and aspirations. It is spiritual." At best, he attained a kind of golden mean. Determined to be candid and considerate after a fashion, he asked Mary's permission to invite Tom to the house on February 1. The young man kept Cheever company while he answered mail in Ben's old room at the top of the house ("[I] didn't realize how much he talked to himself," Tom wrote in his journal), after which the two had sex even though Mary was moving around downstairs. When they joined her later, she didn't seem the least annoyed or suspicious. She asked Tom to carry the dying Edgar into the snow so the dog could pee (nobody mentioned the morbid coincidence), and on parting she warmly thanked him for lifting her husband's spirits. Helping Cheever cope was all part of the same benevolent project.

Perhaps the heaviest burden fell to Max, who in January—with Cheever's encouragement—had tried to find more conventional employment in publishing. Wearing a brand-new Brooks Brothers suit that he'd bought with Cheever's credit card, he walked twenty blocks to the Random House offices ("because all I had in my pocket was a nickel"), only to learn, from Rob Cowley, that the best job he could possibly hope for would be entry-level. That left Max with his work on Cedar Lane, which was more plentiful than ever. In addition to chauffeuring duties, he handled Cheever's business correspondence, serviced his VW Rabbit, ran errands of all kinds, and attended to the usual household chores.* Above all, Cheever depended on his simple physical presence, though he reproached himself for imposing on Max's kindness by asking him to stay overnight—yet again—while knowing full well that Max longed to catch a train but could hardly say no. One night, as Cheever was about to retire, he invited Max to occupy himself by reading a couple of journals. "On the day I left," Max noted, "he told me the reason for letting me read the journals was to give me some notion of cadence."

CHEEVER'S PROGRESS WAS MIXED after the first month of treatment, though he remained determinedly hopeful. The radiation, at least, appeared to be working: he could walk a little better on his left leg, and the burning in his rib cage had decreased somewhat. Over the same period of time, however, he'd lost twenty pounds, and the chemotherapy had done nothing to shrink his tumors. In late January, the oncologist decided to switch Cheever to an experimental treatment of platinum and methotrexate.

The first dose would require a week in the hospital, and Cheever asked whether this (as well as the radiation) might henceforth be administered at Northern Westchester in Mount Kisco, since the long days of convalescence at Sloan-Kettering made him homesick, and never mind the logistical difficulty. He was therefore referred to the thirty-two-year-old Robert Schneider, who'd recently interned with Cheever's regular oncologist. "I am *so* pleased to meet you!" Cheever

*According to a family ledger, Max was paid $4,806 for his services from January to June 1982.

said, springing up from a stretcher (en route to a bone scan) to shake the young man's hand. The two immediately warmed to each other. Schneider was "the only doctor who didn't say it was all right for me to start drinking again," said Cheever, grateful for such manifest faith in his survival. "To Robert Schneider, with whom I share an uncommon hopefulness," he inscribed his most cheerful book, *The Wapshot Chronicle*.

He needed all the reassurance and friendship he could get. Edgar had also been diagnosed with cancer, and if anything the coughing dog regarded Cheever as a bad omen, rather than vice versa. When her master had come home from his kidney operation the previous summer, Edgar had given up her place at the foot of his bed and gone to sleep in the living room. At length Cheever coaxed her back, and later forced himself to crawl painfully under his car to dislodge her when she'd gotten stuck in the snow. Edgar died, finally, in March. "I don't even have a correspondent to whom I can write letters," Cheever lamented afterward. For months he'd been writing little notes to people he cared about, most of them long out of touch; the notes tended to say goodbye, in effect, or else (depending on his mood) that he "fully expect[ed] to recover"—at any rate he let his friends know that he was sick and missed them. A year after his death, Shirley Hazzard found such a note *(Won't you come see us?)* stuck inside a book; she showed it to her husband, Francis Steegmuller, and both were reminded of how they'd meant to visit Cheever but hadn't gotten around to it in time. "We were both so grieved by that," said Hazzard. "We had quite close feelings, though we didn't see a great deal of each other. John's a person I'll always think quite tenderly of."

All too often we are forced to live apart from the people we love most in the world, and this was Cheever's fate to an uncommon degree. His little address book was largely composed of Russian and Bulgarian names—soulmates whose company he'd enjoyed for a few weeks over the course of a lifetime—and one of the first persons he'd called in December, after Mutter had told him the bad news, was a dear friend he hadn't seen in some three years (and rarely before): Saul Bellow. "Since we spoke on the phone I've been thinking incessantly about you," Bellow wrote him a few days later.

> . . . What I would like to tell you is this: we didn't spend much time together but there is a significant attachment between us. I suppose it's in part because we practiced the same self-taught trade. Let me

try to say it better, we put our souls to the same kind of schooling, and it's this esoteric training which we had the gall, under the hostile stare of exoteric America that brings us together. . . . Neither of us had much use for the superficial "given" of social origins. In your origins there were certain advantages; you were too decent to exploit them. . . . You were engaged, as a writer should be, in transforming yourself. When I read your collected stories I was moved to see the transformation taking place on the printed page. There's nothing that counts really except this transforming action of the soul. I loved you for this. I loved you anyway, but for this especially. . . . Love, Saul

The feelings ran even deeper—and far darker—in the case of Maxwell, whom Cheever didn't write until the end of January, when he learned that chemotherapy wasn't working. A few months before, he'd had an erotic dream about his old friend ("I pursue Hope and end up with Bill Maxwell"), which perhaps reflected a few salient if subliminal aspects of their curious relationship: "[Bill] tells me that I am a little mad and that this is the only distinction my style enjoys. He reproves me for my sexual promiscuity . . ." What Cheever finally wrote the man was this: "I have been ill and I wanted to be the one to tell you, I remember so vividly, over the years, your attention. I am quite beyond visits and flowers but I do distribute The Collected Short Stories among the doctors. They seem in the end to be mostly what I've written— even Honora Wapshot is forgotten—and thank you for your help with them." Reading this, Maxwell found himself wishing he'd had the grace years ago "to break through the misunderstanding [before it] was too late," and his reply (and final letter) to Cheever was "written in tears": "The stories are safe," he began, assuring Cheever that his work ranked among the finest of Flaubert, Chekhov, Byron, Yeats; as for what Cheever had called Maxwell's help, it had mostly consisted of the simple "rapture" he'd felt on reading each of Cheever's masterpieces for the first time. He then proceeded to more personal matters. "In recent years"—given Cheever's great success—Maxwell had gotten the impression he'd lost his friend forever: "Your note made it clear that this wasn't true, and I am ashamed of having thought it."

SUSAN HAD BECOME PREGNANT the previous summer, and she and Calvin Tomkins were married a few months later in the library at

Cedar Lane ("It was Tad who suggested that a shot gun might be in order," Cheever wrote Federico, "but if I bring out the old 16-guage [sic] I might be arrested for the possession of an unliscened [sic] fire-arm"). As for Ben, he'd been dating the *New York Times* film critic Janet Maslin, and the two had planned to marry the following June or July; when Ben's father was given six months to live, however, they moved the ceremony to Christmas Eve, 1981. Cheever was delighted by the match, and proved a jolly guest at the wedding (also held in the library), despite his frailty. When the justice of the peace was tardy, Cheever recruited one of the guests, Tony Oursler, to officiate—since, said Cheever, the man's father (Fulton) had written *The Greatest Story Ever Told*, and hence Tony was the closest thing to a clergyman they were likely to find. As the last vows were spoken, the justice of the peace breathlessly arrived, and the couple were married once more.

Whatever its constraints, Cheever's relationship with his older son had become steady and amiable. Ben had persuaded his father to let *Reader's Digest* reprint a few of his old stories (some in condensed form), and Cheever also contributed an essay to the magazine, "Signs of Hope," a rather ponderous homage to his son's long-distance run-ning. "For years, lovers seemed to me to be proof that the world would go on," the piece begins. "Now marathon runners, gathering by thou-sands in cities all over the world to pursue the horizons of fatigue and self-esteem, contribute equally to hopefulness." Cheever had shown the typescript to Tom Smallwood during his February visit, and the young man had permitted himself a quibble or two about this or that line. Cheever erupted: "I was only trying to do something for a place which has gainfully employed my eldest son!" Once he'd calmed down a bit, Cheever fretfully admitted that he was afraid the essay would be the last thing he ever published, as indeed it was.*

Finally, on Valentine's Day, Federico was wed to Mary McNeil in Riverside, California. Only a few weeks before, Cheever had hopefully booked himself an airplane ticket, but when the time came he was sim-ply too ill. "Now this morning Mary and Iole have been driven by Max to take a plane for Fred's California wedding," he noted. "Mary's eyes fill with tears and there is a potential for a tearful scene but we force beyond this." It was a terrible blow, but otherwise the thought of his

---

*Appearing in the May 1982 issue, shortly before Cheever's death.

son gave him nothing but joy: Federico's choice of wife was "highly mature," Cheever reflected, and he was also thrilled that Federico had chosen a sensible profession, law, rather than pursue a Ph.D. in history (or write fiction, for that matter), as he'd once planned. "You have been a splendid son," Cheever wrote, by way of farewell.

CHAPTER FIFTY

{ 1982 }

CHEEVER DESCRIBED *Oh What a Paradise It Seems* as an "eco-logical romance," in which an old man comes to terms with a sense of his own corruption by purifying a pond that has been rezoned as a garbage dump; thus he succeeds "in loving usefulness," as Cheever would have it. Searching for purity, Lemuel Sears is searching for nothing less than an idea of *home* in all its metaphysical grandeur: "Home might be an empty room and an empty bed to many . . . including Sears, but swinging over the black ice [of Beasley's Pond] convinced Sears that he was on his way home. Someone more skeptical might point out that this illuminated how ephemeral is our illusion of homecoming." Home, ideally, is a place where one feels loved, safe, at one with creation, and no wonder it proves ephemeral; yet a yearning for at least some simulacrum of home is part of the human predicament, more so for Cheever than most. Having spent the better part of his life in exile—from a beloved brother, a river, a beach, a fragrance of wood smoke and salt marshes, a village where people knew him and his family—Cheever would pursue this illusion, in art as in life, to the day of his death. His fictional surrogates *ache* for home, and so, in this final novel, the narrator begins and ends with a wish that the reader be, if nothing else, cozy "in bed in an old house on a rainy night."

To be estranged from home is to be lonely and frightened, and of course the only remedy is love, the pursuit of which is problematic. "Sears's sexual demands had given him a great deal of pleasure, some embarrassment and a painful suspicion that the polarities in his constitution were acutely incompatible and that the only myth that suited his

disposition was Dr. Jekyll and Mr. Hyde." Sears fancies himself akin to
Jekyll, on the one hand, because he's a benign, romantic old man "with
loads of friends"; but he is also Mr. Hyde, because women, to him, are
little more than lovely abstractions—the "sunny side of the street"—
whom he can't begin to fathom except through the direct method of
knowing as prescribed in the Bible. "You don't understand the first
thing about women," his lover Renée tells him, again and again,
though Sears's mystification in her case would seem to be understandable. Renée *is* unfathomable. As a character she hardly attains two
dimensions, much less three: we are given only the faintest idea of her
appearance or personality, and she coyly refuses to discuss even her
most telling behavior (attending what are evidently AA meetings). Not
that Sears is particularly curious about her or any of the other women
in his life. After the death of his first wife (the "sainted Amelia"), he
"simply accepted" a marriage proposal from Estelle, the "provincial
sorceress," taking on faith her prediction of future happiness despite
the barren failure of her previous marriage. (The woman's powers of
divination are belied when she doesn't notice the train that wipes her
off the face of the earth.) As for Renée Herndon, pretty much the sum
of what Sears knows about her is that she's willing to sleep with him
despite a thirty-year age difference and scant common interests—
until, just as mysteriously, she won't anymore.

> "I've missed you terribly," [Sears] said. "I'm so hardpacked that I
> can't eat." He unbuckled his trousers and let them fall to his knees.
>   "I'm sorry," she said, "but I cannot help you." . . .
>   "I'll get some flowers," he said. He pulled up and fastened his
> trousers.

One suspects Mr. Hyde had a similar approach, but in Sears's case it
doesn't work (this time), and the lovely Renée simply vanishes from
the book with barely a further word.
    Puzzled and heartbroken, Sears promptly takes up with the elevator
operator in Renée's building, Eduardo, next to whom Renée (as a character) is a triumph of nuanced roundness. The reader has caught a
fleeting glimpse of Eduardo ten pages before, when he gives Sears a
"look of solicitude" that apparently derives from some notion of
Renée's vagaries; when the two meet again, Eduardo wordlessly
embraces the bereft old man: "The stranger's embrace seemed to com-

prehend that newfound province of loneliness that had frightened Sears. . . . The stranger, whose name he hadn't learned, took him downstairs to a small room off the lobby, where he undressed Sears and undressed himself. Sears's next stop, of course, was a psychiatrist." Sears's consternation is not so much due to the fact that he allowed himself to be seduced by an anonymous elevator operator, but rather because his seducer is, after all, a man: "I've never really had any reason to be anxious about money or friends or position or health," Sears "politely" explains to Dr. Palmer, the psychiatrist, "but I did enjoy myself with the elevator man and if I should have to declare myself a homosexual it would be the end of my life." Dr. Palmer informs Sears that he is a "neurotic" who has "invented some ghostly surrogate of a lost school friend or a male relation from [his] early youth." It transpires, however, that Dr. Palmer's views are hardly disinterested, since he himself is a "homosexual spinster" who has spent much of his life in "vigilant repression" of "random erections" suffered because of the odd comely male. We are therefore left with the impression that Sears's "polite" candor is far less neurotic than the shrink's hapless denial, and when the latter accuses Sears, say, of "construct[ing] a carapace of friendliness," it seems merely absurd.

Another aspect of homelessness treated in the novel is the nomadism of modern life, the "converging highways and the gathering whiplike noise of traffic" which conspire to blight the "intrinsic beauty" of the world. Distracted by the mad clamor of it all, Henry and Betsy Logan ruin an idyllic day at the beach by leaving their baby on the shoulder of Route 224—which leads happily, however, to a rare friendship with the baby's savior, Horace Chisholm, who also happens to be the environmentalist Sears has hired to investigate the Beasley's Pond affair. Like Sears, Chisholm seeks in nature a sense of purity—oneness—otherwise lacking in his lonely life: "Nothing waited for him in his apartment. There was no woman, no man, no dog, no cat, and his answering tape would likely be empty and the neighborhood where he lived had become so anonymous and transient that there were no waiters or shopkeepers or bartenders who would greet him." His new friend Betsy assuages her own suburban loneliness by pushing a cart around the Buy Brite ("a massive store in the shopping mall on the four-digit interstate"), to which she vengefully returns when Horace is murdered by the cabal of gangsters and venal public officials who have turned Beasley's Pond into a garbage dump: "Her cart was empty and in her raincoat pocket she carried a bottle of Teriyaki Sauce to which she had added enough ant poison to kill a family. Pasted to this was a message that said: 'Stop poisoning Beasley's Pond or I will poison the food in all 28 Buy Brites.' "

And so the dumping ends, just like that, and Sears is left with the ecstatic task of restoring his skating pond to purity. What this means in metaphorical terms is neatly spelled out for us: "[Sears] had found some sameness in the search for love and the search for potable water. The clearness of Beasley's Pond seemed to have scoured his consciousness of the belief that his own lewdness was a profound contamination." This passage appears on page 99, at which point the reader may indeed be wondering what will happen (with only a page remaining) to the criminals who murdered Chisholm and poisoned the pond. For that matter, what of Renée, who has been missing since the middle of the book? And Eduardo? After that curious tryst in the room off the lobby, he and Sears went on to take a cheerful (and for the most part manly) fishing trip together, after which it was implied that Eduardo would return to his wife and Sears to his pond project, never to meet again, yet mutually refreshed by their harmless encounter. And what, finally, is one to make of the revelation (on page 24) that the book's narrator is a personage from the distant future, lying near a mint-scented stream, "concealed with [his] rifle, waiting to assassinate a pretender who is expected to come here, fishing for trout"? Nothing further is made of this, though one might surmise that the future will be more pastoral (and feudal?) than the blighted, nomadic present, or something like that. But never mind—"this is just a story meant to be read in bed in an old house on a rainy night"—and perhaps Cheever does well to stress the fairy-tale aspect of things. In a fairy tale, elements of conventional narrative can be safely abandoned: women can be bizarrely capricious (whether hot *or* cold); elevator operators can spontaneously offer release from certain "modes of loneliness" before fading back into blessed anonymity, without a trace of the complicated anguish that so-called real life tends to entail. That said, fairy-tale evasions rarely result in good art.

The valedictory themes of the novel were inherently poignant, though, and Cheever addressed them with feeling and an undiminished prose style, such that many reviewers were able to praise *Oh What a Paradise It Seems* with a clear conscience. By the time it was published, in March, Cheever's illness was well known and newspapers were already preparing obituaries. John Leonard, for one, gladly volunteered to write a gentle front-page notice for the *Times Book Review:*

Cheever's "very short and often lovely novel," he said, was a relief after "the heroin addiction, homosexuality and convenient miracles of 'Falconer' [a relief from the heroin addiction anyway]. . . . Certainly, 'Oh What a Paradise It Seems' is minor art, although many of us will never grow up to achieve it." Similarly, in the daily *Times*, Anatole Broyard (who'd been invited to the Cheevers' famous 1969 dinner dance, less than two months after his mixed review of *Bullet Park*) conceded that he wasn't really "comfortable" with the novel's abrupt ending, but then, as he diffidently pointed out, Cheever was the "most spontaneous" of major American writers and doubtless knew what he was doing ("I gave up some time ago the notion that art was a comfortable affair"). Updike, more aware than most of Cheever's recent suffering, wrote perhaps the most elegant tribute of all for *The New Yorker*: "The book is too darting, too gaudy in its deployment of artifice and aside, too disarmingly personal in its voice, to be saddled with the label of novel or novella; it is a parable and a tall tale. . . . [A]ll is fancy, praise, and rue, seamlessly." "Seamlessly" is a long (if heartfelt) stretch, but the opposite view was taken only by a few marginal cranks. "Though Cheever can still turn a phrase with the best of them," wrote a reviewer for *The Village Voice* (also vicious on the subject of Mary's poetry), "*Oh What a Paradise It Seems* is by any and every standard a bad book, worthy of notice only because he put his name to it. Clumsily lurching back and forth between postmodern and realistic techniques, it botches both."

The final verdict was reflected in sales—less than respectable for a writer of Cheever's fame and critical éclat, though not downright disastrous. A rather modest first printing of thirty thousand sold out in a few weeks, perhaps to the mild surprise of Cheever's publisher, as once again a second printing was slow to reach the stores. By then demand had vanished, and there were no further printings. Cheever was not altogether stoical: "That I am not on the best-seller list and that Ann[e] Tyler is* makes me think myself a forgotten creature in the vast cemetery where the living dead of those who have lost their vogue wait out the last, long year of their time on earth. Up yours."

AFTER SIX WEEKS OF PLATINUM, Cheever was told that his tumors were shrinking and that he had a "fifty-fifty chance" of survival. He

---

*With *Dinner at the Homesick Restaurant*.

was naturally elated, and could bear a little better the blow of losing his hair. Almost forty years ago his father had written him, "You were bald as billiard ball, for 6 mo[nth]s as a kid—but you caught up later on hair-game—as all the Cheevers—'wear a lot of hair'—till the final curtain." Cheever had looked forward to the fruits of this inheritance, but one morning in early March he awoke to find most of his hair (only a bit of it gray) on the pillow. Undaunted, he began working again in Ben's room—the best therapy at any time, all the more now that he claimed to be writing stories about cancer survival. Actually, his journal indicates that he was considering a short novel or screenplay ("opening on a slapstick Preston Sturgis tone") about a space-shuttle evacuation of New York resulting from a nuclear accident. An even more compelling theme, however, was yet another apologia "about the sexual enjoyment and sometimes bewilderment men can find with one another": "My determination is to make it clear that in the human condition there are discontents, seizures of loneliness and unease that seem only answered by our homosexual loves."

By the end of March, he was more hopeful than ever ("[I] am determined," he wrote a friend, "to celebrate my 80th birthday by walking to Croton dam"), but a few days later the doctor announced that he was suspending platinum, which Cheever correctly interpreted as an admission that platinum wasn't working. Instead, they gave him shots of "a pollution that is distilled from the Adriatic," as Cheever put it, and within a few days he assured himself, once again, that he was feeling much better. "Gaunt, limping and with much of his hair gone," he gave a clowning interview to the local newspaper, remarking that Dick Cavett had just invited him to do another show: "I asked if I could do it in bed. He didn't think that was funny. I said they could roll the bed out on the set. He thought that was even less funny." A further surge of hope was provided by the birth of his granddaughter, Sarah Liley Cheever Tomkins, on April 12. "I've kicked it," he told Susan the next morning. "It's over."

But more and more he seemed to know better. When his niece Jane Carr sent him a note with a comforting quote from scripture, he took to calling her every so often, mentioning at one point that Fred had died instantly ("what a gift that was"), whereas he himself had to endure this endless agony. Chatting with Hope Lange's brother, David— who owed much of his present sobriety to Cheever—he joked about the hats he wore to cover his baldness, then abruptly became somber: "You know, I can't joke with you," he said. "I only have a few months to live." Lange asked if he'd considered drinking again, and Cheever said no: "When I do [die], I want it to be with dignity." But it was one thing to unburden himself with faraway friends and relations, another to do so with his immediate family, toward whom he maintained a hopeful, humorous façade almost to the end (mixed with pardonable moments of sarcasm or petulance). As much as possible they responded in kind, lest they betray an awful despair toward the whole ghastly ordeal. "[T]here's never a word from the god damn doctors about life or death," Susan wrote Elizabeth Spencer in April—"all they talk about are the miracles of modern medicine and the wonderful thing they are going to try next." Indeed, certain oncologists were not only disingenuous but patronizing: the same doctor who'd told Cheever he had a "fifty-fifty chance" commented to another doctor, in Cheever's presence, that "anything we do from this point on will be palliative"—as if "palliative" were esoteric medical jargon.

"What I am going to write is the last of what I have to say, and Exodus, I think, is what I have in mind," Cheever noted, prior to preparing his remarks for the American Book Awards ceremony at Carnegie Hall on April 27, when he would become the fifteenth recipient of the National Medal for Literature.* Cheever's colleagues—remembering the jaunty man who walked with a quick, seafaring swagger—were aghast at what cancer and its treatment had wrought: wearing a sheepskin cap on his bald head, shrunken into his overcoat, Cheever hobbled along leaning on his wife and a cane—looking, as Max observed, "as though he [were] more in pain from the impression of being lame than of being lame itself." Otherwise he seemed in a fine humor. "Ah, Bill, just tell them I'm short," he quipped to William Styron, when he noticed the two-page panegyric the man had written, which did in fact prove a little on the mawkish side. "In his stories and in his novels," said Styron, "in prose often as sweet and limpid as Mozart but quietly and triumphantly his own, he has told us many things about America in this century: about the untidy lives lived in tidy households, about betrayal and deception and lust and the wounds of the heart, but also about faith and the blessings of simple companionship and the abiding reality of love. . . ." Styron went on like that, then turned to his subject (who'd let go of his cane to cover his ears) and concluded, "You are a

---

*Previous recipients included Nabokov, Auden, Welty, Edmund Wilson, Marianne Moore, Robert Penn Warren, and Robert Lowell.

lord of the language." In the past, Cheever's remarks on these occasions had always been witty, self-deflating, and barely audible, and
after that introduction he might have wished he'd taken such an
approach this time, too—but this was his "Exodus," after all, and he
was entitled to a certain gravitas. "For me, a page of good prose is
where one hears the rain," he said, almost stentorian, startling those
who'd gasped at his frailty when he first appeared on stage. "A page of
good prose is when one hears the noise of battle. . . . A page of good
prose seems to me the most serious dialogue that well-informed and
intelligent men and women carry on today in their endeavor to make
sure that the fires of this planet burn peaceably." Exiting to explosive
applause, Cheever tottered into an otherwise empty hall and was
embraced by his eighty-three-year-old mentor, Malcolm Cowley. "It
was more than fifty years since John first appeared in my office at the
New Republic," Cowley remembered. "John was now older than I and
was leading the way."

AND STILL CHEEVER had days when he seemed quite certain he'd
survive, almost as if it were a kind of mischievous secret. When Gurganus visited for the last time, in May, Cheever met him at the train
station in apparent high spirits, and though he took a long time on the
stairs ("Usually he sort of skipped up and down them like a boy in
loafers"), his deliberation seemed rather graceful. But he soon grew
tired, and rather than walk along the aqueduct as usual, the two sat on
the porch while Cheever spoke of his dogs' private lives ("Maisie
sneaks off in the night and does sad and unspeakable acts with railroad
mongrels, but we are not to know"). Back at the station, Gurganus
said, "I guess I won't be seeing you again"—then added in a rush, as
Cheever's smile died, "until I leave for Yaddo."

It was spring, the dam was in spate, and Cheever's reluctance to
leave the world was keener than ever. "Oh, I wish I were walking across
a field in Ireland!" he sighed, while he and Mary watched a movie
about Parnell and Kitty O'Shea; seeing the lovers walk among flowers
had made him "want to live so." But gradually he let things go. "I
expect we'll renew our connection later," he wrote in a farewell note
to Bellow (having always claimed that they'd met in some other
life, and hence didn't need to spend a lot of time together in this
one). There was a strong sense of parting, too, in his last meeting with

Tom Smallwood. Leafing through an old journal he'd written in Italy, Cheever said, "You might find this interesting"—indicating a passage where he'd described (tormentedly as ever) his arousal at the sight of a handsome soccer player: this, he seemed to suggest, had been part of his life for a very long time. Finally, saying goodbye, he urged Tom to start a family of his own someday, as that was by far the most important aspect of any man's happiness. (Years later, when Tom was reading excerpts from Cheever's journal in *The New Yorker*, he noticed that one of the last entries was about himself: "He [Tom] is a pleasant young man about whose way of life, whose friends, I know nothing and can imagine nothing." "I really regretted that," said Tom, "because I realized I didn't tell him that much about me, because I was so careful to have that relationship exist out of time and out of place. But I adored him, and I miss him a lot. I wish he'd lived and could see the life I live now, because I think he'd be very happy for me.")

Cheever rapidly weakened during the last weeks of his life. "For the first time in forty years I have failed to keep this journal with any care," he wrote. "I am sick. That seems to be my only message." He found himself tiring with "freakish ease" and always felt cold; during a four-hour blood transfusion, he asked Max to hold his hand ("as cold, at first, as any hand I have held"), which gradually warmed as the fresh blood began to circulate. But soon Cheever was beyond such help. He was so exhausted he couldn't bring himself to wind his Rolex (that, too, was Max's job), and when old friends visited, Cheever seemed torn between begging them to stay, lest he never lay eyes on them again, and simply relapsing into blessed oblivion. The last lines of his journal were written in mid- or late May, when he could just muster the strength, still, to drive a guest to the train station:

> I have never known anything like this fatigue. I feel it in the middle of dinner. We have a guest to be driven to the train, and I begin to count the number of times it takes him to empty his dessert plate with a spoon. There is his coffee to finish, but happily he has taken a small cup. Even before this is empty I have him on his feet for the train. It will be for me, I know, twenty-eight steps from the table to the car, and, after he has been abandoned at the station, another twenty-eight steps from the car to my room, where I tear off my clothes, leave them in a heap on the floor, turn out the light, and fall into bed.

His friendship with Max did not become any less complicated. "I have been your Sancho Panza," Max wrote in his journal on May 3, "and I have to stop doing this if I am to get over my longing for your death." Around this time he began seeing a therapist. At first he discussed the fact that he wasn't able to write anymore, and when the therapist asked how he'd managed to support himself, Max mentioned Cheever—circling back, at last, to a moment at the Lake City Motel in 1977, and painfully working his way forward. At some point he began talking about Mary—how ashamed he felt whenever he kissed her. "That was the moment I started crying."

Cheever's own remorse, by then, had mostly to do with his children. He felt particularly obliged to confess things to Ben, who, as a boy, had been the main victim of his self-loathing. "My reluctance to describe to [Ben] my sexual conduct originates in part in my own intolerance," Cheever had written back in November, having spent the previous two years or so talking around the issue of his "difficult propensities." In May, when Ben and Janet were about to leave for a belated honeymoon, Cheever asked if he could speak with his son's therapist in the meantime; when Ben returned from his trip, however, he found that the woman hadn't been contacted. Finally, less than two weeks before his death, Cheever phoned his son at work. "The conversation was brief," Ben remembered in the *Letters*.

 . . . He explained that he hadn't been to see my therapist. This, he said, was "partly because I was busy and partly because I didn't see why I couldn't tell you what I had to tell you face-to-face." He hadn't been busy, he'd been sick, but we both honored this fiction. "What I wanted to tell you," he said, "is that your father has had his cock sucked by quite a few disreputable characters. I thought I'd tell you that, because sooner or later somebody's going to tell you and I'd just as soon it came from me." . . .

 I was forgiving, but mostly I was just bewildered, and I remember now that my reply came almost in a whisper: "I don't mind, Daddy, if you don't mind."

 . . .

TOWARD THE END, after many years, Cheever moved back into the master bedroom with Mary, who devoted almost every waking moment to his care. She cooked three meals a day whether he could eat them or not, and would sometimes crouch over him in bed and shout a little fearfully—"*John! John!*"—when he wouldn't wake up. Once, she stepped outside just long enough to get the mail and check on her garden, and when she came back he was groaning on the floor. While staggering to the bathroom, he'd fallen and broken his leg. With the help of a neighbor, Mary got him back on the bed; then a hospice nurse was summoned to clean him up, put his leg in a splint, and keep him out of pain for the few days he had left. He rarely regained consciousness. One of his last visitors was Don Ettlinger, who found his friend in a fetal position, wizened and comatose ("To see that vital, brilliant, charming man reduced to this was awful, awful"). The nurse asked how long they'd known each other, and Ettlinger murmured, "Forty years," with a touch of wonder at how fast the time had gone by.

Cheever died late in the afternoon on June 18. Susan remembered a peculiar burning odor in the master bedroom—hard to describe, except that it gave her a sense of impending death. When Mary remarked that Federico was about to leave for a ten-day rafting trip in California, Susan called him and burst into tears; he was in the middle of packing, but arranged to take the first flight to New York. Susan then phoned Reverend George Arndt at Trinity Church in Ossining: "I don't think your father wants me," said Arndt, who'd been sent away once before, angrily, since Cheever wasn't ready yet and despised the man besides. Sure enough, he began thrashing when he noticed Arndt standing there in his white robe; Mary, Ben, and Susan joined hands around the bed, reciting the Lord's Prayer, while the priest administered last rites. "[Cheever] was struggling, whether for breath or what, I don't know," Arndt remembered. "He was in physical turmoil. I made the sign of the cross on his forehead and he became absolutely peaceful and took one last breath and that was it." Susan had turned around to give her daughter a bottle, and when she turned back, her father was gone ("like he'd left the room and shut the door"). A shriveled corpse remained. Ben tried mouth-to-mouth resuscitation, then put his arms around the body, with the others, and began to cry.

When the coroner asked the family to leave the room, they refused. Mary went to the closet and picked out her husband's clothes for the funeral: his favorite gray suit with the Academy badge in the buttonhole, a blue shirt, and a pink-and-gray-striped necktie that Alwyn Lee's widow, Essie, had knitted for him. "I just saw him on the Cavett show," the coroner mumbled as he worked. "Gee, it must have been a rerun."

Meanwhile, in Bronxville, Dr. Robert Schneider—the young oncolo-gist who'd forbidden Cheever to drink again—was playing with his three-year-old son when a stream of sunlight gushed into the room and he felt so weak he had to lie down. "I thought something bad had happened to someone, I wasn't sure who. Then Mary called and said John had passed. We had a bond. There are people in your life and you're glad they were part of your life."

EPILOGUE

CHEEVER DIED almost at the pinnacle of his fame, and would have been delighted by all the posthumous applause. "*Front* page, Edgar!" he used to badger his barking dog, when the subject of his own obituary came up. "*Front* page!" The front page is what he got, almost everywhere that mattered. "JOHN CHEEVER IS DEAD AT 70," proclaimed Michiko Kakutani's generous *Times* obituary; "NOVELIST WON PULITZER PRIZE." Cheever's reputation as "a kind of American Chekhov" was duly noted, the big themes of his work were all explored at gratifying length, and a few favorite pensées of the author (*qua* public figure) were quoted in full: "It seems to me that man's inclination toward light, toward brightness, is very near botanical. . . . It seems to me to be that one's total experience is the drive toward light—spiritual light. . . ."

Indeed, it was this Cheever—"A Celebrant of Sunlight," as *Time* hailed him—who received by far the most attention, and never mind that the man and his work were often quite gloomy. The *Boston Globe* mourned Cheever with not only a front-page obituary, but also a fine homage on the editorial page that was intended to fix his fame for all time as both a marvelous writer and a "good and generous man": "Greater authors there are than Cheever, but painfully few of whose work it can be so emphatically said: It delighted us. . . . In a world of Calibans, John Cheever was pure Prospero: He, too, bestowed magic." Even the reclusive William Shawn (whom Cheever always suspected of having it in for him) came forth to praise Cheever as "one of the country's great literary figures of the last fifty years . . . humane, warm-hearted, and brilliant." Perhaps most poignant was a tribute in the Quincy *Patriot Ledger*, which delicately alluded to the author's wayward past: "John Cheever's death Friday at 70 leaves a gap that it would take a very special person to fill—a youngster with a love of writing and the courage to pursue it until maturity brings a mastery of prose and, finally, of personal failings." On the South Shore, at least, neither his courage nor his personal failings were forgotten.*

And to the South Shore he returned at last, for lack of any desirable alternative. Cheever himself used to tell his family to bury him in the backyard, but they couldn't bring themselves to consider the matter until the very end, by which time Cheever was in no condition to say whether that was still his wish. Fortunately, his niece Jane had an appealing solution. Long ago the family had bought a plot in the Norwell Center cemetery, about fifteen miles from where Cheever was born, and a space remained available beside his parents—an eternal proximity that might have given him pause, though it seemed preferable to some obscure spot in Queens. Federico, who'd never set foot on the South Shore until his father's funeral, said, "It was the last place in the *world* he would have wanted to be buried." And yet it's just possible that Cheever might have decided, after all, that death was precisely the right time to go home again. "Nothing seems as genuine and vital to me as the life of the family I have left," he'd reflected back in 1940. "Living in New York I've seen people grow old and buildings torn down, I've seen women cry and funeral processions but when I try to recall the way people live and die I think of my mother and my father and the people who live on our street."

June 22 was a lovely day in Norwell—a "very clear, vertical, Cheever day," as Gurganus put it. The North River sparkled through the trees, their leaves fluttering in a light wind. Perhaps forty people gathered in the pews of the First Parish Church, many of them the same local gentry who'd attended Fred's funeral six years before ("the

---

*It might as well be noted here that Cheever's reputation in the UK never really caught on. Gottlieb mentioned how he'd often try to press Cheever's work on English writers, who tended to say things like "What a discovery! Why isn't he better known?" Part of the answer may be found in the (brief) London *Times* obituary, which sniffishly dismissed Cheever as "a typical graduate of the 'New Yorker' school of writers"— a school the *Times* evidently held in low regard, though the obituarist did see fit to concede that Cheever had written a few "inimitably funny short stories," and proposed that "the best of these are to be found in his earlier collections, notably *The Way Some People Live*." That final observation, all alone, would have soured Cheever's mood for a month.

world into whose umbrella stands my brother used to piss," said Cheever, who'd done much the same thing in a figurative sense). The family entered the church with Updike, the eulogist, and a clamor of creaking wood and clicking cameras was heard from the choir loft, where the press had been crammed. Next came Cheever's almost child-sized, flag-draped coffin, and finally Max arrived, late and a little dazed, whereupon the family insistently made room in their pew.* The three children spoke first. Susan, who didn't feel up to making personal remarks, gave a short reading from Romans ("For I am persuaded that neither death, nor life, nor angels . . . shall be able to separate us from the love of God"); Ben read Leander's advice to his sons from *The Wapshot Chronicle*, and told of how his father had once taught him to use ear wax to oil the joints of a fishing rod. Federico—all the more grieved for having come back too late to say a proper goodbye—reminisced as follows:

> He was forty-five when I was born, an old man nearing the end of his journey, as he said for the last twenty-five years of his life. . . . When I would return home from school after some athletic fiasco or other he would tell me 'Fred, remember you are a Cheever.' I would ask what that meant and he would say 'It means knowing who you are.' . . . What I have discovered is that part of what I am is John Cheever.

Finally Updike rose amid a further racket of picture-taking. "America will miss him, the leading fabulist of his generation," he began, while the congregation shot bitter looks at the choir loft. "His swift rich style never rested to belabor the obvious or to preen," Updike continued, and went on to say many other kind and necessary things, until he made a personal observation that may or may not have surprised those Norwell mourners with their "sailboat tans, white hair and mannered wives": "I saw a lot of him only on two extended occasions: in Boston in the mid-seventies and in Russia in 1964. It was in Russia, strange to say, that he seemed happier and more at home."

There was a lighter side to the proceedings, as Cheever might have

---

*When I reminded Max of this, his voice choked up with emotion. "I was moved by that gesture," he said. "Because at the time I thought they felt, you know, 'Now that he's dead, we no longer have to put up with [Max].' I thought they wanted to write me off."

wished. When Ben's wife began to sniffle, Mary (who'd chosen to forgo the usual widow's weeds in favor of a cheerful beige suit and straw hat) remarked, "She cries easily, doesn't she?" Then, as the pall-bearers followed the hearse across River Street toward the cemetery, the car gained speed and made them break into a staggering trot. "And I wonder whether you saw one touch that was absolutely out of a story by John," observed one of the few writers present, John Hersey, in a subsequent letter to Mary. "While the graveside prayers were being read, a group went over the crest of the hill in the graveyard, and sud-denly a teenage boy, overcome with mysterious exuberance, suddenly tossed off a couple of cartwheels."

The last guest to leave was Gurganus, who sat with his back against a headstone and watched the gravediggers finish their work. He'd heard of Cheever's death on the radio while dressing for breakfast at Yaddo ("In his home in Ossining, New York, beloved novelist and story writer John Cheever succumbed . . ."), and downstairs he found a letter waiting on the mail table: "Dear Allan, Please call or come at once. Something I must tell you. Love J." Sitting in the cemetery, Gur-ganus kept his eye on a particular gravedigger—a gorgeous, strapping, shirtless boy out of a Thomas Eakins painting—which seemed a suit-able way to commune with the dead. "I still find myself suspecting that John actually escaped in some way or other," he wrote a friend. "The baldness of mortality had never registered more graphically for me—than the sight of the decent box going under."

THE OSSINING SERVICE on June 23 was larger (about two hundred mourners, according to the *Times*) though somewhat less satisfying. In the local *Citizen Register*, Cheever had been described as "Ossining's most prominent treasure, our contact with greatness," and the town supervisor had ordered all flags on public buildings to be flown at half-mast for ten days. But the service happened to coincide with the tumultuous reconstruction of Route 9 through downtown Ossining, which almost gave the impression that the world was collapsing out-side the doors of Trinity Church. At a moment's notice, Bellow had agreed to deliver a tribute (pointing out, as he prepared to leave for the church, that Nathanael West had died on his way to Fitzgerald's funeral), which, had it been audible, would have elevated the occasion considerably. While the bulldozers groaned, Bellow spoke of the "dramatic metamorphosis" Cheever had undergone as an artist ("He was one of the self-transformers"), and described their friendship as "a sort of hydroponic plant, flourished in the air": "It was, however, healthy, fed by good elements, and it was a true friendship. Because we met in transit . . . we lost no time in getting down to basics. On both sides there was instant candor."

The other speakers were a little on the vague side, having come to the awkward conclusion that they'd hardly known the man. Burton "Bud" Benjamin, a CBS News producer, had been a neighbor and an occasional backgammon partner; he was surprised when the family asked him to speak. ("I never really had a 'hair-down' talk with John," he later admitted. "I wonder how John would have answered the question, 'Who's your best friend?' Or did he have one?") Cheever had made himself known to the Benjamins largely through the haphazard use of their pool, and so the eulogist tailored his remarks accordingly: "He was marvelous, funny, unpredictable, full-of-life John . . . not a man to test the water's temperature with his toe." Even Eugene Thaw— who'd certainly seen a lot of Cheever in recent years—emphasized that his friend had "lived in a world of imagination that we couldn't completely enter," though he felt safe in adding that Cheever's later fame "never went to his head." Among the mourners leaving the service, one of the most downcast was Dom Anfiteatro: "I was John's mechanic," he announced in the receiving line.

By his own confession, Max was rather drunk and distraught that day, and this time the family did seem to keep him at a distance. "It was just a savage experience," he remembered. "I was all over the place." The most memorable moment, for Max, was when he tried to introduce his would-be *New Yorker* editor, Chip McGrath, to Cheever's widow. "I kept saying to Chip, 'You gotta meet her!' And he's like, 'No no, it's fine.' So finally I introduced him, and she said, 'Hello, it's nice to meet you,' and walked away. *Jesus.*" McGrath demurred when Max tried coaxing him back to Cedar Lane for the reception, which proved the last time certain old friends would gather in one place. Raphael Rudnik was there, struck by the oddly radiant look of bereavement on Sara Spencer's face ("very much as if she had lost her best friend, yet somehow in love with wonder and sociable about the loss itself, as if it were yet another amazing thing"). Zinny's daughters, Annie and Sarah, were there, chatting about the idyllic (in retrospect) Scarborough years; the Ettlingers brought a lot of food and spoke of even more distant times. At Mary's urging, Rob Cowley had come to the house to say goodbye to his and Susan's old retriever, Maisie, so feeble now she could hardly walk; the dog was lying in the master bedroom, where Cheever had died, and began thumping her tail when she saw Cowley. Suddenly remembering many things, he broke down sobbing.

AS A WAY OF COPING with her father's illness and imminent death, Susan had begun a memoir of sorts the previous spring ("a book that would make people love my father and be sad that he was dead"), and by September she had five chapters written. Needing to flesh things out a bit, she decided it was time to have a look at her father's journal, which at Thaw's suggestion had been stored in the Morgan Museum vault on the Upper East Side. Sitting down amid a jumble of exquisite art, Susan was immediately taken aback by what she read; she rented a vault of her own and kept reading for a month or so. It only got worse ("I'd read parts aloud to Calvin and the color just drained out of his face"), and not only because of the gloomy, relentless sexual stuff; there were relatively few references to her own existence, and many of these were scornful. She'd pretty much decided to forget the memoir and write another novel instead, when Cheever's prospective biographer took her to lunch and revealed that he knew all about her father's bisexuality, and naturally would be putting that in his book. Mean- while, too, she'd begun to receive badgering, drunken phone calls from Exley, who appeared to want money for some of Cheever's letters ("John wouldn't have wanted me to be this poor"), which, he implied, were damningly candid. Finally Susan decided to go ahead and write a memoir after all: if anybody was going to tell her father's secrets to the world (the part of it that didn't know them already), it was going to be her. Lovingly. "I don't ever want to go in a grocery store and see a tabloid headline: JOHN CHEEVER A FAG," she said at the time.

Home Before Dark, published in 1984, aroused a certain amount of controversy among those who'd known Cheever principally as a cele- brant of sunlight. As the *Boston Globe* noted—not a little incredulously— Susan had characterized her father as "a sexual omnivore who was attracted to both groupies (female) and protégés (male), and an acerbic and sarcastic husband whose 41-year-old marriage was often filled with resentment." Cheever's old friends in Westchester were, to put it gently, startled: Aline Benjamin (Burton's wife) had always assumed that

Cheever's preoccupation with good and evil was a literary thing ("totally cerebral"), though she and others were bound to admit that the man had, for whatever reason, drunk a great deal for many years. Barrett Clark, an occasional Friday Clubber, remarked that Art Spear would have "dropped John like a hot rock" if he'd known about the bisexuality, and in fact Spear would not stand for any talk of Susan's book around the Friday Club or anywhere else. "Oh, that's just Susie!" he'd say when his daughters mentioned it. Phil Boyer, who'd always considered Cheever his "best friend," was more saddened than resentful— forced to accept that all those years of giddy suburban squirearchy, the martinis and dogs and such, had been something of a sham. The consensus among objective readers, however, was overwhelmingly positive. As Justin Kaplan wrote in the *Times Book Review*, Susan had treated her father "with a quality Walt Whitman once described as 'tenderness, blended with a curious remorseless firmness, as of some surgeon operating on a beloved patient.' "

Asked by the *Boston Globe* what he thought of his sister's book, Federico replied with his usual lucidity: "It's a realistic and sensitive portrait. As far as revelations go, it's all stuff that's going to come out anyway." This would prove prescient, to say the least, as Susan wasn't alone in thinking there had been enough deception while her father was alive. Indeed, the more Ben considered the matter—the sheer breadth of it—the more puzzled and angry he became: "It made me think I must be bisexual, and the only reason I wasn't was because this guy had scared the wits out of me about how dangerous it was, and it turns out *he's* bisexual." As with his sister (and Cheever himself, for that matter), Ben would make peace with his father by writing about him—the first completely successful writing he'd ever managed, what with the daunting standard of his father's work. "It turns out you can write a book without being him," said Ben, who described the commentary he wrote in the *Letters* as "the beginning of identity": "Because I'd write something he'd written, copy it, and then write something I wrote under it. And I could see how I could write something that wasn't as good, but was useful, and belonged there, and could exist on a page with something he'd written." Eventually Ben quit his job at *Reader's Digest* to work full-time on the project, and has been a professional writer ever since.

The Letters of John Cheever appeared four years after *Home Before Dark*, and gave new life to the notion that Cheever's children were bent on defaming his once-beloved memory. "My usual feeling about mail is that it should be received, answered and destroyed on the same day," Cheever had written Litvinov. "I do save yours although I am afraid that, when we are both dust, some damned fool will publish them." Cheever's fears were realized to a degree he could scarcely have anticipated, for his son saw fit to publish even his most graphic letters to lovers of both sexes—since, after all, these reflected an essential part of the man, and besides the cat was out of the bag. "Plus," said Ben, "I thought with some bitterness that if I had had to acknowledge this truth, then others, a lot farther from ground zero, could jolly well come aboard." Among Ben's defenders was William Maxwell, who invoked Voltaire ("we owe nothing to the dead but the truth") in his remarks to the BBC: "Would we like or prefer to know less about Flaubert (who was quite as shocking in his diaries, if not more, than Cheever) in order to find him less upsetting? It is too silly." And really Cheever could hardly have found a more gracious apologist than Ben, who insisted on his father's essential goodness—"his joy and the talent he had for passing that joy on to the people around him"—which was evident, said Ben, even in his cruelty or hypocrisy. Though he could accuse Updike, say, of "exhibitionism" and a "stony heart," his lavish praise on other (more public) occasions was, at bottom, "an attempt to be better than he was." Finally, if Cheever's spirit *hadn't* been so painfully divided, he might well have pursued an easier occupation than writing novels—*Bullet Park*, for instance: "Nailles is too good to be anyone you ever met, and Hammer is too bad," Ben wrote. "By and large his letters convey the sociable lovable side of John Cheever, but the careful reader will see another figure lurking in the background, the vain, ungenerous, ruthless and self-indulgent Paul Hammer. It's like the wolf seen at the edge of an Alpine forest a moment before nightfall. Without that wolf there would have been no sleeping children, no thatched cottage, no village at all."

The question of whether to publish the journal remained, and in this case it was hard to say *what* Cheever had wanted. "I seem unable to read this journal for what it is," he'd written in 1956; "a means of refreshing my memory. I seem to look delightedly at myself in a glass. I think of it as something to be published and studied in libraries and this is not what I want at all." As the years passed, though, and the pages mounted—more than four thousand in all, eventually—Cheever became increasingly convinced that the journal was not only a crucial part of his own oeuvre, but an essential contribution to the genre. At the very least he thought it belonged in a library somewhere. In the sixties he sent an excerpt to his manuscript collection at Brandeis,* and when he received his honorary degree at Harvard, he told Professor Daniel Aaron, in a burst of exuberance, that he wanted to "give [his] papers to Harvard." In a cooler moment, Cheever clarified: by "papers" he meant specifically the journals, and by "give" he meant sell; Rodney Dennis, the curator of manuscripts at Houghton Library, offered five thousand dollars on the spot. "You're not serious," said Cheever, and there the matter rested. After all, it wasn't merely an important literary document that Cheever proposed to part with, but a breathtakingly personal one. "I read last year's journal with the idea of giving it to a library," he noted around this time. "I am shocked at the frequency with which I refer to my member." Also, he couldn't fail to notice that he was awfully hard on his family—incessantly so in Mary's case ("she comes out very poorly and I am quite blameless which cannot be the truth").† But toward the end, in any event, he seemed to make up his mind in favor of posthumous publication—indeed, as Ben remembered, he was "almost gleeful about the prospects."

Susan engineered the journal sale in the late eighties, laying out her father's twenty-eight notebooks on a long table in her apartment and letting various editors spend an hour or two alone with them. The bidding was lively, until Gottlieb offered the rather staggering sum of

---

*I spent the last day of my last research trip to the Boston area at Brandeis, mostly examining the typescripts of Cheever's *New Yorker* stories. With about fifteen minutes to go before the library closed, I glanced at the journal pages Cheever had donated—though there was no need to do this, really, since I had my own copy of the journal. But right away I noticed something amiss: The Brandeis pages were too neatly typed, with a brand-new ribbon, no less. I found a passage on my laptop that I'd transcribed from the original—this about Cheever's meeting with Sophia Loren in the summer of 1967—and compared it with the Brandeis version: Sure enough, they were different! "She seems sincere, magnanimous, lucky and matteroffact," Cheever had (sloppily) typed in the original, followed by a bit of dialogue between the two. "She seems sincere, magnanimous, lucky and intelligent," reads the (immaculate) Brandeis version, and the subsequent dialogue has been deleted. Was it possible that Cheever had not only retyped but substantially *rewritten* many journal pages for the sake of a little academic posterity? I was about to check further when the nice librarian stuck her head in the room and whispered that it was time to go.

†"I'm unable to read the journals," said Mary, "so I didn't have any strong feelings about whether they were published or not. I can't read them. Snatches of them I've read, but I can't sit down and read that stuff. It isn't my life at all. It's him, it's all him. It's all inside him."

$1.2 million to publish excerpts serially in *The New Yorker* (where he'd succeeded Shawn as editor) and finally in a book from Knopf. The critic Ted Solotaroff, for one, was astonished by such largesse; as an editor at Harper & Row, he and a colleague had also examined the notebooks and been distinctly unimpressed. As he later wrote, "The image of Cheever that settled in my mind was of a writer who had just masturbated (he kept a record of that), doodling in the margins of his despair or boredom or occasional euphoria while waiting to hit the bottle." Solotaroff was therefore "very surprised and not a little crest-fallen" to find himself fascinated by the excerpts (perhaps 5 percent of the total journal) that appeared in six installments in *The New Yorker* from August 1990 to August 1991. Gottlieb, too, was satisfied with his selection, though he'd found the work "very, very painful": "The material is *so* dark, and the suffering [Cheever] underwent is so at odds with the polite gentlemanly exterior that I had been exposed to." It was worth it, though, to read mail from so many "mesmerized" readers—mostly. As Gottlieb recalled, "There were also those who thought, 'Why are you doing this stuff? I don't want to read one more *word* about this dopey alcoholic fag.' "

Cheever often worried that, if he were perfectly candid in his work, he would thereby reveal "an almost unremittant depression and a frowsty concern with death," though he liked to think that readers of his journal, at least, would approve of his brave determination to bare even the darkest parts of his soul ("What a good man he is!"). In that respect, he might have been disappointed by the actual response to *The Journals of John Cheever*, published as a book in October 1991. While the beauty of the prose was, as ever, given its due, reviewers tended to be less than admiring about any aspect of the author himself. "For all his vaunted honesty, Cheever had the drunk's habit of evading responsibility and not acknowledging the chaos and pain he caused," Mary Gordon wrote in the *Times Book Review*; "a sad and depressing book," said Jonathan Yardley in the *Washington Post*, "the record of a man so enchained within the prison of self that he was never able to embrace others, even those he most loved." As for Updike, he seemed almost chastened by this final knowledge of the man he used to consider "sprightly, debonair, gracious"; even though he'd once had to dress the drunken, naked Cheever for a night at Symphony Hall, and even though he'd read the man's beyond-the-grave abuse in the *Letters*, Updike was nonetheless shocked by the *Journals*. "Rarely has a gifted and creative life seemed sadder," he wrote in *The New Re-*

public. "[Cheever's] confessions posthumously administer a Christian lesson in the dark gulf between outward appearance and inward condition . . ."

So much for the celebrant of sunlight.

And yet. At least one protesting letter appeared in the *Times Book Review*—this from Thomas J. Sullivan, the Georgetown undergraduate whom Cheever had invited (with his friend George McLoone) to Cedar Lane, sight unseen, some twenty-five years before: "Cheever spent an hour answering our questions and sharing with us numerous anecdotes about his life," Sullivan wrote. "He later took us to his neighbor's pool, where he demonstrated the Australian crawl stroke as he had envisioned it when he wrote the short story, 'The Swimmer.' The John Cheever I visited with was a witty, grinning, intellectually stimulating human being."

A YEAR AFTER THE PUBLICATION of the *Journals*, an episode of *Seinfeld* titled "The Cheever Letters" was aired. The plot is a little hard to explain in so many words. George Costanza is meeting his girlfriend Susan's family for the first time. Susan's crotchety father, meanwhile, has sent George a box of Cuban cigars ("made special for Castro"), which George has dumped on his friend Kramer, who in turn has smoked them in a cabin belonging to Susan's father and burned the place down. When George breaks the news to the father, the man is devastated and takes to his bed. The next day, Jerry and George visit the apartment where Susan's family is gathered, and a doorman appears bearing a charred strongbox: "The only thing left from the remains of the fire," he says. Susan opens the box in front of Jerry, George, and the family (but not her father, who remains in bed): "Letters . . . from John Cheever!" she brightly announces, then reads one aloud:

> Dear Henry [Susan's father],
>   Last night with you was bliss. I fear my orgasm has left me a cripple. I don't know how I shall ever get back to work.
>   I love you madly,
>   John

Amid general consternation, Susan's father shambles in from the bedroom. "The box! My letters! Give me that! Who told you to open this?" The man's grown son, bewildered and almost tearful, exclaims "Dad! You and *John Cheever—?*" "Yes!" the man says defiantly. "Yes! He was the most wonderful person I've ever known! And I loved him deeply"—he turns to his wife (a Waspy, sarcastic ice queen)—"in a way *you* could never understand!" Larry David, the show's writer and co-creator, explained that he'd used Cheever as the lover of Susan's father simply because "he was a well-known writer who was gay."*

One can only imagine how Cheever would have felt about being *primarily* known as a "writer who was gay," but there it is. Because of this—to be exact, because he was a furtively bisexual writer who happened to marry and have children—a BBC documentary titled *John Cheever and Family* appeared in 1994, in which (as the London *Times* put it) "we are given a searing picture of the ripple effects of his life on the lives of his family." Mary's performance is especially noteworthy. Pressed by the soft-voiced, remorseless off-camera interviewer to explain how she felt when she first suspected her husband "was not entirely heterosexual," Mary evenly replied, "It didn't make an awful lot of difference to me." *Why not?* Mary winced slightly, but smiled too, and chose her words with evident care: "By that time, our marriage was not a very *full* relationship . . ." The moment was characteristic. As Cheever's widow, Mary has answered many such questions, a bit grudgingly, and with a kind of bemused insinuation that there are better things to talk about. "What's important is what he wrote, not what he did," she told the *Boston Globe*. "What was important in his life was to go on writing." How important it was to *her* was resoundingly established in 1988, when she undertook what was described in the *Washington Post* as "the most expensive, protracted and vicious court battle to take place in recent years over a book." The book was *The Uncollected Stories of John Cheever*, which had been proposed by a small publisher, Academy Chicago. For the token sum of fifteen hundred dollars, Mary had signed a contract for what she understood to be a *selection* of her husband's uncollected work, arranged in consultation

---

*Larry David seemed a little dismayed by my question, given what we'd discussed a few years earlier in regard to my Richard Yates biography. Back then he'd explained that the *Seinfeld* episode titled "The Jacket" was based on his disastrous, real-life encounter with Yates, whose daughter Monica he'd been dating at the time. When I mentioned that Cheever had a daughter named Susan, and pointed out that George's girlfriend in "The Cheever Letters" is *also* named Susan, David hastened to deny any real-life connection: "Just one of those things!"

with the family. This, however, was not what Academy Chicago (ultimately) had in mind; rather, they preferred a book that included *everything* omitted from *The Stories of John Cheever:* Hemingwayesque juvenilia ("Fall River," "Late Gathering"), Depression-era potboilers ("His Young Wife," "Saratoga"), topical fiction ("Frère Jacques," "Behold a Cloud in the West"), army sketches scribbled at odd moments with a blunt pencil ("Sergeant Limeburner," "The Invisible Ship"), and of course the entirety of *The Way Some People Live*, the very thought of which had never failed to make Cheever cringe in horror. After three years and almost a million dollars in legal fees, Mary "won" the case—that is, the contract was declared invalid—though Academy Chicago was still able to publish a collection of thirteen stories (including the first four mentioned above) whose copyrights had lapsed. "I must miss him, yes," Mary sighs at the end of *John Cheever and Family*, while the old Cedar Lane farmhouse appears onscreen. "I must miss him. Because why am I living this way, if I don't miss him? What's the sense of this? No sense."

And what of the children? Most children are ambivalent about their fathers; Cheever's are more so, as anyone who reads Susan's various memoirs will gather. "[M]y father loved his children," she wrote in the first and most affectionate one. "The three of us were, as he said, 'the roof and settle' of his existence. As individuals we often displeased him, but as a unit we were cherished and indispensable." This is certainly true, though Susan is also eloquent about the damage done by self-absorbed alcoholic parents and John Cheever in particular, writing of her own inherited struggle with alcohol in *Note Found in a Bottle*.* Her mother, however, categorically denies that Susan was ever a *real* alcoholic, regarding such a preposterous (to her) idea as simply "part of [Susan's] identification with her father." And Ben would agree, at least, that his father has cast a long and complicated shadow over Susan's life: "I always feel like she's marrying Daddy," he remarked in *John Cheever and Family*. "First she married the son of the man who published his first story. Then she married a man who was like Daddy appeared to be—went to Princeton, had some money, wrote full-time for *The New Yorker*. Then she married an alcoholic writer at the top of his powers, which is Warren Hinckle." The irony is that Cheever himself would hardly have wanted—very often *did not* want—such an odd, talented,

---

*Susan has been sober since 1992.

challenging daughter, which of course Susan knows better than anyone. As she observed, more or less cheerfully, "In many ways I was a
tremendous disappointment to them"—Mary included—"I'm *proud* to
say, and hope I've continued to be, since what they wanted me to be is
pretty empty."

As for Ben, writing about his father in the *Letters* might have been
the "beginning of identity," but it was hardly the end of it. His first two
novels, *The Plagiarist* and *The Partisan*, were both about domineering
literary father figures, and both reflect something of what it's like to
feel as if one were "a minor character in someone else's book," and
never mind the more fraught sexual issues. That said, Ben has since
written a number of books that have little to do with father figures one
way or the other.

Federico, for his part, feels somewhat fortunate in comparison: "I
think my experience as a child was quite different from Ben and
Susan's, which explains partially our very different trajectories in life.
To some degree, when you're the child of a relatively famous person
you have the choice of going into the family business or not. I decided
not to. But I think he was judgmental with them in a way he wasn't
with me, and as a result they spent a lot of their lives chasing his
approval through proxies, while I haven't." And yet Federico's childhood was far from ideal, given his frequent isolation with a ruinously
alcoholic father; one can't help wondering whether the memories
make him angry or sad sometimes. "I was cast in the role of a helpmate,
and wasn't really entitled to have anger," he explained.

> Sometimes it pisses me off *massively* . . . but what do you do with
> that? There's no help for that. You do what you do.
>
> I don't know what it would be like to come from a normal
> family. I have not a clue. It's interesting because I'm bringing
> up my own children and they have, like most children, space to
> indulge themselves—to be angry without reason, run around and
> do stupid things, to test their parents' love. This was not something
> I ever had.

And what, finally, of Max? A few days after Cheever died, he found
himself alone in his little apartment. There were no more errands to
run, no funerals to attend; his therapist had advised him to stop writing
for a while; he couldn't go back to Utah, what with one thing and
another, and for the moment he was unemployed. Cheever was gone,

and Cheever had dominated his life for the past few years. He began banging his head against the wall. "He had died without ever letting me know if he actually respected me, actually thought I was a talented writer, actually cared about me, actually saw me as something more than a hand-job," said Max. ("If I declare the depth of the love I feel for [Max] I am afraid that he may exploit this," Cheever had noted a year before his death.) "I remember standing there howling because I hurt so much and felt so empty." Then, one night in a bar, he told two of his ex-students what had happened—quite certain their friendship would end as a result. "But they said, 'Jesus Christ, *that's* what you've been going through . . . ?' " Max recalled. "So that's how I started to come back. And finally I told [my girlfriend], just sobbing my eyes out. And I expected her to walk out the door, but she put her arms around me."

Max stayed in the East and picked up the pieces. Falling back on his engineering degree, he supported himself as a freelance technical writer and eventually started his own business. Remarried now, with a family of his own, he lives in a pleasant lake community in New Jersey, and for the most part manages not to dwell on the past. "If there's someone who never loved himself, it was John," Max said twenty-five years ago. Now he says this:

> He was extraordinarily blessed by anyone's standards—fame, wealth, a wonderful wife, great kids who did him proud and loved him, a long and highly successful career, talent, friends, on and on—but he liked to say that all he had in life was an old dog. There was his despair. And then there was his inability to comprehend the despair and self-negation he inflicted on others. He changed the course of my life. I took it from there. Today I look at my own two sons—close in age to my age then—and I can't imagine anyone wanting anything of them except to see that they keep moving forward.

. . .

As Styron gorgeously declaimed at the medal ceremony, "John Cheever's position in literary history is as immovably fixed as one of those huge granite outcroppings which loom over the green lawns and sunlit terraces in the land of his own magic devising." Doubtless Cheever seemed a safe bet in 1982. Three years before, around the time of his Pulitzer, he was ranked third—behind only his eulogists, Bellow and Updike—in a *Philadelphia Inquirer* survey of the living American writers whose work was expected to "endure and be read by future generations."* If Cheever were eligible for such a survey today, some three decades later, it's unlikely he would appear anywhere in the top twenty. One can only hazard a few guesses as to why. It bears repeating that it's hard to determine Cheever's niche in our national literature, and academic canon-makers are fond of niches; in other words, the very fact that he was a "self-transformer," as Bellow put it (speaking only of the quarter-century of Cheever's career contained in the *Stories*), would seem to have worked against him. The scholar Robert Morace covered the spectrum nicely: "Groping about for ways to understand, i.e., pigeonhole, Cheever, reviewers and critics have called him a satirist, a transcendentalist, an existentialist, a social critic, a religious writer, a trenchant moralist, an Enlightened Puritan, an Episcopalian anarch, a suburban surrealist, Ovid in Ossining, the American Chekhov, the American Trollope for an age of angst, a toothless Thurber." Who are Cheever's influences? Arguably too many (and too well assimilated) to say. Whom did he influence? Ditto, and the *manner* of his influence (again, for the very reason of his versatility) is hard to trace. At any rate, academics tend to throw up their hands: Cheever is hardly taught at all in the classroom, where reputations are perpetuated, and dissertations featuring his work have trickled almost to nothing. Odder still: though *The Wapshot Chronicle* appears on the Modern Library's vaunted list of the 100 Best [English-language] Novels [of the Twentieth Century], and *Falconer* appears on the even more recent *Time* list, neither novel (nor any of Cheever's others) is read much anymore. The current Vintage edition of *Falconer* sells about three thousand copies a year, and Harper's handsome 2003 reprints of the *Wapshot* novels—which include adulatory, almost hectoring forewords by Rick Moody and Dave Eggers—have sold fewer than ten thousand copies *combined*. *The Stories of John Cheever* ("They seem in the end to be mostly what I've written") sells about five thousand copies a year—excellent for a book of stories, negligible for a classic of the postwar era.

Even his status as Ossining's "most prominent treasure" (a humble man who used to bring coffee to his barber!) seemed to wane after his

---

*The rest of the top ten: E. B. White, John Gardner, Bernard Malamud, Joseph Heller, Isaac Bashevis Singer, James Michener, and J. D. Salinger. To be ranked so well ahead of Salinger must have pleased Cheever.

death—indeed, Cheever lived just long enough to see the writing on the wall. "Superintendent Wishnie moved at a town meeting that a short street be named John Cheever Street," he wrote the Dirkses in March 1982. "This was stopped by the baglady Jodine Wang. I want to name a street Jodine Wang Street." Twenty-four years would pass before Cheever's name was finally bestowed on the main reading room at the Ossining Public Library, the only memorial in his adopted hometown. That, however, is one more memorial than he's gotten in Quincy or its environs. The house where Cheever was born, at 43 Elm Avenue, is now occupied by one Ronald Goba, who—despite being the retired director of English for Hingham public schools—knew nothing of Cheever's former occupancy until a few years ago, when a lone researcher appeared on his doorstep. "I'll tell you this," said Goba. "There are no Cheever ghosts in here." Nor at Thayer, where only a few of the faculty bother to recall (rather sourly) that Cheever was expelled for smoking and wrote a smart-alecky article about it for some magazine. And finally in Norwell—next to his father for all time ("We are such stuff as dreams are made on")—Cheever's lichen-stained headstone sags a little into the earth. "He's kind of our lost child," said Edward Fitzgerald of the Quincy Historical Society.

"I'm not inclined to think of myself as being remembered for anything," Cheever said with characteristic (if calculated) modesty in 1979. "It seems to me that a writer is obviously mortal, and looking at the history of literature, a great deal that is splendid is splendid only for a very brief period of time." For all the delight he took in his own fame, Cheever's shade just might be pleased with the less-than-general readership he's ended up with (for now): this includes other writers, certainly, as well as discerning people the world over. And no wonder. As Updike wrote in his *New Yorker* obituary, "He was often labelled a writer about suburbia; but many people have written about suburbia, and only Cheever was able to make an archetypal place out of it, a terrain we can recognize within ourselves, wherever we are or have been."* Impervious to trends, Cheever remained true to a highly pecu-

---

*One is reminded of Cheever's vast readership in Russia and Eastern Europe, where the trappings of American suburbia—or postwar Manhattan, or anachronistic New England—are somewhat alien. He might have become the next big thing in China, too: the novelist Wang Meng, minister of culture in the late eighties, spoke of Cheever as his "favorite" Western writer and looked forward to sharing his enthusiasm with the people—but then he was driven from office, post–Tiananmen Square, as a proponent of "bourgeois liberalization."

liar vision, and his archetypal world endures—waiting to be rediscovered by those who remember him, if at all, as a suburban writer or a *New Yorker* writer or, for that matter, "a writer who was gay." In the meantime he will never lack champions among the initiated. In 2004 Jonathan Yardley called *The Stories of John Cheever* an "essential monument of American literature," and Eggers went so far as to insist "that Cheever writes beautifully and with as much lust for words and life as anyone this country has yet produced"—this while imploring a new generation to delight in his *novels* as well: "They are so filled with love that it's hard to believe that a man wrote these sentences, and not some kind of freakish winged book-writing angel-beast."

"Angel-beast" is a useful epithet for the man, whose older son can't help feeling annoyed by strangers who seem "closer to John Cheever than [he] ever did," simply because they happened to read some books. Take the case of Patrick Coyne, a New York cabbie who used to give free rides to people who shared his love of Cheever; when this got back to Liz Smith, the columnist, she asked Coyne to supply her with a "short, pithy, and pointed quote" from his favorite author. Thus Coyne was emboldened to write a note to Cheever, who naturally replied: "I can't imagine what has kept us apart all these years. I gather you are Irish. The Cheevers claim not to be. 'Don't ever wear an overcoat,' my father often said, 'you might be taken for an Irishman.' Only a true Irishman would make such a remark. . . . However, I never wear an overcoat. . . . I would hit any man—or woman—in the nose who called me 'short, pithy, and pointed.' " Well! Coyne was all the more charmed, and on Cheever's death he wrote a letter to the widow about how "characters, out of Cheever, step into [his] cab"—the famous Disco Sally, for instance, "a wizened monkey-skinned woman in her eighties who, in the company of young effetes, made the round of late night discos. Disco Sally died this year. John would have understood the fear that drove her relentlessly from disco to disco." *John* would have understood, all right . . . but still Ben feels a slight impulse to argue with people like Coyne: "I want to ask them where they were when he was drinking, when he needed his eyeglasses found or to be driven to the hospital. This is foolishness. He was at his best on the page."

He was at his best, and worst, on the page—he was *himself*, in short, and hence that massive journal: a monument of tragicomic solipsism, or (to paraphrase one of Cheever's favorite pensées) a history of one man's struggle to be illustrious. "No one, absolutely no one, shared his life with him," said Federico. "There was no one from whom he could get honest advice. Of course, this state of affairs was very much his own doing, but it must have been hard sometimes."

And yet! What of the man who was moved to thank God for the "party" of being alive? The delightful writer who longed, above all, to impart "glad tidings"? He might have chosen to end this story with some happy time in his life—Thanksgiving 1955, say, when his imagination was afire with a joyous first novel, and he'd recently been confirmed in the church, and he'd begun to suspect that he might escape the fate of his "accursed" family after all. That night, Cheever dreamed of sifting among fragments for a clue, perhaps, to the future:

> And at 3am I seem to be walking through Grand Central and the latch on my suitcase gives, spilling out onto the floor the contents of my life and what do we find here? A pint of gin and some contraceptives; the score for Handels Watermusic and a football; the plays of Shakespere, The Brothers Karamazov and Madame Bovary; a sweater, a jockstrap and an old maddar necktie; but also to signify times of irresolution and loss about which I know plenty a daisey for counting and a candle for impotence; but also a hairbrush and a love poem and a photograph of happy times on the deck of the tern and a confirmation certificate and a psychiatrists bill and a yellow leaf or somesuch—the stone from a beach to signify times of solid high spirits.

Acknowledgments

A FEW YEARS AGO, Ben Cheever wrote me a kind note about my biography of Richard Yates, which ultimately led to this book. Technically, I guess, this is an authorized biography, but the usual compromises of authorization don't apply. I was given material—*all* the material—and left alone with it, period. Ben sent letters, clippings, manuscripts, whatever he could find, and during one of my visits to Westchester he drove me and a copy of his father's massive journal to the UPS store. He and Susan also showed me around the Vanderlip estate in Scarborough, the better for me to visualize, say, how the Vanderlip Mansion might have inspired "Clear Haven" in *The Wapshot Chronicle* (think of the naked Moses scampering across the ghastly, sprawling roofs to Melissa's boudoir). Another day, Susan gave me the run of her apartment in Manhattan, refilling my coffee cup while I stood on chairs and rifled boxes in her closets. And I relished my chats with Federico so much that I felt a little bereft once I'd run out of questions to ask. As for Mary Cheever, she submitted to my grinding curiosity with a nice mixture of gaiety and frankness, and was always a gracious hostess during my visits to Cedar Lane—willing to keep me company if necessary, or leave me alone (rather with an old, wheezy black Labrador) in the library while I sorted through papers or photographs. I can hardly find words to thank her for these and so many other kindnesses, and the same goes for her children. The four of them made this project such a pleasure that I have to worry: surely it's downhill from here, at least with regard to writing biographies.

I am beholden to Cheever's niece Jane Carr, who gave me a guided tour of the South Shore and let me rummage through her father's papers. Her brother, David, also sent a pile of Fred's letters from his last five years or so—a fascinating glimpse into the mind of that scrappy, jovial, maddening, lovable man, so like and yet unlike his brother. I also learned a great deal from my interviews with Fred's younger daughters, Sarah Connoway and Ann Adams, whose tender memories of their father are all the more touching in light of the occasional havoc he wreaked in their lives.

Anyone who reads this book will readily grasp why Max Zimmer would prefer to be left alone, and I am very thankful for his cooperation. Once he'd overcome his initial reluctance, he provided me with every pertinent document, no matter how mortifying, in return for which he asked only that I tell the unvarnished truth. We have differed over certain of my conclusions, while respecting the integrity of each other's viewpoint. I'm also grateful to Scott Donaldson, Cheever's first biographer, who was courteous and helpful during the early stages of my research. His papers at William and Mary were indispensable to me—particularly his interview notes, which put me in touch with the various people who have died during the twenty-odd years between his book and mine. Many thanks, too, to Edward Hirsch and G. Thomas Tanselle and everyone else at the Guggenheim Foundation, whose generous fellowship made it possible to persevere after my family and I lost our house and almost everything in it to Hurricane Katrina.

The following people sent letters, photographs, and/or other helpful material, in addition to spending (in many cases) long and perhaps tedious hours in conversation with me: Jennifer Boyer, T. Coraghessan Boyle, Dodie Merwin Captiva, Jane and Barrett Clark, Dennis Coates, Rob Cowley, Larry David, John Dirks, Pamela Spear Goff, Allan Gurganus, Hugh Hennedy, Michael Janeway, James Kaplan, Christopher Lehmann-Haupt, Tanya Litvinov, Ray Mutter, M.D., Nick Puner, Don and Ginger Reiman, Natalie Robins, Ned Rorem, David Rothbart, Raphael Rudnik, Philip Schultz, Rick Siggelkow, Roger Skillings, Clare and Eugene Thaw.

A number of others also granted interviews or else provided written reminiscences: Renata Adler, Martin Amsel, Gino Anelli, Roger Angell, Martin Aronchick, Rollin Bailey, Helen Barolini, Richard Bausch, Marvin Bell, Peter Benelli, Anne Bernays, Simon Michael Bessie, LeClair Bissell, Tina Bourjaily, Vance Bourjaily, Douglas Brayfield, Connie Brothers, Emilie Buchwald, Joseph Caldwell, James Campbell, Susan Colgan, Elizabeth Logan Collins, Evan S. Connell, Molly Cook, Susan Crile, Susan Deakins, Ruth Denney, David Diamond, Dorothy Farrell, Thomas Foley, David Frieze, Linda Gillies, Dana Gioia, Herbert Gold, Ivan Gold, Robert Gottlieb, Christopher Gresov, Piri Halasz, Oakley Hall III, Daniel Halpern, Ron Hansen, Pauline Hanson, Shirley Hazzard, Aurie Henry, Rick Henry, Sandra Hochman, Joseph and Eugenia Hotchkiss, Jeanette Howland, Lee Hyla, Sarah Irwin, Joseph Kahn, Olivia Kahn, Justin Kaplan, Frederica Kaven, Carol Kitman, Arthur Laurents, John Leggett, William Luers, James McConkey, Janet Maslin, Lucy McCord, Charles McGrath, George McLoone, Melissa Meyer, Paul Moor, Lynn Nesbit, Jeffrey Newhouse, Mary Oliver, Anne Palamountain, Anne Peirce, Jean Phillips, Petru Popescu, Robert Ricter, Philip Roth, David Rothbart, Stephen Sandy, Robert Schneider, Grace Schulman, Laurens Schwartz, Joan Silber, J. William Silverberg, M.D., Kate Spear, Elizabeth Spencer, Sol Stein, Toby Stein, Richard Stern, Sarah Stevenson, William Styron, David Swope, Calvin Tomkins, John Updike, Aileen Ward, Mary Weatherall, Maureen and Roger Willson, Bill Winternitz, Tom Winternitz, Virginia Worthen, Ben Yagoda, Yevgeny Yevtushenko, Ethel Zaeder, and Andrew Ziegler.

A veritable army of librarians, friends, and kind strangers helped me with research, and I wish I could eulogize certain individuals at length. However, this book is long enough as it is. Suffice to say, I am *very* grateful to the selfless people listed below: Lillian Wentworth (Thayer Academy); Jennie Rathbun (Houghton Library, Harvard); Eric Esau (Rauner Special Collections Library, Dartmouth); Candace Wait and Elaina Richardson (Yaddo); Stephen Crook (Berg Collection, New York Public Library); Melanie A. Yolles and Raynelda Calderon (Manuscripts and Archives Division, New York Public Library); Susan C. Pyzynksi (Brandeis); Susan Riggs (Swem Library, William and Mary); Jill Gage (Newberry Library); Kathy Kienholz (American Academy of Arts and Letters); Bernard R. Crystal and Jane Gorjevsky (Butler Library, Columbia); Roberta Arminio (Ossining Historical Society); Linda Beeler (Thomas Crane Public Library, Quincy); Barbara Stamos (Quincy Historical Society); Kristen Weiss (Peabody Essex Museum); Marge Motes and Nancy L. Thurlow (Historical Society of Old Newbury); Taran Schindler (Beinecke Rare Book and Manuscript Library, Yale); David Kessler (Bancroft Library, UC-Berkeley); Nicolette Schneider and George Abbott (Syracuse University Library); Beth Alvarez (Hornbake Library, University of Maryland); Jessica Westphal, Daniel Meyer, and Sandra Roscoe (University of Chicago Library); Alice Lotvin Birney and Betty Auman (Library of Congress); Gina P. White (Dacus Library, Winthrop University); Tara Wenger and Tracy Fleischman (Ransom Humanities Research Center, University of Texas); Kris McCusker and Deborah Hollis (University of Colorado Library); Christine Nelson and John Bidwell (Morgan Library); Marianne Hansen (Canaday Library, Bryn Mawr); Phyllis Andrews and Richard Peek (Rhees Library, University of Rochester); Marty Barringer (Georgetown University Library); Sean Noel and Ryan Hendrickson (Gotlieb Archival Research Center, Boston University); Mary S. Presnell and Rebecca C. Cape (Lilly Library, Indiana University); Ron Vanderhye (Copley Library, University of San Diego); Rebecca Melvin (Morris Library, University of Delaware); Ian Graham (Bowdoin Library); Patrick J. Stevens (Kroch Library, Cornell); Amy C. Schindler (Grenander Department of Special Collections, University of Albany); Stephanie Heckaman (Culver Academy); Monique Ostiguy (National Library of Canada); Ellen Welch (University of Virginia); Bethany Holroyd (Union League Club); Sara Seten Berghausen (Duke Library); Carol Leadenham, Elena Danielson, and Robert M. Bulatoff (Hoover Institution, Stanford); Wendy Chmielewski (Swarthmore Library); Elizabeth Rogers and Jared Lewis (University of Utah Library); John B. Straw (Ball State University); Eliza Dame (Thayer Academy); Anita Israel (Longfellow National Historic Site); Judy Englander (Daphne Productions); Terry Karten (HarperCollins); Dwight Garner; Eleanor Munro; Carol Sklenicka.

One of the golden milestones of my life was meeting David McCormick, my agent, at a time when I was still floundering around wondering what to do next. David reassured me with a kind of Jeevesian calm, and ultimately restored me to the middle class. Deb Garrison, my editor, combines an all but infallible sense of literary judgment with a loving heart—in other words, a paragon of her profession and humanity at large. And were it not for the kindness of our mutual friend, Sara Mosle, I wouldn't have met either David or Deb—in which case, well, the mind simply reels. Warm thanks, too, to Deb's excellent assistant, Caroline Zancan, and to my incredibly meticulous copy editor, Terry Zaroff-Evans. At this point I seem to hear the orchestra playing me off the stage, but let me not fail to mention a sweet, supportive family: Kay, Heidi, Chris, Eliza, Emma, Bob, Debra, Jim, Joyce, and of course my wonderful mother, Marlies, whose faith in me has always been disproportionate to the known facts. As for my wife, Mary, and our beautiful Amelia— bottomless love and gratitude to you both.

Notes

For a man who hated to dwell on the past, Cheever left an almost appallingly vast paper trail, and I'm afraid these notes reflect that. His letters are scattered among various libraries and individual recipients all over the world; archives of particular interest are at the New York Public Library, the Morgan Library, the Beinecke Rare Book and Manuscript Library at Yale, and the Swem Library at the College of William and Mary. The largest manuscript archives are at Harvard's Houghton Library and Brandeis, where most of Cheever's *New Yorker* stories are preserved. For a detailed list of items in each of the major archives, I recommend a series of articles by Francis Bosha (two are cited below), which have appeared intermittently in *Resources for American Literary Study*.

I will venture to guess that I am one of perhaps ten people—others include Cheever's children and his editor at Knopf, Robert Gottlieb—who have read all forty-three hundred or so pages (mostly typed, single-spaced) of Cheever's journal. Since 2000, this remarkable document and its attendant detritus (newspaper clippings, train tickets, business cards) have been available to the public at Houghton Library, whose excellent staff have done their best to make sense of it all. And yet it remains somewhat in disarray. A few volumes are haphazardly paginated, others are not, and anyway the pages are badly jumbled. A twenty-three-page segment of handwritten notes from Cheever's 1976 trip to Romania is included with Journal Four, which otherwise is concerned with the years 1955–56; the 242 pages of Journal Two have been shuffled like a deck of cards, skipping around willy-nilly between the years 1947 and 1953. And so on. During my research I compiled the most detailed chronology of Cheever's life that I could manage, and thus was able to restore the page order of the journal with a fair degree of accuracy. Then, once I'd transcribed what I needed, my family was displaced by Hurricane Katrina—whereupon my Xeroxed copy of the journal (or rather Ben Cheever's, alas), which had occupied four linear feet on the bottom shelf of my research cabinet, was drowned in the flood. I repeat that, fortunately, all the necessary parts were already on my computer, but the stately, organized document itself is lost to posterity. In any event, there would be no point in citing the unpublished journal: given the condition of the original, there is no way to cite accurately, and besides these notes are already intolerably swollen. The reader may assume that uncited Cheever quotations are from the unpublished journal at Houghton, or else from a curious memoir fragment that Cheever wrote in two- or three-page increments (double-spaced, perhaps fifty pages in all), sometimes titled "Bloody Papers." This is available at the Berg Collection of the New York Public Library; the better to distinguish it from the Houghton journal, I cite it throughout my first two chapters, where its use is most prevalent.

I did try to avoid repetition in these notes, with indifferent results. Interview subjects are cited initially, and thereafter only when needed for the sake of clarity. I took care to date my interviews—for whatever reason—though I rarely cite separate interviews with a previously cited subject (I conducted some twenty interviews with Mary Cheever alone). The reader may assume that uncited quotations are from personal interviews, and in general, when a source (of *any* kind) is explicitly given in the text, or glaringly obvious, I omit further citation below. Uncollected stories, when quoted, are cited (once) according to their original magazine publication or their appearance in Cheever's disavowed first collection, *The Way Some People Live.** The canonical *Stories of John Cheever* is only cited when its contents are quoted for their biographical (as opposed to critical) interest, and the same applies to the novels. In dating letters, Cheever tended to give the month and day (sometimes only the latter: "Wednesday" or "The Twelfth"), but rarely the year: I supply the missing information in brackets when I'm fairly sure of it, and add a question mark when I'm not. Unless otherwise noted, letters from Cheever are in the hands of the recipients. Cheever's eccentric spelling and punctuation are often retained in quotation, though here and there I've cleaned things up for the sake of clarity. And finally—since I agree with Gerald Clarke that a lot of ellipses "[slow] down a narrative" (and are unsightly to boot)—I occasionally omit extraneous remarks from quotations, silently, without ellipses; when, however, it seems at all important to indicate an omission, I soberly deploy the ellipsis.

The following abbreviations appear in these notes:

Academy	American Academy of Arts and Letters
Albany	Grenander Department of Special Collections, University of Albany
Bancroft	The Bancroft Library, University of California, Berkeley
BC	Benjamin Cheever (JC's older son)
Berg	Henry W. and Albert A. Berg Collection of English and American Literature, New York Public Library
BP	*Bullet Park.* New York: Alfred A. Knopf, 1969.
Bryn Mawr	Canaday Library, Bryn Mawr College

---

*See page 128.

BU	Howard Gotlieb Archival Research Center, Mugar Memorial Library, Boston University
Canada	National Library of Canada
CFP	Cheever Family Papers
Chicago	University of Chicago Library
CJC	Donaldson, Scott, ed. *Conversations with John Cheever.* Jackson: University Press of Mississippi, 1987.
Colorado	Norlin Library, University of Colorado
Columbia	Butler Library, Columbia University
Copley	Helen K. and James S. Copley Library, University of San Diego
Dartmouth	Rauner Special Collections Library, Dartmouth College
Delaware	Morris Library, University of Delaware
F	*Falconer.* New York: Alfred A. Knopf, 1977.
FC	Federico Cheever (JC's younger son)
FLC Jr.	Frederick Lincoln Cheever, Jr. (JC's brother)
FLC Sr.	Frederick Lincoln Cheever, Sr. (JC's father)
GT	Weaver, John D., ed. *Glad Tidings: A Friendship in Letters.* New York: HarperCollins, 1993.
HBD	Cheever, Susan. *Home Before Dark.* Boston: Houghton Mifflin, 1984.
Houghton	Houghton Library, Harvard University
JC	John Cheever
JJC	*The Journals of John Cheever.* New York: Alfred A. Knopf, 1991.
JU	John Updike
LC	Library of Congress
Lilly	The Lilly Library, Indiana University
LJC	Cheever, Benjamin, ed. *The Letters of John Cheever.* New York: Simon & Schuster, 1988.
MC	Mary Cheever (JC's wife)
Morgan	The Morgan Library, New York
MZ	Max Zimmer
Newberry	Newberry Library, Chicago
NFB	Cheever, Susan. *Note Found in a Bottle: My Life as a Drinker.* New York: Simon & Schuster, 1999.
NYPL-MSS	Manuscripts and Archives Division, New York Public Library
OJ	Updike, John. *Odd Jobs.* New York: Alfred A. Knopf, 1991.
OWPS	*Oh What a Paradise It Seems.* New York: Alfred A. Knopf, 1982.
PJC	Papers of Jane Carr (JC's niece)
PRM	Papers of Ray Mutter, M.D. (JC's physician)
Ransom	Harry Ransom Humanities Research Center, University of Texas
Rochester	Rush Rhees Library, University of Rochester
SC	Susan Cheever (JC's daughter)
SJC	*The Stories of John Cheever.* New York: Alfred A. Knopf, 1978.
SD	Scott Donaldson
Swem	Earl Gregg Swem Library, College of William and Mary
TT	Cheever, Susan. *Treetops: A Family Memoir.* New York: Bantam, 1991.
WC	*The Wapshot Chronicle.* New York: Harper & Brothers, 1957.
WM	William Maxwell
WS	*The Wapshot Scandal.* New York: Harper & Row, 1964.
WSPL	*The Way Some People Live.* New York: Random House, 1943.
Yale	Beinecke Rare Book and Manuscript Library, Yale University

PROLOGUE

3   "John had nothing but friends": Malcolm Cowley, "John Cheever: The Novel-
    ist's Life as a Drama," *Sewanee Review* 91, no. 1 (1983), 16.
3   "the salvation of the damned": *JJC*, 393.
3   "A page of good prose": *OJ*, 113.
3   "There were whole areas . . . I couldn't go into": *CJC*, 126.
3   "no more lived-in than a bird perch": *OJ*, 118.
4   "My name is John Cheever": *CJC*, 126.
4   "Displaying much grandiosity and pride": "Patient Progress Notes (4/14/75)"
    from Smithers, Swem.
4   "Cheever's is the triumph of a man in his sixties": quoted in Michiko Kakutani,
    "John Cheever Is Dead at 70; Novelist Won Pulitzer Prize," *New York Times*,
    June 19, 1982, sec. 1, p. 1.
4   "Long before Donald Barthelme": Walter Clemons, "Cheever's Triumph,"
    Newsweek, March 14, 1977, 62.
5   "Grand Old Man of American Letters": *LJC*, 352.
5   "Yankees are distinguished, and tormented as well": Cowley, "Novelist's Life as
    Drama," 15.
6   "His air of seriousness and responsibility": *JJC*, 346.
6   "Life is an improvisation!": author int. BC, June 7, 2004.

CHAPTER ONE: { *1637–1912* }

7   "Many skeletons in family closet": *WC*, 97.
7   "bound to a drunken and tragic destiny": JC memoir fragment, Berg.
7   "We were swapping dirty stories": Alwyn Lee, "Ovid in Ossining," *Time*,
    March 27, 1964, 68.
7   "a half-wit who lived up the road": *JJC*, 189.
8   "his untiring abjuration of the Devil": quoted in Lee, "Ovid in Ossining," 68.
8   "The welfare of the commonwealth": quoted in JC, "My Friend Malcolm Cow-
    ley," *New York Times Book Review*, Aug. 28, 1983, 18.
8   "Old Zeke C.": FLC Sr. to JC and family, Nov. 14, 1943, CFP.
8   "Why tell me?": SD int. Edward Newhouse, June 5, 1984, Swem.
8   "celebrated ship's master": *CJC*, 89.
8   Benjamin Cheever as master at the Newbury North School: *Essex County, Mass-
    achusetts Biographies* (Provo, Utah: Ancestry.com, 2002), 559.
9   "to make them grow": FLC Sr. memoir notes, CFP.
9   "last sailing ship to be made in the Newburyport yards": JC memoir fragment,
    Berg.
9   "playing dominoes with old gent": FLC Sr. memoir notes, CFP.
10 "Mother, saintly old woman": *WC*, 114.
10 "If this were so": JC memoir fragment, Berg.
10 "alcohol & opium—del[irium] tremens": Massachusetts Archives, Death Rec-
    ords, vol. 339, p. 195.
10 "speeches on human ingratitude": JC to Whit Burnett, Nov. 2, 1961, Swem.
10 "[Shakespeare's] plays seemed to light and distinguish: JC, "Homage to Shake-
    speare," *Story*, Nov. 1937, 73–81.
10 "They always begin, as most journals do": *CJC*, 149.

11 "Sturgeon in river then": *WC*, 99.
11 "antic, ungrammatical and . . . vulgar": JC, introduction, *Time* Reading Program Special Edition of *The Wapshot Chronicle* (New York: Time, Inc., 1965), xvii.
11 "makes as little as possible of any event": *CJC*, 207.
11 "Grand sunsets after the daily thunder showers": FLC Sr. memoir notes, CFP.
11 "at the tail of a cart": JC to Tanya Litvinov, May 23, [1965].
11 "A competitor named Pierce": *LJC*, 43.
12 "forgotten and disgraced": JC, "An Afternoon Walk in Iowa City, Iowa," *Travel & Leisure*, Sept. 1974, 50.
12 "black-mouthed old wreck": *SJC*, 634.
13 "a memory I'm inclined to believe": JC memoir fragment, Berg.
14 Cheever claimed his great-grandfather was Sir Percy Devereaux: see JC to WM [c. Jan. 1968], Berg.
14 "He'd ask me if I wanted some cauliflower": author int. SC, Nov. 11, 2004.
14 "a very well-educated English woman": *CJC*, 134.
15 "There was nothing slummy about Aunt Anne": JC to WM [c. Jan. 1968], Berg.
15 "a split personality": *CJC*, 99.
16 "He persuaded her to give up her career": author int. MC, June 19, 2004.
16 Mary Liley Cheever as "quite beautiful": FLC Jr. to Dennis Coates, Oct. 20, 1973, Swem.
16 "He was constantly kissing my mother": JC memoir fragment, Berg.
16 "Madame President" type: Quoted in Dennis Edward Coates, "The Novels of John Cheever," unpublished dissertation, Duke University, 1977, 19. Coates's dissertation is worthy of particular notice as its biographical material is based on a number of personal interviews with Cheever and his brother Fred.
16 like Sarah Wapshot, "had exhausted herself": *WS*, 19.
17 "I was cropped": JC memoir fragment, Berg.
17 "In all the family albums she appeared": *WS*, 23.
17 "Poor Coverly blamed everything": JC, "Mrs. Wapshot," unpublished manuscript, CFP.

CHAPTER TWO { *1912–1926* }

18 "I have no biography": JC memoir fragment, Berg.
18 "no memory for pain": Jesse Kornbluth, "The Cheever Chronicle," *New York Times Magazine*, Oct. 21, 1979, 29.
18 "From somewhere": *OJ*, 108–9.
18 "I always felt there was a blank": SD int. Hortense Calisher, Sept. 17, 1984, Swem.
18 "Life is melancholy": Paul Williams, "John Cheever: Adding Luster to the Stream," *Patriot Ledger*, April 18, 1979.
18 "If you are raised in this atmosphere": *SJC*, 6.
19 "He focused on the surface and texture of life": *HBD*, 77.
19 "I am quite naked to loneliness": Arthur Unger, "John Cheever's First Teleplay—a Parody of Sitcoms," *Christian Science Monitor*, Jan. 11, 1982, 15.
19 "[W]ith dad our sense of his past pain": FC to SC, June 28, 1983, CFP.
20 "Everybody loved [him]": *WS*, 19.
20 "As my mother often pointed out": [MacDowell] *Colony Newsletter* 9, no. 1 (Fall 1979).
20 "I remember my father's detestation": *JJC*, 342.

21   "I assume the factory had not yet been invented": *LJC*, 26.
21   "They were kindly and original people": Earle F. Walbridge, "WLB Biography:
       John Cheever," *Wilson Library Bulletin*, Dec. 1961, 324.
22   "I and the dog walk with him": *JJC*, 180.
22   "pleasant, relaxed": *CJC*, 198.
22   "[W]e were always allowed to play touch football": JC, "Thanks, Too, for Mem-
       ories," *New York Times*, Nov. 22, 1976, C1.
23   "She gathered me in her arms": JC memoir fragment, Berg.
23   "breakdown in service or finance": *JJC*, 90.
23   "sentiments that were . . . too profound": JC, "The Temptations of Emma
       Boynton," *New Yorker*, Nov. 26, 1949, 29–31. The story is a fictionalized portrait
       of Anna Boynton Thompson, and recounts the same fateful Thanksgiving of
       1922 that Cheever remembers in his nonfictional *New York Times* article (cited
       above), "Thanks, Too, for Memories."
24   "the bubbling joie de vivre": *OJ*, 109.
24   "truly halved": *JJC*, 318.
24   "the stoniest glacial and tidal drift": Henry Adams, *The Education of Henry
       Adams* (Boston: Houghton Mifflin Sentry Edition, 1961), 14.
25   "a red-blooded and a splendid inheritance": *JJC*, 41.
25   "I've often wondered": quoted in "Readers' Opinions," *Patriot Ledger*, July 9,
       1982, 18.
25   "jollity and gloom [had contended] for an empire": "The May-Pole of Merry
       Mount," *The Complete Novels and Selected Tales of Nathaniel Hawthorne* (New
       York: Random House, 1937), 882.
25   "[T]he difference between the legend and the present": JC to Reuel Denney
       [c. mid-Aug.? 1934], Dartmouth.
25   "All of Dickens, from beginning to end": *CJC*, 21.
25   "could be called on to recite 'Casey at Bat' ": ibid., 132.
25   "casting around for some way of improving": *LJC*, 264.
26   "That's the way I feel about life": "This Is My Music," WQXR, January 12,
       1980.
26   John "rose glibly to the occasion": Florence M. Varley, "My Most Famous Stu-
       dent: Arithmetic Wasn't His Subject," *NRTA Journal*, March/April 1974, 33.
26   "exaggeration" and "preposterous falsehoods": JC memoir fragment, Berg.
26   "not two faculties but one mega-faculty": *CJC*, 29.
26   "Literature is a force of memory": *GT*, 256.
27   "It's all right with us if you want to be a writer": *CJC*, 208.
27   "When I was small": Rollin Bailey to SD, Aug. 25, 1985, Swem.
27   "I *did* tend to see the bad side": author int. Rollin Bailey, May 18, 2004.
27   propriety was "rigidly observed": *CJC*, 189.
27   "My mother told me to tell you so": [Thayerlands] *Evergreen*, Spring 1926, 26.
27   "she trashed [him] with a belt": JC memoir fragment, Berg.
28   "veered wildly into Christian Science": *CJC*, 218.
28   "enchained by the flesh": *JJC*, 337.
28   "a severe trial for her": FLC Sr. to JC, Feb. 6, 1944, CFP.
28   "[T]hat boy of summer": *JJC*, 235.
29   "To be an American and unable to play baseball": JC, "The National Pastime,"
       New Yorker, Sept. 26, 1953, 29–35.
29   *"Are you men sisters?"*: JC memoir fragment, Berg.
29   "sired a fruit": *JJC*, 219.
30   "merry games of grabarse": quoted in *HBD*, 175.

30 "the authority of an executioner": *LJC*, 350.

30 "It was autumn": *JJC*, 116–17.

31 "the most gratifying and unself-conscious relationship": *SJC*, 685. The narrator of "The Jewels of the Cabots" is referring here to his boyhood chum "DeVarennes"; parallel passages in Cheever's journal clearly indicate that this character is based on Fax.

31 "F[ax] went home and gave it a try": *JJC*, 246. In the published journal, Fax is identified by the initial "F."; his name is given in the original.

31 "When one bed got gummed up": JC memoir fragment, Berg.

32 "Weren't we happy, Johnny?": *JJC*, 359.

32 "Someone called from Thayer last winter": *CJC*, 200.

CHAPTER THREE {1926–1930}

33 "Mr. Forsyth" and "Harry Dobson": *JJC*, 180, 284. On p. 180, the name "Mr. Forsyth" (which appears in the original) has been deleted.

34 "match the purchase to the person": Rollin Bailey to SD, Sept. 4, 1985, Swem.

34 "You can't sell this": *CJC*, 188.

34 "the same exclusiveness and beauty": "Open Little Shop Around the Corner: Mrs. Cheever's New Store Has Atmosphere of French Salon," *Patriot Ledger* (Quincy), Sept. 30, 1929, 2.

35 "They could have their humorless Boston respectability": *HBD*, 16.

35 "My underlying conviction is that any Cheever": FLC Jr. to Sarah Cheever, Dec. 4, 1970, PJC.

36 "I have been a storyteller": *JJC*, 156.

36 "I am Mrs. F. Lincoln Cheever": Henry Allen, "John Cheever: Capturing the Splendors of Suburbia," *Washington Post*, Oct. 8, 1979, B13.

36 "Unclean outcasts whose destiny": notes on *F*, Houghton.

37 "I'm tickled to know that the letters still serve": *LJC*, 221.

37 "the antiques . . . out of Cheever's Yankee past": *CJC*, 204.

37 "dissipation of every kind": Lillian Wentworth, " . . . And Recalled: John Cheever at Prep School," *Parents League of New York Review*, 1984, 1.

38 "a large cast of absolutely naked men": JC, "My Friend Malcolm Cowley," *New York Times Book Review*, Aug. 28, 1983, 7.

38 "What future is there . . . ?": Florence M. Varley, "My Most Famous Student," *NRTA Journal*, March/April 1974, 33.

38 "didn't take well to discipline": *CJC*, 194.

38 "It made me feel good": ibid., 103.

38 "safety-pinned tuxedo": JC to Louis Kronenberger, May 21 [1968?], Copley.

39 "the first account we have of controlled schizophrenia": *CJC*, 25.

39 "My friend, John Cheever, loves it": *New York Times Book Review*, Jan. 15, 1956, 5.

39 "It must sound awfully precocious": *CJC*, 21.

39 "I thought . . . he was a *Charlus*": author int. Litvinov, Dec. 3, 2004.

39 "I remember walking down a street in Boston": *JJC*, 152.

40 "some marble-shooting chum": JC to Frederick Bracher [c. July 1964], Bancroft.

40 "What have you learned from Ernest Hemingway?": Jesse Kornbluth, "The Cheever Chronicle," *New York Times Magazine*, Oct. 21, 1979, 102.

40 "I think it's fine that Bill Faulkner got the Nobel Prize": *LJC*, 142.

40   "enormous confidence in their own genius": Malcolm Cowley, "John Cheever: The Novelist's Life as a Drama," *Sewanee Review*, 91, no. 1 (1983), 12.

40   Manhattan that "was still filled with a river light": *SJC*, vii.

40   Fielding consumed "intravenously": *CJC*, 75.

40   "Oh no, no," he hemmed: author int. George McLoone, July 31, 2004.

41   "For Christ's sake": *JJC*, 152.

41   "The beach was deserted": JC memoir fragment, Berg; see also *F*, 60–62.

42   "drunken, debauched and naked": *LJC*, 338.

42   "He did not even give me bus fare": *JJC*, 242.

43   "I'm a businesswoman!": Alwyn Lee, "Ovid in Ossining," *Time*, March 27, 1964, 68.

43   " 'Polish them Dad' ": FLC Sr. to JC, Oct. 17, 1943, CFP.

43   "Well, she *did* damage my father": *CJC*, 235.

44   "to give some fitness and shape": JC to Bracher, July 15, 1962, Bancroft.

45   "[E]very stranger's face": Marian Christy, "Ben Cheever—a Son in the Shadow," *Boston Globe*, Dec. 25, 1988, A14.

45   "total kook": author int. Anne Peirce, Oct. 27, 2004.

45   "On more than one occasion": Gordon Godfrey to SD [c. Aug. 1985], Swem.

45   "When I told her people laughed at Galsworthy": JC, "Expelled," *New Republic*, Oct. 1, 1930, 172.

45   "existed not to educate us in any way": JC, "My Friend Malcolm Cowley," 18.

46   "I was approached by angry graduates": author int. Peter Benelli, Oct. 10, 2004.

46   "extremely understanding and vastly intelligent": *CJC*, 237.

46   "The young man was not expelled from the Academy": Stacy B. Southworth to Horace Thorner, Oct. 24, 1930, Thayer.

46   Judging from "Expelled": for insight into Cheever's apparent research of *The New Republic*'s pet issues, I'm indebted to Giles Y. Gamble's fascinating paper, "John Cheever's 'Expelled': The Genesis of a Beginning," *American Literary History* 7, no. 4 (1994), 611–32.

47   "alarmingly mature," as Updike put it: *OJ*, 114.

48   "It felt precisely . . . eighty-seven dollars": *CJC*, 45.

48   "Have you been writing today?": *LJC*, 29.

48   Glover had made the front page: "Tired of World, Dartmouth Boy Takes to Woods," *Boston Herald*, Nov. 20, 1928, 1.

49   "Personally, had I the choice": Grace Osgood to Lillian Wentworth [c. spring 1980], Thayer.

49   "His portrait of her dazzles me": Hugh Hennedy to SD, Oct. 9, 1985, Swem.

49   "Without Stacy Baxter Southworth": JC to Robert Mower, Nov. 3, 1981, Thayer.

49   "[He was] wandering under some Elm trees": JC to Hugh Hennedy, Aug. 7, 1980.

CHAPTER FOUR { *1930–1934* }

51   "I was *some* kid in those days": Harvey Breit, "In and Out of Books," *New York Times Book Review*, May 10, 1953, 8.

51   Howard Street—"the arse-end of the city": JC to Denney [c. Aug. 1934], Dartmouth.

52   "It was like a love affair": author int. J. William Silverberg, Sept. 23, 2004.

52 "the erotic romance of his life": author int. Allan Gurganus, Jan. 16, 2005.

52 "I wept for a love": *JJC*, 335.

52 "prescot [sic] townsend will very nearly give me": *LJC*, 29.

53 "lunatic Swiss Family Robinson": quoted in Douglass Shand-Tucci, *The Crimson Letter: Harvard, Homosexuality, and the Shaping of American Culture* (New York: St. Martin's, 2003), 240. I am indebted to this entertaining book for background on the Beacon Hill bohemia of the twenties and thirties, as well as Cheever's friendships with Townsend, Wheelwright, and Dana.

53 "[H]e is very nice, very guarded": JC to Cowley [c. fall 1930], Newberry.

53 "those who split the monism of love": quoted in Shand-Tucci, *Crimson Letter*, 114.

54 "I could not imagine a man so old": JC to Gurganus, March 21 [1974].

54 "Everything I saw meant war": *LJC*, 51.

55 "We had a funny conversation": author int. Sarah Connoway, Jan. 27, 2005.

55 "On the Quai de Louvre, we are told": *New Yorker*, July 25, 1931, 7. This "Talk" item was written by E. B. White and reported by Cheever, as one learns from a visit to *The New Yorker*'s library or from the indispensable DVD set, *The Complete New Yorker* (New York: Random House, 2005).

55 "On the floors and on the beams": JC, "Fall River," *The Left*, Autumn 1931, 70–72.

56 "It had rained hard early in August": JC, "Late Gathering," *Pagany*, Oct.–Dec. 1931, 15–19.

56 "[Amy] thinks about her forty-fifth April": JC, "Bock Beer and Bermuda Onions," *Hound & Horn*, April–June 1932, 411–20.

56 "One could tell it was bath-tub gin": JC to Richard Johns, Oct. 17, 1967, Delaware.

56 Hawthorne was "one of the original beats": quoted in Alwyn Lee, "Ovid in Ossining," *Time*, March 27, 1964, 69.

57 "the Compleat Wasp": Roger Skillings to author, Feb. 14, 2005.

57 "hop along": SD int. Hazel Hawthorne Werner, July 1, 1984, Swem.

57 "Their kindness . . . was exhaustive": JC to Coates, April 22, 1974.

57 "His hair was nearly gone": quoted in Michael Janeway, "Glimpses of Cheever," *Boston Globe*, June 27, 1982, A22.

58 "a wood-burning locomotive": *CJC*, 104.

58 "A writer is a *Prince!*": JC to Laurens Schwartz, Oct. 16 [1975], Swem.

58 "Get out of Boston, Joey!": *CJC*, 206.

58 winning smile and "stubborn jaw": Malcolm Cowley, *Dream of the Golden Mountains* (New York: Viking, 1980), 260.

58 "You taught me to be polite": JC to Cowley, Aug. 20, 1977, Newberry.

58 I was offered two kinds of drinks: quoted in Malcolm Cowley, "John Cheever: The Novelist's Life as a Drama," *Sewanee Review* 91, no. 1 (1983), 2.

59 "human employer of forty-two people": *CJC*, 209–10.

60 "gleaming with tears": ibid., 189.

60 "I still remember": JC to Denney [c. Feb. 1935], Dartmouth.

60 "I can remember night after night": ibid.

61 "Other than Malcolm's word": JC to Elizabeth Ames, April 24, 1933, NYPL-MSS.

61 "I don't expect to do anything worth publishing": *LJC*, 32.

61 "The idea of leaving the city": ibid., 33.

62 "Fred, I'm leaving": *CJC*, 189.

CHAPTER FIVE { *1934–1935* }

63   "Call it Yaddo, Mama, for it makes poetry!": Jean Nathan, "Yaddo," *New York Times*, Sept. 19, 1993, sec. 9, p. 1.

64   "the romantic culmination of a rare triangular friendship": "Historical Note," Yaddo Records, NYPL-MSS.

64   "When a beam of light": JC,"The Hostess of Yaddo," *New York Times Book Review*, May 8, 1977, 3, 35.

64   "When you have a suggestion to make": Ames to Blitzstein, n.d., Yaddo Records, NYPL-MSS.

65   "If Elizabeth Ames was fond of you": SD int. Nellie Shannon, July 17, 1985, Swem.

65   "to a Newport 'cottage' ": quoted in *A Century at Yaddo* (Saratoga Springs, N.Y.: Corporation of Yaddo, 2000), 13.

66   a not-so-subtle "climate of repression": JC to George Biddle [c. Dec. 1954?], LC.

66   "the Yaddo effect": Nathan, "Yaddo," sec. 9, p. 1.

66   "Hooves of fire!": "Hostess of Yaddo," 35.

66   "[M]oving with great Hermian grace": unpublished memoir, courtesy of Allan Gurganus.

66   "I am told that he is twenty-two years old": Ames to William Soskin, Feb. 18, 1930, Yaddo Records, NYPL-MSS.

67   "unwise attachments": JC to Josephine Herbst [c. fall 1938], Yale.

67   " 'I'm glad you did, John' ": JC to Denney, Dec. 15, 1934, Dartmouth.

67   "I realized for the first time": JC to Coates, July 9, 1974.

67   "Only dogs, servants, and children": SD int. Gurganus, Sept. 16, 1984, Swem.

67   "Do you want me to talk to him?": Nellie Shannon to Philippa Walker, May 21, 1993, Yaddo Records, NYPL-MSS.

67   "only place I've ever felt at home": SD int. John Leonard, Oct. 23, 1984, Swem.

68   "a footnote to scholarship history": *New York Times*, May 12, 1995, D17.

68   "I was one of the first to recognize": Tony Quagliano, ed., *Feast of Strangers: Selected Prose and Poetry of Reuel Denney* (Westport, Conn.: Greenwood Press, 1999), 46.

68   "Sympathy and patience": JC to Denney [c. July 1, 1934?], Dartmouth.

69   "[S]eeing the importance you give": JC to Denney [c. Oct. 1934], Dartmouth.

69   "Being likened to a decadent intellectual": JC to Denney [c. Aug. 1934], Dartmouth.

69   "sane conservative" phase: JC to Denney [c. July 1, 1934?], Dartmouth.

69   "There is something immense": JC to Denney, Sept. 20, 1934, Dartmouth.

70   "He's a liberal, a gentleman and a romantic": JC to Denney [c. April 1936], Dartmouth.

70   "I think of Europe as a rat-toothed bitch": JC, "Letter from the Mountains," unpublished manuscript, Newberry. Cowley's halfhearted endorsement of the piece is handwritten on the manuscript itself, as is the reply ("defeatist") of a fellow editor initialed "G.S."

71   "[A]cross the street from me": JC to Denney [c. Aug. 1934], Dartmouth.

71   "I almost destroyed my teeth": *CJC*, 190.

71   "His only capital was a typewriter": Malcolm Cowley, "John Cheever: The Novelist's Life as a Drama," *Sewanee Review* 91, no. 1 (1983), 2.

71 "It was the torpor we objected to": Joseph Barbato int. JC, Oct. 27, 1978, Swem.

72 "Hudson Street is a far cry from . . . Boston": *LJC*, 34.

72 "one of the finest tongues": JC to Denney [c. Nov. 1934], Dartmouth.

72 "On Saturday night Muriel gave a reading": JC to Denney [c. Aug. 1934], Dartmouth.

72 "Nice people to drink beer": JC to Denney [c. Nov. 1934], Dartmouth.

73 "Malcolm produced . . . silver spoons": SD int. Frances Lindley, Sept. 17, 1984, Swem.

73 "I know more about the history of literature": JC to Denney [c. Oct. 1934], Dartmouth.

73 "I've done one lousey detective story": JC to Denney [c. Aug. 1934], Dartmouth.

73 "Silas Crockett, the first in line": JC, "Way Down East," *New Republic*, Dec. 11, 1935, 146.

74 asked to make a "small contribution": Ames to JC, Aug. 23, 1934, Yaddo Records, NYPL-MSS.

74 "It now seems best to set your departure": Ames to JC, Sept. 24, 1934, Yaddo Records, NYPL-MSS.

74 "the lowest of the low": JC to Denney [c. Oct. 1934], Dartmouth.

74 "I have a lot of things to thank you for": JC to Ames [c. Dec. 1934], Yaddo Records, NYPL-MSS.

75 "I am certain of my own voice": JC to Denney [c. Nov. 1934], Dartmouth.

75 "for all of their contempt . . . preciocity": JC to Denney, Aug. 29, 1934, Dartmouth.

75 "I feel confident": *LJC*, 51.

75 "Walker Evans invited me to spend the night": ibid., 304.

76 "We all knew John was sort of gay": author int. Michael Janeway, March 28, 2005.

76 Cowley would later deny having seen "any sign": SD int. Cowley, June 12, 1984, Swem.

76 Cheever's version of Crane's death: author int. SC, Sept. 7, 2004.

76 "Poor Peggy . . . She died": Cowley to JC, Nov. 29, 1979, Newberry.

77 "If I followed my instincts": *JJC*, 219.

77 Denney had never "known or suspected": Quagliano, ed., *Feast of Strangers*, 46.

77 "I wanted to marry almost every girl": *JJC*, 247.

77 "He always had this kind of chuckle": author int. Dodie Merwin Captiva, June 6, 2005.

78 "He would never talk to me about his brother": author int. FC, Aug. 29, 2004.

78 "He wanted to understand the world": WM to SC, n.d., CFP.

CHAPTER SIX {*1935–1938*}

79 "I don't know how I'll get along ": JC to Denney [c. Jan. 1935], Dartmouth.

80 "Tomorrow, try writing a story": Malcolm Cowley, *Dream of the Golden Mountains* (New York: Viking, 1980), 261.

80 "refinement, discretion, excessive detail": *LJC*, 34.

80 "I thought we were taking one": Katharine White to JC, March 22, 1935, NYPL-MSS.

80 "Things got lower and lower": JC to Denney [c. March 1935], Dartmouth.

81   "This story . . . we can't believe is for us": White to Maxim Lieber, April 15, 1935, NYPL-MSS.

81   "She can't ask about her roomers' habits": quoted in White to Lieber, May 2, 1935, NYPL-MSS.

81   "I should be interested to know *how*": White to Lieber, June 18, 1935, NYPL-MSS.

81   "I've never imagined making a living": JC to Denney [c. March 1935], Dartmouth.

82   "Before I left Hanover for the last time": *LJC*, 52.

82   "It would be something as casual": JC, "Of Love: A Testimony," *WSPL*, 43–66.

83   "a story writer and a novelist": *LJC*, 38.

83–84   "While we were talking about Triuna": JC to Ames [c. spring 1935], Yaddo Records, NYPL-MSS.

84   "I have almost always worked": *LJC*, 37.

84   "Yaddo still goes on": JC to Cowleys [c. Sept. 1935?], Newberry.

84   "I can't get a WPA job": *LJC*, 38.

84   "I'm not doing the work I should do": JC to Denney, Nov. 11, 1935, Dartmouth.

85   "[P]oor John can't sit over there in the dark": Walker Evans, *Walker Evans at Work* (New York: Harper & Row, 1982), 117.

85   "C'mon, Cheever, join up!": SD int. Lila Refregier, Jan. 14, 1985, Swem.

85   "nothing in their faces but a love of money": JC, "In Passing," *Atlantic Monthly*, March 1936, 157, 331–43.

86   "I hope he hasn't deserted us entirely": White to Lieber, April 27, 1936, NYPL-MSS.

86   "But it will be ten times as long": JC to Denney [c. Jan. 1936], Dartmouth.

87   "I thought of her not as a distinguished writer": *LJC*, 41.

87   "Poor Nathan": ibid., 152.

87   "I'm not as satisfied with it": JC to Denney [c. April 1936], Dartmouth.

87   "is 'John Cheever' right?": Wolcott Gibbs to JC, June 4, 1936, NYPL-MSS.

87   "It takes almost no gasoline": JC to Denney, Dec. 11, 1935, Dartmouth.

88   discussed their respective "Belle Isles": FLC Jr. to Sarah Cheever, Feb. 22, 1972, PJC.

88   "We disagree on everything": JC to Denney [c. July 1936], Dartmouth.

88   "I'm a stranger here": JC to Denney [c. Jan. 1936], Dartmouth.

88   move to Maine "and have a boat and a girl": JC to Denney [c. May 1936], Dartmouth.

89   "My father keeps telling me": *LJC*, 40.

89   "Daisey MacAfee Bonner": JC to Denney, July 3, 1936, Dartmouth.

90   "I woke one morning with a hangover": *LJC*, 42.

90   "I am sorry that we don't like this story": White to Betty Shalett, Sept. 18, 1936, NYPL-MSS.

90   "interested in the Spanish trouble": "Frère Jacques," *Atlantic Monthly*, March 1938, 161–63.

90–91   "really illuminates the contemporary scene": *New York Times Book Review*, June 4, 1939, 4.

91   "I haven't appreciated anything as much": JC to Gibbs, Oct. 13, 1936, NYPL-MSS.

91   "I've got to go over the whole novel": *LJC*, 42.

91   "I have a chance of a WPA job": JC to Denney [c. Oct. 1936], Dartmouth.

92 "It's the vision of those three sheets": *LJC*, 50.

92 "a good drinking companion": JC to Herbst [c. winter 1937?], Yale.

92 "turned his back on his three beautiful Brooklyn novels": quoted in "Daniel Fuchs," *Independent* (London), Sept. 2, 1993, 30.

92 "It was a pretty idyllic time": Daniel Fuchs to SD, May 8, 1984, Swem.

92 "When I was younger": Barbato int. JC, Oct. 27, 1978, Swem.

93 "He wanted terribly to be respected": SD int. Dorothy Farrell, April 9, 1985, Swem.

93 "crying like a young kid": "His Young Wife," *Collier's*, Jan. 1, 1938, 21–22, 46.

93 "[W]hat's happened between now and then": JC to Denney, Jan. 21, 1938, Dartmouth.

93 "A literary career": "Not for Publication," *Patriot Ledger*, March 17, 1938, 9.

CHAPTER SEVEN { 1938–1939 }

94 with "clarity, ease and meaning": Monty Noam Penkower, *The Federal Writers' Project* (Urbana: University of Illinois Press, 1977), 159.

94 "Every time I saw a beggar in the streets": *LJC*, 48.

94 "a stigma of the lowest order": Jerre Mangione, *The Dream and the Deal* (Boston: Little, Brown, 1972), 119.

95 "Have the Bill Fold and the X [$10] enclosed": FLC Sr. to JC, Dec. 19, 1943, CFP.

95 "an old lady who sits at the head of the table": *LJC*, 45.

95 "under the influence of Fitzgerald": *GT*, 155.

95 "What about John Cheever?": WM to Geraldine Mavor, Sept. 1, 1938, NYPL-MSS.

96 "like pulling a tooth": JC to Ames [c. Oct. 1938], Yaddo Records, NYPL-MSS.

96 "seemed neither interesting nor useful": Penkower, *Federal Writers' Project*, 161.

96 "twisting into order the sentences": *LJC*, 47.

96 "Cheever thinks that the [introduction]": Henry G. Alsberg to Harold Strauss, Jan. 28, 1939, LC.

97 "Hey Johnny . . . it's a long time": Jim McGraw to SD, June 6, 1984, Swem.

97 "dreaming out a book": JC to Denney, July 8, 1939, Dartmouth.

98 "a howling wind that shakes the island": *LJC*, 48.

98 "We got on one another's nerves": JC to Denney [c. Jan. 1940], Dartmouth.

99 "three wonderful writers all named John": *Paris Review* 85 (Fall 1982), 130.

99 "concerning writers and their difficulties": WM to Mavor, Oct. 20, 1939, NYPL-MSS.

99 thought only "half done": WM to JC, Sept. 29, 1939, NYPL-MSS.

99 "This finds me stranded on an island": JC to WM, Oct. 1, 1939, NYPL-MSS.

99 "I appreciate your personal interest": Mavor to WM, Nov. 21, 1939, NYPL-MSS.

100 struck by Cheever's "immense charm": BBC int. WM, April 20, 1993, CFP.

CHAPTER EIGHT { 1939–1941 }

101 "the grey light of New York apartments": JC to Denney [c. Dec. 1939], Dartmouth.

102   "[H]e was kind of slumped over": *LJC*, 53.

102   "That's more or less what I would like": *CJC*, 239.

103   "I was the child she didn't want": *TT*, 31.

103   "Even now, in a family of doctors": ibid., 36.

103   "My own work is extremely confining": MC's Sarah Lawrence application, April 17, 1935, CFP.

103   "very little-girlish speech and behavior": author int. J. William Silverberg, Sept. 23, 2004.

104   "MEDICAL HEAD CRASHES SOCIETY": quoted in *TT*, 42.

104   "Each breath you draw": *LJC*, 51.

104   "I think he avoided France": *TT*, 61.

105   "The folly of a fool": SD int. Sara Spencer, Nov. 10, 1983, Swem.

106   "he would tell a pointless obscene story": quoted in *TT*, 87.

107   "He would like to reduce personality": *LJC*, 66.

107   "Your sweater is on backwards": "Mary—the Other Cheever," *Suburbia Today*, April 19, 1981, 6.

107   "Oh, the Sarah Lawrence girl!": author int. MC, Dec. 13, 2003.

108   "John boy—Quincy your hometown": FLC Sr. to JC, Oct. 2, 1940, CFP.

108   "Dad's just been in telling me about Newburyport": JC to MC [c. summer 1940], Morgan.

108   "Quincy Youth Is Achieving New York Literary Career": *CJC*, 3.

108   "great moodiness and discontent": JC to MC [c. Aug. 1940], Morgan.

109   "a deliberately digressive, episodic . . . work": quoted in Dennis Edward Coates, "The Novels of John Cheever," unpublished dissertation, Duke University, 1977, 35.

110   "Porter is wonderful": *LJC*, 59.

110   "very kind" but "impossible" offer: JC to MC [c. Aug. 1940], Morgan.

110   "If there is anything in my memory": *LJC*, 106.

111   "taken off to the booby-hatch": ibid., 56.

111   dialogue was "beside the point": quoted in *Paris Review* 85 (Fall 1982), 134.

112   " 'I'm going to be a war profiteer' ": JC, "The Happiest Days," *New Yorker*, Nov. 4, 1939, 15–16.

112   lacking "direction or focus": Gustave Lobrano to Lieber, June 20, 1940, NYPL-MSS.

112   "You just sit around here": JC, "I'm Going to Asia," *Harper's Bazaar*, Sept. 1940, 61.

114   "We will have a good life darling": *LJC*, 61

114   "We just decided not to wait much longer": MC to Milton Winternitz, n.d., CFP.

114   "I'm the old one!": author int. Bill Winternitz, June 10, 2004.

114   "My maternal great-grandmother": Lynne Ames, "The View from Ossining: The Solitude of an Author's Wife and a Poet in Her Own Right," *New York Times*, Feb. 19, 1995, Westchester sec. 2, p. 3.

CHAPTER NINE { *1941–1943* }

115   "shopping in Frenchtown": JC to Herbst, Oct. 24, 1942, Yale.

115   "spilling martinis all over the Brevoort": JC to Herbst [c. spring 1942], Yale.

117   "an inability to draw . . . lives together": JC to Herbst [c. Oct. 1954], Yale.

117   "slipped out of the heavy-drinking set": *LJC*, 65.
117   "keep [him] in mind": JC to Cowley, Jan. 3, 1942, Newberry.
117   "All I know about war": *LJC*, 67.
118   "Goodbye, goodbye, goodbye": JC, "Goodbye, Broadway—Hello, Hello," *WSPL*, 224–27.
118   Fort Dix was "like a Boy's Camp": JC to Lobrano [c. May 1942], NYPL-MSS.
118   "razor-back hogs, grits, thin-bloodedness": JC to Herbst [c. 1954?], Yale.
118   "The food is very good": JC to MC [c. May 1942], Morgan.
118   "Our sergeant is a strange and interesting man": *LJC*, 70.
118   "five poisonous gases without [their] masks": ibid., 72.
119   "an ex–smoke eater named Smoko": ibid., 82.
119   "an old ex-prostitute or ex-actress": JC to MC [c. June 1942], Morgan.
119   "[M]ail call is the high point": JC to Lobrano [c. May 1942], NYPL-MSS.
119   "I too have slept with someone else's boot": *LJC*, 83.
119   "Don't bother to answer them": Ibid., 75.
119   "Another grand morning": FLC Sr. to JC and family, Nov. 7, 1943, CFP.
120   "having a lot of trouble with negros": JC to MC [c. Aug. 1942], Morgan.
120   "with his fatigue hat pulled down": JC to MC [c. July 1942], Morgan.
120   "his face sewed up and a pair of dark glasses": *LJC*, 79.
120   "I have a nomination of a writer": Harold Ross to Lt. Col. Egbert White, May 12, 1942, NYPL-MSS.
120   "but Dear Jesus I hope and pray": *LJC*, 75.
121   "[*Yank*] simply got over-manned": Ross to Irwin Shaw, Oct. 1, 1942, NYPL-MSS.
121   "The barracks are white clapboard": JC to WM, Aug. 16, 1942, Berg.
121   "I have never seen such poverty": JC to Ames [c. fall 1942], NYPL-MSS.
121   "homesick for Camp Croft and Sergeant Durham": *LJC*, 77.
121   "southern boys who run around": ibid., 82.
121   "the voluminous correspondence": ibid., 84.
121   "When the conductor shouted 'Columbia'": JC to MC [c. Nov. 1942?], Morgan.
121   "Ain't that pretty?": *LJC*, 91.
122   "the first electrocution in the family": author int. Elizabeth Collins, April 22, 2004.
122   "[We] went to a dance at the Eagle Club": JC to MC [c. Nov. 1942?], Morgan.
122   "[O]h Christ what fun": JC to Herbst, Oct. 24, 1942, Yale.
123   "Just a line to tell you": Bennett Cerf to JC, Oct. 2, 1942, Columbia.
123   "a fact that impresses no one": JC to Cerf, Oct. 15, 1942, Columbia.
123   "I have my schedule down now": JC to MC [c. Oct. 1942], Morgan.
123   "Gordon brought the gun up to the salute": JC, "The Man Who Was Very Homesick for New York," *WSPL*, 248–57.
123   Lobrano thought . . . "really first-rate": Lobrano to JC, Oct. 23, 1942, NYPL-MSS.
123   "There was a nervous, little letter": JC to MC [c. Oct. 1942], Morgan.
124   "You'll appreciate his training": JC, "Sergeant Limeburner," *New Yorker*, March 13, 1943, 19–25.
124   "[The captain] was an odd-looking man": JC, "The Invisible Ship," *New Yorker*, Aug. 7, 1943, 17–21.
124   "[H]e has an up-turned nose": *LJC*, 92.
124   "I feel like a dope": ibid., 86.

125 "Three stripes," wrote his father: FLC Sr. to JC and family, Nov. 14, 1943, CFP.

125 "that the women in Africa": JC to "Gus or Bill," Jan. 9, 1943, NYPL-MSS.

125 "On Lincoln's Birthday": JC to Lobrano, Feb. 14, 1943, NYPL-MSS.

125 "I don't know how the Major will take it": *LJC*, 95.

125 "a special fire issue": ibid., 96.

126 "My family settled in Salem in 1632": JC to Cerf [c. Feb. 1943], Columbia.

126 "I know you have no more illusions": Cerf to JC, Oct. 19, 1942, Columbia.

126–127 Reviews of *The Way Some People Live:* Rose Feld, in *New York Herald Tribune Book Review*, March 14, 1943, 12; William DuBois, in *New York Times Book Review*, March 28, 1943, 10; Weldon Kees, in *New Republic*, April 19, 1943, 516–17; Struthers Burt, in *Saturday Review of Literature*, April 24, 1943, 9.

127 "[A]ll in all—even though they don't like me": *LJC*, 101.

128 "I find all this early work intensely embarrassing": JC to McLoone, March 11 [1968], Georgetown University Library.

128 "were not rueful vignettes": JC, in *Atlantic Brief Lives*, ed. Louis Kronenberger (Boston: Little, Brown, 1971), 275.

CHAPTER TEN {*1943–1945*}

129 the author's "childlike sense of wonder": *GT,* 58.

129 "Between long-distance calls to Frank Capra": ibid., 2.

130 "Kennedy? Kenelly? Kovacs?": *JJC*, 164.

130 "You and I are survivors, of course": JC to David Rothbart, May 9, 1978.

130 "We spend all of our Sundays rooting around": JC to Herbst, May 17 [1943], Yale.

131 "Make it clear, make it logical": Col. Emanuel Cohen, "Film Is a Weapon," *Business Screen* 7, no.1 (1946).

131 *How to Carve a Side of Beef:* author int. Arthur Laurents, April 4, 2005.

131 "lean purity" of his language: Ted Mills to SD, March 19, 1985, Swem.

131 "There wasn't enough work": Leonard Spigelgass to SD, Sept. 11, 1984, Swem.

131 "flatten their backs against the wall": Arthur Laurents, *Original Story By* (New York: Alfred A. Knopf, 2000), 23.

131 "Good John" . . . "Bad John": Caskie Stinnett to SD, Dec. 12, 1985, Swem.

132 "wild and hilarious": SD int. Don Ettlinger, July 6, 1984, Swem.

132 "Lennie, your mascara's running": *GT,* 4.

132 "never been so well regulated, moderate": ibid., 2.

133 remembered how "terribly intolerant": SD int. Ted Mills, Oct. 17, 1985, Swem.

134 refused to let anyone "touch or chastise": SD int. Peggy Murray, June 11, 1984, Swem.

134 "Codfish was not a thing I cooked": author int. Ruth Denney, July 29, 2004.

134 "funny, funny pieces for *The New Yorker*": JC to Herbst, Nov. 1, 1945, Yale.

134 "She ate as though": JC, "Town House II," *New Yorker,* Aug. 11, 1945, 20–25.

135 "It was the naive": JC, "Town House IV," *New Yorker,* Jan. 5, 1946, 23–28.

135 "He used to be president of paramount": *LJC*, 106–7.

135 "hanging out of their windows": JC to MC [c. April 1945], Morgan.

135 "absolutely nothing over waist-high": *CJC*, 50.

135 "crack[ed] coconuts" with a sailor: JC to Coates, April 6, 1974.

136 shouting *La guerre est finie!*: SD int. Katrina Ettlinger, June 4, 1984, Swem.

CHAPTER ELEVEN { *1945–1946* }

137   "saga" of "disorder, hysteria, and vermin": *LJC*, 112.
137   "Here we are . . . living like the wicked rich": MC to Herbst [c. Aug. 1945], Yale.
137   "the interminable funeral procession": *LJC*, 121.
138   "She enjoys herself tremendously": ibid., 123.
138   his "favorite New York": JC, "Moving Out," *Esquire*, July 1960, 67.
138   he thought his parents were "terribly disappointed": SD int. Elizabeth Collins, July 2, 1984, Swem.
139   "on this oblate spheroid": FLC Sr. to JC, Jan. 16, 1944, CFP.
139   "John that's all that makes life worth living": FLC Sr. to JC and family, Oct. 10, 1943, CFP.
139   "its layout sure sparkles": FLC Sr. to JC and family, Nov. 7, 1943, CFP.
140   " 'Too old' as it looks": FLC Sr. to JC, Nov. 21, 1943, CFP.
140   "Got a phone call Th'sgiving": FLC Sr. to JC and family, Nov. 29, 1943, CFP.
140   "They told me to take off my clothes": JC, fragment of *The Holly Tree*, Berg.
140   "My letters from now on": FLC Sr. to JC and family, Nov. 14, 1943, CFP.
141   "excoriating her": *JJC*, 22.
141   "It was a very long association": JC memoir fragment, Berg; also see *WC*, 303.
141   In 1977 he told John Hersey: see *CJC*, 156.
142   "His name is pronounced weasel": JC to WM [c. June 1947], NYPL-MSS.
142   "When I scythe I think of Tolstoy": JC to Litvinov, April 4 [1977].
142   "kind of like a diploma": JC to Herbst [summer 1947?], Yale.
143   "I got too much to do": *SJC*, 31.
143   "There are a lot of Mary's family here": *GT*, 38.
143   "Mary's unstable sister": *LJC*, 117.
144   "I used to put a gin bottle in the window": JC to Ettlingers [c. 1960?], CFP.
144   "Now and then he flashes": *GT*, 62–63.
145   "[T]he cost of this comfortable life": *LJC*, 124.
145   "Last night, folding the bath towel": *JJC*, 16.

CHAPTER TWELVE { *1946–1949* }

146   "I got out of the army in November": *LJC*, 113.
146   "This letter is to thank you": Robert Linscott to JC, July 1, 1946, Columbia.
147   "I like the story but I keep asking myself": *LJC*, 123.
147   "a fairly good chance": JC to Linscott, July 2 [1947], Columbia.
147   "eggs in the city": *GT*, 38.
148   "The writing, or the surface of the book": JC to Linscott, Dec. 16 [1947], Columbia.
149   "That's a wonderful presentation": Linscott to JC, Dec. 22, 1947, Columbia.
149   "the only man in the East Fifties": *GT*, 43.
149   "I want to write short stories": *LJC*, 125.
149   "as long as there wasn't any explicit": *CJC*, 74–75.
149   "It was one of the most felicitous": "Interview with John Cheever," *Contemporary Authors* 5 (Detroit: Gale Publishing, 1981), 110–11.
152   "It will turn out to be a memorable one": Thomas Kunkel, ed., *Letters from the Editor: The New Yorker's Harold Ross* (New York: Modern Library, 2000), 308.
152   "unquestionably excellent": Ross to JC, Oct. 15, 1947, NYPL-MSS.

153 "This story has gone on for 24 hours": *CJC*, 103–4.
153 "I doubt very much if those lunches": quoted in Francis Bosha, "The John Cheever Papers at the New York Public Library's Manuscripts and Archives Division (Part 1)," *Resources for American Literary Study* 27, no. 1 (2001), 83.
153 "I leafed through the Thurber book": JC to WM, Oct. 22, 1959, NYPL-MSS.
153 Ross scribbled, "Eh? What's this?": JC, "Why I Write Short Stories," *Newsweek*, Oct. 30, 1978, 24.
154 "I think Ross's feeling": *CJC*, 123.
154 "[S]he comes home with a briefcase full of themes": *LJC*, 124.
154 "too late for Mary to take up a musical instrument": *GT*, 34.
155 "independence and extraordinary maturity": *LJC*, 132.
155 "Sue is about the same": JC to Ettlingers [c. July 1946], CFP.
155 "[W]hen I picked her up at the party": *LJC*, 136.
155 "We think he's handsome": ibid., 133.
155 "All the people came out of a bad picture": ibid., 121.
155–156 "This maid has a gray uniform": ibid., 134.
156 "saying No thank you very much": ibid., 129.
156 Peter Pan, Voltaire, and Bambi: *CJC*, 5.
156 "From the shelter halves of Guam": JC, "The Origins of 'Town House,' " *Boston Post*, Sept. 5, 1948.
156 "a sentimental and moderately funny piece of bunk": *LJC*, 135.
157 "a thin, loose, mechanical whizzbang": Brooks Atkinson, "At the Theatre: Gertrude Tonkonogy's 'Town House' Is Based on John Cheever's Short Stories in The New Yorker," *New York Times*, Sept. 24, 1948, 31.
157 "I don't quite know who to blame": *LJC*, 136.
157 "We are as poor as we ever have been": *JJC*, 14.
157 "This is a patriarchal relationship": ibid., 15.
157 "[s]corn, ridicule, abuse, and disgust": JC, "The Opportunity," *Cosmopolitan*, Dec. 1949, 44, 174–76.
158 "I keep telling myself that this cannot go on": *JJC*, 20.
158 "Elizabeth [Ames] has closed the door": JC to Denney [c. Jan. 1941], Dartmouth.
158 "[W]henever I heard . . . brilliantly red": Ian Hamilton, *Robert Lowell: A Biography* (New York: Random House, 1982), 146.
159 Yaddo was "permeated with Communists": ibid., 115.
159 "a diseased organ, chronically poisoning": Barry Werth, *The Scarlet Professor* (New York: Doubleday, 2001), 115.
159 "John Cheever was wonderful": SD int. Robert Penn Warren and Eleanor Clark, July 10, 1984, Swem.
159 "We feel that the charge": E. Clark, K. Phelan, J. Cheever, A. Kazin, and H. Breit to the Directors of Yaddo, March 21, 1949, NYPL-MSS.
159 "I do not know how I should have come through": Ames to Herbst, April 3, 1949, Yale.
159 "Nothing that she ever did or said": quoted in Elinor Langer, *Josephine Herbst* (Boston: Little, Brown, 1984), 295.
160 "found so little worthwhile": JC to Naomi Burton, June 3, 1955, Columbia.
160 "I am writing principally to say": JC to Linscott [c. Jan. 1950], Columbia.
161 "I have told you many times": Linscott to JC, Jan. 20, 1950, Columbia.

CHAPTER THIRTEEN {*1949–1951*}

162   "As decadent, I think, as anything": *JJC*, 12.
162   "I can remember walking": ibid., 11.
162   "one of those men who labor": *WS*, 204.
163   "all the characteristics of a failure": *JJC*, 15.
164   "Goddammit, Cheever": *CJC*, 74.
165   "operated in a fantasy world": Michael Shnayerson, *Irwin Shaw: A Biography* (New York: G. P. Putnam's Sons, 1989), 178.
165   "I cannot, in good conscience, accept": JC to Ames, May 21 [1950?], Yaddo Records, NYPL-MSS.
165   "Tonight Ross is giving a party": JC to Herbst [March 18, 1950], Yale.
166   "contemptible smallness": *JJC*, 22.
166   "dread of falling, of loneliness and disgrace": ibid., 32.
167   "It is supposed to operate": JC to WM, July 22, 1953, NYPL-MSS.
167   "like magicians' colored scarves": Anne Tyler, in *New Republic*, Nov. 4, 1978, 46.
168   "the best you have ever written": Linscott to JC, June 7, 1951, Columbia.
168   "pry a saleable story out of [his] head": *LJC*, 147.
168   " 'Eat, eat, eat,' she shouts at them": ibid., 146.
168   "This house is remote and quiet": JC to Lobrano [c. Sept. 1950], NYPL-MSS.
168   "It's been sort of a fuckedup summer": JC to Herbst [c. Aug. 1950], Yale.
169   "Mary's head was light": JC to Cowley [c. 1953?], Newberry.
169   "This is a report on the long-delayed novel": JC to Linscott, Oct. 13, 1950, Columbia.
169   "like some kinds of wine": JC, "What Happened," in *Understanding Fiction*, ed. Cleanth Brooks and R. P. Warren (New York: Appleton-Century-Crofts, 1959), 571.
170   "I had spent the summer in excellent company": ibid., 572.
172   "troublingly uncertain": Cowley to JC, Jan. 22, 1953, Newberry.
172   "The brother story, in its bare outline": *LJC*, 160.
172   "a form with which I seem unable to cope": JC's fellowship application, Nov. 13, 1950, Guggenheim Foundation.
172   "I'm not sanguine": *LJC*, 147.
173   "John seemed to have a joyful knowledge": SD int. WM, Nov. 9, 1983, Swem.
174   "The whole of my youth is in it": quoted in James Campbell, "Secrets of the Confessional," *Guardian* (London), Jan. 11, 2003.
174   "Bill never made a secret": author int. Shirley Hazzard, Aug. 27, 2004.
175   "very remote from [his] life now": ibid.
175   "Mary went wild": *LJC*, 305.
176   "My God, the suburbs!": JC, "Moving Out," *Esquire*, July 1960, 67.
176   "I was standing on the sidewalk [at the time]": WM to SD, April 10, 1985, Swem.
176   "There's this chap named Marples": *JJC*, 211.
176   "There was a paranoid side to him": WM to SC, n.d., CFP.

CHAPTER FOURTEEN {*1951–1952*}

177   "the chicken house in Scarborough": *GT*, 63.
178   "curbed with Italian marble": *LJC*, 150.

178   *"If I can raise six kids"*: SD int. Dudley Schoales Sr., June 25, 1985, Swem.

178   "she played the meanest game of chopanose": *GT,* 132.

178   "Mrs. Vanderlip passed tea and sherry": JC to Eleanor Clark [c. 1954?], CFP.

179   "kind and gentle people": JC to Herbst, July 17 [1951], Yale.

179   Mimi Boyer was from old money: author int. Linda Boyer Gillies, May 29, 2004.

180   "I don't think the Kaiser": SD int. Philip and Mimi Boyer, July 8, 1984, Swem.

180   "fleeting, warm and imperious smile": JC to Litvinov, Jan. 18, 1965.

180   "John, can't you try to be a little neater?": *LJC,* 305.

180   "it wasn't too safe": ibid., 163.

181   "Arthur is a fishing and drinking companion": ibid., 250.

181   "Please don't vote for Goldwater": SD int. Arthur Spear, July 19, 1983, Swem.

182   "I cringe to think how much we drank": SD int. Virginia Kahn, June 5, 1985, Swem.

182   "It wasn't the fall": BC, "My Life with the Bourbon Dynasty: Ben Cheever Recalls Growing Up with an Alcoholic Father . . . ,"*Independent,* Nov. 27, 2000, Features sec., 7.

182–183   "without a leash": *GT,* 55.

183   "[O]n the third play": ibid., 85.

183   "charming, dashing": author int. Joseph Kahn, May 21, 2005.

183   "There has never been a more conscientious": JC to Cowley [c. 1952?], Newberry.

184   "a depressing place to which Jews": JC to Herbst [c. 1952?], Yale.

184   "a man in his shirtsleeves rehearsing": *LJC,* 155.

184   "the peers of Milton": ibid., 212.

184   "When the rich people had left": *TT,* 91.

185   Cheever was almost "stuffy": SD int. Sally Swope, Nov. 8, 1983, Swem.

186   latest effort had "gone very well": JC to Cowley, March 24 [1952], Newberry.

186   "I'd begun to think that the only way": Cowley to JC, March 29, 1952, Newberry.

186   "an all around air of profound embarrassment": JC to Herbst [c. March 1952], Yale.

186   "but it will probably never ring": *LJC,* 151.

187   "When I reached the office": JC to Candida Donadio [c. Jan. 1965], Columbia.

187   "I am like a prisoner who is trying to escape": *JJC,* 5.

188   *"He* was a man of principle": JC to Clark [c. April 1954], CFP.

188   " 'Isn't MaCarthy [sic] wonderful?' ": JC to WM [c. April 1954], Berg.

189   "Just pass the [vermouth] bottle over the gin": *NFB,* 15.

189   "She would take me out to lunch": author int. Jane Carr, May 30, 2004.

190   "an exciting place like New York": FLC Jr. to Sarah Cheever, Feb. 22, 1972, PJC.

190   "Where there's a Cheever, there's *color*": FLC Jr. to David Cheever, July 15, 1970.

190   "Hey, Joey!" Fred would hail him: *HBD,* 203–4.

CHAPTER FIFTEEN { *1952–1954* }

193   "because poor little Benjy is dressed in rags": *GT,* 71.

193   "The only thing to come my way so far": JC to Herbst, July 8 [1952], Yale.

193   "a quiet man with a twinkle": SD int. Ezra Stone, Oct. 11, 1985, Swem.
193   "long-winded suggestions": JC to Mrs. James Byrne, Dec. 17, 1952, Columbia.
193   "I don't recall whether": JC, "Don't Leave the Room During the Commercials," *TV Guide*, Jan. 9, 1982, 20.
194   "stand reading and rereading": Linscott to JC, June 7, 1951, Columbia.
194   "looking around desperately": *LJC*, 159.
194   "to get a clearer idea": JC to Herbst [c. April 1953], Yale.
194   "to old, tender-hearted, soft-brained friends": *GT*, 73.
195   "The short story is determined": quoted in Harvey Breit, "In and Out of Books," *New York Times Book Review*, May 10, 1953, 8.
195   Reviews of *The Enormous Radio*: James Kelly, in *New York Times Book Review*, May 10, 1953, 21; William Peden, in *Saturday Review*, May 11, 1953, 43–44; Arthur Mizener, in *New Republic*, May 25, 1953, 19–20; William DuBois, in *New York Times*, May 1, 1953, 19.
196   "one hell of a story": JC to Lobrano, Jan. 30, 1948, NYPL-MSS.
197   "to find the self-designated intellectuals": quoted in *GT*, 73.
197   "I suppose the happiest days of my life": JC to Natalie Robins, Dec. 3 [1969].
197   "very riveted": author int. Sarah Stevenson, Dec. 6, 2004.
197   "very pleasant ritual": *CJC*, 22.
197   "Almighty God, maker of all things": JC, "Thanks, Too, for Memories," *New York Times*, Nov. 26, 1949, C1.
198   "Physical contact was not encouraged": *HBD*, 36.
200   "[Susan's] smile was broad and forced": *LJC*, 157.
200   "I yearned to discharge": *JJC*, 31.
200   "D-e-r-e daddy, don't leave us": Raymond Carver, *Fires* (Santa Barbara, Calif.: Capra Press, 1983), 200.
201   "I would like to move along": *JJC*, 39.
201   "I keep writing a story": *LJC*, 155.
201   "the theme of aging children": JC to Cowley, Jan. 12 [1953], Newberry.
202   "the rayon blanket tycoon": *LJC*, 174.
203   Fred had fired a secretary: author int. David Cheever, July 15, 2004.
203–204   "by refusing to speak to her for a week or two": *JJC*, 273.
205   "[A]n extraordinary story": WM to JC [c. April 1953], NYPL-MSS.
205   "[She] kept chatting about American poetry": JC to Clark, Aug. 12, 1953, CFP.
205   "I'm going to go as the late Warren G. Harding": *GT*, 77.
205   Mary was "the seven-eyed Sybil": *LJC*, 302.
205   "wire-recording of the 'strange tongues' ": JC to Clark, Nov. 4 [1953], CFP.
206   "comical character": *GT*, 83.
207   "homosexual concerns": Bernard Glueck to SD, March 11, 1985, Swem.
210   "no greater pleasure": JC, "What Happened," *Understanding Fiction*, ed. Cleanth Brooks and R. P. Warren (New York: Appleton-Century-Crofts, 1959), 572.
211   "half-a-dozen particular favorites": Vladimir Nabokov, *Strong Opinions* (New York: Vintage, 1990), 312.
211   "I saw a script before we sailed": JC to Boyers, Nov. 17 [1956].
211   "I read in the newspaper": *CJC*, 190. In the interview, Cheever uses the word "blandly" to describe his mother's dismissive tone of voice. Eleven years before, he'd recorded the exchange in his journal as follows: "I see that you've won a prize, she said. Yes, I said, I didn't write you because it isn't terribly important. I know it isn't she said *harshly* [my italics]."

CHAPTER SIXTEEN {*1954–1956*}

212 "even if I were traveling . . . wrong direction": *LJC*, 165.

212 "Mary thinks that the University called": ibid., 166.

212 "wasn't a crime" to be a writer: author int. Piri Halasz, Sept. 3, 2004.

213 "Most of the girls are so subtle": JC to Clark [c. 1955], CFP.

213 "There is no recorded instance": SD int. Judith Sherwin, Jan. 18, 1985, Swem.

213 "[it] takes the skin off your back": *CJC*, 8.

214 "It was an honor to be sitting there": author int. Toby Stein, Nov. 29, 2004.

214 "It's been my intention": JC to Linscott [c. March 1953], Columbia.

214 he found the genre "bankrupt": *LJC*, 162.

214 "take some situation like the one": Cowley to JC, April 27, 1953, Newberry.

214 "'To my changeling son, Eben'": "The National Pastime," *New Yorker*, Sept. 26, 1953, 29–35.

215 "a model of wrongness": JC to WM, July 14, 1953, NYPL-MSS.

215 "a series of eddies and whirlpools": WM to JC, Nov. 30, 1953, NYPL-MSS.

215–216 "boarding-house widows, seaside girls": JC, "Independence Day at St. Botolph's," *New Yorker*, July 3, 1954, 18–23.

216 "Having revised these lines as Gide": JC, introduction (1965), *WC*, xvii.

216 "So many of my plans": JC to WM [c. Jan. 1955], Berg.

217 "I wonder if any publisher will pay": JC to Naomi Burton, June 3, 1955, Columbia.

217 "Sally was reluctant": author int. David Swope, June 30, 2004.

217 "I am able to spend a good deal": JC to Arthur and Stella Spear, June 30 [1955], papers of Pamela Spear Goff.

217 "When we climbed back to the sand dune": *LJC*, 162.

217 "These old bones are for sale": author int. Simon Michael Bessie, June 4, 2004.

218 "I'm looking for John Cheever!": *HBD*, 104.

218 "ate roast beef and drank India Pale Ale": MC, *The Changing Landscape: A History of Briarcliff Manor–Scarborough* (Kennebunk, Maine: Phoenix Publishing, 1990), 218.

219 "As you can see from the letterhead": JC to Herbst [c. Spring 1956], Yale.

219 "While I was writing the book": JC, introduction (1965), *WC*, xix.

219 "because of an experience of sexual ecstasy": author int. Paul Moor, Jan. 9, 2005.

219 "[T]here is some love in our conception": *JJC*, 47.

219 "[H]aving lived much of my life": *LJC*, 168.

220 "I will not go to church": *JJC*, 209.

220 "I'd ask you to stay for dinner, Bill": SD int. BC, Nov. 8, 1983, Swem.

220 "sufficiently simple . . . gift shop": *HBD*, 168.

220 "a level of introspection": quoted on *The Dick Cavett Show*, Oct. 1981, Daphne Productions.

220 "There has to be *someone*": *GT*, 278.

221 "I am eating a capon": JC to Herbst [c. Nov. 1954], Yale.

221 "a *regular* boy": *JJC*, 65–66.

221 "Who told you?": author int. Elizabeth Collins, May 2, 2004.

222 "[A]lthough she was afraid of many things": *LJC*, 175.

222 "an ugly and useless obscenity": *JJC*, 44.

222 "The Chronicle was not published": *CJC*, 99.

222 A. J. Liebling wrote: Katharine White to JC, June 18, 1956, NYPL-MSS.

222 "one of our most original": White to Nadine Gordimer, Oct. 28, 1957, Lilly.

223   "I guess you and I can look forward": JC to Herbst [c. April 1956], Yale.
223   "You yourself won, didn't you?": author int. Joseph Caldwell, April 5, 2005.
223   "I am crushed and miserable": JC to Hannah Josephson [c. April 1956], Academy.
224   "aimed straight at the cockles": JC to Herbst [c. Oct. 1954], Yale.
224   "I read the Sunday paper while Irwin": *JJC*, 57.
224   Cheever "kept putting it off": John Weaver, "Recollections of a Childlike Imagination," *Los Angeles Times Book Review*, March 13, 1977, 3.
224   "The reason I told the dog about it": *GT*, 90.
224   "which should be spent on gin, shoes": *LJC*, 180.
225   "Bostonians, rocks, sunsets": JC to Jean Stafford, June 26 [1956], Colorado.
225   calling "Yoo hoo, yoo hoo": *LJC*, 184.
225   "The Greatest thing since War and Peace": *GT*, 92.
225   "WELL ROARED LION": *LJC*, 179.
225   "I don't expect to enjoy anything as much": WM to JC [c. July 1956], NYPL-MSS.
226   "between feeling alive": JC to Emily Maxwell, April 5 [1957], Berg.
226   "One of the most cheerful things": White to JC, Aug. 20, 1956, NYPL-MSS.
226   "I seem to get nothing from Harpers": JC to WM, July 30 [1956], Berg.
227   "Harpers *seemed* to like it": JC to White, Aug. 24, 1956, NYPL-MSS.
227   "Bellow . . . first American novelist of parts": SD int. Bessie, June 6, 1984, Swem.
227   "Here is the blend of French and Russian": *JJC*, 20.
228   "had the experience . . . great art": JC, presentation speech, Feb. 23, 1978, National Arts Club, CFP.
228   "At dinner I am conscious": *JJC*, 67.
229   "I loved him": SD int. Saul Bellow, July 10, 1984, Swem.
229   "It fell to John": Saul Bellow, eulogy, June 23, 1982, reprinted in American Academy of Arts and Letters, *Proceedings* (1982), 49–51.

CHAPTER SEVENTEEN { *1956–1957* }

230   "a cross between the Fall River Line": JC to WM [c. Oct. 25, 1956], Berg.
231   "to the noise of smashing flower vases": *JJC*, 71.
231   "Is this all . . . ?": JC to Clark and R. P. Warren, Feb. 28 [1957], Swem.
231   "Mary bought violets": *LJC*, 191.
232   "They talk gaily": JC to WM, Nov. 10 [1956], Berg.
232   "the dash of Roman men": *JJC*, 69.
232   "Scout camp": ibid., 70.
232   "There is only one chair in the salon": *LJC*, 186.
232   "impulsive or hasty guests": JC to Biddle, Oct. 19 [1957?], LC.
233   "a convent where they work the nose off her": *LJC*, 189.
233   Reviews of *Stories*: n.a., in *Time*, Dec. 3, 1956, 106–7; Richard Sullivan, in *New York Times Book Review*, Dec. 23, 1956, 121; William Peden, in *Saturday Review*, Dec. 8, 1956, 52; Orville Prescott, in *New York Times*, Dec. 5, 1956, 37.
233   "The writers explained": JC, "Authors' Note," in *Stories* (New York: Farrar, Straus and Cudahy, 1956).
234   "What a *very* nice idea!": quoted in JC to WM [c. June 1955], NYPL-MSS.
234   "raising great Biblical clouds of dust": *LJC*, 192.

234   *"I Cheevers hanno bisogno di me"*: Elizabeth Spencer to SD, Dec. 11, 1985, Swem.

234   *brutta figura*: HBD, 112.

235   "He studied the dictionary carefully": ibid., 114.

235   "Academy and unAcademy": *LJC*, 187.

235   "old 59th Street cross-town trolley cars": *GT*, 95.

235   Warren as an "academic charlatan": JC to Laurens Schwartz, Oct. 28 [1975], Swem.

236   "about as clear, sweet and blue-sky": *LJC*, 194.

236   cream-colored sedan: Michael Shnayerson, *Irwin Shaw* (New York: G. P. Putnam's Sons, 1989), 250.

236   "Irwin stopped at the [Excelsior] desk": *LJC*, 195.

237   "arsehole jokes and golden piety": *JJC*, 73.

237   "She did this for two weeks": JC to Emily Maxwell, April 5, 1957, Berg.

237   "I went to the zoo for a Campari ": JC to Litvinov, March 8 [1968].

237   found his wife "in great pain": *LJC*, 201.

237   "I don't ever remember loving": *JJC*, 80–81.

238   "a source of boundless pleasure": ibid., 369.

238   *"Il Duce! Il Duce!"*: *LJC*, 201.

CHAPTER EIGHTEEN {*1957*}

240   "Boston trust company": JC to Edith Haggard [c. Nov. 1956], Columbia.

240   "But dizzy with excitement": *JJC*, 78.

240   "the Albany Times-Union": *LJC*, 197.

240   Reviews of *The Wapshot Chronicle*: Maxwell Geismar, in *New York Times Book Review*, March 24, 1957, 5; Charles Poore, in *New York Times*, March 26, 1957, 31; Glendy Culligan, in *Washington Post*, March 24, 1957, E6; Fanny Butcher, in *Chicago Sunday Tribune Book Review*, March 31, 1957, 4; Winfield Townley Scott, in *New York Herald Tribune Book Review*, March 24, 1957, 1, 9; Granville Hicks, in *New Leader*, April 8, 1957, 21–22.

241   "Where did [Cheever] get the confidence": Foreword, *WC* (New York: Perennial Classics Edition, 2003), x.

241   "a freedom to pursue their emotional lives": JC to Frederick Bracher, July 15, 1962, Bancroft.

242   "Perhaps you could have given": Cowley to JC, Jan. 3, 1957, Newberry.

242   "such a pig-headed fool!": *LJC*, 194.

242   "One never, of course, asks is it a novel?": JC, "An Exchange on Fiction," *New York Review of Books*, Feb. 3, 1977, 44.

245   "Mamie is reading the Washington Star": *JJC*, 84.

245   "a vaguely suggestive cover": *HBD*, 176.

246   "just to see how disgusting it was": *GT*, 99.

246   "She likes to take care of [Federico]": JC to WM [c. May 1957], Berg.

247   "The victim lay in a heap": *SJC*, 309; see also *JJC*, 81.

248   "just put . . . in a drawer somewhere": JC to WM, June 7, 1957, NYPL-MSS.

248   "write some more pieces": WM to JC, July 8, 1957, NYPL-MSS.

248   "Yes, the city is dangerous!": *JJC*, 87.

248   "When we arrived here": JC to Peter and Ebie Blume [c. Aug. 1957], Swem.

248   "When Ben walks down the street": JC to WM [c. July 1957], Berg.

249 "And it seems that we cannot reform": *JJC*, 85.
250 Cheever was left feeling "sick with love": ibid., 144.
250 "After having wondered": ibid., 86.

CHAPTER NINETEEN {*1957–1959*}

251 "surly soft-ball games": JC to WM, June 17 [1957], Berg.
251 Melissa modeled after Narcissa: SD int. E. J. Kahn, June 10, 1984, Swem.
251 an "Iagoesque nuisance": *LJC*, 158–59.
252 "I was awfully pleased to have The Wapshot Chronicle": Narcissa Vanderlip to JC, Dec. 3, 1957, CFP.
253 "In an upper-class gathering": *JJC*, 87–88.
253 "Some of the nicest people": author int. Elizabeth Spencer, Jan. 6, 2005.
253 *"Root tee toot, ahhh root tee toot"*: HBD, 105.
253 "I love my colleagues": JC to Schwartz, Oct. 28 [1975], Swem.
253 "When I open my handkerchief drawer": WM to JC, May 9, 1963, NYPL-MSS.
254 "[W]hat is that old man doing?": *LJC*, 212–13.
254 "[H]e would make [one] feel": Stephen Becker to SD, April 30, 1985, Swem.
254 Cheever claimed to have been so appalled: JC to Bracher, June 25, 1963, Bancroft.
254 "Mr. Ross would not have liked": JC to White, March 15 [1958], Bryn Mawr.
254 "at least three good friends": *GT*, 103.
255 "a gathering of nearly 1,000 writers": *New York Times*, March 12, 1958, 26.
255 "in a swift mutter that verged": Becker to SD, April 30, 1985, Swem.
255 "It is very gallant of you to come here": JC, unpublished manuscript, Berg.
255 "Randall Jarrell, who had just washed his beard": *GT*, 104.
256 "rivals but no superiors in the national literature": Jonathan Yardley, "John Cheever's 'Housebreaker,' Welcome as Ever," *Washington Post*, July 20, 2004, C01.
256 Reviews of *The Housebreaker of Shady Hill*: Herbert Mitgang, in *New York Times*, Sept. 6, 1958, 15; William Peden, in *New York Times Book Review*, Sept. 7, 1958, 5; Richard Gilman, in *Commonweal*, Dec. 16, 1958, 320.
257 "to keep a family of five in shoe-leather": *LJC*, 214.
258 "[It] doesn't work, everybody feels": WM to JC, Nov. 5, 1958, NYPL-MSS.
258 "I have not written so feebly": JC to WM, Nov. 24, 1958, NYPL-MSS.
258 "Drank too much; talked too much": JC to Blumes, Oct. 30 [1958?], Swem.
259 "dog-shit all over [his] rugs": *GT*, 106.
259 With a "kind of urgency in his voice": author int. William Styron, Nov. 30, 2004.
259 "I am a solitary drunkard": *JJC*, 94.
260 "I think tonight this fortress": ibid., 104.
260 he detected an "unearthly green light": *LJC*, 213.
260 "The most useful image": quoted in Herbert Gold, ed., *Fiction of the Fifties* (Garden City, N.Y.: Dolphin Books, 1961), 22.
261 " 'The Wrysons' very bad": *JJC*, 131.
261 "in the company of a dozen faded roses": JC to Clark and R. P. Warren, Jan. 1 [1959], Yale.
261 "Mary's love of me does not seem to include": *GT*, 107–8.

261   "He seems to me an unusually gifted young man": JC to Mr. Lemay, Dec. 15 and 31 [1958], Ransom.

262   "the shaven armpits of the poor girls": JC to WM [c. Dec. 1958], Berg.

262   "I thought . . . 'There must be more' ": JU, *More Matter* (New York: Alfred A. Knopf, 1999), 764.

262   "It was nice while you were away": See *F*, 28.

263   "I [used to] sit at a table": FLC Jr. to JC, Dec. 22, 1967, PJC.

263   "corporate freeze": FLC Jr. to Sarah Cheever, Feb. 22, 1972, PJC.

263   "stupid and impenetrable smile on his face": *JJC*, 100.

264   "What are you *doing?*": author int. Halasz, Sept. 3, 2004.

265   "He was happy, high-spirited, and adored": *JJC*, 107.

265   "I look up . . . Alcoholics Anonymous": ibid., 112.

CHAPTER TWENTY { *1959–1960* }

266   he'd throw an "insane tantrum": *JJC*, 126.

267   "some gossip about Philadelphia": ibid., 96.

267   "she cannot, quite understandably, face this": ibid., 103.

267   "This is the *best*": JC to WM [July 1959], Berg.

268   "I began to wave my arms and yell: 'Lennieee, Lennieee' ": *GT*, 114.

269   "another seedy-looking plane": JC to Biddle, Sept. 13 [1959], LC.

269   "to everyone's astonishment": *LJC*, 220.

270   "When Winter died in 1959": *TT*, 61.

270   Cheever described it as a "big blowout": JC to Biddle [c. Oct. 1959], LC.

270   "Winter is dead": JC to WM, Oct. 22, 1959, NYPL-MSS.

270   "Susie is in the throes of adolescence": JC to Warrens, Jan. 1 [1959], Yale.

271   "pushing at the sandwich tables": JC to Biddle, April 30 [1960], LC.

271   "still and patient and watchful": JC to Michael Janeway [c. Sept. 1958].

271   "Susie comes home with the news": *JJC*, 124–25.

272   "Ben, poor Ben, bore the brunt": FC to SC, June 28, 1983, CFP.

274   "rigid with indignation": *GT*, 125.

274   "What I claim to feel": *JJC*, 141.

274   "When I was seven years old": *LJC*, 329.

274   "We'd go outside": BC, "The Boy They Cut," in *Coaches: Twenty-Five Writers Reflect on People Who Made a Difference*, ed. Andrew Blauner (New York: Warner Books, 2005), 199–210.

275   "you could read . . . identity": "John Cheever and Family," TV documentary, BBC *Bookmark* (1994).

275   "talk to [him] through the dust bunnies": BC, "My Life with the Bourbon Dynasty," *Independent*, Nov. 27, 2000, Features sec., 7.

275   "Fred talks on about his trip": *JJC*, 115.

276   "[A]t the moment I have nine dependents": *GT*, 115.

276   "I must realize that the people who read my fiction": *JJC*, 121.

276   "Coverly as Apollo and Moses as Dionysus": ibid., 117.

276   "what with the gin and one thing or another": JC to Biddle, March 7 [1960], LC.

277   "feed, shelter and educate": JC to Henry Allen Moe, March 28, 1960, Guggenheim Foundation Records.

277   "My one New Year resolution": JC to Herbst, Jan. 4, 1960, Yale.

277   "could be employed by [Edward] Teller": manuscript fragment, Berg.

279 "If you don't grow and change": *LJC*, 314.

279 "They thought of it as an art story": ibid., 160.

CHAPTER TWENTY-ONE { *1960–1961* }

281 "There will be the boredom and the bigotry": JC to Biddle, April 30 [1960], LC.

281 "smelled of old poker-decks": JC to Dawn Powell, July 11, 1960, Columbia.

281 "I'm quite pissy about my disappointment": *GT*, 119.

281 "and so handsomely restored by Eric Gugler": JC, "The Second Most Exalted of the Arts," *Journal of Architectural Education* 30, no. 2 (Nov. 1976).

282 "enough bedrooms for us": *LJC*, 224.

282 Greenstein—"a pathological cheapskate": author int. Charles McGrath, Aug. 5, 2004.

282 "and all I have to do now": *LJC*, 226.

283 "It was the general hope that Cheever": Robert Gutwillig, "Dim Views Through Fog," *New York Times Book Review*, Nov. 13, 1960, 68–69.

283 "This is not for publication": JC to Gentlemen, May 20 [1959], LC.

284 "The only writer I meant to attack": JC to Bracher, "Summer 1962," Bancroft.

284 "all autobiographical characters who describe": "Some People, Places, and Things That Will Not Appear in My Next Novel," *New Yorker*, Nov. 12, 1960, 55.

284 "abrasive and faulty surface of the United States": quoted in Gutwillig, "Dim Views," 68.

285 "a sort of apocalyptic poetry": Cowley to JC, Feb. 10, 1961, Newberry.

285 Reviews of *Some People, Places, and Things That Will Not Appear in My Next Novel*: Charles Poore, in *New York Times*, May 16, 1961, 35; David Boroff, in *New York Times Book Review*, April 16, 1961, 34.

286 "[Arvin] was fixed at a prepubertal stage": Barry Werth, *The Scarlet Professor* (New York: Doubleday, 2001), 239.

287 "kind presence will guide [him] away": *GT*, 124.

287 "the magnification of all our vices": *LJC*, 229.

287 "The sensation of my aloneness": *GT*, 234.

287 "fancy hotel apartment" at the Marmont: JC to Arthur and Stella Spear [c. Nov. 1960], courtesy of Pamela Spear Goff.

287 "I ran up a bill of a hundred dollars": JC to WM [c. Feb. 1961], Berg.

288 "My God, John . . . your crotch!": *GT*, 11.

288 "a side-parlor in the Hotel Gladstone": JC to WM [c. Dec. 1960?], Berg.

288 treat Wald "like a demented child": JC to WM [c. Nov. 1960], Berg; the remark is deleted from the letter published in *LJC*, 229.

288 "They talk about Saroyan's tax problems": Weaver to MC, Nov. 29, 1960, CFP.

288 he liked Wald "immensely": Joanne Stang, "Lancaster Swims in Deeper Waters," *New York Times*, Aug. 14, 1966, 101.

288 "literary graveyard": JC to Cowley, Dec. 22, 1960, Newberry.

288 "an old bath-house at the edge of the lot": *LJC*, 229.

289 "curious domestic scenes": JC to the Spears [c. Nov. 1960], courtesy of Pamela Spear Goff.

289 Calvin Kentfield: much of the background derives from my interview with Evan S. Connell, July 21, 2005, as well as correspondence between Kentfield and Katherine Anne Porter on deposit at the University of Maryland.

290 "I spend the night with C.": *JJC*, 143.

290 "When I die you can put on my headstone": *F*, 121.
290 his "seafaring progenitors" had all kept journals: *GT*, 17.
290 "stacks of satisfied starlets": *LJC*, 270.
291 "a big, important film that will explore": JC to WM, May 2, 1961, NYPL-MSS.
291 "or in fact *up* them": Kentfield to Porter, May 20, 1962, University of Maryland.
292 "Kentfield's nude and battered body": *Point Reyes Light*, Sept. 11, 1975, 1.

CHAPTER TWENTY-TWO {*1961*}

293 "We know that it commands the greatest views": quoted in Geoff Walden, "Dealing with Fame and Death," *Ossining Citizen Register*, June 19, 1982.
293 "I feel very much like a bum": quoted in *GT*, 134.
294 "Irwin came for lunch": ibid., 155.
294 "not for her work . . . but for a nonstop": JC to Louise Bogan, May 4, 1959, Academy.
295 "If the knife should slip": *LJC*, 235.
295 "intensely uncomfortable": JC to Herbst [c. June 1964], Yale.
295 "I'm glad you asked": *LJC*, 234.
296 "fire off [his] shotgun at intervals": ibid., 258–59.
296 "immediately thought of John Cheever": author int. Andrew Ziegler, May 4, 2004.
296 "I am loving the Beatles": JC to WM [c. June 1964], Berg.
297 "inhibitive megrims": JC to Herbst, May 6 [1961?], Yale.
297 "I never dreamed I'd take a leak": *GT*, 141.
297 "As he approached the bridge": *JJC*, 148.
298 "marvelous brightness": Alfred Kazin, *Bright Book of Life: American Novelists and Storytellers from Hemingway to Mailer* (Boston: Atlantic–Little, Brown, 1973), 111–14.
298 "Micks in the White House!": JC to Biddle [c. summer 1961], LC.
298 Mrs. Vanderlip had decided to "hydrogen-proof ": *JJC*, 153.
299 "[Bill] was a man who mistook power for love": *LJC*, 314.
300 "Did you know that *The New Yorker*": *CJC*, 107.
300 "[I]t has been my experience": JC to Glenway Wescott, April 28 [1957], Yale.
300 "Don't believe it" . . . "What *is* a shapely day?": manuscripts of "The Bella Lingua" and "The Country Husband," Brandeis.
300 "I kept the conversation": *GT*, 149.
301 "I blundered. I thought there were two endings": *LJC*, 233.
301 "I admire Salinger, of course": ibid.

CHAPTER TWENTY-THREE {*1962–1963*}

302 "I expect that I will continue to report": *JJC*, 168.
303 "Oh, don't worry about me, dear": *HBD*, 67.
304 "What is involved": *JJC*, 150.
305 "His favorite word for me was *diffident*": author int. Ann Adams, July 13, 2004.
305 "He has endured many disappointments": *JJC*, 165.
305 "I love you": Sarah Cheever to FLC Jr., July 12 [1964?], PJC.
306 "I was planning to take him trout fishing": *CJC*, 124.
306 "collection of quaint episodes": Ihab Hassan, *Radical Innocence: Studies in the*

Contemporary American Novel (Princeton, N.J.: Princeton University Press, 1961), 189.

306 "My credentials": Bracher to JC, July 4, 1962, Bancroft.

306 *The Wapshot Chronicle* is loosely situated": Frederick Bracher, "John Cheever and Comedy," *Critique: Studies in Modern Fiction* 6, no. 1 (1963), 66–77.

306 "He's reading Professer Bracher's paper *again*": JC to Bracher, Sept. 20, 1962, Bancroft.

307 "the first I've ever received": Bracher to JC, Oct. 24, 1962, Bancroft.

307 "[C]onsidering the complexity": JC to Bracher, Feb. 13, 1963, Bancroft.

307 "The body of Cummings": Hortense Calisher, in *A Century at Yaddo* (Saratoga Springs, N.Y.: Corporation of Yaddo, 2000), 46.

307 "The force and openness of their affection": *HBD*, 60.

307 "I think of Cummings": *JJC*, 230.

308 "thinking, without censure": JC to James Holmes, April 4, 1979, courtesy of Ned Rorem.

308 "But my itchy member": *JJC*, 171.

308 "to love what is seemly": ibid., 208.

309 "You have two strings to play": ibid., 176.

309 "Bottom-the-Weaver haircut": *GT*, 161.

309 "No necking in the parlor!": *NFB*, 31.

309 "I cannot say truthfully": *JJC*, 167.

310 "beaming like a foolish swain": *GT*, 172.

310 "[L]ast night I dreamed I was a Good Humor man": ibid., 157.

310 "But the middle, aiie, aiie": ibid., 159.

310 "A great many people felt": *JJC*, 179.

311 "This is the small agony": *CJC*, 97.

311 smelling of "cheap handsoap": *GT*, 168.

311 "The initials are intended to represent": JC to WM, Aug. 28, 1963, Berg.

311 "[I]n *The Wapshot Scandal* he began": BBC int. WM, April 20, 1993, CFP.

313 "The death of a child seems to be idle": *JJC*, 113.

314 "side-stepping the Educated woman": Litvinov to JC, Feb. 9, 1965, CFP.

314 "I did go to one or two meetings": Alwyn Lee, "Ovid in Ossining," *Time*, March 27, 1964, 72.

315 "Maybe he *was* wicked": *TT*, 164.

315 intention to "rewrite Bulfinch": SD int. Calisher, Sept. 17, 1984, Swem.

316 "He lived as a child would live": *LJC*, 23.

316 "You can draw a line": *JJC*, 236.

316 "about the irreversibility of human conduct": Joanna Stang, "Lancaster Swims in Deeper Waters," *New York Times*, Aug. 19, 1966, 101.

316 "a perfectly good" novel: Jesse Kornbluth, "The Cheever Chronicle," *New York Times Magazine*, Oct. 21, 1979, 102.

316 "It was growing cold and quiet": *CJC*, 136.

318 " 'The Swimmer' is a masterpiece of mystery": Michael Chabon, "Personal Best," *Salon* (www.salon.com/weekly/cheever960930).

318 "teach fiction . . . veterinary medicine": *CJC*, 69.

318 the magazine was wildly prosperous: J. H. Rutledge and P. B. Bart, "Urbanity, Inc.: How the New Yorker Wins Business Success Despite Air of Disdain," *Wall Street Journal*, June 30, 1958, 1.

319 Maxwell "seemed the gentlest of men": quoted in *Paris Review* 85 (Fall 1982), 109.

319 "[H]e often set it on Christmas Eve": *HBD*, 138.

320   "*The New Yorker* . . . didn't like agents": author int. Lynn Nesbit, April 27, 2005.
320   "I am accused of improvidence": *JJC*, 189.
321   "Cheever didn't realize how low this was": Ben Yagoda, *About Town* (New York: Scribner, 2000), 290.
321   "Whoever was editor of a particular writer": author int. Yagoda, March 4, 2005.

CHAPTER TWENTY-FOUR { 1964 }

322   "That riot of the housewives": Cowley to JC, Oct. 22, 1963, Newberry.
322   Reviews of *The Wapshot Scandal*: Elizabeth Janeway, in *New York Times Book Review*, Jan. 5, 1964, 1, 28; Charles Poore, in *New York Times*, Jan. 7, 1964, 31; Joan Didion, in *National Review*, March 24, 1964, 237–40; Glenway Wescott, in *New York Herald Tribune Book Week*, Jan. 5, 1964, 1, 9; Hilary Corke, in *New Republic*, Jan. 25, 1964, 19–21; Stanley Edgar Hyman, in *New Leader*, Feb. 3, 1964, 23–24; Robert R. Kirsch, in *Los Angeles Times*, Feb. 5, 1964, IV, 6.
323   "[N]ow and then, as it were by chance": Wescott to JC [c. Jan. 1964], Yale.
323   "[H]e forced some perfect stories": Wescott's demurral to Cheever's nomination for the Howells Medal may be found among the Ralph Ellison Papers, LC.
325   most "outstanding" features: George Garrett, reprinted in *Critical Essays on John Cheever*, ed. R. G. Collins (Boston: G. K. Hall & Co., 1982), 51–62.
326   "the lonely and erotic nature of man": notes on *WS*, Brandeis.
328   redeemed at last by "booming" sales: JC to Bracher, Jan. 12, 1964, Bancroft.
328   "They seemed so terribly disappointed": *GT*, 164.
328–329   Lee "had a unique reputation": Paul Moor to SD, Nov. 20, 1984, Swem.
329   "I came home from school": *LJC*, 237.
329   "[Alwyn] had a series of ardent": JC to McLoone, July 29 [1970], Georgetown University Library.
329   "because they seemed . . . to symbolize": "A Letter from the Publisher," *Time*, March 27, 1964.
330   "it's better this way than hiding": *LJC*, 238.
330   "Sally Ziegler, a small-town Georgian": ibid., 239.
331   "John Cheever, almost alone in the field": Alwyn Lee, "Ovid in Ossining," *Time*, March 27, 1964, 72.
331   "I'm frightfully sorry": JC to McLoone, July 29 [1970], Georgetown University Library.
332   his old "boy chum" Fax: JC to WM [c. June 1964], Berg.
332   "two conspicuous lacks": *New York Times*, Dec. 1, 1976, 54.
332   literature . . . a vast impersonal "stream": *CJC*, 185.
333   "serious and likable person": *JJC*, 191.
333   "What are they going to do with it": ibid., 196.
333   "I *am* a Wasp": Peter Costa, "A Wasp Author Discusses Wasps," *Boston Herald American*, May 4, 1977, 15.
334   "more like an upper-class New Yorker": SD int. Philip Roth, July 18, 1984, Swem.
334   "like Thurston Howell III": author int. James Kaplan, Sept. 2, 2004.
334   "I knew John before he had an accent": quoted in Frederick Exley, "That Place," unpublished essay, Rochester.
334   "a suave, fictional dialect": Dana Gioia, "Meeting Mr. Cheever," *Hudson Review* 39, no. 3 (Autumn 1986), 423.

334 "Noble might be a better word": JC, in *Atlantic Brief Lives*, ed. Louis Kronenberger (Boston: Little, Brown, 1971), 275.

335 "I can't connect my life": SD int. John and Mary Dirks, July 16, 1984, Swem.

335 "he had his New England mumble": SD int. Hope Lange, Oct. 24, 1984, Swem.

336 "a writer of consequence, witty": SD int. David Lange, June 6, 1985, Swem.

337 *"Will success spoil John Cheever?"*: HBD, 153.

337 Mary "flash[ed] her rubies and diamonds": JC to Kronenberger [c. July 1964], Copley.

337 "I have the disposition of an adder": JC to Biddle, July 21, 1964, LC.

CHAPTER TWENTY-FIVE { *1964* }

340 "somber and mysterious trip to Russia": *GT*, 172.

341 "I loved the stories so much": Litvinov to JC, April 9, 1961, Columbia.

341 a "lost generation" of Russian youths: Harrison Salisbury, " 'Lost Generation' in Soviet Union, Bored and Nihilistic, Worries Regime," *New York Times*, Feb. 9, 1962, 1, 4.

341 "I was told that my liberty would be in danger": *LJC*, 242.

342 "pour[ing] vodka into [his] ears": *CJC*, 81.

342 "Then a man comes in with the boodle": *GT*, 173–74.

342 "It seemed as if he were in sort of a cloud": SD int. William Luers, Aug. 22, 1985, Swem.

343 neither side wanted any "bad incidents": author int. Luers, July 30, 2004.

343 "through oceans of sheep": JC to Litvinov, Nov. 2 [1965].

343 "Welcome to the house of . . . Chekhov": JC, "The Melancholy of Distance," in *Chekhov and Our Age: Responses to Chekhov by American Writers and Scholars*, ed. James McConkey (Ithaca, N.Y.: Cornell University Center for International Studies, 1984), 126.

344 "How many letters do you get?": *CJC*, 54.

344 "Everybody says that [Voznesensky is] a better poet": JC to Litvinov, May 16 [1967?].

344 "I seem to love him": *JJC*, 201.

344 "You drink like Siberian worker!": author int. Yevgeny Yevtushenko, Oct. 5, 2004.

345 "May I kiss you?" Cheever asked: Litvinov to author, Dec. 22, 2004.

345–346 "I'm getting conditioned to the ads": Litvinov to JC, April 6 [1965?], CFP.

346 "note how this is the dream": SD int. Raymond Carver, Oct. 23, 1984, Swem.

346 "We all enjoy your letters tremendously": JC to Litvinov, March 15 [1965].

346 "on some sort of International Amity Excursion": *LJC*, 250.

346 "heartwarming reunion with the Maxwell's": Litvinov to JC, May 16, 1978, CFP.

347 "I am sure that when I die": *LJC*, 273.

347 "I sincerely admire the brilliance": JC to JU [c. March 1964?], Houghton.

347 "He greeted us with glee": Mary Weatherall to SD, Dec. 17, 1984, Swem.

348 "as gay as an April in Paris": *OJ*, 112.

348 "Cheever's confession made me sad": ibid., 116.

348 "[Updike] tried to upstage me": *LJC*, 248.

349 "At one of our joint appearances": *OJ*, 115.

349 "John [Updike] *loved* Cheever's writing": author int. Mary Weatherall, April 3, 2007.

350   "I would go to considerable expense and inconvenience": *LJC*, 245.

350   "this is nothing you take with you": *LJC*, 242.

351   "As for Paul [Moor]": JC to Litvinov, Sept. 14 [1965].

351   "I would like to live in a world": *LJC*, 264.

352   "fifteen minute impersonation of Yevtushenko": ibid., 246.

352   "I am not a political person": JC to Boris Ryurikov, Jan. 31, 1967, NYPL-MSS. A note is attached: "The following letter was brought to the attention of the FBI on February 28, 1967." The letter is among papers collected by Herbert Mitgang via the Freedom of Information Act for his book *Dangerous Dossiers: Exposing the Secret War Against America's Greatest Authors* (New York: Donald I. Fine, 1988).

352   "My name is mud": JC to Bracher [c. Sept. 1965], Bancroft.

352   "We all miss and love you": Frieda Lurie to JC, Dec. 14, 1964, CFP.

354   "can do the twist beautifully": FLC Jr. to Sarah Cheever, Nov. 16, 1964, PJC.

354   "trying to establish a sales pattern": FLC Jr. to Denise Davidoff, Dec. 4, 1965, PJC.

CHAPTER TWENTY-SIX { *1964–1965* }

355   *"Where the hell are the reviews?"*: JC, on *The Dick Cavett Show*, March 21, 1978, LC.

355   Reviews of *The Brigadier and the Golf Widow*: n.a. in *Newsweek*, Nov. 30, 1964, 104–5; Glendy Culligan, in *Washington Post*, Oct. 16, 1964, A22; Orville Prescott, in *New York Times*, Oct. 14, 1964, 43; John Aldridge, in *New York Herald Tribune Book Week*, Oct. 25, 1964, 3, 19.

356   "toothless Thurber": Irving Howe, in *Partisan Review* 26 (Winter 1959), 131.

356   "At the [Academy] ceremony": JC to WM [c. May 1960], Berg.

356   "I seem neither sane enough nor mad enough": *JJC*, 191.

357   "letting oneself into a labyrinth": JC to Litvinov, March 15 [1965].

357   Cheever and Brodkey: JC's quotes about his flirtation with Brodkey are all from the unpublished journal. The *New Yorker* writer in whom Brodkey confided wishes to remain anonymous; certain others were also privy to such confidences.

358   "[tying] on a can": *JJC*, 198–99.

358   "I felt defensive for him": SD int. Richard Stern, April 23, 1985, Swem.

359   "erudite, bellicose and agile": *LJC*, 245.

359   "Mary flew back on Thursday": *GT*, 180.

359   "May I join you?": Mrs. Donald H. Farquharson to SD, Jan. 19, 1985, Swem.

359   "Mother would have been indignant": JC to WM [c. May 1965], Berg.

359   "I had lunch with Ralph Ellison": *LJC*, 243.

360   "I am very fond of Ralph": JC to Warren, Jan. 12 [1963], Yale.

360   Cheever awoke feeling "crushed": *GT*, 181–82.

360–361   Vietnam War as a "moral outrage": "Academy Speech Angers Benton," *Washington Post*, May 21, 1965, A18.

361   "chaos that we've made of our promise": Ellison Papers, LC.

361   "Thank you very much, Ralph": JC's acceptance remarks, May 19, 1965, Academy.

361   reptile "seemed to possess the world": *JJC*, 200.

361   They decided to "get stoned": *GT*, 183.

362   "I did everything short of kicking him": *LJC*, 249.

362 "banging folding chairs together": JC to Matthew Bruccoli, May 2 [early 1970s?], Morgan.

362 "[Updike] read extracts from three works": quoted in *OJ*, 117.

362 "I am . . . rude, I think, to John": this passage was deleted from the second entry on page 200 in the published *Journals*.

362 "chastening, perhaps edifyingly so": *OJ*, 117.

363 prescribed a "massive tranquilizer": JC to Litvinov [c. Aug. 1965].

364 "People named John and Mary never divorce": *JJC*, 204.

365 "threw in the sponge": WM to SC, n.d., CFP.

365 "I was drinking gin and romping with the dogs": *LJC*, 252.

365 characterizing Cheever as "furious": Wilborn Hampton, "William Maxwell, 91, Author and Legendary Editor, Dies," *New York Times*, Aug. 1, 2000, B9.

366 "I look forward to having the book": JC to WM [c. Jan. 1966], Berg.

367 "the relationship of the novelist": Richard Stern, "Report from the MLA," *New York Review of Books*, Feb. 17, 1966, 26–28.

367 "pleased and excited" by *The Naked and the Dead*: *JJC*, 13.

367 "great affectation of bellicosity": JC to WM [c. May 1960], Berg.

367 "trimmed [his] weight to 138 lbs.": JC to Stern [c. Dec. 1965], Chicago.

367 "Well, you've got to find him!": SD int. Robert F. Lucid, April 2, 1985, Swem.

368 "when he was busily trying to describe": draft of Cheever's MLA remarks, Berg.

368 Mailer was "pissed": SD int. Norman Mailer, March 29, 1985, Swem.

368 "There has been a war": Norman Mailer, *Cannibals and Christians* (New York: Dial Press, 1966), 95.

369 "young women wearing nothing": JC to WM [c. Jan. 1966], Berg.

CHAPTER TWENTY-SEVEN { *1966* }

371 "electrifying conversationalists": Betsy Brown, "The Friday Club, A Cheever Salon," *New York Times*, June 27, 1982, sec. 11, pp. 1, 8.

372 "John called early this AM": Spear to Litvinov, July 12, 1968, courtesy of Pamela Spear Goff.

372 "[John] is in good shape": Spear to Litvinov, April 23, 1974, ibid.

372 "I was dozing in a chair": author int. Raphael Rudnik, Aug. 26, 2004.

373 "glued to the television": author int. Christopher Lehmann-Haupt and Natalie Robins, Aug. 15, 2004.

375 "A man named Exley wrote": *GT*, 187.

375 "Coming in late last night": *LJC*, 247.

375 "tone or volume of my father's farts": ibid., 20.

375 "If my note to you seemed cursory": JC to Exley, Oct. 4 [1965], Rochester.

376 "Environment plays, I hope": JC to McLoone, April 11 [1966], Georgetown University Library.

376 "The old dog; my love": *JJC*, 193–94.

377 "She was a wonderful companion": *LJC*, 261.

377 "teach the Antigone to negroes": JC to Litvinov, May 23 [1965].

378 "My father finally concurred": *NFB*, 51.

379 "Ben, who is my favorite": *LJC*, 249.

379 "I damn near swoon": JC to Herbst [c. June 1965], Yale.

379 "The attachment seems to resist any analysis": *JJC*, 210.

379 "We'd each have a fork": *LJC*, 23.

380   "Christmas . . . not as pleasant": JC to Litvinov, Jan. 7 [1966].
380   "I am teaching Fred": JC to Litvinov, Nov. 2 [1965].
381   "The only one of the children": *TT,* 137.
381   "both young and old, masterful and tearful": *LJC,* 253.
382   "talismanic" cameo: JC to Stern, Aug. 17 [1966], Chicago.
382   "What I was supposed to do": *GT,* 191–92.
382   "into very deep and stormy water": JC to McLoone, Feb. 24 [1967], George-
      town University Library.
383   "Teamster's Union hose-type rainstorm": *CJC,* 64.
383   "It is not a great picture but it is faithful": JC to Litvinov, April 5 [1968].
383   "occasionally gross and mawkish": Vincent Canby, "Cross-County 'Swimmer,' "
      New York Times, May 16, 1968, 53.
383   akin to that of "a shampoo commercial": Joseph Morgenstern, "Puddle
      Jumper," *Newsweek,* May 27, 1968, 94.
383   "Spiegel really fucked it up": JC to William Kennedy, Nov. 21 [1968], Albany.

CHAPTER TWENTY-EIGHT { *1966–1967* }

384   "The mortal boredom of reading": JC to Biddle [c. Nov. 1963], LC.
384   "Oh for heaven's sake, Helen": author int. Helen Barolini, Feb. 27, 2005.
385   "[I] have written two stories": JC to Litvinov [c. June 1966].
386   "written [him] off as an improvident": JC to Bracher, Sept. 14, 1967, Bancroft.
386   "[T]he stuntiness of Barthelme disconcerts me": *LJC,* 270.
386   "Shawn's chosen surrealist": JC memo to grants committee [c. 1980], Academy.
387   Gaddis's *JR* ("less than rubbish"): JC to Laurens Schwartz, Sep. 12 [1977],
      Swem.
387   "That the complexities of contemporary life": JC, "An Exchange on Fiction,"
      New York Review of Books, Feb. 3, 1977, 44.
387   "Jean said, drawing me aside": *CJC,* 169.
387   "[Mailer] is so wonderfully tough": JC to Litvinov, Sept. 25 [1968].
388   "John's new novel (Couples)": JC to Litvinov, May 22 [1968].
388   "It will be miserable and dangerous": JC to WM [c. June 1966], Berg.
389   "I would not make a potholder in the city": *LJC,* 21.
389   "As for Ben he was reclassified 1-A": JC to WM [c. Feb. 1968], Berg.
389   "For no explainable reason": FLC Jr. to JC, Nov. 23, 1966, PJC.
389   "I'm enclosing a small check": JC to FLC Jr., Dec. 1 [1966], PJC.
390   "After twenty-five years of acute alcoholism": *LJC,* 269.
390   "I keep reading biographies of Fitzgerald": JC to Kronenberger, Nov. 3 [1966?],
      Copley.
390   "Shall I dwell on the crucifixion": *JJC,* 213.
391   "hands seem[ed] to drop off ": JC to Robert Gottlieb, Nov. 8 [1968], Swem.
391   "Walking on Madison Avenue": *JJC,* 224.
392   "I can't bear to be gentled by an impotent man": ibid., 223.
392   his wife's "needless darkness": Dr. David C. Hays, notes, Swem.
392   "So I go to the shrink": *JJC,* 213.
393   "We would embrace": ibid., 214.
393   "[I]t was Esquire": *GT,* 193.
393   "Does he know anything about music": *JJC,* 216.
393   "[Hays's] mouth seems a little blubbery": JC to MC [c. July 1966], Swem.

394   "Who profits by concluding that Mrs. Zagreb": *JJC*, 2 1 8.

394   "Some years ago I went to a psychiatrist": *LJC*, 2 6 1.

395   JC and Rorem at Yaddo, 1966: Ned Rorem, *The Nantucket Diary* (New York: North Point, 1987), 2 3 3–3 5.

395   "I've never felt this way before": author int. Rorem, May 9, 2004.

397   "I am weary of being a boy of fifty": *JJC*, 2 2 6.

397   "a little incestuous": JC to Litvinov, Oct. 2 1 [1966].

397   "I seem to know so much": JC to Cowley [c. Oct. 1966], Newberry.

397   "I resolved never to do this again": JC to Rorem, July 7 [1967].

C H A P T E R   T W E N T Y - N I N E   { *1967–1968* }

399   "its annual journey towards the rocks": JC to Litvinov, April 3 [1967].

401   "that if he didn't have a squad of policemen": *GT*, 197.

401   letter to the bishop of New York: author int. Rob Cowley, June 2, 2004.

401   "[made] an exclamation of distaste": *JJC*, 2 3 3.

401   Mrs. Zagreb "raked the male guests": *LJC*, 2 5 8.

402   taking his first "hack job": JC to McLoone, Oct. 18 [1967], Georgetown University Library.

402   Mary . . . "[did] not seem cheered": *JJC*, 2 3 8.

402   seemed to "miss the plane": *LJC*, 2 6 0.

402   "gabbling like a turkey": ibid., 2 5 5.

402   "She has the tact and discretion": JC, "Sophia, Sophia, Sophia," *Saturday Evening Post*, Oct. 2 1, 1967, 3 3–3 5.

402   "She wrote, she wrote, she loves me": JC to WM [c. Oct. 1967], Berg.

403   "suffered from an unstable prostate": JC to Ray Mutter, Nov. 10 [1967].

404   "The admissions committee at the club": *JJC*, 2 4 4.

404   "the narrator isn't a man": WM to JC, April 18, 1967, NYPL-MSS.

404   "They pay well and they are hospitable": JC to McLoone, March 1 1 [1968], Georgetown University Library.

405   "for reasons that I can't recall": *LJC*, 2 6 5.

406   "Of course I cannot judge the book": *JJC*, 2 4 9–5 0.

406   "So off one goes": *LJC*, 2 5 0.

407   "Wipe that artificial smile off your face": ibid., 3 5 8–5 9.

407   "lest [his] smile fall to the bottom of the sea": *GT*, 2 1 0.

C H A P T E R   T H I R T Y   { *1968–1969* }

408   "I'm afraid I was a nuisance about money": JC to Gottlieb [c. July 1968], Swem.

408   "I've changed everything—my doctor": JC to Lindley, Sept. 17, 1968, Swem.

408–409   "I believe we have voted for the swimming pool": JC to Cowley [1962?], Newberry.

409   "*No!*" she shouted into the telephone: author int. Anne Palamountain, June 28, 2004.

409   "This, of course, has nothing to do": JC to Ames, July 28, 1968, NYPL-MSS.

409   "imperturbable, humorous and fair": JC, "Elizabeth Ames," Sept. 7, 1968, Berg.

410   "I've written nothing": *GT*, 209.

410   "Clichés of suburban life!": *CJC*, 36.

410   "After a few more questions have been detonated": ibid., 28.

411   "Guess what the bill is?": ibid., 32.

411   "Perhaps you remember": Gottlieb to JC, Sept. 5, 1968, Swem.

411   *Bullet Park* . . . "better than the Scandal": JC to Bracher, Dec. 11, 1968, Bancroft.

411   "a cast of three characters": *CJC*, 97.

412   the modern world's "living hell": Benjamin DeMott, "The Way We Feel Now," *Harper's*, Feb. 1964, 111–12.

412   "I would rather have an informative [review]": *CJC*, 33.

412   "My father seemed suddenly very frail": *HBD*, 180.

412   Reviews of *Bullet Park*: Benjamin DeMott, in *New York Times Book Review*, April 27, 1969, 1, 40–41; Charles Nicol, in *Atlantic Monthly*, May 1969, 96–98; Guy Davenport, in *National Review*, June 3, 1969, 549–50; Joyce Carol Oates, in *Washington Post Book World*, April 20, 1969, 1, 3; JU, reprinted in *Picked-Up Pieces* (New York: Alfred A. Knopf, 1975), 427–28; John Leonard, in *New York Times*, April 29, 1969, 43; Anatole Broyard, in *New Republic*, April 26, 1969, 36–37.

413   "I count on my experience with Fred": JC, notes on *BP*, Berg.

414   "Neither Hammer nor Nailles": *CJC*, 111.

414   "Nailles's blessing is that he is married": John Gardner, "Witchcraft in Bullet Park," *New York Times Book Review*, Oct. 24, 1971, 2, 24.

416   "I go on about the vulnerability of Nailles": JC, notes on *BP*, Brandeis.

417   "I don't work with plots": *CJC*, 102.

418   "What I wanted was verisimilitude": JC to Litvinov, Feb. 27 [1969].

420   "dumped on [the book] in the *Times*": *CJC*, 97.

420   "and one couldn't ask for more": JC to Bracher, July 21, 1969, Bancroft.

421   "I think something misfired": *LJC*, 278.

421   "plugging for tenure at Amherst": Samuel Coale, "Portrait of John Cheever," unpublished manuscript, Swem.

421   "I aimed for the head": JC to Litvinov, Sept. 1 [1970?].

CHAPTER THIRTY-ONE { *1969–1970* }

422   "We rip off our clothes": *JJC*, 254.

423   "I'll be taking the train": author int. Lehmann-Haupt and Robins, Aug. 15, 2004.

423   "the most beautiful woman": *HBD*, 126.

423   "Swooping (or so I thought) among the trees": *LJC*, 271.

423   "substitute physical pain and infirmity": *JJC*, 254.

423   "I can't write you a story": *LJC*, 270.

424   "the minutiae of upper-middle-class life": *JJC*, 249.

424   "First scoop at half past nine": ibid., 255–56.

424   "[M]any thanks for . . . page numbers": JC to Roth, June 16 [1969], LC.

426   "a little like Zelda": JC to Kronenberger, June 16 [1969], Copley.

427   "he is a kind of prince, scourge, God": JC to Litvinov, Aug. 25 [1969].

427   "I spend a lot of time kissing her": *JJC*, 238.

427   "the two most self-centered animals": ibid., 240.

428   "roughed up by the Man!": *CJC*, 76.

428   "barefoot [with] a fan-shaped beard": *JJC*, 247.

428–429   He found this "wide of the mark": e-mail from Doug Brayfield to author, June 2, 2005.

429   "When did you start wearing a red necktie?": Dick Polman, "John Cheever: The Other Story," *Philadelphia Inquirer,* Dec. 18, 1988, sec. I, pp. 1, 5.

429   "the way suits fit bears and chimpanzees": *LJC,* 279.

430   "My older son seems seriously to have switched": *JJC,* 258.

432   "the peacemaker": Marian Christy, "Ben Cheever—a Son in the Shadow," *Boston Globe,* Dec. 25, 1988, A14.

432   "My dearly beloved son comes in the middle of dinner": *JJC,* 296.

CHAPTER THIRTY-TWO { *1969–1970* }

434   "a little nut-brown guy": SD int. Shana Alexander, Sept. 21, 1984, Swem.

434   "I am a man, a free man": *JJC,* 262–63.

434   his wife's "contemptuous and weary voice": ibid., 263–64.

435   "Hope and Alan are getting a divorce": *GT,* 219.

435   "I don't want to return on these terms": JC to WM [c. Oct. 1969?], Berg.

436   "meant to demolish Barthelme": JC to Stern, Oct. 1 [1970], Chicago.

436   "I am disappointed in Artemis": *JJC,* 270.

437   "Fred is on a diet": *LJC,* 285.

438   "I haven't been as thrilled by anything": author int. Sandra Hochman, Oct. 11, 2004.

439   described the boyfriend as a "gymnast": *LJC,* 283.

440   "implie[d] rapprochement": J. William Silverberg, notes.

440   "What a waste of time to ridicule them": *LJC,* 282.

441   drinking "was beginning to drag on him visibly": JU to SD, June 25, 1984, Swem.

441   "I mount my beloved": *JJC,* 265.

441   "something about a sale at Lord & Taylor's": unpublished chapter of *TT,* CFP.

441   "Water lilies grow at the edge of the pond": *JJC,* 269.

CHAPTER THIRTY-THREE { *1971–1972* }

444   "Is what I have to say urgent": JC, "Fiction Is Our Most Intimate Means of Communication," *U.S. News & World Report,* May 21, 1979, 92.

444   "Esquire wants to buy it": *LJC,* 285.

445   "1. I drink too much": JC to Cowley [c. May 1971], Newberry.

446   "I want a new cadence": JC to Candida Donadio, Jan. 26, 1970, Swem.

446   "I'm happy to have been born in the same century": JC to Donadio [c. June 1971], Swem.

448   "a very wide net": Anatole Broyard, in *New York Times,* Sept. 12, 1973, 45.

448   "My friendship with The New Yorker": JC to Litvinov [c. Nov. 1971].

449   "I didn't go to Sing Sing to gather material": *CJC,* 127.

449   "He was bare-assed and had the shotgun": *LJC,* 369.

449   "exactly twenty-seven details": JC to Cowley [c. May 1971], Newberry.

449   "stamina and courage": JC, "The Melancholy of Distance," in *Chekhov and Our Age,* ed. James McConkey (Ithaca, N.Y.: Cornell University Center for International Studies, 1984), 132.

449   "Tomorrow I go to Sing-Sing": *LJC*, 284.

450   an exercise "in making sense of one's life": *CJC*, 242.

450   "Oh what a cool motherfucker": JC to WM [c. June 1971], Berg.

450   "I had hoped to do something like Camus": quoted in *GT*, 217.

451   ("I thought, 'One *what* . . . ?' "): SD int. Donald Lang, Sept. 20, 1984, Swem.

451   "You'd make a great hostage": *CJC*, 125.

451   "[I]f the cons and I were lined up": ibid., 242.

452   "He explained that his acceptance": Stinnett to SD, Nov. 26, 1985, Swem.

452   "everything but shout 'fire' ": *GT*, 221.

453   "I trust he hasn't heard": JC to McLoone [c. Aug. 1971], Georgetown University Library.

453   "[He] knew I was a fan of . . . Koren": *TT*, 175.

453   "Thirty years ago": *JJC*, 278.

453   "Not often . . . and I can't remember the names": *CJC*, 52.

453–454   "Oh, she writes about men, women, children": ibid., 253.

454   "I have sometimes complained, husband": MC, "Gorgon," in *The Need for Chocolate and Other Poems* (New York: Stein and Day, 1980), 18–19.

455   "Paranoia: The New Urban Life Style": Richard Todd, "Gathering at Bunnymede," *Atlantic Monthly*, Jan. 1972, 86–88.

455   "Not since I came into my inheritance": author int. Herbert Gold, March 5, 2005.

455   "Saul appeared from the clouds": JC, presentation of Gold Medal of Honor to Bellow at National Arts Club, Feb. 23, 1978, CFP.

456   "and ate Homeric feasts": JC, "Melancholy of Distance," 129.

456   "If you think": *GT*, 220.

457   "[I] kept ducking into closets, toilets, etc.": JC to Exley, July 13 [1972], Rochester.

457   "The flight back from Moscow is painful": *JJC*, 280.

457   Zinny's last days: author int. Sarah Stevenson, Dec. 6, 2004, and Annie Thom, Nov. 29, 2004.

458   "I'd like you to meet": SD int. Tom Glazer, Oct. 27, 1983, Swem.

458   "What has happened to this place": *JJC*, 281.

459   "I have entertained John Cheever": Mary Dirks to "Beloved Friends," Sept. 10, 1972, Swem.

459   "Both Susie and I grant [Federico]": *LJC*, 293–94.

460   "Lang called me from jail": ibid., 283.

461   convinced the two were "emotionally involved": SD int. Donadio, June 15, 1984, Swem.

461   "by getting pissed and falling down": JC to MZ, April 23 [1977].

461   "He just burned himself out": Author int. John Dirks, May 9, 2004.

CHAPTER THIRTY-FOUR { *1972–1973* }

462   "The long speech I have prepared": *JJC*, 289.

462   "Hey! There's John Cheever!": *NFB*, 123.

462   "Sauced, I speculate on a homosexual romance": *JJC*, 285.

463   "I think I'd be perfectly capable of killing": quoted in Frederick Exley, "That Place," unpublished essay, Rochester.

463   "You'll be able to lift it to the sound of outboard motors": *CJC*, 52.

463   "I breakfast on scotch and Librium": JC to Exley, July 13 [1972], Rochester.

463 "[A]fter his last story in The New Yorker": JC to grants committee, Jan. 22, 1969, Academy.

463 "didn't find Exley up to his reviews": Felicia Geffen to JC, Jan. 29, 1969, Academy.

464 "[Cheever] sat on his pompous ass": e-mail from Tina Bourjaily to Carol Sklenicka, June 1, 2004.

465 "Hoarseness is not . . . symptom of Clapp": *GT*, 223.

465 "That was great fun": *LJC*, 288.

465 "I don't know what to do about this house": ibid., 289.

465 "Feed me to the pigs": Roger Skillings, journal, April 27, 1973, courtesy of Roger Skillings.

465 "easier to get to Egypt": author int. Molly Cook and Mary Oliver, Feb. 14, 2005.

465 "a kind of nightmare": Skillings to Stanley Kunitz, April 17, 1973, courtesy of Skillings.

467 "a slim collection of the ten stories": *HBD*, 180–81.

467 Reviews of *The World of Apples:* Thomas R. Edwards, in *New York Review of Books*, May 17, 1973, 35; Ronald De Feo, in *National Review*, May 11, 1973, 536–37; Christopher Lehmann-Haupt, in *New York Times*, May 10, 1973, 43; L. Woiwode, in *New York Times Book Review*, May 20, 1973, 1, 26; D. Keith Mano, in *Washington Post Book World*, July 1, 1973, 1, 10.

468 "Apples seems to have done much better": JC to James Valhouli, July 14, 1973, Swem.

468 "All the cardiologists and internists": author int. Ray Mutter, May 12, 2004.

469 "Oxygen: No Smoking": JC to Donadio, May 29 [1973], Swem.

469 "'Are you completely without imagination'": *LJC*, 293.

470 "This brought the cops": *GT*, 225.

470 "Don't be silly": Jack Leggett to SC, June 24, 1982, CFP.

470 the whole "*Death in Venice* plot": SD int. Frank Jewett, June 29, 1984, Swem.

470 "Why did you go and tell 'The Boots'": *HBD*, 165.

470 "There is a sinister shrink in the wings": *GT*, 225.

470 his heart did a "clog dance": JC to Arthur Spear, June 4 [1973], courtesy of Pamela Spear Goff.

472 "The gin bottle, the gin bottle": *JJC*, 290–91.

472 "I'm not at all sure what I'm getting into": JC to Coates, Aug. 23, 1973.

CHAPTER THIRTY-FIVE {*1973*}

473 "He explained the American Academy": Ron Hansen to SD, June 25, 1984, Swem.

474 "when we bring off a seminar": *LJC*, 297.

474 "We were a bunch of ragtag hippies": author int. T. Coraghessan Boyle, July 6, 2004.

475 "If that character is supposed to be *gay*": author int. Hansen, July 10, 2004.

476 "Look in my closet": author int. "Elaine Moody," August 10, 2004.

476 "Ah yes, I loved your book": Michael Ryan, "Meeting Cheever," in *God Hunger* (New York: Viking, 1989), 12–13.

477 "Whatever you do . . . *don't let him drink*": author int. Richard Bausch, July 8, 2004.

477 "I left Iowa never expecting to see him again": *GT*, 230.

477   The "tangible world" was receding: Sarah Irwin to SD, July 18, 1984, Swem.

478   "I shout myself hoarse at football games": *LJC*, 297.

478   "Fellatio is the nicest thing": author int. Sarah Irwin, Oct. 11, 2004.

479   "One way I can find out if I like something": *CJC*, 42.

480   "exercising marital rights": SD int. Leggett, April 28, 1985, Swem.

481   "We part the student and the teacher": *JJC*, 293.

481   "His third marriage, her first": E-mail from Gurganus to author, June 5, 2004.

481   "[Allan] flirts with me": *JJC*, 293.

482   "a truck-driver or master-sergeant type": author int. Leggett, May 23, 2004.

482   "[T]he clerk was just unlocking the front door": Raymond Carver, *Fires* (Santa Barbara, Calif.: Capra Press, 1983), 199.

482   "I'd be very happy to tell the Guggenheims": JC to Ray Carver, Aug. 2 [1977], courtesy of Carol Sklenicka.

482   "The woman was called Miss Dent": Raymond Carver, "The Train," in *Cathedral* (New York: Random House, 1989), 147–56.

483   "Do you know, Mr. Donleavy, that no *major*": Ed Dinger, ed., *Seems like Old Times* (Iowa City: Iowa Writers' Workshop, 1986), 114–16.

483   "Julius Fuck Street": *LJC*, 283.

483   "drab commie suit": author int. Petru Popescu, Nov. 1, 2004.

483   "earthly paradise": Spear to Litvinov, Nov. 28, 1973, courtesy of Pamela Spears Goff.

CHAPTER THIRTY-SIX { *1974* }

486   "she hurled at me the fact": *GT*, 233.

487   *"She's already married! To me!"*: *TT*, 159.

488   "I love you . . . I write an advertisement": *JJC*, 294, 296.

488   "never taken a story about a homosexual": *LJC*, 302.

488   "That was one of the nicest things": JC to WM [c. March 1974], Berg.

488   "kindest thing anybody's ever done": Dwight Garner, "The Salon Interview: Allan Gurganus," *Salon* (www.salon.com/books/int/1997/12/cov_si_08 Gurganus).

488   "the modesty of [his] demands": *LJC*, 303.

489   "appreciate the excellence of your character": JC to Gurganus, March 21 [1974].

490   "a metaphor for something mysterious": JC, "The Leaves, the Lion-Fish and the Bear," *Esquire*, Nov. 1974, 110–11, 192–93, 195–96.

491   *Esquire* had offered "three thousand for anything": JC to Gurganus, April 16 [1974].

491   homosexuality "understandable and valid": SD int. MZ, July 25, 1984, Swem.

491   "[I]n my considered opinion": JC to Stathis Orphanos, May 18, 1979, CFP.

491   it felt "like a gift": author int. Dennis Coates, April 26, 2004.

492   "Your crack about my being unloved": JC to Coates, June 10 [1974].

493   ex-husband . . . found it "kind of appalling": SD int. Rob Cowley, June 20, 1984, Swem.

493   Warren Hinckle . . . a "wretched buffoon": JC to Weaver [c. Sept. 1974], CFP; the remark is deleted from the letter published in *GT*, 237.

493   "People stop me on the street and ask": JC to Cowley, Oct. 1 [1972], Newberry.

493   "He would look hangdog": author int. Lehmann-Haupt and Robins, Aug. 15, 2004.

493   his son called him a "shit": JC to Coates, April 6 [1974].

494 "Why don't you divorce him?": author int. "Elaine Moody," Aug. 10, 2004.

494 "[Elaine] is sulking in Maine": JC to Coates, Aug. 13 [1974].

494 "On return home to a tense emotional atmosphere": Phelps admission report, Aug. 20, 1974, PRM.

CHAPTER THIRTY-SEVEN {1974}

495 Kenmore Square ("part student, part slum"): *LJC*, 307.

495 "end up penniless and naked": *GT*, 237.

495 "I start with the Lief Ericson [sic] monument": JC to Dirkses, Sept. 11 [1974], Swem.

496 "He hasn't sent me a thing": Laurens Schwartz, journal, Swem.

496 "the last pages in Proust": author int. Rick Siggelkow, July 1, 2004.

496 found the administration "quite mysterious": JC to Coates, Sept. 11 [1974].

496 "I did *not* rise to the occasion": George Starbuck to SD, Oct. 28, 1983, Swem.

497 students "responsive and contentious": JC to Coates, Oct. 4 [1974].

497 "It's a found object": author int. Christopher Gresov, July 24, 2005.

497 "Submit it to a New York publisher": author int. Oakley Hall III, June 23, 2005.

498 "had a tendency to walk out . . . nude": author int. Schwartz, June 21, 2004.

499 "We were intimate but not close": John Malcolm Brinnin to SD, May 9, 1984, Swem.

499 "Should I not remember you": JC to Brinnin, Sept. 2, 1978, Delaware.

499 "as if a drink that was merely single": *OJ*, 119.

499 "conspicuous ego clash": *LJC*, 308.

499 "Updike never calls me": Schwartz to SD, March 26, 1986, Swem.

500 "heavily grated corner emporium": *OJ*, 118.

500 Valhouli . . . found them "incoherent": SD int. Valhouli, Oct. 15, 1984, Swem.

500 "Vesuvian maternalism": *LJC*, 308.

501 "She's going to marry a chap": El Borracho [Ivan Gold], "Message in a Bottle," *Boston* magazine, Jan. 1985, 82.

501 "I'd had trouble dissuading him": *LJC*, 307.

502 "Communications Time-peddler, 1970": FLC Jr.'s alumnus file, Dartmouth.

502 "Dear Mr. Nixon (sic)": FLC Jr. to Richard M. Nixon, June 18, 1970, PJC.

502 "no weltgeist, no historical perspective": FLC Jr. to John D. Ehrlichman, Nov. 11, 1972, PJC.

502 "a college drop-out way back in 1926": FLC Jr. to Perry Knowlton, July 20, 1970, Columbia.

502 "potentially an excellent manuscript": Gerald McCauley, Curtis Brown reader, report on *Who Are the Revolutionaries?*, Columbia.

503 "Honolulu is on my itinerary": FLC Jr. to David Cheever, July 15, 1970.

503 "Perhaps I've delineated in non-fiction": FLC Jr. to Knowlton, July 21, 1970, Columbia.

503 "I would hope that it would make McLuhan": FLC Jr. to JC, Aug. 30, 1970, PJC.

503 "or whatever part of that": FLC Jr. to JC, Sept. 14, 1970, PJC.

503 "covered the same ground": FLC Jr. to Knowlton, Oct. 16, 1970, Columbia.

503 "Perhaps . . . 'it should be published'": Knowlton to FLC Jr., April 30, 1971, Columbia.

503 "there is a kind of destiny": FLC Jr. to Sarah Cheever, Feb. 22, 1972, PJC.

503 "Poor Fred began to drink again": JC to Coates, May 23 [1974].

504 "funny and very relevant": FLC Jr. to David Cheever, Oct. 19, 1974.

505 Sexton, whom Cheever found "aggressive": *LJC*, 308.

505 "visceral distaste": author int. Ivan Gold, Sept. 21, 2004.

505 "Did they overhear *that?*": Diane Wood Middlebrook, *Anne Sexton: A Biography* (Boston: Houghton Mifflin, 1991), 394.

505 Cheever "never quite got over this": *LJC*, 310.

505 she'd "never been so happy": JC to Coates, Oct. 14 [1974].

505 "Susie said . . . rather bad show": JC to Coates, Dec. 2 [1974].

505 "extraordinarily bleak" room at Phelps: *CJC*, 65.

506 "you have a father who is dying": *LJC*, 294.

CHAPTER THIRTY-EIGHT { *1975* }

507 "straight asshole": *LJC*, 308–9.

507 "opportunity to ask John *Updike*": author int. David Frieze, March 20, 2005.

508 "I've written more goddamn words": Dean Doner to SD, Oct. 22, 1984, Swem.

509 "I can't think of anything more selfish": JC to Coates, Feb. 10 [1975].

509 "delinquent asshole": JC to Donadio [c. March 1975], Swem.

510 "I'm faring rather poorly": El Borracho [Ivan Gold], "Message in a Bottle," *Boston* magazine, Jan. 1985, 82.

510 "in deep concern" about John: FLC Jr. to David Cheever, March 30, 1975.

510 "I must have been quite drunk and mad": *JJC*, 301.

510–511 a degree of brain damage: Phelps admission summary, April 4, 1975, PRM.

511 "bunch of Christers": *LJC*, 310.

511 memory was "apparently poor": "Patient Progress Notes (4/9/75)" from Smithers, Swem.

511 "A bummer; not really bad, but not good": *JJC*, 298–302.

511 "The indoctrination here is stern": *LJC*, 312.

512 "They don't want me to work": JC to FLC Jr., April 17, 1975, PJC.

513 "almost surreptitiously": SD int. Ruth Maxwell, Sept. 17, 1984, Swem.

513 "I'm really allright but I can't say so": *GT*, 243.

513 "Oh, but of *course* you're right": author int. Carol Kitman, Aug. 16, 2004.

513 "But he was a brilliant poet": JC, to anon., unmailed draft [summer 1975?], Houghton.

513 "Non posso, cara": *HBD*, 194.

514 "Fifteen patients have fled": JC to Spear, April 21 [1975], courtesy of Pamela Spear Goff.

514 "Alcoholism seems to be an infirmity": JC to Clare Thaw, May 11 [1977].

514 "He says that if he were strong enough": *LJC*, 313.

515 "She seems to operate": progress notes, 5/5/75, Swem.

515 a postcard . . . "See?": author int. Oakley Hall III, June 23, 2005.

CHAPTER THIRTY-NINE { *1975* }

516 "To go from continuous drunkenness": *JJC*, 303.

516 "a man of 34 who has been": *CJC*, 113.

516 "This is the one I want!": author int. John Dirks, May 9, 2004.

517   Updike, whose "immense kindness": JC to JU, June 2 [1975], Houghton.
517   "giant martinis in jelly glasses": Betsy Brown, "The Friday Club, A Cheever Salon," *New York Times*, June 27, 1982, sec. 11, pp. 1, 8.
517   "I used to be an alcoholic": SD int. Marion Ascoli, July 5, 1984, Swem.
517   "[If John] can do [AA]": FLC Jr. to David Cheever, May 15, 1975.
517   "lack[ing] the coherence of a redneck cult": JC to Brinnin, Dec. 9 [1975?], Delaware.
518   "My name is Jawn": *GT*, 244.
518   his "wife of a hundred years": author int. Clare Thaw, May 6, 2004.
518   pathetic old man in an "ill-fitting suit": *JJC*, 305.
518   " 'Yesterday was a memory, tomorrow is a dream' ": ibid., 369.
519   "We really need you, Truman": e-mail from Grace Schulman to author, June 29, 2004.
519   "You're an alcoholic like me": SD int. Dudley Schoales, Jr., July 17, 1984, Swem.
520   "I've changed violently": *JJC*, 303.
520   "that the house wasn't cleaned by gremlins": *NFB*, 124.
520   "I lean for a kiss. There is none": *JJC*, 309.
521   "highly polished brown loafer": *BP*, 61.
521   "missed their date at the municipal dump": *JJC*, 314.
521   "Fred got honors at Andover": *GT*, 244.
521   "put her little feet on the path": JC to Schwartz, Oct. 7 [1975], Swem.
522   "Poldark! Poldark!": Steven Hager, "Cheever on Writing for TV," *Horizon*, Dec. 1981, 56.
522   "face of a ferret": JC to Gurganus, May 26 [1976].
522   "the small museum guard in a worn uniform": *JJC*, 330.
523   "without precaution or moderation": Gurganus to JC [c. March 1975], Swem.
523   "A[llan] seems . . . to magnify the incongruities": *JJC*, 306.

CHAPTER FORTY { *1975–1976* }

524   "[his] sordid deliquesence [sic]": JC to anon., unmailed draft [summer 1975?], Houghton.
525   "we were the kind of people": JC, "The Folding-Chair Set," *New Yorker*, Oct. 13, 1975, 38.
525   "finger-exercise" to commemorate: JC to Coates, Oct. 31 [1975].
525   *Do you know who I am?*: author int. Charles McGrath, Aug. 5, 2004.
526   "I am pleased that my work": JC to Siggelkow, Feb. 7 [1976].
526   "We are very grateful to John": WM to Donadio, n.d., NYPL-MSS.
526   "They were all very pleased with it": *CJC*, 118.
526   "brain[ing] Tom Glazer": JC to Coates, Oct. 31 [1975].
526   "Up the river to Yaddo": *JJC*, 311–12.
527   "John! What a *coincidence!*": author int. Gurganus, April 30, 2004.
527   "she decided that the people she loved": JC, "The Hostess of Yaddo," *New York Times Book Review*, May 8, 1977, 3, 35.
527   "POSITIVELY NO SMOKING": author int. Melissa Meyer, Aug. 8, 2004.
527   Gurganus . . . rolled his eyes: author int. Philip Schultz, July 27, 2004.
528   "strike some sort of peace": JC to Brinnin, Sept. 4 [1975], Delaware.
528   "I must repair my farewell scenes": JC to Schwartz, Nov. 17 [1975], Swem.

528   "That place is asshole": JC to Schwartz, Dec. 8 [1975], Swem.

528   " 'Hot shit,' [the cabbie] said": JC to Valhouli, Dec. 6 [1975], Swem.

528   "When you're hot you can write anything": Barbato int. JC, Oct. 27, 1978, Swem.

528   "How like sandpipers were the children": JC, "The President of the Argentine," *Atlantic Monthly*, April 1976, 44.

528   "[T]he piece is shapeless and self-indulgent": *Atlantic* editorial memo, Dec. 29, 1975, courtesy of Michael Janeway.

529   "Intoxicated by the news": Dana Gioia, "Meeting Mr. Cheever," *Hudson Review* 39, no. 3 (Autumn 1986), 421.

530   "All writers suffer terribly from delusions": *LJC*, 319.

531   "He gets out. Farragut gets out": *CJC*, 128.

531   "I think the work is successful": *JJC*, 321.

531   "nearly run over by Donald Lang": JC to Gurganus, April 23 [1976].

531   "[didn't] really give a shit": JC to Coates, May 4 [1976].

532   "It's not very often": McGrath to Donadio, May 25, 1976, NYPL-MSS.

532   "[he] screams a lot, says blah blah blah": JC to Weaver, June 2 [1976], CFP; the remark is deleted from the letter published in *GT*, 264.

532   "My discontents are quite simple": JC to Donadio, Feb. 17 [1977], Swem.

532   "I am the sort of iconoclast": *LJC*, 322.

532   "one of the dandy little apartments": FLC Jr. to David Cheever [c. April 1976?].

532   "Just back from a fine visit with John": FLC Jr. to David Cheever, April 25, 1976.

533   "Fred, I killed you in my novel": *LJC*, 321.

533   "He seems . . . to be suffering a loneliness": *JJC*, 321–22.

533   "Yes, yes, Louisa Hatch did the flowers": *LJC*, 320.

534   "Some clinician would say": *JJC*, 324.

534   "He was . . . a *colleague*": ibid., 323–24.

534   "He is forty-three": JC to Cowley, April 24, 1976, Newberry.

535   "In yesterday's mail I was cordially invited": *LJC*, 355.

535   "most interesting writer of his generation": Michael J. Bandler, ". . . a Conversation with the Storyteller," *Chicago Tribune*, Oct. 22, 1978, sec. 7, p. 1.

535   "Updike's fourth-rate novel": *LJC*, 353.

CHAPTER FORTY-ONE { *1976–1977* }

536   "such a striking example of egocentricity": *GT*, 263.

536   "more readily appreciated": JC to Vance Bourjaily, July 19, 1976, Bowdoin College Library.

536   "an amiable guide who liked to play backgammon": *GT*, 267.

536   "In Romania one drives mostly on such roads": JC, "Romania," *Travel & Leisure*, March 1978, 87.

537   "[T]he Customs man threatened to confiscate": JC to Schwartz, Aug. 7 [1976], Swem.

537   "You are . . . a bore": JC to MZ, April 23 [1977].

538   "went cock-a-hoop over the handlebars": JC to Gurganus [c. Nov. 1976].

538   "looping red trail eight miles long": Philip Schultz, "The Eight-Mile Bike Ride," in *The Holy Worm of Praise* (New York: Harcourt, 2002), 52–53.

539   "quite humorous and innocent": *JJC*, 327.

539   "love of one's neighbor" was a virtue: JC to Sara Spencer, July 4 [1976], Swem.
541   a man "no longer young": Stephen Sandy to SD, Sept. 22, 1984, Swem.
541   "I got into the tub and pretended": *JJC*, 335.
541   "For the master I'll come for bus fare": author int. James McConkey, Feb. 26, 2005.
541   "the Budd Schulberg of New England": JC, "The Melancholy of Distance," in *Chekhov and Our Age*, ed. James McConkey (Ithaca, N.Y.: Cornell University Center for International Studies, 1984), 127.
542   "I can find nothing in Chekov to quote": JC to Gurganus, Nov. 30 [1976].
542   "I'm taking the bus!": author int. Frederica Kaven, Feb. 26, 2005.
543   "some true newness to it": JC to Cowley, Jan. 1 [1977], Newberry.
543   "Cheever's getting out of a seminar": author int. MZ, Dec. 12, 2004.
543   "none of the attributes of a sexual irregular": *JJC*, 343.
544   "difficulty in knowing who the real Max was": SD int. Dave Smith, Jan. 30, 1985, Swem.
544   "It is a story about a man who allies": JC to MZ, n.d.
545   Zimmer felt a "slight hardness": MZ, journal, April 20, 1982, courtesy of MZ.

CHAPTER FORTY-TWO {*1977*}

547   "Firstly this is a no-shit friendship": JC to MZ, Feb. 24 [1977].
547   the "taste of [Hope's] lipstick": JC to MZ [c. Feb. 1977].
547   "That a man of sixty-four": JC to MZ, Feb. 23 [1977].
547   "I don't want to get into your pants": JC to MZ, March 1 [1977].
549   "extraordinarily good detail": Bernard Malamud to JC [c. Dec. 1976], Ransom.
549   "There is some spiritual ungainliness": JC to Malamud, Dec. 14 [1976], Ransom.
549   didn't "seem to [him] all of a piece": Cowley to JC, Nov. 17, 1976, Newberry.
549   "Well, I expected the best": Bellow to JC, Nov. 23, 1976, Swem.
550   "I didn't want them to think I was a rube": *GT*, 277.
550   "Three golden retrievers lie": SC, "A Duet of Cheevers," *Newsweek*, March 14, 1974, reprinted in *CJC*, 121–29.
551   Reviews of *Falconer:* John Gardner, in *Saturday Review of Literature*, April 2, 1977, 20–23; R. Z. Sheppard, in *Time*, Feb. 28, 1977, 79–80; John Leonard, in *Harper's*, April 1977, 88–89; Christopher Lehmann-Haupt, in *New York Times*, March 3, 1977, 31; Joan Didion, in *New York Times Book Review*, March 6, 1977, 1, 22–23.
551   *Time* had "shit on [the book]": *GT*, 279.
551   "[Leonard] is sympathetic": JC to Lehmann-Haupt, Nov. 20 [1976], BU.
552   "It doesn't seem fitting": JC to Lehmann-Haupt, May 1 [1977], BU.
552   "I have neglected to thank you": JC to Donadio, Nov. 27 [1977], Swem.
553   she'd "gone completely insane": JC to Schwartz, April 26 [1978], Swem.
553   "The lesson let us help one another": *HBD*, 39.

CHAPTER FORTY-THREE {*1977*}

560   "Is your father a homosexual drug-addict?": Jesse Kornbluth, "The Cheever Chronicle," *New York Times Magazine*, Oct. 21, 1979, 29.

560   "numerous occurrences of homosexual material": Robert Towers, in *New York Review of Books*, March 17, 1977, 3–4.
560   the sound of his "fruity accent": JC to Valhouli, Dec. 14 [1977], Swem.
561   "I'm having a marvelous time": JC to Gottlieb, March 16, 1977, Swem.
561   "I'd be honored": SD int. John Crutcher, June 22, 1985, Swem.
561   "Mary plans to appear": *GT*, 280.
561   "demonstrating a food-chopper": JC to MZ, April 14 [1978].
561   "My name is John Cheever": *CJC*, 139.
561   "cordial but shy": Peter Benelli to Lillian Wentworth, Aug. 13, 1982, Thayer.
562   return to Thayer and "snatch a smoke": Lillian Wentworth, "And Recalled," *Parents League of New York Review*, 1984, 1.
562   "a delegation of Bulgarians": quoted in *GT*, 283.
562   "the naive optimist": John Koster, "John Cheever Reads, FDU Listens," *Bergen Record*, Sept. 28, 1978, C8.
562   "the first western writer to defect": *HBD*, 157.
562   "Bulgaria seems quite dark": *LJC*, 337.
562   "You may have forgotten what I am like": JC to Litvinov, April 4 [1977].
563   "we embrace and shout in unison": Arthur Unger, "John Cheever's Long View," *Christian Science Monitor*, Oct. 24, 1979, 17.
563   "stupidity and clumsiness and brutality": *CJC*, 79.
563   he "unbuttoned his vest and cut a fart": *GT*, 284.
563   "What political or social significance": JC to Litvinov, June 23, 1977.
564   "We kissed the mayor": *GT*, 287.
564   "Saroyan will be the only one": Gore Vidal to SD, Oct. 16, 1984, Swem.
564   "Women are jealous": Samuel Coale, "Portrait of John Cheever," Swem.
565   "If I sounded sinister yesterday morning": JC to MZ, April 29 [1977].
565   "That one is in conflict with oneself": *CJC*, 158.
565   "Brooding, as I must, about homosexuality": *LJC*, 335.
566   "I love you because so much green[n]ess": JC to MZ [c. May 1977]; the remark is deleted from the letter published in *LJC*, 336–37.
566   he can "kiss Jody passionately, but not tenderly": *F*, 122.
567   "bearass I look like something": JC to MZ, Oct. 20 [1977].
567   "I was delighted to be free of the censure": *JJC*, 347.
567   "Anyone who caressed": ibid., 335.
567   "he suffers acutely from the loss of gravity": *LJC*, 339.
567   "to engage one's interest in the welfare": JC to MZ [c. Aug. 1977?].
568   "something I first got": JC to MZ [c. July 1977].
568   "The contempt you bring to this cast": *LJC*, 357.
568   "With a stiff prick I can read": JC to James Holmes, March 25, 1979, courtesy of Ned Rorem.
568–569   "We would rent a quaint Vermont farmhouse": JC to MZ, May 24 [1977]; the passage is deleted from the letter published in *LJC*, 337.
569   Max was getting "the wretch treatment": Rudnik to Cheevers, Aug. 30, 1977, CFP.
569   "Your description of your love for Marilyn": published, with deletions, in *LJC*, 340.
569   "I'm determined that this should end happily": JC to MZ, Nov. 20 [1977].

CHAPTER FORTY-FOUR { *1977–1978* }

571   "for the first time I feel somewhat estranged": JC to MZ [c. Aug. 1977].

571   "returning to the banks of the Iowa River": JC to Leggett, Sept. 17, 1977, Swem.

572   "I love to see it sitting there": author int. Daniel Halpern, Nov. 16, 2004.

572   "Your psychiatrist and mine can't be the same": JC to Halpern, Nov. 27 [1977], NYPL-MSS.

573   "Some of the Russians": JC to Cowley, March 1, 1978, Newberry.

573   "I wonder what it feels like to die": SD int. Bev Chaney, Jr., June 26, 1984, Swem.

573   "He hinted at the indifference of his marriage": *JJC*, 344.

573   "I would try to buy myself time": e-mail from MZ to author, Aug. 2, 2006.

574   "After spending a night": JC to MZ [c. Feb. 1978].

574   "Neither of us is homosexual": *LJC*, 341.

575   "Old Cheever . . . has gone Gay": quoted in *HBD*, 208.

575   "Every woman needs a man who's a friend": SD int. Palamountain, July 17, 1985, Swem.

575   " 'That,' Anne said sternly, 'is a purely platonic' ": JC to MZ, May 24 [1977]; this passage is deleted from the letter published in *LJC*, 337.

576   wanted to pursue "as a lark": Arthur Unger, "John Cheever's Long View," *Christian Science Monitor*, October 24, 1979, 18.

576   "[spoke] only with a British accent": Richard F. Shepard, "WNET to Do Plays by US Novelists," *New York Times*, Feb. 8, 1979, C13.

576   "I'm really working on the WNET show": *LJC*, 342.

576   writers who were also "acceptable" candidates: Herbert Mitgang, "Saul Bellow Taking Laureateship Lightly," *New York Times*, Nov. 14, 1976, 73.

577   protested as "outrageous": Cowley to Members of the Nominating Committee for the Gold Medal in the Short Story, Feb. 5, 1978, Newberry.

577   "spread the honors around": Richard Wilbur to Cowley, Feb. 20, 1978, Newberry.

577   "The difficulty may be with Bill Maxwell": JC to Cowley, March 1, 1978, Newberry.

577   "This has remained somewhat on my conscience": WM to SD, April 10, 1985, Swem.

578   " 'I recall . . . that at the time of my first novel' ": Jesse Kornbluth, "The Cheever Chronicle," *New York Times Magazine*, Oct. 21, 1979, 29, 102.

580   "John Cheever, the flesh and blood person": Dennis Edward Coates, "The Novels of John Cheever," unpublished dissertation, Duke University, 1977, 11.

580   "My congratulations on having completed": JC to Coates, May 16, 1978.

581   "Oh he's totally discredited": SD int. R. G. Collins, Sept. 27, 1985, Swem.

581   "To have been expelled from Thayer Academy": *JJC*, 348.

581   "revolting invasion of publicity": Israel Shenker, "Solzhenitsyn, in Harvard Speech, Terms West Weak and Cowardly," *New York Times*, June 9, 1978, A8.

581   "Aleksandr brought up the rear": *LJC*, 344.

582   "Your letter was so circumspect": JC to MZ, March 13, 1978.

582   "I don't really know you at all": *LJC*, 342.

582   "Robert Anderson wrote *Tea and Sympathy*": Laurens Schwartz to SD, March 26, 1986, Swem.

CHAPTER FORTY-FIVE { *1978–1979* }

583   "Why do you want to do that?": author int. Gottlieb, June 16, 2004.

584   "totally forgotten some of them": Paul Gray, "Inescapable Conclusions," *Time*, Oct. 16, 1978, 125.

584   "The parturition of a writer": *SJC*, vii.

585   Reviews of *The Stories of John Cheever*: Paul Gray, in *Time*, Oct. 16, 1978, 122, 125; William McPherson, in *Washington Post Book World*, Oct. 22, 1978, E1, 6; John Leonard, in *New York Times*, Nov. 7, 1978, 43; Anne Tyler, in *New Republic*, Nov. 4, 1978, 45–47; John Irving, in *Saturday Review*, Sept. 30, 1978, 44–46; John Gardner, in *Chicago Tribune Book World*, Oct. 22, 1978, 1; Robert Towers in *New York Review of Books*, Nov. 9, 1978, 3–4; Richard Locke, in *New York Times Book Review*, Dec. 3, 1978, 3, 78.

586   "At the risk of sounding pious": Diane White, "John Cheever: Finding Classic Themes in Ordinary Life," *Boston Globe*, Nov. 28, 1978, 21.

587   "Yesterday afternoon Mrs. Vincent Astor": JC to Weaver, Oct. 22 [1978]; this sentence was deleted from the letter published in *GT*, 294–95.

587   "bask[ing] . . . in that fragrance of beaver": *LJC*, 352.

587   "an easy time talking to women": SD int. Lauren Bacall, Jan. 17, 1985, Swem.

587   "I think Betty [Bacall] has got me mixed up": JC to SC, Jan. 13 [1979], Berg.

587   Your mother . . . GARP should have won: JC to SC, Feb. 2 [1979], Berg.

588   "wiping the steam off a windowpane": JC to MZ, Nov. 1 [1978].

588   "I suspect that my tastes ": JC to grants committee, Jan. 15, 1979, Academy.

588   "I don't mean style; I mean voice": JC to Roth, Sept. 17 [1977], LC.

589   "A book comes, of which I'm the subject": *JJC*, 355.

589   "We have never sat at the kitchen table": *GT*, 298.

589   "He is a most judicious": JC to SC, Dec. 31 [1978], Berg.

589   "My enthusiasm for you three is boundless": JC to SC, Sept. 6 [1978], Berg.

591   "I never showed my father anything": *HBD*, 214–15.

591   "We have both agreed that fiction": JC, "My Daughter, the Novelist," *New York*, April 7, 1980, 53.

591   "You finished the marathon?": *LJC*, 357.

592   "a day for athletic-esthetic celebration": Jim Morse, "A Happy Twist to Cheever Chronicle," *Boston Herald American*, April 18, 1979.

592   "I never believed in my childhood days": Paul Williams, "John Cheever: Adding Luster to the Stream," *Patriot Ledger*, April 18, 1979.

592   "[T]his has involved": JC to MZ [c. May 1979].

593   "On Friday I did an ABC tape": JC to MZ, Jan. 6, 1979.

593   Rorem was "the only homosexual": Ned Rorem, *The Nantucket Diary* (New York: North Point, 1987), 233–35.

594   "I like to remember": JC to Holmes, April 4, 1979, courtesy of Ned Rorem.

594   "That the pleasure I take in Jim's company": JC to Rorem, March 3, 1979.

594   "I think I am not particularly susceptible": JC to Holmes, April 12, 1979, courtesy of Ned Rorem.

594   "large orgasims" [sic]: JC to Holmes, Feb. 28, 1979, ibid.

CHAPTER FORTY-SIX { *1979* }

596 "this is the first time . . . view of the park": quoted in Henry Allen, "John Cheever: Capturing the Splendors of Suburbia," *Washington Post*, Oct. 8, 1979, A1, B13.

596 "Some people seem to have a gift": quoted in John Firth, "Talking with John Cheever," *Saturday Review*, April 2, 1977, 23.

597 "he developed another smile for cameras": *HBD*, 37.

597 "There are people who consider me": *CJC*, 243.

598 "I've never been any great shakes": JC to McLoone [c. Jan. 1967], Georgetown University Library.

598 "knock it off about that poetry stuff": author int. Anne Bernays and Justin Kaplan, Feb. 19, 2005.

599 "basking in the reflected light": Spear to Litvinov, March 9, 1979, courtesy of Pamela Spear Goff.

600 "boisterous, leggy, badly bred dog": *HBD*, 147.

600 "When [s]he wakes me, late at night": ibid., 148.

600 "gritty enclave . . . Sing Sing": Martha Smilgis, "The Dark Moments of His Life Rival—and Perhaps Inspire—John Cheever's Stories," *People*, April 23, 1979, 78–79.

600 "Paradise on earth": *Ossining Citizen Register*, April 23, 1979.

601 "I think . . . about the town I came from": JC to Denney [c. March 1935?], Dartmouth.

601 "the village kind of life": Susan Merrill, "The Everyday Ossining Haunts of John Cheever," *Patent Trader* (Mount Kisco, N.Y.), March 14, 1986, B12–13, 34.

602 "Unidentified Flying Object": *LJC*, 323.

602 "I couldn't wait when I'd see him, I'd run out": Merrill, "Everyday Ossining Haunts," B13.

602 speaking of "spiritual things": SD int. John Bukovksy, July 5, 1984, Swem.

603 "*That* I will endorse as you please": Stephen Sandy to SD, Oct. 8 [1984], Swem.

603 "I'm terribly sorry," said Cheever: author int. Martin Amsel, April 24, 2004.

604 "I think we do not know one another": *JJC*, viii.

604 "He had two great fears about me": *LJC*, 327.

604 "I didn't quite get it": *JJC*, ix.

604 a kind of "shorthand": *LJC*, 328.

605 "If the water was right and the tide ebbing": JC to MZ [c. June 1979].

607 Susan "sometimes had a flicker of wondering": *HBD*, 209.

609 "If you would write your fucking homework": JC to MZ, Sept. 27 [1979].

609 reminded Cheever "a little of Beckett": JC to MZ [c. Aug. 1977?].

609 "It reads like a streak": WM to JC, Aug. 22, 1962, NYPL-MSS.

610 "It was written by a guy out fishing": e-mail from MZ to author, Dec. 18, 2004.

610 "I hope Max Zimmer": McGrath to JC, March 6, 1980, NYPL-MSS.

610 "notes scribbled . . . shopping list": Michiko Kakutani, "In a Cheever-Like Setting, John Cheever Gets MacDowell Medal," *New York Times*, Sept. 11, 1979, C7.

610 "The day before yesterday": [MacDowell] *Colony Newsletter* 9, no. 1 (Fall 1979).

611 "Sex is very important to me": SD int. Leonard, Oct. 23, 1984, Swem.

612   "God have mercy on us all": John Koster, "John Cheever Reads, FDU Listens," *Bergen Record*, Sept. 28, 1978, C8.

612   "Any confrontation between": Kay Gardella, "Cheever: The Agonies of Suburbia," *New York Daily News*, Oct. 21, 1979.

612   hard at work on "another bulky book": Jesse Kornbluth, "The Cheever Chronicle," *New York Times Magazine*, Oct. 21, 1979, 102.

613   "That was the year everybody went to China": JC, "The Night Mummy Got the Wrong Mink Coat," *New Yorker*, April 21, 1980, 35.

613   "This cookbook is a pack of lies!": author int. Janet Maslin, Feb. 10, 2005.

615   "We dined with the Ettlingers": *GT*, 156.

615   "You know, you have this whole other life": author int. Joseph Caldwell, April 5, 2005.

617   "I love you very much and my endeavors": JC to MZ, June 11 [1980].

617   "might as well have spent . . . fishing": MZ, journal [c. summer 1981], courtesy of MZ.

618   "in which suppuration, corruption and decay": JC to MZ [c. summer 1977?].

619   "one of the great labors of history": *JJC*, 356.

619   "I mean it's about what it's like to fuck": notes on *OWPS*, Berg.

620   "Richard, have you ever plagiarized?": Mahala Yates Stripling, "Emergency at Yaddo," *Praxis Post: In Person* (on-line), July 11, 2001.

620   "He began an attack in his little bitchy way": Peter Josyph, "The John Cheever Story: A Talk with Richard Selzer," *Twentieth Century Literature* 37, no. 3 (Fall 1991), 335–43.

620   "we watch a ballgame, screw": *JJC*, 362.

620   "I'm working like a streak": JC to MZ, "The Twelfth" [October 12, 1980].

621   "At first I thought it was a joke": author int. Joan Silber, May 9, 2005.

622   "I said that my scrotum hadn't retracted": JC to Bev Chaney, Oct. 21, 1980, Swem.

622   "I'm afraid the seizure jarred": JC to MZ [c. Oct. 1980].

622   "the utter nothingness": *JJC*, 365.

623   "Did you know that I suffer from Grand Mal?": JC to Valhouli, April 9, 1981, Swem.

623   "It's knocked the shit out of ": JC to Philip Schultz, Dec. 17, 1980, Swem.

624   "The need for chocolet is much finer": *LJC*, 360.

625   "I will tell them that our two most conspicuous": JC to MZ [c. Oct. 1980].

626   "These seem never to have enjoyed": quoted in George W. Hunt, *John Cheever: The Hobgoblin Company of Love* (Grand Rapids: William B. Eerdmans, 1983), xiii.

626   "Here they all were—the greatest": JC, "The Island," *New Yorker*, April 27, 1981, 41.

626–627   "in acute distress": Phelps discharge summary, April 25, 1981, PRM.

627   "I felt like a Calla Liley [sic]": *LJC*, 363.

627   "[T]hank you for . . . plumbing": JC to Marvin Schulman, July 3, 1981, Swem.

627   "Yet such was his vitality": *OJ*, 118.

627 "even if [his] prick fell off ": JU to SD, June 25, 1984, Swem.

628 "transitional cell carcinoma": both pathology lab reports are in Cheever's medical file, PRM.

628 "I returned from the hospital": *LJC*, 364.

628 "I'm sure that Schulman ducked it": author int. Mutter, Jan. 8, 2005.

629 "I conclude that these are the last weeks": *JJC*, 379.

629 "I still feel very frail from the defenestration": *LJC*, 365.

629 melancholy but "kind of relieved": SD int. Donald Van Gordon, June 30, 1984, Swem.

630 "[Cheever] looked thin, ashen": Dana Gioia, "Meeting Mr. Cheever," *Hudson Review* 39, no. 3 (Autumn 1986), 434.

632 "well enough to walk to the dam": JC to "Tom Smallwood," Sept. 7, 1981.

633 "The word 'dear' is what I use": *JJC*, 382.

CHAPTER FORTY-NINE { *1981–1982* }

634 "contracted for a full-length novel": e-mail from Gottlieb to author, May 9, 2005.

636 Updike had "described erections": JC to Weaver, Oct. 24, 1981, CFP; this remark was deleted from the letter published in *GT*, 317–18.

636 Updike wrote that he'd "read at a gulp": JU to JC, Nov. 15 [1981], Swem.

636 "a viper who was trying to break wind": *LJC*, 372.

636 "the most ambitious . . . single series": Doug Hill, "Cheever Script Opens 'American Playhouse,' " *New York Times*, Jan. 10, 1982, sec. 2, p. 23.

636 "Hope is out on the coast": JC to SC, Feb. 11 [1979], Berg.

637 "very peculiar" set pieces: SD int. Paul Bogart, Feb. 11, 1985, Swem.

638 "as gooey as a box of Mallomars": Harry F. Waters, "PBS's American Triumph," *Newsweek*, Jan. 11, 1982, 67.

638 "bright, funny, accurate": Jack Thomas, "Cheever Leads Showcase Series," *Boston Globe TV Week*, Jan. 10, 1982, 2.

639 "I am not at all infirm": quoted in Martha Frey, "Achiever (in Memoriam)," *Vassar Quarterly*, Summer 1982, 7–8.

639 "unusually vigorous" bone cancer: *LJC*, 373.

640 "Some parents will do anything": *NFB*, 147.

641 "those rags that are mandatory hospital dress": *JJC*, 385.

641 "While my beloved wife and my good friend": ibid., 386.

641 *"Get out! And don't come back!"*: author int. Robert Schneider, June 29, 2005.

642 "My beloved daughter calls": *JJC*, 385–86.

642 too frail to "throw backgammon dice": JC to Clare Thaw, Jan. 23, 1982.

644 "Since we spoke on the phone": quoted in James Atlas, *Saul Bellow: A Biography* (New York: Random House, 2000), 504–5.

645 "I have been ill and I wanted to be the one": *LJC*, 374.

645 "to break through the misunderstanding": WM to SC, Oct. 16, 1982, CFP.

645 "The stories are safe": WM to JC, n.d., CFP.

646 "It was Tad who suggested": *LJC*, 370.

647 choice of wife was "highly mature": *JJC*, 389.

647 "You have been a splendid son": *LJC*, 373.

CHAPTER FIFTY { *1982* }

648 "ecological romance": *CJC*, 226–28.

651 Reviews of *Oh What a Paradise It Seems:* John Leonard, in *New York Times Book Review*, March 7, 1982, 1; Anatole Broyard, in *New York Times*, March 3, 1982, C28; JU, in *New Yorker*, April 5, 1982, 189; Geoffrey Stokes, in *Village Voice*, March 16, 1982, 93.

653 "You were bald as billiard ball": FLC Sr. to JC and family, Oct. 17, 1943, CFP.

653 "[I] am determined": JC to McConkey, March 31, 1982, Swem.

653 "a pollution that is distilled from the Adriatic": *LJC*, 378.

653 "Gaunt, limping": Geoff Walden, "Illness Aside, Cheever Full of Surprises," *Ossining Citizen Register*, April 25, 1982.

654 "[T]here's never a word": SC to Spencer, April 6 [1982], Canada.

654 "anything we do . . . palliative": *LJC*, 380.

654 "What I am going to write": *JJC*, 393.

655 "It was more than fifty years": Malcolm Cowley, "John Cheever: The Novelist's Life as a Drama," *Sewanee Review* 91, no. 1 (1983), 16.

656 "He [Tom] is a pleasant young man": *JJC*, 394.

656 "I have never known anything like this fatigue": ibid., 394–95.

657 "The conversation was brief": *LJC*, 359.

658 "To see that vital, brilliant, charming": "John Cheever and Family," TV documentary, BBC *Bookmark* (1994).

658 "[Cheever] was struggling": Susan Merrill, "The Everyday Ossining Haunts of John Cheever," *Patent Trader* (Mount Kisco), March 19, 1986, B34.

658 "I just saw him on the Cavett show": Howard Kissell, "Susan Cheever: Crossing a Frail Bridge," *W*, Jan. 25–Feb. 1, 1985, 26.

EPILOGUE

661 "Greater authors there are than Cheever": editorial, *Boston Globe*, June 22, 1982, 18.

662 "John Cheever's death Friday at 70": editorial, *Patriot Ledger*, June 22, 1982, 18.

662 "a typical graduate of the 'New Yorker' school": *Times* (London), June 21, 1982, 12.

664 "And I wonder whether you saw": John Hersey to MC, June 23, 1982, Swem.

664 "Ossining's most prominent treasure": "Ossining Loses Literary Treasure," *Ossining Citizen Register*, June 22, 1982.

665 "I never really had a 'hair-down' talk": SD int. Burton Benjamin, June 19, 1984, Swem.

665 "He was marvelous . . . full-of-life John": Paul L. Montgomery, "Friends and Colleagues Recall Cheever at a Memorial Service," *New York Times*, June 24, 1982, D23.

666 "a book that would make people love my father": Gioia Diliberto, "A new Cheever Chronicle—by John's Daughter, Susan—Reveals His Tormented Life," *People*, Nov. 5, 1984, 46.

666 "JOHN CHEEVER A FAG": *GT*, 18.

666 "a sexual omnivore": Nathan Cobb, "Mixed Reviews from Family and Friends," *Boston Globe*, Oct. 23, 1984, 29–30.

667 "dropped John like a hot rock": author int. Barrett Clark, July 14, 2004.

667 "Oh, that's just Susie!": author int. Pamela Spear Goff, March 26, 2005.

667 "a quality Walt Whitman once described": Justin Kaplan, in *New York Times Book Review*, Oct. 21, 1984, 7.

668 "My usual feeling about mail": JC to Litvinov, March 15 [1965].

668 "I thought with some bitterness": quoted in Charles Baxter, Michael Collier, and Edward Hirsch, eds., *A William Maxwell Portrait* (New York: Norton, 2004), 113.

668 "his joy and the talent he had": *LJC*, 17.

668 "Nailles is too good to be anyone you ever met": ibid., 268.

669 "give [his] papers to Harvard": Francis Bosha, "The John Cheever Manuscript Collection at Harvard," *Resources for American Literary Study* 22, no. 1 (1996), 104.

669 "almost gleeful about the prospects": *JJC*, ix.

670 "The image of Cheever": Ted Solotaroff, in *The Nation*, Nov. 18, 1991, 616–20.

670 "What a good man he is!": *JJC*, 240.

670 Reviews of *The Journals of John Cheever*: Mary Gordon, in *New York Times Book Review*, Oct. 6, 1991, 1; Jonathan Yardley, in *Washington Post*, Sept. 22, 1991, X3; JU, in *New Republic*, reprinted in *More Matter* (New York: Knopf, 1999), 279–86.

671 "Cheever spent an hour": *New York Times Book Review*, Nov. 24, 1991, 37.

672 "a well-known writer who was gay": author int. Larry David, April 5, 2004.

672 "the most expensive, protracted and vicious": quoted in Anita Miller, *Uncollecting Cheever: The Family of John Cheever vs. Academy Chicago Publishers* (New York: Rowman & Littlefield, 1998), ix.

673 "[M]y father loved his children": *HBD*, 218.

674 "a minor character in someone else's book": *TT*, 169.

675 "If there's someone who never loved himself": SD int. MZ, June 27, 1984, Swem.

676 "endure and be read by future generations": "Inquirer Sponsors Poll on Immortal American Authors," *Publishers Weekly*, March 26, 1979.

676 "Groping about for ways to understand": Robert A. Morace, "Long-Distance Thoughts on 'Cheever Studies,'" paper read at Northeast MLA meeting, March 1986, Swem.

677 "Superintendent Wishnie moved": JC to Dirkses, March 13, 1982.

677 "There are no Cheever ghosts": Lane Lambert, "Famous and Forgotten: Cheever's Literary Legacy Unheralded in Quincy," *Patriot Ledger*, June 17, 2000, 1–3.

677 "I'm not inclined to think of myself": John J. Mullins, "Cheever Writes on Matters of Urgency," *Times-Picayune*, Feb. 22, 1979, sec. 4, p. 6.

677 "He was often labelled a writer about suburbia": *OJ*, 109.

677 his "favorite" Western writer: James Kullander, "Why China's Culture Minister Got Sacked," *Christian Science Monitor*, Sept. 15, 1989, 19.

678 "that Cheever writes beautifully": Foreword, *WS* (New York: Perennial Classics Edition, 2003), ix.

678 "short, pithy, and pointed quote": *New York Daily News*, June 23, 1982, 8.

Index

Aaron, Daniel, 669
About Town (Yagoda), 321
Abraham Lincoln Literary Award, 625
Academy Chicago, 672–3
Accidence: A Short Introduction to the Latin Tongue (E. Cheever), 8
Ackerley, J. R., 480*n*
Adams, Henry, 24, 69–70, 502
Addams, Charles, 131, 355, 356
Adventures of Augie March, The (Bellow), 227–8
Aesthetic Realism movement, 560
Agee, James, 57, 72
Aksyonov, Vasily, 342
Albee, Edward, 340
Alcoholics Anonymous (AA), 265, 354, 411, 504, 511, 522, 539
    Cheever's participation in, 462, 517–19, 539, 601
Aldridge, John, 356, 357, 638
Alexander, Shana, 433–4, 436, 455
Alexandra (Bulgarian translator), 604
Aligher, Margaret, 343
All Men Are Mariners (Kentfield), 291
All Saints (Briarcliff Manor, N.Y.), 220
Alsberg, Henry, 94, 96–7
American Academy of Arts and Letters (later American Academy and Institute of Arts and Letters), 97, 223*n*, 367, 469*n*, 473–4, 510, 534
    Cheever's service on grants committee of, 5, 254, 291, 463–4, 587–8
    Gold Medal of, 576, 577–9
    Prix de Rome of, 223, 224*n*, 225, 235–6
    Rosenthal Award of, 463–4
    William Dean Howells Medal of, 323*n*, 359–61, 577
American Book Award, 5, 625, 654–5

American Dream, An (Mailer), 367
American Guide Series, 94–5, 96–7
American Playhouse, 576, 636–9
American Weekly, 276
Amerika Haus (Berlin), 351
Ames, Elizabeth, 83–4, 88–9, 92, 93, 95, 110, 395
    anticommunist witch hunt at Yaddo and, 158–60
    Cheever's first season at Yaddo and, 61, 66–7, 71, 74–5
    Cheever's last visit with (1975), 527
    Cheever's letters to, 72, 74–5, 94, 121
    Cheever's relationship with, 66–7, 84, 91, 158, 159, 165, 409
    removed from Yaddo, 408–9
    Yaddo strictly run by, 64–5, 66
Amnesty International, 562
Amsel, Martin, 603
Anderson, Robert, 582
Anderson, Sherwood, 57, 72
Andover, 465, 487, 493, 501, 521, 529
Anfiteatro, Dominick, 602, 665
"Angel of the Bridge, The," 298
Anna Karenina (Tolstoy), 142
"Another Story," 385, 386, 583*n*
Answered Prayers (Capote), 532
Antioch College, 388–9, 427, 428, 430
anti-Semitism, 102, 184, 344, 349
antiwar movement, 360–1, 387, 388–9, 502
Arendt, Hannah, 312
Armies of the Night, The (Mailer), 387
Armstrong, Anne Liley (aunt), 15, 24
Armstrong, Jim (uncle), 15
Army Signal Corps, 129, 131–2, 133, 134, 135, 145, 335, 615
Arndt, Rev. George, 658
Arnold, Rev. William, 220

"Artemis, the Honest Well Digger," 388, 431*n*, 436, 444–5
Arvin, Newton, 55, 286, 308
Asch, Nathan, 87, 94
Ascoli, Marion, 517
Assistant, The (Malamud), 255
Atlantic Brief Lives, 334, 585
Atlantic Monthly, The, 85–6, 90, 213, 413, 445, 455, 474, 498–9, 528–9
Auden, W. H., 110, 222, 654*n*
Avedon, Richard, 639

"Babi Yar" (Yevtushenko), 344
Bacall, Lauren, 587
"Backgammon Game, The," 169, 171
Bagleigh Chronicle, The (Dirks), 371
Bailey, Rollin "Tifty," 27, 34–5, 51, 378
Baldwin, James, 223, 283, 337
Barbara Frietchie (mouse), 231, 250
Barker's (Ossining, N.Y.), 602
Barnard College, Cheever's teaching job at, 212–14, 261, 262, 264, 585, 617*n*
Barolini, Antonio, 296, 312, 384–5, 397
Barolini, Helen, 312, 384, 385, 633
Barth, John, 4, 365, 387, 476, 586
Barthelme, Donald, 4, 365, 386, 435–6, 463–4, 476, 526, 586
Bathsheba (dog), 589, 590
"Bayonne," 80
BBC documentary on Cheever, 499*n*, 668, 672, 673
Bech: A Book (Updike), 92*n*
Becker, Stephen, 254
Beckett, Samuel, 609, 618
Beechtwig (Scarborough-on-Hudson, N.Y.), 177, 253, 263
Beechwood (Scarborough-on-Hudson, N.Y.), 177, 182–3, 215, 219, 252, 293
Beethoven, Ludwig van, 26*n*, 300
"Behold a Cloud in the West," 673
"Bella Lingua, The," 247–8, 300*n*
Bellow, Alexandra, 530
Bellow, Saul, 81, 94, 222, 227–9, 240, 280, 295, 360, 375, 435, 459, 480, 530, 550*n*, 676
    awards and honors for, 253, 576–7
    Cheever eulogized by, 229, 664–5
    Cheever's assessments of writings of, 227–8, 359, 576

Cheever's relationship with, 228–9, 358–9, 455, 665
Falconer and, 549
farewell notes of Cheever and, 644–5, 655
Benelli, Peter, 46*n*, 49, 508, 561
Benjamin, Aline, 666–7
Benjamin, Burton ("Bud"), 665–6
Benjamin Franklin Magazine Award, 211
Bennington College, 309, 540, 541, 568
Benton, Thomas Hart, 361
Berlin, Cheever's visit to (1964), 351
Berryman, John, 513
Bessie, Simon Michael, 165*n*, 217–18, 225, 226–37, 239–40, 322*n*
Best, Marshall, 101
Best American Short Stories, 152, 164, 211, 448
Best of the Best, 152
Best Short Stories of 1939, The, 90
Bicentennial (1976), 539
Biddle, Francis, 297
Biddle, George, 296–7, 298, 458
Biddle, Helene, 296
Bissell, LeClaire, 512
"Bliss" (Mansfield), 112
Blitzstein, Marc, 64, 67, 308
Bliven, Bruce, 54
Blue Juniata (Cowley), 47, 83
Blume, Ebie, 236, 237, 248, 258, 297
Blume, Peter, 236, 237, 248, 258, 293, 297, 401
Blumenthal, Ann, 638
"Bock Beer and Bermuda Onions," 56
Bogan, Louise, 294
Bogart, Paul, 637
Bomb, Cheever's anxiety about, 260–1
Bonner, Daisey MacAfee, 89
Book-of-the-Month Club, 239–40, 410, 532
Boots Rush (stripper), 51
Borges, Jorge Luis, 526, 586
Boroff, David, 285
Boston, Cheever's promotion of *Falconer* in, 561–2
Boston Globe, 638, 661, 666, 667, 672
Boston Herald, 45, 48
Boston Marathon, 591–2
Boston Post, 156
Boston Tea Party, 8

Boston University (BU), Cheever's
professorship at, 487, 495–510, 581
attempts to make amends after, 517,
528–9
classroom demeanor and, 497, 507
drinking during, 497, 498–9, 501,
505–10, 515
family members' assistance during,
500–1
memories of his miserable youth in
nearby Quincy and, 3, 496
Updike as replacement for, 510, 517
Updike's visit and, 3–4, 507
Bourjaily, Tina, 464
Bourjaily, Vance, 465
Boyd, Willard "Sandy," 478
Boyer, Linda, 270, 271, 309
Boyer, Mimi, 35, 179–80, 190, 211, 230,
280, 298, 450, 458, 571
Boyer, Philip, 35, 179–80, 181–2, 211,
230, 259, 269, 270n, 280, 298, 450,
458, 571, 667
"Boy in Rome," 257–8, 285
Boyle, T. (Tom) Coraghessan, 474, 475,
476, 572, 617n
Boy Scout camp (South Plymouth,
Mass.), 31
"Boy They Cut, The" (B. Cheever),
274–5
Bracher, Frederick, 306–7
Bradford, William, 445
Brandeis University, 669
Brayfield, Doug, 428
Brearley School, 155
Breit, Harvey, 159, 195
Breitburd, Giorgio, 343–4, 345, 346, 456
Brennan, Maeve, 179
Brezhnev, Leonid, 343
Briarcliff Junior College, 311–12, 371,
406, 421, 442
Brigadier and the Golf Widow, The, 314n,
348, 355–6, 435n, 474
"Brigadier and the Golf Widow, The,"
298–301, 355, 365n, 435n
"Brimmer," 435n
Brinnin, John Malcolm, 499
Briscoe, Mary Lavinia, 48
Brodkey, Harold, 321, 357–8, 381, 425n,
541
"Brook, The," 31

"Brooklyn Rooming House," 80n, 81
Brooks, Cleanth, 235
Brooks, Tommy, 218
Brothers Karamazov, The, 679
Brown, Elliot, 508
Brown, Kay, 156
Broyard, Anatole, 413, 448, 551, 552, 652
Buchwald, Emilie, 213n
"Buffalo," 80, 81
Bukovsky, John, 602
Bulfinch, Thomas, 315, 318
Bulgaria:
Cheever's return to (1979), 603–4
International Conference of Writers
in (1977), 562–4
Bullet Park, 257, 407, 410–21, 423, 424n,
521n, 552, 668
advances for, 385, 406, 410
autobiographical elements in, 406,
410, 668
characters and plot of, 414–20
Cheever's assessments of, 421
Cheever's promotional efforts for,
410, 411
ending of, 411, 413, 419–20, 634
excerpts from, published in *The New
Yorker* and *Playboy*, 386, 404–5
Mary's dislike for, 406
reviews of, 411–13, 417, 420–1, 468,
551, 553
sales of, 420
writing of, 357, 384, 404, 405,
413–14, 420
Burt, Struthers, 126, 127, 128
"Bus to St. James's, The," 173, 234
Butcher, Fanny, 240–1
Butler, Thomas (great-uncle), 11, 388,
495–6
By Love Possessed (Cozzens), 254

Cabot, Ned, 377–8, 380
Cairo University, 442
Caldwell, Erskine, 340, 562, 563
Caldwell, Joseph, 223n, 616, 618
Calisher, Hortense, 18, 307, 396, 409n,
475
Camp Croft (Spartanburg, S.C.),
118–20, 121, 125
Camp Gordon (Augusta, Ga.), 121–2,
123, 130

Camus, Albert, 450

Canby, Vincent, 383

Canfield, Cass, 294, 322

Cape and Smith, 83

Capote, Truman, 519, 532

Carr, Jane Cheever (niece). *See* Cheever, Jane

Carr, Sally (grandniece), 49

Carver, Raymond, 200, 345–6

Cassiopeia ("Cassie") (Labrador retriever), 180, 217, 220, 224, 376–7

Catcher in the Rye, The (Salinger), 196, 284n, 341

Cather, Willa, 577

Cavett, Dick, 194, 334, 516, 560, 561, 636, 653, 658

CBS, 144, 665
    Cheever's writing of television pilot for, 193–4
    "The Country Husband" adapted for, 211

Centaur, The (Updike), 315, 347, 348, 349, 362

Century Club (New York City), 175, 299n, 307, 360, 374, 524

Cerf, Bennett, 122, 123, 126, 129, 218, 255, 411

Chabon, Michael, 318

Chagall, Marc, 431

Chaney, Bev, 518, 573, 601, 603

Chase, Mary Ellen, 73–4n

Cheever, Aaron (grandfather), 7, 9–10, 12–13, 254, 468, 495, 608

Cheever, Ann (niece), 88n, 304, 305, 389, 426–7, 532–3

Cheever, Benjamin Hale (great-grandfather), 8–9

Cheever, Benjamin Hale (older son), 8, 21n, 87, 321, 363, 407, 445, 449, 450, 469, 514, 563, 600, 617, 625, 639, 673
    antiwar movement and, 388–9, 428
    birth of, 155
    childhood and adolescence of, 168, 182, 183, 193, 197, 198, 217, 224, 256, 329; Italian sojourn and, 231, 233, 237, 246, 248, 249; psychiatric counseling in, 273; relationship with father in, 272–5, 309–10, 379–80; schooling and, 183, 233, 272, 273, 310, 379
    college education of, 388–9, 427, 428, 430
    father's illness and death and, 628, 630, 639–40, 658, 663
    fathers letters published by, 375n, 667–8, 674
    father's relationship with, 266, 381, 427–32, 501, 521, 646, 667, 674; Ben's defection to his in-laws and, 429–30; Ben's hippie persona and, 428, 430; Ben's placating nature and, 431–2; Ben's requests for money and, 432, 437, 521; in childhood and adolescence, 272–5, 309–10, 379–80; John's attempts at repair of, 591–2, 603–4; John's fear of homosexual tendencies in his son and, 272–5, 604, 667; John's inappropriate social behavior and, 427–9; John's vicarious impulses and, 379–80; John's Yellow Springs visit and, 430–1; lack of physical affection in, 373–4; mutual love of outdoors and, 275, 309; revelations about John's sexual conduct and, 433, 657, 667; sports and, 274–5, 309–10, 379
    girlfriends of, 380, 427, 429
    marathons run by, 589, 591–2, 646
    marriages of: first (Lynda), 380, 427, 429–30, 603, 604; second (Janet), 646
    naming of, 8
    physical appearance of, 379
    psychiatric counseling of, 273, 440, 603, 657
    vision problem diagnosed in, 273
    as writer, 428, 432, 589, 590, 667, 674

Cheever, David (nephew), 88n, 191–2, 263, 305, 503, 510, 517, 532–3

Cheever, Ezekiel (ancestor), 8, 126n

Cheever, Federico ("Fred") (younger son), 7–8, 19, 43, 45, 78, 142, 179, 272, 370, 378, 466, 469, 483, 506, 518, 590, 597, 601, 603, 606, 627, 629, 646, 679
    birth of, 237
    Bullet Park and, 420–1
    childhood and adolescence of, 197, 258, 269, 271, 303, 312, 336, 337, 352, 393, 402, 405, 406, 407,

420–1, 422, 436–8, 440, 441, 450;
Italian sojourn and, 245, 246;
Majorcan sojourn and, 426–7;
overeating in, 437; psychiatric
counseling in, 436–7, 438;
relationship with father in (*see*
Cheever, Federico—father's
relationship with); Russia trip and,
456–7; schooling and, 183, 363,
436, 465, 487, 493, 521, 529
college education of, 524, 529, 537, 546
father's illness and death and, 640,
658, 662, 663
father's relationship with, 237–8,
380–1, 437–8, 456, 459, 492–4,
521, 537, 540, 589, 646–7, 674;
during Boston professorship, 501;
Fred's caretaking role and, 456,
459, 472, 492–3, 494, 674; Fred's
hitting his father and, 437–8
on father's "stream" concept, 332–3
first drinking of, 456, 457
marriage of, 640, 646–7
mother's relationship with, 438, 589
naming of, 237*n*
revelations about father's bisexuality
and, 667
Sing Sing visits and, 450, 451
sports ability lacked by, 380–1
Cheever, Frederick Lincoln (father), 4,
9–13, 19–23, 25, 28, 30, 36, 68, 89,
93, 116, 237*n*, 279, 418
birth and childhood of, 9–10, 11–12
body offered for dissection by, 35
death of, 140–1; burial site and, 222,
662
drinking and odd behavior of, 41–2,
44, 50–1
early manhood of, 12–13
as failure: business losses and, 33, 59;
defeatism and, 41–3; emasculation
by his wife and, 41, 43; John's
sensitivity to, 185
family background of, 7–9, 10–11
fictional characters related to, 525;
Leander Wapshot, 13, 160,
214–15, 216, 245
formal education lacked by, 12, 25
John's comic anecdotes about, 42, 528
John's literary career and, 27, 48, 139
John's novel writing and, 108

John's relationship with, as adult, 7,
60, 95, 108, 138, 139–41
journal or memoir notes of, 11–12,
216, 264
letters to John from, 119–20, 125,
140, 653
living at Hanover farmhouse, 7, 59, 60
marriage of, 16–17, 20, 41, 43, 44, 50,
59, 88, 141
as parent, 19–20, 29, 30, 38*n*, 52, 139;
desire to have John aborted and,
20, 106, 394; John's desire to be
different from, 139, 141, 274
shoe business of, 12–13, 21, 33, 37,
59
Cheever, Frederick Lincoln, Jr.
(brother), 6, 7, 12, 15, 30, 35, 37,
42–3, 56, 57, 60, 61, 69, 71, 74, 87,
108, 114, 189, 221, 237*n*, 316, 320,
394, 509, 581*n*, 601
birth and childhood of, 19–20, 28–9,
265
death and funeral of, 532–4, 653,
662–3
drinking of, 51, 189, 191–2, 262–5,
275, 276, 303–6, 353–4, 389–90,
503–4
fictional characters related to, 20,
203–4, 263–4, 316, 328*n*, 504, 525,
533
Germany trips of, 52, 54–5
John's relationship with, 28–9, 50–1,
52, 55, 61–2, 68, 78, 88, 189–92,
263–5, 275–6, 305–6, 354, 389–90,
501, 503–4, 510, 517, 532–4; John's
financial assistance and, 276, 318,
354, 389, 503; sexual overtones
and, 52, 425*n*
Max as surrogate for, 6, 565
possible homosexual experiences of,
52, 304, 425*n*
reporters' questions and, 330
"The Scarlet Moving Van" and, 264
"The Swimmer" and, 316
transferred to New York and living
near John in Briarcliff Manor,
189–92
wartime activities of, 120
working life of, 51, 263, 275–6, 304,
353–4, 502
writings of, 88, 263, 502–3

Cheever, George Barrell (alleged forebear), 453

Cheever, Iris Gladwin (sister-in-law), 61, 74, 189, 190, 191, 354, 389
  "The Five-Forty-Eight" and, 203–4, 264
  Fred's drinking and, 264, 265, 304, 305, 354

Cheever, Jane (niece) (later Jane Cheever Carr), 88*n*, 138, 189, 190*n*, 191–2, 303, 304–5, 653, 662

Cheever, John:
  accent of, 4, 334, 335, 423, 474, 560, 587
  attractiveness of people important to, 198, 475–6, 602
  awards and honors for: Abraham Lincoln Literary Award, 625; American Book Award, 5, 625; Benjamin Franklin Magazine Award, 211; Edward MacDowell Medal, 610–11; election to National Institute of Arts and Letters, 253; Gold Medal imbroglio and, 577–9; Guggenheim fellowships, 172–3, 276–7; honorary degree from Harvard University, 581, 599, 669; honorary degree from Skidmore, 625; inclusion in *Best American Short Stories*, 152, 164, 211; National Book Award, 254–5, 263, 323, 356, 578; National Book Critics Circle Award, 5, 587; National Medal for Literature, 3, 654–5; O. Henry Awards, 112*n*, 164, 211; Prix de Rome loss and, 223, 224*n*, 225; Pulitzer Prize, 591–2; speeches at ceremonies for, 255, 361, 610–11, 655; William Dean Howells Medal, 323*n*, 359–61, 577
  biography proposal and, 625–6
  birth of, 20
  bisexuality of, 5, 337–8, 351, 466, 467, 512, 553, 622, 626; anxiety about exposure of, 163, 259, 286, 297, 331, 391, 575; appealing aspects of male sex and, 566–7; attempts to tell Ben about, 604, 657; attraction to manly men and, 543–4; Cairo encounter and, 442–3; childhood

experimentation and, 30–1, 274; childhood reading and, 39; Coates's dissertation and, 580–1, 619, 626; concern for social acceptability and, 77, 132; Crane's suicide and, 76–7; drinking motivated by anxiety about, 132, 470; in early years in New York City, 75–6; Ettlinger's revelation of his bisexuality and, 615–17; expressed with Iowa students, 478, 480, 481–2, 488–90; *Falconer* and assumptions about, 550, 560, 619; during final months of his life, 632–3, 642; having sex vs. spending night with a man and, 76, 574; Hollywood sojourn and, 286–7, 289–90, 291, 293; Holmes affair and, 593–5; impotence and, 396; Italian sojourn and, 232, 656; "The Leaves, the Lion-Fish and the Bear" and, 490–2; male prostitutes and, 509, 540, 632; Mary's first inklings of, 162; Maxwell's experiences and writings and, 174–5; mother-in-law's comments and, 142; mother's ambivalence and, 44, 395; near-confessions of, 610–11; New York City apartment and, 611, 618; oral vs. anal intercourse and, 290*n*; posthumous revelations about, 666–7, 668; psychiatric counseling and, 207, 394, 425, 428, 630; relationship with brother and, 52, 304, 534; relationship with former BU student and (*see* Smallwood, Tom); and search for love on college campuses, 540–6 (*see also* Zimmer, Max); *Seinfeld* episode and, 671–2; Signal Corps experiences and, 132, 135–6; Sing Sing inmates and, 452, 460–1, 466; sobriety and, 522–3; Susan's interview with her father and, 550–1; visceral revulsion about, 5, 207; Yaddo visits and, 308, 357–8, 395–6, 397, 398, 409, 478, 526–7
  blurb writing of, 261–2, 384, 397, 438
  cancer and death of, 3, 602, 626–33, 639–47, 651, 652–9; aggressive

treatment, 640–2, 643–4, 652–3; burial site, 662, 677; Cheever's reaction to diagnosis, 629, 640; communication with faraway friends, 644–5, 653–4, 655; friends' farewell visits, 655–6, 658; funeral in Norwell Center, 662–4; initial diagnosis and prognosis, 627–9; memorial service in Ossining, 664–6; National Medal for Literature ceremony, 3, 654–5; obituaries, 661–2; persistence of libido, 632–3, 642; remorse with regard to his children, 657; worsened prognosis, 639–40; writing resumed during last months, 653

childhood and adolescence of, 18–51; cultural upbringing, 25–6; family's affluence, 20–1; family's financial decline in Depression, 33–7, 38; father's lack of closeness, 20, 29, 52; first published story, 46–9; growing up in New England and Quincy in particular, 22, 24–5; last visit to scenes of, 222; misery from, revisited while teaching at BU, 3, 496; mother's lack of tenderness, 27–8; newspaper delivery job, 38; precocity as storyteller, 26–7; psychiatrist's questions about, 394; public manners, 27; pulmonary tuberculosis, 28; reading, 38–41, 45; religious upbringing, 28; schooling, 31–2, 37–8, 45–9; sexual experimentation, 30–1; Thanksgiving celebrations, 23–4; troubled home life, 41–4, 46, 50–1

churchgoing of: regaining of his faith in adulthood, 219–20; religious upbringing, 28

conception of, 20, 106, 219

Coverly as fictional alter ego of, 17, 141n, 162–3, 188, 189n, 245

daily routine of, 92–3, 144, 390, 436, 590

death of. *See* Cheever, John—cancer and death of

dentures of, 407

depression of (*le cafard*), 219n, 311, 363, 370, 390, 392, 402, 423–4, 592, 593; suicidal thoughts and, 101, 154, 165, 187, 518, 573, 629

dogs of, 8, 180–1, 296, 333, 372, 376–7, 380, 597, 600

drinking of, 3–4, 78, 141, 144–5, 166, 191, 198, 258–60, 291, 296, 302–3, 363, 365, 381, 399, 400, 403, 405–6, 410, 411, 420, 425, 426, 441, 449, 458, 459, 464, 466, 467, 491, 608, 667; AA meetings and, 462, 517–19, 539; bloating from, 423–4, 452, 462, 470, 494; Boston professorship and, 497, 498–9, 501, 505–10, 515; brother's example and, 262, 265, 303–6, 504; cancer and, 644, 654; driving under the influence and, 452–3; Federico's caretaking role and, 456, 459, 472, 492–3, 494; furtiveness around family members and, 390, 424, 472; homosexual anxiety as incitement to, 78, 132, 207, 470; hospitalizations necessitated by, 468–71, 494, 505, 510–11; impact on his children of, 270, 673, 674; impotence and, 206, 207, 291, 353; inability to stop, 265, 390–1, 471–2; in Iowa, 477, 479–80, 482, 484, 494; marriage affected by, 259–60, 520; missed during his sobriety, 622–3, 629; near-death experience from, 468–72; "otherness" spells and, 462, 463, 523, 619–20; before public appearances, 332; in Russia, 341, 344, 456, 457; Scarborough social life and, 181–2; start of, 51–2; treatment at Smithers for, 4, 221n, 511–15, 516, 519; in Village hangouts, 115–16; writing hampered by, 445, 462–3; at Yaddo, 66

fame and literary reputation of, 4–5, 222–3, 254–6, 258, 332–5, 586–7, 596–600, 612, 661, 665; admirers' approaches and, 374–6, 596–7, 598–9; book signings and, 561, 597, 602–3; Cheever's attitude about, 330–1, 332; *Falconer* and, 560–2; impact on marriage of, 588–9; *Life* feature and, 410, 516;

Cheever, John (*continued*)
Lutèce gala and, 587; *Newsweek* cover story and, 549–51, 552, 553; owed to stories written early in career, 612–13; public persona and, 108, 332, 333–5, 597, 602, 625; students' correspondence and, 376; *Time* cover story and, 4, 21*n*, 55*n*, 329–32, 333, 356, 359, 366, 368, 550

family background and ancestors of, 7–17, 35–7; "breeding" notion and, 35–6; eccentrics and outcasts in, 36–7; improvised in his storytelling, 36

finances of, 5, 93, 94–5, 146, 149, 154, 155, 157, 165, 176, 186, 193, 215, 225, 302, 408, 420, 524, 589, 596; envy of more prosperous writers and, 145, 165, 173, 223–4, 408; Italian sojourn and, 230, 232; loans to Fred and, 276, 318, 354, 389, 503; Mary's teaching salary and, 311–12; relative wealth of, after *Stories*, 589; repayment of Random House advance and, 216–18; request for raise from *The New Yorker* and, 318–21, 578–9; *Wapshot* movie rights and, 337; writing of second novel and, 276–7; writings motivated by, 257, 258, 276, 277, 285, 524–5, 606–7

flirtations and romances of, 77–8, 89–90, 97, 396–7, 406–7, 427, 433–5, 587, 604; with Iowa student, 479–80, 484–5, 487–8; mentioned to wife and children, 392, 422–3, 433, 493–4, 530, 587; at Yaddo, 399–400, 454–5. *See also* Lange, Hope; Merwin, Dodie; Refregier, Lila; Spencer, Sara; Worthington, Peg

friendships of, 159, 372, 458; literary companionship and, 253–4; profound alienation in his formative years and, 68–9; psychiatrist's characterization as friendless and, 393; in sobriety period, 517, 537–9. *See also specific people*

granddaughter's birth and, 653

illnesses and injuries of: hospitalizations necessitated by his drinking, 468–71, 494, 505, 510–11; knee ligaments torn in skiing injury, 423; prostatitis, 403; pulmonary tuberculosis, 28; seizures, 621–2, 623, 627; urinary problems, 626–7; viral pneumonia, 261, 262. *See also* Cheever, John—cancer and death of

journals of, 678; Cheever family tradition and, 10–11, 290; Cheever's thoughts about fate of, 477, 668–9; earliest surviving pages of, 113; last lines of, 656; literary purposes of, 113; possible rewriting of, 669*n*; publication of, 668–71; references to himself in third person using alter egos in, 220*n*; severe writer's block and, 405; Susan's first encounter with, 666

legacy of, 675–9

marriage of, 101–7, 113–14, 261, 262, 268, 312, 352–3, 397, 407, 425, 437, 441–2, 478, 515, 536, 570, 611, 619; Boston professorship and, 487, 500–1; celebrity and, 333, 588–9; courtship and, 102, 105–7, 113–14; financial responsibility and, 106, 110–11, 113, 165, 282; homosexuality and, 162–3, 207, 440, 580, 672; honeymoon and, 115; impact of drinking on, 182, 259–60, 353, 520; impotence and, 206, 260, 291, 353, 391–2, 484; improved in final years, 624, 633; Iowa teaching stint and, 465, 478, 484, 486; John's consideration of divorce and, 353, 363, 364, 433; John's infidelity and, 422–3, 433; John's relationship with Max and, 548, 606; John's sobriety and, 520–1; John's suspicions about Mary's fidelity and, 329, 353, 364; Mary's consideration of divorce and, 440; Mary's decision never to fight with John again and, 315; Mary's difficult childhood and, 267, 453, 520; Mary's etching studio as sign of gratitude for, 633; Mary's interests outside of marriage and, 206, 311–12, 353, 407; Mary's poem about, 454, 624; Mary's sense of responsibility for caring for potentially great writer and, 152, 440; psychiatric counseling and, 392–5, 439–40, 442; reporters' questions about, 330; resumption of sexual relations and (1970), 441; sleeping separately and, 363, 385, 442; stories related to, 163–4, 312–15, 364–5, 613; tensions in, 133, 269, 353, 358, 363–4, 399, 400, 433, 434, 436, 437, 438–40, 442, 486–7, 581, 589, 608, 613, 666; wedding ceremony and, 114

in military, 117–36, 138, 335; in Asia and Pacific, 135–6; attempts to qualify for Officer Candidate School, 124–5; basic training, 118–20; desk job sought, 120–1; as editor of weekly regimental newspaper, 125; first story collection published during, 122–3, 126–8, 129; as scriptwriter for Army Signal Corps, 129, 131–2, 133, 134, 135; stories based on, 118, 123–4, 126

musical tastes of, 26*n*

naked in less-than-private situations, 3, 66, 409*n*, 459, 492, 498, 501

as parent, 7–8, 27, 43, 130–1, 138, 197–201, 270–5, 308–10, 377–81, 427–8, 437–8, 589–92, 608; aspirations for his children and, 377–8; assessed by his children in their adult years, 666–8, 673–4, 678–9; banter among family members and, 308–9; children's literary ambitions and, 590–1; children's political activism and, 388–9; enjoyment of ritualistic side of family life and, 197, 198; in final days, 657; John's continual presence at home and, 200–1; physical affection and, 27–8, 198, 373–4, 608; sobriety and, 521–2; starting of family and, 125. *See also specific children*

personality and demeanor of: amiable self-absorption, 77–8; blurred sense of identity, 68–9; bon vivant persona, 113; *boulevardier* persona, 107; as conveyed in his journals, 670–1; as conveyed in his letters, 668; cosmopolitan airs, 251; covetousness, 106; desire to identify with group, 69, 70–1; divided nature, 24; drinking's impact on, 259; effects of growing up in New England and Quincy in particular, 24–5; family background and, 15–16, 17; fatalism as member of doomed generation, 70–1, 82; free expression of feelings, 27–8; "Goodbye, My Brother" as exorcism of dour side in, 170–2; impact of upbringing on, 18–19; laughing at odd moments, 4, 513; martyr role and, 303; masculine activities and, 142–3; morbid awareness of other people, 44–5; morbid fears and phobias, 17, 297–8, 388, 391, 403, 425, 601–2; paranoid side, 176, 353; perpetual boyishness, 316; pomposity in later years, 597–8, 603; public persona, 108, 332, 333–5, 597, 602, 625; radical bohemian persona, 51, 69; reluctance to dwell on past, 37, 583–4; shyness in social situations, 51, 332, 517, 596; teachers' reports on, 31–2; traditionalist or conservative phase, 69–70

physical appearance of, 144, 344, 522; public image and, 333; sobriety and, 516

piano lessons taken by, 178

political inclinations of, 85, 92*n*, 388, 562–3; early writings and, 55–6

psychiatrists seen by, 207–8, 392–5, 424–6, 428, 440, 470, 492, 572, 629, 630

scything enjoyed by, 142–3, 303

sexuality of: and belief that stimulation improved his eyesight and concentration, 568; bohemia of Beacon Hill and, 52–4; desire for family and, 77; impotence and, 206, 207, 260, 291, 353, 391–2,

Cheever, John (*continued*)
    396, 422, 484, 572; masturbation
        and, 31, 433, 608, 670; ribald
        anecdotes and, 19; women's
        assessments of, 78, 422; Yaddo
        effect and, 66
    smoking quit by, 592–3, 613
    sobriety of, 516–22; AA and, 517–19;
        boredom of daily life and, 522;
        homosexual urges and, 522–3;
        marital relations and, 520–1;
        obligation to help others and,
        518–19; parental relations and,
        521–2; persistence of "otherness"
        spells in, 523, 619–20; physical
        appearance and energy after, 516;
        urge to mend fences and, 516–17
    sports and, 28–30, 489; baseball, 28–9,
        30, 274–5; bicycling, 516, 538, 602,
        621, 639; relationship with sons
        and, 274–5, 379, 380–1; touch
        football, 145, 183, 373, 410, 478–9
    as storyteller, 18, 26–7, 44; family
        background improvised in, 36;
        going off on tangents and, 151–2,
        315
    travel problematic for, 370, 391
    working people's acceptance enjoyed
        by, 67, 142–3, 219, 600–2
    as writing teacher, 617; at Barnard,
        212–14, 261, 262, 264, 585, 617*n*;
        at Boston University, 495–510 (*see
        also* Boston University, Cheever's
        professorship at); exercises assigned
        by, 210*n*, 474, 497; at Iowa
        Writers' Workshop, 465, 473–85;
        at Sing Sing, 449–52
Cheever, John, writings of:
    arrangements with literary agents for,
        81, 320, 532, 552–3, 596. *See also*
        Donadio, Candida; Lieber, Maxim;
        Nesbit, Lynn
    Coates's dissertation on, 491, 503,
        579–81
    current lack of interest in, 586, 675–6
    first academic study of, 306–7
    first "hack job," 402–3
    journeyman work for newspapers and
        magazines, 60–1, 73–4, 75, 79
    literary influences on, 676; Chekhov,

    111, 112, 167, 584; childhood
        reading and, 38–41; Fielding, 40,
        214; Fitzgerald, 584–5;
        Hemingway, 39–40, 41, 47, 55–6,
        56, 59, 80, 90, 111, 584; Kafka,
        151; O'Hara, 80, 584; "stream"
        concept and, 332–3
    Mrs. Louisa Spingarn as pseudonym
        for, 525, 613
    novels: first unsuccessful attempts at,
        58–9, 61, 82, 83, 86, 87, 88, 90, 91
        (*see also Holly Tree, The; Imposter,
        The*); limitations of literary form
        from Cheever's point of view, 82,
        195, 214, 331, 387, 388. *See also
        Bullet Park; Falconer; Oh What a
        Paradise It Seems; Wapshot Chronicle,
        The; Wapshot Scandal, The*
    playwriting, 277
    plot synopses for M-G-M, 73, 79, 81
    poetry of adolescent years, 31
    in political mode, 55–6, 388
    posthumous publication of
        uncollected work, 672–3
    responses to reviews of, 355–7, 412,
        420–1
    screenplays, 285–6, 288–9, 291
    severe writer's block and, 405, 423–4
    stories: evolving taste of *New Yorker*
        and, 386–7; first published work,
        46–9; with "more size and passion,"
        150–2; short form adopted in,
        80–2; translated into Russian,
        340–1, 345. *See also New Yorker,
        The; specific titles*
    story collections: first (*The Way Some
        People Live*), 122–3, 126–8, 129,
        583, 622*n*, 673; second (*The
        Enormous Radio*), 194–7, 201, 341,
        345; third (*The Housebreaker of
        Shady Hill*), 256–7; fourth (*Some
        People, Places, and Things That Will
        Not Appear in My Next Novel*), 284*n*,
        285, 435*n*; fifth (*The Brigadier and
        the Golf Widow*), 314*n*, 348, 355–6,
        435*n*, 474; sixth (*The World of
        Apples*), 385*n*, 435, 465, 466, 467–8,
        469, 583*n*; seventh (*see Stories of
        John Cheever, The*); *The Uncollected
        Stories of John Cheever*, 672–3

stylistic elements of: absence of plot and conventional narrative, 417–18; drawing together of disparate incidents, 210; episodic structure, 241–2, 490; experimental quality, 4–5, 109, 387, 445–7, 476, 585–6; "predatory women," 313; sexual explicitness and, 385–6, 387–8, 636

for television, 193–4, 277, 575–6, 612, 636–9

for WPA, 94–5, 96–7

writing process and: daily schedule, 92–3, 144, 436, 590; fast pace of work, 81–2; room rented for writing space, 258; unpunctuated, unparagraphed, unrevised draft pages, 500n

Cheever, Lot, 8

Cheever, Lynda (daughter-in-law), 380, 427, 429–32, 469, 603, 604

Cheever, Mary Liley (mother), 3, 16–28, 30, 36, 51, 60, 89, 93, 116, 180, 190n, 303, 359, 503, 514, 601

ambivalent about homosexuality, 44, 395

business ventures of, 139; failures of, 43–4; men of family emasculated by, 41, 43; restaurant, 41, 44; shops, 33–4, 37, 43–4, 138, 188, 189

Christian Science and, 28

death of, 221–2, 533; burial site and, 222, 662

as do-gooder, 15, 16–17, 23, 519

emotional restraint of, 27–8

family background of, 14–16

as grandmother, 189

Honora Wapshot character and, 17, 188, 189n, 215, 222

John's education and, 25–6, 38

John's literary career and, 27, 48

John's psychiatric counseling and, 44, 394

John's relationship with, 27–8, 30–1, 52, 88, 138–9, 188–9, 211, 220–2

John's wife compared to, 44, 392

marriage of, 16–17, 20, 41, 43, 44, 50, 59, 88, 141

pregnancies and childbearing of, 19, 20, 25–6

trained as nurse, 16

Cheever, Mary McNeil (daughter-in-law), 646–7

Cheever, Mary Winternitz (wife), 3, 16, 24, 26n, 31, 37, 40, 44, 96, 102–7, 117, 119, 120, 122, 123, 129, 132–3, 137, 144, 156, 160, 168, 176, 190, 192, 197, 198, 199, 212, 224, 226, 229, 256, 288, 312, 319, 334, 336, 361, 367–8, 373, 374, 381, 382, 383, 402, 423, 458, 466, 472, 504, 538, 561, 563, 564, 565, 568, 598, 629, 639, 666, 669, 674

Bullet Park disliked by, 406

childbearing of: first pregnancy (Susan), 125, 130–1; second pregnancy (Ben), 155; third pregnancy (Federico), 225, 230, 234, 237

childhood and adolescence of, 103–4, 267, 520; father's abusiveness in, 103, 267, 453

courtship and wedding of, 105–7, 113–14; first date, 105; first encounter, 102; honeymoon, 115; wedding ceremony, 114

etching studio built for, 633

family background of, 102–4, 267

father's death and, 269

fictional characters related to, 134–5, 312–15, 364, 570n

as fiction editor for *Westchester Magazine*, 613

inheritance of, 165, 312

John's extramarital flirtations and, 392, 422–3, 433, 587

John's funeral and memorial services and, 664, 665

John's illness and death and, 628, 630–1, 639–40, 641, 642–3, 646–7, 654, 655, 657–8, 659

John's letters to, 108, 109, 110, 118, 121, 123, 124, 127–8, 135, 393

John's Russia trip and, 349, 352

John's treatment for alcoholism and, 511, 514–15

little-girlish speech and youthful looks of, 103

marriage of, 101–7, 113–14, 261, 262, 268, 312, 352–3, 397, 407, 425, 437, 441–2, 478, 515, 536, 570,

Cheever, Mary Winternitz (*continued*)
611, 619; improved in final years,
624, 633; John's Boston
professorship and, 487, 500–1;
John's celebrity and, 333, 588–9;
John's consideration of divorce
and, 353, 363, 364, 433; John's
drinking and, 182, 259–60, 353,
520; John's financial responsibility
and, 106, 110–11, 113; John's
homosexuality and, 162–3, 207,
440, 580, 606, 672; John's
impotence and, 206, 260, 291, 353,
391–2, 484; John's infidelity and,
422–3, 433; John's Iowa teaching
stint and, 465, 478, 484, 486; John's
relationship with Max and, 548,
606; John's sobriety and, 520–1;
John's suspicions about Mary's
fidelity and, 329, 353, 364; Mary's
consideration of divorce and, 440;
Mary's decision never to fight with
John again and, 315; Mary's
difficult childhood and, 267, 453,
520; Mary's etching studio as sign
of gratitude for, 633; Mary's
interests outside of marriage and,
206, 311–12, 353, 407; Mary's
poem about, 454, 624; Mary's sense
of responsibility for caring for
potentially great writer and, 152,
440; psychiatric counseling and,
392–5, 439–40, 442; reporters'
questions about, 330; resumption
of sexual relations and (1970), 441;
sleeping separately and, 363, 385,
442; stories related to, 163–4,
312–15; tensions in, 133, 269, 353,
358, 363–4, 399, 400, 433, 434,
436, 437, 438–40, 442, 486–7, 581,
589, 608, 613, 666
Max's relationship with, 606
move to Ossining and, 281–3
New York City homes of, 105–6, 115,
130, 133–5, 137
poetry writing of, 438, 453–4, 624,
652
publication of husband's uncollected
work and, 672–3
revelations about husband's bisexuality
and, 672

Scarborough home and, 178
Scarborough social life and, 205, 206,
218
Susan's wedding and, 401, 402
as teacher, 154, 311–12, 353, 360, 363,
406, 438, 442, 454, 486–7
vacations of, 328; in Chicago, 358,
359; in Curaçao, 407; in Ireland,
405; Italian sojourn, 230, 231, 233,
234, 237, 246, 247, 248, 251; in
Majorca, 426–7; on Martha's
Vineyard, 168, 169, 170; on
Nantucket, 217, 571; in Russia,
573; in Seoul, 440–1; at Treetops,
337, 393, 453, 459, 471, 494,
520–1, 631; without husband, 439
women's liberation and, 312, 369
Cheever, Sarah (grandmother), 9, 10, 16,
23, 312
Cheever, Sarah (niece), 35, 55*n*, 88*n*,
189, 190, 263, 264*n*, 305, 354
Cheever, Susan Liley (daughter), 4, 14,
19, 35, 103, 104, 220, 306, 319,
321, 363, 389, 412, 423, 438, 441,
459, 469, 492, 493, 505, 520, 531,
533, 534, 538, 563, 587, 597, 600,
605, 666
birth of, 130
boyfriends of, 309, 377–8, 397, 493,
501, 521, 589, 590
childhood and adolescence of, 133,
134, 137, 168, 177, 178, 188, 196,
197–201, 224, 245*n*, 270–2, 303;
grandmother and, 189; Italian
sojourn and, 231, 233, 237, 246–7,
248, 249; psychiatric counseling in,
199; relationship with father in,
155, 198–201, 270–2, 308–9;
schooling and, 138, 155, 183, 199,
233, 251, 270, 271, 272, 307;
summer camp and, 199–200
civil rights movement and, 388, 397
college education of, 309, 361
drinking of, 522, 673
father's bisexuality and, 286, 470,
550–1, 560
father's contract with Knopf and, 635
father's illness and death and, 640,
642, 654, 658, 663
father's journals and, 113, 666, 669
father's relationship with, 246–7,

377–9, 380, 397, 493, 501, 589–91, 673–4; in childhood and adolescence, 155, 198–201, 270–2, 308–9; improved after his sobriety, 521–2; John's occasional efforts to be friends and, 271–2; overeating and attractiveness issues and, 155, 198–9, 270, 271, 272, 308, 309, 378–9; Susan's literary ambitions and, 590–1; Susan's marriage prospects and, 377–9, 397

father's treatment for alcoholism and, 511, 513–14

in Majorca, 426–7

marriages of, 673; first (Cowley), 397, 400–2, 437, 493, 673; second (Tomkins), 590, 645–6; third (Hinckle), 673

Max's relationship with, 607, 642

memoirs written by, 141*n*, 270*n*, 480*n*, 666–7, 673

mother's relationship with, 199, 673, 674

Newsweek cover story on her father and, 549, 550–1

pregnancy of, 642, 645–6, 653

as teacher, 377

twenty-eighth birthday of, 453

Uncle Fred's drinking and, 263, 265

writing career of, 445, 493, 521, 589, 590–1, 596, 673

Cheever, William Hamlet (uncle), 10, 11–12, 20*n*, 29, 30, 35, 241*n*

"Cheever Letters, The" (*Seinfeld* episode), 671–2

Chekhov, Anton, 180, 341, 343, 449
    Cheever compared to, 222, 468, 552, 661
    Cheever's lecture on, 541–2
    as influence on Cheever, 111, 112, 167, 584

Chicago:
    Cheever's vacation in (1965), 358–9
    Modern Language Association meeting in (1965), 367–9
    Playboy writers' gathering in (1971), 455

Chicago Sunday Tribune, 240–1

"Children, The," 187–8

"China Doll, The" (Zimmer), 609–10

China Trade, 8, 9

Christian Scientists, 28, 484

Christmas celebrations, at Cheever's Ossining home, 372–3, 589

Chukovsky, Kornei, 341, 345

Ciardi, John, 223

Civil Rights Act (1964), 337

civil rights movement, 388, 397

Clark, Barrett, 667

Clark, Eleanor (Mrs. Robert Penn Warren), 91–2, 158, 159, 227, 330, 562
    Cheever's Italian sojourn and, 231, 232, 235, 248, 249
    Cheever's letters to, 178, 183, 188, 201, 205, 213, 270

Clarke, Arthur C., 455

Clemons, Walter, 549

Coates, Dennis, 491–2, 494, 503, 505, 509, 531, 538, 565, 579–81, 582, 619, 626

Cocteau, Jean, 26

Cohen, Manny, 135

Collier's, 93, 94, 96

Collinge, Patricia, 193

Collins, Elizabeth ("Lib") Logan, 144, 165, 360

Collins, Loyd ("Pete"), 92, 98, 165

Collins, R. G., 581*n*

Collins, Wilkie, 237, 271

Colorado Rocky Mountain School, 377

Commentary, 254

"Common Day, The," 143, 583*n*

Commonweal, 256–7

Communist Party, 159*n*

Comstock (playboy), 97

Condition humaine, La (Malraux), 70

Congreve, William, 196

Conte Biancamano, 230–1

Cook, Molly, 465–6, 467

Copland, Aaron, 296, 308*n*

Cordelia ("Dilly") (Nantucket babysitter), 217

Corke, Hilary, 323, 325

Cornell University, Cheever's reading at (1976), 540, 541–3

Cosmopolitan, 157

Counterfeiters, The (Gide), 446

"Country Husband, The," 208–11, 217, 222, 234, 256, 269, 300*n*, 403, 586

Coup, The (Updike), 535, 587

Couples (Updike), 388

Cowley, Malcolm, 3, 5, 40, 53, 61, 117, 285, 286, 297, 323, 402, 549, 577, 655
    on Ames's regime at Yaddo, 64, 65
    Blue Juniata by, 47, 83
    Cheever mentored by, 70, 79–80, 81, 82, 127, 186, 201, 214
    Cheever recommended for Guggenheim fellowship by, 172–3
    Cheever's first novel and, 58–9, 109, 186, 214, 241–2
    Cheever's first published story and, 47
    Cheever's letters to, 48, 52, 54, 84, 183–4, 288, 397, 573
    Cheever's relationship with, 72–3, 76
    Cheever's Voice of a Generation potential and, 48, 58, 70–1
    New Republic book reviews assigned by, 73
    as president of National Institute of Arts and Letters, 222–3

Cowley, Muriel, 402

Cowley, Peggy Baird, 58, 76, 297

Cowley, Robert (son-in-law), 79n, 407, 426, 437, 441, 470, 483, 493, 643, 666, 673
    wedding of, 397, 400–2

Coyne, Patrick, 678

Cozzens, James Gould, 254, 355

Craig, Martin, 74

Crane, Hart, 70, 76–7, 291

Cranmer, Thomas, 197, 220, 401

Critique: Studies in Modern Fiction, 307

"Cross-Country Snow" (Hemingway), 59

Croton Aqueduct and Dam, 296, 558–9, 608, 627, 632–3, 653, 655

Crouse, Russel, 193

Culligan, Glendy, 240

Cummings, E. E., 54, 56, 57–8, 69n, 72, 119, 280, 307

Cunard, Victor, 268

Curaçao, Cheever's trip to (1968), 407

"Cure, The," 356–7

Curtis Brown, 320n, 502

Dana, Henry Wadsworth Longfellow, 53–4, 522–3

Dangling Man (Bellow), 227

Davenport, Guy, 413

David (inmate at Sing Sing), 451

David, Larry, 672

Davis, Miles, 383

Davis, Stuart, 91

Day, Clarence, 193–4

"Day the Pig Fell into the Well, The," 166–8, 172, 194n, 234, 584

Death of Bessie Smith (Albee), 340

"Death of Justina, The," 277–9, 284n, 285, 299, 327, 365, 435n, 464–5, 466, 572, 586, 637

De Feo, Ronald, 467

Deland, Margaret, 14–15, 25, 139

DeLay, Dorothy, 117n, 154

Delmore (cat, formerly called Blackie), 294–5

DeMott, Benjamin, 412–13, 417, 420–1

Denney, Randall, 133–4

Denney, Reuel, 70, 80, 228
    on Cheever's bisexuality, 77
    Cheever's letters to, 68–9, 71, 72, 81, 82, 85, 88, 93, 98, 101, 105, 601
    impact on Cheever of, 68
    town house shared by Cheever and, 133–4, 137

Denney, Ruth, 133–4, 137

Dennis, Rodney, 669

Depression, Great, 33–7, 65, 68, 70, 71, 79, 81, 241
    Federal Writers' Project in, 94–5, 96–7

de Veer, Robert, 515

Devereaux, Sir Percy, 14

Devereux, Sir Joseph, 14n

Dial, The, 639

Diamond, David, 308

Dick Cavett Show, The, 194, 334, 516, 560, 561, 636, 653, 658

Dickens, Charles, 25, 41, 271

Didion, Joan, 323, 552

Din, Ronald Aung, 233

Dirks, John, 370–1, 461, 473

Dirks, Mary, 371, 459, 473, 537–8, 602

Doctorow, E. L., 543

Donadio, Candida, 320, 366, 405, 406, 500, 524, 531, 532, 552–3

Doner, Dean, 508

Donleavy, J. P., 482–3

Doria, Principessa, 232, 238

Dos Passos, John, 57, 72

Dostoevski, Feodor, 456, 552, 623

Double Deucer, 125
Douglas, Sharman, 393, 396
Douglass, Jean, 246–7
Dreiser, Theodore, 368
DuBois, William, 127, 196–7
Dudley, Dorothy, 92, 116
Durham, Sergeant, 118–19, 120, 121, 123, 124

Eddy, Mary Baker, 28
Edgar (golden retriever), 600, 626, 629, 632, 642, 644, 661
"Educated American Woman, An," 312–14
Education of Henry Adams, The (Adams), 24, 69–70
Edward MacDowell Medal, 610–11
Edwards, Thomas R., 467
Eggers, Dave, 676, 678
Egypt, Cheever's trip to (1970), 442–3, 483
Ehrlich, Leonard, 66–7, 70, 92, 105, 158
Ehrlichman, John, 502
"Eight-Mile Bike Ride, The" (Schultz), 538
Elaine ("Miss Moody") (Iowa student), 479–80, 484–5, 486, 487–8, 493–4
Eliot, George, 41, 135, 174
Eliot, Justine, 200
Eliot, T. S., 56
Elkin, Stanley, 475
Ellen (sister of Ben's friend), 428
Ellison, Ralph, 235–6, 280, 359–60, 361, 367, 368, 441, 576*n*
Emergency Peace Campaign, 104
Engle, Paul, 212
Enormous Radio, The, 194–7, 201, 583
    Russian translation of, 341, 345
"Enormous Radio, The," 151–2, 194, 586
Ernesta (caretaker at La Rocca), 249
Esquire, 176, 258, 279, 320, 385, 393, 435, 444–5, 491, 532
    symposium in San Francisco sponsored by (1960), 283–5
Ettlinger, Don, 131, 143–4, 145, 147, 154, 157, 517, 589–90, 629, 658, 665–6
    bisexuality of, 615–17
Ettlinger, Katrina Wallingford, 143–4, 145, 147, 615–16, 665–6

Evans, Walker, 57, 71, 75–6, 78, 79, 81, 84–5, 87, 91, 425*n*
"Events of That Easter, The," 276
Evergreen, The, 31, 32
Exley, Frederick, 375–6, 390, 457, 463–5, 499*n*, 523, 619, 666
    Rosenthal Award won by, 463–4
"Expelled from Prep School," 46–9, 271
Ezekiel (Labrador retriever), 8

Fadiman, Clifton, 255
Falconer, 46, 117, 490, 491*n*, 525, 536, 537, 543, 549–58, 563, 570, 583, 625, 652, 676
    advance for, 471, 524
    autobiographical aspects of, 8, 20, 42*n*, 176*n*, 262, 332, 525, 549, 550, 560*n*, 570*n*
    characters and plot of, 553–8
    Cheever's promotional efforts on behalf of, 560–2
    firing of literary agent and, 532, 552–3
    homosexuality in, 5–6, 290*n*, 537, 549–50, 553, 560, 566, 616, 619
    movie option for, 524, 532
    narrative experiments in "The Jewels of the Cabots" and, 447, 448
    Newsweek cover story and, 549–51, 552, 553
    reactions to manuscript of, 531–2
    reviews of, 549, 551–2, 553, 560*n*
    sales of, 552, 553
    Sing Sing experiences and, 449, 450, 452
    writing of, 3, 4, 462–3, 471, 500, 524, 526, 529, 530–1
"Fall River," 55–6, 673
Fan's Notes, A (Exley), 376, 463
Farewell to Arms, A (Hemingway), 55
Farquharson, Sherry, 359
Farrell, Dorothy, 93
Farrell, James, 70
Fast, Betty, 144
Faulkner, William, 40, 577, 586
FBI, 158–9, 352
Federal Art Project, 297
Federal Writers' Project (FWP), 94–5, 96–7
Feld, Rose, 126–7
Felici, Iole, 234, 238, 245, 249, 250, 251, 258, 269, 312, 390, 402, 494, 646

"Fern Hill" (Thomas), 213
Fiedler, Leslie, 306, 315
Field, Brada, 73
Field, Leonard, 131, 165, 168, 268
Fielding, Henry, 40, 214, 242
Filler, Louis, 431
Fine Arts Work Center (Provincetown, Mass.), 465–7
First Love and Other Sorrows (Brodkey), 357
Fish, Melissa, 541
Fitts, Dudley, 438
Fitzgerald, F. Scott, 40, 95, 128, 195, 203, 341–2n, 586, 664
    Cheever's identification with, 334–5, 390
    literary influence on Cheever of, 584–5
"Five-Forty-Eight, The," 203–5, 211, 256, 263–4, 482n, 612
Flato, Charles, 57
Flaubert, Gustave, 39, 474, 668
Florrie (Martha's Vineyard neighbor), 169, 170
Folded Leaf, The (Maxwell), 173–4
"Folding-Chair Set, The," 524–6
Ford, Glenn, 336
Forster, E. M., 313
Fort Dix, 118, 129
"Fourth Alarm, The," 435, 467
France:
    Cheever's avoidance of, 104
    Cheever's trip to (1931), 55
Frankfurt, PEN conference in (1959), 267–8
Franny and Zooey (Salinger), 300
French language, Cheever's everyday speech sprinkled with, 446, 597–8
"Frère Jacques," 90–1, 340n, 673
Freud, Sigmund, 44, 174, 272, 315, 623
Frey, Martha, 639
Friday Club, 370–1, 433, 434–5, 483–4, 491, 517, 526, 595, 599–600, 667
"Friends from Philadelphia" (Updike), 262
Fuchs, Daniel, 92, 93, 233, 234, 288, 290
Fuchs, Sue, 93
"fuck," use of word, 239–40, 387
Fuller, Alvan T., 46
Fullerton, Mabelle, 108, 156

Funaroff, Sol, 72
Funk & Wagnalls, 194

Gaddis, William, 387
Galbraith, John Kenneth, 455
Galsworthy, John, 45, 48, 49n
Ganz, Rudolph, 25
Garbarino, Steve, 383n
Gardner, John, 414, 421, 551, 555, 585, 676n
Garrett, George, 325
Garrison, William Lloyd, 11, 495
Geismar, Maxwell, 240
Gemmel, Harriet, 45, 48–9
"Geometry of Love, The," 364–6, 488, 586
Germany, 86, 97–8, 312, 351
    Cheever brothers' trips to (1930s), 52, 54–5
    Cheever's sojourn in (1959), 267–8
Ghosts (Ibsen), 7
Ghost Writer, The (Roth), 588
Gibbs, Wolcott, 87, 91, 173
Gide, André, 446, 591
Gill, Brendan, 319, 365n
Gilman, Coburn ("Coby"), 116
Gilman, Richard, 256–7
Ginger Man, The (Donleavy), 482
Gioia, Dana, 334, 529, 530, 629–30
Gladwin, Iris. *See* Cheever, Iris Gladwin
Glazer, Nathan, 68
Glazer, Tom, 370–1, 458, 473, 517, 526, 600, 606
Glover, Curtis, 48
Glueck, Bernard, 207–8
Gody, Lou, 96
Goff, Ivan, 288
Gold, Ivan, 496, 510
Goldwyn, Sam, 165, 224
Gollancz, Victor, 194
"Goodbye, Broadway—Hello, Hello," 118, 126
Goodbye, Columbus (Roth), 283
"Goodbye, My Brother," 19, 27, 40, 170–2, 173, 194, 214
Goodman, Benny, 280
Gordon, Mary, 587, 670
Gordon, Max, 155, 156, 157
"Gorgon," 454, 624

Gospel According to St. Luke's, The
  (Stevenson), 73*n*
Gottlieb, Robert, 408, 450, 587, 662*n*,
  669–70
  Bullet Park and, 410, 411, 420
  Falconer and, 471, 531, 553, 561
  The Journals of John Cheever and,
    669–70
  Oh What a Paradise It Seems and, 634–5
  The Stories of John Cheever and, 150*n*,
    385*n*, 448*n*, 583, 584, 635
Gould, Joe, 73
Grant, Cary, 334
Grass, Günter, 563
Graves, Robert, 297, 426, 427
Gravity's Rainbow (Pynchon), 497
Gray, Paul, 585
Great Boston Fire (1872), 9–10
Great Green, The (Kentfield), 291
Great Performances, 612
Greene, Graham, 407
Greenstein, Milton, 282
Grimes, Tammy, 636
Grizzard, George, 637
Grunwald, Henry, 329
Guggenheim fellowships, 172–3, 186,
  276–7, 503
Gugler, Eric, 281*n*, 333
Guinzburg, Tom, 577
Gurganus, Allan, 52, 82, 334, 477, 486,
  487, 496, 523, 543, 546, 576
  Cheever's disdain for supposed
    effeminacy of, 480, 481–2, 489,
    490, 567
  at Cheever's funeral, 662, 664
  Cheever's last visit with, 655
  Cheever's letters to, 54, 533–4, 542*n*
  Cheever's literary patronage of, 488,
    489, 567
  Cheever's sexual advances rejected by,
    480–1, 485, 488–90, 526–7, 567
  as Cheever's student, 474, 475, 476,
    480–1, 617*n*
  at Yaddo, 66, 67, 526–7
Gurney, A. R., 612

"Habit, The," 592*n*
Haggard, Edith, 320*n*
Halasz, Piri, 213*n*
Halpern, Daniel, 572–3

Hamlet (Shakespeare), 325–6*n*
Hamlisch, Marvin, 383
Hanover, Mass., Cheever family's
  farmhouse in, 7, 41, 44, 59, 60,
  65–6, 82, 109
Hansen, Ron, 473–4, 475, 478–9, 483,
  617*n*
"Happiest Days, The," 99, 102, 112
Harding, Warren G., 205*n*
Hardwick, Elizabeth, 159, 610
Harnack, Curtis, 307, 547
Harold Currier, 9
Harout (Hochman's boyfriend), 439
Harper & Brothers (later Harper &
  Row), 670, 676
  ending of Cheever's association with,
    408
  The Wapshot Chronicle and, 217–18,
    225, 226–7, 239–40
  The Wapshot Scandal and, 276, 277,
    322*n*, 408
Harper's, 157*n*, 412, 445, 551–2
Harper's Bazaar, 111, 112*n*
Hart, Bernard, 155
Harvard *Advocate*, 528
Harvard University, 45, 46*n*, 73, 118, 354
  Cheever's honorary degree from, 581,
    599, 669
  Cheever's journals and, 669
  Cheever's readings at, 485, 528, 529
Hassan, Ihab, 306, 315
Hawthorne, Hazel (Mrs. Morris
  Werner), 56–7, 72, 77, 91, 106,
  119, 166, 466, 467
Hawthorne, Nathaniel, 25, 57, 279
Hays, David C., 392–5, 425, 572*n*
Hazzard, Shirley, 174, 235, 255, 321,
  365*n*, 513, 644
Hefner, Hugh, 455
Heller, Joseph, 500, 676*n*
Hellman, Geoffrey, 179
Hellman, Lillian, 374
Hemingway, Ernest, 45, 86, 87, 311,
  342*n*, 356, 451, 483, 586, 622
  Cheever's writings influenced by or
    reminiscent of, 39–40, 41, 47,
    55–6, 56, 59, 80, 90, 111, 584
Hennedy, Hugh, 49*n*
Henry, Richie, 273–4
Hepburn, Katharine, 337*n*

Herbst, Josephine ("Josie"), 86–7, 91,
    126, 158, 159, 159*n*, 179, 401
  Cheever's family visited by, 86–7,
    294–5
  Cheever's financial assistance to, 224*n*,
    294, 295
  Cheever's letters to, 37, 90, 92*n*, 107,
    110, 117, 122, 130, 143, 145, 146,
    154, 166, 168, 183, 184, 186, 193,
    197, 212, 219, 223, 231, 269, 277
  Cheevers' visits to Erwinna home of,
    86, 115, 137, 187
Hermann, John, 159*n*
Herrmann, Edward, 612
Hersey, John, 21, 26*n*, 141*n*, 516, 565,
    664
Herzog (Bellow), 359, 360
Hewling, Betty, 76
Hicks, Granville, 241
Hills, Rust, 283
"Hills Like White Elephants"
    (Hemingway), 90
Hinckle, Warren, 330*n*, 493, 501, 521,
    589, 590, 673
Hiss, Alger, 158
"His Young Wife," 93, 673
Hitler, Adolf, 54, 86, 375
Hochman, Sandra, 438–9
Holly Tree, The, 140*n*
  Cheever's contract with Random
    House and, 146–7, 186–7
  started over and retitled, 185–6. *See
    also Imposter, The*
  writing of, 107–10, 146–9, 160–1,
    166, 169, 172
Hollywood, Cheever's screenwriting job
    in, 285–90
Holm, Celeste, 637
Holmes, Jim, 593–5
"Homage to Shakespeare," 10
Home Before Dark (S. Cheever), 141*n*,
    480*n*, 666–7, 673
homosexuality, 26*n*, 207–8, 283–4
  Aesthetic Realism movement and, 560
  bohemia of Beacon Hill and, 52–4
  first story in *New Yorker* about, 488
  Freudian theory and, 44, 272, 315
  legal sanctions against, 207, 286
  prison life and, 452, 462, 466
  references in Cheever's work to,
    490–2, 560*n*; in *Bullet Park*,

    414–15; in *Falconer*, 5–6, 290*n*, 550,
      553, 560, 566, 616, 619; in *Oh
      What a Paradise It Seems*, 619,
      649–51; in *The Wapshot Chronicle*,
      243
    see also Cheever, John—bisexuality of
Horne, Bob, 381
Horney, Karen, 207
Hotel Earle (New York City), 205
Houghton Library (Harvard College),
    669
Hound & Horn, 56
Housebreaker of Shady Hill, The, 256–7
"Housebreaker of Shady Hill, The,"
    224
Howe, Irving, 356, 638
Huber, Jack, 176
Hudson Review, The, 307
Humboldt, Alexander von, 576
Humboldt's Gift (Bellow), 530, 550*n*,
    576
Hunt, George, 626
Hurt, Mary Beth, 612
Hyla, Lee, 620, 621
Hyman, Stanley Edgar, 323–4

Ibsen, Henrik, 7
"I'm Going to Asia," 112, 340*n*
Imposter, The, 185–7, 194, 214
"Independence Day at St. Botolph's,"
    215–16
Ingersoll, Ralph, 182
"In Passing," 85–6
In Search of Lost Time (Proust), 39,
    396
International Conference of Writers
    (Sofia, Bulgaria; 1977), 562–4
International PEN Congress (Seoul,
    1970), 440–1
Invisible Man (Ellison), 236
"Invisible Ship, The," 124, 673
Iowa Writers' Workshop, 19, 200, 212,
    487–8, 496, 497, 571–2
  Cheever's first visit to (1972), 463,
    464–5
  Cheever's teaching stint at (1973),
    465, 470, 473–85, 486; drills and
    homework assignments in, 474,
    497; drinking during, 477, 479–80,
    482, 484; expressions of his
    homosexuality with students in,

478, 480–1, 481–2, 488–90; fun
  had by Cheever during, 478–82;
  judgments about students' work
  and, 475–6; most constant female
  companion during, 479–80, 484–5
Ireland, Cheever's trip to (1968), 405
Irving, John, 473, 482–3, 585, 587, 588
Irwin, Sarah, 478–9
"Island, The," 626
Italian language, Cheever's attempts at
  learning and speaking, 234–5, 402
Italy:
  Cheever's first sojourn in
    (1956–1957), 225, 230–50, 251,
    355, 656; only story written during,
    247–8; and rental of La Rocca in
    Porto Ercole, 248–9; Venice trip
    and, 245–6. *See also* Rome
  Cheever's returns to: in 1959, 267, 268;
    in 1964, 328, 337, 355; in 1967, 402
Ivory, James, 612

"Jacket, The" (*Seinfeld* episode), 671–2
James, Henry, 57, 63
Janeway, Elizabeth, 322–3, 498
Janeway, Michael, 498–9, 529
Jarrell, Randall, 118*n*, 255, 546
"Jewels of the Cabots, The," 445–8, 467
Jewett, Frank, 470, 492
Joffe, Eugene, 89, 90, 110
"John Cheever and Comedy" (Bracher),
  307
John Cheever and Family (BBC
  documentary), 499*n*, 668, 672, 673
Johns, Richard, 56
Johns Hopkins, 102, 605
Johnson, Elizabeth Ann McMurray, 255
Johnson, Lady Bird, 362
Johnson, Lyndon B., 361, 362
Johnson, Robert, 508
Josephson, Hannah, 223
"Journal of an Old Gent," 216, 264
Journals of John Cheever, The, 668–71
Jowett, Benjamin, 197
Joyce, James, 45
JR (Gaddis), 387
"Just Tell Me Who It Was," 206

Kafka, Franz, 151
Kahn, E. J. ("Jack"), Jr., 176, 179, 182,
  183, 219, 252, 253, 280

Kahn, Joey, 183
Kahn, Virginia ("Ginny"), 182, 280, 523,
  619
Kakutani, Michiko, 661
Kandle, George, 449, 451
Kanin, Garson, 561
Kaplan, James, 334, 598–9
Kaplan, Justin, 667
Kaufman, George S., 155, 156–7
Kaven, Frederica, 542–3
Kay (Mutter's nurse), 602
Kazin, Alfred, 159, 298, 637
Kees, Weldon, 127
Kelly, James, 195
Kennedy, John F., 373, 375
Kentfield, Calvin, 289–90, 291–2, 293,
  297, 357, 425*n*
KGB, 341, 343
Khrushchev, Nikita, 343–4, 444
Kirsch, Robert, 325
Kirstein, Lincoln, 53, 56, 57, 75, 522
Kitman, Carol, 513
Knickerbocker Mortgage Company and
  Bank, 282
Knopf, 261–2, 426, 548, 587, 670
  Bullet Park and, 410, 411, 420
  Cheever's two-book contract with,
    408, 634–5
  Falconer and, 550, 552, 553
  The Journals of John Cheever and,
    669–70
  Oh What a Paradise It Seems and, 596,
    623, 634–5, 652
  The Stories of John Cheever and, 583,
    587, 635
  see also Gottlieb, Robert
Knowles, John, 297
Knowlton, Perry, 502, 503
Koerner, Henry, 329
Kopkind, Andrew, 330, 331
Koren, Edward, 453
Kornbluth, Jesse, 577–9
Kornilov, Vladimir, 562
Kreuger and Toll International Match,
  59
Kronenberger, Louis, 360
Kunitz, Stanley, 465, 466
Kurtz, Irma, 213*n*

Lanahan, Scottie and Jack, 341–2*n*
Lancaster, Burt, 381, 382, 393

Landgard, Janet, 382, 393
Lang, Donald, 451, 452, 459–61, 491,
    522, 531, 606
Lange, David, 336, 519, 653–4
Lange, Hope, 338*n*, 393, 425, 433, 455,
    518–19, 546, 560, 589
  Cheever's first meeting with, 335–6
  Cheever's holding forth about his
    flirtation with, 351, 366, 434–5,
    492, 530, 548, 572*n*; in Mary's
    presence, 422–3
  Cheever's relationship with, 422, 423,
    434–5, 530, 569–70, 582, 593,
    618–19
  Cheever's television project and, 576,
    636–7
La Rocca (Porto Ercole, Italy), Cheever's
    stay at (1957), 248–9
"Late Gathering," 56, 673
Later Diaries, The (Rorem), 396
Laurents, Arthur, 132, 133, 174, 615–16
Lawrence, D. H., 285, 288
League of Women Voters, 206, 314*n*
"Leaves, the Lion-Fish and the Bear,
    The," 490–2, 524
Lee, Alwyn, 55*n*, 328–9, 331–2, 333, 337,
    370–1, 550
Lee, Essie, 337–8, 364, 658
Lee, Peggy, 289, 290
*Left: A Quarterly Review of Radical and
    Experimental Art, The*, 56
Leggett, Jack, 465, 470, 477, 482, 484
Lehmann-Haupt, Christopher, 373–4,
    411–12, 420–1, 437, 468, 538, 551,
    552, 553, 598
Leonard, John, 413, 418, 551–2, 553,
    585, 611, 618, 651–2
"Letter from the Mountains," 70–1
Letters of John Cheever, The, 349, 375*n*,
    469, 499*n*, 657, 667–8, 670
Lewis, Flannery, 110, 116, 228
Lewis, Henry, 224, 285, 288
Lewton, Mrs., 73, 74, 75
Lieber, Maxim, 81, 86, 102, 123, 320
Liebling, A. J., 222
Life, 300, 301, 318, 353
  feature on Cheever in, 410, 516
Life with Father (Day), 193–4, 576
Life with Mother (Day), 193–4
Liley, Anne (aunt). *See* Armstrong, Anne
    Liley

Liley, Florence ("Liley") (aunt), 15–16,
    25, 37, 190*n*, 404
Liley, Mary Devereaux (mother). *See*
    Cheever, Mary Liley
Liley, Sarah (grandmother), 14–15, 16,
    312
Liley, William (grandfather), 14
Lindley, Frances, 73, 90, 92, 322*n*, 408,
    426, 596
Lindsay, Howard, 193
Linscott, Robert, 154, 168, 194
  Cheever's first novel and, 146–7,
    148–9, 160–1, 169, 185, 186–7,
    214, 216–17, 222, 225, 226, 227
Lish, Gordon, 491, 532
Little Shop Around the Corner (Quincy,
    Mass.), 34
Litvinov, Maxim, 340*n*
Litvinov, Tanya, 142, 314*n*, 343, 348,
    349*n*, 372, 457, 573, 599, 623
  boycott of writers' conference in
    Bulgaria and, 562, 563
  Cheever's bisexuality and, 39*n*
  Cheever's correspondence with, 180,
    181, 346, 351, 352, 357, 362, 377,
    380, 383, 385, 387, 394, 399, 402,
    403, 418, 421, 429, 530–1, 532,
    562, 563, 668
  Cheever's relationship with, 345–7
  Cheever's stories translated into
    Russian by, 314*n*, 340–1, 344
  Spear's and Maxwell's friendships
    with, 346–7, 623
Litvinov, Vera, 346
Lobrano, Gustave ("Gus"), 116, 119,
    123, 125, 153, 154, 168, 173, 175,
    196
Lodge, Henry Cabot, 561
Lolita (Nabokov), 269
London *Times*, 413, 662*n*, 672
Lonely Crowd, The (Riesman, Glazer, and
    Denney), 68
Long Madness, A (Barolini), 384
"Long Time Married, A" (earlier title of
    "Gorgon"), 454
Looking for Work (S. Cheever), 591,
    596
Loomis School, 310, 379
Loren, Sophia, 402–3, 669*n*
Los Angeles Times, 325
Lost Girl, The (Lawrence), 285

"Love and Painting" (Kaplan), 599
Lovett, Sidney, 114
Lowell, Robert, 158–9, 160, 654*n*
Lowry, Malcolm, 291
Lucid, Robert, 367–8
Luckinbill, Laurence, 612
Luers, Bill, 342
Lurie, Frieda, 352, 456, 573
Lutèce (New York City), gala dinner for
    Cheever at (1978), 587

MacArthur, Douglas, 158
MacClure, Lavena, 178
Macdonald, Dwight, 254
Macedonia, Cheever's trip to (1977),
    564–5
Machiavelli, Niccolò, 38, 450
Madame Bovary (Flaubert), 39, 679
magical realism, 213, 585
Magician's Own Handbook, The, 13
Mailer, Norman, 367, 368–9, 387, 388,
    576*n*
Maine, Cheever's vacation in (1956), 225,
    226
Maisel, Edward, 159
Maisie (retriever), 655, 666
Majorca, Cheever's trip to (1969), 426–7,
    532–3
Malamud, Ann, 541
Malamud, Bernard, 4, 255, 541, 549,
    568, 676*n*
Malraux, André, 70
Malsin, Art, 298, 337
Mangione, Jerre, 94, 334
Mankiewicz, Herman, 155
Manning, Robert, 499, 528–9
Mano, D. Keith, 468
Mansfield, Katherine, 112
Man Who Loved Children, The (Stead),
    373
Man Who Rented Garter Snakes, The, 436
"Man Who Was Very Homesick for
    New York, The," 123, 126*n*
Marilyn (Zimmer's wife), 566, 569, 605
"Marito in Città," 338
Marquand, John P., 355, 597
Marry Me (Updike), 535
Martha (Mary's student), 406–7
Martha's Vineyard, Cheever's sojourn on
    (1950), 165, 168–9, 173
    story derived from, 169–72

Mary Cheever Gift Shoppe (Quincy,
    Mass.), 33–4
Marymount International (Rome), 233
Maslin, Janet, 646, 657, 664
Masters School (Dobbs Ferry, N.Y.),
    251, 270, 271, 272, 307
Mather, Cotton, 8
Maupassant, Guy de, 474
Mavor, Geraldine, 99
Maxwell, Emily Noyes, 174
Maxwell, Ruth, 513, 515
Maxwell, William, 98–100, 153, 173–5,
    176, 189*n*, 261, 282, 289, 291, 316,
    357, 381, 508*n*, 623, 668
    as author, 98–9, 100, 173–4, 233, 234,
        366
    Bullet Park and, 386, 404
    Cheever's personal correspondence
        with, 142, 199–200, 232, 262, 267,
        287–8, 301, 356*n*, 388, 402–3, 423,
        514
    on Cheever's public image, 334
    Cheever's relationship with, 98,
        99–100, 173, 175, 279, 299–301,
        365–7, 386, 458, 577–9, 582, 599,
        645
    Cheever's stories and, 95, 98, 99, 123,
        167, 173, 205, 208, 248, 258, 277,
        279, 315, 365–6, 386, 406, 435,
        446, 448, 609
    elected to National Institute of Arts
        and Letters, 253–4
    Falconer and, 526, 551
    Gold Medal imbroglio and, 577–9
    Gurganus's story and, 488
    Litvinov's friendship with, 346–7
    National Book Award and, 254, 255,
        578
    payment of fiction writers and, 99,
        319–20, 321
    personality and demeanor of, 174–5,
        229, 319
    retirement of, 525
    Telephone Story and, 578–9
    The Wapshot Chronicle and, 188, 189*n*,
        215, 216, 225–6
    The Wapshot Scandal and, 310, 311,
        324
McCall's, 433, 436
McCarthy, Joseph, 188
McCarthy, Kevin, 636

McCarthy, Mary, 577
McConkey, James, 541
McCullers, Carson, 81, 527
McDonough (shell-shocked veteran in
    Hanover), 59, 60
McGinley, Phyllis, 463
McGrath, Charles ("Chip"), 525–6,
    531–2, 547, 568, 610, 626, 665
McGraw, Jim, 97
McKelway, St. Clair, 179, 193, 270n
McLaughlin, Robert, 149, 150
McLoone, George, 376, 671
McManus, John, 133, 134
McManus, Peggy, 133–4
McNally, Terence, 612
McNeil, Mary, 646–7
McPherson, William, 585
"Meeting Cheever" (Ryan), 476–7
"Melancholy of Distance, The," 541–2
Merwin, Dodie, 77–8, 84, 89, 90, 93, 95,
    96, 130–1, 151, 315
"Metamorphoses," 315
Meyer, Melissa, 527
M-G-M, 73, 79, 81, 129, 224, 230
Miller, Arthur, 563
Millin, Sarah Gertrude, 73, 74
Mills, Ted, 133
Minerva (Labrador retriever), 180
"Mink Decade, The," 154
"Minor Heroism" (Gurganus), 488, 489,
    500, 567
"Miscellany of Characters That Will Not
    Appear, A," 284n, 630n
Mitford, Nancy, 268
Mitgang, Herbert, 256, 599
Mizener, Arthur, 195–6, 222
Modern Language Association (MLA),
    meeting of (Chicago, 1965), 367–9
Modern Library's 100 Best Novels list,
    676
Moe, Henry Allen, 276
"Montraldo," 315
Moody, Rick, 241, 676
Moor, Paul, 351
Moore, Marianne, 56, 362, 654n
Moorehead, Alan, 328, 337
Moorehead, Lucy, 328, 337
Morace, Robert, 676
Moravia, Alberto, 455
Morehouse, Marion, 58

Morgan Museum, 666
Morgenstern, Joseph, 383
Morris, Wright, 530, 576n
Morrow, Margot, 176, 233
Mosel, Tad, 336n
Motherwell, Robert, 105
Moveable Feast, A (Hemingway), 40, 342n
"Mrs. Wapshot," 215
Mulligan, Robert, 335, 337n
Mumford, Lewis, 360–1
Murphy, Michael, 612
Murray, Albert, 360
Murray, Henry A., 498
Museum of Modern Art, 71, 84, 92
Mutter, Ray, 363, 403, 468, 470, 472,
    491, 494, 621–2, 628, 639, 640
"My Daughter, The Novelist," 591
My Father and Myself (Ackerley), 480n
mythography, 315

Nabokov, Vladimir, 99, 149, 211, 269,
    322–3, 599, 654n
Naked and the Dead, The (Mailer), 367
Nantucket, Cheever's vacations on,
    217–18, 253–4, 571
Nash, Ogden, 362
Nation, 91
National Arts Club, 576
National Book Award, 295, 347
    for *The Wapshot Chronicle*, 254–5, 263,
    323, 356, 578
National Book Critics Circle Award, 5,
    587
National Institute of Arts and Letters,
    223, 224n, 235, 253–4, 283, 294,
    295, 297, 323, 347
National Medal for Literature, 3, 654–5
"National Pastime, The," 29, 214–15,
    234, 583n
National Review, 323, 413, 467
National Socialism, 52, 54
Need for Chocolate, The (M. Cheever),
    453, 624, 652
Nemerov, Howard, 53
Nesbit, Lynn, 320n, 596, 635
Newberry, Mrs. (Scarborough heiress),
    184
Newbury North School, 9
Newhouse, Dorothy, 154, 311
Newhouse, Edward, 116–17, 124–5, 153,

165*n*, 173, 223–4, 366, 501, 517, 537, 579, 623

New Leader, 323–4

New Masses, 72

New Republic, The, 51, 54, 58, 71, 72, 80, 111, 585, 655, 670–1
Cheever's book reviews for, 73
Cheever's first published work in, 46–9, 61
Cheever's writings reviewed in, 195–6, 323, 413

Newsweek, 355, 383, 539, 583, 638
cover story on Cheever in, 4, 549–51, 553
Susan's job with, 493, 521, 589, 590

New York, 591

New York City:
Cheever's early years in, 71–86, 91–2, 99–117, 122–3, 130–76; apartments and living arrangements, 71, 79, 105–6, 110, 115, 130, 133–5, 137–8, 175, 176; departure for suburbs, 175–6; drinking during, 115–16
Cheever's solitary stays in, during Westchester years, 205, 611, 618

New York City Guide, The, 96–7

New Yorker, The, 35, 87, 95, 116–17, 119, 139, 145, 179, 183, 212, 213, 248, 267, 289, 291, 346, 348, 351, 357, 358, 405, 463, 490, 503, 547, 598, 599, 673, 677
agents disdained by, 320*n*
anniversary parties of: twenty-fifth, 165–6; fiftieth, 508
Cheever's financial arrangements with, 99, 154, 206, 232, 276; first advance, 111; first-look agreement, 319–21, 525–6, 635; raise request, 318–21, 578–9; request to cosign mortgage, 282
Cheever's label as *"New Yorker* writer" and, 126–7, 222, 276, 368, 662*n*
Cheever's writings in, 105, 107, 338, 578, 607, 609; of thirties, 80–1, 86, 87, 91, 98, 99; of forties, 109, 111–12, 123–4, 134–5, 149–54, 163–4, 166–8; of fifties, 27, 172, 188, 202–5, 208–11, 224, 248, 264; of sixties, 283–4, 299–301, 313, 381,

385, 386, 404, 405, 406, 435, 592*n*; of seventies, 525–6; of eighties, 613, 626; *Bullet Park* excerpts, 386, 404; journal excerpts, 656, 669–70; revision process and, 81, 82*n*, 98, 300*n*; "Talk of the Town" item, 55; "Town House" stories, 134–5, 137, 146, 150; *Wapshot Chronicle* excerpts, 226, 239–40; *Wapshot* stories, 214–16
Cheever's writings rejected by, 81, 90–1, 98, 99, 112, 149, 157, 173, 215, 258, 279, 299, 365–6, 385, 386, 404, 435, 444, 446, 448–9, 526, 531–2
Gurganus's story in, 488, 489, 567
Lobrano's editorship at, 116, 173
Maxwell's editorship at, 95, 98–100, 173–5, 299–301. *See also* Maxwell, William
payment system for fiction in, 319, 320, 321
Ross's editorship at, 152–3, 164
sent to Russia by Cheever, 345–6*n*
style of fiction in, 111–12, 126–7, 166, 240; Cheever's parody of, 528; experimental narrative techniques and, 386–7, 586; low regard among some critics and writers for, 111–12, 369, 662*n*; Mizener's review of, 196
Updike's writings in, 262, 321, 348, 365; review of *Oh What a Paradise It Seems* in, 652
Zimmer's desire to get published in, 567–8, 609, 610, 614

New York Herald Tribune Book Review, 126–7, 356

New York Herald Tribune Book Week, 323

New York Review of Books, 368, 387, 467, 488

New York Times, 22–3, 51, 68, 79, 114, 157, 158, 283, 341, 371, 373, 383, 388, 516, 576, 599, 610–11, 636, 664
best-seller list, 5, 553
Cheever's obituary in, 661
Cheever's writings reviewed in, 90–1, 196–7, 240, 256, 285, 323, 355, 413, 448, 468, 551–2, 585, 652

New York Times Book Review, 195, 667, 670, 671
    Cheever's writings reviewed in, 127, 234, 240, 256, 285, 322–3, 412–13, 420–1, 468, 469, 552, 651–2
New York Times Magazine, 383*n*
    Kornbluth article in, 577–9
Nicol, Charles, 413
"Night Mummy Got the Wrong Mink Coat, The," 613
Nina (Ben's girlfriend), 429
Nine Stories (Salinger), 195, 196
Nixon, Richard M., 213, 502
Nobel Prize, 40*n*, 530, 576
Northern Westchester Hospital Center (Mount Kisco, N.Y.), 643–4
Norwell Center, Mass., cemetery in, 222
    Cheever's burial at, 662–4, 677
Note Found in a Bottle (S. Cheever), 673
"Nothing Has Happened," 99
Novy Mir (The New World), 341
nuclear age:
    Cheever's anxiety about Bomb and, 260–1
    Cheever's teleplay projects and, 277, 637
    paranoia of early sixties and, 298–9
    theme in *The Wapshot Scandal*, 324–6

Oates, Joyce Carol, 413, 417, 420, 550*n*
"Ocean, The," 314, 315, 355, 586
O'Connor, Flannery, 159
O'Faolain, Sean, 455
"Of Love: A Testimony," 82–3, 127, 387
Ogden, Fax, 31, 32, 330, 332, 425*n*, 445
O'Hara, John, 80, 99, 149, 333, 362, 459, 584, 597
Oh! Calcutta!, 435
Oh What a Paradise It Seems, 148*n*, 538*n*, 636, 648–52
    characters, plot, and themes of, 648–51
    contract and advance for, 596, 623, 634–5
    reviews of, 651–2
    sales of, 652
    writing of, 619–21, 622, 623, 626, 627*n*, 634

Old Man at the Railroad Crossing and Other Tales, The (Maxwell), 366
Oliver, Mary, 466, 467
"Opportunity, The," 157
Oribe Tea Barn (Jaffrey, N.H.), 44
Orphanos, Stathis, 491
Osgood, Grace, 31–2, 49
Ossining, N.Y., 257
    admirers invited to Cheever's home in, 374–6
    Cheever's happiness in, 600–2
    Cheever's hikes in, 296
    Cheever's move to, 281–2, 291, 293–4
    Cheever's neighbors and social life in, 295–7, 370–5, 459. *See also* Friday Club
    Cheever's purchase of house in, 281–2
    Cheever's status as "most prominent treasure" of, 664, 676–7
Ossining *Citizen Register*, 600, 664
O'Toole, Johnny, 12
Our Miss Brooks, 144
Oursler, Tony, 646
Overseas School (Rome), 233
"Ovid in Ossining" (Lee), 331–2
"O Youth and Beauty!," 202–3, 204, 214, 256, 262, 586, 612

Pagany, 56
Paige, Satchel, 37
Pakula, Alan, 335, 336, 337*n*, 393, 422, 434–5
Palamountain, Anne, 409, 575, 625
Palamountain, Joseph C., Jr., 409, 625
Palumbo, Angelo, 219, 230
Pantheon, 384
"Parable of the Diligent Novelist, The," 368
Parade (1936 periodical), 80
Paramount Pictures, 524, 532
Paramount Studio (Astoria, Queens), 131
Paris Diary (Rorem), 395
Paris Review, The, 30, 300, 417
Partisan, The (B. Cheever), 674
Partisan Review, 91, 92*n*, 356
Pasternak, Boris, 344–5
PBS, 612, 636–9
Peabody, George Foster, 64
Peabody Essex Museum, 8
Peaches (Lang's girlfriend), 460, 461

Peden, William, 195, 234, 256
Pembroke College, 309, 377
PEN conference (Frankfurt, 1959), 267–8
People, 600
"Percy," 403–4, 406
Perelman, S. J., 173, 321, 361, 362
"Perfect Day for Bananafish, A" (Salinger), 196
"Peril in the Streets, The," 126
Perry, Eleanor, 381, 382–3
Perry, Frank, 381, 382–3
Pettingell, Henry, 8–9
Phelan, Kappo, 159
Phelps Memorial Hospital Center (Sleepy Hollow, N.Y.):
    Cheever's cancer treatments at, 626–9, 630
    Cheever's drinking-related conditions treated at, 468–71, 494, 505, 510–11, 519
"Picture for the Home, A," 91
Pictures from an Institution (Jarrell), 546
Pigeon Feathers (Updike), 347
Pinkham, Mr. (banker), 59
Plagiarist, The (B. Cheever), 674
Plato, 197
"Play a March," 87, 90
Playboy, 404–5, 445, 448, 467n, 491, 524
Playboy International Writers' Convocation (Chicago, 1971), 455
Playhouse 90, 211
"Pleasures of Solitude, The," 340n
Plimpton, George, 334
PM, 182
Pochna, Peter, 541
Podgorny, Nikolai, 457
Poe, Edgar Allan, 70
Poldark, 522
Pollack, Sydney, 383
Pollet, Elizabeth, 295
Poore, Charles, 240, 285, 323
Poorhouse Fair, The (Updike), 261–2
Popescu, Petru, 483, 536
Popov, Lyubomir, 563
Porter, Katherine Anne, 110, 205, 323n, 360
Portnoy's Complaint (Roth), 424
"Pot of Gold, The," 164, 341
Powell, Anthony, 563

Powers, J. F., 530
Prescott, Orville, 234, 355
"President of the Argentine, The," 528–9, 613
Prince, Hezekiah, 181n
Prix de Rome, 223, 224n, 225, 235–6
"Problem No. 4," 126n
Professor of Desire, The (Roth), 588
Proust, Marcel, 39, 45, 396, 468, 496
Provincetown, Mass., Cheever's trips to, 57, 465–7
Pulitzer Prize, 5, 591–2
Puner, Helen, 360
"Pure and Beautiful Story, A," 436
Puritan tradition, 227
Pushcart Prize III, The, 544
Pynchon, Thomas, 4, 347, 497

Quarry West, 547
Quincy, Mass.:
    Cheever's birth and childhood in, 20–51, 677
    Cheever's last visit to, 222
    Cheever's reluctance to return to, 49, 88
Quincy High, 38, 45, 61
Quincy News, 38
Quincy *Patriot Ledger*, 34, 93, 108, 156, 592, 662n

Rabbit Is Rich (Updike), 635–6
racism, 340, 360, 388
Radical Innocence (Hassan), 306
Random House, 643
    Cheever's first novel and, 146–9, 186–7, 216–18. *See also* Linscott, Robert
    Cheever's first story collection and, 122, 123, 126
    Cheever's second story collection and, 194
Reader's Digest, 521, 589, 604, 646, 667
Reader's Digest Condensed Books, 280
"Reasonable Music, The," 157n
Redford, Robert, 337n
Refregier, Anton, 85, 89–90, 91
Refregier, Lila, 89–90, 91, 516
Reik, Theodor, 174
Reiman, Don, 633
"Reunion," 609
Rich Man, Poor Man (Shaw), 286n

Riesman, David, 68
Roberts, Ben, 288
Robins, Natalie, 373–4, 602
Rockland Country Day School, 486–7
Rojack, Stephen, 367
Romania, Cheever's trip to (1976),
   536–7
Rome:
   American colony in, 232, 235–6
   Cheever's first sojourn in
      (1956–1957), 231–40, 246–8;
      children's experiences and, 232–3;
      financial difficulties and, 230, 232;
      inability to work during, 239, 240,
      247; lack of Italian language
      abilities and, 233, 234–5; Mary's
      pregnancy and childbearing in,
      230, 234, 237
   Cheever's return to (1964), 328
Rorem, Ned, 66, 315–18, 395–6, 397–8,
   409, 425n, 433, 593–4, 616
Rosenthal Award, 463–4
Ross, Harold, 81, 120, 121, 145, 152–3,
   164, 165–6, 167, 183, 213, 254, 319
Rossini, Gioacchino, 403
Roth, Philip, 283, 284, 334, 367, 368,
   408, 409, 424, 435, 588
Rothbart, David, 130
Rudnik, Raphael, 372–3, 374, 508, 538,
   569, 606, 665
Rukeyser, Muriel, 70, 72, 110, 158
Rule, Janice, 383
Rules of the Game, The, 277, 576
Russia:
   censorship in, 563
   Cheever's first trip to (1964), 28,
      340–51, 352, 355, 663; Litvinov's
      friendship and, 345–7; Russian
      writers encountered in, 343, 344–5,
      350; State Department and, 340,
      341, 352; story written with
      material from, 388, 444–5;
      Updike's arrival and, 347–50
   Cheever's readership in, 5, 563, 677n
   Cheever's returns to: in 1971, 455–7;
      in 1978, 573
   lofty status of writers in, 342
Russian language, Cheever's writings
   translated into, 340–1, 345
Ryan, Michael, 476–7
Ryurikov, Boris, 345, 352

Sabine (brother Fred's girlfriend), 389
Sacco and Vanzetti, 46–7, 48
Sade, Marquis de, 272
Salinger, J. D., 99, 149, 195, 196, 233–4,
   284n, 300–1, 330, 341, 362, 676n
Sandy, Stephen, 541
San Francisco, *Esquire*-sponsored
   symposium in (1960), 283–5
Sarah Lawrence College, 107, 154,
   546
"Saratoga," 96, 673
Saroyan, William, 131, 288, 564n
Sartre, Jean-Paul, 563
Saturday Evening Post, The, 320, 366,
   402–3, 579
Saturday Review, 126, 195, 551, 585
Saul, Louise, 38
Scarborough Country Day School, 183,
   253, 309–10, 436
Scarborough Fire Company, 218–19
Scarborough-on-Hudson, N.Y.:
   Cheever's dissatisfaction with life in,
      201–2, 280
   Cheever's longings for status and
      acknowledgment in, 185
   Cheever's rented home in, 176, 177–8,
      184
   evolution of suburban life in, 183–4
   Fred's move to nearby Briarcliff
      Manor and, 190–2
   homophobia in, 207
   literary aspirations of Cheever's
      neighbors in, 184
   luxurious lifestyle in, 177–8
   pastoral aspect of, 182–3
   responses to *The Wapshot Chronicle* in,
      251–3
   social life in, 178–83, 218–19,
      280–1
   stories set in suburb similar to (Shady
      Hill), 202–5, 208–11
Scarlet Letter, The (Hawthorne), 279
"Scarlet Moving Van, The," 264, 285,
   415–16
Schary, Dore, 224
Schneider, Robert, 644, 659
Schoales, Annie, 665
Schoales, Dudley, Sr., 177, 182, 198, 201,
   202, 204, 251, 282, 457–8, 519
Schoales, Dudley, Jr., 519
Schoales, Sarah, 197, 198, 270, 665

Schoales, Virginia Vanderlip ("Zinny"), 177, 182, 198, 201, 245, 246, 251, 252, 433
   death of, 457–8, 519
Schulman, Marvin, 627–9, 631–2, 639
Schultz, Philip, 527–8, 529, 533, 539–40, 563, 589, 606
Schwartz, Delmore, 295
Schwartz, Laurens, 497–8, 499, 500–1, 522, 528
Scott, Winfield Townley, 241
Scowcroft, Richard, 530
"Season of Divorce, The," 163–4, 341
Segovia, Andrés, 271
Seinfeld, 671–2
Sekaer, Peter, 84, 85
Selected Stories (Moscow: Progress Publishers), 340*n*
Selzer, Richard, 620, 621, 622
Seoul, Cheever's trip to (1970), 440–1
"Sergeant Limeburner," 124, 673
"Seven Details the Major Critic of the Show Felt to Be Overexplicit" (Gurganus), 474
Sewall, Judge, 8
Sexton, Anne, 505, 511, 529
"Seymour: An Introduction" (Salinger), 196*n*
Shady Hill Kidnapping, The (formerly called *The Hounds of Shady Hill*, then *Kidnapping in Shady Hill*), 575–6, 612, 636–9
"Shady Hill" stories, 202–5, 208–11, 224, 256–7
Shady Lane Farm (Ossining, N.Y.), 296, 312
Shakespeare, William, 10, 12, 13, 26, 36
Shannon, Nellie, 67, 68, 219
Shaw, Irwin, 111, 121, 131, 132, 145, 149, 154, 165, 166, 173*n*, 236, 294
   decline of fiction by, 285–6
   New Yorker contract of, 319, 321
   The Young Lions and, 157–8, 224
Shaw, Mrs. Irwin, 157, 166
Shawn, William, 183, 226, 320, 386, 488, 579, 586, 661–2, 670
Sheed, Wilfrid, 26, 410, 516
Shepherd Company, 46
Sheppard, R. Z., 551
Sherwin, Judith, 213, 585
Ship of Fools (Porter), 323*n*

Siggelkow, Rick, 504, 509
Signal Corps. *See* Army Signal Corps
"Signs of Hope," 646
Silas Crockett (Chase), 73–4*n*
Silber, Joan, 620, 621, 622
Silverberg, J. William, 424–6, 428, 436–7, 438, 439–40, 441, 603
Simon and Schuster, 86, 88, 90, 91, 109
"Simple Life, The," 99
Sinatra, Frank, 435, 492
Sing Sing, 466, 600
   Cheever as teacher at, 449–52
   Cheever's relationship with former inmate at, 459–61. *See also* Lang, Donald
Sitting on the Whorehouse Steps and Empty Bed Blues, 86, 91
Skidmore College, Cheever's honorary degree from, 625
Skillings, Roger, 57, 465–7
Sloan-Kettering (New York City), 640–2, 643
Smallwood, Tom, 607–9, 632, 633, 639, 642–3, 646, 656
Smedley, Agnes, 158
Smith, Dave, 543, 544–5
Smith, Harrison, 83
Smith, Liz, 678
Smith College, 286
Smithers Alcoholism Treatment and Training Center (New York City), 4, 221*n*, 511–15, 516, 519, 630
Sobel, Dr., 199
Social Security, 94, 108
Società Nazionale Dante Alighieri, La (Rome), 234
Sofia, Bulgaria, International Conference of Writers in (1977), 562–4
Solotaroff, Ted, 670
Solzhenitsyn, Aleksandr, 563, 581
Some People, Places, and Things That Will Not Appear in My Next Novel, 284*n*, 285, 435*n*
"Some People, Places, and Things That Will Not Appear in My Next Novel," 283–4
Something Happened (Heller), 500
Song for These States, A (F. Cheever), 88, 263
"Sorrows of Gin, The," 256, 610*n*, 612
Sot-Weed Factor (Barth), 476

Soubletsky (Russian), 342–3
South, Cheever's attitude toward, 118, 121–2
Southworth, Stacy Baxter, 46, 48, 49
Soviet Union. *See* Russia
Soviet Writers' Union, 343, 563
Spanish Civil War, 85, 88
Spear, Arthur Prince ("Art"), 217, 225, 353, 365n, 383, 393, 466, 537, 599, 667
    Cheever's letters to, 478, 511, 514, 628
    Cheever's relationship with, 180–1, 280–1, 370–1, 372, 460–1, 537
    Litvinov's relationship with, 346
Spear, Pammy, 270–1, 309
Spear, Stella, 181, 217, 225, 346
Spencer, Elizabeth, 234, 253, 335, 654
Spencer, Niles, 91, 115–16
Spencer, Sara ("Mrs. Zagreb"), 363n, 369, 374, 376, 383, 394, 401, 456, 471, 493, 630–1, 665
    Cheever's relationship with, 338–9, 396, 433, 539
Spiegel, Sam, 381, 382–3
Spigelgass, Leonard, 129, 131, 132, 195
"Spingarn, Mrs. Louisa," as Cheever pseudonym, 525, 613
Spruces, The (Friendship, Maine), 225
Stacy (Sing Sing inmate), 450–1
Stafford, Jean, 212, 233–4, 387, 496
Stalin, Joseph, 120
Stanford University:
    Cheever's readings at, 529–30, 546
    Federico as student at, 529, 537, 546
Starbuck, George, 487, 496–7
State Department, 159n
    Cheever's Russia trip and, 340, 341, 352
"State of Grace" (Brodkey), 357
Stead, Christina, 373
Steegmuller, Francis, 39n, 254–5, 255, 644
Stein, Gertrude, 356
Stein, Sol, 306
Steinbeck, John, 340
Stern, Richard, 358, 361, 368, 369
Sterne, Laurence, 242
Stevenson, Philip, 73n
Stinnett, Caskie, 451–2, 487
Stockwell, Dean, 289
Stone, Ezra, 193–4
Stories (Cheever, Fuchs, Maxwell, and Stafford), 233–4, 583n

Stories of John Cheever, The, 5, 150, 385, 448n, 467n, 535, 583–6, 587, 589, 592n, 599, 602–3, 629, 635, 673, 676, 678
    awards won by, 5, 587, 591–2, 625
    Cheever's preface to, 584–5
    reviews of, 585–6
Story, 82–3
Stravinsky, Igor, 563
Street, Narcissa, 251, 252
Streetcar Named Desire, A (Williams), 162
Streeter, Lin, 125
Styron, William, 259, 351, 465, 654–5, 675
Suez War (1956), 231–2
Sullivan, Richard, 234
Sullivan, Thomas J., 376, 671
Suntory, 472
SUNY-Oswego, 569, 593, 605, 610
"Superintendent, The," 340, 555
"Sutton Place Story, The," 150–1, 584
Swan Song, 626
"Swimmer, The," 316–18, 345, 355, 365, 459, 577, 586, 602, 671
Swimmer, The (movie), 381–3, 386, 404
Swope, Rod, 206
Swope, Sally, 185, 217n, 429, 509
Synanon, 291–2

Tarrytown Daily News, 445n, 493
Taylor, Peter, 577
Tchaikovsky, Pyotr, 26n
"Teaser, The," 80
Tebaldi, Renata, 246
Telephone Story, 577–9
television:
    Cheever stories adapted for, 211, 612
    Cheever's writings for, 193–4, 277, 575–6, 612, 636–9
Temptation of Roger Heriott, The (Newhouse), 224
Thackeray, William Makepeace, 41
"Thanks, Too, for Memories," 551
Thanksgiving celebrations:
    of Cheever's childhood, 23–4
    at Cheever's Ossining home, 372–4, 505, 589
Thaw, Clare, 539, 571, 589, 617, 642
Thaw, Eugene, 37, 539, 571, 589, 617, 665, 666
Thayer Academy, 24, 37–8, 45–6, 271, 508, 581, 677

"Expelled" based on Cheever's experiences at, 46–9
Falconer book tour and, 561–2
Thayerlands, 31–2, 37
Thomas, Evan, 226–7
Thompson, Anna Boynton, 24, 25, 31, 38
Thompson, Ralph, 239
"Three Stories," 467n
Thurber, James, 153, 356, 638
Time, 133, 134, 314n, 328–30, 661, 676
  cover story on Cheever in, 4, 21n, 55n, 329–32, 333, 356, 359, 366, 368, 550
  reviews of Cheever's work in, 233, 551, 585
Tocqueville, Alexis de, 293
Today, 256
Todd, Richard, 455, 529
Tolstoy, Leo, 142, 551
Tom Jones (Fielding), 40
Tomkins, Calvin ("Tad") (son-in-law), 590, 591, 605, 640, 646, 666, 673
Tomkins, Sarah Liley Cheever (granddaughter), 653
Tonkonogy, Gertrude, 155
"Tony in Bed," 404
"Torch Song," 92n, 152, 172, 586
Towers, Robert, 586
Town House (play), 155–7, 173
"Town House" stories, 134–5, 137, 146, 150
Townsend, Prescott, 52–3
Tracy, Spencer, 337n
"Train, The" (Carver), 482n
Trask, Spencer and Katrina, 63–4, 66, 89
Travel & Leisure, 451–2, 487, 536–7
Treetops (S. Cheever), 103n, 104, 133, 270n
Treetops (Winternitz family's N.H. estate), 110, 133, 139, 166, 187, 205, 219
  Cheever's stays at, 106–7, 141–3, 266–7, 453; after sobriety, 520–1; inability to work during, 166, 168; reveries about, 113
  Mary's trips to, without John, 337, 393, 459, 471, 494, 520, 521, 631
"Triad," 467n
Trilling, Lionel, 222
Trotsky, Leon, 91

Truax, Hawley, 320, 579
Tselkov, Oleg, 350
Tucci, Maria, 587, 636
Turco, Lewis, 569
TV Guide, 193
Twentieth Century–Fox, 131, 285, 288
Twentieth Century Limited, 358, 359
Tyler, Anne, 167, 585, 652

Uncle Vanya (Chekhov), 542
Uncollected Stories of John Cheever, The, 672–3
Underground Railroad, 11
Unger, Mary Ann, 620, 621
Union League Club, 625
United States Information Agency, 572
University of Utah, Cheever's visit to (1977), 6, 543–6
Unspeakable Practices, Unnatural Acts (Barthelme), 463
Updike, Elizabeth, 534, 598
Updike, John, 18, 24, 47, 92n, 99, 315, 351, 354, 368, 375, 408, 435, 441, 459, 480, 610n, 668, 676
  in Boston, 3–4, 499–500, 507, 510, 517
  boycott of writers' conference in Bulgaria and, 562, 563
  Bullet Park reviewed by, 413, 417
  Cheever eulogized by, 663, 677
  Cheever's competitiveness with, 261–2, 348–9, 361–2, 535, 577, 587, 636
  on Cheever's *Journals*, 670–1
  Cheever's relationship with, 347–50, 361–2, 499–500, 534–5
  Cheever's views on writings of, 261–2, 347, 388, 635–6
  Cheever's visited in Ossining by (1981), 627
  false report of death of, 534
  as *New Yorker* writer, 262, 321, 348, 365
  Oh What a Paradise It Seems reviewed by, 652
  in Russia, 347–50
  at White House reception, 361–2
Updike, Mary, 28, 347–8, 349–50, 362, 499, 534n
"Utah Died for Your Sins" (Zimmer), 543, 544, 547, 568
Uzzell, Thomas H., 105

V. (Pynchon), 347
Valhouli, James, 500, 623, 625–6
Vanderlip, Charlotte, 177
Vanderlip, Frank A., 177, 252
Vanderlip, Narcissa, 178, 192, 205, 206, 215, 251, 252, 253, 298
Vanderlip, Virginia ("Zinny"). *See* Schoales, Virginia Vanderlip
Van Gordon, Donald, 629, 630
Van Tassell, Richard, 602
Varley, Florence, 26
"Vega," 157n
Venga (Macedonian prophetess), 564–5
Venice, Cheever's trips to, 245–6, 268
Venza, Jac, 575–6
Vidal, Gore, 286, 563, 564
Vietnam War, 360–1, 387, 388–9, 502
Village Voice, The, 652
Vincent, George, 67
"Vision of the World, A," 303
Vittoria (maid), 234–5
Vonnegut, Kurt, 497, 563
Vorse, Mary Heaton, 66
Voznesensky, Andrei, 344

Waite, Marjorie, 64
Wald, Jerry, 285, 288, 290, 291
Walking Papers (Hochman), 438
Wall Street Journal, 318
Walt Whitman School (New York), 138
Wang Meng, 677n
Wapshot Chronicle, The, 181n, 188–9n, 202, 239–45, 247, 276, 277n, 311, 323, 355, 394, 425, 555, 644, 663, 676
    autobiographical aspects of, 7, 10, 12, 13, 15, 17, 20, 42n, 53, 141n, 162–3, 241, 245
    as Book-of-the-Month Club selection, 239–40
    characters and plot of, 241–5
    Cheever's "woolgathering" about, 239, 240, 245
    elements of *The Holly Tree* incorporated into, 147, 148, 149, 160
    father's memoir notes incorporated into, 11, 216, 264
    first academic study of, 306–7
    literary experimentation of late sixties and seventies and, 241

National Book Award won by, 254–5, 263, 323, 356, 578
    not published until after Cheever's mother's death, 222
    precursors to. *See Holly Tree, The; Imposter, The*
    Random House contract and advance and, 146, 216–18
    reviews of, 240–1
    sales of, 245, 257
    sensuality in, 244
    "smells" in, 226, 243–4
    structural approach in, 214, 240, 241–2
    Vanderlip family's responses to, 251–2
    writing of, 213–18, 222, 225, 230, 241, 420
Wapshot novels, 22, 552, 601, 676
    literary influences on, 40
    movie rights to, 335–7
Wapshot Scandal, The, 222, 322–8, 331, 355, 411, 603
    characters and plot of, 324–8
    Cheever's dissatisfaction with, 310–11, 322, 359–61
    dedicated to Maxwell, 311
    Lindley's editing of, 322n, 408
    Maxwell's reaction to, 310, 311
    reviews of, 322–4, 412
    sales of, 328n
    structure of, 324, 325
    William Dean Howells Medal awarded to, 323n, 359–61, 577
    writing of, 276–7, 302, 307, 310, 315, 372
War Department, 158
Warhol, Andy, 157n
Warren, Mrs. Robert Penn. *See* Clark, Eleanor
Warren, Robert Penn ("Red"), 235, 248, 255–6, 270, 280, 295, 330, 360, 497–8, 562, 654n
Washington, D.C.:
    Cheever's FWP stint in (1938–1939), 94–7
    USIA videotaping in (1977), 572–3
"Washington Boarding House," 98
Washington Post, 240, 355, 670, 672
Washington Post Book World, 413, 468, 585
Wasserstein, Wendy, 612
Waters, Harry F., 638
Waters, John, 53n
Watson, Mrs. Thomas A., 165

Watson, Thomas A., 102, 106
Way Some People Live, The, 122–3, 126–8, 129, 583, 662n, 673
Way We Were, The, 616
Weaver, Harriett, 133, 287, 288, 289, 290, 530
Weaver, John, 131, 133, 224, 287, 477, 530
   Cheever's letters to, 143, 144, 261, 268, 328, 342, 359, 360, 375, 382, 393, 470, 488, 513, 521, 561, 587, 636
Weaver, Sigourney, 612
Webster (Susan's boyfriend), 309
Welty, Eudora, 99, 541, 577, 629, 654n
Werner, Morris, 56, 57, 72, 87, 91, 106, 119, 166
Werner, Mrs. Morris. *See* Hawthorne, Hazel
Werth, Barry, 286n
Wescott, Glenway, 297, 323, 360
West, Nathanael, 81, 664
Westchester County, N.Y.:
   Cheever's dissatisfaction with social milieu of, 184–5, 201–2, 280–2, 352
   Cheever's move to, 175–6, 177–85
   see also Ossining, N.Y.; Scarborough-on-Hudson, N.Y.
Westchester Magazine, 613
Wesul, Peter, 142–3, 157n, 219, 266, 602
Whedon, John, 193–4
Wheelwright, John, 53
Where Angels Fear to Tread (Forster), 313
Whiskey Island, Cheever's visits to Boyers' compound on, 35, 179–80, 454, 571
White, Egbert, 120
White, Katharine, 58, 80, 81, 86, 90, 98, 222, 226, 227, 254
White House, reception at (1965), 361–2
Whitney, Freddy, 104, 142, 143
Whitney, Janie, 104, 143
Whitney, Louisa, 104, 143
Whitney, Stephen, 104, 143
Who Are the Revolutionaries? (F. Cheever), 502, 503
Wilder, Clinton, 155
William Dean Howells Medal, 323n, 359–61, 577
Willson, Roger, 623
Wilson, Edmund, 57, 72, 654n
Wilson, Kenneth, 280
Winternitz, Bill (brother-in-law), 103, 104, 114, 143, 265, 453, 628, 640, 641

Winternitz, Elizabeth "Buff" (sister-in-law), 104, 114, 143, 266, 267, 392, 402
   death of, 520–1
Winternitz, Helen Watson (Mary's mother), 102, 103
Winternitz, Mary (wife). *See* Cheever, Mary Winternitz
Winternitz, Milton ("Winter") (father-in-law), 102–4, 116, 129, 139, 155, 183, 303, 521
   as abusive parent, 103, 267, 453
   career and accomplishments of, 102, 103, 185, 266
   Cheever's relationship with, 107, 141–2, 266–7, 269–70
   death of, 269–70, 337
   Mary's relationship with Cheever and, 107, 110, 114
   personality and demeanor of, 106, 107, 141–2, 266–7
   wardrobe bequeathed to Cheever by, 270
Winternitz, Pauline Whitney ("Polly") (mother-in-law), 103–4, 108, 143, 155, 187, 475
   Cheever's relationship with, 107, 141, 142, 190, 266, 267, 270
   Mary's relationship with Cheever and, 107, 110, 114, 267
   personality and demeanor of, 104, 106, 142
Winternitz, Tom (brother-in-law), 103, 104, 267
WNET, 575–6, 612, 639
Woiwode, Larry, 468, 469
Wolk, Seymour, 601
Wollaston Grammar, 26
Woman in White, The (Collins), 237
women's movement, 312, 369, 438–9
Woodstock (school in Vermont), 272
Wordsworth, William, 45, 598
Work for the Night Is Coming, 626
Works Progress Administration (WPA), 94–5, 297
World According to Garp, The (Irving), 587, 588
World of Apples, The, 385n, 435, 465, 466, 467–8, 469, 583n
"World of Apples, The," 385–6, 387, 467, 616

World War I, 16, 24
World War II, 24, 97–8, 101, 104,
115–16, 441
Cheever's military service in, 117–36,
138, 335. *See also* Cheever, John—
in military
"Worm in the Apple, The," 257
Worthington, Peg, 97, 101
"Writing in America Today" (San
Francisco, 1960), 283–5
"Wrysons, The," 261, 285

Yaddo artists' colony, 63–71, 85, 105,
113, 141, 165, 201, 289, 294
Ames regime at, 64–5, 66, 409
Ames removed as director of, 408–9
anticommunist witch hunt at, 158–60
Cheever's interest in moving to
vicinity of, 281
Cheever's last visit to (1980), 620–2
Cheever's relationships with young
writers and artists met at, 372–3,
399–400, 527–8
Cheever's service on board of
directors of, 5, 68, 228, 286; named
vice-president, 587; visits related
to, 260, 307, 308, 315–18, 357–8,
372–3, 395–6, 397, 398, 424,
454–5, 478, 526–7
Cheever's youthful sojourns at: in
1934, 61–3, 66–71, 74–5; in 1935,
83–4; in 1936, 86–7, 88–91; in
1937, 92–3; in 1939, 97–8, 99; in
1940, 110; permission to come and
go as he pleased and, 91, 92, 93;
warm relations with servants and,
67, 219; work arrangements and,
65–6, 74, 83–4, 87, 88–9
homosexuals at, 308, 357–8, 395, 399,
409, 478
Lake George facility of, 83–4, 88–9, 97
origins of, 63–4
"Yaddo effect" and, 66
Zimmer at, 545, 547, 549, 565, 566,
568–9
Yagoda, Ben, 321
Yale University, 565
Yale Younger Poets Award, 68, 438
Yank, 120–1, 135
Yardley, Jonathan, 256, 670, 678

Yates, Richard, 177*n*, 371*n*, 672*n*
Years with Ross, The (Thurber), 153
"Yellow Room, The," 404–5
Yevtushenko, Yevgeny ("Zhenya"), 344–5,
350, 352, 456–7, 483, 563, 564
Young, Florence Liley ("Liley") (aunt),
15–16, 25, 37, 190*n*, 404
Young, Randall (cousin), 25, 37, 215
Young, Robert Devereaux (cousin), 190*n*
Young Lions, The (Shaw), 157–8, 224

Zagreb, Mrs., 338*n*
see also Spencer, Sara
Zhivkov, Todor, 562
Ziegler, Andrew, 296, 361
Ziegler, Sally, 295, 330
Ziegler, Ted, 295–6
Zimmer, Max, 6, 543–9, 558–9, 565–9,
573–5, 594, 595, 604–7, 609–11,
617–18, 618, 654
after Cheever's death, 674–5
background of, 544
Cheever assisted during his illness by,
630–2, 639, 640, 641, 642, 643,
646–7, 656, 657
Cheever's first encounters with, 543–6
at Cheever's funeral and memorial
services, 663, 665
Cheever's letters to, 547–8, 565, 568–9,
571, 574–5, 582, 587, 593, 621,
625
Cheever's literary patronage of,
567–8, 573–4, 609–10, 614, 617
Cheever's mentorship of, 545, 568,
609, 617–18
Cheever's sexual experiences with,
545–6, 558–9, 566, 568, 574–5, 623
engagement and first marriage of,
566, 569, 573, 574, 605
living near Cheever's Ossining home,
605–7, 609–10, 614
physical appearance and demeanor of,
543
as surrogate for Cheever's dead
brother, 6, 565
teaching jobs of, 569, 605
writer's block of, 568, 614, 657
at Yaddo, 545, 547, 549, 565, 566,
568–9, 620
Znamya (The Banner), 341

BLAKE BAILEY edited a two-volume edition of Cheever's work, published in 2009 by The Library of America. His last book, *A Tragic Honesty: The Life and Work of Richard Yates*, was a finalist for the National Book Critics Circle Award. He received a Guggenheim fellowship in 2005, and his articles and reviews have appeared in *Slate*, the *New York Times*, the *New York Observer*, and elsewhere. He lives in Virginia with his wife and daughter.

A NOTE ON THE TYPE

This book was set in Janson, a typeface long thought to have been made by the Dutchman Anton Janson, who was a practicing typefounder in Leipzig during the years 1668–1687. However, it has been conclusively demonstrated that these types are actually the work of Nicholas Kis (1650–1702), a Hungarian, who most probably learned his trade from the master Dutch typefounder Dirk Voskens. The type is an excellent example of the influential and sturdy Dutch types that prevailed in England up to the time William Caslon (1692–1766) developed his own incomparable designs from them.

Composed by Creative Graphics, Inc.,
Allentown, Pennsylvania
Printed and bound by Berryville Graphics,
Berryville, Virginia
Designed by Virginia Tan